God grant me the serenity to
accept the things I cannot change,
courage to change the things I can,
and wisdom to know the difference.

Living one day at a time,
enjoying one moment at a time,
accepting hardship as the pathway to peace.

Taking, as He did, this sinful world
as it is, not as I would have it.

Trusting that He will make all things right
if I surrender to His will,
that I may be reasonably happy in this life
and supremely happy with Him forever in the next.

Amen
—Reinhold Niebuhr

To _____

From _____

Date _____

Recovery®

NEW TESTAMENT
with Psalms and Proverbs

Tyndale House Publishers, Inc.
CAROL STREAM, ILLINOIS

CONTRIBUTORS

CONTENTS

THE BOOKS OF THE NEW TESTAMENT with Psalms and Proverbs

ALPHABETICAL LISTING

A NOTE TO READERS

SINCE its early years, Tyndale House Publishers has been committed to publishing editions of the Bible in the language of the people. With over forty million copies in print, *The Living Bible* represented this tradition well for more than thirty years. More recently, Tyndale has continued this tradition by commissioning ninety evangelical scholars to produce the *Holy Bible,* New Living Translation. This general-purpose translation is accurate and excellent for study, while also being easy to read. The NLT is helping many discover, and rediscover, the power of God's living Word. The goal of any translation of the Scriptures is to convey the meaning of the ancient Hebrew and Greek texts as accurately as possible to the contemporary reader.

The challenge for our translators was to create a text that would make the same impact in the lives of modern readers that the original text did in the lives of readers in its ancient context. In the New Living Translation, this has been accomplished by translating entire thoughts (rather than just words) into natural, everyday English. The end result is a translation that is easy to read and understand and that accurately communicates the meaning of the original texts.

We believe that the New Living Translation, which combines the latest in scholarship with the best in translation style, will speak to your heart. We publish it with the prayer that God will use it to speak his timeless truth to the church and to the world in a fresh and powerful way.

The Publishers
July 1996

INTRODUCTION TO THE NEW LIVING TRANSLATION

TRANSLATION PHILOSOPHY AND METHODOLOGY

There are two general theories or methods of Bible translation. The first has been called "formal equivalence." According to this theory, the translator attempts to render each word of the original language into the receptor language and seeks to preserve the original word order and sentence structure as much as possible. The second has been called "dynamic equivalence" or "functional equivalence." The goal of this translation theory is to produce in the receptor language the closest natural equivalent of the message expressed by the original-language text—both in meaning and in style. Such a translation attempts to have the same impact on modern readers as the original had on its own audience.

A dynamic-equivalence translation can also be called a thought-for-thought translation, as contrasted with a formal-equivalence or word-for-word translation. Of course, to translate the thought of the original language requires that the text be interpreted accurately and then be rendered in understandable idiom. So the goal of any thought-for-thought translation is to be both reliable and eminently readable. Thus, as a thought-for-thought translation, the New Living Translation seeks to be both exegetically accurate and idiomatically powerful.

In making a thought-for-thought translation, the translators must do their best to enter into the thought patterns of the ancient authors and to present the same ideas, connotations, and effects in the receptor language. In order to guard against personal biases and to ensure the accuracy of the message, a thought-for-thought translation should be created by a group of scholars who employ the best exegetical tools and who also understand the receptor language very well. With these concerns in mind, the Bible Translation Committee assigned each book of the Bible to three different scholars. Each scholar made a thorough review of the assigned book and submitted suggested revisions to the appropriate general reviewer. The general reviewer reviewed and summarized these suggestions and then proposed a first-draft revision of the text. This draft served as the basis for several additional phases of exegetical and stylistic committee review. Then the Bible Translation Committee jointly reviewed and approved every verse in the final translation.

A thought-for-thought translation prepared by a group of capable scholars has the potential to represent the intended meaning of the original text even more accurately than a word-for-word translation. This is illustrated by the various renderings of the Greek word *dikaiosune*. This term cannot be adequately translated by any single English word because it can connote human righteousness, God's righteousness, doing what is right, justice, being made right in God's sight, goodness, etc. The context—not the lexicon—must determine which English term is selected for translation.

The value of a thought-for-thought translation can be illustrated by comparing 2 Corinthians 9:1 in the King James Version, the New International Version, and the New Living Translation. "For as touching the ministering to the saints, it is superfluous for me to write to you" (KJV). "There is no need for me to write to you about this service to the saints" (NIV). "I really don't need to write to you about this gift for the Christians in Jerusalem" (NLT). Only the New Living Translation clearly translates the real meaning of the Greek idiom "service to the saints" into contemporary English.

WRITTEN TO BE READ ALOUD

It is evident in Scripture that the biblical documents were written to be read aloud, often in public worship (see Luke 4:16-20; 1 Timothy 4:13; Revelation 1:3). It is still the case today that more people will hear the Bible read aloud in church than are likely to read it for themselves. Therefore, a new translation must communicate with clarity and power when it is read aloud. For this reason, the New Living Translation is recommended as a Bible to be used for public reading. Its living language is not only easy to understand, but it also has an emotive quality that will make an impact on the listener.

THE TEXTS BEHIND THE NEW LIVING TRANSLATION

The translators of the Old Testament used the Masoretic Text of the Hebrew Bible as their standard text. They used the edition known as *Biblia Hebraica Stuttgartensia* (1977) with its up-to-date textual apparatus, a revision of Rudolf Kittel's *Biblia Hebraica* (Stuttgart, 1937). The translators also compared the Dead Sea Scrolls, the Septuagint and other Greek manuscripts, the Samaritan Pentateuch, the Syriac Peshitta, the Latin Vulgate, and any other versions or manuscripts that shed light on textual problems.

The translators of the New Testament used the two standard editions of the Greek New Testament: the *Greek New Testament,* published by the United Bible Societies (fourth revised edition, 1993), and *Novum Testamentum Graece,* edited by Nestle and Aland (twenty-seventh edition, 1993). These two editions, which have the same text but differ in punctuation and textual notes, represent the best in modern textual scholarship.

TRANSLATION ISSUES

The translators have made a conscious effort to provide a text that can be easily understood by the average reader of modern English. To this end, we have used the vocabulary and language structures commonly used by the average person. The result is a translation of the Scriptures written generally at the reading level of a junior high school student. We have avoided using language that is likely to become quickly dated or that reflects a narrow subdialect of English, with the goal of making the New Living Translation as broadly useful as possible.

But our concern for readability goes beyond the concerns of vocabulary and sentence structure. We are also concerned about historical and cultural barriers to understanding the Bible, and we have sought to translate terms shrouded in history or culture in ways that can be immediately understood by the contemporary reader. Thus, our goal of easy readability expresses itself in a number of other ways:

* Rather than translating ancient weights and measures literally, which communicates little to the modern reader, we have expressed them by means of recognizable contemporary equivalents. We have converted ancient weights and measures to modern English (American) equivalents, and we have rendered the literal Hebrew or Greek measures, along with metric equivalents, in textual footnotes.

* Instead of translating ancient currency values literally, we have generally expressed them in terms of weights in precious metals. In some cases we have used other common terms to communicate the message effectively. For example, "three shekels of silver" might become "three silver coins" or "three pieces of silver" to convey the intended message. Again, a rendering of the literal Hebrew or Greek is given in textual footnotes.

* Since ancient references to the time of day differ from our modern methods of denoting time, we used renderings that are instantly understandable to the modern reader. Accordingly, we have rendered specific times of day by using approximate equivalents in terms of our common "o'clock" system. On occasion, translations such as "at dawn the next morn-

ing" or "as the sun began to set" have been used when the biblical reference is general.

* Many words in the original texts made sense to the original audience but communicate something quite different to the modern reader. In such cases, some liberty must be allowed in translation to communicate what was intended. Places identified by the term normally translated "city," for example, are often better identified as "towns" or "villages." Similarly, the term normally translated "mountain" is often better rendered "hill."

* Many words and phrases carry a great deal of cultural meaning that was obvious to the original readers but needs explanation in our own culture. For example, the phrase "they beat their breasts" (Luke 23:48) in ancient times meant that people were very upset. In our translation we chose to translate this phrase dynamically: "They went home *in deep sorrow.*" In some cases, however, we have simply illuminated the existing expression to make it immediately understandable. For example, we might have expanded the literal phrase to read "they beat their breasts *in sorrow.*"

* Metaphorical language is often difficult for contemporary readers to understand, so at times we have chosen to translate or illuminate the metaphor. For example, the ancient poet writes, "Their throat is an open grave" (Psalm 5:9, and quoted in Romans 3:13). To help the modern reader, who might be confused or distracted by a literal visualization of this image, we converted the metaphor to a simile to make the meaning immediately clear: "Their talk is foul, *like* the stench from an open grave." Here we also translated "throat" as "talk" to help the modern reader catch the significance of the metaphoric expression.

* One challenge we faced was in determining how to translate accurately the ancient biblical text that was originally written in a context where male-oriented terms were used to refer to humanity generally. We needed to respect the nature of the ancient context while also trying to make the translation clear to a modern audience that tends to read male-oriented language as applying only to males. Often the original text, though using masculine nouns and pronouns, clearly intends that the message be applied to both men and women. One example is found in the New Testament epistles, where the believers are called "brothers" *(adelphoi).* Yet it is clear that these epistles were addressed to all the believers—male and female. Thus, we have usually translated this Greek word "brothers and sisters" in order to represent the historical situation more accurately.

We have also been sensitive to passages where the text applies generally to human beings or to the human condition. In many instances we have used plural pronouns (they, them) in place of the masculine singular (he, him). For example, a traditional rendering of Proverbs 22:6 is: "Train up a child in the way he should go, and when he is old he will not turn from it." We have rendered it: "Teach your children to choose the right path, and when they are older, they will remain upon it." At times, we have also replaced third person pronouns with the second person to ensure clarity. A traditional rendering of Proverbs 26:27 is: "He who digs a pit will fall into it, and he who rolls a stone, it will come back on him." We have rendered it: "If you set a trap for others, you will get caught in it yourself. If you roll a boulder down on others, it will roll back and crush you." All such decisions were driven by the concern to reflect accurately the intended meaning of the original texts of Scripture.

We should emphasize, however, that all masculine nouns and pronouns used to represent God (for example, "Father") have been maintained without exception. We believe that essential traits of God's revealed character can only be conveyed through the masculine language expressed in the original texts of Scripture.

LEXICAL CONSISTENCY IN TERMINOLOGY

For the sake of clarity, we have maintained lexical consistency in areas such as divine names, synoptic passages, rhetorical structures, and nontheological technical terms (i.e., liturgical, cultic, zoological, botanical, cultural, and legal terms). For theological terms, we have allowed a greater semantic range of acceptable English words or phrases for a single Hebrew or Greek word. We avoided weighty theological terms that do not readily communicate to many modern readers. For example, we avoided using words such as "justification," "sanctification," and "regeneration." In place of these words (which are carryovers from Latin), we provided renderings such as "we are made right with God," "we are made holy," and "we are born anew."

THE RENDERING OF DIVINE NAMES

All appearances of *'el, 'elohim,* or *'eloah* have been translated "God," except where the context demands the translation "god(s)." We have rendered the tetragrammaton *(YHWH)* consistently as "the LORD," utilizing a form with small capitals that is common among English translations. This will distinguish it from the name *'adonai,* which we render "Lord." When *'adonai* and *YHWH* appear in conjunction, we have rendered it "Sovereign LORD." This also distinguishes *'adonai YHWH* from cases where *YHWH* appears with *'elohim,* which is rendered "LORD God." When *YH* (the short form of *YHWH*) and *YHWH* appear together, we have rendered it "LORD GOD." The Hebrew word *'adon* is rendered "lord," or "master," or sometimes "sir."

In the New Testament, the Greek word *christos* has been translated as "Messiah" when the context assumes a Jewish audience. When a Gentile audience can be assumed, *christos* has been translated as "Christ." The Greek word *kurios* is consistently translated "Lord," except in four quotations of Psalm 110:1, where it is translated "LORD."

TEXTUAL FOOTNOTES

The New Living Translation provides several kinds of textual footnotes:

* All Old Testament passages that are clearly quoted in the New Testament are identified in a textual footnote in the New Testament.
* Some textual footnotes provide cultural and historical information on places, things, and people in the Bible that are probably obscure to modern readers. Such notes should aid the reader in understanding the message of the text. For example, in Acts 12:1, "King Herod" is named in this translation as "King Herod Agrippa" and is identified in a footnote as being "the nephew of Herod Antipas and a grandson of Herod the Great."
* When various ancient manuscripts contain different readings, these differences are often documented in footnotes. For instance, textual variants are footnoted when the variant reading is very familiar (usually through the King James Version). We have used footnotes when we have selected variant readings that differ from the Hebrew and Greek editions normally followed.
* Textual footnotes are also used to show alternative renderings. These are prefaced with the word "Or."

AS WE SUBMIT this translation of the Bible for publication, we recognize that any translation of the Scriptures is subject to limitations and imperfections. Anyone who has attempted to communicate the richness of God's Word into another language will realize it is impossible to make a perfect translation. Recognizing these limitations, we sought God's guidance and wisdom throughout this project. Now we pray that he will accept our efforts and use this translation for the benefit of the church and of all people.

We pray that the New Living Translation will overcome some of the barriers of history, culture, and language that have kept people from reading and understanding God's Word. We hope that readers unfamiliar with the Bible will find the words clear and easy to understand and that readers well versed in the Scriptures will gain a fresh perspective. We pray that readers will gain insight and wisdom for living but most of all that they will meet the God of the Bible and be forever changed by knowing him.

The Bible Translation Committee
July 1996

HOLY BIBLE
NEW LIVING TRANSLATION
BIBLE TRANSLATION TEAM

PENTATEUCH

Daniel I. Block,
General Reviewer
*The Southern Baptist
Theological Seminary*

GENESIS
Allen Ross, *Trinity Episcopal
Seminary*
John Sailhamer, *Northwestern
College*
Gordon Wenham, *The
Cheltenham and Gloucester
College of Higher Education*

EXODUS
Robert Bergen, *Hannibal-
LaGrange College*
Daniel I. Block, *The Southern
Baptist Theological Seminary*
Eugene Carpenter, *Bethel
College, Mishawaka,
Indiana*

LEVITICUS
David Baker, *Ashland
Theological Seminary*
Victor Hamilton, *Asbury
College*
Kenneth Mathews, *Beeson
Divinity School, Samford
University*

NUMBERS
Dale A. Brueggemann,
*Assemblies of God, Division
of Foreign Missions*
Roland K. Harrison (deceased),
Wycliffe College
Gerald L. Mattingly, *Johnson
Bible College*

DEUTERONOMY
J. Gordon McConville, *The
Cheltenham and Gloucester
College of Higher Education*
Eugene H. Merrill, *Dallas
Theological Seminary*

John A. Thompson, *University
of Melbourne*

HISTORICAL BOOKS

Barry J. Beitzel,
General Reviewer
*Trinity Evangelical Divinity
School*

JOSHUA/JUDGES
Carl E. Armerding, *Schloss
Mittersill Study Centre*
Barry J. Beitzel, *Trinity
Evangelical Divinity School*
Lawson Stone, *Asbury
Theological Seminary*

1 & 2 SAMUEL
Barry J. Beitzel, *Trinity
Evangelical Divinity School*
V. Philips Long, *Covenant
Theological Seminary*
J. Robert Vannoy, *Biblical
Theological Seminary*

1 & 2 KINGS
Bill T. Arnold, *Asbury
Theological Seminary*
William H. Barnes, *North
Central University*
Frederic W. Bush, *Fuller
Theological Seminary*

1 & 2 CHRONICLES
Raymond B. Dillard
(deceased), *Westminster
Theological Seminary*
David A. Dorsey, *Evangelical
School of Theology*
Terry Eves, *Calvin College*

EZRA/NEHEMIAH/
ESTHER/RUTH
William C. Williams, *Southern
California College*
Hugh G. M. Williamson,
Oxford University

POETRY

Tremper Longman III,
General Reviewer
*Westminster Theological
Seminary*

JOB
August Konkel, *Providence
Theological Seminary*
Tremper Longman III,
*Westminster Theological
Seminary*
Al Wolters, *Redeemer College*

PSALMS 1–75
Mark D. Futato, *Westminster
Theological Seminary in
California*
Douglas Green, *Westminster
Theological Seminary*
Richard Pratt, *Reformed
Theological Seminary*

PSALMS 76–150
David M. Howard Jr., *Trinity
Evangelical Divinity School*
Raymond C. Ortlund Jr.,
*Trinity Evangelical Divinity
School*
Willem VanGemeren, *Trinity
Evangelical Divinity School*

PROVERBS
Ted Hildebrandt, *Grace College*
Richard Schultz, *Wheaton
College*
Raymond C. Van Leeuwen,
Eastern College

ECCLESIASTES/
SONG OF SONGS
Daniel C. Fredericks, *Belhaven
College*
David Hubbard (deceased),
Fuller Theological Seminary
Tremper Longman III,
*Westminster Theological
Seminary*

PROPHETS

John N. Oswalt,
General Reviewer
Asbury Theological Seminary

ISAIAH

John N. Oswalt, *Asbury Theological Seminary*

Gary Smith, *Bethel Theological Seminary*

John Walton, *Moody Bible Institute*

JEREMIAH/LAMENTATIONS

G. Herbert Livingston, *Asbury Theological Seminary*

Elmer A. Martens, *Mennonite Brethren Biblical Seminary*

EZEKIEL

Daniel I. Block, *The Southern Baptist Theological Seminary*

David H. Engelhard, *Calvin Theological Seminary*

David Thompson, *Asbury Theological Seminary*

DANIEL/HAGGAI/ ZECHARIAH/MALACHI

Joyce Baldwin Caine (deceased), *Trinity College, Bristol*

Douglas Gropp, *Catholic University of America*

Roy Hayden, *Oral Roberts School of Theology*

HOSEA–ZEPHANIAH

Joseph Coleson, *Nazarene Theological Seminary*

Andrew Hill, *Wheaton College*

Richard Patterson, *Professor Emeritus, Liberty University*

GOSPELS AND ACTS

Grant R. Osborne,
General Reviewer
Trinity Evangelical Divinity School

MATTHEW

Craig Blomberg, *Denver Conservative Baptist Seminary*

Donald A. Hagner, *Fuller Theological Seminary*

David Turner, *Grand Rapids Baptist Seminary*

MARK

Robert Guelich (deceased), *Fuller Theological Seminary*

Grant R. Osborne, *Trinity Evangelical Divinity School*

LUKE

Darrel Bock, *Dallas Theological Seminary*

Scot McKnight, *North Park College*

Robert Stein, *Bethel Theological Seminary*

JOHN

Gary M. Burge, *Wheaton College*

Philip W. Comfort, *Wheaton College*

Marianne Meye Thompson, *Fuller Theological Seminary*

ACTS

D. A. Carson, *Trinity Evangelical Divinity School*

William J. Larkin, *Columbia Biblical Seminary*

Roger Mohrlang, *Whitworth College*

LETTERS AND REVELATION

Norman R. Ericson,
General Reviewer
Wheaton College

ROMANS/GALATIANS

Gerald Borchert, *The Southern Baptist Theological Seminary*

Douglas J. Moo, *Trinity Evangelical Divinity School*

Thomas R. Schreiner, *Bethel Theological Seminary*

1 & 2 CORINTHIANS

Joseph Alexanian, *Trinity International University*

Linda Belleville, *North Park Theological Seminary*

Douglas A. Oss, *Central Bible College*

Robert Sloan, *Baylor University*

EPHESIANS–PHILEMON

Harold W. Hoehner, *Dallas Theological Seminary*

Moises Silva, *Gordon-Conwell Theological Seminary*

Klyne Snodgrass, *North Park Theological Seminary*

HEBREWS/JAMES/ 1 & 2 PETER/JUDE

Peter Davids, *Canadian Theological Seminary*

Norman R. Ericson, *Wheaton College*

William Lane (deceased), *Seattle Pacific University*

J. Ramsey Michaels, *S.W. Missouri State University*

1–3 JOHN/REVELATION

Greg Beale, *Gordon-Conwell Theological Seminary*

Robert Mounce, *Whitworth College*

M. Robert Mulholland Jr., *Asbury Theological Seminary*

SPECIAL REVIEWERS

F. F. Bruce (deceased), *University of Manchester*

Kenneth N. Taylor (deceased), *Tyndale House Publishers*

COORDINATING TEAM

Mark R. Norton,
Managing Editor and O.T. Coordinating Editor

Philip W. Comfort, *N.T. Coordinating Editor*

Ronald A. Beers, *Executive Director and Stylist*

Mark D. Taylor, *Director and Chief Stylist*

Daniel W. Taylor, *Consultant*

THE NEW TESTAMENT is a book about recovery. It looks back to the Old Testament Scriptures, which record God's good creation of our world, but then sin's entrance on the scene through the bad choices of God's highest creation—the human race. The Old Testament reveals the painful consequences of sin and the fall and the beginnings of God's plan for our recovery from its powerful grip. The New Testament completes this story through the amazing life and sacrificial death of God's son, Jesus Christ. It is through him that we can discover the source and power for our own deliverance. The Scriptures provide us with the only real pathway to wholeness—God's program for forgiveness, reconciliation, and healing.

Each feature in the *Life Recovery New Testament* leads to the powerful resources for recovery found in the New Testament Scriptures:

DEVOTIONAL READING PLANS

Each devotional is set near the Scripture it comments on and directs the reader to the next devotional in the reading chain. To get a bird's-eye view of each of these reading plans, turn to the indexes at the back of this Bible.

* The **Twelve Step Devotional Reading Plan** includes fifty-two Bible-based devotionals built around the Twelve Steps.
To begin this reading plan, turn to page 73.
* The **Recovery Principle Devotional Reading Plan** is composed of forty Bible-based devotionals shaped around principles important in the recovery process.
To begin this reading plan, turn to page 7.
* The **Serenity Prayer Devotional Reading Plan** is made up of sixteen Bible-based devotionals related to the Serenity Prayer.
To begin this reading plan, turn to page 13.

RECOVERY PROFILES

In this feature twenty individuals and relationships are profiled, and important recovery lessons are drawn from their lives. For a quick view of the profiles included, see the Index to Recovery Profiles on page 642.

INTRODUCTORY MATERIAL FOR BIBLE BOOKS

Each book of the Bible is preceded by a number of helpful features.

✻ **Book Introduction** presents the content and themes from the standpoint of recovery.

✻ **The Big Picture** gives a panoramic view of the book in outline form.

✻ **The Bottom Line** provides vital historical information for the book.

✻ **Recovery Themes** present and discuss important themes for people in recovery.

RECOVERY COMMENTARY NOTES

The Bible text is supported by numerous **Recovery Notes** that pinpoint passages and thoughts important to recovery. The notes appear at the foot of each page and are indexed in the Life Recovery Topical Index beginning on page 613.

✻ Additional commentary material is provided in the **Recovery Reflections** that follow many of the Bible books. The notes in these sections are arranged topically. The topics discussed are indexed in the Index to Recovery Reflections on page 647.

INDEXES

The **Life Recovery Topical Index** guides the reader to the important notes, profiles, devotionals, and recovery themes related to more than a hundred terms important to issues in the recovery process.

✻ The **Index to Recovery Profiles** lists and locates the twenty Recovery Profiles in the order they appear.

✻ The **Index to Twelve Step Devotionals** lists and locates the fifty-two Twelve Step devotionals.

✻ The **Index to Recovery Principle Devotionals** lists and locates the forty Recovery Principle devotionals.

✻ The **Index to Serenity Prayer Devotionals** lists and locates the sixteen Serenity Prayer devotionals.

✻ The **Index to Recovery Reflections** lists and locates the various topics discussed in the Reflections feature of this Bible.

v

STEPS FOR RECOVERY

The 12 Steps have long been of great help to people in recovery. Much of their power comes from the fact that they capture principles evident in the Bible. The following chart lists the 12 Steps and connects them to various Scriptures that support them. A third column ties the 12 Steps to the 8 Recovery Principles of the Celebrate Recovery program. This will enable users of this New Testament who are familiar with the 8 Recovery Principles to relate quickly to content tied to the 12 Steps.

The 12 Steps	Help from the Scriptures	8 Recovery Principles
Step 1: We admitted that we were powerless over our dependencies— that our lives had become unmanageable.	*"I know that I am rotten through and through. . . . I can't make myself do right. I want to, but I can't"* (Romans 7:18; see also John 8:31-36; Romans 7:14-25).	**Principle 1: R**ealize I'm not God. I admit that I am powerless to control my tendency to do the wrong thing and that my life is unmanageable.
Step 2: We came to believe that a Power greater than ourselves could restore us to sanity.	*"God is working in you, giving you the desire to obey him and the power to do what pleases him"* (Philippians 2:13; see also Romans 4:6-8; Ephesians 1:6-8; Colossians 1:21-22; Hebrews 11:1-10).	**Principle 2: E**arnestly believe that God exists, that I matter to Him, and that He has the power to help me to recover.
Step 3: We made a decision to turn our wills and our lives over to the care of God.	*"Dear brothers and sisters, I plead with you to give your bodies to God. Let them be a living and holy sacrifice—the kind he will accept"* (Romans 12:1; see also Matthew 11:28-30; Mark 10:14-16; James 4:7-10).	**Principle 3: C**onsciously choose to commit all my life and will to Christ's care and control.
Step 4: We made a searching and fearless moral inventory of our-selves.	*"God can use sorrow in our lives to help us turn away from sin and seek salvation"* (2 Corinthians 7:10; see also Lamentations 3:40; Matthew 7:1-5).	**Principle 4: O**penly examine and confess my faults to myself, to God, and to someone I trust.
Step 5: We admitted to God, to ourselves, and to another human being the exact nature of our wrongs.	*"Confess your sins to each other and pray for each other so that you may be healed"* (James 5:16; see also Psalm 32:1-5; 51:1-3; 1 John 1:2-6).	
Step 6: We were entirely ready to have God remove all these defects of character.	*"When you bow down before the Lord and admit your dependence on him, he will lift you up and give you honor"* (James 4:10; see also Romans 6:5-11; Philippians 3:12-14).	**Principle 5: V**oluntarily submit to every change God wants to make in my life, and humbly ask Him to remove my character defects.
Step 7: We humbly asked God to remove our shortcomings.	*"If we confess our sins to him, he is faithful and just to forgive us our sins and to cleanse us from every wrong"* (1 John 1:9; see also Luke 18:9-14; 1 John 5:13-15).	

The 12 Steps	Help from the Scriptures	8 Recovery Principles
Step 8: We made a list of all the persons we had harmed and became willing to make amends to them all.	*"Do for others as you would like them to do for you"* (Luke 6:31; see also Colossians 3:12-15; 1 John 3:10-20).	**Principle 6: E**valuate all my relationships. Offer forgiveness to those who have hurt me and make amends for harm I've done to others, except when to do so would harm them or others.
Step 9: We made direct amends to such people wherever possible, except when to do so would injure them or others.	*"If you are standing before the altar in the Temple, offering a sacrifice to God, and . . . someone has something against you, leave your sacrifice there beside the altar. Go and be reconciled to that person. Then come and offer your sacrifice to God"* (Matthew 5:23-24; see also Luke 19:1-10; 1 Peter 2:21-25).	
Step 10: We continued to take personal inventory, and when we were wrong, promptly admitted it.	*"If you think you are standing strong, be careful, for you, too, may fall into the same sin"* (1 Corinthians 10:12; see also Romans 5:3-6; 2 Timothy 2:1-7; 1 John 1:8-10).	**Principle 7: R**eserve a daily time with God for self-examination, Bible reading, and prayer in order to know God and His will for my life and to gain the power to follow His will.
Step 11: We sought through prayer and meditation to improve our conscious contact with God, praying only for knowledge of His will for us and the power to carry that out.	*"Devote yourselves to prayer with an alert mind and a thankful heart"* (Colossians 4:2; see also Isaiah 40:28-31; 1 Timothy 4:7-8).	
Step 12: Having had a spiritual awakening as the result of these steps, we tried to carry this message to others and to practice these principles in all our affairs.	*"Dear brothers and sisters, if another Christian is overcome by some sin, you who are godly should gently and humbly help that person back onto the right path. And be careful not to fall into the same temptation yourself"* (Galatians 6:1; see also Isaiah 61:1-3; Titus 3:3-7; 1 Peter 4:1-5).	**Principle 8: Y**ield myself to God to be used to bring this Good News to others, both by my example and by my words.

THE NEW TESTAMENT is the greatest book on recovery ever written. In its pages we meet numerous individuals whose hurting lives are restored through the wisdom and power of God. We meet the God who is waiting with arms outstretched for all of us to turn back to him, seek after his will, and recover the wonderful plan he has for each of us.

Many of us are just waking up to the fact that recovery is an essential part of life for everyone. It is the simple but challenging process of daily seeking God's will for our life instead of demanding to go our own way. Recovery is letting God do for us what we cannot do for ourself, while also taking the steps necessary to draw closer to our Creator and Redeemer. It is a process of allowing God to heal our wounded soul so we can help others in the process of healing. All of us need to take part in this process; it is an inherent part of being human.

Let us set out together on the journey toward healing and newfound strength—not strength found within ourself, but strength found through trusting God and allowing him to direct our decisions and plans. This journey will take us through the Twelve Steps and other materials designed to help us focus on the provisions our powerful God offers for recovery. The *Life Recovery New Testament* will enrich our experience and expand our understanding of the God who loves us and sent his Son to die that we might be made whole.

Without God there is no recovery, only disappointing substitutions and repeated failure. We pray that the resources within these pages will help us all better understand who God is and how he wants to heal our brokenness and set us on the path toward wholeness.

MATTHEW

THE BIG PICTURE

Many Jews of Jesus' day harbored some form of "messianic hope." They were suffering at the hands of their Roman oppressors and clung to the belief that a Savior would emerge to deliver them. Based on the Old Testament promises of a delivering king, they eagerly awaited the Messiah's coming.

God wanted the world to accept Jesus as the Messiah and Savior. Through Jesus' ancestry, virgin birth, fulfillment of Old Testament prophecies, teachings, and miracles, God demonstrated who Jesus was. But during Jesus' earthly ministry, most people were unwilling to face the reality of who he was. Instead of looking to him as their long-awaited Messiah, they crucified him. And instead of finding deliverance, they remained in a state of oppression.

To deal with our problems, we may have focused our hopes on various "deliverers." Some of us are still looking to our addiction for deliverance from inner pain, a choice that only leads to greater suffering. Some of us hope for "freedom" through recovery programs that emphasize "self-actualization," but these programs only lead us away from our true Deliverer. The Gospel of Matthew makes it clear that our only hope for recovery lies in Jesus the Messiah.

Jesus deserves our trust and commitment as we seek recovery from our dependency and sins. When we rely on the power of forgiveness gained through his death and the hope for new life found in his resurrection, we have true hope for genuine recovery. But it is up to us to place our hope in God. We must let go of our selfish denial and make Jesus the king of our life. He alone is worthy of that honor and responsibility.

THE BOTTOM LINE

PURPOSE: To prove that Jesus was the promised Messiah and to show that God offers recovery to anyone through him. AUTHOR: Matthew, the apostle and former tax collector. AUDIENCE: Matthew wrote primarily for Jewish readers. DATE WRITTEN: Probably between A.D. 60 and 65. SETTING: Matthew emphasized the fulfillment of Old Testament prophecy in the person of Jesus Christ, making this Gospel the connecting link between Old and New Testaments. KEY VERSE: "Don't misunderstand why I have come. I did not come to abolish the law of Moses or the writings of the prophets. No, I came to fulfill them" (5:17). KEY PEOPLE AND RELATIONSHIPS: Jesus in relationship with his ancestors, Mary and Joseph, John the Baptist, Jesus' disciples, and the Jewish and Roman leaders.

RECOVERY THEMES

The Power of the Resurrection: Sometimes we look for the power for recovery within ourself. We don't want to depend on a power that is outside of us. But the power within us can be only as strong as we are, and we have already recognized that we are powerless. In the Gospels God demonstrated his power in many ways, but the ultimate example was in the resurrection of Jesus Christ. In his victory over sin and death, Jesus established his credentials as king and his power and authority over all evil. That's the kind of power we need in recovery. It is available to us when we turn our life over to him.

The Importance of Hope: Without hope we are miserable; hope is the driving force behind all recovery. If we had no hope, there would be no possibility of recovery. Understanding who Jesus is gives each of us a hope that can transcend even our deepest despair. In the Gospel of Matthew, we see and hear the message of hope that is available to everyone, not just to a select group of people. Jesus' resurrection forms the basis of our hope because in it God demonstrated his power over death.

The Dangers of Denial: Often people say that if they could just see a miracle, they would believe. But as we see in Matthew, many people denied the truth about Jesus despite the miracles he did for them. Our denial system is well entrenched. God can handle our doubts and fears, but cynicism and unbelief shut us off from his transforming power. Let us be like the disciples, who stood in awe on the Mount of Transfiguration and wondered what kind of man Jesus was. That kind of openness facilitates the recovery process.

God's Kingdom—A Model for Recovery: Jesus came to earth to inaugurate his Kingdom. His complete rule, however, will be realized only when he returns. His Kingdom will be made up of all those who, in faith, have turned their lives over to God and sought to follow him. We begin the recovery process by believing in him. But living as children of the King requires moment-by-moment acts of faith and trust. Recovery works the same way. Just as in this life we never fully enter into God's Kingdom, we never really finish recovery. We look forward to that day when we will see Jesus face to face and know that our recovery is complete—in him.

CHAPTER 1
The Record of Jesus' Ancestors

This is a record of the ancestors of Jesus the Messiah, a descendant of King David and of Abraham:

2 Abraham was the father of Isaac.
Isaac was the father of Jacob.
Jacob was the father of Judah and his
brothers.
3 Judah was the father of Perez and Zerah
(their mother was Tamar).
Perez was the father of Hezron.
Hezron was the father of Ram.*
4 Ram was the father of Amminadab.
Amminadab was the father of Nahshon.
Nahshon was the father of Salmon.

5 Salmon was the father of Boaz (his
mother was Rahab).
Boaz was the father of Obed (his
mother was Ruth).
Obed was the father of Jesse.
6 Jesse was the father of King David.
David was the father of Solomon (his
mother was Bathsheba, the widow
of Uriah).
7 Solomon was the father of
Rehoboam.
Rehoboam was the father of Abijah.
Abijah was the father of Asaph.*
8 Asaph was the father of Jehoshaphat.
Jehoshaphat was the father of
Jehoram.*
Jehoram was the father* of Uzziah.

1:3 Greek *Aram;* also in 1:4. See 1 Chr 2:9-10. **1:7** *Asaph* is the same person as Asa; also in 1:8. See 1 Chr 3:10. **1:8a** Greek *Joram.* See 1 Kgs 22:50 and note at 1 Chr 3:11. **1:8b** Or *ancestor;* also in 1:11.

1:1-16 The family tree of Jesus, the sinless God-man, was far from perfect. Judah fathered Perez with his daughter-in-law Tamar, thinking she was a prostitute (1:3; Genesis 38); Salmon married Rahab, a former prostitute in Jericho (1:5; Joshua 6); and David had an adulterous affair with Uriah's wife, Bathsheba (1:6; 2 Samuel 11). Throughout history God has used imperfect people to work his will. He was more concerned about the attitude of their heart than about the mistakes they made. God is never fooled or discouraged by people's past mistakes. This should give us hope that God can give us a productive future no matter how destructive our past has been. For a new start, we must admit our sins and commit our life to God.

JOSEPH & MARY

Trust can be rebuilt when it has been broken, but this does not happen automatically. Such a process takes work and commitment, especially when a relationship has been threatened by unfaithfulness. This was the challenge that Joseph and Mary faced.

Months before their planned wedding, Mary became pregnant. Because Joseph knew that this was not his child, he assumed that she had been unfaithful to him. Though he was troubled by doubts and anger, he chose to break off the engagement as inconspicuously as possible. He was a man of integrity and mercy, so he did not want to hurt or embarrass Mary.

God had other plans, however. He sent an angel to speak to Joseph and assured him that Mary's baby had been supernaturally conceived by the Holy Spirit. The child's name would be Jesus, and he would be the Savior of the world, the one who would offer spiritual recovery to all. Because Joseph believed God, his perspective changed. Mary and Joseph's mutual commitment to and trust in God served as the foundation upon which their trust in each other could be reestablished.

Mary and Joseph humbly and joyfully entered a new life together. Joseph did all that was possible to protect Mary and the baby Jesus when he was born. He became a loving father who carefully taught his son the carpentry trade. Mary was an attentive and caring mother. This relationship demonstrates that it is possible to rebuild trust and repair love in relationships that were once very fragile.

The story of Joseph and Mary is told in the Gospels, notably in Matthew 1–2 and Luke 1–2. Mary is also mentioned in Acts 1:14.

STRENGTHS AND ACCOMPLISHMENTS:
- Joseph and Mary's relationship was founded on their commitment to God.
- They were open to God's will and willing to change their opinions.
- They obeyed God despite the embarrassment they would suffer.

WEAKNESSES AND MISTAKES:
- Joseph did not give Mary the benefit of the doubt early in her pregnancy.
- They failed to understand Jesus' need to spend time in his Father's house.

LESSONS FROM THEIR LIVES:
- Relationships should not be destroyed by unsubstantiated doubts.
- Trust can always be rebuilt if God is at the center of a relationship.
- Things are not always what they seem to be.
- Trust in God is foundational for trust between people.

KEY VERSES:
"Joseph . . . decided to break the engagement quietly, so as not to disgrace her publicly. As he considered this, he fell asleep, and an angel of the Lord appeared to him in a dream. 'Joseph, son of David,' the angel said, 'do not be afraid to go ahead with your marriage to Mary. For the child within her has been conceived by the Holy Spirit'" (Matthew 1:19-20).

---

⁹ Uzziah was the father of Jotham.
Jotham was the father of Ahaz.
Ahaz was the father of Hezekiah.
¹⁰ Hezekiah was the father of Manasseh.
Manasseh was the father of Amos.*
Amos was the father of Josiah.
¹¹ Josiah was the father of Jehoiachin*
and his brothers (born at the time of the exile to Babylon).
¹² After the Babylonian exile:
Jehoiachin was the father of Shealtiel.
Shealtiel was the father of Zerubbabel.
¹³ Zerubbabel was the father of Abiud.
Abiud was the father of Eliakim.
Eliakim was the father of Azor.

¹⁴ Azor was the father of Zadok.
Zadok was the father of Akim.
Akim was the father of Eliud.
¹⁵ Eliud was the father of Eleazar.
Eleazar was the father of Matthan.
Matthan was the father of Jacob.
¹⁶ Jacob was the father of Joseph, the husband of Mary.
Mary was the mother of Jesus, who is called the Messiah.

¹⁷All those listed above include fourteen generations from Abraham to King David, and fourteen from David's time to the Babylonian exile, and fourteen from the Babylonian exile to the Messiah.

1:10 *Amos* is the same person as Amon. See 1 Chr 3:14. **1:11** Greek *Jeconiah;* also in 1:12. See 2 Kgs 24:6 and note at 1 Chr 3:16.

The Birth of Jesus the Messiah

18Now this is how Jesus the Messiah was born. His mother, Mary, was engaged to be married to Joseph. But while she was still a virgin, she became pregnant by the Holy Spirit. 19Joseph, her fiancé, being a just man, decided to break the engagement quietly, so as not to disgrace her publicly.

20As he considered this, he fell asleep, and an angel of the Lord appeared to him in a dream. "Joseph, son of David," the angel said, "do not be afraid to go ahead with your marriage to Mary. For the child within her has been conceived by the Holy Spirit. 21And she will have a son, and you are to name him Jesus,* for he will save his people from their sins." 22All of this happened to fulfill the Lord's message through his prophet:

23 "Look! The virgin will conceive a child!
    She will give birth to a son,
    and he will be called Immanuel*
    (meaning, God is with us)."

24When Joseph woke up, he did what the angel of the Lord commanded. He brought Mary home to be his wife, 25but she remained a virgin until her son was born. And Joseph named him Jesus.

CHAPTER 2
The Visit of the Wise Men

Jesus was born in the town of Bethlehem in Judea, during the reign of King Herod. About that time some wise men* from eastern lands arrived in Jerusalem, asking, 2"Where is the newborn king of the Jews? We have seen his star as it arose,* and we have come to worship him."

3Herod was deeply disturbed by their question, as was all of Jerusalem. 4He called a meeting of the leading priests and teachers of religious law. "Where did the prophets say the Messiah would be born?" he asked them.

5"In Bethlehem," they said, "for this is what the prophet wrote:

6 'O Bethlehem of Judah,
    you are not just a lowly village in Judah,
for a ruler will come from you
    who will be the shepherd for my people
        Israel.'*"

7Then Herod sent a private message to the wise men, asking them to come see him. At this meeting he learned the exact time when they first saw the star. 8Then he told them, "Go to Bethlehem and search carefully for the child. And when you find him, come back and tell me so that I can go and worship him, too!"

9After this interview the wise men went their way. Once again the star appeared to them, guiding them to Bethlehem. It went ahead of them and stopped over the place where the child was. 10When they saw the star, they were filled with joy! 11They entered the house where the child and his mother, Mary, were, and they fell down before him and worshiped him. Then they opened their treasure chests and gave him gifts of gold, frankincense, and myrrh. 12But when it was time to leave, they went home another way, because God had warned them in a dream not to return to Herod.

The Escape to Egypt

13After the wise men were gone, an angel of the Lord appeared to Joseph in a dream. "Get

1:21 *Jesus* means "The LORD saves." **1:23** Isa 7:14; 8:8, 10. **2:1** Or *royal astrologers;* Greek reads *magi;* also in 2:7, 16. **2:2** Or *in the east.* **2:6** Mic 5:2; 2 Sam 5:2.

1:18-19 Joseph reacted to the implications of Mary's pregnancy by deciding to break their engagement. Although he was a man of principle and well intentioned, his choice was still shortsighted (see 1:20-23). Attitudes and decisions based on incomplete understandings are significant problems related to recovery. Patience, honesty, and perseverance in communication are crucial to preventing far-reaching mistakes, such as broken relationships.

2:3-8, 12-18 King Herod was a tyrant who could charm and manipulate others to achieve his ends. Herod thought he could get information about the identity and whereabouts of the Messiah from the wise men by feigning interest in and a desire to worship him. Frequently, abusive or oppressive personalities will "play along" in the earliest stages of recovery, hoping to crush any resistance to their domination later. We need to be careful to avoid such people, as did the wise men and Joseph.

3:1-2 John the Baptist preached a centuries-old message: repentance. People could easily have dismissed his message by saying, "I've heard this before" or "I'll quit sinning tomorrow." But John presented the need for an immediate moral U-turn with fresh urgency: "The Kingdom of Heaven is near." Repentance requires honest self-examination. The sense of urgency in John's message is similar to the urgency for recovery. There is no time like the present to face reality and turn from our self-destructive behavior.

up and flee to Egypt with the child and his mother," the angel said. "Stay there until I tell you to return, because Herod is going to try to kill the child." ¹⁴That night Joseph left for Egypt with the child and Mary, his mother, ¹⁵and they stayed there until Herod's death. This fulfilled what the Lord had spoken through the prophet: "I called my Son out of Egypt."*

¹⁶Herod was furious when he learned that the wise men had outwitted him. He sent soldiers to kill all the boys in and around Bethlehem who were two years old and under, because the wise men had told him the star first appeared to them about two years earlier.* ¹⁷Herod's brutal action fulfilled the prophecy of Jeremiah:

¹⁸ "A cry of anguish is heard in Ramah—
     weeping and mourning unrestrained.
  Rachel weeps for her children,
     refusing to be comforted—for they are
       dead."*

The Return to Nazareth

¹⁹When Herod died, an angel of the Lord appeared in a dream to Joseph in Egypt and told him, ²⁰"Get up and take the child and his mother back to the land of Israel, because those who were trying to kill the child are dead." ²¹So Joseph returned immediately to Israel with Jesus and his mother. ²²But when he learned that the new ruler was Herod's son Archelaus, he was afraid. Then, in another dream, he was warned to go to Galilee. ²³So they went and lived in a town called Nazareth. This fulfilled what was spoken by the prophets concerning the Messiah: "He will be called a Nazarene."

CHAPTER 3
John the Baptist Prepares the Way
In those days John the Baptist began preaching in the Judean wilderness. His message was, ²"Turn from your sins and turn to God, because the Kingdom of Heaven is near.*" ³Isaiah had spoken of John when he said,

"He is a voice shouting in the wilderness:
  'Prepare a pathway for the Lord's coming!
    Make a straight road for him!'"*

⁴John's clothes were woven from camel hair, and he wore a leather belt; his food was locusts and wild honey. ⁵People from Jerusalem and from every section of Judea and from all

2:15 Hos 11:1. **2:16** Or *according to the time he calculated from the wise men.* **2:18** Jer 31:15. **3:2** Or *has come* or *is coming soon.* **3:3** Isa 40:3.

▶ The recovery principle devotional reading plan begins here.

Delayed Gratification

READ MATTHEW 4:1-11

We may be searching for shortcuts to happiness. The road of life often takes us through painful places we would rather avoid. Some of us have gotten off the right track, lured away by hopes of faster and easier ways to "the good life."

Jesus faced this same temptation. He was destined to become the King of all the earth. The plan was that he would come to earth as a man, live a sinless life, die to pay for our sins, rise from the dead, and return to heaven to wait for those who would be his. Then he would return to earth to claim his people and his rightful place as King of kings. Satan offered Jesus a shortcut. "The Devil . . . showed him the nations of the world and all their glory. 'I will give it all to you,' he said, 'if you will only kneel down and worship me.' 'Get out of here, Satan,' Jesus told him. 'For the Scriptures say, "You must worship the Lord your God; serve only him"'" (Matthew 4:8-10). If Jesus had fallen for this trick, he would have sinned and lost everything.

We need to beware of "shortcuts" that take us even one step outside of God's will. We are warned: "Resist the Devil, and he will flee from you" (James 4:7). We can show this resistance by ignoring offers that are "too good to be true." There are really no quick fixes in life. The path of recovery can be long and hard, but many have gone before us and have been successful. As we stay on the path, taking one step at a time, we'll find the good things in life God has for us.
Turn to page 11, Matthew 6.

over the Jordan Valley went out to the wilderness to hear him preach. 6And when they confessed their sins, he baptized them in the Jordan River.

7But when he saw many Pharisees and Sadducees coming to be baptized, he denounced them. "You brood of snakes!" he exclaimed. "Who warned you to flee God's coming judgment? 8Prove by the way you live that you have really turned from your sins and turned to God. 9Don't just say, 'We're safe—we're the descendants of Abraham.' That proves nothing. God can change these stones here into children of Abraham. 10Even now the ax of God's judgment is poised, ready to sever your roots. Yes, every tree that does not produce good fruit will be chopped down and thrown into the fire.

11"I baptize with* water those who turn from their sins and turn to God. But someone is coming soon who is far greater than I am—so much greater that I am not even worthy to be his slave.* He will baptize you with the Holy Spirit and with fire.* 12He is ready to separate the chaff from the grain with his winnowing fork. Then he will clean up the threshing area, storing the grain in his barn but burning the chaff with never-ending fire."

The Baptism of Jesus

13Then Jesus went from Galilee to the Jordan River to be baptized by John. 14But John didn't want to baptize him. "I am the one who needs to be baptized by you," he said, "so why are you coming to me?"

15But Jesus said, "It must be done, because we must do everything that is right.*" So then John baptized him.

16After his baptism, as Jesus came up out of the water, the heavens were opened and he saw the Spirit of God descending like a dove and settling on him. 17And a voice from heaven said, "This is my beloved Son, and I am fully pleased with him."

CHAPTER 4

The Temptation of Jesus

Then Jesus was led out into the wilderness by the Holy Spirit to be tempted there by the Devil. 2For forty days and forty nights he ate nothing and became very hungry. 3Then the Devil* came and said to him, "If you are the Son of God, change these stones into loaves of bread."

4But Jesus told him, "No! The Scriptures say,

'People need more than bread for their life;
    they must feed on every word of God.'*"

5Then the Devil took him to Jerusalem, to the highest point of the Temple, 6and said, "If you are the Son of God, jump off! For the Scriptures say,

'He orders his angels to protect you.
And they will hold you with their hands
    to keep you from striking your foot on
    a stone.'*"

7Jesus responded, "The Scriptures also say, 'Do not test the Lord your God.'*"

8Next the Devil took him to the peak of a very high mountain and showed him the nations of the world and all their glory. 9"I will give it all to you," he said, "if you will only kneel down and worship me."

10"Get out of here, Satan," Jesus told him. "For the Scriptures say,

3:11a Or *in.* **3:11b** Greek *to carry his sandals.* **3:11c** Or *in the Holy Spirit and in fire.* **3:15** Or *we must fulfill all righteousness.* **4:3** Greek *the tempter.* **4:4** Deut 8:3. **4:6** Ps 91:11-12. **4:7** Deut 6:16.

3:16-17 After Jesus' baptism, the Holy Spirit was seen in visible form, and the Father commended his Son. Jesus is thus shown to be in perfect harmony with his Father and the Holy Spirit. While those of us seeking recovery will never have perfect unity in our relationships, we can draw support from those who affirm us. As we study the Bible, God's love letter to the human race, we see numerous evidences of God's unlimited love for us. Knowing how much our heavenly Father loves us can help offset the lack of love and affirmation from our earthly relationships.

4:3-7 Satan did not doubt that Jesus was the Son of God. Satan appealed to real needs and possible doubts that were common to all humanity. Like us, Jesus needed food, security, protection, significance, and achievement. Had Jesus faltered in his humanity, Satan could have called into question Jesus' right to rule and his perfection as the unique God-man. Similarly, Satan and his forces will attack those of us pursuing recovery at our most vulnerable points. It is important that we be on guard against these attacks.

4:12-16 The way of recovery through Jesus Christ is open to everyone, not just the "religious." Jesus can heal anyone, regardless of past history, religious affiliation, or nationality. Jesus himself proved this by spending his early years in the cosmopolitan region of Galilee. The Jews in this area were not considered "good Jews" by those in Judea because of their contact with the many Gentiles who lived there. But Jesus showed God's love for them. And he continues to show his love to all who trust him, no matter who we are or how great our past sins.

'You must worship the Lord your God; serve only him.'*"

[11]Then the Devil went away, and angels came and cared for Jesus.

The Ministry of Jesus Begins

[12]When Jesus heard that John had been arrested, he left Judea and returned to Galilee. [13]But instead of going to Nazareth, he went to Capernaum, beside the Sea of Galilee, in the region of Zebulun and Naphtali. [14]This fulfilled Isaiah's prophecy:

[15] "In the land of Zebulun and of Naphtali,
    beside the sea, beyond the Jordan
        River—
    in Galilee where so many Gentiles live—
[16]the people who sat in darkness
    have seen a great light.
And for those who lived in the land where
        death casts its shadow,
    a light has shined."*

[17]From then on, Jesus began to preach, "Turn from your sins and turn to God, because the Kingdom of Heaven is near.*"

The First Disciples

[18]One day as Jesus was walking along the shore beside the Sea of Galilee, he saw two brothers—Simon, also called Peter, and Andrew—fishing with a net, for they were commercial fishermen. [19]Jesus called out to them, "Come, be my disciples, and I will show you how to fish for people!" [20]And they left their nets at once and went with him.

[21]A little farther up the shore he saw two other brothers, James and John, sitting in a boat with their father, Zebedee, mending their nets. And he called them to come, too. [22]They immediately followed him, leaving the boat and their father behind.

The Ministry of Jesus in Galilee

[23]Jesus traveled throughout Galilee teaching in the synagogues, preaching everywhere the Good News about the Kingdom. And he healed people who had every kind of sickness and disease. [24]News about him spread far beyond the borders of Galilee so that the sick were soon coming to be healed from as far away as Syria. And whatever their illness and pain, or if they were possessed by demons, or were epileptics, or were paralyzed—he healed them all. [25]Large crowds followed him wherever he went—people from Galilee, the Ten Towns,* Jerusalem,

4:10 Deut 6:13. **4:15-16** Isa 9:1-2. **4:17** Or *has come* or *is coming soon.* **4:25** Greek *Decapolis.*

STEP 9

Making Peace

BIBLE READING: Matthew 5:23-25

We made direct amends to such people wherever possible, except when to do so would injure them or others.

We all suffer brokenness in our life, in our relationship with God, and in our relationships with others. Brokenness tends to weigh us down and can easily lead us back into our addiction. Recovery isn't complete until all areas of brokenness are mended.

Jesus taught: "So if you are standing before the altar in the Temple, offering a sacrifice to God, and you suddenly remember that someone has something against you, leave your sacrifice there beside the altar. Go and be reconciled to that person. Then come and offer your sacrifice to God" (Matthew 5:23-24). The apostle John wrote: "If someone says, 'I love God,' but hates a Christian brother or sister, that person is a liar; for if we don't love people we can see, how can we love God, whom we have not seen?" (1 John 4:20).

Much of recovery involves repairing the brokenness in our life. This requires that we make peace with God, with ourself, and with others whom we have alienated. Unresolved issues in relationships can keep us from being at peace with God and ourself. Once we go through the process of making amends, we must keep our mind and heart open to anyone we may have overlooked. God will often remind us of relationships that need attention. We should not delay going to those we have offended and seeking to repair the damage we have caused. *Turn to page 129, Luke 19.*

from all over Judea, and from east of the Jordan River.

CHAPTER 5
The Sermon on the Mount
One day as the crowds were gathering, Jesus went up the mountainside with his disciples and sat down to teach them.

The Beatitudes
²This is what he taught them:

³"God blesses those who realize their need
      for him,*
   for the Kingdom of Heaven is given
      to them.
⁴God blesses those who mourn,
   for they will be comforted.
⁵God blesses those who are gentle and lowly,
   for the whole earth will belong to them.
⁶God blesses those who are hungry and
      thirsty for justice,
   for they will receive it in full.
⁷God blesses those who are merciful,
   for they will be shown mercy.
⁸God blesses those whose hearts are pure,
   for they will see God.
⁹God blesses those who work for peace,
   for they will be called the children of God.
¹⁰God blesses those who are persecuted
      because they live for God,
   for the Kingdom of Heaven is theirs.

¹¹"God blesses you when you are mocked and persecuted and lied about because you are my followers. ¹²Be happy about it! Be very glad! For a great reward awaits you in heaven. And remember, the ancient prophets were persecuted, too.

Teaching about Salt and Light
¹³"You are the salt of the earth. But what good is salt if it has lost its flavor? Can you make it useful again? It will be thrown out and trampled underfoot as worthless. ¹⁴You are the light of the world—like a city on a mountain, glowing in the night for all to see. ¹⁵Don't hide your light under a basket! Instead, put it on a stand and let it shine for all. ¹⁶In the same way, let your good deeds shine out for all to see, so that everyone will praise your heavenly Father.

Teaching about the Law
¹⁷"Don't misunderstand why I have come. I did not come to abolish the law of Moses or the writings of the prophets. No, I came to fulfill them. ¹⁸I assure you, until heaven and earth disappear, even the smallest detail of God's law will remain until its purpose is achieved. ¹⁹So if you break the smallest commandment and teach others to do the same, you will be the least in the Kingdom of Heaven. But anyone who obeys God's laws and teaches them will be great in the Kingdom of Heaven.

²⁰"But I warn you—unless you obey God better than the teachers of religious law and the Pharisees do, you can't enter the Kingdom of Heaven at all!

Teaching about Anger
²¹"You have heard that the law of Moses says, 'Do not murder. If you commit murder, you are subject to judgment.'* ²²But I say, if you are angry with someone,* you are subject to judgment! If you call someone an idiot,* you are in danger of being brought before the high council. And if you curse someone,* you are in danger of the fires of hell.

²³"So if you are standing before the altar in the Temple, offering a sacrifice to God, and you suddenly remember that someone has something against you, ²⁴leave your sacrifice there beside the altar. Go and be reconciled to that person. Then come and offer your sacrifice to God. ²⁵Come to terms quickly with your enemy before it is too late and you

---

5:3 Greek *the poor in spirit.* **5:21** Exod 20:13; Deut 5:17. **5:22a** Greek *your brother;* also in 5:23. Some manuscripts add *without cause.* **5:22b** Greek uses an Aramaic term of contempt: *If you say to your brother, 'Raca.'* **5:22c** Greek *if you say, 'You fool.'*

5:3-5 We cannot experience God-blessed recovery without true humility. Pride often stands in the way of our dealing with painful problems and a destructive dependency. If we cannot admit our problems and sins, there can be no real cure for us. When we humble ourself before God, we mourn and grieve over our mistakes and losses. As we do this, we will experience the wonderful comfort that only God can offer (see 2 Corinthians 1:3-5).
5:21-22, 27-29 Anger and lust are two dangerous pitfalls that threaten all of us in one way or another. Intense emotions and desires must be dealt with from the inside out. Those of us burning with rage, lust, or some other addictive behavior generally think we can control it. But we eventually and invariably lose control. Jesus shows how the patterns of anger and lust are serious and far too powerful for us to control alone. We can begin the path toward victory by admitting that we are powerless and looking to our powerful God for help.

are dragged into court, handed over to an officer, and thrown in jail. ²⁶I assure you that you won't be free again until you have paid the last penny.

Teaching about Adultery

²⁷"You have heard that the law of Moses says, 'Do not commit adultery.'* ²⁸But I say, anyone who even looks at a woman with lust in his eye has already committed adultery with her in his heart. ²⁹So if your eye—even if it is your good eye*—causes you to lust, gouge it out and throw it away. It is better for you to lose one part of your body than for your whole body to be thrown into hell. ³⁰And if your hand—even if it is your stronger hand*—causes you to sin, cut it off and throw it away. It is better for you to lose one part of your body than for your whole body to be thrown into hell.

Teaching about Divorce

³¹"You have heard that the law of Moses says, 'A man can divorce his wife by merely giving her a letter of divorce.'* ³²But I say that a man who divorces his wife, unless she has been unfaithful, causes her to commit adultery. And anyone who marries a divorced woman commits adultery.

Teaching about Vows

³³"Again, you have heard that the law of Moses says, 'Do not break your vows; you must carry out the vows you have made to the Lord.'* ³⁴But I say, don't make any vows! If you say, 'By heaven!' it is a sacred vow because heaven is God's throne. ³⁵And if you say, 'By the earth!' it is a sacred vow because the earth is his footstool. And don't swear, 'By Jerusalem!' for Jerusalem is the city of the great King. ³⁶Don't even swear, 'By my head!' for you can't turn one hair white or black. ³⁷Just say a simple, 'Yes, I will,' or 'No, I won't.' Your word is enough. To strengthen your promise with a vow shows that something is wrong.*

Teaching about Revenge

³⁸"You have heard that the law of Moses says, 'If an eye is injured, injure the eye of the person who did it. If a tooth gets knocked out, knock out the tooth of the person who did it.'* ³⁹But I say, don't resist an evil person! If you are slapped on the right cheek, turn the other, too. ⁴⁰If you are ordered to court and

5:27 Exod 20:14; Deut 5:18. **5:29** Greek *your right eye*. **5:30** Greek *your right hand*. **5:31** Deut 24:1. **5:33** Num 30:2. **5:37** Or *Anything beyond this is from the evil one*. **5:38** Greek *'An eye for an eye and a tooth for a tooth.'* Exod 21:24; Lev 24:20; Deut 19:21.

Forgiveness

READ MATTHEW 6:9-15

Some of us become so focused on our personal failures in recovery that we don't deal with the pain we have suffered at the hands of others. Some of us, on the other hand, focus too much on the ways we have been mistreated and use these as excuses for our behavior. Either approach to past abuse leaves us with emotional baggage that will hinder our progress in recovery. Forgiving others is an important part of turning our will over to God.

Jesus taught his disciples: "Pray like this: Our Father in heaven, may your name be honored. May your Kingdom come soon. May your will be done here on earth, just as it is in heaven. Give us our food for today, and forgive us our sins, just as we have forgiven those who have sinned against us. And don't let us yield to temptation, but deliver us from the evil one. If you forgive those who sin against you, your heavenly Father will forgive you. But if you refuse to forgive others, your Father will not forgive your sins" (Matthew 6:9-15).

Being forgiven for the wrongs we have done to others does not excuse us from our actions or make our actions right. When we forgive others of the wrongs they have committed against us, we do not excuse what they have done. We simply recognize that we have been hurt unjustly and turn the matter over to God. This helps us face the truth about our own pain. It also rids us of any excuse to continue our compulsive behavior because of what has been done to us. *Turn to page 29, Matthew 15.*

your shirt is taken from you, give your coat, too. ⁴¹If a soldier demands that you carry his gear for a mile,* carry it two miles. ⁴²Give to those who ask, and don't turn away from those who want to borrow.

Teaching about Love for Enemies

⁴³"You have heard that the law of Moses says, 'Love your neighbor'ᴧ and hate your enemy. ⁴⁴But I say, love your enemies!* Pray for those who persecute you! ⁴⁵In that way, you will be acting as true children of your Father in heaven. For he gives his sunlight to both the evil and the good, and he sends rain on the just and on the unjust, too. ⁴⁶If you love only those who love you, what good is that? Even corrupt tax collectors do that much. ⁴⁷If you are kind only to your friends,* how are you different from anyone else? Even pagans do that. ⁴⁸But you are to be perfect, even as your Father in heaven is perfect.

CHAPTER 6
Teaching about Giving to the Needy

"Take care! Don't do your good deeds publicly, to be admired, because then you will lose the reward from your Father in heaven. ²When you give a gift to someone in need, don't shout about it as the hypocrites do—blowing trumpets in the synagogues and streets to call attention to their acts of charity! I assure you, they have received all the reward they will ever get. ³But when you give to someone, don't tell your left hand what your right hand is doing. ⁴Give your gifts in secret, and your Father, who knows all secrets, will reward you.

Teaching about Prayer and Fasting

⁵"And now about prayer. When you pray, don't be like the hypocrites who love to pray publicly on street corners and in the synagogues where everyone can see them. I assure you, that is all the reward they will ever get. ⁶But when you pray, go away by yourself, shut the door behind you, and pray to your Father secretly. Then your Father, who knows all secrets, will reward you.

⁷"When you pray, don't babble on and on as people of other religions do. They think their prayers are answered only by repeating their words again and again. ⁸Don't be like them, because your Father knows exactly what you need even before you ask him! ⁹Pray like this:

Our Father in heaven,
may your name be honored.
¹⁰ May your Kingdom come soon.
May your will be done here on earth,
just as it is in heaven.
¹¹ Give us our food for today,*
¹² and forgive us our sins,
just as we have forgiven those who
have sinned against us.
¹³ And don't let us yield to temptation,
but deliver us from the evil one.*

¹⁴"If you forgive those who sin against you, your heavenly Father will forgive you. ¹⁵But if you refuse to forgive others, your Father will not forgive your sins.

¹⁶"And when you fast, don't make it obvious, as the hypocrites do, who try to look pale and disheveled so people will admire them

---

5:41 Greek *milion* [4,854 feet or 1,478 meters]. **5:43** Lev 19:18. **5:44** Some manuscripts add *Bless those who curse you, do good to those who hate you.* **5:47** Greek *your brothers.* **6:11** Or *for tomorrow.* **6:13** Or *from evil.* Some manuscripts add *For yours is the kingdom and the power and the glory forever. Amen.*

5:43-48 When we love our enemies, we can be sure that we are making progress in recovery. Loving our enemies doesn't mean we have to like them, but it does mean we must forgive them and desire what is best for them. If we harbor anger and bitterness toward others, we hurt only ourself; such emotions keep us from making progress in recovery. God loved us while we were still his enemies (see Romans 5:8); he loves us even though we are far from perfect. Recovery is not perfectionism; it is developing the ability to follow God and shape our decisions and actions according to his will for us.

6:5-8 Public prayer is open to many distortions and abuses. Some individuals use majestic-sounding, churchy jargon that impresses people, but not God. Others think that the key to answered prayer is repetition, thus reducing it almost to a chant or mantra. Both attitudes miss the mark because they assume prayer has more to do with technique than internal attitudes and realities. True heart-to-heart communication with God, whether private or public, is rewarded and will have a profound effect on our progress in recovery.

6:12, 14-15 True forgiveness is an essential part of any recovery program. We often have difficulty getting past our anger and bitterness toward those who have mistreated or abused us. However, asking God's forgiveness for our personal shortcomings and sins is hypocritical unless we are willing to forgive others. We forfeit forgiveness from God by denying forgiveness to others, to the detriment of our recovery program. This is not only selfish but also self-destructive.

READ MATTHEW 6:25-34

▶ **The Serenity Prayer devotional reading plan begins here.**

GOD grant me the serenity to accept the things I cannot change the courage to change the things I can and the wisdom to know the difference AMEN

Living one day at a time is a discipline we all have to focus on when we are in recovery.

It is easy to slip back into worrying about tomorrow, dwelling on the "what ifs" and the "if onlys." Each day brings a host of things we cannot change; there will always be circumstances beyond our control. We must also face the reality of who we are—human beings confined within the slice of life we call today. It is tempting to deny the present, but escaping reality is part of the insanity of our addictive way of life.

Jesus said, "Can all your worries add a single moment to your life? . . . Don't worry about tomorrow, for tomorrow will bring its own worries. Today's trouble is enough for today" (Matthew 6:27, 34). The prophet Jeremiah said, "The unfailing love of the LORD never ends! By his mercies we have been kept from complete destruction. Great is his faithfulness; his mercies begin afresh each day" (Lamentations 3:22-23). Since God's grace comes in daily doses, that's the best way to face life.

We need to ask ourself at every turn in life, Am I accepting this present moment, or am I pretending—trying to escape into the past or the future? Each day there is something to find joy in, and there is strength promised for the troubles of that day. The psalmist wrote, "This is the day the LORD has made. We will rejoice and be glad in it" (Psalm 118:24). We, too, can choose to find joy, strength, and sanity when we accept each day's realities. *Turn to page 27, Matthew 14.*

---

for their fasting. I assure you, that is the only reward they will ever get. [17]But when you fast, comb your hair and wash your face. [18]Then no one will suspect you are fasting, except your Father, who knows what you do in secret. And your Father, who knows all secrets, will reward you.

Teaching about Money and Possessions

[19]"Don't store up treasures here on earth, where they can be eaten by moths and get rusty, and where thieves break in and steal. [20]Store your treasures in heaven, where they will never become moth-eaten or rusty and where they will be safe from thieves. [21]Wherever your treasure is, there your heart and thoughts will also be.

[22]"Your eye is a lamp for your body. A pure eye lets sunshine into your soul. [23]But an evil eye shuts out the light and plunges you into darkness. If the light you think you have is really darkness, how deep that darkness will be!

[24]"No one can serve two masters. For you will hate one and love the other, or be devoted to one and despise the other. You cannot serve both God and money.

[25]"So I tell you, don't worry about everyday life—whether you have enough food, drink, and clothes. Doesn't life consist of more than food and clothing? [26]Look at the birds. They don't need to plant or harvest or put food in barns because your heavenly Father feeds them. And you are far more valuable to him than they are. [27]Can all your worries add a single moment to your life? Of course not.

[28]"And why worry about your clothes? Look at the lilies and how they grow. They don't work or make their clothing, [29]yet Solomon in all his glory was not dressed as beautifully as they are. [30]And if God cares so wonderfully for flowers that are here today and gone tomorrow, won't he more surely care for you? You have so little faith! [31]"So don't worry about having enough

food or drink or clothing. ³²Why be like the pagans who are so deeply concerned about these things? Your heavenly Father already knows all your needs, ³³and he will give you all you need from day to day if you live for him and make the Kingdom of God your primary concern.

³⁴"So don't worry about tomorrow, for tomorrow will bring its own worries. Today's trouble is enough for today.

CHAPTER 7

Don't Condemn Others

"Stop judging others, and you will not be judged. ²For others will treat you as you treat them.* Whatever measure you use in judging others, it will be used to measure how you are judged. ³And why worry about a speck in your friend's eye* when you have a log in your own? ⁴How can you think of saying, 'Let me help you get rid of that speck in your eye,' when you can't see past the log in your own eye? ⁵Hypocrite! First get rid of the log from your own eye; then perhaps you will see well enough to deal with the speck in your friend's eye.

⁶"Don't give what is holy to unholy people.* Don't give pearls to swine! They will trample the pearls, then turn and attack you.

Effective Prayer

⁷"Keep on asking, and you will be given what you ask for. Keep on looking, and you will find. Keep on knocking, and the door will be opened. ⁸For everyone who asks, receives. Everyone who seeks, finds. And the door is opened to everyone who knocks. ⁹You parents—if your children ask for a loaf of bread, do you give them a stone instead? ¹⁰Or if they ask for a fish, do you give them a snake? Of course not! ¹¹If you sinful people know how to give good gifts to your children, how much more will your heavenly Father give good gifts to those who ask him.

The Golden Rule

¹²"Do for others what you would like them to do for you. This is a summary of all that is taught in the law and the prophets.

The Narrow Gate

¹³"You can enter God's Kingdom only through the narrow gate. The highway to hell* is broad, and its gate is wide for the many who choose the easy way. ¹⁴But the gateway to life is small, and the road is narrow, and only a few ever find it.

The Tree and Its Fruit

¹⁵"Beware of false prophets who come disguised as harmless sheep, but are really wolves that will tear you apart. ¹⁶You can detect them by the way they act, just as you can identify a tree by its fruit. You don't pick grapes from thornbushes, or figs from thistles. ¹⁷A healthy tree produces good fruit, and

---

7:2 Or *For God will treat you as you treat others;* Greek reads *For with the judgment you judge you will be judged.* **7:3** Greek *your brother's eye;* also in 7:5. **7:6** Greek *Don't give the sacred to dogs.* **7:13** Greek *The way that leads to destruction.*

7:7-11 Prayer can teach us perseverance. These three commands ("keep on asking," "keep on looking," and "keep on knocking") are positive habits we should develop. We will persist in prayer with realistic hopes once we fully appreciate the kind of father who hears our prayers. Many of us in recovery have suffered because of dysfunctional, even abusive, parents who often gave us "stones" and "snakes." Thus, often we must completely rethink our concept of God as a father who gives good gifts to his children. As we discover God's loving character, we will be encouraged to ask him for the gift of recovery.

7:15-20 The good fruit that our life should be producing is "love, joy, peace, patience, kindness, goodness, faithfulness, gentleness, and self-control" (Galatians 5:22-23). In the throes of an addiction, however, we are without peace and totally out of control. If we take an honest moral inventory, we will admit that the fruits of our life are not those that God intends for us. Once we admit our failures, we can enter recovery and work to produce the fruit that God wants for us.

8:2-4 Jesus' healing of the leper demonstrated his ability to bring about instant physical recovery in response to faith. Jesus then directed the grateful leper to be examined immediately, calling him to display his deliverance and faith publicly. Emotional and spiritual recovery generally involves a longer process than was the leper's physical healing. Yet both timetables for recovery have the same starting and ending points. The same Jesus who healed instantly is also the originator and perfecter of the recovery process (see Hebrews 12:2).

8:5-13 The healing of the Roman officer's servant has much to teach all of us who are in recovery. The officer understood and humbly admitted his need, believing that Jesus could heal his young servant even from a distance. Jesus marveled because such faith was rare, even among God's chosen people, the Jews. We see here that Jesus came to bring deliverance to all people, Jew or Gentile, man or woman, rich or poor, religious or nonreligious. With God's help we can all have hope for recovery, no matter who we are or what we have done.

an unhealthy tree produces bad fruit. [18]A good tree can't produce bad fruit, and a bad tree can't produce good fruit. [19]So every tree that does not produce good fruit is chopped down and thrown into the fire. [20]Yes, the way to identify a tree or a person is by the kind of fruit that is produced.

True Disciples

[21]"Not all people who sound religious are really godly. They may refer to me as 'Lord,' but they still won't enter the Kingdom of Heaven. The decisive issue is whether they obey my Father in heaven. [22]On judgment day many will tell me, 'Lord, Lord, we prophesied in your name and cast out demons in your name and performed many miracles in your name.' [23]But I will reply, 'I never knew you. Go away; the things you did were unauthorized.*'

Building on a Solid Foundation

[24]"Anyone who listens to my teaching and obeys me is wise, like a person who builds a house on solid rock. [25]Though the rain comes in torrents and the floodwaters rise and the winds beat against that house, it won't collapse, because it is built on rock. [26]But anyone who hears my teaching and ignores it is foolish, like a person who builds a house on sand. [27]When the rains and floods come and the winds beat against that house, it will fall with a mighty crash."

[28]After Jesus finished speaking, the crowds were amazed at his teaching, [29]for he taught as one who had real authority—quite unlike the teachers of religious law.

CHAPTER 8
Jesus Heals a Man with Leprosy

Large crowds followed Jesus as he came down the mountainside. [2]Suddenly, a man with leprosy approached Jesus. He knelt before him, worshiping. "Lord," the man said, "if you want to, you can make me well again."

[3]Jesus touched him. "I want to," he said. "Be healed!" And instantly the leprosy disappeared. [4]Then Jesus said to him, "Go right over to the priest and let him examine you. Don't talk to anyone along the way. Take along the offering required in the law of Moses for those who have been healed of leprosy, so everyone will have proof of your healing."

Faith of the Roman Officer

[5]When Jesus arrived in Capernaum, a Roman officer came and pleaded with him, [6]"Lord,

7:23 Or *unlawful*.

STEP 4

Finger Pointing

BIBLE READING: Matthew 7:1-5
We made a searching and fearless moral inventory of ourselves.
There have probably been times when we have ignored our own sins and problems and pointed a finger at someone else. We may be out of touch with our internal affairs because we are still blaming others for our moral choices. Or perhaps we avoid self-examination by making moral inventories of the people around us.

When God asked Adam and Eve about their sin, they each pointed a finger at someone else. "'Have you eaten the fruit I commanded you not to eat?' 'Yes,' Adam admitted, 'but it was the woman you gave me who brought me the fruit, and I ate it.' Then the Lord God asked the woman, 'How could you do such a thing?' 'The serpent tricked me,' she replied" (Genesis 3:11-13). It seems to be human nature to blame others as our first line of defense.

We also may avoid our own problems by evaluating and criticizing others. Jesus tells us, "And why worry about a speck in your friend's eye when you have a log in your own? . . . Hypocrite! First get rid of the log from your own eye; then perhaps you will see well enough to deal with the speck in your friend's eye" (Matthew 7:3, 5).

While doing this step, we must constantly remember that this is a season of *self*-examination. We must guard against blaming and examining the lives of others. There will be time in the future for helping others after we have taken responsibility for our own life. *Turn to page 291, 2 Corinthians 7.*

my young servant lies in bed, paralyzed and racked with pain."

⁷Jesus said, "I will come and heal him."

⁸Then the officer said, "Lord, I am not worthy to have you come into my home. Just say the word from where you are, and my servant will be healed! ⁹I know, because I am under the authority of my superior officers and I have authority over my soldiers. I only need to say, 'Go,' and they go, or 'Come,' and they come. And if I say to my slaves, 'Do this or that,' they do it."

¹⁰When Jesus heard this, he was amazed. Turning to the crowd, he said, "I tell you the truth, I haven't seen faith like this in all the land of Israel! ¹¹And I tell you this, that many Gentiles will come from all over the world and sit down with Abraham, Isaac, and Jacob at the feast in the Kingdom of Heaven. ¹²But many Israelites—those for whom the Kingdom was prepared—will be cast into outer darkness, where there will be weeping and gnashing of teeth."

¹³Then Jesus said to the Roman officer, "Go on home. What you have believed has happened." And the young servant was healed that same hour.

Jesus Heals Many People

¹⁴When Jesus arrived at Peter's house, Peter's mother-in-law was in bed with a high fever. ¹⁵But when Jesus touched her hand, the fever left her. Then she got up and prepared a meal for him.

¹⁶That evening many demon-possessed people were brought to Jesus. All the spirits fled when he commanded them to leave; and he healed all the sick. ¹⁷This fulfilled the word of the Lord through Isaiah, who said, "He took our sicknesses and removed our diseases."*

The Cost of Following Jesus

¹⁸When Jesus noticed how large the crowd was growing, he instructed his disciples to cross to the other side of the lake.

¹⁹Then one of the teachers of religious law said to him, "Teacher, I will follow you no matter where you go!"

²⁰But Jesus said, "Foxes have dens to live in, and birds have nests, but I, the Son of Man, have no home of my own, not even a place to lay my head."

²¹Another of his disciples said, "Lord, first let me return home and bury my father."

²²But Jesus told him, "Follow me now! Let those who are spiritually dead care for their own dead."*

Jesus Calms the Storm

²³Then Jesus got into the boat and started across the lake with his disciples. ²⁴Suddenly, a terrible storm came up, with waves breaking into the boat. But Jesus was sleeping. ²⁵The disciples went to him and woke him up, shouting, "Lord, save us! We're going to drown!"

²⁶And Jesus answered, "Why are you afraid? You have so little faith!" Then he stood up and rebuked the wind and waves, and suddenly all was calm. ²⁷The disciples just sat there in awe. "Who is this?" they asked themselves. "Even the wind and waves obey him!"

Jesus Heals Two Demon-Possessed Men

²⁸When Jesus arrived on the other side of the lake in the land of the Gadarenes,* two men who were possessed by demons met him. They lived in a cemetery and were so dangerous that no one could go through that area. ²⁹They began screaming at him, "Why are you bothering us, Son of God? You have no right to torture us before God's appointed time!" ³⁰A large herd of pigs was feeding in the distance, ³¹so the demons begged, "If you cast us out, send us into that herd of pigs."

³²"All right, go!" Jesus commanded them. So the demons came out of the men and entered the pigs, and the whole herd plunged down the steep hillside into the lake and drowned in the water. ³³The herdsmen fled to the nearby city, telling everyone what happened to the demon-possessed men. ³⁴The entire town came out to meet Jesus, but they begged him to go away and leave them alone.

8:17 Isa 53:4. **8:22** Greek *Let the dead bury their own dead.* **8:28** Some manuscripts read *Gerasenes;* other manuscripts read *Gergesenes.* See Mark 5:1; Luke 8:26.

8:23-32 In this passage Jesus exhibited power over both the weather and the demonic realm. In both cases his disciples learned about faith in the incredible power of God. Since Jesus has the ability to calm a mighty storm and rid people of demonic influence, he can certainly empower us in the recovery process. We can experience God's power by first recognizing how powerless we are and then by giving our life to him.

CHAPTER 9

Jesus Heals a Paralyzed Man

Jesus climbed into a boat and went back across the lake to his own town. ²Some people brought to him a paralyzed man on a mat. Seeing their faith, Jesus said to the paralyzed man, "Take heart, son! Your sins are forgiven."

³"Blasphemy! This man talks like he is God!" some of the teachers of religious law said among themselves.

⁴Jesus knew what they were thinking, so he asked them, "Why are you thinking such evil thoughts? ⁵Is it easier to say, 'Your sins are forgiven' or 'Get up and walk'? ⁶I will prove that I, the Son of Man, have the authority on earth to forgive sins." Then Jesus turned to the paralyzed man and said, "Stand up, take your mat, and go on home, because you are healed!"

⁷And the man jumped up and went home! ⁸Fear swept through the crowd as they saw this happen right before their eyes. They praised God for sending a man with such great authority.

Jesus Calls Matthew

⁹As Jesus was going down the road, he saw Matthew sitting at his tax-collection booth. "Come, be my disciple," Jesus said to him. So Matthew got up and followed him.

¹⁰That night Matthew invited Jesus and his disciples to be his dinner guests, along with his fellow tax collectors and many other notorious sinners. ¹¹The Pharisees were indignant. "Why does your teacher eat with such scum*?" they asked his disciples.

¹²When he heard this, Jesus replied, "Healthy people don't need a doctor—sick people do." ¹³Then he added, "Now go and learn the meaning of this Scripture: 'I want you to be merciful; I don't want your sacrifices.'* For I have come to call sinners, not those who think they are already good enough."

A Discussion about Fasting

¹⁴One day the disciples of John the Baptist came to Jesus and asked him, "Why do we and the Pharisees fast, but your disciples don't fast?"

¹⁵Jesus responded, "Should the wedding guests mourn while celebrating with the groom? Someday he will be taken from them, and then they will fast. ¹⁶And who would patch an old garment with unshrunk cloth? For the patch shrinks and pulls away from the old cloth, leaving an even bigger hole than before. ¹⁷And no one puts new wine into old wineskins. The old skins would burst from the pressure, spilling the wine and ruining the skins. New wine must be stored in new wineskins. That way both the wine and the wineskins are preserved."

Jesus Heals in Response to Faith

¹⁸As Jesus was saying this, the leader of a synagogue came and knelt down before him. "My daughter has just died," he said, "but you can bring her back to life again if you just come and lay your hand upon her."

¹⁹As Jesus and the disciples were going to the official's home, ²⁰a woman who had had a hemorrhage for twelve years came up behind him. She touched the fringe of his robe, ²¹for she thought, "If I can just touch his robe, I will be healed."

9:11 Greek *with tax collectors and sinners.* **9:13** Hos 6:6.

9:1-7 The Jewish religious leaders thought it blasphemous that Jesus claimed to forgive sins, but they considered it just as impossible for him to heal the paralyzed man. By doing the impossible—healing the paralytic—Jesus made it clear to his critics that he also had the power to forgive sins. Implicit in his actions was his claim to deity, because only God can forgive sins. Knowing this truth should give us the courage to turn to Jesus for help. As God's own Son, Jesus has the power to offer forgiveness and recovery to all who trust in him.

9:14-17 Using two analogies, Jesus contrasted religious ritualism that cannot save with true spiritual power that can transform a life. The unshrunk cloth and new wine represent the power for recovery that Jesus offers. The old garment and wineskins refer to the ritualistic lifestyles and outward appearances characteristic of many Jews in Jesus' day. Jesus could just as easily be speaking directly to us who need recovery today. Small, external adjustments will not bring relief from our addiction. We need the newness of full recovery in Jesus Christ.

9:18-33 More miracles prove that Jesus is the Messiah and the source of recovery for all kinds of hurting people. Jesus restored life to a dead girl and stopped a woman's chronic hemorrhage. Then he healed two blind men and a demon-possessed man who was unable to speak. Jesus showed his power to help people who were living, or even dying, under the power of personal demons. No matter what the issue, recognizing our need and turning to God in faith are the first steps to recovery.

22Jesus turned around and said to her, "Daughter, be encouraged! Your faith has made you well." And the woman was healed at that moment.

23When Jesus arrived at the official's home, he noticed the noisy crowds and heard the funeral music. 24He said, "Go away, for the girl isn't dead; she's only asleep." But the crowd laughed at him. 25When the crowd was finally outside, Jesus went in and took the girl by the hand, and she stood up! 26The report of this miracle swept through the entire countryside.

Jesus Heals the Blind and Mute

27After Jesus left the girl's home, two blind men followed along behind him, shouting, "Son of David, have mercy on us!"

28They went right into the house where he was staying, and Jesus asked them, "Do you believe I can make you see?"

"Yes, Lord," they told him, "we do."

29Then he touched their eyes and said, "Because of your faith, it will happen." 30And suddenly they could see! Jesus sternly warned them, "Don't tell anyone about this." 31But instead, they spread his fame all over the region.

32When they left, some people brought to him a man who couldn't speak because he was possessed by a demon. 33So Jesus cast out the demon, and instantly the man could talk. The crowds marveled. "Nothing like this has ever happened in Israel!" they exclaimed.

34But the Pharisees said, "He can cast out demons because he is empowered by the prince of demons."

The Need for Workers

35Jesus traveled through all the cities and villages of that area, teaching in the synagogues and announcing the Good News about the Kingdom. And wherever he went, he healed people of every sort of disease and illness. 36He felt great pity for the crowds that came, because their problems were so great and they didn't know where to go for help. They were like sheep without a shepherd. 37He said to his disciples, "The harvest is so great, but the workers are so few. 38So pray to the Lord who is in charge of the harvest; ask him to send out more workers for his fields."

CHAPTER 10
Jesus Sends Out the Twelve Apostles

Jesus called his twelve disciples to him and gave them authority to cast out evil spirits and to heal every kind of disease and illness. 2Here are the names of the twelve apostles:

first Simon (also called Peter),
then Andrew (Peter's brother),
James (son of Zebedee),
John (James's brother),
3 Philip,
Bartholomew,
Thomas,
Matthew (the tax collector),
James (son of Alphaeus),
Thaddaeus,
4 Simon (the Zealot*),
Judas Iscariot (who later betrayed him).

5Jesus sent the twelve disciples out with these instructions: "Don't go to the Gentiles or the Samaritans, 6but only to the people of Israel—God's lost sheep. 7Go and announce to them that the Kingdom of Heaven is near.* 8Heal the sick, raise the dead, cure those with leprosy, and cast out demons. Give as freely as you have received!

9"Don't take any money with you. 10Don't carry a traveler's bag with an extra coat and sandals or even a walking stick. Don't hesitate to accept hospitality, because those who work deserve to be fed.* 11Whenever you enter a city or village, search for a worthy man and stay in his home until you leave for the next town. 12When you are invited into someone's home, give it your blessing. 13If it turns out to be a worthy home, let your blessing stand; if it is not, take back the blessing. 14If a village doesn't welcome you or listen to you, shake off the dust of that place from your feet as you leave. 15I assure you, the wicked cities of Sodom and Gomorrah will be better off on the judgment day than that place will be.

16"Look, I am sending you out as sheep among wolves. Be as wary as snakes and harmless as doves. 17But beware! For you will be handed over to the courts and beaten in the synagogues. 18And you must stand trial before governors and kings because you are my followers. This will be your opportunity

10:4 Greek the Cananean. 10:7 Or has come or is coming soon. 10:10 Or the worker is worthy of support.

10:16-26 Those of us living for God and pursuing recovery may feel like sheep in the presence of wolves. But when wisdom and honesty define our behavior and relationships, we can face the inevitable misunderstandings and persecutions. Jesus suffered much at the hands of godless men, and those who are committed to him often receive similar treatment. If we persevere in following God's will for us, we will receive a great reward in heaven (see 5:11-12).

MATTHEW & SIMON THE ZEALOT

It has been said that opposites attract; just as often, however, opposites repel. The differences between people often result in complementary relationships in which the strengths of one make up for the weaknesses of the other. But in some cases the differences lead only to continual strife. Marriage relationships are often comprised of two opposites, resulting in either great teamwork or terrible conflict.

Two of Jesus' twelve disciples, Matthew and Simon the Zealot, were opposites. Matthew was a Jew who worked for the Roman government as a tax collector. People of this occupation were known for their corruption. They grew rich by extorting excess taxes from their own oppressed people. These tax collectors were nonreligious and, needless to say, were hated and despised as traitors by their countrymen.

As indicated by his title "the Zealot," Simon, at the very least, was a religious fanatic. This term was sometimes used to label people with intense zeal for the law of Moses and Jewish religious tradition. It could also identify someone who belonged to the religious-political party known as the Zealots, which wanted to overthrow the Roman government. If Simon was a member, he would have been strongly opposed to the Roman occupation of Judea, while Matthew was an integral part of its government. Clearly, these men were opposites.

Both Matthew and Simon met Jesus and realized the emptiness and futility of their former pursuits. Both gave up what they had been to follow Christ in faith and experience new life—life that developed from the inside out. Both were transformed by the God of recovery into people who could love and accept those who were very different from themselves.

STRENGTHS AND ACCOMPLISHMENTS:
- Matthew and Simon both apparently were capable men.
- Both men were willing to recognize that they needed to change.
- Both men made Jesus the center of their life, enabling them to work with people quite different from themselves.

WEAKNESSES AND MISTAKES:
- Both had been driven by shortsighted motivations before following Jesus.
- As a tax collector, Matthew had probably used his position to extort money from the poor.
- As a Zealot, Simon probably condoned the use of violence for achieving his political ends.

LESSONS FROM THEIR LIVES:
- Financial success cannot replace the need for a relationship with God.
- If Christ is at the center of a relationship, no difference is too great to overcome.
- Differences can be used to strengthen relationships and should not be used as an excuse to destroy them.

KEY VERSES:
"[The disciples] went to the upstairs room of the house where they were staying. Here is the list of those who were present: . . . Matthew, . . . Simon (the Zealot)" (Acts 1:13).

The story of the apostles Matthew and Simon the Zealot is found in the Gospels. Both men are also mentioned in Acts 1:13.

---

to tell them about me—yes, to witness to the world. [19]When you are arrested, don't worry about what to say in your defense, because you will be given the right words at the right time. [20]For it won't be you doing the talking—it will be the Spirit of your Father speaking through you.

[21]"Brother will betray brother to death, fathers will betray their own children, and children will rise against their parents and cause them to be killed. [22]And everyone will hate you because of your allegiance to me. But

those who endure to the end will be saved. [23]When you are persecuted in one town, flee to the next. I assure you that I, the Son of Man, will return before you have reached all the towns of Israel.

[24]"A student is not greater than the teacher. A servant is not greater than the master. [25]The student shares the teacher's fate. The servant shares the master's fate. And since I, the master of the household, have been called the prince of demons,* how much more will it happen to you, the members of the

10:25 Greek *Beelzeboul*.

household! ²⁶But don't be afraid of those who threaten you. For the time is coming when everything will be revealed; all that is secret will be made public. ²⁷What I tell you now in the darkness, shout abroad when daybreak comes. What I whisper in your ears, shout from the housetops for all to hear!

²⁸"Don't be afraid of those who want to kill you. They can only kill your body; they cannot touch your soul. Fear only God, who can destroy both soul and body in hell. ²⁹Not even a sparrow, worth only half a penny, can fall to the ground without your Father knowing it. ³⁰And the very hairs on your head are all numbered. ³¹So don't be afraid; you are more valuable to him than a whole flock of sparrows.

³²"If anyone acknowledges me publicly here on earth, I will openly acknowledge that person before my Father in heaven. ³³But if anyone denies me here on earth, I will deny that person before my Father in heaven.

³⁴"Don't imagine that I came to bring peace to the earth! No, I came to bring a sword. ³⁵I have come to set a man against his father, and a daughter against her mother, and a daughter-in-law against her mother-in-law. ³⁶Your enemies will be right in your own household! ³⁷If you love your father or mother more than you love me, you are not worthy of being mine; or if you love your son or daughter more than me, you are not worthy of being mine. ³⁸If you refuse to take up your cross and follow me, you are not worthy of being mine. ³⁹If you cling to your life, you will lose it; but if you give it up for me, you will find it.

⁴⁰"Anyone who welcomes you is welcoming me, and anyone who welcomes me is welcoming the Father who sent me. ⁴¹If you welcome a prophet as one who speaks for God,* you will receive the same reward a prophet gets. And if you welcome good and godly people because of their godliness, you will be given a reward like theirs. ⁴²And if you give even a cup of cold water to one of the least of my followers, you will surely be rewarded."

CHAPTER 11
Jesus and John the Baptist

When Jesus had finished giving these instructions to his twelve disciples, he went off teaching and preaching in towns throughout the country.

²John the Baptist, who was now in prison, heard about all the things the Messiah was doing. So he sent his disciples to ask Jesus, ³"Are you really the Messiah we've been waiting for, or should we keep looking for someone else?"

⁴Jesus told them, "Go back to John and tell him about what you have heard and seen— ⁵the blind see, the lame walk, the lepers are cured, the deaf hear, the dead are raised to life, and the Good News is being preached to the poor. ⁶And tell him: 'God blesses those who are not offended by me.*'"

⁷When John's disciples had gone, Jesus began talking about him to the crowds. "Who is this man in the wilderness that you went out to see? Did you find him weak as a reed, moved by every breath of wind? ⁸Or were you expecting to see a man dressed in expensive clothes? Those who dress like that live in palaces, not out in the wilderness. ⁹Were you looking for a prophet? Yes, and he is more than a prophet. ¹⁰John is the man to whom the Scriptures refer when they say,

'Look, I am sending my messenger before you,
	and he will prepare your way before you.'*

10:41 Greek *welcome a prophet in the name of a prophet.* **11:6** Or *who don't fall away because of me.* **11:10** Mal 3:1.

10:39 The only way to find life (and get control of it) is to submit to God through Jesus Christ. Living for self, we become a slave to material success, work, alcohol, illicit sex, or any number of other destructive behaviors. We have lost control of our life and are in trouble. By turning to Jesus, we allow him to cleanse us of our addiction and show us the way to real life—a life free of any destructive dependency. As we obey God, we will find meaning in our present life and eternal peace with God.

11:2-6 Doubt is a troubling reality for those of us in recovery. We doubt ourself, and we doubt others. Even John the Baptist doubted that Jesus was the promised Messiah, the one who would come to offer physical and spiritual healing to his people. Jesus answered John's doubts by pointing to his miraculous healings and restorations. Such an impressive résumé should also convince us that Jesus is willing and able to meet even our greatest needs for recovery and restoration.

11:16-19 When we are in denial, we tend to resist those who challenge our comfort zones. We find excuses not to accept the good advice of others no matter what they do or say. We become cynical and try to justify our inconsistencies. The message of recovery is too joyful and hopeful for some, or it is too realistic and direct for others. Recovery is too structured for those of us who are used to doing our own thing; it is too liberating for those of us from a legalistic background. But such perspectives are only blind excuses that keep us from facing our need for recovery.

[11]"I assure you, of all who have ever lived, none is greater than John the Baptist. Yet even the most insignificant person in the Kingdom of Heaven is greater than he is! [12]And from the time John the Baptist began preaching and baptizing until now, the Kingdom of Heaven has been forcefully advancing, and violent people attack it.* [13]For before John came, all the teachings of the Scriptures looked forward to this present time. [14]And if you are willing to accept what I say, he is Elijah, the one the prophets said would come.* [15]Anyone who is willing to hear should listen and understand!

[16]"How shall I describe this generation? These people are like a group of children playing a game in the public square. They complain to their friends, [17]'We played wedding songs, and you weren't happy, so we played funeral songs, but you weren't sad.' [18]For John the Baptist didn't drink wine and he often fasted, and you say, 'He's demon possessed.' [19]And I, the Son of Man, feast and drink, and you say, 'He's a glutton and a drunkard, and a friend of the worst sort of sinners!' But wisdom is shown to be right by what results from it."

Judgment for the Unbelievers

[20]Then Jesus began to denounce the cities where he had done most of his miracles, because they hadn't turned from their sins and turned to God. [21]"What horrors await you, Korazin and Bethsaida! For if the miracles I did in you had been done in wicked Tyre and Sidon, their people would have sat in deep repentance long ago, clothed in sackcloth and throwing ashes on their heads to show their remorse. [22]I assure you, Tyre and Sidon will be better off on the judgment day than you! [23]And you people of Capernaum, will you be exalted to heaven? No, you will be brought down to the place of the dead.* For if the miracles I did for you had been done in Sodom, it would still be here today. [24]I assure you, Sodom will be better off on the judgment day than you."

Jesus' Prayer of Thanksgiving

[25]Then Jesus prayed this prayer: "O Father, Lord of heaven and earth, thank you for hiding the truth from those who think themselves so wise and clever, and for revealing it to the childlike. [26]Yes, Father, it pleased you to do it this way!

[27]"My Father has given me authority over

11:12 Or *until now, eager multitudes have been pressing into the Kingdom of Heaven.* **11:14** See Mal 4:5.
11:23 Greek *to Hades.*

STEP 3

Submission and Rest

BIBLE READING: Matthew 11:27-30
We made a decision to turn our will and our life over to the care of God.
When our burdens become heavy and we find that our way of life is leading us toward death, we may finally be willing to let someone else do the driving. We may have worked hard at getting our life on the right track but still feel as if we always end up on dead-end streets.

Proverbs tells us, "There is a path before each person that seems right, but it ends in death" (Proverbs 14:12). When we began our addictive behavior, we were probably seeking pleasure or looking for a way to overcome our pain. The way seemed right at first, but it wasn't long before it became clear that we were on the wrong track. By then we were unable to turn around on our own. Jesus said, "Come to me, all of you who are weary and carry heavy burdens, and I will give you rest. Take my yoke upon you. Let me teach you, because I am humble and gentle, and you will find rest for your souls" (Matthew 11:28-29).

Taking on a yoke implies being united to another in order to work together. Those who are yoked together must go in the same direction; by doing so, their work is made considerably easier. When we finally decide to submit our life and our will to God's direction, our burdens will become manageable. When we let him do the driving, we will "find rest" for our soul. He knows the way and has the strength to turn us around and get us on the road toward recovery. *Turn to page 213, Acts 17.*

everything. No one really knows the Son except the Father, and no one really knows the Father except the Son and those to whom the Son chooses to reveal him."

28Then Jesus said, "Come to me, all of you who are weary and carry heavy burdens, and I will give you rest. 29Take my yoke upon you. Let me teach you, because I am humble and gentle, and you will find rest for your souls. 30For my yoke fits perfectly, and the burden I give you is light."

CHAPTER 12
Controversy about the Sabbath

At about that time Jesus was walking through some grainfields on the Sabbath. His disciples were hungry, so they began breaking off heads of wheat and eating the grain. 2Some Pharisees saw them do it and protested, "Your disciples shouldn't be doing that! It's against the law to work by harvesting grain on the Sabbath."

3But Jesus said to them, "Haven't you ever read in the Scriptures what King David did when he and his companions were hungry? 4He went into the house of God, and they ate the special bread reserved for the priests alone. That was breaking the law, too. 5And haven't you ever read in the law of Moses that the priests on duty in the Temple may work on the Sabbath? 6I tell you, there is one here who is even greater than the Temple! 7But you would not have condemned those who aren't guilty if you knew the meaning of this Scripture: 'I want you to be merciful; I don't want your sacrifices.'* 8For I, the Son of Man, am master even of the Sabbath."

9Then he went over to the synagogue, 10where he noticed a man with a deformed hand. The Pharisees asked Jesus, "Is it legal to work by healing on the Sabbath day?" (They were, of course, hoping he would say yes, so they could bring charges against him.)

11And he answered, "If you had one sheep, and it fell into a well on the Sabbath, wouldn't you get to work and pull it out? Of course you would. 12And how much more valuable is a person than a sheep! Yes, it is right to do good on the Sabbath." 13Then he said to the man, "Reach out your hand." The man reached out his hand, and it became normal, just like the other one. 14Then the Pharisees called a meeting and discussed plans for killing Jesus.

Jesus, God's Chosen Servant

15But Jesus knew what they were planning. He left that area, and many people followed him. He healed all the sick among them, 16but he warned them not to say who he was. 17This fulfilled the prophecy of Isaiah concerning him:

18 "Look at my Servant,
   whom I have chosen.
He is my Beloved,
   and I am very pleased with him.
I will put my Spirit upon him,
   and he will proclaim justice to the nations.
19 He will not fight or shout;
   he will not raise his voice in public.
20 He will not crush those who are weak,
   or quench the smallest hope,
   until he brings full justice with his final victory.
21 And his name will be the hope
   of all the world."*

Jesus and the Prince of Demons

22Then a demon-possessed man, who was both blind and unable to talk, was brought to

12:7 Hos 6:6. 12:18-21 Isa 42:1-4.

12:1-8 God's standards were intended for our good—to mercifully meet his people's needs. But legalism abuses his laws. Following God's laws to the letter can easily violate the very reasons that God gave them in the first place. God gave the Sabbath laws to protect his people from overwork, but the Pharisees applied this law so rigidly that the Sabbath became a day of rigorous self-denial—the opposite of what God intended. The Pharisees employed God's Word for restrictive and enslaving purposes rather than for spiritual freedom and balance. In his mercy, God offers us recovery and hope instead of condemnation. If God had wanted to crush us with legalism, he would never have sent Jesus to die for us. He would have let us die in our sins.
12:17-21 Centuries earlier the prophet Isaiah had described the Messiah (Isaiah 42:1-4); Matthew recognized how Jesus fulfilled that prophecy. This passage offers a powerful message of hope for those of us in recovery. Jesus the Messiah is both our servant and our leader. He is strong enough to lead and judge the nations, yet tender enough to care for the weak and helpless. He is the world's hope for salvation and our hope for recovery.
12:22-32 Only God through Jesus Christ can offer us the power we need for recovery. If we look to any other source for help, our recovery will be limited at best. Secular, New Age, and even

Jesus. He healed the man so that he could both speak and see. ²³The crowd was amazed. "Could it be that Jesus is the Son of David, the Messiah?" they wondered out loud.

²⁴But when the Pharisees heard about the miracle, they said, "No wonder he can cast out demons. He gets his power from Satan,* the prince of demons."

²⁵Jesus knew their thoughts and replied, "Any kingdom at war with itself is doomed. A city or home divided against itself is doomed. ²⁶And if Satan is casting out Satan, he is fighting against himself. His own kingdom will not survive. ²⁷And if I am empowered by the prince of demons,* what about your own followers? They cast out demons, too, so they will judge you for what you have said. ²⁸But if I am casting out demons by the Spirit of God, then the Kingdom of God has arrived among you. ²⁹Let me illustrate this. You can't enter a strong man's house and rob him without first tying him up. Only then can his house be robbed!* ³⁰Anyone who isn't helping me opposes me, and anyone who isn't working with me is actually working against me.

³¹"Every sin or blasphemy can be forgiven— except blasphemy against the Holy Spirit, which can never be forgiven. ³²Anyone who blasphemes against me, the Son of Man, can be forgiven, but blasphemy against the Holy Spirit will never be forgiven, either in this world or in the world to come.

³³"A tree is identified by its fruit. Make a tree good, and its fruit will be good. Make a tree bad, and its fruit will be bad. ³⁴You brood of snakes! How could evil men like you speak what is good and right? For whatever is in your heart determines what you say. ³⁵A good person produces good words from a good heart, and an evil person produces evil words from an evil heart. ³⁶And I tell you this, that you must give an account on judgment day of every idle word you speak. ³⁷The words you say now reflect your fate then; either you will be justified by them or you will be condemned."

The Sign of Jonah

³⁸One day some teachers of religious law and Pharisees came to Jesus and said, "Teacher, we want you to show us a miraculous sign to prove that you are from God."

³⁹But Jesus replied, "Only an evil, faithless generation would ask for a miraculous sign; but the only sign I will give them is the sign of the prophet Jonah. ⁴⁰For as Jonah was in the belly of the great fish for three days and three nights, so I, the Son of Man, will be in the heart of the earth for three days and three nights. ⁴¹The people of Nineveh will rise up against this generation on judgment day and condemn it, because they repented at the preaching of Jonah. And now someone greater than Jonah is here—and you refuse to repent. ⁴²The queen of Sheba* will also rise up against this generation on judgment day and condemn it, because she came from a distant land to hear the wisdom of Solomon. And now someone greater than Solomon is here—and you refuse to listen to him.

⁴³"When an evil spirit leaves a person, it goes into the desert, seeking rest but finding none. ⁴⁴Then it says, 'I will return to the person I came from.' So it returns and finds its former home empty, swept, and clean. ⁴⁵Then the spirit finds seven other spirits more evil than itself, and they all enter the person and live there. And so that person is worse off than before. That will be the experience of this evil generation."

The True Family of Jesus

⁴⁶As Jesus was speaking to the crowd, his mother and brothers were outside, wanting to talk with him. ⁴⁷Someone told Jesus, "Your mother and your brothers are outside, and they want to speak to you."

⁴⁸Jesus asked, "Who is my mother? Who are my brothers?" ⁴⁹Then he pointed to his disciples and said, "These are my mother and brothers. ⁵⁰Anyone who does the will of my Father in heaven is my brother and sister and mother!"

12:24 Greek *Beelzeboul*. **12:27** Greek *by Beelzeboul*. **12:29** Or *One cannot rob Satan's kingdom without first tying him up. Only then can his demons be cast out.* **12:42** Greek *The queen of the south.*

---

occult approaches to recovery are available. It is tragic that Christ-centered recovery is often doubted by many who need it the most, but it is even more tragic when people who find deliverance through Christ are later told that it is all a lie. God's way of recovery is the way of Jesus Christ; through him we receive the power we need for recovery and restoration.
12:43-45 Incomplete recovery can leave a person "worse off than before." To be rid of what afflicts us is only half the battle. Once we kick an addiction or dependency, there is a void in our life that was once filled with our old behavior. We must fill that emptiness with God's Spirit and godly attitudes and actions through prayer and reading God's Word. Otherwise, a new addiction or dependency can move in and cause further problems in our life.

CHAPTER 13
Story of the Farmer Scattering Seed

Later that same day, Jesus left the house and went down to the shore, ²where an immense crowd soon gathered. He got into a boat, where he sat and taught as the people listened on the shore. ³He told many stories such as this one:

"A farmer went out to plant some seed. ⁴As he scattered it across his field, some seeds fell on a footpath, and the birds came and ate them. ⁵Other seeds fell on shallow soil with underlying rock. The plants sprang up quickly, ⁶but they soon wilted beneath the hot sun and died because the roots had no nourishment in the shallow soil. ⁷Other seeds fell among thorns that shot up and choked out the tender blades. ⁸But some seeds fell on fertile soil and produced a crop that was thirty, sixty, and even a hundred times as much as had been planted. ⁹Anyone who is willing to hear should listen and understand!"

¹⁰His disciples came and asked him, "Why do you always tell stories when you talk to the people?"

¹¹Then he explained to them, "You have been permitted to understand the secrets of the Kingdom of Heaven, but others have not. ¹²To those who are open to my teaching, more understanding will be given, and they will have an abundance of knowledge. But to those who are not listening, even what they have will be taken away from them. ¹³That is why I tell these stories, because people see what I do, but they don't really see. They hear what I say, but they don't really hear, and they don't understand. ¹⁴This fulfills the prophecy of Isaiah, which says:

'You will hear my words,
   but you will not understand;
you will see what I do,
   but you will not perceive its meaning.
¹⁵For the hearts of these people are
   hardened,
   and their ears cannot hear,
   and they have closed their eyes—
so their eyes cannot see,
   and their ears cannot hear,
   and their hearts cannot understand,
and they cannot turn to me
   and let me heal them.'*

¹⁶"But blessed are your eyes, because they see; and your ears, because they hear. ¹⁷I assure you, many prophets and godly people have longed to see and hear what you have seen and heard, but they could not.

¹⁸"Now here is the explanation of the story I told about the farmer sowing grain: ¹⁹The seed that fell on the hard path represents those who hear the Good News about the Kingdom and don't understand it. Then the evil one comes and snatches the seed away from their hearts. ²⁰The rocky soil represents those who hear the message and receive it with joy. ²¹But like young plants in such soil, their roots don't go very deep. At first they get along fine, but they wilt as soon as they have problems or are persecuted because they believe the word. ²²The thorny ground represents those who hear and accept the Good News, but all too quickly the message is crowded out by the cares of this life and the lure of wealth, so no crop is produced. ²³The good soil represents the hearts of those who truly accept God's message and produce a huge harvest—thirty, sixty, or even a hundred times as much as had been planted."

Story of the Wheat and Weeds

²⁴Here is another story Jesus told: "The Kingdom of Heaven is like a farmer who planted good seed in his field. ²⁵But that night as everyone slept, his enemy came and planted weeds among the wheat. ²⁶When the crop

13:14-15 Isa 6:9-10.

13:1-9, 18-23 The story about the farmer and the four soils applies directly to recovery. The varied responses to the "seed" of the gospel are like the many responses to recovery. Some embrace recovery wholeheartedly, some only halfheartedly or temporarily, and some pass up the opportunity, denying they need it. Generally, various trials clarify which recovery category we fit into. If we hope to succeed in recovery and experience new life, we must allow God to prepare the soil of our heart, making it ready to receive his healing message.

13:10-17 Jesus' explanation for teaching with stories and illustrations fits well with the dynamics of recovery and denial. Those of us who respond in faith to what we already know will be given more insight as we progress in recovery. Those who do not respond properly will become more and more spiritually blind and hardened in denial. Amazingly, God continues to offer recovery even to those who have turned their back on him in denial. When we are ready to ask God what to do, he will be there with the answer (see James 1:5).

began to grow and produce grain, the weeds also grew. ²⁷The farmer's servants came and told him, 'Sir, the field where you planted that good seed is full of weeds!'

²⁸"'An enemy has done it!' the farmer exclaimed.

"'Shall we pull out the weeds?' they asked.

²⁹"He replied, 'No, you'll hurt the wheat if you do. ³⁰Let both grow together until the harvest. Then I will tell the harvesters to sort out the weeds and burn them and to put the wheat in the barn.'"

Illustration of the Mustard Seed

³¹Here is another illustration Jesus used: "The Kingdom of Heaven is like a mustard seed planted in a field. ³²It is the smallest of all seeds, but it becomes the largest of garden plants and grows into a tree where birds can come and find shelter in its branches."

Illustration of the Yeast

³³Jesus also used this illustration: "The Kingdom of Heaven is like yeast used by a woman making bread. Even though she used a large amount* of flour, the yeast permeated every part of the dough."

³⁴Jesus always used stories and illustrations like these when speaking to the crowds. In fact, he never spoke to them without using such parables. ³⁵This fulfilled the prophecy that said,

"I will speak to you in parables.
    I will explain mysteries hidden since
        the creation of the world."*

The Wheat and Weeds Explained

³⁶Then, leaving the crowds outside, Jesus went into the house. His disciples said, "Please explain the story of the weeds in the field."

³⁷"All right," he said. "I, the Son of Man, am the farmer who plants the good seed. ³⁸The field is the world, and the good seed represents the people of the Kingdom. The weeds are the people who belong to the evil one. ³⁹The enemy who planted the weeds among the wheat is the Devil. The harvest is the end of the world, and the harvesters are the angels.

⁴⁰"Just as the weeds are separated out and burned, so it will be at the end of the world. ⁴¹I, the Son of Man, will send my angels, and they will remove from my Kingdom everything that causes sin and all who do evil, ⁴²and they will throw them into the furnace and burn them. There will be weeping and gnashing of teeth. ⁴³Then the godly will shine like the sun in their Father's Kingdom. Anyone who is willing to hear should listen and understand!

Illustration of the Hidden Treasure

⁴⁴"The Kingdom of Heaven is like a treasure that a man discovered hidden in a field. In his excitement, he hid it again and sold everything he owned to get enough money to buy the field—and to get the treasure, too!

Illustration of the Pearl Merchant

⁴⁵"Again, the Kingdom of Heaven is like a pearl merchant on the lookout for choice pearls. ⁴⁶When he discovered a pearl of great value, he sold everything he owned and bought it!

Illustration of the Fishing Net

⁴⁷"Again, the Kingdom of Heaven is like a fishing net that is thrown into the water and gathers fish of every kind. ⁴⁸When the net is full, they drag it up onto the shore, sit down, sort the good fish into crates, and throw the bad ones away. ⁴⁹That is the way it will be at the end of the world. The angels will come and separate the wicked people from the godly, ⁵⁰throwing the wicked into the fire. There will be weeping and gnashing of teeth. ⁵¹Do you understand?"

"Yes," they said, "we do."

⁵²Then he added, "Every teacher of religious law who has become a disciple in the Kingdom of Heaven is like a person who brings out of the storehouse the new teachings as well as the old."

13:33 Greek *3 measures*. **13:35** Ps 78:2.

13:24-30, 36-43 The story about the wheat and the weeds applies to those of us considering recovery. Ultimately, there are two kinds of people in the world: Some submit to God's will and experience the restoration he offers in Jesus Christ; the others, whether they realize it or not, have submitted to the control of Satan. This stark but realistic contrast shows us that if we do not choose God, we choose Satan by default. If we have already undertaken a form of recovery but have not yet committed our life to Jesus Christ, we still have one more step to go before experiencing the victory available in God's recovery program.

Jesus Rejected at Nazareth

⁵³When Jesus had finished telling these stories, he left that part of the country. ⁵⁴He returned to Nazareth, his hometown. When he taught there in the synagogue, everyone was astonished and said, "Where does he get his wisdom and his miracles? ⁵⁵He's just a carpenter's son, and we know Mary, his mother, and his brothers—James, Joseph, Simon, and Judas. ⁵⁶All his sisters live right here among us. What makes him so great?" ⁵⁷And they were deeply offended and refused to believe in him.

Then Jesus told them, "A prophet is honored everywhere except in his own hometown and among his own family." ⁵⁸And so he did only a few miracles there because of their unbelief.

CHAPTER 14
The Death of John the Baptist

When Herod Antipas* heard about Jesus, ²he said to his advisers, "This must be John the Baptist come back to life again! That is why he can do such miracles." ³For Herod had arrested and imprisoned John as a favor to his wife Herodias (the former wife of Herod's brother Philip). ⁴John kept telling Herod, "It is illegal for you to marry her." ⁵Herod would have executed John, but he was afraid of a riot, because all the people believed John was a prophet.

⁶But at a birthday party for Herod, Herodias's daughter performed a dance that greatly pleased him, ⁷so he promised with an oath to give her anything she wanted. ⁸At her mother's urging, the girl asked, "I want the head of John the Baptist on a tray!" ⁹The king was sorry, but because of his oath and because he didn't want to back down in front of his guests, he issued the necessary orders. ¹⁰So John was beheaded in the prison, ¹¹and his head was brought on a tray and given to the girl, who took it to her mother. ¹²John's disciples came for his body and buried it. Then they told Jesus what had happened.

Jesus Feeds Five Thousand

¹³As soon as Jesus heard the news, he went off by himself in a boat to a remote area to be alone. But the crowds heard where he was headed and followed by land from many villages. ¹⁴A vast crowd was there as he stepped from the boat, and he had compassion on them and healed their sick.

¹⁵That evening the disciples came to him and said, "This is a desolate place, and it is getting late. Send the crowds away so they can go to the villages and buy food for themselves."

¹⁶But Jesus replied, "That isn't necessary—you feed them."

¹⁷"Impossible!" they exclaimed. "We have only five loaves of bread and two fish!"

¹⁸"Bring them here," he said. ¹⁹Then he told the people to sit down on the grass. And he took the five loaves and two fish, looked up toward heaven, and asked God's blessing on the food. Breaking the loaves into pieces, he gave some of the bread and fish to each disciple, and the disciples gave them to the people. ²⁰They all ate as much as they wanted, and they picked up twelve baskets of leftovers. ²¹About five thousand men had eaten from those five loaves, in addition to all the women and children!

14:1 Greek *Herod the tetrarch.* He was a son of King Herod and was ruler over one of the four districts in Palestine.

13:53-58 We must always fight the preconceived notions that others have of us. We might leave our dysfunctional family or group of friends and enter a successful recovery program. When we return, we shouldn't be surprised to find that others will ignore our message of recovery, saying that we are *just* so-and-so or *just* the kid they went to school with. They won't listen to us because they are too close to who we were and cannot see who we have become through God's grace. As we share our recovery story with those who know our past, it may take time to convince them of our sincerity and our new life.

14:15-21 Jesus fed multitudes of hungry people on more than one occasion (see also 15:32-39). Jesus is not only able to do the impossible, but he is also concerned with our pressing human needs. He is committed to meeting our most basic physical needs, but how much more is he committed to meeting our emotional needs related to recovery! Jesus did not do everything himself; his disciples helped meet the people's needs. Jesus often meets our needs through human instruments. God may be working our recovery through concerned friends or others who are hurting like us. We should never refuse help from godly friends. As we have opportunities to encourage others in recovery, we can be thankful that God has chosen to use us.

14:22-23 Time alone to focus on our tasks and pray is necessary if we are engaged in any form of prolonged recovery program. Although we may feel we are wasting time, it is important to recharge our battery—physically, emotionally, and spiritually. If we don't, we will burn out. Since Jesus took time out to pray and recharge, we should follow his example.

READ MATTHEW 14:23-33

GOD grant me the serenity to accept the things I cannot change the courage to change the things I can and the wisdom to know the difference AMEN

Having God deal with our defects can be frightening. We may stay trapped in destructive life patterns because we fear change.

If we wait for all our fears to go away before we take steps, we will never make significant progress in recovery. Courage isn't the absence of fear. Courage means that we take advantage of the little strength we find within ourself, that we find little ways to encourage ourself, and that we stubbornly stick to God's program for us. Courage doesn't mean being free of fear. It means finding enough strength to take the next step.

The disciples were terrified when they saw Jesus walk on water. "Then Peter called to him, 'Lord, if it's really you, tell me to come to you by walking on water.' 'All right, come,' Jesus said. So Peter went over the side of the boat and walked on the water toward Jesus. But when he looked around at the high waves, he was terrified and began to sink. 'Save me, Lord!' he shouted. Instantly Jesus reached out his hand and grabbed him" (Matthew 14:28-31).

Peter gathered up enough courage to take one step and venture out into a new experience. When he got in over his head, he called out to Jesus and found the help he needed. We only need to summon the courage to take the next step. This doesn't mean that we won't be afraid or don't need help. It does mean that with God's help, we can make it. All we need is the courage to take just one more step. *Turn to page 45, Matthew 26.*

Jesus Walks on Water

²²Immediately after this, Jesus made his disciples get back into the boat and cross to the other side of the lake while he sent the people home. ²³Afterward he went up into the hills by himself to pray. Night fell while he was there alone. ²⁴Meanwhile, the disciples were in trouble far away from land, for a strong wind had risen, and they were fighting heavy waves.

²⁵About three o'clock in the morning* Jesus came to them, walking on the water. ²⁶When the disciples saw him, they screamed in terror, thinking he was a ghost. ²⁷But Jesus spoke to them at once. "It's all right," he said. "I am here! Don't be afraid."

²⁸Then Peter called to him, "Lord, if it's really you, tell me to come to you by walking on water."

²⁹"All right, come," Jesus said.

So Peter went over the side of the boat and walked on the water toward Jesus. ³⁰But when he looked around at the high waves, he was terrified and began to sink. "Save me, Lord!" he shouted.

³¹Instantly Jesus reached out his hand and grabbed him. "You don't have much faith," Jesus said. "Why did you doubt me?" ³²And when they climbed back into the boat, the wind stopped.

³³Then the disciples worshiped him. "You really are the Son of God!" they exclaimed.

³⁴After they had crossed the lake, they landed at Gennesaret. ³⁵The news of their arrival spread quickly throughout the whole surrounding area, and soon people were bringing all their sick to be healed. ³⁶The sick begged him to let them touch even the fringe of his robe, and all who touched it were healed.

14:25 Greek *In the fourth watch of the night.*

CHAPTER 15
Jesus Teaches about Inner Purity
Some Pharisees and teachers of religious law now arrived from Jerusalem to interview Jesus. [2]"Why do your disciples disobey our age-old traditions?" they demanded. "They ignore our tradition of ceremonial hand washing before they eat."

[3]Jesus replied, "And why do you, by your traditions, violate the direct commandments of God? [4]For instance, God says, 'Honor your father and mother,' and 'Anyone who speaks evil of father or mother must be put to death.'* [5]But you say, 'You don't need to honor your parents by caring for their needs if you give the money to God instead.' [6]And so, by your own tradition, you nullify the direct commandment of God. [7]You hypocrites! Isaiah was prophesying about you when he said,

[8]'These people honor me with their lips,
    but their hearts are far away.
[9]Their worship is a farce,
    for they replace God's commands
    with their own man-made
    teachings.'*"

[10]Then Jesus called to the crowds and said, "Listen to what I say and try to understand. [11]You are not defiled by what you eat; you are defiled by what you say and do.*"

[12]Then the disciples came to him and asked, "Do you realize you offended the Pharisees by what you just said?"

[13]Jesus replied, "Every plant not planted by my heavenly Father will be rooted up, [14]so ignore them. They are blind guides leading the blind, and if one blind person guides another, they will both fall into a ditch."

[15]Then Peter asked Jesus, "Explain what you meant when you said people aren't defiled by what they eat."

[16]"Don't you understand?" Jesus asked him. [17]"Anything you eat passes through the stomach and then goes out of the body. [18]But evil words come from an evil heart and defile the person who says them. [19]For from the heart come evil thoughts, murder, adultery, all other sexual immorality, theft, lying, and slander. [20]These are what defile you. Eating with unwashed hands could never defile you and make you unacceptable to God!"

The Faith of a Gentile Woman
[21]Jesus then left Galilee and went north to the region of Tyre and Sidon. [22]A Gentile* woman who lived there came to him, pleading, "Have mercy on me, O Lord, Son of David! For my daughter has a demon in her, and it is severely tormenting her."

[23]But Jesus gave her no reply—not even a word. Then his disciples urged him to send her away. "Tell her to leave," they said. "She is bothering us with all her begging."

[24]Then he said to the woman, "I was sent only to help the people of Israel—God's lost sheep—not the Gentiles."

[25]But she came and worshiped him and pleaded again, "Lord, help me!"

[26]"It isn't right to take food from the children and throw it to the dogs," he said.

15:4 Exod 20:12; 21:17; Lev 20:9; Deut 5:16. **15:8-9** Isa 29:13. **15:11** Or *what comes out of the mouth defiles a person.* **15:22** Greek *Canaanite.*

15:1-20 Some people will look down on us and criticize us for our dependency and our need for recovery. They will assume a self-righteous posture because they are fulfilling all their proper "religious" obligations, while we are far from being a model church member. Jesus says that outward activities don't necessarily correspond to inner righteousness. If we do all the right things with a proud and selfish heart, we will be judged by God. If we have accepted Jesus into our heart and are humbly trying to recover, God is pleased with us, no matter what others may say.

15:32-38 The feeding of the four thousand is both similar to and different from the previous feeding of the five thousand (see 14:15-21). In both cases Jesus cared about those in need; he took a small amount of food and fed a large number of people; he used the disciples to distribute the resources; and much more was left over at the end than they had in the beginning. Since the reason for concern was somewhat different, as were the location and the number of people fed, we see that Jesus tailored his resources to meet the various situations and needs. We can count on God to show similar concern and unlimited power to support us in our recovery process.

16:1-4 The Pharisees had the kind of attitude that often hinders recovery. They wanted Jesus to show them miraculous signs to prove that he was the Messiah. We make the same mistake when we expect an instant cure or supernatural intervention in our life. Looking for quick fixes to lifelong problems is tantamount to seeking "a sign from heaven." It often takes a lifetime of hard work to remain victorious over our addiction. When we recognize this truth, we will be less likely to be disappointed by the difficulties of the recovery process. We will also be more aware of the small victories that God gives us along the way.

²⁷"Yes, Lord," she replied, "but even dogs are permitted to eat crumbs that fall beneath their master's table."

²⁸"Woman," Jesus said to her, "your faith is great. Your request is granted." And her daughter was instantly healed.

Jesus Heals Many People

²⁹Jesus returned to the Sea of Galilee and climbed a hill and sat down. ³⁰A vast crowd brought him the lame, blind, crippled, mute, and many others with physical difficulties, and they laid them before Jesus. And he healed them all. ³¹The crowd was amazed! Those who hadn't been able to speak were talking, the crippled were made well, the lame were walking around, and those who had been blind could see again! And they praised the God of Israel.

Jesus Feeds Four Thousand

³²Then Jesus called his disciples to him and said, "I feel sorry for these people. They have been here with me for three days, and they have nothing left to eat. I don't want to send them away hungry, or they will faint along the road."

³³The disciples replied, "And where would we get enough food out here in the wilderness for all of them to eat?"

³⁴Jesus asked, "How many loaves of bread do you have?"

They replied, "Seven, and a few small fish." ³⁵So Jesus told all the people to sit down on the ground. ³⁶Then he took the seven loaves and the fish, thanked God for them, broke them into pieces, and gave them to the disciples, who distributed the food to the crowd.

³⁷They all ate until they were full, and when the scraps were picked up, there were seven large baskets of food left over! ³⁸There were four thousand men who were fed that day, in addition to all the women and children. ³⁹Then Jesus sent the people home, and he got into a boat and crossed over to the region of Magadan.

CHAPTER 16
Leaders Demand a Miraculous Sign

One day the Pharisees and Sadducees came to test Jesus' claims by asking him to show them a miraculous sign from heaven.

²He replied, "You know the saying, 'Red sky at night means fair weather tomorrow, ³red sky in the morning means foul weather all day.' You are good at reading the weather signs in the sky, but you can't read the obvious

Faith

READ MATTHEW 15:22-28

Sometimes the insanity of living with our own addiction or with people who are acting in bizarre ways can cause us to become desperate for help. Jesus once dealt with a woman who was driven to him out of desperation.

"A Gentile woman who lived there came to him, pleading, 'Have mercy on me, O Lord, Son of David! For my daughter has a demon in her, and it is severely tormenting her.' But Jesus gave her no reply—not even a word. . . . Then he said to the woman, 'I was sent only to help the people of Israel—God's lost sheep—not the Gentiles.' But she came and worshiped him and pleaded again, 'Lord, help me!' 'It isn't right to take food from the children and throw it to the dogs,' he said. 'Yes, Lord,' she replied, 'but even dogs are permitted to eat crumbs that fall beneath their master's table.' 'Woman,' Jesus said to her, 'your faith is great. Your request is granted.' And her daughter was instantly healed" (Matthew 15:22-28).

It took a lot of courage for this woman to even speak to Jesus because of the racism of their time. She was despised and ridiculed for seeking an end to her family's torment, but she didn't give up. She believed God was the only one who could help her, and she would not be deterred. Our own desperation can lead to sincere faith that can be of tremendous help to us in recovery. *Turn to page 31, Matthew 16.*

signs of the times!* ⁴Only an evil, faithless generation would ask for a miraculous sign, but the only sign I will give them is the sign of the prophet Jonah." Then Jesus left them and went away.

Yeast of the Pharisees and Sadducees

⁵Later, after they crossed to the other side of the lake, the disciples discovered they had forgotten to bring any food. ⁶"Watch out!" Jesus warned them. "Beware of the yeast of the Pharisees and Sadducees."

⁷They decided he was saying this because they hadn't brought any bread. ⁸Jesus knew what they were thinking, so he said, "You have so little faith! Why are you worried about having no food? ⁹Won't you ever understand? Don't you remember the five thousand I fed with five loaves, and the baskets of food that were left over? ¹⁰Don't you remember the four thousand I fed with seven loaves, with baskets of food left over? ¹¹How could you even think I was talking about food? So again I say, 'Beware of the yeast of the Pharisees and Sadducees.'"

¹²Then at last they understood that he wasn't speaking about yeast or bread but about the false teaching of the Pharisees and Sadducees.

Peter's Declaration about Jesus

¹³When Jesus came to the region of Caesarea Philippi, he asked his disciples, "Who do people say that the Son of Man is?"

¹⁴"Well," they replied, "some say John the Baptist, some say Elijah, and others say Jeremiah or one of the other prophets."

¹⁵Then he asked them, "Who do you say I am?"

¹⁶Simon Peter answered, "You are the Messiah, the Son of the living God."

¹⁷Jesus replied, "You are blessed, Simon son of John,* because my Father in heaven has revealed this to you. You did not learn this from any human being. ¹⁸Now I say to you that you are Peter,* and upon this rock I will build my church, and all the powers of hell* will not conquer it. ¹⁹And I will give you the keys of the Kingdom of Heaven. Whatever you lock on earth will be locked in heaven, and whatever you open on earth will be opened in heaven." ²⁰Then he sternly warned them not to tell anyone that he was the Messiah.

Jesus Predicts His Death

²¹From then on Jesus began to tell his disciples plainly that he had to go to Jerusalem, and he told them what would happen to him there. He would suffer at the hands of the leaders and the leading priests and the teachers of religious law. He would be killed, and he would be raised on the third day.

²²But Peter took him aside and corrected him. "Heaven forbid, Lord," he said. "This will never happen to you!"

²³Jesus turned to Peter and said, "Get away from me, Satan! You are a dangerous trap to me. You are seeing things merely from a human point of view, and not from God's."

²⁴Then Jesus said to the disciples, "If any of you wants to be my follower, you must put aside your selfish ambition, shoulder your cross, and follow me. ²⁵If you try to keep your life for yourself, you will lose it. But if you give up your life for me, you will find true life. ²⁶And how do you benefit if you gain the

16:2-3 Several manuscripts do not include any of the words in 16:2-3 after *He replied.* **16:17** Greek *Simon son of Jonah;* see John 1:42; 21:15-17. **16:18a** *Peter* means "stone" or "rock." **16:18b** Greek *and the gates of Hades.*

16:13-17 There are many answers to the question, Who is Jesus? but only one of them is correct. The insight that Jesus is the promised Messiah and the Son of God comes from God himself, not from any human source. Likewise, the realization that the God of the Bible is the higher power we need for recovery is a revelation from God's Word. To put our trust in any other power for recovery will only lead to disappointment and failure.

17:1-8 Even before Jesus' transfiguration, Jesus was the glorious Son of God. But Peter, James, and John had never seen Jesus in that way. After their experience on the Mount of Transfiguration, these disciples would never again consider Jesus as anything less than God's Son without being in full-scale denial. Through the words of Matthew and the testimony of other believers, we too are witnesses of God's glory in Jesus Christ. To deny his authority over our life is to assure the failure of any recovery program. Jesus is the only one who can transform our broken life.

17:14-21 This account of the disciples' failure to cast out a demon teaches us a crucial lesson about the role of faith in recovery. Jesus criticized the disciples for their lack of faith in God's power to heal the boy. We don't need a large amount of faith to begin the healing process in our life; we need "faith as small as a mustard seed" to effect change. Prayer and faith in God are the tools for recovery; with these we can move mountains!

whole world but lose your own soul* in the process? Is anything worth more than your soul? 27For I, the Son of Man, will come in the glory of my Father with his angels and will judge all people according to their deeds. 28And I assure you that some of you standing here right now will not die before you see me, the Son of Man, coming in my Kingdom."

CHAPTER 17
The Transfiguration
Six days later Jesus took Peter and the two brothers, James and John, and led them up a high mountain. 2As the men watched, Jesus' appearance changed so that his face shone like the sun, and his clothing became dazzling white. 3Suddenly, Moses and Elijah appeared and began talking with Jesus. 4Peter blurted out, "Lord, this is wonderful! If you want me to, I'll make three shrines,* one for you, one for Moses, and one for Elijah."

5But even as he said it, a bright cloud came over them, and a voice from the cloud said, "This is my beloved Son, and I am fully pleased with him. Listen to him." 6The disciples were terrified and fell face down on the ground.

7Jesus came over and touched them. "Get up," he said, "don't be afraid." 8And when they looked, they saw only Jesus with them. 9As they descended the mountain, Jesus commanded them, "Don't tell anyone what you have seen until I, the Son of Man, have been raised from the dead."

10His disciples asked, "Why do the teachers of religious law insist that Elijah must return before the Messiah comes*?"

11Jesus replied, "Elijah is indeed coming first to set everything in order. 12But I tell you, he has already come, but he wasn't recognized, and he was badly mistreated. And soon the Son of Man will also suffer at their hands." 13Then the disciples realized he had been speaking of John the Baptist.

Jesus Heals a Demon-Possessed Boy
14When they arrived at the foot of the mountain, a huge crowd was waiting for them. A man came and knelt before Jesus and said, 15"Lord, have mercy on my son, because he has seizures and suffers terribly. He often falls into the fire or into the water. 16So I brought him to your disciples, but they couldn't heal him."

17Jesus replied, "You stubborn, faithless people! How long must I be with you until

16:26 Or *your life;* also in 16:26b. **17:4** Or *shelters;* Greek reads *tabernacles.* **17:10** Greek *that Elijah must come first.*

D elayed Gratification
READ MATTHEW 16:24-26
Some of us are addicted to chaos. We may be so used to crisis that we don't know how to enjoy the calm. Life in recovery may seem boring in comparison to our old ways. We may even miss the excitement and danger. The rewards may seem too slow in coming.

The apostle Paul said, "So don't get tired of doing what is good. Don't get discouraged and give up, for we will reap a harvest of blessing at the appropriate time" (Galatians 6:9). Weeds spring up quickly. Good crops grow more slowly and must be tended steadily, even before we can see anything sprout. It's only in time that we will enjoy the fruit.

Jesus suggested that we expand our perspective even further, with a view toward eternity. "Jesus said to the disciples, 'If any of you wants to be my follower, you must put aside your selfish ambition, shoulder your cross, and follow me. If you try to keep your life for yourself, you will lose it. But if you give up your life for me, you will find true life. And how do you benefit if you gain the whole world but lose your own soul in the process?'" (Matthew 16:24-26).

It is God's will for us to have a rewarding and fulfilled life. It may be easier to adjust to our new way of life if we remember that denying ourself immediate pleasures will bring a harvest of rich rewards in this life and in the life to come. *Turn to page 43, Matthew 25.*

you believe? How long must I put up with you? Bring the boy to me." 18Then Jesus rebuked the demon in the boy, and it left him. From that moment the boy was well.

19Afterward the disciples asked Jesus privately, "Why couldn't we cast out that demon?"

20"You didn't have enough faith," Jesus told them. "I assure you, even if you had faith as small as a mustard seed you could say to this mountain, 'Move from here to there,' and it would move. Nothing would be impossible."*

Jesus Again Predicts His Death

22One day after they had returned to Galilee, Jesus told them, "The Son of Man is going to be betrayed. 23He will be killed, but three days later he will be raised from the dead." And the disciples' hearts were filled with grief.

Payment of the Temple Tax

24On their arrival in Capernaum, the tax collectors for the Temple tax came to Peter and asked him, "Doesn't your teacher pay the Temple tax?"

25"Of course he does," Peter replied. Then he went into the house to talk to Jesus about it.

But before he had a chance to speak, Jesus asked him, "What do you think, Peter*? Do kings tax their own people or the foreigners they have conquered?"

26"They tax the foreigners," Peter replied.

"Well, then," Jesus said, "the citizens are free! 27However, we don't want to offend them, so go down to the lake and throw in a line. Open the mouth of the first fish you catch, and you will find a coin. Take the coin and pay the tax for both of us."

CHAPTER 18
The Greatest in the Kingdom

About that time the disciples came to Jesus and asked, "Which of us is greatest in the Kingdom of Heaven?"

2Jesus called a small child over to him and put the child among them. 3Then he said, "I assure you, unless you turn from your sins and become as little children, you will never get into the Kingdom of Heaven. 4Therefore, anyone who becomes as humble as this little child is the greatest in the Kingdom of Heaven. 5And anyone who welcomes a little child like this on my behalf is welcoming me. 6But if anyone causes one of these little ones who trusts in me to lose faith, it would be better for that person to be thrown into the sea with a large millstone tied around the neck.

7"How terrible it will be for anyone who causes others to sin. Temptation to do wrong is inevitable, but how terrible it will be for the person who does the tempting. 8So if your hand or foot causes you to sin, cut it off and throw it away. It is better to enter heaven* crippled or lame than to be thrown into the unquenchable fire with both of your hands and feet. 9And if your eye causes you to sin, gouge it out and throw it away. It is better to enter heaven half blind than to have two eyes and be thrown into hell.

10"Beware that you don't despise a single one of these little ones. For I tell you that in heaven their angels are always in the presence of my heavenly Father.*

Story of the Lost Sheep

12"If a shepherd has one hundred sheep, and one wanders away and is lost, what will he do? Won't he leave the ninety-nine others and go out into the hills to search for the lost one? 13And if he finds it, he will surely rejoice over it more than over the ninety-nine that

---

17:20 Some manuscripts add verse 21, *But this kind of demon won't leave unless you have prayed and fasted.*
17:25 Greek *Simon.* **18:8** Greek *enter life;* also in 18:9. **18:10** Some manuscripts add verse 11, *And I, the Son of Man, have come to save the lost.*

18:2-6 By calling the little children to come to him, Jesus revealed his love for each of us. He warned that terrible judgment would come upon those who harm his followers or cause them to lose faith. This is encouraging for those of us who have suffered injustices or abuse from others, especially when we were children. We don't have to carry our hate with us or waste our energy dreaming of revenge. God will judge those who have harmed us. We should focus on recovery, not on the punishment of the people who have hurt us.
18:10-14 Many children and adults believe the lie that they are worthless to other people and insignificant to God. Jesus indicated that he came to save the lost, no matter how few or how "insignificant" they seemed. God the Father does not want anyone to miss the opportunity for salvation or recovery in Jesus Christ. God values each one of us, no matter how painful our past or how far we have strayed. If we admit our need for him and seek to follow his will for us, we will discover how very important we are to God and the people close to us.

didn't wander away! [14]In the same way, it is not my heavenly Father's will that even one of these little ones should perish.

Correcting a Fellow Believer

[15]"If another believer* sins against you, go privately and point out the fault. If the other person listens and confesses it, you have won that person back. [16]But if you are unsuccessful, take one or two others with you and go back again, so that everything you say may be confirmed by two or three witnesses. [17]If that person still refuses to listen, take your case to the church. If the church decides you are right, but the other person won't accept it, treat that person as a pagan or a corrupt tax collector. [18]I tell you this: Whatever you prohibit on earth is prohibited in heaven, and whatever you allow on earth is allowed in heaven.

[19]"I also tell you this: If two of you agree down here on earth concerning anything you ask, my Father in heaven will do it for you. [20]For where two or three gather together because they are mine,* I am there among them."

Story of the Unforgiving Debtor

[21]Then Peter came to him and asked, "Lord, how often should I forgive someone* who sins against me? Seven times?"

[22]"No!" Jesus replied, "seventy times seven!*

[23]"For this reason, the Kingdom of Heaven can be compared to a king who decided to bring his accounts up to date with servants who had borrowed money from him. [24]In the process, one of his debtors was brought in who owed him millions of dollars.* [25]He couldn't pay, so the king ordered that he, his wife, his children, and everything he had be sold to pay the debt. [26]But the man fell down before the king and begged him, 'Oh, sir, be patient with me, and I will pay it all.' [27]Then the king was filled with pity for him, and he released him and forgave his debt.

[28]"But when the man left the king, he went to a fellow servant who owed him a few thousand dollars.* He grabbed him by the throat and demanded instant payment. [29]His fellow servant fell down before him and begged for a little more time. 'Be patient and I will pay it,' he pleaded. [30]But his creditor wouldn't wait. He had the man arrested and jailed until the debt could be paid in full.

18:15 Greek *your brother.* **18:20** Greek *gather together in my name.* **18:21** Greek *my brother.* **18:22** Or *77 times.* **18:24** Greek *10,000 talents.* **18:28** Greek *100 denarii.* A denarius was the equivalent of a full day's wage.

STEP 8

Forgiven to Forgive

BIBLE READING: Matthew 18:23-35

We made a list of all persons we had harmed and became willing to make amends to them all.

Listing all the people we have harmed will probably trigger a natural defensiveness. With each name we write down, another mental list may begin to form—a list of the wrongs that have been done to us. How can we deal with the resentment we hold toward others so we can move toward making amends?

Jesus told this story: "A king . . . decided to bring his accounts up to date with servants who had borrowed money from him. In the process, one of his debtors was brought in who owed him millions of dollars" (Matthew 18:23-24). The man begged for forgiveness because he couldn't pay. "The king was filled with pity for him, and he released him and forgave his debt. But when the man left the king, he went to a fellow servant who owed him a few thousand dollars. He grabbed him by the throat and demanded instant payment" (18:27-28). This was reported to the king. "Then the king called in the man he had forgiven and said, 'You evil servant! I forgave you that tremendous debt because you pleaded with me. Shouldn't you have mercy on your fellow servant . . . ?' Then the angry king sent the man to prison until he had paid every penny. That's what my heavenly Father will do to you if you refuse to forgive your brothers and sisters" (18:32-35).

When we look at all that God has forgiven us, it makes sense to choose to forgive others. This also frees us from the torture of festering resentment. We can't change what others have done to us, but we can write off their debts and become willing to make amends. *Turn to page 283, 2 Corinthians 2.*

³¹"When some of the other servants saw this, they were very upset. They went to the king and told him what had happened. ³²Then the king called in the man he had forgiven and said, 'You evil servant! I forgave you that tremendous debt because you pleaded with me. ³³Shouldn't you have mercy on your fellow servant, just as I had mercy on you?' ³⁴Then the angry king sent the man to prison until he had paid every penny.

³⁵"That's what my heavenly Father will do to you if you refuse to forgive your brothers and sisters* in your heart."

CHAPTER 19
Discussion about Divorce and Marriage
After Jesus had finished saying these things, he left Galilee and went southward to the region of Judea and into the area east of the Jordan River. ²Vast crowds followed him there, and he healed their sick.

³Some Pharisees came and tried to trap him with this question: "Should a man be allowed to divorce his wife for any reason?"

⁴"Haven't you read the Scriptures?" Jesus replied. "They record that from the beginning 'God made them male and female.'* ⁵And he said, 'This explains why a man leaves his father and mother and is joined to his wife, and the two are united into one.'* ⁶Since they are no longer two but one, let no one separate them, for God has joined them together."

⁷"Then why did Moses say a man could merely write an official letter of divorce and send her away?"* they asked.

⁸Jesus replied, "Moses permitted divorce as a concession to your hard-hearted wickedness, but it was not what God had origi-

nally intended. ⁹And I tell you this, a man who divorces his wife and marries another commits adultery—unless his wife has been unfaithful.*"

¹⁰Jesus' disciples then said to him, "Then it is better not to marry!"

¹¹"Not everyone can accept this statement," Jesus said. "Only those whom God helps. ¹²Some are born as eunuchs, some have been made that way by others, and some choose not to marry for the sake of the Kingdom of Heaven. Let anyone who can, accept this statement."

Jesus Blesses the Children
¹³Some children were brought to Jesus so he could lay his hands on them and pray for them. The disciples told them not to bother him. ¹⁴But Jesus said, "Let the children come to me. Don't stop them! For the Kingdom of Heaven belongs to such as these." ¹⁵And he put his hands on their heads and blessed them before he left.

The Rich Young Man
¹⁶Someone came to Jesus with this question: "Teacher,* what good things must I do to have eternal life?"

¹⁷"Why ask me about what is good?" Jesus replied. "Only God is good. But to answer your question, you can receive eternal life if you keep the commandments."

¹⁸"Which ones?" the man asked.

And Jesus replied: "'Do not murder. Do not commit adultery. Do not steal. Do not testify falsely. ¹⁹Honor your father and mother. Love your neighbor as yourself.'*"

²⁰"I've obeyed all these commandments," the young man replied. "What else must I do?"

18:35 Greek *your brother.* **19:4** Gen 1:27; 5:2. **19:5** Gen 2:24. **19:7** Deut 24:1. **19:9** Some manuscripts add *And the man who marries a divorced woman commits adultery.* **19:16** Some manuscripts read *Good Teacher.* **19:18-19** Exod 20:12-16; Lev 19:18; Deut 5:16-20.

19:3-12 Jesus affirmed the importance of the marriage relationship. We may find it confining to be without an "escape hatch" in marriage, but God has always intended that marriage be a life-long commitment. Realizing that marriage is permanent and that a husband and wife are one through marriage should make us consider how much our sins and dependency harm our spouse. Even though divorce may end the conflict between a couple, it will not correct the attitudes or behaviors that brought about the conflict. Unless we correct the root problems in ourself, we will have the same conflicts in future relationships.

19:16-24 The rich young man was trying to work (and buy) his way to heaven. Jesus played along with this man's shortsighted attempt to claim he was perfect. But it soon became clear that the man was addicted to his material wealth and the security it bought him. His possessions had a higher priority in his life than God did. Materialism is a form of addiction or compulsion that makes it nearly impossible to be humble and trust Jesus Christ alone for salvation and recovery. As long as we believe we can buy our way out of our problems, we will never achieve lasting recovery.

²¹Jesus told him, "If you want to be perfect, go and sell all you have and give the money to the poor, and you will have treasure in heaven. Then come, follow me." ²²But when the young man heard this, he went sadly away because he had many possessions.

²³Then Jesus said to his disciples, "I tell you the truth, it is very hard for a rich person to get into the Kingdom of Heaven. ²⁴I say it again—it is easier for a camel to go through the eye of a needle than for a rich person to enter the Kingdom of God!"

²⁵The disciples were astounded. "Then who in the world can be saved?" they asked.

²⁶Jesus looked at them intently and said, "Humanly speaking, it is impossible. But with God everything is possible."

²⁷Then Peter said to him, "We've given up everything to follow you. What will we get out of it?"

²⁸And Jesus replied, "I assure you that when I, the Son of Man, sit upon my glorious throne in the Kingdom,* you who have been my followers will also sit on twelve thrones, judging the twelve tribes of Israel. ²⁹And everyone who has given up houses or brothers or sisters or father or mother or children or property, for my sake, will receive a hundred times as much in return and will have eternal life. ³⁰But many who seem to be important now will be the least important then, and those who are considered least here will be the greatest then.*

CHAPTER 20
Story of the Vineyard Workers

"For the Kingdom of Heaven is like the owner of an estate who went out early one morning to hire workers for his vineyard. ²He agreed to pay the normal daily wage* and sent them out to work.

³"At nine o'clock in the morning he was passing through the marketplace and saw some people standing around doing nothing. ⁴So he hired them, telling them he would pay them whatever was right at the end of the day. ⁵At noon and again around three o'clock he did the same thing. ⁶At five o'clock that evening he was in town again and saw some more people standing around. He asked them, 'Why haven't you been working today?'

⁷"They replied, 'Because no one hired us.'

"The owner of the estate told them, 'Then go on out and join the others in my vineyard.'

⁸"That evening he told the foreman to call the workers in and pay them, beginning with the last workers first. ⁹When those hired at five o'clock were paid, each received a full day's wage. ¹⁰When those hired earlier came to get their pay, they assumed they would receive more. But they, too, were paid a day's wage. ¹¹When they received their pay, they protested, ¹²'Those people worked only one hour, and yet you've paid them just as much as you paid us who worked all day in the scorching heat.'

¹³"He answered one of them, 'Friend, I haven't been unfair! Didn't you agree to work all day for the usual wage? ¹⁴Take it and go. I wanted to pay this last worker the same as you. ¹⁵Is it against the law for me to do what I want with my money? Should you be angry because I am kind?'

¹⁶"And so it is, that many who are first now will be last then; and those who are last now will be first then."

Jesus Again Predicts His Death

¹⁷As Jesus was on the way to Jerusalem, he took the twelve disciples aside privately and told them what was going to happen to him. ¹⁸"When we get to Jerusalem," he said, "the Son of Man will be betrayed to the leading priests and the teachers of religious law. They will sentence him to die. ¹⁹Then they will hand him over to the Romans to be mocked, whipped, and crucified. But on the third day he will be raised from the dead."

19:28 Greek *in the regeneration.* **19:30** Greek *But many who are first will be last; and the last, first.* **20:2** Greek *a denarius,* the payment for a full day's labor; also in 20:9, 10, 13.

19:25-26 These verses are true not only for salvation but also for recovery. Left on our own, we would fall deeper into the pit of our addiction, never gaining control over it. But with God's help, the inconceivable is possible. He can turn our life around, bringing hope and health where once despair and pain had reigned. Giving God control of our life is the only way to regain independence from our addiction and other compulsive behaviors.

20:1-16 The story about the workers and their pay speaks strongly about God's grace. No matter when we begin to follow Jesus, we receive the same amount of grace from God. That may seem unfair to some; but God in his mercy accepts all people who turn to him for salvation and recovery, no matter how early or late in life. It is never too late to begin the process of recovery!

Jesus Teaches about Serving Others

[20]Then the mother of James and John, the sons of Zebedee, came to Jesus with her sons. She knelt respectfully to ask a favor. [21]"What is your request?" he asked.

She replied, "In your Kingdom, will you let my two sons sit in places of honor next to you, one at your right and the other at your left?"

[22]But Jesus told them, "You don't know what you are asking! Are you able to drink from the bitter cup of sorrow I am about to drink?"

"Oh yes," they replied, "we are able!"

[23]"You will indeed drink from it," he told them. "But I have no right to say who will sit on the thrones next to mine. My Father has prepared those places for the ones he has chosen."

[24]When the ten other disciples heard what James and John had asked, they were indignant. [25]But Jesus called them together and said, "You know that in this world kings are tyrants, and officials lord it over the people beneath them. [26]But among you it should be quite different. Whoever wants to be a leader among you must be your servant, [27]and whoever wants to be first must become your slave. [28]For even I, the Son of Man, came here not to be served but to serve others, and to give my life as a ransom for many."

Jesus Heals Two Blind Men

[29]As Jesus and the disciples left the city of Jericho, a huge crowd followed behind. [30]Two blind men were sitting beside the road. When they heard that Jesus was coming that way, they began shouting, "Lord, Son of David, have mercy on us!" [31]The crowd told them to be quiet, but they only shouted louder, "Lord, Son of David, have mercy on us!"

[32]Jesus stopped in the road and called, "What do you want me to do for you?"

[33]"Lord," they said, "we want to see!" [34]Jesus felt sorry for them and touched their eyes. Instantly they could see! Then they followed him.

CHAPTER 21
The Triumphal Entry

As Jesus and the disciples approached Jerusalem, they came to the town of Bethphage on the Mount of Olives. Jesus sent two of them on ahead. [2]"Go into the village over there," he said, "and you will see a donkey tied there, with its colt beside it. Untie them and bring them here. [3]If anyone asks what you are doing, just say, 'The Lord needs them,' and he will immediately send them." [4]This was done to fulfill the prophecy,

[5]"Tell the people of Israel,*
  'Look, your King is coming to you.
He is humble, riding on a donkey—
  even on a donkey's colt.'"*

[6]The two disciples did as Jesus said. [7]They brought the animals to him and threw their garments over the colt, and he sat on it.* [8]Most of the crowd spread their coats on the road ahead of Jesus, and others cut branches from the trees and spread them on the road. [9]He was in the center of the procession, and the crowds all around him were shouting,

"Praise God* for the Son of David!
Bless the one who comes in the name
  of the Lord!
Praise God in highest heaven!"*

[10]The entire city of Jerusalem was stirred as he entered. "Who is this?" they asked.

[11]And the crowds replied, "It's Jesus, the prophet from Nazareth in Galilee."

21:5a Greek *Tell the daughter of Zion.* Isa 62:11. 21:5b Zech 9:9. 21:7 Greek *over them, and he sat on them.* 21:9a Greek *Hosanna,* an exclamation of praise that literally means "save now"; also in 21:9b, 15. 21:9b Pss 118:25-26; 148:1.

20:20-28 The other disciples were indignant at the request for special recognition made by James's and John's mother because they, too, wanted positions of honor in God's Kingdom. This prideful attitude contradicted what Jesus taught and is always detrimental to recovery. Becoming great in God's sight is achieved through humbly serving others. This is also one of our goals in recovery. As we receive God's grace and restoration, we are called to carry God's message to others and to help them in the recovery process.

20:29-34 Jesus' sensitivity to the needs of two blind men in a huge crowd shows that God cares very much for individuals who hurt. Jesus healed them because they asked him to. They believed in him and did not listen to the bystanders' discouraging remarks. They persevered despite opposition and continued with their humble pleas for help. In recovery we may encounter opposition; we may need to swallow our pride and just keep going. We can be sure that even if others laugh at us or discourage us, God is listening and will help us in the recovery process.

Jesus Clears the Temple

¹²Jesus entered the Temple and began to drive out the merchants and their customers. He knocked over the tables of the money changers and the stalls of those selling doves. ¹³He said, "The Scriptures declare, 'My Temple will be called a place of prayer,' but you have turned it into a den of thieves!"*

¹⁴The blind and the lame came to him, and he healed them there in the Temple. ¹⁵The leading priests and the teachers of religious law saw these wonderful miracles and heard even the little children in the Temple shouting, "Praise God for the Son of David." But they were indignant ¹⁶and asked Jesus, "Do you hear what these children are saying?"

"Yes," Jesus replied. "Haven't you ever read the Scriptures? For they say, 'You have taught children and infants to give you praise.'*" ¹⁷Then he returned to Bethany, where he stayed overnight.

Jesus Curses the Fig Tree

¹⁸In the morning, as Jesus was returning to Jerusalem, he was hungry, ¹⁹and he noticed a fig tree beside the road. He went over to see if there were any figs on it, but there were only leaves. Then he said to it, "May you never bear fruit again!" And immediately the fig tree withered up.

²⁰The disciples were amazed when they saw this and asked, "How did the fig tree wither so quickly?"

²¹Then Jesus told them, "I assure you, if you have faith and don't doubt, you can do things like this and much more. You can even say to this mountain, 'May God lift you up and throw you into the sea,' and it will happen. ²²If you believe, you will receive whatever you ask for in prayer."

The Authority of Jesus Challenged

²³When Jesus returned to the Temple and began teaching, the leading priests and other leaders came up to him. They demanded, "By whose authority did you drive out the merchants from the Temple?* Who gave you such authority?"

²⁴"I'll tell you who gave me the authority to do these things if you answer one question," Jesus replied. ²⁵"Did John's baptism come from heaven or was it merely human?"

They talked it over among themselves. "If we say it was from heaven, he will ask why we didn't believe him. ²⁶But if we say it was merely human, we'll be mobbed, because the people think he was a prophet." ²⁷So they finally replied, "We don't know."

And Jesus responded, "Then I won't answer your question either.

Story of the Two Sons

²⁸"But what do you think about this? A man with two sons told the older boy, 'Son, go out and work in the vineyard today.' ²⁹The son answered, 'No, I won't go,' but later he changed his mind and went anyway. ³⁰Then the father told the other son, 'You go,' and he said, 'Yes, sir, I will.' But he didn't go. ³¹Which of the two was obeying his father?"

They replied, "The first, of course."

Then Jesus explained his meaning: "I assure you, corrupt tax collectors and prostitutes will get into the Kingdom of God before you do. ³²For John the Baptist came and showed you the way to life, and you didn't believe him, while tax collectors and prostitutes did. And even when you saw this happening, you refused to turn from your sins and believe him.

Story of the Evil Farmers

³³"Now listen to this story. A certain landowner planted a vineyard, built a wall around it, dug a pit for pressing out the grape juice, and built a lookout tower. Then he leased the vineyard to tenant farmers and moved to another country. ³⁴At the time of

21:13 Isa 56:7; Jer 7:11. **21:16** Ps 8:2. **21:23** Or *By whose authority do you do these things?*

21:18-22 Jesus again commented on the power of faith. Seemingly impossible answers to prayer, including life-transforming recovery, can occur as we live by faith and grow in commitment to God. This passage does not suggest that we pray for the withering of a fig tree or the actual relocation of a mountain. It tells us, however, that incredible answers are given when we pray to God and believe that he will answer.

21:28-32 Before we began the recovery process, we were like the first son, saying no to his father's wishes. We turned our back to God and indulged our selfish desires. But later we saw where we were headed, changed our mind, and followed our Father. Although we have messed up our life, we are now obeying God. This is in sharp contrast to the son who said he would obey and then didn't. People like this may be part of the established "church" and think they are following God but are far from his ways. Our change of heart and lifestyle will gain us eternal life; their denial will earn them eternal punishment.

the grape harvest he sent his servants to collect his share of the crop. 35But the farmers grabbed his servants, beat one, killed one, and stoned another. 36So the landowner sent a larger group of his servants to collect for him, but the results were the same.

37"Finally, the owner sent his son, thinking, 'Surely they will respect my son.'

38"But when the farmers saw his son coming, they said to one another, 'Here comes the heir to this estate. Come on, let's kill him and get the estate for ourselves!' 39So they grabbed him, took him out of the vineyard, and murdered him.

40"When the owner of the vineyard returns," Jesus asked, "what do you think he will do to those farmers?"

41The religious leaders replied, "He will put the wicked men to a horrible death and lease the vineyard to others who will give him his share of the crop after each harvest."

42Then Jesus asked them, "Didn't you ever read this in the Scriptures?

'The stone rejected by the builders
    has now become the cornerstone.
This is the Lord's doing,
    and it is marvelous to see.'*

43What I mean is that the Kingdom of God will be taken away from you and given to a nation that will produce the proper fruit. 44Anyone who stumbles over that stone will be broken to pieces, and it will crush anyone on whom it falls.*"

45When the leading priests and Pharisees heard Jesus, they realized he was pointing at them—that they were the farmers in his story. 46They wanted to arrest him, but they were afraid to try because the crowds considered Jesus to be a prophet.

CHAPTER 22
Story of the Great Feast
Jesus told them several other stories to illustrate the Kingdom. He said, 2"The Kingdom of Heaven can be illustrated by the story of a king who prepared a great wedding feast for his son. 3Many guests were invited, and when the banquet was ready, he sent his servants to notify everyone that it was time to come. But they all refused! 4So he sent other servants to tell them, 'The feast has been prepared, and choice meats have been cooked. Everything is ready. Hurry!' 5But the guests he had invited ignored them and went about their business, one to his farm, another to his store. 6Others seized his messengers and treated them shamefully, even killing some of them.

7"Then the king became furious. He sent out his army to destroy the murderers and burn their city. 8And he said to his servants, 'The wedding feast is ready, and the guests I invited aren't worthy of the honor. 9Now go out to the street corners and invite everyone you see.'

10"So the servants brought in everyone they could find, good and bad alike, and the banquet hall was filled with guests. 11But when the king came in to meet the guests, he noticed a man who wasn't wearing the proper clothes for a wedding. 12'Friend,' he asked, 'how is it that you are here without wedding clothes?' And the man had no reply. 13Then the king said to his aides, 'Bind him hand and foot and throw him out into the outer darkness, where there is weeping and gnashing of teeth.' 14For many are called, but few are chosen."

Taxes for Caesar
15Then the Pharisees met together to think of a way to trap Jesus into saying something for which they could accuse him. 16They decided to send some of their disciples, along with the supporters of Herod, to ask him this question: "Teacher, we know how honest you are. You teach about the way of God regardless of the consequences. You are impartial and don't play favorites. 17Now tell us what you think about this: Is it right to pay taxes to the Roman government or not?"

18But Jesus knew their evil motives. "You hypocrites!" he said. "Whom are you trying to fool with your trick questions? 19Here, show me the Roman coin used for the tax." When they handed him the coin,* 20he asked, "Whose picture and title are stamped on it?"

21:42 Ps 118:22-23. 21:44 This verse is omitted in some early manuscripts. 22:19 Greek a denarius.

22:1-10 When the king's servants brought everyone they could find to the wedding feast, there were good and bad people. The offer was open to anyone who wanted to come. So it is with heaven: Everyone is invited, and anyone can refuse the offer. The same principles apply to recovery. God wants everyone to lead a healthy, productive, godly life; but anyone can refuse to start the recovery process. Will we be like the first group of guests and suffer for our decision, or will we be like the second group and enjoy what God offers us?

²¹"Caesar's," they replied.

"Well, then," he said, "give to Caesar what belongs to him. But everything that belongs to God must be given to God." ²²His reply amazed them, and they went away.

Discussion about Resurrection

²³That same day some Sadducees stepped forward—a group of Jews who say there is no resurrection after death. They posed this question: ²⁴"Teacher, Moses said, 'If a man dies without children, his brother should marry the widow and have a child who will be the brother's heir.'* ²⁵Well, there were seven brothers. The oldest married and then died without children, so the second brother married the widow. ²⁶This brother also died without children, and the wife was married to the next brother, and so on until she had been the wife of each of them. ²⁷And then she also died. ²⁸So tell us, whose wife will she be in the resurrection? For she was the wife of all seven of them!"

²⁹Jesus replied, "Your problem is that you don't know the Scriptures, and you don't know the power of God. ³⁰For when the dead rise, they won't be married. They will be like the angels in heaven. ³¹But now, as to whether there will be a resurrection of the dead—haven't you ever read about this in the Scriptures? Long after Abraham, Isaac, and Jacob had died, God said,* ³²'I am the God of Abraham, the God of Isaac, and the God of Jacob.'* So he is the God of the living, not the dead."

³³When the crowds heard him, they were impressed with his teaching.

The Most Important Commandment

³⁴But when the Pharisees heard that he had silenced the Sadducees with his reply, they thought up a fresh question of their own to ask him. ³⁵One of them, an expert in religious law, tried to trap him with this question: ³⁶"Teacher, which is the most important commandment in the law of Moses?"

³⁷Jesus replied, "'You must love the Lord your God with all your heart, all your soul, and all your mind.'* ³⁸This is the first and greatest commandment. ³⁹A second is equally important: 'Love your neighbor as yourself.'* ⁴⁰All the other commandments and all the demands of the prophets are based on these two commandments."

Whose Son Is the Messiah?

⁴¹Then, surrounded by the Pharisees, Jesus asked them a question: ⁴²"What do you think about the Messiah? Whose son is he?"

They replied, "He is the son of David."

⁴³Jesus responded, "Then why does David, speaking under the inspiration of the Holy Spirit, call him Lord? For David said,

⁴⁴ 'The LORD said to my Lord,
  Sit in honor at my right hand
    until I humble your enemies beneath
      your feet.'*

⁴⁵Since David called him Lord, how can he be his son at the same time?"

⁴⁶No one could answer him. And after that, no one dared to ask him any more questions.

CHAPTER 23
Jesus Warns the Religious Leaders

Then Jesus said to the crowds and to his disciples, ²"The teachers of religious law and the Pharisees are the official interpreters of the Scriptures. ³So practice and obey whatever they say to you, but don't follow their example. For they don't practice what they teach. ⁴They crush you with impossible religious demands and never lift a finger to help ease the burden.

22:24 Deut 25:5-6. **22:31** Greek *in the Scriptures? God said.* **22:32** Exod 3:6. **22:37** Deut 6:5. **22:39** Lev 19:18. **22:44** Ps 110:1.

22:33-40 To simplify our priorities, Jesus narrowed the six hundred–plus regulations of the law of Moses into two foundational commandments: Love God with everything we are and have; love our neighbors as ourself. To do these is to obey every other law. A better two-point summary of the Twelve Steps could not be found. When we love God with our very life, we will not want to do anything to disgrace him or make him angry. Loving others should make us aware of the pain others feel when we engage in our addiction; our concern and love for them should make us think twice before causing them to suffer.

23:1-12 The Pharisees and Jewish leaders are classic examples of people who live by a double standard. They made the standards of behavior for others impossibly difficult, but they failed to keep these stipulations themselves. In spite of their shortcomings, they demanded to be called by titles fit only for God. They did not realize that true greatness begins with humility and is proven by a willingness to help others. The Pharisees' pride kept them from seeing their true need for God.

5"Everything they do is for show. On their arms they wear extra wide prayer boxes with Scripture verses inside,* and they wear extra long tassels on their robes. 6And how they love to sit at the head table at banquets and in the most prominent seats in the synagogue! 7They enjoy the attention they get on the streets, and they enjoy being called 'Rabbi.'* 8Don't ever let anyone call you 'Rabbi,' for you have only one teacher, and all of you are on the same level as brothers and sisters.* 9And don't address anyone here on earth as 'Father,' for only God in heaven is your spiritual Father. 10And don't let anyone call you 'Master,' for there is only one master, the Messiah. 11The greatest among you must be a servant. 12But those who exalt themselves will be humbled, and those who humble themselves will be exalted.

13"How terrible it will be for you teachers of religious law and you Pharisees. Hypocrites! For you won't let others enter the Kingdom of Heaven, and you won't go in yourselves.* 15Yes, how terrible it will be for you teachers of religious law and you Pharisees. For you cross land and sea to make one convert, and then you turn him into twice the son of hell as you yourselves are.

16"Blind guides! How terrible it will be for you! For you say that it means nothing to swear 'by God's Temple'—you can break that oath. But then you say that it is binding to swear 'by the gold in the Temple.' 17Blind fools! Which is greater, the gold, or the Temple that makes the gold sacred? 18And you say that to take an oath 'by the altar' can be broken, but to swear 'by the gifts on the altar' is binding! 19How blind! For which is greater, the gift on the altar, or the altar that makes the gift sacred? 20When you swear 'by the altar,' you are swearing by it and by everything on it. 21And when you swear 'by the Temple,' you are swearing by it and by God, who lives in it. 22And when you swear 'by heaven,' you are swearing by the throne of God and by God, who sits on the throne.

23"How terrible it will be for you teachers of religious law and you Pharisees. Hypocrites! For you are careful to tithe even the tiniest part of your income,* but you ignore the important things of the law—justice, mercy, and faith. You should tithe, yes, but you should not leave undone the more important things. 24Blind guides! You strain your water so you won't accidentally swallow a gnat; then you swallow a camel!

25"How terrible it will be for you teachers of religious law and you Pharisees. Hypocrites! You are so careful to clean the outside of the cup and the dish, but inside you are filthy—full of greed and self-indulgence! 26Blind Pharisees! First wash the inside of the cup, and then the outside will become clean, too.

27"How terrible it will be for you teachers of religious law and you Pharisees. Hypocrites! You are like whitewashed tombs—beautiful on the outside but filled on the inside with dead people's bones and all sorts of impurity. 28You try to look like upright people outwardly, but inside your hearts are filled with hypocrisy and lawlessness.

29"How terrible it will be for you teachers of religious law and you Pharisees. Hypocrites! For you build tombs for the prophets your ancestors killed and decorate the graves of the godly people your ancestors destroyed. 30Then you say, 'We never would have joined them in killing the prophets.'

31"In saying that, you are accusing yourselves of being the descendants of those who murdered the prophets. 32Go ahead. Finish what they started. 33Snakes! Sons of vipers! How will you escape the judgment of hell? 34I will send you prophets and wise men and teachers of religious law. You will kill some by crucifixion and whip others in your synagogues, chasing them from city to city. 35As a result, you will become guilty of murdering all the godly people from righteous Abel to Zechariah son of Barachiah, whom you murdered in the Temple between the altar and the sanctuary. 36I assure you, all the accumulated judgment of the centuries will break upon the heads of this very generation.

23:5 Greek *They enlarge their phylacteries.* 23:7 *Rabbi,* from Aramaic, means "master" or "teacher." 23:8 Greek *brothers.* 23:13 Some manuscripts add verse 14, *How terrible it will be for you teachers of religious law and you Pharisees. Hypocrites! You shamelessly cheat widows out of their property, and then, to cover up the kind of people you really are, you make long prayers in public. Because of this, your punishment will be the greater.* 23:23 Greek *to tithe the mint, the dill, and the cumin.*

23:13-36 Jesus gave warnings of judgment to all the spiritually blind religious leaders because of their hypocrisy. Their external rhetoric and ritualism were shams, all show with no inner reality. Such people cause others great pain and are far from recovery themselves. However, there is hope for everyone—even hypocrites! Joseph of Arimathea and Nicodemus, once numbered among the hypocrites, eventually found recovery through belief in Jesus (see John 19:38-42). If we search for Jesus, we will find him, and he will help us in the recovery process.

Jesus Grieves over Jerusalem

37"O Jerusalem, Jerusalem, the city that kills the prophets and stones God's messengers! How often I have wanted to gather your children together as a hen protects her chicks beneath her wings, but you wouldn't let me. 38And now look, your house is left to you, empty and desolate. 39For I tell you this, you will never see me again until you say, 'Bless the one who comes in the name of the Lord!'*"

CHAPTER 24
Jesus Foretells the Future

As Jesus was leaving the Temple grounds, his disciples pointed out to him the various Temple buildings. 2But he told them, "Do you see all these buildings? I assure you, they will be so completely demolished that not one stone will be left on top of another!"

3Later, Jesus sat on the slopes of the Mount of Olives. His disciples came to him privately and asked, "When will all this take place? And will there be any sign ahead of time to signal your return and the end of the world*?"

4Jesus told them, "Don't let anyone mislead you. 5For many will come in my name, saying, 'I am the Messiah.' They will lead many astray. 6And wars will break out near and far, but don't panic. Yes, these things must come, but the end won't follow immediately. 7The nations and kingdoms will proclaim war against each other, and there will be famines and earthquakes in many parts of the world. 8But all this will be only the beginning of the horrors to come.

9"Then you will be arrested, persecuted, and killed. You will be hated all over the world because of your allegiance to me. 10And many will turn away from me and betray and hate each other. 11And many false prophets will appear and will lead many people astray. 12Sin will be rampant everywhere, and the love of many will grow cold. 13But those who endure to the end will be saved. 14And the Good News about the Kingdom will be preached throughout the whole world, so that all nations will hear it; and then, finally, the end will come.

15"The time will come when you will see what Daniel the prophet spoke about: the sacrilegious object that causes desecration* standing in the Holy Place"—reader, pay attention! 16"Then those in Judea must flee to the hills. 17A person outside the house* must not go inside to pack. 18A person in the field must not return even to get a coat. 19How terrible it will be for pregnant women and for mothers nursing their babies in those days. 20And pray that your flight will not be in winter or on the Sabbath. 21For that will be a time of greater horror than anything the world has ever seen or will ever see again. 22In fact, unless that time of calamity is shortened, the entire human race will be destroyed. But it will be shortened for the sake of God's chosen ones.

23"Then if anyone tells you, 'Look, here is the Messiah,' or 'There he is,' don't pay any attention. 24For false messiahs and false prophets will rise up and perform great miraculous signs and wonders so as to deceive, if possible, even God's chosen ones. 25See, I have warned you.

26"So if someone tells you, 'Look, the Messiah is out in the desert,' don't bother to go and look. Or, 'Look, he is hiding here,' don't believe it! 27For as the lightning lights up the entire sky, so it will be when the Son of Man comes. 28Just as the gathering of vultures shows there is a carcass nearby, so these signs indicate that the end is near.*

29"Immediately after those horrible days end,

the sun will be darkened,
 the moon will not give light,
the stars will fall from the sky,
 and the powers of heaven will be shaken.*

23:39 Ps 118:26. 24:3 Or *the age.* 24:15 Greek *the abomination of desolation.* See Dan 9:27; 11:31; 12:11. 24:17 Greek *on the roof.* 24:28 Greek *Wherever the carcass is, the vultures gather.* 24:29 See Isa 13:10; 34:4; Joel 2:10.

24:2-8 Many people needing or seeking recovery are greatly discouraged by the fear that things will go on indefinitely in the same miserable, dysfunctional way they are now. As Jesus began his Olivet discourse (Matthew 24–25), he looked ahead to events surrounding his return to earth, and he promised that someday true recovery would take place (24:13). But things may get worse before they get better, which parallels the normal course for recovery. We need to hang in there until our program is complete and we are restored.

24:14 Because God loves everyone, he is delaying the world's judgment until all parts of the world have heard the message of salvation. This does not mean that everyone will accept the gospel; but every group will have had a chance to respond. As we get closer to world evangelization, we get closer to Christ's second coming. Have we accepted Jesus and his plan for salvation and recovery? If not, time is running out.

³⁰And then at last, the sign of the coming of the Son of Man will appear in the heavens, and there will be deep mourning among all the nations of the earth. And they will see the Son of Man arrive on the clouds of heaven with power and great glory.* ³¹And he will send forth his angels with the sound of a mighty trumpet blast, and they will gather together his chosen ones from the farthest ends of the earth and heaven.

³²"Now learn a lesson from the fig tree. When its buds become tender and its leaves begin to sprout, you know without being told that summer is near. ³³Just so, when you see the events I've described beginning to happen, you can know his return is very near, right at the door. ³⁴I assure you, this generation* will not pass from the scene before all these things take place. ³⁵Heaven and earth will disappear, but my words will remain forever.

³⁶"However, no one knows the day or the hour when these things will happen, not even the angels in heaven or the Son himself.* Only the Father knows.

³⁷"When the Son of Man returns, it will be like it was in Noah's day. ³⁸In those days before the Flood, the people were enjoying banquets and parties and weddings right up to the time Noah entered his boat. ³⁹People didn't realize what was going to happen until the Flood came and swept them all away. That is the way it will be when the Son of Man comes.

⁴⁰"Two men will be working together in the field; one will be taken, the other left. ⁴¹Two women will be grinding flour at the mill; one will be taken, the other left. ⁴²So be prepared, because you don't know what day your Lord is coming.

⁴³"Know this: A homeowner who knew exactly when a burglar was coming would stay alert and not permit the house to be broken into. ⁴⁴You also must be ready all the time. For the Son of Man will come when least expected.

⁴⁵"Who is a faithful, sensible servant, to whom the master can give the responsibility of managing his household and feeding his family? ⁴⁶If the master returns and finds that the servant has done a good job, there will be a reward. ⁴⁷I assure you, the master will put that servant in charge of all he owns. ⁴⁸But if the servant is evil and thinks, 'My master won't be back for a while,' ⁴⁹and begins oppressing the other servants, partying, and getting drunk—⁵⁰well, the master will return unannounced and unexpected. ⁵¹He will tear the servant apart and banish him with the hypocrites. In that place there will be weeping and gnashing of teeth.

CHAPTER 25
Story of the Ten Bridesmaids

"The Kingdom of Heaven can be illustrated by the story of ten bridesmaids* who took their lamps and went to meet the bridegroom. ²Five of them were foolish, and five were wise. ³The five who were foolish took no oil for their lamps, ⁴but the other five were wise enough to take along extra oil. ⁵When the bridegroom was delayed, they all lay down and slept. ⁶At midnight they were roused by the shout, 'Look, the bridegroom is coming! Come out and welcome him!'

⁷"All the bridesmaids got up and prepared their lamps. ⁸Then the five foolish ones asked the others, 'Please give us some of your oil because our lamps are going out.' ⁹But the others replied, 'We don't have enough for all of us. Go to a shop and buy some for yourselves.'

¹⁰"But while they were gone to buy oil, the bridegroom came, and those who were ready went in with him to the marriage feast, and the door was locked. ¹¹Later, when the other five bridesmaids returned, they stood outside, calling, 'Sir, open the door for us!' ¹²But he called back, 'I don't know you!'

¹³"So stay awake and be prepared, because you do not know the day or hour of my return.

24:30 See Dan 7:13. 24:34 Or *this age,* or *this nation.* 24:36 Some manuscripts omit the phrase *or the Son himself.*
25:1 Or *virgins;* also in 25:7, 11.

24:36-51 Jesus did not tell us when the final redemption of this evil world will come. In the same way, we may not know when our personal recovery is to be complete. All of us are still recovering, one day at a time. None of us has arrived. Not until Christ's second coming will we be relieved of daily working, watching, and recovering.
25:1-13 The story of the ten bridesmaids reinforces the need for wise preparation and readiness for Christ's coming. Those who have not readied themselves for the return of Jesus, the heavenly bridegroom—by faith, commitment, and responsible living—will be left behind. For those of us who have suffered from a dysfunctional background, recovery is a very important part of that preparation.

Story of the Three Servants

14"Again, the Kingdom of Heaven can be illustrated by the story of a man going on a trip. He called together his servants and gave them money to invest for him while he was gone. 15He gave five bags of gold* to one, two bags of gold to another, and one bag of gold to the last—dividing it in proportion to their abilities—and then left on his trip. 16The servant who received the five bags of gold began immediately to invest the money and soon doubled it. 17The servant with two bags of gold also went right to work and doubled the money. 18But the servant who received the one bag of gold dug a hole in the ground and hid the master's money for safekeeping.

19"After a long time their master returned from his trip and called them to give an account of how they had used his money. 20The servant to whom he had entrusted the five bags of gold said, 'Sir, you gave me five bags of gold to invest, and I have doubled the amount.' 21The master was full of praise. 'Well done, my good and faithful servant. You have been faithful in handling this small amount, so now I will give you many more responsibilities. Let's celebrate together!'

22"Next came the servant who had received the two bags of gold, with the report, 'Sir, you gave me two bags of gold to invest, and I have doubled the amount.' 23The master said, 'Well done, my good and faithful servant. You have been faithful in handling this small amount, so now I will give you many more responsibilities. Let's celebrate together!'

24"Then the servant with the one bag of gold came and said, 'Sir, I know you are a hard man, harvesting crops you didn't plant and gathering crops you didn't cultivate. 25I was afraid I would lose your money, so I hid it in the earth and here it is.'

26"But the master replied, 'You wicked and lazy servant! You think I'm a hard man, do you, harvesting crops I didn't plant and gathering crops I didn't cultivate? 27Well, you should at least have put my money into the bank so I could have some interest. 28Take the money from this servant and give it to the one with the ten bags of gold. 29To those who use well what they are given, even more will be given, and they will have an abundance. But from those who are unfaithful,* even what little they have will be taken away. 30Now throw this useless servant into outer darkness, where there will be weeping and gnashing of teeth.'

25:15 Greek *talents;* also throughout the story. A talent is equal to 75 pounds or 34 kilograms. 25:29 Or *who have nothing.*

Perfectionism

READ MATTHEW 25:14-30

Perfectionism can paralyze us. Perhaps we have been shamed for not being exactly what others wanted us to be. Now the shadow of unrealistic expectations is cast over how we see ourself, creating unrealistic expectations for our progress.

Jesus told the story of a man who loaned three servants money to invest for him while he was away. The first two men invested and doubled the money; the third hid his money in a hole. The third servant saw the master through the eyes of fear. He "came and said, 'Sir, I know you are a hard man, harvesting crops you didn't plant and gathering crops you didn't cultivate. I was afraid I would lose your money, so I hid it in the earth and here it is.' But the master replied, ' . . . Well, you should at least have put my money into the bank so I could have some interest'" (Matthew 25:24-27).

When we measure ourself by the expectations of others or by our own need to be perfect, we may fall so short that we may not even try to succeed. All God asks of us is that we try to do something with our abilities and resources. When we allow ourself the option of just making modest progress, we will find the courage to progress in recovery. Even the least improvement is better than not trying at all or being doomed to complete failure by our perfectionism. ***Turn to page 103, Luke 6.***

The Final Judgment

[31]"But when the Son of Man comes in his glory, and all the angels with him, then he will sit upon his glorious throne. [32]All the nations will be gathered in his presence, and he will separate them as a shepherd separates the sheep from the goats. [33]He will place the sheep at his right hand and the goats at his left. [34]Then the King will say to those on the right, 'Come, you who are blessed by my Father, inherit the Kingdom prepared for you from the foundation of the world. [35]For I was hungry, and you fed me. I was thirsty, and you gave me a drink. I was a stranger, and you invited me into your home. [36]I was naked, and you gave me clothing. I was sick, and you cared for me. I was in prison, and you visited me.'

[37]"Then these righteous ones will reply, 'Lord, when did we ever see you hungry and feed you? Or thirsty and give you something to drink? [38]Or a stranger and show you hospitality? Or naked and give you clothing? [39]When did we ever see you sick or in prison, and visit you?' [40]And the King will tell them, 'I assure you, when you did it to one of the least of these my brothers and sisters,* you were doing it to me!'

[41]"Then the King will turn to those on the left and say, 'Away with you, you cursed ones, into the eternal fire prepared for the Devil and his demons! [42]For I was hungry, and you didn't feed me. I was thirsty, and you didn't give me anything to drink. [43]I was a stranger, and you didn't invite me into your home. I was naked, and you gave me no clothing. I was sick and in prison, and you didn't visit me.'

[44]"Then they will reply, 'Lord, when did we ever see you hungry or thirsty or a stranger or naked or sick or in prison, and not help you?' [45]And he will answer, 'I assure you, when you refused to help the least of these my brothers and sisters, you were refusing to help me.' [46]And they will go away into eternal punishment, but the righteous will go into eternal life."

CHAPTER 26
The Plot to Kill Jesus

When Jesus had finished saying these things, he said to his disciples, [2]"As you know, the Passover celebration begins in two days, and I, the Son of Man, will be betrayed and crucified."

[3]At that same time the leading priests and other leaders were meeting at the residence of Caiaphas, the high priest, [4]to discuss how to capture Jesus secretly and put him to death. [5]"But not during the Passover," they agreed, "or there will be a riot."

Jesus Anointed at Bethany

[6]Meanwhile, Jesus was in Bethany at the home of Simon, a man who had leprosy. [7]During supper, a woman came in with a beautiful jar* of expensive perfume and poured it over his head. [8]The disciples were indignant when they saw this. "What a waste of money," they said. [9]"She could have sold it for a fortune and given the money to the poor."

[10]But Jesus replied, "Why berate her for doing such a good thing to me? [11]You will always have the poor among you, but I will not be here with you much longer. [12]She has poured this perfume on me to prepare my body for burial. [13]I assure you, wherever the Good News is preached throughout the

25:40 Greek *my brothers.* 26:7 Greek *an alabaster jar.*

25:31-46 Ultimately we will all be accountable to God on judgment day. We will be responsible not only for our own recovery but also for how we have helped others. The last step in recovery is to tell others about our recovery and encourage them in the recovery process. Since Jesus identifies himself with those who suffer, we should follow his example and be especially alert to the needs of others.

26:6-13 This woman expressed her love for Jesus the best way she knew how. The disciples criticized her wastefulness, but Jesus commended her action. There will always be someone who thinks we are foolish for expressing our gratitude to God. But we should continue to praise him because he is the one who is working our recovery, and it gives us a chance to tell others what God has done for us. God loves our praise.

26:14-16, 20-25 Judas thought he could hide his dealings with the chief priests, but Jesus saw right through his false front. Jesus discreetly yet openly made Judas aware that he knew exactly what was going on. Judas, however, passed up an opportunity to confess his actions and restore his relationship with Jesus. When we are confronted with our sins, will we do as Judas did and deny our involvement, or will we use the chance to turn to God?

GOD grant me the serenity to accept the things I cannot change the courage to change the things I can and the wisdom to know the difference AMEN

Although we know our goal of recovery is worthy of our commitment, we often find the challenge of working through the process overwhelming. As God deals with our defects, we may wish there were some other way. We may feel fear, a lack of confidence, deep anguish, or a host of other emotions that threaten to stop us in our tracks.

Jesus understands how we feel. He had similar emotions the night he was arrested. His friends were nearby, but when he needed them, they were asleep. He told his friends, "My soul is crushed with grief to the point of death" (Matthew 26:38). As he realized the enormity of the pain he would face, he looked for some other way. He was not immediately able to accept the path set before him. He struggled and prayed the same thing three times: "My Father! If it is possible, let this cup of suffering be taken away from me. Yet I want your will, not mine" (26:39). Finally Jesus found the grace to accept God's plan.

We may be overwhelmed as we face our own cross on the way to our new life. But during times of stress, we can go to Jesus for encouragement and express our deepest emotions about our struggles. As we cry out for help, we can be confident that he will give us the strength we need for the next step. *Turn to page 81, Mark 14.*

As we work through the steps of recovery, we look up a long, difficult road toward a better life.

---

world, this woman's deed will be talked about in her memory."

Judas Agrees to Betray Jesus

¹⁴Then Judas Iscariot, one of the twelve disciples, went to the leading priests ¹⁵and asked, "How much will you pay me to betray Jesus to you?" And they gave him thirty pieces of silver. ¹⁶From that time on, Judas began looking for the right time and place to betray Jesus.

The Last Supper

¹⁷On the first day of the Festival of Unleavened Bread, the disciples came to Jesus and asked, "Where do you want us to prepare the Passover supper?"

¹⁸"As you go into the city," he told them, "you will see a certain man. Tell him, 'The Teacher says, My time has come, and I will eat the Passover meal with my disciples at your house.'" ¹⁹So the disciples did as Jesus told them and prepared the Passover supper there.

²⁰When it was evening, Jesus sat down at the table with the twelve disciples. ²¹While they were eating, he said, "The truth is, one of you will betray me."

²²Greatly distressed, one by one they began to ask him, "I'm not the one, am I, Lord?"

²³He replied, "One of you who is eating with me now* will betray me. ²⁴For I, the Son of Man, must die, as the Scriptures declared long ago. But how terrible it will be for my betrayer. Far better for him if he had never been born!"

²⁵Judas, the one who would betray him, also asked, "Teacher, I'm not the one, am I?"

And Jesus told him, "You have said it yourself."

26:23 Or *The one who has dipped his hand in the bowl with me.*

26As they were eating, Jesus took a loaf of bread and asked God's blessing on it. Then he broke it in pieces and gave it to the disciples, saying, "Take it and eat it, for this is my body." 27And he took a cup of wine and gave thanks to God for it. He gave it to them and said, "Each of you drink from it, 28for this is my blood, which seals the covenant* between God and his people. It is poured out to forgive the sins of many. 29Mark my words—I will not drink wine again until the day I drink it new with you in my Father's Kingdom." 30Then they sang a hymn and went out to the Mount of Olives.

Jesus Predicts Peter's Denial

31"Tonight all of you will desert me," Jesus told them. "For the Scriptures say,

'God* will strike the Shepherd,
and the sheep of the flock will be scattered.'*

32But after I have been raised from the dead, I will go ahead of you to Galilee and meet you there."

33Peter declared, "Even if everyone else deserts you, I never will."

34"Peter," Jesus replied, "the truth is, this very night, before the rooster crows, you will deny me three times."

35"No!" Peter insisted. "Not even if I have to die with you! I will never deny you!" And all the other disciples vowed the same.

Jesus Prays in Gethsemane

36Then Jesus brought them to an olive grove called Gethsemane, and he said, "Sit here while I go on ahead to pray." 37He took Peter and Zebedee's two sons, James and John, and he began to be filled with anguish and deep distress. 38He told them, "My soul is crushed with grief to the point of death. Stay here and watch with me."

39He went on a little farther and fell face down on the ground, praying, "My Father! If it is possible, let this cup of suffering be taken away from me. Yet I want your will, not mine." 40Then he returned to the disciples and found them asleep. He said to Peter, "Couldn't you stay awake and watch with me even one hour? 41Keep alert and pray. Otherwise temptation will overpower you. For though the spirit is willing enough, the body is weak!"

42Again he left them and prayed, "My Father! If this cup cannot be taken away until I drink it, your will be done." 43He returned to them again and found them sleeping, for they just couldn't keep their eyes open.

44So he went back to pray a third time, saying the same things again. 45Then he came to the disciples and said, "Still sleeping? Still resting?* Look, the time has come. I, the Son of Man, am betrayed into the hands of sinners. 46Up, let's be going. See, my betrayer is here!"

Jesus Is Arrested

47And even as he said this, Judas, one of the twelve disciples, arrived with a mob that was armed with swords and clubs. They had been sent out by the leading priests and other leaders of the people. 48Judas had given them a prearranged signal: "You will know which one to arrest when I go over and give him the kiss of greeting." 49So Judas came straight to Jesus. "Greetings, Teacher!" he exclaimed and gave him the kiss.

50Jesus said, "My friend, go ahead and do what you have come for." Then the others grabbed Jesus and arrested him. 51One of the men with Jesus pulled out a sword and slashed off an ear of the high priest's servant.

52"Put away your sword," Jesus told him. "Those who use the sword will be killed by the sword. 53Don't you realize that I could ask my Father for thousands* of angels to protect us, and he would send them instantly? 54But if

---

26:28 Some manuscripts read *the new covenant.* **26:31a** Greek *I.* **26:31b** Zech 13:7. **26:45** Or *Sleep on, take your rest.* **26:53** Greek *12 legions.*

26:26-28 Through the Last Supper, Jesus communicated why he came to earth to die on the cross. His body would be broken, like the bread, so we could receive continued spiritual sustenance. His blood, represented by the wine, was the eternal payment for our sins. When we acknowledge Jesus as the Lord of our life, we become a member of his body, forgiven because of his blood. There are no restrictions based on race, sex, occupation, or past failures. All who look to Jesus are forgiven through the blood he shed on the cross.

26:31-75 Like Peter, we often go through stages as we give in to our weaknesses. First we claim that we will never fail in a certain way (26:31-35). Then we do what we promised we wouldn't do (26:56, 69-74). Next we realize that we have failed miserably (26:75). From there we have two options: We can work to overcome our weakness and learn from the experience, as Peter did; or we can wallow in our sins and never grow spiritually, as Judas did (27:5).

I did, how would the Scriptures be fulfilled that describe what must happen now?"

⁵⁵Then Jesus said to the crowd, "Am I some dangerous criminal, that you have come armed with swords and clubs to arrest me? Why didn't you arrest me in the Temple? I was there teaching every day. ⁵⁶But this is all happening to fulfill the words of the prophets as recorded in the Scriptures." At that point, all the disciples deserted him and fled.

Jesus before the Council

⁵⁷Then the people who had arrested Jesus led him to the home of Caiaphas, the high priest, where the teachers of religious law and other leaders had gathered. ⁵⁸Meanwhile, Peter was following far behind and eventually came to the courtyard of the high priest's house. He went in, sat with the guards, and waited to see what was going to happen to Jesus.

⁵⁹Inside, the leading priests and the entire high council* were trying to find witnesses who would lie about Jesus, so they could put him to death. ⁶⁰But even though they found many who agreed to give false witness, there was no testimony they could use. Finally, two men were found ⁶¹who declared, "This man said, 'I am able to destroy the Temple of God and rebuild it in three days.'"

⁶²Then the high priest stood up and said to Jesus, "Well, aren't you going to answer these charges? What do you have to say for yourself?" ⁶³But Jesus remained silent. Then the high priest said to him, "I demand in the name of the living God that you tell us whether you are the Messiah, the Son of God."

⁶⁴Jesus replied, "Yes, it is as you say. And in the future you will see me, the Son of Man, sitting at God's right hand in the place of power and coming back on the clouds of heaven."*

⁶⁵Then the high priest tore his clothing to show his horror, shouting, "Blasphemy! Why do we need other witnesses? You have all heard his blasphemy. ⁶⁶What is your verdict?"

"Guilty!" they shouted. "He must die!"

⁶⁷Then they spit in Jesus' face and hit him with their fists. And some slapped him, ⁶⁸saying, "Prophesy to us, you Messiah! Who hit you that time?"

Peter Denies Jesus

⁶⁹Meanwhile, as Peter was sitting outside in the courtyard, a servant girl came over and said to him, "You were one of those with Jesus the Galilean."

⁷⁰But Peter denied it in front of everyone. "I don't know what you are talking about," he said.

⁷¹Later, out by the gate, another servant girl noticed him and said to those standing around, "This man was with Jesus of Nazareth."

⁷²Again Peter denied it, this time with an oath. "I don't even know the man," he said.

⁷³A little later some other bystanders came over to him and said, "You must be one of them; we can tell by your Galilean accent."

⁷⁴Peter said, "I swear by God, I don't know the man." And immediately the rooster crowed. ⁷⁵Suddenly, Jesus' words flashed through Peter's mind: "Before the rooster crows, you will deny me three times." And he went away, crying bitterly.

CHAPTER 27
Judas Hangs Himself

Very early in the morning, the leading priests and other leaders met again to discuss how to persuade the Roman government to sentence Jesus to death. ²Then they bound him and took him to Pilate, the Roman governor.

³When Judas, who had betrayed him, realized that Jesus had been condemned to die, he was filled with remorse. So he took the thirty pieces of silver back to the leading priests and other leaders. ⁴"I have sinned," he declared, "for I have betrayed an innocent man."

"What do we care?" they retorted. "That's your problem." ⁵Then Judas threw the money onto the floor of the Temple and went out and hanged himself. ⁶The leading priests picked up the money. "We can't put it in the Temple treasury," they said, "since it's against the law to accept money paid for murder." ⁷After some discussion they finally decided to buy the potter's field, and they made it into a cemetery for foreigners. ⁸That is why the field is still called the Field of Blood. ⁹This fulfilled the prophecy of Jeremiah that says,

26:59 Greek *the Sanhedrin.* **26:64** See Ps 110:1; Dan 7:13.

27:3-8 The religious leaders refused to accept the blood money that Judas tried to return. It may have been their way of denying that they were responsible for the death of Jesus. If we are not careful, we can fall into this kind of hypocrisy and denial. Sometimes we hide behind righteous activities to conceal terrible sins. We should take moral inventory of our whole life and see which of our actions do not align with God's desires. Denying even one area of sin can jeopardize our entire recovery.

"They took* the thirty pieces of silver—
the price at which he was valued by the
people of Israel—
[10] and purchased the potter's field,
as the Lord directed.*"

Jesus' Trial before Pilate

[11] Now Jesus was standing before Pilate, the
Roman governor. "Are you the King of the
Jews?" the governor asked him.

Jesus replied, "Yes, it is as you say."

[12] But when the leading priests and other
leaders made their accusations against him,
Jesus remained silent. [13]"Don't you hear
their many charges against you?" Pilate demanded. [14]But Jesus said nothing, much to
the governor's great surprise.

[15] Now it was the governor's custom to release one prisoner to the crowd each year
during the Passover celebration—anyone
they wanted. [16]This year there was a notorious criminal in prison, a man named Barabbas.* [17]As the crowds gathered before Pilate's
house that morning, he asked them,
"Which one do you want me to release to
you—Barabbas, or Jesus who is called the
Messiah?" [18](He knew very well that the
Jewish leaders had arrested Jesus out of
envy.)

[19] Just then, as Pilate was sitting on the
judgment seat, his wife sent him this message: "Leave that innocent man alone, because I had a terrible nightmare about him
last night."

[20] Meanwhile, the leading priests and
other leaders persuaded the crowds to ask
for Barabbas to be released and for Jesus to
be put to death. [21]So when the governor
asked again, "Which of these two do you
want me to release to you?" the crowd
shouted back their reply: "Barabbas!"

[22]"But if I release Barabbas," Pilate asked
them, "what should I do with Jesus who is
called the Messiah?"

And they all shouted, "Crucify him!"

[23]"Why?" Pilate demanded. "What crime
has he committed?"

But the crowd only roared the louder,
"Crucify him!"

[24]Pilate saw that he wasn't getting anywhere and that a riot was developing. So he
sent for a bowl of water and washed his
hands before the crowd, saying, "I am innocent of the blood of this man. The responsibility is yours!"

[25]And all the people yelled back, "We will
take responsibility for his death—we and our
children!"*

[26]So Pilate released Barabbas to them. He
ordered Jesus flogged with a lead-tipped
whip, then turned him over to the Roman
soldiers to crucify him.

The Soldiers Mock Jesus

[27]Some of the governor's soldiers took Jesus
into their headquarters and called out the
entire battalion. [28]They stripped him and
put a scarlet robe on him. [29]They made a
crown of long, sharp thorns and put it on
his head, and they placed a stick in his right
hand as a scepter. Then they knelt before
him in mockery, yelling, "Hail! King of the
Jews!" [30]And they spit on him and grabbed
the stick and beat him on the head with it.
[31]When they were finally tired of mocking
him, they took off the robe and put his own
clothes on him again. Then they led him
away to be crucified.

The Crucifixion

[32]As they were on the way, they came across a
man named Simon, who was from Cyrene,*
and they forced him to carry Jesus' cross.
[33]Then they went out to a place called Gol-

27:9 Or *I took.* **27:9-10** Greek *as the Lord directed me.* Zech 11:12-13; Jer 32:6-9. **27:16** Some manuscripts read *Jesus Barabbas;* also in 27:17. **27:25** Greek *"His blood be on us and on our children."* **27:32** *Cyrene* was a city in northern Africa.

27:11-26 Pontius Pilate's handling of Jesus' trial indicates that he was a man consumed with pleasing others. Although he was convinced that Jesus was innocent and righteous (27:23-24), he bowed to public opinion. Pilate exemplifies someone in need of recovery who knows the right thing to do but does not have the courage to follow through and risk angering others. Since it is impossible to please everyone all the time, we must make sure that what we do is honest and pleasing to God. We should be more concerned about sinning against God than about angering other people.

27:26-54 The narrative of Jesus' crucifixion and death records one act of brutal abuse after another. Jesus was beaten, ridiculed, tortured, and killed. Thus, he can understand the feelings of those who have been abused or oppressed. Jesus can also redeem oppressors or abusers who come to faith, as did the Roman officer and other soldiers at the cross. Jesus' death and resurrection were intended to bring deliverance for everyone.

gotha (which means Skull Hill). ³⁴The soldiers gave him wine mixed with bitter gall, but when he had tasted it, he refused to drink it.

³⁵After they had nailed him to the cross, the soldiers gambled for his clothes by throwing dice.* ³⁶Then they sat around and kept guard as he hung there. ³⁷A signboard was fastened to the cross above Jesus' head, announcing the charge against him. It read: "This is Jesus, the King of the Jews."

³⁸Two criminals were crucified with him, their crosses on either side of his. ³⁹And the people passing by shouted abuse, shaking their heads in mockery. ⁴⁰"So! You can destroy the Temple and build it again in three days, can you? Well then, if you are the Son of God, save yourself and come down from the cross!"

⁴¹The leading priests, the teachers of religious law, and the other leaders also mocked Jesus. ⁴²"He saved others," they scoffed, "but he can't save himself! So he is the king of Israel, is he? Let him come down from the cross, and we will believe in him! ⁴³He trusted God—let God show his approval by delivering him! For he said, 'I am the Son of God.'" ⁴⁴And the criminals who were crucified with him also shouted the same insults at him.

The Death of Jesus

⁴⁵At noon, darkness fell across the whole land until three o'clock. ⁴⁶At about three o'clock, Jesus called out with a loud voice, *"Eli, Eli, lema sabachthani?"* which means, "My God, my God, why have you forsaken me?"*

⁴⁷Some of the bystanders misunderstood and thought he was calling for the prophet Elijah. ⁴⁸One of them ran and filled a sponge with sour wine, holding it up to him on a stick so he could drink. ⁴⁹But the rest said, "Leave him alone. Let's see whether Elijah will come and save him."*

⁵⁰Then Jesus shouted out again, and he gave up his spirit. ⁵¹At that moment the curtain in the Temple was torn in two, from top to bottom. The earth shook, rocks split apart, ⁵²and tombs opened. The bodies of many godly men and women who had died were raised from the dead ⁵³after Jesus' resurrection. They left the cemetery, went into the holy city of Jerusalem, and appeared to many people.*

⁵⁴The Roman officer and the other soldiers at the crucifixion were terrified by the earthquake and all that had happened. They said, "Truly, this was the Son of God!"

⁵⁵And many women who had come from Galilee with Jesus to care for him were watching from a distance. ⁵⁶Among them were Mary Magdalene, Mary (the mother of James and Joseph), and Zebedee's wife, the mother of James and John.

The Burial of Jesus

⁵⁷As evening approached, Joseph, a rich man from Arimathea who was one of Jesus' followers, ⁵⁸went to Pilate and asked for Jesus' body. And Pilate issued an order to release it to him. ⁵⁹Joseph took the body and wrapped it in a long linen cloth. ⁶⁰He placed it in his own new tomb, which had been carved out of the rock. Then he rolled a great stone across the entrance as he left. ⁶¹Both Mary Magdalene and the other Mary were sitting nearby watching.

The Guard at the Tomb

⁶²The next day—on the first day of the Passover ceremonies*—the leading priests and Pharisees went to see Pilate. ⁶³They told him, "Sir, we remember what that deceiver once said while he was still alive: 'After three days I will be raised from the dead.' ⁶⁴So we request that you seal the tomb until the third day. This will prevent his disciples from coming and stealing his body and

---

27:35 Greek *by casting lots.* A few late manuscripts add *This fulfilled the word of the prophet: "They divided my clothes among themselves and cast lots for my robe."* See Ps 22:18. **27:46** Ps 22:1. **27:49** Some manuscripts add *And another took a spear and pierced his side, and out came water and blood.* **27:51-53** Or *The earth shook, rocks split apart, tombs opened, and the bodies of many godly men and women who had died were raised from the dead. After Jesus' resurrection, they left the cemetery, went into the holy city of Jerusalem, and appeared to many people.* **27:62** Or *On the next day, which is after the Preparation.*

27:57-60 Joseph of Arimathea was a secret disciple (see John 19:38) who revealed his faith at a crisis point. He was like the people who toy with recovery in a limited and private sense, but then come to the point of decision where they either have to reject their program or make a deeper commitment to it. Joseph's willingness to approach Pilate, as well as his generous burial of Jesus, indicates that he took a step of faith toward a stronger commitment to the Lord. What kind of crisis will it take to inspire us to devote our life wholeheartedly to God and his program of recovery?

then telling everyone he came back to life! If that happens, we'll be worse off than we were at first."

⁶⁵Pilate replied, "Take guards and secure it the best you can." ⁶⁶So they sealed the tomb and posted guards to protect it.

CHAPTER 28
The Resurrection

Early on Sunday morning,* as the new day was dawning, Mary Magdalene and the other Mary went out to see the tomb. ²Suddenly there was a great earthquake, because an angel of the Lord came down from heaven and rolled aside the stone and sat on it. ³His face shone like lightning, and his clothing was as white as snow. ⁴The guards shook with fear when they saw him, and they fell into a dead faint.

⁵Then the angel spoke to the women. "Don't be afraid!" he said. "I know you are looking for Jesus, who was crucified. ⁶He isn't here! He has been raised from the dead, just as he said would happen. Come, see where his body was lying. ⁷And now, go quickly and tell his disciples he has been raised from the dead, and he is going ahead of you to Galilee. You will see him there. Remember, I have told you."

⁸The women ran quickly from the tomb. They were very frightened but also filled with great joy, and they rushed to find the disciples to give them the angel's message. ⁹And as they went, Jesus met them. "Greetings!" he said. And they ran to him, held his feet, and worshiped him. ¹⁰Then Jesus said to them, "Don't be afraid! Go tell my brothers to leave for Galilee, and they will see me there."

The Report of the Guard

¹¹As the women were on their way into the city, some of the men who had been guarding the tomb went to the leading priests and told them what had happened. ¹²A meeting of all the religious leaders was called, and they decided to bribe the soldiers. ¹³They told the soldiers, "You must say, 'Jesus' disciples came during the night while we were sleeping, and they stole his body.' ¹⁴If the governor hears about it, we'll stand up for you and everything will be all right." ¹⁵So the guards accepted the bribe and said what they were told to say. Their story spread widely among the Jews, and they still tell it today.

The Great Commission

¹⁶Then the eleven disciples left for Galilee, going to the mountain where Jesus had told them to go. ¹⁷When they saw him, they worshiped him—but some of them still doubted!

¹⁸Jesus came and told his disciples, "I have been given complete authority in heaven and on earth. ¹⁹Therefore, go and make disciples of all the nations, baptizing them in the name of the Father and the Son and the Holy Spirit. ²⁰Teach these new disciples to obey all the commands I have given you. And be sure of this: I am with you always, even to the end of the age."

28:1 Greek *After the Sabbath, on the first day of the week.*

27:62–28:15 The religious leaders went to a lot of trouble to be free of Jesus' message. They discredited him in front of the crowds and plotted his murder. When they caught him, they tried to come up with witnesses and had to convince Rome that Jesus should be killed. After Jesus' death, the leaders feared he would come back to life, so they sealed and guarded the tomb. Finally, they invented a story to explain the disappearance of Jesus' body. It would have been easier to accept Jesus' message and make appropriate changes in their lives and beliefs. We must not become so hardened by denial that we, like the Jewish leaders, go to great lengths to avoid accepting the lifesaving message of the gospel.

28:16-20 Some disciples adjusted to the reality of Jesus' resurrection quite readily, while others still doubted. But Jesus' resurrection was not an end in itself, nor was it for just his closest disciples. This new life through faith in the crucified and resurrected Christ is offered to all the people of the world. Those who by faith enter true spiritual recovery are baptized to show their commitment. Studying God's Word and regular instruction in the faith help those in recovery grow spiritually. Recovery is available through God's power until Jesus returns at the end of the age.

REFLECTIONS ON *M*ATTHEW

✷*insights* ABOUT THE PERSON OF JESUS

The mention of Tamar, Rahab, Ruth, and Bathsheba in Jesus' lineage in **Matthew 1:1-16** is significant. Each of these women was almost certainly non-Jewish in ethnic background. Yet God used them along the way to prepare for the coming of the Jewish Messiah. Similarly, God often employs people from diverse and unusual backgrounds to accomplish his purposes. His grace is stronger than the presumed limitations of our past. He can use us regardless of our background.

In **Matthew 3:13-15** Jesus was baptized by John the Baptist. Jesus had no real reason to follow John's call to baptism because Jesus had never sinned and had no reason to repent. Jesus was baptized anyway because it was the right thing to do, and his actions modeled the importance of baptism to others. We who seek recovery need examples of those who do the right things for the right reasons, thus modeling a balanced life. As we proceed in the recovery process, we can become a model for others in need of recovery. Being an example for others through our words and deeds will not only help others but also encourage us to persevere in our own recovery.

In **Matthew 4:23-25** Jesus offered healing and restoration—physically, spiritually, and interpersonally. He provides recovery from the pain of abuse and dysfunctional relationships, areas that trouble an ever-increasing number of people. Such recovery is extended through faith in Jesus Christ. Through him, true recovery is open to all who believe in him. No part of our life is beyond his healing touch.

✷*insights* CONCERNING OBSTACLES TO RECOVERY

In **Matthew 1:18-25** Joseph was in a difficult predicament. His fiancée, Mary, had become pregnant, so he was considering how he could break their engagement quietly. But when Joseph was shown that the Holy Spirit was responsible for the pregnancy, he immediately changed his decision about breaking the engagement and obeyed God. He married her as the angel of the Lord commanded, despite the rumors that would surely surround their marriage. Pride can easily become an obstacle to the restoration of our damaged relationships. We should resist pride and obey God as Joseph did.

When we enter recovery, we should not mistakenly think that our faith and spiritual growth will insulate us from temptation. On the contrary, in **Matthew 4:1-2** Jesus was actually led into the wilderness by the Holy Spirit for a prolonged siege of temptation. This should serve as a fair warning that temptation may follow quickly on the heels of a spiritual high. God often uses such trials in our life to remind us of how helpless we are without him.

In **Matthew 5:10-12** we are reminded that persecution can be a real problem for us as we try to live by God's principles. Old friends may try to intimidate us into giving up on recovery. Family members may be threatened by the changes we are making and try to discourage us. We must realize that it is more important to please God than other people. As we do things God's way, we will be set free from our destructive and codependent relationships. Then we can build healthy relationships with others and continue to strengthen our all-important relationship with God.

In **Matthew 6:19-34** Jesus made it clear that living for personal gain will only lead to great anxiety. Materialism and anxiety are two enemies of recovery. They often work together to lead us away from a balanced life. We need to realize that the essence of life is not found in the possession of things and that worry about the future availability of material things is never helpful. We are powerless to change the future and must trust God to take care of us and empower us in recovery. As we entrust our life to him, we will no longer need to worry about what is around the corner.

People who refuse to admit they need recovery are usually the first to stand in the way of someone else's recovery. Instead of praising God for the miracle that Jesus performed, in **Matthew 12:9-12** the Pharisees judged Jesus for breaking the Sabbath laws. To the Pharisees, it was more important to preserve their legalistic observances than to see a man healed of his deformity. They chose to be ruled by their interpretations of the law and rejected the rule of the compassionate Messiah-King. There will be people who oppose our recovery, doing anything they can to keep us enslaved to our addiction. We should make every effort to overcome our dependency, regardless of the pressures from those around us. With God's help, no obstacle is too great to overcome.

In **Matthew 14:1-11** John the Baptist was arrested because he had condemned Herod Antipas for marrying his brother's wife, Herodias. Rather than admit his sin, Herod put John in prison, hoping to silence him. Herodias wanted John silenced too, but she was more vicious than her husband and wanted John executed. In the end, Herod was too weak to refuse his wife's request, and the prophet was beheaded. Our shame from one sin often leads us to commit greater sins. To avoid the downward spiral, we must have the courage to admit our smaller sins and problems before they grow larger. As we turn our sins and failures over to God, we can be confident that we will receive his healing help.

insights ABOUT HONESTY AND DENIAL

It is clear from **Matthew 3:5-9** that not everyone who listened to John the Baptist wanted to repent and find a new life. John saw that the Pharisees and others like them were merely going through the motions, trusting external appearances for their salvation. Similarly, some of us who claim to be in recovery are simply going through the motions, appearing to work on the addiction while not having changed our heart through repentance. If this is the case, we are headed for painful relapses. We need to begin with an honest assessment of our weaknesses and failures before we can receive God's help and forgiveness.

In **Matthew 3:7-11** John the Baptist confronted the Pharisees with their denial. These religious leaders were blind to the sins of their hearts and believed they were beyond the reach of God's judgment. Perhaps we have acted as if the consequences of our actions would never catch up with us. Our denial may have been so deep that we weren't even aware of the serious consequences we would have to face. It is only a matter of time before God will take his ax of judgment to "unproductive trees"—those who are not following him. For those of us who truly repent, God fuels our recovery with the power of his Holy Spirit. The choice is ours: Either we continue as we are and await God's judgment, or we turn from our present lifestyle and enter recovery, depending on God's Spirit to help us change.

In **Matthew 7:1-5** Jesus warned against our tendency of being critical of others. It is easy to hide from the sins and dependency ("logs") in our own life by pointing out the small failures ("specks") in the lives of others. This kind of denial destroys the relationships we need for recovery and blinds us to our own sins and their destructive consequences. To be truly helpful to others, we must first recognize sin in our own life and deal with it. After humbling ourself in this way, we will be ready to confront others about their need for recovery.

The tax collectors in Judea during Jesus' time were Jews who had sold out to the oppressive Roman government. They used their position to extort money from their own people. They were hated by the Jewish population, who considered them traitors to God and their homeland. In **Matthew 9:9-13** the Jews were surprised that Jesus would even speak to such people. Matthew, the author of this Gospel, and his friends were surprisingly open to grace and forgiveness. As dysfunctional as they were, they admitted their need and responded to Jesus with humility. On the other hand, the Pharisees clung to their self-righteous denial, not recognizing their own desperate need for recovery. It is not how we appear to others that matters; it is whether or not we are willing to let God free us from the power of sin in our life.

In **Matthew 10:14-15** we discover that denial has eternal ramifications. Those who refuse the offer of recovery in Christ are making an eternal mistake. This message may seem threatening at the moment, but it is meant to bring peace and serenity. In the end, we who have become comfortable in our ever-increasing denial will have to answer to God at the time of our final judgment.

insights ABOUT GOD'S PRIORITIES

The Beatitudes in **Matthew 5:1-12** contain much of what God desires of us as we seek to follow his will for our life. This lifestyle affirms God's perspective, priorities, and boundaries. As we look over God's program in this passage, we may wonder how anyone could live up to it. The truth is, no one can do it without God's help. Following God's program requires wisdom and grace from above. But the lifestyle found in these verses can replace our warped human outlook with God's enduring perspective.

In **Matthew 6:1-4** we see that God's priorities are very different from ours. God is more interested in our quiet service to others than our outward worldly success. Each of us has a public and a private life, but the reward systems for each are very different. While we may succeed in the world by becoming famous or wealthy, we will never receive further reward from God for our public success. If we humbly seek to help others, we will be openly rewarded by our heavenly Father. What seems private and unnoticed by other people is public, even center stage, before God.

*insights INTO SHARING THE GOOD NEWS

In **Matthew 5:13-16** Jesus described what we should be like. If we have been delivered by God's power, we are witnesses to his power to save. We are to carry the light of his good news to people imprisoned in the darkness of addiction and sin. Dysfunctional behavior and warped relationships abound, in part due to our lack of healthy, Christian role models. People are desperate for seasoning and light. We can make a significant impact on individuals, relationships, and even societal structures if we let our spiritual light shine for others to see. As we experience God's deliverance, we are called to share our recovery with others. This will not only extend hope to hurting people, but it will also encourage us as we face new trials ahead.

Jesus had great compassion for those who had no protection or guidance. So in **Matthew 9:36–10:8** Jesus began training his closest disciples to help fill the need. They were to go out and use God's power to heal and encourage those needing physical or spiritual recovery. They were not expected to reach everyone, but they were to make a difference in at least one needy group. As we share our story of recovery with others, we cannot expect to reach everyone with the good news of recovery. We can, however, share the message with a few, who will also share their story with others. As we use our own recovery to encourage the recovery of others, we will start a chain reaction that will touch the lives of many.

Matthew 25:14-30 is about using our gifts wisely, and it provides needed encouragement and sobering reality to those of us in recovery. Even though this parable is about money, it can, by extension, also refer to God-given abilities. Everyone has been given various abilities by God; no one is untalented or worthless. That should encourage us. On the other hand, we are each responsible to use our abilities for God. After suffering for years as a slave to our destructive addiction, some of us may wonder if we have anything to offer. Yet even if we have nothing else, we have something to tell others. As we share our experiences of deliverance, we will give others hope for recovery. Our years of suffering may become the gift of life to someone in need.

*insights ABOUT PRAYER

In **Matthew 6:9-13** Jesus gave his disciples a model prayer to follow. This prayer is more than just a model for our prayers; it is a model for our life in recovery. We are to acknowledge God in our life and honor his name. Our greatest desire should be to see his Kingdom established and his will done on earth, both in our life and in the world in general. God's daily provision for us is another petition important for recovery. We must ask for forgiveness of our sins and forgive those who have wronged us. Finally, God wants us to ask for protection from Satan's temptations we face each day. If we are praying these things and living them in our walk with God, we are truly on the path of recovery.

*insights CONCERNING TRUE FAITH

In **Matthew 7:24-27** we are told that two kinds of life-building foundations are available. One foundation is as solid as rock—the foundation of faith in Jesus Christ. The other foundation is like shifting sand—the foundation of human pride and selfish endeavor. Our life might be outwardly impressive, but if it is built on the wrong foundation, difficult circumstances will soon level what we have built. Like a fragile house of cards, our life will come crashing down. How much better to build our life on the solid foundation of faith in Jesus Christ. Then when the inevitable storms of life come, we will not be destroyed.

In **Matthew 11:25-30** we are told of the importance of childlike faith. Only when we come to Jesus as little children can we find recovery and relief for our emotional pain. Many of us think we can work things out our own way. In doing this, we miss this simple truth: God alone has the power to enable us in recovery. We cannot even begin recovery until we are willing to admit how powerless we are; this is the importance of childlike faith. Children are powerless and are very aware of that fact; they entrust themselves to their parents each and every day. As we recognize how powerless we are over our dependency, we can entrust ourself to God's loving care. He has all the power we need for full recovery.

In **Matthew 14:25-33** Jesus walked on water and then enabled Peter, through faith, to do the same. Before we began the process of recovery, our life was as turbulent as a stormy sea. When we trusted God for recovery, we, like Peter, stepped out in faith into that storm-tossed sea. As long as we hold on to our faith and keep our eyes on Jesus, we will succeed over the waves of life. When we focus on the troubled waters around us and forget God's assistance, we start to sink and are overwhelmed by our dependency and character flaws. If we want to make continued progress, we need to focus on Christ.

In **Matthew 15:21-28** a Gentile woman showed great perseverance and faith, and Jesus rewarded her for it. When we seek recovery, we must truly believe that God is able to effect our recovery. We also must be prepared to persist in our program, not giving up even when there seems to be little hope for success. God will reward our efforts if we are fully committed to following his will and prove it by our actions.

MARK

THE BIG PICTURE

A. JESUS PREPARES FOR SERVICE (1:1-13)
B. JESUS SERVES THROUGH WORD AND DEED (1:14–13:37)
   1. Jesus Serves in Galilee (1:14–9:50)
   2. Jesus Serves beyond Jerusalem (10:1-45)
   3. Jesus Serves in Jerusalem (10:46–13:37)
C. JESUS SERVES THROUGH SELF-SACRIFICE (14:1–16:20)

When our life was out of control, we responded to our trials in various ways—with anger, bitterness, or rebellion. Our addiction determined our behavior and attitudes. We eventually realized that our life had become unmanageable and that we were destroying not only ourself but our loved ones, too. We needed to break the cycle, but we were powerless to do so.

The Gospel of Mark is written for people like us; it shows that Jesus is powerful and wants to help us. In this Gospel we see Jesus' power displayed again and again: He raised the dead, gave sight to the blind, restored deformed limbs, made lame people walk, cast out demons, healed incurable skin diseases, and quieted stormy waters. Although Mark is the shortest Gospel, it records more miracles than any of the others. It proves that Jesus is a powerful Savior and is more than able to help suffering people.

This Gospel also emphasizes the fact that Jesus wants to help us. Jesus spent his energy to the point of exhaustion healing those who came to him for help. By recording a rapid succession of vivid pictures of Jesus in action, the Gospel writer has shown that Jesus came to help us. This truth is driven home by Jesus' willingness to suffer a painful death to free us from our bondage to sin.

Jesus has power over the problems that bind us. He is more powerful than our dependency, problems, and weaknesses. He has the power to help us all with recovery, no matter how terrible our past experiences. All we have to do is look to him and admit that we need his help.

THE BOTTOM LINE

PURPOSE: To encourage us to continue trusting and serving God, especially through life's difficulties. AUTHOR: John Mark. AUDIENCE: The Christians in Rome. DATE WRITTEN: Probably between A.D. 55 and 65. SETTING: The Roman Empire had unified the known world, and its use of a common language made conditions ideal for the spread of the gospel in written form. KEY VERSE: "For even I, the Son of Man, came here not to be served but to serve others, and to give my life as a ransom for many" (10:45). SPECIAL FEATURES: The Gospel of Mark is characterized by its fast-paced narrative. KEY PEOPLE AND RELATIONSHIPS: Jesus with his disciples, especially Peter.

RECOVERY THEMES

Jesus as the Servant: The Twelfth Step tells us that our recovery should lead us to be servants and share our story of deliverance with others. Real greatness in God's eyes is demonstrated by a willingness to serve and sacrifice for others. Jesus didn't come as a conquering king; he came as a servant. He chose to obey his Father and die for us. When personal ambition and hunger for power control our life, we live in contradiction to the principles of recovery and to God's will for our life.

The Power of God: The Gospel of Mark is filled with amazing events that display the awesome power of God in Jesus. Mark recorded more of Jesus' miracles than his sermons. He wanted us to see God's power in action. The more we are convinced that Jesus is God, the more we will see his power and his love in action in our own life. His greatest miracles are still those that involve forgiveness, healing of relationships, and the restoration of lost or wasted pasts. The same power we see in Mark's Gospel is available to us today.

Recovery Is Not the Goal: Some people are afraid of recovery because it seems all-consuming. They have a distorted image of what recovery is all about. Our goal is not recovery; our goal is spiritual and emotional growth, demonstrated by sacrificial service. That is one reason we can never claim to have recovered. Jesus set the pace for us with his example of service. His whole purpose in coming was to serve, not to be served. That principle—that we seek to give away what we have gained—is an essential part of the recovery process.

Sharing the Message: There is no such thing as a secret disciple or a private recovery. Discipleship and recovery take place within relationships. God's good news is meant to be shared. As we share the joys and struggles of our own experiences in recovery, we encourage others in recovery. The message transcends national, racial, and economic barriers, reaching out to all those who are willing to admit their powerlessness. The message of recovery is worth sharing with others.

CHAPTER 1
John the Baptist Prepares the Way

Here begins the Good News about Jesus the Messiah, the Son of God.*

²In the book of the prophet Isaiah, God said,

"Look, I am sending my messenger before you,
and he will prepare your way.*
³He is a voice shouting in the wilderness:
'Prepare a pathway for the Lord's coming!
Make a straight road for him!'*"

⁴This messenger was John the Baptist. He lived in the wilderness and was preaching that people should be baptized to show that they had turned from their sins and turned to God to be forgiven.* ⁵People from Jerusalem and from all over Judea traveled out into the wilderness to see and hear John. And when they confessed their sins, he baptized them in the Jordan River. ⁶His clothes were woven from camel hair, and he wore a leather belt; his food was locusts and wild honey. ⁷He announced: "Someone is coming soon who is far greater than I am—so much greater that I am not even worthy to be his slave.* ⁸I baptize you with* water, but he will baptize you with the Holy Spirit!"

The Baptism of Jesus

⁹One day Jesus came from Nazareth in Galilee, and he was baptized by John in the Jordan River. ¹⁰And when Jesus came up out of the water, he saw the heavens split open and the Holy Spirit descending like a dove on him. ¹¹And a voice came from heaven saying, "You are my beloved Son, and I am fully pleased with you."

The Temptation of Jesus

¹²Immediately the Holy Spirit compelled Jesus to go into the wilderness. ¹³He was there for forty days, being tempted by Satan. He was out among the wild animals, and angels took care of him.

1:1 Some manuscripts do not include *the Son of God.* **1:2** Mal 3:1. **1:3** Isa 40:3. **1:4** Greek *preaching a baptism of repentance for the forgiveness of sins.* **1:7** Greek *to stoop down and untie his sandals.* **1:8** Or *in;* also in 1:8b.

1:1-13 Only belief in a Power greater than ourself can restore us to sanity. That's how John the Baptist saw Jesus—as one far greater than he was. Jesus demonstrated his great power through victory over Satan and his temptations. This should encourage us as we face our own temptations. With his help, we can stand up to anything. Under our own power, we are helpless against the power of our dependency. We can tap into God's power by making a conscious decision to turn our back on sin (1:4) and by entrusting our life to God's care.

SIMON PETER

Simon the fisherman was reckless, vacillating, and often thoughtless. We would never nickname such a person *Peter,* which means "rock." Jesus did. What greater evidence could there be that Jesus not only accepted Simon as he was but also envisioned what he would become? By the end of his life Simon's nickname, Peter, appropriately described his steadfast maturity. What an amazing transformation took place in that burly fisherman!

Most of us readily identify with Simon Peter. His intentions were usually good, but he was impetuous in speech and impulsive in action. Instead of standing in awe at the Transfiguration, he blurted out the first idea that came into his head. When Jesus revealed that his divine mission would involve a painful death, Peter rashly told Jesus to stop talking that way. At the Last Supper he brazenly objected to Jesus washing his feet. When Jesus was arrested, Peter bravely but brashly cut off the ear of the high priest's servant. Finally, at a critical point in his life, Peter denied Jesus three times. Even as Jesus was restoring Peter from this failure, Peter's attention was on John rather than on what God was doing for him.

Later in Simon's life we see what Jesus saw when he called him "Rock." Peter presided over the meeting to select a successor to Judas. At Pentecost he preached publicly about Jesus despite the opposition he knew he would face. Peter performed several miracles and was himself miraculously rescued from prison. Peter was the apostle who had the spiritual insight to proclaim the great confession at Caesarea Philippi, stating clearly that Jesus Christ is the only means to salvation.

In Simon Peter's life we see hope for our transformation and recovery. He was amazingly transformed by God, but we should remember that he was never made perfect. The apostle Paul described in Galatians 2:11-14 how Peter acted hypocritically. Despite his imperfections, however, his transformation had a profound effect on the world around him; his words, actions, and letters became a significant part of the early church's spiritual foundation.

STRENGTHS AND ACCOMPLISHMENTS:
- Simon's natural boldness was used to spread the good news of Jesus Christ.
- He was the recognized leader and spokesman for the twelve disciples.
- He was inspired to write letters to encourage believers (1 and 2 Peter).
- His natural enthusiasm was later channeled into disciplined courage.

WEAKNESSES AND MISTAKES:
- Simon often spoke and acted before he thought about the consequences.
- His temperament was mercurial; he quickly moved from professed loyalty to betrayal.
- Even after his transformation, he allowed a situation to govern his actions at least once (Galatians 2:11-14).

LESSONS FROM HIS LIFE:
- Jesus Christ has enough power to transform even the most unlikely people.
- God can transform our faults into powerful tools for use in his Kingdom.
- When people make themselves available, they can always be used by God.

KEY VERSE:
"Now I say to you that you are Peter, and upon this rock I will build my church, and all the powers of hell will not conquer it" (Matthew 16:18).

There is extensive biblical material on Simon Peter in the Gospels and Acts 1–15. In Paul's letters, Peter is mentioned in 1 Corinthians 1:12; 3:22; 9:5; 15:5; and Galatians 1:18; 2:7-14. Some material about him may also be gleaned from his two letters, 1 and 2 Peter.

The First Disciples

[14]Later on, after John was arrested by Herod Antipas, Jesus went to Galilee to preach God's Good News. [15]"At last the time has come!" he announced. "The Kingdom of God is near! Turn from your sins and believe this Good News!"

[16]One day as Jesus was walking along the shores of the Sea of Galilee, he saw Simon* and his brother, Andrew, fishing with a net, for they were commercial fishermen. [17]Jesus called out to them, "Come, be my disciples, and I will show you how to fish for people!" [18]And they left their nets at once and went with him.

[19]A little farther up the shore Jesus saw Zebedee's sons, James and John, in a boat mending their nets. [20]He called them, too, and

1:16 *Simon* is called *Peter* in 3:16 and thereafter.

immediately they left their father, Zebedee, in the boat with the hired men and went with him.

Jesus Casts Out an Evil Spirit

[21]Jesus and his companions went to the town of Capernaum, and every Sabbath day he went into the synagogue and taught the people. [22]They were amazed at his teaching, for he taught as one who had real authority—quite unlike the teachers of religious law.

[23]A man possessed by an evil spirit was in the synagogue, [24]and he began shouting, "Why are you bothering us, Jesus of Nazareth? Have you come to destroy us? I know who you are—the Holy One sent from God!"

[25]Jesus cut him short. "Be silent! Come out of the man." [26]At that, the evil spirit screamed and threw the man into a convulsion, but then he left him.

[27]Amazement gripped the audience, and they began to discuss what had happened. "What sort of new teaching is this?" they asked excitedly. "It has such authority! Even evil spirits obey his orders!" [28]The news of what he had done spread quickly through that entire area of Galilee.

Jesus Heals Many People

[29]After Jesus and his disciples left the synagogue, they went over to Simon and Andrew's home, and James and John were with them. [30]Simon's mother-in-law was sick in bed with a high fever. They told Jesus about her right away. [31]He went to her bedside, and as he took her by the hand and helped her to sit up, the fever suddenly left, and she got up and prepared a meal for them.

[32]That evening at sunset, many sick and demon-possessed people were brought to Jesus. [33]And a huge crowd of people from all over Capernaum gathered outside the door to watch. [34]So Jesus healed great numbers of sick people who had many different kinds of diseases, and he ordered many demons to come out of their victims. But because they knew who he was, he refused to allow the demons to speak.

Jesus Preaches in Galilee

[35]The next morning Jesus awoke long before daybreak and went out alone into the wilderness to pray. [36]Later Simon and the others went out to find him. [37]They said, "Everyone is asking for you."

[38]But he replied, "We must go on to other towns as well, and I will preach to them, too, because that is why I came." [39]So he traveled throughout the region of Galilee, preaching in the synagogues and expelling demons from many people.

Jesus Heals a Man with Leprosy

[40]A man with leprosy came and knelt in front of Jesus, begging to be healed. "If you want to, you can make me well again," he said.

[41]Moved with pity,* Jesus touched him. "I want to," he said. "Be healed!" [42]Instantly the leprosy disappeared—the man was healed. [43]Then Jesus sent him on his way and told him sternly, [44]"Go right over to the priest and let him examine you. Don't talk to anyone along the way. Take along the offering required in the law of Moses for those who have been healed of leprosy, so everyone will have proof of your healing."

[45]But as the man went on his way, he spread the news, telling everyone what had happened to him. As a result, such crowds soon surrounded Jesus that he couldn't enter a town anywhere publicly. He had to stay out in the secluded places, and people from everywhere came to him there.

CHAPTER 2
Jesus Heals a Paralyzed Man

Several days later Jesus returned to Capernaum, and the news of his arrival spread

---

1:41 Some manuscripts read *Moved with anger.*

1:35-39 If Jesus, the Son of God, took time from his busy schedule to pray to his Father, how much more do we need to do so. By placing a high priority on prayer, Jesus could persevere in his ministry and keep from burning out. We who seek recovery for ourself and for others cannot get by without prayer. The busier the day ahead, the more we need to meditate on God's Word and pray for his strength and wisdom.

2:1-12 Jesus came not only to heal physical problems but also to solve the sin problem. If we do not know Jesus yet, we are paralyzed in spirit, as powerless to help ourselves as was this paralytic. If our faith is still too weak to carry us to the point of healing, the faith of "four friends" may be enough to get us there. Notice that it was not enough for Jesus to mouth the words of forgiveness; he proved his authority and intent with action. In the same way, it is not enough for us to mouth words of faith. We must take responsible action if we expect spiritual cleansing and physical healing.

quickly through the town. ²Soon the house where he was staying was so packed with visitors that there wasn't room for one more person, not even outside the door. And he preached the word to them. ³Four men arrived carrying a paralyzed man on a mat. ⁴They couldn't get to Jesus through the crowd, so they dug through the clay roof above his head. Then they lowered the sick man on his mat, right down in front of Jesus. ⁵Seeing their faith, Jesus said to the paralyzed man, "My son, your sins are forgiven."

⁶But some of the teachers of religious law who were sitting there said to themselves, ⁷"What? This is blasphemy! Who but God can forgive sins!"

⁸Jesus knew what they were discussing among themselves, so he said to them, "Why do you think this is blasphemy? ⁹Is it easier to say to the paralyzed man, 'Your sins are forgiven' or 'Get up, pick up your mat, and walk'? ¹⁰I will prove that I, the Son of Man, have the authority on earth to forgive sins." Then Jesus turned to the paralyzed man and said, ¹¹"Stand up, take your mat, and go on home, because you are healed!"

¹²The man jumped up, took the mat, and pushed his way through the stunned onlookers. Then they all praised God. "We've never seen anything like this before!" they exclaimed.

Jesus Calls Levi (Matthew)

¹³Then Jesus went out to the lakeshore again and taught the crowds that gathered around him. ¹⁴As he walked along, he saw Levi son of Alphaeus sitting at his tax-collection booth. "Come, be my disciple," Jesus said to him. So Levi got up and followed him.

¹⁵That night Levi invited Jesus and his disciples to be his dinner guests, along with his fellow tax collectors and many other notorious sinners. (There were many people of this kind among the crowds that followed Jesus.) ¹⁶But when some of the teachers of religious law who were Pharisees* saw him eating with people like that, they said to his disciples, "Why does he eat with such scum*?"

¹⁷When Jesus heard this, he told them, "Healthy people don't need a doctor—sick people do. I have come to call sinners, not those who think they are already good enough."

A Discussion about Fasting

¹⁸John's disciples and the Pharisees sometimes fasted. One day some people came to Jesus and asked, "Why do John's disciples and the Pharisees fast, but your disciples don't fast?"

¹⁹Jesus replied, "Do wedding guests fast while celebrating with the groom? Of course not. They can't fast while they are with the groom. ²⁰But someday he will be taken away from them, and then they will fast. ²¹And who would patch an old garment with unshrunk cloth? For the new patch shrinks and pulls away from the old cloth, leaving an even bigger hole than before. ²²And no one puts new wine into old wineskins. The wine would burst the wineskins, spilling the wine and ruining the skins. New wine needs new wineskins."

A Discussion about the Sabbath

²³One Sabbath day as Jesus was walking through some grainfields, his disciples began breaking off heads of wheat. ²⁴But the Pharisees said to Jesus, "They shouldn't be doing that! It's against the law to work by harvesting grain on the Sabbath."

2:16a Greek *the scribes of the Pharisees.* 2:16b Greek *with tax collectors and sinners.*

2:13-17 Because of their reputed cheating and support of pagan Rome, tax collectors were considered notorious sinners by the Jews, especially the self-righteous religious leaders. But it was for people like this that Jesus came to bring salvation. Levi (Matthew) proved he meant business with Jesus by immediately witnessing to his friends, colleagues, and collaborators in sin. Some may question whether a person so new and immature in his faith should be telling his story to others. But the account here illustrates the truth that we are strengthened in recovery when we share our story with others, no matter the extent of our knowledge, skills, or experiences.

2:18-22 The old wineskins of Jewish religious practice were too rigid to carry the expansive, life-changing message of God's love in Jesus Christ. Religious activities are never enough unless they are coupled with genuine repentance. We must start by recognizing the sins in our life and then look to the only one who can make things right again—God in Jesus Christ. If we repent and look to him for help, he will forgive us and get us back on the right track. God will make our hard heart open and pliable like a fresh wineskin, so we can receive his gift of grace.

25But Jesus replied, "Haven't you ever read in the Scriptures what King David did when he and his companions were hungry? 26He went into the house of God (during the days when Abiathar was high priest), ate the special bread reserved for the priests alone, and then gave some to his companions. That was breaking the law, too." 27Then he said to them, "The Sabbath was made to benefit people, and not people to benefit the Sabbath. 28And I, the Son of Man, am master even of the Sabbath!"

CHAPTER 3
Jesus Heals on the Sabbath

Jesus went into the synagogue again and noticed a man with a deformed hand. 2Since it was the Sabbath, Jesus' enemies watched him closely. Would he heal the man's hand on the Sabbath? If he did, they planned to condemn him. 3Jesus said to the man, "Come and stand in front of everyone." 4Then he turned to his critics and asked, "Is it legal to do good deeds on the Sabbath, or is it a day for doing harm? Is this a day to save life or to destroy it?" But they wouldn't answer him. 5He looked around at them angrily, because he was deeply disturbed by their hard hearts. Then he said to the man, "Reach out your hand." The man reached out his hand, and it became normal again! 6At once the Pharisees went away and met with the supporters of Herod to discuss plans for killing Jesus.

Crowds Follow Jesus

7Jesus and his disciples went out to the lake, followed by a huge crowd from all over Galilee, Judea, 8Jerusalem, Idumea, from east of the Jordan River, and even from as far away as Tyre and Sidon. The news about his miracles had spread far and wide, and vast numbers of people came to see him for themselves.

9Jesus instructed his disciples to bring around a boat and to have it ready in case he was crowded off the beach. 10There had been many healings that day. As a result, many sick people were crowding around him, trying to touch him. 11And whenever those possessed by evil spirits caught sight of him, they would fall down in front of him shrieking, "You are the Son of God!" 12But Jesus strictly warned them not to say who he was.

Jesus Chooses the Twelve Apostles

13Afterward Jesus went up on a mountain and called the ones he wanted to go with him. And they came to him. 14Then he selected twelve of them to be his regular companions, calling them apostles.* He sent them out to preach, 15and he gave them authority to cast out demons. 16These are the names of the twelve he chose:

Simon (he renamed him Peter),
17 James and John (the sons of Zebedee, but Jesus nicknamed them "Sons of Thunder"*),
18 Andrew,
Philip,
Bartholomew,
Matthew,
Thomas,
James (son of Alphaeus),
Thaddaeus,
Simon (the Zealot*),
19 Judas Iscariot (who later betrayed him).

Jesus and the Prince of Demons

20When Jesus returned to the house where he was staying, the crowds began to gather again, and soon he and his disciples couldn't even find time to eat. 21When his family heard what was happening, they tried to

3:14 Some manuscripts do not include *calling them apostles.* 3:17 Greek *whom he named Boanerges, which means Sons of Thunder.* 3:18 Greek *the Cananean.*

3:7-19 Despite rejection by the religious establishment, Jesus enjoyed an ever-growing following, even from places he had not yet ministered in. Nearly halfway through three years of public ministry, Jesus' popularity peaked. The great demands on Jesus for service may have prompted him to appoint the twelve members of his close support group. Not even Jesus attempted to minister alone. We need to surround ourself with those who will support us and help us maintain what we have gained through recovery.

3:20-30 Although Satan causes a great deal of trouble in our world, God has power over him. Since Jesus is God, he has the power to work his will with Satan. Binding Satan's stronghold of demons and loosening his grip on our life is the solemn work of recovery. Not one of our past sins is so heinous that it cannot be forgiven, no hurt so deep that it cannot be healed. The one exception to this is blasphemy against the Holy Spirit, which is denying God's power through his Son, Jesus Christ.

JAMES & JOHN

Sons of Thunder! Why would Jesus use such a powerful description for two Galilean fishermen, James and John? We are given a glimpse of their fiery personalities when, after they were rejected by the people of a Samaritan village, James and John asked Jesus if they should call down fire from heaven to consume the village. Jesus rebuked them for their impulse to retaliate.

Jesus worked in these brothers' lives so that they became men known for their love and forgiveness, not for their anger and revenge. John, "the disciple Jesus loved," wrote powerful words on the importance of love. He had discovered that he didn't have to earn God's love but that he could freely receive it and pass it on to others.

James was the first of the twelve disciples to give his life for his faith. He was killed in Jerusalem by order of Herod Agrippa. John became an important leader in the church of Asia Minor and was later exiled to the island of Patmos, where he wrote the book of Revelation. He apparently outlived the rest of the twelve disciples.

Although the two brothers had once been ambitious for personal advancement, they became ambitious to advance the lives of others by sharing God's love with them. The brothers had discovered the important truth that when we understand and experience God's love, we are free to live and grow. And as we grow and share our discovery with others, God can use us to touch the lives of many in need of his help and healing.

STRENGTHS AND ACCOMPLISHMENTS:
- With Peter, James and John formed the inner circle of Jesus' disciples.
- Both men were important leaders in the early church.
- John was inspired to write five New Testament books (the Gospel of John; 1, 2, & 3 John; and Revelation).

WEAKNESSES AND MISTAKES:
- They apparently had a tendency to react angrily to anyone who opposed them.
- They selfishly tried to promote themselves ahead of the other disciples.

LESSONS FROM THEIR LIVES:
- It is important to experience God's love and act with love toward others.
- God can take our weaknesses and change them into strengths.

KEY VERSES:
"Then [Jesus] selected twelve of them to be his regular companions. . . . These are the names of the twelve he chose: . . . James and John (the sons of Zebedee, but Jesus nicknamed them 'Sons of Thunder')" (Mark 3:14-17).

The stories of James and John are told in Matthew 4:21-22; 20:20-28; Mark 1:19; 3:13-19; 9:1-9; 10:35-40; Luke 9:49-56; John 13:23-25; 19:26-27; 21:20-24; Acts 4:1-23; 8:14-25; 12:2; and Revelation 1:1-2, 9; 22:8.

---

take him home with them. "He's out of his mind," they said. 22But the teachers of religious law who had arrived from Jerusalem said, "He's possessed by Satan,* the prince of demons. That's where he gets the power to cast out demons."

23Jesus called them over and said to them by way of illustration, "How can Satan cast out Satan? 24A kingdom at war with itself will collapse. 25A home divided against itself is doomed. 26And if Satan is fighting against himself, how can he stand? He would never survive. 27Let me illustrate this. You can't enter a strong man's house and rob him without first tying him up. Only then can his house be robbed!* 28"I assure you that any sin can be forgiven, including blasphemy; 29but anyone who blasphemes against the Holy Spirit will never be forgiven. It is an eternal sin." 30He told them this because they were saying he had an evil spirit.

The True Family of Jesus

31Jesus' mother and brothers arrived at the house where he was teaching. They stood outside and sent word for him to come out and talk with them. 32There was a crowd around Jesus, and someone said, "Your mother and your brothers and sisters* are outside, asking for you."

33Jesus replied, "Who is my mother? Who are my brothers?" 34Then he looked at those around him and said, "These are my mother and brothers. 35Anyone who does God's will is my brother and sister and mother."

3:22 Greek *Beelzeboul.* **3:27** Or *One cannot rob Satan's kingdom without first tying him up. Only then can his demons be cast out.* **3:32** Some manuscripts do not include *and sisters.*

CHAPTER 4

Story of the Farmer Scattering Seed

Once again Jesus began teaching by the lakeshore. There was such a large crowd along the shore that he got into a boat and sat down and spoke from there. ²He began to teach the people by telling many stories such as this one:

³"Listen! A farmer went out to plant some seed. ⁴As he scattered it across his field, some seed fell on a footpath, and the birds came and ate it. ⁵Other seed fell on shallow soil with underlying rock. The plant sprang up quickly, ⁶but it soon wilted beneath the hot sun and died because the roots had no nourishment in the shallow soil. ⁷Other seed fell among thorns that shot up and choked out the tender blades so that it produced no grain. ⁸Still other seed fell on fertile soil and produced a crop that was thirty, sixty, and even a hundred times as much as had been planted." Then he said, ⁹"Anyone who is willing to hear should listen and understand!"

¹⁰Later, when Jesus was alone with the twelve disciples and with the others who were gathered around, they asked him, "What do your stories mean?"

¹¹He replied, "You are permitted to understand the secret about the Kingdom of God. But I am using these stories to conceal everything about it from outsiders, ¹²so that the Scriptures might be fulfilled:

'They see what I do,
 but they don't perceive its meaning.
They hear my words,
 but they don't understand.

4:12 Isa 6:9-10.

So they will not turn from their sins
 and be forgiven.'*

¹³"But if you can't understand this story, how will you understand all the others I am going to tell? ¹⁴The farmer I talked about is the one who brings God's message to others. ¹⁵The seed that fell on the hard path represents those who hear the message, but then Satan comes at once and takes it away from them. ¹⁶The rocky soil represents those who hear the message and receive it with joy. ¹⁷But like young plants in such soil, their roots don't go very deep. At first they get along fine, but they wilt as soon as they have problems or are persecuted because they believe the word. ¹⁸The thorny ground represents those who hear and accept the Good News, ¹⁹but all too quickly the message is crowded out by the cares of this life, the lure of wealth, and the desire for nice things, so no crop is produced. ²⁰But the good soil represents those who hear and accept God's message and produce a huge harvest—thirty, sixty, or even a hundred times as much as had been planted."

Illustration of the Lamp

²¹Then Jesus asked them, "Would anyone light a lamp and then put it under a basket or under a bed to shut out the light? Of course not! A lamp is placed on a stand, where its light will shine.

²²"Everything that is now hidden or secret will eventually be brought to light. ²³Anyone who is willing to hear should listen and understand! ²⁴And be sure to pay attention to

4:1-20 Some welcome recovery, while others reject it. The mystery of this is revealed in the stories Jesus tells about the Kingdom, four of which are given in 4:1-34. God's Kingdom refers to God's hidden reign in the world that will be made visible at the return of Christ. This first story dramatizes varying responses to God's message in the hearts of his people. As we proceed with recovery and learn to seek out God's will for us, we are placing ourself under the just and loving rule of God. And we can be sure that as we plow the soil of our heart through self-examination, we will experience a fruitful and meaningful life.

4:21-25 The lamp represents the truth about Jesus. We hide that light every time we put a box over it. As we progress in recovery, it is important that we remove the boxes of guilt, bitterness, anger, shame, or denial that we hide behind. It is extremely important that we humbly share our story of pain and deliverance with others. We may need to start by taking moral inventory of our life to uncover the attitudes that keep us from sharing who we are and what God has done for us. As we discover the things that cause us to hide the light, we can give them to God and ask for his help in removing them. We must let God's truth shine from our life.

4:35-41 The disciples were awed when Jesus demonstrated his power over nature; even the wind and the waves obeyed him! Seeing this incredible display of power should strengthen our faith in God. Just as he was able to calm the stormy sea, he has the power to calm our storm-tossed life. With Jesus in our boat, we need not fear the storms of life that threaten to drown us. No storm is too violent or powerful for Jesus to calm. We should never hesitate to cry out, "Teacher, don't you even care that we are going to drown?" (4:38).

what you hear. The more you do this, the more you will understand—and even more, besides. ²⁵To those who are open to my teaching, more understanding will be given. But to those who are not listening, even what they have will be taken away from them."

Illustration of the Growing Seed

²⁶Jesus also said, "Here is another illustration of what the Kingdom of God is like: A farmer planted seeds in a field, ²⁷and then he went on with his other activities. As the days went by, the seeds sprouted and grew without the farmer's help, ²⁸because the earth produces crops on its own. First a leaf blade pushes through, then the heads of wheat are formed, and finally the grain ripens. ²⁹And as soon as the grain is ready, the farmer comes and harvests it with a sickle."

Illustration of the Mustard Seed

³⁰Jesus asked, "How can I describe the Kingdom of God? What story should I use to illustrate it? ³¹It is like a tiny mustard seed. Though this is one of the smallest of seeds, ³²it grows to become one of the largest of plants, with long branches where birds can come and find shelter."

³³He used many such stories and illustrations to teach the people as much as they were able to understand. ³⁴In fact, in his public teaching he taught only with parables, but afterward when he was alone with his disciples, he explained the meaning to them.

Jesus Calms the Storm

³⁵As evening came, Jesus said to his disciples, "Let's cross to the other side of the lake." ³⁶He was already in the boat, so they started out, leaving the crowds behind (although other boats followed). ³⁷But soon a fierce storm arose. High waves began to break into the boat until it was nearly full of water.

³⁸Jesus was sleeping at the back of the boat with his head on a cushion. Frantically they woke him up, shouting, "Teacher, don't you even care that we are going to drown?"

³⁹When he woke up, he rebuked the wind and said to the water, "Quiet down!" Suddenly the wind stopped, and there was a great calm. ⁴⁰And he asked them, "Why are you so afraid? Do you still not have faith in me?"

⁴¹And they were filled with awe and said among themselves, "Who is this man, that even the wind and waves obey him?"

STEP 2

Internal Bondage

BIBLE READING: Mark 5:1-13
We came to believe that a Power greater than ourselves could restore us to sanity. When we are under the influence of our addiction, its hold may seem to have supernatural force. We may give up on living and throw ourself into self-destructive behaviors with reckless abandon. People may also give up on us. They may distance themselves from us, as though we were already dead. Whether our "insanity" is self-induced or has a more sinister origin, there is power available to restore us to sanity and wholeness.

Jesus helped a man who was acting insanely. "This man lived among the tombs and could not be restrained, even with a chain. Whenever he was put into chains and shackles—as he often was—he snapped the chains from his wrists and smashed the shackles. No one was strong enough to control him. All day long and throughout the night, he would wander among the tombs and in the hills, screaming and hitting himself with stones" (Mark 5:3-5). Jesus went into the graveyard and assessed the situation. He dealt with the forces of darkness that were afflicting the man and restored him to sanity. He then sent him home to his friends to tell them what God had done for him.

We may have gone so far into our addiction that we have broken all restraints. We struggle to be free from the control of society and loved ones, only to discover that our bondage doesn't come from outside sources. All hope seems lost, but where there is still life, there is still hope. God can touch our insanity and restore us to sanity. *Turn to page 109, Luke 8.*

CHAPTER 5

Jesus Heals a Demon-Possessed Man

So they arrived at the other side of the lake, in the land of the Gerasenes.* ²Just as Jesus was climbing from the boat, a man possessed by an evil spirit ran out from a cemetery to meet him. ³This man lived among the tombs and could not be restrained, even with a chain. ⁴Whenever he was put into chains and shackles—as he often was—he snapped the chains from his wrists and smashed the shackles. No one was strong enough to control him. ⁵All day long and throughout the night, he would wander among the tombs and in the hills, screaming and hitting himself with stones.

⁶When Jesus was still some distance away, the man saw him. He ran to meet Jesus and fell down before him. ⁷He gave a terrible scream, shrieking, "Why are you bothering me, Jesus, Son of the Most High God? For God's sake, don't torture me!" ⁸For Jesus had already said to the spirit, "Come out of the man, you evil spirit."

⁹Then Jesus asked, "What is your name?"

And the spirit replied, "Legion, because there are many of us here inside this man." ¹⁰Then the spirits begged him again and again not to send them to some distant place. ¹¹There happened to be a large herd of pigs feeding on the hillside nearby. ¹²"Send us into those pigs," the evil spirits begged. ¹³Jesus gave them permission. So the evil spirits came out of the man and entered the pigs, and the entire herd of two thousand pigs plunged down the steep hillside into the lake, where they drowned.

¹⁴The herdsmen fled to the nearby city and the surrounding countryside, spreading the news as they ran. Everyone rushed out to see for themselves. ¹⁵A crowd soon gathered around Jesus, but they were frightened when they saw the man who had been demon possessed, for he was sitting there fully clothed and perfectly sane. ¹⁶Those who had seen what happened to the man and to the pigs told everyone about it, ¹⁷and the crowd began pleading with Jesus to go away and leave them alone.

¹⁸When Jesus got back into the boat, the man who had been demon possessed begged to go, too. ¹⁹But Jesus said, "No, go home to your friends, and tell them what wonderful things the Lord has done for you and how merciful he has been." ²⁰So the man started off to visit the Ten Towns* of that region and began to tell everyone about the great things Jesus had done for him; and everyone was amazed at what he told them.

Jesus Heals in Response to Faith

²¹When Jesus went back across to the other side of the lake, a large crowd gathered around him on the shore. ²²A leader of the local synagogue, whose name was Jairus, came and fell down before him, ²³pleading with him to heal his little daughter. "She is about to die," he said in desperation. "Please come and place your hands on her; heal her so she can live."

²⁴Jesus went with him, and the crowd thronged behind. ²⁵And there was a woman in the crowd who had had a hemorrhage for twelve years. ²⁶She had suffered a great deal from many doctors through the years and had spent everything she had to pay them, but she had gotten no better. In fact, she was worse. ²⁷She had heard about Jesus, so she came up behind him through the crowd and touched the fringe of his robe. ²⁸For she thought to herself, "If I can just touch his clothing, I will be healed." ²⁹Immediately the bleeding stopped, and she could feel that she had been healed!

³⁰Jesus realized at once that healing power had gone out from him, so he turned around in the crowd and asked, "Who touched my clothes?"

5:1 Some manuscripts read *Gadarenes;* others read *Gergesenes.* See Matt 8:28; Luke 8:26. 5:20 Greek *Decapolis.*

5:21-43 Jairus was among a minority of Jewish leaders who responded positively to Jesus. Driven by love for his daughter and faith that Jesus could help her, Jairus risked the scorn of his peers by publicly seeking Jesus' help. In the end, we see that his humble faith paid off. Some of us avoid recovery because we are too ashamed to admit publicly that we have problems. But if we cannot humbly confess our sins, there is little hope for our healing. Like Jairus, we must risk the scorn of friends and enemies and admit our failures. If we do, we can be sure that Jesus will be there to help us. No problem is too great for him to solve; no wound is too deep for him to heal.

5:25-34 Sometimes we feel so ashamed of our sins that we think God's opinion of us must mirror the social ostracism or self-loathing we have experienced. Such was the case with the woman who had been bleeding for twelve years and probably lived as an outcast. This hemorrhage was likely a menstrual or uterine disorder, which would have made her ritually "unclean" (Leviticus 15:25-27). According to Jewish law, anyone who touched her would also be rendered unclean. But instead of shrinking back from touching Jesus, she reached out in faith and was miraculously healed. We must never allow fear or shame to keep us from approaching God for forgiveness and healing. He is waiting for us to reach out and touch him.

³¹His disciples said to him, "All this crowd is pressing around you. How can you ask, 'Who touched me?'"

³²But he kept on looking around to see who had done it. ³³Then the frightened woman, trembling at the realization of what had happened to her, came and fell at his feet and told him what she had done. ³⁴And he said to her, "Daughter, your faith has made you well. Go in peace. You have been healed."

³⁵While he was still speaking to her, messengers arrived from Jairus's home with the message, "Your daughter is dead. There's no use troubling the Teacher now."

³⁶But Jesus ignored their comments and said to Jairus, "Don't be afraid. Just trust me." ³⁷Then Jesus stopped the crowd and wouldn't let anyone go with him except Peter and James and John. ³⁸When they came to the home of the synagogue leader, Jesus saw the commotion and the weeping and wailing. ³⁹He went inside and spoke to the people. "Why all this weeping and commotion?" he asked. "The child isn't dead; she is only asleep."

⁴⁰The crowd laughed at him, but he told them all to go outside. Then he took the girl's father and mother and his three disciples into the room where the girl was lying. ⁴¹Holding her hand, he said to her, "Get up, little girl!"* ⁴²And the girl, who was twelve years old, immediately stood up and walked around! Her parents were absolutely overwhelmed. ⁴³Jesus commanded them not to tell anyone what had happened, and he told them to give her something to eat.

CHAPTER 6
Jesus Rejected at Nazareth

Jesus left that part of the country and returned with his disciples to Nazareth, his hometown. ²The next Sabbath he began teaching in the synagogue, and many who heard him were astonished. They asked, "Where did he get all his wisdom and the power to perform such miracles? ³He's just the carpenter, the son of Mary and brother of James, Joseph,* Judas, and Simon. And his sisters live right here

among us." They were deeply offended and refused to believe in him.

⁴Then Jesus told them, "A prophet is honored everywhere except in his own hometown and among his relatives and his own family." ⁵And because of their unbelief, he couldn't do any mighty miracles among them except to place his hands on a few sick people and heal them. ⁶And he was amazed at their unbelief.

Jesus Sends Out the Twelve Apostles

Then Jesus went out from village to village, teaching. ⁷And he called his twelve disciples together and sent them out two by two, with authority to cast out evil spirits. ⁸He told them to take nothing with them except a walking stick—no food, no traveler's bag, no money. ⁹He told them to wear sandals but not to take even an extra coat. ¹⁰"When you enter each village, be a guest in only one home," he said. ¹¹"And if a village won't welcome you or listen to you, shake off its dust from your feet as you leave. It is a sign that you have abandoned that village to its fate."

¹²So the disciples went out, telling all they met to turn from their sins. ¹³And they cast out many demons and healed many sick people, anointing them with olive oil.

The Death of John the Baptist

¹⁴Herod Antipas, the king, soon heard about Jesus, because people everywhere were talking about him. Some were saying,* "This must be John the Baptist come back to life again. That is why he can do such miracles." ¹⁵Others thought Jesus was the ancient prophet Elijah. Still others thought he was a prophet like the other great prophets of the past. ¹⁶When Herod heard about Jesus, he said, "John, the man I beheaded, has come back from the dead." ¹⁷For Herod had sent soldiers to arrest and imprison John as a favor to Herodias. She had been his brother Philip's wife, but Herod had married her. ¹⁸John kept telling Herod, "It is illegal for you to marry your brother's wife." ¹⁹Herodias was enraged and wanted John killed in revenge,

---

5:41 Greek text uses Aramaic *"Talitha cumi"* and then translates it as "Get up, little girl." **6:3** Greek *Joses;* see Matt 13:55. **6:14** Some manuscripts read *He was saying.*

6:7-13 When we experience the joy of recovery, we naturally want to share the good news of the Messiah's coming with others. Yet we are not always well received. The disciples faced rejection as they traveled, healed people, and preached repentance and deliverance. They were paired off and told what to take, where to stay and for how long, and what to do when rejected. As we share the healing we have experienced in the recovery process, not everyone will be responsive. When ridiculed or rejected, we must press on to share our hope with the next fellow struggler we meet. Sharing our message may be the difference between life and death for someone in need.

but without Herod's approval she was powerless. [20]And Herod respected John, knowing that he was a good and holy man, so he kept him under his protection. Herod was disturbed whenever he talked with John, but even so, he liked to listen to him.

[21]Herodias's chance finally came. It was Herod's birthday, and he gave a party for his palace aides, army officers, and the leading citizens of Galilee. [22]Then his daughter, also named Herodias,* came in and performed a dance that greatly pleased them all. "Ask me for anything you like," the king said to the girl, "and I will give it to you." [23]Then he promised, "I will give you whatever you ask, up to half of my kingdom!"

[24]She went out and asked her mother, "What should I ask for?"

Her mother told her, "Ask for John the Baptist's head!"

[25]So the girl hurried back to the king and told him, "I want the head of John the Baptist, right now, on a tray!"

[26]Then the king was very sorry, but he was embarrassed to break his oath in front of his guests. [27]So he sent an executioner to the prison to cut off John's head and bring it to him. The soldier beheaded John in the prison, [28]brought his head on a tray, and gave it to the girl, who took it to her mother. [29]When John's disciples heard what had happened, they came for his body and buried it in a tomb.

Jesus Feeds Five Thousand

[30]The apostles returned to Jesus from their ministry tour and told him all they had done and what they had taught. [31]Then Jesus said, "Let's get away from the crowds for a while and rest." There were so many people coming and going that Jesus and his apostles didn't even have time to eat. [32]They left by boat for a quieter spot. [33]But many people saw them leaving, and people from many towns ran ahead along the shore and met them as they landed. [34]A vast crowd was there as he stepped from the boat, and he had compassion on them because they were like sheep without a shepherd. So he taught them many things.

[35]Late in the afternoon his disciples came to him and said, "This is a desolate place, and it is getting late. [36]Send the crowds away so they can go to the nearby farms and villages and buy themselves some food."

[37]But Jesus said, "You feed them."

"With what?" they asked. "It would take a small fortune* to buy food for all this crowd!"

[38]"How much food do you have?" he asked. "Go and find out."

They came back and reported, "We have five loaves of bread and two fish." [39]Then Jesus told the crowd to sit down in groups on the green grass. [40]So they sat in groups of fifty or a hundred.

[41]Jesus took the five loaves and two fish, looked up toward heaven, and asked God's blessing on the food. Breaking the loaves into pieces, he kept giving the bread and fish to the disciples to give to the people. [42]They all ate as much as they wanted, [43]and they picked up twelve baskets of leftover bread and fish. [44]Five thousand men had eaten from those five loaves!

Jesus Walks on Water

[45]Immediately after this, Jesus made his disciples get back into the boat and head out across the lake to Bethsaida, while he sent the people home. [46]Afterward he went up into the hills by himself to pray.

[47]During the night, the disciples were in their boat out in the middle of the lake, and Jesus was alone on land. [48]He saw that they

6:22 Some manuscripts read *the daughter of Herodias herself.* **6:37** Greek *200 denarii.* A denarius was the equivalent of a full day's wage.

6:30-32 The disciples demonstrated accountability to Jesus by reporting their activities to him. At the same time, Jesus encouraged them to take care of themselves by drawing them away for rest and solitude. To continue helping others, the disciples needed time apart for personal reflection and refreshment. Unfortunately, their time apart was delayed by the many who followed them. We must balance our life too, taking time apart to recharge our spiritual and emotional batteries. As we take time to reflect, we will learn the lessons of humility and dependence on God that are necessary for our progress in recovery.

6:45-52 We may lose sight of Jesus, but Jesus never loses sight of us. That's the lesson for people in "deep water" who appreciate his threefold miracle: (1) Jesus walked on water; (2) he calmed the storm; and (3) he saw the disciples' boat safely to shore (see John 6:21). Despite many such miracles, the disciples still had not realized how powerful Jesus was. All of us can recall some time when Jesus intervened in our life to show us how much he cares. When we begin to waver in our faith, we should recall the times when he has helped us in the past. This should give us the courage to continue in his loving care.

HEROD & FAMILY

Certain names in history immediately bring to mind images of horror, violence, greed, and cruelty. Several Herods are mentioned in the New Testament. The first, Herod the Great, was called "great" because of his ambitious and lavish building projects, including the rebuilding of the Temple in Jerusalem. His character, however, was anything but great. He was known for his cruelty, jealousy, and insatiable lust for power and wealth.

Herod was appointed king by the Romans, but many of his Jewish subjects never really accepted him as a legitimate ruler. Herod was not really of Jewish descent; he was actually an Idumean from the land south of Judea. Because of this, Herod was uneasy about any threat to his position and responded with swift cruelty to the slightest rumor of disloyalty. The Herods didn't hesitate to have even their own family members murdered if it would be to their own advantage.

Herod Antipas, Herod the Great's son, is well known for his role in killing John the Baptist. Another descendant, Herod Agrippa I, was responsible for the death of the apostle James. A grandson, Agrippa II, heard the truth of the gospel directly from the apostle Paul. In fact, each of the Herods had an encounter with a messenger from God but refused to respond to the truth.

Herod the Great's failure to respond to God's truth grew out of his greed and insecurity. As a result, Herod left his children and grandchildren a heritage of greed and cruelty. It is important that we seriously consider what heritage we are leaving our children. We can either remain in our denial and pass on our dysfunctions, or we can choose the path of recovery and build happy and meaningful futures for our children and grandchildren. There is a great deal at stake in recovery. We are fighting for more than just our own life; we are fighting for the lives of countless descendants as well.

STRENGTHS AND ACCOMPLISHMENTS:
- Herod and his family were industrious builders.
- They were extremely clever at political maneuvering.

WEAKNESSES AND MISTAKES:
- Herod and his family lusted for power and possessions.
- They didn't hesitate to destroy innocent people who stood in their way.
- They were extremely insecure and suspicious of the people around them.

LESSONS FROM THEIR LIVES:
- Having power and wealth doesn't guarantee success and happiness.
- We must carefully consider the heritage we will leave our children.
- Those who live for themselves at the expense of others will pay the price in the end.

KEY VERSE:
"Herod was furious when he learned that the wise men had outwitted him. He sent soldiers to kill all the boys in and around Bethlehem who were two years old and under" (Matthew 2:16).

Herod and members of his family are mentioned in Matthew 2:1-11; Mark 6:14-29; Luke 1:5; and Acts 4:27; 12:1-23; 13:1; and 25:13–26:32.

---

were in serious trouble, rowing hard and struggling against the wind and waves. About three o'clock in the morning* he came to them, walking on the water. He started to go past them, [49]but when they saw him walking on the water, they screamed in terror, thinking he was a ghost. [50]They were all terrified when they saw him. But Jesus spoke to them at once. "It's all right," he said. "I am here! Don't be afraid." [51]Then he climbed into the boat, and the wind stopped. They were astonished at what they saw. [52]They still didn't understand the significance of the miracle of the multiplied loaves, for their hearts were hard and they did not believe.

[53]When they arrived at Gennesaret on the other side of the lake, they anchored the boat [54]and climbed out. The people standing there recognized him at once, [55]and they ran throughout the whole area and began carrying sick people to him on mats. [56]Wherever he went—in villages and cities and out on the farms—they laid the sick in the market plazas and streets. The sick begged him to let them at least touch the fringe of his robe, and all who touched it were healed.

6:48 Greek *About the fourth watch of the night.*

CHAPTER 7

Jesus Teaches about Inner Purity

One day some Pharisees and teachers of religious law arrived from Jerusalem to confront Jesus. [2]They noticed that some of Jesus' disciples failed to follow the usual Jewish ritual of hand washing before eating. [3](The Jews, especially the Pharisees, do not eat until they have poured water over their cupped hands,* as required by their ancient traditions. [4]Similarly, they eat nothing bought from the market unless they have immersed their hands in water. This is but one of many traditions they have clung to—such as their ceremony of washing cups, pitchers, and kettles.*) [5]So the Pharisees and teachers of religious law asked him, "Why don't your disciples follow our age-old customs? For they eat without first performing the hand-washing ceremony."

[6]Jesus replied, "You hypocrites! Isaiah was prophesying about you when he said,

[7]'These people honor me with their lips,
     but their hearts are far away.
  Their worship is a farce,
     for they replace God's commands with
        their own man-made teachings.'*

[8]For you ignore God's specific laws and substitute your own traditions."

[9]Then he said, "You reject God's laws in order to hold on to your own traditions. [10]For instance, Moses gave you this law from God: 'Honor your father and mother,' and 'Anyone who speaks evil of father or mother must be put to death.'* [11]But you say it is all right for people to say to their parents, 'Sorry, I can't help you. For I have vowed to give to God what I could have given to you.'* [12]You let them disregard their needy parents. [13]As such, you break the law of God in order to protect your own tradition. And this is only one example. There are many, many others."

[14]Then Jesus called to the crowd to come and hear. "All of you listen," he said, "and try to understand. [15]You are not defiled by what you eat; you are defiled by what you say and do!*"

[17]Then Jesus went into a house to get away from the crowds, and his disciples asked him what he meant by the statement he had made. [18]"Don't you understand either?" he asked. "Can't you see that what you eat won't defile you? [19]Food doesn't come in contact with your heart, but only passes through the stomach and then comes out again." (By saying this, he showed that every kind of food is acceptable.)

[20]And then he added, "It is the thought-life that defiles you. [21]For from within, out of a person's heart, come evil thoughts, sexual immorality, theft, murder, [22]adultery, greed, wickedness, deceit, eagerness for lustful pleasure, envy, slander, pride, and foolishness. [23]All these vile things come from within; they are what defile you and make you unacceptable to God."

The Faith of a Gentile Woman

[24]Then Jesus left Galilee and went north to the region of Tyre.* He tried to keep it secret that he was there, but he couldn't. As usual, the news of his arrival spread fast. [25]Right away a woman came to him whose little girl

7:3 Greek *washed with the fist.* **7:4** Some Greek manuscripts add *and dining couches.* **7:7** Isa 29:13. **7:10** Exod 20:12; 21:17; Lev 20:9; Deut 5:16. **7:11** Greek *'What I could have given to you is Corban' (that is, a gift).* **7:15** Some manuscripts add verse 16, *Anyone who is willing to hear should listen and understand.* **7:24** Some Greek manuscripts add *and Sidon.*

7:1-13 For many of the Jewish leaders, man-made tradition had begun to supersede God's revealed Word. Ritual had begun to replace a relationship with God; reputation had become more important than godliness. Jesus called this hypocrisy, and it is a dangerous form of denial. If we hide the pain we feel and the mistakes we make, we will never be able to deal with them and experience healing. Recovery can succeed only if we are willing to be honest in taking our moral inventory, using God's Word as our standard. As we seek to follow God's will for our life, we will experience his powerful help and direction.

7:14-23 Jesus explained that defilement does not come from our external behavior, but that it comes from within our heart. Most of us have tried to control our dependency by changing various aspects of our external behavior. The fact that this never worked for long is clear evidence that our real problems lie within. We should find it encouraging that God goes right to the root of our problems; he works his healing from the inside out. By recognizing our need for internal healing, we open our life to God's healing power.

7:24-30 By helping this Gentile woman, Jesus made it clear that his message of hope was for everyone, not just a privileged few. Jesus responded not only to the woman's humility and accurate self-perception but also to her great faith and perseverance. The more we trust God, the more he can do for us and through us. Conversely, a lack of faith and perseverance will prevent God from working his healing in our life and in the lives of our loved ones.

was possessed by an evil spirit. She had heard about Jesus, and now she came and fell at his feet. 26She begged him to release her child from the demon's control.

Since she was a Gentile, born in Syrian Phoenicia, 27Jesus told her, "First I should help my own family, the Jews.* It isn't right to take food from the children and throw it to the dogs."

28She replied, "That's true, Lord, but even the dogs under the table are given some crumbs from the children's plates."

29"Good answer!" he said. "And because you have answered so well, I have healed your daughter." 30And when she arrived home, her little girl was lying quietly in bed, and the demon was gone.

Jesus Heals a Deaf and Mute Man

31Jesus left Tyre and went to Sidon, then back to the Sea of Galilee and the region of the Ten Towns.* 32A deaf man with a speech impediment was brought to him, and the people begged Jesus to lay his hands on the man to heal him. 33Jesus led him to a private place away from the crowd. He put his fingers into the man's ears. Then, spitting onto his own fingers, he touched the man's tongue with the spittle. 34And looking up to heaven, he sighed and commanded, "Be opened!"* 35Instantly the man could hear perfectly and speak plainly!

36Jesus told the crowd not to tell anyone, but the more he told them not to, the more they spread the news, 37for they were completely amazed. Again and again they said, "Everything he does is wonderful. He even heals those who are deaf and mute."

CHAPTER 8
Jesus Feeds Four Thousand

About this time another great crowd had gathered, and the people ran out of food again. Jesus called his disciples and told them, 2"I feel sorry for these people. They have been here with me for three days, and they have nothing left to eat. 3And if I send them home without feeding them, they will faint along the road. For some of them have come a long distance."

4"How are we supposed to find enough food for them here in the wilderness?" his disciples asked.

5"How many loaves of bread do you have?" he asked.

"Seven," they replied. 6So Jesus told all the people to sit down on the ground. Then he took the seven loaves, thanked God for them, broke them into pieces, and gave them to his disciples, who distributed the bread to the crowd. 7A few small fish were found, too, so Jesus also blessed these and told the disciples to pass them out.

8They ate until they were full, and when the scraps were picked up, there were seven large baskets of food left over! 9There were about four thousand people in the crowd that day, and he sent them home after they had eaten. 10Immediately after this, he got into a boat with his disciples and crossed over to the region of Dalmanutha.

Pharisees Demand a Miraculous Sign

11When the Pharisees heard that Jesus had arrived, they came to argue with him. Testing him to see if he was from God, they

---

7:27 Greek *Let the children eat first.* **7:31** Greek *Decapolis.* **7:34** Greek text uses Aramaic *"Ephphatha"* and then translates it as "Be opened."

7:31-37 One key to recovery can be other people who lead us to the help we need. In this account, a group of people apparently cared enough for this deaf man to do something about his problem. They brought their friend to Jesus and begged Jesus to heal him. We may be the one God will use to give other hurting people hope and direction for recovery. As we share our story of deliverance and God's power for bringing recovery, we can give others the gift of life and health. We will not only give hope to others, but we will also experience a renewed commitment to our own recovery.

8:1-9 We sometimes feel like our prayers never get beyond the ceiling. We wonder if the hot line to God is busy and if we have been left indefinitely on hold. The truth is, God is never too busy to concern himself with the daily needs of his people. Jesus was moved by pity to feed four thousand hungry people, even though he was busy with a preaching and healing campaign. There is no need too small or request too large that God will not hear and respond to.

8:10-21 Jesus was troubled by his disciples' lack of faith and their seeming inability to learn the basic lessons he was trying to teach them. As slow to catch on as they were, Jesus still nurtured them in faith. We may tend to progress in recovery in a series of lurches and falls. When we fail, we can recover by quickly admitting our limitations, accepting God's forgiveness, and continuing to depend on his power, day by day. God will be patient with us if we are willing to stick with his program for recovery.

demanded, "Give us a miraculous sign from heaven to prove yourself."

12When he heard this, he sighed deeply and said, "Why do you people keep demanding a miraculous sign? I assure you, I will not give this generation any such sign." 13So he got back into the boat and left them, and he crossed to the other side of the lake.

Yeast of the Pharisees and Herod

14But the disciples discovered they had forgotten to bring any food, so there was only one loaf of bread with them in the boat. 15As they were crossing the lake, Jesus warned them, "Beware of the yeast of the Pharisees and of Herod."

16They decided he was saying this because they hadn't brought any bread. 17Jesus knew what they were thinking, so he said, "Why are you so worried about having no food? Won't you ever learn or understand? Are your hearts too hard to take it in? 18'You have eyes—can't you see? You have ears—can't you hear?'* Don't you remember anything at all? 19What about the five thousand men I fed with five loaves of bread? How many baskets of leftovers did you pick up afterward?"

"Twelve," they said.

20"And when I fed the four thousand with seven loaves, how many large baskets of leftovers did you pick up?"

"Seven," they said.

21"Don't you understand even yet?" he asked them.

Jesus Heals a Blind Man

22When they arrived at Bethsaida, some people brought a blind man to Jesus, and they begged him to touch and heal the man. 23Jesus took the blind man by the hand and led him out of the village. Then, spitting on the man's eyes, he laid his hands on him and asked, "Can you see anything now?"

24The man looked around. "Yes," he said, "I see people, but I can't see them very clearly. They look like trees walking around."

25Then Jesus placed his hands over the man's eyes again. As the man stared intently, his sight was completely restored, and he could see everything clearly. 26Jesus sent him home, saying, "Don't go back into the village on your way home."

Peter's Declaration about Jesus

27Jesus and his disciples left Galilee and went up to the villages of Caesarea Philippi. As they were walking along, he asked them, "Who do people say I am?"

28"Well," they replied, "some say John the Baptist, some say Elijah, and others say you are one of the other prophets."

29Then Jesus asked, "Who do you say I am?"

Peter replied, "You are the Messiah." 30But Jesus warned them not to tell anyone about him.

Jesus Predicts His Death

31Then Jesus began to tell them that he, the Son of Man, would suffer many terrible things and be rejected by the leaders, the leading priests, and the teachers of religious law. He would be killed, and three days later he would rise again. 32As he talked about this openly with his disciples, Peter took him aside and told him he shouldn't say things like that.*

33Jesus turned and looked at his disciples and then said to Peter very sternly, "Get away from me, Satan! You are seeing things merely from a human point of view, not from God's."

34Then he called his disciples and the crowds to come over and listen. "If any of you wants to be my follower," he told them, "you must put aside your selfish ambition, shoulder your cross, and follow me. 35If you try to keep your life for yourself, you will lose it. But if you give up your life for my sake and for the sake of the Good News, you will find true life. 36And how do you benefit if you gain the whole world but lose your own soul* in the process? 37Is anything worth more than your soul? 38If a person is ashamed of me and my message in these adulterous and sinful days, I, the Son of Man, will be ashamed of that person when I return in the glory of my Father with the holy angels."

8:18 Jer 5:21. 8:32 Or *and began to correct him.* 8:36 Or *your life;* also in 8:37.

8:31–9:1 When Jesus told his disciples that his ministry would lead to suffering and death, he was sharing a basic truth about life. When we are dealing with the destructive effects of sin, victory usually comes only after pain and tears. No cross, no resurrection. No pain, no gain. Jesus had to suffer in order to overcome the destructive power of sin in our world. Recovery from our destructive habits will also involve pain, but we should not let this discourage us. Jesus has already paid the price for our sins. If we confess our sins and accept God's forgiveness, we can be sure of victory over our addiction with God's daily help.

CHAPTER 9

Jesus went on to say, "I assure you that some of you standing here right now will not die before you see the Kingdom of God arrive in great power!"

The Transfiguration

[2]Six days later Jesus took Peter, James, and John to the top of a mountain. No one else was there. As the men watched, Jesus' appearance changed, [3]and his clothing became dazzling white, far whiter than any earthly process could ever make it. [4]Then Elijah and Moses appeared and began talking with Jesus.

[5]"Teacher, this is wonderful!" Peter exclaimed. "We will make three shrines*—one for you, one for Moses, and one for Elijah." [6]He didn't really know what to say, for they were all terribly afraid.

[7]Then a cloud came over them, and a voice from the cloud said, "This is my beloved Son. Listen to him." [8]Suddenly they looked around, and Moses and Elijah were gone, and only Jesus was with them. [9]As they descended the mountainside, he told them not to tell anyone what they had seen until he, the Son of Man, had risen from the dead. [10]So they kept it to themselves, but they often asked each other what he meant by "rising from the dead."

[11]Now they began asking him, "Why do the teachers of religious law insist that Elijah must return before the Messiah comes?"

[12]Jesus responded, "Elijah is indeed coming first to set everything in order. Why then is it written in the Scriptures that the Son of Man must suffer and be treated with utter contempt? [13]But I tell you, Elijah has already come, and he was badly mistreated, just as the Scriptures predicted."

Jesus Heals a Boy Possessed by an Evil Spirit

[14]At the foot of the mountain they found a great crowd surrounding the other disciples, as some teachers of religious law were arguing with them. [15]The crowd watched Jesus in awe as he came toward them, and then they ran to greet him. [16]"What is all this arguing about?" he asked.

[17]One of the men in the crowd spoke up and said, "Teacher, I brought my son for you to heal him. He can't speak because he is possessed by an evil spirit that won't let him talk. [18]And whenever this evil spirit seizes him, it throws him violently to the ground and makes him foam at the mouth and grind his teeth and become rigid.* So I asked your disciples to cast out the evil spirit, but they couldn't do it."

[19]Jesus said to them, "You faithless people! How long must I be with you until you believe? How long must I put up with you? Bring the boy to me." [20]So they brought the boy. But when the evil spirit saw Jesus, it threw the child into a violent convulsion, and he fell to the ground, writhing and foaming at the mouth. [21]"How long has this been happening?" Jesus asked the boy's father.

He replied, "Since he was very small. [22]The evil spirit often makes him fall into the fire or into water, trying to kill him. Have mercy on us and help us. Do something if you can."

[23]"What do you mean, 'If I can'?" Jesus asked. "Anything is possible if a person believes."

[24]The father instantly replied, "I do believe, but help me not to doubt!"

[25]When Jesus saw that the crowd of onlookers was growing, he rebuked the evil spirit. "Spirit of deafness and muteness," he said, "I command you to come out of this child and never enter him again!" [26]Then the spirit screamed and threw the boy into another violent convulsion and left him. The boy lay there motionless, and he appeared to be dead. A murmur ran through the crowd, "He's dead." [27]But Jesus took him by the hand and helped him to his feet, and he stood up.

[28]Afterward, when Jesus was alone in the house with his disciples, they asked him, "Why couldn't we cast out that evil spirit?"

[29]Jesus replied, "This kind can be cast out only by prayer.*"

9:5 Or *shelters;* Greek reads *tabernacles.* **9:18** Or *become weak.* **9:29** Some manuscripts add *and fasting.*

9:14-29 Through honest self-examination, the father of the demon-possessed boy acknowledged both belief and doubt. He believed that Jesus could restore his son to health, but he questioned whether Jesus would do so. Sometimes we feel the same way. We see how God has delivered others and believe that God can help, but we fear that he will refuse to help us. Perhaps we are afraid that God will think us unworthy of his deliverance. God never works that way. Not only is he *able* to help us, but he also *wants* to help us. We must turn to him in faith, ask for his help and forgiveness, and follow his revealed will for us. God will do the rest.

Jesus Again Predicts His Death

[30]Leaving that region, they traveled through Galilee. Jesus tried to avoid all publicity [31]in order to spend more time with his disciples and teach them. He said to them, "The Son of Man is going to be betrayed. He will be killed, but three days later he will rise from the dead." [32]But they didn't understand what he was saying, and they were afraid to ask him what he meant.

The Greatest in the Kingdom

[33]After they arrived at Capernaum, Jesus and his disciples settled in the house where they would be staying. Jesus asked them, "What were you discussing out on the road?" [34]But they didn't answer, because they had been arguing about which of them was the greatest. [35]He sat down and called the twelve disciples over to him. Then he said, "Anyone who wants to be the first must take last place and be the servant of everyone else."

[36]Then he put a little child among them. Taking the child in his arms, he said to them, [37]"Anyone who welcomes a little child like this on my behalf welcomes me, and anyone who welcomes me welcomes my Father who sent me."

Using the Name of Jesus

[38]John said to Jesus, "Teacher, we saw a man using your name to cast out demons, but we told him to stop because he isn't one of our group."

[39]"Don't stop him!" Jesus said. "No one who performs miracles in my name will soon be able to speak evil of me. [40]Anyone who is not against us is for us. [41]If anyone gives you even a cup of water because you belong to the Messiah, I assure you, that person will be rewarded.

[42]"But if anyone causes one of these little ones who trusts in me to lose faith, it would be better for that person to be thrown into the sea with a large millstone tied around the neck. [43]If your hand causes you to sin, cut it off. It is better to enter heaven* with only one hand than to go into the unquenchable fires of hell with two hands.* [45]If your foot causes you to sin, cut it off. It is better to enter heaven with only one foot than to be thrown into hell with two feet.* [47]And if your eye causes you to sin, gouge it out. It is better to enter the Kingdom of God half blind than to have two eyes and be thrown into hell, [48]'where the worm never dies and the fire never goes out.'*

9:43a Greek *enter life;* also in 9:45. **9:43b** Some manuscripts add verse 44 (which is identical with 9:48). **9:45** Some manuscripts add verse 46 (which is identical with 9:48). **9:48** Isa 66:24.

9:30-37 The argument over who would be the greatest in God's Kingdom ran counter to everything Jesus stood for. True greatness is measured by how we serve others. That service, for the disciples, included showing love for all people, even a little child. We may not be tempted to turn away from needy children, but what about the many adults who need our help? Do we turn away people who are poor, homeless, hungry, or addicted? God heals our hurts so we can help others get the healing they need, not so we can rise to a higher position in society. If we fail to help needy people, we are pushing Jesus right out of our life.

9:38-42 Cooperation and peace, not cutthroat competition, must characterize our interpersonal relationships. Jesus instructed his disciples to fully and peacefully accept others who ministered in his name. He accepted those not under his own direct authority but who were building up the Kingdom of God. So must we. If we fail to do so and cause others to lose their faith, we will suffer the painful consequences.

9:43-50 Through a series of startling statements, Jesus admonished his disciples to get rid of anything in their lives that might draw them away from God. For us, this could refer to our besetting addiction and the emotional baggage that supports it. We can identify our weaknesses by making an honest moral inventory of our life and then take action to "cut off" our offensive parts so we can begin the process of healing. It is usually wise to have the help of a support group as we follow through on such drastic measures.

10:1-12 The Pharisees were not looking for guidance when they asked Jesus about divorce; they were looking for a means to trap him. Jesus offered no grounds for divorce, with the possible exception of infidelity (see Matthew 19:9). Today many believe divorce is a good way to deal with conflict. Most of us have discovered, however, that interpersonal conflicts follow us wherever we go because they are only evidence of much deeper problems. These same problems may also drive our dependency. Marriage is not always easy; neither is recovery. But both can be of great help to each other. Marriage gives us a context of accountability and loving support to help us through recovery. Recovery gives us the program for personal growth and reestablishing our family and marriage relationships.

⁴⁹"For everyone will be purified with fire.* ⁵⁰Salt is good for seasoning. But if it loses its flavor, how do you make it salty again? You must have the qualities of salt among yourselves and live in peace with each other."

CHAPTER 10
Discussion about Divorce and Marriage
Then Jesus left Capernaum and went southward to the region of Judea and into the area east of the Jordan River. As always there were the crowds, and as usual he taught them.

²Some Pharisees came and tried to trap him with this question: "Should a man be allowed to divorce his wife?"

³"What did Moses say about divorce?" Jesus asked them.

⁴"Well, he permitted it," they replied. "He said a man merely has to write his wife an official letter of divorce and send her away."*

⁵But Jesus responded, "He wrote those instructions only as a concession to your hard-hearted wickedness. ⁶But God's plan was seen from the beginning of creation, for 'He made them male and female.'* ⁷'This explains why a man leaves his father and mother and is joined to his wife,* ⁸and the two are united into one.'* Since they are no longer two but one, ⁹let no one separate them, for God has joined them together."

¹⁰Later, when he was alone with his disciples in the house, they brought up the subject again. ¹¹He told them, "Whoever divorces his wife and marries someone else commits adultery against her. ¹²And if a woman divorces her husband and remarries, she commits adultery."

Jesus Blesses the Children
¹³One day some parents brought their children to Jesus so he could touch them and bless them, but the disciples told them not to bother him. ¹⁴But when Jesus saw what was happening, he was very displeased with his disciples. He said to them, "Let the children come to me. Don't stop them! For the Kingdom of God belongs to such as these. ¹⁵I assure you, anyone who doesn't have their kind of faith will never get into the Kingdom of God." ¹⁶Then he took the children into his arms and placed his hands on their heads and blessed them.

9:49 Greek *salted with fire.* Some manuscripts add *and every sacrifice will be salted with salt.* **10:4** Deut 24:1. **10:6** Gen 1:27; 5:2. **10:7** Some manuscripts do not include *and is joined to his wife.* **10:7-8** Gen 2:24.

▶ **The Twelve Step devotional reading plan begins here.**

S T E P 1

Like Little Children
BIBLE READING: Mark 10:13-16
We admitted that we were powerless over our dependencies—that our life had become unmanageable.
For many of us in recovery, memories of childhood are full of the terrors associated with being powerless. If we were raised in a family that was out of control, where we were neglected, abused, or exposed to domestic violence and dysfunctional behavior, the thought of being powerless might be very frightening. We may have silently vowed never again to be as vulnerable as we were when we were children.

Jesus tells us that in order to enter the Kingdom of God we must become like little children, and this involves being powerless. He said, "I assure you, anyone who doesn't have their kind of faith will never get into the Kingdom of God" (Mark 10:15).

In any society, children are the most dependent members. They have no inherent power for self-protection—no means to ensure that their lives will be safe, comfortable, or fulfilling. Little children are singularly reliant on the love, care, and nurture of others for their most basic needs. They *must* cry out even though they may not know exactly what they need. They *must* trust their lives to someone who is more powerful than they, and, hopefully, they will be heard and lovingly cared for.

We, too, must admit that we are truly powerless if our life is to become healthy. This doesn't mean we have to become victims again. Admitting our powerlessness is an honest appraisal of our situation in life and a positive step toward recovery. *Turn to page 199, Acts 9.*

The Rich Man

17As he was starting out on a trip, a man came running up to Jesus, knelt down, and asked, "Good Teacher, what should I do to get eternal life?"

18"Why do you call me good?" Jesus asked. "Only God is truly good. 19But as for your question, you know the commandments. 'Do not murder. Do not commit adultery. Do not steal. Do not testify falsely. Do not cheat. Honor your father and mother.'*"

20"Teacher," the man replied, "I've obeyed all these commandments since I was a child."

21Jesus felt genuine love for this man as he looked at him. "You lack only one thing," he told him. "Go and sell all you have and give the money to the poor, and you will have treasure in heaven. Then come, follow me." 22At this, the man's face fell, and he went sadly away because he had many possessions.

23Jesus looked around and said to his disciples, "How hard it is for rich people to get into the Kingdom of God!" 24This amazed them. But Jesus said again, "Dear children, it is very hard* to get into the Kingdom of God. 25It is easier for a camel to go through the eye of a needle than for a rich person to enter the Kingdom of God!"

26The disciples were astounded. "Then who in the world can be saved?" they asked.

27Jesus looked at them intently and said, "Humanly speaking, it is impossible. But not with God. Everything is possible with God."

28Then Peter began to mention all that he and the other disciples had left behind. "We've given up everything to follow you," he said.

29And Jesus replied, "I assure you that everyone who has given up house or brothers or sisters or mother or father or children or property, for my sake and for the Good News, 30will receive now in return, a hundred times over, houses, brothers, sisters, mothers, children, and property—with persecutions. And in the world to come they will have eternal life. 31But many who seem to be important now will be the least important then, and those who are considered least here will be the greatest then.*"

Jesus Again Predicts His Death

32They were now on the way to Jerusalem, and Jesus was walking ahead of them. The disciples were filled with dread and the people following behind were overwhelmed with fear. Taking the twelve disciples aside, Jesus once more began to describe everything that was about to happen to him in Jerusalem. 33"When we get to Jerusalem," he told them, "the Son of Man will be betrayed to the leading priests and the teachers of religious law. They will sentence him to die and hand him over to the Romans. 34They will mock him, spit on him, beat him with their whips, and kill him, but after three days he will rise again."

Jesus Teaches about Serving Others

35Then James and John, the sons of Zebedee, came over and spoke to him. "Teacher," they said, "we want you to do us a favor."

36"What is it?" he asked.

37"In your glorious Kingdom, we want to sit in places of honor next to you," they said, "one at your right and the other at your left."

38But Jesus answered, "You don't know what you are asking! Are you able to drink from the bitter cup of sorrow I am about to drink? Are you able to be baptized with the baptism of suffering I must be baptized with?"

39"Oh yes," they said, "we are able!"

And Jesus said, "You will indeed drink from my cup and be baptized with my baptism, 40but I have no right to say who will sit on the thrones next to mine. God has prepared those places for the ones he has chosen."

10:19 Exod 20:12-16; Deut 5:16-20. 10:24 Some manuscripts add *for those who trust in riches.* 10:31 Greek *But many who are first will be last; and the last, first.*

10:23-31 Most people in Jesus' day believed that wealth was a reward from God for being good. Thus, the wealthy usually enjoyed a measure of prestige. Jesus amazed his audience by showing how very difficult it was for the rich to enter God's Kingdom. Wealthy people have a hard time recognizing their need for anything, and the only way to receive God's help is by recognizing how much we need him. The rich young man needed to see his helplessness before he could be helped. But even this problem is not too big for God; he gets the attention of even the proud and self-sufficient. Many of us have learned through painful experiences that we are helpless and need God's intervention in our life. God often lets us hit bottom so we can begin to experience his healing and forgiveness.

⁴¹When the ten other disciples discovered what James and John had asked, they were indignant. ⁴²So Jesus called them together and said, "You know that in this world kings are tyrants, and officials lord it over the people beneath them. ⁴³But among you it should be quite different. Whoever wants to be a leader among you must be your servant, ⁴⁴and whoever wants to be first must be the slave of all. ⁴⁵For even I, the Son of Man, came here not to be served but to serve others, and to give my life as a ransom for many."

Jesus Heals Blind Bartimaeus

⁴⁶And so they reached Jericho. Later, as Jesus and his disciples left town, a great crowd was following. A blind beggar named Bartimaeus (son of Timaeus) was sitting beside the road as Jesus was going by. ⁴⁷When Bartimaeus heard that Jesus from Nazareth was nearby, he began to shout out, "Jesus, Son of David, have mercy on me!"

⁴⁸"Be quiet!" some of the people yelled at him.

But he only shouted louder, "Son of David, have mercy on me!"

⁴⁹When Jesus heard him, he stopped and said, "Tell him to come here."

So they called the blind man. "Cheer up," they said. "Come on, he's calling you!" ⁵⁰Bartimaeus threw aside his coat, jumped up, and came to Jesus.

⁵¹"What do you want me to do for you?" Jesus asked.

"Teacher," the blind man said, "I want to see!"

⁵²And Jesus said to him, "Go your way. Your faith has healed you." And instantly the blind man could see! Then he followed Jesus down the road.*

CHAPTER 11
The Triumphal Entry

As Jesus and his disciples approached Jerusalem, they came to the towns of Bethphage and Bethany, on the Mount of Olives. Jesus sent two of them on ahead. ²"Go into that village over there," he told them, "and as soon as you enter it, you will see a colt tied there that has never been ridden. Untie it and bring it here. ³If anyone asks what you are doing, just say, 'The Lord needs it and will return it soon.'"

⁴The two disciples left and found the colt standing in the street, tied outside a house. ⁵As they were untying it, some bystanders demanded, "What are you doing, untying that colt?" ⁶They said what Jesus had told them to say, and they were permitted to take it. ⁷Then they brought the colt to Jesus and threw their garments over it, and he sat on it.

⁸Many in the crowd spread their coats on the road ahead of Jesus, and others cut leafy branches in the fields and spread them along the way. ⁹He was in the center of the procession, and the crowds all around him were shouting,

"Praise God!*
  Bless the one who comes in the name
    of the Lord!
¹⁰ Bless the coming kingdom of our
    ancestor David!
  Praise God in highest heaven!"*

¹¹So Jesus came to Jerusalem and went into the Temple. He looked around carefully at everything, and then he left because it was late in the afternoon. Then he went out to Bethany with the twelve disciples.

10:52 Or *on the way.* **11:9** Greek *Hosanna,* an exclamation of praise that literally means "save now"; also in 11:10. **11:9-10** Pss 118:25-26; 148:1.

10:46-52 Faith brought sight to blind Bartimaeus. He persevered in faith despite the initial opposition he experienced from Jesus' followers. In Jesus' day, blindness was considered a divine curse for sin (see John 9:2), but Jesus refuted this notion by both word and deed. We sometimes face opposition in our recovery process. Sometimes those who claim to be God's people reject us and make us feel unwelcome because we are trapped by our dependency. Even when others reject us, we can be sure that Jesus will never turn us away. We should persevere like Bartimaeus did, knowing that Jesus has the power and the desire to help us overcome our besetting weaknesses.

11:1-10 As we suffer the pain of our addiction, we often look for instant relief. We wish someone would come and sweep all our problems away. The Judeans were expecting the same kind of deliverance from their Messiah. They wanted a glorious political king on a warhorse to ride into Jerusalem and sweep the Romans out of power. Instead, Jesus came riding on a lowly donkey, in peace. God does not offer instant cures; he works our recovery through a process of personal growth, from the inside out. He helps us recognize our sins and our need for help, and he gives us the strength to take the necessary steps toward recovery.

Jesus Curses the Fig Tree

¹²The next morning as they were leaving Bethany, Jesus felt hungry. ¹³He noticed a fig tree a little way off that was in full leaf, so he went over to see if he could find any figs on it. But there were only leaves because it was too early in the season for fruit. ¹⁴Then Jesus said to the tree, "May no one ever eat your fruit again!" And the disciples heard him say it.

Jesus Clears the Temple

¹⁵When they arrived back in Jerusalem, Jesus entered the Temple and began to drive out the merchants and their customers. He knocked over the tables of the money changers and the stalls of those selling doves, ¹⁶and he stopped everyone from bringing in merchandise. ¹⁷He taught them, "The Scriptures declare, 'My Temple will be called a place of prayer for all nations,' but you have turned it into a den of thieves."*

¹⁸When the leading priests and teachers of religious law heard what Jesus had done, they began planning how to kill him. But they were afraid of him because the people were so enthusiastic about Jesus' teaching. ¹⁹That evening Jesus and the disciples* left the city.

²⁰The next morning as they passed by the fig tree he had cursed, the disciples noticed it was withered from the roots. ²¹Peter remembered what Jesus had said to the tree on the previous day and exclaimed, "Look, Teacher! The fig tree you cursed has withered!"

²²Then Jesus said to the disciples, "Have faith in God. ²³I assure you that you can say to this mountain, 'May God lift you up and throw you into the sea,' and your command will be obeyed. All that's required is that you really believe and do not doubt in your heart. ²⁴Listen to me! You can pray for anything, and if you believe, you will have it. ²⁵But when you are praying, first forgive anyone you are holding a grudge against, so that your Father in heaven will forgive your sins, too.*"

The Authority of Jesus Challenged

²⁷By this time they had arrived in Jerusalem again. As Jesus was walking through the Temple area, the leading priests, the teachers of religious law, and the other leaders came up to him. They demanded, ²⁸"By whose authority did you drive out the merchants from the Temple?* Who gave you such authority?"

²⁹"I'll tell who gave me authority to do these things if you answer one question," Jesus replied. ³⁰"Did John's baptism come from heaven or was it merely human? Answer me!"

³¹They talked it over among themselves. "If we say it was from heaven, he will ask why we didn't believe him. ³²But do we dare say it was merely human?" For they were afraid that the people would start a riot, since everyone thought that John was a prophet. ³³So they finally replied, "We don't know."

And Jesus responded, "Then I won't answer your question either."

CHAPTER 12

Story of the Evil Farmers

Then Jesus began telling them stories: "A man planted a vineyard, built a wall around

---

11:17 Isa 56:7; Jer 7:11. **11:19** Greek *they;* some manuscripts read *he.* **11:25** Some manuscripts add verse 26, *But if you do not forgive, neither will your Father who is in heaven forgive your sins.* **11:28** Or *By whose authority do you do these things?*

11:12-19 The barren fig tree is analogous to spiritually bankrupt people. If the fig tree did not produce fruit, as it was designed to do, then it had no real reason to exist. If the Temple did not produce true worship and prayer but only ill-gotten gain for the money changers, then the Temple had to be judged and cleansed as well. So also in recovery. If our life in recovery is not bearing the fruit of new behavior patterns, then it must be overhauled. If we only go through the motions of recovery, then our faith has no substance, and our attempts to recover are only pretenses.

11:20-25 God wants us to pray for his will to be done in our life as much as he wants us to pray for fruitfulness in his Kingdom work. It is God's will, however, to remove mountains of resistance or denial from our life. God has the power to do miracles—but not if we doubt him. The God of the Kingdom and of recovery is the God of the impossible. If we want God to work a miracle of healing in our life, we must pray and believe that he will. We need to admit our helplessness and put our life into God's hands. He will then walk with us as we face each new step in recovery.

12:1-12 Jesus confronted the religious leaders with their hypocrisy and denial with this story. The leaders were the wicked farmers who had rejected God, the owner of his people (who were represented by the vineyard). These leaders pretended to be in touch with God, but their actions and attitudes proved otherwise. Jesus confronted them, hoping they would listen and change. We also need to be awakened from our denial if we hope to recover. God often brings people into our life to wake us up. We must not be like the proud Pharisees. If we refuse to admit our sins, we will never receive God's help for recovery.

it, dug a pit for pressing out the grape juice, and built a lookout tower. Then he leased the vineyard to tenant farmers and moved to another country. ²At grape-picking time he sent one of his servants to collect his share of the crop. ³But the farmers grabbed the servant, beat him up, and sent him back empty-handed.

⁴"The owner then sent another servant, but they beat him over the head and treated him shamefully. ⁵The next servant he sent was killed. Others who were sent were either beaten or killed, ⁶until there was only one left—his son whom he loved dearly. The owner finally sent him, thinking, 'Surely they will respect my son.'

⁷"But the farmers said to one another, 'Here comes the heir to this estate. Let's kill him and get the estate for ourselves!' ⁸So they grabbed him and murdered him and threw his body out of the vineyard.

⁹"What do you suppose the owner of the vineyard will do?" Jesus asked. "I'll tell you—he will come and kill them all and lease the vineyard to others. ¹⁰Didn't you ever read this in the Scriptures?

'The stone rejected by the builders
     has now become the cornerstone.
¹¹This is the Lord's doing,
     and it is marvelous to see.'*"

¹²The Jewish leaders wanted to arrest him for using this illustration because they realized he was pointing at them—they were the wicked farmers in his story. But they were afraid to touch him because of the crowds. So they left him and went away.

Taxes for Caesar

¹³The leaders sent some Pharisees and supporters of Herod to try to trap Jesus into saying something for which he could be arrested. ¹⁴"Teacher," these men said, "we know how honest you are. You are impartial and don't play favorites. You sincerely teach the ways of God. Now tell us—is it right to pay taxes to the Roman government or not? ¹⁵Should we pay them, or should we not?"

Jesus saw through their hypocrisy and said, "Whom are you trying to fool with your trick questions? Show me a Roman coin,* and I'll tell you." ¹⁶When they handed it to him, he asked, "Whose picture and title are stamped on it?"

"Caesar's," they replied.

¹⁷"Well, then," Jesus said, "give to Caesar what belongs to him. But everything that belongs to God must be given to God." This reply completely amazed them.

Discussion about Resurrection

¹⁸Then the Sadducees stepped forward—a group of Jews who say there is no resurrection after death. They posed this question: ¹⁹"Teacher, Moses gave us a law that if a man dies, leaving a wife without children, his brother should marry the widow and have a child who will be the brother's heir.* ²⁰Well, there were seven brothers. The oldest of them married and then died without children. ²¹So the second brother married the widow, but soon he too died and left no children. Then the next brother married her and died without children. ²²This continued until all the brothers had married her and died, and still there were no children. Last of all, the woman died, too. ²³So tell us, whose wife will she be in the resurrection? For all seven were married to her."

²⁴Jesus replied, "Your problem is that you don't know the Scriptures, and you don't know the power of God. ²⁵For when the dead rise, they won't be married. They will be like the angels in heaven. ²⁶But now, as to whether the dead will be raised—haven't you ever read about this in the writings of Moses, in the story of the burning bush? Long after Abraham, Isaac, and Jacob had died, God said to Moses,* 'I am the God of Abraham, the God of Isaac, and the God of Jacob.'* ²⁷So he is the God of the living, not the dead. You have made a serious error."

12:10-11 Ps 118:22-23. **12:15** Greek *a denarius.* **12:19** Deut 25:5-6. **12:26a** Greek *in the story of the bush? God said to him.* **12:26b** Exod 3:6.

12:18-27 Jesus avoided another trick question, this one by the Sadducees, who did not believe in the resurrection after death. Again Jesus cleverly exposed the moral shortcomings of those who had the form of religion but denied its power. Book learning, even Scripture memory, is not enough to keep us from sin or help us recover from our dependency. We must know the living God personally and accept the help he offers as our Savior. The God of the patriarchs is not the God of philosophical speculation. He is our God, active today in our recovery. He is the God of hope and resurrection.

The Most Important Commandment

²⁸One of the teachers of religious law was standing there listening to the discussion. He realized that Jesus had answered well, so he asked, "Of all the commandments, which is the most important?"

²⁹Jesus replied, "The most important commandment is this: 'Hear, O Israel! The Lord our God is the one and only Lord. ³⁰And you must love the Lord your God with all your heart, all your soul, all your mind, and all your strength.'* ³¹The second is equally important: 'Love your neighbor as yourself.'* No other commandment is greater than these."

³²The teacher of religious law replied, "Well said, Teacher. You have spoken the truth by saying that there is only one God and no other. ³³And I know it is important to love him with all my heart and all my understanding and all my strength, and to love my neighbors as myself. This is more important than to offer all of the burnt offerings and sacrifices required in the law."

³⁴Realizing this man's understanding, Jesus said to him, "You are not far from the Kingdom of God." And after that, no one dared to ask him any more questions.

Whose Son Is the Messiah?

³⁵Later, as Jesus was teaching the people in the Temple, he asked, "Why do the teachers of religious law claim that the Messiah will be the son of David? ³⁶For David himself, speaking under the inspiration of the Holy Spirit, said,

'The LORD said to my Lord,
Sit in honor at my right hand
 until I humble your enemies beneath
  your feet.'*

³⁷Since David himself called him Lord, how can he be his son at the same time?" And the crowd listened to him with great interest.

³⁸Here are some of the other things he taught them at this time: "Beware of these teachers of religious law! For they love to parade in flowing robes and to have everyone bow to them as they walk in the marketplaces. ³⁹And how they love the seats of honor in the synagogues and at banquets. ⁴⁰But they shamelessly cheat widows out of their property, and then, to cover up the kind of people they really are, they make long prayers in public. Because of this, their punishment will be the greater."

The Widow's Offering

⁴¹Jesus went over to the collection box in the Temple and sat and watched as the crowds dropped in their money. Many rich people put in large amounts. ⁴²Then a poor widow came and dropped in two pennies.* ⁴³He called his disciples to him and said, "I assure you, this poor widow has given more than all the others have given. ⁴⁴For they gave a tiny part of their surplus, but she, poor as she is, has given everything she has."

CHAPTER 13
Jesus Foretells the Future

As Jesus was leaving the Temple that day, one of his disciples said, "Teacher, look at these tremendous buildings! Look at the massive stones in the walls!"

²Jesus replied, "These magnificent buildings will be so completely demolished that not one stone will be left on top of another."

³Later, Jesus sat on the slopes of the Mount of Olives across the valley from the Temple. Peter, James, John, and Andrew came to him privately and asked him, ⁴"When will all this take place? And will there be any sign ahead of time to show us when all this will be fulfilled?"

12:29-30 Deut 6:4-5. **12:31** Lev 19:18. **12:36** Ps 110:1. **12:42** Greek *2 lepta, which is a kodrantes.*

12:28-34 Many think of religion, with all its commandments, as a burdensome straitjacket, antithetical to true recovery. This may have been true, in some sense, of the Judaism in Jesus' day, and it is sometimes true today among people who claim to belong to God. Jesus wanted to correct this false understanding of true faith. He summed up the numerous Jewish laws in two simple but profound commandments: Love God totally and love others as much as we love ourself. If these two thoughts rule our heart and mind, we will be well along the path toward recovery.
13:1-20 The Olivet discourse (13:1-37) speaks to the all-too-human preoccupation with the uncertainty of the future. The disciples worried about the future of their nation after Jesus predicted the destruction of the Temple that was then being rebuilt. We may worry about whether or not we will survive future conflicts and temptations. As we face an uncertain future, we are encouraged to live one day at a time. God makes it clear that despite our trials, we should not worry. If we entrust our life to God, his Spirit will be with us during our difficult times. Recovery is never easy, but it is always possible with God's help.

5Jesus replied, "Don't let anyone mislead you, 6because many will come in my name, claiming to be the Messiah.* They will lead many astray. 7And wars will break out near and far, but don't panic. Yes, these things must come, but the end won't follow immediately. 8Nations and kingdoms will proclaim war against each other, and there will be earthquakes in many parts of the world, and famines. But all this will be only the beginning of the horrors to come. 9But when these things begin to happen, watch out! You will be handed over to the courts and beaten in the synagogues. You will be accused before governors and kings of being my followers. This will be your opportunity to tell them about me.* 10And the Good News must first be preached to every nation. 11But when you are arrested and stand trial, don't worry about what to say in your defense. Just say what God tells you to. Then it is not you who will be speaking, but the Holy Spirit.

12"Brother will betray brother to death, fathers will betray their own children, and children will rise against their parents and cause them to be killed. 13And everyone will hate you because of your allegiance to me. But those who endure to the end will be saved.

14"The time will come when you will see the sacrilegious object that causes desecration* standing where it should not be"— reader, pay attention! "Then those in Judea must flee to the hills. 15A person outside the house* must not go back into the house to pack. 16A person in the field must not return even to get a coat. 17How terrible it will be for pregnant women and for mothers nursing their babies in those days. 18And pray that your flight will not be in winter. 19For those will be days of greater horror than at any time since God created the world. And it will never happen again. 20In fact, unless the Lord shortens that time of calamity, the entire human race will be destroyed. But for the sake of his chosen ones he has shortened those days.

21"And then if anyone tells you, 'Look, here is the Messiah,' or, 'There he is,' don't pay any attention. 22For false messiahs and false prophets will rise up and perform miraculous signs and wonders so as to deceive, if possible, even God's chosen ones. 23Watch out! I have warned you!

24"At that time, after those horrible days end,

the sun will be darkened,
    the moon will not give light,
25 the stars will fall from the sky,
    and the powers of heaven will be
        shaken.*

26Then everyone will see the Son of Man arrive on the clouds with great power and glory.* 27And he will send forth his angels to gather together his chosen ones from all over the world—from the farthest ends of the earth and heaven.

28"Now, learn a lesson from the fig tree. When its buds become tender and its leaves begin to sprout, you know without being told that summer is near. 29Just so, when you see the events I've described beginning to happen, you can be sure that his return is very near, right at the door. 30I assure you, this generation* will not pass from the scene until all these events have taken place. 31Heaven and earth will disappear, but my words will remain forever.

32"However, no one knows the day or hour when these things will happen, not even the angels in heaven or the Son himself. Only the Father knows. 33And since you don't know when they will happen, stay alert and keep watch.*

34"The coming of the Son of Man can be compared with that of a man who left home to go on a trip. He gave each of his employees instructions about the work they were to do, and he told the gatekeeper to watch for his return. 35So keep a sharp lookout! For you do not know when the homeowner will return—at evening, midnight, early dawn, or late daybreak. 36Don't let him find you

---

13:6 Greek *name, saying, 'I am.'* **13:9** Or *This will be your testimony against them.* **13:14** Greek *the abomination of desolation.* See Dan 9:27; 11:31; 12:11. **13:15** Greek *on the roof.* **13:24-25** See Isa 13:10; 34:4; Joel 2:10. **13:26** See Dan 7:13. **13:30** Or *this age,* or *this nation.* **13:33** Some manuscripts add *and pray.*

13:21-37 Jesus did not reveal when the end would come, but this should motivate us to remain alert and watchful from now until the end. As we are unsure of the future of our world, we are also uncertain about the timing and difficulties we will face in recovery. We are never completely recovered; we are always in recovery. We will experience total victory only after Jesus has returned to make us into new people. Preparation for his return must be made one day at a time. We cannot calculate the day of his return and plan to change just before he comes. Our daily preparation and actions are important keys to our spiritual health and recovery.

sleeping when he arrives without warning. [37]What I say to you I say to everyone: Watch for his return!"

CHAPTER 14

Jesus Anointed at Bethany

It was now two days before the Passover celebration and the Festival of Unleavened Bread. The leading priests and the teachers of religious law were still looking for an opportunity to capture Jesus secretly and put him to death. [2]"But not during the Passover," they agreed, "or there will be a riot."

[3]Meanwhile, Jesus was in Bethany at the home of Simon, a man who had leprosy. During supper, a woman came in with a beautiful jar of expensive perfume.* She broke the seal and poured the perfume over his head. [4]Some of those at the table were indignant. "Why was this expensive perfume wasted?" they asked. [5]"She could have sold it for a small fortune* and given the money to the poor!" And they scolded her harshly.

[6]But Jesus replied, "Leave her alone. Why berate her for doing such a good thing to me? [7]You will always have the poor among you, and you can help them whenever you want to. But I will not be here with you much longer. [8]She has done what she could and has anointed my body for burial ahead of time. [9]I assure you, wherever the Good News is preached throughout the world, this woman's deed will be talked about in her memory."

Judas Agrees to Betray Jesus

[10]Then Judas Iscariot, one of the twelve disciples, went to the leading priests to arrange to betray Jesus to them. [11]The leading priests were delighted when they heard why he had come, and they promised him a reward. So he began looking for the right time and place to betray Jesus.

The Last Supper

[12]On the first day of the Festival of Unleavened Bread (the day the Passover lambs were sacrificed), Jesus' disciples asked him, "Where do you want us to go to prepare the Passover supper?"

[13]So Jesus sent two of them into Jerusalem to make the arrangements. "As you go into the city," he told them, "a man carrying a pitcher of water will meet you. Follow him. [14]At the house he enters, say to the owner, 'The Teacher asks, Where is the guest room where I can eat the Passover meal with my disciples?' [15]He will take you upstairs to a large room that is already set up. That is the place; go ahead and prepare our supper there." [16]So the two disciples went on ahead into the city and found everything just as Jesus had said, and they prepared the Passover supper there.

[17]In the evening Jesus arrived with the twelve disciples. [18]As they were sitting around the table eating, Jesus said, "The truth is, one of you will betray me, one of you who is here eating with me."

[19]Greatly distressed, one by one they began to ask him, "I'm not the one, am I?"

[20]He replied, "It is one of you twelve, one who is eating with me now.* [21]For I, the Son of Man, must die, as the Scriptures declared long ago. But how terrible it will be for my betrayer. Far better for him if he had never been born!"

14:3 Greek *an alabaster jar of expensive ointment, pure nard.* **14:5** Greek *300 denarii.* A denarius was the equivalent of a full day's wage. **14:20** Or *one who is dipping bread into the bowl with me.*

14:10-26 We are often shocked by Judas's betrayal of Jesus. Since Judas had spent about three years in close friendship with Jesus, we wonder what could have prompted him to act as he did. Yet if we are truly honest with ourself, we may see the same potential in our own heart. Whenever we refuse to give Jesus authority over a certain area of our life, we act like Judas. Whenever we promise to do one thing and then do another, we act like Judas. We all have betrayed God in some way or another. We should use Judas's failure as an opportunity to take a hard look at our own life. In what ways are we betraying God?

14:27-31 Peter wasn't honest with himself when he promised to stay with Jesus no matter what the cost. He still did not realize that following Jesus would lead him to the foot of the cross. When things got tough, Peter backed out of his commitment (see 14:66-71). We often do the same thing in recovery. We determine to escape the pain of our addiction and commit ourself to recovery. But we may be unaware of the hard times we must face along the way. As recovery becomes difficult and we experience opposition, we are tempted to give up and fall back into our destructive habits. We should consider the difficulties we may face before we start the journey. Then we won't be devastated when we have to face them.

GOD grant me the serenity to accept the things I cannot change the courage to change the things I can and the wisdom to know the difference AMEN

As we pray the serenity prayer, we learn to think in new ways. We learn to ask questions that will lead us away from our destructive past and into a productive future.

We begin to ask, What can we change in our situation? What things are beyond our control? What are our responsibilities in the situations we face? As we develop these new thought processes, we may lack confidence in our own wisdom and common sense. We may hesitate to carry out God's will if we are afraid of the criticism of the people around us.

Common sense could be defined as our ability to figure out in advance what the likely consequences of our choices and actions will be. We are told that "Getting wisdom is the most important thing you can do! And whatever else you do, get good judgment" (Proverbs 4:7). We can exercise our common sense by thinking about what we can do and then doing the things that we can.

A woman wanted to do something to demonstrate her love for Jesus, so she poured some expensive perfume on his head. The disciples criticized her for doing this. Jesus came to her defense with these words: "Leave her alone. Why berate her for doing such a good thing to me? . . . She has done what she could" (Mark 14:6-8). These are words we can cling to.

God wants to renew our mind and help us develop wisdom and common sense. As we try to sort out our choices and develop common sense, people may criticize us. But we can trust that God will come to our defense, as long as we do what Scripture directs us to do. *Turn to page 117, Luke 11.*

---

²²As they were eating, Jesus took a loaf of bread and asked God's blessing on it. Then he broke it in pieces and gave it to the disciples, saying, "Take it, for this is my body."

²³And he took a cup of wine and gave thanks to God for it. He gave it to them, and they all drank from it. ²⁴And he said to them, "This is my blood, poured out for many, sealing the covenant* between God and his people. ²⁵I solemnly declare that I will not drink wine again until that day when I drink it new in the Kingdom of God." ²⁶Then they sang a hymn and went out to the Mount of Olives.

Jesus Predicts Peter's Denial

²⁷"All of you will desert me," Jesus told them. "For the Scriptures say,

'God* will strike the Shepherd,
    and the sheep will be scattered.'*

²⁸But after I am raised from the dead, I will go ahead of you to Galilee and meet you there."

²⁹Peter said to him, "Even if everyone else deserts you, I never will."

³⁰"Peter," Jesus replied, "the truth is, this very night, before the rooster crows twice, you will deny me three times."

³¹"No!" Peter insisted. "Not even if I have to die with you! I will never deny you!" And all the others vowed the same.

Jesus Prays in Gethsemane

³²And they came to an olive grove called Gethsemane, and Jesus said, "Sit here while I

14:24 Some manuscripts read *the new covenant.* **14:27a** Greek *I.* **14:27b** Zech 13:7.

go and pray." [33]He took Peter, James, and John with him, and he began to be filled with horror and deep distress. [34]He told them, "My soul is crushed with grief to the point of death. Stay here and watch with me."

[35]He went on a little farther and fell face down on the ground. He prayed that, if it were possible, the awful hour awaiting him might pass him by. [36]"Abba,* Father," he said, "everything is possible for you. Please take this cup of suffering away from me. Yet I want your will, not mine."

[37]Then he returned and found the disciples asleep. "Simon!" he said to Peter. "Are you asleep? Couldn't you stay awake and watch with me even one hour? [38]Keep alert and pray. Otherwise temptation will overpower you. For though the spirit is willing enough, the body is weak."

[39]Then Jesus left them again and prayed, repeating his pleadings. [40]Again he returned to them and found them sleeping, for they just couldn't keep their eyes open. And they didn't know what to say.

[41]When he returned to them the third time, he said, "Still sleeping? Still resting?* Enough! The time has come. I, the Son of Man, am betrayed into the hands of sinners. [42]Up, let's be going. See, my betrayer is here!"

Jesus Is Betrayed and Arrested

[43]And immediately, as he said this, Judas, one of the twelve disciples, arrived with a mob that was armed with swords and clubs. They had been sent out by the leading priests, the teachers of religious law, and the other leaders. [44]Judas had given them a prearranged signal: "You will know which one to arrest when I go over and give him the kiss of greeting. Then you can take him away under guard."

[45]As soon as they arrived, Judas walked up to Jesus. "Teacher!" he exclaimed, and gave him the kiss. [46]Then the others grabbed Jesus and arrested him. [47]But someone pulled out a sword and slashed off an ear of the high priest's servant.

[48]Jesus asked them, "Am I some dangerous criminal, that you come armed with swords and clubs to arrest me? [49]Why didn't you arrest me in the Temple? I was there teaching every day. But these things are happening to fulfill what the Scriptures say about me."

[50]Meanwhile, all his disciples deserted him and ran away. [51]There was a young man following along behind, clothed only in a linen nightshirt. When the mob tried to grab him, [52]they tore off his clothes, but he escaped and ran away naked.

Jesus before the Council

[53]Jesus was led to the high priest's home where the leading priests, other leaders, and teachers of religious law had gathered. [54]Meanwhile, Peter followed far behind and then slipped inside the gates of the high priest's courtyard. For a while he sat with the guards, warming himself by the fire.

[55]Inside, the leading priests and the entire high council* were trying to find witnesses who would testify against Jesus, so they could put him to death. But their efforts were in vain. [56]Many false witnesses spoke against him, but they contradicted each other. [57]Finally, some men stood up to testify against him with this lie: [58]"We heard him say, 'I will destroy this Temple made with human hands, and in three days I will build another, made without human hands.'" [59]But even then they didn't get their stories straight!

[60]Then the high priest stood up before the others and asked Jesus, "Well, aren't you going to answer these charges? What do you have to say for yourself?" [61]Jesus made no reply. Then the high priest asked him, "Are you the Messiah, the Son of the blessed God?"

14:36 *Abba* is an Aramaic term for "father." **14:41** Or *Sleep on, take your rest.* **14:55** Greek *the Sanhedrin.*

14:32-42 Jesus opened his heart to Peter, James, and John: "My soul is crushed with grief to the point of death. Stay here and watch with me" (14:34). Jesus demonstrated qualities that are important for us in recovery: honesty, transparency, and trust. Jesus evidently needed others for support in this hour of agony shortly before his death. If Jesus needed human support to face his trials, we must need it even more. It is important that we develop a support group that will hold us accountable to our commitment to recovery. Unless we can develop and maintain meaningful human relationships, it will be nearly impossible to continue in recovery.
14:53-65 Jesus was a victim of abuse and injustice: He was lied about, falsely accused and convicted, and physically assaulted. But instead of returning words or blows in kind, he entrusted himself to his Father's care (1 Peter 2:23). Jesus modeled the kind of trust that a person with a history of abuse might emulate. As we remember the pain of past abuses in our life, we can turn all the hurtful events and vengeful feelings over to God. We can then focus on our own problems and dependency, knowing that God will deal justly with the people who have hurt us in the past.

⁶²Jesus said, "I am, and you will see me, the Son of Man, sitting at God's right hand in the place of power and coming back on the clouds of heaven."*

⁶³Then the high priest tore his clothing to show his horror and said, "Why do we need other witnesses? ⁶⁴You have all heard his blasphemy. What is your verdict?" And they all condemned him to death.

⁶⁵Then some of them began to spit at him, and they blindfolded him and hit his face with their fists. "Who hit you that time, you prophet?" they jeered. And even the guards were hitting him as they led him away.

Peter Denies Jesus

⁶⁶Meanwhile, Peter was below in the courtyard. One of the servant girls who worked for the high priest ⁶⁷noticed Peter warming himself at the fire. She looked at him closely and then said, "You were one of those with Jesus, the Nazarene."

⁶⁸Peter denied it. "I don't know what you're talking about," he said, and he went out into the entryway. Just then, a rooster crowed.*

⁶⁹The servant girl saw him standing there and began telling the others, "That man is definitely one of them!" ⁷⁰Peter denied it again.

A little later some other bystanders began saying to Peter, "You must be one of them because you are from Galilee."

⁷¹Peter said, "I swear by God, I don't know this man you're talking about." ⁷²And immediately the rooster crowed the second time. Suddenly, Jesus' words flashed through Peter's mind: "Before the rooster crows twice, you will deny me three times." And he broke down and cried.

CHAPTER 15
Jesus' Trial before Pilate

Very early in the morning the leading priests, other leaders, and teachers of religious law—the entire high council*—met to discuss their next step. They bound Jesus and took him to Pilate, the Roman governor.

²Pilate asked Jesus, "Are you the King of the Jews?"

Jesus replied, "Yes, it is as you say."

³Then the leading priests accused him of many crimes, ⁴and Pilate asked him, "Aren't you going to say something? What about all these charges against you?" ⁵But Jesus said nothing, much to Pilate's surprise.

⁶Now it was the governor's custom to release one prisoner each year at Passover time—anyone the people requested. ⁷One of the prisoners at that time was Barabbas, convicted along with others for murder during an insurrection. ⁸The mob began to crowd in toward Pilate, asking him to release a prisoner as usual. ⁹"Should I give you the King of the Jews?" Pilate asked. ¹⁰(For he realized by now that the leading priests had arrested Jesus out of envy.) ¹¹But at this point the leading priests stirred up the mob to demand the release of Barabbas instead of Jesus. ¹²"But if I release Barabbas," Pilate asked them, "what should I do with this man you call the King of the Jews?"

¹³They shouted back, "Crucify him!"

¹⁴"Why?" Pilate demanded. "What crime has he committed?"

But the crowd only roared the louder, "Crucify him!"

¹⁵So Pilate, anxious to please the crowd, released Barabbas to them. He ordered Jesus flogged with a lead-tipped whip, then turned him over to the Roman soldiers to crucify him.

14:62 See Ps 110:1; Dan 7:13. **14:68** Some manuscripts do not include *Just then, a rooster crowed.* **15:1** Greek *the Sanhedrin;* also in 15:43.

14:66-72 Peter apparently didn't know himself as well as he thought he did. Earlier he had claimed that he would never deny Jesus (14:29, 31); here he denied his Master three times. Peter could have profited from Jesus' earlier prediction of his denial (14:30). Instead of shrugging it off, he should have responded to Jesus' words with honest self-examination. Denying the sad truth about ourself usually leads to the loss of important opportunities to correct our character flaws. This, in turn, stops our progress in recovery and stunts our spiritual growth.

15:1-15 Pilate told Jesus' accusers that he found no guilt in Jesus, yet he handed him over for execution. The Jews' strong emotions and Pilate's desire to pacify them at all costs led to the death of an innocent man. We have a lot in common with Pilate. When we sacrifice the truth in order to please the crowd, we crucify Jesus. Our challenge in recovery is to stand firm in our faith and not succumb to cynicism, compromises, or moral laxity. When we take the first step toward relapse, we must recover our footing with courage and wisdom.

The Soldiers Mock Jesus

[16]The soldiers took him into their headquarters* and called out the entire battalion. [17]They dressed him in a purple robe and made a crown of long, sharp thorns and put it on his head. [18]Then they saluted, yelling, "Hail! King of the Jews!" [19]And they beat him on the head with a stick, spit on him, and dropped to their knees in mock worship. [20]When they were finally tired of mocking him, they took off the purple robe and put his own clothes on him again. Then they led him away to be crucified.

The Crucifixion

[21]A man named Simon, who was from Cyrene,* was coming in from the country just then, and they forced him to carry Jesus' cross. (Simon is the father of Alexander and Rufus.) [22]And they brought Jesus to a place called Golgotha (which means Skull Hill). [23]They offered him wine drugged with myrrh, but he refused it. [24]Then they nailed him to the cross. They gambled for his clothes, throwing dice* to decide who would get them.

[25]It was nine o'clock in the morning when the crucifixion took place. [26]A signboard was fastened to the cross above Jesus' head, announcing the charge against him. It read: "The King of the Jews." [27]Two criminals were crucified with him, their crosses on either side of his.* [29]And the people passing by shouted abuse, shaking their heads in mockery. "Ha! Look at you now!" they yelled at him. "You can destroy the Temple and rebuild it in three days, can you? [30]Well then, save yourself and come down from the cross!"

[31]The leading priests and teachers of religious law also mocked Jesus. "He saved others," they scoffed, "but he can't save himself! [32]Let this Messiah, this king of Israel, come down from the cross so we can see it and believe him!" Even the two criminals who were being crucified with Jesus ridiculed him.

The Death of Jesus

[33]At noon, darkness fell across the whole land until three o'clock. [34]Then, at that time Jesus called out with a loud voice, *"Eloi, Eloi, lema sabachthani?"* which means, "My God, my God, why have you forsaken me?"*

[35]Some of the bystanders misunderstood and thought he was calling for the prophet Elijah. [36]One of them ran and filled a sponge with sour wine, holding it up to him on a stick so he could drink. "Leave him alone. Let's see whether Elijah will come and take him down!" he said.

[37]Then Jesus uttered another loud cry and breathed his last. [38]And the curtain in the Temple was torn in two, from top to bottom. [39]When the Roman officer who

---

15:16 Greek *the courtyard, which is the praetorium.* **15:21** *Cyrene* was a city in northern Africa. **15:24** Greek *casting lots.* See Ps 22:18. **15:27** Some manuscripts add verse 28, *And the Scripture was fulfilled that said, "He was counted among those who were rebels."* See Isa 53:12. **15:34** Ps 22:1.

15:16-32 Jesus suffered verbal and physical abuse when he was spat upon, beaten, mocked, and nailed to a cross. Knowing that Jesus did all this to provide a powerful means for recovery should give us hope. No matter how terrible our past actions or how great our mistakes, Jesus has paid the penalty for our sins. Because of his suffering, we can each have a true relationship with our powerful God. As we grow in our relationship with him, we will discover that there is sufficient power available for the recovery of all who truly desire it.

15:33-41 Jesus' purpose in coming to earth was to serve others and to give his life as payment for our sins; this is a key thought in Mark's Gospel (10:45). At this excruciating moment, the Savior bore the pain and punishment for all the sins ever committed (1 Peter 2:24). This is truly good news! Although we are never good enough to gain God's favor, Jesus' sacrifice provides the eternal security necessary for complete recovery. No matter how hard we try, we can never attain recovery from sin and its effects under our own power or effort. But with God's help we can overcome even the most terrible sin, dependency, or compulsion.

16:1-7 These women were wondering how they could ever roll the great stone from the tomb entrance, when, to their amazement, they found it already gone. The tomb was empty! The women had only wanted to roll back the stone, but God had accomplished so much more: He had raised Jesus from the dead! If God can give life to a dead body, he surely can restore our life to wholeness. We must put our trust in him. There is always hope. With God, all things are possible! He specializes in rolling away burdens too great for our feeble human strength to handle. And, if we set out to do what we can in the recovery process, we will likely discover that God has already accomplished our goals—and even more!

stood facing him saw how he had died, he exclaimed, "Truly, this was the Son of God!"

⁴⁰Some women were there, watching from a distance, including Mary Magdalene, Mary (the mother of James the younger and of Joseph*), and Salome. ⁴¹They had been followers of Jesus and had cared for him while he was in Galilee. Then they and many other women had come with him to Jerusalem.

The Burial of Jesus
⁴²This all happened on Friday, the day of preparation,* the day before the Sabbath. As evening approached, ⁴³an honored member of the high council, Joseph from Arimathea (who was waiting for the Kingdom of God to come), gathered his courage and went to Pilate to ask for Jesus' body. ⁴⁴Pilate couldn't believe that Jesus was already dead, so he called for the Roman military officer in charge and asked him. ⁴⁵The officer confirmed the fact, and Pilate told Joseph he could have the body. ⁴⁶Joseph bought a long sheet of linen cloth, and taking Jesus' body down from the cross, he wrapped it in the cloth and laid it in a tomb that had been carved out of the rock. Then he rolled a stone in front of the entrance. ⁴⁷Mary Magdalene and Mary the mother of Joseph saw where Jesus' body was laid.

CHAPTER 16
The Resurrection
The next evening, when the Sabbath ended, Mary Magdalene and Salome and Mary the mother of James went out and purchased burial spices to put on Jesus' body. ²Very early on Sunday morning,* just at sunrise, they came to the tomb. ³On the way they were discussing who would roll the stone away from the entrance to the tomb. ⁴But when they arrived, they looked up and saw that the stone—a very large one—had already been rolled aside. ⁵So they entered the tomb, and there on the right sat a young man clothed in a white robe. The women were startled, ⁶but the angel said, "Do not be so surprised. You are looking for Jesus, the Nazarene, who was crucified. He isn't here! He has been raised from the dead! Look, this is where they laid his body. ⁷Now go and give this message to his disciples, including Peter: Jesus is going ahead of you to Galilee.

15:40 Greek *Joses;* also in 15:47. See Matt 27:56.
15:42 Greek *on the day of preparation.* **16:2** Greek *on the first day of the week;* also in 16:9.

STEP 12

Our Story
BIBLE READING: Mark 16:14-18
Having had a spiritual awakening as the result of these steps, we tried to carry this message to others and to practice these principles in all our affairs.
Each one of us has a valuable story to tell. We may be shy and feel awkward about speaking. We may think that what we have to share is too trivial. Is it actually going to help anyone else? We may struggle to get beyond the shame of our past experiences. But our recovery story can help others who are trapped back where we were. Are we willing to allow God to use us to help free others?

Jesus left us with this vital task: "Go into all the world and preach the Good News [of salvation from the bondage and penalty of sin] to everyone, everywhere" (Mark 16:15). The apostle Paul traveled the world over telling everyone of his conversion. He ended up in chains, but his spirit was free. He presented his defense (and his own story of redemption) before kings. King Agrippa interrupted him to say, "'Do you think you can make me a Christian so quickly?' Paul replied, 'Whether quickly or not, I pray to God that both you and everyone here in this audience might become the same as I am, except for these chains'" (Acts 26:28-29).

Within each personal journey from bondage to freedom is a microcosm of the gospel. When people hear our story, even if it seems trivial, we are offering them the chance to loosen their chains and begin their own recovery. *Turn to page 171, John 15.*

You will see him there, just as he told you before he died!" [8]The women fled from the tomb, trembling and bewildered, saying nothing to anyone because they were too frightened to talk.*

[Shorter Ending of Mark]

Then they reported all these instructions briefly to Peter and his companions. Afterward Jesus himself sent them out from east to west with the sacred and unfailing message of salvation that gives eternal life. Amen.

[Longer Ending of Mark]

[9]It was early on Sunday morning when Jesus rose from the dead, and the first person who saw him was Mary Magdalene, the woman from whom he had cast out seven demons. [10]She went and found the disciples, who were grieving and weeping. [11]But when she told them that Jesus was alive and she had seen him, they didn't believe her. [12]Afterward he appeared to two who were walking from Jerusalem into the country, but they didn't recognize him at first because he had changed his appearance. [13]When they realized who he was, they rushed back to tell the others, but no one believed them.

[14]Still later he appeared to the eleven disciples as they were eating together. He rebuked them for their unbelief—their stubborn refusal to believe those who had seen him after he had risen.

[15]And then he told them, "Go into all the world and preach the Good News to everyone, everywhere. [16]Anyone who believes and is baptized will be saved. But anyone who refuses to believe will be condemned. [17]These signs will accompany those who believe: They will cast out demons in my name, and they will speak new languages.* [18]They will be able to handle snakes with safety, and if they drink anything poisonous, it won't hurt them. They will be able to place their hands on the sick and heal them."

[19]When the Lord Jesus had finished talking with them, he was taken up into heaven and sat down in the place of honor at God's right hand. [20]And the disciples went everywhere and preached, and the Lord worked with them, confirming what they said by many miraculous signs.

16:8 The most reliable early manuscripts conclude the Gospel of Mark at verse 8. Other manuscripts include various endings to the Gospel. Two of the more noteworthy endings are printed here. **16:17** Or *new tongues.* Some manuscripts omit *new*.

16:9-20 Many of the disciples had a hard time believing that Jesus had risen from the dead. When they finally met the resurrected Jesus, he rebuked them for their unbelief. Then Jesus rewarded his followers as they came to believe. Faith is foundational for salvation and recovery; unbelief leads to condemnation and relapse. As we grow in our faith in Jesus, we will discover that the power of his resurrection can touch and transform our life. Then we can become a source of encouragement to others as we share how God has delivered us.

REFLECTIONS ON

MARK

insights CONCERNING TRUE FAITH

In **Mark 1:16-20** Jesus called four burly fishermen to be his disciples. We are not sure how many times Jesus called Simon Peter, Andrew, James, and John to follow him. On two other occasions, a similar call went out to these four fishermen (see Luke 5:1-11; John 1:35-42). Their response to Jesus' call on any one occasion, as here, seems to have been "immediate." But it seems that they soon went back to their old occupation and way of life. So it is in recovery. Our faith in God will grow over time, at an uneven rate and with uncertain steps. Each step of faith we take requires that we drop whatever else we are doing and follow Jesus wholeheartedly.

In **Mark 10:13-22** two kinds of people are contrasted: the little children, who came to Jesus with innocent trust; and a wealthy young man, who trusted in his wealth and was unwilling to give it up to follow Jesus. The only way to enter the Kingdom of God is through childlike trust. This is also the only way we can enter recovery. As long as we think we can make it on our own, we are hopelessly entrapped by our dependency. Anyone who has tried to recover alone has discovered that it is a losing battle. We must begin by admitting that we are helpless, just like little children. Then we must put our life into God's hands and do what we can to follow his program for us. If we trust in our abilities or wealth for deliverance, we are doomed to self-inflicted destruction.

The women who followed Jesus to the cross in **Mark 15:47–16:11** were not in a position to stop the Crucifixion. But instead of running away, they stayed at the foot of the cross, watched to see where Jesus would be buried, and prepared spices to embalm his body. They were willing to do this even though the twelve disciples had run for their lives. Their resourcefulness and faithful devotion to the very end were honored by an opportunity to see the risen Jesus. As we continue in the process of recovery, we should never waste time waiting for something to happen. We need to take full advantage of the opportunities God gives us for recovery.

*insights ABOUT GOD'S POWER TO SAVE

In **Mark 1:40-45** Jesus displayed his power by healing a man with leprosy. Leprosy is a progressive, contagious, and crippling skin disease. In ancient times it was often considered a form of divine retribution (see Numbers 12:9-10; 2 Chronicles 26:16-23). Since there was no cure, except by a miracle from God, a person with leprosy was socially ostracized (see Leviticus 13). Modern medicine has all but eliminated this disease, but we must consider what it must have been like. We all are "lepers," infected by the incurable disease of sin, which has made us ugly and separated us from the people we love. Yet there is hope for us. We can be restored to healthy living and fellowship by the healing touch of Jesus. First we must realize our inability to cure ourself. Then we can trust Jesus' power and love for cleansing and recovery.

In **Mark 4:26-29** Jesus used an illustration to show how God works in the recovery process. Just as seeds silently grow in the soil, God gradually and relentlessly changes us from the inside out. We have come to recognize how helpless we are against our dependency. We already know that we are powerless to change alone. We have already failed many times by trying to participate in the right activities and behaviors. We know we can't change from the outside in. Here we are given a wonderful message of hope! God changes us from the inside out! He has the power to make us into new people and will sustain us in the recovery process.

The miracle of **Mark 6:35-44** displays an important recovery principle: Our needs are never greater than God's supply. That's the lesson for people in recovery who appreciate Jesus' miraculous supply of food for more than five thousand people. The twelve disciples should have learned this lesson through Jesus' ample provision but failed to do so (6:52). They should have learned that when confronted with impossible situations, Jesus could be trusted. We also need to remember that no obstacle to recovery is too great for God. He is sufficient to meet all of our needs.

In **Mark 9:2-13** Jesus was transfigured on the mountain. In this amazing event, we are given a picture of what we can hope for in our own life. Someday we will be changed; we will be made perfect. We may be struggling with destructive dependency, in despair about our devastated life. At such times, it might help to reflect on who we will become if we entrust our life to God through Jesus Christ. God wants to begin the process of leading us toward a healthy and productive life now. When he returns in glory, he will restore us and his entire creation to perfection. With this hope in mind, let us start the process of recovery now.

*insights ABOUT GOD'S PRIORITIES

God gave the Sabbath laws (Exodus 34:21) to protect his people from overwork and keep their lives in proper balance. Like all of God's laws, these laws were intended for the good of his people. When the disciples picked grain at the edge of a farmer's field in **Mark 2:23-28,** they were actually following one of the provisions God had prescribed in his law (Leviticus 19:9-10). Yet the Pharisees, with their man-made rules and false assumptions, accused Jesus of breaking the law by working on the Sabbath. Sadly, as they pretended to uphold the law, the Pharisees actually stood counter to God's intentions. Today our preconceptions about disease, sin, or God's plan can cause us to block the path of recovery for others. We must never set up roadblocks to the healing of hurting people, especially by using God's Word. It is part of God's plan that people should live healthy lives; we should do all we can to support his plan.

We find in **Mark 10:32-45** that immediately after Jesus warned his disciples of his impending suffering and death, James and John requested positions of honor and authority. They were blind to the fact that the call to follow Jesus would involve suffering and persecution. Following Jesus on the road to recovery is never easy. It demands that we swallow our pride and admit our mistakes. It calls us to give up the dependency that we have used to try to escape our inner pain. It means that we have to come out of hiding and show the world how ugly we are inside. We must humble ourself before the people we have wronged. Following Jesus is never the easiest path, but it is the only path that will lead us to restoration, joy, and fulfillment.

Jesus expressed his true feelings in **Mark 14:35-36,** as he begged his Father to remove the cup of suffering before him, but he never rebelled against God's will. He was willing to suffer and die so that all of us could experience forgiveness from sin and recovery from its painful effects. As much as we might want to escape certain unpleasant tasks in the recovery process, we must submit all such desires to God's will. God may lead us into some tough experiences, but, as painful as they may be, we can be assured that he has our best in mind. We can also be sure that he will stand with us throughout the process.

insights CONCERNING OBSTACLES TO RECOVERY

The Sabbath controversy recorded in **Mark 3:1-6** reveals two ways of dealing with anger. Anger itself is a normal human emotion; it is morally neutral. What we do with our anger is what counts. Jesus was angry at the Pharisees for making up rules about the Sabbath that stood counter to God's real intentions in the law. Jesus used his anger constructively—not to tear people down, but to heal a man's deformed hand. Jesus' enemies, in their anger, plotted to kill him. Anger expressed in selfish or harmful ways will always stand in the way of recovery.

After healing a demon-possessed man, Jesus faced opposition from the people of the nearby town in **Mark 5:1-20.** The demons left the man and entered a herd of pigs, causing them to run wildly into the lake and drown. The people of the town did not like losing their source of livelihood and felt threatened when the status quo of their world was disturbed. We may experience similar opposition when God begins to change us. Friends and family members may feel threatened by the changes and try to stop us. If we experience opposition from codependents, we should be neither surprised nor discouraged. We should simply continue trusting God to change us so we can help our friends and families.

In **Mark 14:1-9** a woman showed her devotion to Jesus by anointing him with expensive perfume (equal in value to a year's wages), as if preparing a king for burial. Her devotion was mocked by some of the disciples, but it was praised by Jesus as an example for all believers to follow. Our faith in God and commitment to recovery often receive the criticism of others. Sometimes family members have a hard time believing we are sincere. Our friends may even feel threatened by the changes they see in us. We can be sure, however, that no matter what others might say, Jesus is pleased with the steps we are taking. If we persevere, we will discover that others will someday praise our efforts, too.

insights ABOUT THE PERSON OF JESUS

In **Mark 6:1-6** Jesus visited his hometown of Nazareth, where he was looked upon as a mere man, a carpenter, Mary's boy. The people's unbelief kept Jesus from performing "mighty miracles" in Nazareth. Unfortunately for the people of Nazareth, their familiarity with Jesus bred contempt. Fortunately for us, Jesus left and went elsewhere to minister to those who would believe in his miracles and message. Our world has tried to pass Jesus off as just another man, a good teacher, or a wise prophet. Anyone who focuses on Jesus' humanity to the exclusion of his divinity makes a grave mistake. If Jesus were not the Son of God, there would be little hope for any recovery, including our own.

insights ABOUT HONESTY AND DENIAL

Herod Antipas did not like being corrected. So in **Mark 6:14-29,** when John the Baptist confronted him concerning his immoral marriage to his brother's wife, the prophet paid for it with his life. Herod denied his sin and did not like to be reminded of what he had done. But his denial only led to an even greater sin—murder. We are guilty of the same thing when we refuse to listen to warnings about our destructive behavior. We need to learn that our denial will never help things; it will only lead to greater suffering and devastation. We must act immediately and heed the warnings we receive. If we don't, we are headed for even greater trouble.

LUKE

THE BIG PICTURE

A. THE SAVIOR'S BIRTH AND PREPARATION (1:1–4:13)
B. THE SAVIOR'S MINISTRY IN WORD AND DEED (4:14–21:38)
  1. Jesus' Ministry in Galilee (4:14–9:50)
  2. Jesus' Ministry on the Way to Jerusalem (9:51–19:27)
  3. Jesus' Ministry in Jerusalem (19:28–21:38)
C. THE SAVIOR'S DEATH AND RESURRECTION (22:1–24:53)

Luke was a physician and a historian. He presented Jesus as a man who cared greatly for suffering and downtrodden people, a man who brought healing to the hurting. In the genealogy of Jesus, Luke traced Jesus' human ancestors back to Adam, the father of the human race. Luke's stories about Jesus focused on his relationships with individual people. Jesus paid special attention to people who were often ignored in society—women, children, the poor, prostitutes, despised tax collectors, and sinners of every sort.

Jesus offered salvation, strength, and spiritual recovery to everyone he met, but his greatest concern was for the outcasts of society. Luke stressed Jesus' humanity and compassion more than any of the other Gospel writers did. His narrative made it clear that God, through his Son Jesus, reaches out in love to the unlovable of our world. Ever since Adam and Eve's first sin in the Garden of Eden, God has passionately desired and pursued the recovery of broken people. His love and concern for us are unstoppable!

As we work through the process of recovery, many of us discover just how terrible and destructive our sins have been. As the levels of denial peel away, we begin to see how sick and broken we really are. We may wonder whether there is any hope for us. How could God care for us after all we have done? In reading the Gospel of Luke, we can gain hope from the compassion God showed toward people who were a lot like us. God wants to show us how much he loves us, regardless of our past mistakes. He wants to have an active role in our recovery.

THE BOTTOM LINE

PURPOSE: To confirm the historical record of the life of Jesus Christ, whose universal message offers hope and salvation to all who turn to him. AUTHOR: Luke, the physician. AUDIENCE: Theophilus, whose name means "lover of God." DATE WRITTEN: Probably about A.D. 60. KEY VERSES: "Jesus responded, 'Salvation has come to this home today, for this man has shown himself to be a son of Abraham. And I, the Son of Man, have come to seek and save those like him who are lost'" (19:9-10). SPECIAL FEATURES: Luke focused on Jesus' relationships with people, particularly those who were in need, and he placed special emphasis on the role of women. KEY PEOPLE AND RELATIONSHIPS: Jesus and his disciples, Zechariah and Elizabeth, Mary, Mary Magdalene, and John the Baptist.

RECOVERY THEMES

Jesus Loves the Outcast: Jesus paid special attention to the poor, the despised, the hurt, and the sinful. He rejected no one; he ignored no one. No one today is beyond the scope of his love or beyond his ability to help—including us. He cares for us no matter what we have done or what we have suffered. Only this kind of deep love can satisfy our deepest needs and mobilize us to recovery. When our life is most unmanageable and we are faced with our powerlessness, we often feel that no one can understand or care. Luke shows us that God understands and cares. We can safely turn our life over to him!

The Power of the Resurrection: Paul wrote to the Philippians and told them that he longed to "experience the mighty power that raised [Jesus] from the dead" (Philippians 3:10). Like the other Gospel writers, Luke showed in detail the events surrounding the death and resurrection of Jesus. There is no greater example of God's power at work than that which can bring the dead back to life again. God specializes in demonstrating that kind of power. In recovery, we experience his power at work within us, bringing our soul and body back to life. With God, nothing is too difficult.

God's Passion for Our Recovery: God wants us to experience recovery even more than we do because he loves and cares about us. Jesus showed this by revealing his intense interest in people and relationships. He cared for his followers and friends. He was interested in all types of people—men, women, and children. His concern transcended all barriers and extended to all he met. He longed to see people whole, well, and growing in their knowledge of God. As we come to know him and share his heart, we experience his passion for our wholeness and recovery.

The Power of the Holy Spirit: Jesus lived in complete dependence on the Holy Spirit. The Holy Spirit was present at the birth of Jesus, at his baptism, in his ministry, and in his resurrection. The Holy Spirit was sent by the Father to confirm Jesus' authority. Today the Holy Spirit is given to empower us to live as God wants us to live. By faith, we can receive the Holy Spirit's presence and power within us, enabling us in the recovery process and in our spiritual growth.

CHAPTER 1
Introduction

Most honorable Theophilus:

Many people have written accounts about the events that took place* among us. ²They used as their source material the reports circulating among us from the early disciples and other eyewitnesses of what God has done in fulfillment of his promises. ³Having carefully investigated all of these accounts from the beginning, I have decided to write a careful summary for you, ⁴to reassure you of the truth of all you were taught.

1:1 Or *have been fulfilled.*

The Birth of John the Baptist Foretold

⁵It all begins with a Jewish priest, Zechariah, who lived when Herod was king of Judea. Zechariah was a member of the priestly order of Abijah. His wife, Elizabeth, was also from the priestly line of Aaron. ⁶Zechariah and Elizabeth were righteous in God's eyes, careful to obey all of the Lord's commandments and regulations. ⁷They had no children because Elizabeth was barren, and now they were both very old.

⁸One day Zechariah was serving God in the Temple, for his order was on duty that

---

1:1-4 In this preface Luke testified that the gospel of Jesus is based upon historical facts and not theories or myths. Speculative religions, secular philosophies, or political leaders do not meet the deepest needs of the human heart. History is filled with people who aspired to be gods, but only one is truly God. All the other would-be "messiahs" or gods—Alexander the Great, King Tut, Julius Caesar, Napoleon, Adolf Hitler—fell short. Jesus alone can meet our deepest needs.
1:5-7 Zechariah and Elizabeth were godly people. They were childless, and Elizabeth was well past the childbearing years. Their situation was discouraging, even depressing, as many couples in our society can testify. In their society childlessness was taken as a sign of God's curse or displeasure. But Zechariah and Elizabeth remained faithful in trusting God. This was a key to the blessings they received later on. Their faithfulness and patient perseverance are good examples for those of us in recovery.
1:16-17 John the Baptist's ministry would turn the hearts of parents to their children (Malachi 4:5-6). This need is felt by many in recovery. John the Baptist called for personal repentance and the restoration of broken family relationships. Even though the complete fulfillment of these words is still in the future, the principle has always been true. Spiritual cleansing by God is the first foundational step toward the rebuilding of hurting and broken family relationships. When God is at work, even the most resistant hearts can be softened and the most dysfunctional families restored.

LUKE

Luke wrote more of the New Testament than did any other author. He gave a detailed account of the life of Jesus in his Gospel and a description of the early church in Acts. He was a physician by profession, and his writing reveals his compassion for people. Even his efforts to write his two books were motivated by a concern to help a friend grow in faith. Consistent with this, Luke pointed his readers to the healing work and person of Jesus, the Great Physician.

Luke's concern for the spiritual health of others was matched by his compassion for their physical well-being. Throughout his books he noted the physical suffering of people and the care that those people received. He recounted many times how Jesus and his apostles brought physical and spiritual healing into hurting and broken lives. Luke also noticed how Jesus paid special attention to the helpless in society. Jesus helped not only the wealthy or religious but also the outcasts, lepers, prostitutes, and hated tax collectors. Luke's compassionate heart led him to emphasize Jesus' compassion for the rejects of society.

Luke was also noted for his commitment and loyalty to the apostle Paul as they traveled together spreading the gospel in Asia Minor and Greece. In prison, near the end of his life, Paul wrote of his appreciation for Luke. He called Luke a beloved friend, for he had stayed with Paul even when most of Paul's friends had deserted him. Luke was willing to follow God, even when it led him to share in Paul's sufferings.

Luke did not aspire to greatness or try to grab the spotlight. His goal in life was to serve and care for others. We need people like Luke in our life and should do what we can to build relationships with compassionate, godly people. Perhaps an even greater need, however, is for us to learn how we can become an instrument of healing in the lives of the people around us. Sharing what Christ has done in our life can help others and is one of the important goals of recovery.

STRENGTHS AND ACCOMPLISHMENTS:
- Luke proclaimed the merits of Jesus without promoting himself.
- He used his talents in medicine and writing to help others.
- He had great compassion for those with physical and spiritual needs.
- He was a loyal and faithful friend to the apostle Paul.
- He persevered in following God, even when he encountered tough times.

LESSONS FROM HIS LIFE:
- Our care for others should meet spiritual, emotional, and physical needs.
- Being loyal to our friends during hard times is very important.
- God's good will for us sometimes leads us through difficult times.
- If we offer our abilities to God, he will use them to do something of eternal significance.

KEY VERSES:
"Demas has deserted me because he loves the things of this life and has gone to Thessalonica. Crescens has gone to Galatia, and Titus has gone to Dalmatia. Only Luke is with me" (2 Timothy 4:10-11).

Luke included himself in the "we" sections of Acts 16–28. He is also mentioned in Luke 1:3; Acts 1:1-2; Colossians 4:14; 2 Timothy 4:11; and Philemon 1:24.

---

week. ⁹As was the custom of the priests, he was chosen by lot to enter the sanctuary and burn incense in the Lord's presence. ¹⁰While the incense was being burned, a great crowd stood outside, praying.

¹¹Zechariah was in the sanctuary when an angel of the Lord appeared, standing to the right of the incense altar. ¹²Zechariah was overwhelmed with fear. ¹³But the angel said, "Don't be afraid, Zechariah! For God has heard your prayer, and your wife, Elizabeth, will bear you a son! And you are to name him John. ¹⁴You will have great joy and gladness, and many will rejoice with you at his birth, ¹⁵for he will be great in the eyes of the Lord. He must never touch wine or hard liquor, and he will be filled with the Holy Spirit, even before his birth.* ¹⁶And he will persuade many Israelites to turn to the Lord their God. ¹⁷He will be a man with the spirit and power of Elijah, the prophet of old. He will precede the coming of the Lord, preparing the people for his arrival. He will turn the hearts of the fathers to their children, and he will change disobedient minds to accept godly wisdom."*

1:15 Or *even from birth.* **1:17** See Mal 4:5-6.

¹⁸Zechariah said to the angel, "How can I know this will happen? I'm an old man now, and my wife is also well along in years."

¹⁹Then the angel said, "I am Gabriel! I stand in the very presence of God. It was he who sent me to bring you this good news! ²⁰And now, since you didn't believe what I said, you won't be able to speak until the child is born. For my words will certainly come true at the proper time."

²¹Meanwhile, the people were waiting for Zechariah to come out, wondering why he was taking so long. ²²When he finally did come out, he couldn't speak to them. Then they realized from his gestures that he must have seen a vision in the Temple sanctuary.

²³He stayed at the Temple until his term of service was over, and then he returned home. ²⁴Soon afterward his wife, Elizabeth, became pregnant and went into seclusion for five months. ²⁵"How kind the Lord is!" she exclaimed. "He has taken away my disgrace of having no children!"

The Birth of Jesus Foretold

²⁶In the sixth month of Elizabeth's pregnancy, God sent the angel Gabriel to Nazareth, a village in Galilee, ²⁷to a virgin named Mary. She was engaged to be married to a man named Joseph, a descendant of King David. ²⁸Gabriel appeared to her and said, "Greetings, favored woman! The Lord is with you!*"

²⁹Confused and disturbed, Mary tried to think what the angel could mean. ³⁰"Don't be frightened, Mary," the angel told her, "for God has decided to bless you! ³¹You will become pregnant and have a son, and you are to name him Jesus. ³²He will be very great and will be called the Son of the Most High. And the Lord God will give him the throne of his ancestor David. ³³And he will reign over Israel* forever; his Kingdom will never end!"

³⁴Mary asked the angel, "But how can I have a baby? I am a virgin."

³⁵The angel replied, "The Holy Spirit will come upon you, and the power of the Most High will overshadow you. So the baby born to you will be holy, and he will be called the Son of God. ³⁶What's more, your relative Elizabeth has become pregnant in her old age! People used to say she was barren, but she's already in her sixth month. ³⁷For nothing is impossible with God."

³⁸Mary responded, "I am the Lord's servant, and I am willing to accept whatever he wants. May everything you have said come true." And then the angel left.

Mary Visits Elizabeth

³⁹A few days later Mary hurried to the hill country of Judea, to the town ⁴⁰where Zechariah lived. She entered the house and greeted Elizabeth. ⁴¹At the sound of Mary's greeting, Elizabeth's child leaped within her, and Elizabeth was filled with the Holy Spirit.

⁴²Elizabeth gave a glad cry and exclaimed to Mary, "You are blessed by God above all other women, and your child is blessed. ⁴³What an honor this is, that the mother of my Lord should visit me! ⁴⁴When you came in and greeted me, my baby jumped for joy the instant I heard your voice! ⁴⁵You are blessed, because you believed that the Lord would do what he said."

The Magnificat: Mary's Song of Praise

⁴⁶Mary responded,

"Oh, how I praise the Lord.
⁴⁷   How I rejoice in God my Savior!
⁴⁸ For he took notice of his lowly servant girl,
   and now generation after generation
   will call me blessed.
⁴⁹ For he, the Mighty One, is holy,
   and he has done great things for me.
⁵⁰ His mercy goes on from generation to generation,
   to all who fear him.
⁵¹ His mighty arm does tremendous things!
   How he scatters the proud and haughty ones!

1:28 Some manuscripts add *Blessed are you among women.* 1:33 Greek *over the house of Jacob.*

1:18-20 As godly as Zechariah was, he still did not believe the angel Gabriel's promise. From a natural frame of reference, it seemed impossible that he and Elizabeth could conceive a child in their old age. The consequence of even this short-term unbelief was substantial—Zechariah could not speak during Elizabeth's miraculous pregnancy. Unbelief can have a numbing effect on our recovery as well. Confession of faith before God and others, as Zechariah was eventually able to do (1:63-64), will help us along the path of recovery. Honestly admitting our doubts is a good place to start.

52 He has taken princes from their thrones
and exalted the lowly.
53 He has satisfied the hungry with good
things
and sent the rich away with empty
hands.
54 And how he has helped his servant Israel!
He has not forgotten his promise to be
merciful.
55 For he promised our ancestors—Abraham
and his children—
to be merciful to them forever."

56Mary stayed with Elizabeth about three months and then went back to her own home.

The Birth of John the Baptist

57Now it was time for Elizabeth's baby to be born, and it was a boy. 58The word spread quickly to her neighbors and relatives that the Lord had been very kind to her, and everyone rejoiced with her.

59When the baby was eight days old, all the relatives and friends came for the circumcision ceremony. They wanted to name him Zechariah, after his father. 60But Elizabeth said, "No! His name is John!"

61"What?" they exclaimed. "There is no one in all your family by that name." 62So they asked the baby's father, communicating to him by making gestures. 63He motioned for a writing tablet, and to everyone's surprise he wrote, "His name is John!" 64Instantly Zechariah could speak again, and he began praising God.

65Wonder fell upon the whole neighborhood, and the news of what had happened spread throughout the Judean hills. 66Everyone who heard about it reflected on these events and asked, "I wonder what this child will turn out to be? For the hand of the Lord is surely upon him in a special way."

Zechariah's Prophecy

67Then his father, Zechariah, was filled with the Holy Spirit and gave this prophecy:

68 "Praise the Lord, the God of Israel,
because he has visited his people and
redeemed them.

69 He has sent us a mighty Savior
from the royal line of his servant
David,
70 just as he promised
through his holy prophets long ago.
71 Now we will be saved from our enemies
and from all who hate us.
72 He has been merciful to our ancestors
by remembering his sacred covenant
with them,
73   the covenant he gave to our ancestor
Abraham.
74 We have been rescued from our
enemies,
so we can serve God without fear,
75   in holiness and righteousness
forever.

76 "And you, my little son,
will be called the prophet of the Most
High,
because you will prepare the way for
the Lord.
77 You will tell his people how to find
salvation
through forgiveness of their sins.
78 Because of God's tender mercy,
the light from heaven is about to break
upon us,
79 to give light to those who sit in darkness
and in the shadow of death,
and to guide us to the path of peace."

80John grew up and became strong in spirit. Then he lived out in the wilderness until he began his public ministry to Israel.

CHAPTER 2
The Birth of Jesus

At that time the Roman emperor, Augustus, decreed that a census should be taken throughout the Roman Empire. 2(This was the first census taken when Quirinius was governor of Syria.) 3All returned to their own towns to register for this census. 4And because Joseph was a descendant of King David, he had to go to Bethlehem in Judea, David's ancient home. He traveled there from the village of Nazareth in Galilee. 5He took with him Mary, his fiancée, who was obviously pregnant by this time.

1:51-55 These words from Mary's song present God's priorities in stark contrast to the way our world thinks. When life seems unfair and does not turn out the way we might have chosen, it is important to realize that God's ways are not our ways. Personal fulfillment and genuine recovery do not come through human greatness and success, but through repentance and sincere humility. The most important relationships in life are not with the rich and famous but often with the lowly, the needy, and those in recovery.

⁶And while they were there, the time came for her baby to be born. ⁷She gave birth to her first child, a son. She wrapped him snugly in strips of cloth and laid him in a manger, because there was no room for them in the village inn.

The Shepherds and Angels

⁸That night some shepherds were in the fields outside the village, guarding their flocks of sheep. ⁹Suddenly, an angel of the Lord appeared among them, and the radiance of the Lord's glory surrounded them. They were terribly frightened, ¹⁰but the angel reassured them. "Don't be afraid!" he said. "I bring you good news of great joy for everyone! ¹¹The Savior—yes, the Messiah, the Lord—has been born tonight in Bethlehem, the city of David! ¹²And this is how you will recognize him: You will find a baby lying in a manger, wrapped snugly in strips of cloth!"

¹³Suddenly, the angel was joined by a vast host of others—the armies of heaven—praising God:

¹⁴ "Glory to God in the highest heaven,
    and peace on earth to all whom God
    favors.*"

¹⁵When the angels had returned to heaven, the shepherds said to each other, "Come on, let's go to Bethlehem! Let's see this wonderful thing that has happened, which the Lord has told us about."

¹⁶They ran to the village and found Mary and Joseph. And there was the baby, lying in the manger. ¹⁷Then the shepherds told everyone what had happened and what the angel had said to them about this child. ¹⁸All who heard the shepherds' story were astonished, ¹⁹but Mary quietly treasured these things in her heart and thought about them often. ²⁰The shepherds went back to their fields and flocks, glorifying and praising God for what the angels had told them, and because they had seen the child, just as the angel had said.

Jesus Is Presented in the Temple

²¹Eight days later, when the baby was circumcised, he was named Jesus, the name given him by the angel even before he was conceived.

²²Then it was time for the purification offering, as required by the law of Moses after the birth of a child; so his parents took him to Jerusalem to present him to the Lord. ²³The law of the Lord says, "If a woman's first child is a boy, he must be dedicated to the Lord."* ²⁴So they offered a sacrifice according to what was required in the law of the Lord—"either a pair of turtledoves or two young pigeons."*

2:14 Or *and peace on earth for all those pleasing God.* Some manuscripts read *and peace on earth, goodwill among people.* **2:23** Exod 13:2. **2:24** Lev 12:8.

2:6-7 Jesus' welcome in Bethlehem illustrates how most people respond to him today. Jesus' birthplace was hardly an idyllic place like the ones pictured on our Christmas cards. It was probably a cold, damp, dark, dirty cave with a hollowed-out feeding trough or manger. Jesus entered a world unfit for his royal presence. God's willingness to enter our world, darkened and dirtied by sin, is a reason to be thankful. We don't have to clean up our act first in order to make room for him. When Jesus comes into our life, he accepts us as we are—that's when the real housecleaning and moral inventory begin. Thankfully, he is there to help us with the process.

2:8-12 Encounters with the living God inevitably elicit fear. The angels reassured the shepherds: "Don't be afraid!" Once the shepherds realized that God accepted them and wanted to communicate with them, they were free to worship the Christ child. Jesus' coming in the flesh reassures us that our holy and almighty God is also a personal God. God is with us and for us. We need not fear the unknown future or the all-too-familiar past. When we put our faith in the living God of yesterday, today, and tomorrow, his perfect love expels all fear (see 1 John 4:18).

2:19 In recovery painful thoughts of a guilt-ridden past or an uncertain future often intrude and disrupt the present and sometimes cause us to feel depressed. Certainly these darker issues must be faced for us to break free from the patterns of the past. But Mary shows us how thoughts about God can lift our spirits and give us the courage to take the next step. She meditated on the things God was doing and wanted to do in her life. When we do the same, we take a step toward recovery and wholeness. Pondering the joy with the sorrow, the awesome with the awful, the gain with the pain will lead to emotional and spiritual healing.

2:29-32 Simeon's words reveal the universality of God's plan of salvation. It was a rare thing for a Jew to declare that the Messiah would bring deliverance to the whole world, not just the Jews. God reaches out to all people, not just one ethnic group. He gives light, life, and contentment to all who put their faith in him through Jesus Christ. God will accept any who turn to him for help, regardless of background or situation in life. He is the universal Savior. With faith in Jesus we can go through life and death "in peace," as did Simeon.

ELIZABETH & ZECHARIAH

Many loving couples who long for children are unable to have them. Often their attempts to conceive a child go on for years. As each month passes, they go through a painful progression from hope, to fear, to terrible disappointment. Through the years all their lingering hopes disappear; they are left with shattered dreams and empty resignation.

This was what it must have been like for Elizabeth and Zechariah. Their desire for children had not been fulfilled, and they concluded that they would remain childless for the rest of their lives. But suddenly life changed for them. While serving in the Jerusalem Temple, an angel visited Zechariah and announced that he and Elizabeth would have a son. He was to be called John and would become the forerunner of the Messiah.

Understandably shocked, Zechariah doubted the angel's words. Because of his unbelief, he was rendered speechless until the child's birth. When Elizabeth heard the news, she believed the angel's message and was excited about her forthcoming pregnancy. When she was six months pregnant, Elizabeth was visited by her cousin, Mary, who was pregnant with the child Jesus. Filled with the Holy Spirit, Elizabeth praised Mary's faith.

When Elizabeth's baby was born, Zechariah, who still could not speak, wrote down the name the angel had given him—John. At that point, God restored his voice. With his first joyful words, Zechariah praised God for his loving concern for them in giving them this wonderful son. God can bless the childless with children or give the helpless his powerful presence. We see from the lives of Elizabeth and Zechariah that God is intimately involved in our pain and that he desires to fill the empty places in our life.

STRENGTHS AND ACCOMPLISHMENTS:
- Zechariah and Elizabeth were known as godly people.
- Zechariah overcame his doubt and praised God for his power.
- Zechariah obeyed the angel and named his son John.
- Elizabeth commended Mary for her role as the Messiah's mother.

WEAKNESSES AND MISTAKES:
- Zechariah doubted God's ability to give them a child in their older years.

LESSONS FROM THEIR LIVES:
- God is fully aware of the painful disappointment of childless people.
- God is intimately aware of the pain of hurting people.
- All things are possible with God.
- God can use older people to make significant contributions to his plan.

KEY VERSE:
"Zechariah and Elizabeth were righteous in God's eyes, careful to obey all of the Lord's commandments and regulations" (Luke 1:6).

The story of Elizabeth and Zechariah is told in Luke 1:5-80.

The Prophecy of Simeon
25Now there was a man named Simeon who lived in Jerusalem. He was a righteous man and very devout. He was filled with the Holy Spirit, and he eagerly expected the Messiah to come and rescue Israel. 26The Holy Spirit had revealed to him that he would not die until he had seen the Lord's Messiah. 27That day the Spirit led him to the Temple. So when Mary and Joseph came to present the baby Jesus to the Lord as the law required, 28Simeon was there. He took the child in his arms and praised God, saying,

29"Lord, now I can die in peace!
　As you promised me,
30I have seen the Savior
31　you have given to all people.
32He is a light to reveal God to the nations,
　and he is the glory of your people Israel!"

33Joseph and Mary were amazed at what was being said about Jesus. 34Then Simeon blessed them, and he said to Mary, "This child will be rejected by many in Israel, and it will be their undoing. But he will be the greatest joy to many others. 35Thus, the deepest thoughts of many hearts will be revealed. And a sword will pierce your very soul."

The Prophecy of Anna

36Anna, a prophet, was also there in the Temple. She was the daughter of Phanuel, of the tribe of Asher, and was very old. She was a widow, for her husband had died when they had been married only seven years. 37She was now eighty-four years old. She never left the Temple but stayed there day and night, worshiping God with fasting and prayer. 38She came along just as Simeon was talking with Mary and Joseph, and she began praising God. She talked about Jesus to everyone who had been waiting for the promised King to come and deliver Jerusalem.

39When Jesus' parents had fulfilled all the requirements of the law of the Lord, they returned home to Nazareth in Galilee. 40There the child grew up healthy and strong. He was filled with wisdom beyond his years, and God placed his special favor upon him.

Jesus Speaks with the Teachers

41Every year Jesus' parents went to Jerusalem for the Passover festival. 42When Jesus was twelve years old, they attended the festival as usual. 43After the celebration was over, they started home to Nazareth, but Jesus stayed behind in Jerusalem. His parents didn't miss him at first, 44because they assumed he was with friends among the other travelers. But when he didn't show up that evening, they started to look for him among their relatives and friends. 45When they couldn't find him, they went back to Jerusalem to search for him there. 46Three days later they finally discovered him. He was in the Temple, sitting among the religious teachers, discussing deep questions with them. 47And all who heard him were amazed at his understanding and his answers.

48His parents didn't know what to think.

"Son!" his mother said to him. "Why have you done this to us? Your father and I have been frantic, searching for you everywhere."

49"But why did you need to search?" he asked. "You should have known that I would be in my Father's house."* 50But they didn't understand what he meant.

51Then he returned to Nazareth with them and was obedient to them; and his mother stored all these things in her heart. 52So Jesus grew both in height and in wisdom, and he was loved by God and by all who knew him.

CHAPTER 3
John the Baptist Prepares the Way

It was now the fifteenth year of the reign of Tiberius, the Roman emperor. Pilate was governor over Judea; Herod Antipas was ruler* over Galilee; his brother Philip was ruler* over Iturea and Traconitis; Lysanias was ruler over Abilene. 2Annas and Caiaphas were the high priests. At this time a message from God came to John son of Zechariah, who was living out in the wilderness. 3Then John went from place to place on both sides of the Jordan River, preaching that people should be baptized to show that they had turned from their sins and turned to God to be forgiven.* 4Isaiah had spoken of John when he said,

"He is a voice shouting in the wilderness:
'Prepare a pathway for the Lord's coming!
    Make a straight road for him!
5 Fill in the valleys,
    and level the mountains and hills!
Straighten the curves,
    and smooth out the rough places!
6 And then all people will see
    the salvation sent from God.'"*

2:49 Or *"Didn't you realize that I should be involved with my Father's affairs?"* 3:1a Greek *Herod was tetrarch.* Herod Antipas was a son of King Herod. 3:1b Greek *tetrarch;* also in 3:1c, 19. 3:3 Greek *preaching a baptism of repentance for the forgiveness of sins.* 3:4-6 Isa 40:3-5.

2:36-38 Anna modeled how the power of faith can bring meaning to life for people in recovery. After many years of widowhood, Anna did not allow bitterness to set in. Instead, she found that her singleness gave her more opportunities to serve God in the Temple. She overcame adversity by drawing closer to God through prayer and fasting, and she was given the gift of prophecy. Anna accepted God's plan for her, which included a glimpse of the Messiah she had been longing for. Decades of unwanted singleness can drive many of us to find love in all the wrong places. We must trust God in that area of life as well.

3:1-6 The road to recovery can be as treacherous, fatiguing, dry, and deserted as a trek through the Judean wilderness. John knew that, so he preached a discomforting message about God's "bulldozer" preparing the way for the world's Savior. Those who were honest with themselves in their immermost heart knew that John was right. All that remained was a public confession of faith. Those of us in recovery need to take responsibility for our sinful actions, turn our life over to God, and experience God's power to "smooth out" our life.

7Here is a sample of John's preaching to the crowds that came for baptism: "You brood of snakes! Who warned you to flee God's coming judgment? 8Prove by the way you live that you have really turned from your sins and turned to God. Don't just say, 'We're safe—we're the descendants of Abraham.' That proves nothing. God can change these stones here into children of Abraham. 9Even now the ax of God's judgment is poised, ready to sever your roots. Yes, every tree that does not produce good fruit will be chopped down and thrown into the fire."

10The crowd asked, "What should we do?"

11John replied, "If you have two coats, give one to the poor. If you have food, share it with those who are hungry."

12Even corrupt tax collectors came to be baptized and asked, "Teacher, what should we do?"

13"Show your honesty," he replied. "Make sure you collect no more taxes than the Roman government requires you to."

14"What should we do?" asked some soldiers.

John replied, "Don't extort money, and don't accuse people of things you know they didn't do. And be content with your pay."

15Everyone was expecting the Messiah to come soon, and they were eager to know whether John might be the Messiah. 16John answered their questions by saying, "I baptize with* water; but someone is coming soon who is greater than I am—so much greater that I am not even worthy to be his slave.* He will baptize you with the Holy Spirit and with fire.* 17He is ready to separate the chaff from the grain with his winnowing fork. Then he will clean up the threshing area, storing the grain in his barn but burning the chaff with never-ending fire." 18John used many such warnings as he announced the Good News to the people.

19John also publicly criticized Herod Antipas, ruler of Galilee, for marrying Herodias, his brother's wife, and for many other wrongs he had done. 20So Herod put John in prison, adding this sin to his many others.

The Baptism of Jesus

21One day when the crowds were being baptized, Jesus himself was baptized. As he was praying, the heavens opened, 22and the Holy Spirit descended on him in the form of a dove. And a voice from heaven said, "You are my beloved Son, and I am fully pleased with you.*"

The Record of Jesus' Ancestors

23Jesus was about thirty years old when he began his public ministry.

Jesus was known as the son of Joseph.
Joseph was the son of Heli.
24 Heli was the son of Matthat.
Matthat was the son of Levi.
Levi was the son of Melki.
Melki was the son of Jannai.
Jannai was the son of Joseph.
25 Joseph was the son of Mattathias.
Mattathias was the son of Amos.
Amos was the son of Nahum.
Nahum was the son of Esli.
Esli was the son of Naggai.

3:16a Or *in.* **3:16b** Greek *to untie his sandals.* **3:16c** Or *in the Holy Spirit and in fire.* **3:22** Some manuscripts read *and today I have become your Father.*

3:21-22 By settling upon him in the form of a dove, God the Holy Spirit visibly showed not only that he identified with Jesus but that God's power was with him. God the Father showed how pleased he was with his Son by speaking directly from heaven. If we are trusting Christ through recovery, we will experience God's heavenly power in us, his fatherly love for us, and his supreme identification with us. We, too, are God's "beloved children," and he loves us very much.
3:23 Even though Jesus knew from his youth what his mission on earth would be, this "son of Joseph" patiently persevered as an obscure carpenter in Nazareth until the age of thirty. He never rushed to accomplish his ambitious God-given task. He modeled for us the patience and trust in God's timing that we need as we progress through recovery. As we are faithful, God will work his healing power within us over time.
3:23-38 Jesus' genealogy is rooted in the very beginning of the human race, showing his close identification with all humanity. Jesus' genealogy is sprinkled with people known for their mistakes. Judah fathered Perez through an illicit relationship with his daughter Tamar. Salmon fathered Boaz through his marriage with Rahab, a former prostitute from Jericho. Boaz fathered Obed through his marriage with the Moabitess, Ruth. David fathered Solomon through Bathsheba, the wife of another man. Jesus is clearly "one of us." No problem in our life is "foreign" to him. By becoming flesh, God in Jesus Christ was subject to the weaknesses of humanity and even suffered death for us. Jesus truly understands the difficulties we face in recovery.

26 Naggai was the son of Maath.
Maath was the son of Mattathias.
Mattathias was the son of Semein.
Semein was the son of Josech.
Josech was the son of Joda.
27 Joda was the son of Joanan.
Joanan was the son of Rhesa.
Rhesa was the son of Zerubbabel.
Zerubbabel was the son of Shealtiel.
Shealtiel was the son of Neri.
28 Neri was the son of Melki.
Melki was the son of Addi.
Addi was the son of Cosam.
Cosam was the son of Elmadam.
Elmadam was the son of Er.
29 Er was the son of Joshua.
Joshua was the son of Eliezer.
Eliezer was the son of Jorim.
Jorim was the son of Matthat.
Matthat was the son of Levi.
30 Levi was the son of Simeon.
Simeon was the son of Judah.
Judah was the son of Joseph.
Joseph was the son of Jonam.
Jonam was the son of Eliakim.
31 Eliakim was the son of Melea.
Melea was the son of Menna.
Menna was the son of Mattatha.
Mattatha was the son of Nathan.
Nathan was the son of David.
32 David was the son of Jesse.
Jesse was the son of Obed.
Obed was the son of Boaz.
Boaz was the son of Salmon.*
Salmon was the son of Nahshon.
33 Nahshon was the son of Amminadab.
Amminadab was the son of Admin.
Admin was the son of Arni.*
Arni was the son of Hezron.
Hezron was the son of Perez.
Perez was the son of Judah.
34 Judah was the son of Jacob.
Jacob was the son of Isaac.
Isaac was the son of Abraham.
Abraham was the son of Terah.
Terah was the son of Nahor.
35 Nahor was the son of Serug.

Serug was the son of Reu.
Reu was the son of Peleg.
Peleg was the son of Eber.
Eber was the son of Shelah.
36 Shelah was the son of Cainan.
Cainan was the son of Arphaxad.
Arphaxad was the son of Shem.
Shem was the son of Noah.
Noah was the son of Lamech.
37 Lamech was the son of Methuselah.
Methuselah was the son of Enoch.
Enoch was the son of Jared.
Jared was the son of Mahalalel.
Mahalalel was the son of Kenan.
38 Kenan was the son of Enosh.*
Enosh was the son of Seth.
Seth was the son of Adam.
Adam was the son of God.

CHAPTER 4
The Temptation of Jesus

Then Jesus, full of the Holy Spirit, left the Jordan River. He was led by the Spirit to go out into the wilderness, 2where the Devil tempted him for forty days. He ate nothing all that time and was very hungry.

3Then the Devil said to him, "If you are the Son of God, change this stone into a loaf of bread."

4But Jesus told him, "No! The Scriptures say, 'People need more than bread for their life.'*"

5Then the Devil took him up and revealed to him all the kingdoms of the world in a moment of time. 6The Devil told him, "I will give you the glory of these kingdoms and authority over them—because they are mine to give to anyone I please. 7I will give it all to you if you will bow down and worship me."

8Jesus replied, "The Scriptures say,

'You must worship the Lord your God;
    serve only him.'*"

9Then the Devil took him to Jerusalem, to the highest point of the Temple, and said, "If you are the Son of God, jump off! 10For the Scriptures say,

---

3:32 Greek *Sala;* see Ruth 4:22. **3:33** *Arni* is the same person as Ram; see 1 Chr 2:9-10. **3:38** Greek *Enos;* see Gen 5:6.
4:4 Deut 8:3. **4:8** Deut 6:13.

4:1-2 Alone in the Judean wastelands, Jesus was sorely tempted for forty days. Here, as in every aspect of his life, he overcame adversity by depending on the power of the Holy Spirit working through him. This same power is available for us today. Believers have immediate access to this power through God's Holy Spirit dwelling within them. This power within our heart is great enough to help us resist the most tempting sins the world, the flesh, or the Devil has to throw at us (1 John 2:16; 4:4). Even the most powerful addiction is no match for the Holy Spirit.

'He orders his angels to protect and
    guard you.
[11] And they will hold you with their
    hands
    to keep you from striking your foot
    on a stone.'*"

[12]Jesus responded, "The Scriptures also
say, 'Do not test the Lord your God.'*"
[13]When the Devil had finished tempting
Jesus, he left him until the next opportunity
came.

Jesus Rejected at Nazareth

[14]Then Jesus returned to Galilee, filled with
the Holy Spirit's power. Soon he became well
known throughout the surrounding country. [15]He taught in their synagogues and was
praised by everyone.
[16]When he came to the village of Nazareth,
his boyhood home, he went as usual to the
synagogue on the Sabbath and stood up to
read the Scriptures. [17]The scroll containing
the messages of Isaiah the prophet was
handed to him, and he unrolled the scroll to
the place where it says:

[18] "The Spirit of the Lord is upon me,
    for he has appointed me to preach
        Good News to the poor.
He has sent me to proclaim
    that captives will be released,
    that the blind will see,
    that the downtrodden will be freed
        from their oppressors,
[19]   and that the time of the Lord's favor
    has come.*"

[20]He rolled up the scroll, handed it back to
the attendant, and sat down. Everyone in the
synagogue stared at him intently. [21]Then he
said, "This Scripture has come true today before your very eyes!"
[22]All who were there spoke well of him and
were amazed by the gracious words that fell
from his lips. "How can this be?" they asked.
"Isn't this Joseph's son?"
[23]Then he said, "Probably you will quote
me that proverb, 'Physician, heal yourself'—
meaning, 'Why don't you do miracles here
in your hometown like those you did in Capernaum?' [24]But the truth is, no prophet is
accepted in his own hometown.
[25]"Certainly there were many widows in
Israel who needed help in Elijah's time,
when there was no rain for three and a half
years and hunger stalked the land. [26]Yet Elijah was not sent to any of them. He was sent
instead to a widow of Zarephath—a foreigner in the land of Sidon. [27]Or think of the
prophet Elisha, who healed Naaman, a Syrian, rather than the many lepers in Israel
who needed help."
[28]When they heard this, the people in the
synagogue were furious. [29]Jumping up, they
mobbed him and took him to the edge of
the hill on which the city was built. They intended to push him over the cliff, [30]but he
slipped away through the crowd and left them.

Jesus Casts Out a Demon

[31]Then Jesus went to Capernaum, a town in
Galilee, and taught there in the synagogue
every Sabbath day. [32]There, too, the people

4:10-11 Ps 91:11-12. 4:12 Deut 6:16. 4:18-19 Or *and to proclaim the acceptable year of the Lord.* Isa 61:1-2.

4:13 Temptation by the Devil is an ongoing reality. After unsuccessfully tempting Jesus in
the wilderness, Satan gave up, but only temporarily. He would save his best punch for later
(at the cross). Satan exhausted his most compelling temptations to no avail and left defeated.
But he continued to try to undermine Jesus' ministry, especially through the people around him
(see Luke 11:14-22). If we in recovery withstand temptation at one point, Satan will eventually
try again, either in the same area or in another. We must be on guard against Satan's repeated
attacks.
4:18-21 When Jesus claimed to fulfill the words of Isaiah 61, he was directly claiming to be
Israel's long-awaited Messiah. Isaiah beautifully characterized a major focus of the Messiah's
ministry. The Messiah would deliver those who were captives to the power of sin and spiritual
discouragement. He would give sight to the physically and spiritually blind. He would bring freedom from their oppressors to the downtrodden. A relationship with God through Jesus Christ
provides these limitless resources to all of us in recovery.
4:28-30 The response of this hard-hearted, hometown crowd in Nazareth to Jesus' remarks is an
example of what happens when denial is mixed with anger. When Jesus challenged their unbelief,
their surface appreciation of his ministry turned to outrage. They wondered how this hometown
boy could claim to be a prophet. Their attempt at mob violence showed how hysterical and resistant to the truth even religious people can be. We need to overcome the areas of denial in our life
if we want God to step in and transform us into new and healthy people. God cannot heal us
until we are willing to recognize our problems and our unbelief.

were amazed at the things he said, because he spoke with authority.

³³Once when he was in the synagogue, a man possessed by a demon began shouting at Jesus, ³⁴"Go away! Why are you bothering us, Jesus of Nazareth? Have you come to destroy us? I know who you are—the Holy One sent from God."

³⁵Jesus cut him short. "Be silent!" he told the demon. "Come out of the man!" The demon threw the man to the floor as the crowd watched; then it left him without hurting him further.

³⁶Amazed, the people exclaimed, "What authority and power this man's words possess! Even evil spirits obey him and flee at his command!" ³⁷The story of what he had done spread like wildfire throughout the whole region.

Jesus Heals Many People

³⁸After leaving the synagogue that day, Jesus went to Simon's home, where he found Simon's mother-in-law very sick with a high fever. "Please heal her," everyone begged. ³⁹Standing at her bedside, he spoke to the fever, rebuking it, and immediately her temperature returned to normal. She got up at once and prepared a meal for them.

⁴⁰As the sun went down that evening, people throughout the village brought sick family members to Jesus. No matter what their diseases were, the touch of his hand healed everyone. ⁴¹Some were possessed by demons; and the demons came out at his command, shouting, "You are the Son of God." But because they knew he was the Messiah, he stopped them and told them to be silent.

Jesus Continues to Preach

⁴²Early the next morning Jesus went out into the wilderness. The crowds searched everywhere for him, and when they finally found him, they begged him not to leave them. ⁴³But he replied, "I must preach the Good News of the Kingdom of God in other places, too, because that is why I was sent." ⁴⁴So he continued to travel around, preaching in synagogues throughout Judea.*

CHAPTER 5
The First Disciples

One day as Jesus was preaching on the shore of the Sea of Galilee,* great crowds pressed in on him to listen to the word of God. ²He noticed two empty boats at the water's edge, for the fishermen had left them and were washing their nets. ³Stepping into one of the boats, Jesus asked Simon,* its owner, to push it out into the water. So he sat in the boat and taught the crowds from there.

⁴When he had finished speaking, he said to Simon, "Now go out where it is deeper and let down your nets, and you will catch many fish."

⁵"Master," Simon replied, "we worked hard all last night and didn't catch a thing. But if you say so, we'll try again." ⁶And this time their nets were so full they began to tear! ⁷A shout for help brought their partners in the other boat, and soon both boats were filled with fish and on the verge of sinking.

⁸When Simon Peter realized what had happened, he fell to his knees before Jesus and said, "Oh, Lord, please leave me—I'm too much of a sinner to be around you." ⁹For he was awestruck by the size of their catch, as were the others with him. ¹⁰His partners, James and John, the sons of Zebedee, were also amazed.

Jesus replied to Simon, "Don't be afraid! From now on you'll be fishing for people!" ¹¹And as soon as they landed, they left everything and followed Jesus.

Jesus Heals a Man with Leprosy

¹²In one of the villages, Jesus met a man with an advanced case of leprosy. When the man saw Jesus, he fell to the ground, face down in the dust, begging to be healed. "Lord," he said, "if you want to, you can make me well again."

¹³Jesus reached out and touched the man. "I want to," he said. "Be healed!" And instantly the leprosy disappeared. ¹⁴Then Jesus instructed him not to tell anyone what had happened. He said, "Go right to the priest

---

4:44 Some manuscripts read *Galilee.* **5:1** Greek *Lake Gennesaret,* another name for the Sea of Galilee. **5:3** *Simon* is called *Peter* in 6:14 and thereafter.

5:4-11 The disciples were certainly persistent in their fishing, but doing things their way just wasn't enough. As soon as they followed Jesus' advice, they experienced success. We may be struggling to attain recovery on our own. We may be diligent, hardworking, and disciplined. But if we aren't doing things God's way, no amount of hard work will bring success. Following God's will for our life will lead to healing and success. Some may think the truth found in God's Word seems crazy. But as we follow God's program obediently and seek his gracious help, we will experience his powerful deliverance.

and let him examine you. Take along the offering required in the law of Moses for those who have been healed of leprosy, so everyone will have proof of your healing." [15]Yet despite Jesus' instructions, the report of his power spread even faster, and vast crowds came to hear him preach and to be healed of their diseases. [16]But Jesus often withdrew to the wilderness for prayer.

Jesus Heals a Paralyzed Man

[17]One day while Jesus was teaching, some Pharisees and teachers of religious law were sitting nearby. (It seemed that these men showed up from every village in all Galilee and Judea, as well as from Jerusalem.) And the Lord's healing power was strongly with Jesus. [18]Some men came carrying a paralyzed man on a sleeping mat. They tried to push through the crowd to Jesus, [19]but they couldn't reach him. So they went up to the roof, took off some tiles, and lowered the sick man down into the crowd, still on his mat, right in front of Jesus. [20]Seeing their faith, Jesus said to the man, "Son, your sins are forgiven."

[21]"Who does this man think he is?" the Pharisees and teachers of religious law said to each other. "This is blasphemy! Who but God can forgive sins?"

[22]Jesus knew what they were thinking, so he asked them, "Why do you think this is blasphemy? [23]Is it easier to say, 'Your sins are forgiven' or 'Get up and walk'? [24]I will prove that I, the Son of Man, have the authority on earth to forgive sins." Then Jesus turned to the paralyzed man and said, "Stand up, take your mat, and go on home, because you are healed!"

[25]And immediately, as everyone watched, the man jumped to his feet, picked up his mat, and went home praising God. [26]Everyone was gripped with great wonder and awe. And they praised God, saying over and over again, "We have seen amazing things today."

Jesus Calls Levi (Matthew)

[27]Later, as Jesus left the town, he saw a tax collector named Levi sitting at his tax-collection booth. "Come, be my disciple!" Jesus said to him. [28]So Levi got up, left everything, and followed him.

[29]Soon Levi held a banquet in his home with Jesus as the guest of honor. Many of Levi's fellow tax collectors and other guests were there. [30]But the Pharisees and their teachers of religious law complained bitterly to Jesus' disciples, "Why do you eat and drink with such scum*?"

[31]Jesus answered them, "Healthy people don't need a doctor—sick people do. [32]I have come to call sinners to turn from their sins, not to spend my time with those who think they are already good enough."

A Discussion about Fasting

[33]The religious leaders complained that Jesus' disciples were feasting instead of fasting. "John the Baptist's disciples always fast and pray," they declared, "and so do the disciples of the Pharisees. Why are yours always feasting?"

[34]Jesus asked, "Do wedding guests fast while celebrating with the groom? [35]Someday he will be taken away from them, and then they will fast."

[36]Then Jesus gave them this illustration: "No one tears a piece of cloth from a new garment and uses it to patch an old garment. For then the new garment would be torn, and the patch wouldn't even match the old garment. [37]And no one puts new wine into old wineskins. The new wine would burst the old skins, spilling the wine and ruining the skins. [38]New wine must be put into new wineskins. [39]But no one who drinks the old wine seems to want the fresh and the new. 'The old is better,' they say."

CHAPTER 6

A Discussion about the Sabbath

One Sabbath day as Jesus was walking through some grainfields, his disciples broke off heads of wheat, rubbed off the husks in their hands, and ate the grains. [2]But some Pharisees said, "You shouldn't be doing that! It's against the law to work by harvesting grain on the Sabbath."

5:30 Greek *with tax collectors and sinners.*

5:30-32 To receive Jesus' help and begin recovery, we must first recognize and admit how helpless we are. Jesus' greatest priority was ministering to the so-called notorious sinners (social outcasts) because they admitted their lowly, helpless position. The Pharisees were also sinners, but they denied their sins. Because of their self-righteousness and self-sufficiency, Jesus could do nothing for them. When we recognize our need for help and admit our failures to God and others, Jesus will reach out and help us.

[3]Jesus replied, "Haven't you ever read in the Scriptures what King David did when he and his companions were hungry? [4]He went into the house of God, ate the special bread reserved for the priests alone, and then gave some to his friends. That was breaking the law, too." [5]And Jesus added, "I, the Son of Man, am master even of the Sabbath."

Jesus Heals on the Sabbath

[6]On another Sabbath day, a man with a deformed right hand was in the synagogue while Jesus was teaching. [7]The teachers of religious law and the Pharisees watched closely to see whether Jesus would heal the man on the Sabbath, because they were eager to find some legal charge to bring against him. [8]But Jesus knew their thoughts. He said to the man with the deformed hand, "Come and stand here where everyone can see." So the man came forward. [9]Then Jesus said to his critics, "I have a question for you. Is it legal to do good deeds on the Sabbath, or is it a day for doing harm? Is this a day to save life or to destroy it?" [10]He looked around at them one by one and then said to the man, "Reach out your hand." The man reached out his hand, and it became normal again! [11]At this, the enemies of Jesus were wild with rage and began to discuss what to do with him.

Jesus Chooses the Twelve Apostles

[12]One day soon afterward Jesus went to a mountain to pray, and he prayed to God all night. [13]At daybreak he called together all of his disciples and chose twelve of them to be apostles. Here are their names:

[14] Simon (he also called him Peter),
Andrew (Peter's brother),
James,
John,
Philip,
Bartholomew,
[15] Matthew,
Thomas,
James (son of Alphaeus),
Simon (the Zealot),
[16] Judas (son of James),
Judas Iscariot (who later betrayed him).

Crowds Follow Jesus

[17]When they came down the slopes of the mountain, the disciples stood with Jesus on a large, level area, surrounded by many of his followers and by the crowds. There were people from all over Judea and from Jerusalem and from as far north as the seacoasts of Tyre and Sidon. [18]They had come to hear him and to be healed, and Jesus cast out many evil spirits. [19]Everyone was trying to touch him, because healing power went out from him, and they were all cured.

The Beatitudes

[20]Then Jesus turned to his disciples and said,

"God blesses you who are poor,
for the Kingdom of God is given to you.
[21]God blesses you who are hungry now,
for you will be satisfied.
God blesses you who weep now,
for the time will come when you will
laugh with joy.
[22]God blesses you who are hated and
excluded and mocked and cursed
because you are identified with me, the
Son of Man.

[23]"When that happens, rejoice! Yes, leap for joy! For a great reward awaits you in heaven. And remember, the ancient prophets were also treated that way by your ancestors.

Sorrows Foretold

[24]"What sorrows await you who are rich,
for you have your only happiness now.
[25]What sorrows await you who are satisfied
and prosperous now,
for a time of awful hunger is before
you.

6:6-11 Jesus routinely healed people on the Sabbath. This angered his opponents, especially the Pharisees. Not everyone will be pleased with our recovery. Friends also caught in the trap of addiction may be threatened by the changes in us and become angry. People who have used our addiction to gain power over us may also be upset as they lose their ability to manipulate us. These friends may resemble the scribes and Pharisees. No matter how great the opposition to our recovery, Jesus wants us to be healed. As we trust in him and obey him, we will experience healing.
6:20-26 When Jesus spoke about Kingdom values, he was speaking about the importance of following God's priorities in life. He pronounced blessings and joy for those who follow him and hunger for God. But he pronounced sorrows on those who selfishly seek to be rich and live for the moment. By his strong words, Jesus was creating a crisis intervention of sorts. Those who put their greatest trust in money and material goods and do not realize their need for God will one day meet the great Equalizer. Those who trust in God will be rewarded.

What sorrows await you who laugh
carelessly,
for your laughing will turn to mourning
and sorrow.
26 What sorrows await you who are praised
by the crowds,
for their ancestors also praised false
prophets.

Love for Enemies

27"But if you are willing to listen, I say, love
your enemies. Do good to those who hate
you. 28Pray for the happiness of those who
curse you. Pray for those who hurt you. 29If
someone slaps you on one cheek, turn the
other cheek. If someone demands your coat,
offer your shirt also. 30Give what you have
to anyone who asks you for it; and when
things are taken away from you, don't try to
get them back. 31Do for others as you would
like them to do for you.

32"Do you think you deserve credit merely
for loving those who love you? Even the sinners do that! 33And if you do good only to
those who do good to you, is that so wonderful? Even sinners do that much! 34And if
you lend money only to those who can repay you, what good is that? Even sinners
will lend to their own kind for a full return.

35"Love your enemies! Do good to them!
Lend to them! And don't be concerned that
they might not repay. Then your reward
from heaven will be very great, and you
will truly be acting as children of the Most
High, for he is kind to the unthankful and
to those who are wicked. 36You must be compassionate, just as your Father is compassionate.

Don't Condemn Others

37"Stop judging others, and you will not be
judged. Stop criticizing others, or it will all
come back on you. If you forgive others,
you will be forgiven. 38If you give, you will
receive. Your gift will return to you in full
measure, pressed down, shaken together to
make room for more, and running over.
Whatever measure you use in giving—large
or small—it will be used to measure what is
given back to you."

39Then Jesus gave the following illustration: "What good is it for one blind person
to lead another? The first one will fall into a
ditch and pull the other down also. 40A student is not greater than the teacher. But the
student who works hard will become like
the teacher.

Forgiveness

READ LUKE 6:27-36

As we set out to mend relationships, there
may be some things that are beyond our
control. Some people may refuse to be
reconciled, even when we do our best to
make amends. This may leave us feeling
like victims. Once again we are stuck with
the pain of unresolved issues. We may be
left with negative feelings that continue
to surface. What can we do to gain control
in these situations?

Jesus said, "But if you are willing to
listen, I say, love your enemies. Do good
to those who hate you. Pray for the happiness of those who curse you. Pray for those
who hurt you. . . . Love your enemies! Do
good to them! Lend to them! And don't
be concerned that they might not repay.
Then your reward from heaven will be very
great, and you will truly be acting as children of the Most High, for he is kind to the
unthankful and to those who are wicked"
(Luke 6:27-28, 35).

We no longer need to be controlled by
other people's dispositions and actions.
Even when we have done our best to
make amends for the wrongs we have
done, the situation may not change. And
even when we have come to terms with
the wrongs that have been done against
us, our feelings may not change. But we
don't have to be held captive by our feelings or the feelings of others. We can
choose to forgive and act in loving ways.
This will free us from being controlled by
anyone other than God. As we choose to
forgive others and do good, our feelings
will change with time. *Turn to page 125,
Luke 17.*

[41]"And why worry about a speck in your friend's eye* when you have a log in your own? [42]How can you think of saying, 'Friend,* let me help you get rid of that speck in your eye,' when you can't see past the log in your own eye? Hypocrite! First get rid of the log from your own eye; then perhaps you will see well enough to deal with the speck in your friend's eye.

The Tree and Its Fruit

[43]"A good tree can't produce bad fruit, and a bad tree can't produce good fruit. [44]A tree is identified by the kind of fruit it produces. Figs never grow on thornbushes or grapes on bramble bushes. [45]A good person produces good deeds from a good heart, and an evil person produces evil deeds from an evil heart. Whatever is in your heart determines what you say.

Building on a Solid Foundation

[46]"So why do you call me 'Lord,' when you won't obey me? [47]I will show you what it's like when someone comes to me, listens to my teaching, and then obeys me. [48]It is like a person who builds a house on a strong foundation laid upon the underlying rock. When the floodwaters rise and break against the house, it stands firm because it is well built. [49]But anyone who listens and doesn't obey is like a person who builds a house without a foundation. When the floods sweep down against that house, it will crumble into a heap of ruins."

CHAPTER 7
Faith of the Roman Officer

When Jesus had finished saying all this, he went back to Capernaum. [2]Now the highly valued slave of a Roman officer was sick and near death. [3]When the officer heard about Jesus, he sent some respected Jewish leaders to ask him to come and heal his slave. [4]So they earnestly begged Jesus to come with them and help the man. "If anyone deserves your help, it is he," they said, [5]"for he loves the Jews and even built a synagogue for us."

[6]So Jesus went with them. But just before they arrived at the house, the officer sent some friends to say, "Lord, don't trouble yourself by coming to my home, for I am not worthy of such an honor. [7]I am not even worthy to come and meet you. Just say the word from where you are, and my servant will be healed. [8]I know because I am under the authority of my superior officers, and I have authority over my soldiers. I only need to say, 'Go,' and they go, or 'Come,' and they come. And if I say to my slaves, 'Do this or that,' they do it."

[9]When Jesus heard this, he was amazed. Turning to the crowd, he said, "I tell you, I haven't seen faith like this in all the land of Israel!" [10]And when the officer's friends returned to his house, they found the slave completely healed.

Jesus Raises a Widow's Son

[11]Soon afterward Jesus went with his disciples to the village of Nain, with a great crowd following him. [12]A funeral procession was coming out as he approached the village gate. The boy who had died was the only son of a widow, and many mourners from the village were with her. [13]When the Lord saw her, his heart overflowed with compassion. "Don't cry!" he said. [14]Then he walked over to the coffin and touched it, and the bearers stopped. "Young man," he said, "get up." [15]Then the dead boy sat up and began to talk to those around him! And Jesus gave him back to his mother.

[16]Great fear swept the crowd, and they praised God, saying, "A mighty prophet has risen among us," and "We have seen the hand of God at work today." [17]The report of what Jesus had done that day spread all over Judea and even out across its borders.

6:41 Greek *your brother's eye;* also in 6:42. **6:42** Greek *Brother.*

7:1-10 The Roman officer demonstrated qualities that are key elements in receiving God's greatest blessings. The officer showed compassion to people of a lower social class and people of another race and religion. He was humble and recognized his own unworthiness despite being a man of authority. He wholeheartedly placed his faith in Jesus to heal his valued slave. Jesus marveled at such faith and answered his request. Those who have been raised in religious circles are expected to have faith but very often do not. Sometimes true faith is found in places we least expect—among the unchurched and the outcasts, who recognize their need for help and cry out to God in their helplessness. This kind of faith is necessary to the recovery process.

7:11-15 By raising the young boy from the dead, Jesus showed his compassion for people experiencing great loss. This woman had previously lost her husband, and now her only son was dead. This miracle shows us that no situation in our life is beyond the restoring power of God. Even in the midst of what seems like a dead end, God is not limited. This same power that can raise the dead can certainly bring health for the sick and freedom for the addicted.

Jesus and John the Baptist

[18]The disciples of John the Baptist told John about everything Jesus was doing. So John called for two of his disciples, [19]and he sent them to the Lord to ask him, "Are you the Messiah we've been expecting, or should we keep looking for someone else?"

[20]John's two disciples found Jesus and said to him, "John the Baptist sent us to ask, 'Are you the Messiah we've been expecting, or should we keep looking for someone else?'"

[21]At that very time, he cured many people of their various diseases, and he cast out evil spirits and restored sight to the blind. [22]Then he told John's disciples, "Go back to John and tell him what you have seen and heard—the blind see, the lame walk, the lepers are cured, the deaf hear, the dead are raised to life, and the Good News is being preached to the poor. [23]And tell him, 'God blesses those who are not offended by me.*'"

[24]After they left, Jesus talked to the crowd about John. "Who is this man in the wilderness that you went out to see? Did you find him weak as a reed, moved by every breath of wind? [25]Or were you expecting to see a man dressed in expensive clothes? No, people who wear beautiful clothes and live in luxury are found in palaces, not in the wilderness. [26]Were you looking for a prophet? Yes, and he is more than a prophet. [27]John is the man to whom the Scriptures refer when they say,

'Look, I am sending my messenger before
    you,
    and he will prepare your way before
    you.'*

[28]I tell you, of all who have ever lived, none is greater than John. Yet even the most insignificant person in the Kingdom of God is greater than he is!"

[29]When they heard this, all the people, including the unjust tax collectors, agreed that God's plan was right,* for they had been baptized by John. [30]But the Pharisees and experts in religious law had rejected God's plan for them, for they had refused John's baptism.

[31]"How shall I describe this generation?" Jesus asked. "With what will I compare them? [32]They are like a group of children playing a game in the public square. They complain to their friends, 'We played wedding songs, and you weren't happy, so we played funeral songs, but you weren't sad.' [33]For John the Baptist didn't drink wine and he often fasted, and you say, 'He's demon possessed.' [34]And I, the Son of Man, feast and drink, and you say, 'He's a glutton and a drunkard, and a friend of the worst sort of sinners!' [35]But wisdom is shown to be right by the lives of those who follow it.*"

Jesus Anointed by a Sinful Woman

[36]One of the Pharisees asked Jesus to come to his home for a meal, so Jesus accepted the invitation and sat down to eat. [37]A certain immoral woman heard he was there and brought a beautiful jar* filled with expensive perfume. [38]Then she knelt behind him at his feet, weeping. Her tears fell on his feet, and she wiped them off with her hair. Then she kept kissing his feet and putting perfume on them.

[39]When the Pharisee who was the host saw what was happening and who the woman was, he said to himself, "This proves that Jesus is no prophet. If God had really sent him, he would know what kind of woman is touching him. She's a sinner!"

[40]Then Jesus spoke up and answered his thoughts. "Simon," he said to the Pharisee, "I have something to say to you."

7:23 Or *who don't fall away because of me.* **7:27** Mal 3:1. **7:29** Or *praised God.* **7:35** Or *But wisdom is justified by all her children.* **7:37** Greek *an alabaster jar.*

7:18-23 John the Baptist's experience shows that even the strongest believers will go through times of discouragement and doubt. John had been imprisoned and was facing death (Matthew 11:2). Jesus' seeming inability or unwillingness to set up his Kingdom led John to send these inquirers. Jesus deeply respected John (Luke 7:28), even with his doubts. John's questions were honestly asked in a time of acute suffering, so Jesus affirmed him and answered him accordingly. God invites us to bring our doubts to him, and he will gently move us along the path of discovery and recovery.

7:24-28 Because of his strength of character, John the Baptist did not allow himself to be squeezed into anyone else's mold. He committed himself to fulfill his God-given role as a prophet and forerunner of the Messiah. Just as he did for John, God has a purpose for each one of us. As we discover what our role in his plan is, he will reveal his will to us and bring us joy. As we obey him, he will always be with us, guiding and strengthening us along the way. Trying to be someone we were never intended to be only slows our spiritual growth and our progress in recovery.

"All right, Teacher," Simon replied, "go ahead."

[41]Then Jesus told him this story: "A man loaned money to two people—five hundred pieces of silver* to one and fifty pieces to the other. [42]But neither of them could repay him, so he kindly forgave them both, canceling their debts. Who do you suppose loved him more after that?"

[43]Simon answered, "I suppose the one for whom he canceled the larger debt."

"That's right," Jesus said. [44]Then he turned to the woman and said to Simon, "Look at this woman kneeling here. When I entered your home, you didn't offer me water to wash the dust from my feet, but she has washed them with her tears and wiped them with her hair. [45]You didn't give me a kiss of greeting, but she has kissed my feet again and again from the time I first came in. [46]You neglected the courtesy of olive oil to anoint my head, but she has anointed my feet with rare perfume. [47]I tell you, her sins—and they are many—have been forgiven, so she has shown me much love. But a person who is forgiven little shows only little love." [48]Then Jesus said to the woman, "Your sins are forgiven."

[49]The men at the table said among themselves, "Who does this man think he is, going around forgiving sins?"

[50]And Jesus said to the woman, "Your faith has saved you; go in peace."

CHAPTER 8
Women Who Followed Jesus
Not long afterward Jesus began a tour of the nearby cities and villages to announce the Good News concerning the Kingdom of God. He took his twelve disciples with him, [2]along with some women he had healed and from whom he had cast out evil spirits. Among them were Mary Magdalene, from whom he had cast out seven demons; [3]Joanna, the wife of Chuza, Herod's business manager; Susanna; and many others who were contributing from their own resources to support Jesus and his disciples.

Story of the Farmer Scattering Seed
[4]One day Jesus told this story to a large crowd that had gathered from many towns to hear him: [5]"A farmer went out to plant some seed. As he scattered it across his field, some seed fell on a footpath, where it was stepped on, and the birds came and ate it. [6]Other seed fell on shallow soil with underlying rock. This seed began to grow, but soon it withered and died for lack of moisture. [7]Other seed fell among thorns that shot up and choked out the tender blades. [8]Still other seed fell on fertile soil. This seed grew and produced a crop one hundred times as much as had been planted." When he had said this, he called out, "Anyone who is willing to hear should listen and understand!"

[9]His disciples asked him what the story meant. [10]He replied, "You have been permitted to understand the secrets of the Kingdom of God. But I am using these stories to conceal everything about it from outsiders, so that the Scriptures might be fulfilled:

'They see what I do,
  but they don't really see;
they hear what I say,
  but they don't understand.'*

[11]"This is the meaning of the story: The seed is God's message. [12]The seed that fell on the hard path represents those who hear the message, but then the Devil comes and steals it away and prevents them from believing and being saved. [13]The rocky soil represents those who hear the message with joy. But like young plants in such soil, their roots don't go very deep. They believe for a while, but they wilt when the hot winds of testing blow. [14]The thorny ground represents those who hear and accept the message, but all too quickly the message is crowded out by the cares and riches and pleasures of this life. And so they never grow into maturity. [15]But the good soil represents honest, good-hearted people who hear God's message, cling to it, and steadily produce a huge harvest.

7:41 Greek *500 denarii*. A denarius was the equivalent of a full day's wage. **8:10** Isa 6:9.

8:4-15 This story about the farmer and the soils emphasizes accountability and discipleship in our relationship with God. The attitudes and condition of our heart matter more than our outward profession of faith. The pressures that draw us back into addiction are well known to those of us in recovery. We face continual temptation to give in to our destructive habit, so we must be consistent and watchful in the recovery process. Taking regular moral inventory helps us avoid the problems that tend to creep into our life through the back door. As we keep our heart focused on God, he will give us a new lease on life.

Illustration of the Lamp

[16]"No one would light a lamp and then cover it up or put it under a bed. No, lamps are mounted in the open, where they can be seen by those entering the house. [17]For everything that is hidden or secret will eventually be brought to light and made plain to all. [18]So be sure to pay attention to what you hear. To those who are open to my teaching, more understanding will be given. But to those who are not listening, even what they think they have will be taken away from them."

The True Family of Jesus

[19]Once when Jesus' mother and brothers came to see him, they couldn't get to him because of the crowds. [20]Someone told Jesus, "Your mother and your brothers are outside, and they want to see you."

[21]Jesus replied, "My mother and my brothers are all those who hear the message of God and obey it."

Jesus Calms the Storm

[22]One day Jesus said to his disciples, "Let's cross over to the other side of the lake." So they got into a boat and started out. [23]On the way across, Jesus lay down for a nap, and while he was sleeping the wind began to rise. A fierce storm developed that threatened to swamp them, and they were in real danger.

[24]The disciples woke him up, shouting, "Master, Master, we're going to drown!"

So Jesus rebuked the wind and the raging waves. The storm stopped and all was calm! [25]Then he asked them, "Where is your faith?"

And they were filled with awe and amazement. They said to one another, "Who is this man, that even the winds and waves obey him?"

Jesus Heals a Demon-Possessed Man

[26]So they arrived in the land of the Gerasenes,* across the lake from Galilee. [27]As Jesus was climbing out of the boat, a man who was possessed by demons came out to meet him. Homeless and naked, he had lived in a cemetery for a long time. [28]As soon as he saw Jesus, he shrieked and fell to the ground before him, screaming, "Why are you bothering me, Jesus, Son of the Most High God? Please, I beg you, don't torture me!" [29]For Jesus had already commanded the evil spirit to come out of him. This spirit had often taken control of the man. Even when he was shackled with chains, he simply broke them and rushed out into the wilderness, completely under the demon's power.

[30]"What is your name?" Jesus asked.

"Legion," he replied—for the man was filled with many demons. [31]The demons kept begging Jesus not to send them into the Bottomless Pit. [32]A large herd of pigs was feeding on the hillside nearby, and the demons pleaded with him to let them enter into the pigs. Jesus gave them permission. [33]So the demons came out of the man and entered the pigs, and the whole herd plunged down the steep hillside into the lake, where they drowned.

[34]When the herdsmen saw it, they fled to the nearby city and the surrounding countryside, spreading the news as they ran. [35]A crowd soon gathered around Jesus, for they wanted to see for themselves what had happened. And they saw the man who had been possessed by demons sitting quietly at Jesus' feet, clothed and sane. And the whole crowd was afraid. [36]Then those who had seen what happened told the others how the demon-possessed man had been healed. [37]And all the people in that region begged Jesus to go away and leave them alone, for a great wave of fear swept over them.

So Jesus returned to the boat and left, crossing back to the other side of the lake. [38]The man who had been demon possessed begged to go, too, but Jesus said, [39]"No, go back to

8:26 Some manuscripts read *Gadarenes;* other manuscripts read *Gergesenes.* See Matt 8:28; Mark 5:1.

8:16-17 Just as lamps expose everything else to the light, so God will someday bring our thoughts out into the open. Our thoughts and habits are already known to God (see Psalm 139:1-4); someday others will know them, too. As we are open, honest, and transparent in confessing our sins, God can work his plan of recovery and healing in us.

8:26-37 The life of this demon-possessed man was a complete disaster. Desperately in need of healing, he was a physical and emotional wreck, an embarrassing social outcast. But only Jesus had, and still has, the power to break satanic bondage and bring recovery. Yet the people of the community were more concerned about their loss of a herd of pigs than they were with the healing of this helpless and broken man. Regrettably, we sometimes experience opposition to recovery. No matter what obstacles we face, however, Jesus desires to deliver us from bondage and will help us progress toward recovery.

your family and tell them all the wonderful things God has done for you." So he went all through the city telling about the great thing Jesus had done for him.

Jesus Heals in Response to Faith
⁴⁰On the other side of the lake the crowds received Jesus with open arms because they had been waiting for him. ⁴¹And now a man named Jairus, a leader of the local synagogue, came and fell down at Jesus' feet, begging him to come home with him. ⁴²His only child was dying, a little girl twelve years old.

As Jesus went with him, he was surrounded by the crowds. ⁴³And there was a woman in the crowd who had had a hemorrhage for twelve years. She had spent everything she had on doctors* and still could find no cure. ⁴⁴She came up behind Jesus and touched the fringe of his robe. Immediately, the bleeding stopped.

⁴⁵"Who touched me?" Jesus asked.

Everyone denied it, and Peter said, "Master, this whole crowd is pressing up against you."

⁴⁶But Jesus told him, "No, someone deliberately touched me, for I felt healing power go out from me." ⁴⁷When the woman realized that Jesus knew, she began to tremble and fell to her knees before him. The whole crowd heard her explain why she had touched him and that she had been immediately healed. ⁴⁸"Daughter," he said to her, "your faith has made you well. Go in peace."

⁴⁹While he was still speaking to her, a messenger arrived from Jairus's home with the message, "Your little girl is dead. There's no use troubling the Teacher now."

⁵⁰But when Jesus heard what had happened, he said to Jairus, "Don't be afraid. Just trust me, and she will be all right."

⁵¹When they arrived at the house, Jesus wouldn't let anyone go in with him except Peter, James, John, and the little girl's father and mother. ⁵²The house was filled with people weeping and wailing, but he said, "Stop the weeping! She isn't dead; she is only asleep."

⁵³But the crowd laughed at him because they all knew she had died. ⁵⁴Then Jesus took her by the hand and said in a loud voice, "Get up, my child!" ⁵⁵And at that moment her life returned, and she immediately stood up! Then Jesus told them to give her something to eat. ⁵⁶Her parents were overwhelmed, but Jesus insisted that they not tell anyone what had happened.

CHAPTER 9
Jesus Sends Out the Twelve Apostles
One day Jesus called together his twelve apostles and gave them power and authority to cast out demons and to heal all diseases. ²Then he sent them out to tell everyone about the coming of the Kingdom of God and to heal the sick. ³"Don't even take along a walking stick," he instructed them, "nor a traveler's bag, nor food, nor money. Not even an extra coat. ⁴When you enter each village, be a guest in only one home. ⁵If the people of the village won't receive your message when you enter it, shake off its dust from your feet as you leave. It is a sign that you have abandoned that village to its fate."

⁶So they began their circuit of the villages, preaching the Good News and healing the sick.

Herod's Confusion
⁷When reports of Jesus' miracles reached Herod Antipas,* he was worried and puzzled because some were saying, "This is John the Baptist come back to life again." ⁸Others

---

8:43 Some manuscripts omit *She had spent everything she had on doctors.* 9:7 Greek *Herod the tetrarch.* He was a son of King Herod and was ruler over one of the four districts in Palestine.

8:43-44 Luke, with his background in medicine, noted that medical doctors had been able to do nothing for this woman's chronic illness. By faith, God's power did the impossible. As with many of Jesus' miracles, this incident shows that one who trusts in God can experience hope where previously there had been only despair. Recovery may seem beyond the scope of most doctors, but it is well within the miraclous works that God does for people who look to him in faith.

9:10-20 Once again Jesus demonstrated his desire to meet needs at various levels. In feeding the five thousand he supplied a basic need—food. Earlier Jesus had been dealing primarily with various problems that called for physical healing. Here Jesus met the intellectual and emotional needs of his disciples as well as the crowd's physical need. As God helps us toward recovery, he ultimately meets our spiritual need for a right relationship with God. Jesus the Messiah offers recovery that touches every area of our life. With his help we can take steps to live in harmony with God, the people around us, and the world.

were saying, "It is Elijah or some other ancient prophet risen from the dead."

⁹"I beheaded John," Herod said, "so who is this man about whom I hear such strange stories?" And he tried to see him.

Jesus Feeds Five Thousand

¹⁰When the apostles returned, they told Jesus everything they had done. Then he slipped quietly away with them toward the town of Bethsaida. ¹¹But the crowds found out where he was going, and they followed him. And he welcomed them, teaching them about the Kingdom of God and curing those who were ill. ¹²Late in the afternoon the twelve disciples came to him and said, "Send the crowds away to the nearby villages and farms, so they can find food and lodging for the night. There is nothing to eat here in this deserted place."

¹³But Jesus said, "You feed them."

"Impossible!" they protested. "We have only five loaves of bread and two fish. Or are you expecting us to go and buy enough food for this whole crowd?" ¹⁴For there were about five thousand men there.

"Just tell them to sit down on the ground in groups of about fifty each," Jesus replied. ¹⁵So the people all sat down. ¹⁶Jesus took the five loaves and two fish, looked up toward heaven, and asked God's blessing on the food. Breaking the loaves into pieces, he kept giving the bread and fish to the disciples to give to the people. ¹⁷They all ate as much as they wanted, and they picked up twelve baskets of leftovers!

Peter's Declaration about Jesus

¹⁸One day as Jesus was alone, praying, he came over to his disciples and asked them, "Who do people say I am?"

¹⁹"Well," they replied, "some say John the Baptist, some say Elijah, and others say you are one of the other ancient prophets risen from the dead."

²⁰Then he asked them, "Who do you say I am?"

Peter replied, "You are the Messiah sent from God!"

Jesus Predicts His Death

²¹Jesus warned them not to tell anyone about this. ²²"For I, the Son of Man, must suffer many terrible things," he said. "I will be rejected by the leaders, the leading priests, and the teachers of religious law. I will be killed, but three days later I will be raised from the dead."

STEP 2

Healing Faith

BIBLE READING: Luke 8:43-48

We came to believe that a Power greater than ourselves could restore us to sanity. Faith is a key to successfully working the second step. For some of us faith comes easily. For others, especially if we have experienced betrayal, it may be more difficult. Sometimes we must exhaust all of our own resources in trying to overcome our addictive "disease" before we will risk believing in a higher Power.

When Jesus lived on earth, he was so renowned for his healing power that crowds of sick people constantly pressed in on him. One day "there was a woman in the crowd who had had a hemorrhage for twelve years. She had spent everything she had on doctors and still could find no cure. She came up behind Jesus and touched the fringe of his robe. Immediately, the bleeding stopped." Jesus realized that someone had deliberately touched him, because he felt healing power go out from him. When the woman confessed that she was the one who had been healed, Jesus said, "Your faith has made you well. Go in peace" (Luke 8:43-44, 48).

In order to recover we must follow the example of this woman. We cannot afford to stand back, hoping for "cures," and avoid deliberate action because of our lack of faith. We may have lived with our condition for many years, spending our resources on promising "cures" without success. When we can come to believe in God, a power greater than ourself, and have the faith to take hold of our own recovery, we will find the healing power we have been looking for. *Turn to page 123, Luke 15.*

[23]Then he said to the crowd, "If any of you wants to be my follower, you must put aside your selfish ambition, shoulder your cross daily, and follow me. [24]If you try to keep your life for yourself, you will lose it. But if you give up your life for me, you will find true life. [25]And how do you benefit if you gain the whole world but lose or forfeit your own soul in the process? [26]If a person is ashamed of me and my message, I, the Son of Man, will be ashamed of that person when I return in my glory and in the glory of the Father and the holy angels. [27]And I assure you that some of you standing here right now will not die before you see the Kingdom of God."

The Transfiguration

[28]About eight days later Jesus took Peter, James, and John to a mountain to pray. [29]And as he was praying, the appearance of his face changed, and his clothing became dazzling white. [30]Then two men, Moses and Elijah, appeared and began talking with Jesus. [31]They were glorious to see. And they were speaking of how he was about to fulfill God's plan by dying in Jerusalem.

[32]Peter and the others were very drowsy and had fallen asleep. Now they woke up and saw Jesus' glory and the two men standing with him. [33]As Moses and Elijah were starting to leave, Peter, not even knowing what he was saying, blurted out, "Master, this is wonderful! We will make three shrines*—one for you, one for Moses, and one for Elijah." [34]But even as he was saying this, a cloud came over them; and terror gripped them as it covered them.

[35]Then a voice from the cloud said, "This is my Son, my Chosen One.* Listen to him." [36]When the voice died away, Jesus was there alone. They didn't tell anyone what they had seen until long after this happened.

Jesus Heals a Demon-Possessed Boy

[37]The next day, after they had come down the mountain, a huge crowd met Jesus. [38]A man in the crowd called out to him, "Teacher, look at my boy, who is my only son. [39]An evil spirit keeps seizing him, making him scream. It throws him into convulsions so that he foams at the mouth. It is always hitting and injuring him. It hardly ever leaves him alone. [40]I begged your disciples to cast the spirit out, but they couldn't do it."

[41]"You stubborn, faithless people," Jesus said, "how long must I be with you and put up with you? Bring him here." [42]As the boy came forward, the demon knocked him to the ground and threw him into a violent convulsion. But Jesus rebuked the evil spirit and healed the boy. Then he gave him back to his father. [43]Awe gripped the people as they saw this display of God's power.

Jesus Again Predicts His Death

While everyone was marveling over all the wonderful things he was doing, Jesus said to his disciples, [44]"Listen to me and remember what I say. The Son of Man is going to be betrayed." [45]But they didn't know what he meant. Its significance was hidden from them, so they could not understand it, and they were afraid to ask him about it.

The Greatest in the Kingdom

[46]Then there was an argument among them as to which of them would be the greatest. [47]But Jesus knew their thoughts, so he brought a little child to his side. [48]Then he said to them, "Anyone who welcomes a little child like this on my behalf welcomes me, and anyone who welcomes me welcomes my Father who sent me. Whoever is the least among you is the greatest."

9:33 Or *shelters;* Greek reads *tabernacles.* **9:35** Some manuscripts read *This is my beloved Son.*

9:23-27 In this confrontation of wills, Jesus shows the critical importance of submitting our will to God's will. Jesus has a prior claim on our life that supersedes our personal conveniences or desires. Clinging to selfish ambition and worldly desires will destroy us. Paradoxically, "giving up one's life" in a relationship with God through Jesus is the only sure way of finding ultimate meaning and purpose. This teaching opposes our natural inclinations and can only be accepted by faith. But if we submit our will to God's will, we will begin to experience the meaningful life that God wants us to have.

9:28-36 While initial impressions mean a lot and many judge others based on appearances, things often are not as they seem to be. Peter relied too much on first impressions and outward appearances, so he jumped to some foolish conclusions. To Peter, these two great Old Testament prophets appeared to be on a par with Jesus. Yet God's voice and later events confirmed that Jesus was God's Son. If we are to progress in recovery, we need to stop judging on outward appearances, explore spiritual realities, and always listen to God.

Using the Name of Jesus

⁴⁹John said to Jesus, "Master, we saw someone using your name to cast out demons. We tried to stop him because he isn't in our group."

⁵⁰But Jesus said, "Don't stop him! Anyone who is not against you is for you."

Opposition from Samaritans

⁵¹As the time drew near for his return to heaven, Jesus resolutely set out for Jerusalem. ⁵²He sent messengers ahead to a Samaritan village to prepare for his arrival. ⁵³But they were turned away. The people of the village refused to have anything to do with Jesus because he had resolved to go to Jerusalem. ⁵⁴When James and John heard about it, they said to Jesus, "Lord, should we order down fire from heaven to burn them up*?" ⁵⁵But Jesus turned and rebuked them.* ⁵⁶So they went on to another village.

The Cost of Following Jesus

⁵⁷As they were walking along someone said to Jesus, "I will follow you no matter where you go."

⁵⁸But Jesus replied, "Foxes have dens to live in, and birds have nests, but I, the Son of Man, have no home of my own, not even a place to lay my head."

⁵⁹He said to another person, "Come, be my disciple."

The man agreed, but he said, "Lord, first let me return home and bury my father."

⁶⁰Jesus replied, "Let those who are spiritually dead care for their own dead.* Your duty is to go and preach the coming of the Kingdom of God."

⁶¹Another said, "Yes, Lord, I will follow you, but first let me say good-bye to my family."

⁶²But Jesus told him, "Anyone who puts a hand to the plow and then looks back is not fit for the Kingdom of God."

CHAPTER 10

Jesus Sends Out His Disciples

The Lord now chose seventy-two* other disciples and sent them on ahead in pairs to all the towns and villages he planned to visit. ²These were his instructions to them: "The harvest is so great, but the workers are so few. Pray to the Lord who is in charge of the harvest, and ask him to send out more workers for his fields. ³Go now, and remember that I am sending you out as lambs among wolves. ⁴Don't take along any money, or a traveler's bag, or even an extra pair of sandals. And don't stop to greet anyone on the road.

⁵"Whenever you enter a home, give it your blessing. ⁶If those who live there are worthy, the blessing will stand; if they are not, the blessing will return to you. ⁷When you enter a town, don't move around from home to home. Stay in one place, eating and drinking what they provide you. Don't hesitate to accept hospitality, because those who work deserve their pay.

⁸"If a town welcomes you, eat whatever is set before you ⁹and heal the sick. As you heal them, say, 'The Kingdom of God is near you now.' ¹⁰But if a town refuses to welcome you, go out into its streets and say, ¹¹'We wipe the dust of your town from our feet as a public announcement of your doom. And don't forget the Kingdom of God is near!' ¹²The truth is, even wicked Sodom will be better off than such a town on the judgment day.

¹³"What horrors await you, Korazin and Bethsaida! For if the miracles I did in you had been done in wicked Tyre and Sidon, their people would have sat in deep repentance long ago, clothed in sackcloth and throwing ashes on their heads to show their remorse. ¹⁴Yes, Tyre and Sidon will be better off on the judgment day than you. ¹⁵And you people of Capernaum, will you be exalted to heaven? No, you will be brought down to the place of the dead.*"

¹⁶Then he said to the disciples, "Anyone who accepts your message is also accepting me. And anyone who rejects you is rejecting me. And anyone who rejects me is rejecting God who sent me."

¹⁷When the seventy-two disciples returned, they joyfully reported to him, "Lord, even the demons obey us when we use your name!"

9:54 Some manuscripts add *as Elijah did.* **9:55** Some manuscripts add *And he said, "You don't realize what your hearts are like.* ⁵⁶*For the Son of Man has not come to destroy men's lives, but to save them."* **9:60** Greek *Let the dead bury their own dead.* **10:1** Some manuscripts read *70;* also in 10:17. **10:15** Greek *to Hades.*

10:8-16 The disciples were given the ambitious task and privilege of sharing the message of the Messiah throughout the land. Their ministry would not always be well received. One who follows Jesus toward recovery will encounter similar setbacks, such as rejection and ridicule. As we share our story of deliverance with others, we may find we are not always welcome in our old stomping grounds. When we experience rejection, we should be prepared to make a timely exit, go in peace, and find a more receptive audience.

¹⁸"Yes," he told them, "I saw Satan falling from heaven as a flash of lightning! ¹⁹And I have given you authority over all the power of the enemy, and you can walk among snakes and scorpions and crush them. Nothing will injure you. ²⁰But don't rejoice just because evil spirits obey you; rejoice because your names are registered as citizens of heaven."

Jesus' Prayer of Thanksgiving

²¹Then Jesus was filled with the joy of the Holy Spirit and said, "O Father, Lord of heaven and earth, thank you for hiding the truth from those who think themselves so wise and clever, and for revealing it to the childlike. Yes, Father, it pleased you to do it this way.

²²"My Father has given me authority over everything. No one really knows the Son except the Father, and no one really knows the Father except the Son and those to whom the Son chooses to reveal him."

²³Then when they were alone, he turned to the disciples and said, "How privileged you are to see what you have seen. ²⁴I tell you, many prophets and kings have longed to see and hear what you have seen and heard, but they could not."

The Most Important Commandment

²⁵One day an expert in religious law stood up to test Jesus by asking him this question: "Teacher, what must I do to receive eternal life?"

²⁶Jesus replied, "What does the law of Moses say? How do you read it?"

²⁷The man answered, "'You must love the Lord your God with all your heart, all your soul, all your strength, and all your mind.' And, 'Love your neighbor as yourself.'"*

²⁸"Right!" Jesus told him. "Do this and you will live!"

²⁹The man wanted to justify his actions, so he asked Jesus, "And who is my neighbor?"

Story of the Good Samaritan

³⁰Jesus replied with an illustration: "A Jewish man was traveling on a trip from Jerusalem to Jericho, and he was attacked by bandits. They stripped him of his clothes and money, beat him up, and left him half dead beside the road.

³¹"By chance a Jewish priest came along; but when he saw the man lying there, he crossed to the other side of the road and passed him by. ³²A Temple assistant* walked over and looked at him lying there, but he also passed by on the other side.

³³"Then a despised Samaritan came along, and when he saw the man, he felt deep pity. ³⁴Kneeling beside him, the Samaritan soothed his wounds with medicine and bandaged them. Then he put the man on his own donkey and took him to an inn, where he took care of him. ³⁵The next day he handed the innkeeper two pieces of silver* and told him to take care of the man. 'If his bill runs higher than that,' he said, 'I'll pay the difference the next time I am here.'

10:27 Deut 6:5; Lev 19:18. **10:32** Greek *A Levite.* **10:35** Greek *2 denarii.* A denarius was the equivalent of a full day's wage.

10:25-37 The story of the Good Samaritan teaches that true love for God expresses itself in caring for others' needs. In Jesus' day the Jews and Samaritans hated each other. So when the despised Samaritan proved to be the good neighbor to the wounded Jew, Jesus was showing that concern for others has no boundaries. When God has brought us healing and recovery, we become an effective instrument in reaching others with similar needs. Sharing the good news of our deliverance is a responsibility we receive from God. As we share, we will experience great joy as others gain hope for recovery. Our own faith and recovery are also strengthened as we remember what God has done on our behalf.

10:38-42 There is a difference between being spiritually committed to recovery and being preoccupied with recovery. This story about Mary and Martha illustrates the difference. Martha was so busy "doing for others" that she had no time or energy left for simply being with Jesus. In all her doing, Martha even became irritated at Mary for not being equally busy. Mary, on the other hand, took time out to listen to Jesus. Recovery must be a recovery from the heart, not just a recovery where we act compulsively to look the part.

11:2 The opening of this prayer, "Father," describes the attitude and relationship with which we are to approach God. Luke used an intimate word that a child might use in speaking to an earthly father. The equivalent in our everyday speech would be addressing God as "Daddy." Only through this kind of intimate prayer relationship with our heavenly Father can we find strength to tackle the big challenges of lifelong recovery.

MARY & MARTHA

As with all siblings, Mary and Martha each had unique gifts and personality. Martha was industrious and concerned about detail, while Mary, the contemplative one, treasured sitting at his feet and being a student of Jesus.

We are given a glimpse into the heart of Mary when we see her anoint Jesus with costly perfume shortly before his death. Mary's extravagant act of love and devotion was hypocritically criticized by Judas. In the process of recovery it may be necessary to take steps that others will criticize, but we must remember that the bottom line is whether or not God is pleased with our actions.

When their brother Lazarus died, the events that followed allowed both sisters to grow in their understanding of Jesus. Jesus knew that if he delayed coming to them, he wouldn't arrive until after Lazarus's death. If he had come before Lazarus died, he certainly could have healed him; but by coming later, Jesus was able to do something even more glorious—raise him from the dead!

For Mary and Martha, the delay was painful. The ultimate outcome, however, was a deeper faith and a fuller experience of the joy that comes from trusting God with the details of life. As we go through difficult times, we may not always understand what God is doing, but we will grow in strength and faith as we patiently endure. There is always hope when the God who can raise the dead is on our side.

STRENGTHS AND ACCOMPLISHMENTS:
- Both were devoted followers of Jesus.
- Martha was hardworking, efficient, and conscientious.
- Mary had a heart that was devoted to God.

WEAKNESSES AND MISTAKES:
- Martha was so worried about details that she missed spending time with Jesus.

LESSONS FROM THEIR LIVES:
- We may get so busy doing things in the recovery process—even good things—that we forget to spend time with Jesus.
- Jesus valued the contribution of these women among his followers.
- It is important to see each of our children as a unique individual.

KEY VERSES:
"Martha. . . . came to Jesus and said, 'Lord, doesn't it seem unfair to you that my sister just sits here while I do all the work? Tell her to come and help me.' But the Lord said to her, 'My dear Martha, you are so upset over all these details! There is really only one thing worth being concerned about. Mary has discovered it—and I won't take it away from her'" (Luke 10:40-42).

The story of Mary and Martha is found in Matthew 26:6-13; Luke 10:38-42; and John 11:1-45; 12:1-8.

---

³⁶"Now which of these three would you say was a neighbor to the man who was attacked by bandits?" Jesus asked.

³⁷The man replied, "The one who showed him mercy."

Then Jesus said, "Yes, now go and do the same."

Jesus Visits Martha and Mary
³⁸As Jesus and the disciples continued on their way to Jerusalem, they came to a village where a woman named Martha welcomed them into her home. ³⁹Her sister, Mary, sat at the Lord's feet, listening to what he taught. ⁴⁰But Martha was worrying over the big dinner she was preparing. She came to Jesus and said, "Lord, doesn't it seem unfair to you that my sister just sits here while I do all the work? Tell her to come and help me."

⁴¹But the Lord said to her, "My dear Martha, you are so upset over all these details! ⁴²There is really only one thing worth being concerned about. Mary has discovered it— and I won't take it away from her."

CHAPTER 11
Teaching about Prayer
Once when Jesus had been out praying, one of his disciples came to him as he finished and said, "Lord, teach us to pray, just as John taught his disciples."

²He said, "This is how you should pray:

"Father, may your name be honored.
May your Kingdom come soon.
³Give us our food day by day.

⁴And forgive us our sins—
just as we forgive those who have
sinned against us.
And don't let us yield to temptation.*"

⁵Then, teaching them more about prayer, he used this illustration: "Suppose you went to a friend's house at midnight, wanting to borrow three loaves of bread. You would say to him, ⁶'A friend of mine has just arrived for a visit, and I have nothing for him to eat.' ⁷He would call out from his bedroom, 'Don't bother me. The door is locked for the night, and we are all in bed. I can't help you this time.' ⁸But I tell you this—though he won't do it as a friend, if you keep knocking long enough, he will get up and give you what you want so his reputation won't be damaged.*

⁹"And so I tell you, keep on asking, and you will be given what you ask for. Keep on looking, and you will find. Keep on knocking, and the door will be opened. ¹⁰For everyone who asks, receives. Everyone who seeks, finds. And the door is opened to everyone who knocks.

¹¹"You fathers—if your children ask* for a fish, do you give them a snake instead? ¹²Or if they ask for an egg, do you give them a scorpion? Of course not! ¹³If you sinful people know how to give good gifts to your children, how much more will your heavenly Father give the Holy Spirit to those who ask him."

Jesus and the Prince of Demons

¹⁴One day Jesus cast a demon out of a man who couldn't speak, and the man's voice returned to him. The crowd was amazed, ¹⁵but some said, "No wonder he can cast out demons. He gets his power from Satan,* the prince of demons!" ¹⁶Trying to test Jesus, others asked for a miraculous sign from heaven to see if he was from God.

¹⁷He knew their thoughts, so he said, "Any kingdom at war with itself is doomed. A divided home is also doomed. ¹⁸You say I am empowered by the prince of demons.* But if Satan is fighting against himself by empowering me to cast out his demons, how can his kingdom survive? ¹⁹And if I am empowered by the prince of demons, what about your own followers? They cast out demons, too, so they will judge you for what you have said. ²⁰But if I am casting out demons by the power of God, then the Kingdom of God has arrived among you. ²¹For when Satan,* who is completely armed, guards his palace, it is safe—²²until someone who is stronger attacks and overpowers him, strips him of his weapons, and carries off his belongings.

²³"Anyone who isn't helping me opposes me, and anyone who isn't working with me is actually working against me.

²⁴"When an evil spirit leaves a person, it goes into the desert, searching for rest. But when it finds none, it says, 'I will return to the person I came from.' ²⁵So it returns and finds that its former home is all swept and clean. ²⁶Then the spirit finds seven other spirits more evil than itself, and they all enter the person and live there. And so that person is worse off than before."

²⁷As he was speaking, a woman in the crowd called out, "God bless your mother—the womb from which you came, and the breasts that nursed you!"

²⁸He replied, "But even more blessed are all who hear the word of God and put it into practice."

The Sign of Jonah

²⁹As the crowd pressed in on Jesus, he said, "These are evil times, and this evil genera-

---

11:2-4 Some manuscripts add additional portions of the Lord's Prayer as it reads in Matt 6:9-13. **11:8** Greek *in order to avoid shame,* or *because of [your] persistence.* **11:11** Some manuscripts add *for bread, do you give them a stone? Or if they ask.* **11:15** Greek *Beelzeboul.* **11:18** Greek *by Beelzeboul;* also in 11:19. **11:21** Greek *the strong one.*

11:4 God's forgiveness of us and our forgiveness of others are inextricably linked together. Jesus said that if we refuse to forgive others, God will not forgive our sins (Matthew 6:14-15). To fully experience God's forgiveness, we must be willing to forgive others. Conversely, unforgiving spirits hinder our ability to enjoy the freedom found in God's forgiveness. To harbor anger and an unforgiving spirit when God has forgiven us so much is hypocritical and a roadblock to recovery.

11:4 The honesty of this prayer recognizes our own weakness and vulnerability to temptation. The prayer of faith asks God to help us to not yield to temptation. As a model prayer, this principle is especially important when we seek victory over areas of our life where sin has gained a stronghold. The recovery process involves not only recognizing our own sins and character defects but also avoiding situations that might lead to temptation and a fall.

tion keeps asking me to show them a miraculous sign. But the only sign I will give them is the sign of the prophet Jonah. ³⁰What happened to him was a sign to the people of Nineveh that God had sent him. What happens to me will be a sign that God has sent me, the Son of Man, to these people.

³¹"The queen of Sheba* will rise up against this generation on judgment day and condemn it, because she came from a distant land to hear the wisdom of Solomon. And now someone greater than Solomon is here—and you refuse to listen to him. ³²The people of Nineveh, too, will rise up against this generation on judgment day and condemn it, because they repented at the preaching of Jonah. And now someone greater than Jonah is here—and you refuse to repent.

Receiving the Light

³³"No one lights a lamp and then hides it or puts it under a basket. Instead, it is put on a lampstand to give light to all who enter the room. ³⁴Your eye is a lamp for your body. A pure eye lets sunshine into your soul. But an evil eye shuts out the light and plunges you into darkness. ³⁵Make sure that the light you think you have is not really darkness. ³⁶If you are filled with light, with no dark corners, then your whole life will be radiant, as though a floodlight is shining on you."

Jesus Criticizes the Religious Leaders

³⁷As Jesus was speaking, one of the Pharisees invited him home for a meal. So he went in and took his place at the table. ³⁸His host was amazed to see that he sat down to eat without first performing the ceremonial washing required by Jewish custom. ³⁹Then the Lord said to him, "You Pharisees are so careful to clean the outside of the cup and the dish, but inside you are still filthy—full of greed and wickedness! ⁴⁰Fools! Didn't God make the inside as well as the outside? ⁴¹So give to the needy what you greedily possess, and you will be clean all over.

⁴²"But how terrible it will be for you Pharisees! For you are careful to tithe even the tiniest part of your income,* but you completely forget about justice and the love of God. You should tithe, yes, but you should not leave undone the more important things.

⁴³"How terrible it will be for you Pharisees! For how you love the seats of honor in the

11:31 Greek *the queen of the south.* **11:42** Greek *to tithe the mint and the rue and every herb.*

STEP 7

Pride Born of Hurt

BIBLE READING: Luke 11:5-13
We humbly asked him to remove our shortcomings.

Our pride can keep us from asking for what we need. We may have grown up in a family where we were consistently ignored or disappointed. Perhaps our needs were seldom met. Some of us may have reacted by becoming self-sufficient. We determined never to ask anyone for help. In fact, we were going to strive to never need anyone's help ever again!

It is this type of pride, born of hurt, that will hold us back from asking God to help us deal with our shortcomings. Jesus said, "And so I tell you, keep on asking, and you will be given what you ask for. Keep on looking, and you will find. Keep on knocking, and the door will be opened. For everyone who asks, receives. Everyone who seeks, finds. And the door is opened to everyone who knocks" (Luke 11:9-10). "You parents—if your children ask for a loaf of bread, do you give them a stone instead? Or if they ask for a fish, do you give them a snake? Of course not! If you sinful people know how to give good gifts to your children, how much more will your heavenly Father give good gifts to those who ask him" (Matthew 7:9-11).

We must come to the place of giving up our prideful self-sufficiency; we must be willing to ask for help. And we can't ask for help just once and be done with it. We must be persistent and ask repeatedly as the needs arise. When we practice Step Seven in this way, we can be assured that our loving heavenly Father will respond by giving us good gifts and removing our shortcomings. *Turn to page 127, Luke 18.*

synagogues and the respectful greetings from everyone as you walk through the markets! ⁴⁴Yes, how terrible it will be for you. For you are like hidden graves in a field. People walk over them without knowing the corruption they are stepping on."

⁴⁵"Teacher," said an expert in religious law, "you have insulted us, too, in what you just said."

⁴⁶"Yes," said Jesus, "how terrible it will be for you experts in religious law! For you crush people beneath impossible religious demands, and you never lift a finger to help ease the burden. ⁴⁷How terrible it will be for you! For you build tombs for the very prophets your ancestors killed long ago. ⁴⁸Murderers! You agree with your ancestors that what they did was right. You would have done the same yourselves. ⁴⁹This is what God in his wisdom said about you:* 'I will send prophets and apostles to them, and they will kill some and persecute the others.'

⁵⁰"And you of this generation will be held responsible for the murder of all God's prophets from the creation of the world— ⁵¹from the murder of Abel to the murder of Zechariah, who was killed between the altar and the sanctuary. Yes, it will surely be charged against you.

⁵²"How terrible it will be for you experts in religious law! For you hide the key to knowledge from the people. You don't enter the Kingdom yourselves, and you prevent others from entering."

⁵³As Jesus finished speaking, the Pharisees and teachers of religious law were furious. From that time on they grilled him with many hostile questions, ⁵⁴trying to trap him into saying something they could use against him.

11:49 Greek *Therefore, the wisdom of God said.*

CHAPTER 12

A Warning against Hypocrisy

Meanwhile, the crowds grew until thousands were milling about and crushing each other. Jesus turned first to his disciples and warned them, "Beware of the yeast of the Pharisees— beware of their hypocrisy. ²The time is coming when everything will be revealed; all that is secret will be made public. ³Whatever you have said in the dark will be heard in the light, and what you have whispered behind closed doors will be shouted from the housetops for all to hear!

⁴"Dear friends, don't be afraid of those who want to kill you. They can only kill the body; they cannot do any more to you. ⁵But I'll tell you whom to fear. Fear God, who has the power to kill people and then throw them into hell.

⁶"What is the price of five sparrows? A couple of pennies? Yet God does not forget a single one of them. ⁷And the very hairs on your head are all numbered. So don't be afraid; you are more valuable to him than a whole flock of sparrows.

⁸"And I assure you of this: If anyone acknowledges me publicly here on earth, I, the Son of Man, will openly acknowledge that person in the presence of God's angels. ⁹But if anyone denies me here on earth, I will deny that person before God's angels. ¹⁰Yet those who speak against the Son of Man may be forgiven, but anyone who speaks blasphemies against the Holy Spirit will never be forgiven.

¹¹"And when you are brought to trial in the synagogues and before rulers and authorities, don't worry about what to say in your defense, ¹²for the Holy Spirit will teach you what needs to be said even as you are standing there."

12:6-7 If God cares for even the smallest sparrow, then he cares even more for us. If he cares enough to count the hairs on our head, then he cares even more about our thoughts and feelings. Dwelling on this reality can help us when we feel depressed or lonely. The most powerful and important person in the universe cares deeply and personally about us.

12:13-21 Jesus continually emphasized the dangers of materialism. Materialism was not just a problem for the rich people Jesus encountered or for the characters in his stories. The tendency to desire more of everything is endemic to human nature. Jesus was concerned not so much with how much we possess but with how much our wealth possesses us. True freedom and contentment cannot be found in the things we own; recovery can never be bought. These gifts are freely given to us as we humbly turn to God for his gracious help.

12:22-31 True freedom and contentment are found by depending exclusively on God and obeying him. Jesus pointed out the worthlessness of spending time worrying about things God has already taken care of. Since neither animals nor plants worry about food and clothing, neither should we. As God takes care of them while they live from day to day, so also will God take care of us if we make his Kingdom our primary concern. Trusting God's supreme providential care enables people in recovery to live one day at a time.

READ LUKE 11:37-44

GOD grant me the serenity to accept the things I cannot change the courage to change the things I can and the wisdom to know the difference AMEN

We often protect ourself by focusing our attention on other people and their behaviors. That way we don't have to examine our own.

We often stay in relationships in which we seem powerless, for in doing so, we maintain built-in excuses for failure. We may also spend time looking down on others who are "worse" than we are, thus avoiding an examination of our own corruption. But in doing these things, we fail to take responsibility for our own life through honest self-examination.

Jesus confronted the Pharisees, saying, "You Pharisees are so careful to clean the outside of the cup and the dish, but inside you are still filthy—full of greed and wickedness!" (Luke 11:39). Can you imagine washing only the outside of a cup that is moldy on the inside and then drinking from it? Of course not! But we do this in a spiritual sense because it is hard to deal with the "dirt" inside our heart.

Changing those things in our life that we can change involves taking steps to clean the inside of our "cup," our heart. We must begin by turning our eyes away from everyone around us, including those we blame for our condition in life or those we condemn to make our wrongs seem less in comparison. Then we can get back to looking within ourself. We all contain some residue of wrongdoing. When we admit this to God, to ourself, and to others, we will experience the cleansing of humility and forgiveness. Then we will have a life that can bring refreshment to others. *Turn to page 271, 1 Corinthians 10.*

Story of the Rich Fool

¹³Then someone called from the crowd, "Teacher, please tell my brother to divide our father's estate with me."

¹⁴Jesus replied, "Friend, who made me a judge over you to decide such things as that?" ¹⁵Then he said, "Beware! Don't be greedy for what you don't have. Real life is not measured by how much we own."

¹⁶And he gave an illustration: "A rich man had a fertile farm that produced fine crops. ¹⁷In fact, his barns were full to overflowing. ¹⁸So he said, 'I know! I'll tear down my barns and build bigger ones. Then I'll have room enough to store everything. ¹⁹And I'll sit back and say to myself, My friend, you have enough stored away for years to come. Now take it easy! Eat, drink, and be merry!'

²⁰"But God said to him, 'You fool! You will die this very night. Then who will get it all?'

²¹"Yes, a person is a fool to store up earthly wealth but not have a rich relationship with God."

Teaching about Money and Possessions

²²Then turning to his disciples, Jesus said, "So I tell you, don't worry about everyday life—whether you have enough food to eat or clothes to wear. ²³For life consists of far more than food and clothing. ²⁴Look at the ravens. They don't need to plant or harvest or put food in barns because God feeds them. And you are far more valuable to him than any birds! ²⁵Can all your worries add a single moment to your life? Of course not! ²⁶And if worry can't do little things like that, what's the use of worrying over bigger things?

²⁷"Look at the lilies and how they grow. They don't work or make their clothing, yet

Solomon in all his glory was not dressed as beautifully as they are. 28And if God cares so wonderfully for flowers that are here today and gone tomorrow, won't he more surely care for you? You have so little faith! 29And don't worry about food—what to eat and drink. Don't worry whether God will provide it for you. 30These things dominate the thoughts of most people, but your Father already knows your needs. 31He will give you all you need from day to day if you make the Kingdom of God your primary concern.

32"So don't be afraid, little flock. For it gives your Father great happiness to give you the Kingdom.

33"Sell what you have and give to those in need. This will store up treasure for you in heaven! And the purses of heaven have no holes in them. Your treasure will be safe—no thief can steal it and no moth can destroy it. 34Wherever your treasure is, there your heart and thoughts will also be.

Be Ready for the Lord's Coming

35"Be dressed for service and well prepared, 36as though you were waiting for your master to return from the wedding feast. Then you will be ready to open the door and let him in the moment he arrives and knocks. 37There will be special favor for those who are ready and waiting for his return. I tell you, he himself will seat them, put on an apron, and serve them as they sit and eat! 38He may come in the middle of the night or just before dawn.* But whenever he comes, there will be special favor for his servants who are ready!

39"Know this: A homeowner who knew exactly when a burglar was coming would not permit the house to be broken into. 40You must be ready all the time, for the Son of Man will come when least expected."

41Peter asked, "Lord, is this illustration just for us or for everyone?"

42And the Lord replied, "I'm talking to any faithful, sensible servant to whom the master gives the responsibility of managing his household and feeding his family. 43If the master returns and finds that the servant has done a good job, there will be a reward. 44I assure you, the master will put that servant in charge of all he owns. 45But if the servant thinks, 'My master won't be back for a while,' and begins oppressing the other servants, partying, and getting drunk—46well, the master will return unannounced and unexpected. He will tear the servant apart and banish him with the unfaithful. 47The servant will be severely punished, for though he knew his duty, he refused to do it.

48"But people who are not aware that they are doing wrong will be punished only lightly. Much is required from those to whom much is given, and much more is required from those to whom much more is given.

Jesus Causes Division

49"I have come to bring fire to the earth, and I wish that my task were already completed! 50There is a terrible baptism ahead of me, and I am under a heavy burden until it is accomplished. 51Do you think I have come to bring peace to the earth? No, I have come to bring strife and division! 52From now on families will be split apart, three in favor of me, and two against—or the other way around. 53There will be a division between father and son, mother and daughter, mother-in-law and daughter-in-law."

54Then Jesus turned to the crowd and said, "When you see clouds beginning to form in the west, you say, 'Here comes a shower.' And you are right. 55When the south wind blows, you say, 'Today will be a scorcher.' And it is. 56You hypocrites! You know how to interpret the appearance of the earth and the sky, but you can't interpret these present times.

57"Why can't you decide for yourselves what is right? 58If you are on the way to court and you meet your accuser, try to settle the matter before it reaches the judge, or you may be sentenced and handed over to an officer and thrown in jail. 59And if that happens, you won't be free again until you have paid the last penny."

12:38 Greek *in the second or third watch.*

12:32-34 The heart represents all that motivates us—our thoughts, ideals, inclinations, priorities, convictions, worries, and fears. If we want genuine recovery in problem areas of our life, we must first release our heartfelt attachments to the dependency or compulsion we are struggling with. The things we value most and spend time and money pursuing—that's where our deep attachments and personal identity can be found. Our checkbook and date book are barometers of our heart condition and our progress in recovery.

CHAPTER 13
A Call to Repentance
About this time Jesus was informed that Pilate had murdered some people from Galilee as they were sacrificing at the Temple in Jerusalem. ²"Do you think those Galileans were worse sinners than other people from Galilee?" he asked. "Is that why they suffered? ³Not at all! And you will also perish unless you turn from your evil ways and turn to God. ⁴And what about the eighteen men who died when the Tower of Siloam fell on them? Were they the worst sinners in Jerusalem? ⁵No, and I tell you again that unless you repent, you will also perish."

Illustration of the Barren Fig Tree
⁶Then Jesus used this illustration: "A man planted a fig tree in his garden and came again and again to see if there was any fruit on it, but he was always disappointed. ⁷Finally, he said to his gardener, 'I've waited three years, and there hasn't been a single fig! Cut it down. It's taking up space we can use for something else.'

⁸"The gardener answered, 'Give it one more chance. Leave it another year, and I'll give it special attention and plenty of fertilizer. ⁹If we get figs next year, fine. If not, you can cut it down.'"

Jesus Heals on the Sabbath
¹⁰One Sabbath day as Jesus was teaching in a synagogue, ¹¹he saw a woman who had been crippled by an evil spirit. She had been bent double for eighteen years and was unable to stand up straight. ¹²When Jesus saw her, he called her over and said, "Woman, you are healed of your sickness!" ¹³Then he touched her, and instantly she could stand straight. How she praised and thanked God!

¹⁴But the leader in charge of the synagogue was indignant that Jesus had healed her on the Sabbath day. "There are six days of the week for working," he said to the crowd. "Come on those days to be healed, not on the Sabbath."

¹⁵But the Lord replied, "You hypocrite! You work on the Sabbath day! Don't you untie your ox or your donkey from their stalls on the Sabbath and lead them out for water? ¹⁶Wasn't it necessary for me, even on the Sabbath day, to free this dear woman* from the bondage in which Satan has held her for eighteen years?" ¹⁷This shamed his enemies. And all the people rejoiced at the wonderful things he did.

Illustration of the Mustard Seed
¹⁸Then Jesus said, "What is the Kingdom of God like? How can I illustrate it? ¹⁹It is like a tiny mustard seed planted in a garden; it grows and becomes a tree, and the birds come and find shelter among its branches."

Illustration of the Yeast
²⁰He also asked, "What else is the Kingdom of God like? ²¹It is like yeast used by a woman making bread. Even though she used a large amount* of flour, the yeast permeated every part of the dough."

The Narrow Door
²²Jesus went through the towns and villages, teaching as he went, always pressing on toward Jerusalem. ²³Someone asked him, "Lord, will only a few be saved?"

He replied, ²⁴"The door to heaven is narrow. Work hard to get in, because many will try to enter, ²⁵but when the head of the house has locked the door, it will be too late. Then you will stand outside knocking and pleading, 'Lord, open the door for us!' But he will reply, 'I do not know you.' ²⁶You will say, 'But we ate and drank with you, and you taught in our streets.' ²⁷And he will reply, 'I tell you, I don't know you. Go away, all you who do evil.'

13:16 Greek *this woman, a daughter of Abraham.* 13:21 Greek *3 measures.*

13:10-13 Jesus cared for social outcasts, emotional and physical cripples, and those in spiritual bondage. This handicapped woman was hurting in all three respects. In eighteen years she had probably tried everything to be healed, but now was resigned to her painful limitations. The power of an evil spirit had crippled her. But the power of Jesus Christ knows no limitations. Jesus healed this woman who had given up all hope for a new life. He can do the same for us by bringing us healing and deliverance.

13:22-30 Appearances can be deceiving. But God is not fooled—he knows the real intent of our heart. We can go to church, teach Sunday school, or sing in the choir and, like the religious hypocrites of Jesus' day, still lack a real relationship with God. Being sincere, not merely religious, is crucial to recovery. God will judge religious hypocrisy, and he will honor honest attempts to obey him and know him better—no matter how many times we fail.

28"And there will be great weeping and gnashing of teeth, for you will see Abraham, Isaac, Jacob, and all the prophets within the Kingdom of God, but you will be thrown out. 29Then people will come from all over the world to take their places in the Kingdom of God. 30And note this: Some who are despised now will be greatly honored then; and some who are greatly honored now will be despised then.*"

Jesus Grieves over Jerusalem

31A few minutes later some Pharisees said to him, "Get out of here if you want to live, because Herod Antipas wants to kill you!"

32Jesus replied, "Go tell that fox that I will keep on casting out demons and doing miracles of healing today and tomorrow; and the third day I will accomplish my purpose. 33Yes, today, tomorrow, and the next day I must proceed on my way. For it wouldn't do for a prophet of God to be killed except in Jerusalem!

34"O Jerusalem, Jerusalem, the city that kills the prophets and stones God's messengers! How often I have wanted to gather your children together as a hen protects her chicks beneath her wings, but you wouldn't let me. 35And now look, your house is left to you empty. And you will never see me again until you say, 'Bless the one who comes in the name of the Lord!'*"

CHAPTER 14
Jesus Heals on the Sabbath

One Sabbath day Jesus was in the home of a leader of the Pharisees. The people were watching him closely, 2because there was a man there whose arms and legs were swollen.* 3Jesus asked the Pharisees and experts in religious law, "Well, is it permitted in the law to heal people on the Sabbath day, or not?" 4When they refused to answer, Jesus touched the sick man and healed him and sent him away. 5Then he turned to them and asked, "Which of you doesn't work on the Sabbath? If your son* or your cow falls into a pit, don't you proceed at once to get him out?" 6Again they had no answer.

Jesus Teaches about Humility

7When Jesus noticed that all who had come to the dinner were trying to sit near the head of the table, he gave them this advice: 8"If you are invited to a wedding feast, don't always head for the best seat. What if someone more respected than you has also been invited? 9The host will say, 'Let this person sit here instead.' Then you will be embarrassed and will have to take whatever seat is left at the foot of the table!

10"Do this instead—sit at the foot of the table. Then when your host sees you, he will come and say, 'Friend, we have a better place than this for you!' Then you will be honored in front of all the other guests. 11For the proud will be humbled, but the humble will be honored."

12Then he turned to his host. "When you put on a luncheon or a dinner," he said, "don't invite your friends, brothers, relatives, and rich neighbors. For they will repay you by inviting you back. 13Instead, invite the poor, the crippled, the lame, and the blind. 14Then at the resurrection of the godly, God will reward you for inviting those who could not repay you."

Story of the Great Feast

15Hearing this, a man sitting at the table with Jesus exclaimed, "What a privilege it would be to have a share in the Kingdom of God!"

16Jesus replied with this illustration: "A man prepared a great feast and sent out many invitations. 17When all was ready, he sent his servant around to notify the guests that it was time for them to come. 18But they all began making excuses. One said he had just bought a field and wanted to inspect it, so he asked to be excused. 19Another said he had just bought five pair of oxen and wanted to try them out. 20Another had just been married, so he said he couldn't come.

21"The servant returned and told his master what they had said. His master was angry and said, 'Go quickly into the streets and alleys of the city and invite the poor, the crippled, the lame, and the blind.' 22After the

13:30 Greek *Some are last who will be first, and some are first who will be last.* 13:35 Ps 118:26. 14:2 Traditionally translated *who had dropsy.* 14:5 Some manuscripts read *donkey.*

14:12-24 This story about the great feast illustrates one of the major themes in Luke's Gospel. God extends his saving grace and blessing to all people, including the poor and the handicapped of society, who in almost every case are ignored, even abused. Extending mercy to such people will be rewarded by God. An important step in following Jesus and in our own recovery program is our willingness to help others less fortunate than we.

servant had done this, he reported, 'There is still room for more.' 23So his master said, 'Go out into the country lanes and behind the hedges and urge anyone you find to come, so that the house will be full. 24For none of those I invited first will get even the smallest taste of what I had prepared for them.'"

The Cost of Being a Disciple

25Great crowds were following Jesus. He turned around and said to them, 26"If you want to be my follower you must love me more than* your own father and mother, wife and children, brothers and sisters—yes, more than your own life. Otherwise, you cannot be my disciple. 27And you cannot be my disciple if you do not carry your own cross and follow me.

28"But don't begin until you count the cost. For who would begin construction of a building without first getting estimates and then checking to see if there is enough money to pay the bills? 29Otherwise, you might complete only the foundation before running out of funds. And then how everyone would laugh at you! 30They would say, 'There's the person who started that building and ran out of money before it was finished!'

31"Or what king would ever dream of going to war without first sitting down with his counselors and discussing whether his army of ten thousand is strong enough to defeat the twenty thousand soldiers who are marching against him? 32If he is not able, then while the enemy is still far away, he will send a delegation to discuss terms of peace. 33So no one can become my disciple without giving up everything for me.

34"Salt is good for seasoning. But if it loses its flavor, how do you make it salty again? 35Flavorless salt is good neither for the soil nor for fertilizer. It is thrown away. Any-

one who is willing to hear should listen and understand!"

CHAPTER 15
Story of the Lost Sheep

Tax collectors and other notorious sinners often came to listen to Jesus teach. 2This made the Pharisees and teachers of religious law complain that he was associating with such despicable people—even eating with them!

3So Jesus used this illustration: 4"If you had one hundred sheep, and one of them strayed away and was lost in the wilderness, wouldn't you leave the ninety-nine others to go and search for the lost one until you found it? 5And then you would joyfully carry it home on your shoulders. 6When you arrived, you would call together your friends and neighbors to rejoice with you because your lost sheep was found. 7In the same way, heaven will be happier over one lost sinner who returns to God than over ninety-nine others who are righteous and haven't strayed away!

Story of the Lost Coin

8"Or suppose a woman has ten valuable silver coins* and loses one. Won't she light a lamp and look in every corner of the house and sweep every nook and cranny until she finds it? 9And when she finds it, she will call in her friends and neighbors to rejoice with her because she has found her lost coin. 10In the same way, there is joy in the presence of God's angels when even one sinner repents."

Story of the Lost Son

11To illustrate the point further, Jesus told them this story: "A man had two sons. 12The younger son told his father, 'I want my share of your estate now, instead of waiting until you die.' So his father agreed to divide his wealth between his sons.

14:26 Greek *you must hate.* **15:8** Greek *10 drachmas.* A drachma was the equivalent of a full day's wage.

14:26-33 "Counting the cost" applies not only to the decision to follow Jesus, but it also speaks of our need to weigh the cost of recovery. A searching and fearless moral inventory of our life is required in both cases. If commitment to Jesus and recovery are more valuable to us than our compulsion, addiction, or dysfunctional behavior, then recovery in the fullest sense will be realized. If we cannot give up the pleasures of our sinful lifestyle, our recovery will be short-lived. We will compromise our commitment and remain enslaved to our dependency and its painful consequences.
15:3-10 The stories of the lost coin and the lost sheep show God's grace toward those who have strayed and his great joy in finding them. Though our past may be tarnished, we are extremely valuable in God's eyes, which is reflected symbolically by the coin and sheep (valuable commodities in that day). That the owner would stop everything to search for the lost sheep or coin shows how valuable we are to the one who owns us.

¹³"A few days later this younger son packed all his belongings and took a trip to a distant land, and there he wasted all his money on wild living. ¹⁴About the time his money ran out, a great famine swept over the land, and he began to starve. ¹⁵He persuaded a local farmer to hire him to feed his pigs. ¹⁶The boy became so hungry that even the pods he was feeding the pigs looked good to him. But no one gave him anything.

¹⁷"When he finally came to his senses, he said to himself, 'At home even the hired men have food enough to spare, and here I am, dying of hunger! ¹⁸I will go home to my father and say, "Father, I have sinned against both heaven and you, ¹⁹and I am no longer worthy of being called your son. Please take me on as a hired man."'

²⁰"So he returned home to his father. And while he was still a long distance away, his father saw him coming. Filled with love and compassion, he ran to his son, embraced him, and kissed him. ²¹His son said to him, 'Father, I have sinned against both heaven and you, and I am no longer worthy of being called your son.*'

²²"But his father said to the servants, 'Quick! Bring the finest robe in the house and put it on him. Get a ring for his finger, and sandals for his feet. ²³And kill the calf we have been fattening in the pen. We must celebrate with a feast, ²⁴for this son of mine was dead and has now returned to life. He was lost, but now he is found.' So the party began.

²⁵"Meanwhile, the older son was in the fields working. When he returned home, he heard music and dancing in the house, ²⁶and he asked one of the servants what was going on. ²⁷'Your brother is back,' he was told, 'and your father has killed the calf we were fattening and has prepared a great feast. We are celebrating because of his safe return.'

²⁸"The older brother was angry and wouldn't go in. His father came out and begged him, ²⁹but he replied, 'All these years I've worked hard for you and never once refused to do a single thing you told me to. And in all that time you never gave me even one young goat for a feast with my friends. ³⁰Yet when this son of yours comes back after squandering your money on prostitutes, you celebrate by killing the finest calf we have.'

³¹"His father said to him, 'Look, dear son, you and I are very close, and everything I have is yours. ³²We had to celebrate this happy day. For your brother was dead and has come back to life! He was lost, but now he is found!'"

CHAPTER 16

Story of the Shrewd Manager

Jesus told this story to his disciples: "A rich man hired a manager to handle his affairs, but soon a rumor went around that the manager was thoroughly dishonest. ²So his employer called him in and said, 'What's this I hear about your stealing from me? Get your report in order, because you are going to be dismissed.'

³"The manager thought to himself, 'Now what? I'm through here, and I don't have the strength to go out and dig ditches, and I'm too proud to beg. ⁴I know just the thing! And

15:21 Some manuscripts add *Please take me on as a hired man.*

15:20-24 The father's great compassion for his returning son portrays God's response to a repentant sinner. Like the father in this story, God waits for the sinner to come to return to him of his own volition. Our heavenly Father does not wait for total amends or cleanup acts. (Those steps in the recovery process can wait.) The father in the story ran to his penitent son, hugged and kissed him, and threw a party—thus relieving him of all shame and guilt. In the same way, God actively seeks those of us who have strayed in our walk of faith as well as those who do not have a personal relationship with him.
15:25-30 God asks us to share his love with those who are helpless and lost and to carry the message of salvation and hope to them. The older brother's selfish attitude is shown to be sinful and self-centered. He represents the religious leadership of that time, as well as those of us who still cling to our own self-sufficiency. The father in this story demonstrates God's willingness to accept repentant sinners. God desires our restoration, whether the people around us like it or not. He also wants to use us to support, not hinder, fellow strugglers in the recovery process.
16:1-13 This story teaches the importance of using our material possessions to help bring eternal life and spiritual blessing to others. If the shrewd accountant is commended for cleverly using his talent for winning friends and influencing people, how much more the honest steward who dedicates all to God. Using material possessions and God-given talent merely for personal enjoyment, with no concern for others, is wrong. That may mean that our possessions have possessed us or that our goods have become our gods. Serving God alone will lead us to recovery.

then I'll have plenty of friends to take care of me when I leave!'

⁵"So he invited each person who owed money to his employer to come and discuss the situation. He asked the first one, 'How much do you owe him?' ⁶The man replied, 'I owe him eight hundred gallons of olive oil.' So the manager told him, 'Tear up that bill and write another one for four hundred gallons.*'

⁷"'And how much do you owe my employer?' he asked the next man. 'A thousand bushels of wheat,' was the reply. 'Here,' the manager said, 'take your bill and replace it with one for only eight hundred bushels.*'

⁸"The rich man had to admire the dishonest rascal for being so shrewd. And it is true that the citizens of this world are more shrewd than the godly are. ⁹I tell you, use your worldly resources to benefit others and make friends. In this way, your generosity stores up a reward for you in heaven.*

¹⁰"Unless you are faithful in small matters, you won't be faithful in large ones. If you cheat even a little, you won't be honest with greater responsibilities. ¹¹And if you are untrustworthy about worldly wealth, who will trust you with the true riches of heaven? ¹²And if you are not faithful with other people's money, why should you be trusted with money of your own?

¹³"No one can serve two masters. For you will hate one and love the other, or be devoted to one and despise the other. You cannot serve both God and money."

¹⁴The Pharisees, who dearly loved their money, naturally scoffed at all this. ¹⁵Then he said to them, "You like to look good in public, but God knows your evil hearts. What this world honors is an abomination in the sight of God.

¹⁶"Until John the Baptist began to preach, the laws of Moses and the messages of the prophets were your guides. But now the Good News of the Kingdom of God is preached, and eager multitudes are forcing their way in. ¹⁷But that doesn't mean that the law has lost its force in even the smallest point. It is stronger and more permanent than heaven and earth.

¹⁸"Anyone who divorces his wife and marries someone else commits adultery, and anyone who marries a divorced woman commits adultery."

16:6 Greek *100 baths . . . 50 [baths].* **16:7** Greek *100 korous . . . 80 [korous].* **16:9** Or *Then when you run out at the end of this life, your friends will welcome you into eternal homes.*

STEP 2

Restoration

BIBLE READING: Luke 15:11-24

We came to believe that a Power greater than ourselves could restore us to sanity.
In the natural progression of addiction, life degenerates. In one way or another, many of us wake up one day to realize that we are living like an animal. How true this is depends on the nature of our addiction. Some of us may be living like an animal in terms of our physical surroundings. Others of us may be a slave to our animal passions—powerful emotions that dehumanize us and others.

A young man took an early inheritance and traveled away from home. When the money was spent, the women just a memory, and the "high" long gone, he resorted to slopping pigs to earn a meager living. When he became so hungry that he eyed the pigs' slop with envy, he realized he had a problem. "When he finally came to his senses, he said to himself, 'At home even the hired men have food enough to spare, and here I am, dying of hunger! I will go home to my father. . . .' So he returned home to his father. And while he was still a long distance away, his father saw him coming. Filled with love and compassion, he ran to his son, embraced him, and kissed him" (Luke 15:17-18, 20).

The fact that we are able to recognize our life as degenerate or insane proves that there is hope for a better way of life. We are reminded of times when life was good, and we long to have that goodness restored. When we turn to God, who is powerful enough to help us build something better, we will discover that his power can restore us to sanity. *Turn to page 233, Romans 1.*

The Rich Man and Lazarus

¹⁹Jesus said, "There was a certain rich man who was splendidly clothed and who lived each day in luxury. ²⁰At his door lay a diseased beggar named Lazarus. ²¹As Lazarus lay there longing for scraps from the rich man's table, the dogs would come and lick his open sores. ²²Finally, the beggar died and was carried by the angels to be with Abraham.* The rich man also died and was buried, ²³and his soul went to the place of the dead.* There, in torment, he saw Lazarus in the far distance with Abraham.

²⁴"The rich man shouted, 'Father Abraham, have some pity! Send Lazarus over here to dip the tip of his finger in water and cool my tongue, because I am in anguish in these flames.'

²⁵"But Abraham said to him, 'Son, remember that during your lifetime you had everything you wanted, and Lazarus had nothing. So now he is here being comforted, and you are in anguish. ²⁶And besides, there is a great chasm separating us. Anyone who wanted to cross over to you from here is stopped at its edge, and no one there can cross over to us.'

²⁷"Then the rich man said, 'Please, Father Abraham, send him to my father's home. ²⁸For I have five brothers, and I want him to warn them about this place of torment so they won't have to come here when they die.'

²⁹"But Abraham said, 'Moses and the prophets have warned them. Your brothers can read their writings anytime they want to.'

³⁰"The rich man replied, 'No, Father Abraham! But if someone is sent to them from the dead, then they will turn from their sins.'

³¹"But Abraham said, 'If they won't listen to Moses and the prophets, they won't listen even if someone rises from the dead.'"

CHAPTER 17
Teachings about Forgiveness and Faith

One day Jesus said to his disciples, "There will always be temptations to sin, but how terrible it will be for the person who does the tempting. ²It would be better to be thrown into the sea with a large millstone around the neck than to face the punishment in store for harming one of these little ones. ³I am warning you! If another believer* sins, rebuke him; then if he repents, forgive him. ⁴Even if he wrongs you seven times a day and each time turns again and asks forgiveness, forgive him."

⁵One day the apostles said to the Lord, "We need more faith; tell us how to get it."

⁶"Even if you had faith as small as a mustard seed," the Lord answered, "you could say to this mulberry tree, 'May God uproot you and throw you into the sea,' and it would obey you!

⁷"When a servant comes in from plowing or taking care of sheep, he doesn't just sit down and eat. ⁸He must first prepare his master's meal and serve him his supper before eating his own. ⁹And the servant is not even thanked, because he is merely doing what he is supposed to do. ¹⁰In the same way, when you obey me you should say, 'We are not worthy of praise. We are servants who have simply done our duty.'"

16:22 Greek *into Abraham's bosom.* **16:23** Greek *to Hades.* **17:3** Greek *your brother.*

16:19-31 Here we see the consequences of selfishness. Insulated by all the material comforts of life, this rich man never took inventory of his deepest needs and sins. Because he was hardhearted and selfish, refusing to feed the beggar Lazarus, he was consigned to hell. Lazarus, on the other hand, lacked basic material needs and suffered physical pain in his lifetime, but he was prepared for eternity. Death proved to be the great equalizer, effecting a reversal of fortune for these two. God wants us to have the proper attitude toward money and possessions and to use them unselfishly to help others.

17:1-4 Knowing when to forgive and when to confront is critical to the recovery process. Jesus taught that forgiveness is to be freely and frequently extended to others with no strings attached. On the other hand, the recovery process sometimes calls for tough love. If our friends are clearly acting counter to God's Word, we need to confront them for their own good. Woe to the person, however, who tempts a person in recovery. Strong drink or drugs, for example, should never be offered to people in recovery. Those who offer such temptations will pay dearly when they stand before God.

17:11-19 These ten lepers illustrate Jesus' great compassion for the hurting and his desire to make them whole. Only one of the ten lepers returned to say thanks, and that one was a Samaritan. In recovery most people will not appreciate our efforts to intervene on their behalf. Those few who are grateful are the faithful ones who get well.

Ten Healed of Leprosy

[11]As Jesus continued on toward Jerusalem, he reached the border between Galilee and Samaria. [12]As he entered a village there, ten lepers stood at a distance, [13]crying out, "Jesus, Master, have mercy on us!"

[14]He looked at them and said, "Go show yourselves to the priests." And as they went, their leprosy disappeared.

[15]One of them, when he saw that he was healed, came back to Jesus, shouting, "Praise God, I'm healed!" [16]He fell face down on the ground at Jesus' feet, thanking him for what he had done. This man was a Samaritan.

[17]Jesus asked, "Didn't I heal ten men? Where are the other nine? [18]Does only this foreigner return to give glory to God?" [19]And Jesus said to the man, "Stand up and go. Your faith has made you well."

The Coming of the Kingdom

[20]One day the Pharisees asked Jesus, "When will the Kingdom of God come?"

Jesus replied, "The Kingdom of God isn't ushered in with visible signs.* [21]You won't be able to say, 'Here it is!' or 'It's over there!' For the Kingdom of God is among you.*"

[22]Later he talked again about this with his disciples. "The time is coming when you will long to share in the days of the Son of Man, but you won't be able to," he said. [23]"Reports will reach you that the Son of Man has returned and that he is in this place or that. Don't believe such reports or go out to look for him. [24]For when the Son of Man returns, you will know it beyond all doubt. It will be as evident as the lightning that flashes across the sky. [25]But first the Son of Man must suffer terribly* and be rejected by this generation.

[26]"When the Son of Man returns, the world will be like the people were in Noah's day. [27]In those days before the flood, the people enjoyed banquets and parties and weddings right up to the time Noah entered his boat and the flood came to destroy them all.

[28]"And the world will be as it was in the days of Lot. People went about their daily business—eating and drinking, buying and selling, farming and building—[29]until the morning Lot left Sodom. Then fire and burning sulfur rained down from heaven and destroyed them all. [30]Yes, it will be 'business as usual' right up to the hour when the Son of Man returns.* [31]On that day a person outside the house* must not go into the house to

17:20 Or by your speculations. 17:21 Or within you. 17:25 Or suffer many things. 17:30 Or on the day the Son of Man is revealed. 17:31 Greek on the roof.

F aith

READ LUKE 17:1-10

How many times have we wished that we could overcome the addiction or compulsion that keeps us in bondage? We know what it is like to struggle with the effects of addiction and the craziness this brings to our life. We may feel despair and wonder if there really is any way out of the insanity of our current circumstances. Maybe our plight is impossible, at least without God's help, but faith can make even the impossible happen.

"One day the apostles said to the Lord, 'We need more faith; tell us how to get it.' 'Even if you had faith as small as a mustard seed,' the Lord answered, 'you could say to this mulberry tree, "May God uproot you and throw you into the sea," and it would obey you!'" (Luke 17:5-6). Matthew also recorded Jesus' words: "I assure you, even if you had faith as small as a mustard seed you could say to this mountain, 'Move from here to there,' and it would move. Nothing would be impossible" (Matthew 17:20).

Faith is a mysterious commodity. Jesus says that if we have faith, real faith, it only takes a small amount to make a big difference. We may be exercising faith without even realizing it. It takes faith to believe that a Power greater than ourself could restore us to sanity. It takes faith to work through the steps of a recovery program. It is comforting to know that God only needs a tiny bit of faith in order to work in powerful ways to restore our sanity.

Turn to page 135, Luke 22.

pack. A person in the field must not return to town. ³²Remember what happened to Lot's wife! ³³Whoever clings to this life will lose it, and whoever loses this life will save it. ³⁴That night two people will be asleep in one bed; one will be taken away, and the other will be left. ³⁵Two women will be grinding flour together at the mill; one will be taken, the other left.*"

³⁷"Lord, where will this happen?" the disciples asked.

Jesus replied, "Just as the gathering of vultures shows there is a carcass nearby, so these signs indicate that the end is near."*

CHAPTER 18
Story of the Persistent Widow
One day Jesus told his disciples a story to illustrate their need for constant prayer and to show them that they must never give up. ²"There was a judge in a certain city," he said, "who was a godless man with great contempt for everyone. ³A widow of that city came to him repeatedly, appealing for justice against someone who had harmed her. ⁴The judge ignored her for a while, but eventually she wore him out. 'I fear neither God nor man,' he said to himself, ⁵'but this woman is driving me crazy. I'm going to see that she gets justice, because she is wearing me out with her constant requests!'"

⁶Then the Lord said, "Learn a lesson from this evil judge. ⁷Even he rendered a just decision in the end, so don't you think God will surely give justice to his chosen people who plead with him day and night? Will he keep putting them off? ⁸I tell you, he will

grant justice to them quickly! But when I, the Son of Man, return, how many will I find who have faith?"

Story of the Pharisee and Tax Collector
⁹Then Jesus told this story to some who had great self-confidence and scorned everyone else: ¹⁰"Two men went to the Temple to pray. One was a Pharisee, and the other was a dishonest tax collector. ¹¹The proud Pharisee stood by himself and prayed this prayer: 'I thank you, God, that I am not a sinner like everyone else, especially like that tax collector over there! For I never cheat, I don't sin, I don't commit adultery, ¹²I fast twice a week, and I give you a tenth of my income.'

¹³"But the tax collector stood at a distance and dared not even lift his eyes to heaven as he prayed. Instead, he beat his chest in sorrow, saying, 'O God, be merciful to me, for I am a sinner.' ¹⁴I tell you, this sinner, not the Pharisee, returned home justified before God. For the proud will be humbled, but the humble will be honored."

Jesus Blesses the Children
¹⁵One day some parents brought their little children to Jesus so he could touch them and bless them, but the disciples told them not to bother him. ¹⁶Then Jesus called for the children and said to the disciples, "Let the children come to me. Don't stop them! For the Kingdom of God belongs to such as these. ¹⁷I assure you, anyone who doesn't have their kind of faith will never get into the Kingdom of God."

17:35 Some manuscripts add verse 36, *Two men will be working in the field; one will be taken, the other left.* **17:37** Greek *Wherever the carcass is, the vultures gather.*

18:1-8 Many of us have experienced injustice at the hands of authority figures, such as family-court judges, mean bosses, or parole officers. This story contrasts God with the unfair judge and makes the point that even if life is unfair, God is fair. If an evil judge finally answers the pleas of a persistent widow, how much more will a just God respond to those in need who pray to him in faith. When trials and challenges make life seem unfair, we can still trust God to deliver us. Seeking God in prayer requires patience and persistence, but he always answers.
18:15-17 Children trust naturally; God wants our relationship with him to be driven by that kind of simple trust. Any other kind of "faith" is inappropriate, unnatural, and ineffective. If we are unable to trust, it may help to understand the hurts in our past that make it so difficult to do this. Childlike faith is itself a gift from God that may take time for him to restore in us, especially if we have been abused (spiritually, emotionally, sexually, or physically). In recovery we are told to keep it simple; a simple faith in an almighty God is necessary for a successful recovery.
18:31-34 Jesus predicted the suffering he would endure on his way to the cross. While his pain and disgrace would be extreme, he was willing to accept it as a necessary part of the process toward the goal of salvation. In recovery the process of spiritual growth often involves pain and sacrifice. Reversing patterns of sinful or addictive behavior can be extremely difficult and discouraging; so it is essential that we keep our focus on the goal—recovery—which is worth the sacrifice.

The Rich Man

¹⁸Once a religious leader asked Jesus this question: "Good teacher, what should I do to get eternal life?"

¹⁹"Why do you call me good?" Jesus asked him. "Only God is truly good. ²⁰But as for your question, you know the commandments: 'Do not commit adultery. Do not murder. Do not steal. Do not testify falsely. Honor your father and mother.'*"

²¹The man replied, "I've obeyed all these commandments since I was a child."

²²"There is still one thing you lack," Jesus said. "Sell all you have and give the money to the poor, and you will have treasure in heaven. Then come, follow me." ²³But when the man heard this, he became sad because he was very rich.

²⁴Jesus watched him go and then said to his disciples, "How hard it is for rich people to get into the Kingdom of God! ²⁵It is easier for a camel to go through the eye of a needle than for a rich person to enter the Kingdom of God!"

²⁶Those who heard this said, "Then who in the world can be saved?"

²⁷He replied, "What is impossible from a human perspective is possible with God."

²⁸Peter said, "We have left our homes and followed you."

²⁹"Yes," Jesus replied, "and I assure you, everyone who has given up house or wife or brothers or parents or children, for the sake of the Kingdom of God, ³⁰will be repaid many times over in this life, as well as receiving eternal life in the world to come."

Jesus Again Predicts His Death

³¹Gathering the twelve disciples around him, Jesus told them, "As you know, we are going to Jerusalem. And when we get there, all the predictions of the ancient prophets concerning the Son of Man will come true. ³²He will be handed over to the Romans to be mocked, treated shamefully, and spit upon. ³³They will whip him and kill him, but on the third day he will rise again."

³⁴But they didn't understand a thing he said. Its significance was hidden from them, and they failed to grasp what he was talking about.

Jesus Heals a Blind Beggar

³⁵As they approached Jericho, a blind beggar was sitting beside the road. ³⁶When he heard the noise of a crowd going past, he

18:20 Exod 20:12-16; Deut 5:16-20.

STEP 7

A Humble Heart

BIBLE READING: Luke 18:10-14
We humbly asked him to remove our shortcomings.
After examining our life closely (as we did in Steps Four, Five, and Six), we may feel cut off from God. Considering the scope of what we have done, we may feel unworthy to ask God for anything. Maybe our sinful behaviors are despised as the lowest kind of evil by those whom we consider respectable. We may struggle with self-hatred. Our genuine remorse may cause us to wonder if we even dare approach God to ask for his help.

God welcomes us, even when we feel this way. Jesus told this story: "Two men went to the Temple to pray. One was a Pharisee, and the other was a dishonest tax collector. The proud Pharisee stood by himself and prayed this prayer: 'I thank you, God, that I am not a sinner like everyone else, especially like that tax collector over there! For I never cheat, I don't sin, I don't commit adultery, I fast twice a week, and I give you a tenth of my income.' But the tax collector stood at a distance and dared not even lift his eyes to heaven as he prayed. Instead, he beat his chest in sorrow, saying, 'O God, be merciful to me, for I am a sinner.' I tell you, this sinner, not the Pharisee, returned home justified before God. For the proud will be humbled, but the humble will be honored" (Luke 18:10-14).

Tax collectors were among the most despised citizens in Jewish society. Pharisees, on the other hand, commanded the highest respect. Jesus purposely chose this illustration to show that it doesn't matter where we fit in society's hierarchy. It is the humble heart that opens the door to God's forgiveness. *Turn to page 239, Romans 3.*

asked what was happening. ³⁷They told him that Jesus of Nazareth was going by. ³⁸So he began shouting, "Jesus, Son of David, have mercy on me!" ³⁹The crowds ahead of Jesus tried to hush the man, but he only shouted louder, "Son of David, have mercy on me!"

⁴⁰When Jesus heard him, he stopped and ordered that the man be brought to him. ⁴¹Then Jesus asked the man, "What do you want me to do for you?"

"Lord," he pleaded, "I want to see!"

⁴²And Jesus said, "All right, you can see! Your faith has healed you." ⁴³Instantly the man could see, and he followed Jesus, praising God. And all who saw it praised God, too.

CHAPTER 19
Jesus and Zacchaeus

Jesus entered Jericho and made his way through the town. ²There was a man there named Zacchaeus. He was one of the most influential Jews in the Roman tax-collecting business, and he had become very rich. ³He tried to get a look at Jesus, but he was too short to see over the crowds. ⁴So he ran ahead and climbed a sycamore tree beside the road, so he could watch from there.

⁵When Jesus came by, he looked up at Zacchaeus and called him by name. "Zacchaeus!" he said. "Quick, come down! For I must be a guest in your home today."

⁶Zacchaeus quickly climbed down and took Jesus to his house in great excitement and joy. ⁷But the crowds were displeased. "He has gone to be the guest of a notorious sinner," they grumbled.

⁸Meanwhile, Zacchaeus stood there and said to the Lord, "I will give half my wealth to the poor, Lord, and if I have overcharged people on their taxes, I will give them back four times as much!"

⁹Jesus responded, "Salvation has come to this home today, for this man has shown himself to be a son of Abraham. ¹⁰And I, the Son of Man, have come to seek and save those like him who are lost."

Story of the Ten Servants

¹¹The crowd was listening to everything Jesus said. And because he was nearing Jerusalem, he told a story to correct the impression that the Kingdom of God would begin right away. ¹²He said, "A nobleman was called away to a distant empire to be crowned king and then return. ¹³Before he left, he called together ten servants and gave them ten pounds of silver* to invest for him while he was gone. ¹⁴But his people hated him and sent a delegation after him to say they did not want him to be their king.

¹⁵"When he returned, the king called in the servants to whom he had given the money. He wanted to find out what they had done with the money and what their profits were. ¹⁶The first servant reported a tremendous gain—ten times as much as the original amount! ¹⁷'Well done!' the king exclaimed. 'You are a trustworthy servant. You have been faithful with the little I entrusted to you, so you will be governor of ten cities as your reward.'

¹⁸"The next servant also reported a good gain—five times the original amount. ¹⁹'Well done!' the king said. 'You can be governor over five cities.'

²⁰"But the third servant brought back only the original amount of money and said, 'I hid it and kept it safe. ²¹I was afraid because you are a hard man to deal with, taking what isn't yours and harvesting crops you didn't plant.'

²²'You wicked servant!' the king roared. 'Hard, am I? If you knew so much about me and how tough I am, ²³why didn't you deposit the money in the bank so I could at least get some interest on it?' ²⁴Then turning to the others standing nearby, the king ordered, 'Take the money from this servant, and give it to the one who earned the most.'

²⁵'But, master,' they said, 'that servant has enough already!'

²⁶'Yes,' the king replied, 'but to those who use well what they are given, even more will be given. But from those who are

19:13 Greek *10 minas;* 1 mina was was worth about 3 months' wages.

19:11-27 This story teaches stewardship—accountability before God to use wisely the gifts, abilities, and possessions he has entrusted to us. Wisely using what God has given will result in generous rewards; refusing to do so will bring a stern reprimand from God. Whatever opportunities and resources God gives us—time, money, talents, or relationships—we are to use in the lives of others. After years of pain and devastation, we may wonder what we have to offer. Our story of deliverance may be all someone needs to take a step toward God and recovery. Sharing ourself with others may help save the life of a needy person.

unfaithful,* even what little they have will be taken away. ²⁷And now about these enemies of mine who didn't want me to be their king—bring them in and execute them right here in my presence.'"

The Triumphal Entry

²⁸After telling this story, Jesus went on toward Jerusalem, walking ahead of his disciples. ²⁹As they came to the towns of Bethphage and Bethany, on the Mount of Olives, he sent two disciples ahead. ³⁰"Go into that village over there," he told them, "and as you enter it, you will see a colt tied there that has never been ridden. Untie it and bring it here. ³¹If anyone asks what you are doing, just say, 'The Lord needs it.'"

³²So they went and found the colt, just as Jesus had said. ³³And sure enough, as they were untying it, the owners asked them, "Why are you untying our colt?"

³⁴And the disciples simply replied, "The Lord needs it." ³⁵So they brought the colt to Jesus and threw their garments over it for him to ride on.

³⁶Then the crowds spread out their coats on the road ahead of Jesus. ³⁷As they reached the place where the road started down from the Mount of Olives, all of his followers began to shout and sing as they walked along, praising God for all the wonderful miracles they had seen.

³⁸"Bless the King who comes in the name of
    the Lord!
  Peace in heaven
    and glory in highest heaven!"*

³⁹But some of the Pharisees among the crowd said, "Teacher, rebuke your followers for saying things like that!"

⁴⁰He replied, "If they kept quiet, the stones along the road would burst into cheers!"

Jesus Weeps over Jerusalem

⁴¹But as they came closer to Jerusalem and Jesus saw the city ahead, he began to cry. ⁴²"I wish that even today you would find the way of peace. But now it is too late, and peace is hidden from you. ⁴³Before long your enemies will build ramparts against your walls and encircle you and close in on you. ⁴⁴They will crush you to the ground, and your children with you. Your enemies will not leave a single stone in place, because you have rejected the opportunity God offered you."

19:26 Or *who have nothing.* **19:38** Pss 118:26; 148:1.

From Taker to Giver

BIBLE READING: Luke 19:1-10

We made direct amends to such people wherever possible, except when to do so would injure them or others.

When we are feeding our addiction, it is easy to become consumed by our own needs. Nothing matters except getting what we crave so desperately. We may have to lie, cheat, kill, or steal; but that doesn't stop us. Within our family and community we become known as "takers," trampling over the feelings and needs of others.

Zacchaeus had the same problem. His hunger for riches drove him to betray his own people by collecting taxes for the oppressive Roman government. He was hated by his own people and considered a thief, an extortioner, and a traitor. But when Jesus reached out to him, he changed dramatically. "Meanwhile, Zacchaeus stood there and said to the Lord, 'I will give half my wealth to the poor, Lord, and if I have overcharged people on their taxes, I will give them back four times as much!' Jesus responded, 'Salvation has come to this home today'" (Luke 19:8-9).

Zacchaeus went beyond just paying back what he had taken. For the first time in a long time, he saw the needs of others and wanted to be a "giver." Making amends includes paying back what we have taken whenever possible. Some of us may even seize the opportunity to go further, giving more than we took. As we begin to see the needs of others and respond by choice, our self-esteem will rise. We will realize that we can give to others, instead of just being a burden. *Turn to page 377, Philemon 1.*

Jesus Clears the Temple

45Then Jesus entered the Temple and began to drive out the merchants from their stalls. 46He told them, "The Scriptures declare, 'My Temple will be a place of prayer,' but you have turned it into a den of thieves."*

47After that, he taught daily in the Temple, but the leading priests, the teachers of religious law, and the other leaders of the people began planning how to kill him. 48But they could think of nothing, because all the people hung on every word he said.

CHAPTER 20
The Authority of Jesus Challenged

One day as Jesus was teaching and preaching the Good News in the Temple, the leading priests and teachers of religious law and other leaders came up to him. 2They demanded, "By whose authority did you drive out the merchants from the Temple?* Who gave you such authority?"

3"Let me ask you a question first," he replied. 4"Did John's baptism come from heaven, or was it merely human?"

5They talked it over among themselves. "If we say it was from heaven, he will ask why we didn't believe him. 6But if we say it was merely human, the people will stone us, because they are convinced he was a prophet." 7Finally they replied, "We don't know."

8And Jesus responded, "Then I won't answer your question either."

Story of the Evil Farmers

9Now Jesus turned to the people again and told them this story: "A man planted a vineyard, leased it out to tenant farmers, and moved to another country to live for several years. 10At grape-picking time, he sent one of his servants to collect his share of the crop. But the farmers attacked the servant, beat him up, and sent him back empty-handed.

11So the owner sent another servant, but the same thing happened; he was beaten up and treated shamefully, and he went away empty-handed. 12A third man was sent and the same thing happened. He, too, was wounded and chased away.

13"'What will I do?' the owner asked himself. 'I know! I'll send my cherished son. Surely they will respect him.'

14"But when the farmers saw his son, they said to each other, 'Here comes the heir to this estate. Let's kill him and get the estate for ourselves!' 15So they dragged him out of the vineyard and murdered him.

"What do you suppose the owner of the vineyard will do to those farmers?" Jesus asked. 16"I'll tell you—he will come and kill them all and lease the vineyard to others."

"But God forbid that such a thing should ever happen," his listeners protested.

17Jesus looked at them and said, "Then what do the Scriptures mean?

'The stone rejected by the builders
　　has now become the cornerstone.'*

18All who stumble over that stone will be broken to pieces, and it will crush anyone on whom it falls."

19When the teachers of religious law and the leading priests heard this story, they wanted to arrest Jesus immediately because they realized he was pointing at them—that they were the farmers in the story. But they were afraid there would be a riot if they arrested him.

Taxes for Caesar

20Watching for their opportunity, the leaders sent secret agents pretending to be honest men. They tried to get Jesus to say something that could be reported to the Roman governor so he would arrest Jesus. 21They said, "Teacher, we know that you speak and teach

---

19:46 Isa 56:7; Jer 7:11. **20:2** Or *By whose authority do you do these things?* **20:17** Ps 118:22.

19:45-48 The people's worship had become so dysfunctional that Jesus became angry and drove the merchants out of God's Temple. Correcting this gross perversion was not appreciated and did not produce the desired change in the worshipers. Instead, the priests, religious teachers, and leaders were angry and desired vengeance. Change, even much-needed change for the better, is resisted by those in denial.

20:9-18 This story is unmistakably blunt. No one likes being confronted with their denial and blindness. The farmers rejected the messages of the servants and killed the owner's son. Jesus' audience, especially the priests and religious teachers, did the same; they didn't like the message, so they killed the messenger (Jesus). When we deny the truth, there is not much God or others can do. Sometimes the truth can penetrate our denial when someone speaks plainly but indirectly as Nathan did with David in the Old Testament by telling him a story, which motivated David to repent of his sin (2 Samuel 12). Yet some people in denial, like the ones Jesus was speaking to, will resist to their dying day.

what is right and are not influenced by what others think. You sincerely teach the ways of God. ²²Now tell us—is it right to pay taxes to the Roman government or not?"

²³He saw through their trickery and said, ²⁴"Show me a Roman coin.* Whose picture and title are stamped on it?"

"Caesar's," they replied.

²⁵"Well then," he said, "give to Caesar what belongs to him. But everything that belongs to God must be given to God." ²⁶So they failed to trap him in the presence of the people. Instead, they were amazed by his answer, and they were silenced.

Discussion about Resurrection

²⁷Then some Sadducees stepped forward—a group of Jews who say there is no resurrection after death. ²⁸They posed this question: "Teacher, Moses gave us a law that if a man dies, leaving a wife but no children, his brother should marry the widow and have a child who will be the brother's heir.* ²⁹Well, there were seven brothers. The oldest married and then died without children. ³⁰His brother married the widow, but he also died. Still no children. ³¹And so it went, one after the other, until each of the seven had married her and died, leaving no children. ³²Finally, the woman died, too. ³³So tell us, whose wife will she be in the resurrection? For all seven were married to her!"

³⁴Jesus replied, "Marriage is for people here on earth. ³⁵But that is not the way it will be in the age to come. For those worthy of being raised from the dead won't be married then. ³⁶And they will never die again. In these respects they are like angels. They are children of God raised up to new life. ³⁷But now, as to whether the dead will be raised—even Moses proved this when he wrote about the burning bush. Long after Abraham, Isaac, and Jacob had died, he referred to the Lord* as 'the God of Abraham, the God of Isaac, and the God of Jacob.'* ³⁸So he is the God of the living, not the dead. They are all alive to him."

³⁹"Well said, Teacher!" remarked some of the teachers of religious law who were standing there. ⁴⁰And that ended their questions; no one dared to ask any more.

Whose Son Is the Messiah?

⁴¹Then Jesus presented them with a question. "Why is it," he asked, "that the Messiah is said to be the son of David? ⁴²For David himself wrote in the book of Psalms:

'The LORD said to my Lord,
 Sit in honor at my right hand
⁴³   until I humble your enemies,
    making them a footstool under your
      feet.'*

⁴⁴Since David called him Lord, how can he be his son at the same time?"

⁴⁵Then, with the crowds listening, he turned to his disciples and said, ⁴⁶"Beware of these teachers of religious law! For they love to parade in flowing robes and to have everyone bow to them as they walk in the marketplaces. And how they love the seats of honor in the synagogues and at banquets. ⁴⁷But they shamelessly cheat widows out of their property, and then, to cover up the kind of people they really are, they make long prayers in public. Because of this, their punishment will be the greater."

CHAPTER 21
The Widow's Offering

While Jesus was in the Temple, he watched the rich people putting their gifts into the collection box. ²Then a poor widow came by and dropped in two pennies.* ³"I assure you," he said, "this poor widow has given more than all the rest of them. ⁴For they have given a tiny part of their surplus, but she, poor as she is, has given everything she has."

Jesus Foretells the Future

⁵Some of his disciples began talking about the beautiful stonework of the Temple and the memorial decorations on the walls. But Jesus said, ⁶"The time is coming when all these things will be so completely demolished that not one stone will be left on top of another."

20:24 Greek *a denarius.* **20:28** Deut 25:5-6. **20:37a** Greek *when he wrote about the bush. He referred to the Lord.* **20:37b** Exod 3:6. **20:42-43** Ps 110:1. **21:2** Greek *2 lepta.*

21:1-4 God has a unique standard by which he measures giving and givers. With God, attitude counts more than amount, so Jesus praised this widow. A generous person is not one who gives conveniently and comfortably out of abundance. A generous person in God's eyes risks all, sacrifices cheerfully, and gives without demanding attention or expecting a reward. Whether it's our time, talents, or money, God wants us to turn everything in our life over to his care. One small step in giving may become one giant leap toward recovery.

7"Teacher," they asked, "when will all this take place? And will there be any sign ahead of time?"

8He replied, "Don't let anyone mislead you. For many will come in my name, claiming to be the Messiah* and saying, 'The time has come!' But don't believe them. 9And when you hear of wars and insurrections, don't panic. Yes, these things must come, but the end won't follow immediately." 10Then he added, "Nations and kingdoms will proclaim war against each other. 11There will be great earthquakes, and there will be famines and epidemics in many lands, and there will be terrifying things and great miraculous signs in the heavens.

12"But before all this occurs, there will be a time of great persecution. You will be dragged into synagogues and prisons, and you will be accused before kings and governors of being my followers. 13This will be your opportunity to tell them about me. 14So don't worry about how to answer the charges against you, 15for I will give you the right words and such wisdom that none of your opponents will be able to reply! 16Even those closest to you—your parents, brothers, relatives, and friends—will betray you. And some of you will be killed. 17And everyone will hate you because of your allegiance to me. 18But not a hair of your head will perish! 19By standing firm, you will win your souls.

20"And when you see Jerusalem surrounded by armies, then you will know that the time of its destruction has arrived. 21Then those in Judea must flee to the hills. Let those in Jerusalem escape, and those outside the city should not enter it for shelter. 22For those will be days of God's vengeance, and the prophetic words of the Scriptures will be fulfilled. 23How terrible it will be for pregnant women and for mothers nursing their babies. For there will be great distress in the land and wrath upon this people. 24They will be brutally killed by the sword or sent away as captives to all the nations of the world. And Jerusalem will be conquered and trampled down by the Gentiles until the age of the Gentiles comes to an end.

25"And there will be strange events in the skies—signs in the sun, moon, and stars. And down here on earth the nations will be in turmoil, perplexed by the roaring seas and strange tides. 26The courage of many people will falter because of the fearful fate they see coming upon the earth, because the stability of the very heavens will be broken up. 27Then everyone will see the Son of Man arrive on the clouds with power and great glory.* 28So when all these things begin to happen, stand straight and look up, for your salvation is near!"

29Then he gave them this illustration: "Notice the fig tree, or any other tree. 30When the leaves come out, you know without being told that summer is near. 31Just so, when you see the events I've described taking place, you can be sure that the Kingdom of God is near. 32I assure you, this generation* will not pass from the scene until all these events have taken place. 33Heaven and earth will disappear, but my words will remain forever.

34"Watch out! Don't let me find you living in careless ease and drunkenness, and filled with the worries of this life. Don't let that day catch you unaware, 35as in a trap. For that day will come upon everyone living on the earth. 36Keep a constant watch. And pray that, if possible, you may escape these horrors and stand before the Son of Man."

37Every day Jesus went to the Temple to teach, and each evening he returned to spend the night on the Mount of Olives. 38The crowds gathered early each morning to hear him.

21:8 Greek *name, saying, 'I am.'* 21:27 See Dan 7:13. 21:32 Or *this age,* or *this nation.*

21:16-17 What happened to Jesus leading up to the cross and what would happen to his disciples afterward illustrate an important principle in recovery. Family members and friends are not always overjoyed at our changed life. Faith in Jesus, as well as freedom from sin and addiction, often threatens the status quo. Often those closest to us become the greatest hindrances to our healing and recovery as they resist what we know is best for us. As we become aware of this, we cannot allow them to impede our progress. In time they will discover that the recovery process is good for us and for them.

21:34-36 This charge follows a lengthy prophecy about the coming days of destruction (21:5-31), and it illustrates the biblical purpose of prophecy. Prophecy is never given simply to satisfy the curiosity of those who wonder about God's plan for the future. Prophecy is primarily a call for believers to repent, stay alert, and prepare spiritually for the coming of God's Kingdom. As we await the triumphant return of Christ, or even the recovery of sanity, God warns about the dangers of being controlled by sin. We only fool ourself if we think we have all the time in the world to get ready. If we continue to put off recovery until tomorrow, one day tomorrow will not come!

CHAPTER 22
Judas Agrees to Betray Jesus

The Festival of Unleavened Bread, which begins with the Passover celebration, was drawing near. ²The leading priests and teachers of religious law were actively plotting Jesus' murder. But they wanted to kill him without starting a riot, a possibility they greatly feared.

³Then Satan entered into Judas Iscariot, who was one of the twelve disciples, ⁴and he went over to the leading priests and captains of the Temple guard to discuss the best way to betray Jesus to them. ⁵They were delighted that he was ready to help them, and they promised him a reward. ⁶So he began looking for an opportunity to betray Jesus so they could arrest him quietly when the crowds weren't around.

The Last Supper

⁷Now the Festival of Unleavened Bread arrived, when the Passover lambs were sacrificed. ⁸Jesus sent Peter and John ahead and said, "Go and prepare the Passover meal, so we can eat it together."

⁹"Where do you want us to go?" they asked him.

¹⁰He replied, "As soon as you enter Jerusalem, a man carrying a pitcher of water will meet you. Follow him. At the house he enters, ¹¹say to the owner, 'The Teacher asks, Where is the guest room where I can eat the Passover meal with my disciples?' ¹²He will take you upstairs to a large room that is already set up. That is the place. Go ahead and prepare our supper there." ¹³They went off to the city and found everything just as Jesus had said, and they prepared the Passover supper there.

¹⁴Then at the proper time Jesus and the twelve apostles sat down together at the table. ¹⁵Jesus said, "I have looked forward to this hour with deep longing, anxious to eat this Passover meal with you before my suffering begins. ¹⁶For I tell you now that I won't eat it again until it comes to fulfillment in the Kingdom of God."

¹⁷Then he took a cup of wine, and when he had given thanks for it, he said, "Take this and share it among yourselves. ¹⁸For I will not drink wine again until the Kingdom of God has come."

¹⁹Then he took a loaf of bread; and when he had thanked God for it, he broke it in pieces and gave it to the disciples, saying, "This is my body, given for you. Do this in remembrance of me." ²⁰After supper he took another cup of wine and said, "This wine is the token of God's new covenant to save you—an agreement sealed with the blood I will pour out for you.*

²¹"But here at this table, sitting among us as a friend, is the man who will betray me. ²²For I, the Son of Man, must die since it is part of God's plan. But how terrible it will be for my betrayer!" ²³Then the disciples began to ask each other which of them would ever do such a thing.

²⁴And they began to argue among themselves as to who would be the greatest in the coming Kingdom. ²⁵Jesus told them, "In this world the kings and great men order their people around, and yet they are called 'friends of the people.' ²⁶But among you, those who are the greatest should take the lowest rank, and the leader should be like a servant. ²⁷Normally the master sits at the table and is served by his servants. But not here! For I am your servant. ²⁸You have remained true to me in my time of trial. ²⁹And just as my Father has granted me a Kingdom, I now grant you the right ³⁰to eat and drink at my table in that Kingdom. And you will sit on thrones, judging the twelve tribes of Israel.

22:19-20 Some manuscripts omit 22:19b-20, *given for you . . . I will pour out for you.*

22:3-6 At the deepest level, the brokenness, the bondage, and the uncontrolled nature of our life is due to Satan. Spiritual warfare plays itself out in personal relationships—in Judas's betrayal of Jesus and in the breakup of our own relationships. Spiritual warfare undermines and destroys relational boundaries and renders our life unmanageable. (Judas would later commit suicide.) But Satan's involvement does not excuse human sin, addiction, and betrayal; we are responsible for our behavior. God is in control of every situation. Jesus' death (at the hands of Satan) was part of God's plan all along. No matter how Satan harms us, God can use Satan's evil plans to work his good for us (Romans 8:28) when we trust and obey him.

22:24-30 This upper-room discourse contrasts Jesus' humility and servant's heart with the selfish intentions of his twelve closest followers. In going to the cross, Jesus showed his disciples what it meant to be a servant-leader. The disciples' desire for a special place at God's table was not what Jesus had intended to teach them. Jesus calls us to put the needs of others before our own and serve others rather than expecting to be served. Our life should be defined and motivated by humility.

Jesus Predicts Peter's Denial

31"Simon, Simon, Satan has asked to have all of you, to sift you like wheat. 32But I have pleaded in prayer for you, Simon, that your faith should not fail. So when you have repented and turned to me again, strengthen and build up your brothers."

33Peter said, "Lord, I am ready to go to prison with you, and even to die with you."

34But Jesus said, "Peter, let me tell you something. The rooster will not crow tomorrow morning until you have denied three times that you even know me."

35Then Jesus asked them, "When I sent you out to preach the Good News and you did not have money, a traveler's bag, or extra clothing, did you lack anything?"

"No," they replied.

36"But now," he said, "take your money and a traveler's bag. And if you don't have a sword, sell your clothes and buy one! 37For the time has come for this prophecy about me to be fulfilled: 'He was counted among those who were rebels.'* Yes, everything written about me by the prophets will come true."

38"Lord," they replied, "we have two swords among us."

"That's enough," he said.

Jesus Prays on the Mount of Olives

39Then, accompanied by the disciples, Jesus left the upstairs room and went as usual to the Mount of Olives. 40There he told them, "Pray that you will not be overcome by temptation."

41He walked away, about a stone's throw, and knelt down and prayed, 42"Father, if you are willing, please take this cup of suffering away from me. Yet I want your will, not mine." 43Then an angel from heaven appeared and strengthened him. 44He prayed more fervently, and he was in such agony of spirit that his sweat fell to the ground like great drops of blood.* 45At last he stood up again and returned to the disciples, only to find them asleep, exhausted from grief. 46"Why are you sleeping?" he asked. "Get up and pray. Otherwise temptation will overpower you."

Jesus Is Betrayed and Arrested

47But even as he said this, a mob approached, led by Judas, one of his twelve disciples. Judas walked over to Jesus and greeted him with a kiss. 48But Jesus said, "Judas, how can you betray me, the Son of Man, with a kiss?"

49When the other disciples saw what was about to happen, they exclaimed, "Lord, should we fight? We brought the swords!" 50And one of them slashed at the high priest's servant and cut off his right ear.

51But Jesus said, "Don't resist anymore." And he touched the place where the man's ear had been and healed him. 52Then Jesus spoke to the leading priests and captains of the Temple guard and the other leaders who headed the mob. "Am I some dangerous criminal," he asked, "that you have come armed with swords and clubs to arrest me? 53Why didn't you arrest me in the Temple? I was there every day. But this is your moment, the time when the power of darkness reigns."

22:37 Isa 53:12. 22:43-44 These verses are not included in many ancient manuscripts.

22:39-46 Jesus' prayer on the Mount of Olives reflected the awesome task before him: He was about to shoulder the sins of the world. He persevered through fear and agony of spirit and submitted to God's sovereign will. His absolute commitment to God's will is an example for us to follow. Jesus could have selfishly seized the privileges of deity and avoided the cross (see Philippians 2:6-8), but he willingly delayed the gratification of heaven's glory to accomplish the task set before him by his Father. Although our challenges in life are not of this magnitude, God enables us to persevere through the tough stages of recovery to reap the rewards that follow.

22:54-62 Peter's denial of Jesus is a classic story of recovery. Although Peter believed he could never stoop so low (22:31-34), he denied Jesus completely when the heat was on. Peter disappointed Jesus and himself, but even then, all was not lost. His experience led to genuine sorrow and healthy repentance. Peter's threefold denial was followed by a threefold affirmation and his restoration to full-fledged service (John 21:15-19). Later Peter became the leading spokesman for the early church, powerfully proclaiming the message of the risen Christ. Only through God's complete forgiveness could Peter have so effectively recovered from the depths of despair.

23:1-5 The Jewish council attempted to manipulate Pilate's verdict about Jesus by telling half-truths, even outright lies. In denial, the subtle (and not-so-subtle) lies we tell ourself and others keep us from making progress in recovery. Lying is often used by others to knock us off track and to maintain the status quo. Often others are not even aware of their need to keep everything, including us, in place. Recovery is based on the principles of truth and honesty.

Peter Denies Jesus

[54]So they arrested him and led him to the high priest's residence, and Peter was following far behind. [55]The guards lit a fire in the courtyard and sat around it, and Peter joined them there. [56]A servant girl noticed him in the firelight and began staring at him. Finally she said, "This man was one of Jesus' followers!"

[57]Peter denied it. "Woman," he said, "I don't even know the man!"

[58]After a while someone else looked at him and said, "You must be one of them!"

"No, man, I'm not!" Peter replied.

[59]About an hour later someone else insisted, "This must be one of Jesus' disciples because he is a Galilean, too."

[60]But Peter said, "Man, I don't know what you are talking about." And as soon as he said these words, the rooster crowed. [61]At that moment the Lord turned and looked at Peter. Then Peter remembered that the Lord had said, "Before the rooster crows tomorrow morning, you will deny me three times." [62]And Peter left the courtyard, crying bitterly.

[63]Now the guards in charge of Jesus began mocking and beating him. [64]They blindfolded him; then they hit him and asked, "Who hit you that time, you prophet?" [65]And they threw all sorts of terrible insults at him.

Jesus before the Council

[66]At daybreak all the leaders of the people assembled, including the leading priests and the teachers of religious law. Jesus was led before this high council,* [67]and they said, "Tell us if you are the Messiah."

But he replied, "If I tell you, you won't believe me. [68]And if I ask you a question, you won't answer. [69]But the time is soon coming when I, the Son of Man, will be sitting at God's right hand in the place of power."*

[70]They all shouted, "Then you claim you are the Son of God?"

And he replied, "You are right in saying that I am."

[71]"What need do we have for other witnesses?" they shouted. "We ourselves heard him say it."

CHAPTER 23
Jesus' Trial before Pilate

Then the entire council took Jesus over to Pilate, the Roman governor. [2]They began at once to state their case: "This man has been leading our people to ruin by telling them not to pay their taxes to the Roman government and by claiming he is the Messiah, a king."

22:66 Greek *before their Sanhedrin.* **22:69** See Ps 110:1.

Faith

READ LUKE 22:31-34

It is easy to lose faith when we are troubled. As we are buffeted about by the storms of life, we may feel like the faith we once had has slipped away. We may begin to feel anger toward God.

Simon Peter had his ups and downs with God. On the night Simon Peter would deny him, Jesus said to him, "Simon, Simon, Satan has asked to have all of you, to sift you like wheat. But I have pleaded in prayer for you, Simon, that your faith should not fail. So when you have repented and turned to me again, strengthen and build up your brothers" (Luke 22:31-32).

Jesus pointed out that Simon had an assailant in the spiritual realm. Jesus knew Peter would be attacked and "sifted," but he also was confident that afterward Peter would return to God. Wheat is sifted by throwing it repeatedly into the air. The kernels are separated from the chaff as the lighter chaff is carried away by the wind. All that remain are the good, solid wheat kernels.

We should not be surprised that we face times when our faith seems to disappear. We may feel as if we are being ripped open and our faith is being blown away like chaff. But we needn't worry. We will find the core of our faith again. And when we do, we will be all the better for it—and better able to encourage others, too.

Turn to page 159, John 8.

³So Pilate asked him, "Are you the King of the Jews?"

Jesus replied, "Yes, it is as you say."

⁴Pilate turned to the leading priests and to the crowd and said, "I find nothing wrong with this man!"

⁵Then they became desperate. "But he is causing riots everywhere he goes, all over Judea, from Galilee to Jerusalem!"

⁶"Oh, is he a Galilean?" Pilate asked. ⁷When they answered that he was, Pilate sent him to Herod Antipas, because Galilee was under Herod's jurisdiction, and Herod happened to be in Jerusalem at the time.

⁸Herod was delighted at the opportunity to see Jesus, because he had heard about him and had been hoping for a long time to see him perform a miracle. ⁹He asked Jesus question after question, but Jesus refused to answer. ¹⁰Meanwhile, the leading priests and the teachers of religious law stood there shouting their accusations. ¹¹Now Herod and his soldiers began mocking and ridiculing Jesus. Then they put a royal robe on him and sent him back to Pilate. ¹²Herod and Pilate, who had been enemies before, became friends that day.

¹³Then Pilate called together the leading priests and other religious leaders, along with the people, ¹⁴and he announced his verdict. "You brought this man to me, accusing him of leading a revolt. I have examined him thoroughly on this point in your presence and find him innocent. ¹⁵Herod came to the same conclusion and sent him back to us. Nothing this man has done calls for the death penalty. ¹⁶So I will have him flogged, but then I will release him."*

¹⁸Then a mighty roar rose from the crowd, and with one voice they shouted, "Kill him, and release Barabbas to us!" ¹⁹(Barabbas was in prison for murder and for taking part in an in-surrection in Jerusalem against the government.) ²⁰Pilate argued with them, because he wanted to release Jesus. ²¹But they shouted, "Crucify him! Crucify him!"

²²For the third time he demanded, "Why? What crime has he committed? I have found no reason to sentence him to death. I will therefore flog him and let him go."

²³But the crowd shouted louder and louder for Jesus' death, and their voices prevailed. ²⁴So Pilate sentenced Jesus to die as they demanded. ²⁵As they had requested, he released Barabbas, the man in prison for insurrection and murder. But he delivered Jesus over to them to do as they wished.

The Crucifixion

²⁶As they led Jesus away, Simon of Cyrene,* who was coming in from the country just then, was forced to follow Jesus and carry his cross. ²⁷Great crowds trailed along behind, including many grief-stricken women. ²⁸But Jesus turned and said to them, "Daughters of Jerusalem, don't weep for me, but weep for yourselves and for your children. ²⁹For the days are coming when they will say, 'Fortunate indeed are the women who are child-less, the wombs that have not borne a child and the breasts that have never nursed.' ³⁰People will beg the mountains to fall on them and the hills to bury them. ³¹For if these things are done when the tree is green, what will happen when it is dry?*"

³²Two others, both criminals, were led out to be executed with him. ³³Finally, they came to a place called The Skull.* All three were crucified there—Jesus on the center cross, and the two criminals on either side.

³⁴Jesus said, "Father, forgive these people, because they don't know what they are doing."* And the soldiers gambled for his clothes by throwing dice.*

23:16 Some manuscripts add verse 17, *For it was necessary for him to release one [prisoner] for them during the feast.* **23:26** *Cyrene* was a city in northern Africa. **23:31** Or *If these things are done to me, the living tree, what will happen to you, the dry tree?* **23:33** Sometimes rendered *Calvary*, which comes from the Latin word for "skull." **23:34a** This sentence is not included in many ancient manuscripts. **23:34b** Greek *by casting lots.* See Ps 22:18.

23:13-25 Pilate initially saw through all the lies of Jesus' accusers. That is an indictment of his accusers, not Jesus. Yet Pilate could not follow through on his convictions. He acquiesced to political expediency and moral compromise to save his job. In seeing Jesus as a political threat, Pilate denied him his human dignity and rights. Often the truth does come out, vindicating the innocent person, but not before a price has been paid. In the recovery process, telling the truth and doing the right thing are always crucial.

23:32-34 Jesus forgave those who nailed him to the cross. Here in the most unjust situation in history, unlimited forgiveness was extended. If Christ forgave in this way from the cross, no sin we've committed is too great for his forgiveness. As we accept his forgiveness, we are freed to forgive those who have sinned against us. Christ helps us release our bitterness and resentment, which only imprison us. His forgiveness empowers us to be forgiving people—forgiving ourself and those who have hurt us.

35The crowd watched, and the leaders laughed and scoffed. "He saved others," they said, "let him save himself if he is really God's Chosen One, the Messiah." 36The soldiers mocked him, too, by offering him a drink of sour wine. 37They called out to him, "If you are the King of the Jews, save yourself!" 38A signboard was nailed to the cross above him with these words: "This is the King of the Jews."

39One of the criminals hanging beside him scoffed, "So you're the Messiah, are you? Prove it by saving yourself—and us, too, while you're at it!"

40But the other criminal protested, "Don't you fear God even when you are dying? 41We deserve to die for our evil deeds, but this man hasn't done anything wrong." 42Then he said, "Jesus, remember me when you come into your Kingdom."

43And Jesus replied, "I assure you, today you will be with me in paradise."

The Death of Jesus

44By this time it was noon, and darkness fell across the whole land until three o'clock. 45The light from the sun was gone. And suddenly, the thick veil hanging in the Temple was torn apart. 46Then Jesus shouted, "Father, I entrust my spirit into your hands!"* And with those words he breathed his last.

47When the captain of the Roman soldiers handling the executions saw what had happened, he praised God and said, "Surely this man was innocent.*" 48And when the crowd that came to see the crucifixion saw all that had happened, they went home in deep sorrow.* 49But Jesus' friends, including the women who had followed him from Galilee, stood at a distance watching.

The Burial of Jesus

50Now there was a good and righteous man named Joseph. He was a member of the Jewish high council, 51but he had not agreed with the decision and actions of the other religious leaders. He was from the town of Arimathea in Judea, and he had been waiting for the Kingdom of God to come. 52He went to Pilate and asked for Jesus' body. 53Then he took the body down from the cross and wrapped it in a long linen cloth and laid it in a new tomb that had been carved out of rock. 54This was done late on Friday afternoon, the day of preparation* for the Sabbath.

55As his body was taken away, the women from Galilee followed and saw the tomb where they placed his body. 56Then they went home and prepared spices and ointments to embalm him. But by the time they were finished it was the Sabbath, so they rested all that day as required by the law.

CHAPTER 24
The Resurrection

But very early on Sunday morning* the women came to the tomb, taking the spices they had prepared. 2They found that the stone covering the entrance had been rolled aside. 3So they went in, but they couldn't find the body of the Lord Jesus. 4They were puzzled, trying to think what could have happened to it. Suddenly, two men appeared to them, clothed in dazzling robes. 5The women were terrified and bowed low before them. Then the men asked, "Why are you looking in a tomb for someone who is alive? 6He isn't here! He has risen from the dead! Don't you remember what he told you back in Galilee, 7that the Son of Man must be betrayed into the hands of sinful men and be crucified, and that he would rise again the third day?"

8Then they remembered that he had said this. 9So they rushed back to tell his eleven disciples—and everyone else—what had happened. 10The women who went to the

23:46 Ps 31:5. 23:47 Or *righteous.* 23:48 Greek *beating their breasts.* 23:54 Greek *on the day of preparation.* 24:1 Greek *But on the first day of the week, very early in the morning.*

23:40-43 The piercing self-examination of the criminal crucified next to Jesus was the prelude to his salvation. His attitude stands in stark contrast to the self-sufficient bitterness and cynicism of the other criminal, who died in bondage to sin and despair. God always preserves the element of choice in the recovery process, right up to the end of life. It is not too late to begin the process!
24:1-12 During Jesus' arrest and trial, the disciples showed complete helplessness in dealing with the circumstances at hand. But after the Resurrection, in the book of Acts, a new Power enabled them to recover their courage and go into the world with the message of God's good news. The Resurrection is both a historical fact and an experiential power. This power is greater than death itself and can help us overcome our dependency or compulsion. The Resurrection is the very source of recovery. As we experience the power of Christ's resurrection in our life, we will enjoy victory over temptation and freedom from the bondage of our addiction.

tomb were Mary Magdalene, Joanna, Mary the mother of James, and several others. They told the apostles what had happened, [11]but the story sounded like nonsense, so they didn't believe it. [12]However, Peter ran to the tomb to look. Stooping, he peered in and saw the empty linen wrappings; then he went home again, wondering what had happened.*

The Walk to Emmaus

[13]That same day two of Jesus' followers were walking to the village of Emmaus, seven miles* out of Jerusalem. [14]As they walked along they were talking about everything that had happened. [15]Suddenly, Jesus himself came along and joined them and began walking beside them. [16]But they didn't know who he was, because God kept them from recognizing him.

[17]"You seem to be in a deep discussion about something," he said. "What are you so concerned about?"

They stopped short, sadness written across their faces. [18]Then one of them, Cleopas, replied, "You must be the only person in Jerusalem who hasn't heard about all the things that have happened there the last few days."

[19]"What things?" Jesus asked.

"The things that happened to Jesus, the man from Nazareth," they said. "He was a prophet who did wonderful miracles. He was a mighty teacher, highly regarded by both God and all the people. [20]But our leading priests and other religious leaders arrested him and handed him over to be condemned to death, and they crucified him. [21]We had thought he was the Messiah who had come to rescue Israel. That all happened three days ago. [22]Then some women from our group of his followers were at his tomb early this morning, and they came back with an amazing report. [23]They said his body was missing, and they had seen angels who told them

Jesus is alive! [24]Some of our men ran out to see, and sure enough, Jesus' body was gone, just as the women had said."

[25]Then Jesus said to them, "You are such foolish people! You find it so hard to believe all that the prophets wrote in the Scriptures. [26]Wasn't it clearly predicted by the prophets that the Messiah would have to suffer all these things before entering his time of glory?" [27]Then Jesus quoted passages from the writings of Moses and all the prophets, explaining what all the Scriptures said about himself.

[28]By this time they were nearing Emmaus and the end of their journey. Jesus would have gone on, [29]but they begged him to stay the night with them, since it was getting late. So he went home with them. [30]As they sat down to eat, he took a small loaf of bread, asked God's blessing on it, broke it, then gave it to them. [31]Suddenly, their eyes were opened, and they recognized him. And at that moment he disappeared!

[32]They said to each other, "Didn't our hearts feel strangely warm as he talked with us on the road and explained the Scriptures to us?" [33]And within the hour they were on their way back to Jerusalem, where the eleven disciples and the other followers of Jesus were gathered. When they arrived, they were greeted with the report, [34]"The Lord has really risen! He appeared to Peter*!"

Jesus Appears to the Disciples

[35]Then the two from Emmaus told their story of how Jesus had appeared to them as they were walking along the road and how they had recognized him as he was breaking the bread. [36]And just as they were telling about it, Jesus himself was suddenly standing there among them. He said, "Peace be with you."* [37]But the whole group was terribly frightened, thinking they were seeing a ghost! [38]"Why are you frightened?" he asked. "Why

24:12 Some manuscripts do not include this verse. 24:13 Greek *60 stadia* [11.1 kilometers]. 24:34 Greek *Simon*. 24:36 Some manuscripts do not include *He said, "Peace be with you."*

24:13-24 The two followers on the road to Emmaus were deeply discouraged and grieved by the events of the past few days. They did not fully comprehend who Jesus was nor the kind of faith needed to recover from their pain. Through a step of faith, however, they were lifted from their grief to become people who would help change the world. By meeting and speaking with Jesus, the road from the cross to Emmaus became their path of recovery and wholeness.

24:36-49 Jesus is alive and well, yet this was not immediately evident to his followers in the upper room. As they were banded together in their grief and pain, the living Christ appeared. This living Christ, the Holy Spirit, is present in us; only he can calm our fears and doubts. The task of spreading the good news of resurrection and recovery was overwhelming. Through the promised Holy Spirit (see Acts 2), Jesus gave them the peace and power to do all things through Christ. He can do the same for anyone in recovery who trusts in him.

do you doubt who I am? ³⁹Look at my hands. Look at my feet. You can see that it's really me. Touch me and make sure that I am not a ghost, because ghosts don't have bodies, as you see that I do!" ⁴⁰As he spoke, he held out his hands for them to see, and he showed them his feet.*

⁴¹Still they stood there doubting, filled with joy and wonder. Then he asked them, "Do you have anything here to eat?" ⁴²They gave him a piece of broiled fish, ⁴³and he ate it as they watched.

⁴⁴Then he said, "When I was with you before, I told you that everything written about me by Moses and the prophets and in the Psalms must all come true." ⁴⁵Then he opened their minds to understand these many Scriptures. ⁴⁶And he said, "Yes, it was written long ago that the Messiah must suf-fer and die and rise again from the dead on the third day. ⁴⁷With my authority, take this message of repentance to all the nations, beginning in Jerusalem: 'There is forgiveness of sins for all who turn to me.' ⁴⁸You are witnesses of all these things.

⁴⁹"And now I will send the Holy Spirit, just as my Father promised. But stay here in the city until the Holy Spirit comes and fills you with power from heaven."

The Ascension

⁵⁰Then Jesus led them to Bethany, and lifting his hands to heaven, he blessed them. ⁵¹While he was blessing them, he left them and was taken up to heaven.* ⁵²They worshiped him and* then returned to Jerusalem filled with great joy. ⁵³And they spent all of their time in the Temple, praising God.

24:40 Some manuscripts do not include this verse. **24:51** Some manuscripts do not include *and was taken up to heaven.* **24:52** Some manuscripts do not include *worshiped him and.*

REFLECTIONS ON LUKE

✳*insights* ABOUT THE PERSON OF JESUS

Jesus Christ is portrayed in **Luke 1:76-79** as light shining on those living in darkness. This meta-phor might have reminded the original readers of a group of travelers overtaken by darkness, who were left in danger by the roadside all night. Such people, helpless to defend themselves against the attacks of robbers, would have welcomed the light of the rising sun. This is a picture of what Jesus can do for any of us who are "in darkness," helpless to defend ourself against the draw of our powerful dependency. We move from darkness into light as we receive God's gift of forgive-ness and make a personal commitment to him. As we experience new hope in Jesus, we can tell fellow strugglers about the "sunrise" that is just around the corner when they accept Christ as their Savior.

Jesus, of course, did not need recovery because he was the sinless God-man. From **Luke 2:52** it is clear that from childhood to adulthood Jesus was a perfect model of balanced growth as he developed physically, intellectually, spiritually, and socially. He displayed both personal and inter-personal growth. No dimension of his growth was overemphasized, underdeveloped, or rejected. Our own life needs to be balanced in a similar way as we work through the process of recovery.

Jesus did not succumb to temptation, yet he fully experienced, in one form or another, every temptation known to humanity. The Bible clearly affirms that Jesus was vulnerable to sin because of his humanity, yet he did not sin. If Jesus would have been unable to sin because of his deity, then the temptations given by Satan in **Luke 4:3-13** would have been meaningless. If Jesus was beyond temptation, he would be unable to sympathize with our weaknesses (see Hebrews 4:15). When we experience temptation, especially from our injuries or addiction of the past, we can remember that Jesus understands.

*insights ABOUT GOD'S POWER TO SAVE

In **Luke 4:33-37** Jesus displayed his ability to deliver people from demon possession. Luke and the other Gospel writers repeatedly affirmed Jesus' power in this arena. In Jesus' day, being possessed by a demon was believed to be the greatest adversity one could suffer. By his absolute control over demons, Jesus proved his sovereignty over all the adversity that this world and the world below could heap on humanity. To this day, no evil or adversity in life is too great for God's power to overcome.

The story of Zacchaeus in **Luke 19:1-10** beautifully illustrates God's acceptance and restoration of repentant sinners. After admitting his sins to God, to himself, and to others, Zacchaeus was willing to repay the people he had wronged. Making restitution to those we have harmed or cheated is crucial to repentance and recovery, unless the process of making amends will only cause further injury to people we have wronged. In such cases, it is enough to admit our wrongdoings to God, to ourself, and to another person.

Luke 19:9-10 captures the central theme of Luke's Gospel: Jesus' passion to find and restore those who are lost and alienated from God. This priority has been on the heart of God since the first sin in the Garden of Eden. Immediately after Adam and Eve sinned, God sought them out as they hid in fear. He restored fellowship with them and offered them a way of recovery from their sin (Genesis 3). The work of Jesus on the cross represents the culmination of God's plan for forgiveness, hope, and restored fellowship with God.

The cup of wine shared by Jesus and his disciples in **Luke 22:20** symbolized the blood of Jesus, which would institute the New Covenant. Jesus Christ was the ultimate sacrificial Lamb of God, who has taken away the sins of the world (see John 1:29). Without this provision for sin once and for all, we have no peace or serenity. Without the cup of God's salvation, we are still in sin and insecurity, and many will keep looking for salvation in a bottle. We have an open invitation to receive God's gracious forgiveness. Through Christ we can now rest secure in God's grace, which allows us to escape the guilt of our past.

*insights ABOUT PRAYER

In **Luke 6:12-16** Jesus spent an entire night in prayer before choosing his twelve disciples. Despite the care he took, however, among them was Judas Iscariot, who would betray him. Jesus did not make a mistake; Judas was chosen purposely and prayerfully. Unlike Jesus, we make foolish choices no matter how careful we are. Yet we are like Jesus in that the prayerful choices we make in recovery may still result in betrayal. Even though we may still be betrayed through no fault of our own, we can take comfort from the fact that God can and will use this for good in our life.

Luke 11:5-13 emphasizes that God wants us to approach him with shameless persistence. The commands to ask, seek, and knock are all given in the present tense, emphasizing continuous, persistent action on our part. It is the persistence of the seeker, not necessarily the kindness of the giver, that gets results. To practice this quality in our prayer life and recovery program, we must first have a personal relationship with the giver of all good gifts. Through faith, we can expect that God, who is kinder than any human father, wants us to experience wholeness and will answer our prayers for recovery.

*insights CONCERNING TRUE FAITH

Luke 10:21 tells us where to look for true wisdom. Many of us have spent years looking for wisdom that will help us in the recovery process. We may have begun to think it is hard, if not impossible, to come by. Often the reason we find true wisdom so elusive is that it is divinely and simply revealed to "the childlike." True wisdom does not come from the worldly wise or from ivory-tower intellectuals. God's wisdom for recovery comes from reading his Word and simply trusting him, one day at a time. People in recovery can gain a great deal by following God's leading in childlike simplicity and trust.

In **Luke 15:1-2** we see that Jesus attracted many of the outcasts of Jewish religious and social life. Perhaps this was because he was the only one who did not despise and reject them. Jesus preferred these downcast people because they were aware of their sinfulness and they approached God with humble attitudes. In contrast, the religious leaders, who were outwardly moral but inwardly proud, were not at all attracted to Jesus. To this day, religion can still hinder recovery. But an admission of powerlessness and a relationship with Jesus will help the recovery process.

The story of the lost son in **Luke 15:11-32** wonderfully illustrates the theme of Luke's Gospel (Luke 19:9-10) and the steps of recovery. Like the younger son, we have been guilty of choosing a life of pleasure. With time, however, we discovered that we had become a slave to our selfish lifestyle. Some of us never even saw how lost we were until we hit bottom. The bottom for this son was his realization that the pigs were eating better than he was. When we realize that our life is hopelessly out of control, we have made the first step toward recovery. When we are humbled by our helplessness, we are in the best situation to establish a healthy relationship with our gracious God.

In **Luke 18:40-43** Jesus miraculously healed a blind man. Jesus would not have healed this man, however, had the man not trusted in Jesus' power to do so. On the other hand, it was not simply the blind man's faith that healed him. Faith heals to the extent that it is clearly focused on the proper and powerful object of faith—God in Jesus Christ. Recovery is based not on our own power or our faith, but on our loving God, who has the power and desire to heal us. Our part is to look to him for help.

insights CONCERNING OBSTACLES TO RECOVERY

In **Luke 11:14-23** Jesus was accused of being an ally of Satan. Through Jesus' words and actions, however, it became clear that these accusations were false. Unseen powers of darkness are agents of Satan's kingdom and are behind a great deal of human bondage. When we understand this, then "riding the fence" between living for God and living for ourself is no longer an option. Our success in recovery leaves no room for neutrality or moral compromise. Not to decide for God in Jesus Christ is to decide for Satan and his world of bondage. Only through uncompromising faith in Jesus Christ can we achieve victory and lifelong recovery.

We see in **Luke 22:31-34** that Simon Peter was influenced by Satan to break his commitment to Jesus and found his life careening out of control. While it pained Peter to hear that he would betray Jesus, Jesus held out to him the hope of repentance and restoration. Jesus knows when we will betray or deny him, and he makes gracious provision for that. Though we may have been "sifted by Satan," it is never too late to turn back to Jesus. By continuing to take personal moral inventory, our relapses from recovery will become shorter in duration and fewer in number.

insights ABOUT HONESTY AND DENIAL

The Pharisee in **Luke 18:10-14** did not have an accurate self-perception. He looked upon himself as better than others; his pride hindered his ability to see himself or others as God did. He is a good example of what we are like when we are in denial. Most of us are guilty of ignoring our own dependency by pointing a hypocritical finger at others worse off than we are. Some of us have hidden behind the respectable image we hold in our community. God sees our heart and will reward us (forgive us, heal us, aid us in recovery) according to our humble faith. The tax collector, with humble and honest self-awareness, was well on his way to recovery; the Pharisee was headed for spiritual disaster.

Our true spiritual condition is evidenced not so much by our religious activities as it is by what we depend on for security. In **Luke 18:18-23** Jesus exposed a wealthy young man's dependence on his possessions. Jesus brought him face to face with a common human problem—misplaced devotion. We don't know whether or not this young man ever repented of his attachment to his belongings, but each of us is faced with the same choice. Only by renouncing our unhealthy dependency can we receive lasting spiritual treasure—a healthy, fulfilling relationship with God, ourself, and others.

JOHN

THE BIG PICTURE

A. THE GLORIOUS SOURCE OF RECOVERY IS REVEALED (1:1-18)

B. JESUS GIVES NEW LIFE (1:19–3:36)

C. SATISFYING THE LONGINGS OF THE SOUL (4:1–7:53)

D. COMING INTO THE LIGHT TO BE FREED FROM A PAINFUL PAST (8:1–9:41)

E. EMBRACING AND CELEBRATING AN ABUNDANT LIFE (10:1–12:50)

F. LOVING OTHERS AS JESUS HAS LOVED US (13:1–17:26)

G. THE CRUCIFIXION: EVERYTHING SEEMS TO FALL APART (18:1–19:42)

H. THE RESURRECTION: MIRACULOUS RECOVERY (20:1–21:25)

From the vast stretches of eternity to the confines of time—so the Son of God entered into this world. Jesus was the Creator of this world, but then he immersed himself in his creation. God became a man and willingly sacrificed himself so that all who would receive him could have forgiveness and redemption.

John used a number of images to illustrate who Jesus is and how he gives us eternal life: Jesus is the unblemished Lamb of God who is sacrificed for us; the bread of life who satisfies our spiritual hunger; the living water who satisfies our spiritual thirst; the light who guides us; the good shepherd who leads us; the true vine who gives us life; and the counselor who comforts and teaches us. Through these images, John demonstrated that Jesus can give us all we need for a new, abundant life.

John also used the miracles Jesus performed to show us Jesus' power to transform lives. This Gospel is filled with examples of the power of God in lives needing recovery. With God's help, we can drink the new wine of a changed life; take responsibility to walk away from the sins that paralyze us; recover from our sicknesses; be healed of our blindness to the truth; escape from our sinful addictions and the people who condemn us; and be raised to new life from a dead and empty existence.

John collected this series of images and miracles to help us recognize who Jesus is—the Son of God. When we accept Jesus as our Lord and Savior, we can begin to experience the new life that he offers to all who believe in him.

THE BOTTOM LINE

PURPOSE: To reveal Jesus as the Son of God and show that by faith in him we can experience true love, forgiveness, and recovery. AUTHOR: John the apostle, brother of James, called a "Son of Thunder." AUDIENCE: All people everywhere. DATE WRITTEN: Probably between A.D. 80 and 90. SETTING: After many years of reflecting on his experience as a disciple of Jesus, the apostle John recorded his unique perspective on the gospel. KEY VERSE: "These [things] are written so that you may believe that Jesus is the Messiah, the Son of God, and that by believing in him you will have life" (20:31). KEY PEOPLE AND RELATIONSHIPS: Jesus with John the Baptist, the disciples, Mary, Martha, Lazarus, the religious leaders, Pilate, and Mary Magdalene.

RECOVERY THEMES

The Power of God: Each of the miracles recorded by John, six of which are not recorded in the other Gospels, clearly demonstrates God's power. Jesus healed a man born blind; he walked on water and then calmed a storm; he healed a nobleman's son without even being there; he raised Lazarus from the dead after the man had been dead for more than three days. John did not simply tell us about the life of Christ—he made the important point that Jesus is the embodiment of all of God's power. That power is promised to us when we come to him in our powerlessness and turn our life over to him.

God's Power Can Be within Us: Recovery is based on God's power at work within us. Jesus gave us several pictures of how we can have God's power. He described how the branch abides in the vine and draws life and power from the vine. He told us that he is the bread of life, and that we are to eat that bread. He said that he has water for us to drink that will quench our thirst forever. Each of these images illustrates the promise he made in the upper room: The Holy Spirit would be available to teach us, comfort us, and empower us daily. When we turn our life over to God, the Holy Spirit comes to live within us and take us step-by-step to wholeness and healing.

The Dangers of Denial: In Jesus' early ministry, large crowds followed him. But as Jesus confronted the people with the truth of their sins, the crowds gradually dwindled. Eventually, as people were unwilling to face the realities Jesus exposed in their lives, they rejected the only one who could help them. Times have changed, but the pattern of denial remains the same: We begin with some question about the truth and over time develop rigid resistance to it. Gradually our heart becomes hardened, and we no longer see the obvious truth. Just as he confronted the crowds, Jesus also confronts us with the changes we need to make. It takes courage to be open and willing to face the truth; admitting the truth is the first step toward recovery.

The Invitation to Relationship: Although each of the Gospels shows us the love of Jesus, John presented it as a central theme. In the upper room, Jesus said that the mark of following him is loving others. He prayed that we would be united in love as he and the Father are. John referred to himself in this Gospel as "the disciple Jesus loved" (21:20). In one of his later letters, John wrote that the greatest evidence of God's presence in our life is our love for others (see 1 John 4:11-12, 20-21). Central to the recovery process and to our relationship with God is our recognition of God's love for us and our willingness to value and respect others.

CHAPTER 1
Christ, the Eternal Word

In the beginning the Word already existed. He was with God, and he was God. ²He was in the beginning with God. ³He created everything there is. Nothing exists that he didn't make. ⁴Life itself was in him, and this life gives light to everyone. ⁵The light shines through the darkness, and the darkness can never extinguish it.

⁶God sent John the Baptist ⁷to tell everyone about the light so that everyone might believe because of his testimony. ⁸John himself was not the light; he was only a witness to the light. ⁹The one who is the true light, who gives light to everyone, was going to come into the world.

¹⁰But although the world was made through him, the world didn't recognize him when he came. ¹¹Even in his own land

---

1:1-13 The same Power that created the universe is available to create a new life from our shattered hopes. The light of life that exposes and drives away the darkness of the human race is the same light that brightens the dark corners of our world. This source of all life and true light of the world is the source of all recovery. Eternal life and true recovery are ours when we believe what God says, renounce our tendency to do things our way, and receive the one whom God sent to help us.

1:14-18 The true light of the world became a human being known to us as Jesus Christ, who was full of God's unfailing love and faithfulness. Through Jesus, who was both fully God and fully human, we can know what God is like and enjoy a relationship with him. Jesus Christ came to bring us God's unfailing love and forgiveness and to reveal God's faithfulness to us. God's forgiving grace says, "I forgive you for your wrongs; I love and accept you freely for the person you are." His faithfulness says, "I will follow through on all I have promised."

JOHN THE BAPTIST

A thunderstorm swept in from the wilderness of Judea, stirring many from their slumber, demolishing old structures and soaking the moisture-starved fields. Many were afraid of the fierce deluge, but others were thankful for the future bounty its rain would provide. In the same way, John the Baptist broke onto the scene in Judea. He challenged the power structure of the Jewish leadership and paved the way for what was to come.

From the day an angel appeared to John's father to announce his birth, it was clear that John was special, set aside for a unique purpose. John boldly preached a clear and powerful message: The Kingdom of God was coming, and people were called to turn from their sins and be baptized as a sign of their repentance.

Some were deeply moved by John's words and humbly sought to change their lives; others were hardened in their pride and arrogance. When King Herod married Herodias, his brother's wife, John did not remain silent but pointed out the king's neglect of God's law. Herodias was angered by John's words of condemnation and had him killed. She was able to stomp out the messenger but not the message. The way had been prepared; the Messiah had broken onto the scene. John had done his job.

John felt he was not worthy even to be Jesus' slave. Jesus, however, said that there was no one greater than John in the history of the human race. John did not have a self-esteem problem; he had appropriate humility. When we truly understand the greatness of Jesus, our own self-importance, pride, and self-sufficiency will be transformed into humble gratitude and a desire to please him.

STRENGTHS AND ACCOMPLISHMENTS:
- John spoke the truth no matter what the cost.
- He cared about God's opinion, not what others thought.
- He fulfilled God's will for him by preparing the way for the Messiah.
- He put God first in everything he did and said.
- He honestly expressed his feelings of confusion and doubt.

LESSONS FROM HIS LIFE:
- Standing for the truth may be costly, but it is worthwhile in the end.
- There is joy in telling others about God's Kingdom and Jesus the King.
- An accurate self-perception is a key to faithful service.

KEY VERSE:
"John replied in the words of Isaiah: 'I am a voice shouting in the wilderness, "Prepare a straight pathway for the Lord's coming!"'" (John 1:23).

John's story is found in Matthew 3:1-17; 11:18-19; 14:1-12; Mark 1:1-11; 6:14-29; Luke 1:5-25, 39-45, 57-80; 3:1-22; 7:18-35; 9:7-9; John 1:6-9, 19-37. He is also mentioned in Acts 1:5, 21-22; 10:36-37; 11:16; 13:24-25; 18:25-26; 19:3-4.

---

and among his own people, he was not accepted. ¹²But to all who believed him and accepted him, he gave the right to become children of God. ¹³They are reborn! This is not a physical birth resulting from human passion or plan—this rebirth comes from God.

¹⁴So the Word became human and lived here on earth among us. He was full of unfailing love and faithfulness.* And we have seen his glory, the glory of the only Son of the Father.

¹⁵John pointed him out to the people. He shouted to the crowds, "This is the one I was talking about when I said, 'Someone is coming who is far greater than I am, for he existed long before I did.'"

¹⁶We have all benefited from the rich blessings he brought to us—one gracious blessing after another.* ¹⁷For the law was given through Moses; God's unfailing love and faithfulness came through Jesus Christ. ¹⁸No one has ever seen God. But his only Son, who is himself God,* is near to the Father's heart; he has told us about him.

The Testimony of John the Baptist

¹⁹This was the testimony of John when the Jewish leaders sent priests and Temple

1:14 Greek *grace and truth;* also in 1:17. **1:16** Greek *grace upon grace.* **1:18** Some manuscripts read *his one and only Son.*

assistants* from Jerusalem to ask John whether he claimed to be the Messiah. [20]He flatly denied it. "I am not the Messiah," he said.

[21]"Well then, who are you?" they asked. "Are you Elijah?"

"No," he replied.

"Are you the Prophet?"*

"No."

[22]"Then who are you? Tell us, so we can give an answer to those who sent us. What do you have to say about yourself?"

[23]John replied in the words of Isaiah:

"I am a voice shouting in the wilderness,
     'Prepare a straight pathway for the
         Lord's coming!'"*

[24]Then those who were sent by the Pharisees [25]asked him, "If you aren't the Messiah or Elijah or the Prophet, what right do you have to baptize?"

[26]John told them, "I baptize with* water, but right here in the crowd is someone you do not know, [27]who will soon begin his ministry. I am not even worthy to be his slave.*" [28]This incident took place at Bethany, a village east of the Jordan River, where John was baptizing.

Jesus, the Lamb of God

[29]The next day John saw Jesus coming toward him and said, "Look! There is the Lamb of God who takes away the sin of the world! [30]He is the one I was talking about when I said, 'Soon a man is coming who is far greater than I am, for he existed long before I did.' [31]I didn't know he was the one, but I have been baptizing with water in order to point him out to Israel."

[32]Then John said, "I saw the Holy Spirit descending like a dove from heaven and resting upon him. [33]I didn't know he was the one, but when God sent me to baptize with water, he told me, 'When you see the Holy Spirit descending and resting upon someone, he is the one you are looking for. He is the one who baptizes with the Holy Spirit.' [34]I saw this happen to Jesus, so I testify that he is the Son of God.*"

The First Disciples

[35]The following day, John was again standing with two of his disciples. [36]As Jesus walked by, John looked at him and then declared, "Look! There is the Lamb of God!" [37]Then John's two disciples turned and followed Jesus.

[38]Jesus looked around and saw them following. "What do you want?" he asked them.

They replied, "Rabbi" (which means Teacher), "where are you staying?"

[39]"Come and see," he said. It was about four o'clock in the afternoon when they went with him to the place, and they stayed there the rest of the day.

[40]Andrew, Simon Peter's brother, was one of these men who had heard what John said and then followed Jesus. [41]The first thing Andrew did was to find his brother, Simon, and tell him, "We have found the Messiah" (which means the Christ).

[42]Then Andrew brought Simon to meet Jesus. Looking intently at Simon, Jesus said, "You are Simon, the son of John—but you will be called Cephas" (which means Peter*).

[43]The next day Jesus decided to go to Galilee. He found Philip and said to him, "Come, be my disciple." [44]Philip was from Bethsaida, Andrew and Peter's hometown.

[45]Philip went off to look for Nathanael and told him, "We have found the very person Moses and the prophets wrote about! His name is Jesus, the son of Joseph from Nazareth."

[46]"Nazareth!" exclaimed Nathanael. "Can anything good come from there?"

"Just come and see for yourself," Philip said.

[47]As they approached, Jesus said, "Here comes an honest man—a true son of Israel."

[48]"How do you know about me?" Nathanael asked.

And Jesus replied, "I could see you under the fig tree before Philip found you."

[49]Nathanael replied, "Teacher, you are the Son of God—the King of Israel!"

1:19 Greek *and Levites*. **1:21** See Deut 18:15, 18; Mal 4:5-6. **1:23** Isa 40:3. **1:26** Or *in;* also in 1:31, 33. **1:27** Greek *to untie his sandals.* **1:34** Some manuscripts read *the chosen One of God.* **1:42** The names *Cephas* and *Peter* both mean "rock."

1:19-28 John the Baptist was an original messenger of repentance and recovery. He was not the true light or source of recovery; he merely pointed to the one who was. Likewise, those of us in recovery reflect God's light and merely point the way to recovery. We should not draw followers to ourself any more than John did. We are mere beggars telling other beggars where to find food. When we lay aside pride in our achievements and abilities as John the Baptist did, we are better able to serve Christ by showing fellow strugglers the way to recovery.

50Jesus asked him, "Do you believe all this just because I told you I had seen you under the fig tree? You will see greater things than this." 51Then he said, "The truth is, you will all see heaven open and the angels of God going up and down upon the Son of Man."*

CHAPTER 2
The Wedding at Cana

The next day* Jesus' mother was a guest at a wedding celebration in the village of Cana in Galilee. 2Jesus and his disciples were also invited to the celebration. 3The wine supply ran out during the festivities, so Jesus' mother spoke to him about the problem. "They have no more wine," she told him.

4"How does that concern you and me?" Jesus asked. "My time has not yet come."

5But his mother told the servants, "Do whatever he tells you."

6Six stone waterpots were standing there; they were used for Jewish ceremonial purposes and held twenty to thirty gallons* each. 7Jesus told the servants, "Fill the jars with water." When the jars had been filled to the brim, 8he said, "Dip some out and take it to the master of ceremonies." So they followed his instructions.

9When the master of ceremonies tasted the water that was now wine, not knowing where it had come from (though, of course, the servants knew), he called the bridegroom over. 10"Usually a host serves the best wine first," he said. "Then, when everyone is full and doesn't care, he brings out the less expensive wines. But you have kept the best until now!"

11This miraculous sign at Cana in Galilee was Jesus' first display of his glory. And his disciples believed in him.

12After the wedding he went to Capernaum for a few days with his mother, his brothers, and his disciples.

Jesus Clears the Temple

13It was time for the annual Passover celebration, and Jesus went to Jerusalem. 14In the Temple area he saw merchants selling cattle, sheep, and doves for sacrifices; and he saw money changers behind their counters. 15Jesus made a whip from some ropes and chased them all out of the Temple. He drove out the sheep and oxen, scattered the money changers' coins over the floor, and turned over their tables. 16Then, going over to the people who sold doves, he told them, "Get these things out of here. Don't turn my Father's house into a marketplace!"

17Then his disciples remembered this prophecy from the Scriptures: "Passion for God's house burns within me."*

18"What right do you have to do these things?" the Jewish leaders demanded. "If you have this authority from God, show us a miraculous sign to prove it."

19"All right," Jesus replied. "Destroy this temple, and in three days I will raise it up."

20"What!" they exclaimed. "It took forty-six years to build this Temple, and you can do it in three days?" 21But by "this temple," Jesus meant his body. 22After he was raised from the dead, the disciples remembered that he had said this. And they believed both Jesus and the Scriptures.

23Because of the miraculous signs he did in Jerusalem at the Passover celebration, many people were convinced that he was indeed the Messiah. 24But Jesus didn't trust them, because he knew what people were really like. 25No one needed to tell him about human nature.

1:51 See Gen 28:10-17, the account of Jacob's ladder. **2:1** Greek *On the third day;* see 1:35, 43. **2:6** Greek *2 or 3 measures* [75 to 113 liters]. **2:17** Or *"Concern for God's house will be my undoing."* Ps 69:9.

2:1-12 Jesus was at a wedding celebration with family and friends when the wine ran out. So Jesus turned the water in six stone waterpots into enough wine for the rest of the celebration. If we are in recovery, this abundance of wine would be dangerous. But one truth should be encouraging to us all: Jesus valued the celebration of people at a wedding feast. God is concerned about the seemingly mundane needs we have and has the power to meet those needs. He may call us to do some painful things in the process of recovery, but his ultimate goal for us is a life of peace and wholeness.

2:13-16 Jesus was angry at those who turned the Temple courts into a marketplace of unjust profit. The merchants forced the people to buy "approved" sacrificial animals at exorbitant prices and exchanged their currency for Temple currency at inflated rates. They abused the public trust and mocked holy worship. Anger that is measured and authorized by God's purposes is justified. Sometimes this kind of anger can play an important role in our spiritual, emotional, and physical recovery. We may need to stand up to the abusive forces in our life and make changes that will set us free from their grip. As we do, God will stand by us.

CHAPTER 3
Jesus and Nicodemus

After dark one evening, a Jewish religious leader named Nicodemus, a Pharisee, ²came to speak with Jesus. "Teacher," he said, "we all know that God has sent you to teach us. Your miraculous signs are proof enough that God is with you."

³Jesus replied, "I assure you, unless you are born again,* you can never see the Kingdom of God."

⁴"What do you mean?" exclaimed Nicodemus. "How can an old man go back into his mother's womb and be born again?"

⁵Jesus replied, "The truth is, no one can enter the Kingdom of God without being born of water and the Spirit.* ⁶Humans can reproduce only human life, but the Holy Spirit gives new life from heaven. ⁷So don't be surprised at my statement that you* must be born again. ⁸Just as you can hear the wind but can't tell where it comes from or where it is going, so you can't explain how people are born of the Spirit."

⁹"What do you mean?" Nicodemus asked.

¹⁰Jesus replied, "You are a respected Jewish teacher, and yet you don't understand these things? ¹¹I assure you, I am telling you what we know and have seen, and yet you won't believe us. ¹²But if you don't even believe me when I tell you about things that happen here on earth, how can you possibly believe if I tell you what is going on in heaven? ¹³For only I, the Son of Man,* have come to earth and will return to heaven again. ¹⁴And as Moses lifted up the bronze snake on a pole in the wilderness, so I, the Son of Man, must be lifted up on a pole,* ¹⁵so that everyone who believes in me will have eternal life.

¹⁶"For God so loved the world that he gave his only Son, so that everyone who believes in him will not perish but have eternal life. ¹⁷God did not send his Son into the world to condemn it, but to save it.

¹⁸"There is no judgment awaiting those who trust him. But those who do not trust him have already been judged for not believing in the only Son of God. ¹⁹Their judgment is based on this fact: The light from heaven came into the world, but they loved the darkness more than the light, for their actions were evil. ²⁰They hate the light because they want to sin in the darkness. They stay away from the light for fear their sins will be exposed and they will be punished. ²¹But those who do what is right come to the light gladly, so everyone can see that they are doing what God wants."

John the Baptist Exalts Jesus

²²Afterward Jesus and his disciples left Jerusalem, but they stayed in Judea for a while and baptized there.

²³At this time John the Baptist was baptizing at Aenon, near Salim, because there was plenty of water there and people kept coming to him for baptism. ²⁴This was before John was put into prison. ²⁵At that time a certain Jew began an argument with John's disciples over ceremonial cleansing. ²⁶John's disciples came to him and said, "Teacher, the man you met on the other

---

3:3 Or *born from above;* also in 3:7. **3:5** Or *spirit.* The Greek word for *Spirit* can also be translated *wind;* see 3:8. **3:7** The Greek word for *you* is plural; also in 3:12. **3:13** Some manuscripts add *who lives in heaven.* **3:14** Greek *must be lifted up.*

3:1-12 Spiritual rebirth is as necessary to the recovery process as it is to entering God's Kingdom. Being born again is the beginning—a baby step in the process. The hard part comes each subsequent day as we submit our stubborn heart and will to the control of God's Spirit. True recovery is not attained by our trying harder to live a better life. As we repent, entrust our life to God, and seek to obey him, we will receive forgiveness and true recovery.

3:16-18 Faith says yes to God's loving overtures to us. God cared enough to send his own Son, Jesus Christ, to pay for our sins. True faith has nothing to do with our human efforts, social achievements, or material wealth. True faith says to God, "I'm a helpless sinner, unable to effect my own recovery. I trust your forgiveness, which you freely offer me in Jesus Christ." This faith delivers us from the ultimate consequence of our sins—eternal separation from God. It also empowers us to make changes in the present that will plant the seeds for a new life.

4:4-27 The disciples were surprised to find Jesus speaking with the woman at the well: She was a Samaritan (half Jew and half Gentile), she was a woman, and she had a questionable past. Any one of these factors would have disqualified her from speaking with a "righteous" Jewish man. Jesus broke down the traditional barriers, accepting her as she was and giving her a fresh start in life. Jesus demonstrated God's love for all who have been rejected, condemned, or shunned, which should encourage us. No matter what we have done, God offers us his unconditional acceptance in Jesus. With his powerful help, nothing can stand between us and recovery.

side of the Jordan River, the one you said was the Messiah, is also baptizing people. And everybody is going over there instead of coming here to us."

²⁷John replied, "God in heaven appoints each person's work. ²⁸You yourselves know how plainly I told you that I am not the Messiah. I am here to prepare the way for him—that is all. ²⁹The bride will go where the bridegroom is. A bridegroom's friend rejoices with him. I am the bridegroom's friend, and I am filled with joy at his success. ³⁰He must become greater and greater, and I must become less and less.

³¹"He has come from above and is greater than anyone else. I am of the earth, and my understanding is limited to the things of earth, but he has come from heaven.* ³²He tells what he has seen and heard, but how few believe what he tells them! ³³Those who believe him discover that God is true. ³⁴For he is sent by God. He speaks God's words, for God's Spirit is upon him without measure or limit. ³⁵The Father loves his Son, and he has given him authority over everything. ³⁶And all who believe in God's Son have eternal life. Those who don't obey the Son will never experience eternal life, but the wrath of God remains upon them."

CHAPTER 4
Jesus and the Samaritan Woman

Jesus* learned that the Pharisees had heard, "Jesus is baptizing and making more disciples than John" ²(though Jesus himself didn't baptize them—his disciples did). ³So he left Judea to return to Galilee.

⁴He had to go through Samaria on the way. ⁵Eventually he came to the Samaritan village of Sychar, near the parcel of ground that Jacob gave to his son Joseph. ⁶Jacob's well was there; and Jesus, tired from the long walk, sat wearily beside the well about noontime. ⁷Soon a Samaritan woman came to draw water, and Jesus said to her, "Please give me a drink." ⁸He was alone at the time because his disciples had gone into the village to buy some food.

⁹The woman was surprised, for Jews refuse to have anything to do with Samaritans. She said to Jesus, "You are a Jew, and I am a Samaritan woman. Why are you asking me for a drink?"

¹⁰Jesus replied, "If you only knew the gift God has for you and who I am, you would ask me, and I would give you living water."

3:31 Some manuscripts omit *but he has come from heaven.* **4:1** Some manuscripts read *The Lord.*

STEP 11

Friends of the Light

BIBLE READING: John 3:18-21

We sought through prayer and meditation to improve our conscious contact with God, praying only for knowledge of his will for us and the power to carry that out.

Sometimes we don't want to know God's will because there are areas in our life that we aren't ready to deal with yet. Recovery is a process for us. We may be ready to pray for God's will in some areas but feel uncomfortable having God's light shine into the areas that are still hidden in shame.

When talking about those who refuse to trust him with their life, Jesus said, "The light from heaven came into the world, but they loved the darkness more than the light, for their actions were evil. . . . They stay away from the light for fear their sins will be exposed and they will be punished" (John 3:19-20). Later, in one of his talks, Jesus said to the people, "I am the light of the world. If you follow me, you won't be stumbling through the darkness, because you will have the light that leads to life" (John 8:12).

Darkness is great when we are trying to hide something, but light is needed when we are trying to walk without falling. When we were hiding our shameful behavior and holding on to our addiction, the darkness seemed like our friend. Now that we are trying to walk toward recovery, we need the light to keep us from stumbling. We don't have to be afraid of God's light anymore since we have his forgiveness through Christ. He wants to safely guide us on the right path. *Turn to page 493, Psalm 27.*

¹¹"But sir, you don't have a rope or a bucket," she said, "and this is a very deep well. Where would you get this living water? ¹²And besides, are you greater than our ancestor Jacob who gave us this well? How can you offer better water than he and his sons and his cattle enjoyed?"

¹³Jesus replied, "People soon become thirsty again after drinking this water. ¹⁴But the water I give them takes away thirst altogether. It becomes a perpetual spring within them, giving them eternal life."

¹⁵"Please, sir," the woman said, "give me some of that water! Then I'll never be thirsty again, and I won't have to come here to haul water."

¹⁶"Go and get your husband," Jesus told her.

¹⁷"I don't have a husband," the woman replied.

Jesus said, "You're right! You don't have a husband—¹⁸for you have had five husbands, and you aren't even married to the man you're living with now."

¹⁹"Sir," the woman said, "you must be a prophet. ²⁰So tell me, why is it that you Jews insist that Jerusalem is the only place of worship, while we Samaritans claim it is here at Mount Gerizim,* where our ancestors worshiped?"

²¹Jesus replied, "Believe me, the time is coming when it will no longer matter whether you worship the Father here or in Jerusalem. ²²You Samaritans know so little about the one you worship, while we Jews know all about him, for salvation comes through the Jews. ²³But the time is coming and is already here when true worshipers will worship the Father in spirit and in truth. The Father is looking for anyone who will worship him that way. ²⁴For God is Spirit, so those who worship him must worship in spirit and in truth."

²⁵The woman said, "I know the Messiah will come—the one who is called Christ. When he comes, he will explain everything to us."

²⁶Then Jesus told her, "I am the Messiah!"*

²⁷Just then his disciples arrived. They were astonished to find him talking to a woman, but none of them asked him why he was doing it or what they had been discussing. ²⁸The woman left her water jar beside the well and went back to the village and told everyone, ²⁹"Come and meet a man who told me everything I ever did! Can this be the Messiah?" ³⁰So the people came streaming from the village to see him.

³¹Meanwhile, the disciples were urging Jesus to eat. ³²"No," he said, "I have food you don't know about."

³³"Who brought it to him?" the disciples asked each other.

³⁴Then Jesus explained: "My nourishment comes from doing the will of God, who sent me, and from finishing his work. ³⁵Do you think the work of harvesting will not begin until the summer ends four months from now? Look around you! Vast fields are ripening all around us and are ready now for the harvest. ³⁶The harvesters are paid good wages, and the fruit they harvest is people brought to eternal life. What joy awaits both the planter and the harvester alike! ³⁷You know the saying, 'One person plants and someone else harvests.' And it's true. ³⁸I sent you to harvest where you didn't plant; others had already done the work, and you will gather the harvest."

Many Samaritans Believe

³⁹Many Samaritans from the village believed in Jesus because the woman had said, "He told me everything I ever did!" ⁴⁰When they came out to see him, they begged him to stay at their village. So he stayed for two days, ⁴¹long enough for many of them to hear his message and believe. ⁴²Then they said to the woman, "Now we believe because we have heard him ourselves, not just because of what you told us. He is indeed the Savior of the world."

4:20 Greek *on this mountain.* **4:26** Greek *"I am, the one speaking to you."*

4:39-42 The Samaritan woman put her faith in Jesus, who knew all her faults yet loved and respected her. She responded to God's gracious forgiveness by immediately telling her neighbors about the Messiah who had given her a new life. As a result, many were blessed with faith in Jesus Christ. As we experience God's powerful deliverance, it is important that we share the good news with others. It may be the difference between life and death for people we know. As we share what God has done for us, we will experience anew the great joy of victory in Christ.

4:46-53 The government official demonstrated faith in Jesus by humbly asking him to heal his son. He believed Jesus' word to be true even though he hadn't yet seen the results. Our faith is expressed in similar ways. We can begin by humbly and honestly seeking God's help. He will help us even though we may not see immediate results. The recovery process takes time. We can believe that God is working and persevere, even when the results are not immediately evident.

Jesus Heals an Official's Son

⁴³At the end of the two days' stay, Jesus went on into Galilee. ⁴⁴He had previously said, "A prophet is honored everywhere except in his own country." ⁴⁵The Galileans welcomed him, for they had been in Jerusalem at the Passover celebration and had seen all his miraculous signs.

⁴⁶In the course of his journey through Galilee, he arrived at the town of Cana, where he had turned the water into wine. There was a government official in the city of Capernaum whose son was very sick. ⁴⁷When he heard that Jesus had come from Judea and was traveling in Galilee, he went over to Cana. He found Jesus and begged him to come to Capernaum with him to heal his son, who was about to die.

⁴⁸Jesus asked, "Must I do miraculous signs and wonders before you people will believe in me?"

⁴⁹The official pleaded, "Lord, please come now before my little boy dies."

⁵⁰Then Jesus told him, "Go back home. Your son will live!" And the man believed Jesus' word and started home.

⁵¹While he was on his way, some of his servants met him with the news that his son was alive and well. ⁵²He asked them when the boy had begun to feel better, and they replied, "Yesterday afternoon at one o'clock his fever suddenly disappeared!" ⁵³Then the father realized it was the same time that Jesus had told him, "Your son will live." And the officer and his entire household believed in Jesus. ⁵⁴This was Jesus' second miraculous sign in Galilee after coming from Judea.

CHAPTER 5
Jesus Heals a Lame Man

Afterward Jesus returned to Jerusalem for one of the Jewish holy days. ²Inside the city, near the Sheep Gate, was the pool of Bethesda,* with five covered porches. ³Crowds of sick people—blind, lame, or paralyzed—lay on the porches.* ⁵One of the men lying there had been sick for thirty-eight years. ⁶When Jesus saw him and knew how long he had been ill, he asked him, "Would you like to get well?"

⁷"I can't, sir," the sick man said, "for I have no one to help me into the pool when

5:2 Some manuscripts read *Beth-zatha;* other manuscripts read *Bethsaida.* **5:3** Some manuscripts add *waiting for a certain movement of the water,* ⁴*for an angel of the Lord came from time to time and stirred up the water. And the first person to step down into it afterward was healed.*

S T E P

Discovering Hope

BIBLE READING: John 5:1-15

We were entirely ready to have God remove all these defects of character.
How can we honestly say that we are entirely ready for God to remove our defects of character? If we think in terms of all or nothing, we may get stuck here because we will never feel entirely ready. It is important to keep in mind that the Twelve Steps are guiding ideals. No one can work them perfectly. Our part is to keep moving, to get as close as we can to being ready.

In Jesus' day there was a pool where people went, hoping to experience miraculous healing. "One of the men lying there had been sick for thirty-eight years. When Jesus saw him and knew how long he had been ill, he asked him, 'Would you like to get well?' 'I can't, sir,' the sick man said, 'for I have no one to help me into the pool when the water is stirred up. While I am trying to get there, someone else always gets in ahead of me.' Jesus told him, 'Stand up, pick up your sleeping mat, and walk!' Instantly, the man was healed! He rolled up the mat and began walking!" (John 5:5-9).

This man was so crippled that he couldn't go any farther on his own. He camped as near as he could to a place where there was hope for recovery. God met him there and brought him the rest of the way. For us, "entirely ready" may mean getting as close to the hope of healing as we can in our crippled condition. When we do, God will meet us there and take us the rest of the way. *Turn to page 245, Romans 6.*

the water is stirred up. While I am trying to get there, someone else always gets in ahead of me."

8Jesus told him, "Stand up, pick up your sleeping mat, and walk!"

9Instantly, the man was healed! He rolled up the mat and began walking! But this miracle happened on the Sabbath day. 10So the Jewish leaders objected. They said to the man who was cured, "You can't work on the Sabbath! It's illegal to carry that sleeping mat!"

11He replied, "The man who healed me said to me, 'Pick up your sleeping mat and walk.'"

12"Who said such a thing as that?" they demanded.

13The man didn't know, for Jesus had disappeared into the crowd. 14But afterward Jesus found him in the Temple and told him, "Now you are well; so stop sinning, or something even worse may happen to you."

15Then the man went to find the Jewish leaders and told them it was Jesus who had healed him.

Jesus Claims to Be the Son of God

16So the Jewish leaders began harassing Jesus for breaking the Sabbath rules. 17But Jesus replied, "My Father never stops working, so why should I?" 18So the Jewish leaders tried all the more to kill him. In addition to disobeying the Sabbath rules, he had spoken of God as his Father, thereby making himself equal with God.

19Jesus replied, "I assure you, the Son can do nothing by himself. He does only what he sees the Father doing. Whatever the Father does, the Son also does. 20For the Father loves the Son and tells him everything he is doing, and the Son will do far greater things than healing this man. You will be astonished at what he does. 21He will even raise from the dead anyone he wants to, just as the Father does. 22And the Father leaves all judgment to his Son, 23so that everyone will honor the Son, just as they honor the Father. But if you refuse to honor the Son, then you are certainly not honoring the Father who sent him.

24"I assure you, those who listen to my message and believe in God who sent me have eternal life. They will never be condemned for their sins, but they have already passed from death into life.

25"And I assure you that the time is coming, in fact it is here, when the dead will hear my voice—the voice of the Son of God. And those who listen will live. 26The Father has life in himself, and he has granted his Son to have life in himself. 27And he has given him authority to judge all mankind because he is the Son of Man. 28Don't be so surprised! Indeed, the time is coming when all the dead in their graves will hear the voice of God's Son, 29and they will rise again. Those who have done good will rise to eternal life, and those who have continued in evil will rise to judgment. 30But I do nothing without consulting the Father. I judge as I am told. And my judgment is absolutely just, because it is according to the will of God who sent me; it is not merely my own.

Witnesses to Jesus

31"If I were to testify on my own behalf, my testimony would not be valid. 32But someone else is also testifying about me, and I can assure you that everything he says about me is true. 33In fact, you sent messengers to listen to John the Baptist, and he preached the truth. 34But the best testimony about me is not from a man, though I have reminded you about John's testimony so you might be saved. 35John shone brightly for a while, and you benefited and rejoiced. 36But I have a greater witness than John—my teachings and my miracles. They have been assigned to me by the Father, and they testify that the Father has sent me. 37And the Father himself has also testified about me. You have never heard his voice or seen him face to face, 38and you do not have his message in your hearts, because you do not believe me—the one he sent to you.

39"You search the Scriptures because you believe they give you eternal life. But the Scriptures point to me! 40Yet you refuse to come to me so that I can give you this eternal life.

5:39-40 The Jewish leaders knew the Scriptures backward and forward, yet they were spiritually dead. They missed the whole purpose of the Scriptures—to bring people into a vital relationship with the God of grace. Intellectual knowledge about the Bible does not bring us into a transforming relationship with God unless we act on that knowledge. Knowing about God's truth concerning recovery without applying it personally only results in failure. Real growth and recovery come through knowing God through Jesus Christ.

⁴¹"Your approval or disapproval means nothing to me, ⁴²because I know you don't have God's love within you. ⁴³For I have come to you representing my Father, and you refuse to welcome me, even though you readily accept others who represent only themselves. ⁴⁴No wonder you can't believe! For you gladly honor each other, but you don't care about the honor that comes from God alone.

⁴⁵"Yet it is not I who will accuse you of this before the Father. Moses will accuse you! Yes, Moses, on whom you set your hopes. ⁴⁶But if you had believed Moses, you would have believed me because he wrote about me. ⁴⁷And since you don't believe what he wrote, how will you believe what I say?"

CHAPTER 6
Jesus Feeds Five Thousand

After this, Jesus crossed over the Sea of Galilee, also known as the Sea of Tiberias. ²And a huge crowd kept following him wherever he went, because they saw his miracles as he healed the sick. ³Then Jesus went up into the hills and sat down with his disciples around him. ⁴(It was nearly time for the annual Passover celebration.) ⁵Jesus soon saw a great crowd of people climbing the hill, looking for him. Turning to Philip, he asked, "Philip, where can we buy bread to feed all these people?" ⁶He was testing Philip, for he already knew what he was going to do.

⁷Philip replied, "It would take a small fortune* to feed them!"

⁸Then Andrew, Simon Peter's brother, spoke up. ⁹"There's a young boy here with five barley loaves and two fish. But what good is that with this huge crowd?"

¹⁰"Tell everyone to sit down," Jesus ordered. So all of them—the men alone numbered five thousand—sat down on the grassy slopes. ¹¹Then Jesus took the loaves, gave thanks to God, and passed them out to the people. Afterward he did the same with the fish. And they all ate until they were full. ¹²"Now gather the leftovers," Jesus told his disciples, "so that nothing is wasted." ¹³There were only five barley loaves to start with, but twelve baskets were filled with the pieces of bread the people did not eat!

¹⁴When the people saw this miraculous sign, they exclaimed, "Surely, he is the Prophet* we have been expecting!" ¹⁵Jesus saw that they were ready to take him by force and make him king, so he went higher into the hills alone.

Jesus Walks on Water

¹⁶That evening his disciples went down to the shore to wait for him. ¹⁷But as darkness fell and Jesus still hadn't come back, they got into the boat and headed out across the lake toward Capernaum. ¹⁸Soon a gale swept down upon them as they rowed, and the sea grew very rough. ¹⁹They were three or four miles* out when suddenly they saw Jesus walking on the water toward the boat. They were terrified, ²⁰but he called out to them, "I am here! Don't be afraid." ²¹Then they were eager to let him in, and immediately the boat arrived at their destination!

Jesus, the Bread of Life

²²The next morning, back across the lake, crowds began gathering on the shore, waiting to see Jesus. For they knew that he and his

6:7 Greek *200 denarii.* A denarius was the equivalent of a full day's wage. **6:14** See Deut 18:15, 18. **6:19** Greek *25 or 30 stadia* [4.6 or 5.5 kilometers].

5:41-44 Jesus called the Pharisees to task for being more concerned about what others thought of them than about what God thought. At times during recovery it may be necessary to do things that are neither understood nor approved of by those around us. The bottom line for us is whether or not God approves of what we are doing, not what others think. As we take our moral inventory, God and his Word—not the opinions of others—are the standards for our behavior.
6:1-15 Jesus often used people as channels of his grace. In feeding 5,000 hungry men (plus women and children), Jesus used a young boy's provisions. In effecting our recovery—or others' recovery—God allows us to have a part in what he does. When we willingly dedicate our own small resources—time, talents, or possessions—to God, he can work a miracle of recovery for us and others. God can take our limited resources and multiply them beyond our wildest expectations.
6:16-21 It was a dark and stormy night on Lake Galilee. The disciples were cold, wet, and exhausted from rowing almost four miles in storm-tossed waters. They had been impatient and left safe shores without Jesus, but he came to their rescue anyway—walking on the stormy sea toward their boat! When Jesus got in the boat, he brought them safely to shore. We would be wise to stay with Jesus and his plan for us. Going off on our own will inevitably lead us into some stormy situations. When we leave Jesus behind, however, he will still rescue us if we look to him for help.

disciples had come over together and that the disciples had gone off in their boat, leaving him behind. 23Several boats from Tiberias landed near the place where the Lord had blessed the bread and the people had eaten. 24When the crowd saw that Jesus wasn't there, nor his disciples, they got into the boats and went across to Capernaum to look for him. 25When they arrived and found him, they asked, "Teacher, how did you get here?"

26Jesus replied, "The truth is, you want to be with me because I fed you, not because you saw the miraculous sign. 27But you shouldn't be so concerned about perishable things like food. Spend your energy seeking the eternal life that I, the Son of Man, can give you. For God the Father has sent me for that very purpose."

28They replied, "What does God want us to do?"

29Jesus told them, "This is what God wants you to do: Believe in the one he has sent."

30They replied, "You must show us a miraculous sign if you want us to believe in you. What will you do for us? 31After all, our ancestors ate manna while they journeyed through the wilderness! As the Scriptures say, 'Moses gave them bread from heaven to eat.'*"

32Jesus said, "I assure you, Moses didn't give them bread from heaven. My Father did. And now he offers you the true bread from heaven. 33The true bread of God is the one who comes down from heaven and gives life to the world."

34"Sir," they said, "give us that bread every day of our lives."

35Jesus replied, "I am the bread of life. No one who comes to me will ever be hungry again. Those who believe in me will never thirst. 36But you haven't believed in me even though you have seen me. 37However, those the Father has given me will come to me, and I will never reject them. 38For I have come down from heaven to do the will of God who sent me, not to do what I want. 39And this is the will of God, that I should not lose even one of all those he has given me, but that I should raise them to eternal life at the last day. 40For it is my Father's will that all who see his Son and believe in him should have eternal life—that I should raise them at the last day."

41Then the people* began to murmur in disagreement because he had said, "I am the bread from heaven." 42They said, "This is Jesus, the son of Joseph. We know his father and mother. How can he say, 'I came down from heaven'?"

43But Jesus replied, "Don't complain about what I said. 44For people can't come to me unless the Father who sent me draws them to me, and at the last day I will raise them from the dead. 45As it is written in the Scriptures, 'They will all be taught by God.'* Everyone who hears and learns from the Father comes to me. 46(Not that anyone has ever seen the Father; only I, who was sent from God, have seen him.)

47"I assure you, anyone who believes in me already has eternal life. 48Yes, I am the bread of life! 49Your ancestors ate manna in the wilderness, but they all died. 50However, the bread from heaven gives eternal life to everyone who eats it. 51I am the living bread that came down out of heaven. Anyone who eats this bread will live forever; this bread is my flesh, offered so the world may live."

52Then the people began arguing with each other about what he meant. "How can this man give us his flesh to eat?" they asked.

53So Jesus said again, "I assure you, unless you eat the flesh of the Son of Man and drink his blood, you cannot have eternal

6:31 Exod 16:4; Ps 78:24. 6:41 Greek *Jewish people;* also in 6:52. 6:45 Isa 54:13.

6:32-40 After feeding more than 5,000 hungry people with five loaves of bread and two fish, Jesus explained that he himself was the bread of life. Jesus feeds the hungry with himself. His is a perfect love that never rejects us, no matter what our past sins are. He satisfies the deepest hungers of our soul and wants to help us complete our recovery. Until the end of time, Jesus will work toward the healing and recovery of all the broken people in his world. Our part is to turn to him and believe in his power to help us.

6:53-58 Jesus' words here are jarring. In saying we need to eat his flesh and drink his blood to have eternal life, Jesus offended many people, but he made some important points. Jesus' flesh reminds us that he was fully human so he understands our temptations and struggles. Jesus' mention of his blood anticipated his death on the cross—in our place, for our sins. To "eat" his flesh and "drink" his blood was a call to make him and his teachings our very life, not just an intellectual activity. We are to make Jesus the core of our being—emotional, spiritual, and physical. As we feed our body with food, we are to feed our soul with the spiritual reality represented by the body and blood of Christ.

life within you. 54But those who eat my flesh and drink my blood have eternal life, and I will raise them at the last day. 55For my flesh is the true food, and my blood is the true drink. 56All who eat my flesh and drink my blood remain in me, and I in them. 57I live by the power of the living Father who sent me; in the same way, those who partake of me will live because of me. 58I am the true bread from heaven. Anyone who eats this bread will live forever and not die as your ancestors did, even though they ate the manna."

59He said these things while he was teaching in the synagogue in Capernaum.

Many Disciples Desert Jesus

60Even his disciples said, "This is very hard to understand. How can anyone accept it?"

61Jesus knew within himself that his disciples were complaining, so he said to them, "Does this offend you? 62Then what will you think if you see me, the Son of Man, return to heaven again? 63It is the Spirit who gives eternal life. Human effort accomplishes nothing. And the very words I have spoken to you are spirit and life. 64But some of you don't believe me." (For Jesus knew from the beginning who didn't believe, and he knew who would betray him.) 65Then he said, "That is what I meant when I said that people can't come to me unless the Father brings them to me."

66At this point many of his disciples turned away and deserted him. 67Then Jesus turned to the Twelve and asked, "Are you going to leave, too?"

68Simon Peter replied, "Lord, to whom would we go? You alone have the words that give eternal life. 69We believe them, and we know you are the Holy One of God."

70Then Jesus said, "I chose the twelve of you, but one is a devil." 71He was speaking of Judas, son of Simon Iscariot, one of the Twelve, who would betray him.

CHAPTER 7

Jesus and His Brothers

After this, Jesus stayed in Galilee, going from village to village. He wanted to stay out of Judea where the Jewish leaders were plotting his death. 2But soon it was time for the Festival of Shelters, 3and Jesus' brothers urged him to go to Judea for the celebration. "Go where your followers can see your miracles!" they scoffed. 4"You can't become a public figure if you hide like this! If you can do such wonderful things, prove it to the world!" 5For even his brothers didn't believe in him.

6Jesus replied, "Now is not the right time for me to go. But you can go anytime, and it will make no difference. 7The world can't hate you, but it does hate me because I accuse it of sin and evil. 8You go on. I am not yet* ready to go to this festival, because my time has not yet come." 9So Jesus remained in Galilee.

Jesus Teaches Openly at the Temple

10But after his brothers had left for the festival, Jesus also went, though secretly, staying out of public view. 11The Jewish leaders tried to find him at the festival and kept asking if

7:8 Some manuscripts omit *yet*.

6:68-69 Sales pitches for enticing products assault us daily. Publishers' sweepstakes, lottery games, television specials, political causes, religious gurus all call for our time, money, and devotion. They promise to give us what we need and desire. When all is said and done, however, we are left with Peter's question, "Lord, to whom would we go?" Jesus is the answer to our every need—including recovery. He alone can deliver us from our powerful addiction or compulsion. He alone deserves our total commitment.

7:3-10 Jesus experienced firsthand the ridicule and rejection from family that many of us in recovery have experienced. Jesus knew what was right and when to act. He resisted the timetables, agendas, and expectations that others—even his own brothers—foisted upon him. Timetables for recovery, going public, or staging a comeback will vary for each person. Premature publicity of our conversion to Christ or commitment to recovery may lead to unnecessary attacks from others or inflated pride about our personal successes. Either will stand in the way of what God is trying to accomplish in and through our life. Often it is best to remain anonymous until the time is right.

7:10-15, 25-27, 40-49 In this chapter the author polled the audience for opinions about who Jesus actually is. Some believed he was a wonderful teacher. Others thought he was a fraud or a madman. Still others conceded he might be the Messiah or at least a prophet. The religious authorities saw him as a political threat and wanted him arrested, even killed. We, too, must decide who Jesus is and what he means to us. Our decision about Jesus is very important. It will not only affect our recovery; it will have eternal consequences as well (see 8:24).

anyone had seen him. [12]There was a lot of discussion about him among the crowds. Some said, "He's a wonderful man," while others said, "He's nothing but a fraud, deceiving the people." [13]But no one had the courage to speak favorably about him in public, for they were afraid of getting in trouble with the Jewish leaders.

[14]Then, midway through the festival, Jesus went up to the Temple and began to teach. [15]The Jewish leaders were surprised when they heard him. "How does he know so much when he hasn't studied everything we've studied?" they asked.

[16]So Jesus told them, "I'm not teaching my own ideas, but those of God who sent me. [17]Anyone who wants to do the will of God will know whether my teaching is from God or is merely my own. [18]Those who present their own ideas are looking for praise for themselves, but those who seek to honor the one who sent them are good and genuine. [19]None of you obeys the law of Moses! In fact, you are trying to kill me."

[20]The crowd replied, "You're demon possessed! Who's trying to kill you?"

[21]Jesus replied, "I worked on the Sabbath by healing a man, and you were offended. [22]But you work on the Sabbath, too, when you obey Moses' law of circumcision. (Actually, this tradition of circumcision is older than the law of Moses; it goes back to Abraham.) [23]For if the correct time for circumcising your son falls on the Sabbath, you go ahead and do it, so as not to break the law of Moses. So why should I be condemned for making a man completely well on the Sabbath? [24]Think this through and you will see that I am right."

Is Jesus the Messiah?

[25]Some of the people who lived there in Jerusalem said among themselves, "Isn't this the man they are trying to kill? [26]But here he is, speaking in public, and they say nothing to him. Can it be that our leaders know that he really is the Messiah? [27]But how could he be? For we know where this man comes from.

When the Messiah comes, he will simply appear; no one will know where he comes from."

[28]While Jesus was teaching in the Temple, he called out, "Yes, you know me, and you know where I come from. But I represent one you don't know, and he is true. [29]I know him because I have come from him, and he sent me to you." [30]Then the leaders tried to arrest him; but no one laid a hand on him, because his time had not yet come.

[31]Many among the crowds at the Temple believed in him. "After all," they said, "would you expect the Messiah to do more miraculous signs than this man has done?"

[32]When the Pharisees heard that the crowds were murmuring such things, they and the leading priests sent Temple guards to arrest Jesus. [33]But Jesus told them, "I will be here a little longer. Then I will return to the one who sent me. [34]You will search for me but not find me. And you won't be able to come where I am."

[35]The Jewish leaders were puzzled by this statement. "Where is he planning to go?" they asked. "Maybe he is thinking of leaving the country and going to the Jews in other lands, or maybe even to the Gentiles! [36]What does he mean when he says, 'You will search for me but not find me,' and 'You won't be able to come where I am'?"

Jesus Promises Living Water

[37]On the last day, the climax of the festival, Jesus stood and shouted to the crowds, "If you are thirsty, come to me! [38]If you believe in me, come and drink! For the Scriptures declare that rivers of living water will flow out from within."* [39](When he said "living water," he was speaking of the Spirit, who would be given to everyone believing in him. But the Spirit had not yet been given, because Jesus had not yet entered into his glory.)

Division and Unbelief

[40]When the crowds heard him say this, some of them declared, "This man surely is the Prophet."* [41]Others said, "He is the Mes-

---

7:37-38 Or *"Let anyone who is thirsty come to me and drink.* [38]*For the Scriptures declare that rivers of living water will flow from the heart of those who believe in me."* **7:40** See Deut 18:15, 18.

7:37-39 Jesus is the living water who satisfies our thirst. When we believe in him, he gives us his Spirit. The Holy Spirit becomes an inexhaustible river of living water, welling up in us and flowing through us. The indwelling and eternal Holy Spirit goes with us wherever we go and can quench even our strongest spiritual thirsts and meet our deepest needs. Having this water "on tap" is the key to resisting the temptation of alcohol, food, sex, work, a codependent relationship, or any other compulsion.

siah." Still others said, "But he can't be! Will the Messiah come from Galilee? ⁴²For the Scriptures clearly state that the Messiah will be born of the royal line of David, in Bethlehem, the village where King David was born."* ⁴³So the crowd was divided in their opinion about him. ⁴⁴And some wanted him arrested, but no one touched him.

⁴⁵The Temple guards who had been sent to arrest him returned to the leading priests and Pharisees. "Why didn't you bring him in?" they demanded.

⁴⁶"We have never heard anyone talk like this!" the guards responded.

⁴⁷"Have you been led astray, too?" the Pharisees mocked. ⁴⁸"Is there a single one of us rulers or Pharisees who believes in him? ⁴⁹These ignorant crowds do, but what do they know about it? A curse on them anyway!"

⁵⁰Nicodemus, the leader who had met with Jesus earlier, then spoke up. ⁵¹"Is it legal to convict a man before he is given a hearing?" he asked.

⁵²They replied, "Are you from Galilee, too? Search the Scriptures and see for yourself—no prophet ever comes from Galilee!"

[*The most ancient Greek manuscripts do not include John 7:53–8:11.*]

⁵³Then the meeting broke up and everybody went home.

CHAPTER 8
A Woman Caught in Adultery

Jesus returned to the Mount of Olives, ²but early the next morning he was back again at the Temple. A crowd soon gathered, and he sat down and taught them. ³As he was speaking, the teachers of religious law and Pharisees brought a woman they had caught in the act of adultery. They put her in front of the crowd.

⁴"Teacher," they said to Jesus, "this woman was caught in the very act of adultery. ⁵The law of Moses says to stone her. What do you say?"

⁶They were trying to trap him into saying something they could use against him, but Jesus stooped down and wrote in the dust with his finger. ⁷They kept demanding an answer, so he stood up again and said, "All right, stone her. But let those who have never sinned throw the first stones!" ⁸Then he stooped down again and wrote in the dust.

7:42 See Mic 5:2.

S T E P

Feelings of Shame

BIBLE READING: John 8:3-11

We admitted to God, to ourselves, and to another human being the exact nature of our wrongs.

Shame has kept many of us in hiding. The thought of admitting our sins and revealing ourself to other human beings stirs up feelings of shame and the fear of being publicly exposed.

"The teachers of religious law and Pharisees brought a woman they had caught in the act of adultery. They put her in front of the crowd. 'Teacher,' they said to Jesus, '. . . the law of Moses says to stone her. What do you say?' . . . Jesus stooped down and wrote in the dust with his finger. They kept demanding an answer, so he stood up again and said, 'All right, stone her. But let those who have never sinned throw the first stones!' Then he stooped down again and wrote in the dust. When the accusers heard this, they slipped away one by one . . . until only Jesus was left in the middle of the crowd with the woman" (John 8:3-9).

Many believe that it was Jesus' writing in the dust that caused the accusers to leave. Perhaps he was listing the secret sins of the Jewish leaders. If this is true, it gives us a beautiful picture of the kind of person Jesus is—a person to whom we can safely expose our secrets. Our confessor needs to be someone who is not surprised by sin and will not be waiting to condemn us. Such a person needs to take private note of our wrongs, writing them in the soft dust, not etching them in stone and posting them in public. Since shame can be a trigger for addictive behavior, we need to be careful about whom we choose to confide in. *Turn to page 225, Acts 26.*

⁹When the accusers heard this, they slipped away one by one, beginning with the oldest, until only Jesus was left in the middle of the crowd with the woman. ¹⁰Then Jesus stood up again and said to her, "Where are your accusers? Didn't even one of them condemn you?"

¹¹"No, Lord," she said.

And Jesus said, "Neither do I. Go and sin no more."

Jesus, the Light of the World

¹²Jesus said to the people, "I am the light of the world. If you follow me, you won't be stumbling through the darkness, because you will have the light that leads to life."

¹³The Pharisees replied, "You are making false claims about yourself!"

¹⁴Jesus told them, "These claims are valid even though I make them about myself. For I know where I came from and where I am going, but you don't know this about me. ¹⁵You judge me with all your human limitations,* but I am not judging anyone. ¹⁶And if I did, my judgment would be correct in every respect because I am not alone—I have with me the Father who sent me. ¹⁷Your own law says that if two people agree about something, their witness is accepted as fact.* ¹⁸I am one witness, and my Father who sent me is the other."

¹⁹"Where is your father?" they asked.

Jesus answered, "Since you don't know who I am, you don't know who my Father is. If you knew me, then you would know my Father, too." ²⁰Jesus made these statements while he was teaching in the section of the Temple known as the Treasury. But he was not arrested, because his time had not yet come.

The Unbelieving People Warned

²¹Later Jesus said to them again, "I am going away. You will search for me and die in your sin. You cannot come where I am going."

²²The Jewish leaders asked, "Is he planning to commit suicide? What does he mean, 'You cannot come where I am going'?"

²³Then he said to them, "You are from below; I am from above. You are of this world; I am not. ²⁴That is why I said that you will die in your sins; for unless you believe that I am who I say I am, you will die in your sins."

²⁵"Tell us who you are," they demanded.

Jesus replied, "I am the one I have always claimed to be.* ²⁶I have much to say about you and much to condemn, but I won't. For I say only what I have heard from the one who sent me, and he is true." ²⁷But they still didn't understand that he was talking to them about his Father.

²⁸So Jesus said, "When you have lifted up the Son of Man on the cross, then you will realize that I am he and that I do nothing on my own, but I speak what the Father taught me. ²⁹And the one who sent me is with me—he has not deserted me. For I always do those things that are pleasing to him." ³⁰Then many who heard him say these things believed in him.

Jesus and Abraham

³¹Jesus said to the people* who believed in him, "You are truly my disciples if you keep obeying my teachings. ³²And you will know the truth, and the truth will set you free."

³³"But we are descendants of Abraham," they said. "We have never been slaves to anyone on earth. What do you mean, 'set free'?"

³⁴Jesus replied, "I assure you that everyone who sins is a slave of sin. ³⁵A slave is not a permanent member of the family, but a son is part of the family forever. ³⁶So if the Son sets you free, you will indeed be free. ³⁷Yes, I realize that you are descendants of Abraham. And yet some of you are trying to kill me because my message does not find a place in your hearts. ³⁸I am telling you what I saw when I

8:15 Or *judge me by human standards.* **8:17** See Deut 19:15. **8:25** Or *"Why do I speak to you at all?"* **8:31** Greek *Jewish people;* also in 8:48, 52, 57.

8:12 As the light of the world, Jesus exposes what has been hidden and guides us down the path of life and recovery. In part, to walk in the light means to be honest and vulnerable with others and to walk in fellowship with God (see 1 John 1:5-7). As we express our needs and feelings, our sins and struggles, with the people we trust, light will fall on our failures and strengths. This will give us the direction we need to make significant progress in recovery.

8:31-36 To be "set free" is to know the truth—the truth about ourself and about Jesus our liberator. The truth is this: We are a slave to sin and powerless to manage our life effectively. With God's truth as a standard for our moral inventory, we can recognize and confess our needs and struggles, our sins and addiction. As we confess these to God, to ourself, and to at least one other person, we share the truth about our life. When we turn our broken life over to God, who alone can make us whole, we are again acknowledging the truth. These different applications of the truth can combine to set us free from sinful habits, chemical dependencies, and emotional bondage.

was with my Father. But you are following the advice of your father."

³⁹"Our father is Abraham," they declared.

"No," Jesus replied, "for if you were children of Abraham, you would follow his good example.* ⁴⁰I told you the truth I heard from God, but you are trying to kill me. Abraham wouldn't do a thing like that. ⁴¹No, you are obeying your real father when you act that way."

They replied, "We were not born out of wedlock! Our true Father is God himself."

⁴²Jesus told them, "If God were your Father, you would love me, because I have come to you from God. I am not here on my own, but he sent me. ⁴³Why can't you understand what I am saying? It is because you are unable to do so! ⁴⁴For you are the children of your father the Devil, and you love to do the evil things he does. He was a murderer from the beginning and has always hated the truth. There is no truth in him. When he lies, it is consistent with his character; for he is a liar and the father of lies. ⁴⁵So when I tell the truth, you just naturally don't believe me! ⁴⁶Which of you can truthfully accuse me of sin? And since I am telling you the truth, why don't you believe me? ⁴⁷Anyone whose Father is God listens gladly to the words of God. Since you don't, it proves you aren't God's children."

⁴⁸The people retorted, "You Samaritan devil! Didn't we say all along that you were possessed by a demon?"

⁴⁹"No," Jesus said, "I have no demon in me. For I honor my Father—and you dishonor me. ⁵⁰And though I have no wish to glorify myself, God wants to glorify me. Let him be the judge. ⁵¹I assure you, anyone who obeys my teaching will never die!"

⁵²The people said, "Now we know you are possessed by a demon. Even Abraham and the prophets died, but you say that those who obey your teaching will never die! ⁵³Are you greater than our father Abraham, who died? Are you greater than the prophets, who died? Who do you think you are?"

⁵⁴Jesus answered, "If I am merely boasting about myself, it doesn't count. But it is my Father who says these glorious things about me. You say, 'He is our God,' ⁵⁵but you do not even know him. I know him. If I said otherwise, I would be as great a liar as you! But it is true—I know him and obey him. ⁵⁶Your ancestor Abraham rejoiced as he looked forward to my coming. He saw it and was glad."

Honesty

READ JOHN 8:30-36

Living in denial is living dishonestly. How many times have we lied to ourself and others, saying, "I can stop any time I want to!" or "I have the right to choose how I live my own life!" or "My behavior doesn't affect anyone but me!" Ironically, as we asserted our freedom to live as we chose, we soon lost the freedom to choose anything other than our dependency; we became enslaved to it.

Jesus said to some people who believed in him: "You are truly my disciples if you keep obeying my teachings. And you will know the truth, and the truth will set you free. . . . I assure you that everyone who sins is a slave of sin. A slave is not a permanent member of the family, but a son is part of the family forever. So if the Son sets you free, you will indeed be free. . . . Why can't you understand what I am saying? It is because you are unable to do so! For you are the children of your father the Devil. . . . He was a murderer from the beginning and has always hated the truth. There is no truth in him. When he lies, it is consistent with his character; for he is a liar and the father of lies" (John 8:31-36, 43-44).

The spiritual forces that sway our life have roots in either truth or deceit. Truth leads to freedom; deceit leads to bondage and death. Denial is a lie that keeps us in slavery. When we are a slave to our addiction, we lose the right to choose any other way of life. It is only when we break the cycle of denial, when we become brutally honest about our bondage, that there is any chance for real freedom. *Turn to page 169, John 14.*

8:39 Some manuscripts read *if you are children of Abraham, follow his example.*

[57]The people said, "You aren't even fifty years old. How can you say you have seen Abraham?*"

[58]Jesus answered, "The truth is, I existed before Abraham was even born!"* [59]At that point they picked up stones to kill him. But Jesus hid himself from them and left the Temple.

CHAPTER 9
Jesus Heals a Man Born Blind

As Jesus was walking along, he saw a man who had been blind from birth. [2]"Teacher," his disciples asked him, "why was this man born blind? Was it a result of his own sins or those of his parents?"

[3]"It was not because of his sins or his parents' sins," Jesus answered. "He was born blind so the power of God could be seen in him. [4]All of us must quickly carry out the tasks assigned us by the one who sent me, because there is little time left before the night falls and all work comes to an end. [5]But while I am still here in the world, I am the light of the world."

[6]Then he spit on the ground, made mud with the saliva, and smoothed the mud over the blind man's eyes. [7]He told him, "Go and wash in the pool of Siloam" (Siloam means Sent). So the man went and washed, and came back seeing!

[8]His neighbors and others who knew him as a blind beggar asked each other, "Is this the same man—that beggar?" [9]Some said he was, and others said, "No, but he surely looks like him!"

And the beggar kept saying, "I am the same man!"

[10]They asked, "Who healed you? What happened?"

[11]He told them, "The man they call Jesus made mud and smoothed it over my eyes and told me, 'Go to the pool of Siloam and wash off the mud.' I went and washed, and now I can see!"

[12]"Where is he now?" they asked.

"I don't know," he replied.

[13]Then they took the man to the Pharisees. [14]Now as it happened, Jesus had healed the man on a Sabbath. [15]The Pharisees asked the man all about it. So he told them, "He smoothed the mud over my eyes, and when it was washed away, I could see!"

[16]Some of the Pharisees said, "This man Jesus is not from God, for he is working on the Sabbath." Others said, "But how could an ordinary sinner do such miraculous signs?" So there was a deep division of opinion among them.

[17]Then the Pharisees once again questioned the man who had been blind and demanded, "This man who opened your eyes—who do you say he is?"

The man replied, "I think he must be a prophet."

[18]The Jewish leaders wouldn't believe he had been blind, so they called in his parents. [19]They asked them, "Is this your son? Was he born blind? If so, how can he see?"

[20]His parents replied, "We know this is our son and that he was born blind, [21]but we don't know how he can see or who healed him. He is old enough to speak for himself. Ask him." [22]They said this because they were afraid of the Jewish leaders, who had announced that anyone saying Jesus was the Messiah would be expelled from the synagogue. [23]That's why they said, "He is old enough to speak for himself. Ask him."

[24]So for the second time they called in the man who had been blind and told him, "Give glory to God by telling the truth,* because we know Jesus is a sinner."

8:57 Some manuscripts read *How can you say Abraham has seen you?* 8:58 Or *"Truly, truly, before Abraham was, I am."* 9:24 Or *Give glory to God, not to Jesus;* Greek reads *Give glory to God.*

9:1-12, 35-41 Imagine being blind from birth, not being able to see the people we love and the world around us. Then imagine people insinuating that we are blind because of our personal sins or the sins of our parents! Jesus healed this man's blindness, but the real miracle occurred later when the man's spiritual blindness was healed. He saw through eyes of faith that Jesus truly was the Messiah, the Savior of the world. We, too, must recognize that God has the power and the desire to free us from habitual sins, chemical dependencies, and character flaws. Recognizing Jesus as our deliverer is the beginning of our spiritual sight.

9:13-34 The Pharisees were so blinded by their legalistic attitudes that they could not see a wonderful miracle of healing taking place right in front of them. They were more concerned about the letter of the law and the threat Jesus posed to their authority than the amazing healing. They were exposed to the power of God but chose to remain blind to the truth. Those who are teachable and humble will discover that God can heal even the most terrible affliction. Often the people we think least likely to make progress in recovery experience healing and deliverance because they are humble enough to ask God for help.

²⁵"I don't know whether he is a sinner," the man replied. "But I know this: I was blind, and now I can see!"

²⁶"But what did he do?" they asked. "How did he heal you?"

²⁷"Look!" the man exclaimed. "I told you once. Didn't you listen? Why do you want to hear it again? Do you want to become his disciples, too?"

²⁸Then they cursed him and said, "You are his disciple, but we are disciples of Moses. ²⁹We know God spoke to Moses, but as for this man, we don't know anything about him."

³⁰"Why, that's very strange!" the man replied. "He healed my eyes, and yet you don't know anything about him! ³¹Well, God doesn't listen to sinners, but he is ready to hear those who worship him and do his will. ³²Never since the world began has anyone been able to open the eyes of someone born blind. ³³If this man were not from God, he couldn't do it."

³⁴"You were born in sin!" they answered. "Are you trying to teach us?" And they threw him out of the synagogue.

Spiritual Blindness

³⁵When Jesus heard what had happened, he found the man and said, "Do you believe in the Son of Man*?"

³⁶The man answered, "Who is he, sir, because I would like to."

³⁷"You have seen him," Jesus said, "and he is speaking to you!"

³⁸"Yes, Lord," the man said, "I believe!" And he worshiped Jesus.

³⁹Then Jesus told him, "I have come to judge the world. I have come to give sight to the blind and to show those who think they see that they are blind."

⁴⁰The Pharisees who were standing there heard him and asked, "Are you saying we are blind?"

⁴¹"If you were blind, you wouldn't be guilty," Jesus replied. "But you remain guilty because you claim you can see.

CHAPTER 10
The Good Shepherd and His Sheep

"I assure you, anyone who sneaks over the wall of a sheepfold, rather than going through the gate, must surely be a thief and a robber! ²For a shepherd enters through the gate. ³The gatekeeper opens the gate for him, and the sheep hear his voice and come to him. He calls his own sheep by name and leads them out. ⁴After he has gathered his own flock, he walks ahead of them, and they follow him because they recognize his voice. ⁵They won't follow a stranger; they will run from him because they don't recognize his voice."

⁶Those who heard Jesus use this illustration didn't understand what he meant, ⁷so he explained it to them. "I assure you, I am the gate for the sheep," he said. ⁸"All others who came before me were thieves and robbers. But the true sheep did not listen to them. ⁹Yes, I am the gate. Those who come in through me will be saved. Wherever they go, they will find green pastures. ¹⁰The thief's purpose is to steal and kill and destroy. My purpose is to give life in all its fullness.

¹¹"I am the good shepherd. The good shepherd lays down his life for the sheep. ¹²A hired hand will run when he sees a wolf coming. He will leave the sheep because they aren't his and he isn't their shepherd. And so the wolf attacks them and scatters the flock. ¹³The hired hand runs away because he is merely hired and has no real concern for the sheep.

¹⁴"I am the good shepherd; I know my own sheep, and they know me, ¹⁵just as my Father knows me and I know the Father. And I lay down my life for the sheep. ¹⁶I have other sheep, too, that are not in this sheepfold. I

9:35 Some manuscripts read *the Son of God.*

10:1-5 The shepherd knows each of his sheep by name, and they know and respond only to his voice. In like manner, Jesus knows our personality, needs, feelings, and desires. He even knows our faults and our sins, yet he still loves us! He calls out to us and leads us in the way that is best for us. To be set free from the pain of our past, we must respond to the guiding voice of our shepherd, who knows us fully and loves us completely.

10:7-18 At night shepherds in Bible times led their flocks to lie down in a sheepfold (an area boxed in by brush or rock). The shepherd slept in the opening and literally became the gate to the sheepfold. He protected the sheep from wild animals and robbers with his own body. Jesus, our gate and good shepherd, does this for us. By sacrificing his life he has provided the means for our salvation and protection from temptations and addictions. In Christ we can find security and serenity, even when we fail. God is able to use our sins and failures to bring about our ultimate good if we trust him and obey his plan for our life.

must bring them also, and they will listen to my voice; and there will be one flock with one shepherd.

[17]"The Father loves me because I lay down my life that I may have it back again. [18]No one can take my life from me. I lay down my life voluntarily. For I have the right to lay it down when I want to and also the power to take it again. For my Father has given me this command."

[19]When he said these things, the people* were again divided in their opinions about him. [20]Some of them said, "He has a demon, or he's crazy. Why listen to a man like that?" [21]Others said, "This doesn't sound like a man possessed by a demon! Can a demon open the eyes of the blind?"

Jesus Claims to Be the Son of God

[22]It was now winter, and Jesus was in Jerusalem at the time of Hanukkah.* [23]He was at the Temple, walking through the section known as Solomon's Colonnade. [24]The Jewish leaders surrounded him and asked, "How long are you going to keep us in suspense? If you are the Messiah, tell us plainly."

[25]Jesus replied, "I have already told you, and you don't believe me. The proof is what I do in the name of my Father. [26]But you don't believe me because you are not part of my flock. [27]My sheep recognize my voice; I know them, and they follow me. [28]I give them eternal life, and they will never perish. No one will snatch them away from me, [29]for my Father has given them to me, and he is more powerful than anyone else. So no one can take them from me. [30]The Father and I are one."

[31]Once again the Jewish leaders picked up stones to kill him. [32]Jesus said, "At my Father's direction I have done many things to help the people. For which one of these good deeds are you killing me?"

[33]They replied, "Not for any good work, but for blasphemy, because you, a mere man, have made yourself God."

[34]Jesus replied, "It is written in your own law that God said to certain leaders of the people, 'I say, you are gods!'* [35]And you know that the Scriptures cannot be altered. So if those people, who received God's message, were called 'gods,' [36]why do you call it blasphemy when the Holy One who was sent into the world by the Father says, 'I am the Son of God'? [37]Don't believe me unless I carry out my Father's work. [38]But if I do his work, believe in what I have done, even if you don't believe me. Then you will realize that the Father is in me, and I am in the Father."

[39]Once again they tried to arrest him, but he got away and left them. [40]He went beyond the Jordan River to stay near the place where John was first baptizing. [41]And many followed him. "John didn't do miracles," they remarked to one another, "but all his predictions about this man have come true." [42]And many believed in him there.

CHAPTER 11
The Death of Lazarus

A man named Lazarus was sick. He lived in Bethany with his sisters, Mary and Martha. [2]This is the Mary who poured the expensive perfume on the Lord's feet and wiped them with her hair.* Her brother, Lazarus, was sick.

10:19 Greek *Jewish people.* **10:22** Or *the Festival of Dedication.* **10:34** Ps 82:6. **11:2** This incident is recorded in chapter 12.

10:27-29 When we entrust ourself to Jesus, we can feel safe and secure. No one can take us away from him and his care, not even the Devil! Such security is sometimes hard for us to grasp emotionally, especially if we have been a victim of abuse; we may have been so emotionally damaged that life can seem very unsafe. Unsure of whom we can trust and not wanting to be hurt again, we keep everyone at a distance—even God. Recovery from abuse can occur only in a safe relationship that God offers to us in which divine love and protection are expressed.
10:30-38 Jesus said that he and the Father are one; this was a clear claim to divinity. Jesus was God in human flesh (1:14). He was one with his Father in essence, in purpose, in words, and in thoughts. All of Jesus' miracles attest to his divine authority (10:37-38), as do the Scriptures (5:39). Only a God-man could perfectly understand our human weaknesses yet command our complete trust. Only the divine miracle worker, Jesus, can effect the everyday and everlasting recovery that we need.
11:3-4 When faced with a critical illness or a hopeless situation, we have options. We can whine and look for pity, we can complain and blame God, or we can see the crisis as an opportunity to make requests of God. Mary and Martha asked Jesus to help them with their sick brother. Then they gave him the glory for the amazing miracle he did—raising their brother, Lazarus, from the dead. If we can learn to humbly ask God for help, we will make progress in recovery. If he can raise someone from the dead, he is powerful enough to help us overcome our dependency and character flaws.

³So the two sisters sent a message to Jesus telling him, "Lord, the one you love is very sick."

⁴But when Jesus heard about it he said, "Lazarus's sickness will not end in death. No, it is for the glory of God. I, the Son of God, will receive glory from this." ⁵Although Jesus loved Martha, Mary, and Lazarus, ⁶he stayed where he was for the next two days and did not go to them. ⁷Finally after two days, he said to his disciples, "Let's go to Judea again."

⁸But his disciples objected. "Teacher," they said, "only a few days ago the Jewish leaders in Judea were trying to kill you. Are you going there again?"

⁹Jesus replied, "There are twelve hours of daylight every day. As long as it is light, people can walk safely. They can see because they have the light of this world. ¹⁰Only at night is there danger of stumbling because there is no light." ¹¹Then he said, "Our friend Lazarus has fallen asleep, but now I will go and wake him up."

¹²The disciples said, "Lord, if he is sleeping, that means he is getting better!" ¹³They thought Jesus meant Lazarus was having a good night's rest, but Jesus meant Lazarus had died.

¹⁴Then he told them plainly, "Lazarus is dead. ¹⁵And for your sake, I am glad I wasn't there, because this will give you another opportunity to believe in me. Come, let's go see him."

¹⁶Thomas, nicknamed the Twin,* said to his fellow disciples, "Let's go, too—and die with Jesus."

¹⁷When Jesus arrived at Bethany, he was told that Lazarus had already been in his grave for four days. ¹⁸Bethany was only a few miles* down the road from Jerusalem, ¹⁹and many of the people* had come to pay their respects and console Martha and Mary on their loss. ²⁰When Martha got word that Jesus was coming, she went to meet him. But Mary stayed at home. ²¹Martha said to Jesus, "Lord, if you had been here, my brother would not have died. ²²But even now I know that God will give you whatever you ask."

²³Jesus told her, "Your brother will rise again."

²⁴"Yes," Martha said, "when everyone else rises, on resurrection day."

²⁵Jesus told her, "I am the resurrection and the life.* Those who believe in me, even though they die like everyone else, will live again. ²⁶They are given eternal life for believing in me and will never perish. Do you believe this, Martha?"

²⁷"Yes, Lord," she told him. "I have always believed you are the Messiah, the Son of God, the one who has come into the world from God." ²⁸Then she left him and returned to Mary. She called Mary aside from the mourners and told her, "The Teacher is here and wants to see you." ²⁹So Mary immediately went to him.

³⁰Now Jesus had stayed outside the village, at the place where Martha met him. ³¹When the people who were at the house trying to console Mary saw her leave so hastily, they assumed she was going to Lazarus's grave to weep. So they followed her there. ³²When Mary arrived and saw Jesus, she fell down at his feet and said, "Lord, if you had been here, my brother would not have died."

³³When Jesus saw her weeping and saw the other people wailing with her, he was moved with indignation and was deeply troubled. ³⁴"Where have you put him?" he asked them.

They told him, "Lord, come and see." ³⁵Then Jesus wept. ³⁶The people who were standing nearby said, "See how much he loved him." ³⁷But some said, "This man healed a blind man. Why couldn't he keep Lazarus from dying?"

Jesus Raises Lazarus from the Dead

³⁸And again Jesus was deeply troubled. Then they came to the grave. It was a cave with a stone rolled across its entrance. ³⁹"Roll the stone aside," Jesus told them.

But Martha, the dead man's sister, said, "Lord, by now the smell will be terrible because he has been dead for four days."

⁴⁰Jesus responded, "Didn't I tell you that you will see God's glory if you believe?" ⁴¹So they rolled the stone aside. Then Jesus looked up to heaven and said, "Father, thank you for hearing me. ⁴²You always hear me,

---

11:16 Greek *the one who was called Didymus.* **11:18** Greek *was about 15 stadia* [about 2.8 kilometers]. **11:19** Greek *Jewish people;* also 11:31, 33, 36, 45, 54. **11:25** Some manuscripts do not include *and the life.*

11:37-44 Imagine being there when Jesus raised Lazarus from the dead. The man had been dead for four days, and his body had begun to smell. Suddenly he responded to Jesus' voice and walked out of the grave wrapped up like a mummy! Lazarus was alive! The one who has power over the grave has power to bring new life to us (11:25-27). Jesus Christ has set us free from the bondage of sin and death, but our "graveclothes"—destructive habits and dependencies—have got to go!

but I said it out loud for the sake of all these people standing here, so they will believe you sent me." [43]Then Jesus shouted, "Lazarus, come out!" [44]And Lazarus came out, bound in graveclothes, his face wrapped in a headcloth. Jesus told them, "Unwrap him and let him go!"

The Plot to Kill Jesus

[45]Many of the people who were with Mary believed in Jesus when they saw this happen. [46]But some went to the Pharisees and told them what Jesus had done. [47]Then the leading priests and Pharisees called the high council* together to discuss the situation. "What are we going to do?" they asked each other. "This man certainly performs many miraculous signs. [48]If we leave him alone, the whole nation will follow him, and then the Roman army will come and destroy both our Temple and our nation."

[49]And one of them, Caiaphas, who was high priest that year, said, "How can you be so stupid? [50]Why should the whole nation be destroyed? Let this one man die for the people."

[51]This prophecy that Jesus should die for the entire nation came from Caiaphas in his position as high priest. He didn't think of it himself; he was inspired to say it. [52]It was a prediction that Jesus' death would be not for Israel only, but for the gathering together of all the children of God scattered around the world.

[53]So from that time on the Jewish leaders began to plot Jesus' death. [54]As a result, Jesus stopped his public ministry among the people and left Jerusalem. He went to a place near the wilderness, to the village of Ephraim, and stayed there with his disciples.

[55]It was now almost time for the celebration of Passover, and many people from the country arrived in Jerusalem several days early so they could go through the cleansing ceremony before the Passover began. [56]They wanted to see Jesus, and as they talked in the Temple, they asked each other, "What do you think? Will he come for the Passover?" [57]Meanwhile, the leading priests and Pharisees had publicly announced that anyone seeing Jesus must report him immediately so they could arrest him.

CHAPTER 12
Jesus Anointed at Bethany

Six days before the Passover ceremonies began, Jesus arrived in Bethany, the home of Lazarus—the man he had raised from the dead. [2]A dinner was prepared in Jesus' honor. Martha served, and Lazarus sat at the table with him. [3]Then Mary took a twelve-ounce jar* of expensive perfume made from essence of nard, and she anointed Jesus' feet with it and wiped his feet with her hair. And the house was filled with fragrance.

[4]But Judas Iscariot, one of his disciples—the one who would betray him—said, [5]"That perfume was worth a small fortune.* It should have been sold and the money given to the poor." [6]Not that he cared for the poor—he was a thief who was in charge of the disciples' funds, and he often took some for his own use.

[7]Jesus replied, "Leave her alone. She did it in preparation for my burial. [8]You will always have the poor among you, but I will not be here with you much longer."

[9]When all the people* heard of Jesus' arrival, they flocked to see him and also to see Lazarus, the man Jesus had raised from the dead. [10]Then the leading priests decided to kill Lazarus, too, [11]for it was because of him that many of the people had deserted them and believed in Jesus.

11:47 Greek *the Sanhedrin.* **12:3** Greek *took 1 litra* [327 grams]. **12:5** Greek *300 denarii.* A denarius was equivalent to a full day's wage. **12:9** Greek *Jewish people;* also in 12:11.

12:1-8 Mary's faith in Jesus is a testimony to us all. Scripture records that she knelt in humble faith at Jesus' feet three times: She sat at Jesus' feet listening to his every word (Luke 10:39); she fell at his feet crying and seeking comfort (John 11:32); and here she knelt to anoint his feet with expensive perfume. Jesus was first in her heart, and she surrendered herself to him. The decision to surrender all we are and have to God is a crucial step in the recovery process. When we do, God will help us with our problems.

12:12-19 The crowds hailed Jesus as the promised Messiah, but his days of popularity would be few. He had just raised Lazarus from the dead in front of many witnesses. In a few days, however, the people would do nothing as the Jewish leaders and Roman governors crowned Jesus with thorns and executed him as a pretentious "King of the Jews" (18:39–19:21). The recovery process can be like that for us—full of heated curiosity one week and hollow commitment the next. If we hope to benefit from our recovery program, our commitment must be wholehearted. A half-hearted commitment to recovery could leave us worse off than we were before we started.

JUDAS ISCARIOT

In the life of Judas we find a terrible tragedy—the tragedy of having been so close to Jesus yet never really knowing him. For Judas the bottom line was profit. He was always looking for a way to gain something for himself. In following Jesus, Judas thought he was on a sure road to political and financial success. Indeed, Judas was excited about the role he would have in the Kingdom that Jesus would set up.

Listening to Jesus talk of death and sacrifice, Judas, as well as the other disciples, couldn't see how that could be part of God's plan. In his disappointment, Judas failed to perceive that Jesus would do much more than simply challenge the political system in one corner of the world and dispose of the hated Roman oppressors. Instead, by his sacrificial death, Jesus would bring true freedom—freedom from spiritual oppression, freedom from the darkness of sin.

Judas betrayed Jesus with a kiss, turning a sign of affection and respect into a token of betrayal. Judas did feel great remorse for his actions, but his feelings of guilt never led to true repentance. In contrast to Peter, who also betrayed Jesus, Judas destroyed himself instead of turning to the mercy and forgiveness of God. For those of us in recovery, it is vital to remember that Jesus waits for us with open arms, wanting to give us the gifts of mercy and forgiveness. We can run to him in times of need because he does not condemn us—he longs to change us, heal the pain, and take away the guilt in our life.

The story of Judas Iscariot is found in the Gospels; see especially Luke 22:3-6 and John 12:4-6. He is also mentioned in Acts 1:16-19.

STRENGTHS AND ACCOMPLISHMENTS:
- He was the only non-Galilean disciple.
- He was trusted enough to be made treasurer of the group.
- He recognized how wrong his betrayal of Jesus was.

WEAKNESSES AND MISTAKES:
- Judas valued material wealth over spiritual wealth.
- He was more interested in what he could get from Jesus than in who Jesus was.

LESSONS FROM HIS LIFE:
- Spiritual wealth is more valuable than material wealth.
- God always offers us what is best for us, not always what we want.
- It is easy to underestimate the value of spiritual growth when we are preoccupied with material gain.
- We cannot stop at admitting our sins; we must also turn to God for healing and forgiveness.

KEY VERSES:
"Then Satan entered into Judas Iscariot, who was one of the twelve disciples, and he went over to the leading priests and captains of the Temple guard to discuss the best way to betray Jesus to them" (Luke 22:3-4).

The Triumphal Entry

¹²The next day, the news that Jesus was on the way to Jerusalem swept through the city. A huge crowd of Passover visitors ¹³took palm branches and went down the road to meet him. They shouted,

"Praise God!*
Bless the one who comes in the name
    of the Lord!
Hail to the King of Israel!"*

¹⁴Jesus found a young donkey and sat on it, fulfilling the prophecy that said:

¹⁵ "Don't be afraid, people of Israel.*
Look, your King is coming,
    sitting on a donkey's colt."*

¹⁶His disciples didn't realize at the time that this was a fulfillment of prophecy. But after Jesus entered into his glory, they remembered that these Scriptures had come true before their eyes.

¹⁷Those in the crowd who had seen Jesus call Lazarus back to life were telling others all about it. ¹⁸That was the main reason so many went out to meet him—because they had heard about this mighty miracle. ¹⁹Then the Pharisees said to each other, "We've lost. Look, the whole world has gone after him!"

Jesus Predicts His Death

²⁰Some Greeks who had come to Jerusalem to attend the Passover ²¹paid a visit to Philip,

12:13a Greek *Hosanna*, an exclamation of praise that literally means "save now." **12:13b** Ps 118:25-26; Zeph 3:15.
12:15a Greek *daughter of Zion.* **12:15b** Zech 9:9.

who was from Bethsaida in Galilee. They said, "Sir, we want to meet Jesus." [22]Philip told Andrew about it, and they went together to ask Jesus.

[23]Jesus replied, "The time has come for the Son of Man to enter into his glory. [24]The truth is, a kernel of wheat must be planted in the soil. Unless it dies it will be alone—a single seed. But its death will produce many new kernels—a plentiful harvest of new lives. [25]Those who love their life in this world will lose it. Those who despise their life in this world will keep it for eternal life. [26]All those who want to be my disciples must come and follow me, because my servants must be where I am. And if they follow me, the Father will honor them. [27]Now my soul is deeply troubled. Should I pray, 'Father, save me from what lies ahead'? But that is the very reason why I came! [28]Father, bring glory to your name."

Then a voice spoke from heaven, saying, "I have already brought it glory, and I will do it again." [29]When the crowd heard the voice, some thought it was thunder, while others declared an angel had spoken to him.

[30]Then Jesus told them, "The voice was for your benefit, not mine. [31]The time of judgment for the world has come, when the prince of this world* will be cast out. [32]And when I am lifted up on the cross,* I will draw everyone to myself." [33]He said this to indicate how he was going to die.

[34]"Die?" asked the crowd. "We understood from Scripture that the Messiah would live forever. Why are you saying the Son of Man will die? Who is this Son of Man you are talking about?"

[35]Jesus replied, "My light will shine out for you just a little while longer. Walk in it while you can, so you will not stumble when the darkness falls. If you walk in the darkness, you cannot see where you are going. [36]Believe in the light while there is still time; then you will become children of the light." After saying these things, Jesus went away and was hidden from them.

The Unbelief of the People

[37]But despite all the miraculous signs he had done, most of the people did not believe in him. [38]This is exactly what Isaiah the prophet had predicted:

"Lord, who has believed our message?
To whom will the Lord reveal his saving power?"*

[39]But the people couldn't believe, for as Isaiah also said,

[40]"The Lord has blinded their eyes
and hardened their hearts—
so their eyes cannot see,
and their hearts cannot understand,
and they cannot turn to me
and let me heal them."*

[41]Isaiah was referring to Jesus when he made this prediction, because he was given a vision of the Messiah's glory. [42]Many people, including some of the Jewish leaders, believed in him. But they wouldn't admit it to anyone because of their fear that the Pharisees would expel them from the synagogue. [43]For they loved human praise more than the praise of God.

[44]Jesus shouted to the crowds, "If you trust me, you are really trusting God who sent me. [45]For when you see me, you are seeing the one who sent me. [46]I have come as a light to shine in this dark world, so that all who put their trust in me will no longer remain in the darkness. [47]If anyone hears me and doesn't obey me, I am not his judge—for I have come to save the world and not to judge it. [48]But all

---

12:31 *The prince of this world* is a name for Satan. **12:32** Greek *lifted up from the earth.* **12:38** Isa 53:1. **12:40** Isa 6:10.

12:23-25 Instead of giving a king's acceptance speech, Jesus explained why he would have to die. He said, in effect: "I must die so that I can bring new life to you. If you want this new life, then turn away from your current way of living!" This message can be hard for us to accept, just as it was for the Jews of Jesus' day. But in order to move through recovery—from addiction to freedom, from brokenness to healing, from guilt to forgiveness, or from isolation to intimacy—we must accept it. No longer can we embrace lives of escapism and denial. We must honestly embrace the painful realities in our life and patiently allow God's love to make us whole.

12:42-43 Many of the Jewish leaders believed in Jesus, but their faith was rendered ineffective by fear and isolation. They were more concerned about what their peers thought of them than about what God thought. This weak faith will never take us far in recovery. If we want real progress in recovery, we need to share our belief in God with at least one other person. When we tell others about our belief and change in our life, we are inviting them to hold us accountable. Accountability for our intentions, attitudes, and actions is a necessary part of recovery. Making others a significant part of our life is crucial to the recovery process and our growth; we cannot do it alone.

who reject me and my message will be judged at the day of judgment by the truth I have spoken. ⁴⁹I don't speak on my own authority. The Father who sent me gave me his own instructions as to what I should say. ⁵⁰And I know his instructions lead to eternal life; so I say whatever the Father tells me to say!"

CHAPTER 13
Jesus Washes His Disciples' Feet
Before the Passover celebration, Jesus knew that his hour had come to leave this world and return to his Father. He now showed the disciples the full extent of his love.* ²It was time for supper, and the Devil had already enticed Judas, son of Simon Iscariot, to carry out his plan to betray Jesus. ³Jesus knew that the Father had given him authority over everything and that he had come from God and would return to God. ⁴So he got up from the table, took off his robe, wrapped a towel around his waist, ⁵and poured water into a basin. Then he began to wash the disciples' feet and to wipe them with the towel he had around him.

⁶When he came to Simon Peter, Peter said to him, "Lord, why are you going to wash my feet?"

⁷Jesus replied, "You don't understand now why I am doing it; someday you will."

⁸"No," Peter protested, "you will never wash my feet!"

Jesus replied, "But if I don't wash you, you won't belong to me."

⁹Simon Peter exclaimed, "Then wash my hands and head as well, Lord, not just my feet!"

¹⁰Jesus replied, "A person who has bathed all over does not need to wash, except for the feet,* to be entirely clean. And you are clean, but that isn't true of everyone here." ¹¹For Jesus knew who would betray him. That

is what he meant when he said, "Not all of you are clean."

¹²After washing their feet, he put on his robe again and sat down and asked, "Do you understand what I was doing? ¹³You call me 'Teacher' and 'Lord,' and you are right, because it is true. ¹⁴And since I, the Lord and Teacher, have washed your feet, you ought to wash each other's feet. ¹⁵I have given you an example to follow. Do as I have done to you. ¹⁶How true it is that a servant is not greater than the master. Nor are messengers more important than the one who sends them. ¹⁷You know these things—now do them! That is the path of blessing.

Jesus Predicts His Betrayal
¹⁸"I am not saying these things to all of you; I know so well each one of you I chose. The Scriptures declare, 'The one who shares my food has turned against me,'* and this will soon come true. ¹⁹I tell you this now, so that when it happens you will believe I am the Messiah. ²⁰Truly, anyone who welcomes my messenger is welcoming me, and anyone who welcomes me is welcoming the Father who sent me."

²¹Now Jesus was in great anguish of spirit, and he exclaimed, "The truth is, one of you will betray me!"

²²The disciples looked at each other, wondering whom he could mean. ²³One of Jesus' disciples, the one Jesus loved, was sitting next to Jesus at the table.* ²⁴Simon Peter motioned to him to ask who would do this terrible thing. ²⁵Leaning toward Jesus, he asked, "Lord, who is it?"

²⁶Jesus said, "It is the one to whom I give the bread dipped in the sauce." And when he had dipped it, he gave it to Judas, son of Simon Iscariot. ²⁷As soon as Judas had eaten the bread, Satan entered into him. Then Jesus

---

13:1 Or *He loved his disciples to the very end.* **13:10** Some manuscripts do not include *except for the feet.* **13:18** Ps 41:9. **13:23** Greek *was reclining on Jesus' bosom.* The "disciple whom Jesus loved" was probably John.

13:1-7 The Son of God came not as a proud master who demanded service from others but as a humble servant who delighted in helping others. In stooping down to do the most menial job (washing his disciples' feet), Jesus showed them that true leaders serve their followers. To follow Jesus' example and serve others, we start by allowing him to serve us. As we experience his cleansing power in our life, we can serve others—sharing our story, listening to their confessions, feeling their pain, and standing by them in the tough times. As we support others in the recovery process, we will be strengthened as we continue toward recovery.
13:20 One way God speaks to us is through his chosen messengers. We may experience God's love and healing through the godly people he sends into our life. This may be very difficult for us if we have been a victim of abuse. We may feel that we never want to be close to other people. But as we allow godly people into our life, we learn that they bring the healing touch of Jesus with them. As we reach out to others in Jesus' name, we in turn become his messenger. God will use us to bring his powerful deliverance into others' lives.

told him, "Hurry. Do it now." [28]None of the others at the table knew what Jesus meant. [29]Since Judas was their treasurer, some thought Jesus was telling him to go and pay for the food or to give some money to the poor. [30]So Judas left at once, going out into the night.

Jesus Predicts Peter's Denial

[31]As soon as Judas left the room, Jesus said, "The time has come for me, the Son of Man, to enter into my glory, and God will receive glory because of all that happens to me. [32]And God will bring* me into my glory very soon. [33]Dear children, how brief are these moments before I must go away and leave you! Then, though you search for me, you cannot come to me—just as I told the Jewish leaders. [34]So now I am giving you a new commandment: Love each other. Just as I have loved you, you should love each other. [35]Your love for one another will prove to the world that you are my disciples."

[36]Simon Peter said, "Lord, where are you going?"

And Jesus replied, "You can't go with me now, but you will follow me later."

[37]"But why can't I come now, Lord?" he asked. "I am ready to die for you."

[38]Jesus answered, "Die for me? No, before the rooster crows tomorrow morning, you will deny three times that you even know me.

CHAPTER 14

Jesus, the Way to the Father

"Don't be troubled. You trust God, now trust in me. [2]There are many rooms in my Father's home, and I am going to prepare a place for you. If this were not so, I would tell you plainly. [3]When everything is ready, I will come and get you, so that you will always be with me where I am. [4]And you know where I am going and how to get there."

[5]"No, we don't know, Lord," Thomas said. "We haven't any idea where you are going, so how can we know the way?"

[6]Jesus told him, "I am the way, the truth, and the life. No one can come to the Father except through me. [7]If you had known who I am, then you would have known who my Father is.* From now on you know him and have seen him!"

[8]Philip said, "Lord, show us the Father and we will be satisfied."

[9]Jesus replied, "Philip, don't you even yet know who I am, even after all the time I have been with you? Anyone who has seen me has seen the Father! So why are you asking to see him? [10]Don't you believe that I am in the Father and the Father is in me? The words I say are not my own, but my Father who lives in me does his work through me. [11]Just believe that I am in the Father and the Father is in me. Or at least believe because of what you have seen me do.

13:32 Some manuscripts read *And if God is glorified in him [the Son of Man], God will bring.* **14:7** Some manuscripts read *If you really have known me, you will know who my Father is.*

13:34-35 Our ability to love others (and ourself) is based on the degree to which we have received God's love (most often through other people). When we try to love others without God's love, we try to give what we don't have; we end up giving to others in hopes of receiving something in return. This kind of selfish gift never feels good to us or to the person we are trying to help. When we love one another out of the overflow of God's love, our witness and service can be effective toward recovery.

14:1-4 We receive lasting comfort by putting our trust in God. Sometimes God gives us immediate deliverance from a painful situation. More often, he walks with us as we struggle with problems that never seem to end. Our struggles may be direct consequences of our past mistakes; they may be the result of other people's failures. God allows us to experience such trying circumstances to build character in us and strengthen our faith. When we place our trust in Jesus, we receive his peace in this life and the promise of a home with him in eternity.

14:5-11 Faith in Jesus is the only way to truly know God and receive the meaningful life that God wants for each of us. Despite living with Jesus for many months, Thomas and Philip did not yet know God through his Son, Jesus. Many people know about God and Jesus Christ, but they don't know God personally. Genuine faith is personal and relational and based upon the truths about God found in Scripture. Jesus Christ is the way, the truth, and the life for anyone going through recovery. He has the power to forgive our sins, help us overcome our addiction, and give us a new life.

14:27 Many of us are dealing with stress and anxiety, grief and loss; we long for peace of mind and heart. So did the early disciples—they were about to lose their best friend and their Messiah. Their souls were indeed troubled, like many of us recovering from the loss of a job, a spouse, or children, or from a chemical addiction. They were looking for something to fill the void. Yet Jesus said he was leaving them with wholesome, fulfilling peace—*shalom*—unlike worldly peace, which is merely an absence of conflict. God can bring us peace even in the midst of our troubles (see 16:33).

[12]"The truth is, anyone who believes in me will do the same works I have done, and even greater works, because I am going to be with the Father. [13]You can ask for anything in my name, and I will do it, because the work of the Son brings glory to the Father. [14]Yes, ask anything in my name, and I will do it!

Jesus Promises the Holy Spirit

[15]"If you love me, obey my commandments. [16]And I will ask the Father, and he will give you another Counselor,* who will never leave you. [17]He is the Holy Spirit, who leads into all truth. The world at large cannot receive him, because it isn't looking for him and doesn't recognize him. But you do, because he lives with you now and later will be in you. [18]No, I will not abandon you as orphans—I will come to you. [19]In just a little while the world will not see me again, but you will. For I will live again, and you will, too. [20]When I am raised to life again, you will know that I am in my Father, and you are in me, and I am in you. [21]Those who obey my commandments are the ones who love me. And because they love me, my Father will love them, and I will love them. And I will reveal myself to each one of them."

[22]Judas (not Judas Iscariot, but the other disciple with that name) said to him, "Lord, why are you going to reveal yourself only to us and not to the world at large?"

[23]Jesus replied, "All those who love me will do what I say. My Father will love them, and we will come to them and live with them. [24]Anyone who doesn't love me will not do what I say. And remember, my words are not my own. This message is from the Father who sent me. [25]I am telling you these things now while I am still with you. [26]But when the Father sends the Counselor as my representative—and by the Counselor I mean the Holy Spirit—he will teach you everything and will remind you of everything I myself have told you.

[27]"I am leaving you with a gift—peace of mind and heart. And the peace I give isn't like the peace the world gives. So don't be troubled or afraid. [28]Remember what I told you: I am going away, but I will come back to you again. If you really love me, you will be very happy for me, because now I can go to the Father, who is greater than I am. [29]I have told you these things before they happen so that you will believe when they do happen.

14:16 Or *Comforter,* or *Encourager,* or *Advocate.* Greek *Paraclete;* also in 14:26.

Love

■ READ JOHN 14:15-26

Real love brings security into our life. For many of us, feelings of insecurity contribute to the power of our dependency. Believing that love can bring lasting security may be hard for those of us who have been abandoned. Maybe someone we loved betrayed our trust. Perhaps someone turned away from us when we betrayed theirs. It could be that someone we needed died, leaving us permanently.

Jesus promised, "No, I will not abandon you as orphans—I will come to you" (John 14:18). We may ask, How can I trust in God's love when it feels like all I've ever known is love that disappoints? Here's the difference: Jesus is the only one who entered our life through the "one way" door of death. "God showed how much he loved us by sending his only Son into the world so that we might have eternal life through him. This is real love. It is not that we loved God, but that he loved us and sent his Son as a sacrifice to take away our sins" (1 John 4:9-10). The psalmist wrote, "For he understands how weak we are; he knows we are only dust. . . . The wind blows, and we are gone . . . But the love of the LORD remains forever with those who fear him" (Psalm 103:14-18).

God's love is unconditional and always waiting for us. Turning our life over to God involves opening the door of our heart to his love. Filling up on God's love helps us to avoid relapses. It meets us at our deepest need and overcomes our most powerful insecurities. *Turn to page 179, John 21.*

30"I don't have much more time to talk to you, because the prince of this world approaches. He has no power over me, 31but I will do what the Father requires of me, so that the world will know that I love the Father. Come, let's be going.

CHAPTER 15
Jesus, the True Vine

"I am the true vine, and my Father is the gardener. 2He cuts off every branch that doesn't produce fruit, and he prunes the branches that do bear fruit so they will produce even more. 3You have already been pruned for greater fruitfulness by the message I have given you. 4Remain in me, and I will remain in you. For a branch cannot produce fruit if it is severed from the vine, and you cannot be fruitful apart from me.

5"Yes, I am the vine; you are the branches. Those who remain in me, and I in them, will produce much fruit. For apart from me you can do nothing. 6Anyone who parts from me is thrown away like a useless branch and withers. Such branches are gathered into a pile to be burned. 7But if you stay joined to me and my words remain in you, you may ask any request you like, and it will be granted! 8My true disciples produce much fruit. This brings great glory to my Father.

9"I have loved you even as the Father has loved me. Remain in my love. 10When you obey me, you remain in my love, just as I obey my Father and remain in his love. 11I have told you this so that you will be filled with my joy. Yes, your joy will overflow! 12I command you to love each other in the same way that I love you. 13And here is how to measure it—the greatest love is shown when people lay down their lives for their friends. 14You are my friends if you obey me. 15I no longer call you servants, because a master doesn't confide in his servants. Now you are my friends, since I have told you everything the Father told me. 16You didn't choose me. I chose you. I appointed you to go and produce fruit that will last, so that the Father will give you whatever you ask for, using my name. 17I command you to love each other.

The World's Hatred

18"When the world hates you, remember it hated me before it hated you. 19The world would love you if you belonged to it, but you don't. I chose you to come out of the world, and so it hates you. 20Do you remember what I told you? 'A servant is not greater than the master.' Since they persecuted me, naturally they will persecute you. And if they had listened to me, they would listen to you! 21The people of the world will hate you because you belong to me, for they don't know God who sent me. 22They would not be guilty if I had not come and spoken to them. But now they have no excuse for their sin. 23Anyone who hates me hates my Father, too. 24If I hadn't done such miraculous signs among them that no one else could do, they would not be counted guilty. But as it is, they saw all that I did and yet hated both of us—me and my Father. 25This has fulfilled what the Scriptures said: 'They hated me without cause.'*

26"But I will send you the Counselor*—the Spirit of truth. He will come to you from the Father and will tell you all about me. 27And you must also tell others about me because you have been with me from the beginning.

15:25 Pss 35:19; 69:4. **15:26** Or *Comforter*, or *Encourager*, or *Advocate*. Greek *Paraclete*.

15:1-8 God desires that our life be like the fruitful branches of a grapevine. The only way to be fruitful is to remain connected to Jesus, the vine, and to allow God, the gardener, to prune our life to stimulate growth and fruitfulness. It is God's cultivating, weeding, and pruning in our life that brings forth spiritual fruit, character development, and progress in recovery. Just as sustenance for the desired fruit comes through the vine, so fullness of life comes through faith in Jesus Christ. We need to stay close to Jesus, the source of power and practical help for recovery.

15:15 Jesus demonstrated God's desire to be our friend, not our taskmaster. Many of us in recovery have never experienced God on such friendly, intimate terms. Rare in our experience is the authority figure who actually seeks to confide in us and befriend us, rather than lording his power over us. So we find it hard to imagine God as a friend. Jesus urges us to trust in him. By becoming our friend, God, through Jesus, empowers us and enables us to become accountable, responsible, and trustworthy.

16:20-22 Jesus' followers certainly grieved the imminent loss of their friend and master. Losing a loved one is a painful and universal experience. We may grieve the loss of our childhood, our innocence, our spouse, or our only means of livelihood. We even grieve the loss of our addiction that we have used to numb our pain. Abuse, abandonment, or neglect by someone we trust is painful. But there is no pain so great that Jesus cannot heal it. When we find the courage to honestly face and grieve over our losses and injuries, we can discover what lies beyond grief—freedom and joy!

CHAPTER 16

"I have told you these things so that you won't fall away. [2]For you will be expelled from the synagogues, and the time is coming when those who kill you will think they are doing God a service. [3]This is because they have never known the Father or me. [4]Yes, I'm telling you these things now, so that when they happen, you will remember I warned you. I didn't tell you earlier because I was going to be with you for a while longer.

The Work of the Holy Spirit

[5]"But now I am going away to the one who sent me, and none of you has asked me where I am going. [6]Instead, you are very sad. [7]But it is actually best for you that I go away, because if I don't, the Counselor* won't come. If I do go away, he will come because I will send him to you. [8]And when he comes, he will convince the world of its sin, and of God's righteousness, and of the coming judgment. [9]The world's sin is unbelief in me. [10]Righteousness is available because I go to the Father, and you will see me no more. [11]Judgment will come because the prince of this world has already been judged.

[12]"Oh, there is so much more I want to tell you, but you can't bear it now. [13]When the Spirit of truth comes, he will guide you into all truth. He will not be presenting his own ideas; he will be telling you what he has heard. He will tell you about the future. [14]He will bring me glory by revealing to you whatever he receives from me. [15]All that the Father has is mine; this is what I mean when I say that the Spirit will reveal to you whatever he receives from me.

Sadness Will Be Turned to Joy

[16]"In just a little while I will be gone, and you won't see me anymore. Then, just a little while after that, you will see me again."

[17]The disciples asked each other, "What does he mean when he says, 'You won't see me, and then you will see me'? And what does he mean when he says, 'I am going to the Father'? [18]And what does he mean by 'a little while'? We don't understand."

[19]Jesus realized they wanted to ask him, so he said, "Are you asking yourselves what I meant? I said in just a little while I will be gone, and you won't see me anymore. Then, just a little while after that, you will see me again. [20]Truly, you will weep and mourn over what is going to happen to me, but the world

16:7 Or *Comforter*, or *Encourager*, or *Advocate*. Greek *Paraclete*.

STEP 12

Sharing Together

BIBLE READING: John 15:5-15

Having had a spiritual awakening as the result of these steps, we tried to carry this message to others and to practice these principles in all our affairs.

Since we have worked through the Twelve Steps, we are in a special position to carry the message to others. We can recognize the warning signs of addictive/compulsive tendencies in those around us, as well as in ourself. When touching on such deep and sensitive issues, it is important to speak in the language of love, not condemnation.

The Bible tells us that if someone "is overcome by some sin, you who are godly should gently and humbly help that person back onto the right path. And be careful not to fall into the same temptation yourself. Share each other's troubles and problems, and in this way obey the law of Christ" (Galatians 6:1-2). The command was the one Jesus taught his disciples: "So now I am giving you a new commandment: Love each other. Just as I have loved you, you should love each other" (John 13:34). "I command you to love each other in the same way that I love you. And here is how to measure it—the greatest love is shown when people lay down their lives for their friends" (15:12-13).

We are not the Savior, but we can love others as he has loved us. Love goes beyond mere words. Sometimes it is spoken in silence, when we don't condemn someone who comes to us looking for help. Love doesn't just tell them what the problems are. It helps carry the weight of their burdens. We can be part of a support network to help carry our friends until they are able to take steps toward recovery on their own initiative. *Turn to page 197, Acts 8.*

will rejoice. You will grieve, but your grief will suddenly turn to wonderful joy when you see me again. ²¹It will be like a woman experiencing the pains of labor. When her child is born, her anguish gives place to joy because she has brought a new person into the world. ²²You have sorrow now, but I will see you again; then you will rejoice, and no one can rob you of that joy. ²³At that time you won't need to ask me for anything. The truth is, you can go directly to the Father and ask him, and he will grant your request because you use my name. ²⁴You haven't done this before. Ask, using my name, and you will receive, and you will have abundant joy.

²⁵"I have spoken of these matters in parables, but the time will come when this will not be necessary, and I will tell you plainly all about the Father. ²⁶Then you will ask in my name. I'm not saying I will ask the Father on your behalf, ²⁷for the Father himself loves you dearly because you love me and believe that I came from God. ²⁸Yes, I came from the Father into the world, and I will leave the world and return to the Father."

²⁹Then his disciples said, "At last you are speaking plainly and not in parables. ³⁰Now we understand that you know everything and don't need anyone to tell you anything.* From this we believe that you came from God."

³¹Jesus asked, "Do you finally believe? ³²But the time is coming—in fact, it is already here—when you will be scattered, each one going his own way, leaving me alone. Yet I am not alone because the Father is with me. ³³I have told you all this so that you may have peace in me. Here on earth you will have many trials and sorrows. But take heart, because I have overcome the world."

CHAPTER 17
The Prayer of Jesus

When Jesus had finished saying all these things, he looked up to heaven and said, "Father, the time has come. Glorify your Son so he can give glory back to you. ²For you have given him authority over everyone in all the earth. He gives eternal life to each one you have given him. ³And this is the way to have eternal life—to know you, the only true God, and Jesus Christ, the one you sent to earth. ⁴I brought glory to you here on earth by doing everything you told me to do. ⁵And now, Father, bring me into the glory we shared before the world began.

⁶"I have told these men about you. They were in the world, but then you gave them to me. Actually, they were always yours, and you gave them to me; and they have kept your word. ⁷Now they know that everything I have is a gift from you, ⁸for I have passed on to them the words you gave me; and they accepted them and know that I came from you, and they believe you sent me.

⁹"My prayer is not for the world, but for those you have given me, because they belong to you. ¹⁰And all of them, since they are mine, belong to you; and you have given them back to me, so they are my glory! ¹¹Now I am departing the world; I am leaving them behind and coming to you. Holy Father, keep them and care for them—all those you have given me—so that they will be united just as we are. ¹²During my time here, I have kept them safe.* I guarded them so that not one was lost, except the one headed for destruction, as the Scriptures foretold.

¹³"And now I am coming to you. I have told them many things while I was with them so they would be filled with my joy. ¹⁴I have given them your word. And the world

16:30 Or *don't need that anyone should ask you anything.* **17:12** Greek *I have kept in your name those whom you have given me.*

16:33 In this world, especially in recovery, we encounter "many trials and sorrows," many of them beyond our control. These can be endured with God's help. On the other hand, some of our suffering is self-inflicted and can be avoided. In such situations, God still offers us peace as we muster the courage to make needed changes in our life. God's forgiveness and loving acceptance can give us peace as we face all of our our trials and sorrows. God's power can lead us through recovery; he has already overcome all the obstacles that stand in our way!

17:1-26 Jesus is our high priest and intercessor (Hebrews 8:1-6). He makes God's will known to us and our heartfelt needs known to God. Jesus' words and deeds reveal God's mercy, justice, glory, truth, and his desire to establish a personal relationship with each of us. Jesus intercedes with God the Father on our behalf, bringing our needs and requests continually before God. He prays that we would know his perfect joy, be protected from all evil, grow in truth and holiness, and show love toward all people. Jesus prayed this prayer for his twelve disciples as they faced his imminent death. Yet this prayer is for all of us as we follow Jesus through the process of recovery.

hates them because they do not belong to the world, just as I do not. ¹⁵I'm not asking you to take them out of the world, but to keep them safe from the evil one. ¹⁶They are not part of this world any more than I am. ¹⁷Make them pure and holy by teaching them your words of truth. ¹⁸As you sent me into the world, I am sending them into the world. ¹⁹And I give myself entirely to you so they also might be entirely yours.

²⁰"I am praying not only for these disciples but also for all who will ever believe in me because of their testimony. ²¹My prayer for all of them is that they will be one, just as you and I are one, Father—that just as you are in me and I am in you, so they will be in us, and the world will believe you sent me.

²²"I have given them the glory you gave me, so that they may be one, as we are—²³I in them and you in me, all being perfected into one. Then the world will know that you sent me and will understand that you love them as much as you love me. ²⁴Father, I want these whom you've given me to be with me, so they can see my glory. You gave me the glory because you loved me even before the world began!

²⁵"O righteous Father, the world doesn't know you, but I do; and these disciples know you sent me. ²⁶And I have revealed you to them and will keep on revealing you. I will do this so that your love for me may be in them and I in them."

CHAPTER 18

Jesus Is Betrayed and Arrested

After saying these things, Jesus crossed the Kidron Valley with his disciples and entered a grove of olive trees. ²Judas, the betrayer, knew this place, because Jesus had gone there many times with his disciples. ³The leading priests and Pharisees had given Judas a battalion of Roman soldiers and Temple guards to accompany him. Now with blazing torches, lanterns, and weapons, they arrived at the olive grove.

⁴Jesus fully realized all that was going to happen to him. Stepping forward to meet them, he asked, "Whom are you looking for?"

⁵"Jesus of Nazareth," they replied.

"I am he,"* Jesus said. Judas was standing there with them when Jesus identified himself. ⁶And as he said, "I am he," they all fell backward to the ground! ⁷Once more he asked them, "Whom are you searching for?"

And again they replied, "Jesus of Nazareth."

⁸"I told you that I am he," Jesus said. "And since I am the one you want, let these others go." ⁹He did this to fulfill his own statement: "I have not lost a single one of those you gave me."*

¹⁰Then Simon Peter drew a sword and slashed off the right ear of Malchus, the high priest's servant. ¹¹But Jesus said to Peter, "Put your sword back into its sheath. Shall I not drink from the cup the Father has given me?"

Annas Questions Jesus

¹²So the soldiers, their commanding officer, and the Temple guards arrested Jesus and tied him up. ¹³First they took him to Annas, the father-in-law of Caiaphas, the high priest that year. ¹⁴Caiaphas was the one who had told the other Jewish leaders, "Better that one should die for all."

Peter's First Denial

¹⁵Simon Peter followed along behind, as did another of the disciples. That other disciple was acquainted with the high priest, so he was allowed to enter the courtyard with Jesus. ¹⁶Peter stood outside the gate. Then the other disciple spoke to the woman watching at the gate, and she let Peter in. ¹⁷The woman asked Peter, "Aren't you one of Jesus' disciples?"

"No," he said, "I am not."

¹⁸The guards and the household servants were standing around a charcoal fire they had made because it was cold. And Peter stood there with them, warming himself.

The High Priest Questions Jesus

¹⁹Inside, the high priest began asking Jesus about his followers and what he had been teaching them. ²⁰Jesus replied, "What I teach is widely known, because I have preached regularly in the synagogues and the Temple. I have been heard by people* everywhere,

---

18:5 Greek *I am;* also in 18:6, 8. **18:9** See John 6:39 and 17:12. **18:20** Greek *Jewish people;* also in 18:38.

18:15-18, 25-27 Peter denied Jesus not only once but three times, despite his earlier assurances of loyalty. We have often done the same thing. We have professed our faith, only to turn around and deny Christ's lordship over crucial areas of our life. Peter meant well when he assured Jesus of his loyalty, but he still failed. Yet his relapse was not the end of the story (see 21:15-19), just as our relapses don't have to be the end of our recovery. With Jesus Christ, there is always hope for restoration.

and I teach nothing in private that I have not said in public. ²¹Why are you asking me this question? Ask those who heard me. They know what I said."

²²One of the Temple guards standing there struck Jesus on the face. "Is that the way to answer the high priest?" he demanded.

²³Jesus replied, "If I said anything wrong, you must give evidence for it. Should you hit a man for telling the truth?"

²⁴Then Annas bound Jesus and sent him to Caiaphas, the high priest.

Peter's Second and Third Denials

²⁵Meanwhile, as Simon Peter was standing by the fire, they asked him again, "Aren't you one of his disciples?"

"I am not," he said.

²⁶But one of the household servants of the high priest, a relative of the man whose ear Peter had cut off, asked, "Didn't I see you out there in the olive grove with Jesus?" ²⁷Again Peter denied it. And immediately a rooster crowed.

Jesus' Trial before Pilate

²⁸Jesus' trial before Caiaphas ended in the early hours of the morning. Then he was taken to the headquarters of the Roman governor. His accusers didn't go in themselves because it would defile them, and they wouldn't be allowed to celebrate the Passover feast. ²⁹So Pilate, the governor, went out to them and asked, "What is your charge against this man?"

³⁰"We wouldn't have handed him over to you if he weren't a criminal!" they retorted.

³¹"Then take him away and judge him by your own laws," Pilate told them.

"Only the Romans are permitted to execute someone," the Jewish leaders replied. ³²This

18:32 See John 12:32-33.

fulfilled Jesus' prediction about the way he would die.*

³³Then Pilate went back inside and called for Jesus to be brought to him. "Are you the King of the Jews?" he asked him.

³⁴Jesus replied, "Is this your own question, or did others tell you about me?"

³⁵"Am I a Jew?" Pilate asked. "Your own people and their leading priests brought you here. Why? What have you done?"

³⁶Then Jesus answered, "I am not an earthly king. If I were, my followers would have fought when I was arrested by the Jewish leaders. But my Kingdom is not of this world."

³⁷Pilate replied, "You are a king then?"

"You say that I am a king, and you are right," Jesus said. "I was born for that purpose. And I came to bring truth to the world. All who love the truth recognize that what I say is true."

³⁸"What is truth?" Pilate asked. Then he went out again to the people and told them, "He is not guilty of any crime. ³⁹But you have a custom of asking me to release someone from prison each year at Passover. So if you want me to, I'll release the King of the Jews."

⁴⁰But they shouted back, "No! Not this man, but Barabbas!" (Barabbas was a criminal.)

CHAPTER 19
Jesus Sentenced to Death

Then Pilate had Jesus flogged with a lead-tipped whip. ²The soldiers made a crown of long, sharp thorns and put it on his head, and they put a royal purple robe on him. ³"Hail! King of the Jews!" they mocked, and they hit him with their fists.

⁴Pilate went outside again and said to the people, "I am going to bring him out to you now, but understand clearly that I find him not guilty." ⁵Then Jesus came out wearing the

---

18:28-38 Many people believe that truth is relative, as did Pilate. Modern moral relativists live without absolute guidelines for right and wrong, not realizing how destructive even the most private sins can be. Since we are all tempted at times to disregard God's guidelines for healthy living, we need to be held accountable to God's truth. We need godly people who can help us measure our attitudes and actions against the truth of God's Word. If we try to write our own rules for recovery, we are headed for painful relapses.

19:4-16 The people shouting "Crucify! Crucify!" had hailed Jesus as their king just days before (12:12-13). Perhaps we have done a similar thing. We may have entrusted our life to God only to discover that his recovery program wasn't quite what we had in mind. We may have wanted a quick fix for our problems or an easy way out of our pain. When we realized that recovery was painful and laborious, even with God's help, we turned against him. The people in Jerusalem, even Jesus' twelve disciples, lost hope as Jesus hung on the cross. But three days later they discovered that even death gave way to God's power! The path of pain and death led to the greatest of victories—the Resurrection! The same is true in recovery.

MARY MAGDALENE

The people who have been healed of the worst afflictions are often the most grateful for their new lease on life. Once enslaved by seven demons but freed by Jesus, Mary Magdalene became a shining example of a life filled with gratitude and loyalty to Jesus.

We know few details of Mary's life. She was apparently from Magdala in Galilee and was an early follower of Jesus. Her life was dramatically changed by Jesus when he released her from demons. She traveled with Jesus and the disciples and helped meet the practical needs of the group. During Jesus' crucifixion, when many of the disciples were not to be found, she was one of the few courageous ones to stay at the foot of the cross. She was also one of the women who wanted to make sure Jesus had a proper burial.

Some have suggested that since the twelve disciples were all men, Jesus must not have considered women very important to his ministry. But the role of Mary Magdalene and the other women who followed Jesus shows that this was definitely not the case. Jesus treated women in a manner far beyond the cultural expectation of the day, respecting them fully as persons and considering them a necessary part of his ministry.

We may identify with Mary Magdalene, either as a woman or as one who has been delivered from a life of total bondage. She was an outcast in society, a woman of ill repute. But through her desire for healing and her trusting obedience to Jesus, she became a significant person in the history of our world. Her life gives us the courage to come boldly before God, knowing that his love extends to all of us, regardless of our situation. He specializes in tough cases.

STRENGTHS AND ACCOMPLISHMENTS:
- Mary supported the work of Jesus and his disciples.
- She was present at Jesus' death.
- She was the first to see the risen Jesus.
- She was given the responsibility of telling the disciples about the Resurrection.

WEAKNESSES AND MISTAKES:
- Mary had somehow become enslaved by demonic forces.

LESSONS FROM HER LIFE:
- Those who have been forgiven much by God are often the most grateful.
- God intends women to play essential roles in his ministry.
- The forgiveness we experience can motivate us to live our life for God.

KEY VERSE:
"It was early on Sunday morning when Jesus rose from the dead, and the first person who saw him was Mary Magdalene, the woman from whom he had cast out seven demons" (Mark 16:9).

Mary Magdalene's story is found in Matthew 27:55–28:10; Mark 15:40–16:11; Luke 8:1-3; and John 20:1-18.

---

crown of thorns and the purple robe. And Pilate said, "Here is the man!"

⁶When they saw him, the leading priests and Temple guards began shouting, "Crucify! Crucify!"

"You crucify him," Pilate said. "I find him not guilty."

⁷The Jewish leaders replied, "By our laws he ought to die because he called himself the Son of God."

⁸When Pilate heard this, he was more frightened than ever. ⁹He took Jesus back into the headquarters again and asked him, "Where are you from?" But Jesus gave no answer. ¹⁰"You won't talk to me?" Pilate demanded. "Don't you realize that I have the power to release you or to crucify you?"

¹¹Then Jesus said, "You would have no power over me at all unless it were given to you from above. So the one who brought me to you has the greater sin."

¹²Then Pilate tried to release him, but the Jewish leaders told him, "If you release this man, you are not a friend of Caesar. Anyone who declares himself a king is a rebel against Caesar."

¹³When they said this, Pilate brought Jesus out to them again. Then Pilate sat down on the judgment seat on the platform that is called the Stone Pavement (in Hebrew, *Gabbatha*). ¹⁴It was now about noon of the day of preparation for the Passover. And Pilate said to the people,* "Here is your king!"

19:14 Greek *Jewish people;* also in 19:20.

15"Away with him," they yelled. "Away with him—crucify him!"

"What? Crucify your king?" Pilate asked.

"We have no king but Caesar," the leading priests shouted back.

16Then Pilate gave Jesus to them to be crucified.

The Crucifixion

So they took Jesus and led him away. 17Carrying the cross by himself, Jesus went to the place called Skull Hill (in Hebrew, *Golgotha*). 18There they crucified him. There were two others crucified with him, one on either side, with Jesus between them. 19And Pilate posted a sign over him that read, "Jesus of Nazareth, the King of the Jews." 20The place where Jesus was crucified was near the city; and the sign was written in Hebrew, Latin, and Greek, so that many people could read it.

21Then the leading priests said to Pilate, "Change it from 'The King of the Jews' to 'He said, I am King of the Jews.'"

22Pilate replied, "What I have written, I have written. It stays exactly as it is."

23When the soldiers had crucified Jesus, they divided his clothes among the four of them. They also took his robe, but it was seamless, woven in one piece from the top. 24So they said, "Let's not tear it but throw dice* to see who gets it." This fulfilled the Scripture that says, "They divided my clothes among themselves and threw dice for my robe."* So that is what they did.

25Standing near the cross were Jesus' mother, and his mother's sister, Mary (the wife of Clopas), and Mary Magdalene. 26When Jesus saw his mother standing there beside the disciple he loved, he said to her, "Woman, he is your son." 27And he said to this disciple, "She is your mother." And from then on this disciple took her into his home.

The Death of Jesus

28Jesus knew that everything was now finished, and to fulfill the Scriptures he said, "I am thirsty."* 29A jar of sour wine was sitting there, so they soaked a sponge in it, put it on a hyssop branch, and held it up to his lips. 30When Jesus had tasted it, he said, "It is finished!" Then he bowed his head and gave up his spirit.

31The Jewish leaders didn't want the victims hanging there the next day, which was the Sabbath (and a very special Sabbath at that, because it was the Passover), so they asked Pilate to hasten their deaths by ordering that their legs be broken. Then their bodies could be taken down. 32So the soldiers came and broke the legs of the two men crucified with Jesus. 33But when they came to Jesus, they saw that he was dead already, so they didn't break his legs. 34One of the soldiers, however, pierced his side with a spear, and blood and water flowed out. 35This report is from an eyewitness giving an accurate account; it is presented so that you also can believe. 36These things happened in fulfillment of the Scriptures that say, "Not one of his bones will be broken,"* 37and "They will look on him whom they pierced."*

The Burial of Jesus

38Afterward Joseph of Arimathea, who had been a secret disciple of Jesus (because he feared the Jewish leaders), asked Pilate for permission to take Jesus' body down. When Pilate gave him permission, he came and took the body away. 39Nicodemus, the man who had come to Jesus at night, also came, bringing about seventy-five pounds* of embalming ointment made from myrrh and aloes. 40Together they wrapped Jesus' body in a long linen cloth with the spices, as is the Jewish custom of burial. 41The place of crucifixion was near a garden, where there was a new tomb, never used before. 42And so, because it was the day of preparation before the Passover and since the tomb was close at hand, they laid Jesus there.

CHAPTER 20

The Resurrection

Early Sunday morning,* while it was still dark, Mary Magdalene came to the tomb and

19:24a Greek *cast lots.* **19:24b** Ps 22:18. **19:28** See Pss 22:15; 69:21. **19:36** Exod 12:46; Num 9:12; Ps 34:20. **19:37** Zech 12:10. **19:39** Greek *100 litras* [32.7 kilograms]. **20:1** Greek *On the first day of the week.*

19:28-30 What did Jesus finish? On the cross Jesus finished the work he was sent to do (17:4) and fully paid for our sins (1 Peter 3:18). In the greatest act of love in history and in fulfillment of a complicated, centuries-old system of sacrifices, he became the perfect sacrificial Lamb of God (see 1:29; Hebrews 9:11-12). The miracle of the Resurrection (20:1-9) confirmed that Jesus is the Savior who can bring salvation and forgiveness, new life, and recovery to all of us.

THOMAS

Although distrust or wavering faith is a reality for most of us, it is painful to be labeled a "doubting Thomas." We might wonder what it was like for Thomas, the disciple of Jesus who became known for his doubting. He simply did not believe that Jesus had risen from the dead. But that is not the end of his story.

Didymus was the other name given for Thomas in the Gospels; it means "twin." Like most twins, Thomas was probably compared to, often in conflict with, and forced to share with his twin sibling. This background could easily have instilled a habit of doubt or distrust into his outlook on life. In spite of this, however, Thomas became one of the inner circle of Jesus' followers and at times exhibited great courage. When Jesus went with his disciples to Bethany to raise Lazarus from the dead, they were walking into a dangerous situation. The religious leaders were actively plotting to kill Jesus. Thomas and the other disciples bravely chose to go along.

Thomas did not doubt Jesus' resurrection out of fear. He continued to meet with the followers of Jesus in the upper room. He just happened to be absent when the risen Jesus first appeared to them. Thomas wanted some kind of proof that his companions had not just been seeing things. Thomas was given the undeniable evidence that he needed when Jesus appeared a second time, permanently dispelling his doubts.

We also have undeniable evidence for the Resurrection. As we trust in Jesus as our Savior, we will experience his power to transform our life, giving us firsthand knowledge of his power. We can overcome our troubling doubts as we continue to trust God to show his power in our life. When Thomas overcame his doubts, he set out on a ministry that exhibited extraordinary faith. As we experience God's power in deliverance, we, too, can minister to others through the power of the Holy Spirit.

STRENGTHS AND ACCOMPLISHMENTS:
• Thomas was willing to give up everything to follow Jesus.
• He was a man of conviction and courage.
• He was a keen thinker and analyst of events.
• He was willing to admit his mistake.

WEAKNESSES AND MISTAKES:
• Thomas discounted the supernatural explanation of the Resurrection.
• He wanted unquestionable evidence before he was willing to believe.

LESSONS FROM HIS LIFE:
• People from difficult family backgrounds can recover by following Jesus.
• Doubt can lead to deeper faith if faced honestly.
• Undeniable evidence is not necessary to begin a life of faith.
• God's work in our life can lead to deeper faith.

KEY VERSE:
"Then Jesus told [Thomas], 'You believe because you have seen me. Blessed are those who haven't seen me and believe anyway'" (John 20:29).

Thomas's story is told in several passages in the Gospels. He is also mentioned in Acts 1:14.

---

found that the stone had been rolled away from the entrance. ²She ran and found Simon Peter and the other disciple, the one whom Jesus loved. She said, "They have taken the Lord's body out of the tomb, and I don't know where they have put him!"

³Peter and the other disciple ran to the tomb to see. ⁴The other disciple outran Peter and got there first. ⁵He stooped and looked in and saw the linen cloth lying there, but he didn't go in. ⁶Then Simon Peter arrived and went inside. He also noticed the linen wrappings lying there, ⁷while the cloth that had covered Jesus' head was folded up and lying to

the side. ⁸Then the other disciple also went in, and he saw and believed—⁹for until then they hadn't realized that the Scriptures said he would rise from the dead. ¹⁰Then they went home.

Jesus Appears to Mary Magdalene

¹¹Mary was standing outside the tomb crying, and as she wept, she stooped and looked in. ¹²She saw two white-robed angels sitting at the head and foot of the place where the body of Jesus had been lying. ¹³"Why are you crying?" the angels asked her.

"Because they have taken away my Lord,"

she replied, "and I don't know where they have put him."

[14]She glanced over her shoulder and saw someone standing behind her. It was Jesus, but she didn't recognize him. [15]"Why are you crying?" Jesus asked her. "Who are you looking for?"

She thought he was the gardener. "Sir," she said, "if you have taken him away, tell me where you have put him, and I will go and get him."

[16]"Mary!" Jesus said.

She turned toward him and exclaimed, "Teacher!"*

[17]"Don't cling to me," Jesus said, "for I haven't yet ascended to the Father. But go find my brothers and tell them that I am ascending to my Father and your Father, my God and your God."

[18]Mary Magdalene found the disciples and told them, "I have seen the Lord!" Then she gave them his message.

Jesus Appears to His Disciples

[19]That evening, on the first day of the week, the disciples were meeting behind locked doors because they were afraid of the Jewish leaders. Suddenly, Jesus was standing there among them! "Peace be with you," he said. [20]As he spoke, he held out his hands for them to see, and he showed them his side. They were filled with joy when they saw their Lord! [21]He spoke to them again and said, "Peace be with you. As the Father has sent me, so I send you." [22]Then he breathed on them and said to them, "Receive the Holy Spirit. [23]If you forgive anyone's sins, they are forgiven. If you refuse to forgive them, they are unforgiven."

Jesus Appears to Thomas

[24]One of the disciples, Thomas (nicknamed the Twin*), was not with the others when Jesus came. [25]They told him, "We have seen the Lord!" But he replied, "I won't believe it unless I see the nail wounds in his hands, put my fingers into them, and place my hand into the wound in his side."

[26]Eight days later the disciples were together again, and this time Thomas was with them. The doors were locked; but suddenly, as before, Jesus was standing among them. He said, "Peace be with you." [27]Then he said to Thomas, "Put your finger here and see my hands. Put your hand into the wound in my side. Don't be faithless any longer. Believe!"

[28]"My Lord and my God!" Thomas exclaimed.

[29]Then Jesus told him, "You believe because you have seen me. Blessed are those who haven't seen me and believe anyway."

20:16 Greek *and said in Hebrew, "Rabboni," which means "Teacher."* 20:24 Greek *the one who was called Didymus.*

20:11-18 Mary Magdalene modeled an essential part of the recovery process—telling others the good news. Once healed of seven demons (Mark 16:9), Mary had supported the ministry of Jesus financially (Luke 8:2-3) and was a faithful follower from early in his ministry. Her faithfulness was honored when the risen Christ appeared and spoke to her before he spoke to anyone else! After seeing the resurrected Jesus, she went immediately and told the disciples. When we realize the power that the risen Christ can bring us through the recovery process, we can show our gratitude by doing as Mary did—carrying the message to others.

20:22-23 The risen Christ did as he had promised (see 14:16-17; 15:26; 16:7) and breathed his Holy Spirit on his disciples. This life-bringing, truth-revealing, sin-convicting, comfort-giving Spirit is also a Spirit of forgiveness. Just as we receive God's forgiveness for our sins, so we are exhorted and enabled to forgive those who sin against us. If we refuse to forgive others, we will miss the blessed freedom that God offers. He wants us to experience the emotional healing that comes only from working through our anger and hurt to the point of releasing it to God. By God's Spirit, recovery from our painful past can be completed.

20:24-29 Here doubting Thomas earned his reputation. He refused to believe in Jesus' resurrection until he saw and felt the risen Christ with his own eyes and hands. In recovery we often experience doubts. We have a hard time believing that God is at work in our life when we don't see immediate changes or miraculous results. Recovery can be a painstaking process without much to show for it at first. Even when evidence of God's power is not immediate, if we persevere in faith, we will experience the peace that comes from trusting God with our present problems and the unknown future.

21:1-14 Imagine what the disciples must have felt! These professional fishermen had spent an entire night fishing and hadn't caught anything. Then Jesus called to them and told them to throw the net on the other side of the boat. The disciples' first response must have been to laugh. But when they obeyed Jesus, they caught so many fish that the net began to break. As strange as it may sound, that is how the recovery process works. When we have tried everything and finally realize our helplessness, we need to follow God's instructions for healthy living. It may seem foolish at first, but as we trust God and obey his will, we learn that God's power can rebuild our life.

Purpose of the Book

[30]Jesus' disciples saw him do many other miraculous signs besides the ones recorded in this book. [31]But these are written so that you may believe* that Jesus is the Messiah, the Son of God, and that by believing in him you will have life.

CHAPTER 21
Jesus Appears to Seven Disciples

Later Jesus appeared again to the disciples beside the Sea of Galilee.* This is how it happened. [2]Several of the disciples were there—Simon Peter, Thomas (nicknamed the Twin*), Nathanael from Cana in Galilee, the sons of Zebedee, and two other disciples.

[3]Simon Peter said, "I'm going fishing."

"We'll come, too," they all said. So they went out in the boat, but they caught nothing all night.

[4]At dawn the disciples saw Jesus standing on the beach, but they couldn't see who he was. [5]He called out, "Friends, have you caught any fish?"

"No," they replied.

[6]Then he said, "Throw out your net on the right-hand side of the boat, and you'll get plenty of fish!" So they did, and they couldn't draw in the net because there were so many fish in it.

[7]Then the disciple whom Jesus loved said to Peter, "It is the Lord!" When Simon Peter heard that it was the Lord, he put on his tunic (for he had stripped for work), jumped into the water, and swam ashore. [8]The others stayed with the boat and pulled the loaded net to the shore, for they were only out about three hundred feet.* [9]When they got there, they saw that a charcoal fire was burning and fish were frying over it, and there was bread.

[10]"Bring some of the fish you've just caught," Jesus said. [11]So Simon Peter went aboard and dragged the net to the shore. There were 153 large fish, and yet the net hadn't torn.

[12]"Now come and have some breakfast!" Jesus said. And no one dared ask him if he really was the Lord because they were sure of it. [13]Then Jesus served them the bread and the fish. [14]This was the third time Jesus had appeared to his disciples since he had been raised from the dead.

20:31 Some manuscripts read *may continue to believe.*
21:1 Greek *Sea of Tiberias,* another name for the Sea of Galilee. **21:2** Greek *the one who was called Didymus.*
21:8 Greek *200 cubits* [90 meters].

Love

READ JOHN 21:14-25

We may wonder how we can love people but still hurt them. This paradox causes shame and sometimes erects barriers between us and the ones we love. We may be afraid to say that we love them, thinking, *If I really loved them, I wouldn't let them down the way I have.*

Peter had once sworn his love for Jesus. But after Jesus was arrested, Peter protected himself by denying that he even knew Jesus. Jesus wasn't surprised, but Peter had a hard time forgiving himself. After Jesus rose from the dead, he talked with Peter: "Jesus said to Simon Peter, 'Simon son of John, do you love me more than these?' 'Yes, Lord,' Peter replied, 'you know I love you.' . . . Jesus repeated the question: 'Simon son of John, do you love me?' 'Yes, Lord,' Peter said, 'you know I love you.' . . . Once more he asked him, 'Simon son of John, do you love me?' Peter was grieved that Jesus asked the question a third time. He said, 'Lord, you know everything. You know I love you'" (John 21:15-17).

Jesus allowed Peter to affirm his love the best he could and accepted Peter as he was. In this way Jesus reduced the shame and restored the relationship. Shame and isolation can lead us back to our addiction. For the sake of recovery, we must not let our shame cause us to avoid the people we love. It is all right if we love others imperfectly—no one is perfect. But we must keep our love relationships together until we have had time to heal. ***Turn to page 237, Romans 3.***

Jesus Challenges Peter

[15]After breakfast Jesus said to Simon Peter, "Simon son of John, do you love me more than these?"

"Yes, Lord," Peter replied, "you know I love you."

"Then feed my lambs," Jesus told him.

[16]Jesus repeated the question: "Simon son of John, do you love me?"

"Yes, Lord," Peter said, "you know I love you."

"Then take care of my sheep," Jesus said.

[17]Once more he asked him, "Simon son of John, do you love me?"

Peter was grieved that Jesus asked the question a third time. He said, "Lord, you know everything. You know I love you."

Jesus said, "Then feed my sheep. [18]The truth is, when you were young, you were able to do as you liked and go wherever you wanted to. But when you are old, you will stretch out your hands, and others will direct you and take you where you don't want to go." [19]Jesus said this to let him know what kind of death he would die to glorify God. Then Jesus told him, "Follow me."

[20]Peter turned around and saw the disciple Jesus loved following them—the one who had leaned over to Jesus during supper and asked, "Lord, who among us will betray you?" [21]Peter asked Jesus, "What about him, Lord?"

[22]Jesus replied, "If I want him to remain alive until I return, what is that to you? You follow me." [23]So the rumor spread among the community of believers* that that disciple wouldn't die. But that isn't what Jesus said at all. He only said, "If I want him to remain alive until I return, what is that to you?"

Conclusion

[24]This is that disciple who saw these events and recorded them here. And we all know that his account of these things is accurate.

[25]And I suppose that if all the other things Jesus did were written down, the whole world could not contain the books.

21:23 Greek *the brothers.*

21:15-17 Peter had denied Jesus three times, so Jesus allowed Peter to declare his love for him three times. Each time Jesus affirmed his confidence in Peter by commissioning him to feed his flock. Later Peter fulfilled this commission when he was filled with the mighty power of the Holy Spirit at Pentecost. He became a key leader in the early church. Although we may experience failures and relapses, when we open our heart to God, he can and will restore us—even to the point where our life becomes a model of recovery to others.

REFLECTIONS ON

JOHN

✳*insights* FROM JESUS' WORDS AND DEEDS

Jesus was a perfect picture of God and a perfect teacher of God's truth. In **John 1:29-31** we find that he was also the perfect sacrifice—the Lamb of God. The Old Testament sacrificial system required that an unblemished lamb be slain on the altar in place of the people on at least a yearly basis. Through its death the people could be forgiven of their sins and given a fresh start. By dying on the cross, Jesus fulfilled the requirements of that sacrificial system completely and forever. He is the Lamb of God who deals with our sins, our powerlessness, and our shortcomings. He gives each of us a chance for a new start, no matter how terrible our past has been.

Those who witnessed Jesus' actions and heard his words had to choose between belief and unbelief. Our choice, like that of the Pharisees in **John 2:17-25,** is to accept or reject Jesus' claims about his mission and authority. Was he just a fascinating man who did amazing deeds? Was he just a good teacher with an interesting message? Was he a madman with delusions of grandeur?

Or was Jesus actually God, who came to live among us? According to the Bible, Jesus is God, and he has the power to offer each of us a new life. The disciples discovered this truth and were transformed from rough, inexperienced men into some of the greatest leaders of their day. God has the power to transform us, too.

The paralyzed man in **John 5:1-15** had waited at the pool of Bethesda for many years, hoping to be healed. He was as hopelessly trapped by his physical handicap as we are by our dependency. He was full of excuses for why things weren't working out for him. He couldn't stand up and walk until he took responsibility for his life and put his faith in Jesus' power to heal him. After Jesus healed him, he stood up to Jesus' critics and witnessed to others about God's power to save. Recovery does not come to those who wallow in the blame game but only to those who are willing to take small steps of faith.

In **John 8:1-11** the Pharisees brought to Jesus a woman who had been caught in the act of adultery. Jewish law required that she be stoned to death (Leviticus 20:10; Deuteronomy 22:22). The Pharisees hoped to trap him by asking him to judge the situation. If Jesus said to stone her, they could have brought him before the Roman authorities. The Romans did not allow the Jews to implement their own death sentences. If Jesus had pardoned this woman, the Pharisees could have claimed he was a false prophet for ignoring God's law. Jesus wisely escaped the trap by showing the Pharisees that they had no grounds for judging since they sinned too. Then Jesus told the woman to go and sin no more. Jesus did not ignore this woman's sin, but he forgave her and gave her a new start in life. Jesus can give each of us a new life, no matter how terrible our past.

When we are ridiculed, rejected, or abused, we should look to Jesus' experiences leading to the cross. In **John 19:1-3** Jesus suffered the pain and humiliation of being whipped, mocked, crowned with thorns, and struck in the face. He was shamefully exposed on the cross yet held his head high enough to shout, "It is finished!" (19:30). Because of the shame Jesus suffered, we can hold our heads high as we look to God. We have been forgiven. Through Jesus, our sins and shames are removed, and we have been offered another chance at life.

✳*insights* FROM THE DISCIPLES' LIVES

Once Andrew had met Jesus and realized who he was, he was quick to carry the saving message to others. In **John 1:40-42** he rushed off to find his brother, Simon, whom he immediately brought to Jesus. When we experience God's power in our life, we will be just as eager to share our newfound hope with others. This is an essential part of the recovery process. As we share the good news of God's power to deliver, we will give great hope to fellow strugglers. We will also be encouraged to persevere when we remember all the great things God has done for us.

Throughout his Gospel (see **John 13:23; 19:26; 21:20**), the apostle John referred to himself as "the disciple Jesus loved." John was probably Jesus' closest friend during the years of his ministry, but John was not boasting about this. The apostle was basing his self-perception solely upon God's unconditional love for him. When we see ourself as God does—deeply loved—we will have an accurate self-image and make healthy progress toward recovery.

It is easy to fall into the trap of comparing ourself to others, as Peter did with John in **John 21:20-25.** We sometimes take solace in comparing ourself to people who are still in bondage to an addiction. Or we may look at others in recovery and become jealous of how quickly they seem to progress. Focusing on the failures and successes of others in recovery is an easy distraction from our own life and recovery. Our challenge is to make a searching inventory of our own life, not the lives of others. When we focus on our own issues, we will soon begin to make progress in recovery.

✳*insights* ABOUT OUR RELATIONSHIP WITH GOD

In **John 6:28-29** the people asked Jesus, "What does God want us to do?" That question has plagued the human race since Adam and Eve first sinned. Many of us live by a list of shoulds and shouldn'ts in our efforts to earn God's acceptance. Some of us learned this as children, when our parents persistently pressured us to measure up to their ideals. In turn, we may do this to our own children. The good news is that we can receive God's help and forgiveness! God in Jesus Christ has taken the initiative; we simply need to repent and receive him by faith. Our growth begins as we respond to God's love for us.

As we see in **John 15:9-12**, the ability to show genuine, unconditional love to others comes from the abundant love God gives us. Conversely, unhealthy, selfish, codependent love starts with our emptiness and need for love. We may try to love others in an attempt to earn their love in return. Only when we experience and remain in God's love (shared by godly people we trust and respect) can we genuinely love ourself and others. God's joy is made complete in us when we experience his love in our life. Then we can offer his unselfish love to others out of an over-flowing heart (see also 13:34-35).

✳*insights* CONCERNING THE HOLY SPIRIT

God desires a special kind of relationship with us. When Jesus ascended to the Father in heaven, he sent his Spirit to live within his followers. In **John 14:15-18** the Holy Spirit is called the Coun-selor. Other translations call him the Comforter or Advocate. By whatever name, he ministers God's compassion to us, brings to mind Jesus' teachings, guides us into doing justice and know-ing all truth, and brings our needs before God the Father (see 14:26; 15:26; 16:5-15). Many of us in recovery feel like emotional orphans or cripples who have been abandoned or neglected. God, the Holy Spirit, will never leave us. He is with us at all times, and he has the power to help us overcome our sins and dependency.

In recovery it is crucial that we learn to depend on the Holy Spirit. In **John 15:26-27** we find that the Holy Spirit reveals the truth of God's Word, holds us accountable to other believers, and helps us conform to the image of his Son. As the "Spirit of truth," he gives wisdom to help us examine our life; he helps us see past our denial and self-deception. The Holy Spirit can guide us to an accurate perception of ourself, just like an unflattering mirror. The result will be convicting, but fulfilling—so much so that we cannot help but share the good news with others.

ACTS

THE BIG PICTURE

A. TO JERUSALEM: TELLING THEIR STORY AT HOME (1:1–8:40)
B. TO JUDEA AND SAMARIA: TRANSITION TO OUTSIDERS (9:1–12:25)
C. TO THE WHOLE WORLD: HOW OUTSIDERS BECOME INSIDERS (13:1–21:40)
D. JERUSALEM TO ROME: THE COST OF FOLLOWING JESUS (22:1–28:31)

What occurred during Jesus' brief earthly life was limited to a small corner of the world. Most of civilization never noticed Jesus bringing hope to a hurting and seemingly forsaken group of people. But just as Jesus predicted, the small band of disciples that met in Jerusalem following his death and resurrection turned the world upside down. Life on planet earth hasn't been the same since.

Written by Luke as a sequel to his Gospel, Acts records the history of the early believers and the church. Through the examples of these early believers, we see that the Holy Spirit has the power to change lives. We learn that God can transform our life and help us live at peace with him and with others.

The first half of this book focuses on the ministry of Peter—how he was transformed from an impulsive and unreliable, though well-intentioned, follower of Jesus to a bold and dedicated leader. The second half of the book presents us with the life and ministry of Paul. Paul and his companions faced all kinds of difficulties and opposition, but through the power of God they spread the good news about Jesus throughout the Mediterranean world.

These men should be an encouragement to us. Both made serious mistakes as younger men, but as they turned their lives over to God, they were gradually changed. Paul, who as an angry young man helped to kill the first Christian martyr, Stephen, later became a selfless and dedicated missionary. Peter, whose cockiness often prevented him from overcoming his weaknesses, became a humble and effective leader. The changes in both men demonstrate what God can do in our life, too.

THE BOTTOM LINE

PURPOSE: To trace how the Jewish Jesus movement became a worldwide movement through the impetus of the Holy Spirit. AUTHOR: Luke, the physician. AUDIENCE: Theophilus, whose name means "lover of God." DATE WRITTEN: Sometime between A.D. 63 and 70. SETTING: Acts provides a history of the events that followed the resurrection of Jesus. KEY VERSE: "But when the Holy Spirit has come upon you, you will receive power and will tell people about me everywhere—in Jerusalem, throughout Judea, in Samaria, and to the ends of the earth" (1:8). SPECIAL FEATURES: The book of Acts is a sequel to the Gospel of Luke. KEY PEOPLE: Peter, John, Stephen, Philip, Paul, Barnabas, Silas, Timothy, and Luke.

RECOVERY THEMES

The Power of the Holy Spirit: Jesus promised the disciples that after he left, the Holy Spirit would bring them power. Little did they know just what kind of power! As they learned firsthand, the Holy Spirit and his power are real. When we compare Peter in the Gospels with Peter in the book of Acts, we see that his life was changed. When we look at Saul doing his utmost to destroy the early church and then see his dedicated missionary service, we can tell that he was radically transformed by God. The power of God changed their hearts and gave them confidence to tell the truth about him. In our powerlessness, God makes his power available to us through the Holy Spirit. With his help, no problem is too great to overcome; no life is so far gone that it cannot be made new.

Commitment That Overcomes Opposition: Luke did not idealize the people of the early church. They did not have an easy task that swiftly and smoothly moved to its objective. Instead, they struggled with controversy, opposition, and discouragement. They were misunderstood by religious and irreligious people alike. But their common bond was a commitment to God at any cost. As we commit our life to God and to recovery, we can expect to face obstacles, but we can also expect to overcome any problems or opposing forces with God's power.

Living beyond Circumstances: When we read about the early Christians and how they shared what they had and took care of each other, it is easy to think that somehow they did not experience the kinds of problems we do. This was not the case. They learned how to live above their circumstances. They weren't in denial; they were more conscious of God than they were of their problems. When we focus on our problems, we lose sight of our source of power. We try to generate the power from within, only to fail and become discouraged. It does no good to deny or ignore our circumstances, but it does a world of good to trust God and turn our life and our circumstances over to him.

Sharing the Message: As Peter, John, Philip, Paul, Barnabas, and others came to faith in Jesus, they shared the Good News with others. God's healing power is good news! As we share the message of our own spiritual awakening with others in need, we share the good news of God's healing power, as did those early disciples. In so doing, we become stronger in our own recovery and stronger in our faith in God.

CHAPTER 1
The Promise of the Holy Spirit
Dear Theophilus:

In my first book* I told you about everything Jesus began to do and teach ²until the day he ascended to heaven after giving his chosen apostles further instructions from the Holy Spirit. ³During the forty days after his crucifixion, he appeared to the apostles from time to time and proved to them in many ways that he was actually alive. On these occasions he talked to them about the Kingdom of God.

⁴In one of these meetings as he was eating a meal with them, he told them, "Do not leave Jerusalem until the Father sends you what he promised. Remember, I have told you about this before. ⁵John baptized with* water, but in just a few days you will be baptized with the Holy Spirit."

The Ascension of Jesus
⁶When the apostles were with Jesus, they kept asking him, "Lord, are you going to free Israel now and restore our kingdom?"

⁷"The Father sets those dates," he replied,

1:1 The reference is to the book of Luke. 1:5 Or *in;* also in 1:5b.

1:1-5 This sequel to Luke's Gospel picks up where the Gospel left off. It records the activities of the apostles soon after Jesus' resurrection. Before ascending to heaven, Jesus assured his followers that the Holy Spirit he had promised to send would come upon them as they waited in Jerusalem (Luke 24:49). At the appointed time, the early Christians received the power they needed to reach the world with the good news of Jesus Christ. God offers us this same power through the Holy Spirit to overcome the barriers in our recovery process.

1:6-11 When the disciples asked Jesus about the coming of his earthly Kingdom, they yearned for the Messiah's reign of freedom and peace. But Jesus turned their eyes to the present. With the power of the Holy Spirit, they were to share the good news of salvation through Jesus Christ with others. Sometimes we do what the disciples did, looking forward to a time of complete freedom and peace, while we should be taking productive steps of action here and now. The Holy Spirit gives us the power necessary for a successful recovery. An important part of that recovery process is to share the Good News with others.

"and they are not for you to know. [8]But when the Holy Spirit has come upon you, you will receive power and will tell people about me everywhere—in Jerusalem, throughout Judea, in Samaria, and to the ends of the earth."

[9]It was not long after he said this that he was taken up into the sky while they were watching, and he disappeared into a cloud. [10]As they were straining their eyes to see him, two white-robed men suddenly stood there among them. [11]They said, "Men of Galilee, why are you standing here staring at the sky? Jesus has been taken away from you into heaven. And someday, just as you saw him go, he will return!"

Matthias Replaces Judas

[12]The apostles were at the Mount of Olives when this happened, so they walked the half mile* back to Jerusalem. [13]Then they went to the upstairs room of the house where they were staying. Here is the list of those who were present:

Peter,
John,
James,
Andrew,
Philip,
Thomas,
Bartholomew,
Matthew,
James (son of Alphaeus),
Simon (the Zealot),
and Judas (son of James).

[14]They all met together continually for prayer, along with Mary the mother of Jesus, several other women, and the brothers of Jesus.

[15]During this time, on a day when about 120 believers* were present, Peter stood up and addressed them as follows:

[16]"Brothers, it was necessary for the Scriptures to be fulfilled concerning Judas, who guided the Temple police to arrest Jesus. This was predicted long ago by the Holy Spirit, speaking through King David. [17]Judas was one of us, chosen to share in the ministry with us."

[18](Judas bought a field with the money he received for his treachery, and falling there, he burst open, spilling out his intestines. [19]The news of his death spread rapidly among all the people of Jerusalem, and they gave the place the Aramaic name *Akeldama*, which means "Field of Blood.")

[20]Peter continued, "This was predicted in the book of Psalms, where it says, 'Let his home become desolate, with no one living in it.' And again, 'Let his position be given to someone else.'*

[21]"So now we must choose another man to take Judas's place. It must be someone who has been with us all the time that we were with the Lord Jesus—[22]from the time he was baptized by John until the day he was taken from us into heaven. Whoever is chosen will join us as a witness of Jesus' resurrection."

[23]So they nominated two men: Joseph called Barsabbas (also known as Justus) and Matthias. [24]Then they all prayed for the right man to be chosen. "O Lord," they said, "you know every heart. Show us which of these men you have chosen [25]as an apostle to replace Judas the traitor in this ministry, for he has deserted us and gone where he belongs." [26]Then they cast lots, and in this way Matthias was chosen and became an apostle with the other eleven.

CHAPTER 2
The Holy Spirit Comes

On the day of Pentecost, seven weeks after Jesus' resurrection,* the believers were meeting together in one place. [2]Suddenly, there was a sound from heaven like the roaring of a mighty windstorm in the skies above them, and it filled the house where they were meeting. [3]Then, what looked like flames or tongues of fire appeared and settled on each of them. [4]And everyone present was filled with the Holy Spirit and began speaking in other languages,* as the Holy Spirit gave them this ability.

[5]Godly Jews from many nations were living in Jerusalem at that time. [6]When they heard this sound, they came running to see what it was all about, and they were bewildered to

---

1:12 Greek *a Sabbath day's journey.* **1:15** Greek *brothers.* **1:20** Pss 69:25; 109:8. **2:1** Greek *When the day of Pentecost arrived.* This annual celebration came 50 days after the Passover ceremonies. See Lev 23:16. **2:4** Or *in other tongues.*

2:1-4 On the day of Pentecost, the disciples obeyed Jesus and waited in Jerusalem. Suddenly the Holy Spirit manifested his presence by sound (wind), sight (fire), and speech (new languages). The believers were filled with the Holy Spirit, and God's renewing power began its work of transforming them from the inside out. This marked a new era in history as God's powerful presence entered the hearts of all believers. God's powerful presence can still indwell us, transforming our life and healing our wounds. As we trust God, his Spirit empowers us in recovery.

hear their own languages being spoken by the believers.

[7]They were beside themselves with wonder. "How can this be?" they exclaimed. "These people are all from Galilee, [8]and yet we hear them speaking the languages of the lands where we were born! [9]Here we are—Parthians, Medes, Elamites, people from Mesopotamia, Judea, Cappadocia, Pontus, the province of Asia, [10]Phrygia, Pamphylia, Egypt, and the areas of Libya toward Cyrene, visitors from Rome (both Jews and converts to Judaism), [11]Cretans, and Arabians. And we all hear these people speaking in our own languages about the wonderful things God has done!" [12]They stood there amazed and perplexed. "What can this mean?" they asked each other. [13]But others in the crowd were mocking. "They're drunk, that's all!" they said.

Peter Preaches to a Crowd

[14]Then Peter stepped forward with the eleven other apostles and shouted to the crowd, "Listen carefully, all of you, fellow Jews and residents of Jerusalem! Make no mistake about this. [15]Some of you are saying these people are drunk. It isn't true! It's much too early for that. People don't get drunk by nine o'clock in the morning. [16]No, what you see this morning was predicted centuries ago by the prophet Joel:

[17]'In the last days, God said,
   I will pour out my Spirit upon all people.
Your sons and daughters will prophesy,
   your young men will see visions,
   and your old men will dream dreams.
[18]In those days I will pour out my Spirit
   upon all my servants, men and women
      alike,
   and they will prophesy.
[19]And I will cause wonders in the heavens
      above
   and signs on the earth below—
   blood and fire and clouds of smoke.
[20]The sun will be turned into darkness,
   and the moon will turn bloodred,
   before that great and glorious day of
      the Lord arrives.

[21]And anyone who calls on the name of the
      Lord
   will be saved.'*

[22]"People of Israel, listen! God publicly endorsed Jesus of Nazareth by doing wonderful miracles, wonders, and signs through him, as you well know. [23]But you followed God's prearranged plan. With the help of lawless Gentiles, you nailed him to the cross and murdered him. [24]However, God released him from the horrors of death and raised him back to life again, for death could not keep him in its grip. [25]King David said this about him:

'I know the Lord is always with me.
   I will not be shaken, for he is right
      beside me.
[26]No wonder my heart is filled with joy,
   and my mouth shouts his praises!
   My body rests in hope.
[27]For you will not leave my soul among the
      dead*
   or allow your Holy One to rot in the
      grave.
[28]You have shown me the way of life,
   and you will give me wonderful joy in
      your presence.'*

[29]"Dear brothers, think about this! David wasn't referring to himself when he spoke these words I have quoted, for he died and was buried, and his tomb is still here among us. [30]But he was a prophet, and he knew God had promised with an oath that one of David's own descendants would sit on David's throne as the Messiah. [31]David was looking into the future and predicting the Messiah's resurrection. He was saying that the Messiah would not be left among the dead and that his body would not rot in the grave. [32]"This prophecy was speaking of Jesus, whom God raised from the dead, and we all are witnesses of this. [33]Now he sits on the throne of highest honor in heaven, at God's right hand. And the Father, as he had promised, gave him the Holy Spirit to pour out upon us, just as you see and hear today. [34]For David himself never ascended into heaven, yet he said,

2:17-21 Joel 2:28-32. **2:27** Greek *in Hades;* also in 2:31. **2:25-28** Ps 16:8-11.

2:14-21 After asserting the sobriety of the believers, Peter told the crowd about the power they just witnessed. The amazing power of the Holy Spirit had been promised by the prophet Joel centuries earlier. By quoting Joel 2:28-32, Peter stressed the universal impact of the Holy Spirit; it would be given to all God's people—young and old, men and women, masters and servants. God's power is available to everyone—regardless of race, gender, or social class—who recognizes his or her helpless state and asks for God's mercy (2:21). No one with a humble heart is beyond the reach of God's power.

'The LORD said to my Lord,
Sit in honor at my right hand
35   until I humble your enemies,
     making them a footstool under your feet.'*

36So let it be clearly known by everyone in Israel that God has made this Jesus whom you crucified to be both Lord and Messiah!"

37Peter's words convicted them deeply, and they said to him and to the other apostles, "Brothers, what should we do?"

38Peter replied, "Each of you must turn from your sins and turn to God, and be baptized in the name of Jesus Christ for the forgiveness of your sins. Then you will receive the gift of the Holy Spirit. 39This promise is to you and to your children, and even to the Gentiles*—all who have been called by the Lord our God." 40Then Peter continued preaching for a long time, strongly urging all his listeners, "Save yourselves from this generation that has gone astray!"

41Those who believed what Peter said were baptized and added to the church—about three thousand in all. 42They joined with the other believers and devoted themselves to the apostles' teaching and fellowship, sharing in the Lord's Supper and in prayer.

The Believers Meet Together

43A deep sense of awe came over them all, and the apostles performed many miraculous signs and wonders. 44And all the believers met together constantly and shared everything they had. 45They sold their possessions and shared the proceeds with those in need. 46They worshiped together at the Temple each day, met in homes for the Lord's Supper, and shared their meals with great joy and generosity—47all the while praising God and enjoying the goodwill of all the people. And each day the Lord added to their group those who were being saved.

CHAPTER 3
Peter Heals a Crippled Beggar

Peter and John went to the Temple one afternoon to take part in the three o'clock prayer service. 2As they approached the Temple, a man lame from birth was being carried in. Each day he was put beside the Temple gate, the one called the Beautiful Gate, so he could beg from the people going into the Temple. 3When he saw Peter and John about to enter, he asked them for some money.

4Peter and John looked at him intently, and Peter said, "Look at us!" 5The lame man looked at them eagerly, expecting a gift. 6But Peter said, "I don't have any money for you. But I'll give you what I have. In the name of Jesus Christ of Nazareth, get up and walk!"

7Then Peter took the lame man by the right hand and helped him up. And as he did, the man's feet and anklebones were healed and strengthened. 8He jumped up, stood on his feet, and began to walk! Then, walking, leaping, and praising God, he went into the Temple with them.

9All the people saw him walking and heard him praising God. 10When they realized he was the lame beggar they had seen so often at the Beautiful Gate, they were absolutely astounded! 11They all rushed out to Solomon's Colonnade, where he was holding tightly to Peter and John. Everyone stood there in awe of the wonderful thing that had happened.

2:34-35 Ps 110:1. 2:39 Greek *to those far away.*

2:37-39 Peter's preaching led the people to examine their lives, and they readily recognized their need for salvation in Christ. Peter assured them that by turning from their sins and entrusting their lives to God, they would be forgiven and receive gift of the Holy Spirit. We can expect the same blessings if we bring our sins before God. His forgiveness will set us free from bondage to our sins of the past. The presence of his Holy Spirit will give us the power to persevere through hard times. If God is in our life, he will lead us to successful recovery.
2:42-47 Luke mentioned the activities that characterized the early Christian community. They committed themselves to spiritual growth by studying the Scriptures together, sharing together, and praying together. They helped those in need by selling their possessions and generously sharing the proceeds with them. Their faith, joy, and loving support were so contagious that many more became believers. Recovery follows the same pattern as we grow in faith—it is never done in isolation. We need people to walk with us, encouraging us when we become discouraged and holding us accountable when we stray.
3:1-11 This crippled man was truly helpless; he was a prime candidate for God's powerful help. Notice the steps in this healing. Peter established personal contact by asking the man to look at him. Then Peter told him to get up and walk in Jesus' name. Peter helped the man up, and suddenly he was walking, leaping, and praising God! Healing can come as God touches our life through the ministry of others. As we experience healing and share our story, we can bless others by leading them to Jesus Christ.

Peter Preaches in the Temple

¹²Peter saw his opportunity and addressed the crowd. "People of Israel," he said, "what is so astounding about this? And why look at us as though we had made this man walk by our own power and godliness? ¹³For it is the God of Abraham, the God of Isaac, the God of Jacob, the God of all our ancestors who has brought glory to his servant Jesus by doing this. This is the same Jesus whom you handed over and rejected before Pilate, despite Pilate's decision to release him. ¹⁴You rejected this holy, righteous one and instead demanded the release of a murderer. ¹⁵You killed the author of life, but God raised him to life. And we are witnesses of this fact!

¹⁶"The name of Jesus has healed this man— and you know how lame he was before. Faith in Jesus' name has caused this healing before your very eyes.

¹⁷"Friends,* I realize that what you did to Jesus was done in ignorance; and the same can be said of your leaders. ¹⁸But God was fulfilling what all the prophets had declared about the Messiah beforehand— that he must suffer all these things. ¹⁹Now turn from your sins and turn to God, so you can be cleansed of your sins. ²⁰Then wonderful times of refreshment will come from the presence of the Lord, and he will send Jesus your Messiah to you again. ²¹For he must remain in heaven until the time for the final restoration of all things, as God promised long ago through his prophets. ²²Moses said, 'The Lord your God will raise up a Prophet like me from among your own people. Listen carefully to everything he tells you.'* ²³Then Moses said, 'Anyone who will not listen to that Prophet will be cut off from God's people and utterly destroyed.'*

²⁴"Starting with Samuel, every prophet spoke about what is happening today. ²⁵You are the children of those prophets, and you are included in the covenant God promised to your ancestors. For God said to Abraham, 'Through your descendants all the families on earth will be blessed.'* ²⁶When God raised up his servant, he sent him first to you people of Israel, to bless you by turning each of you back from your sinful ways."

CHAPTER 4
Peter and John before the Council

While Peter and John were speaking to the people, the leading priests, the captain of the Temple guard, and some of the Sadducees came over to them. ²They were very disturbed that Peter and John were claiming, on the authority of Jesus, that there is a resurrection of the dead. ³They arrested them and, since it was already evening, jailed them until morning. ⁴But many of the people who heard their message believed it, so that the number of believers totaled about five thousand men, not counting women and children.*

⁵The next day the council of all the rulers and elders and teachers of religious law met in Jerusalem. ⁶Annas the high priest was there, along with Caiaphas, John, Alexander, and other relatives of the high priest. ⁷They brought in the two disciples and demanded, "By what power, or in whose name, have you done this?"

⁸Then Peter, filled with the Holy Spirit, said to them, "Leaders and elders of our nation, ⁹are we being questioned because we've done a good deed for a crippled man? Do you want to know how he was healed? ¹⁰Let me clearly state to you and to all the people of Israel that he was healed in the name and power of Jesus Christ from Nazareth, the man you crucified, but whom God raised from the dead. ¹¹For Jesus is the one referred to in the Scriptures, where it says,

'The stone that you builders rejected
    has now become the cornerstone.'*

¹²There is salvation in no one else! There is no other name in all of heaven for people to call on to save them."

¹³The members of the council were amazed when they saw the boldness of Peter and John, for they could see that they were ordi-

---

3:17 Greek *Brothers.* **3:22** Deut 18:15. **3:23** Deut 18:19; Lev 23:29. **3:25** Gen 22:18. **4:4** Greek *5,000 adult males.* **4:11** Ps 118:22.

4:10-12 Peter consistently held his listeners accountable for their actions (4:10; see 2:36; 3:12-23), but he never concluded his messages negatively. He always declared that God can do what we are powerless to do—deliver us from the destructive grip of sin. We all need the forgiveness and recovery offered only by Jesus Christ. Jesus desires complete recovery for us—spiritual, emotional, and physical—and he has the power to bring it about.

4:13-22 Peter's boldness and power took the religious leaders by surprise, and they were uncertain about how they should proceed. They commanded Peter to stop preaching and healing, but Peter refused to obey, affirming his commitment to an even higher Power. The leaders could not stop the spread of Jesus' message in Jerusalem and beyond. God wants people the world over to find forgive-

nary men who had had no special training. They also recognized them as men who had been with Jesus. [14]But since the man who had been healed was standing right there among them, the council had nothing to say. [15]So they sent Peter and John out of the council chamber* and conferred among themselves.

[16]"What should we do with these men?" they asked each other. "We can't deny they have done a miraculous sign, and everybody in Jerusalem knows about it. [17]But perhaps we can stop them from spreading their propaganda. We'll warn them not to speak to anyone in Jesus' name again." [18]So they called the apostles back in and told them never again to speak or teach about Jesus.

[19]But Peter and John replied, "Do you think God wants us to obey you rather than him? [20]We cannot stop telling about the wonderful things we have seen and heard."

[21]The council then threatened them further, but they finally let them go because they didn't know how to punish them without starting a riot. For everyone was praising God [22]for this miraculous sign—the healing of a man who had been lame for more than forty years.

The Believers Pray for Courage

[23]As soon as they were freed, Peter and John found the other believers and told them what the leading priests and elders had said. [24]Then all the believers were united as they lifted their voices in prayer: "O Sovereign Lord, Creator of heaven and earth, the sea, and everything in them—[25]you spoke long ago by the Holy Spirit through our ancestor King David, your servant, saying,

'Why did the nations rage?
Why did the people waste their time
with futile plans?

[26]The kings of the earth prepared
for battle;
the rulers gathered together
against the Lord
and against his Messiah.'*

[27]"That is what has happened here in this city! For Herod Antipas, Pontius Pilate the governor, the Gentiles, and the people of Israel were all united against Jesus, your holy servant, whom you anointed. [28]In fact, everything they did occurred according to your eternal will and plan. [29]And now, O Lord, hear their threats, and give your servants great boldness in their preaching. [30]Send your healing power; may miraculous signs and wonders be done through the name of your holy servant Jesus."

[31]After this prayer, the building where they were meeting shook, and they were all filled with the Holy Spirit. And they preached God's message with boldness.

The Believers Share Their Possessions

[32]All the believers were of one heart and mind, and they felt that what they owned was not their own; they shared everything they had. [33]And the apostles gave powerful witness to the resurrection of the Lord Jesus, and God's great favor was upon them all. [34]There was no poverty among them, because people who owned land or houses sold them [35]and brought the money to the apostles to give to others in need.

[36]For instance, there was Joseph, the one the apostles nicknamed Barnabas (which means "Son of Encouragement"). He was from the tribe of Levi and came from the island of Cyprus. [37]He sold a field he owned and brought the money to the apostles for those in need.

4:15 Greek *the Sanhedrin.* **4:25-26** Ps 2:1-2.

---

ness and freedom, despite what government authorities might say. Once we have experienced the reality of God's power and guidance in our life, we won't want to return to our old way of life.
4:23-31 Peter and John were released by the religious leaders and returned to their support group. They dealt with their difficulties by discussing the issues, worshiping God, and praying. This resulted in a new manifestation of God's presence among them and a new boldness empowered by the Holy Spirit. We can learn from these early believers. We can find help in support groups, where our problems can safely be discussed and prayed over. As we depend on God, he gives us the power to persevere despite difficulties. When we bring our problems to God, he can turn seemingly devastating circumstances into occasions for joy.
4:32-37 The early Christians were growing spiritually by caring for each other, by meeting each other's basic needs, and by carrying the Good News to people who hadn't yet heard. Barnabas was a good example. His name was Joseph, but the apostles nicknamed him Barnabas, meaning "Son of Encouragement." He sold a field he owned to help those in need. As a part of the recovery process, we may need to give ourself a new name that reflects what we are becoming in Christ. Who knows? We might also become sons or daughters of encouragement.

CHAPTER 5
Ananias and Sapphira

There was also a man named Ananias who, with his wife, Sapphira, sold some property. [2]He brought part of the money to the apostles, but he claimed it was the full amount. His wife had agreed to this deception.

[3]Then Peter said, "Ananias, why has Satan filled your heart? You lied to the Holy Spirit, and you kept some of the money for yourself. [4]The property was yours to sell or not sell, as you wished. And after selling it, the money was yours to give away. How could you do a thing like this? You weren't lying to us but to God."

[5]As soon as Ananias heard these words, he fell to the floor and died. Everyone who heard about it was terrified. [6]Then some young men wrapped him in a sheet and took him out and buried him.

[7]About three hours later his wife came in, not knowing what had happened. [8]Peter asked her, "Was this the price you and your husband received for your land?"

"Yes," she replied, "that was the price."

[9]And Peter said, "How could the two of you even think of doing a thing like this—conspiring together to test the Spirit of the Lord? Just outside that door are the young men who buried your husband, and they will carry you out, too."

[10]Instantly, she fell to the floor and died. When the young men came in and saw that she was dead, they carried her out and buried her beside her husband. [11]Great fear gripped the entire church and all others who heard what had happened.

The Apostles Heal Many

[12]Meanwhile, the apostles were performing many miraculous signs and wonders among the people. And the believers were meeting regularly at the Temple in the area known as Solomon's Colonnade. [13]No one else dared to join them, though everyone had high regard for them. [14]And more and more people believed and were brought to the Lord—crowds of both men and women. [15]As a result of the apostles' work, sick people were brought out into the streets on beds and mats so that Peter's shadow might fall across some of them as he went by. [16]Crowds came in from the villages around Jerusalem, bringing their sick and those possessed by evil spirits, and they were all healed.

The Apostles Meet Opposition

[17]The high priest and his friends, who were Sadducees, reacted with violent jealousy. [18]They arrested the apostles and put them in the jail. [19]But an angel of the Lord came at night, opened the gates of the jail, and brought them out. Then he told them, [20]"Go to the Temple and give the people this message of life!" [21]So the apostles entered the Temple about daybreak and immediately began teaching.

5:1-11 God's judgment of Ananias and Sapphira is a unique event in the history of the church but universal in its application. God does not normally punish denial and misrepresentation with immediate death. We all are guilty of denial and trying to impress others with lies and half-truths. Although the consequences may not be as serious today, lying is sinful and destructive to the recovery process. Our regular moral inventory needs to focus on our destructive tendency toward deceit and denial. Then we can take the necessary steps to root it out.

5:9-11 Peter confronted Ananias and Sapphira about their dishonesty, holding them accountable for their sins. Honest confrontation is essential for recovery today, just as it was necessary for maintaining the spiritual health of this early Christian community. Confrontation and discipline are vital in any community, whether a Christian church, a recovery group, or a family. As we are confronted with the truth about ourself, we need to humbly and honestly admit our sins and defects of character. As we do this, God will help us overcome them.

5:12-16 We may wonder how God could possibly do anything for us. We may have never seen, heard, or felt him. In the activities of the early church, we are shown the primary means that God uses to work in people's lives. He touches hurting people through the help of other hurting people. God channels his power through people like us so others can experience his power for healing and recovery. God has probably touched our life through the help of individuals or groups. As we carry the Good News to others through our words and deeds, God can use us to bring hope and healing to others.

5:17-42 This power struggle between the religious establishment and the apostles is instructive for recovery. We may have already faced opposition. People may have tried to stand in our way as we grew in our relationship with God or participated in recovery activities. They may have sought to impose their will on us, hindering us from following God's will. Recovery must be centered around God and his will for us; then nothing can stop our progress. The key is to obey God rather than other people.

When the high priest and his officials arrived, they convened the high council,* along with all the elders of Israel. Then they sent for the apostles to be brought for trial. ²²But when the Temple guards went to the jail, the men were gone. So they returned to the council and reported, ²³"The jail was locked, with the guards standing outside, but when we opened the gates, no one was there!"

²⁴When the captain of the Temple guard and the leading priests heard this, they were perplexed, wondering where it would all end. ²⁵Then someone arrived with the news that the men they had jailed were out in the Temple, teaching the people.

²⁶The captain went with his Temple guards and arrested them, but without violence, for they were afraid the people would kill them if they treated the apostles roughly. ²⁷Then they brought the apostles in before the council. ²⁸"Didn't we tell you never again to teach in this man's name?" the high priest demanded. "Instead, you have filled all Jerusalem with your teaching about Jesus, and you intend to blame us for his death!"

²⁹But Peter and the apostles replied, "We must obey God rather than human authority. ³⁰The God of our ancestors raised Jesus from the dead after you killed him by crucifying him. ³¹Then God put him in the place of honor at his right hand as Prince and Savior. He did this to give the people of Israel an opportunity to turn from their sins and turn to God so their sins would be forgiven. ³²We are witnesses of these things and so is the Holy Spirit, who is given by God to those who obey him."

³³At this, the high council was furious and decided to kill them. ³⁴But one member had a different perspective. He was a Pharisee named Gamaliel, who was an expert on religious law and was very popular with the people. He stood up and ordered that the apostles be sent outside the council chamber for a while. ³⁵Then he addressed his colleagues as follows: "Men of Israel, take care what you are planning to do to these men! ³⁶Some time ago there was that fellow Theudas, who pretended to be someone great. About four hundred others joined him, but he was killed, and his followers went their various ways. The whole movement came to nothing. ³⁷After him, at the time of the census, there was Judas of Galilee. He got some people to follow him, but he was killed, too, and all his followers were scattered.

³⁸"So my advice is, leave these men alone. If they are teaching and doing these things merely on their own, it will soon be overthrown. ³⁹But if it is of God, you will not be able to stop them. You may even find yourselves fighting against God."

⁴⁰The council accepted his advice. They called in the apostles and had them flogged. Then they ordered them never again to speak in the name of Jesus, and they let them go. ⁴¹The apostles left the high council rejoicing that God had counted them worthy to suffer dishonor for the name of Jesus. ⁴²And every day, in the Temple and in their homes,* they continued to teach and preach this message: "The Messiah you are looking for is Jesus."

CHAPTER 6
Seven Men Chosen to Serve

But as the believers* rapidly multiplied, there were rumblings of discontent. Those who spoke Greek complained against those who spoke Hebrew, saying that their widows were being discriminated against in the daily distribution of food. ²So the Twelve called a meeting of all the believers.

"We apostles should spend our time preaching and teaching the word of God, not administering a food program," they said. ³"Now look around among yourselves, brothers, and select seven men who are well respected and are full of the Holy Spirit and wisdom. We will put them in charge of this business. ⁴Then we can spend our time in prayer and preaching and teaching the word."

5:21 Greek *Sanhedrin;* also in 5:27, 41. 5:42 Greek *from house to house.* 6:1 Greek *disciples;* also in 6:2, 7.

6:2-6 Conflict resolution is vital to recovery today, just as it was to the early church. The early believers acknowledged their limitations, set their priorities, and laid out specific tasks that would fulfill their needs. In this case they sought God's wisdom and selected seven Spirit-filled, well-respected leaders to administer the food program. No problem in recovery is insurmountable. With God's wisdom, together with a network of godly support, we can work through old dysfunctional patterns and find healthy, balanced ways to rebuild our life and meet the needs of the people around us.

5This idea pleased the whole group, and they chose the following: Stephen (a man full of faith and the Holy Spirit), Philip, Procorus, Nicanor, Timon, Parmenas, and Nicolas of Antioch (a Gentile convert to the Jewish faith, who had now become a Christian). 6These seven were presented to the apostles, who prayed for them as they laid their hands on them.

7God's message was preached in everwidening circles. The number of believers greatly increased in Jerusalem, and many of the Jewish priests were converted, too.

Stephen Is Arrested

8Stephen, a man full of God's grace and power, performed amazing miracles and signs among the people. 9But one day some men from the Synagogue of Freed Slaves, as it was called, started to debate with him. They were Jews from Cyrene, Alexandria, Cilicia, and the province of Asia. 10None of them was able to stand against the wisdom and Spirit by which Stephen spoke.

11So they persuaded some men to lie about Stephen, saying, "We heard him blaspheme Moses, and even God." 12Naturally, this roused the crowds, the elders, and the teachers of religious law. So they arrested Stephen and brought him before the high council.* 13The lying witnesses said, "This man is always speaking against the Temple and against the law of Moses. 14We have heard him say that this Jesus of Nazareth will destroy the Temple and change the customs Moses handed down to us." 15At this point everyone in the council stared at Stephen because his face became as bright as an angel's.

CHAPTER 7
Stephen Addresses the Council

Then the high priest asked Stephen, "Are these accusations true?"

2This was Stephen's reply: "Brothers and honorable fathers, listen to me. Our glorious God appeared to our ancestor Abraham in Mesopotamia before he moved to Haran.* 3God told him, 'Leave your native land and your relatives, and come to the land that I will show you.'* 4So Abraham left the land of the Chaldeans and lived in Haran until his father died. Then God brought him here to the land where you now live. 5But God gave him no inheritance here, not even one square foot of land. God did promise, however, that eventually the whole country would belong to Abraham and his descendants—though he had no children yet. 6But God also told him that his descendants would live in a foreign country where they would be mistreated as slaves for four hundred years. 7But I will punish the nation that enslaves them,' God told him, 'and in the end they will come out and worship me in this place.'* 8God also gave Abraham the covenant of circumcision at that time. And so Isaac, Abraham's son, was circumcised when he was eight days old. Isaac became the father of Jacob, and Jacob was the father of the twelve patriarchs of the Jewish nation.

9"These sons of Jacob were very jealous of their brother Joseph, and they sold him to be a slave in Egypt. But God was with him 10and delivered him from his anguish. And God gave him favor before Pharaoh, king of Egypt. God also gave Joseph unusual wisdom, so that Pharaoh appointed him governor over all of Egypt and put him in charge of all the affairs of the palace.

11"But a famine came upon Egypt and Canaan. There was great misery for our ancestors, as they ran out of food. 12Jacob heard that there was still grain in Egypt, so he sent his sons* to buy some. 13The second time they went, Joseph revealed his identity to his brothers, and they were introduced to Pharaoh. 14Then Joseph sent for his father,

---

6:12 Greek *Sanhedrin;* also in 6:15. 7:2 *Mesopotamia* was the region now called Iraq. *Haran* was a city in what is now called Syria. 7:3 Gen 12:1. 7:5-7 Gen 12:7; 15:13-14; Exod 3:12. 7:12 Greek *our fathers;* also in 7:15.

6:8-15 Stephen was "a man full of God's grace and power" and performed amazing miracles among the people. The Jewish establishment falsely accused Stephen of attacking the law of Moses and the Jerusalem Temple. Stephen confronted them with their false religion and denial and called them to face the truth. We may need to do the same for our fellow strugglers. This requires God's wisdom and power. We can receive God's wisdom and power by entrusting our life to God and faithfully obeying his Word.

7:1-53 Stephen did not get defensive about or take personally the accusations of his fellow Jews. Instead, he took control of the situation and boldly defended his faith. Like Stephen, we do not need to be ashamed about our faith or recovery. When we are experiencing God's healing power in our life, we can boldly carry that message to others without apology, fear, or shame. Others may try to harm us, as they did Stephen, but that does not negate the reality of God's power in our life.

STEPHEN

Stephen was a man filled with the Holy Spirit, exhibiting God's power and love in everything he did. He was known for performing amazing miracles and helping people in need. He was called to be one of the first deacons, and it was his job to make sure that no one (especially widows) was overlooked in the distribution of food. Stephen also proclaimed the good news of Jesus with boldness and power. Even as he was stoned to death by the religious leaders, God's hand was clearly upon him.

Stephen demonstrated God's message publicly through the miracles he did in Jesus' name. Those who tried to disprove the truth about Jesus Christ were not able to stand against his wisdom and spirit. So they lied about him in order to have him arrested and brought before the council of Jewish leaders.

Stephen responded to the inquisition by telling the history of the Jewish people, beginning with Abraham, progressing through Moses, and ending with the coming of Jesus the Messiah. He concluded with a scathing attack on the religious leaders who, like many of their ancestors, resisted the essential message of God's revealed Word and the leading of the Holy Spirit.

Stephen's words angered the Jewish leaders so much that they rushed him out of the city and stoned him to death. As he stumbled under the rain of stones, Stephen called upon God to receive his spirit and to forgive the people who were killing him. Unlike Stephen, many of us hold on to grudges and past hurts and allow them to control our life. This makes complete healing and recovery impossible. If we entrust our life to God, we can live and die with joy, knowing that God will take care of the details we cannot control or change.

STRENGTHS AND ACCOMPLISHMENTS:
- Stephen really knew God, both personally and through the Scriptures.
- Because he trusted God, he was able to rise above his circumstances.
- He had a passion for God and compassion for others.
- He used his many gifts to serve the poor and helpless.

LESSONS FROM HIS LIFE:
- Serving others becomes natural when we have given our life to God.
- If we can trust God in daily life, we will be able to face death with joy.
- We can face even the most terrible circumstances if God is with us.

KEY VERSE:
"Stephen, a man full of God's grace and power, performed amazing miracles and signs among the people" (Acts 6:8).

Stephen's story is told in Acts 6–8, 11, and 22.

Jacob, and all his relatives to come to Egypt, seventy-five persons in all. [15]So Jacob went to Egypt. He died there, as did all his sons. [16]All of them were taken to Shechem and buried in the tomb Abraham had bought from the sons of Hamor in Shechem.

[17]"As the time drew near when God would fulfill his promise to Abraham, the number of our people in Egypt greatly increased. [18]But then a new king came to the throne of Egypt who knew nothing about Joseph. [19]This king plotted against our people and forced parents to abandon their newborn babies so they would die.

[20]"At that time Moses was born—a beautiful child in God's eyes. His parents cared for him at home for three months. [21]When at last they had to abandon him, Pharaoh's daughter found him and raised him as her own son. [22]Moses was taught all the wisdom of the Egyptians, and he became mighty in both speech and action.

[23]"One day when he was forty years old, he decided to visit his relatives, the people of Israel. [24]During this visit, he saw an Egyptian mistreating a man of Israel. So Moses came to his defense and avenged him, killing the Egyptian. [25]Moses assumed his brothers would realize that God had sent him to rescue them, but they didn't.

[26]"The next day he visited them again and saw two men of Israel fighting. He tried to be a peacemaker. 'Men,' he said, 'you are brothers. Why are you hurting each other?'

²⁷"But the man in the wrong pushed Moses aside and told him to mind his own business. 'Who made you a ruler and judge over us?' he asked. ²⁸'Are you going to kill me as you killed that Egyptian yesterday?' ²⁹When Moses heard that, he fled the country and lived as a foreigner in the land of Midian, where his two sons were born.

³⁰"Forty years later, in the desert near Mount Sinai, an angel appeared to Moses in the flame of a burning bush. ³¹Moses saw it and wondered what it was. As he went to see, the voice of the Lord called out to him, ³²'I am the God of your ancestors—the God of Abraham, Isaac, and Jacob.' Moses shook with terror and dared not look.

³³"And the Lord said to him, 'Take off your sandals, for you are standing on holy ground. ³⁴You can be sure that I have seen the misery of my people in Egypt. I have heard their cries. So I have come to rescue them. Now go, for I will send you to Egypt.'* ³⁵And so God sent back the same man his people had previously rejected by demanding, 'Who made you a ruler and judge over us?' Through the angel who appeared to him in the burning bush, Moses was sent to be their ruler and savior. ³⁶And by means of many miraculous signs and wonders, he led them out of Egypt, through the Red Sea, and back and forth through the wilderness for forty years.

³⁷"Moses himself told the people of Israel, 'God will raise up a Prophet like me from among your own people.'* ³⁸Moses was with the assembly of God's people in the wilderness. He was the mediator between the people of Israel and the angel who gave him life-giving words on Mount Sinai to pass on to us.

³⁹"But our ancestors rejected Moses and wanted to return to Egypt. ⁴⁰They told Aaron, 'Make us some gods who can lead us, for we don't know what has become of this Moses, who brought us out of Egypt.' ⁴¹So they made an idol shaped like a calf, and they sacrificed to it and rejoiced in this thing they had made. ⁴²Then God turned away from them and gave them up to serve the sun, moon, and stars as their gods! In the book of the prophets it is written,

'Was it to me you were bringing
    sacrifices
    during those forty years in the
      wilderness, Israel?
⁴³No, your real interest was in your pagan
    gods—
    the shrine of Molech,
    the star god Rephan,
    and the images you made to worship
      them.
So I will send you into captivity
    far away in Babylon.'*

⁴⁴"Our ancestors carried the Tabernacle* with them through the wilderness. It was constructed in exact accordance with the plan shown to Moses by God. ⁴⁵Years later, when Joshua led the battles against the Gentile nations that God drove out of this land, the Tabernacle was taken with them into their new territory. And it was used there until the time of King David.

⁴⁶"David found favor with God and asked for the privilege of building a permanent Temple for the God of Jacob.* ⁴⁷But it was Solomon who actually built it. ⁴⁸However, the Most High doesn't live in temples made by human hands. As the prophet says,

⁴⁹'Heaven is my throne,
    and the earth is my footstool.
Could you ever build me a temple as
      good as that?'
    asks the Lord.
'Could you build a dwelling place
    for me?
⁵⁰   Didn't I make everything in heaven
      and earth?'*

⁵¹"You stubborn people! You are heathen at heart and deaf to the truth. Must you forever resist the Holy Spirit? But your ancestors

---

7:31-34 Exod 3:5-10. **7:37** Deut 18:15. **7:42-43** Amos 5:25-27. **7:44** Greek *the tent of witness.* **7:46** Some manuscripts read *the house of Jacob.* **7:49-50** Isa 66:1-2.

7:44-50 Stephen referred to the Temple to make a point that is important to us in recovery. Israel had limited God to the Temple and the institutions that surrounded the worship there. They had taken the eternal God—the Master of the universe—and had figuratively bound him inside the Temple walls. Sometimes we define God in ways we can understand and control. We shape and limit him with our theological systems, our church dogmas, our political presuppositions, and our personal experiences. God is much bigger than any concept we could ever have of him. His omnipresence and abundant grace fill the entire universe! As we more accurately understand God and his power, we will discover that he is far bigger than our problems.

did, and so do you! [52]Name one prophet your ancestors didn't persecute! They even killed the ones who predicted the coming of the Righteous One—the Messiah whom you betrayed and murdered. [53]You deliberately disobeyed God's law, though you received it from the hands of angels.*"

[54]The Jewish leaders were infuriated by Stephen's accusation, and they shook their fists in rage.* [55]But Stephen, full of the Holy Spirit, gazed steadily upward into heaven and saw the glory of God, and he saw Jesus standing in the place of honor at God's right hand. [56]And he told them, "Look, I see the heavens opened and the Son of Man standing in the place of honor at God's right hand!"

[57]Then they put their hands over their ears, and drowning out his voice with their shouts, they rushed at him. [58]They dragged him out of the city and began to stone him. The official witnesses took off their coats and laid them at the feet of a young man named Saul.*

[59]And as they stoned him, Stephen prayed, "Lord Jesus, receive my spirit." [60]And he fell to his knees, shouting, "Lord, don't charge them with this sin!" And with that, he died.

CHAPTER 8
Saul was one of the official witnesses at the killing of Stephen.

Persecution Scatters the Believers

A great wave of persecution began that day, sweeping over the church in Jerusalem, and all the believers except the apostles fled into Judea and Samaria. [2](Some godly men came and buried Stephen with loud weeping.) [3]Saul was going everywhere to devastate the church. He went from house to house, dragging out both men and women to throw them into jail.

Philip Preaches in Samaria

[4]But the believers who had fled Jerusalem went everywhere preaching the Good News about Jesus. [5]Philip, for example, went to the city of Samaria and told the people there about the Messiah. [6]Crowds listened intently to what he had to say because of the miracles he did. [7]Many evil spirits were cast out, screaming as they left their victims. And many who had been paralyzed or lame were healed. [8]So there was great joy in that city.

[9]A man named Simon had been a sorcerer there for many years, claiming to be someone great. [10]The Samaritan people, from the least to the greatest, often spoke of him as "the Great One—the Power of God." [11]He was very influential because of the magic he performed. [12]But now the people believed Philip's message of Good News concerning the Kingdom of God and the name of Jesus

7:53 Greek *received the Law as it was ordained by angels.* 7:54 Greek *they were grinding their teeth against him.*
7:58 *Saul* is later called Paul; see 13:9.

7:51-60 Stephen confronted the religious leaders about their stubborn denial. They were resisting the Holy Spirit and didn't like being rebuked. We would think that as mature adults, these leaders would have pondered Stephen's words and made some kind of honest self-assessment. But they were infuriated and set out to kill Stephen. Despite their rage, Stephen did not desire revenge or harbor a grudge. He kept his focus on Christ, forgiving the people even as they killed him. Stephen's peace and self-control are gifts of the Holy Spirit that are available to us all through faith.
8:1-3 The people who seem the most unlikely candidates for recovery are often at the top of God's list. Saul (later called Paul; see 13:9) was one such candidate. Saul witnessed Stephen's death and was one of the dreaded enemies of the fledgling Christian movement. He went from house to house, dragging believers to jail. Yet Saul's story is really a story of God's amazing grace. Saul the persecutor became Paul the apostle, one of the greatest leaders in Christian history. Many of us began the recovery process as unlikely candidates, but there is no limit to what we can become with God's powerful and gracious help.
8:1-3 God used the terrible circumstances of persecution for his glory. The believers were driven from their homes in Jerusalem, but they shared the Good News wherever they went. God often uses painful circumstances for his glory. Many of us would not be in recovery were it not for the suffering caused by our addiction. Our pain has awakened us to the opportunity to build a new life of faith. We can rebuild our broken relationships and make amends with the people we have hurt. God has used our painful circumstances to give each of us a second chance.
8:4-17 Philip had preached boldly to the Samaritans, whom the Jews considered no better than Gentiles because of the Samaritans' mixed ancestry. The Samaritans responded to the gospel message in great numbers, and many were baptized. Hearing about the successful ministry there, Peter and John joined Philip and prayed for the Samaritan believers to receive the Holy Spirit. The Good News of salvation in Christ was not just for the Jews—it was for all people, including the Samaritans. The Good News of Jesus Christ is for us, too, no matter who we are or what we have done.

Christ. As a result, many men and women were baptized. ¹³Then Simon himself believed and was baptized. He began following Philip wherever he went, and he was amazed by the great miracles and signs Philip performed.

¹⁴When the apostles back in Jerusalem heard that the people of Samaria had accepted God's message, they sent Peter and John there. ¹⁵As soon as they arrived, they prayed for these new Christians to receive the Holy Spirit. ¹⁶The Holy Spirit had not yet come upon any of them, for they had only been baptized in the name of the Lord Jesus. ¹⁷Then Peter and John laid their hands upon these believers, and they received the Holy Spirit.

¹⁸When Simon saw that the Holy Spirit was given when the apostles placed their hands upon people's heads, he offered money to buy this power. ¹⁹"Let me have this power, too," he exclaimed, "so that when I lay my hands on people, they will receive the Holy Spirit!"

²⁰But Peter replied, "May your money perish with you for thinking God's gift can be bought! ²¹You can have no part in this, for your heart is not right before God. ²²Turn from your wickedness and pray to the Lord. Perhaps he will forgive your evil thoughts, ²³for I can see that you are full of bitterness and held captive by sin."

²⁴"Pray to the Lord for me," Simon exclaimed, "that these terrible things won't happen to me!"

²⁵After testifying and preaching the word of the Lord in Samaria, Peter and John returned to Jerusalem. And they stopped in many Samaritan villages along the way to preach the Good News to them, too.

Philip and the Ethiopian Eunuch

²⁶As for Philip, an angel of the Lord said to him, "Go south* down the desert road that runs from Jerusalem to Gaza." ²⁷So he did, and he met the treasurer of Ethiopia, a eunuch of great authority under the queen of Ethiopia.* The eunuch had gone to Jerusalem to worship, ²⁸and he was now returning. Seated in his carriage, he was reading aloud from the book of the prophet Isaiah.

²⁹The Holy Spirit said to Philip, "Go over and walk along beside the carriage."

³⁰Philip ran over and heard the man reading from the prophet Isaiah; so he asked, "Do you understand what you are reading?"

³¹The man replied, "How can I, when there is no one to instruct me?" And he begged Philip to come up into the carriage and sit with him. ³²The passage of Scripture he had been reading was this:

"He was led as a sheep to the slaughter.
    And as a lamb is silent before the
        shearers,
    he did not open his mouth.
³³ He was humiliated and received no
        justice.
    Who can speak of his descendants?
    For his life was taken from the earth."*

³⁴The eunuch asked Philip, "Was Isaiah talking about himself or someone else?" ³⁵So Philip began with this same Scripture and then used many others to tell him the Good News about Jesus.

³⁶As they rode along, they came to some water, and the eunuch said, "Look! There's some water! Why can't I be baptized?"* ³⁸He ordered the carriage to stop, and they went down into the water, and Philip baptized him.

8:26 Or *Go at noon.* **8:27** Greek *under the Candace, the queen of Ethiopia.* **8:32-33** Isa 53:7-8. **8:36** Some manuscripts add verse 37, *"You can," Philip answered, "if you believe with all your heart." And the eunuch replied, "I believe that Jesus Christ is the Son of God."*

8:18-25 When Simon the sorcerer saw the ministry of Peter and John, he offered to buy the secret of their power. This showed Peter that Simon did not understand his relationship with God; he only sought God for what he might get out of the relationship. Perhaps he wanted to gain back the prestige he had lost when Philip came to town (see 8:9-13). Peter warned Simon that he needed to examine himself and repent. This problem of impure motives also applies to recovery. If we are in recovery just to look good, we are in it for the wrong reason. When we look to God for help, we are making his will our own. We succeed in recovery only as we submit completely to God's will for our life.

9:10-16 During Saul's intense self-examination, God sent Ananias to befriend him, pray for him, and restore his sight. Ananias was afraid at first because he wasn't sure that Saul had really changed. When he met with Saul, however, Ananias discovered that no one is beyond God's help. By coming to help Saul, Ananias discovered a truth that we learn in recovery. When we reach out to others and share the Good News, God not only uses us to help others, he also strengthens our own faith.

39When they came up out of the water, the Spirit of the Lord caught Philip away. The eunuch never saw him again but went on his way rejoicing. 40Meanwhile, Philip found himself farther north at the city of Azotus! He preached the Good News there and in every city along the way until he came to Caesarea.

CHAPTER 9
Saul's Conversion

Meanwhile, Saul was uttering threats with every breath. He was eager to destroy the Lord's followers,* so he went to the high priest. 2He requested letters addressed to the synagogues in Damascus, asking their cooperation in the arrest of any followers of the Way he found there. He wanted to bring them—both men and women—back to Jerusalem in chains.

3As he was nearing Damascus on this mission, a brilliant light from heaven suddenly beamed down upon him! 4He fell to the ground and heard a voice saying to him, "Saul! Saul! Why are you persecuting me?"

5"Who are you, sir?" Saul asked.

And the voice replied, "I am Jesus, the one you are persecuting! 6Now get up and go into the city, and you will be told what you are to do."

7The men with Saul stood speechless with surprise, for they heard the sound of someone's voice, but they saw no one! 8As Saul picked himself up off the ground, he found that he was blind. 9So his companions led him by the hand to Damascus. He remained there blind for three days. And all that time he went without food and water.

10Now there was a believer* in Damascus named Ananias. The Lord spoke to him in a vision, calling, "Ananias!"

"Yes, Lord!" he replied.

11The Lord said, "Go over to Straight Street, to the house of Judas. When you arrive, ask for Saul of Tarsus. He is praying to me right now. 12I have shown him a vision of a man named Ananias coming in and laying his hands on him so that he can see again."

13"But Lord," exclaimed Ananias, "I've heard about the terrible things this man has done to the believers in Jerusalem! 14And we hear that he is authorized by the leading priests to arrest every believer in Damascus."

9:1 Greek *disciples*. **9:10** Greek *disciple;* also in 9:36.

STEP 12

Listening First

BIBLE READING: Acts 8:26-40

Having had a spiritual awakening as the result of these steps, we tried to carry this message to others and to practice these principles in all our affairs.

We may be so excited about what God has done for us that we want to rush right out and tell everyone our story. Or we may be very shy and hesitate to tell people, especially if we think they are better than we are. We all have a valuable story to tell; we just need to discover the best way to communicate it.

God led the evangelist Philip to meet an influential traveler who "had gone to Jerusalem to worship, and he was now returning . . . reading aloud from the book of the prophet Isaiah. The Holy Spirit said to Philip, 'Go over and walk along beside the carriage.' Philip ran over and heard the man reading from the prophet Isaiah; so he asked, 'Do you understand what you are reading?' The man replied, 'How can I, when there is no one to instruct me?' . . . So Philip began with this same Scripture and then used many others to tell him the Good News about Jesus" (Acts 8:27-31, 35).

The way Philip communicated is a model for us. He was sensitive to allow God to lead him to someone who was ready. He wasn't intimidated by the man's status and did not hesitate to tell him the Good News about Jesus. Philip began by listening carefully. He tuned into the man's need and interests and then explained their relationship to the message he was prepared to share. Whether we are zealous or shy, following this model can help us communicate our message in a way that people can understand and receive it. *Turn to page 357, 1 Timothy 4.*

¹⁵But the Lord said, "Go and do what I say. For Saul is my chosen instrument to take my message to the Gentiles and to kings, as well as to the people of Israel. ¹⁶And I will show him how much he must suffer for me."

¹⁷So Ananias went and found Saul. He laid his hands on him and said, "Brother Saul, the Lord Jesus, who appeared to you on the road, has sent me so that you may get your sight back and be filled with the Holy Spirit." ¹⁸Instantly something like scales fell from Saul's eyes, and he regained his sight. Then he got up and was baptized. ¹⁹Afterward he ate some food and was strengthened.

Saul in Damascus and Jerusalem

Saul stayed with the believers* in Damascus for a few days. ²⁰And immediately he began preaching about Jesus in the synagogues, saying, "He is indeed the Son of God!"

²¹All who heard him were amazed. "Isn't this the same man who persecuted Jesus' followers with such devastation in Jerusalem?" they asked. "And we understand that he came here to arrest them and take them in chains to the leading priests."

²²Saul's preaching became more and more powerful, and the Jews in Damascus couldn't refute his proofs that Jesus was indeed the Messiah. ²³After a while the Jewish leaders decided to kill him. ²⁴But Saul was told about their plot, and that they were watching for him day and night at the city gate so they could murder him. ²⁵So during the night, some of the other believers* let him down in a large basket through an opening in the city wall.

²⁶When Saul arrived in Jerusalem, he tried to meet with the believers, but they were all afraid of him. They thought he was only pretending to be a believer! ²⁷Then Barnabas brought him to the apostles and told them how Saul had seen the Lord on the way to Damascus. Barnabas also told them what the Lord had said to Saul and how he boldly preached in the name of Jesus in Damascus. ²⁸Then the apostles accepted Saul, and after that he was constantly with them in Jerusalem, preaching boldly in the name of the Lord. ²⁹He debated with some Greek-speaking Jews, but they plotted to murder him. ³⁰When the believers* heard about it, however, they took him to Caesarea and sent him on to his hometown of Tarsus.

³¹The church then had peace throughout Judea, Galilee, and Samaria, and it grew in strength and numbers. The believers were walking in the fear of the Lord and in the comfort of the Holy Spirit.

Peter Heals Aeneas and Raises Dorcas

³²Peter traveled from place to place to visit the believers, and in his travels he came to the Lord's people in the town of Lydda. ³³There he met a man named Aeneas, who had been paralyzed and bedridden for eight years. ³⁴Peter said to him, "Aeneas, Jesus Christ heals you! Get up and make your bed!" And he was healed instantly. ³⁵Then

9:19 Greek *disciples;* also in 9:26. **9:25** Greek *his disciples.* **9:30** Greek *brothers.*

9:20-25 Saul stayed with the Christians in Damascus for a few days and shared the Good News of salvation in Jesus Christ, demonstrating that his transformation was real. Both Jews and Christians were astounded at the changes in Saul. The Jews turned against him and plotted to kill him, but his new Christian friends helped him escape. We may also experience opposition from our old friends when we enter the recovery process. They may feel guilty about their own dependency, or they may be afraid they will lose a friend. Whatever the reason, our old friends may try to thwart our recovery. This is where our new support groups take on an essential role, protecting and guiding us through these difficult times.

9:26-30 Saul returned to Jerusalem and tried to meet with the Christian believers there. He immediately met skepticism. They couldn't believe that such a cruel enemy could have changed so quickly. In time Saul proved his sincerity and was accepted. When we enter recovery, we may meet skepticism for a while. Friends and family members may turn away. In time, however, if we continue to follow God's will for our life and seek to make amends, broken relationships will begin to heal. Our broken relationships, like our addiction, took time to develop. Recovery also will take time.

9:36-43 Peter received a call for help from grieving friends in Joppa. Dorcas, a believer who had served other widows and helped the poor, had just died, and those who loved her had sent for Peter. Implementing God's power over death (see Luke 8:41-42, 49-56), Peter prayed and brought this woman back to life. When God's power is at work within us, nothing is impossible. God's power can pull us out of our addiction, as if from death, and give us a new life in Jesus Christ.

the whole population of Lydda and Sharon turned to the Lord when they saw Aeneas walking around.

³⁶There was a believer in Joppa named Tabitha (which in Greek is Dorcas*). She was always doing kind things for others and helping the poor. ³⁷About this time she became ill and died. Her friends prepared her for burial and laid her in an upstairs room. ³⁸But they had heard that Peter was nearby at Lydda, so they sent two men to beg him, "Please come as soon as possible!"

³⁹So Peter returned with them; and as soon as he arrived, they took him to the upstairs room. The room was filled with widows who were weeping and showing him the coats and other garments Dorcas had made for them. ⁴⁰But Peter asked them all to leave the room; then he knelt and prayed. Turning to the body he said, "Get up, Tabitha." And she opened her eyes! When she saw Peter, she sat up! ⁴¹He gave her his hand and helped her up. Then he called in the widows and all the believers, and he showed them that she was alive.

⁴²The news raced through the whole town, and many believed in the Lord. ⁴³And Peter stayed a long time in Joppa, living with Simon, a leatherworker.

CHAPTER 10
Cornelius Calls for Peter

In Caesarea there lived a Roman army officer named Cornelius, who was a captain of the Italian Regiment. ²He was a devout man who feared the God of Israel, as did his entire household. He gave generously to charity and was a man who regularly prayed to God. ³One afternoon about three o'clock, he had a vision in which he saw an angel of God coming toward him. "Cornelius!" the angel said.

⁴Cornelius stared at him in terror. "What is it, sir?" he asked the angel.

And the angel replied, "Your prayers and gifts to the poor have not gone unnoticed by God! ⁵Now send some men down to Joppa to find a man named Simon Peter. ⁶He is staying with Simon, a leatherworker who lives near the shore. Ask him to come and visit you."

⁷As soon as the angel was gone, Cornelius called two of his household servants and a devout soldier, one of his personal attendants. ⁸He told them what had happened and sent them off to Joppa.

9:36 The names *Tabitha* in Aramaic and *Dorcas* in Greek both mean "gazelle."

STEP 1

A Time to Choose

BIBLE READING: Acts 9:1-9

We admitted that we were powerless over our dependencies—that our life had become unmanageable.

There are important moments in life that can change our destiny. These are often times when we are confronted with how powerless we are over the events of our life. These moments can either destroy us or forever set the course of our life in a much better direction.

Saul of Tarsus (later called Paul; see 13:9) had such a moment. After Jesus' ascension, Saul took it upon himself to rid the world of Christians. As he headed to Damascus on this mission, "a brilliant light from heaven suddenly beamed down upon him! He fell to the ground and heard a voice saying to him, 'Saul! Saul! Why are you persecuting me? . . . I am Jesus, the one you are persecuting! Now get up and go into the city, and you will be told what you are to do.' . . . As Saul picked himself up off the ground, he found that he was blind. So his companions led him by the hand to Damascus. He remained there blind for three days. And all that time he went without food and water" (Acts 9:3-6, 8-9).

Saul was suddenly confronted with the fact that his life wasn't as perfect as he had thought. Self-righteousness had been his trademark. By letting go of his illusions of power, however, he became one of the most powerful men ever—the apostle Paul. When we are confronted with the knowledge that our life isn't under our control, we have a choice. We can continue in denial and self-righteousness, or we can face the fact that we have been blind to some important issues. If we become willing to be led into recovery and into a whole new way of life, we will find true power. *Turn to page 285, 2 Corinthians 4.*

Peter Visits Cornelius

⁹The next day as Cornelius's messengers were nearing the city, Peter went up to the flat roof to pray. It was about noon, ¹⁰and he was hungry. But while lunch was being prepared, he fell into a trance. ¹¹He saw the sky open, and something like a large sheet was let down by its four corners. ¹²In the sheet were all sorts of animals, reptiles, and birds. ¹³Then a voice said to him, "Get up, Peter; kill and eat them."

¹⁴"Never, Lord," Peter declared. "I have never in all my life eaten anything forbidden by our Jewish laws.*"

¹⁵The voice spoke again, "If God says something is acceptable, don't say it isn't."* ¹⁶The same vision was repeated three times. Then the sheet was pulled up again to heaven.

¹⁷Peter was very perplexed. What could the vision mean? Just then the men sent by Cornelius found the house and stood outside at the gate. ¹⁸They asked if this was the place where Simon Peter was staying. ¹⁹Meanwhile, as Peter was puzzling over the vision, the Holy Spirit said to him, "Three men have come looking for you. ²⁰Go down and go with them without hesitation. All is well, for I have sent them."

²¹So Peter went down and said, "I'm the man you are looking for. Why have you come?"

²²They said, "We were sent by Cornelius, a Roman officer. He is a devout man who fears the God of Israel and is well respected by all the Jews. A holy angel instructed him to send for you so you can go to his house and give him a message." ²³So Peter invited the men to be his guests for the night. The next day he went with them, accompanied by some other believers* from Joppa.

²⁴They arrived in Caesarea the following day. Cornelius was waiting for him and had called together his relatives and close friends to meet Peter. ²⁵As Peter entered his home, Cornelius fell to the floor before him in worship. ²⁶But Peter pulled him up and said, "Stand up! I'm a human being like you!" ²⁷So Cornelius got up, and they talked together and went inside where the others were assembled.

²⁸Peter told them, "You know it is against the Jewish laws for me to come into a Gentile home like this. But God has shown me that I should never think of anyone as impure. ²⁹So I came as soon as I was sent for. Now tell me why you sent for me."

³⁰Cornelius replied, "Four days ago I was praying in my house at three o'clock in the afternoon. Suddenly, a man in dazzling clothes was standing in front of me. ³¹He told me, 'Cornelius, your prayers have been heard, and your gifts to the poor have been noticed by God! ³²Now send some men to Joppa and summon Simon Peter. He is staying in the home of Simon, a leatherworker who lives near the shore.' ³³So I sent for you at once, and it was good of you to come. Now here we are, waiting before God to hear the message the Lord has given you."

The Gentiles Hear the Good News

³⁴Then Peter replied, "I see very clearly that God doesn't show partiality. ³⁵In every nation he accepts those who fear him and do what is right. ³⁶I'm sure you have heard about the Good News for the people of Israel—that there is peace with God through Jesus Christ, who is Lord of all. ³⁷You know what happened

---

10:14 Greek *anything common and unclean.* 10:15 Greek *"What God calls clean you must not call unclean."* 10:23 Greek *brothers.*

10:9-20 God sent a special vision to Peter to reveal to him some of his hidden prejudices. Peter saw a large sheet covered with animals that according to Jewish law were unclean. At first Peter refused to have anything to do with them. But God sent the vision three times, challenging Peter's view of what was clean or unclean. God was preparing Peter to carry the Good News to the "unclean" Gentiles and to the home of Cornelius. Peter needed to realize that God accepts people of all backgrounds. This truth is important for us as well. As we share the Good News with others, we must not allow our prejudices to stand in the way of God's will. If God opens a door to share the gospel with someone, we need to step through it in faith. God will go with us as we spread his message of hope.

10:21-33 Peter didn't want to visit the home of this "unclean" Gentile. But when Peter and Cornelius met, they excitedly shared the unusual things they had just seen and heard. God had worked to remove the prejudices that would have kept them from speaking to each other. As a result, the Holy Spirit filled all the Gentiles who were in Cornelius's home. God drew people close who had once been separated by immense barriers. We may have relationships that seem broken beyond repair. Harsh emotions and the prejudices formed during our years in bondage have made communication almost impossible. As hopeless as such relationships seem, God can work to soften our defenses and enhance communication. He will do this as we entrust our life to him and seek to follow his will.

CORNELIUS & FAMILY

Recovery usually doesn't happen overnight; it is a process. When Cornelius and his family came into the spotlight in Acts 10, the process of their recovery had already begun. From a Roman religious and a military background, this army officer and his family "feared the God of Israel." They prayed to the God of Israel and gave generously to charity.

Cornelius's family had undoubtedly changed many of the habitual patterns and perspectives that had come from their Roman background. At this point God intervened and allowed them to proceed to a deeper understanding of God, which led to eternal life. God met them by sending the apostle Peter who came to them with the needed spiritual insight.

The scene in Cornelius's home is a model of family recovery. As Cornelius and his family came to believe in the redemptive work of Jesus, they also entered a phase of spiritual recovery augmented by the power of the Holy Spirit. This wasn't the end of their recovery process by any means. But they were well on their way because they had established healthy relationships with each other and with God.

When the family of Cornelius received the gift of the Holy Spirit, a new era of history was born. For the first time God showed that *all* people were acceptable to God through Jesus Christ—even "unclean" Gentiles. Because of his cultural prejudices, Peter had a hard time accepting this truth, but when Cornelius and his family received the Holy Spirit, Peter could no longer deny it. God desires to make the Holy Spirit's power a part of all our life. If we repent of our sins and accept God's forgiveness on the basis of the work of Jesus Christ, we can experience God's power in our life. With God's help, no problem or dependency is too great to overcome.

STRENGTHS AND ACCOMPLISHMENTS:
- Cornelius believed God to the degree that he understood him.
- He led his family to know God the best way he knew how.
- He was not satisfied with his level of maturity and sought to grow further.
- He and his family were open to change and embraced new life in Jesus Christ.

WEAKNESSES AND MISTAKES:
- Cornelius's understanding was limited, and he initially worshiped Peter.

LESSONS FROM THEIR LIVES:
- God reaches out to all those who want to know him better.
- The power of Jesus is for everyone, regardless of race or background.
- Recovery often requires guidance from others who have already been there.

KEY VERSE:
"Everyone who believes in [Jesus Christ] will have their sins forgiven through his name" (Acts 10:43).

The story of Cornelius and his family is told in Acts 10–11.

---

all through Judea, beginning in Galilee after John the Baptist began preaching. [38]And no doubt you know that God anointed Jesus of Nazareth with the Holy Spirit and with power. Then Jesus went around doing good and healing all who were oppressed by the Devil, for God was with him.

[39]"And we apostles are witnesses of all he did throughout Israel and in Jerusalem. They put him to death by crucifying him, [40]but God raised him to life three days later. Then God allowed him to appear, [41]not to the general public,* but to us whom God had chosen beforehand to be his witnesses. We were those who ate and drank with him after he rose from the dead. [42]And he ordered us to preach everywhere and to testify that Jesus is ordained of God to be the judge of all—the living and the dead. [43]He is the one all the prophets testified about, saying that everyone who believes in him will have their sins forgiven through his name."

The Gentiles Receive the Holy Spirit
[44]Even as Peter was saying these things, the Holy Spirit fell upon all who had heard the message. [45]The Jewish believers who came with Peter were amazed that the gift of the Holy Spirit had been poured out upon the Gentiles, too. [46]And there could be no doubt about it, for they heard them speaking in tongues and praising God.

10:41 Greek *the people.*

Then Peter asked, [47]"Can anyone object to their being baptized, now that they have received the Holy Spirit just as we did?" [48]So he gave orders for them to be baptized in the name of Jesus Christ. Afterward Cornelius asked him to stay with them for several days.

CHAPTER 11
Peter Explains His Actions

Soon the news reached the apostles and other believers* in Judea that the Gentiles had received the word of God. [2]But when Peter arrived back in Jerusalem, some of the Jewish believers* criticized him. [3]"You entered the home of Gentiles* and even ate with them!" they said.

[4]Then Peter told them exactly what had happened. [5]"One day in Joppa," he said, "while I was praying, I went into a trance and saw a vision. Something like a large sheet was let down by its four corners from the sky. And it came right down to me. [6]When I looked inside the sheet, I saw all sorts of small animals, wild animals, reptiles, and birds that we are not allowed to eat. [7]And I heard a voice say, 'Get up, Peter; kill and eat them.'

[8]"'Never, Lord,' I replied. 'I have never eaten anything forbidden by our Jewish laws.*'

[9]"But the voice from heaven came again, 'If God says something is acceptable, don't say it isn't.'*

[10]"This happened three times before the sheet and all it contained was pulled back up to heaven. [11]Just then three men who had been sent from Caesarea arrived at the house where I was staying. [12]The Holy Spirit told me to go with them and not to worry about their being Gentiles. These six brothers here accompanied me, and we soon arrived at the home of the man who had sent for us. [13]He told us how an angel had appeared to him in his home and had told him, 'Send messengers to Joppa to find Simon Peter. [14]He will tell you how you and all your household will be saved!'

[15]"Well, I began telling them the Good News, but just as I was getting started, the Holy Spirit fell on them, just as he fell on us at the beginning. [16]Then I thought of the Lord's words when he said, 'John baptized with* water, but you will be baptized with the Holy Spirit.' [17]And since God gave these Gentiles the same gift he gave us when we believed in the Lord Jesus Christ, who was I to argue?"

[18]When the others heard this, all their objections were answered and they began praising God. They said, "God has also given the Gentiles the privilege of turning from sin and receiving eternal life."

The Church in Antioch of Syria

[19]Meanwhile, the believers who had fled from Jerusalem during the persecution after Stephen's death traveled as far as Phoenicia, Cyprus, and Antioch of Syria. They preached the Good News, but only to Jews. [20]However, some of the believers who went to Antioch from Cyprus and Cyrene began preaching to Gentiles* about the Lord Jesus. [21]The power of the Lord was upon them, and large numbers of these Gentiles believed and turned to the Lord.

[22]When the church at Jerusalem heard what had happened, they sent Barnabas to

11:1 Greek *brothers.* **11:2** Greek *those of the circumcision.* **11:3** Greek *of uncircumcised men.* **11:8** Greek *anything common or unclean.* **11:9** Greek *'What God calls clean you must not call unclean.'* **11:16** Or *in;* also in 11:16b. **11:20** Greek *the Greeks;* other manuscripts read *the Hellenists.*

11:1-3 Even before Peter arrived home, the Jewish believers heard that Gentiles had believed in Christ. Because of their prejudice, they did not accept what they had heard, so they immediately confronted Peter. Earlier, when faced with opposition before Christ's death (Luke 22:54-62), Peter had denied his faith. But he did not fold this time; God had made some amazing changes in him since that painful failure. Peter defended the truth that had been revealed to him without concern for the cost to himself. Sometimes we may be surprised by the changes that God has worked in our life. Recognizing how far we have already come can encourage us to persevere in the process.

11:4-18 The Jewish believers were slow to accept Gentile believers into their fellowship. They criticized an event that actually was reason for rejoicing. They had succeeded in obeying Jesus' mandate to testify about him "in Jerusalem, throughout Judea, in Samaria, and to the ends of the earth" (1:8). Numerous Samaritans had already believed in Christ (8:1-25), and now Gentiles from the ends of the earth had joined the Christian community (see also 8:26-40). We may have friends who cannot recognize our moments of triumph in recovery. They may try to discourage us as we take significant steps to follow God's will. We must not allow them to dampen our faith or discourage our progress.

Antioch. 23When he arrived and saw this proof of God's favor, he was filled with joy, and he encouraged the believers to stay true to the Lord. 24Barnabas was a good man, full of the Holy Spirit and strong in faith. And large numbers of people were brought to the Lord.

25Then Barnabas went on to Tarsus to find Saul. 26When he found him, he brought him back to Antioch. Both of them stayed there with the church for a full year, teaching great numbers of people. (It was there at Antioch that the believers* were first called Christians.)

27During this time, some prophets traveled from Jerusalem to Antioch. 28One of them named Agabus stood up in one of the meetings to predict by the Spirit that a great famine was coming upon the entire Roman world. (This was fulfilled during the reign of Claudius.) 29So the believers in Antioch decided to send relief to the brothers and sisters* in Judea, everyone giving as much as they could. 30This they did, entrusting their gifts to Barnabas and Saul to take to the elders of the church in Jerusalem.

CHAPTER 12
James Is Killed and Peter Is Imprisoned
About that time King Herod Agrippa* began to persecute some believers in the church. 2He had the apostle James (John's brother) killed with a sword. 3When Herod saw how much this pleased the Jewish leaders, he arrested Peter during the Passover celebration* 4and imprisoned him, placing him under the guard of four squads of four soldiers each. Herod's intention was to bring Peter out for public trial after the Passover. 5But while Peter was in prison, the church prayed very earnestly for him.

Peter's Miraculous Escape from Prison
6The night before Peter was to be placed on trial, he was asleep, chained between two soldiers, with others standing guard at the prison gate. 7Suddenly, there was a bright light in the cell, and an angel of the Lord stood before Peter. The angel tapped him on the side to awaken him and said, "Quick! Get up!" And the chains fell off his wrists. 8Then the angel told him, "Get dressed and put on your sandals." And he did. "Now put on your coat and follow me," the angel ordered.

9So Peter left the cell, following the angel. But all the time he thought it was a vision. He didn't realize it was really happening. 10They passed the first and second guard posts and came to the iron gate to the street, and this opened to them all by itself. So they passed through and started walking down the street, and then the angel suddenly left him.

11Peter finally realized what had happened. "It's really true!" he said to himself. "The Lord has sent his angel and saved me from Herod and from what the Jews were hoping to do to me!"

12After a little thought, he went to the home of Mary, the mother of John Mark, where many were gathered for prayer. 13He knocked at the door in the gate, and a servant girl named Rhoda came to open it. 14When she recognized Peter's voice, she was so overjoyed that, instead of opening the door, she ran back inside and told everyone, "Peter is standing at the door!"

15"You're out of your mind," they said. When she insisted, they decided, "It must be his angel."

16Meanwhile, Peter continued knocking. When they finally went out and opened the door, they were amazed. 17He motioned for them to quiet down and told them what had happened and how the Lord had led him out of jail. "Tell James and the other brothers what happened," he said. And then he went to another place.

18At dawn, there was a great commotion among the soldiers about what had happened to Peter. 19Herod Agrippa ordered a thorough search for him. When he couldn't be found, Herod interrogated the guards and sentenced them to death. Afterward Herod left Judea to stay in Caesarea for a while.

11:26 Greek *disciples;* also in 11:29. **11:29** Greek *the brothers.* **12:1** Greek *Herod the king.* He was the nephew of Herod Antipas and a grandson of Herod the Great. **12:3** Greek *the days of unleavened bread.*

12:1-11 Peter's miraculous escape from prison shows that nothing can thwart God's plans. In response to prayer, God can always overcome the obstacles that stand in our way. He may even use supernatural means to deliver us. This does not mean we will never face difficulties in our walk with God. Even as the early church enjoyed phenomenal success, it still suffered severe trials. We will always face obstacles as we seek to live out God's plan for our life. But since God wants us to succeed in recovery, nothing can stand in the way of our success if we entrust our life to his care.

The Death of Herod Agrippa

[20]Now Herod was very angry with the people of Tyre and Sidon. So they sent a delegation to make peace with him because their cities were dependent upon Herod's country for their food. They made friends with Blastus, Herod's personal assistant, [21]and an appointment with Herod was granted. When the day arrived, Herod put on his royal robes, sat on his throne, and made a speech to them. [22]The people gave him a great ovation, shouting, "It is the voice of a god, not of a man!"

[23]Instantly, an angel of the Lord struck Herod with a sickness, because he accepted the people's worship instead of giving the glory to God. So he was consumed with worms and died.

[24]But God's Good News was spreading rapidly, and there were many new believers.

[25]When Barnabas and Saul had finished their mission in Jerusalem, they returned to Antioch, taking John Mark with them.

CHAPTER 13
Barnabas and Saul Are Sent Out

Among the prophets and teachers of the church at Antioch of Syria were Barnabas, Simeon (called "the black man"*), Lucius (from Cyrene), Manaen (the childhood companion of King Herod Antipas*), and Saul. [2]One day as these men were worshiping the Lord and fasting, the Holy Spirit said, "Dedicate Barnabas and Saul for the special work I have for them." [3]So after more fasting and prayer, the men laid their hands on them and sent them on their way.

Paul's First Missionary Journey

[4]Sent out by the Holy Spirit, Saul and Barnabas went down to the seaport of Seleucia and then sailed for the island of Cyprus. [5]There, in the town of Salamis, they went to the Jewish synagogues and preached the word of God. (John Mark went with them as their assistant.)

[6]Afterward they preached from town to town across the entire island until finally they reached Paphos, where they met a Jewish sorcerer, a false prophet named Bar-Jesus. [7]He had attached himself to the governor, Sergius Paulus, a man of considerable insight and understanding. The governor invited Barnabas and Saul to visit him, for he wanted to hear the word of God. [8]But Elymas, the sorcerer (as his name means in Greek), interfered and urged the governor to pay no attention to what Saul and Barnabas said. He was trying to turn the governor away from the Christian faith.

[9]Then Saul, also known as Paul, filled with the Holy Spirit, looked the sorcerer in the eye and said, [10]"You son of the Devil, full of every sort of trickery and villainy, enemy of all that is good, will you never stop perverting the true ways of the Lord? [11]And now the Lord has laid his hand of punishment upon you, and you will be stricken awhile with blindness." Instantly mist and darkness fell upon him, and he began wandering around begging for someone to take his hand and

---

13:1a Greek *who was called Niger.* **13:1b** Greek *Herod the tetrarch.*

12:20-24 Herod Agrippa pompously considered himself entirely self-sufficient; he saw no need for others, much less any higher Power. He enjoyed the worship he received from his people, playing the role of a god in their lives. What a contrast to the helpless way he died. Death is the great leveler of the whole human race. God will not be mocked; he will judge those who try to displace him on the throne of their life. When we give up our self-sufficiency and turn to God, our true king, we learn that his mercy and justice are sufficient for each day and for eternity.

13:1-3 However reluctant the church in Antioch may have been to lose Paul and Barnabas, they immediately submitted to the voice of the Holy Spirit. Although it meant a major change, they released and commissioned these key leaders to missionary service. Before sending them on their way, the people fasted, prayed, and laid their hands on them. In like manner, we can support one another in recovery. If God is number one in our life, we must be willing to give up our possessions, lifestyle, or codependent relationship to obey God. Although this may include personal sacrifice, it will lead us to joy and serenity.

13:13-14 John Mark left the missionary team and returned to Jerusalem. We aren't sure why he deserted the team; perhaps it was due to lack of faith, disappointment in Paul's leadership, culture shock, homesickness, or fear. His failure here may remind us of our experiences of relapse. It is encouraging to see that later John Mark was restored to fellowship with Barnabas and Paul. Barnabas took John Mark under his wing, even when Paul rejected him (15:37-39). From Paul's letters a decade later (Colossians 4:10; 2 Timothy 4:11), we know that John Mark became a faithful minister in the early church. Our failures can become opportunities to start over and to keep learning and growing.

PAUL

Saul the Pharisee (later called Paul) was exemplary in his religious fervor, and he backed up his convictions with immediate and decisive action. No one could doubt his sincerity. His number one priority was to wipe out the church of Jesus Christ—and he thought this was what God wanted him to do. He pursued the first Christians with a vengeance.

One day Jesus Christ confronted this proud religious leader on the road to Damascus. He intervened in Saul's life when Saul was driven by an angry religious fanaticism. Although God blinded Saul physically, he gave him clear spiritual insight. In one moment Saul was broken, humbled, and set on the road to recovery. He was freed from the legalistic mind-set that had controlled his life. Saul had experienced the transforming power of God.

With the same kind of commitment and intensity that he had displayed as a Pharisee, Saul, now called Paul, set out to tell the world about Jesus Christ. He endured sickness, rejection, and repeated attacks on his life to bring the message of God's forgiveness to needy people. He spoke before Jews, Greeks, and Romans. He defended his faith before kings and emperors. By the end of his life, much of the Mediterranean world had been reached with the gospel. This former Pharisee became the greatest missionary of the early church.

As we rejoice in the transformation of Paul's life, it is important to remember that this change took place because of the marvelous grace of God. Originally he was highly dysfunctional, driven by his misplaced passion. As a result of his conversion, however, he was set free from his unhealthy attitudes and behaviors. We can also experience this freeing and transforming grace of God. We can be healed and transformed, no matter how dark our past or how great our mistakes.

STRENGTHS AND ACCOMPLISHMENTS:
- Paul displayed great commitment to the causes he pursued.
- He was a brilliant spokesperson for Jesus Christ.
- He was no longer driven to self-serving achievement after his conversion.
- Paul was largely responsible for the dramatic spread of the gospel.

WEAKNESSES AND MISTAKES:
- Before his conversion, Paul sought to destroy the church of Jesus Christ.
- Before he came to believe, Paul vehemently denied the truth about Jesus.

LESSONS FROM HIS LIFE:
- Zeal and energy alone do not impress God or make a person successful.
- A person can be healed from the past and find hope for the future.
- No matter when we begin recovery, we can still make an impact on others.

KEY VERSES:
"No, dear brothers and sisters, I am still not all I should be, but I am focusing all my energies on this one thing: Forgetting the past and looking forward to what lies ahead, I strain to reach the end of the race and receive the prize for which God, through Christ Jesus, is calling us up to heaven" (Philippians 3:13-14).

Paul's story is told in Acts 7–28. Additional information can be found in the various letters he wrote. He is also mentioned in 2 Peter 3:15-16.

---

lead him. ¹²When the governor saw what had happened, he believed and was astonished at what he learned about the Lord.

Paul Preaches in Antioch of Pisidia

¹³Now Paul and those with him left Paphos by ship for Pamphylia,* landing at the port town of Perga. There John Mark left them and returned to Jerusalem. ¹⁴But Barnabas and Paul traveled inland to Antioch of Pisidia.*

On the Sabbath they went to the synagogue for the services. ¹⁵After the usual readings from the books of Moses and from the Prophets, those in charge of the service sent them this message: "Brothers, if you have any word of encouragement for us, come and give it!"

¹⁶So Paul stood, lifted his hand to quiet them, and started speaking. "People of Israel," he said, "and you devout Gentiles who fear the God of Israel, listen to me.

¹⁷"The God of this nation of Israel chose our ancestors and made them prosper in Egypt. Then he powerfully led them out of their slavery. ¹⁸He put up with them* through forty years of wandering around in the wilderness. ¹⁹Then he destroyed seven

13:13-14 *Pamphylia* and *Pisidia* were districts in the land now called Turkey. **13:18** Other manuscripts read *He cared for them;* compare Deut 1:31.

nations in Canaan and gave their land to Israel as an inheritance. ²⁰All this took about 450 years. After that, judges ruled until the time of Samuel the prophet. ²¹Then the people begged for a king, and God gave them Saul son of Kish, a man of the tribe of Benjamin, who reigned for forty years. ²²But God removed him from the kingship and replaced him with David, a man about whom God said, 'David son of Jesse is a man after my own heart, for he will do everything I want him to.'*

²³"And it is one of King David's descendants, Jesus, who is God's promised Savior of Israel! ²⁴But before he came, John the Baptist preached the need for everyone in Israel to turn from sin and turn to God and be baptized. ²⁵As John was finishing his ministry he asked, 'Do you think I am the Messiah? No! But he is coming soon—and I am not even worthy to be his slave.*'

²⁶"Brothers—you sons of Abraham, and also all of you devout Gentiles who fear the God of Israel—this salvation is for us! ²⁷The people in Jerusalem and their leaders fulfilled prophecy by condemning Jesus to death. They didn't recognize him or realize that he is the one the prophets had written about, though they hear the prophets' words read every Sabbath. ²⁸They found no just cause to execute him, but they asked Pilate to have him killed anyway.

²⁹"When they had fulfilled all the prophecies concerning his death, they took him down from the cross and placed him in a tomb. ³⁰But God raised him from the dead! ³¹And he appeared over a period of many days to those who had gone with him from Galilee to Jerusalem—these are his witnesses to the people of Israel.

³²"And now Barnabas and I are here to bring you this Good News. God's promise to our ancestors has come true in our own time, ³³in that God raised Jesus. This is what the second psalm is talking about when it says concerning Jesus,

'You are my Son.
Today I have become your Father.*'

³⁴For God had promised to raise him from the dead, never again to die. This is stated in the Scripture that says, 'I will give you the sacred blessings I promised to David.'* ³⁵Another psalm explains more fully, saying, 'You will not allow your Holy One to rot in the grave.'* ³⁶Now this is not a reference to David, for after David had served his generation according to the will of God, he died and was buried, and his body decayed. ³⁷No, it was a reference to someone else—someone whom God raised and whose body did not decay.

³⁸"Brothers, listen! In this man Jesus there is forgiveness for your sins. ³⁹Everyone who believes in him is freed from all guilt and declared right with God—something the Jewish law could never do. ⁴⁰Be careful! Don't let the prophets' words apply to you. For they said,

⁴¹'Look, you mockers,
    be amazed and die!
For I am doing something in your own
        day,
    something you wouldn't believe
    even if someone told you about it.'*"

⁴²As Paul and Barnabas left the synagogue that day, the people asked them to return again and speak about these things the next week. ⁴³Many Jews and godly converts to Judaism who worshiped at the synagogue followed Paul and Barnabas, and the two men urged them, "By God's grace, remain faithful."

Paul Turns to the Gentiles

⁴⁴The following week almost the entire city turned out to hear them preach the word of the Lord. ⁴⁵But when the Jewish leaders saw the crowds, they were jealous; so they slandered Paul and argued against whatever he said.

⁴⁶Then Paul and Barnabas spoke out boldly and declared, "It was necessary that this Good News from God be given first to you Jews. But since you have rejected it and judged yourselves unworthy of eternal life—well, we will offer it to Gentiles. ⁴⁷For this is as the Lord commanded us when he said,

13:22 1 Sam 13:14. **13:25** Greek *to untie his sandals.* **13:33** Or *Today I reveal you as my Son.* Ps 2:7. **13:34** Isa 55:3. **13:35** Ps 16:10. **13:41** Hab 1:5.

13:44–14:6 Jealousy, rejection, ridicule, revenge, physical abuse, murder plots—Paul and Barnabas experienced all that and more as they preached the Good News to others. Sometimes Paul and Barnabas stayed in a town for weeks; other times they had to run for their lives after a short stay. When we reach out to others in recovery, we may need courage to hang in there with unreceptive people who present challenges to our message. In other cases we may need to cut our losses and run. It takes wisdom from above to know how to react in any given situation.

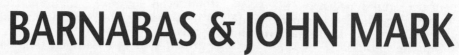

BARNABAS & JOHN MARK

Discouragement often drains our energy, especially when we face the trials of recovery. At such times it is very helpful to spend time with people who know how to encourage. Some people know just what to do or say to remind us that life is worthwhile, even in the midst of pain and failure. They know how to inspire hope when there seems to be nothing to hope for. Barnabas, whose name means "Son of Encouragement," was just that kind of person.

Barnabas's gift of encouragement was demonstrated through his financial generosity, his leadership, his teaching of new believers at Antioch, and his acceptance of Paul when others were afraid of him and doubted his conversion. It is probably accurate to say that Barnabas changed the course of church history and even the shape of the New Testament itself by persevering in his encouragement of John Mark.

Unfortunately, John Mark bailed out of his responsibilities on the first missionary journey with Paul and Barnabas. Later Barnabas was willing to give the younger man an opportunity for recovery by including him in a second journey, but Paul wouldn't hear of it. The disagreement between Paul and Barnabas was so great that they parted company. Paul went back to Asia Minor with his new partner, Silas; Barnabas went on his own missionary journey with John Mark at his side.

With Barnabas's encouragement, Mark was faithful in his missionary ministry and soon regained Paul's respect. Later Mark would also work with the apostle Peter. He is the author of the Gospel of Mark, written to encourage others to consider faith in Jesus Christ. As was true for John Mark, failure need not be the end for us. The recovery offered by Jesus Christ gives each of us the chance for a new start. As we recover, we also have the privilege of encouraging others along the way.

STRENGTHS AND ACCOMPLISHMENTS:
- Barnabas was a gifted encourager.
- Barnabas was willing to invest in John Mark even after his failure.
- John Mark became a great minister and writer.

WEAKNESSES AND MISTAKES:
- John Mark gave up and went home during Paul's first missionary journey.

LESSONS FROM THEIR LIVES:
- As we work through the process of recovery, we need encouragers to give us perspective.
- At times we may need to make personal sacrifices to encourage others.
- Although it can lead to disappointment, encouragement can pay huge dividends.

KEY VERSES:
"Barnabas . . . wanted to take along John Mark. But Paul disagreed strongly, since John Mark had deserted them in Pamphylia and had not shared in their work. Their disagreement over this was so sharp that they separated. Barnabas took John Mark with him and sailed for Cyprus" (Acts 15:37-39).

The story of Barnabas and John Mark is told in Acts 12:25–15:39. Both are also mentioned in Colossians 4:10. Barnabas is referred to in Acts 4, 9, and 11; 1 Corinthians 9; and Galatians 2. John Mark is referred to in 2 Timothy 4; Philemon 1:24; and 1 Peter 5.

'I have made you a light to the Gentiles,
to bring salvation to the farthest
corners of the earth.'*"

48When the Gentiles heard this, they were very glad and thanked the Lord for his message; and all who were appointed to eternal life became believers. 49So the Lord's message spread throughout that region.

50Then the Jewish leaders stirred up both the influential religious women and the leaders of the city, and they incited a mob against Paul and Barnabas and ran them out of town. 51But they shook off the dust of their feet against them and went to the city of Iconium. 52And the believers* were filled with joy and with the Holy Spirit.

CHAPTER 14
Paul and Barnabas in Iconium
In Iconium,* Paul and Barnabas went together to the synagogue and preached with such power that a great number of both Jews and Gentiles believed. 2But the Jews who spurned God's message stirred up distrust among the Gentiles against Paul and Barnabas, saying all sorts of evil things about them. 3The apostles stayed there a

13:47 Isa 49:6. **13:52** Greek *the disciples.* **14:1** *Iconium,* as well as *Lystra* and *Derbe* (14:6), were cities in the land now called Turkey.

long time, preaching boldly about the grace of the Lord. The Lord proved their message was true by giving them power to do miraculous signs and wonders. 4But the people of the city were divided in their opinion about them. Some sided with the Jews, and some with the apostles.

5A mob of Gentiles and Jews, along with their leaders, decided to attack and stone them. 6When the apostles learned of it, they fled for their lives. They went to the region of Lycaonia, to the cities of Lystra and Derbe and the surrounding area, 7and they preached the Good News there.

Paul and Barnabas in Lystra and Derbe

8While they were at Lystra, Paul and Barnabas came upon a man with crippled feet. He had been that way from birth, so he had never walked. 9He was listening as Paul preached, and Paul noticed him and realized he had faith to be healed. 10So Paul called to him in a loud voice, "Stand up!" And the man jumped to his feet and started walking.

11When the listening crowd saw what Paul had done, they shouted in their local dialect, "These men are gods in human bodies!" 12They decided that Barnabas was the Greek god Zeus and that Paul, because he was the chief speaker, was Hermes. 13The temple of Zeus was located on the outskirts of the city. The priest of the temple and the crowd brought oxen and wreaths of flowers, and they prepared to sacrifice to the apostles at the city gates.

14But when Barnabas and Paul heard what was happening, they tore their clothing in dismay and ran out among the people, shouting, 15"Friends,* why are you doing this? We are merely human beings like yourselves! We have come to bring you the Good News that you should turn from these worthless things to the living God, who made heaven and earth, the sea, and everything in them. 16In earlier days he permitted all the nations to go their own ways, 17but he never left himself without a witness. There were always his reminders, such as sending you rain and good crops and giving you food and joyful hearts." 18But even so, Paul and Barnabas could scarcely restrain the people from sacrificing to them.

19Now some Jews arrived from Antioch and Iconium and turned the crowds into a murderous mob. They stoned Paul and dragged him out of the city, apparently dead. 20But as the believers* stood around him, he got up and went back into the city. The next day he left with Barnabas for Derbe.

Paul and Barnabas Return to Antioch of Syria

21After preaching the Good News in Derbe and making many disciples, Paul and Barnabas returned again to Lystra, Iconium, and Antioch of Pisidia, 22where they strengthened the believers. They encouraged them to continue in the faith, reminding them that they must enter into the Kingdom of God through many tribulations. 23Paul and Barnabas also appointed elders in every church and prayed for them with fasting, turning them over to the care of the Lord, in whom they had come to trust. 24Then they traveled back through Pisidia to Pamphylia. 25They preached again in Perga, then went on to Attalia.

26Finally, they returned by ship to Antioch of Syria, where their journey had begun and where they had been committed to the grace of God for the work they had now completed. 27Upon arriving in Antioch, they called the church together and reported about their trip, telling all that God had done and how he had opened the door of faith to the Gentiles, too. 28And they stayed there with the believers in Antioch for a long time.

CHAPTER 15
The Council at Jerusalem

While Paul and Barnabas were at Antioch of Syria, some men from Judea arrived and

14:15 Greek Men. 14:20 Greek disciples; also in 14:22, 28.

14:14-20 The crowds at Lystra erroneously thought Paul and Barnabas were Greek gods. The missionaries were horrified by such sadly misplaced worship. They quickly sought to clear up the misunderstanding. Soon after this, Jews from the neighboring towns of Antioch and Iconium persuaded the crowds that Paul was a charlatan. As a result, Paul was nearly killed, but God intervened to spare his life. The people at Lystra changed their attitudes and opinions about God very quickly and on very little evidence. The result was destructive. If we persevere in our faith and commitment to God, we will enjoy long-term recovery.

began to teach the Christians*: "Unless you keep the ancient Jewish custom of circumcision taught by Moses, you cannot be saved." [2]Paul and Barnabas, disagreeing with them, argued forcefully and at length. Finally, Paul and Barnabas were sent to Jerusalem, accompanied by some local believers, to talk to the apostles and elders about this question. [3]The church sent the delegates to Jerusalem, and they stopped along the way in Phoenicia and Samaria to visit the believers.* They told them—much to everyone's joy—that the Gentiles, too, were being converted.

[4]When they arrived in Jerusalem, Paul and Barnabas were welcomed by the whole church, including the apostles and elders. They reported on what God had been doing through their ministry. [5]But then some of the men who had been Pharisees before their conversion stood up and declared that all Gentile converts must be circumcised and be required to follow the law of Moses.

[6]So the apostles and church elders got together to decide this question. [7]At the meeting, after a long discussion, Peter stood and addressed them as follows: "Brothers, you all know that God chose me from among you some time ago to preach to the Gentiles so that they could hear the Good News and believe. [8]God, who knows people's hearts, confirmed that he accepts Gentiles by giving them the Holy Spirit, just as he gave him to us. [9]He made no distinction between us and them, for he also cleansed their hearts through faith. [10]Why are you now questioning God's way by burdening the Gentile believers* with a yoke that neither we nor our ancestors were able to bear? [11]We believe that we are all saved the same way, by the special favor of the Lord Jesus."

[12]There was no further discussion, and everyone listened as Barnabas and Paul told about the miraculous signs and wonders God had done through them among the Gentiles.

[13]When they had finished, James stood and said, "Brothers, listen to me. [14]Peter* has told you about the time God first visited the Gentiles to take from them a people for himself. [15]And this conversion of Gentiles agrees with what the prophets predicted. For instance, it is written:

[16]'Afterward I will return,
and I will restore the fallen kingdom
of David.
From the ruins I will rebuild it,
and I will restore it,
[17]so that the rest of humanity might find
the Lord,
including the Gentiles—
all those I have called to be mine.
This is what the Lord says,
[18]he who made these things known
long ago.'*

[19]And so my judgment is that we should stop troubling the Gentiles who turn to God, [20]except that we should write to them and tell them to abstain from eating meat sacrificed to idols, from sexual immorality, and from consuming blood or eating the meat of strangled animals. [21]For these laws of Moses have been preached in Jewish synagogues in every city on every Sabbath for many generations."

The Letter for Gentile Believers

[22]Then the apostles and elders and the whole church in Jerusalem chose delegates, and they

---

15:1 Greek *brothers;* also in 15:32, 33. **15:3** Greek *brothers;* also in 15:23, 36, 40. **15:10** Greek *disciples.* **15:14** Greek *Simon.* **15:16-18** Amos 9:11-12; Isa 45:21.

15:1-5 The Jerusalem Council marked a crisis point in the history of Christianity. At the center of this crisis was the Jewish law. Jewish Christians thought Gentile Christians should be required to keep the law of Moses, including the rite of circumcision. The council's answer would affect the basis for faith, fellowship, outreach, and leadership in the church. The very gospel of grace was at stake. Is Christ's work alone sufficient for salvation? Or do we also have to follow the law of Moses? In the end, the sufficiency of Christ was defended. Self-examination and crisis intervention were essential to the health of the early church, just as they are to recovery today. Reaffirming the basis of our faith regularly and at crucial moments is important to the recovery and renewal process.

15:12-21 At this council meeting James concluded the discussion and confirmed Peter's view that Gentiles were acceptable to God through Christ without adhering to Jewish law. James defended his view using the Scriptures as his final authority for faith and practice. Gentile believers did not have to keep the Jewish law in order to be accepted in the Christian community. Just as the Jews wisely did not add unnecessary requirements for salvation in Christ, we must be careful to keep the requirements for involvement in recovery simple. God is the ultimate director of recovery. As we continue to submit to his will, he will show us what is essential.

sent them to Antioch of Syria with Paul and Barnabas to report on this decision. The men chosen were two of the church leaders*—Judas (also called Barsabbas) and Silas. 23This is the letter they took along with them:

"This letter is from the apostles and elders, your brothers in Jerusalem. It is written to the Gentile believers in Antioch, Syria, and Cilicia. Greetings!

24"We understand that some men from here have troubled you and upset you with their teaching, but they had no such instructions from us. 25So it seemed good to us, having unanimously agreed on our decision, to send you these official representatives, along with our beloved Barnabas and Paul, 26who have risked their lives for the sake of our Lord Jesus Christ. 27So we are sending Judas and Silas to tell you what we have decided concerning your question.

28"For it seemed good to the Holy Spirit and to us to lay no greater burden on you than these requirements: 29You must abstain from eating food offered to idols, from consuming blood or eating the meat of strangled animals, and from sexual immorality. If you do this, you will do well. Farewell."

30The four messengers went at once to Antioch, where they called a general meeting of the Christians and delivered the letter. 31And there was great joy throughout the church that day as they read this encouraging message.

32Then Judas and Silas, both being prophets, spoke extensively to the Christians, encouraging and strengthening their faith. 33They stayed for a while, and then Judas and Silas were sent back to Jerusalem, with the blessings of the Christians, to those who had sent them.* 35Paul and Barnabas stayed in Antioch to assist many others who were teaching and preaching the word of the Lord there.

Paul and Barnabas Separate

36After some time Paul said to Barnabas, "Let's return to each city where we previously preached the word of the Lord, to see how the new believers are getting along." 37Barnabas agreed and wanted to take along John Mark. 38But Paul disagreed strongly, since John Mark had deserted them in Pamphylia and had not shared in their work. 39Their disagreement over this was so sharp that they separated. Barnabas took John Mark with him and sailed for Cyprus. 40Paul chose Silas, and the believers sent them off, entrusting them to the Lord's grace. 41So they traveled throughout Syria and Cilicia to strengthen the churches there.

CHAPTER 16
Paul's Second Missionary Journey

Paul and Silas went first to Derbe and then on to Lystra. There they met Timothy, a young disciple whose mother was a Jewish believer, but whose father was a Greek. 2Timothy was well thought of by the believers* in Lystra and Iconium, 3so Paul wanted him to join them on their journey. In deference to the Jews of the area, he arranged for Timothy to be circumcised before they left, for everyone knew that his father was a Greek. 4Then they went from town to town, explaining the decision regarding the commandments that were to be obeyed, as decided by the apostles and elders in Jerusalem. 5So the churches were strengthened in their faith and grew daily in numbers.

15:22 Greek *were leaders among the brothers.* 15:33 Some manuscripts add verse 34, *But Silas decided to stay there.* 16:2 Greek *brothers;* also in 16:40.

15:36-41 Recovery and spiritual growth are processes we never complete—a fact demonstrated in the conflict between Paul and Barnabas over John Mark. Paul could not forgive John Mark for abandoning them on the first missionary journey (see 13:13-14). This resulted in a sharp disagreement and split between Paul and Barnabas. Even as mature men of faith, Paul and Barnabas had to deal with conflict and anger. They still needed to examine their motives and make amends. We know from Paul's letters that all three later reconciled, due in part to Barnabas's willingness to take John Mark with him. Like these godly men, we are never beyond the need for recovery and restoration.

16:1-3 Paul advised Timothy to submit to the Jewish practice of circumcision, even though it wasn't necessary for his salvation—the Jerusalem Council had established that fact (see 15:12-21). Timothy voluntarily followed Paul's advice in order to remove any possible stumbling block to his communicating with a Jewish audience. As we seek to share the Good News of God's powerful deliverance, we must remove any cultural or social barriers to effective communication. In this way we can get the message out to as many people in need of recovery as possible.

A Call from Macedonia

⁶Next Paul and Silas traveled through the area of Phrygia and Galatia, because the Holy Spirit had told them not to go into the province of Asia at that time. ⁷Then coming to the borders of Mysia, they headed for the province of Bithynia,* but again the Spirit of Jesus did not let them go. ⁸So instead, they went on through Mysia to the city of Troas.

⁹That night Paul had a vision. He saw a man from Macedonia in northern Greece, pleading with him, "Come over here and help us." ¹⁰So we* decided to leave for Macedonia at once, for we could only conclude that God was calling us to preach the Good News there.

Lydia of Philippi Believes in Jesus

¹¹We boarded a boat at Troas and sailed straight across to the island of Samothrace, and the next day we landed at Neapolis. ¹²From there we reached Philippi, a major city of the district of Macedonia and a Roman colony; we stayed there several days.

¹³On the Sabbath we went a little way outside the city to a riverbank, where we supposed that some people met for prayer, and we sat down to speak with some women who had come together. ¹⁴One of them was Lydia from Thyatira, a merchant of expensive purple cloth. She was a worshiper of God. As she listened to us, the Lord opened her heart, and she accepted what Paul was saying. ¹⁵She was baptized along with other members of her household, and she asked us to be her guests. "If you agree that I am faithful to the Lord," she said, "come and stay at my home." And she urged us until we did.

Paul and Silas in Prison

¹⁶One day as we were going down to the place of prayer, we met a demon-possessed slave girl. She was a fortune-teller who earned a lot of money for her masters. ¹⁷She followed along behind us shouting, "These men are servants of the Most High God, and they have come to tell you how to be saved."

¹⁸This went on day after day until Paul got so exasperated that he turned and spoke to the demon within her. "I command you in the name of Jesus Christ to come out of her," he said. And instantly it left her.

¹⁹Her masters' hopes of wealth were now shattered, so they grabbed Paul and Silas and dragged them before the authorities at the marketplace. ²⁰"The whole city is in an uproar because of these Jews!" they shouted. ²¹"They are teaching the people to do things that are against Roman customs."

²²A mob quickly formed against Paul and Silas, and the city officials ordered them stripped and beaten with wooden rods. ²³They were severely beaten, and then they were thrown into prison. The jailer was ordered to make sure they didn't escape. ²⁴So he took no chances but put them into the inner dungeon and clamped their feet in the stocks.

²⁵Around midnight, Paul and Silas were praying and singing hymns to God, and the other prisoners were listening. ²⁶Suddenly, there was a great earthquake, and the prison was shaken to its foundations. All the doors flew open, and the chains of every prisoner fell off! ²⁷The jailer woke up to see the prison doors wide open. He assumed the prisoners had escaped, so he drew his sword to kill himself. ²⁸But Paul shouted to him, "Don't do it! We are all here!"

²⁹Trembling with fear, the jailer called for lights and ran to the dungeon and fell down before Paul and Silas. ³⁰He brought them out and asked, "Sirs, what must I do to be saved?"

16:6-7 *Phrygia, Galatia, Asia, Mysia,* and *Bithynia* were all districts in the land now called Turkey. **16:10** Luke, the writer of this book, here joined Paul and accompanied him on his journey.

16:11-18 In Macedonia Paul's first converts were women. One was a businesswoman named Lydia, who sold expensive purple cloth to the wealthy. Another convert was a demon-possessed slave girl. These two females from entirely different economic and social levels in society both played key roles in the growth of the Philippian church. We are all welcome into the throne room of God through our relationship with Christ. We may be tempted to discriminate against others on the basis of gender, age, social class, employment status, marital status, or handicap. But God's power for recovery is available to everyone who believes in him.

16:25-34 Paul and Silas had been beaten and jailed. Yet they sang praises to God despite the painful circumstances they faced. God was not finished with Paul and Silas, and he delivered them from this abusive situation. In so doing he taught a clear lesson to the Philippian rulers: God can deliver and sustain us in even the most abusive circumstances. When our focus is on God and all he has done for us, our identity and inner strength will be sustained. Our inner joy and ability to praise God in the midst of persecution and hardship are signs of God's power in us and may even result in our enemies believing in God, as the jailer did.

³¹They replied, "Believe on the Lord Jesus and you will be saved, along with your entire household." ³²Then they shared the word of the Lord with him and all who lived in his household. ³³That same hour the jailer washed their wounds, and he and everyone in his household were immediately baptized. ³⁴Then he brought them into his house and set a meal before them. He and his entire household rejoiced because they all believed in God.

³⁵The next morning the city officials sent the police to tell the jailer, "Let those men go!" ³⁶So the jailer told Paul, "You and Silas are free to leave. Go in peace."

³⁷But Paul replied, "They have publicly beaten us without trial and jailed us—and we are Roman citizens. So now they want us to leave secretly? Certainly not! Let them come themselves to release us!"

³⁸When the police made their report, the city officials were alarmed to learn that Paul and Silas were Roman citizens. ³⁹They came to the jail and apologized to them. Then they brought them out and begged them to leave the city. ⁴⁰Paul and Silas then returned to the home of Lydia, where they met with the believers and encouraged them once more before leaving town.

CHAPTER 17
Paul Preaches in Thessalonica
Now Paul and Silas traveled through the towns of Amphipolis and Apollonia and came to Thessalonica, where there was a Jewish synagogue. ²As was Paul's custom, he went to the synagogue service, and for three Sabbaths in a row he interpreted the Scriptures to the people. ³He was explaining and proving the prophecies about the sufferings of the Messiah and his rising from the dead. He said, "This Jesus I'm telling you about is the Messiah." ⁴Some who listened were persuaded and became converts, including a large number of godly Greek men and also many important women of the city.*

⁵But the Jewish leaders were jealous, so they gathered some worthless fellows from the streets to form a mob and start a riot. They attacked the home of Jason, searching for Paul and Silas so they could drag them out to the crowd.* ⁶Not finding them there, they dragged out Jason and some of the other believers* instead and took them before the city council. "Paul and Silas have turned the rest of the world upside down, and now they are here disturbing our city," they shouted. ⁷"And Jason has let them into his home. They are all guilty of treason against Caesar, for they profess allegiance to another king, Jesus."

⁸The people of the city, as well as the city officials, were thrown into turmoil by these reports. ⁹But the officials released Jason and the other believers after they had posted bail.

Paul and Silas in Berea
¹⁰That very night the believers sent Paul and Silas to Berea. When they arrived there, they went to the synagogue. ¹¹And the people of Berea were more open-minded than those in Thessalonica, and they listened eagerly to Paul's message. They searched the Scriptures day after day to check up on Paul and Silas,

17:4 Some manuscripts read *many of the wives of the leading men.* 17:5 Or *the city council.* 17:6 Greek *brothers;* also in 17:10, 14.

17:1-9 At Thessalonica Paul interpreted Scriptures and explained prophecies to his largely Jewish audience. As a result, many Jews and Gentiles turned their lives over to God. Nevertheless, many more Jews objected to Paul's message. So they stirred up the crowds and city officials to run Paul out of town. This mixed response is similar to the response generated by the recovery movement. Just because some people do not agree with our God-centered approach to recovery doesn't mean it is wrong. We must keep God central to our program and persevere in the face of opposition, just as Paul and Silas did.

17:10-12 At Berea Paul enjoyed a most eager response from the Jewish community. The Bereans searched the Scriptures to see if Paul and Silas were really teaching the truth. How exciting when someone is eager to hear the Good News of God's plan of salvation and recovery. But no one should simply take our word alone as truth. Fortunately, we have the Scriptures to back up every claim we make about God's grace and his power to deliver.

17:22-31 In Athens Paul preached in the synagogue as he normally did upon entering a new town. But then he also shared the Good News with intellectuals and philosophers in the public square. Paul began by acknowledging their belief in an unnamed higher Power—the "Unknown God." Then he identified that higher Power as the heavenly Father, the Creator, the risen Lord, and the future Judge. Thanks to Jesus Christ, we can know God personally (see 1 John 1:1-3). We don't have to look to some unnamed or unknowable higher power for help in recovery. We can trust in a powerful, loving, and personal God.

to see if they were really teaching the truth. [12]As a result, many Jews believed, as did some of the prominent Greek women and many men.

[13]But when some Jews in Thessalonica learned that Paul was preaching the word of God in Berea, they went there and stirred up trouble. [14]The believers acted at once, sending Paul on to the coast, while Silas and Timothy remained behind. [15]Those escorting Paul went with him to Athens; then they returned to Berea with a message for Silas and Timothy to hurry and join him.

Paul Preaches in Athens

[16]While Paul was waiting for them in Athens, he was deeply troubled by all the idols he saw everywhere in the city. [17]He went to the synagogue to debate with the Jews and the God-fearing Gentiles, and he spoke daily in the public square to all who happened to be there.

[18]He also had a debate with some of the Epicurean and Stoic philosophers. When he told them about Jesus and his resurrection, they said, "This babbler has picked up some strange ideas." Others said, "He's pushing some foreign religion."

[19]Then they took him to the Council of Philosophers.* "Come and tell us more about this new religion," they said. [20]"You are saying some rather startling things, and we want to know what it's all about." [21](It should be explained that all the Athenians as well as the foreigners in Athens seemed to spend all their time discussing the latest ideas.)

[22]So Paul, standing before the Council,* addressed them as follows: "Men of Athens, I notice that you are very religious, [23]for as I was walking along I saw your many altars. And one of them had this inscription on it—'To an Unknown God.' You have been worshiping him without knowing who he is, and now I wish to tell you about him.

[24]"He is the God who made the world and everything in it. Since he is Lord of heaven and earth, he doesn't live in man-made temples, [25]and human hands can't serve his needs—for he has no needs. He himself gives life and breath to everything, and he satisfies every need there is. [26]From one man he created all the nations throughout the whole earth. He decided beforehand which should rise and fall, and he determined their boundaries.

17:19 Greek *the Areopagus.* **17:22** Or *in the middle of Mars Hill;* Greek reads *in the middle of the Areopagus.*

S T E P

3

Discovering God

BIBLE READING: Acts 17:23-28

We made a decision to turn our will and our life over to the care of God.

Before we can turn our life over to God, we need to have an accurate understanding of who he is. It is crucial that we entrust ourself to the God who loves us and not to the "god" of this world, who seeks only to deceive and destroy us. The apostle Paul described the deceiver this way: "Satan, the god of this evil world, has blinded the minds of those who don't believe, so they are unable to see the glorious light of the Good News that is shining upon them. They don't understand the message we preach about the glory of Christ, who is the exact likeness of God" (2 Corinthians 4:4). Has Satan deceived us? How can we be sure that we have a true understanding of God?

When Paul addressed the men of Athens, he said, "I saw your many altars. And one of them had this inscription on it—'To an Unknown God.' You have been worshiping him without knowing who he is, and now I wish to tell you about him. . . . His purpose in all of this was that the nations should seek after God and perhaps feel their way toward him and find him— though he is not far from any one of us. For in him we live and move and exist" (Acts 17:23, 27-28).

Even though God may be unknown to us, he is near and willing to reveal himself. God promised through the prophet Jeremiah, "If you look for me in earnest, you will find me when you seek me" (Jeremiah 29:13). Turning over our will involves accepting God as he is instead of insisting on creating him in our own image. When we seek God with an open heart and mind, we will find him. *Turn to page 409, James 4.*

27"His purpose in all of this was that the nations should seek after God and perhaps feel their way toward him and find him—though he is not far from any one of us. 28For in him we live and move and exist. As one of your own poets says, 'We are his offspring.' 29And since this is true, we shouldn't think of God as an idol designed by craftsmen from gold or silver or stone. 30God overlooked people's former ignorance about these things, but now he commands everyone everywhere to turn away from idols and turn to him.* 31For he has set a day for judging the world with justice by the man he has appointed, and he proved to everyone who this is by raising him from the dead."

32When they heard Paul speak of the resurrection of a person who had been dead, some laughed, but others said, "We want to hear more about this later." 33That ended Paul's discussion with them, 34but some joined him and became believers. Among them were Dionysius, a member of the Council,* a woman named Damaris, and others.

CHAPTER 18
Paul Meets Priscilla and Aquila in Corinth

Then Paul left Athens and went to Corinth.* 2There he became acquainted with a Jew named Aquila, born in Pontus, who had recently arrived from Italy with his wife, Priscilla. They had been expelled from Italy as a result of Claudius Caesar's order to deport all Jews from Rome. 3Paul lived and worked with them, for they were tentmakers* just as he was.

4Each Sabbath found Paul at the synagogue, trying to convince the Jews and Greeks alike. 5And after Silas and Timothy came down from Macedonia, Paul spent his full time preaching and testifying to the Jews, telling them, "The Messiah you are looking for is Jesus." 6But when the Jews opposed him and insulted him, Paul shook the dust from his robe and said, "Your blood be upon your own heads—I am innocent. From now on I will go to the Gentiles."

7After that he stayed with Titius Justus, a Gentile who worshiped God and lived next door to the synagogue. 8Crispus, the leader of the synagogue, and all his household believed in the Lord. Many others in Corinth also became believers and were baptized.

9One night the Lord spoke to Paul in a vision and told him, "Don't be afraid! Speak out! Don't be silent! 10For I am with you, and no one will harm you because many people here in this city belong to me." 11So Paul stayed there for the next year and a half, teaching the word of God.

12But when Gallio became governor of Achaia, some Jews rose in concerted action against Paul and brought him before the governor for judgment. 13They accused Paul of "persuading people to worship God in ways that are contrary to the law." 14But just as Paul started to make his defense, Gallio turned to Paul's accusers and said, "Listen, you Jews, if this were a case involving some wrongdoing or a serious crime, I would be obliged to listen to you. 15But since it is merely a question of words and names and your Jewish laws, you take care of it. I refuse to judge such matters." 16And he drove them out of the courtroom. 17The mob had grabbed Sosthenes, the leader of the synagogue, and had beaten him right there in the courtroom. But Gallio paid no attention.

Paul Returns to Antioch of Syria

18Paul stayed in Corinth for some time after that and then said good-bye to the brothers and sisters* and sailed for the coast of Syria,

17:30 Greek *everywhere to repent.* 17:34 Greek *an Areopagite.* 18:1 *Athens* and *Corinth* were major cities in Achaia, the region on the southern end of the Greek peninsula. 18:3 Or *leatherworkers.* 18:18 Greek *brothers;* also in 18:27.

18:1-9 Perhaps Paul was discouraged because his Athens ministry had resulted in very few converts. That might explain his discouragement in Corinth and account for the direct encouragement he received from God while there. We all go through hard times, especially as we pursue recovery. If we follow God's will, however, he will be there to encourage us when times get tough. God doesn't help us along to a certain point just to leave us to be destroyed.

18:24-28 Apollos was very well educated in philosophy and the Scriptures, and he was a skilled orator. Yet after hearing him speak in the synagogue, Priscilla and Aquila realized that his knowledge of Scripture was incomplete. They took him aside and explained the gospel to him more accurately, filling him in on the things he didn't yet know or understand. We may know people who seem to have it all together, yet they are missing an essential truth in their understanding of the gospel and their relationship with God. Their giftedness need not intimidate us from sharing the truth with them. We may find that they sense the need for recovery in their life and are ready to respond to our message.

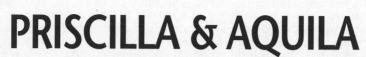

PRISCILLA & AQUILA

Priscilla and Aquila were united not only in marriage but also in ministry. In writing of this godly couple, Paul and Luke never mentioned them apart from each other. Their abilities and talents were complementary; together they were able to enrich the lives of the people around them.

Priscilla and Aquila moved to Corinth, Greece, to build a new life after the Jews were commanded to leave the city of Rome. While adjusting to this change, they opened their home to the apostle Paul. He had recently experienced intense trials in his ministry and needed a place to rest and recuperate. In the home of Priscilla and Aquila, Paul found not only acceptance and love but a livelihood as well. Paul joined them in their tent-making business.

Paul rested and was greatly encouraged from his time with Priscilla and Aquila. Refreshed from his visit in this godly home, Paul responded to God's challenge and entered new territories of ministry. Aquila and Priscilla moved to Ephesus with Paul and helped him in the ministry. Their faithful friendship provided Paul with a relationship of accountability and encouragement.

When Paul left Ephesus, Aquila and Priscilla stayed and oversaw the ministry there. They became aware that a young Jew, Apollos, was speaking with great zeal but with incomplete knowledge of the truth. They patiently explained the things of God to him more accurately. Apollos soon became one of the most gifted preachers in the early church.

As a result of their perseverance in God's work, Priscilla and Aquila eventually had a church meeting in their home. Their strong relationship with God and godly example made them ideal leaders in the early church. Though they never became famous preachers or leaders themselves, they were used by God to minister to some great leaders of the early church.

STRENGTHS AND ACCOMPLISHMENTS:
- Priscilla and Aquila shared responsibilities in their marriage.
- They enjoyed a marriage built on respect and love.
- They were willing to take risks and accept new challenges.
- They opened their home to help and encourage others.

LESSONS FROM THEIR LIVES:
- A healthy marriage allows both husband and wife the opportunity to exercise their gifts.
- A godly and healthy home is always open to minister to others in need.
- Rest is often needed before and after times of stress and change.

KEY VERSES:
"Greet Priscilla and Aquila. They have been co-workers in my ministry for Christ Jesus. In fact, they risked their lives for me. I am not the only one who is thankful to them; so are all the Gentile churches" (Romans 16:3-4).

Priscilla and Aquila's story is told in Acts 18. Both are also mentioned in Romans 16:3; 1 Corinthians 16:19; and 2 Timothy 4:19.

---

taking Priscilla and Aquila with him. (Earlier, at Cenchrea, Paul had shaved his head according to Jewish custom, for he had taken a vow.) [19]When they arrived at the port of Ephesus, Paul left the others behind. But while he was there, he went to the synagogue to debate with the Jews. [20]They asked him to stay longer, but he declined. [21]So he left, saying, "I will come back later,* God willing." Then he set sail from Ephesus. [22]The next stop was at the port of Caesarea. From there he went up and visited the church at Jerusalem* and then went back to Antioch.

[23]After spending some time in Antioch, Paul went back to Galatia and Phrygia, visiting all the believers,* encouraging them and helping them to grow in the Lord.

Apollos Instructed at Ephesus
[24]Meanwhile, a Jew named Apollos, an eloquent speaker who knew the Scriptures well, had just arrived in Ephesus from Alexandria

18:21 Some manuscripts read *"I must by all means be at Jerusalem for the upcoming festival, but I will come back later."* **18:22** Greek *the church.* **18:23** Greek *disciples;* also in 18:27.

in Egypt. [25]He had been taught the way of the Lord and talked to others with great enthusiasm and accuracy about Jesus. However, he knew only about John's baptism. [26]When Priscilla and Aquila heard him preaching boldly in the synagogue, they took him aside and explained the way of God more accurately.

[27]Apollos had been thinking about going to Achaia, and the brothers and sisters in Ephesus encouraged him in this. They wrote to the believers in Achaia, asking them to welcome him. When he arrived there, he proved to be of great benefit to those who, by God's grace, had believed. [28]He refuted all the Jews with powerful arguments in public debate. Using the Scriptures, he explained to them, "The Messiah you are looking for is Jesus."

CHAPTER 19
Paul's Third Missionary Journey

While Apollos was in Corinth, Paul traveled through the interior provinces. Finally, he came to Ephesus, where he found several believers.* [2]"Did you receive the Holy Spirit when you believed?" he asked them.

"No," they replied, "we don't know what you mean. We haven't even heard that there is a Holy Spirit."

[3]"Then what baptism did you experience?" he asked.

And they replied, "The baptism of John."

[4]Paul said, "John's baptism was to demonstrate a desire to turn from sin and turn to God. John himself told the people to believe in Jesus, the one John said would come later."

[5]As soon as they heard this, they were baptized in the name of the Lord Jesus. [6]Then when Paul laid his hands on them, the Holy Spirit came on them, and they spoke in other tongues and prophesied. [7]There were about twelve men in all.

Paul Ministers in Ephesus

[8]Then Paul went to the synagogue and preached boldly for the next three months, arguing persuasively about the Kingdom of God. [9]But some rejected his message and publicly spoke against the Way, so Paul left the synagogue and took the believers with him. Then he began preaching daily at the lecture hall of Tyrannus. [10]This went on for the next two years, so that people throughout the province of Asia—both Jews and Greeks—heard the Lord's message.

[11]God gave Paul the power to do unusual miracles, [12]so that even when handkerchiefs or cloths that had touched his skin were placed on sick people, they were healed of their diseases, and any evil spirits within them came out.

[13]A team of Jews who were traveling from town to town casting out evil spirits tried to use the name of the Lord Jesus. The incantation they used was this: "I command you by Jesus, whom Paul preaches, to come out!" [14]Seven sons of Sceva, a leading priest, were doing this. [15]But when they tried it on a man possessed by an evil spirit, the spirit replied, "I know Jesus, and I know Paul. But who are you?" [16]And he leaped on them and attacked them with such violence that they fled from the house, naked and badly injured.

[17]The story of what happened spread quickly all through Ephesus, to Jews and Greeks alike. A solemn fear descended on the city, and the name of the Lord Jesus was greatly honored. [18]Many who became believers confessed their sinful practices. [19]A number of them who had been practicing magic brought their incantation books and burned them at a public bonfire. The value of the books was several million dollars.* [20]So the message about the Lord spread widely and had a powerful effect.

The Riot in Ephesus

[21]Afterward Paul felt impelled by the Holy Spirit* to go over to Macedonia and Achaia before returning to Jerusalem. "And after that," he said, "I must go on to Rome!" [22]He sent his two assistants, Timothy and Erastus, on ahead to Macedonia while he stayed awhile longer in the province of Asia.

19:1 Greek *disciples;* also in 19:9, 30. **19:19** Greek *50,000 pieces of silver,* each of which was the equivalent of a day's wage. **19:21** Or *purposed in his spirit.*

19:11-20 The people of Ephesus were in bondage to their fear of the spiritual realm, and the seven sons of Sceva made their living by allaying those fears. When they were confronted by a real demon, however, these men were powerless. But the demon recognized the authority of Jesus Christ and Paul because they were representatives of God himself. When the people heard this story that proved God's sovereignty over the demonic realm, they were filled with a healthy awe of Jesus Christ and his true representatives. Like the evil spirits, our compulsions and addictions are more powerful than we are. We need God's power to work in our life because no other power can overcome our destructive habits and sustain us in recovery.

APOLLOS

Apollos was a Jewish Bible teacher and skilled orator from Alexandria. He had heard about John the Baptist's message concerning the coming Messiah. Because he had studied the Scriptures seriously, he knew John's message was true. Apollos traveled north to Ephesus, preaching the message of God's Kingdom and zealously debating the skeptics.

Priscilla and Aquila heard Apollos preach in Ephesus. They were two devoted followers of Christ who had been greatly impacted by Paul's ministry. Although they appreciated his zeal, they discerned that he had incomplete knowledge of the Scriptures. So they took him aside and more fully explained the truth about Jesus Christ, the salvation he brought, and the Holy Spirit who indwelt and empowered believers. For the first time, Apollos was able to put it all together!

With this new understanding, Apollos went to minister in the city of Corinth. His ministry was so effective that Paul had to warn the believers there to keep their eyes on Christ, rather than on Apollos or himself. Apollos continued to travel and speak throughout Greece. Paul appreciated him so much that he encouraged Titus to support Apollos as much as possible.

The story of Apollos demonstrates the tremendous value of wise counsel in our life. Unfortunately, the counsel many seek lacks true spiritual insight. Some of us stumble through life with a very limited view of the love and power available to us in Jesus Christ. The more we are exposed to truth through wise counsel, the more we will fully comprehend Christ's work on our behalf. As this occurs, we can internalize the healing nature of the gospel and become better equipped to minister to others in need.

STRENGTHS AND ACCOMPLISHMENTS:
- Apollos believed God and was committed to him.
- He used his strengths and abilities for the Kingdom of God.
- He was teachable when confronted with the truth.

WEAKNESSES AND MISTAKES:
- Initially, Apollos was operating on an incomplete understanding of the truth.

LESSONS FROM HIS LIFE:
- God's wisdom and truth are available for our personal healing.
- As we discover God's truth and experience his power, we are better able to help our fellow strugglers.
- If we are willing to act on the little we do know, God will make it possible for us to learn the full truth.

KEY VERSES:
"Meanwhile, a Jew named Apollos, an eloquent speaker who knew the Scriptures well. . . . talked to others with great enthusiasm and accuracy about Jesus. However, he knew only about John's baptism. When Priscilla and Aquila heard him preaching boldly in the synagogue, they took him aside and explained the way of God more accurately" (Acts 18:24-26).

The story of Apollos is told in Acts 18:24-28. He is also mentioned in 1 Corinthians 1:12; 3:4-6, 22; 4:1, 6; 16:12; and Titus 3:13.

---

[23]But about that time, serious trouble developed in Ephesus concerning the Way. [24]It began with Demetrius, a silversmith who had a large business manufacturing silver shrines of the Greek goddess Artemis.* He kept many craftsmen busy. [25]He called the craftsmen together, along with others employed in related trades, and addressed them as follows:

"Gentlemen, you know that our wealth comes from this business. [26]As you have seen and heard, this man Paul has persuaded many people that handmade gods aren't gods at all. And this is happening not only here in Ephesus but throughout the entire province! [27]Of course, I'm not just talking about the loss of public respect for our business. I'm also con-

cerned that the temple of the great goddess Artemis will lose its influence and that Artemis—this magnificent goddess worshiped throughout the province of Asia and all around the world—will be robbed of her prestige!"

[28]At this their anger boiled, and they began shouting, "Great is Artemis of the Ephesians!" [29]A crowd began to gather, and soon the city was filled with confusion. Everyone rushed to the amphitheater, dragging along Gaius and Aristarchus, who were Paul's traveling companions from Macedonia. [30]Paul wanted to go in, but the believers wouldn't let him. [31]Some of the officials of the province, friends of Paul, also sent a message to him, begging him not to risk his life by entering the amphitheater.

19:24 *Artemis* is otherwise known as Diana.

32Inside, the people were all shouting, some one thing and some another. Everything was in confusion. In fact, most of them didn't even know why they were there. 33Alexander was thrust forward by some of the Jews, who encouraged him to explain the situation. He motioned for silence and tried to speak in defense. 34But when the crowd realized he was a Jew, they started shouting again and kept it up for two hours: "Great is Artemis of the Ephesians! Great is Artemis of the Ephesians!"

35At last the mayor was able to quiet them down enough to speak. "Citizens of Ephesus," he said. "Everyone knows that Ephesus is the official guardian of the temple of the great Artemis, whose image fell down to us from heaven. 36Since this is an indisputable fact, you shouldn't be disturbed, no matter what is said. Don't do anything rash. 37You have brought these men here, but they have stolen nothing from the temple and have not spoken against our goddess. 38If Demetrius and the craftsmen have a case against them, the courts are in session and the judges can take the case at once. Let them go through legal channels. 39And if there are complaints about other matters, they can be settled in a legal assembly. 40I am afraid we are in danger of being charged with rioting by the Roman government, since there is no cause for all this commotion. And if Rome demands an explanation, we won't know what to say." 41Then he dismissed them, and they dispersed.

CHAPTER 20
Paul Goes to Macedonia and Greece

When it was all over, Paul sent for the believers* and encouraged them. Then he said good-bye and left for Macedonia. 2Along the way, he encouraged the believers in all the towns he passed through. Then he traveled down to Greece, 3where he stayed for three months. He was preparing to sail back to Syria when he discovered a plot by some Jews against his life, so he decided to return through Macedonia.

4Several men were traveling with him. They were Sopater of Berea, the son of Pyrrhus; Aristarchus and Secundus, from Thessalonica; Gaius, from Derbe; Timothy; and Tychicus and Trophimus, who were from the province of Asia. 5They went ahead and waited for us at Troas. 6As soon as the Passover season* ended, we boarded a ship at Philippi in Macedonia and five days later arrived in Troas, where we stayed a week.

Paul's Final Visit to Troas

7On the first day of the week, we gathered to observe the Lord's Supper.* Paul was preaching; and since he was leaving the next day, he talked until midnight. 8The upstairs room where we met was lighted with many flickering lamps. 9As Paul spoke on and on, a young man named Eutychus, sitting on the windowsill, became very drowsy. Finally, he sank into a deep sleep and fell three stories to his death below. 10Paul went down, bent over him, and took him into his arms. "Don't worry," he said, "he's alive!" 11Then they all went back upstairs and ate the Lord's Supper together.* And Paul continued talking to them until dawn; then he left. 12Meanwhile, the young man was taken home unhurt, and everyone was greatly relieved.

Paul Meets the Ephesian Elders

13Paul went by land to Assos, where he had arranged for us to join him, and we went on

20:1 Greek *disciples*. 20:6 Greek *the days of unleavened bread*. 20:7 Greek *to break bread*. 20:11 Greek *broke the bread*.

20:1-6 Paul did not operate as a lone ranger; he traveled with other godly men to whom he was accountable. He was responsible to and for others. He didn't just make converts; he cared for them and helped them to grow spiritually. When we share our message of hope and recovery with others, it is important to do more than just share the Good News. We need to walk through each new step in recovery with those who desire to change. Paul's entourage worked as a team for the welfare of the believers. So we also can join hands with other believers to help hurting people make progress and to receive encouragement for our own daily struggles.
20:7-12 Eutychus fell asleep while Paul was preaching and fell to his death. But Paul brought him back to life. When we know the happy outcome, this story can seem somewhat humorous—especially since we sense a kindred spirit with Eutychus. (Who among us has not fallen asleep during a sermon?) Luke recounts this event to remind us that God has the power to restore the dead to new life. God works beyond our own natural laws and capabilities, doing what we would consider impossible. He can do the same for those of us who are dead in sin and gripped by addictions. We can find hope for restoration in this amazing story of resurrection.

ahead by ship. [14]He joined us there and we sailed together to Mitylene. [15]The next day we passed the island of Kios. The following day, we crossed to the island of Samos. And a day later we arrived at Miletus.

[16]Paul had decided against stopping at Ephesus this time because he didn't want to spend further time in the province of Asia. He was hurrying to get to Jerusalem, if possible, for the Festival of Pentecost. [17]But when we landed at Miletus, he sent a message to the elders of the church at Ephesus, asking them to come down to meet him.

[18]When they arrived he declared, "You know that from the day I set foot in the province of Asia until now [19]I have done the Lord's work humbly—yes, and with tears. I have endured the trials that came to me from the plots of the Jews. [20]Yet I never shrank from telling you the truth, either publicly or in your homes. [21]I have had one message for Jews and Gentiles alike—the necessity of turning from sin and turning to God, and of faith in our Lord Jesus.

[22]"And now I am going to Jerusalem, drawn there irresistibly by the Holy Spirit,* not knowing what awaits me, [23]except that the Holy Spirit has told me in city after city that jail and suffering lie ahead. [24]But my life is worth nothing unless I use it for doing the work assigned me by the Lord Jesus—the work of telling others the Good News about God's wonderful kindness and love.

[25]"And now I know that none of you to whom I have preached the Kingdom will ever see me again. [26]Let me say plainly that I have been faithful. No one's damnation can be blamed on me,* [27]for I didn't shrink from declaring all that God wants for you.

[28]"And now beware! Be sure that you feed and shepherd God's flock—his church, purchased with his blood—over whom the Holy Spirit has appointed you as elders.* [29]I know full well that false teachers, like vicious wolves, will come in among you after I leave, not sparing the flock. [30]Even some of you will distort the truth in order to draw a following. [31]Watch out! Remember the three years I was with you—my constant watch and care over you night and day, and my many tears for you.

[32]"And now I entrust you to God and the word of his grace—his message that is able to build you up and give you an inheritance with all those he has set apart for himself.

[33]"I have never coveted anyone's money or fine clothing. [34]You know that these hands of mine have worked to pay my own way, and I have even supplied the needs of those who were with me. [35]And I have been a constant example of how you can help the poor by working hard. You should remember the words of the Lord Jesus: 'It is more blessed to give than to receive.'"

[36]When he had finished speaking, he knelt and prayed with them. [37]They wept aloud as they embraced him in farewell, [38]sad most of all because he had said that they would never see him again. Then they accompanied him down to the ship.

CHAPTER 21
Paul's Journey to Jerusalem

After saying farewell to the Ephesian elders, we sailed straight to the island of Cos. The next day we reached Rhodes and then went to Patara. [2]There we boarded a ship sailing for the Syrian province of Phoenicia. [3]We sighted the island of Cyprus, passed it on our left, and landed at the harbor of Tyre, in Syria, where the ship was to unload. [4]We went ashore, found the local believers,* and stayed with them a week. These disciples prophesied through the Holy Spirit that Paul should not go on to Jerusalem. [5]When we returned to the ship at the end of the week, the entire congregation, including wives and children, came down to the shore with us. There we knelt, prayed, [6]and said our farewells. Then we went aboard, and they returned home.

[7]The next stop after leaving Tyre was

20:22 Or *by my spirit,* or *by an inner compulsion.* Greek reads *by the spirit.* 20:26 Greek *I am innocent of the blood of all.* 20:28 Greek *overseers.* 21:4 Greek *disciples;* also in 21:16.

20:22-38 As Paul met with the Ephesian elders, he told them of his plans to return to Jerusalem. Paul sensed a clear leading by the Holy Spirit and was determined to follow it. Apparently, Paul was aware that God's plan would lead him through difficult circumstances. Yet he felt compelled to do the work God assigned him. Following God's will in recovery is not easy. Sometimes it leads to loneliness and loss. Sometimes it causes conflict with our friends and family. Even though following God's will can be hard at times, it is always the best way. Paul's example encourages us to pray for clear knowledge of God's will and the power to obey it.

Ptolemais, where we greeted the brothers and sisters* but stayed only one day. [8]Then we went on to Caesarea and stayed at the home of Philip the Evangelist, one of the seven men who had been chosen to distribute food. [9]He had four unmarried daughters who had the gift of prophecy.

[10]During our stay of several days, a man named Agabus, who also had the gift of prophecy, arrived from Judea. [11]When he visited us, he took Paul's belt and bound his own feet and hands with it. Then he said, "The Holy Spirit declares, 'So shall the owner of this belt be bound by the Jewish leaders in Jerusalem and turned over to the Romans.'" [12]When we heard this, we who were traveling with him, as well as the local believers, begged Paul not to go on to Jerusalem.

[13]But he said, "Why all this weeping? You are breaking my heart! For I am ready not only to be jailed at Jerusalem but also to die for the sake of the Lord Jesus." [14]When it was clear that we couldn't persuade him, we gave up and said, "The will of the Lord be done."

Paul Arrives at Jerusalem

[15]Shortly afterward we packed our things and left for Jerusalem. [16]Some believers from Caesarea accompanied us, and they took us to the home of Mnason, a man originally from Cyprus and one of the early disciples. [17]All the brothers and sisters in Jerusalem welcomed us cordially.

[18]The next day Paul went in with us to meet with James, and all the elders of the Jerusalem church were present. [19]After greetings were exchanged, Paul gave a detailed account of the things God had accomplished among the Gentiles through his ministry.

[20]After hearing this, they praised God. But then they said, "You know, dear brother, how many thousands of Jews have also believed, and they all take the law of Moses

very seriously. [21]Our Jewish Christians here at Jerusalem have been told that you are teaching all the Jews living in the Gentile world to turn their backs on the laws of Moses. They say that you teach people not to circumcise their children or follow other Jewish customs. [22]Now what can be done? For they will certainly hear that you have come.

[23]"Here's our suggestion. We have four men here who have taken a vow and are preparing to shave their heads. [24]Go with them to the Temple and join them in the purification ceremony, and pay for them to have their heads shaved. Then everyone will know that the rumors are all false and that you yourself observe the Jewish laws.

[25]"As for the Gentile Christians, all we ask of them is what we already told them in a letter: They should not eat food offered to idols, nor consume blood, nor eat meat from strangled animals, and they should stay away from all sexual immorality."

Paul Is Arrested

[26]So Paul agreed to their request, and the next day he went through the purification ritual with the men and went to the Temple. Then he publicly announced the date when their vows would end and sacrifices would be offered for each of them.

[27]The seven days were almost ended when some Jews from the province of Asia saw Paul in the Temple and roused a mob against him. They grabbed him, [28]yelling, "Men of Israel! Help! This is the man who teaches against our people and tells everybody to disobey the Jewish laws. He speaks against the Temple—and he even defiles it by bringing Gentiles in!" [29](For earlier that day they had seen him in the city with Trophimus, a Gentile from Ephesus,* and they assumed Paul had taken him into the Temple.)

21:7 Greek *brothers;* also in 21:17. **21:29** Greek *Trophimus, the Ephesian.*

21:7-9 The last recorded event involving Philip had taken place some twenty-five years earlier while he traveled to Caesarea (8:40). After that time, Philip had not only a continuing ministry but also a godly family with four daughters gifted in prophecy. Philip had instilled in them his faith in Christ and God's power for life and ministry. This indicates that Christianity, though new, had the power to transform lives on a permanent basis. Philip demonstrated the kind of perseverance and fruitfulness we can have as we work our recovery program today.

21:18-26 Paul had been accused of encouraging Jews to live a Gentile lifestyle. So James suggested that Paul participate in a special vow to show the Jews that he was still one of them. Paul's love for his brothers and sisters led him to do what he could to remove anything that might destroy the faith of a Jewish believer. Thus, Paul followed James's advice and participated in the prescribed Temple worship. Like Paul, we may need to make some personal sacrifices in order to encourage someone in the recovery process. As we learn to give up our own rights for the sake of others, we will discover the joy of serving God and his people.

[30]The whole population of the city was rocked by these accusations, and a great riot followed. Paul was dragged out of the Temple, and immediately the gates were closed behind him. [31]As they were trying to kill him, word reached the commander of the Roman regiment that all Jerusalem was in an uproar. [32]He immediately called out his soldiers and officers and ran down among the crowd. When the mob saw the commander and the troops coming, they stopped beating Paul. [33]The commander arrested him and ordered him bound with two chains. Then he asked the crowd who he was and what he had done. [34]Some shouted one thing and some another. He couldn't find out the truth in all the uproar and confusion, so he ordered Paul to be taken to the fortress. [35]As they reached the stairs, the mob grew so violent the soldiers had to lift Paul to their shoulders to protect him. [36]And the crowd followed behind shouting, "Kill him, kill him!"

Paul Speaks to the Crowd

[37]As Paul was about to be taken inside, he said to the commander, "May I have a word with you?"

"Do you know Greek?" the commander asked, surprised. [38]"Aren't you the Egyptian who led a rebellion some time ago and took four thousand members of the Assassins out into the desert?"

[39]"No," Paul replied, "I am a Jew from Tarsus in Cilicia, which is an important city. Please, let me talk to these people." [40]The commander agreed, so Paul stood on the stairs and motioned to the people to be quiet. Soon a deep silence enveloped the crowd, and he addressed them in their own language, Aramaic.*

CHAPTER 22
"Brothers and esteemed fathers," Paul said, "listen to me as I offer my defense." [2]When they heard him speaking in their own language,* the silence was even greater. [3]"I am a Jew, born in Tarsus, a city in Cilicia, and I was brought up and educated here in Jerusalem under Gamaliel. At his feet I learned to follow our Jewish laws and customs very carefully. I became very zealous to honor God in everything I did, just as all of you are today. [4]And I persecuted the followers of the Way, hounding some to death, binding and delivering both men and women to prison. [5]The high priest and the whole council of leaders can testify that this is so. For I received letters from them to our Jewish brothers in Damascus, authorizing me to bring the Christians from there to Jerusalem, in chains, to be punished.

[6]"As I was on the road, nearing Damascus, about noon a very bright light from heaven suddenly shone around me. [7]I fell to the ground and heard a voice saying to me, 'Saul, Saul, why are you persecuting me?'

[8]"'Who are you, sir?' I asked. And he replied, 'I am Jesus of Nazareth, the one you are persecuting.' [9]The people with me saw the light but didn't hear the voice.

[10]"I said, 'What shall I do, Lord?' And the Lord told me, 'Get up and go into Damascus, and there you will be told all that you are to do.'

[11]"I was blinded by the intense light and had to be led into Damascus by my companions. [12]A man named Ananias lived there. He was a godly man in his devotion to the law, and he was well thought of by all the Jews of Damascus. [13]He came to me and stood beside me and said, 'Brother Saul, receive your sight.' And that very hour I could see him!

[14]"Then he told me, 'The God of our ancestors has chosen you to know his will and to see the Righteous One and hear him speak. [15]You are to take his message everywhere, telling the whole world what you have seen and heard. [16]And now, why delay? Get up and be baptized, and have your sins washed away, calling on the name of the Lord.'

[17]"One day after I returned to Jerusalem, I was praying in the Temple, and I fell into a trance. [18]I saw a vision of Jesus saying to me, 'Hurry! Leave Jerusalem, for the people here won't believe you when you give them your testimony about me.'

21:40 Or *Hebrew.* 22:2 Greek *in Aramaic.*

22:1-21 In this second account of Paul's conversion (see 9:1-18), we learn one additional detail: Paul studied under the great rabbinic scholar, Gamaliel. We are reminded of Paul's rage against the believers prior to his conversion. But despite Paul's former self-sufficiency, he quickly admitted his helplessness when Christ appeared to him in a blinding light. His powerless state was so complete that others had to lead him by the hand due to his temporary blindness. Fortunately, we don't all need such a dramatic event to force us to face our powerlessness. But we must all realize that without God we cannot overcome our compulsion or addiction. When we understand this truth, we have started down the road of recovery.

19"'But Lord,' I argued, 'they certainly know that I imprisoned and beat those in every synagogue who believed on you. 20And when your witness Stephen was killed, I was standing there agreeing. I kept the coats they laid aside as they stoned him.'

21"But the Lord said to me, 'Leave Jerusalem, for I will send you far away to the Gentiles!'"

22The crowd listened until Paul came to that word; then with one voice they shouted, "Away with such a fellow! Kill him! He isn't fit to live!" 23They yelled, threw off their coats, and tossed handfuls of dust into the air.

Paul Reveals His Roman Citizenship

24The commander brought Paul inside and ordered him lashed with whips to make him confess his crime. He wanted to find out why the crowd had become so furious. 25As they tied Paul down to lash him, Paul said to the officer standing there, "Is it legal for you to whip a Roman citizen who hasn't even been tried?"

26The officer went to the commander and asked, "What are you doing? This man is a Roman citizen!"

27So the commander went over and asked Paul, "Tell me, are you a Roman citizen?"

"Yes, I certainly am," Paul replied.

28"I am, too," the commander muttered, "and it cost me plenty!"

"But I am a citizen by birth!"

29The soldiers who were about to interrogate Paul quickly withdrew when they heard he was a Roman citizen, and the commander was frightened because he had ordered him bound and whipped.

Paul before the High Council

30The next day the commander freed Paul from his chains and ordered the leading priests into session with the Jewish high council.* He had Paul brought in before them to try to find out what the trouble was all about.

CHAPTER 23
Gazing intently at the high council,* Paul began: "Brothers, I have always lived before God in all good conscience!"

2Instantly Ananias the high priest commanded those close to Paul to slap him on the mouth. 3But Paul said to him, "God will slap you, you whitewashed wall! What kind of judge are you to break the law yourself by ordering me struck like that?"

4Those standing near Paul said to him, "Is that the way to talk to God's high priest?"

5"I'm sorry, brothers. I didn't realize he was the high priest," Paul replied, "for the Scriptures say, 'Do not speak evil of anyone who rules over you.'*"

6Paul realized that some members of the high council were Sadducees and some were Pharisees, so he shouted, "Brothers, I am a Pharisee, as were all my ancestors! And I am on trial because my hope is in the resurrection of the dead!"

7This divided the council—the Pharisees against the Sadducees—8for the Sadducees say there is no resurrection or angels or spirits, but the Pharisees believe in all of these. 9So a great clamor arose. Some of the teachers of religious law who were Pharisees jumped up to argue that Paul was all right. "We see nothing wrong with him," they shouted. "Perhaps a spirit or an angel spoke to him." 10The shouting grew louder and louder, and the men were tugging at Paul from both sides, pulling him this way and that. Finally, the commander, fearing they would tear him apart, ordered his soldiers to take him away from them and bring him back to the fortress.

11That night the Lord appeared to Paul and said, "Be encouraged, Paul. Just as you have told the people about me here in Jerusalem, you must preach the Good News in Rome."

The Plan to Kill Paul

12The next morning a group of Jews got together and bound themselves with an oath to neither eat nor drink until they had killed Paul. 13There were more than forty of them. 14They went to the leading priests and other leaders and told them what they had done. "We have bound ourselves under oath to neither eat nor drink until we have killed Paul. 15You and the high council should tell the commander to bring Paul back to the

22:30 Greek *Sanhedrin*. **23:1** Greek *Sanhedrin;* also in 23:6, 15, 20, 28. **23:5** Exod 22:28.

23:12-35 Paul's brave, young nephew risked his life to warn his uncle of a plot against his life. With this intelligence information, the Roman commander made adjustments in his plan and moved Paul safely to Caesarea. A military escort accompanied Paul on his journey that very night, and a cover letter to Governor Felix won Paul another chance to speak for himself and for God. Thus God providentially worked through various people to move Paul one step closer to Rome. God uses people—little children and governors alike—to accomplish his divine will.

council again," they requested. "Pretend you want to examine his case more fully. We will kill him on the way."

16But Paul's nephew heard of their plan and went to the fortress and told Paul. 17Paul called one of the officers and said, "Take this young man to the commander. He has something important to tell him."

18So the officer did, explaining, "Paul, the prisoner, called me over and asked me to bring this young man to you because he has something to tell you."

19The commander took him by the arm, led him aside, and asked, "What is it you want to tell me?"

20Paul's nephew told him, "Some Jews are going to ask you to bring Paul before the Jewish high council tomorrow, pretending they want to get some more information. 21But don't do it! There are more than forty men hiding along the way ready to jump him and kill him. They have vowed not to eat or drink until they kill him. They are ready, expecting you to agree to their request."

22"Don't let a soul know you told me this," the commander warned the young man as he sent him away.

Paul Is Sent to Caesarea

23Then the commander called two of his officers and ordered, "Get two hundred soldiers ready to leave for Caesarea at nine o'clock tonight. Also take two hundred spearmen and seventy horsemen. 24Provide horses for Paul to ride, and get him safely to Governor Felix." 25Then he wrote this letter to the governor:

26"From Claudius Lysias, to his Excellency, Governor Felix. Greetings! 27This man was seized by some Jews, and they were about to kill him when I arrived with the troops. When I learned that he was a Roman citizen, I removed him to safety. 28Then I took him to their high council to try to find out what he had done. 29I soon discovered it was something regarding their religious law—certainly nothing worthy of imprisonment or death. 30But when I was informed of a plot to kill him, I immediately sent him on to you. I have

told his accusers to bring their charges before you."

31So that night, as ordered, the soldiers took Paul as far as Antipatris. 32They returned to the fortress the next morning, while the horsemen took him on to Caesarea. 33When they arrived in Caesarea, they presented Paul and the letter to Governor Felix. 34He read it and then asked Paul what province he was from. "Cilicia," Paul answered.

35"I will hear your case myself when your accusers arrive," the governor told him. Then the governor ordered him kept in the prison at Herod's headquarters.

CHAPTER 24
Paul Appears before Felix

Five days later Ananias, the high priest, arrived with some of the Jewish leaders and the lawyer* Tertullus, to press charges against Paul. 2When Paul was called in, Tertullus laid charges against Paul in the following address to the governor:

"Your Excellency, you have given peace to us Jews and have enacted reforms for us. 3And for all of this we are very grateful to you. 4But lest I bore you, kindly give me your attention for only a moment as I briefly outline our case against this man. 5For we have found him to be a troublemaker, a man who is constantly inciting the Jews throughout the world to riots and rebellions against the Roman government. He is a ringleader of the sect known as the Nazarenes. 6Moreover he was trying to defile the Temple when we arrested him.* 8You can find out the truth of our accusations by examining him yourself." 9Then the other Jews chimed in, declaring that everything Tertullus said was true.

10Now it was Paul's turn. The governor motioned for him to rise and speak. Paul said, "I know, sir, that you have been a judge of Jewish affairs for many years, and this gives me confidence as I make my defense. 11You can quickly discover that it was no more than twelve days ago that I arrived in Jerusalem to worship at the Temple. 12I didn't argue with anyone in the Temple, nor did I incite a riot in any synagogue or on the streets of the city.

24:1 Greek *some elders and an orator.* **24:6** Some manuscripts add *We would have judged him by our law,* 7*but Lysias, the commander of the garrison, came and took him violently away from us,* 8*commanding his accusers to come before you.*

24:26-27 Felix made no decision on Paul's case. He probably was afraid that if he set Paul free, the Jews would rebel. Felix left Paul in prison for two years. Perhaps he hoped Paul would bribe him to buy his release. No doubt the miserable prison conditions challenged Paul to the depth of his being. By the grace of God he patiently endured his years in bondage. Paul depended on God to help him one day at a time; we can do the same.

[13]These men certainly cannot prove the things they accuse me of doing.

[14]"But I admit that I follow the Way, which they call a sect. I worship the God of our ancestors, and I firmly believe the Jewish law and everything written in the books of prophecy. [15]I have hope in God, just as these men do, that he will raise both the righteous and the ungodly. [16]Because of this, I always try to maintain a clear conscience before God and everyone else.

[17]"After several years away, I returned to Jerusalem with money to aid my people and to offer sacrifices to God. [18]My accusers saw me in the Temple as I was completing a purification ritual. There was no crowd around me and no rioting. [19]But some Jews from the province of Asia were there—and they ought to be here to bring charges if they have anything against me! [20]Ask these men here what wrongdoing the Jewish high council* found in me, [21]except for one thing I said when I shouted out, 'I am on trial before you today because I believe in the resurrection of the dead!'"

[22]Felix, who was quite familiar with the Way, adjourned the hearing and said, "Wait until Lysias, the garrison commander, arrives. Then I will decide the case." [23]He ordered an officer to keep Paul in custody but to give him some freedom and allow his friends to visit him and take care of his needs.

[24]A few days later Felix came with his wife, Drusilla, who was Jewish. Sending for Paul, they listened as he told them about faith in Christ Jesus. [25]As he reasoned with them about righteousness and self-control and the judgment to come, Felix was terrified. "Go away for now," he replied. "When it is more convenient, I'll call for you again." [26]He also hoped that Paul would bribe him, so he sent for him quite often and talked with him.

[27]Two years went by in this way; then Felix was succeeded by Porcius Festus. And because Felix wanted to gain favor with the Jewish leaders, he left Paul in prison.

CHAPTER 25
Paul Appears before Festus

Three days after Festus arrived in Caesarea to take over his new responsibilities, he left for Jerusalem, [2]where the leading priests and other Jewish leaders met with him and made their accusations against Paul. [3]They asked Festus as a favor to transfer Paul to Jerusalem. (Their plan was to waylay and kill him.) [4]But Festus replied that Paul was at Caesarea and he himself would be returning there soon. [5]So he said, "Those of you in authority can return with me. If Paul has done anything wrong, you can make your accusations."

[6]Eight or ten days later he returned to Caesarea, and on the following day Paul's trial began. [7]On Paul's arrival in court, the Jewish leaders from Jerusalem gathered around and made many serious accusations they couldn't prove. [8]Paul denied the charges. "I am not guilty," he said. "I have committed no crime against the Jewish laws or the Temple or the Roman government."

[9]Then Festus, wanting to please the Jews, asked him, "Are you willing to go to Jerusalem and stand trial before me there?"

[10]But Paul replied, "No! This is the official Roman court, so I ought to be tried right here. You know very well I am not guilty. [11]If I have done something worthy of death, I don't refuse to die. But if I am innocent, neither you nor anyone else has a right to turn me over to these men to kill me. I appeal to Caesar!"

[12]Festus conferred with his advisers and then replied, "Very well! You have appealed to Caesar, and to Caesar you shall go!"

[13]A few days later King Agrippa arrived with his sister, Bernice,* to pay their respects to Festus. [14]During their stay of several days, Festus discussed Paul's case with the king. "There is a prisoner here," he told him, "whose case was left for me by Felix. [15]When I was in Jerusalem, the leading priests and other Jewish leaders pressed charges against him and asked me to sentence him. [16]Of course, I quickly pointed out to them that Roman law does not

24:20 Greek *Sanhedrin.* 25:13 Greek *Agrippa the king and Bernice arrived.*

26:1-23 This is the third account of Paul's conversion in the book of Acts (see 9:1-20; 22:1-21). Paul had become quite skilled at sharing his story with anyone who would listen. Before meeting Christ, Paul was a powerful enemy of the Christian faith and did horrible things to try and stop its growth. When Paul met Jesus in a dramatic way, it led to his painful spiritual awakening. After his conversion Paul preached to others who needed to hear the message of God's salvation. If we aren't sure how to share our story with others, it might help to follow Paul's example by telling others what happened in our life before, during, and after we experienced God's deliverance.

convict people without a trial. They are given an opportunity to defend themselves face to face with their accusers.

17"When they came here for the trial, I called the case the very next day and ordered Paul brought in. 18But the accusations made against him weren't at all what I expected. 19It was something about their religion and about someone called Jesus who died, but whom Paul insists is alive. 20I was perplexed as to how to conduct an investigation of this kind, and I asked him whether he would be willing to stand trial on these charges in Jerusalem. 21But Paul appealed to the emperor. So I ordered him back to jail until I could arrange to send him to Caesar."

22"I'd like to hear the man myself," Agrippa said.

And Festus replied, "You shall—tomorrow!"

Paul Speaks to Agrippa

23So the next day Agrippa and Bernice arrived at the auditorium with great pomp, accompanied by military officers and prominent men of the city. Festus ordered that Paul be brought in. 24Then Festus said, "King Agrippa and all present, this is the man whose death is demanded both by the local Jews and by those in Jerusalem. 25But in my opinion he has done nothing worthy of death. However, he appealed his case to the emperor, and I decided to send him. 26But what shall I write the emperor? For there is no real charge against him. So I have brought him before all of you, and especially you, King Agrippa, so that after we examine him, I might have something to write. 27For it doesn't seem reasonable to send a prisoner to the emperor without specifying the charges against him!"

CHAPTER 26
Then Agrippa said to Paul, "You may speak in your defense."

So Paul, with a gesture of his hand, started his defense: 2"I am fortunate, King Agrippa, that you are the one hearing my defense against all these accusations made by the Jewish leaders, 3for I know you are an expert on Jewish customs and controversies. Now please listen to me patiently!

4"As the Jewish leaders are well aware, I was given a thorough Jewish training from my earliest childhood among my own people and in Jerusalem. 5If they would admit it, they know that I have been a member of the Pharisees, the strictest sect of our religion.

STEP 5

Receiving Forgiveness

BIBLE READING: Acts 26:12-18

We admitted to God, to ourselves, and to another human being the exact nature of our wrongs.

As we work our recovery program, we go through a process of accepting the truth about our life and the consequences of our choices. We may feel that we have to earn forgiveness instead of just receiving it. We may find it easier to forgive others who have hurt us than to forgive ourself for the hurts we have caused.

When Jesus confronted the apostle Paul, he gave him this mission: "Now stand up! For I have appeared to you to appoint you as my servant and my witness. . . . Yes, I am going to send you to the Gentiles, to open their eyes so they may turn from darkness to light, and from the power of Satan to God. Then they will receive forgiveness for their sins and be given a place among God's people, who are set apart by faith in me" (Acts 26:16-18).

God's goal in sending his Word to us is that we may receive forgiveness. The process involves first opening our eyes to our true condition, which happens in Steps One, Two, and Four. This allows us the opportunity to repent, changing our mind so that we are in agreement with God and ready to admit our sins. God wants us to receive immediate forgiveness based on the finished work of Jesus Christ. We are not second-class citizens in the Kingdom of God. We don't have to work the rest of the Twelve Steps as a form of penance. Forgiveness awaits us right now if we will only receive it. *Turn to page 235, Romans 2.*

⁶Now I am on trial because I am looking forward to the fulfillment of God's promise made to our ancestors. ⁷In fact, that is why the twelve tribes of Israel worship God night and day, and they share the same hope I have. Yet, O king, they say it is wrong for me to have this hope! ⁸Why does it seem incredible to any of you that God can raise the dead?

⁹"I used to believe that I ought to do everything I could to oppose the followers of Jesus of Nazareth.* ¹⁰Authorized by the leading priests, I caused many of the believers in Jerusalem to be sent to prison. And I cast my vote against them when they were condemned to death. ¹¹Many times I had them whipped in the synagogues to try to get them to curse Christ. I was so violently opposed to them that I even hounded them in distant cities of foreign lands.

¹²"One day I was on such a mission to Damascus, armed with the authority and commission of the leading priests. ¹³About noon, Your Majesty, a light from heaven brighter than the sun shone down on me and my companions. ¹⁴We all fell down, and I heard a voice saying to me in Aramaic,* 'Saul, Saul, why are you persecuting me? It is hard for you to fight against my will.*'

¹⁵"'Who are you, sir?' I asked.

"And the Lord replied, 'I am Jesus, the one you are persecuting. ¹⁶Now stand up! For I have appeared to you to appoint you as my servant and my witness. You are to tell the world about this experience and about other times I will appear to you. ¹⁷And I will protect you from both your own people and the Gentiles. Yes, I am going to send you to the Gentiles, ¹⁸to open their eyes so they may turn from darkness to light, and from the power of Satan to God. Then they will receive forgiveness for their sins and be given a place among God's people, who are set apart by faith in me.'

¹⁹"And so, O King Agrippa, I was not disobedient to that vision from heaven. ²⁰I preached first to those in Damascus, then in Jerusalem and throughout all Judea, and also to the Gentiles, that all must turn from their sins and turn to God—and prove they have changed by the good things they do. ²¹Some Jews arrested me in the Temple for preaching this, and they tried to kill me. ²²But God protected me so that I am still alive today to tell these facts to everyone, from the least to the greatest. I teach nothing except what the prophets and Moses said would happen— ²³that the Messiah would suffer and be the first to rise from the dead as a light to Jews and Gentiles alike."

²⁴Suddenly, Festus shouted, "Paul, you are insane. Too much study has made you crazy!"

²⁵But Paul replied, "I am not insane, Most Excellent Festus. I am speaking the sober truth. ²⁶And King Agrippa knows about these things. I speak frankly, for I am sure these events are all familiar to him, for they were not done in a corner! ²⁷King Agrippa, do you believe the prophets? I know you do—"

²⁸Agrippa interrupted him. "Do you think you can make me a Christian so quickly?"*

²⁹Paul replied, "Whether quickly or not, I pray to God that both you and everyone here in this audience might become the same as I am, except for these chains."

³⁰Then the king, the governor, Bernice, and all the others stood and left. ³¹As they talked it over they agreed, "This man hasn't done anything worthy of death or imprisonment." ³²And Agrippa said to Festus, "He could be set free if he hadn't appealed to Caesar!"

CHAPTER 27
Paul Sails for Rome

When the time came, we set sail for Italy. Paul and several other prisoners were placed in the custody of an army officer named Julius, a captain of the Imperial Regiment.

26:9 Greek *oppose the name of Jesus the Nazarene.* **26:14a** Or *Hebrew.* **26:14b** Greek *It is hard for you to kick against the oxgoads.* **26:28** Or *"A little more, and your arguments would make me a Christian."*

26:19-23 Paul assured King Agrippa that he was suffering persecution, not because he had done anything wrong but because he was preaching the faith he had once tried to destroy. Paul showed that his preaching was in agreement with the Old Testament Scriptures. The basic teaching of the Old and New Testaments is that God desires to deliver all people from the power of sin and has done so perfectly through the work of God's anointed one—the Messiah. Knowing that God desires to save us is essential to the recovery process.

26:24-29 Paul was so concerned about the salvation of other people that he had little time to worry about his own problems. Here he risked his life to share his testimony with a man who had the power to have him killed. This conversation with King Agrippa shows Paul's burning desire to soften and reclaim even the most hardened hearts. For everyone in recovery it is helpful to get our eyes off our own afflictions and focus on the needs of others. As we help others discover the way to recovery, we will be freed from our self-centeredness and strengthened in our own recovery.

²And Aristarchus, a Macedonian from Thessalonica, was also with us. We left on a boat whose home port was Adramyttium; it was scheduled to make several stops at ports along the coast of the province of Asia.

³The next day when we docked at Sidon, Julius was very kind to Paul and let him go ashore to visit with friends so they could provide for his needs. ⁴Putting out to sea from there, we encountered headwinds that made it difficult to keep the ship on course, so we sailed north of Cyprus between the island and the mainland. ⁵We passed along the coast of the provinces of Cilicia and Pamphylia, landing at Myra, in the province of Lycia. ⁶There the officer found an Egyptian ship from Alexandria that was bound for Italy, and he put us on board.

⁷We had several days of rough sailing, and after great difficulty we finally neared Cnidus. But the wind was against us, so we sailed down to the leeward side of Crete, past the cape of Salmone. ⁸We struggled along the coast with great difficulty and finally arrived at Fair Havens, near the city of Lasea. ⁹We had lost a lot of time. The weather was becoming dangerous for long voyages by then because it was so late in the fall,* and Paul spoke to the ship's officers about it.

¹⁰"Sirs," he said, "I believe there is trouble ahead if we go on—shipwreck, loss of cargo, injuries, and danger to our lives." ¹¹But the officer in charge of the prisoners listened more to the ship's captain and the owner than to Paul. ¹²And since Fair Havens was an exposed harbor—a poor place to spend the winter—most of the crew wanted to go to Phoenix, farther up the coast of Crete, and spend the winter there. Phoenix was a good harbor with only a southwest and northwest exposure.

The Storm at Sea

¹³When a light wind began blowing from the south, the sailors thought they could make it. So they pulled up anchor and sailed along close to shore. ¹⁴But the weather changed abruptly, and a wind of typhoon strength (a "northeaster," they called it) caught the ship and blew it out to sea. ¹⁵They couldn't turn the ship into the wind, so they gave up and let it run before the gale.

¹⁶We sailed behind a small island named Cauda,* where with great difficulty we hoisted aboard the lifeboat that was being towed behind us. ¹⁷Then we banded the ship with ropes to strengthen the hull. The sailors were afraid of being driven across to the sandbars of Syrtis off the African coast, so they lowered the sea anchor and were thus driven before the wind.

¹⁸The next day, as gale-force winds continued to batter the ship, the crew began throwing the cargo overboard. ¹⁹The following day they even threw out the ship's equipment and anything else they could lay their hands on. ²⁰The terrible storm raged unabated for many days, blotting out the sun and the stars, until at last all hope was gone.

²¹No one had eaten for a long time. Finally, Paul called the crew together and said, "Men, you should have listened to me in the first place and not left Fair Havens. You would have avoided all this injury and loss. ²²But take courage! None of you will lose your lives, even though the ship will go down. ²³For last night an angel of the God to whom I belong and whom I serve stood beside me, ²⁴and he said, 'Don't be afraid, Paul, for you will surely stand trial before Caesar! What's more, God in his goodness has granted safety to everyone sailing with you.' ²⁵So take courage! For I believe God. It will be just as

27:9 Greek *because the fast was now already gone by*. This fast happened on the Day of Atonement (*Yom Kippur*), which occurred in late September or early October. **27:16** Some manuscripts read *Clauda*.

27:1-15 It was God's plan that Paul go to Rome, but his journey there was hardly straightforward. After years in prison, Paul was finally put on a ship bound for Rome; he arrived there only after surviving a life-threatening storm and shipwreck. Paul had no control over the means or timing of getting to his destination. But Paul knew God wanted him in Rome and was confident he would eventually get there. We can be sure that God wants us to make progress in recovery. Yet, like Paul, we don't have complete control over the route we will take to get there. Faithfulness does not ensure a life without storms or shipwrecks. Yet God guarantees that his presence and power will be with us and that we will arrive at our ultimate destination.
27:13-26 After two storm-tossed weeks, the sailors had given up hope, and everyone was hungry and terrified. Yet Paul urged all to believe his promise from God that they would survive. The fate of 276 people—passengers and crew—hung in the balance. Paul's courageous faith was met with assurances that he would reach Rome, yet not without hardships. Life in recovery is often like that. We are assured by faith of a positive outcome, but it is usually attained by persevering through difficult times.

he said. [26]But we will be shipwrecked on an island."

The Shipwreck

[27]About midnight on the fourteenth night of the storm, as we were being driven across the Sea of Adria,* the sailors sensed land was near. [28]They took soundings and found the water was only 120 feet deep. A little later they sounded again and found only 90 feet.* [29]At this rate they were afraid we would soon be driven against the rocks along the shore, so they threw out four anchors from the stern and prayed for daylight. [30]Then the sailors tried to abandon the ship; they lowered the lifeboat as though they were going to put out anchors from the prow. [31]But Paul said to the commanding officer and the soldiers, "You will all die unless the sailors stay aboard." [32]So the soldiers cut the ropes and let the boat fall off.

[33]As the darkness gave way to the early morning light, Paul begged everyone to eat. "You haven't touched food for two weeks," he said. [34]"Please eat something now for your own good. For not a hair of your heads will perish." [35]Then he took some bread, gave thanks to God before them all, and broke off a piece and ate it. [36]Then everyone was encouraged, [37]and all 276 of us began eating—for that is the number we had aboard. [38]After eating, the crew lightened the ship further by throwing the cargo of wheat overboard.

[39]When morning dawned, they didn't recognize the coastline, but they saw a bay with a beach and wondered if they could get between the rocks and get the ship safely to shore. [40]So they cut off the anchors and left them in the sea. Then they lowered the rudders, raised the foresail, and headed toward shore. [41]But the ship hit a shoal and ran aground. The bow of the ship stuck fast, while the stern was repeatedly smashed by the force of the waves and began to break apart.

[42]The soldiers wanted to kill the prisoners to make sure they didn't swim ashore and escape. [43]But the commanding officer wanted to spare Paul, so he didn't let them carry out their plan. Then he ordered all who could swim to jump overboard first and make for land, [44]and he told the others to try for it on planks and debris from the broken ship. So everyone escaped safely ashore!

CHAPTER 28
Paul on the Island of Malta

Once we were safe on shore, we learned that we were on the island of Malta. [2]The people of the island were very kind to us. It was cold and rainy, so they built a fire on the shore to welcome us and warm us.

[3]As Paul gathered an armful of sticks and was laying them on the fire, a poisonous snake, driven out by the heat, fastened itself onto his hand. [4]The people of the island saw it hanging there and said to each other, "A murderer, no doubt! Though he escaped the sea, justice will not permit him to live." [5]But Paul shook off the snake into the fire and was unharmed. [6]The people waited for him to swell up or suddenly drop dead. But when they had waited a long time and saw no harm come to him, they changed their minds and decided he was a god.

[7]Near the shore where we landed was an estate belonging to Publius, the chief official of the island. He welcomed us courteously and fed us for three days. [8]As it happened, Publius's father was ill with fever and dysentery. Paul went in and prayed for him, and laying his hands on him, he healed him. [9]Then all the other sick people on the island came and were cured. [10]As a result we were showered with honors, and when the time came to sail, people put on board all sorts of things we would need for the trip.

27:27 The *Sea of Adria* is in the central Mediterranean; it is not to be confused with the Adriatic Sea. **27:28** Greek *20 fathoms . . . 15 fathoms* [37 meters . . . 27 meters].

27:27-42 Earlier the ship's captain and owner had ignored Paul (27:9-12), but this time they listened carefully (27:30-32). Paul assured them that even though the ship would be destroyed, all the passengers would reach land safely. The next day the ship ran aground and was destroyed by the winds and waves. But all the passengers were safe. Few of us have an awareness of the future like Paul did. But we can have the same confidence in God's power to protect us when we follow his will. We can have success in recovery by walking obediently by faith, one step at a time.
28:1-10 The ship's crew and passengers spent the winter safely on the island of Malta. If stormy seas and a shipwreck couldn't thwart God's plan for Paul, neither would the bite of a poisonous snake. Paul was bitten by a deadly snake, yet he suffered no ill effects. While Paul was deterred from reaching Rome, he helped the people around him. To Paul, even obstacles were opportunities to serve others and share his faith. As we work through the process of recovery, we too can turn our obstacles into wonderful opportunities for growth and service.

Paul Arrives at Rome

¹¹It was three months after the shipwreck that we set sail on another ship that had wintered at the island—an Alexandrian ship with the twin gods* as its figurehead. ¹²Our first stop was Syracuse,* where we stayed three days. ¹³From there we sailed across to Rhegium.* A day later a south wind began blowing, so the following day we sailed up the coast to Puteoli. ¹⁴There we found some believers,* who invited us to stay with them seven days. And so we came to Rome.

¹⁵The brothers and sisters* in Rome had heard we were coming, and they came to meet us at the Forum* on the Appian Way. Others joined us at The Three Taverns.* When Paul saw them, he thanked God and took courage.

¹⁶When we arrived in Rome, Paul was permitted to have his own private lodging, though he was guarded by a soldier.

Paul Preaches at Rome under Guard

¹⁷Three days after Paul's arrival, he called together the local Jewish leaders. He said to them, "Brothers, I was arrested in Jerusalem and handed over to the Roman government, even though I had done nothing against our people or the customs of our ancestors. ¹⁸The Romans tried me and wanted to release me, for they found no cause for the death sentence. ¹⁹But when the Jewish leaders protested the decision, I felt it necessary to appeal to Caesar, even though I had no desire to press charges against my own people. ²⁰I asked you to come here today so we could get acquainted and so I could tell you that I am bound with this chain because I believe that the hope of Israel—the Messiah—has already come."

²¹They replied, "We have heard nothing against you. We have had no letters from Judea or reports from anyone who has arrived here. ²²But we want to hear what you believe, for the only thing we know about these Christians* is that they are denounced everywhere."

²³So a time was set, and on that day a large number of people came to Paul's house. He told them about the Kingdom of God and taught them about Jesus from the Scriptures—from the five books of Moses and the books of the prophets. He began lecturing in the morning and went on into the evening. ²⁴Some believed and some didn't. ²⁵But after they had argued back and forth among themselves, they left with this final word from Paul: "The Holy Spirit was right when he said to our ancestors through Isaiah the prophet,

²⁶ 'Go and say to my people,
You will hear my words,
    but you will not understand;
you will see what I do,
    but you will not perceive its meaning.
²⁷ For the hearts of these people are hardened,
    and their ears cannot hear,
    and they have closed their eyes—
so their eyes cannot see,
    and their ears cannot hear,
    and their hearts cannot understand,
and they cannot turn to me
    and let me heal them.'*

²⁸So I want you to realize that this salvation from God is also available to the Gentiles, and they will accept it."*

³⁰For the next two years, Paul lived in his own rented house.* He welcomed all who visited him, ³¹proclaiming the Kingdom of God with all boldness and teaching about the Lord Jesus Christ. And no one tried to stop him.

28:11 The *twin gods* were the Roman gods Castor and Pollux. **28:12** *Syracuse* was on the island of Sicily. **28:13** *Rhegium* was on the southern tip of Italy. **28:14** Greek *brothers*. **28:15a** Greek *brothers*. **28:15b** *The Forum* was about 43 miles (70 kilometers) from Rome. **28:15c** *The Three Taverns* was about 35 miles (57 kilometers) from Rome. **28:22** Greek *this sect*. **28:26-27** Isa 6:9-10. **28:28** Some manuscripts add verse 29, *And when he had said these words, the Jews departed, greatly disagreeing with each other.* **28:30** Or *at his own expense.*

28:30-31 Even under house arrest, Paul experienced the peace and contentment that come only by following God's will. Paul carried the message of salvation to people in need through all circumstances in his life. His life is an example to each of us, showing the importance and benefits of persisting in our relationship with God and sharing our faith. As we know God better, learn to trust in his love and power, and share this power for recovery with others, we can live each new day with serenity and courage.

REFLECTIONS ON ACTS

*insights CONCERNING THE HOLY SPIRIT

In **Acts 2:5-15,** when the Holy Spirit came in power, the results were immediately apparent in the believers, especially Peter. This man, who had previously failed to live up to his commitment to Christ (Luke 22:54-62), was now confidently preaching and helping others discover this new power for living. When we experience God's power in our life, we will never be the same, nor will we be able to keep the Good News to ourself.

*insights FROM THE EARLY CHRISTIAN COMMUNITY

As the Christian community grew, various problems arose. One such problem is mentioned in **Acts 6:1** concerning the distribution of food to needy widows. The conflict was apparently rooted in the cultural differences between the various church members. Most of the church members were Hebrew-speaking Palestinian Jews, but there were also Greek-speaking Jews among them who had been raised outside of Palestine. Apparently, the Greek-speaking Jews were being neglected by the Jews native to Palestine. Relationships within the church, as well as in the recovery movement, can be stretched, even broken, if members refuse to accept each other. As we humbly recognize our own need for God's gracious forgiveness, we will have less trouble accepting others who are different from us.

*insights FROM PHILIP'S LIFE

In **Acts 8:26-40** Philip was called to share the Good News with an Ethiopian eunuch. Philip is an excellent model of how we can effectively engage in this important recovery activity. He didn't rush in and start preaching. He took time to understand where the Ethiopian was concerning his faith. Then he proceeded humbly and confidently to share God's truth—that Jesus is the Messiah and that through him we can experience deliverance from sin and its power. Sharing our faith as Philip did takes time; it requires patience and sensitivity. But as we follow Philip's example, we will learn to share our faith with not only words but also with deeds.

*insights FROM PAUL'S LIFE

In **Acts 9:3-9** Paul is traveling to Damascus to persecute the Christians there. As he neared his destination, he was suddenly struck down by a brilliant light from heaven. Blind and helpless, Paul was led to Damascus to await further instructions from God. For three days he ate and drank nothing. He was forced into a period of rigorous self-examination. This kind of experience is often helpful in recovery. Some of us may have been confronted suddenly and dramatically with the painful truth about our life. But whether it happened with a bang or with a whisper, we all have come face to face with our sins and character flaws. Recovery begins as we discover our helplessness; it continues with honest self-examination and continued dependence on God's power.

ROMANS

THE BIG PICTURE

The church in Rome was a testimony to God's power. It had flourished despite the obstacles posed by the surrounding pagan culture. Yet these believers were not perfect; in fact, they had some serious problems. Though they were well established in their faith, their convictions and unity as a group were threatened by racial and cultural division.

The main topic in this letter is the gospel—the good news that salvation from sin is available through Jesus Christ. At the core of the gospel is the truth that God is bigger than the past. No matter who we are or what we have done, we can be saved by grace (undeserved favor from God) through faith (complete trust) in Christ. We can stand before God, justified—declared "not guilty." That's good news!

In Romans Paul explains four major points. First, God makes no distinction between us as individuals—we are all guilty, and we are all offered his free gift of salvation. Second, we can all be freed from sin's power through God's grace and the Holy Spirit within us. Third, we are all "in recovery" and therefore have no grounds for arrogance. And fourth, because of God's mercy we all must respect one another, despite our differences.

Many people have called this letter the greatest theological treatise ever written, but it's really a letter about how to live. It teaches us how to deal with our sinful attitudes and behaviors and tells us how to get back on the right track. Paul's letter applies directly to us, showing us how to recover from the effects of sin and dysfunction in our life.

THE BOTTOM LINE

PURPOSE: To introduce Paul to the church at Rome and summarize his message before he arrived there. AUTHOR: The apostle Paul. AUDIENCE: The church at Rome. DATE WRITTEN: A.D. 57, from Corinth, just before Paul's return to Jerusalem. SETTING: Paul wrote this letter in anticipation of a future visit to the believers in Rome. KEY VERSES: "And I am convinced that nothing can ever separate us from his love. Death can't, and life can't. The angels can't, and the demons can't. Our fears for today, our worries about tomorrow, and even the powers of hell can't keep God's love away. . . . Nothing in all creation will ever be able to separate us from the love of God" (8:38-39). KEY PEOPLE AND RELATIONSHIPS: Paul with the believers in Rome and with Phoebe, who helped Paul in his ministry.

RECOVERY THEMES

Our Universal Need: All of us have sinned; we have all fallen short of God's glorious standard. Regardless of whether we have fallen deeply into a controlling addiction, been abused by dysfunctional family members, or escaped severe trauma—we are all in need of recovery from sin of one kind or another. Ever since Adam and Eve rebelled against God, our nature has been to disobey him; we have been addicted to ignoring God's will. We are all powerless in our sin and need God to save us.

God's Power to Deliver: Our need for recovery involves the need to be forgiven and to forgive, as well as to be cleansed from the effects of the past. Although we are powerless to help ourself and don't really deserve to be helped, God, in his great love, reaches out to us, offering to forgive us, cleanse us, and empower us to become what he wants us to be. This is truly good news! Our part is to admit our powerlessness and turn our life and will over to this powerful, loving God.

Recovery Leads to Freedom: Because God has attacked our problems at the roots—that is, he has made it possible for us to be freed from our sins—we can be free from our controlling addiction. Through God's power, our life can become manageable. Although the process is never easy, over time we can become more and more like Christ as we walk one day at a time with him. The better we know him, the more empowered we can be. By continuing to take inventory, confessing our sins, asking for his forgiveness, and seeking to make amends to those whom we have wronged, we can experience true freedom.

The Role of Faith: Much of this letter describes the importance of faith or trust in God. "It is through faith that a righteous person has life" (1:17). There is no other way to recovery; the role of faith is central. The recovery process began with faith when we turned our will and our life over to God, and each step of the way built on that first step of faith. There is no magic formula for this—it is a daily act of trusting our all-powerful God, who promises never to forsake us and to always love us no matter how unlovable we are.

CHAPTER 1
Greetings from Paul
This letter is from Paul, Jesus Christ's slave, chosen by God to be an apostle and sent out to preach his Good News. ²This Good News was promised long ago by God through his prophets in the holy Scriptures. ³It is the Good News about his Son, Jesus, who came as a man, born into King David's royal family line. ⁴And Jesus Christ our Lord was shown to be the Son of God when God powerfully raised him from the dead by means of the Holy Spirit.* ⁵Through Christ, God has given us the privilege and authority to tell Gentiles everywhere what God has done for them, so that they will believe and obey him, bringing glory to his name.

⁶You are among those who have been called to belong to Jesus Christ, ⁷dear friends in Rome. God loves you dearly, and he has called you to be his very own people.

May grace and peace be yours from God our Father and the Lord Jesus Christ.

God's Good News
⁸Let me say first of all that your faith in God is becoming known throughout the world. How I thank God through Jesus Christ for

1:4 Or *the Spirit of holiness.*

1:1 In this letter Paul introduced himself as a slave of Jesus Christ. Paul was a Roman citizen; for him to choose a life of slavery was unthinkable. But Paul purposely used this word to demonstrate his humility and dependence upon God. Paul demonstrated the type of humility we need in recovery. We make progress in recovery when we recognize how helpless we are and how much we need God. Only when we joyfully submit to God's will for our life can we begin the recovery process.
1:16-17 All of us have failed in one way or another, and we all know what shame feels like. We are ashamed of our past failures, our bad habits, or even the abuses we have suffered. Paul tells us that the Good News of Jesus Christ is God's power to deliver us from all the shameful things in our life. And it's for everyone! God has the power to deliver and transform us when we turn our life over to him. The Good News of salvation is certainly nothing to be ashamed of!
1:21-32 When we refuse to admit our powerlessness and hold on to our self-sufficiency, we follow the downward path that Paul describes here. First, we exchange worship of God for worship of things—our addiction or compulsion. Second, we exchange our worship of the living God for a willful form of sin. Third, we move beyond these forms of sin to deep denial—we believe lies and reject truth. This passage describes lives that have become totally unmanageable, the natural consequence of refusing to acknowledge God. The only way to escape such destruction is to recognize our powerlessness and turn our life over to God.

each one of you. ⁹God knows how often I pray for you. Day and night I bring you and your needs in prayer to God, whom I serve with all my heart* by telling others the Good News about his Son.

¹⁰One of the things I always pray for is the opportunity, God willing, to come at last to see you. ¹¹For I long to visit you so I can share a spiritual blessing with you that will help you grow strong in the Lord. ¹²I'm eager to encourage you in your faith, but I also want to be encouraged by yours. In this way, each of us will be a blessing to the other.

¹³I want you to know, dear brothers and sisters,* that I planned many times to visit you, but I was prevented until now. I want to work among you and see good results, just as I have done among other Gentiles. ¹⁴For I have a great sense of obligation to people in our culture and to people in other cultures,* to the educated and uneducated alike. ¹⁵So I am eager to come to you in Rome, too, to preach God's Good News.

¹⁶For I am not ashamed of this Good News about Christ. It is the power of God at work, saving everyone who believes—Jews first and also Gentiles. ¹⁷This Good News tells us how God makes us right in his sight. This is accomplished from start to finish by faith. As the Scriptures say, "It is through faith that a righteous person has life."*

God's Anger at Sin

¹⁸But God shows his anger from heaven against all sinful, wicked people who push the truth away from themselves.* ¹⁹For the truth about God is known to them instinctively.* God has put this knowledge in their hearts. ²⁰From the time the world was created, people have seen the earth and sky and all that God made. They can clearly see his invisible qualities—his eternal power and divine nature. So they have no excuse whatsoever for not knowing God.

²¹Yes, they knew God, but they wouldn't worship him as God or even give him thanks. And they began to think up foolish ideas of what God was like. The result was that their minds became dark and confused. ²²Claiming to be wise, they became utter fools instead. ²³And instead of worshiping the glorious, ever-living God, they worshiped idols made to look like mere people, or birds and animals and snakes.

1:9 Or *in my spirit.* **1:13** Greek *brothers.* **1:14** Greek *to Greeks and to barbarians.* **1:17** Hab 2:4. **1:18** Or *who prevent the truth from being known.* **1:19** Greek *is manifest in them.*

STEP 2

Coming to Believe

BIBLE READING: Romans 1:18-20

We came to believe that a Power greater than ourselves could restore us to sanity. Saying that we "came to believe" suggests a process. Belief is the result of consideration, doubt, reasoning, and concluding. The ability to form beliefs is part of what it means to be made in God's image. It involves emotion and logic. It leads to action. What, then, is the process that leads us to solid belief and changes our life?

We start with our own experiences, and we see what doesn't work. Looking at the condition of our life, we realize that we don't have enough power to overcome our dependency. We try with all our might, but to no avail. When we are quiet enough to listen, we hear that still, small voice inside us saying, "There is a God, and he is extremely powerful." The apostle Paul said it this way: "For the truth about God is known to [all people] instinctively. God has put this knowledge in their hearts" (Romans 1:19).

Recognizing our internal weaknesses is the first step toward recovery. When we look beyond ourself, we see that there are others who have struggled with an addiction and recovered. We know that they, too, were unable to heal themselves, yet they now live free of addictive behaviors. We conclude that there must be a greater Power that helped them. Since we can see the similarities between their struggles and our own, we come to believe that our powerful God can restore us to sanity. This is where many people are when they get to Step Two, and it's a good place to be on the way to recovery. *Turn to page 391, Hebrews 11.*

²⁴So God let them go ahead and do whatever shameful things their hearts desired. As a result, they did vile and degrading things with each other's bodies. ²⁵Instead of believing what they knew was the truth about God, they deliberately chose to believe lies. So they worshiped the things God made but not the Creator himself, who is to be praised forever. Amen.

²⁶That is why God abandoned them to their shameful desires. Even the women turned against the natural way to have sex and instead indulged in sex with each other. ²⁷And the men, instead of having normal sexual relationships with women, burned with lust for each other. Men did shameful things with other men and, as a result, suffered within themselves the penalty they so richly deserved.

²⁸When they refused to acknowledge God, he abandoned them to their evil minds and let them do things that should never be done. ²⁹Their lives became full of every kind of wickedness, sin, greed, hate, envy, murder, fighting, deception, malicious behavior, and gossip. ³⁰They are backstabbers, haters of God, insolent, proud, and boastful. They are forever inventing new ways of sinning and are disobedient to their parents. ³¹They refuse to understand, break their promises, and are heartless and unforgiving. ³²They are fully aware of God's death penalty for those who do these things, yet they go right ahead and do them anyway. And, worse yet, they encourage others to do them, too.

CHAPTER 2
God's Judgment of Sin

You may be saying, "What terrible people you have been talking about!" But you are just as bad, and you have no excuse! When you say they are wicked and should be punished, you are condemning yourself, for you do these very same things. ²And we know that God, in his justice, will punish anyone who does such things. ³Do you think that God will judge and condemn others for doing them and not judge you when you do them, too? ⁴Don't you realize how kind, tolerant, and patient God is with you? Or don't you care? Can't you see how kind he has been in giving you time to turn from your sin?

⁵But no, you won't listen. So you are storing up terrible punishment for yourself because of your stubbornness in refusing to turn from your sin. For there is going to come a day of judgment when God, the just judge of all the world, ⁶will judge all people according to what they have done. ⁷He will give eternal life to those who persist in doing what is good, seeking after the glory and honor and immortality that God offers. ⁸But he will pour out his anger and wrath on those who live for themselves, who refuse to obey the truth and practice evil deeds. ⁹There will be trouble and calamity for everyone who keeps on sinning—for the Jew first and also for the Gentile. ¹⁰But there will be glory and honor and peace from God for all who do good—for the Jew first and also for the Gentile. ¹¹For God does not show favoritism.

¹²God will punish the Gentiles when they sin, even though they never had God's written law. And he will punish the Jews when they sin, for they do have the law. ¹³For it is not merely knowing the law that brings God's approval. Those who obey the law will be declared right in

---

2:1-4 As we see people whose lives are wicked and completely out of control, it is easy to feel superior and point a finger at them. Paul quickly corrects the tendency to do this by showing that everyone is in the same boat. We all do things that are wrong; we hide all kinds of problems, habits, and sins in the dark recesses of our life. If we often apply this passage to other people, we probably really need to apply it to ourself. Recovery begins with an honest personal inventory.

2:5-16 God is impartial. He doesn't forgive us because we are members of a special group of people. He doesn't judge us by the way we talk, walk, or dress. He judges us by whether or not we obey and believe in him. The Jews of Paul's day believed that they had special privileges from God, but here we find that God treats all people the same. If we admit our failures and seek to follow God's will for us, we are his special people. We are also on the way to recovery. Some of us have felt like an outsider all our life, having been rejected by others because of our problems or failures. God will never reject us if we confess our sins, accept his forgiveness, and humbly obey him.

2:28-29 Paul made an important point very clear in these verses: God is concerned that our heart be open and obedient to him. Our outward religious or recovery activities are important only if they reflect our love for God and others. We can always fake recovery, just as we can fake our relationship with God. If we just go through the motions and make no real commitment to God, we cannot make progress for long. But if we are filled with his Spirit and motivated by our love for God and other people, no obstacle to recovery is too great to overcome.

God's sight. ¹⁴Even when Gentiles, who do not have God's written law, instinctively follow what the law says, they show that in their hearts they know right from wrong. ¹⁵They demonstrate that God's law is written within them, for their own consciences either accuse them or tell them they are doing what is right. ¹⁶The day will surely come when God, by Jesus Christ, will judge everyone's secret life. This is my message.

The Jews and the Law

¹⁷If you are a Jew, you are relying on God's law for your special relationship with him. You boast that all is well between yourself and God. ¹⁸Yes, you know what he wants; you know right from wrong because you have been taught his law. ¹⁹You are convinced that you are a guide for the blind and a beacon light for people who are lost in darkness without God. ²⁰You think you can instruct the ignorant and teach children the ways of God. For you are certain that in God's law you have complete knowledge and truth.

²¹Well then, if you teach others, why don't you teach yourself? You tell others not to steal, but do you steal? ²²You say it is wrong to commit adultery, but do you do it? You condemn idolatry, but do you steal from pagan temples? ²³You are so proud of knowing the law, but you dishonor God by breaking it. ²⁴No wonder the Scriptures say, "The world blasphemes the name of God because of you."*

²⁵The Jewish ceremony of circumcision is worth something only if you obey God's law. But if you don't obey God's law, you are no better off than an uncircumcised Gentile. ²⁶And if the Gentiles obey God's law, won't God give them all the rights and honors of being his own people? ²⁷In fact, uncircumcised Gentiles who keep God's law will be much better off than you Jews who are circumcised and know so much about God's law but don't obey it.

²⁸For you are not a true Jew just because you were born of Jewish parents or because you have gone through the Jewish ceremony of circumcision. ²⁹No, a true Jew is one whose heart is right with God. And true circumcision is not a cutting of the body but a change of heart produced by God's Spirit. Whoever has that kind of change seeks praise from God, not from people.

2:24 Isa 52:5.

STEP 5

Freedom through Confession

BIBLE READING: Romans 2:12-15

We admitted to God, to ourselves, and to another human being the exact nature of our wrongs.

All of us struggle with our conscience, trying to make peace within our own heart. We may deny what we have done, find excuses, or try to squirm out from beneath the full weight of our conduct. We may work hard to be "good," trying to counteract our wrongs. We do everything we can to even out the score. In order to put the past to rest, however, we must stop rationalizing our sins and admit the truth.

We are all born with a built-in alarm that alerts us when we do wrong. God holds everyone accountable: "In their hearts they know right from wrong. They demonstrate that God's law is written within them, for their own consciences either accuse them or tell them they are doing what is right" (Romans 2:14-15).

In Step Five we set out to stop this internal struggle and admit that wrong is wrong. It is time to be honest with God and ourself about our cover-ups and the exact nature of our wrongs. We need to admit the sins we have committed and the pain we have caused others. We may have spent years constructing alibis, coming up with excuses, and trying to plea-bargain. It is time to come clean. It is time to admit what we know deep down inside to be true: "Yes, I'm guilty as charged."

There is no real freedom without confession. What a relief it is to finally give up the weight of our lies and excuses. When we confess our sins, we will find the internal peace we lost so long ago. We will also be one step closer to recovery. *Turn to page 305, Galatians 6.*

CHAPTER 3
God Remains Faithful

Then what's the advantage of being a Jew? Is there any value in the Jewish ceremony of circumcision? ²Yes, being a Jew has many advantages. First of all, the Jews were entrusted with the whole revelation of God.*

³True, some of them were unfaithful; but just because they broke their promises, does that mean God will break his promises? ⁴Of course not! Though everyone else in the world is a liar, God is true. As the Scriptures say, "He will be proved right in what he says, and he will win his case in court."*

⁵"But," some say, "our sins serve a good purpose, for people will see God's goodness when he declares us sinners to be innocent. Isn't it unfair, then, for God to punish us?" (That is actually the way some people talk.) ⁶Of course not! If God is not just, how is he qualified to judge the world? ⁷"But," some might still argue, "how can God judge and condemn me as a sinner if my dishonesty highlights his truthfulness and brings him more glory?" ⁸If you follow that kind of thinking, however, you might as well say that the more we sin the better it is! Those who say such things deserve to be condemned, yet some slander me by saying this is what I preach!

All People Are Sinners

⁹Well then, are we Jews better than others?* No, not at all, for we have already shown that all people, whether Jews or Gentiles, are under the power of sin. ¹⁰As the Scriptures say,

"No one is good—
not even one.
¹¹No one has real understanding;
no one is seeking God.
¹²All have turned away from God;
all have gone wrong.
No one does good,
not even one."*
¹³"Their talk is foul, like the stench from an open grave.
Their speech is filled with lies."
"The poison of a deadly snake drips from their lips."*
¹⁴"Their mouths are full of cursing and bitterness."*
¹⁵"They are quick to commit murder.
¹⁶Wherever they go, destruction and misery follow them.
¹⁷They do not know what true peace is."*
¹⁸"They have no fear of God to restrain them."*

¹⁹Obviously, the law applies to those to whom it was given, for its purpose is to keep people from having excuses and to bring the entire world into judgment before God. ²⁰For no one can ever be made right in God's sight by doing what his law commands. For the more we know God's law, the clearer it becomes that we aren't obeying it.

3:2 Greek *the oracles of God.* 3:4 Ps 51:4. 3:9 Greek *Are we better?* 3:10-12 Pss 14:1-3; 53:1-3. 3:13 Pss 5:9; 140:3. 3:14 Ps 10:7. 3:15-17 Isa 59:7-8. 3:18 Ps 36:1.

3:20 The more we know about God's laws, God's heart, and God's claim on our life, the clearer it becomes that we don't measure up. God's Old Testament laws represent his will for us; following them leads to a godly life. But none of us can follow these ideals with our own power. We must recognize our need for God's gracious forgiveness and his power on a daily basis to help us follow his program for healthy living. When we fail in our walk with God, we can remind ourself that we are powerless without him. This is the first step back into the process of recovery.
3:21-26 This portion of Scripture clearly states why Jesus died on the cross. We are all made right with God through faith in Jesus Christ. None of us are so good that we don't need God; none of us are so bad that we are beyond the reach of God's loving grace. Jesus has declared us not guilty and set us free from God's anger. Salvation is freely given, but it was expensively purchased by God!
3:27 God deals with all people on the same basis, regardless of race or social class. In our day Paul might have said that God gives the same attention to the cry of the homeless alcoholic as he does to that of the richest person in the world. No one can earn God's acceptance. All must come to recovery through faith and trust in God. This leaves us nothing to boast about; none of us can be saved by anything we do or say. But there is no reason for us to hide from God either; nothing is so bad in our life that it cannot be forgiven completely by our gracious and loving God.
4:6-8 Many of us have failed desperately; we have hurt others in ways that cannot easily be repaired. What can we do about our guilt? King David was guilty of serious sins—adultery, deceit, and murder—yet when he acknowledged his guilt, confessed his sins to God, and experienced God's forgiveness, he found joy. Each of these steps was an act of faith, but the result was joy. Each of the steps we take in recovery is also an act of faith, but as we faithfully work each step, we will also experience God's forgiveness and joy.

Christ Took Our Punishment

²¹But now God has shown us a different way of being right in his sight—not by obeying the law but by the way promised in the Scriptures long ago. ²²We are made right in God's sight when we trust in Jesus Christ to take away our sins. And we all can be saved in this same way, no matter who we are or what we have done.

²³For all have sinned; all fall short of God's glorious standard. ²⁴Yet now God in his gracious kindness declares us not guilty. He has done this through Christ Jesus, who has freed us by taking away our sins. ²⁵For God sent Jesus to take the punishment for our sins and to satisfy God's anger against us. We are made right with God when we believe that Jesus shed his blood, sacrificing his life for us. God was being entirely fair and just when he did not punish those who sinned in former times. ²⁶And he is entirely fair and just in this present time when he declares sinners to be right in his sight because they believe in Jesus.

²⁷Can we boast, then, that we have done anything to be accepted by God? No, because our acquittal is not based on our good deeds. It is based on our faith. ²⁸So we are made right with God through faith and not by obeying the law.

²⁹After all, God is not the God of the Jews only, is he? Isn't he also the God of the Gentiles? Of course he is. ³⁰There is only one God, and there is only one way of being accepted by him. He makes people right with himself only by faith, whether they are Jews or Gentiles. ³¹Well then, if we emphasize faith, does this mean that we can forget about the law? Of course not! In fact, only when we have faith do we truly fulfill the law.

CHAPTER 4
The Faith of Abraham

Abraham was, humanly speaking, the founder of our Jewish nation. What were his experiences concerning this question of being saved by faith? ²Was it because of his good deeds that God accepted him? If so, he would have had something to boast about. But from God's point of view Abraham had no basis at all for pride. ³For the Scriptures tell us, "Abraham believed God, so God declared him to be righteous."*

⁴When people work, their wages are not a gift. Workers earn what they receive. ⁵But people are declared righteous because of their faith, not because of their work.

⁶King David spoke of this, describing the

Self-Perception

READ ROMANS 3:10-12

We may feel that we are different from other people—either much worse or much better. We may look down on ourself and continually compare ourself with "good" people. Or perhaps our addiction seems more socially acceptable than others. So we console ourself by looking down on others whose sins seem worse than ours.

"As the Scriptures say, 'No one is good—not even one. No one has real understanding; no one is seeking God. All have turned away from God; all have gone wrong'" (Romans 3:10-12).

The first chapter of Romans is often used to condemn sexual sins or sexual addictions. People tend to skip over the last few verses, which condemn the more "acceptable" sins such as backbiting, disobeying parents, or bragging. In the second chapter the apostle Paul speaks to people who see themselves as better than others: "You may be saying, 'What terrible people you have been talking about!' But you are just as bad, and you have no excuse! When you say they are wicked and should be punished, you are condemning yourself, for you do these very same things" (Romans 2:1).

Every one of us is made of the same stuff—both good and bad. We may act out in different ways, but in God's eyes we are all the same. When we focus on admitting our wrongs, it helps us remember that we are not so different from others after all. As we call on God and admit our helplessness, we can begin the steps toward healing and recovery. *Turn to page 241, Romans 4.*

happiness of an undeserving sinner who is declared to be righteous:

7 "Oh, what joy for those whose
    disobedience is forgiven,
  whose sins are put out of sight.
8 Yes, what joy for those
  whose sin is no longer counted against
    them by the Lord."*

9 Now then, is this blessing only for the Jews, or is it for Gentiles, too? Well, what about Abraham? We have been saying he was declared righteous by God because of his faith. 10 But how did his faith help him? Was he declared righteous only after he had been circumcised, or was it before he was circumcised? The answer is that God accepted him first, and then he was circumcised later!

11 The circumcision ceremony was a sign that Abraham already had faith and that God had already accepted him and declared him to be righteous—even before he was circumcised. So Abraham is the spiritual father of those who have faith but have not been circumcised. They are made right with God by faith. 12 And Abraham is also the spiritual father of those who have been circumcised, but only if they have the same kind of faith Abraham had before he was circumcised.

13 It is clear, then, that God's promise to give the whole earth to Abraham and his descendants was not based on obedience to God's law, but on the new relationship with God that comes by faith. 14 So if you claim that God's promise is for those who obey God's law and think they are "good enough" in God's sight, then you are saying that faith is useless. And in that case, the promise is also meaningless. 15 But the law brings punishment on those who try to obey it. (The only way to avoid breaking the law is to have no law to break!)

16 So that's why faith is the key! God's promise is given to us as a free gift. And we are certain to receive it, whether or not we follow Jewish customs, if we have faith like Abraham's. For Abraham is the father of all who believe. 17 That is what the Scriptures mean when God told him, "I have made you the father of many nations."* This happened because Abraham believed in the God who brings the dead back to life and who brings into existence what didn't exist before.

18 When God promised Abraham that he would become the father of many nations, Abraham believed him. God had also said, "Your descendants will be as numerous as the stars,"* even though such a promise seemed utterly impossible! 19 And Abraham's faith did not weaken, even though he knew that he was too old to be a father at the age of one hundred and that Sarah, his wife, had never been able to have children.

20 Abraham never wavered in believing God's promise. In fact, his faith grew stronger, and in this he brought glory to God. 21 He was absolutely convinced that God was able to do anything he promised. 22 And because of Abraham's faith, God declared him to be righteous.

23 Now this wonderful truth—that God declared him to be righteous—wasn't just for Abraham's benefit. 24 It was for us, too, assuring us that God will also declare us to be righteous if we believe in God, who brought Jesus our Lord back from the dead. 25 He was handed over to die because of our sins, and he was raised from the dead to make us right with God.

4:7-8 Ps 32:1-2. 4:17 Gen 17:5. 4:18 Gen 15:5.

4:23-25 When we believe in God and the restoration he offers in Jesus Christ, an exchange takes place. We turn our unmanageable life over to God, including all our sins and guilt, and he gives us his goodness and forgiveness in return. When Jesus died on the cross, he took our sins and guilt away. When Jesus rose from the grave, God demonstrated his power to transform us and fill us with his goodness. As we follow God's program for restoration, we die to our sins and failures and experience a new and better life through God's power.
5:12-14 How can we be judged for something Adam did thousands of years ago? It doesn't seem fair. Many of us find it easy to blame others for our problems, citing our parents or even Adam and Eve as the cause of our failures and sins. Paul made it clear that Adam's sin and the sins of our ancestors are not our primary concern. Our problems may have started with the mistakes of others, but we have all solidly aligned ourselves with Adam by repeatedly making the same mistakes. We are made of the same stuff, prone to rebel against God and his ways. We will suffer the consequences for our sins if God doesn't intervene. We don't need fairness from God; we need his mercy. And that is what God provides for all who believe in him.

CHAPTER 5
Faith Brings Joy

Therefore, since we have been made right in God's sight by faith, we have peace with God because of what Jesus Christ our Lord has done for us. ²Because of our faith, Christ has brought us into this place of highest privilege where we now stand, and we confidently and joyfully look forward to sharing God's glory.

³We can rejoice, too, when we run into problems and trials, for we know that they are good for us—they help us learn to endure. ⁴And endurance develops strength of character in us, and character strengthens our confident expectation of salvation. ⁵And this expectation will not disappoint us. For we know how dearly God loves us, because he has given us the Holy Spirit to fill our hearts with his love.

⁶When we were utterly helpless, Christ came at just the right time and died for us sinners. ⁷Now, no one is likely to die for a good person, though someone might be willing to die for a person who is especially good. ⁸But God showed his great love for us by sending Christ to die for us while we were still sinners. ⁹And since we have been made right in God's sight by the blood of Christ, he will certainly save us from God's judgment. ¹⁰For since we were restored to friendship with God by the death of his Son while we were still his enemies, we will certainly be delivered from eternal punishment by his life. ¹¹So now we can rejoice in our wonderful new relationship with God—all because of what our Lord Jesus Christ has done for us in making us friends of God.

Adam and Christ Contrasted

¹²When Adam sinned, sin entered the entire human race. Adam's sin brought death, so death spread to everyone, for everyone sinned. ¹³Yes, people sinned even before the law was given. And though there was no law to break, since it had not yet been given, ¹⁴they all died anyway—even though they did not disobey an explicit commandment of God, as Adam did. What a contrast between Adam and Christ, who was yet to come! ¹⁵And what a difference between our sin and God's generous gift of forgiveness. For this one man, Adam, brought death to many through his sin. But this other man, Jesus Christ, brought forgiveness to many through God's bountiful gift. ¹⁶And the

STEP 7

Declared "Not Guilty"

BIBLE READING: Romans 3:23-28
We humbly asked him to remove our shortcomings.

What are our shortcomings? We all realize that we have them. Is this just another way of saying that we have fallen short of our personal ideals? At some time all of us have held high ideals to define what we think our life should be like. But most of us learned early on that we couldn't measure up to them. Worse yet, we have often fallen short of the expectations of others and the standards of God. Oh, the weight of guilt we carry! Oh, the pain to think of how we have disappointed those we love! Oh, the longing for some way to be what we should be!

The apostle Paul wrote: "For all have sinned; all fall short of God's glorious standard. Yet now God in his gracious kindness declares us not guilty. He has done this through Christ Jesus, who has freed us by taking away our sins" (Romans 3:23-24). Paul goes on to ask, "Can we boast, then, that we have done anything to be accepted by God? No, because our acquittal is not based on our good deeds. It is based on our faith. So we are made right with God through faith and not by obeying the law" (3:27-28).

When God removes our sins, he does a great job! "He has removed our rebellious acts as far away from us as the east is from the west" (Psalm 103:12). We can trust God to remove our shortcomings, moment by moment, if we humble ourself to obey his Word. That means having faith in Jesus Christ to make up for our weaknesses in both character and action. *Turn to page 325, Philippians 2.*

result of God's gracious gift is very different from the result of that one man's sin. For Adam's sin led to condemnation, but we have the free gift of being accepted by God, even though we are guilty of many sins. [17]The sin of this one man, Adam, caused death to rule over us, but all who receive God's wonderful, gracious gift of righteousness will live in triumph over sin and death through this one man, Jesus Christ.

[18]Yes, Adam's one sin brought condemnation upon everyone, but Christ's one act of righteousness makes all people right in God's sight and gives them life. [19]Because one person disobeyed God, many people became sinners. But because one other person obeyed God, many people will be made right in God's sight.

[20]God's law was given so that all people could see how sinful they were. But as people sinned more and more, God's wonderful kindness became more abundant. [21]So just as sin ruled over all people and brought them to death, now God's wonderful kindness rules instead, giving us right standing with God and resulting in eternal life through Jesus Christ our Lord.

CHAPTER 6
Sin's Power Is Broken

Well then, should we keep on sinning so that God can show us more and more kindness and forgiveness? [2]Of course not! Since we have died to sin, how can we continue to live in it? [3]Or have you forgotten that when we became Christians and were baptized to become one with Christ Jesus, we died with him? [4]For we died and were buried with Christ by baptism. And just as Christ was raised from the dead by the glorious power of the Father, now we also may live new lives.

[5]Since we have been united with him in his death, we will also be raised as he was. [6]Our old sinful selves were crucified with Christ so that sin might lose its power in our lives. We are no longer slaves to sin. [7]For when we died with Christ we were set free from the power of sin. [8]And since we died with Christ, we know we will also share his new life. [9]We are sure of this because Christ rose from the dead, and he will never die again. Death no longer has any power over him. [10]He died once to defeat sin, and now he lives for the glory of God. [11]So you should consider yourselves dead to sin and

---

5:15-21 Paul had already asserted that we stand forgiven and joyful in God's grace (5:2), and here he elaborated on that reality. The essential nature of God's grace is that it rules over sin and death in our world. While Adam's sin brought sin and death, Jesus Christ has brought life through his grace for all who are willing to receive it. Our old sinful life represents the rule of death through Adam. Our life in recovery through Jesus Christ represents the rule of God's grace, kindness, and love. When we turn our life over to God, we can begin to receive the wonderful joy and forgiveness that he offers.

6:1-3 If God loves to forgive, why not sin to give him added opportunities to forgive us? We may not admit it, but we act on this principle all too often. Paul's response to this excuse for sin is an emphatic *no!* Such an attitude presumes upon God's grace and is clear evidence that we are in denial. When we knowingly continue to sin, we are making light of the tremendous cost of our salvation. It is unthinkable to continue to allow sin to be our master when we have turned our life over to God.

6:12-14 As we recover from our addiction or compulsive behaviors, we may become very discouraged because the old desires still tempt us. Paul recognized that temptation would be an ongoing problem, so he gave us this warning: "Do not give in." The temptations we face are extensions of the defects of character that exist in each of us. Though we cannot overcome our sinful nature alone, we can ask God to help us. As God helps us clear the destructive patterns from our life, we can replace them with healthy patterns and desires. As we are transformed with God's help, we will overcome the powerful temptations in our life.

6:19-22 It is impossible to be neutral. We all have a master—either sin or God. Making sin our master may seem easier and fun for a while, but it will lead only to pain and destruction. When we turn our life over to God and work on recovery, we are affirming that God is our master. This is the only way we can experience restoration for our life. At first God's way may look harder than the way of sin, but in time we will discover that God's way is the only way to a joyful and meaningful life.

7:1-6 Paul used a marriage analogy to clarify his reasoning. If the person we have married dies, the laws of marriage no longer apply to us. We are not bound to the dead spouse. In the same way, when we turn our life over to God, our old bondage to sin no longer applies. We now are "married" to God, giving him a position of power and authority in our life. If we are willing to live under God's authority, we will experience the meaningful life that he wants for every one of his people.

able to live for the glory of God through Christ Jesus.

¹²Do not let sin control the way you live;* do not give in to its lustful desires. ¹³Do not let any part of your body become a tool of wickedness, to be used for sinning. Instead, give yourselves completely to God since you have been given new life. And use your whole body as a tool to do what is right for the glory of God. ¹⁴Sin is no longer your master, for you are no longer subject to the law, which enslaves you to sin. Instead, you are free by God's grace.

Freedom to Obey God

¹⁵So since God's grace has set us free from the law, does this mean we can go on sinning? Of course not! ¹⁶Don't you realize that whatever you choose to obey becomes your master? You can choose sin, which leads to death, or you can choose to obey God and receive his approval. ¹⁷Thank God! Once you were slaves of sin, but now you have obeyed with all your heart the new teaching God has given you. ¹⁸Now you are free from sin, your old master, and you have become slaves to your new master, righteousness.

¹⁹I speak this way, using the illustration of slaves and masters, because it is easy to understand. Before, you let yourselves be slaves of impurity and lawlessness. Now you must choose to be slaves of righteousness so that you will become holy. ²⁰In those days, when you were slaves of sin, you weren't concerned with doing what was right. ²¹And what was the result? It was not good, since now you are ashamed of the things you used to do, things that end in eternal doom. ²²But now you are free from the power of sin and have become slaves of God. Now you do those things that lead to holiness and result in eternal life. ²³For the wages of sin is death, but the free gift of God is eternal life through Christ Jesus our Lord.

CHAPTER 7
No Longer Bound to the Law

Now, dear brothers and sisters*—you who are familiar with the law—don't you know that the law applies only to a person who is still living? ²Let me illustrate. When a woman marries, the law binds her to her husband as long as he is alive. But if he dies, the laws of marriage no longer apply to her. ³So while her husband is alive, she would be committing adultery if she married another

6:12 Or *Do not let sin reign in your body, which is subject to death.* **7:1** Greek *brothers.*

Faith

READ ROMANS 4:1-5

Our addictive patterns are "sinful," so it is common to feel awkward about getting close to God. We may feel ineligible to receive God's love and, instead, expect his angry judgment. We might feel guilty and be afraid that God will reject us. Secretly we wish that we could have a loving relationship with God, but we are afraid we could never be good enough.

The apostle Paul has shown us that we can have the love and acceptance we desire: "For the Scriptures tell us, 'Abraham believed God, so God declared him to be righteous.' When people work, their wages are not a gift. Workers earn what they receive. But people are declared righteous because of their faith, not because of their work. . . . Now this wonderful truth—that God declared him to be righteous—wasn't just for Abraham's benefit. It was for us, too, assuring us that God will also declare us to be righteous if we believe in God, who brought Jesus our Lord back from the dead. He was handed over to die because of our sins, and he was raised from the dead to make us right with God" (Romans 4:3-5, 23-25).

There are free gifts waiting for us that are essential to the recovery process: God's forgiveness, acceptance, and powerful support. God makes it clear that we have been declared "not guilty" in his court of justice if we have trusted Christ. He has promised to give us a special home in heaven with our name on it. There is no need for us to do anything but accept his free gifts. When we turn our life over to God, we gain far more than we could ever lose! *Turn to page 247, Romans 7.*

man. But if her husband dies, she is free from that law and does not commit adultery when she remarries.

⁴So this is the point: The law no longer holds you in its power, because you died to its power when you died with Christ on the cross. And now you are united with the one who was raised from the dead. As a result, you can produce good fruit, that is, good deeds for God. ⁵When we were controlled by our old nature, sinful desires were at work within us, and the law aroused these evil desires that produced sinful deeds, resulting in death. ⁶But now we have been released from the law, for we died with Christ, and we are no longer captive to its power. Now we can really serve God, not in the old way by obeying the letter of the law, but in the new way, by the Spirit.

God's Law Reveals Our Sin

⁷Well then, am I suggesting that the law of God is evil? Of course not! The law is not sinful, but it was the law that showed me my sin. I would never have known that coveting is wrong if the law had not said, "Do not covet."* ⁸But sin took advantage of this law and aroused all kinds of forbidden desires

7:7 Exod 20:17; Deut 5:21.

within me! If there were no law, sin would not have that power.

⁹I felt fine when I did not understand what the law demanded. But when I learned the truth, I realized I had broken the law and was a sinner, doomed to die. ¹⁰So the good law, which was supposed to show me the way of life, instead gave me the death penalty. ¹¹Sin took advantage of the law and fooled me; it took the good law and used it to make me guilty of death. ¹²But still, the law itself is holy and right and good.

¹³But how can that be? Did the law, which is good, cause my doom? Of course not! Sin used what was good to bring about my condemnation. So we can see how terrible sin really is. It uses God's good commandment for its own evil purposes.

Struggling with Sin

¹⁴The law is good, then. The trouble is not with the law but with me, because I am sold into slavery, with sin as my master. ¹⁵I don't understand myself at all, for I really want to do what is right, but I don't do it. Instead, I do the very thing I hate. ¹⁶I know perfectly well that what I am doing is wrong, and my

---

7:13 Paul didn't want to leave us with the impression that God's laws are bad. They were meant to help us lead a godly life in close fellowship with him. The real problem is our inability to live up to the standard God has set. By nature we are flawed and sinful creatures. Few of us set out to become enslaved to a destructive substance or relationship, but we are overcome by our inherent tendency to sin. We can be thankful that God has made a provision for our sin through the death and resurrection of Jesus Christ. Now if we turn our life over to God, we can experience his transforming power. He will help us overcome our destructive behaviors.

7:14-17 We can all identify with the struggle Paul described. We long to do what is good, healthy, and right, but we end up doing the same old destructive things. As we take personal inventory, we admit our failures and seek to change, but then we fall right back into our destructive habits. We are not alone in this struggle—it is part of being human. We must not become discouraged. Instead, we must use our failures to inspire new moral inventory and then get on with recovery once again. In time our sins and failures will become fewer as God begins to transform us.

8:1 This is one of the great affirmations of Scripture. We will never be condemned by God for our sins, because Jesus Christ has paid the price once and for all. When we decide to turn our life over to God's care, we can be confident that we will not be condemned by him. If we have confessed our sins and accepted God's forgiveness in Christ, there is "no condemnation."

8:2-4 Once we recognize how helpless we are to fight our dependency, we must look outside ourself to God for the power we need. The life-giving Spirit that Paul mentioned here is the Holy Spirit. He was present at the creation of the world (Genesis 1–2) and is available to help us as we seek to rebuild our life. We cannot overcome our addiction or compulsion alone, but God is more than able to help us. He sent his Son and destroyed the power of sin through his death and resurrection. Now we can follow God's program for godly living through the power of the Holy Spirit within us.

8:5-6 Paul puts people in two categories—those who let themselves be controlled by their self-serving "sinful natures" and those who are controlled by the Holy Spirit. Once we have made the decision to turn our life over to God, we must consciously choose to follow his way for continued recovery daily. We need to continually reassess our progress, taking a regular moral inventory of our life.

bad conscience shows that I agree that the law is good. [17]But I can't help myself, because it is sin inside me that makes me do these evil things.

[18]I know I am rotten through and through so far as my old sinful nature is concerned. No matter which way I turn, I can't make myself do right. I want to, but I can't. [19]When I want to do good, I don't. And when I try not to do wrong, I do it anyway. [20]But if I am doing what I don't want to do, I am not really the one doing it; the sin within me is doing it.

[21]It seems to be a fact of life that when I want to do what is right, I inevitably do what is wrong. [22]I love God's law with all my heart. [23]But there is another law at work within me that is at war with my mind. This law wins the fight and makes me a slave to the sin that is still within me. [24]Oh, what a miserable person I am! Who will free me from this life that is dominated by sin?* [25]Thank God! The answer is in Jesus Christ our Lord. So you see how it is: In my mind I really want to obey God's law, but because of my sinful nature I am a slave to sin.

CHAPTER 8
Life in the Spirit

So now there is no condemnation for those who belong to Christ Jesus. [2]For the power* of the life-giving Spirit has freed you* through Christ Jesus from the power of sin that leads to death. [3]The law of Moses could not save us, because of our sinful nature. But God put into effect a different plan to save us. He sent his own Son in a human body like ours, except that ours are sinful. God destroyed sin's control over us by giving his Son as a sacrifice for our sins. [4]He did this so that the requirement of the law would be fully accomplished for us* who no longer follow our sinful nature but instead follow the Spirit.

[5]Those who are dominated by the sinful nature think about sinful things, but those who are controlled by the Holy Spirit think about things that please the Spirit. [6]If your sinful nature controls your mind, there is death. But if the Holy Spirit controls your mind, there is life and peace. [7]For the sinful nature is always hostile to God. It never did obey God's laws, and it never will. [8]That's why those who are still under the control of their sinful nature can never please God.

7:24 Greek *from this body of death?* **8:2a** Greek *the law;* also in 8:2b. **8:2b** Some manuscripts read *me.* **8:4** Or *accomplished by us.*

S T E P

10

Repeated Forgiveness

BIBLE READING: Romans 5:3-5

We continued to take personal inventory and when we were wrong promptly admitted it.

We may grow impatient with ourself when we continue to commit the same sins over and over again. This may cause us to get discouraged, or we may be afraid that we are doomed to relapse.

Peter asked Jesus, "'Lord, how often should I forgive someone who sins against me? Seven times?' 'No!' Jesus replied, 'seventy times seven!'" (Matthew 18:21-22). If this is to be our attitude toward others, doesn't it make sense that we should extend the same grace to ourself? We need to be as patient with ourself as God expects us to be with others.

Paul wrote: "We can rejoice, too, when we run into problems and trials, for we know that they are good for us—they help us learn to endure. And endurance develops strength of character in us, and character strengthens our confident expectation of salvation. . . . For we know how dearly God loves us, because he has given us the Holy Spirit to fill our hearts with his love" (Romans 5:3-5).

Learning to wait patiently is an important characteristic for us to develop. Each time we admit sin and accept God's forgiveness, our hope and faith have a chance to be exercised and grow stronger. We no longer have to hide in shame every time we slip. We can admit our wrongs and move on. God's love for us is reaffirmed every time we rely on it. In this way God helps us hold our head high no matter what happens. *Turn to page 319, Ephesians 4.*

9But you are not controlled by your sinful nature. You are controlled by the Spirit if you have the Spirit of God living in you. (And remember that those who do not have the Spirit of Christ living in them are not Christians at all.) 10Since Christ lives within you, even though your body will die because of sin, your spirit is alive* because you have been made right with God. 11The Spirit of God, who raised Jesus from the dead, lives in you. And just as he raised Christ from the dead, he will give life to your mortal body by this same Spirit living within you.

12So, dear brothers and sisters,* you have no obligation whatsoever to do what your sinful nature urges you to do. 13For if you keep on following it, you will perish. But if through the power of the Holy Spirit you turn from it* and its evil deeds, you will live. 14For all who are led by the Spirit of God are children* of God.

15So you should not be like cowering, fearful slaves. You should behave instead like God's very own children, adopted into his family*—calling him "Father, dear Father."* 16For his Holy Spirit speaks to us deep in our hearts and tells us that we are God's children. 17And since we are his children, we will share his treasures—for everything God gives to his Son, Christ, is ours, too. But if we are to share his glory, we must also share his suffering.

The Future Glory

18Yet what we suffer now is nothing compared to the glory he will give us later. 19For all creation is waiting eagerly for that future day when God will reveal who his children really are. 20Against its will, everything on earth was subjected to God's curse. 21All creation anticipates the day when it will join God's children in glorious freedom from death and decay. 22For we know that all creation has been groaning as in the pains of childbirth right up to the present time. 23And even we Christians, although we have the Holy Spirit within us as a foretaste of future glory, also groan to be released from pain and suffering. We, too, wait anxiously for that day when God will give us our full rights as his children,* including the new bodies he has promised us. 24Now that we are saved, we eagerly look forward to this freedom. For if you already have something, you don't need to hope for it. 25But if we look forward to something we don't have yet, we must wait patiently and confidently.

26And the Holy Spirit helps us in our distress. For we don't even know what we should pray for, nor how we should pray. But the Holy Spirit prays for us with groanings that cannot be expressed in words. 27And the Father who knows all hearts knows what the Spirit is saying, for the Spirit pleads for us believers in harmony with God's own will. 28And we know that God causes everything to work together* for the good of those who love God and are called according to his purpose for them. 29For God knew his people in advance, and he chose them to become like his Son, so that his Son would be the firstborn, with many brothers and sisters. 30And having chosen them, he called them to come to him. And he gave them right standing with himself, and he promised them his glory.

Nothing Can Separate Us from God's Love

31What can we say about such wonderful things as these? If God is for us, who can ever be against us? 32Since God did not spare even his own Son but gave him up for us all, won't God, who gave us Christ, also give us everything else?

33Who dares accuse us whom God has chosen for his own? Will God? No! He is the one who has given us right standing with himself. 34Who then will condemn us? Will Christ Jesus? No, for he is the one who died for us

---

8:10 Or *the Spirit will bring you eternal life.* 8:12 Greek *brothers;* also in 8:29. 8:13 Greek *put it to death.* 8:14 Greek *sons;* also in 8:19. 8:15a Greek *You received a spirit of sonship.* 8:15b Greek *"Abba, Father." Abba* is an Aramaic term for "father." 8:23 Greek *wait anxiously for sonship.* 8:28 Some manuscripts read *And we know that everything works together.*

8:9-11 Either we have the Spirit of God living in us, or we don't. How does the Spirit of God come to live within us? By our act of faith in turning our life over to God and by our acceptance of the work of Christ on our behalf. Can we feel the Spirit of God within us? Sometimes, but we can know he is there whether we feel his presence or not. God has promised to give us the Holy Spirit when we ask. We receive the same Holy Spirit who raised Jesus from the dead. God will use this same power in us to bring about our recovery.

8:31-39 Our security in life and in recovery is based on God's unshakable love for us. The love God has for us is not just an emotion but a matter of historical record. God proved his love for us by willingly sending his Son to suffer and die. So why would he hold back any lesser gift? In fact, there is nothing in the whole universe that can separate us from God's love! What more could God say or do to us to make us more secure in his love?

and was raised to life for us and is sitting at the place of highest honor next to God, pleading for us.

³⁵Can anything ever separate us from Christ's love? Does it mean he no longer loves us if we have trouble or calamity, or are persecuted, or are hungry or cold or in danger or threatened with death? ³⁶(Even the Scriptures say, "For your sake we are killed every day; we are being slaughtered like sheep."*) ³⁷No, despite all these things, overwhelming victory is ours through Christ, who loved us.

³⁸And I am convinced that nothing can ever separate us from his love. Death can't, and life can't. The angels can't, and the demons can't. Our fears for today, our worries about tomorrow, and even the powers of hell can't keep God's love away. ³⁹Whether we are high above the sky or in the deepest ocean, nothing in all creation will ever be able to separate us from the love of God that is revealed in Christ Jesus our Lord.

CHAPTER 9
God's Selection of Israel

In the presence of Christ, I speak with utter truthfulness—I do not lie—and my conscience and the Holy Spirit confirm that what I am saying is true. ²My heart is filled with bitter sorrow and unending grief ³for my people, my Jewish brothers and sisters.* I would be willing to be forever cursed—cut off from Christ!—if that would save them. ⁴They are the people of Israel, chosen to be God's special children.* God revealed his glory to them. He made covenants with them and gave his law to them. They have the privilege of worshiping him and receiving his wonderful promises. ⁵Their ancestors were great people of God, and Christ himself was a Jew as far as his human nature is concerned. And he is God, who rules over everything and is worthy of eternal praise! Amen.*

⁶Well then, has God failed to fulfill his promise to the Jews? No, for not everyone born into a Jewish family is truly a Jew! ⁷Just the fact that they are descendants of Abraham doesn't make them truly Abraham's children. For the Scriptures say, "Isaac is the son through whom your descendants will be counted,"* though Abraham had other children, too. ⁸This means that Abraham's physical descendants are not necessarily children of God. It is the children of the promise who

8:36 Ps 44:22. **9:3** Greek *my brothers.* **9:4** Greek *chosen for sonship.* **9:5** Or *May God, who rules over everything, be praised forever. Amen.* **9:7** Gen 21:12.

Removed, Not Improved

BIBLE READING: Romans 6:5-11

We were entirely ready to have God remove all these defects of character.
Most of us have made numerous attempts at self-improvement. Perhaps we have consciously tried to improve our attitudes, our education, our appearance, or our habits. We may have had success in self-improvement on some level. However, when it comes to our struggles with defects of character, chances are we have experienced only deep frustration.

There is a reason for our frustration. These character defects can only be removed, never improved! The illustration given us in the Bible is that our sins and defects of character must be put to death, as Jesus was, with the hope of new life to follow. The apostle Paul wrote: "Our old sinful selves were crucified with Christ so that sin might lose its power in our lives. We are no longer slaves to sin" (Romans 6:6). "Those who belong to Christ Jesus have nailed the passions and desires of their sinful nature to his cross and crucified them there" (Galatians 5:24).

There is no Band-Aid cure for our sins and defects of character. They have been fatally wounded and must die on the cross. This process is never easy. Who goes to a crucifixion without some measure of anxiety? But when we accept this and allow God to remove our defects, we will be pleasantly surprised by the new life that awaits us. *Turn to page 327, Philippians 3.*

are considered to be Abraham's children. [9]For God had promised, "Next year I will return, and Sarah will have a son."*

[10]This son was our ancestor Isaac. When he grew up, he married Rebekah, who gave birth to twins. [11]But before they were born, before they had done anything good or bad, she received a message from God. (This message proves that God chooses according to his own plan, [12]not according to our good or bad works.) She was told, "The descendants of your older son will serve the descendants of your younger son."* [13]In the words of the Scriptures, "I loved Jacob, but I rejected Esau."*

[14]What can we say? Was God being unfair? Of course not! [15]For God said to Moses,

"I will show mercy to anyone I choose,
    and I will show compassion to anyone I
    choose."*

[16]So receiving God's promise is not up to us. We can't get it by choosing it or working hard for it. God will show mercy to anyone he chooses.

[17]For the Scriptures say that God told Pharaoh, "I have appointed you for the very purpose of displaying my power in you, and so that my fame might spread throughout the earth."* [18]So you see, God shows mercy to some just because he wants to, and he chooses to make some people refuse to listen.

[19]Well then, you might say, "Why does God blame people for not listening? Haven't they simply done what he made them do?"

[20]No, don't say that. Who are you, a mere human being, to criticize God? Should the thing that was created say to the one who made it, "Why have you made me like this?" [21]When a potter makes jars out of clay, doesn't he have a right to use the same lump of clay to make one jar for decoration and an-other to throw garbage into? [22]God has every right to exercise his judgment and his power, but he also has the right to be very patient with those who are the objects of his judgment and are fit only for destruction. [23]He also has the right to pour out the riches of his glory upon those he prepared to be the objects of his mercy—[24]even upon us, whom he selected, both from the Jews and from the Gentiles.

[25]Concerning the Gentiles, God says in the prophecy of Hosea,

"Those who were not my people,
    I will now call my people.
And I will love those
    whom I did not love before."*

[26]And,

"Once they were told,
    'You are not my people.'
But now he will say,
    'You are children of the living God.'*"

[27]Concerning Israel, Isaiah the prophet cried out,

"Though the people of Israel are as
        numerous as the sand on the
        seashore,
    only a small number will be saved.
[28] For the Lord will carry out his sentence
        upon the earth
    quickly and with finality."*

[29]And Isaiah said in another place,

"If the Lord Almighty
    had not spared a few of us,
we would have been wiped out
    as completely as Sodom and
    Gomorrah."*

9:9 Gen 18:10, 14. **9:12** Gen 25:23. **9:13** Mal 1:2-3. **9:15** Exod 33:19. **9:17** Exod 9:16. **9:25** Hos 2:23. **9:26** Greek *You are sons of the living God.* Hos 1:10. **9:27-28** Isa 10:22-23. **9:29** Isa 1:9.

9:25-26 God specializes in loving those who are unlovely and undeserving. None of us deserve God's love, and those of us who think we do are in denial. God's love is bestowed on all who admit their need and respond to his love for them. Sometimes the most undeserving are the first to admit their need for God. No one is entirely innocent of wrongdoing; yet no sin is too great for God to forgive. Thus, desperate addicts who have confessed their sins are better off than "respectable" people who deny their need for God. Admitting that we have failed and that we need God is an essential part of the recovery process.

10:8-15 Salvation comes by trusting Jesus Christ; we can do nothing to earn it. Many of us have spent our entire life trying to earn the approval of others. Perhaps the pain we feel at our failure to achieve perfection is at the heart of our compulsive behavior. We can be thankful that God does not accept us on the basis of our performance. He accepts us because of what Christ has done on our behalf, no matter how great our sins have been. We have no reason to hide our sins from God; he wants only to relieve us of our burdens. He invites us to entrust our life to him and seek to follow his will.

Israel's Unbelief

30Well then, what shall we say about these things? Just this: The Gentiles have been made right with God by faith, even though they were not seeking him. 31But the Jews, who tried so hard to get right with God by keeping the law, never succeeded. 32Why not? Because they were trying to get right with God by keeping the law and being good instead of by depending on faith. They stumbled over the great rock in their path. 33God warned them of this in the Scriptures when he said,

"I am placing a stone in Jerusalem* that
    causes people to stumble,
and a rock that makes them fall.*
But anyone who believes in him
    will not be disappointed.*"

CHAPTER 10

Dear brothers and sisters,* the longing of my heart and my prayer to God is that the Jewish people might be saved. 2I know what enthusiasm they have for God, but it is misdirected zeal. 3For they don't understand God's way of making people right with himself. Instead, they are clinging to their own way of getting right with God by trying to keep the law. They won't go along with God's way. 4For Christ has accomplished the whole purpose* of the law. All who believe in him are made right with God.

Salvation Is for Everyone

5For Moses wrote that the law's way of making a person right with God requires obedience to all of its commands.* 6But the way of getting right with God through faith says, "You don't need to go to heaven" (to find Christ and bring him down to help you). 7And it says, "You don't need to go to the place of the dead" (to bring Christ back to life again). 8Salvation that comes from trusting Christ— which is the message we preach—is already within easy reach. In fact, the Scriptures say, "The message is close at hand; it is on your lips and in your heart."*

9For if you confess with your mouth that Jesus is Lord and believe in your heart that God raised him from the dead, you will be saved. 10For it is by believing in your heart that you are made right with God, and it is by confessing with your mouth that you are saved. 11As the Scriptures tell us,

---

Self-Perception

READ ROMANS 7:18-25

We may have begun to realize that we have character flaws that are beyond our control. Deep down inside there is a sense of brokenness that is a constant reminder of our humanity. Hopefully, we will get to a place where our behavior is under control, and we will be able to maintain sobriety. But as long as we are in a human body, we will have to contend with our sinful nature.

Paul said of himself, "I know I am rotten through and through so far as my old sinful nature is concerned. No matter which way I turn, I can't make myself do right. I want to, but I can't. . . . There is another law at work within me that is at war with my mind. This law wins the fight and makes me a slave to the sin that is still within me" (Romans 7:18, 23). King David described God's tenderness toward us because of our human condition: "The Lord is like a father to his children, tender and compassionate to those who fear him. For he understands how weak we are; he knows we are only dust" (Psalm 103:13-15).

No matter how far we progress, our sinful nature will always incline toward and be susceptible to the lure of our addiction. We can't afford to forget this or let down our guard. Maintaining sobriety is something we will need to nurture for the rest of our life, one day at a time. But we also have a reason for great hope. By trusting Christ and recognizing our helplessness against the power of sin, we open our life to the transforming power of God. *Turn to page 251, Romans 12.*

9:33a Greek *in Zion.* **9:33b** Isa 8:14. **9:33c** Or *will not be put to shame.* Isa 28:16. **10:1** Greek *Brothers.* **10:4** Or *the end.* **10:5** Lev 18:5. **10:6-8** Deut 30:12-14.

"Anyone who believes in him will not be disappointed."* [12]Jew and Gentile are the same in this respect. They all have the same Lord, who generously gives his riches to all who ask for them. [13]For "Anyone who calls on the name of the Lord will be saved."*

[14]But how can they call on him to save them unless they believe in him? And how can they believe in him if they have never heard about him? And how can they hear about him unless someone tells them? [15]And how will anyone go and tell them without being sent? That is what the Scriptures mean when they say, "How beautiful are the feet of those who bring good news!"*

[16]But not everyone welcomes the Good News, for Isaiah the prophet said, "Lord, who has believed our message?"* [17]Yet faith comes from listening to this message of good news—the Good News about Christ.

[18]But what about the Jews? Have they actually heard the message? Yes, they have:

"The message of God's creation has gone
    out to everyone,
  and its words to all the world."*

[19]But did the people of Israel really understand? Yes, they did, for even in the time of Moses, God had said,

"I will rouse your jealousy by blessing
    other nations.
  I will make you angry by blessing the
    foolish Gentiles."*

[20]And later Isaiah spoke boldly for God:

"I was found by people
    who were not looking for me.
  I showed myself to those
    who were not asking for me."*

[21]But regarding Israel, God said,

"All day long I opened my arms
    to them,
  but they kept disobeying me and
    arguing with me."*

CHAPTER 11
God's Mercy on Israel

I ask, then, has God rejected his people, the Jews? Of course not! Remember that I myself am a Jew, a descendant of Abraham and a member of the tribe of Benjamin.

[2]No, God has not rejected his own people, whom he chose from the very beginning. Do you remember what the Scriptures say about this? Elijah the prophet complained to God about the people of Israel and said, [3]"Lord, they have killed your prophets and torn down your altars. I alone am left, and now they are trying to kill me, too."*

[4]And do you remember God's reply? He said, "You are not the only one left. I have seven thousand others who have never bowed down to Baal!"*

[5]It is the same today, for not all the Jews have turned away from God. A few* are being saved as a result of God's kindness in choosing them. [6]And if they are saved by God's kindness, then it is not by their good works. For in that case, God's wonderful kindness would not be what it really is—free and undeserved.

[7]So this is the situation: Most of the Jews have not found the favor of God they are looking for so earnestly. A few have—the ones God has chosen—but the rest were made unresponsive. [8]As the Scriptures say,

"God has put them into a deep sleep.
To this very day he has shut their eyes so
    they do not see,
  and closed their ears so they do not hear."*

[9]David spoke of this same thing when he said,

"Let their bountiful table become a snare,
    a trap that makes them think all is well.
  Let their blessings cause them to
    stumble.
[10] Let their eyes go blind so they cannot see,
  and let their backs grow weaker and
    weaker."*

[11]Did God's people stumble and fall beyond recovery? Of course not! His purpose

10:11 Or *will not be put to shame.* Isa 28:16. **10:13** Joel 2:32. **10:15** Isa 52:7. **10:16** Isa 53:1. **10:18** Ps 19:4. **10:19** Deut 32:21. **10:20** Isa 65:1. **10:21** Isa 65:2. **11:3** 1 Kgs 19:10, 14. **11:4** 1 Kgs 19:18. **11:5** Greek *A remnant.* **11:8** Deut 29:4; Isa 29:10. **11:9-10** Ps 69:22-23.

11:1-10 Paul asked, "Has God rejected his people, the Jews?" The apostle answered his own question with a resounding *no!* Even though a majority of Jews had rejected Jesus' messianic claims, there was still hope for them. It is never too late to turn our life over to God and experience his healing power and grace. As long as we have breath, we can still ask for God's help and forgiveness. Even though this is true, however, an extended period of denial is always costly. We may cause great pain to others, and the longer we wait, the more difficult it will be to change. The time to seek change is now!

was to make his salvation available to the Gentiles, and then the Jews would be jealous and want it for themselves. [12]Now if the Gentiles were enriched because the Jews turned down God's offer of salvation, think how much greater a blessing the world will share when the Jews finally accept it.

[13]I am saying all of this especially for you Gentiles. God has appointed me as the apostle to the Gentiles. I lay great stress on this, [14]for I want to find a way to make the Jews want what you Gentiles have, and in that way I might save some of them. [15]For since the Jews' rejection meant that God offered salvation to the rest of the world, how much more wonderful their acceptance will be. It will be life for those who were dead! [16]And since Abraham and the other patriarchs were holy, their children will also be holy.* For if the roots of the tree are holy, the branches will be, too.

[17]But some of these branches from Abraham's tree, some of the Jews, have been broken off. And you Gentiles, who were branches from a wild olive tree, were grafted in. So now you also receive the blessing God has promised Abraham and his children, sharing in God's rich nourishment of his special olive tree. [18]But you must be careful not to brag about being grafted in to replace the branches that were broken off. Remember, you are just a branch, not the root.

[19]"Well," you may say, "those branches were broken off to make room for me." [20]Yes, but remember—those branches, the Jews, were broken off because they didn't believe God, and you are there because you do believe. Don't think highly of yourself, but fear what could happen. [21]For if God did not spare the branches he put there in the first place, he won't spare you either.

[22]Notice how God is both kind and severe. He is severe to those who disobeyed, but kind to you as you continue to trust in his kindness. But if you stop trusting, you also will be cut off. [23]And if the Jews turn from their unbelief, God will graft them back into the tree again. He has the power to do it.

[24]For if God was willing to take you who were, by nature, branches from a wild olive tree and graft you into his own good tree—a very unusual thing to do—he will be far more eager to graft the Jews back into the tree where they belong.

God's Mercy Is for Everyone

[25]I want you to understand this mystery, dear brothers and sisters,* so that you will not feel proud and start bragging. Some of the Jews have hard hearts, but this will last only until the complete number of Gentiles comes to Christ. [26]And so all Israel will be saved. Do you remember what the prophets said about this?

"A Deliverer will come from Jerusalem,*
    and he will turn Israel* from all
        ungodliness.
[27] And then I will keep my covenant with them
    and take away their sins."*

[28]Many of the Jews are now enemies of the Good News. But this has been to your benefit, for God has given his gifts to you Gentiles. Yet the Jews are still his chosen people because of his promises to Abraham, Isaac, and Jacob. [29]For God's gifts and his call can never be withdrawn. [30]Once, you Gentiles were rebels against God, but when the Jews refused his mercy, God was merciful to you instead. [31]And now, in the same way, the Jews are the rebels, and God's mercy has come to you. But someday they,* too, will share in God's mercy. [32]For God has imprisoned all people in their own disobedience so he could have mercy on everyone.

[33]Oh, what a wonderful God we have! How great are his riches and wisdom and knowledge! How impossible it is for us to understand his decisions and his methods! [34]For who can know what the Lord is thinking? Who knows enough to be his counselor?* [35]And who could ever give him so much that he would have to pay it back? [36]For everything comes from him; everything exists by his power and is intended for his glory. To him be glory evermore. Amen.

11:16 Greek *If the dough offered as firstfruits is holy, so is the whole lump.* **11:25** Greek *brothers.* **11:26a** Greek *from Zion.* **11:26b** Greek *Jacob.* **11:26-27** Isa 59:20-21. **11:31** Some manuscripts read *But now they;* other manuscripts read *But they.* **11:34** See Isa 40:13.

11:33-36 After sketching out the broad contours of God's plan for us, Paul could only worship God's majesty. God's plan, wisdom, knowledge, and ways are all so far beyond ours that we have only one option: to humbly give him the praise he deserves! For those of us who recognize how limited and helpless we are, the fact that God's power and wisdom are great can be an encouragement, especially since he loves us and wants to help us.

CHAPTER 12

A Living Sacrifice to God

And so, dear brothers and sisters,* I plead with you to give your bodies to God. Let them be a living and holy sacrifice—the kind he will accept. When you think of what he has done for you, is this too much to ask? 2Don't copy the behavior and customs of this world, but let God transform you into a new person by changing the way you think. Then you will know what God wants you to do, and you will know how good and pleasing and perfect his will really is.

3As God's messenger, I give each of you this warning: Be honest in your estimate of yourselves, measuring your value by how much faith God has given you. 4Just as our bodies have many parts and each part has a special function, 5so it is with Christ's body. We are all parts of his one body, and each of us has different work to do. And since we are all one body in Christ, we belong to each other, and each of us needs all the others.

6God has given each of us the ability to do certain things well. So if God has given you the ability to prophesy, speak out when you have faith that God is speaking through you. 7If your gift is that of serving others, serve them well. If you are a teacher, do a good job of teaching. 8If your gift is to encourage others, do it! If you have money, share it generously. If God has given you leadership ability, take the responsibility seriously. And if you have a gift for showing kindness to others, do it gladly.

9Don't just pretend that you love others. Really love them. Hate what is wrong. Stand on the side of the good. 10Love each other with genuine affection,* and take delight in honoring each other. 11Never be lazy in your work, but serve the Lord enthusiastically.

12Be glad for all God is planning for you. Be patient in trouble, and always be prayerful. 13When God's children are in need, be the one to help them out. And get into the habit of inviting guests home for dinner or, if they need lodging, for the night.

12:1 Greek *brothers.* 12:10 Greek *with brotherly love.*

12:3 This verse is a call to honesty and true humility. We are to take personal inventory of our life, making an honest assessment of both our strengths and weaknesses and measuring our value by our faith. This will teach us humility as we uncover our sins and faults. It will also help us develop a grateful attitude toward God as we discover the many gifts he has given us.

12:4-8 God has an important role for each of us, even though we may wonder how he could use us significantly. Our addiction may have decimated our resources and destroyed our relationships. We may feel useless, isolated, and alone. But we are all given special gifts that are needed by others. Paul mentioned the gift of encouraging others—something we in recovery are especially suited to do. Who could better help a person devastated by addiction than someone who has already been there? Part of recovery involves sharing our story of deliverance with others. It could mean the difference between life and death for someone in need. As we reach out to encourage others, our isolation will give way to fellowship.

12:9-21 God tells us to let love govern all our attitudes and actions; this certainly applies to the process of recovery. We are called to even love our enemies. We have all been wronged by others. God's love allows us to forgive them and seek reconciliation. All of us have hurt others. Love enables us to ask for their forgiveness and seek to make amends for the trouble and pain we have caused. Often we need to make a special effort to reach out to immediate family members—parents, siblings, children, spouse. Love in action is not easy; it demands that we swallow our pride and admit our wrongs to others. As painful as love may be, however, it is the only way to experience the joy of rebuilding our relationships and progressing in recovery.

13:1-7 Our lifestyle in recovery includes the way we relate to governmental authorities. Paul pointed out that government exists because God put it there. Therefore, we need to submit to the government as we would submit to God himself. Some of us may have suffered great abuse by people in authority over us. How could God want us to submit to authorities who do not act wisely or justly? Elsewhere in Scripture we find that there is a place for civil disobedience (see Acts 4:13-22). Sometimes we need to resist the injustices that are being done against us. We can do this by communicating with trustworthy people about the abuses we have suffered. We are called to support and obey authorities that seek to uphold justice. But when they stand in direct contradiction to God's will, we need to seek the support of others and try to change the situation.

¹⁴If people persecute you because you are a Christian, don't curse them; pray that God will bless them. ¹⁵When others are happy, be happy with them. If they are sad, share their sorrow. ¹⁶Live in harmony with each other. Don't try to act important, but enjoy the company of ordinary people. And don't think you know it all!

¹⁷Never pay back evil for evil to anyone. Do things in such a way that everyone can see you are honorable. ¹⁸Do your part to live in peace with everyone, as much as possible.

¹⁹Dear friends, never avenge yourselves. Leave that to God. For it is written,

"I will take vengeance;
  I will repay those who deserve it,"*
  says the Lord.

²⁰Instead, do what the Scriptures say:

"If your enemies are hungry, feed them.
  If they are thirsty, give them something
    to drink,
    and they will be ashamed of what they
      have done to you."*

²¹Don't let evil get the best of you, but conquer evil by doing good.

CHAPTER 13
Respect for Authority

Obey the government, for God is the one who put it there. All governments have been placed in power by God. ²So those who refuse to obey the laws of the land are refusing to obey God, and punishment will follow. ³For the authorities do not frighten people who are doing right, but they frighten those who do wrong. So do what they say, and you will get along well. ⁴The authorities are sent by God to help you. But if you are doing something wrong, of course you should be afraid, for you will be punished. The authorities are established by God for that very purpose, to punish those who do wrong. ⁵So you must obey the government for two reasons: to keep from being punished and to keep a clear conscience.

⁶Pay your taxes, too, for these same reasons. For government workers need to be paid so they can keep on doing the work God intended them to do. ⁷Give to everyone what you owe them: Pay your taxes and import duties, and give respect and honor to all to whom it is due.

12:19 Deut 32:35. **12:20** Greek *and you will heap burning coals on their heads*. Prov 25:21-22.

Self-Perception

READ ROMANS 12:1-2

How many times have we wished that we could be someone else? Perhaps one reason we act out our addiction is that we hate ourself. Self-hatred is often associated with an addictive/compulsive personality. If we don't like who we are and feel helpless to change, we can be reassured in knowing that God has the power to change us dramatically.

The apostle Paul wrote: "I plead with you to give your bodies to God. Let them be a living and holy sacrifice—the kind he will accept. When you think of what he has done for you, is this too much to ask? Don't copy the behavior and customs of this world, but let God transform you into a new person by changing the way you think. Then you will know what God wants you to do, and you will know how good and pleasing and perfect his will really is" (Romans 12:1-2).

Paul tells us to avoid being like the world around us. If we copy the behavior and customs of this world, we will head straight toward selfish ways and destructive dependencies. Our part is to turn our will and our life over to the care of God. As we trust and obey him, he will work changes in us and make us new people. God wants to change us from the inside out. As we are changed on the inside, we will begin to evidence those changes in our external attitudes and actions.

We all have great potential for change, but we cannot do it under our own power. As we yield our life and will to God, we can depend on him to renew our mind and heart. He will help us overcome our defects of character, transforming us from the inside out. *Turn to page 265, 1 Corinthians 6.*

Love Fulfills God's Requirements

[8]Pay all your debts, except the debt of love for others. You can never finish paying that! If you love your neighbor, you will fulfill all the requirements of God's law. [9]For the commandments against adultery and murder and stealing and coveting—and any other commandment—are all summed up in this one commandment: "Love your neighbor as yourself."* [10]Love does no wrong to anyone, so love satisfies all of God's requirements.

[11]Another reason for right living is that you know how late it is; time is running out. Wake up, for the coming of our salvation is nearer now than when we first believed. [12]The night is almost gone; the day of salvation will soon be here. So don't live in darkness. Get rid of your evil deeds. Shed them like dirty clothes. Clothe yourselves with the armor of right living, as those who live in the light. [13]We should be decent and true in everything we do, so that everyone can approve of our behavior. Don't participate in wild parties and getting drunk, or in adultery and immoral living, or in fighting and jealousy. [14]But let the Lord Jesus Christ take control of you, and don't think of ways to indulge your evil desires.

CHAPTER 14
The Danger of Criticism

Accept Christians who are weak in faith, and don't argue with them about what they think is right or wrong. [2]For instance, one person believes it is all right to eat anything. But another believer who has a sensitive conscience will eat only vegetables. [3]Those who think it is all right to eat anything must not look down on those who won't. And those who won't eat certain foods must not condemn those who do, for God has accepted them. [4]Who are you to condemn God's servants? They are responsible to the Lord, so let him tell them whether they are right or wrong. The Lord's power will help them do as they should.

[5]In the same way, some think one day is more holy than another day, while others think every day is alike. Each person should have a personal conviction about this matter. [6]Those who have a special day for worshiping the Lord are trying to honor him. Those who eat all kinds of food do so to honor the Lord, since they give thanks to God before eating. And those who won't eat everything also want to please the Lord and give thanks to God. [7]For we are not our own masters when we live or when we die. [8]While we live, we live to please the Lord. And when we die, we go to be with the Lord. So in life and in death, we belong to the Lord. [9]Christ died and rose again for this very purpose, so that he might be Lord of those who are alive and of those who have died.

[10]So why do you condemn another Christian*? Why do you look down on another

13:9 Lev 19:18. 14:10 Greek *your brother;* also in 14:10b, 13, 15, 21.

13:8-10 Progress in recovery can take place only as we learn to love others. Love is not an emotion we feel; it is an attitude and ourpouring of unselfish concern for others. If we love God and the people around us, we will treat others with respect. We would never steal from or harm them in any way to satisfy our own selfish desires. As we continue to take regular personal inventory, we can use love as the standard by which we judge our behavior. Do we act with the best interests of others in mind? If we measure all our actions against God's standard of love, we will experience great progress in recovery and in our relationships.

13:12-14 When we turn our life over to God, we are given a new identity; we become children of the light. People who live in the light are awake—their eyes are open. They are not in the darkness of denial; they have the ability to see and admit the truth about themselves. One way to make sure we are walking in the light is to take regular moral inventory. This will help us shed our evil deeds and be "decent and true in everything we do."

14:1-4 We may have a tendency to judge others who are still struggling in recovery, with one foot still in the old patterns of the past. We might even be tempted to show them how "strong" we are by participating in activities that would still lead them into destructive falls. Even if we have progressed in recovery to the point that certain circumstances no longer tempt us, we still need to be sensitive to the fact that our friends may be led astray by our activities. Our love for others will lead us to avoid activities that might lead to their downfall. The more mature we are, the more responsible we will be in responding to others in loving ways.

14:10-12 Paul reminds us that we are not to take inventory for others. Many of us find it easier to point out the failures of others than to look critically and honestly at our own life. But it isn't our primary responsibility to straighten out other people's lives. We must remember that all of us will be personally accountable before God for our actions. If we spend our time pointing a finger at others, we will never clean up our own act and progress in our own recovery.

Christian? Remember, each of us will stand personally before the judgment seat of God. [11]For the Scriptures say,

> "'As surely as I live,' says the Lord,
> 'every knee will bow to me
>   and every tongue will confess allegiance
>   to God.'"*

[12]Yes, each of us will have to give a personal account to God. [13]So don't condemn each other anymore. Decide instead to live in such a way that you will not put an obstacle in another Christian's path.

[14]I know and am perfectly sure on the authority of the Lord Jesus that no food, in and of itself, is wrong to eat. But if someone believes it is wrong, then for that person it is wrong. [15]And if another Christian is distressed by what you eat, you are not acting in love if you eat it. Don't let your eating ruin someone for whom Christ died. [16]Then you will not be condemned for doing something you know is all right.

[17]For the Kingdom of God is not a matter of what we eat or drink, but of living a life of goodness and peace and joy in the Holy Spirit. [18]If you serve Christ with this attitude, you will please God. And other people will approve of you, too. [19]So then, let us aim for harmony in the church and try to build each other up.

[20]Don't tear apart the work of God over what you eat. Remember, there is nothing wrong with these things in themselves. But it is wrong to eat anything if it makes another person stumble. [21]Don't eat meat or drink wine or do anything else if it might cause another Christian to stumble. [22]You may have the faith to believe that there is nothing wrong with what you are doing, but keep it between yourself and God. Blessed are those who do not condemn themselves by doing something they know is all right. [23]But if people have doubts about whether they should eat something, they shouldn't eat it. They would be condemned for not acting in faith before God. If you do anything you believe is not right, you are sinning.

CHAPTER 15
Living to Please Others

We may know that these things make no difference, but we cannot just go ahead and do them to please ourselves. We must be considerate of the doubts and fears of those who think these things are wrong. [2]We should please others. If we do what helps them, we will build them up in the Lord. [3]For even Christ didn't please himself. As the Scriptures say, "Those who insult you are also insulting me."* [4]Such things were written in the Scriptures long ago to teach us. They give us hope and encouragement as we wait patiently for God's promises.

[5]May God, who gives this patience and encouragement, help you live in complete harmony with each other—each with the attitude of Christ Jesus toward the other. [6]Then all of you can join together with one voice, giving praise and glory to God, the Father of our Lord Jesus Christ.

[7]So accept each other just as Christ has accepted you; then God will be glorified. [8]Remember that Christ came as a servant to the Jews to show that God is true to the promises he made to their ancestors. [9]And he came so the Gentiles might also give glory to God for his mercies to them. That is what the psalmist meant when he wrote:

> "I will praise you among the Gentiles;
>   I will sing praises to your name."*

14:11 Isa 45:23. **15:3** Ps 69:9. **15:9** Ps 18:49.

14:22-23 In the process of recovery we sometimes are tempted to do things that are not necessarily wrong but could lead us toward a fall. We know such activities are dangerous, but it is hard to turn away, especially if our friends are involved. We need to learn that when we *feel* something is wrong for us, it *is* wrong for us. If we do it anyway, we are sinning. Many activities are wrong, purely and simply. But the activities or thoughts that are not specifically sinful are the ones we need to be especially careful of. If we have any doubts about something, we shouldn't do it. We must ask God for wisdom and the power to resist it.

15:1-6 Showing consideration to others is crucial for successful recovery. Our human relationships are second in importance only to our relationship with God. If we are not at peace with others, we will be at war within ourself. And that is a perfect recipe for relapse. We need to learn to delay our personal gratification for the sake of others. This will help us form healthy relationships with the significant people in our life, a necessity for progress in any recovery program. Such relationships will help us to find balance between meeting the needs of others and finding healthy ways to meet our own needs.

[10]And in another place it is written,

"Rejoice, O you Gentiles,
along with his people, the Jews."*

[11]And yet again,

"Praise the Lord, all you Gentiles;
praise him, all you people of the earth."*

[12]And the prophet Isaiah said,

"The heir to David's throne* will come,
and he will rule over the Gentiles.
They will place their hopes on him."*

[13]So I pray that God, who gives you hope, will keep you happy and full of peace as you believe in him. May you overflow with hope through the power of the Holy Spirit.

Paul's Reason for Writing

[14]I am fully convinced, dear brothers and sisters,* that you are full of goodness. You know these things so well that you are able to teach others all about them. [15]Even so, I have been bold enough to emphasize some of these points, knowing that all you need is this reminder from me. For I am, by God's grace, [16]a special messenger from Christ Jesus to you Gentiles. I bring you the Good News and offer you up as a fragrant sacrifice to God so that you might be pure and pleasing to him by the Holy Spirit. [17]So it is right for me to be enthusiastic about all Christ Jesus has done through me in my service to God. [18]I dare not boast of anything else. I have brought the Gentiles to God by my message and by the way I lived before them. [19]I have won them over by the miracles done through me as signs from God—all by the power of God's Spirit. In this way, I have fully presented the Good News of Christ all the way from Jerusalem clear over into Illyricum.*

[20]My ambition has always been to preach the Good News where the name of Christ has never been heard, rather than where a church has already been started by someone else. [21]I have been following the plan spoken of in the Scriptures, where it says,

"Those who have never been told about
him will see,
and those who have never heard of him
will understand."*

[22]In fact, my visit to you has been delayed so long because I have been preaching in these places.

Paul's Travel Plans

[23]But now I have finished my work in these regions, and after all these long years of waiting, I am eager to visit you. [24]I am planning to go to Spain, and when I do, I will stop off in Rome. And after I have enjoyed your fellowship for a little while, you can send me on my way again.

[25]But before I come, I must go down to Jerusalem to take a gift to the Christians there. [26]For you see, the believers in Greece* have eagerly taken up an offering for the Christians in Jerusalem, who are going through such hard times. [27]They were very glad to do this because they feel they owe a real debt to them. Since the Gentiles received the wonderful spiritual blessings of the Good News from the Jewish Christians, they feel the least they can do in return is help them financially. [28]As soon as I have delivered this money and completed this good deed of theirs, I will come to see you on my way to Spain. [29]And I am sure that when I come, Christ will give me a great blessing for you.

[30]Dear brothers and sisters, I urge you in the name of our Lord Jesus Christ to join me in my struggle by praying to God for me. Do this because of your love for me, given to you by the Holy Spirit. [31]Pray that I will be rescued from those in Judea who refuse to obey God. Pray also that the Christians there will be willing to accept the donation I am bringing them. [32]Then, by the will of God, I will be able to come to you with a happy heart, and we will be an encouragement to each other.

[33]And now may God, who gives us his peace, be with you all. Amen.

CHAPTER 16
Paul Greets His Friends

Our sister Phoebe, a deacon in the church in Cenchrea, will be coming to see you soon. [2]Receive her in the Lord, as one who is worthy of high honor. Help her in every way you can, for she has helped many in their needs, including me.

[3]Greet Priscilla and Aquila. They have been co-workers in my ministry for Christ Jesus. [4]In fact, they risked their lives for me. I am not the only one who is thankful to them; so are all the Gentile churches. [5]Please give my greetings to the church that meets in their home.

Greet my dear friend Epenetus. He was the very first person to become a Christian in the province of Asia. [6]Give my greetings to Mary,

---

15:10 Deut 32:43. **15:11** Ps 117:1. **15:12a** Greek *The root of Jesse.* **15:12b** Isa 11:10. **15:14** Greek *brothers;* also in 15:30. **15:19** *Illyricum* was a region northeast of Italy. **15:21** Isa 52:15. **15:26** Greek *Macedonia and Achaia,* the northern and southern regions of Greece.

who has worked so hard for your benefit. ⁷Then there are Andronicus and Junia,* my relatives,* who were in prison with me. They are respected among the apostles and became Christians before I did. Please give them my greetings. ⁸Say hello to Ampliatus, whom I love as one of the Lord's own children, ⁹and Urbanus, our co-worker in Christ, and beloved Stachys.

¹⁰Give my greetings to Apelles, a good man whom Christ approves. And give my best regards to the members of the household of Aristobulus. ¹¹Greet Herodion, my relative.* Greet the Christians in the household of Narcissus. ¹²Say hello to Tryphena and Tryphosa, the Lord's workers, and to dear Persis, who has worked so hard for the Lord. ¹³Greet Rufus, whom the Lord picked out to be his very own; and also his dear mother, who has been a mother to me.

¹⁴And please give my greetings to Asyncritus, Phlegon, Hermes, Patrobas, Hermas, and the brothers and sisters* who are with them. ¹⁵Give my greetings to Philologus, Julia, Nereus and his sister, and to Olympas and all the other believers who are with them. ¹⁶Greet each other in Christian love.* All the churches of Christ send you their greetings.

Paul's Final Instructions

¹⁷And now I make one more appeal, my dear brothers and sisters. Watch out for people who cause divisions and upset people's faith by teaching things that are contrary to what you have been taught. Stay away from them. ¹⁸Such people are not serving Christ our Lord; they are serving their own personal interests. By smooth talk and glowing words they deceive innocent people. ¹⁹But everyone knows that you are obedient to the Lord. This makes me very happy. I want you to see clearly what is right and to stay innocent of any wrong. ²⁰The God of peace will soon crush Satan under your feet. May the grace of our Lord Jesus Christ be with you.

²¹Timothy, my fellow worker, and Lucius, Jason, and Sosipater, my relatives, send you their good wishes.

²²I, Tertius, the one who is writing this letter for Paul, send my greetings, too, as a Christian brother.

²³Gaius says hello to you. I am his guest, and the church meets here in his home. Erastus, the city treasurer, sends you his greetings, and so does Quartus, a Christian brother.*

²⁵God is able to make you strong, just as the Good News says. It is the message about Jesus Christ and his plan for you Gentiles, a plan kept secret from the beginning of time. ²⁶But now as the prophets* foretold and as the eternal God has commanded, this message is made known to all Gentiles everywhere, so that they might believe and obey Christ. ²⁷To God, who alone is wise, be the glory forever through Jesus Christ. Amen.

16:7a Or *Junias;* some manuscripts read *Julia.* **16:7b** Or *compatriots;* also in 16:21. **16:11** Or *compatriot.* **16:14** Greek *brothers;* also in 16:17. **16:16** Greek *with a sacred kiss.* **16:23** Some manuscripts add verse 24, *May the grace of our Lord Jesus Christ be with you all. Amen.* **16:26** Greek *the prophetic writings.*

REFLECTIONS ON ROMANS

*insights ABOUT THE POWER OF CHRIST'S RESURRECTION

In **Romans 6:2-11** Paul examined how we can receive new life through the death and resurrection of Jesus Christ. He traced the history of Jesus' life: (1) his earthly body subjected to death; (2) his death, burial, and resurrection; (3) his resurrection body that was no longer under the power of death. Next Paul showed how our own life can be parallel to that of Jesus: (1) we begin under the mastery of sin and death; (2) we identify with Jesus' death, burial, and resurrection; (3) we receive new life, with the power to overcome sin and death. God has the power to take a life headed for destruction and set it on the road to new life.

✳*insights* ABOUT OUR HELPLESSNESS

In **Romans 3:9-10** Paul summarized his earlier discussion by concluding that "all people . . . are under the power of sin." No one is exempt—we are all fallen and dysfunctional; we are all in need of salvation and recovery. If we pretend to be healthy and without sin, we only prove that we are in denial. Recovery can begin only after we have admitted this truth. When we recognize that we are broken and helpless and turn to God, he steps in and provides the power we need for recovery.

In **Romans 5:1-11** Paul used several phrases to describe our painful condition: "we were utterly helpless" (5:6); we were "sinners" (5:6, 8-9); and we were God's "enemies" (5:10). It was precisely when we were in this condition that God decided to solve our sin problem for us. He loved us so much that he sent his Son to die on the cross to set us free from the power of sin. We cannot be any worse than the way Paul described us here, so God's love and acceptance of us can never be negated by mistakes in our past! With a Savior like that, we can confidently turn our life over to him.

In **Romans 7:18-20** Paul recognized the power of sin in his life and admitted how helpless he was against its persistence and strength. As he admitted his powerlessness, he was starting down the lifelong road toward recovery from his illusion that he could be saved by doing all the right things. When we can admit how powerless we are over our dependency, we will have made a significant step toward recovery. Only then will we be ready to accept God's help; only with God's power will we be able to overcome the temptations we face.

✳*insights* ABOUT FAITH

In **Romans 4:1-3** Paul showed how Abraham was accepted by God and declared righteous because of his faith. As we look at Abraham in the book of Genesis, we find a man who was set apart for God. Despite his mistakes, he could be considered a person who had it all together. But Abraham had to come to God the same way we do—through faith. He did nothing to deserve the special promises that God gave him. In the same way, we can do nothing to deserve the promises of forgiveness and recovery that God offers us. No social status or good deed can make us deserving of God's gracious forgiveness; yet no failure is too great an obstacle for God's restoring power. When we entrust our life to God and believe that he can help us, God gives us the power and courage to move forward one step at a time.

✳*insights* ABOUT PRAYER

Prayer is listed in **Romans 8:26-28** as one of the ways we improve our conscious contact with God. Paul assures us that the indwelling Holy Spirit is at work within us as we pray. We are not left alone to work out our problems. As we entrust our life to God, he allows the events of our life, even the painful ones, for our good. He can turn even our sins and mistakes into the means for our growth and blessing.

✳*insights* ABOUT THE BENEFITS OF SUBMISSION TO GOD

In **Romans 12:1-2** we are told to offer our life to God as a living and holy sacrifice. We are exhorted to turn our life and will over to God so he can transform us into the godly person he wants us to be. We are called to follow God's program for our life, utilizing the power he offers. As we do this, we will become an example to others of what God's transforming power can do. And as we grow, we will discover the joy and meaning that can be experienced when we offer our life to God. When we sacrifice all we are and have to God, he will return what we gave up, multiplied many times over.

FIRST CORINTHIANS

THE BIG PICTURE

The Greek city of Corinth was known for its corruption, immorality, and pagan religion. Following Christ in that setting meant leaving behind many of the practices accepted by the larger culture. This presented the new believers there with all kinds of temptations and problems.

Although the Corinthian believers had received new life in Christ, they had much to learn. It would take time for them to mature in their faith. In short, their intentions were fine, but they needed further instruction about following Christ. They needed to get a handle on God's perspectives concerning right and wrong. Paul wrote this letter to help them make progress— to give them advice about how to change.

The recovery process often requires a similar struggle against the surrounding environment. Though we determine to change, the world in which we live stays much the same. We live and work with the same people, go to many of the same places, and do many of the same things—all while trying to make radical changes in our life. The feelings of loneliness that result can make us as vulnerable as the Corinthian believers once were.

Despite the difficulties we face, God understands our struggle. That is why he has given us his Word, his power, and his people; they are all available to help us take one step at a time. This letter alone contains numerous insights for recovery. Through it we can learn how to separate ourself from our old way of life and open ourself to God's new standard. The transformation may be slow or even painful, but by God's grace and our commitment, it will happen.

THE BOTTOM LINE

PURPOSE: To encourage the believers living in Corinth to resolve their problems and honor God. AUTHOR: The apostle Paul. AUDIENCE: The church at Corinth, a city in Greece. DATE WRITTEN: Around A.D. 55, near the end of Paul's three-year stay in Ephesus. SETTING: Corinth was a large cosmopolitan city that teemed with idolatry and immorality. The church in Corinth was fairly new and made up primarily of non-Jewish (Gentile) believers. KEY VERSE: "But whatever I am now, it is all because God poured out his special favor on me—and not without results. For I have worked harder than all the other apostles, yet it was not I but God who was working through me by his grace" (15:10). KEY PEOPLE AND RELATIONSHIPS: Paul with Timothy, Chloe's household, and the Corinthian believers.

RECOVERY THEMES

Jesus Is the Center of Recovery: The believers in Corinth show us what happens when we take our eyes off Jesus Christ. Though they were followers of Christ, they identified themselves primarily with their various teachers. This caused unnecessary divisions among them and kept them from growing spiritually. While the support and advice of others are important, our Savior is Jesus Christ. He is the center of all our efforts; we must focus on him. People and recovery techniques are his tools, not ours.

Freedom with Loving Restraint: The new believers in Corinth had to make a clean break with their past. Some of these believers were quite mature and were no longer bothered by the temptations that had plagued them before. But others were not so secure. Paul therefore instructed the more mature ones not to flaunt their freedom around those who still struggled. Successful recovery or spiritual maturity doesn't give us license to be inconsiderate or insensitive to others. We can support one another by being careful how we use our freedom. We will always have this responsibility to look out for one another.

Life Is to Be Enjoyed Responsibly: The believers in Corinth lived in a very immoral, pleasure-seeking society. The standards of conduct that God had for them were quite different from what they were used to in their culture. But if those believers thought those standards seemed too restrictive, they were mistaken. Longing for "freedom" from God's laws is like longing for the "fun" of being an alcoholic. It is like wanting to be trapped in a life of addiction, compulsion, or other destructive behaviors, reasoning that turning our life over to God would keep us from having fun. On the contrary, God challenges us to live an uncompromising life because that is the way to enjoy life at its fullest. The same is true for us in recovery—we are discovering what life was meant to be!

The Invitation to Love: One of the most beautiful passages on love ever written is found in chapter 13 of this letter to the Corinthians. Paul points out that love is more than an emotion; it is selfless action. If we love, then we will act in selfless ways. When we don't feel loving or don't feel loved, 1 Corinthians 13 is a wonderful reminder of how God loves us and how we can show love to others.

CHAPTER 1
Greetings from Paul

This letter is from Paul, chosen by the will of God to be an apostle of Christ Jesus, and from our brother Sosthenes.

²We are writing to the church of God in Corinth, you who have been called by God to be his own holy people. He made you holy by means of Christ Jesus, just as he did all Christians everywhere—whoever calls upon the name of Jesus Christ, our Lord and theirs.

³May God our Father and the Lord Jesus Christ give you his grace and peace.

Paul Gives Thanks to God

⁴I can never stop thanking God for all the generous gifts he has given you, now that you belong to Christ Jesus. ⁵He has enriched your church with the gifts of eloquence and every kind of knowledge. ⁶This shows that what I told you about Christ is true. ⁷Now you have every spiritual gift you need as you eagerly wait for the return of our Lord Jesus Christ. ⁸He will keep you strong right up to the end, and he will keep you free from all blame on the great day when our Lord Jesus Christ returns. ⁹God will surely do this for you, for he always does just what he says,

---

1:2 Corinth was a giant cultural melting pot with a great diversity of ethnic groups, religions, intellectual perspectives, and moral standards. It had a reputation for being fiercely independent and decadent. Idolatry flourished; more than a dozen pagan temples at one time had employed at least a thousand religious prostitutes. The new believers in Corinth had to deal with many deep-rooted habits and attitudes as they sought to nurture their new lives in Christ. Temptations of all kinds abounded throughout the city. Corinth was not unlike our world today. The apostle Paul's advice to these early believers will touch on many of the issues we face today.

1:4-9 Although there were problems among the Corinthian believers, Paul began his letter to them on a positive note. He understood that confronting others about their failures is more effective when we approach them diplomatically. We need to gain a hearing by recognizing the good things in the lives of those we need to confront. In this way, we show that we are concerned about them and value them as people. Our intervention will be effective only when we first show that we love the people we want to help.

and he is the one who invited you into this wonderful friendship with his Son, Jesus Christ our Lord.

Divisions in the Church

¹⁰Now, dear brothers and sisters,* I appeal to you by the authority of the Lord Jesus Christ to stop arguing among yourselves. Let there be real harmony so there won't be divisions in the church. I plead with you to be of one mind, united in thought and purpose. ¹¹For some members of Chloe's household have told me about your arguments, dear brothers and sisters. ¹²Some of you are saying, "I am a follower of Paul." Others are saying, "I follow Apollos," or "I follow Peter,*" or "I follow only Christ." ¹³Can Christ be divided into pieces?

Was I, Paul, crucified for you? Were any of you baptized in the name of Paul? ¹⁴I thank God that I did not baptize any of you except Crispus and Gaius, ¹⁵for now no one can say they were baptized in my name. ¹⁶(Oh yes, I also baptized the household of Stephanas. I don't remember baptizing anyone else.) ¹⁷For Christ didn't send me to baptize, but to preach the Good News—and not with clever speeches and high-sounding ideas, for fear that the cross of Christ would lose its power.

The Wisdom of God

¹⁸I know very well how foolish the message of the cross sounds to those who are on the road to destruction. But we who are being saved recognize this message as the very power of God. ¹⁹As the Scriptures say,

"I will destroy human wisdom
and discard their most brilliant ideas."*

²⁰So where does this leave the philosophers, the scholars, and the world's brilliant debaters? God has made them all look foolish and has shown their wisdom to be useless nonsense. ²¹Since God in his wisdom saw to it that the world would never find him through human wisdom, he has used our foolish preaching to save all who believe. ²²God's way seems foolish to the Jews because they want a sign from heaven to prove it is true. And it is foolish to the Greeks because they believe only what agrees with their own wisdom. ²³So when we preach that Christ was crucified, the Jews are offended, and the Gentiles say it's all nonsense. ²⁴But to those called by God to salvation, both Jews and Gentiles,* Christ is the mighty power of God and the wonderful wisdom of God. ²⁵This "foolish" plan of God is far wiser than the wisest of human plans, and God's weakness is far stronger than the greatest of human strength.

²⁶Remember, dear brothers and sisters, that few of you were wise in the world's eyes, or powerful, or wealthy when God called you. ²⁷Instead, God deliberately chose things the world considers foolish in order to shame those who think they are wise. And he chose those who are powerless to shame those who are powerful. ²⁸God chose things despised by the world, things counted as nothing at all, and used them to bring to nothing what the world considers important, ²⁹so that no one can ever boast in the presence of God.

³⁰God alone made it possible for you to be in Christ Jesus. For our benefit God made Christ to be wisdom itself. He is the one who made us acceptable to God. He made us pure and holy, and he gave himself to purchase our freedom. ³¹As the Scriptures say,

"The person who wishes to boast
should boast only of what the Lord
has done."*

1:10 Greek *brothers;* also in 1:11, 26. **1:12** Greek *Cephas.* **1:19** Isa 29:14. **1:24** Greek *Greeks.* **1:31** Jer 9:24.

1:12 The Corinthian believers had begun to elevate various leaders to unhealthy positions in their lives. They were attributing power and wisdom to these people that no one but God could legitimately claim. This is a form of idolatry—a sin God forbids in the Ten Commandments (Exodus 20:3). All too often we give people, perhaps religious leaders or the leaders of recovery movements, positions of gods in our life. We believe everything they say and are willing to do anything they ask us to do. This is dangerous. We must remember that all people are powerless—the only one worthy of worship is Christ himself. We must measure everything we hear against the eternal truth of God's Word.
1:18-19 Some Corinthian believers followed the human wisdom of the day, which called the idea of salvation in Christ into question. It seemed too simple! How could God forgive us through what Christ did on the cross? Surely we need to do something special or know something special to be saved! Paul made it clear that we need nothing but a willing heart to receive God's power and forgiveness. We have no power or ability that can overcome the power of sin in our life. In fact, a life of self-sufficiency is ultimately self-destructive. When we turn our life over to God, we accept his way—the way of the cross. Only then can we experience God's power.

CHAPTER 2
Paul Preaches Wisdom

Dear brothers and sisters,* when I first came to you I didn't use lofty words and brilliant ideas to tell you God's message.* ²For I decided to concentrate only on Jesus Christ and his death on the cross. ³I came to you in weakness—timid and trembling. ⁴And my message and my preaching were very plain. I did not use wise and persuasive speeches, but the Holy Spirit was powerful among you. ⁵I did this so that you might trust the power of God rather than human wisdom.

⁶Yet when I am among mature Christians, I do speak with words of wisdom, but not the kind of wisdom that belongs to this world, and not the kind that appeals to the rulers of this world, who are being brought to nothing. ⁷No, the wisdom we speak of is the secret wisdom of God,* which was hidden in former times, though he made it for our benefit before the world began. ⁸But the rulers of this world have not understood it; if they had, they would never have crucified our glorious Lord. ⁹That is what the Scriptures mean when they say,

"No eye has seen, no ear has heard,
and no mind has imagined
what God has prepared
for those who love him."*

¹⁰But we know these things because God has revealed them to us by his Spirit, and his Spirit searches out everything and shows us even God's deep secrets. ¹¹No one can know what anyone else is really thinking except that person alone, and no one can know God's thoughts except God's own Spirit. ¹²And God has actually given us his Spirit (not the world's spirit) so we can know the wonderful things God has freely given us. ¹³When we tell you this, we do not use words of human wisdom. We speak words given to us by the Spirit, using the Spirit's words to explain spiritual truths.* ¹⁴But people who aren't Christians can't understand these truths from God's Spirit. It all sounds foolish to them because only those who have the Spirit can understand what the Spirit means. ¹⁵We who have the Spirit understand these things, but others can't understand us at all. ¹⁶How could they? For,

"Who can know what the Lord is thinking?
Who can give him counsel?"*

But we can understand these things, for we have the mind of Christ.

CHAPTER 3
Paul and Apollos, Servants of Christ

Dear brothers and sisters,* when I was with you I couldn't talk to you as I would to mature Christians. I had to talk as though you

---

2:1a Greek *Brothers.* **2:1b** Greek *mystery;* other manuscripts read *testimony.* **2:7** Greek *we speak God's wisdom in a mystery.* **2:9** Isa 64:4. **2:13** Or *explaining spiritual truths in spiritual language,* or *explaining spiritual truths to spiritual people.* **2:16** Isa 40:13. **3:1a** Greek *Brothers.*

2:1-5 Many times when we seek to help others, we overwhelm them with complicated theories and instructions. Paul realized that doing this would only confuse the Corinthians, making them think that salvation was dependent on some kind of special wisdom or knowledge. So he brought them the plain, simple message of the gospel: There is nothing we can do to save ourself, for God has done everything necessary for our deliverance. As we share our story of deliverance with others, we need to keep things simple and trust the power of the Holy Spirit to work in their lives.
2:7 God has had a good plan for us from the beginning of time. If we allow him to work in our life, that plan will come about. No matter how badly we have sinned, God can still turn things around so they work out according to his will. Our part is to entrust our life to him and seek to follow his will as he reveals it to us. No matter what we have done in the past, God still chooses to love us and to work his restoration within us.
2:9-10 When our life is unmanageable and we feel as if we have lost direction, we often blame God or feel that somehow he is making things worse. Paul reminded the Corinthians that God had wonderful things planned for them, things even more wonderful than they could imagine. This message is for us, too. If we turn our life and will over to God, he can build a new life for us that is beyond our wildest dreams.
2:14-15 People who refuse to turn their life over to the care of God cannot understand God's truth or his plan. That's why recovery begins not with understanding but with a decision to follow God. Prior to that decision, God's way may seem like madness. Only when we face the fact that our life is insane can we open ourself to God and his good plan for us.
3:1-4 Part of maturing is realizing that following our own desires leads down a dead-end street. We remain "infants" as long as we try to do things our own way. Maturity occurs only as we begin to follow God's will for our life. Then we will consider what God wants and what others

belonged to this world or as though you were infants in the Christian life.* ²I had to feed you with milk and not with solid food, because you couldn't handle anything stronger. And you still aren't ready, ³for you are still controlled by your own sinful desires. You are jealous of one another and quarrel with each other. Doesn't that prove you are controlled by your own desires? You are acting like people who don't belong to the Lord. ⁴When one of you says, "I am a follower of Paul," and another says, "I prefer Apollos," aren't you acting like those who are not Christians?*

⁵Who is Apollos, and who is Paul, that we should be the cause of such quarrels? Why, we're only servants. Through us God caused you to believe. Each of us did the work the Lord gave us. ⁶My job was to plant the seed in your hearts, and Apollos watered it, but it was God, not we, who made it grow. ⁷The ones who do the planting or watering aren't important, but God is important because he is the one who makes the seed grow. ⁸The one who plants and the one who waters work as a team with the same purpose. Yet they will be rewarded individually, according to their own hard work. ⁹We work together as partners who belong to God. You are God's field, God's building—not ours.

¹⁰Because of God's special favor to me, I have laid the foundation like an expert builder. Now others are building on it. But whoever is building on this foundation must be very careful. ¹¹For no one can lay any other foundation than the one we already have—Jesus Christ. ¹²Now anyone who builds on that foundation may use gold, silver, jewels, wood, hay, or straw. ¹³But there is going to come a time of testing at the judgment day to see what kind of work each builder has done. Everyone's work will be put through the fire to see whether or not it keeps its value. ¹⁴If the work survives the fire, that builder will receive a reward. ¹⁵But if the work is burned up, the builder will suffer great loss. The builders themselves will be saved, but like someone escaping through a wall of flames.

¹⁶Don't you realize that all of you together are the temple of God and that the Spirit of God lives in* you? ¹⁷God will bring ruin upon anyone who ruins this temple. For God's temple is holy, and you Christians are that temple.

¹⁸Stop fooling yourselves. If you think you are wise by this world's standards, you will have to become a fool so you can become wise by God's standards. ¹⁹For the wisdom of this world is foolishness to God. As the Scriptures say,

"God catches those who think they
    are wise
    in their own cleverness."*

3:1b Greek *in Christ.* 3:4 Greek *aren't you merely human?* 3:16 Or *among.* 3:19 Job 5:13.

---

need before we act. To do this we have to give the control of our life and will over to God. It may also mean that we have to delay self-gratification at times for the sake of others. This is not easy, but when we do it, we will experience the meaningful life that God wants for each of us.

3:5-6 As we progress in recovery, we are to reach out to others. As we tell them about our deliverance, hoping to help them turn their lives around, these verses should encourage us. Even when the message doesn't seem to be getting through, we can leave the results in God's hands. Sometimes people respond to our story immediately and enter recovery. At other times our words are only seeds that over time will grow and lead someone to be changed by God's power. Perhaps we are just one of many people God will use to change someone's life. One thing is sure: If we speak out, God will use us to change lives.

3:13-15 Many of us struggle with denial because the truth is so painful. We avoid the truth about our sins so we won't have to make difficult changes in our life. But no matter how much we hide from our mistakes, in time they will come back to haunt us. Allowing our dependency to continue unchecked will lead to painful consequences. Here we are reminded that those consequences continue into eternity. A day of reckoning will come! Have we put our life in God's hands? As we turn our life over to him, he will help us build on a solid foundation. When the day of reckoning arrives, we will still be standing.

3:18-20 It is possible for intelligence to hinder progress in recovery. As we analyze the steps we are asked to take, we may find them somewhat foolish or demeaning. The truth is, sometimes following God's plan will not make perfect sense to us. We may wonder how entrusting our life to God can change anything. We might even find that following God's will is embarrassing at times. True understanding often happens only as we take steps to obey God's program for healing. We may be better off throwing aside our need to analyze and understand so that we can experience God's healing power through simple faith and obedience.

²⁰And again,

"The Lord knows the thoughts of the wise,
    that they are worthless."*

²¹So don't take pride in following a particular leader. Everything belongs to you: ²²Paul and Apollos and Peter*; the whole world and life and death; the present and the future. Everything belongs to you, ²³and you belong to Christ, and Christ belongs to God.

CHAPTER 4
Paul and the Corinthians

So look at Apollos and me as mere servants of Christ who have been put in charge of explaining God's secrets. ²Now, a person who is put in charge as a manager must be faithful. ³What about me? Have I been faithful? Well, it matters very little what you or anyone else thinks. I don't even trust my own judgment on this point. ⁴My conscience is clear, but that isn't what matters. It is the Lord himself who will examine me and decide.

⁵So be careful not to jump to conclusions before the Lord returns as to whether or not someone is faithful. When the Lord comes, he will bring our deepest secrets to light and will reveal our private motives. And then God will give to everyone whatever praise is due.

⁶Dear brothers and sisters,* I have used Apollos and myself to illustrate what I've been saying. If you pay attention to the Scriptures,* you won't brag about one of your leaders at the expense of another. ⁷What makes you better than anyone else? What do you have that God hasn't given you? And if all you have is from God, why boast as though you have accomplished something on your own?

⁸You think you already have everything you need! You are already rich! Without us you have become kings! I wish you really were on your thrones already, for then we would be reigning with you! ⁹But sometimes I think God has put us apostles on display, like prisoners of war at the end of a victor's parade, condemned to die. We have become a spectacle to the entire world—to people and angels alike.

¹⁰Our dedication to Christ makes us look like fools, but you are so wise! We are weak, but you are so powerful! You are well thought of, but we are laughed at. ¹¹To this very hour we go hungry and thirsty, without enough clothes to keep us warm. We have endured many beatings, and we have no homes of our own. ¹²We have worked wearily with our own hands to earn our living. We bless those who curse us. We are patient with those who abuse us. ¹³We respond gently when evil things are said about us. Yet we are treated like the world's garbage, like everybody's trash—right up to the present moment.

¹⁴I am not writing these things to shame you, but to warn you as my beloved children. ¹⁵For even if you had ten thousand others to teach you about Christ, you have only one spiritual father. For I became your father in Christ Jesus when I preached the Good News to you. ¹⁶So I ask you to follow my example and do as I do.

¹⁷That is the very reason I am sending Timothy—to help you do this. For he is my beloved and trustworthy child in the Lord. He will remind you of what I teach about Christ Jesus in all the churches wherever I go.

¹⁸I know that some of you have become arrogant, thinking I will never visit you again. ¹⁹But I will come—and soon—if the Lord will let me, and then I'll find out whether these arrogant people are just big

3:20 Ps 94:11. **3:22** Greek *Cephas*. **4:6a** Greek *Brothers*. **4:6b** Or *You must learn not to go beyond "what is written," so that.*

4:6-13 How easy it is to become puffed up about our success and forget that pride leads to a fall. The Corinthian believers were very self-sufficient, looking down on Paul and his ministry among them. Their prideful attitudes led them away from Paul's teachings about Christ, a dangerous thing for anyone living in a diverse religious environment like theirs. It is just as dangerous for us to become proud about our success in recovery. We forget that it was God's power that delivered us and that we continue to need his help. If we allow pride to get a foothold in our life, we will discover that self-sufficiency leads to relapse.

4:17 Paul sent Timothy to remind the Corinthian believers of what Paul had taught them. The apostle realized that they needed someone to hold them accountable to the truth they had been taught and to encourage them to persevere in their faith. One of the best ways to protect ourself from self-sufficiency is to be accountable to others. Mentors and sponsors are there to help us remember what works in recovery. They are also there to help us learn how to develop faithfulness in our life, an essential part of our spiritual growth.

talkers or whether they really have God's power. [20]For the Kingdom of God is not just fancy talk; it is living by God's power. [21]Which do you choose? Should I come with punishment and scolding, or should I come with quiet love and gentleness?

CHAPTER 5
Paul Condemns Spiritual Pride

I can hardly believe the report about the sexual immorality going on among you, something so evil that even the pagans don't do it. I am told that you have a man in your church who is living in sin with his father's wife. [2]And you are so proud of yourselves! Why aren't you mourning in sorrow and shame? And why haven't you removed this man from your fellowship?

[3]Even though I am not there with you in person, I am with you in the Spirit.* Concerning the one who has done this, I have already passed judgment [4]in the name of the Lord Jesus. You are to call a meeting of the church,* and I will be there in spirit, and the power of the Lord Jesus will be with you as you meet. [5]Then you must cast this man out of the church and into Satan's hands, so that his sinful nature will be destroyed* and he himself* will be saved when the Lord returns.

[6]How terrible that you should boast about your spirituality, and yet you let this sort of thing go on. Don't you realize that if even one person is allowed to go on sinning, soon all will be affected? [7]Remove this wicked person from among you so that you can stay pure.* Christ, our Passover Lamb, has been sacrificed for us. [8]So let us celebrate the festival, not by eating the old bread* of wickedness and evil, but by eating the new bread* of purity and truth.

[9]When I wrote to you before, I told you not to associate with people who indulge in sexual sin. [10]But I wasn't talking about unbelievers who indulge in sexual sin, or who are greedy or are swindlers or idol worshipers. You would have to leave this world to avoid people like that. [11]What I meant was that you are not to associate with anyone who claims to be a Christian* yet indulges in sexual sin, or is greedy, or worships idols, or is abusive, or a drunkard, or a swindler. Don't even eat with such people.

[12]It isn't my responsibility to judge outsiders, but it certainly is your job to judge those inside the church who are sinning in these ways. [13]God will judge those on the outside; but as the Scriptures say, "You must remove the evil person from among you."*

5:3 Or *in spirit.* **5:4** Or *In the name of the Lord Jesus, you are to call a meeting of the church.* **5:5a** Or *so that he will die;* Greek reads *for the destruction of the flesh.* **5:5b** Greek *and the spirit.* **5:6-7** Greek *Don't you realize that even a little leaven spreads quickly through the whole batch of dough?* [7]*Purge out the old leaven so that you can be a new batch of dough, just as you are already unleavened.* **5:8a** Greek *not with old leaven.* **5:8b** Greek *but with unleavened [bread].* **5:11** Greek *a brother.* **5:13** Deut 17:7.

5:1-5 We face many of the same forms of sexual immorality that the Corinthians faced. Like the believers in Corinth, we tend to put on a blindfold and tell ourself that everything is all right. Our denial of illicit sexual activity and sexual abuse, however, only builds barriers between us and others. In time we even grow distant from God. Such denial allows the problems in our churches and communities to fester until individuals and families are torn apart. We need to open our eyes to the problems around us and confront them together as a community, as Paul advised the Corinthians to do.

5:6-8 Paul called the Corinthian believers to remove the unrepentant sinner from their fellowship. If they didn't, his destructive activities would eat away at their church fellowship like a cancer. This principle is important in recovery. As we begin our program, we need to give up the relationships and activities that are likely to lead to our downfall. When Paul called the Corinthians to excommunicate this unrepentant sinner, he also instructed them to take part in wholesome activities. Likewise, when we give up our destructive activities and relationships, we must replace them with wholesome activities and godly people who will encourage us in the recovery process.

5:9-13 Paul warned his people to avoid close relationships with other believers who were in denial about their sins. But they were not to totally isolate themselves from unbelievers either. They were still to share the Good News with people who needed to hear the message. We also need to avoid close relationships with people who will drag us down and try to hinder our recovery. Yet as we experience God's power in our life, we need to share this news with others. Our story of deliverance may save the lives of others in bondage. As we share the message, not only will we be a source of hope to others, but we will also find renewed strength to continue our own recovery.

CHAPTER 6
Avoiding Lawsuits with Christians

When you have something against another Christian, why do you file a lawsuit and ask a secular court to decide the matter, instead of taking it to other Christians to decide who is right? ²Don't you know that someday we Christians are going to judge the world? And since you are going to judge the world, can't you decide these little things among yourselves? ³Don't you realize that we Christians will judge angels? So you should surely be able to resolve ordinary disagreements here on earth. ⁴If you have legal disputes about such matters, why do you go to outside judges who are not respected by the church? ⁵I am saying this to shame you. Isn't there anyone in all the church who is wise enough to decide these arguments? ⁶But instead, one Christian* sues another—right in front of unbelievers!

⁷To have such lawsuits at all is a real defeat for you. Why not just accept the injustice and leave it at that? Why not let yourselves be cheated? ⁸But instead, you yourselves are the ones who do wrong and cheat even your own Christian brothers and sisters.*

Avoiding Sexual Sin

⁹Don't you know that those who do wrong will have no share in the Kingdom of God? Don't fool yourselves. Those who indulge in sexual sin, who are idol worshipers, adulterers, male prostitutes, homosexuals, ¹⁰thieves, greedy people, drunkards, abusers, and swindlers—none of these will have a share in the Kingdom of God. ¹¹There was a time when some of you were just like that, but now your sins have been washed away,* and you have been set apart for God. You have been made right with God because of what the Lord Jesus Christ and the Spirit of our God have done for you.

¹²You may say, "I am allowed to do anything." But I reply, "Not everything is good for you." And even though "I am allowed to do anything," I must not become a slave to anything. ¹³You say, "Food is for the stomach, and the stomach is for food." This is true, though someday God will do away with both of them. But our bodies were not made for sexual immorality. They were made for the Lord, and the Lord cares about our bodies. ¹⁴And God will raise our bodies from the dead by his marvelous power, just as he raised our Lord from the dead. ¹⁵Don't you realize that your bodies

6:6 Greek *one brother.* **6:8** Greek *brothers.* **6:11** Or *you have been cleansed.*

6:1-6 Taking someone to court, as painful as it may be, is often the easy way out of a conflict. Instead of working our problems out, we hand them over to an impartial judge. Dealing with conflict in such an indirect way usually leads to separation rather than reconciliation. Paul warned the Corinthian believers not to go to unbelieving judges to settle their disputes. If God's power is at work within us, we can use the wisdom and guidance of the Holy Spirit to settle our conflicts. We need to keep this in mind as we seek to make amends with those we have harmed.

6:18-20 Sexual sin affects us like no other sin. It isn't that it is the heaviest on some imaginary sin scale, but its effects are broad and devastating. In sexual sin, we sin not only against ourself but also against other people and against God. Our body is the dwelling place of God's Holy Spirit, and it belongs to God. This is a convincing reason for taking care of our body and seeking a new life in recovery.

7:2-5 Marriage is the God-given place for sexual expression and fulfillment. Our body doesn't belong to us; it belongs to God. But here Paul is saying that our body also belongs to our spouse. If we seek sexual fulfillment outside of marriage, we will be trapped by selfish pleasure seeking. Only in marriage can our sexuality be acted out with concern for and commitment to the other person involved. If we belong to God and to our spouse, we have the potential to act in ways to bring them great joy. Our challenge is to not seek only our personal gratification. As we keep our sexuality within the bounds of marriage, we experience the joy that comes from living faithfully with another person before God.

7:8-9 If we are single, we may feel that recovery would be easier if we had the help of a spouse. If we are married, we may think we could focus more on recovery if we were unmarried. Whether we are single or married, there are difficulties that we must deal with. When we wish we were in a different situation, we are usually wanting to avoid the responsibilities of our present situation. We should seek ways to improve the situation we are in rather than abandoning it for something else. Abandoning relationships or desperately grasping at new ones will never solve our problems.

are actually parts of Christ? Should a man take his body, which belongs to Christ, and join it to a prostitute? Never! ¹⁶And don't you know that if a man joins himself to a prostitute, he becomes one body with her? For the Scriptures say, "The two are united into one."* ¹⁷But the person who is joined to the Lord becomes one spirit with him.

¹⁸Run away from sexual sin! No other sin so clearly affects the body as this one does. For sexual immorality is a sin against your own body. ¹⁹Or don't you know that your body is the temple of the Holy Spirit, who lives in you and was given to you by God? You do not belong to yourself, ²⁰for God bought you with a high price. So you must honor God with your body.

CHAPTER 7
Instruction on Marriage
Now about the questions you asked in your letter. Yes, it is good to live a celibate life. ²But because there is so much sexual immorality, each man should have his own wife, and each woman should have her own husband.

³The husband should not deprive his wife of sexual intimacy, which is her right as a married woman, nor should the wife deprive her husband. ⁴The wife gives authority over her body to her husband, and the husband also gives authority over his body to his wife. ⁵So do not deprive each other of sexual relations. The only exception to this rule would be the agreement of both husband and wife to refrain from sexual intimacy for a limited time, so they can give themselves more completely to prayer. Afterward they should come together again so that Satan won't be able to tempt them because of their lack of self-control. ⁶This is only my suggestion. It's not meant to be an absolute rule. ⁷I wish everyone could get along without marrying, just as I do. But we are not all the same. God gives some the gift of marriage, and to others he gives the gift of singleness.

⁸Now I say to those who aren't married and to widows—it's better to stay unmarried, just as I am. ⁹But if they can't control themselves, they should go ahead and marry. It's better to marry than to burn with lust.

¹⁰Now, for those who are married I have a command that comes not from me, but from

Delayed Gratification

READ 1 CORINTHIANS 6:1-13
Our appetites can overtake and enslave us. Perfectly good activities can get us into trouble when we fail to practice them in moderation. Or there may be times when we don't feed our appetites in balanced ways. Then we become so starved that we fall to the temptation of our addiction at the first opportunity.

This happened to Esau in the Old Testament book of Genesis. One day he came home so hungry that he promised his birthright to his younger brother in exchange for a bowl of porridge. We are warned: "Make sure that no one is immoral or godless like Esau. He traded his birthright as the oldest son for a single meal. And afterward, when he wanted his father's blessing, he was rejected. It was too late for repentance, even though he wept bitter tears" (Hebrews 12:16-17). The apostle Paul wrote: "You may say, 'I am allowed to do anything.' But I reply, 'Not everything is good for you.' And even though 'I am allowed to do anything,' I must not become a slave to anything" (1 Corinthians 6:12).

We need to satisfy our appetites in appropriate ways so we don't become starved and thus more susceptible to temptation. There may be some good things that have such control over us that it's best to avoid them altogether. If we allow the demands of our appetites to become overpowering, we might risk losing things (or people) that we might never get back. *Turn to page 275, 1 Corinthians 13.*

the Lord.* A wife must not leave her husband. [11]But if she does leave him, let her remain single or else go back to him. And the husband must not leave his wife.

[12]Now, I will speak to the rest of you, though I do not have a direct command from the Lord. If a Christian man* has a wife who is an unbeliever and she is willing to continue living with him, he must not leave her. [13]And if a Christian woman has a husband who is an unbeliever, and he is willing to continue living with her, she must not leave him. [14]For the Christian wife brings holiness to her marriage, and the Christian husband brings holiness to his marriage. Otherwise, your children would not have a godly influence, but now they are set apart for him. [15](But if the husband or wife who isn't a Christian insists on leaving, let them go. In such cases the Christian husband or wife is not required to stay with them, for God wants his children to live in peace.) [16]You wives must remember that your husbands might be converted because of you. And you husbands must remember that your wives might be converted because of you.

[17]You must accept whatever situation the Lord has put you in, and continue on as you were when God first called you. This is my rule for all the churches. [18]For instance, a man who was circumcised before he became a believer should not try to reverse it. And the man who was uncircumcised when he became a believer should not be circumcised now. [19]For it makes no difference whether or not a man has been circumcised. The important thing is to keep God's commandments. [20]You should continue on as you were when God called you. [21]Are you a slave? Don't let that worry you—but if you get a chance to be free, take it. [22]And remember, if you were a slave when the Lord called you, the Lord has now set you free from the awful power of sin. And if you were free when the Lord called you, you are now a slave of Christ. [23]God purchased you at a high price. Don't be enslaved by the world.* [24]So, dear brothers and sisters,* whatever situation you were in when you became a believer, stay there in your new relationship with God.

[25]Now, about the young women who are not yet married. I do not have a command from the Lord for them. But the Lord in his kindness has given me wisdom that can be trusted, and I will share it with you. [26]Because of the present crisis,* I think it is best to remain just as you are. [27]If you have a wife, do not end the marriage. If you do not have a wife, do not get married. [28]But if you do get married, it is not a sin. And if a young woman gets married, it is not a sin. However, I am trying to spare you the extra problems that come with marriage.

[29]Now let me say this, dear brothers and sisters: The time that remains is very short, so husbands should not let marriage be their major concern. [30]Happiness or sadness or wealth should not keep anyone from doing God's work. [31]Those in frequent contact with the things of the world should make good use of them without becoming attached to them, for this world and all it contains will pass away. [32]In everything you do, I want you to be free from the concerns of this life. An unmarried man can spend his time doing the Lord's work and thinking how to please him. [33]But a married man can't do that so well. He has to think about his earthly responsibilities and how to please his wife. [34]His interests are divided. In the same way, a

---

7:10 See Matt 5:32; 19:9; Mark 10:11-12; Luke 16:18. **7:12** Greek *a brother.* **7:23** Greek *don't become slaves of people.* **7:24** Greek *brothers;* also in 7:29. **7:26** Or *pressures of life.*

7:10-15 Many of us have been hurt by divorce, either as participants or as children of divorced parents. Paul firmly reminded his readers of God's command to avoid divorce at all cost. Yet he recognized that there are situations in which divorce is a legitimate option. God wants us to live in harmony with one another. When we are not experiencing harmony, we need to examine our life to see where we might need to change. If, after making appropriate changes, we still face significant problems, we may need to help our spouse through a similar process. Often a marriage counselor can facilitate this process. Divorce is an option only when one of the partners refuses to remain faithful to the marriage commitment.

7:20-24 The Roman world was filled with oppressed people, many of whom had been taken as children to a foreign land to serve as slaves. Some of these slaves came to believe in Christ, and, naturally, they yearned for freedom. They may have thought they could be better Christians if they were free. We may fall into the same trap. We look at others and think that different circumstances would make recovery easier for us. Instead of wishing for miracles, we can start the recovery process no matter what our situation. When we turn our will and our life over to God, we have a new power at work within us—regardless of our outward circumstances.

woman who is no longer married or has never been married can be more devoted to the Lord in body and in spirit, while the married woman must be concerned about her earthly responsibilities and how to please her husband.

³⁵I am saying this for your benefit, not to place restrictions on you. I want you to do whatever will help you serve the Lord best, with as few distractions as possible. ³⁶But if a man thinks he ought to marry his fiancée because he has trouble controlling his passions and time is passing, it is all right; it is not a sin. Let them marry. ³⁷But if he has decided firmly not to marry and there is no urgency and he can control his passion, he does well not to marry. ³⁸So the person who marries does well, and the person who doesn't marry does even better.

³⁹A wife is married to her husband as long as he lives. If her husband dies, she is free to marry whomever she wishes, but this must be a marriage acceptable to the Lord.* ⁴⁰But in my opinion it will be better for her if she doesn't marry again, and I think I am giving you counsel from God's Spirit when I say this.

CHAPTER 8
Food Sacrificed to Idols

Now let's talk about food that has been sacrificed to idols. You think that everyone should agree with your perfect knowledge. While knowledge may make us feel important, it is love that really builds up the church. ²Anyone who claims to know all the answers doesn't really know very much. ³But the person who loves God is the one God knows and cares for.

⁴So now, what about it? Should we eat meat that has been sacrificed to idols? Well, we all know that an idol is not really a god and that there is only one God and no other.

⁵According to some people, there are many so-called gods and many lords, both in heaven and on earth. ⁶But we know that there is only one God, the Father, who created everything, and we exist for him. And there is only one Lord, Jesus Christ, through whom God made everything and through whom we have been given life.

⁷However, not all Christians realize this. Some are accustomed to thinking of idols as being real, so when they eat food that has been offered to idols, they think of it as the worship of real gods, and their weak consciences are violated. ⁸It's true that we can't win God's approval by what we eat. We don't miss out on anything if we don't eat it, and we don't gain anything if we do. ⁹But you must be careful with this freedom of yours. Do not cause a brother or sister with a weaker conscience to stumble.

¹⁰You see, this is what can happen: Weak Christians who think it is wrong to eat this food will see you eating in the temple of an idol. You know there's nothing wrong with it, but they will be encouraged to violate their conscience by eating food that has been dedicated to the idol. ¹¹So because of your superior knowledge, a weak Christian,* for whom Christ died, will be destroyed. ¹²And you are sinning against Christ when you sin against other Christians* by encouraging them to do something they believe is wrong. ¹³If what I eat is going to make another Christian sin, I will never eat meat again as long as I live—for I don't want to make another Christian stumble.

CHAPTER 9
Paul Gives Up His Rights

Do I not have as much freedom as anyone else?* Am I not an apostle? Haven't I seen Jesus our Lord with my own eyes? Isn't it because of my hard work that you are in the

---

7:39 Or *but only to a Christian;* Greek reads *but only in the Lord.* **8:11** Greek *brother;* also in 8:13. **8:12** Greek *brothers.* **9:1** Greek *Am I not free?*

8:1-3 Love is a lifestyle in which all our thoughts and actions are guided by our concern for others. Most of us need recovery because we have lived for our own gratification. As we sought to escape our inner pain through the fleeting pleasures of addictive activities or substances, we became blind to the needs of the people around us. That lifestyle left our past littered with hurt people and broken relationships. A life governed by selfless love is the only path to rebuilding our broken past. Knowing that God loves us no matter what our past is the place to start recovery.
8:10-13 Our personal freedom is a precious right until it deprives someone else of his or her personal freedom. We can try to justify our actions by intellectualizing them, but love is the only principle that will guide us to make legitimate moral choices. When we love, our freedom to do certain things will not be as important as our relationships with others. We must learn to put the needs of others before our own desires. Love is to be the standard for our moral inventory and the motivation for making amends with the people we have wronged.

Lord? ²Even if others think I am not an apostle, I certainly am to you, for you are living proof that I am the Lord's apostle.

³This is my answer to those who question my authority as an apostle.* ⁴Don't we have the right to live in your homes and share your meals? ⁵Don't we have the right to bring a Christian wife* along with us as the other disciples and the Lord's brothers and Peter* do? ⁶Or is it only Barnabas and I who have to work to support ourselves? ⁷What soldier has to pay his own expenses? And have you ever heard of a farmer who harvests his crop and doesn't have the right to eat some of it? What shepherd takes care of a flock of sheep and isn't allowed to drink some of the milk? ⁸And this isn't merely human opinion. Doesn't God's law say the same thing? ⁹For the law of Moses says, "Do not keep an ox from eating as it treads out the grain."* Do you suppose God was thinking only about oxen when he said this? ¹⁰Wasn't he also speaking to us? Of course he was. Just as farm workers who plow fields and thresh the grain expect a share of the harvest, Christian workers should be paid by those they serve.

¹¹We have planted good spiritual seed among you. Is it too much to ask, in return, for mere food and clothing? ¹²If you support others who preach to you, shouldn't we have an even greater right to be supported? Yet we have never used this right. We would rather put up with anything than put an ob-

stacle in the way of the Good News about Christ.

¹³Don't you know that those who work in the Temple get their meals from the food brought to the Temple as offerings? And those who serve at the altar get a share of the sacrificial offerings. ¹⁴In the same way, the Lord gave orders that those who preach the Good News should be supported by those who benefit from it. ¹⁵Yet I have never used any of these rights. And I am not writing this to suggest that I would like to start now. In fact, I would rather die than lose my distinction of preaching without charge. ¹⁶For preaching the Good News is not something I can boast about. I am compelled by God to do it. How terrible for me if I didn't do it!

¹⁷If I were doing this of my own free will, then I would deserve payment. But God has chosen me and given me this sacred trust, and I have no choice. ¹⁸What then is my pay? It is the satisfaction I get from preaching the Good News without expense to anyone, never demanding my rights as a preacher.

¹⁹This means I am not bound to obey people just because they pay me, yet I have become a servant of everyone so that I can bring them to Christ. ²⁰When I am with the Jews, I become one of them so that I can bring them to Christ. When I am with those who follow the Jewish laws, I do the same, even though I am not subject to the law, so

9:3 Greek *those who examine me.* 9:5a Greek *a sister, a wife.* 9:5b Greek *Cephas.* 9:9 Deut 25:4.

9:4-12 Paul modeled giving up personal freedom to show love toward others. Paul had all the rights we have, but he willingly gave them up because of his relationship with Jesus Christ and his desire to help others. We may feel that we have certain freedoms and rights, but if we desire to make progress in recovery, we may have to give up some of those rights. We may have the right to take part in certain activities or frequent certain places, but we probably know that some of these things will lead to a fall. We need to give up activities and relationships that will lead to relapse. We may also need to relinquish some of our rights to support others in recovery.

9:15-18 Paul gave up his right to be paid for his work in the ministry, choosing instead to support himself. The point wasn't whether or not he should have been paid. He was illustrating the principle that when God has called us to do something, we may have to give up some of our rights and freedoms to accomplish it. If we hope to progress in recovery, our relationship with Jesus Christ and adherence to his program need to take the central place in our life. We may need to give up some of our possessions, activities, and codependent relationships to achieve the freedom that we long for.

9:19-23 An essential part of recovery is sharing the Good News of God's forgiveness and help. Paul shows us that if we want to communicate to others, we must first take the time to understand where they are coming from. Paul listened to his audience and found common ground with them before he helped them change. As we seek to help others, we begin by gaining their confidence. We don't need to be good at winning arguments; we need to be good at listening and showing that we care. Paul listened to the needs of people and then presented his message in a way that met their specific needs. We can do the same as we carry the message of hope to hurting people.

that I can bring them to Christ. 21When I am with the Gentiles who do not have the Jewish law,* I fit in with them as much as I can. In this way, I gain their confidence and bring them to Christ. But I do not discard the law of God; I obey the law of Christ.

22When I am with those who are oppressed, I share their oppression so that I might bring them to Christ. Yes, I try to find common ground with everyone so that I might bring them to Christ. 23I do all this to spread the Good News, and in doing so I enjoy its blessings.

24Remember that in a race everyone runs, but only one person gets the prize. You also must run in such a way that you will win. 25All athletes practice strict self-control. They do it to win a prize that will fade away, but we do it for an eternal prize. 26So I run straight to the goal with purpose in every step. I am not like a boxer who misses his punches.* 27I discipline my body like an athlete, training it to do what it should. Otherwise, I fear that after preaching to others I myself might be disqualified.

CHAPTER 10
Warnings against Idolatry

I don't want you to forget, dear brothers and sisters,* what happened to our ancestors in the wilderness long ago. God guided all of them by sending a cloud that moved along ahead of them, and he brought them all safely through the waters of the sea on dry ground. 2As followers of Moses, they were all baptized in the cloud and the sea. 3And all of them ate the same miraculous* food, 4and all of them drank the same miraculous water. For they all drank from the miraculous rock that traveled with them, and that rock was

Christ. 5Yet after all this, God was not pleased with most of them, and he destroyed them in the wilderness.

6These events happened as a warning to us, so that we would not crave evil things as they did 7or worship idols as some of them did. For the Scriptures say, "The people celebrated with feasting and drinking, and they indulged themselves in pagan revelry."* 8And we must not engage in sexual immorality as some of them did, causing 23,000 of them to die in one day. 9Nor should we put Christ* to the test, as some of them did and then died from snakebites. 10And don't grumble as some of them did, for that is why God sent his angel of death to destroy them. 11All these events happened to them as examples for us. They were written down to warn us, who live at the time when this age is drawing to a close.

12If you think you are standing strong, be careful, for you, too, may fall into the same sin. 13But remember that the temptations that come into your life are no different from what others experience. And God is faithful. He will keep the temptation from becoming so strong that you can't stand up against it. When you are tempted, he will show you a way out so that you will not give in to it.

14So, my dear friends, flee from the worship of idols. 15You are reasonable people. Decide for yourselves if what I am about to say is true. 16When we bless the cup at the Lord's Table, aren't we sharing in the benefits of the blood of Christ? And when we break the loaf of bread, aren't we sharing in the benefits of the body of Christ? 17And we all eat from one loaf, showing that we are one body. 18And think about the nation of Israel; all who eat the sacrifices are united by that act.

9:21 Greek *those without the law.* 9:26 Or *I am not just shadowboxing.* 10:1 Greek *brothers.* 10:3 Greek *spiritual;* also in 10:4. 10:7 Exod 32:6. 10:9 Some manuscripts read *the Lord.*

9:24-27 The process of recovery is a lot like training for a title bout in boxing or preparing for a marathon. These activities require a great deal of endurance and strict discipline for those who want to win. No one ever said recovery would be easy, and Paul makes it clear that growing in our relationship with God can be tough. If we want to succeed in recovery and grow spiritually, we need to focus on those goals. We need to give up the destructive activities that will slow us down and train rigorously. If we recognize that things won't be easy at the outset of our program and persevere toward our eternal prize, we will experience God's power and the freedom of recovery.

10:1-13 Paul had just used himself as an example of the disciplined, vigilant athlete. Here he used the history of Israel to show us what not to be like. The Israelites' lack of self-discipline and vigilance against temptation led them into sin. They were overconfident, and that attitude led them to disobey God's good instructions for them. Paul held up Israel's failure as a warning to us. If we follow their example, we will suffer the same painful consequences that they did.

¹⁹What am I trying to say? Am I saying that the idols to whom the pagans bring sacrifices are real gods and that these sacrifices are of some value? ²⁰No, not at all. What I am saying is that these sacrifices are offered to demons, not to God. And I don't want any of you to be partners with demons. ²¹You cannot drink from the cup of the Lord and from the cup of demons, too. You cannot eat at the Lord's Table and at the table of demons, too. ²²What? Do you dare to rouse the Lord's jealousy as Israel did? Do you think we are stronger than he is?

²³You say, "I am allowed to do anything"— but not everything is helpful. You say, "I am allowed to do anything"—but not everything is beneficial. ²⁴Don't think only of your own good. Think of other Christians and what is best for them.

²⁵Here's what you should do. You may eat any meat that is sold in the marketplace. Don't ask whether or not it was offered to idols, and then your conscience won't be bothered. ²⁶For "the earth is the Lord's, and everything in it."*

²⁷If someone who isn't a Christian asks you home for dinner, go ahead; accept the invitation if you want to. Eat whatever is offered to you and don't ask any questions about it. Your conscience should not be bothered by this. ²⁸But suppose someone warns you that this meat has been offered to an idol. Don't eat it, out of consideration for the conscience of the one who told you. ²⁹It might not be a matter of conscience for you, but it is for the other person.

Now, why should my freedom be limited by what someone else thinks? ³⁰If I can thank God for the food and enjoy it, why should I be condemned for eating it? ³¹Whatever you eat or drink or whatever you do, you must do all for the glory of God. ³²Don't give offense to Jews or Gentiles or the church of God. ³³That is the plan I follow, too. I try to please everyone in everything I do. I don't just do what I like or what is best for me, but what is best for them so they may be saved.

CHAPTER 11

And you should follow my example, just as I follow Christ's.

Instructions for Public Worship

²I am so glad, dear friends, that you always keep me in your thoughts and you are following the Christian teaching I passed on to you. ³But there is one thing I want you to know: A man is responsible to Christ, a woman is responsible to her husband, and Christ is responsible to God. ⁴A man dishonors Christ* if he covers his head while praying or prophesying. ⁵But a woman dishonors her husband* if she prays or prophesies without a covering on her head, for this is the same as shaving her head. ⁶Yes, if she refuses to wear a head covering, she should cut off all her hair. And since it is shameful for a woman to have her hair cut or her head shaved, then she should wear a covering.* ⁷A man should not wear anything on his head

---

10:26 Ps 24:1. **11:4** Greek *his head.* **11:5** Greek *her head.* **11:6** Or *then she should have long hair.*

10:19-22 We cannot serve both Christ and the devil. We cannot be in recovery and dabble in our old lifestyle. Compromising our personal standards to please those who represent our dysfunctional past is walking on dangerous ground. If we continue in this pattern, our relationship with God will soon falter, and our recovery will be in jeopardy. Recovery requires a choice, and that choice means we have to leave some things behind.

10:23-33 Paul sought to balance his argument here, for it is easy to become too legalistic as we work through the recovery process. The balance can be found by being willing to give up any of our rights that might cause others to fall while also not forcing our standards on anyone else. This does not lead to codependency, where we seek to please others for unhealthy reasons. Paul sought to please others for the specific purpose of leading them to salvation. If our actions are governed by our love for others, we will be well on the way to developing strong relationships and overcoming the problems that drive our addiction or compulsion. God will also use us as powerful instruments to help other hurting people.

11:17-22 Paul tried to solve a problem in the Corinthian church. Apparently some of the wealthier believers looked down on the poorer members and refused to share from their abundance at the communion meal. Paul made it clear that a superior attitude is extremely destructive. As we undergo recovery, we must share the process with others. There may be people in our groups whom we feel are below us, but this kind of attitude is destructive. In God's eyes, no one is better than anyone else. We are all broken by sin and need God's transforming power. Our material well-being or educational level does not make us better. When we recognize this and humbly share our failures with others, we can make progress in recovery.

GOD grant me the serenity to accept the things I cannot change the courage to change the things I can and the wisdom to know the difference A M E N

Unfortunately, temptation is a permanent part of our sinful world and of human experience. The Bible says, "The temptations that come into your life are no different from what others experience" (1 Corinthians 10:13). Not only is temptation all around us; it is within us as well. "Temptation comes from the lure of our own evil desires" (James 1:14). Even if we could rid ourself of all external temptations, we would still have to live with the destructive desires within our old nature.

Belief in an instant cure for addiction will put our recovery at risk; on the other hand, belief that we will someday be beyond the reach of temptation is also dangerous.

Even Jesus Christ faced temptation, and yet he never sinned. Before he was tempted, he spent an extended period of time alone in the wilderness, and he went without food. We are usually tempted the most when we are lonely or hungry.

Facing temptation is part of accepting reality. We need to accept the fact that we will always be susceptible to temptation in our areas of weakness and predisposition. When we receive Christ as our Savior, God gives us a new nature, but it is unrealistic to believe that our old sinful nature will ever disappear. When we put away the false belief that temptation will magically disappear when we turn to God, we will be more aware and better able to avoid yielding to temptation's power. We need to prayerfully seek God's help in dealing with this reality of life. ***Turn to page 329, Philippians 4.***

---

when worshiping, for man is God's glory, made in God's own image, but woman is the glory of man. [8]For the first man didn't come from woman, but the first woman came from man. [9]And man was not made for woman's benefit, but woman was made for man. [10]So a woman should wear a covering on her head as a sign of authority because the angels are watching.

[11]But in relationships among the Lord's people, women are not independent of men, and men are not independent of women. [12]For although the first woman came from man, all men have been born from women ever since, and everything comes from God.

[13]What do you think about this? Is it right for a woman to pray to God in public without covering her head? [14]Isn't it obvious that it's disgraceful for a man to have long hair? [15]And isn't it obvious that long hair is a woman's pride and joy? For it has been given

to her as a covering. [16]But if anyone wants to argue about this, all I can say is that we have no other custom than this, and all the churches of God feel the same way about it.

Order at the Lord's Supper

[17]But now when I mention this next issue, I cannot praise you. For it sounds as if more harm than good is done when you meet together. [18]First of all, I hear that there are divisions among you when you meet as a church, and to some extent I believe it. [19]But, of course, there must be divisions among you so that those of you who are right will be recognized!

[20]It's not the Lord's Supper you are concerned about when you come together. [21]For I am told that some of you hurry to eat your own meal without sharing with others. As a result, some go hungry while others get drunk. [22]What? Is this really true? Don't you have your own homes for eating and

drinking? Or do you really want to disgrace the church of God and shame the poor? What am I supposed to say about these things? Do you want me to praise you? Well, I certainly do not!

²³For this is what the Lord himself said, and I pass it on to you just as I received it. On the night when he was betrayed, the Lord Jesus took a loaf of bread, ²⁴and when he had given thanks, he broke it and said, "This is my body, which is given* for you. Do this in remembrance of me." ²⁵In the same way, he took the cup of wine after supper, saying, "This cup is the new covenant between God and you, sealed by the shedding of my blood. Do this in remembrance of me as often as you drink it." ²⁶For every time you eat this bread and drink this cup, you are announcing the Lord's death until he comes again.

²⁷So if anyone eats this bread or drinks this cup of the Lord unworthily, that person is guilty of sinning against the body and the blood of the Lord. ²⁸That is why you should examine yourself before eating the bread and drinking from the cup. ²⁹For if you eat the bread or drink the cup unworthily, not honoring the body of Christ,* you are eating and drinking God's judgment upon yourself. ³⁰That is why many of you are weak and sick and some have even died.

³¹But if we examine ourselves, we will not be examined by God and judged in this way. ³²But when we are judged and disciplined by the Lord, we will not be condemned with the world. ³³So, dear brothers and sisters,* when you gather for the Lord's Supper, wait for each other. ³⁴If you are really hungry, eat at home so you won't bring judgment upon yourselves when you meet together.

I'll give you instructions about the other matters after I arrive.

CHAPTER 12
Spiritual Gifts
And now, dear brothers and sisters,* I will write about the special abilities the Holy Spirit gives to each of us, for I must correct your misunderstandings about them. ²You know that when you were still pagans you were led astray and swept along in worshiping speechless idols. ³So I want you to know how to discern what is truly from God: No one speaking by the Spirit of God can curse Jesus, and no one is able to say, "Jesus is Lord," except by the Holy Spirit.

⁴Now there are different kinds of spiritual gifts, but it is the same Holy Spirit who is the source of them all. ⁵There are different kinds of service in the church, but it is the same Lord we are serving. ⁶There are different ways God works in our lives, but it is the same God who does the work through all of us. ⁷A spiritual gift is given to each of us as a means of helping the entire church.

⁸To one person the Spirit gives the ability to give wise advice; to another he gives the gift of special knowledge. ⁹The Spirit gives special faith to another, and to someone else he gives the power to heal the sick. ¹⁰He gives one person the power to perform miracles, and to another the ability to prophesy. He gives someone else the ability to know whether it is really the Spirit of God or another spirit that is speaking. Still another person is given the ability to speak in unknown languages,* and another is given the ability to interpret what is being said. ¹¹It is the one and only Holy Spirit who distributes these gifts. He alone decides which gift each person should have.

One Body with Many Parts
¹²The human body has many parts, but the many parts make up only one body. So it is

11:24 Some manuscripts read *broken.* 11:29 Greek *the body;* some manuscripts read *the Lord's body.* 11:33 Greek *brothers.* 12:1 Greek *brothers.* 12:10 Or *in tongues;* also in 12:28, 30.

11:27-30 In these verses Paul called the Corinthians to make a searching and fearless moral inventory of their lives. Some of them needed to recognize their pride and take steps to remove it. This is something we all need to do regularly; it must be a way of life for us. Spiritual growth, emotional growth, and recovery depend on our faithfulness in taking our personal inventory. Paul noted here that even physical illness can be the result of not examining our life before taking Communion. When we take the time for a regular moral inventory we will gain victory over the destructive forces in our life.

12:4-11 God has gifted each of us in some way. No one is without talents and special abilities. When we put ourself down, we are rejecting these gifts from God rather than delighting in them. We don't need to build up our self-esteem; we just need to see more accurately who we are and how God has gifted us. Whether we have recognized it or not, being in recovery is a unique gift in itself. Having suffered through the process of failure and deliverance, we are uniquely gifted to help others struggling in similar ways. By sharing what God has done for us, we may be giving the gift of life to someone else in need.

with the body of Christ. [13]Some of us are Jews, some are Gentiles, some are slaves, and some are free. But we have all been baptized into Christ's body by one Spirit, and we have all received the same Spirit.*

[14]Yes, the body has many different parts, not just one part. [15]If the foot says, "I am not a part of the body because I am not a hand," that does not make it any less a part of the body. [16]And if the ear says, "I am not part of the body because I am only an ear and not an eye," would that make it any less a part of the body? [17]Suppose the whole body were an eye—then how would you hear? Or if your whole body were just one big ear, how could you smell anything?

[18]But God made our bodies with many parts, and he has put each part just where he wants it. [19]What a strange thing a body would be if it had only one part! [20]Yes, there are many parts, but only one body. [21]The eye can never say to the hand, "I don't need you." The head can't say to the feet, "I don't need you."

[22]In fact, some of the parts that seem weakest and least important are really the most necessary. [23]And the parts we regard as less honorable are those we clothe with the greatest care. So we carefully protect from the eyes of others those parts that should not be seen, [24]while other parts do not require this special care. So God has put the body together in such a way that extra honor and care are given to those parts that have less dignity. [25]This makes for harmony among the members, so that all the members care for each other equally. [26]If one part suffers, all the parts suffer with it, and if one part is honored, all the parts are glad.

[27]Now all of you together are Christ's body, and each one of you is a separate and necessary part of it. [28]Here is a list of some of the members that God has placed in the body of Christ:

first are apostles,
second are prophets,
third are teachers,
then those who do miracles,
those who have the gift of healing,
those who can help others,
those who can get others to work together,
those who speak in unknown languages.

[29]Is everyone an apostle? Of course not. Is everyone a prophet? No. Are all teachers? Does everyone have the power to do miracles? [30]Does everyone have the gift of healing? Of course not. Does God give all of us the ability to speak in unknown languages? Can everyone interpret unknown languages? No! [31]And in any event, you should desire the most helpful gifts.

Love Is the Greatest

First, however, let me tell you about something else that is better than any of them!

CHAPTER 13

If I could speak in any language in heaven or on earth* but didn't love others, I would only be making meaningless noise like a loud gong or a clanging cymbal. [2]If I had the gift of prophecy, and if I knew all the mysteries of the future and knew everything about everything, but didn't love others, what good would I be? And if I had the gift of faith so that I could speak to a mountain and make it move, without love I would be no good to anybody. [3]If I gave everything I have to the poor and even sacrificed my body, I could boast about it;* but if I didn't love others, I would be of no value whatsoever.

[4]Love is patient and kind. Love is not jealous or boastful or proud [5]or rude. Love does not demand its own way. Love is not irritable, and it keeps no record of when it has

12:13 Greek *we were all given one Spirit to drink.* **13:1** Greek *in tongues of people and angels.* **13:3** Some manuscripts read *and even gave my body to be burned.*

12:12-26 When we become proud of our gifts and accomplishments, we invariably end up hurting ourself and others. God has gifted all of us in some way or another. If we do not recognize this truth, we may take credit for our progress in recovery and flaunt our success. This kind of pride causes pain to others and leads us toward a fall. When we have an accurate view of ourself, we will give God the credit for the gifts he has given us and be thankful for his help in recovery. If we cannot do this, we need to go back to Step One and once again admit how powerless we really are.

13:1-3 Paul was writing to a group of believers who had started to forget what real love is. He showed them that all their abilities, talents, and spiritual gifts amounted to nothing if they didn't love each other. Without selfless love, we have nothing. Loving relationships are also essential to the recovery process.

been wronged. ⁶It is never glad about injustice but rejoices whenever the truth wins out. ⁷Love never gives up, never loses faith, is always hopeful, and endures through every circumstance.

⁸Love will last forever, but prophecy and speaking in unknown languages* and special knowledge will all disappear. ⁹Now we know only a little, and even the gift of prophecy reveals little! ¹⁰But when the end comes, these special gifts will all disappear.

¹¹It's like this: When I was a child, I spoke and thought and reasoned as a child does. But when I grew up, I put away childish things. ¹²Now we see things imperfectly as in a poor mirror, but then we will see everything with perfect clarity.* All that I know now is partial and incomplete, but then I will know everything completely, just as God knows me now.

¹³There are three things that will endure—faith, hope, and love—and the greatest of these is love.

CHAPTER 14
The Gifts of Tongues and Prophecy
Let love be your highest goal, but also desire the special abilities the Spirit gives, especially the gift of prophecy. ²For if your gift is the ability to speak in tongues,* you will be talking to God but not to people, since they won't be able to understand you. You will be speaking by the power of the Spirit, but it will all be mysterious. ³But one who prophesies is helping others grow in the Lord, encouraging and comforting them. ⁴A person who speaks in tongues is strengthened personally in the Lord, but one who speaks a word of prophecy strengthens the entire church.

⁵I wish you all had the gift of speaking in tongues, but even more I wish you were all able to prophesy. For prophecy is a greater and more useful gift than speaking in tongues, unless someone interprets what you are saying so that the whole church can get some good out of it.

⁶Dear brothers and sisters,* if I should come to you talking in an unknown language,* how would that help you? But if I bring you some revelation or some special knowledge or some prophecy or some teaching—that is what will help you. ⁷Even musical instruments like the flute or the harp, though they are lifeless, are examples of the need for speaking in plain language. For no one will recognize the melody unless the notes are played clearly. ⁸And if the bugler doesn't sound a clear call, how will the soldiers know they are being called to battle? ⁹And it's the same for you. If you talk to people in a language they don't understand, how will they know what you mean? You might as well be talking to an empty room.

¹⁰There are so many different languages in the world, and all are excellent for those who understand them, ¹¹but to me they mean nothing. I will not understand people who

---

13:8 Or *in tongues*. **13:12** Greek *see face to face*. **14:2** Or *in unknown languages;* also in 14:4, 5, 13, 14, 18, 22, 28, 39. **14:6a** Greek *brothers;* also in 14:20, 26, 39. **14:6b** Or *in tongues;* also in 14:19, 23, 26, 27.

13:11-13 Recovery and growth are never complete in this life; we are always in recovery—always growing. We are still like children, needing to mature. Only when we see God face to face will we be complete and whole. Paul shares this truth not to discourage us, but to give us hope that someday we will be made perfect. We will persevere in the process of recovery if we have *faith* in God and those around us. We need *hope* to endure and be healed from our painful problems and addiction. Most of all we need genuine *love* to conquer the barriers and bondage of our past. Faith, hope, and love are all necessary to successful recovery. Genuine love, however, is the greatest healer of all.

14:1-12 Paul returned to the subject of spiritual gifts. He warned us not to use our gifts to build ourself up or to reinforce our own sense of self-sufficiency. All spiritual gifts are just that—gifts. They are given to us by God to be used to build others up and encourage them in their spiritual growth. Using our God-given gifts for our own purposes shows that we have forgotten the one who gave the gifts in the first place—God. This kind of attitude invariably leads to failure. We will succeed as we acknowledge that we are powerless and in need of God's powerful help.

14:26-39 Paul summarized his teachings on relationships, especially those characterized by healthy interdependence. We are to live in community with others, building them up and meeting their needs. It is important to distinguish between this kind of relationship and a codependent relationship, in which we relate to others for an ulterior motive, perhaps seeking to meet our own lack or need. Healthy interdependent relationships attempt to meet others' needs without seeking some hidden reward. When we learn to love selflessly as Paul proposed, the physical and emotional needs of everyone in our community will be met. One of the goals of recovery is restoring our broken, dysfunctional relationships, turning them into healthy, interdependent ones.

speak those languages, and they will not understand me. 12Since you are so eager to have spiritual gifts, ask God for those that will be of real help to the whole church.

13So anyone who has the gift of speaking in tongues should pray also for the gift of interpretation in order to tell people plainly what has been said. 14For if I pray in tongues, my spirit is praying, but I don't understand what I am saying.

15Well then, what shall I do? I will do both. I will pray in the spirit,* and I will pray in words I understand. I will sing in the spirit, and I will sing in words I understand. 16For if you praise God only in the spirit, how can those who don't understand you praise God along with you? How can they join you in giving thanks when they don't understand what you are saying? 17You will be giving thanks very nicely, no doubt, but it doesn't help the other people present.

18I thank God that I speak in tongues more than all of you. 19But in a church meeting I would much rather speak five understandable words that will help others than ten thousand words in an unknown language.

20Dear brothers and sisters, don't be childish in your understanding of these things. Be innocent as babies when it comes to evil, but be mature and wise in understanding matters of this kind. 21It is written in the Scriptures,*

"I will speak to my own people
through unknown languages
and through the lips of foreigners.
But even then, they will not listen
to me,"*
says the Lord.

22So you see that speaking in tongues is a sign, not for believers, but for unbelievers; prophecy, however, is for the benefit of believers, not unbelievers. 23Even so, if unbelievers or people who don't understand these things come into your meeting and hear everyone talking in an unknown language, they will think you are crazy. 24But if all of you are prophesying, and unbelievers or people who don't understand these things come into your meeting, they will be convicted of sin, and they will be condemned by what you say. 25As they listen, their secret thoughts will be laid bare, and they will fall down on their knees and worship God, declaring, "God is really here among you."

14:15 Or *in the Spirit;* also in 14:15b, 16. **14:21a** Greek *in the law.* **14:21b** Isa 28:11-12.

Love

READ 1 CORINTHIANS 13:1-7

We may have given up on love. Perhaps we have waited for love to find us, only to be disappointed. Maybe our loved ones have hurt us so badly that we needed to numb ourself from the pain. In the past our addiction helped to keep us numb, but now that we are in recovery, we have to find ways to deal with the issue of love once again.

It is God's will that we love others; without love nothing else matters (see 1 Corinthians 13:1-3). Love is more than a feeling; it is choosing to behave in loving ways. It is a fruit of the Holy Spirit, produced in our life as we yield to God. The Bible defines it this way: "Love is patient and kind. Love is not jealous or boastful or proud or rude. . . . Love never gives up, never loses faith, is always hopeful, and endures through every circumstance" (1 Corinthians 13:4-7).

This passage is a description of how God loves us. As we begin to absorb his love, we will find ourself reaching out to love again. No one loves perfectly, but we must learn how to love. We can ask God to help us love others and stop waiting for them to love us. We cannot expect to be good at loving right away; we should be patient as God's love grows within us and he teaches us how to love. When we choose to act in loving ways, the emotions will follow, and we will find that our love will be returned. *Turn to page 287, 2 Corinthians 5.*

A Call to Orderly Worship

²⁶Well, my brothers and sisters, let's summarize what I am saying. When you meet, one will sing, another will teach, another will tell some special revelation God has given, one will speak in an unknown language, while another will interpret what is said. But everything that is done must be useful to all and build them up in the Lord. ²⁷No more than two or three should speak in an unknown language. They must speak one at a time, and someone must be ready to interpret what they are saying. ²⁸But if no one is present who can interpret, they must be silent in your church meeting and speak in tongues to God privately.

²⁹Let two or three prophesy, and let the others evaluate what is said. ³⁰But if someone is prophesying and another person receives a revelation from the Lord, the one who is speaking must stop. ³¹In this way, all who prophesy will have a turn to speak, one after the other, so that everyone will learn and be encouraged. ³²Remember that people who prophesy are in control of their spirit and can wait their turn. ³³For God is not a God of disorder but of peace, as in all the other churches.*

³⁴Women should be silent during the church meetings. It is not proper for them to speak. They should be submissive, just as the law says. ³⁵If they have any questions to ask, let them ask their husbands at home, for it is improper for women to speak in church meetings.*

³⁶Do you think that the knowledge of God's word begins and ends with you Corinthians? Well, you are mistaken! ³⁷If you claim to be a prophet or think you are very spiritual, you should recognize that what I am saying is a command from the Lord himself. ³⁸But if you do not recognize this, you will not be recognized.*

³⁹So, dear brothers and sisters, be eager to prophesy, and don't forbid speaking in tongues. ⁴⁰But be sure that everything is done properly and in order.

CHAPTER 15

The Resurrection of Christ

Now let me remind you, dear brothers and sisters,* of the Good News I preached to you before. You welcomed it then and still do now, for your faith is built on this wonderful message. ²And it is this Good News that saves you if you firmly believe it—unless, of course, you believed something that was never true in the first place.

³I passed on to you what was most important and what had also been passed on to me—that Christ died for our sins, just as the Scriptures said. ⁴He was buried, and he was raised from the dead on the third day, as the Scriptures said. ⁵He was seen by Peter* and then by the twelve apostles. ⁶After that, he was seen by more than five hundred of his followers* at one time, most of whom are still alive, though some have died by now. ⁷Then he was seen by James and later by all the apostles. ⁸Last of all, I saw him, too, long after the others, as though I had been born at the wrong time. ⁹For I am the least of all the apostles, and I am not worthy to be called an apostle after the way I persecuted the church of God.

¹⁰But whatever I am now, it is all because God poured out his special favor on me—and not without results. For I have worked harder than all the other apostles, yet it was not I but God who was working through me by his grace. ¹¹So it makes no difference whether I preach or they preach. The important thing is that you believed what we preached to you.

The Resurrection of the Dead

¹²But tell me this—since we preach that Christ rose from the dead, why are some of you say-

---

14:33 The phrase *as in all the other churches* could be joined to the beginning of 14:34. **14:35** Some manuscripts place verses 34-35 after 14:40. **14:38** Some manuscripts read *If you are ignorant of this, stay in your ignorance.*
15:1 Greek *brothers;* also in 15:31, 50, 58. **15:5** Greek *Cephas.* **15:6** Greek *the brothers.*

15:10 In recovery we often say something beginning with "But for the grace of God, I . . ." Such statements started with Paul as he recognized that without God's grace, he never would have achieved any of his success. We must recognize that our success in recovery is from God. When we fail to give the credit to God for what has happened in our life, we negate our progress by forgetting the lessons of its earliest steps. Notice, however, that Paul also recognized his own hard work in the process. Recovery is based on the grace of God and his desire to help us, but we still have a part in the equation: We have to work hard! Recovery takes a combination of God's power and our faithful willingness to obey him.
15:12-20 Some of the Corinthian believers had begun to question the hope of being resurrected to new life at Christ's second coming. So Paul reemphasized the importance of the resurrection

ing there will be no resurrection of the dead? [13]For if there is no resurrection of the dead, then Christ has not been raised either. [14]And if Christ was not raised, then all our preaching is useless, and your trust in God is useless. [15]And we apostles would all be lying about God, for we have said that God raised Christ from the grave, but that can't be true if there is no resurrection of the dead. [16]If there is no resurrection of the dead, then Christ has not been raised. [17]And if Christ has not been raised, then your faith is useless, and you are still under condemnation for your sins. [18]In that case, all who have died believing in Christ have perished! [19]And if we have hope in Christ only for this life, we are the most miserable people in the world.

[20]But the fact is that Christ has been raised from the dead. He has become the first of a great harvest of those who will be raised to life again.

[21]So you see, just as death came into the world through a man, Adam, now the resurrection from the dead has begun through another man, Christ. [22]Everyone dies because all of us are related to Adam, the first man. But all who are related to Christ, the other man, will be given new life. [23]But there is an order to this resurrection: Christ was raised first; then when Christ comes back, all his people will be raised.

[24]After that the end will come, when he will turn the Kingdom over to God the Father, having put down all enemies of every kind.* [25]For Christ must reign until he humbles all his enemies beneath his feet. [26]And the last enemy to be destroyed is death. [27]For the Scriptures say, "God has given him authority over all things."* (Of course, when it says "authority over all things," it does not include God himself, who gave Christ his authority.) [28]Then, when he has conquered all things, the Son will present himself to God, so that God, who gave his Son authority over all things, will be utterly supreme over everything everywhere.

[29]If the dead will not be raised, then what point is there in people being baptized for those who are dead? Why do it unless the dead will someday rise again?

[30]And why should we ourselves be continually risking our lives, facing death hour by hour? [31]For I swear, dear brothers and sisters, I face death daily. This is as certain as my pride in what the Lord Jesus Christ has done in you. [32]And what value was there in fighting wild beasts—those men of Ephesus*—if there will be no resurrection from the dead? If there is no resurrection,

"Let's feast and get drunk,
for tomorrow we die!"*

[33]Don't be fooled by those who say such things, for "bad company corrupts good character." [34]Come to your senses and stop sinning. For to your shame I say that some of you don't even know God.

The Resurrection Body

[35]But someone may ask, "How will the dead be raised? What kind of bodies will they have?" [36]What a foolish question! When you put a seed into the ground, it doesn't grow into a plant unless it dies first. [37]And what you put in the ground is not the plant that will grow, but only a dry little seed of wheat or whatever it is you are planting. [38]Then God gives it a new body—just the kind he wants it

15:24 Greek *every ruler and every authority and power.* **15:27** Ps 8:6. **15:32a** Greek *fighting wild beasts in Ephesus.* **15:32b** Isa 22:13.

and the hope it offers to all, even those who are already dead. The greatest expression of God's power was raising Jesus from the dead. If God could do that, then he has the power to do anything! If God did not raise Jesus from the grave, however, then our God is powerless, and we are lost. Paul affirmed the truth that Jesus did rise from the dead; in so doing, he also affirmed that we have access to the greatest power in the universe—God himself.

15:29-34 If death is the end of everything, then a selfish, pleasure-seeking lifestyle may be a justifiable alternative. But Paul reminds us that our hope and our recovery lead to an existence beyond the grave. It is this truth about the resurrection that motivates us to make right choices and leave behind our old way of life. If we do things God's way, we have an eternity of joy and peace to look forward to. If we do things our own way, we face an eternity of suffering.

15:35-58 No matter how terrifying our dependency may have become, death is probably still our greatest fear. Sometimes fear of death can motivate us to seek God for help with our destructive problems. Yet our fear of death can also lead us to despair and may actually feed our dependency. Paul reminds us of a fact that can remove our fear of death: Jesus Christ has conquered death. His resurrection conquered death and the "sting" of death, which is sin. With the resurrection power of Jesus Christ at work within us, nothing we do is ever wasted. God can use even our failures and relapses to teach us something for his glory.

to have. A different kind of plant grows from each kind of seed. [39]And just as there are different kinds of seeds and plants, so also there are different kinds of flesh—whether of humans, animals, birds, or fish.

[40]There are bodies in the heavens, and there are bodies on earth. The glory of the heavenly bodies is different from the beauty of the earthly bodies. [41]The sun has one kind of glory, while the moon and stars each have another kind. And even the stars differ from each other in their beauty and brightness.

[42]It is the same way for the resurrection of the dead. Our earthly bodies, which die and decay, will be different when they are resurrected, for they will never die. [43]Our bodies now disappoint us, but when they are raised, they will be full of glory. They are weak now, but when they are raised, they will be full of power. [44]They are natural human bodies now, but when they are raised, they will be spiritual bodies. For just as there are natural bodies, so also there are spiritual bodies.

[45]The Scriptures tell us, "The first man, Adam, became a living person."* But the last Adam—that is, Christ—is a life-giving Spirit. [46]What came first was the natural body, then the spiritual body comes later. [47]Adam, the first man, was made from the dust of the earth, while Christ, the second man, came from heaven. [48]Every human being has an earthly body just like Adam's, but our heavenly bodies will be just like Christ's. [49]Just as we are now like Adam, the man of the earth, so we will someday be like Christ, the man from heaven.

[50]What I am saying, dear brothers and sisters, is that flesh and blood cannot inherit the Kingdom of God. These perishable bodies of ours are not able to live forever.

[51]But let me tell you a wonderful secret God has revealed to us. Not all of us will die, but we will all be transformed. [52]It will happen in a moment, in the blinking of an eye, when the last trumpet is blown. For when the trumpet sounds, the Christians who have died* will be raised with transformed bodies. And then we who are living will be transformed so that we will never die. [53]For our perishable earthly bodies must be transformed into heavenly bodies that will never die.

[54]When this happens—when our perishable earthly bodies have been transformed into heavenly bodies that will never die—then at last the Scriptures will come true:

"Death is swallowed up in victory.*
[55]O death, where is your victory?
O death, where is your sting?"*

[56]For sin is the sting that results in death, and the law gives sin its power. [57]How we thank God, who gives us victory over sin and death through Jesus Christ our Lord!

[58]So, my dear brothers and sisters, be strong and steady, always enthusiastic about the Lord's work, for you know that nothing you do for the Lord is ever useless.

CHAPTER 16
The Collection for Jerusalem

Now about the money being collected for the Christians in Jerusalem: You should follow the same procedures I gave to the churches in Galatia. [2]On every Lord's Day,* each of you should put aside some amount of money in relation to what you have earned and save it for this offering. Don't wait until I get there and then try to collect it all at once. [3]When I come I will write letters of recommendation for the messengers you choose to deliver your gift to Jerusalem. [4]And if it seems appropriate for me also to go along, then we can travel together.

Paul's Final Instructions

[5]I am coming to visit you after I have been to Macedonia, for I am planning to travel through Macedonia. [6]It could be that I will stay awhile with you, perhaps all winter, and then you can send me on my way to the next destination. [7]This time I don't want to make just a short visit and then go right on. I want to come and stay awhile, if the Lord will let me. [8]In the meantime, I will be staying here at Ephesus until the Festival of Pentecost, [9]for there is a wide-open door for a great work here, and many people are responding. But there are many who oppose me.

[10]When Timothy comes, treat him with respect. He is doing the Lord's work, just as I am. [11]Don't let anyone despise him. Send him on his way with your blessings when he

---

15:45 Gen 2:7. **15:52** Greek *the dead*. **15:54** Isa 25:8. **15:55** Hos 13:14. **16:2** Greek *every first day of the week*.

16:5-18 Throughout this letter Paul encouraged the Corinthians in their recovery and spiritual growth. In closing Paul revealed his love and trust in them by making personal requests. There is always a balance between caring for the hurts and needs of others and being able to ask for what we need as well. Healthy relationships are characterized by this kind of balanced give-and-take.

returns to me. I am looking forward to seeing him soon, along with the other brothers.

¹²Now about our brother Apollos—I urged him to join the other brothers when they visit you, but he was not willing to come right now. He will be seeing you later, when the time is right.

¹³Be on guard. Stand true to what you believe. Be courageous. Be strong. ¹⁴And everything you do must be done with love.

¹⁵You know that Stephanas and his household were the first to become Christians in Greece,* and they are spending their lives in service to other Christians. I urge you, dear brothers and sisters,* ¹⁶to respect them fully and others like them who serve with such real devotion. ¹⁷I am so glad that Stephanas, Fortunatus, and Achaicus have come here. They have been making up for the help you weren't here to give me. ¹⁸They have been a wonderful encouragement to me, as they have been to you, too. You must give proper honor to all who serve so well.

Paul's Final Greetings

¹⁹The churches here in the province of Asia* greet you heartily in the Lord, along with Aquila and Priscilla and all the others who gather in their home for church meetings. ²⁰All the brothers and sisters here have asked me to greet you for them. Greet each other in Christian love.*

²¹Here is my greeting, which I write with my own hand—PAUL.

²²If anyone does not love the Lord, that person is cursed. Our Lord, come!*

²³May the grace of the Lord Jesus be with you.

²⁴My love to all of you in Christ Jesus.*

16:15a Greek *were the firstfruits in Achaia,* the southern region of the Greek peninsula. **16:15b** Greek *brothers;* also in 16:20. **16:19** *Asia* was a Roman province in what is now western Turkey. **16:20** Greek *with a sacred kiss.* **16:22** From Aramaic, *Marana tha.* **16:24** Some manuscripts add *Amen.*

REFLECTIONS ON

FIRST

CORINTHIANS

✳insights ABOUT OUR POWERLESSNESS AND GOD'S POWER

Through a series of illustrations in **1 Corinthians 1:26-31,** Paul pointed out that God's plan for recovery doesn't utilize our human wisdom, strength, or skill. We don't have to be famous or rich to receive God's forgiveness and power. For self-sufficient people this may be hard to accept. We want to feel worthy of our salvation or recovery. But until we can admit that we are powerless to change without God's help, we are doomed to cycles of painful failure. God's free gifts of forgiveness and the power to live a new life may appear foolish to us. But when we accept Christ as our Savior and we turn our will and our life over to him, we will discover genuine power and release from the bondage of our past.

✳insights INTO FINDING GOD'S WILL

Some of us may wonder how we could ever know God's will for our life. In **1 Corinthians 2:11-12** we find that we can know God's mind and heart because he has placed his Holy Spirit within us to communicate these things to us. Often the Holy Spirit uses God's Word to communicate with us. What a privilege to read God's thoughts and feelings! God's presence in us will help us know how to deal with our painful past as he helps us make an accurate personal inventory. This will lead to a healthy view of ourself and the restoration of our broken life and relationships. If we consistently follow God's direction in our life through the Holy Spirit, our recovery is assured.

✳insights INTO HEALTHY RELATIONSHIPS

In **1 Corinthians 6:12** Paul told the Corinthian believers to avoid involvement in activities that could likely seduce them back into their old way of life. This warning is important for us in recovery, too. Many of our old activities and relationships are not wrong in themselves, but staying involved in those things will naturally lead us toward relapses. If this is the case, these activities are not good for us or our recovery. We need to avoid anything that might stop or hinder our spiritual growth in any way.

✳insights ABOUT LOVE

Most of us define love as an emotion and stop there. But in **1 Corinthians 13:4-7** Paul defined love as a commitment to act a certain way toward others. We may not always be able to conjure up the emotions and feelings of love, but we can certainly choose to practice the behaviors he listed in these verses. The apostle knew that when we behave in loving ways, feelings of love soon follow. As we seek to restore our broken relationships and make amends, we will find that Paul's description of loving action is a powerful prescription for restoration and healing.

SECOND CORINTHIANS

THE BIG PICTURE

A. PAUL DISCUSSES HIS MOTIVES AND ACTIONS (1:1–2:13)
B. PAUL RELATES HIS MINISTRY TO THE NEW COVENANT (2:14–7:16)
C. PAUL APPEALS TO HIS READERS FOR SUPPORT (8:1–9:15)
D. PAUL DEFENDS HIS APOSTOLIC AUTHORITY (10:1–13:13)

Paul wrote this letter mainly to defend the authority of his teachings about Christ. The church at Corinth was struggling, and one of its problems was the presence of members who openly challenged Paul's authority. These challengers slandered Paul's character and questioned the message he preached. They also introduced a number of dangerous false teachings. Since the believers in Corinth had come to faith through Paul's ministry, this put the entire church at risk.

The false teachers claimed that following the Jewish laws was a requirement for salvation. To counteract this false teaching, Paul emphasized the truth that God changes us from the inside out. We cannot change ourself by changing our external behavior. As we are reconciled to God, he transforms us into entirely new people; our old self is fundamentally changed.

Of course, change is never easy when it involves our lifestyle. Old habits die hard, and positive habits have a way of falling prey to neglect. Typically the habits that die hardest are our negative or unhealthy thoughts and behavioral patterns. "Out with the old; in with the new!" sounds simple, but even as we long for an end to our bad habits, we cling to them.

Fortunately, God has done something about our helpless situation. That is why we can admit our powerlessness and come to him for help. It is essential for recovery that we turn our life over to God. Through Christ's death and resurrection, God made it possible for us to experience the changes we long for. By being reconciled to him, we can have a new life in Christ, transformed from the inside out.

THE BOTTOM LINE

PURPOSE: To explain new life in Christ while also defending Paul's authority to preach. AUTHOR: The apostle Paul. AUDIENCE: The church at Corinth, a city in Greece. DATE WRITTEN: About A.D. 55 from Macedonia. SETTING: After hearing several accusations against himself circulating in Corinth, Paul wrote to the Corinthian believers to correct their misunderstandings and help them with other problems. KEY VERSE: "Those who become Christians become new persons. They are not the same anymore, for the old life is gone. A new life has begun!" (5:17). KEY PLACES: Corinth, Macedonia, Troas, Jerusalem. KEY PEOPLE AND RELATIONSHIPS: Paul with Timothy, Titus, the Corinthian believers, and some false apostles.

RECOVERY THEMES

God's Power for Our Recovery: All of us have made resolutions about how we are going to change. The results are usually the same—we end up falling back into the same old bad habits we promised to stop. The Corinthians were apparently doing the same thing, with the same results. What they failed to grasp as they listened to the false teachers was that only God's power could enable them to make changes in their lives. Likewise, our own efforts always fall short. Instead of merely making resolutions, we need to admit our powerlessness and turn our life over to God. Then we can allow his power to change us from within.

Learning to Accept Criticism: One of Paul's purposes in writing this letter was to discipline those who needed to be corrected. Criticism usually hurts. Yet it also forces us to face our problems and helps us see what we need to change. If we are going to be successful in recovery, we must confront and solve problems, not ignore them. That means being open to criticism.

Conflict Can Inspire Growth: Interpersonal conflicts are an inevitable part of being human. They can also be so discouraging that they cause us to give in to failure. But what conflicts do to us depends on how we handle them. If we view them as opportunities for growth, as Paul urged the Corinthians to do, they can urge us into being productive. If we face them and try to solve them in loving ways, they can motivate us to make progress in recovery and recommitment to one another. If we ignore them, they can eat away at us like a cancer, destroying the work of recovery not only within us but also in others around us. Conflicts are opportunities for growth if we use them as such.

God's Strength in Our Weakness: In this letter of Paul's, he told about a particular "thorn" in his flesh (12:7). We don't know what this problem was because he didn't tell us. Some have suggested that it was a physical ailment or even a disease affecting his eyes. Whatever it was, it was debilitating and chronic, and at times, it interfered with his work. It also kept Paul humble because it forced him to depend on God. Through this hardship, Paul learned to thank God for his weakness. In each of us there will always be weaknesses holding us back and bogging us down. But our weaknesses have a purpose—to bring us to God. To what better place can our weaknesses take us?

CHAPTER 1
Greetings from Paul

This letter is from Paul, appointed by God to be an apostle of Christ Jesus, and from our dear brother Timothy.

We are writing to God's church in Corinth and to all the Christians throughout Greece.*

²May God our Father and the Lord Jesus Christ give you his grace and peace.

God Offers Comfort to All

³All praise to the God and Father of our Lord Jesus Christ. He is the source* of every mercy and the God who comforts us. ⁴He comforts us in all our troubles so that we can comfort others. When others are troubled, we will be able to give them the same comfort God has given us. ⁵You can be sure that the more we suffer for Christ, the more God will shower us with his comfort through Christ. ⁶So when we

1:1 Greek *Achaia*, the southern region of the Greek peninsula. **1:3** Greek *the Father*.

1:1-7 Not only is God the God of peace, but he is also the God of mercy and comfort. That's good news, both when we are going through particular trials and when we are trying to recover from dysfunctional or abusive situations. Jesus Christ suffered greatly and unjustly when he went to the cross. He fully understands and identifies with our suffering, and he knows the kind of comfort we need. He is worthy of our trust and able to deliver us from our painful circumstances.

1:8-10 Paul wrote of his own recent need for comfort from God (see 1:3-7). Apparently, Paul and his missionary group had been almost killed as they ministered in the Roman province of Asia, now southwestern Turkey. Even though Paul and his companions thought the end had come, God delivered them. Many of us have experienced God's delivering power in our own life. Even when everything seems to be coming apart, God can rescue us from what appears to be sure destruction.

1:23–2:4 For all of his strength of personality, Paul was not insensitive to the pain of his readers. The apostle knew that the strong rebuke he needed to give these people would be devastating. He truly wanted to be positive, but he concluded that there was no way to avoid honestly confronting them about their responsibilities before God and others. Sometimes we need to be comforted; sometimes we need to be confronted. When we confront others about their failures, we must make sure that we are seeking their best, just as Paul did. It is sometimes tempting to judge others in order to cover up our own shortcomings.

are weighed down with troubles, it is for your benefit and salvation! For when God comforts us, it is so that we, in turn, can be an encouragement to you. Then you can patiently endure the same things we suffer. ⁷We are confident that as you share in suffering, you will also share God's comfort.

⁸I think you ought to know, dear brothers and sisters,* about the trouble we went through in the province of Asia. We were crushed and completely overwhelmed, and we thought we would never live through it. ⁹In fact, we expected to die. But as a result, we learned not to rely on ourselves, but on God who can raise the dead. ¹⁰And he did deliver us from mortal danger. And we are confident that he will continue to deliver us. ¹¹He will rescue us because you are helping by praying for us. As a result, many will give thanks to God because so many people's prayers for our safety have been answered.

Paul's Change of Plans

¹²We can say with confidence and a clear conscience that we have been honest* and sincere in all our dealings. We have depended on God's grace, not on our own earthly wisdom. That is how we have acted toward everyone, and especially toward you. ¹³My letters have been straightforward, and there is nothing written between the lines and nothing you can't understand. I hope someday you will fully understand us, ¹⁴even if you don't fully understand us now. Then on the day when our Lord Jesus comes back again, you will be proud of us in the same way we are proud of you.

¹⁵Since I was so sure of your understanding and trust, I wanted to give you a double blessing. ¹⁶I wanted to stop and see you on my way to Macedonia and again on my return trip. Then you could send me on my way to Judea.

¹⁷You may be asking why I changed my plan. Hadn't I made up my mind yet? Or am I like people of the world who say yes when they really mean no? ¹⁸As surely as God is true, I am not that sort of person. My yes means yes ¹⁹because Jesus Christ, the Son of God, never wavers between yes and no. He is the one whom Timothy, Silas,* and I preached to you, and he is the divine Yes— God's affirmation. ²⁰For all of God's promises have been fulfilled in him. That is why we say "Amen" when we give glory to God through Christ. ²¹It is God who gives us, along with you, the ability to stand firm for Christ.* He has commissioned

1:8 Greek *brothers.* 1:12 Some manuscripts read *holy.*
1:19 Greek *Silvanus.* 1:21 Or *who has identified us and you as genuine Christians.*

STEP 8

The Fruit of Forgiveness

BIBLE READING: 2 Corinthians 2:5-8
We made a list of all persons we had harmed and became willing to make amends to them all.
Some of the things we have done have earned us disapproval and possibly loss of love. We have found that some people love us only if they can approve of our behavior. We may have struggled with bitterness toward them because we feel as if they have been trying to punish us. If our "sins" have been made public, we may assume that we have lost the love of everyone who disapproves of our actions. This fear of rejection might deter us from reaching out to make amends.

In the young Corinthian church, a man was cut off from church fellowship when his sins were made public. After he turned around and tried to make amends, some people refused to welcome him back into the church. The apostle Paul told the believers: "The man who caused all the trouble . . . was punished enough when most of you were united in your judgment against him. Now it is time to forgive him and comfort him. Otherwise he may become so discouraged that he won't be able to recover. Now show him that you still love him" (2 Corinthians 2:5-8). Some people will follow this advice and reaffirm their love for you when you go to them.

There will be some people who will respond with forgiveness, comfort, acceptance, and love. This will help us overcome the grief, the bitterness, and the discouragement we may feel. Their forgiveness will help us move on with recovery. *Turn to page 307, Galatians 6.*

us, 22and he has identified us as his own by placing the Holy Spirit in our hearts as the first installment of everything he will give us.

23Now I call upon God as my witness that I am telling the truth. The reason I didn't return to Corinth was to spare you from a severe rebuke. 24But that does not mean we want to tell you exactly how to put your faith into practice.* We want to work together with you so you will be full of joy as you stand firm in your faith.

CHAPTER 2
So I said to myself, "No, I won't do it. I won't make them unhappy with another painful visit." 2For if I cause you pain and make you sad, who is going to make me glad? 3That is why I wrote as I did in my last letter, so that when I do come, I will not be made sad by the very ones who ought to give me the greatest joy. Surely you know that my happiness depends on your happiness. 4How painful it was to write that letter! Heartbroken, I cried over it. I didn't want to hurt you, but I wanted you to know how very much I love you.

Forgiveness for the Sinner
5I am not overstating it when I say that the man who caused all the trouble hurt your entire church more than he hurt me. 6He was punished enough when most of you were united in your judgment against him. 7Now it is time to forgive him and comfort him. Otherwise he may become so discouraged that he won't be able to recover. 8Now show him that you still love him.

1:24 Greek *want to lord it over your faith.*

9I wrote to you as I did to find out how far you would go in obeying me. 10When you forgive this man, I forgive him, too. And when I forgive him (for whatever is to be forgiven), I do so with Christ's authority for your benefit, 11so that Satan will not outsmart us. For we are very familiar with his evil schemes.

Ministers of the New Covenant
12Well, when I came to the city of Troas to preach the Good News of Christ, the Lord gave me tremendous opportunities. 13But I couldn't rest because my dear brother Titus hadn't yet arrived with a report from you. So I said good-bye and went on to Macedonia to find him.

14But thanks be to God, who made us his captives and leads us along in Christ's triumphal procession. Now wherever we go he uses us to tell others about the Lord and to spread the Good News like a sweet perfume. 15Our lives are a fragrance presented by Christ to God. But this fragrance is perceived differently by those being saved and by those perishing. 16To those who are perishing we are a fearful smell of death and doom. But to those who are being saved we are a life-giving perfume. And who is adequate for such a task as this? 17You see, we are not like those hucksters—and there are many of them—who preach just to make money. We preach God's message with sincerity and with Christ's authority. And we know that the God who sent us is watching us.

2:14-17 Continued recovery is based on sharing the Good News of God's deliverance. For some of us, this may seem impossible and terrifying. Paul shows us here that it is a natural outworking of God's grace in our life. As God transforms us, giving us victory over our dependency, we begin to reflect his grace in our life. The fragrance of God's transforming work will be a "life-giving perfume" to others if we are open and transparent with them. We don't have to be an eloquent speaker to share our story and the Good News of salvation. Our humble message passed along by our words and deeds may encourage someone who needs to get his or her life back on track.

3:4-5 In his letters Paul frequently comes across as a very confident person. He explained here, however, that his confidence was not so much self-confidence as it was "God-inspired" confidence. If we trust God to work in and through us, we can know with confidence that the resources are available to overcome any problems we might face. The most healthy foundation for self-esteem is the knowledge that we are made in God's image (Genesis 1:26-27) and that we are competent because of Christ's work on our behalf.

3:6-16 Paul's contrast between the old covenant (the law of Moses) and the new covenant (salvation through Jesus Christ) is applicable to the recovery process. The glory of the law, as well as the glory of God shining on Moses' face, faded, implying that the law was not a long-term solution to the sin problem. Likewise, the many humanistic recovery programs and other means for dealing with pain and dependencies may seem "gloriously" effective in the short run, but success through them rapidly fades. The new life that God offers through an ongoing relationship with Jesus Christ is the only means to a permanent recovery.

CHAPTER 3

Are we beginning again to tell you how good we are? Some people need to bring letters of recommendation with them or ask you to write letters of recommendation for them. ²But the only letter of recommendation we need is you yourselves! Your lives are a letter written in our* hearts, and everyone can read it and recognize our good work among you. ³Clearly, you are a letter from Christ prepared by us. It is written not with pen and ink, but with the Spirit of the living God. It is carved not on stone, but on human hearts.

⁴We are confident of all this because of our great trust in God through Christ. ⁵It is not that we think we can do anything of lasting value by ourselves. Our only power and success come from God. ⁶He is the one who has enabled us to represent his new covenant. This is a covenant, not of written laws, but of the Spirit. The old way ends in death; in the new way, the Holy Spirit gives life.

The Glory of the New Covenant

⁷That old system of law etched in stone led to death, yet it began with such glory that the people of Israel could not bear to look at Moses' face. For his face shone with the glory of God, even though the brightness was already fading away. ⁸Shouldn't we expect far greater glory when the Holy Spirit is giving life? ⁹If the old covenant, which brings condemnation, was glorious, how much more glorious is the new covenant, which makes us right with God! ¹⁰In fact, that first glory was not glorious at all compared with the overwhelming glory of the new covenant. ¹¹So if the old covenant, which has been set aside, was full of glory, then the new covenant, which remains forever, has far greater glory.

¹²Since this new covenant gives us such confidence, we can be very bold. ¹³We are not like Moses, who put a veil over his face so the people of Israel would not see the glory fading away. ¹⁴But the people's minds were hardened, and even to this day whenever the old covenant is being read, a veil covers their minds so they cannot understand the truth. And this veil can be removed only by believing in Christ. ¹⁵Yes, even today when they read Moses' writings, their hearts are covered with that veil, and they do not understand.

3:2 Some manuscripts read *your*.

The Paradox of Powerlessness

BIBLE READING: 2 Corinthians 4:7-10
We admitted that we were powerless over our dependencies—that our life had become unmanageable.
We may be afraid to admit that we are powerless and that our life is unmanageable. If we admit that we are powerless, won't we be tempted to give up completely in the struggle against our addiction? It doesn't seem to make sense that we can admit powerlessness and still find the power to go on. This paradox will be dealt with as we go on to Steps Two and Three.

Life is full of paradoxes. The apostle Paul tells us, "This precious treasure—this light and power that now shine within us—is held in perishable containers, that is, in our weak bodies. So everyone can see that our glorious power is from God and is not our own. We are pressed on every side by troubles, but we are not crushed and broken" (2 Corinthians 4:7-8).

The picture here contrasts a precious treasure and the simple container in which the treasure is stored. The living power poured into our life from above is the treasure. Our human body, with all its flaws and weaknesses, is the perishable container. As human beings, we are imperfect.

Once we recognize the paradox of powerlessness, we can be quite relieved. We don't have to always be strong or pretend to be perfect. We can live a real life, with its daily struggles, in a human body beset with weakness and still find the power from above to keep going without being crushed and broken. *Turn to Step Two, page 63, Mark 5.*

¹⁶But whenever anyone turns to the Lord, then the veil is taken away. ¹⁷Now, the Lord is the Spirit, and wherever the Spirit of the Lord is, he gives freedom. ¹⁸And all of us have had that veil removed so that we can be mirrors that brightly reflect* the glory of the Lord. And as the Spirit of the Lord works within us, we become more and more like him and reflect his glory even more.

CHAPTER 4
Treasure in Perishable Containers

And so, since God in his mercy has given us this wonderful ministry, we never give up. ²We reject all shameful and underhanded methods. We do not try to trick anyone, and we do not distort the word of God. We tell the truth before God, and all who are honest know that.

³If the Good News we preach is veiled from anyone, it is a sign that they are perishing. ⁴Satan, the god of this evil world, has blinded the minds of those who don't believe, so they are unable to see the glorious light of the Good News that is shining upon them. They don't understand the message we preach about the glory of Christ, who is the exact likeness of God.

⁵We don't go around preaching about ourselves; we preach Christ Jesus, the Lord. All we say about ourselves is that we are your servants because of what Jesus has done for us. ⁶For God, who said, "Let there be light in the darkness," has made us understand that this light is the brightness of the glory of God that is seen in the face of Jesus Christ.

⁷But this precious treasure—this light and power that now shine within us—is held in perishable containers, that is, in our weak bodies.* So everyone can see that our glorious power is from God and is not our own.

⁸We are pressed on every side by troubles, but we are not crushed and broken. We are perplexed, but we don't give up and quit. ⁹We are hunted down, but God never abandons us. We get knocked down, but we get up again and keep going. ¹⁰Through suffering, these bodies of ours constantly share in the death of Jesus so that the life of Jesus may also be seen in our bodies.

¹¹Yes, we live under constant danger of death because we serve Jesus, so that the life of Jesus will be obvious in our dying bodies. ¹²So we live in the face of death, but it has resulted in eternal life for you.

3:18 Or *so that we can see in a mirror.* **4:7** Greek *But we have this treasure in earthen vessels.*

3:17-18 The glory of God is seen in the new covenant as well as the old. But rather than being reflected on the outside, as with Moses' face, the glory of the new covenant is a transformation from the inside out. This glory shines through the lives of all who trust Jesus Christ and pursue true recovery in the power of the Holy Spirit. The further we progress in our relationship with God, the more visible God's glory becomes in our life.

4:3-4 If we will not recognize the sins in our life, we are in denial and are headed for destruction. If Satan has blinded us to our sins and addiction, we cannot accept the gift of forgiveness that God offers us through a relationship with Jesus Christ. The only way to overcome the powerful effects of our sins is to admit our helplessness and entrust our life to God. He will help us take an honest inventory of our life and empower us to change. But we begin the process by shedding our denial and accepting the Good News of salvation through Jesus Christ.

4:16-18 When we entrust our life to God, two opposite and somewhat confusing processes are simultaneously at work. On the one hand, the body's physical deterioration and eventual death are inevitable, as are the distressing trials that accompany life on this earth. On the other hand, our spirit is being renewed, preparing us day-by-day for the overwhelming glory and blessing we will experience in the presence of God throughout eternity. If we trust God to help us in our troubles now, we can look beyond those troubles to the everlasting joy he has for us in eternity.

5:6-9 The fact that God is preparing a new body and a better home for us at the end of our life cannot be proven scientifically; it must be accepted by faith because God told us so (see Hebrews 11:1). Such faith always pleases God, and it helps us overcome our great fear of death—the doorway to eternal life with God (see John 14:2-3). It is important in recovery that we entrust our life to God and seek to please him. Knowing that God wants to give us something special after this life can give us confidence and motivate us to trust him now.

5:10-11 Consequences and motives are major issues in the recovery process. Consequences for selfish and destructive actions reach even beyond the boundaries of this life. All of us will have to stand before Christ and receive his piercing evaluation. For those of us who have believed in Jesus Christ for salvation, this judgment will also include the giving of rewards. Understanding that our actions and commitments have eternal consequences can help us think twice before we act and motivate us to live according to God's program.

¹³But we continue to preach because we have the same kind of faith the psalmist had when he said, "I believed in God, and so I speak."* ¹⁴We know that the same God who raised our Lord Jesus will also raise us with Jesus and present us to himself along with you. ¹⁵All of these things are for your benefit. And as God's grace brings more and more people to Christ, there will be great thanksgiving, and God will receive more and more glory.

¹⁶That is why we never give up. Though our bodies are dying, our spirits are* being renewed every day. ¹⁷For our present troubles are quite small and won't last very long. Yet they produce for us an immeasurably great glory that will last forever! ¹⁸So we don't look at the troubles we can see right now; rather, we look forward to what we have not yet seen. For the troubles we see will soon be over, but the joys to come will last forever.

CHAPTER 5
New Bodies

For we know that when this earthly tent we live in is taken down—when we die and leave these bodies—we will have a home in heaven, an eternal body made for us by God himself and not by human hands. ²We grow weary in our present bodies, and we long for the day when we will put on our heavenly bodies like new clothing. ³For we will not be spirits without bodies, but we will put on new heavenly bodies. ⁴Our dying bodies make us groan and sigh, but it's not that we want to die and have no bodies at all. We want to slip into our new bodies so that these dying bodies will be swallowed up by everlasting life. ⁵God himself has prepared us for this, and as a guarantee he has given us his Holy Spirit.

⁶So we are always confident, even though we know that as long as we live in these bodies we are not at home with the Lord. ⁷That is why we live by believing and not by seeing. ⁸Yes, we are fully confident, and we would rather be away from these bodies, for then we will be at home with the Lord. ⁹So our aim is to please him always, whether we are here in this body or away from this body. ¹⁰For we must all stand before Christ to be judged. We will each receive whatever we deserve for the good or evil we have done in our bodies.

We Are God's Ambassadors

¹¹It is because we know this solemn fear of the Lord that we work so hard to persuade others. God knows we are sincere, and I hope you know this, too. ¹²Are we trying to

4:13 Ps 116:10. **4:16** Greek *our inner being is.*

Self-Perception

READ 2 CORINTHIANS 5:12-21

Our addiction may be so ingrained in us that we define our identity by it. We may even begin to feel that we are predisposed to behave as we do. We may grow discouraged as we are condemned for behaviors that seem beyond our control. How can we escape our self-perception that causes us to define ourself in terms of the addiction that dominates our life?

One passage in Scripture seems to identify people by their behavior: "Those who indulge in sexual sin, who are idol worshipers, adulterers, male prostitutes, homosexuals, thieves, greedy people, drunkards, abusers, and swindlers—none of these will have a share in the Kingdom of God" (1 Corinthians 6:9-10). This doesn't seem fair. We feel like we will never be able to escape our addictive nature. But the passage continues: "There was a time when some of you were just like that, but now your sins have been washed away, and you have been set apart for God. You have been made right with God because of what the Lord Jesus Christ and the Spirit of our God have done for you" (6:11). "Those who become Christians become new persons. They are not the same anymore, for the old life is gone. A new life has begun!" (2 Corinthians 5:17).

God doesn't just erase our sinful behaviors. When we identify ourself with Christ, he gives us a new identity. We will always remember what we were and realize that our sinful nature and our body may always be predisposed to a particular addiction. We may even still slip up at times, but we need no longer define ourself by our addiction. In Christ we are all the forgiven, cleansed, and holy children of God. *Turn to page 303, Galatians 5.*

pat ourselves on the back again? No, we are giving you a reason to be proud of us, so you can answer those who brag about having a spectacular ministry rather than having a sincere heart before God. [13]If it seems that we are crazy, it is to bring glory to God. And if we are in our right minds, it is for your benefit. [14]Whatever we do, it is because Christ's love controls us.* Since we believe that Christ died for everyone, we also believe that we have all died to the old life we used to live.* [15]He died for everyone so that those who receive his new life will no longer live to please themselves. Instead, they will live to please Christ, who died and was raised for them.

[16]So we have stopped evaluating others by what the world thinks about them. Once I mistakenly thought of Christ that way, as though he were merely a human being. How differently I think about him now! [17]What this means is that those who become Christians become new persons. They are not the same anymore, for the old life is gone. A new life has begun!

[18]All this newness of life is from God, who brought us back to himself through what Christ did. And God has given us the task of reconciling people to him. [19]For God was in Christ, reconciling the world to himself, no longer counting people's sins against them. This is the wonderful message he has given us to tell others. [20]We are Christ's ambassadors, and God is using us to speak to you. We urge you, as though Christ himself were here pleading with you, "Be reconciled to God!" [21]For God made Christ, who never sinned, to be the offering for our sin, so that we could be made right with God through Christ.

CHAPTER 6
As God's partners,* we beg you not to reject this marvelous message of God's great kindness. [2]For God says,

"At just the right time, I heard you.
On the day of salvation, I helped you."*

Indeed, God is ready to help you right now. Today is the day of salvation.

Paul's Hardships
[3]We try to live in such a way that no one will be hindered from finding the Lord by the way we act, and so no one can find fault with our ministry. [4]In everything we do we try to show that we are true ministers of God. We patiently endure troubles and hardships and calamities of every kind. [5]We have been beaten, been put in jail, faced angry mobs, worked to exhaustion, endured sleepless nights, and gone without food. [6]We have proved ourselves by our purity, our understanding, our patience, our kindness, our sincere love, and the power of the Holy Spirit.* [7]We have faithfully preached the truth. God's power has been working in us. We have righteousness as our weapon, both to attack and to defend ourselves. [8]We serve God whether people honor us or despise us, whether they slander us or

5:14a Or *urges us on.* 5:14b Greek *Since one died on behalf of all, then all died.* 6:1 Or *As we work together.* 6:2 Isa 49:8. 6:6 Or *the holiness of spirit.*

5:17 The new life we experience in Jesus Christ is so far-reaching and complete that we become a brand-new person through him. That does not mean that our thoughts and habits, including our compulsion or addiction, will automatically vanish. But it does mean that from God's point of view, we have been forgiven—we are a new creature in his sight. And through the power of God's Holy Spirit, we have all the power necessary for complete transformation in every area of our life.
5:18-21 One of the great needs in most recovery contexts is the reconciliation of dysfunctional or fractured relationships. At the human level, this is very difficult to do. But in the case of our broken relationship with God, he has already met us more than halfway by offering us reconciliation through Jesus Christ. God's work of reconciliation is even more profound since God committed none of the wrongs in our relationship with him. By accepting the forgiveness he offers, our relationship with God can be restored. We are also called to follow God and forgive others. If the gift of forgiveness is offered by someone else, we can humbly accept it. In this way we can begin rebuilding our relationships and making amends to the people we have wronged.
6:8-10 When we live for God and follow his program for godly living, others will react to us in one of two ways. Some honor us as genuine and support what we are trying to do; others will malign and dishonor us. If we are trying to impress others to bolster our self-esteem, we will be devastated when people react negatively. This may lead us to give up on what we have started. Paul received his self-esteem from his relationship with God and did not need to be honored by others. He knew that he could never please everyone anyway. If we live to please God, we will find that as we build healthy relationships with others we will have joy.

praise us. We are honest, but they call us impostors. [9]We are well known, but we are treated as unknown. We live close to death, but here we are, still alive. We have been beaten within an inch of our lives. [10]Our hearts ache, but we always have joy. We are poor, but we give spiritual riches to others. We own nothing, and yet we have everything.

[11]Oh, dear Corinthian friends! We have spoken honestly with you. Our hearts are open to you. [12]If there is a problem between us, it is not because of a lack of love on our part, but because you have withheld your love from us. [13]I am talking now as I would to my own children. Open your hearts to us!

The Temple of the Living God

[14]Don't team up with those who are unbelievers. How can goodness be a partner with wickedness? How can light live with darkness? [15]What harmony can there be between Christ and the Devil*? How can a believer be a partner with an unbeliever? [16]And what union can there be between God's temple and idols? For we are the temple of the living God. As God said:

"I will live in them
   and walk among them.
I will be their God,
   and they will be my people.*
[17]Therefore, come out from them
   and separate yourselves from them, says
      the Lord.

Don't touch their filthy things,
   and I will welcome you.*
[18]And I will be your Father,
   and you will be my sons and daughters,
      says the Lord Almighty.*"

CHAPTER 7

Because we have these promises, dear friends, let us cleanse ourselves from everything that can defile our body or spirit. And let us work toward complete purity because we fear God.

Paul's Joy at the Church's Repentance

[2]Please open your hearts to us. We have not done wrong to anyone. We have not led anyone astray. We have not taken advantage of anyone. [3]I'm not saying this to condemn you, for I said before that you are in our hearts forever. We live or die together with you. [4]I have the highest confidence in you, and my pride in you is great. You have greatly encouraged me; you have made me happy despite all our troubles.

[5]When we arrived in Macedonia there was no rest for us. Outside there was conflict from every direction, and inside there was fear. [6]But God, who encourages those who are discouraged, encouraged us by the arrival of Titus. [7]His presence was a joy, but so was the news he brought of the encouragement he received from you. When he told me how much you were looking forward to my visit,

6:15 Greek *and Beliar.* **6:16** Lev 26:12; Ezek 37:27. **6:17** Isa 52:11; Ezek 20:34. **6:18** 2 Sam 7:14.

6:11-13 Paul went the extra mile to reconcile with the Corinthians. Having defended his sincerity toward them earlier (see 1:12-23), he again pledged his honest affection to his readers, challenging them to do the same for him. In recovering relationships, one party often withholds affection to childishly punish the other. This only leads to deeper alienation and loss. We may not be able to control how other people act in a broken relationship, but we can control how *we* act. We should never withhold forgiveness. Like Paul, we should extend the invitation of reconciliation to others, humbly and without reservation.

6:14-18 Since we started the recovery process, we may have struggled with our past friendships. Some old friends may be uncomfortable with us because they feel guilty about their own dependency. Others may be threatened by the changes we are making because they can no longer control us. These people may try to stop us from making progress. Very often we need to put our codependent relationships on hold for a time, sometimes even permanently. This does not mean we do not reach out to unbelievers; it only means that we do not become too close to people who could lead us away from God and the recovery he desires for us. Our primary relationships need to be with unselfish, godly people who will support our recovery.

7:5-7 For all his determined and aggressive style of ministry, Paul was definitely a man with emotions. Here he freely admitted his fears during a very difficult time. But he was greatly comforted by God through the arrival of Titus from Corinth. Titus brought news that the Corinthian believers had changed their negative attitudes toward Paul. In recovery it is important that we keep a similar balance between our personal tasks and our relationships. If we get so focused on the recovery tasks that we undervalue our relationships, our recovery is at risk. One of the most important parts of recovery is reconciliation with other people, without which long-term success is impossible.

and how sorry you were about what had happened, and how loyal your love is for me, I was filled with joy!

⁸I am no longer sorry that I sent that letter to you, though I was sorry for a time, for I know that it was painful to you for a little while. ⁹Now I am glad I sent it, not because it hurt you, but because the pain caused you to have remorse and change your ways. It was the kind of sorrow God wants his people to have, so you were not harmed by us in any way. ¹⁰For God can use sorrow in our lives to help us turn away from sin and seek salvation. We will never regret that kind of sorrow. But sorrow without repentance is the kind that results in death.

¹¹Just see what this godly sorrow produced in you! Such earnestness, such concern to clear yourselves, such indignation, such alarm, such longing to see me, such zeal, and such a readiness to punish the wrongdoer. You showed that you have done everything you could to make things right. ¹²My purpose was not to write about who did the wrong or who was wronged. I wrote to you so that in the sight of God you could show how much you really do care for us. ¹³We have been encouraged by this.

In addition to our own encouragement, we were especially delighted to see how happy Titus was at the way you welcomed him and set his mind at ease. ¹⁴I had told him how proud I was of you—and you didn't dis-

appoint me. I have always told you the truth, and now my boasting to Titus has also proved true! ¹⁵Now he cares for you more than ever when he remembers the way you listened to him and welcomed him with such respect and deep concern. ¹⁶I am very happy now because I have complete confidence in you.

CHAPTER 8
A Call to Generous Giving

Now I want to tell you, dear brothers and sisters,* what God in his kindness has done for the churches in Macedonia. ²Though they have been going through much trouble and hard times, their wonderful joy and deep poverty have overflowed in rich generosity. ³For I can testify that they gave not only what they could afford but far more. And they did it of their own free will. ⁴They begged us again and again for the gracious privilege of sharing in the gift for the Christians in Jerusalem. ⁵Best of all, they went beyond our highest hopes, for their first action was to dedicate themselves to the Lord and to us for whatever directions God might give them.

⁶So we have urged Titus, who encouraged your giving in the first place, to return to you and encourage you to complete your share in this ministry of giving. ⁷Since you excel in so many ways—you have so much faith, such gifted speakers, such knowledge, such enthusiasm, and such love for us*—now I want

8:1 Greek *brothers.* **8:7** Some manuscripts read *love from us to you.*

7:11-13 When we admit our sins to God and others and do what we can to follow God's will, wonderful changes take place in our life. In these verses we see that such repentance produces fruit on three fronts: (1) it purifies and revitalizes our life and emotions in a remarkable way; (2) it renews our relationship with God; and (3) it has an amazing effect for good on our relationships with other people, both those we have wronged and onlookers who are encouraged by the refreshing changes that have taken place.

7:15 For all the mistakes the Corinthians made in their relationship with Paul, they did do one thing right. They listened when Titus presented Paul's version of some earlier events that they had misinterpreted. This teachability and lack of defensiveness drew great admiration and love from both Titus and Paul. A willingness to listen and be teachable is necessary for a successful recovery. It will help us take honest moral inventory and follow God's good plan for our life.

8:9 Jesus Christ is the perfect model for graciously helping others. He became a lowly human being and died like a criminal on a cross to conquer our enemies—sin and death. He gave up his heavenly glory and willingly suffered on our behalf (see Philippians 2:6-8). Thus, besides enriching our life spiritually, Christ can also strongly identify with our pain and temptation (see Hebrews 4:15). He is available and able to help us in recovery. As we receive his help, we can then reach out helping hands to others in need.

8:10-12 It is much easier to start something than to finish it. This is especially true as we work through the recovery process. Thus, perseverance is crucial for those of us with the tendency to "run out of gas." The Corinthians had enthusiastically started a relief fund for the Jerusalem church but failed to follow through on their commitment. Paul confronted them and encouraged them to persevere in this worthy task. Recovery is no less worthy of perseverance. We need to do more than make promises and verbal commitments to recovery; we need to follow through on them as well.

you to excel also in this gracious ministry of giving. [8]I am not saying you must do it, even though the other churches are eager to do it. This is one way to prove your love is real.

[9]You know how full of love and kindness our Lord Jesus Christ was. Though he was very rich, yet for your sakes he became poor, so that by his poverty he could make you rich.

[10]I suggest that you finish what you started a year ago, for you were the first to propose this idea, and you were the first to begin doing something about it. [11]Now you should carry this project through to completion just as enthusiastically as you began it. Give whatever you can according to what you have. [12]If you are really eager to give, it isn't important how much you are able to give. God wants you to give what you have, not what you don't have. [13]Of course, I don't mean you should give so much that you suffer from having too little. I only mean that there should be some equality. [14]Right now you have plenty and can help them. Then at some other time they can share with you when you need it. In this way, everyone's needs will be met. [15]Do you remember what the Scriptures say about this? "Those who gathered a lot had nothing left over, and those who gathered only a little had enough."*

Titus and His Companions

[16]I am thankful to God that he has given Titus the same enthusiasm for you that I have. [17]He welcomed our request that he visit you again. In fact, he himself was eager to go and see you. [18]We are also sending another brother with Titus. He is highly praised in all the churches as a preacher of the Good News. [19]He was appointed by the churches to accompany us as we take the offering to Jerusalem*—a service that glorifies the Lord and shows our eagerness to help. [20]By traveling together we will guard against any suspicion, for we are anxious that no one should find fault with the way we are handling this generous gift. [21]We are careful to be honorable before the Lord, but we also want everyone else to know we are honorable.

[22]And we are also sending with them another brother who has been thoroughly tested and has shown how earnest he is on many occasions. He is now even more enthusiastic because of his increased confidence in you. [23]If anyone asks about Titus, say that he is my partner who works with me to help

STEP 4

Constructive Sorrow

BIBLE READING: 2 Corinthians 7:8-11
We made a searching and fearless moral inventory of ourselves.
We all have to deal with sorrow. We may try to stuff it down and ignore it. We may try to drown it by giving in to our addiction or avoid feeling it by intellectualizing. But sorrow doesn't go away. We need to accept the sorrow that will be a part of the inventory process.

Not all sorrow is bad for us. The apostle Paul had written a letter to the church in Corinth that made them very sad because Paul confronted them about something they were doing wrong. At first he was sorry that he had hurt them, but later he said, "Now I am glad I sent it, not because it hurt you, but because the pain caused you to have remorse and change your ways. It was the kind of sorrow God wants his people to have. . . . For God can use sorrow in our lives to help us turn away from sin and seek salvation. We will never regret that kind of sorrow. . . . Just see what this godly sorrow produced in you! . . . You showed that you have done everything you could to make things right" (2 Corinthians 7:9-11).

Jeremiah said, "Though [God] brings grief, he also shows compassion according to the greatness of his unfailing love. For he does not enjoy hurting people or causing them sorrow" (Lamentations 3:32-33).

The Corinthians' grief was good—it came from honest self-evaluation, not morbid self-condemnation. We can learn to accept our sorrow as a positive part of recovery, not as punishment. *Turn to page 467, Revelation 20.*

you. And these brothers are representatives*
of the churches. They are splendid examples
of those who bring glory to Christ. 24So show
them your love, and prove to all the churches
that our boasting about you is justified.

CHAPTER 9
The Collection for Christians in Jerusalem

I really don't need to write to you about this
gift for the Christians in Jerusalem.* 2For I
know how eager you are to help, and I have
been boasting to our friends in Macedonia
that you Christians in Greece* were ready to
send an offering a year ago. In fact, it was
your enthusiasm that stirred up many of
them to begin helping. 3But I am sending
these brothers just to be sure that you really
are ready, as I told them you would be, with
your money all collected. I don't want it to
turn out that I was wrong in my boasting
about you. 4I would be humiliated—and so
would you—if some Macedonian Christians
came with me, only to find that you still
weren't ready after all I had told them! 5So I
thought I should send these brothers ahead of
me to make sure the gift you promised is
ready. But I want it to be a willing gift, not
one given under pressure.

6Remember this—a farmer who plants
only a few seeds will get a small crop. But the
one who plants generously will get a generous crop. 7You must each make up your own
mind as to how much you should give.
Don't give reluctantly or in response to pressure. For God loves the person who gives
cheerfully. 8And God will generously provide
all you need. Then you will always have
everything you need and plenty left over to
share with others. 9As the Scriptures say,

"Godly people give generously to the poor.
  Their good deeds will never be
    forgotten."*

10For God is the one who gives seed to the
farmer and then bread to eat. In the same
way, he will give you many opportunities to
do good, and he will produce a great harvest
of generosity* in you.

11Yes, you will be enriched so that you can
give even more generously. And when we
take your gifts to those who need them,
they will break out in thanksgiving to God.
12So two good things will happen—the
needs of the Christians in Jerusalem will be
met, and they will joyfully express their
thanksgiving to God. 13You will be glorifying God through your generous gifts. For
your generosity to them will prove that you
are obedient to the Good News of Christ.
14And they will pray for you with deep affection because of the wonderful grace of God
shown through you.

15Thank God for his Son—a gift too wonderful for words!*

CHAPTER 10
Paul Defends His Authority

Now I, Paul, plead with you. I plead with
the gentleness and kindness that Christ
himself would use, even though some of
you say I am bold in my letters but timid in
person. 2I hope it won't be necessary, but
when I come I may have to be very bold
with those who think we act from purely
human motives. 3We are human, but we
don't wage war with human plans and
methods. 4We use God's mighty weapons,
not mere worldly weapons, to knock down
the Devil's strongholds. 5With these weapons we break down every proud argument
that keeps people from knowing God. With
these weapons we conquer their rebellious
ideas, and we teach them to obey Christ.
6And we will punish those who remained
disobedient after the rest of you became
loyal and obedient.

7The trouble with you is that you make
your decisions on the basis of appearance.*
You must recognize that we belong to Christ
just as much as those who proudly declare
that they belong to Christ. 8I may seem to

8:23 Greek *apostles.* **9:1** Greek *about the offering for the saints.* **9:2** Greek *Achaia,* the southern region of the Greek peninsula. **9:9** Ps 112:9. **9:10** Greek *righteousness.* **9:15** Greek *Thank God for his indescribable gift.* **10:7** Or *Look at the obvious facts.*

9:6-9 The more spiritual seeds we plant by generously helping others, the greater will be our harvest of spiritual fruit. God never forces us to give; he wants us to give with willing hearts. God is not only interested in what we do; he is also interested in the attitudes and motives behind our actions. Some of us may feel that we don't have much to offer people in need. Our life may be in ruins; we may have gone into debt to support destructive habits. But even if we have nothing else to give, we can share our story of how God gave us a second chance. As little as this may seem to us, it may be the gift of life to someone in the throes of an addiction.

be boasting too much about the authority given to us by the Lord. But this authority is to build you up, not to tear you down. And I will not be put to shame by having my work among you destroyed.

⁹Now this is not just an attempt to frighten you by my letters. ¹⁰For some say, "Don't worry about Paul. His letters are demanding and forceful, but in person he is weak, and his speeches are really bad!" ¹¹The ones who say this must realize that we will be just as demanding and forceful in person as we are in our letters.

¹²Oh, don't worry; I wouldn't dare say that I am as wonderful as these other men who tell you how important they are! But they are only comparing themselves with each other, and measuring themselves by themselves. What foolishness!

¹³But we will not boast of authority we do not have. Our goal is to stay within the boundaries of God's plan for us, and this plan includes our working there with you. ¹⁴We are not going too far when we claim authority over you, for we were the first to travel all the way to you with the Good News of Christ. ¹⁵Nor do we claim credit for the work someone else has done. Instead, we hope that your faith will grow and that our work among you will be greatly enlarged. ¹⁶Then we will be able to go and preach the Good News in other places that are far beyond you, where no one else is working. Then there will be no question about being in someone else's territory. ¹⁷As the Scriptures say,

"The person who wishes to boast
should boast only of what the Lord has
done."*

10:17 Jer 9:24. **11:2** Greek *a virgin*. **11:10** Greek *Achaia*.

¹⁸When people boast about themselves, it doesn't count for much. But when the Lord commends someone, that's different!

CHAPTER 11
Paul and the False Apostles

I hope you will be patient with me as I keep on talking like a fool. Please bear with me. ²I am jealous for you with the jealousy of God himself. For I promised you as a pure bride* to one husband, Christ. ³But I fear that somehow you will be led away from your pure and simple devotion to Christ, just as Eve was deceived by the serpent. ⁴You seem to believe whatever anyone tells you, even if they preach about a different Jesus than the one we preach, or a different Spirit than the one you received, or a different kind of gospel than the one you believed. ⁵But I don't think I am inferior to these "super apostles." ⁶I may not be a trained speaker, but I know what I am talking about. I think you realize this by now, for we have proved it again and again.

⁷Did I do wrong when I humbled myself and honored you by preaching God's Good News to you without expecting anything in return? ⁸I "robbed" other churches by accepting their contributions so I could serve you at no cost. ⁹And when I was with you and didn't have enough to live on, I did not ask you to help me. For the brothers who came from Macedonia brought me another gift. I have never yet asked you for any support, and I never will. ¹⁰As surely as the truth of Christ is in me, I will never stop boasting about this all over Greece.* ¹¹Why? Because I don't love you? God knows I do.

¹²But I will continue doing this to cut the

10:13-15 From a recovery perspective, it is illuminating to note that Paul had set limits on his ministry based on his understanding of God's will for him. Our recovery activities also need to be in line with God's plan. We must concentrate our limited energy on priorities that reflect God's will. Paul was sensitive to God's will for his life, and he was confident that his leadership over the Corinthian church was a part of that plan. We can be sure that recovery is part of God's plan for us. We need to learn what activities he wants us to be involved in on a daily basis. Insight concerning God's will for us is likely to come through prayer, study of the Scriptures, the help of godly friends, or the guidance from the Holy Spirit.

11:2-4 Paul was worried that the Corinthian believers would replace their faith in Jesus with a false faith. Corinth was a cosmopolitan city; numerous pagan religions and cults were practiced there. Paul also was concerned because rejecting Christ would lead to painful consequences. Believers might reject the abundant life offered by Jesus Christ for lives of ultimate disaster. We also live in a world of multiple religions; recovery programs can be found that represent most of them. But true recovery is possible only through the work of Jesus Christ and the power of the Holy Spirit. Rejecting the hope offered in Christ is rejecting the only real power available for recovery. Looking to any other power will lead to disappointment and failure.

ground out from under the feet of those who boast that their work is just like ours. ¹³These people are false apostles. They have fooled you by disguising themselves as apostles of Christ. ¹⁴But I am not surprised! Even Satan can disguise himself as an angel of light. ¹⁵So it is no wonder his servants can also do it by pretending to be godly ministers. In the end they will get every bit of punishment their wicked deeds deserve.

Paul's Many Trials

¹⁶Once again, don't think that I have lost my wits to talk like this. But even if you do, listen to me, as you would to a foolish person, while I also boast a little. ¹⁷Such bragging is not something the Lord wants, but I am acting like a fool. ¹⁸And since others boast about their human achievements, I will, too. ¹⁹After all, you, who think you are so wise, enjoy listening to fools! ²⁰You put up with it when they make you their slaves, take everything you have, take advantage of you, put on airs, and slap you in the face. ²¹I'm ashamed to say that we were not strong enough to do that!

But whatever they dare to boast about— I'm talking like a fool again—I can boast about it, too. ²²They say they are Hebrews, do they? So am I. And they say they are Israelites? So am I. And they are descendants of Abraham? So am I. ²³They say they serve Christ? I know I sound like a madman, but I have served him far more! I have worked harder, been put in jail more often, been whipped times without number, and faced death again and again. ²⁴Five different times the Jews gave me thirty-nine lashes. ²⁵Three times I was beaten with rods. Once I was stoned. Three times I was shipwrecked. Once I spent a whole night and a day adrift at sea. ²⁶I have traveled many weary miles. I have faced danger from flooded rivers and from robbers. I have faced danger from my own people, the Jews, as well as from the Gentiles. I have faced danger in the cities, in the deserts, and on the stormy seas. And I have faced danger from men who claim to be Christians but are not.* ²⁷I have lived with weariness and pain and sleepless nights. Often I have been hungry and thirsty and have gone without food. Often I have shivered with cold, without enough clothing to keep me warm.

²⁸Then, besides all this, I have the daily burden of how the churches are getting along. ²⁹Who is weak without my feeling that weakness? Who is led astray, and I do not burn with anger?

³⁰If I must boast, I would rather boast about the things that show how weak I am. ³¹God, the Father of our Lord Jesus, who is to be praised forever, knows I tell the truth. ³²When I was in Damascus, the governor under King Aretas kept guards at the city gates to catch me. ³³But I was lowered in a basket through a window in the city wall, and that's how I got away!

11:26 Greek *from false brothers.*

11:13-15 The Corinthian believers had apparently rejected Paul's teachings in order to follow a number of false teachers who had twisted the Christian message. These false leaders were probably Judaizers who taught that salvation came through faith in Christ plus adherence to the Jewish law (see 11:22). Sometimes we are tempted to follow the same heresy. We want to earn our recovery by working hard. This approach, however, is powerless over our dependency. We need God's help. Paul made it clear in all of his letters that salvation is a free gift, paid for by the sacrificial work of Jesus Christ. Without God, we are helpless against the power of sin in our life. But with his help, we can overcome our dependency.

11:23-29 Paul demonstrated his commitment to Jesus Christ by listing the tremendous hardships he had suffered. If nothing else, such ongoing mistreatment, deprivation, and the burden of his ministry responsibility revealed his perseverance. Paul was definitely no fairweather minister or friend. If we display the kind of commitment to recovery that Paul had for his ministry, we will receive the same kind of powerful help that Paul experienced in his service for Christ.

11:30; 12:1-10 Paul's "boasting" was not intended to make him look better than he really was. He boasted about his weakness so Christ could work through him (see 12:9). Even though the apostle told of his incredible vision of heaven (12:1-4), he quickly admitted his own weaknesses (11:30; 12:5). He recounted how he sensed God's grace even through his chronic physical suffering and spiritual warfare (12:9-10). Paul honestly assessed his life, recognizing both his strengths and weaknesses. Then he accepted and received the power that God offers to all who look to him. Paul is a good model for us to follow. When we make an honest assessment of our life and learn to depend upon God's infinite resources, we will make significant progress in recovery.

CHAPTER 12
Paul's Vision and His Thorn in the Flesh
This boasting is all so foolish, but let me go on. Let me tell about the visions and revelations I received from the Lord. [2]I* was caught up into the third heaven fourteen years ago. [3]Whether my body was there or just my spirit, I don't know; only God knows. [4]But I do know that I* was caught up into paradise and heard things so astounding that they cannot be told. [5]That experience is something worth boasting about, but I am not going to do it. I am going to boast only about my weaknesses. [6]I have plenty to boast about and would be no fool in doing it, because I would be telling the truth. But I won't do it. I don't want anyone to think more highly of me than what they can actually see in my life and my message, [7]even though I have received wonderful revelations from God. But to keep me from getting puffed up, I was given a thorn in my flesh, a messenger from Satan to torment me and keep me from getting proud.

[8]Three different times I begged the Lord to take it away. [9]Each time he said, "My gracious favor is all you need. My power works best in your weakness." So now I am glad to boast about my weaknesses, so that the power of Christ may work through me. [10]Since I know it is all for Christ's good, I am quite content with my weaknesses and with insults, hardships, persecutions, and calamities. For when I am weak, then I am strong.

Paul's Concern for the Corinthians
[11]You have made me act like a fool—boasting like this. You ought to be writing commendations for me, for I am not at all inferior to these "super apostles," even though I am nothing at all. [12]When I was with you, I certainly gave you every proof that I am truly an apostle, sent to you by God himself. For I patiently did many signs and wonders and miracles among you.

[13]The only thing I didn't do, which I do in the other churches, was to become a burden to you. Please forgive me for this wrong!

[14]Now I am coming to you for the third time, and I will not be a burden to you. I don't want what you have; I want you. And anyway, little children don't pay for their parents' food. It's the other way around; parents supply food for their children. [15]I will gladly spend myself and all I have for your spiritual good, even though it seems that the more I love you, the less you love me.

[16]Some of you admit I was not a burden to you. But they still think I was sneaky and took advantage of you by trickery. [17]But how? Did any of the men I sent to you take advantage of you? [18]When I urged Titus to visit you and sent our other brother with him, did Titus take advantage of you? No, of course not! For we both have the same Spirit and walk in each other's steps, doing things the same way.

[19]Perhaps you think we are saying all this just to defend ourselves. That isn't it at all. We tell you this as Christ's servants, and we know that God is listening. Everything we do, dear friends, is for your benefit. [20]For I am afraid that when I come to visit you I won't like what I find, and then you won't like my response. I am afraid that I will find quarreling, jealousy, outbursts of anger, selfishness, backstabbing, gossip, conceit, and disorderly behavior. [21]Yes, I am afraid that when I come, God will humble me again because of you. And I will have to grieve because many of you who sinned earlier have not repented of your impurity, sexual immorality, and eagerness for lustful pleasure.

CHAPTER 13
Paul's Final Advice
This is the third time I am coming to visit you. As the Scriptures say, "The facts of every case must be established by the testimony of two or three witnesses."* [2]I have

12:2 Greek *I know a man in Christ who.* **12:4** Greek *he.* **13:1** Deut 19:15.

12:19-21 Everything that Paul said to the Corinthians, both negative and positive, was intended for their good. Paul was concerned that they mature in their faith, and he did what he could to encourage their spiritual growth. The demands he made on these believers were motivated by his love and concern for them. Many of us have realized that we often communicate with others for selfish reasons. When we compliment people, we are looking for something in return rather than trying to honestly build them up. When we criticize others, we are seeking to destroy rather than correct. As we take moral inventory, we need to be aware of our tendency to use others for our own ends. As we seek to restore our damaged relationships, the apostle Paul is an excellent model to follow.

already warned those who had been sinning when I was there on my second visit. Now I again warn them and all others, just as I did before, that this next time I will not spare them.

³I will give you all the proof you want that Christ speaks through me. Christ is not weak in his dealings with you; he is a mighty power among you. ⁴Although he died on the cross in weakness, he now lives by the mighty power of God. We, too, are weak, but we live in him and have God's power—the power we use in dealing with you.

⁵Examine yourselves to see if your faith is really genuine. Test yourselves. If you cannot tell that Jesus Christ is among you,* it means you have failed the test. ⁶I hope you recognize that we have passed the test and are approved by God.

⁷We pray to God that you will not do anything wrong. We pray this, not to show that our ministry to you has been successful, but because we want you to do right even if we ourselves seem to have failed. ⁸Our responsibility is never to oppose the truth, but to stand for the truth at all times. ⁹We are glad to be weak, if you are really strong. What we pray for is your restoration to maturity.

¹⁰I am writing this to you before I come, hoping that I won't need to deal harshly with you when I do come. For I want to use the authority the Lord has given me to build you up, not to tear you down.

Paul's Final Greetings

¹¹Dear brothers and sisters,* I close my letter with these last words: Rejoice. Change your ways. Encourage each other. Live in harmony and peace. Then the God of love and peace will be with you.

¹²Greet each other in Christian love.* All the Christians here send you their greetings.

¹³May the grace of our Lord Jesus Christ, the love of God, and the fellowship of the Holy Spirit be with you all.*

13:5 Or *in you.* **13:11** Greek *Brothers.* **13:12** Greek *with a sacred kiss.* **13:12-13** Some English versions divide verse 12 into verses 12 and 13, and then verse 13 becomes verse 14.

13:2-3 Paul had warned the Corinthians earlier that discipline would be forthcoming if they did not face their personal and interpersonal sins. Here he gave them an additional warning because he had been away from Corinth for longer than he had intended. He wanted to make sure that the people knew his warning was not hollow. Paul would indeed follow through forcefully and hold the Corinthian believers accountable to their commitments to God. We all need people like Paul in our life—godly people who can hold us accountable to our recovery commitments and our obedience to God.

13:5-6 Paul urged the Corinthian believers to seriously examine themselves. He wanted them to assess the nature of their commitment to God by looking closely at their own lives. This is an essential part of the recovery process. We need to engage in honest self-examination if we hope to uncover the problems that tear down our relationships and drive our dependency. As we admit our failures to God, he will forgive us and help us make progress in recovery.

13:11 As Paul closed this letter to the Corinthians, he left them with some worthy challenges and goals to pursue. In essence, he admonished the people to open their minds and hearts to personal change and the healing of their relationships. Such spiritual growth and interpersonal harmony can be fueled by faith in God, the ultimate source of healing love and peace. As modern readers of this letter, we, too, can benefit by acting on Paul's wise counsel.

REFLECTIONS ON

SECOND

CORINTHIANS

*insights ABOUT PRAYER

It is essential that we learn to encourage others in recovery without giving up the balance in our own life. That is exactly what Paul was asking the Corinthians to do in **2 Corinthians 1:11** when he requested their prayers. By praying for the needs of the apostle and his companions, the Corinthian believers would be helping and strengthening them from a distance. Because of our own weaknesses, we sometimes are unable to help some of the people we care about. To maintain our own recovery, we have to keep our distance. But this does not mean that we need to forget about them. We can help them by praying that they will discover how helpless they are without God and that they will turn to him for help. God has the power to do for them what we may not be able to do through direct contact.

*insights ABOUT RESTORING RELATIONSHIPS

A problem in the Corinthian church (probably the one described in 1 Corinthians 5:1-11) was the basis for Paul's rebuke in **2 Corinthians 2:5-11.** When the troublemaker in question repented of his sin and honestly faced the consequences of his behavior, the Corinthian believers refused to forgive him. Paul pointed out how cruel it was to withhold forgiveness. The apostle explained that through their lack of forgiveness they were actually playing right into Satan's hands by discouraging the repentant party. We need to make sure that when others repent of their sins, we do our part to encourage the process of restoration and healing. Most of us have experienced the pain of being rejected, even after admitting our mistakes and trying to change. We should be the last to cause the same kind of pain to others.

*insights FOR SURVIVAL DURING TOUGH TIMES

In **2 Corinthians 4:8-11** Paul reflects on the value of suffering. The hard times in life tend to either crush and disillusion or challenge and stimulate us. It is hard for us to keep going when the going gets tough. But it can be a real encouragement to know that God is with us in the midst of the trials we face, and that he can use even our weaknesses for his glory. In fact, our perseverance in recovery from our addiction may be the gift of life to other people in bondage to a powerful dependency. As they see God's work in our life, they may gain the courage to face and conquer their own addiction with God's powerful help.

In **2 Corinthians 5:1-5** Paul reminded his readers that their weak bodies would someday be replaced by glorious new ones. To many of us, the aging process is a depressing reality—one we'd like to avoid. The fact that we pay great sums of money for cosmetic surgery, hair coloring, and the like is evidence of that. But there is a comforting side to aging if we trust Jesus Christ for our salvation and recovery. Before long, we will "check in" our present physical body and receive a glorified eternal body. The Holy Spirit's presence in our life is the guarantee that we are drawing ever closer to that point.

*insights ABOUT SHARING THE GOOD NEWS

We find in **2 Corinthians 6:3-4** that Paul sought to live in such a way that no one would be offended or kept away from God on his account. He was a model for other believers to look up to and follow. Some of us who have been in recovery for a while may have found it exhausting to be a model for the recovery of others. We have felt the burdens of numerous expectations. As a result, some of us may have quit trying to help others in recovery. As we grow spiritually, the responsibility to help others will always be there. The apostle Paul took this responsibility very seriously and acted out of concern for the well-being of others. Though this may be a difficult burden for some of us, it may help us to realize that being a model for others in recovery is one of the ways that God keeps us on the road toward wholeness.

*insights ABOUT CONFRONTATION

Paul had apparently written a short letter between 1 and 2 Corinthians that was not included among the New Testament books. From his mention of the letter in **2 Corinthians 7:8-10,** it must have been quite sharp in tone. He admits that he had mixed feelings about sending that letter. But because of the Corinthians' positive response to his tough love, all his regrets had vanished. In recovery situations, we must realize that when we confront others, we are taking a calculated risk that might lead to either healing or alienation. When we do confront people about their problems, we must do so with humility and love, and entrust the situation to God. If we do this, God will work things out according to his perfect will.

GALATIANS

THE BIG PICTURE

Paul planted the churches in Galatia during his first missionary journey in Asia Minor. But within months of Paul's ministry there, certain people began to contradict the Good News Paul had preached. These teachers claimed that non-Jewish converts to Christ had to keep the Jewish law in order to be saved. This meant that all Gentiles who sought membership in the church would have to be circumcised.

This alternative gospel was very enticing to the Galatian believers. For one thing, its proponents claimed to have the direct blessing of the apostles back in Jerusalem. Their arguments from the Old Testament seemed flawless and irrefutable. But because Paul knew how destructive this teaching could be, he wrote this letter to correct them.

Paul made it clear to the Galatians that in Christ they were truly free. They were free from the demands of the Jewish law, free from the power of sin, and free to live under God's grace. We may wonder why the Galatians would ever want to give up the freedom they had in Christ. But bondage is subtle. No one ever starts drinking with a determination to become an alcoholic. We slowly become dependent on certain behaviors, substances, or attitudes. And, in a pathetic sort of way, our bondage gives us security.

This letter to the Galatian believers challenges us to hold on to our freedom. Being controlled by alcohol or drugs means living in slavery. So does being involved in any recovery program that is based on our own abilities and strengths. We cannot escape the grip of addiction and sin alone, but as we turn our life over to God, he will graciously give us the power we need to overcome our dependency.

THE BOTTOM LINE

PURPOSE: To encourage readers to depend on Christ alone for salvation and daily strength. AUTHOR: The apostle Paul. AUDIENCE: Several churches in southern Galatia. DATE WRITTEN: Probably around A.D. 49. SETTING: The most pressing controversy in the early church was whether new non-Jewish converts needed to accept Jewish laws to be a part of the church. Paul wrote this letter to answer that question. KEY VERSE: "So Christ has really set us free. Now make sure that you stay free, and don't get tied up again in slavery to the law" (5:1). KEY PEOPLE AND RELATIONSHIPS: Paul with the Galatian believers and with the Jerusalem apostles, as well as the false teachers.

RECOVERY THEMES

The Seduction of the Law: For some of us, following a set of rules may seem easier than working on a personal inventory, praying, meditating on Scripture, or engaging in other activities that lead to a deeper relationship with God. We would rather have someone tell us what to do. Perhaps the Galatians felt the same way. They may have said, "Just give us some rules to follow, like the Mosaic law." Just following a set of rules for recovery is never the way to success. It is impossible for us to do by ourself, and it also leads us away from our dependence on God, the only real source for success.

Recovery Leads to True Freedom: This letter was written to show us how to find true spiritual freedom. Paul's advice to the Galatians applies to us as we search for freedom from our addiction, dysfunctional family, compulsive behavior, or codependent relationship. True freedom is found as we turn our life over to God, depending not on our own self-sufficiency but on his powerful and firm intervention. Having faith in Christ is the only way we can have true freedom from sin and its consequences, and from bondage to our defects of character.

The Power of the Holy Spirit: We become believers through the work of the Holy Spirit, the personal expression of the power of God. We also are empowered in recovery by the Holy Spirit. He brings new life to us; even the faith to believe and the courage to admit our own powerlessness are gifts from him. The Holy Spirit instructs, guides, leads, and gives us power. It is he who delivers us from our bondage to evil desires and addictive patterns and creates in us love, joy, peace, and serenity.

The Necessity of Faith: Many of us have been frustrated, even discouraged to the point of giving up, by our failed efforts to change. Recovery from sin and its destructive effects, including our dependency, is only possible through trust in Jesus Christ. Turning our will and our life over to God does not miraculously and instantly transform us (though some changes may happen right away). But by placing our trust and confidence in Jesus Christ, we experience God's forgiveness and unconditional acceptance. Then his power begins to work within us to enable our continued growth and recovery.

CHAPTER 1
Greetings from Paul

This letter is from Paul, an apostle. I was not appointed by any group or by human authority. My call is from Jesus Christ himself and from God the Father, who raised Jesus from the dead.

²All the brothers and sisters* here join me in sending greetings to the churches of Galatia.

³May grace and peace be yours from God our Father and from the Lord Jesus Christ. ⁴He died for our sins, just as God our Father planned, in order to rescue us from this evil world in which we live. ⁵That is why all glory belongs to God through all the ages of eternity. Amen.

1:2 Greek *brothers;* also in 1:11.

There Is Only One Good News

⁶I am shocked that you are turning away so soon from God, who in his love and mercy called you to share the eternal life he gives through Christ. You are already following a different way ⁷that pretends to be the Good News but is not the Good News at all. You are being fooled by those who twist and change the truth concerning Christ.

⁸Let God's curse fall on anyone, including myself, who preaches any other message than the one we told you about. Even if an angel comes from heaven and preaches any other message, let him be forever cursed. ⁹I will say it again: If anyone preaches any other gospel than the one you welcomed, let God's curse fall upon that person.

1:1-5 In this letter Paul gave much more than the brief, customary greeting. He introduced the main themes: his God-given apostolic authority, and clear teachings about the fatherhood of God and the delivering power of Jesus Christ. God, our loving Father, had a plan to rescue us from this evil world through the death of his Son. When we turn our life over to him, God is able to help us overcome our problems and shortcomings.
1:6-10 The Galatians faced a choice between the true gospel Paul preached and the false gospel preached by his opponents. The choice we face as we look for a way to deal with our sins and failures is just as clear. We can listen to those who offer us amazing and easy recovery fads. Or we can yield to a legalistic system that manipulates us through our guilt to effect our own recovery by adhering to a set of rules. Or we can accept what God says about the power of sin and his ability to set us free if we focus on him. Only God through Jesus Christ can offer us the power we need for true recovery. No other solution to our problems and dependency will ever lead to real or permanent change.

[10]Obviously, I'm not trying to be a people pleaser! No, I am trying to please God. If I were still trying to please people, I would not be Christ's servant.

Paul's Message Comes from Christ

[11]Dear brothers and sisters, I solemnly assure you that the Good News of salvation which I preach is not based on mere human reasoning or logic. [12]For my message came by a direct revelation from Jesus Christ himself. No one else taught me.

[13]You know what I was like when I followed the Jewish religion—how I violently persecuted the Christians.* I did my best to get rid of them. [14]I was one of the most religious Jews of my own age, and I tried as hard as possible to follow all the old traditions of my religion.

[15]But then something happened! For it pleased God in his kindness to choose me and call me, even before I was born! What undeserved mercy! [16]Then he revealed his Son to me* so that I could proclaim the Good News about Jesus to the Gentiles. When all this happened to me, I did not rush out to consult with anyone else; [17]nor did I go up to Jerusalem to consult with those who were apostles before I was. No, I went away into Arabia and later returned to the city of Damascus. [18]It was not until three years later that I finally went to Jerusalem for a visit with Peter* and stayed there with him for fifteen days. [19]And the only other apostle I met at that time was James, our Lord's brother. [20]You must believe what I am saying, for I declare before God that I am not lying. [21]Then after this visit, I went north into the provinces of Syria and Cilicia. [22]And still the Christians in the churches in Judea didn't know me personally. [23]All they knew was that people were saying, "The one who used to persecute us now preaches the very faith he tried to destroy!" [24]And they gave glory to God because of me.

CHAPTER 2
The Apostles Accept Paul

Then fourteen years later I went back to Jerusalem again, this time with Barnabas; and Titus came along, too. [2]I went there because God revealed to me that I should go. While I was there I talked privately with the leaders of the church. I wanted them to understand what I had been preaching to the Gentiles. I wanted to make sure they did not disagree, or my ministry would have been useless. [3]And they did agree. They did not even demand that my companion Titus be circumcised, though he was a Gentile.*

[4]Even that question wouldn't have come up except for some so-called Christians there—false ones, really*—who came to spy on us and see our freedom in Christ Jesus. They wanted to force us, like slaves, to follow their Jewish regulations. [5]But we refused to listen to them for a single moment. We wanted to preserve the truth of the Good News for you.

[6]And the leaders of the church who were there had nothing to add to what I was preaching. (By the way, their reputation as great leaders made no difference to me, for God has no favorites.) [7]They saw that God had given me the responsibility of preaching the Good News to the Gentiles, just as he had given Peter the responsibility of preaching to the Jews. [8]For the same God who worked through Peter for the benefit of the

1:13 Greek *the church of God.* **1:16** Or *in me.* **1:18** Greek *Cephas.* **2:3** Greek *a Greek.* **2:4** Greek *some false brothers.*

1:11-24 As Paul looked back on his conversion, he recalled how he had once been an extremely religious Jew. He had actively worked to defend his faith against the threat of Christianity. But by grace, God reached out and radically transformed him. Paul recognized that all his religious activities were ultimately fruitless; they could never deliver him from the power of sin. Only God could forgive his sins and give him the power to start over again. If we have tried to overcome our dependency through behavior modification or religious activities, we already know what it means to fail. But if we have entrusted our life to God and are living by his power, we know the secret of victory. God's power through Jesus Christ is the only means to lasting recovery.

2:1-10 Paul presented a clear argument against the teachings of the Judaizers. These people recognized that God's work through Jesus Christ was important, but they also believed that people were required to follow the Jewish laws to obtain salvation. For them, salvation was based on actions, not solely on God's gracious gift. Paul wanted the Galatians to realize that none of us can follow God's laws adequately on our own. Christ alone has the power to release us from sin and its destructive consequences. Most of us have already discovered how powerless we are against sin. We know that we need God's power to help us overcome our addictions and compulsions. Paul's message of grace is a source of hope for us as we trust God to help us overcome our dependency.

Jews worked through me for the benefit of the Gentiles. ⁹In fact, James, Peter,* and John, who were known as pillars of the church, recognized the gift God had given me, and they accepted Barnabas and me as their co-workers. They encouraged us to keep preaching to the Gentiles, while they continued their work with the Jews. ¹⁰The only thing they suggested was that we remember to help the poor, and I have certainly been eager to do that.

Paul Confronts Peter

¹¹But when Peter came to Antioch, I had to oppose him publicly, speaking strongly against what he was doing, for it was very wrong. ¹²When he first arrived, he ate with the Gentile Christians, who don't bother with circumcision. But afterward, when some Jewish friends of James came, Peter wouldn't eat with the Gentiles anymore because he was afraid of what these legalists would say. ¹³Then the other Jewish Christians followed Peter's hypocrisy, and even Barnabas was influenced to join them in their hypocrisy.

¹⁴When I saw that they were not following the truth of the Good News, I said to Peter in front of all the others, "Since you, a Jew by birth, have discarded the Jewish laws and are living like a Gentile, why are you trying to make these Gentiles obey the Jewish laws you abandoned? ¹⁵You and I are Jews by birth, not 'sinners' like the Gentiles. ¹⁶And yet we Jewish Christians know that we become right with God, not by doing what the law commands, but by faith in Jesus Christ. So we have believed in Christ Jesus, that we might be accepted by God because of our faith in Christ—and not because we have obeyed the law. For no one will ever be saved by obeying the law."*

¹⁷But what if we seek to be made right with God through faith in Christ and then find out that we are still sinners? Has Christ led us into sin? Of course not! ¹⁸Rather, I make myself guilty if I rebuild the old system I already tore down. ¹⁹For when I tried to keep the law, I realized I could never earn God's approval. So I died to the law so that I might live for God. I have been crucified with Christ. ²⁰I myself no longer live, but Christ lives in me. So I live my life in this earthly body by trusting in the Son of God, who loved me and gave himself for me. ²¹I am not one of those who treats the grace of God as meaningless. For if we could be saved by keeping the law, then there was no need for Christ to die.

CHAPTER 3
The Law and Faith in Christ

Oh, foolish Galatians! What magician has cast an evil spell on you? For you used to see

2:9 Greek *Cephas;* also in 2:11, 14. **2:16** Some translators hold that the quotation extends through verse 14; others through verse 16; and still others through verse 21.

2:11-16 The apostle Peter, a Jewish Christian, knew that salvation is a free gift of grace. While in Antioch, he freely associated with the Gentile Christians, even though they had not fulfilled the Jewish law of circumcision. When other Jewish Christian leaders arrived, however, Peter stopped associating with the Gentile believers. He was influenced by his Jewish peers and began to act as if obeying the Jewish laws was necessary for salvation. Paul confronted Peter about his prejudice, and the problem was resolved. Some of us know how Peter felt when his Jewish friends arrived. As we became involved in recovery, we may have been embarrassed among our old friends. We may have succumbed to the pressure to turn from our commitment to the truth about our need for recovery. Like Peter, we can humbly assess our failures and get back on the right track.

2:20-21 Paul showed that our old lifestyle died on the cross with Jesus Christ. The Jewish Christians had to give up trying to earn salvation by following the Jewish law. Many of us have struggled with this very problem. Some of us have worked very hard to overcome our addiction but have achieved no real freedom. Paul wanted the Jewish believers to realize that they could gain nothing by trying harder. They had to give up control and allow God to heal them and empower them in battling sin. We must give up our old ways of looking for deliverance and accept God's grace—the free gift of forgiveness and healing offered by Jesus Christ.

3:1-14 Paul appealed to the clear evidence seen among the Galatians when they received the Holy Spirit upon believing in Christ. We become children of Abraham, as the Bible says, when we receive the redemption available to us through the sacrifice of Jesus Christ. The evidence of becoming Abraham's sons and daughters is not circumcision but the presence of the Holy Spirit in our life. We can be sure of the Holy Spirit's presence when we begin to change. Knowing God and being in a right relationship with him enables us to know his will and follow it. But trying to follow God's laws in our human strength will never bring us into right relationship with God.

the meaning of Jesus Christ's death as clearly as though I had shown you a signboard with a picture of Christ dying on the cross. ²Let me ask you this one question: Did you receive the Holy Spirit by keeping the law? Of course not, for the Holy Spirit came upon you only after you believed the message you heard about Christ. ³Have you lost your senses? After starting your Christian lives in the Spirit, why are you now trying to become perfect by your own human effort? ⁴You have suffered so much for the Good News. Surely it was not in vain, was it? Are you now going to just throw it all away?

⁵I ask you again, does God give you the Holy Spirit and work miracles among you because you obey the law of Moses? Of course not! It is because you believe the message you heard about Christ.

⁶In the same way, "Abraham believed God, so God declared him righteous because of his faith."* ⁷The real children of Abraham, then, are all those who put their faith in God.

⁸What's more, the Scriptures looked forward to this time when God would accept the Gentiles, too, on the basis of their faith. God promised this good news to Abraham long ago when he said, "All nations will be blessed through you."* ⁹And so it is: All who put their faith in Christ share the same blessing Abraham received because of his faith.

¹⁰But those who depend on the law to make them right with God are under his curse, for the Scriptures say, "Cursed is everyone who does not observe and obey all these commands that are written in God's Book of the Law."* ¹¹Consequently, it is clear that no one can ever be right with God by trying to keep the law. For the Scriptures say, "It is through faith that a righteous person has life."* ¹²How different from this way of faith is the way of law, which says, "If you wish to find life by obeying the law, you must obey all of its commands."* ¹³But Christ has rescued us from the curse pronounced by the law. When he was hung on the cross, he took upon himself the curse for our wrongdoing. For it is written in the Scriptures, "Cursed is everyone who is hung on a tree."* ¹⁴Through the work of Christ Jesus, God has blessed the Gentiles with the same blessing he promised to Abraham, and we Christians receive the promised Holy Spirit through faith.

Self-Control

READ GALATIANS 5:16-23

There's a struggle going on inside of us—a fight for control. Our willpower fails us repeatedly. Where can we turn when we realize that we can't get control of our life?

The apostle Paul said: "I advise you to live according to your new life in the Holy Spirit. Then you won't be doing what your sinful nature craves. The old sinful nature loves to do evil, which is just opposite from what the Holy Spirit wants. And the Spirit gives us desires that are opposite from what the sinful nature desires. These two forces are constantly fighting each other, and your choices are never free from this conflict. . . . But when the Holy Spirit controls our lives, he will produce this kind of fruit in us: love, joy, peace, patience, kindness, goodness, faithfulness, gentleness, and self-control" (Galatians 5:16-17, 22-23).

Self-control is not willpower. It is not something we get by gritting our teeth and forcing ourselves to "just say no." Self-control is called a fruit. Fruit doesn't instantly pop out on the tree. As the tree grows and seasons pass, the fruit naturally develops. As we continue to follow God's guidance, taking one step at a time, our self-control will gradually grow. Our job is to stay connected to God. It is the Holy Spirit's job to produce the fruit of self-control in our life. *Turn to page 315, Ephesians 2.*

3:6 Gen 15:6. 3:8 Gen 12:3; 18:18; 22:18. 3:10 Deut 27:26. 3:11 Hab 2:4. 3:12 Lev 18:5. 3:13 Deut 21:23.

The Law and God's Promises

15Dear brothers and sisters,* here's an example from everyday life. Just as no one can set aside or amend an irrevocable agreement, so it is in this case. 16God gave the promise to Abraham and his child.* And notice that it doesn't say the promise was to his children,* as if it meant many descendants. But the promise was to his child—and that, of course, means Christ. 17This is what I am trying to say: The agreement God made with Abraham could not be canceled 430 years later when God gave the law to Moses. God would be breaking his promise. 18For if the inheritance could be received only by keeping the law, then it would not be the result of accepting God's promise. But God gave it to Abraham as a promise.

19Well then, why was the law given? It was given to show people how guilty they are. But this system of law was to last only until the coming of the child to whom God's promise was made. And there is this further difference. God gave his laws to angels to give to Moses, who was the mediator between God and the people. 20Now a mediator is needed if two people enter into an agreement, but God acted on his own when he made his promise to Abraham.

21Well then, is there a conflict between God's law and God's promises? Absolutely not! If the law could have given us new life, we could have been made right with God by obeying it. 22But the Scriptures have declared that we are all prisoners of sin, so the only way to receive God's promise is to believe in Jesus Christ.

23Until faith in Christ was shown to us as the way of becoming right with God, we were guarded by the law. We were kept in protective custody, so to speak, until we could put our faith in the coming Savior.

God's Children through Faith

24Let me put it another way. The law was our guardian and teacher to lead us until Christ came. So now, through faith in Christ, we are made right with God. 25But now that faith in Christ has come, we no longer need the law as our guardian. 26So you are all children* of God through faith in Christ Jesus. 27And all who have been united with Christ in baptism have been made like him. 28There is no longer Jew or Gentile,* slave or free, male or female. For you are all Christians—you are one in Christ Jesus. 29And now that you belong to Christ, you are the true children of Abraham. You are his heirs, and now all the promises God gave to him belong to you.

3:15 Greek *Brothers.* 3:16a Greek *seed;* also in 3:16c, 19. See Gen 12:7. 3:16b Greek *seeds.* 3:26 Greek *sons.* 3:28 Greek *Jew or Greek.*

3:15-29 God's relationship with us is not based on our keeping the law but on the promises made to Abraham to bless all humanity through his offspring, Jesus Christ. The law shows us that we are sinners deserving punishment and in need of a Savior. Following the law is not the solution to the sin problem; the law is a measuring stick that reveals the sin problem. None of us are capable of true and complete obedience. Despite our helplessness God desires to bless us when we trust in his promises, not when we perform according to his perfect standards. Knowing that God loves us enough to pay for our sins can help us be more fearless as we take our moral inventory. When we confess our sins to God, he will set us free from their destructive power.

3:26-29 When we entrust our life to God through Jesus Christ, we become his children. What an amazing truth! We are each given a place in God's family, no matter what our past sins, no matter how dysfunctional our family, no matter how deeply we have been hurt. He has a plan for each of us, and like any parent, he wants to help us succeed. Faith in Christ is all we need to enter into this privileged status. Each one of us is important to God, and he loves us enough to help us overcome our weaknesses and character flaws.

4:8-11 If we are not willing to trust and obey God, we soon become enslaved to other things. We turn to other activities or substances to help us deal with our problems. Most of us realize that this often leads to various forms of addiction. We have discovered that drugs, alcohol, sexual immorality, work, or even religious activities can never solve our problems. In fact, depending on anything other than God himself leads to even deeper problems. Only God offers us the power to be delivered from bondage to build a new life. Turning to him for help is really the only valid option we have.

4:17-20 Paul was trying to help the Galatians experience the new life that God offers through Jesus Christ. The false teachers were trying to lead the people back into bondage under the Jewish law. There was a distinct contrast between Paul's attitudes and actions and those of the false teachers. The false teachers were not concerned about the people's good; Paul was. We have all seen recovery fads that promise amazing results. These programs usually cost a lot of money and yield, at best, only temporary results. The only real means to recovery is God's power—and it's free of charge! All we have to do is accept it.

CHAPTER 4

Think of it this way. If a father dies and leaves great wealth for his young children, those children are not much better off than slaves until they grow up, even though they actually own everything their father had. ²They have to obey their guardians until they reach whatever age their father set.

³And that's the way it was with us before Christ came. We were slaves to the spiritual powers of this world. ⁴But when the right time came, God sent his Son, born of a woman, subject to the law. ⁵God sent him to buy freedom for us who were slaves to the law, so that he could adopt us as his very own children.* ⁶And because you Gentiles have become his children, God has sent the Spirit of his Son into your hearts, and now you can call God your dear Father.* ⁷Now you are no longer a slave but God's own child.* And since you are his child, everything he has belongs to you.

Paul's Concern for the Galatians

⁸Before you Gentiles knew God, you were slaves to so-called gods that do not even exist. ⁹And now that you have found God (or should I say, now that God has found you), why do you want to go back again and become slaves once more to the weak and useless spiritual powers of this world? ¹⁰You are trying to find favor with God by what you do or don't do on certain days or months or seasons or years. ¹¹I fear for you. I am afraid that all my hard work for you was worth nothing. ¹²Dear brothers and sisters,* I plead with you to live as I do in freedom from these things, for I have become like you Gentiles were—free from the law.

You did not mistreat me when I first preached to you. ¹³Surely you remember that I was sick when I first brought you the Good News of Christ. ¹⁴But even though my sickness was revolting to you, you did not reject me and turn me away. No, you took me in and cared for me as though I were an angel from God or even Christ Jesus himself. ¹⁵Where is that joyful spirit we felt together then? In those days, I know you would gladly have taken out your own eyes and given them to me if it had been possible. ¹⁶Have I now become your enemy because I am telling you the truth?

¹⁷Those false teachers who are so anxious

4:5 Greek *sons;* also in 4:6. **4:6** Greek *into your hearts, crying, "Abba, Father." Abba* is an Aramaic term for "father." **4:7** Greek *son;* also in 4:7b. **4:12** Greek *brothers;* also in 4:28, 31.

s T E P

5

Escaping Self-Deception

BIBLE READING: Galatians 6:7-10

We admitted to God, to ourselves, and to another human being the exact nature of our wrongs.

We may fool ourself into believing that we can simply bury our wrongs and go on without ever having to admit them. In time, we all discover that those deeds we thought were buried once and for all were actually seeds. They grow and bear fruit. Eventually we have to deal with a crop of consequences and face the fact that self-deception doesn't work to our advantage.

"You will always reap what you sow! Those who live only to satisfy their own sinful desires will harvest the consequences of decay and death. But those who live to please the Spirit will harvest everlasting life from the Spirit" (Galatians 6:7-8). "If we say we have no sin, we are only fooling ourselves and refusing to accept the truth. But if we confess our sins to [God], he is faithful and just to forgive us and to cleanse us from every wrong" (1 John 1:8-9).

Step Five says good-bye to self-deception and hello to forgiveness and cleansing. We should note that there is cleansing from every wrong, not from "wrongdoing" in a general sense. Admitting the exact nature of our wrongs includes giving our accounts in exact and specific terms. It is only when we get specific that we will no longer be able to fool ourself about the nature of our wrongs. Since we cannot ignore God and get away with it anyway, we might as well come clean and be forgiven. *Turn to Step Six, page 151, John 5.*

to win your favor are not doing it for your good. They are trying to shut you off from me so that you will pay more attention to them. [18]Now it's wonderful if you are eager to do good, and especially when I am not with you. [19]But oh, my dear children! I feel as if I am going through labor pains for you again, and they will continue until Christ is fully developed in your lives. [20]How I wish I were there with you right now, so that I could be more gentle with you. But at this distance I frankly don't know what else to do.

Abraham's Two Children
[21]Listen to me, you who want to live under the law. Do you know what the law really says? [22]The Scriptures say that Abraham had two sons, one from his slave-wife and one from his freeborn wife.* [23]The son of the slave-wife was born in a human attempt to bring about the fulfillment of God's promise. But the son of the freeborn wife was born as God's own fulfillment of his promise.

[24]Now these two women serve as an illustration of God's two covenants. Hagar, the slave-wife, represents Mount Sinai where people first became enslaved to the law. [25]And now Jerusalem is just like Mount Sinai in Arabia, because she and her children live in slavery. [26]But Sarah, the free woman, represents the heavenly Jerusalem. And she is our mother. [27]That is what Isaiah meant when he prophesied,

"Rejoice, O childless woman!
Break forth into loud and joyful song,
   even though you never gave birth to a child.
For the woman who could bear no children
   now has more than all the other women!"*

[28]And you, dear brothers and sisters, are children of the promise, just like Isaac. [29]And we who are born of the Holy Spirit are persecuted by those who want us to keep the law, just as Isaac, the child of promise, was persecuted by Ishmael, the son of the slave-wife.

[30]But what do the Scriptures say about that? "Get rid of the slave and her son, for the son of the slave woman will not share the family inheritance with the free woman's son."* [31]So, dear brothers and sisters, we are not children of the slave woman, obligated to the law. We are children of the free woman, acceptable to God because of our faith.

CHAPTER 5
Freedom in Christ
So Christ has really set us free. Now make sure that you stay free, and don't get tied up again in slavery to the law.

[2]Listen! I, Paul, tell you this: If you are counting on circumcision to make you right with God, then Christ cannot help you. [3]I'll say it again. If you are trying to find favor with God by being circumcised, you must obey all of the regulations in the whole law of Moses. [4]For if you are trying to make yourselves right with God by keeping the law, you have been cut off from Christ! You have fallen away from God's grace.

[5]But we who live by the Spirit eagerly wait to receive everything promised to us who are right with God through faith. [6]For when we place our faith in Christ Jesus, it makes no difference to God whether we are circumcised or not circumcised. What is important is faith expressing itself in love.

[7]You were getting along so well. Who has interfered with you to hold you back from following the truth? [8]It certainly isn't God, for he is the one who called you to free-

4:22 See Gen 16:15; 21:2-3. **4:27** Isa 54:1. **4:30** Gen 21:10.

5:1-12 The Galatians faced the same basic choice that all of us face. Should we choose power and freedom in Christ or slavery through useless and destructive solutions? If we make a bad choice, we risk being cut off from the deliverance available to God's people. There is no deliverance from the power of sin except through Christ and his powerful presence within us. Only his power can restore us.

5:22-24 These qualities are produced by the Holy Spirit's work in a life submitted to God. Just as a tree bears fruit by means of God's silent work in nature, we experience these fruits of the Spirit by means of God's power alone. Our part is to entrust our life to him. When the Holy Spirit begins to bear these fruits in our life, our dependency loses its power. With *joy* and *peace* we overcome the pain of our broken past. With *love, kindness, goodness, faithfulness,* and *gentleness* we restore our relationships and make amends. With *patience* we persevere through the difficult times. With *self-control* we stand against our tendency to relapse. God's Spirit can supply everything necessary for a successful recovery.

dom. ⁹But it takes only one wrong person among you to infect all the others—a little yeast spreads quickly through the whole batch of dough! ¹⁰I am trusting the Lord to bring you back to believing as I do about these things. God will judge that person, whoever it is, who has been troubling and confusing you.

¹¹Dear brothers and sisters,* if I were still preaching that you must be circumcised— as some say I do—why would the Jews persecute me? The fact that I am still being persecuted proves that I am still preaching salvation through the cross of Christ alone. ¹²I only wish that those troublemakers who want to mutilate you by circumcision would mutilate themselves.*

¹³For you have been called to live in freedom—not freedom to satisfy your sinful nature, but freedom to serve one another in love. ¹⁴For the whole law can be summed up in this one command: "Love your neighbor as yourself."* ¹⁵But if instead of showing love among yourselves you are always biting and devouring one another, watch out! Beware of destroying one another.

Living by the Spirit's Power
¹⁶So I advise you to live according to your new life in the Holy Spirit. Then you won't be doing what your sinful nature craves. ¹⁷The old sinful nature loves to do evil, which is just opposite from what the Holy Spirit wants. And the Spirit gives us desires that are opposite from what the sinful nature desires. These two forces are constantly fighting each other, and your choices are never free from this conflict. ¹⁸But when you are directed by the Holy Spirit, you are no longer subject to the law.

¹⁹When you follow the desires of your sinful nature, your lives will produce these evil results: sexual immorality, impure thoughts, eagerness for lustful pleasure, ²⁰idolatry, participation in demonic activities, hostility, quarreling, jealousy, outbursts of anger, selfish ambition, divisions, the feeling that everyone is wrong except those in your own little group, ²¹envy, drunkenness, wild parties, and other kinds of sin. Let me tell you again, as I have before, that anyone living that sort of life will not inherit the Kingdom of God.

²²But when the Holy Spirit controls our lives, he will produce this kind of fruit in us: love, joy, peace, patience, kindness,

5:11 Greek *Brothers*. **5:12** Or *castrate themselves;* Greek reads *cut themselves off*. **5:14** Lev 19:18.

STEP 8

Reaping Goodness

BIBLE READING: Galatians 6:7-10

We made a list of all persons we had harmed and became willing to make amends to them all.

While in recovery, we learn to accept responsibility for our actions, even when we are powerless over our addiction. We come to realize that all our actions yield consequences. Some of us may have fooled ourself into thinking we could escape the consequences of the things we did. But with time, it has become clear that God has made accountability a necessary element of healthy living.

"You will always reap what you sow! Those who live only to satisfy their own sinful desires will harvest the consequences of decay and death. But those who live to please the Spirit will harvest everlasting life from the Spirit" (Galatians 6:7-8).

The law of sowing and reaping can also work for us. God spoke through the prophet Hosea: "Plant the good seeds of righteousness, and you will harvest a crop of my love. Plow up the hard ground of your hearts, for now is the time to seek the LORD, that he may come and shower righteousness upon you" (Hosea 10:12).

God says we *always* reap what we have sown. Even after we have been forgiven, we must deal with the consequences of our actions. It may take time to finish harvesting the negative consequences from our past, but we don't have to let this discourage us. Making our list of those we have harmed is a step toward planting good seeds. In time we will see a good crop begin to grow. *Turn to Step Nine, page 9, Matthew 5.*

goodness, faithfulness, ²³gentleness, and self-control. Here there is no conflict with the law.

²⁴Those who belong to Christ Jesus have nailed the passions and desires of their sinful nature to his cross and crucified them there. ²⁵If we are living now by the Holy Spirit, let us follow the Holy Spirit's leading in every part of our lives. ²⁶Let us not become conceited, or irritate one another, or be jealous of one another.

CHAPTER 6
We Reap What We Sow

Dear brothers and sisters, if another Christian* is overcome by some sin, you who are godly should gently and humbly help that person back onto the right path. And be careful not to fall into the same temptation yourself. ²Share each other's troubles and problems, and in this way obey the law of Christ. ³If you think you are too important to help someone in need, you are only fooling yourself. You are really a nobody.

⁴Be sure to do what you should, for then you will enjoy the personal satisfaction of having done your work well, and you won't need to compare yourself to anyone else. ⁵For we are each responsible for our own conduct.

⁶Those who are taught the word of God should help their teachers by paying them.

⁷Don't be misled. Remember that you can't ignore God and get away with it. You will always reap what you sow! ⁸Those who live only to satisfy their own sinful desires will harvest the consequences of decay and death. But those who live to please the Spirit will harvest everlasting life from the Spirit. ⁹So don't get tired of doing what is good. Don't get discouraged and give up, for we will reap a harvest of blessing at the appropriate time. ¹⁰Whenever we have the opportunity, we should do good to everyone, especially to our Christian brothers and sisters.

Paul's Final Advice

¹¹Notice what large letters I use as I write these closing words in my own handwriting. ¹²Those who are trying to force you to be circumcised are doing it for just one reason. They don't want to be persecuted for teaching that the cross of Christ alone can save. ¹³And even those who advocate circumcision don't really keep the whole law. They only want you to be circumcised so they can brag about it and claim you as their disciples.

¹⁴As for me, God forbid that I should boast about anything except the cross of our Lord Jesus Christ. Because of that cross,* my interest in this world died long ago, and the world's interest in me is also long dead. ¹⁵It doesn't make any difference now whether we have been circumcised or not. What counts is whether we really have been changed into new and different people. ¹⁶May God's mercy and peace be upon all those who live by this principle. They are the new people of God.*

¹⁷From now on, don't let anyone trouble me with these things. For I bear on my body the scars that show I belong to Jesus.

¹⁸My dear brothers and sisters,* may the grace of our Lord Jesus Christ be with you all. Amen.

6:1 Greek *Brothers, if a man.* **6:14** Or *Because of him.* **6:16** Greek *the Israel of God.* **6:18** Greek *Brothers.*

6:1-3 Paul told the Galatians to share their troubles with one another. This would bring healing to hurting people and provide opportunities for the believers to help each other. Paul included a special note to encourage those who might be too proud to admit their problems. An essential part of recovery is admitting to others the exact nature of our wrongs. As we share with others, we will discover that much of the burden of our painful past or our addictive tendency will be lifted. With their encouragement and call to accountability, we can shed our painful past and move on to a productive future.

6:11-18 In these closing verses Paul recapped his major arguments with an emotional appeal to stand firm against false teachers who try to attract people away from the liberating message of the gospel. Admitting that we are helpless to overcome our sins and accepting God's help are responsible decisions. Rather than humiliating us, God bestows dignity and healing upon us when we enter the process of recovery through faith in Christ. As God heals us, we can take the Good News to others as Paul did with the Galatian believers.

REFLECTIONS ON

GALATIANS

insights INTO GOD'S WILL

Very often God's will for us stands in direct opposition to our natural desires. Recovery depends on our accepting the fact that following our own selfish desires is destructive. In **Galatians 5:16-21** we find a whole list of destructive behaviors that flow out of a self-centered life. When we turn our life over to God, however, we allow his Spirit to help us control those evil desires, and God's desires become our own desires more and more. Submitting our life to God's will is the best choice we can make.

insights ABOUT CONSEQUENCES

In **Galatians 6:7-10** Paul left an important reminder for us all. We will always reap what we have sown. In other words, sins and addictions have painful consequences. For a while we might be able to fool ourself into thinking that certain activities and relationships are all right. But when the consequences catch up with us, there will be no denying the facts. We need to take this warning seriously and take steps to change now. We don't have to wait to hit bottom before we act. Using God's Word as our standard, we can take a fearless moral inventory and work toward a godly life before it's too late.

EPHESIANS

THE BIG PICTURE

A. GREETINGS (1:1-2)
B. ASSURANCE OF GOD'S PROGRAM FOR SPIRITUAL WHOLENESS (1:3–3:21)
C. ACCEPTANCE OF OUR RESPONSIBILITY FOR SPIRITUAL WHOLENESS (4:1–6:9)
D. AWARENESS OF OUR ROLE IN SPIRITUAL WARFARE (6:10-20)
E. CLOSING REMARKS (6:21-24)

The Ephesian church had been planted through Paul's influence, and for a few years he had served as its pastor. This church thrived in a city renowned as a center for the worship of the goddess Artemis (also known as Diana). While Paul was there, the Ephesian believers maintained a strong attachment to him, and when he left they openly expressed their sorrow.

How could the Ephesian church survive for the long haul in its hostile environment? They could not depend on Paul's presence forever; with God's help they would have to learn to stand on their own. Paul wrote this letter to remind the Ephesian believers to place their faith in the only solid foundation for healthy living—God.

How can we maintain our recovery in a hostile environment? None of us have the resources or strength to initiate and sustain our recovery alone. Paul asserted one important fact: We can change! But our transformation is possible only on God's terms. We can recover if we break with our former way of life and depend on God's power to help us change. While programs and supportive people are helpful, lasting recovery happens only when we recognize our need for a higher power—the God who created us and sustains our life.

Belief in God and obedience to his will are keys to a genuine, stable recovery. If we adopt an attitude of submission to God's authority and care, and our attitudes and actions reflect God's truth, we will indeed make progress. Recovery that ignores God is doomed to failure; recovery that depends on God will succeed.

THE BOTTOM LINE

PURPOSE: To strengthen the believers in Ephesus in their relationships with God and with each other. AUTHOR: The apostle Paul. AUDIENCE: The believers in Ephesus, a city in western Asia Minor, and all believers everywhere. DATE WRITTEN: Around A.D. 60, during Paul's imprisonment in Rome. SETTING: This letter was not sent to solve any particular problem. Rather, it was a somewhat personal message from Paul to some dear friends in the mother church of Asia. Paul probably intended this to be a circular letter passed from church to church for encourage- ment. KEY VERSE: "A final word: Be strong with the Lord's mighty power" (6:10). KEY PEOPLE AND RELATIONSHIPS: Paul with Tychicus, and with his close friends in the Ephesian church.

RECOVERY THEMES

God Desires Recovery for Us: God has had a plan for each of us since the beginning of time. His plan doesn't include bondage to sin or the past. He wants us to have a relationship with him so we can enjoy his love and presence. He wants us to recover even more than we do! Many of us have a distorted image of God based on painful images of authority figures in our past. This letter shows us that God is a father who has loved us from the beginning of time. He will continue to love us, no matter what we do.

The Importance of Jesus Christ: In the New Testament and especially in Ephesians, Jesus Christ is exalted as the focus of all history and as the only means for experiencing a meaningful life. Only through God's Son, Jesus Christ, can the power of sin be overcome. This letter urges us to keep Christ at the center of all we do, maintaining conscious contact with him on a daily basis.

True Recovery Leads to Wise Conduct: It is easy to think of recovery only in terms of stopping destructive behavior patterns. But it is important to see that the best way to stop destructive habits is to build constructive ones to replace them. We are able to lay aside old patterns when we consciously repent, turn our life over to God, and seek his will for us each day. As we begin to obey God's will for our life, we will find we are no longer following the path toward destruction.

Adoption into God's Family: Many of us have painful memories from the past, particularly from the experiences we had in our family. Some of us have no positive memories of family life at all. The letter to the Ephesians reminds us that when we trust God as our Savior, he adopts us into a new family. In this family, God is our perfect and loving father. Even God's family, the church, has its limitations and imperfections. But our Father is perfect, and becoming a part of his family is an all-important step in recovery.

CHAPTER 1
Greetings from Paul

This letter is from Paul, chosen by God to be an apostle of Christ Jesus.

It is written to God's holy people in Ephesus,* who are faithful followers of Christ Jesus.

²May grace and peace be yours, sent to you from God our Father and Jesus Christ our Lord.

Spiritual Blessings

³How we praise God, the Father of our Lord Jesus Christ, who has blessed us with every spiritual blessing in the heavenly realms because we belong to Christ. ⁴Long ago, even before he made the world, God loved us and chose us in Christ to be holy and without fault in his eyes. ⁵His unchanging plan has always been to adopt us into his own family by bringing us to himself through Jesus Christ. And this gave him great pleasure.

⁶So we praise God for the wonderful kindness he has poured out on us because we belong to his dearly loved Son. ⁷He is so rich in kindness that he purchased our freedom through the blood of his Son, and our sins are forgiven. ⁸He has showered his kindness on us, along with all wisdom and understanding.

⁹God's secret plan has now been revealed to us; it is a plan centered on Christ, designed long ago according to his good pleasure. ¹⁰And this is his plan: At the right

1:1 Some manuscripts do not include *in Ephesus*.

1:3-6 Recovery cannot begin until we admit that our life is unmanageable and that we are powerless over our circumstances. The apostle Paul reminds us that God is sovereign over all the details of our life. God has a special plan for each of us, and that unchanging plan includes adopting us into his family. We have already realized that doing things our way leads to painful consequences. With this in mind, we can be motivated to submit to God's perfect will for our life. God wants only what is best for us. It is always God's will for us to find new life in him.

1:11-12 Some of us may wonder how we can know God's will for our life. While there are details we may never know in advance, God's Word points us in the right direction. God desires many things for all of us, and these are revealed in Scripture. God wants us to experience an intimate relationship with him through Christ. In this relationship, God will delight in us and we will praise him in return. This is an amazing truth: God wants to have a close relationship with us, no matter who we are or what we have done. Because of what God has done for us through Jesus Christ, we can praise him and share the Good News with others in need.

time he will bring everything together under the authority of Christ—everything in heaven and on earth. [11]Furthermore, because of Christ, we have received an inheritance from God,* for he chose us from the beginning, and all things happen just as he decided long ago. [12]God's purpose was that we who were the first to trust in Christ should praise our glorious God. [13]And now you also have heard the truth, the Good News that God saves you. And when you believed in Christ, he identified you as his own by giving you the Holy Spirit, whom he promised long ago. [14]The Spirit is God's guarantee that he will give us everything he promised and that he has purchased us to be his own people. This is just one more reason for us to praise our glorious God.

Paul's Prayer for Spiritual Wisdom

[15]Ever since I first heard of your strong faith in the Lord Jesus and your love for Christians everywhere, [16]I have never stopped thanking God for you. I pray for you constantly, [17]asking God, the glorious Father of our Lord Jesus Christ, to give you spiritual wisdom and understanding, so that you might grow in your knowledge of God. [18]I pray that your hearts will be flooded with light so that you can understand the wonderful future he has promised to those he called. I want you to realize what a rich and glorious inheritance he has given to his people.*

[19]I pray that you will begin to understand the incredible greatness of his power for us who believe him. This is the same mighty power [20]that raised Christ from the dead and seated him in the place of honor at God's right hand in the heavenly realms.

[21]Now he is far above any ruler or authority or power or leader or anything else in this world or in the world to come. [22]And God has put all things under the authority of Christ, and he gave him this authority for the benefit of the church. [23]And the church is his body; it is filled by Christ, who fills everything everywhere with his presence.

CHAPTER 2
Made Alive with Christ

Once you were dead, doomed forever because of your many sins. [2]You used to live just like the rest of the world, full of sin, obeying Satan, the mighty prince of the power of the air. He is the spirit at work in the hearts of those who refuse to obey God. [3]All of us used to live that way, following the passions and desires of our evil nature. We were born with an evil nature, and we were under God's anger just like everyone else.

[4]But God is so rich in mercy, and he loved us so very much, [5]that even while we were dead because of our sins, he gave us life when he raised Christ from the dead. (It is only by God's special favor that you have been saved!) [6]For he raised us from the dead along with Christ, and we are seated with him in the heavenly realms—all because we are one with Christ Jesus. [7]And so God can always point to us as examples of the incredible wealth of his favor and kindness toward us, as shown in all he has done for us through Christ Jesus.

[8]God saved you by his special favor when you believed. And you can't take credit for this; it is a gift from God. [9]Salvation is not a reward for the good things we have done, so none of us can boast about it. [10]For we are

---

1:11 Or *we have become God's inheritance.* 1:18 Or *realize how much God has been honored by acquiring his people.*

1:13-14 God's plan for our salvation is continued by the sealing work of the Holy Spirit. Just as an official marks a document as genuine, so the Holy Spirit's work within us guarantees our identity as God's adopted child. This is all made possible by Jesus Christ and his saving work on our behalf. It becomes a reality in our life when we place our faith in him. Our knowledge of God's love for us and the help he offers gives us reason for hope as we seek to overcome our problems and dependency. When we trust God, we become part of his powerful solution to deal with sin in our world.

2:1-10 Here Paul affirms two essential truths related to recovery: (1) we are all born with an evil nature, powerless to stand against our tendency toward sin and failure; (2) God is rich in mercy and love, and even though we are far from him and entrapped by sin, God graciously reaches out to us. God wants to forgive us and give us the power to rebuild our life. Through the work of Jesus Christ, God has already conquered the power of sin and death. When we admit that we need God's help and ask him to act on our behalf, God empowers us to overcome our problems and dependency.

God's masterpiece. He has created us anew in Christ Jesus, so that we can do the good things he planned for us long ago.

Oneness and Peace in Christ

[11]Don't forget that you Gentiles used to be outsiders by birth. You were called "the uncircumcised ones" by the Jews, who were proud of their circumcision, even though it affected only their bodies and not their hearts. [12]In those days you were living apart from Christ. You were excluded from God's people, Israel, and you did not know the promises God had made to them. You lived in this world without God and without hope. [13]But now you belong to Christ Jesus. Though you once were far away from God, now you have been brought near to him because of the blood of Christ.

[14]For Christ himself has made peace between us Jews and you Gentiles by making us all one people. He has broken down the wall of hostility that used to separate us. [15]By his death he ended the whole system of Jewish law that excluded the Gentiles. His purpose was to make peace between Jews and Gentiles by creating in himself one new person from the two groups. [16]Together as one body, Christ reconciled both groups to God by means of his death, and our hostility toward each other was put to death. [17]He has brought this Good News of peace to you Gentiles who were far away from him, and to us Jews who were near. [18]Now all of us, both Jews and Gentiles, may come to the Father through the same Holy Spirit because of what Christ has done for us.

A Temple for the Lord

[19]So now you Gentiles are no longer strangers and foreigners. You are citizens along with all of God's holy people. You are members of God's family. [20]We are his house, built on the foundation of the apostles and the prophets. And the cornerstone is Christ Jesus himself. [21]We who believe are carefully joined together, becoming a holy temple for the Lord. [22]Through him you Gentiles are also joined together as part of this dwelling where God lives by his Spirit.

CHAPTER 3
God's Secret Plan Revealed

I, Paul, am a prisoner of Christ Jesus because of my preaching to you Gentiles. [2]As you already know, God has given me this special ministry of announcing his favor to you Gentiles. [3]As I briefly mentioned earlier in this letter, God himself revealed his secret plan to me. [4]As you read what I have written, you will understand what I know about this plan regarding Christ. [5]God did not reveal it to previous generations, but now he has revealed it by the Holy Spirit to his holy apostles and prophets.

[6]And this is the secret plan: The Gentiles have an equal share with the Jews in all the riches inherited by God's children. Both

2:14-19 Through Jesus Christ, the barrier between God and his sinful creatures has been removed. But Christ's work of reconciliation does not stop there. He can also remove the obstacles that alienate us from other people. In Christ we can have peace with God and with others. Restoration of our broken relationships is a necessary part of the recovery process. Some of us may feel that our relationships could never be salvaged. But realizing that Christ can give us the power to live at peace with others gives us new hope. His power will enable us to make amends to people we have wronged. All who believe in Christ are made brothers and sisters in him.

3:1-13 In these verses one truth stands out: God accepts all of us through faith. Race, reputation, and position have no bearing on God's forgiveness. Paul wrote these words to convince the believers of their oneness in Christ. Apparently some of the Jewish believers claimed superiority because of their relationship to God in the Old Testament Scriptures. Paul refuted their view by reminding them that our relationship with God is based on our trust in Jesus Christ, not our personal history or position in society. This important truth is encouraging for us in recovery. Our addiction may have destroyed the reputation we once commanded. None of this matters to God. If we seek his forgiveness, he will accept us and help us make a new start.

3:14-21 For churches or small groups to function effectively as vehicles for recovery, they must be driven by God's dynamic and unlimited love. Paul prayed that his friends might be deeply anchored and rooted in the soil of God's love. As we learn how much God loves us, we will become confident that he is able to do far more in and through us than we could ever imagine! We can bank our recovery on this truth! We may feel that our life is hopeless and beyond recovery. But through God restoration and healing are possible. When we are grounded in God's love, recovery will follow.

groups have believed the Good News, and both are part of the same body and enjoy together the promise of blessings through Christ Jesus. ⁷By God's special favor and mighty power, I have been given the wonderful privilege of serving him by spreading this Good News.

⁸Just think! Though I did nothing to deserve it, and though I am the least deserving Christian there is, I was chosen for this special joy of telling the Gentiles about the endless treasures available to them in Christ. ⁹I was chosen to explain to everyone this plan that God, the Creator of all things, had kept secret from the beginning.

¹⁰God's purpose was to show his wisdom in all its rich variety to all the rulers and authorities in the heavenly realms. They will see this when Jews and Gentiles are joined together in his church. ¹¹This was his plan from all eternity, and it has now been carried out through Christ Jesus our Lord.

¹²Because of Christ and our faith in him, we can now come fearlessly into God's presence, assured of his glad welcome. ¹³So please don't despair because of what they are doing to me here. It is for you that I am suffering, so you should feel honored and encouraged.

Paul's Prayer for Spiritual Empowering

¹⁴When I think of the wisdom and scope of God's plan, I fall to my knees and pray to the Father,* ¹⁵the Creator of everything in heaven and on earth. ¹⁶I pray that from his glorious, unlimited resources he will give you mighty inner strength through his Holy Spirit. ¹⁷And I pray that Christ will be more and more at home in your hearts as you trust in him. May your roots go down deep into the soil of God's marvelous love. ¹⁸And may you have the power to understand, as all God's people should, how wide, how long, how high, and how deep his love really is. ¹⁹May you experience the love of Christ, though it is so great you will never fully understand it. Then you will be filled with the fullness of life and power that comes from God.

²⁰Now glory be to God! By his mighty power at work within us, he is able to accomplish infinitely more than we would ever dare to ask or hope. ²¹May he be given glory in the church and in Christ Jesus forever and ever through endless ages. Amen.

3:14 Some manuscripts read *the Father of our Lord Jesus Christ.*

Self-Perception

READ EPHESIANS 2:1-13

We may feel like we are not good enough to be an example for others. We may realize that we need other people but find it hard to believe that our story of deliverance could help anyone else.

The apostle Paul said, "Just as our bodies have many parts and each part has a special function, so it is with Christ's body. We are all parts of his one body, and each of us has different work to do. And since we are all one body in Christ, we belong to each other, and each of us needs all the others" (Romans 12:4-5). "We are God's masterpiece. He has created us anew in Christ Jesus, so that we can do the good things he planned for us long ago" (Ephesians 2:10).

To have a true view of where we fit in the scheme of things, we need to see that God has a purpose for our life. God created each of us with abilities and talents. He likens us to a part of a body where every part is needed for the proper working of the whole. If you isolate any one part of a body and examine it apart from its proper place among the other members, it may seem odd and useless. Only when it is connected to the body and doing its appointed job is its usefulness realized. And so it is with us.

We need to find places where our talents and abilities can be used to help others. Doing this will show that we have gained an honest understanding of who God created us to be. He loves us and wants to help each of us realize our place in the body of Christ and our unique purpose in life. ***Turn to page 317, Ephesians 4.***

CHAPTER 4

Unity in the Body

Therefore I, a prisoner for serving the Lord, beg you to lead a life worthy of your calling, for you have been called by God. ²Be humble and gentle. Be patient with each other, making allowance for each other's faults because of your love. ³Always keep yourselves united in the Holy Spirit, and bind yourselves together with peace.

⁴We are all one body, we have the same Spirit, and we have all been called to the same glorious future. ⁵There is only one Lord, one faith, one baptism, ⁶and there is only one God and Father, who is over us all and in us all and living through us all. ⁷However, he has given each one of us a special gift according to the generosity of Christ. ⁸That is why the Scriptures say,

"When he ascended to the heights,
he led a crowd of captives
and gave gifts to his people."*

⁹Notice that it says "he ascended." This means that Christ first came down to the lowly world in which we live.* ¹⁰The same one who came down is the one who ascended higher than all the heavens, so that his rule might fill the entire universe.

¹¹He is the one who gave these gifts to the church: the apostles, the prophets, the evangelists, and the pastors and teachers. ¹²Their responsibility is to equip God's people to do his work and build up the church, the body of Christ, ¹³until we come to such unity in our faith and knowledge of God's Son that we will be mature and full grown in the Lord, measuring up to the full stature of Christ.

¹⁴Then we will no longer be like children, forever changing our minds about what we believe because someone has told us something different or because someone has cleverly lied to us and made the lie sound like the truth. ¹⁵Instead, we will hold to the truth in love, becoming more and more in every way like Christ, who is the head of his body, the church. ¹⁶Under his direction, the whole body is fitted together perfectly. As each part does its own special work, it helps the other parts grow, so that the whole body is healthy and growing and full of love.

Living as Children of Light

¹⁷With the Lord's authority let me say this: Live no longer as the ungodly* do, for they are hopelessly confused. ¹⁸Their closed minds are full of darkness; they are far away from the life of God because they have shut their minds

4:8 Ps 68:18. 4:9 Or *to the lowest parts of the earth.* 4:17 Greek *Gentiles.*

4:1-6 Even though God's program for recovery is centered on his sovereign purposes and power, we have important responsibilities as well. What we believe about God is crucial, but so is the manner in which we live. For many of us, the recovery process is hindered by our faults, especially our stubborn pride that prevents us from taking searching and fearless inventory of our life. Recovery is impossible until we humbly admit that we are powerless and need God's help. As we trust God to help us, his Holy Spirit will replace our character flaws with humility, love, and patience. When God asks us to live a certain way, he provides the power we need to succeed.

4:7-16 We have been gifted in ways that make us necessary to others. Others have been gifted in ways that make them necessary to us. Some of us have special gifts for teaching others about God. Others may have the gift of caring for hurting people. Our individual gifts are important for the emotional and spiritual growth of others. God has a purpose for each of us, so we must strive to know him better through prayer and meditation on his Word. He will show us what our gifts are and how we can use them to help others. As we share our gifts and receive the benefits of other people's gifts, we will find the body of Christ growing stronger and full of love.

4:31-32 A life of recovery is committed to knowing God better through prayer and meditation on his Word. In examining our life, we realize just how demanding God's standards for righteous living are, but since it is God's grace that helps us conform to his will, we need not despair. As we obey him, he will teach us to live without bitterness, anger, or harsh words. God is in the business of healing our relationships. When we do things his way, we are well on the way to reconciling with our alienated friends and building solid foundations for recovery.

5:1-7 In recovery we are told to follow God's example in all we do. God wants us to be like Jesus Christ—to think and act like him. We are to love our enemies. We are to avoid sexual immorality, greed, and obscene language, since they stand counter to God's character. These requirements are right in line with what is needed in recovery. We are to seek to rebuild our broken relationships, avoid destructive behaviors, admit our wrongs, and seek to make amends for the pain we have caused. As difficult as imitating Christ might sound, anything is possible with God's powerful help.

and hardened their hearts against him. ¹⁹They don't care anymore about right and wrong, and they have given themselves over to immoral ways. Their lives are filled with all kinds of impurity and greed.

²⁰But that isn't what you were taught when you learned about Christ. ²¹Since you have heard all about him and have learned the truth that is in Jesus, ²²throw off your old evil nature and your former way of life, which is rotten through and through, full of lust and deception. ²³Instead, there must be a spiritual renewal of your thoughts and attitudes. ²⁴You must display a new nature because you are a new person, created in God's likeness—righteous, holy, and true.

²⁵So put away all falsehood and "tell your neighbor the truth"* because we belong to each other. ²⁶And "don't sin by letting anger gain control over you."* Don't let the sun go down while you are still angry, ²⁷for anger gives a mighty foothold to the Devil.

²⁸If you are a thief, stop stealing. Begin using your hands for honest work, and then give generously to others in need. ²⁹Don't use foul or abusive language. Let everything you say be good and helpful, so that your words will be an encouragement to those who hear them.

³⁰And do not bring sorrow to God's Holy Spirit by the way you live. Remember, he is the one who has identified you as his own, guaranteeing that you will be saved on the day of redemption.

³¹Get rid of all bitterness, rage, anger, harsh words, and slander, as well as all types of malicious behavior. ³²Instead, be kind to each other, tenderhearted, forgiving one another, just as God through Christ has forgiven you.

CHAPTER 5
Living in the Light
Follow God's example in everything you do, because you are his dear children. ²Live a life filled with love for others, following the example of Christ, who loved you and gave himself as a sacrifice to take away your sins. And God was pleased, because that sacrifice was like sweet perfume to him.

³Let there be no sexual immorality, impurity, or greed among you. Such sins have no place among God's people. ⁴Obscene stories, foolish talk, and coarse jokes—these are not for you. Instead, let there be thankfulness to God. ⁵You can be sure that no immoral, impure, or greedy person will inherit the Kingdom of Christ and of God. For a greedy person

Honesty
READ EPHESIANS 4:12-27

We may have grown up believing lies about life, about ourself, about our family. We may still experience confusion and uncertainty because we don't have a strong sense of what is really true. The lies we believe can contribute to our addictive ways, so we need to reexamine our life in the light of what is true.

The apostle Paul talked about how the people who believed in Christ were to function like a single body. Each member is to be "mature and full grown in the Lord" (Ephesians 4:13), offering the gifts he or she has to help the whole body mature. Since Jesus described himself as "the truth" (John 14:6) and we are to be filled with him, the recovery process involves becoming "truth-full." Paul continued: "Then we will no longer be like children, forever changing our minds about what we believe because someone has told us something different or because someone has cleverly lied to us and made the lie sound like the truth. Instead, we will hold to the truth in love, becoming more and more in every way like Christ" (Ephesians 4:14-15).

Recovery can be like growing up all over again. As we grow, we are to continue to aim for what is true. In the past we measured truth against whatever sounded right to us at the time. Now we can have the sure measurement of God's Word and Jesus Christ himself. From this perspective we can reevaluate our beliefs. What is true about God? What is true about me? What is right? What is wrong? *Turn to page 323, Philippians 1.*

is really an idolater who worships the things of this world. 6Don't be fooled by those who try to excuse these sins, for the terrible anger of God comes upon all those who disobey him. 7Don't participate in the things these people do. 8For though your hearts were once full of darkness, now you are full of light from the Lord, and your behavior should show it! 9For this light within you produces only what is good and right and true.

10Try to find out what is pleasing to the Lord. 11Take no part in the worthless deeds of evil and darkness; instead, rebuke and expose them. 12It is shameful even to talk about the things that ungodly people do in secret. 13But when the light shines on them, it becomes clear how evil these things are. 14And where your light shines, it will expose their evil deeds. This is why it is said,

> "Awake, O sleeper,
>   rise up from the dead,
>   and Christ will give you light."

Living by the Spirit's Power

15So be careful how you live, not as fools but as those who are wise. 16Make the most of every opportunity for doing good in these evil days. 17Don't act thoughtlessly, but try to understand what the Lord wants you to do. 18Don't be drunk with wine, because that will ruin your life. Instead, let the Holy Spirit fill and control you. 19Then you will sing psalms and hymns and spiritual songs among yourselves, making music to the Lord in your hearts. 20And you will always give thanks for everything to God the Father in the name of our Lord Jesus Christ.

Spirit-Guided Relationships: Wives and Husbands

21And further, you will submit to one another out of reverence for Christ. 22You wives will submit to your husbands as you do to the Lord. 23For a husband is the head of his wife as Christ is the head of his body, the church; he gave his life to be her Savior. 24As the church submits to Christ, so you wives must submit to your husbands in everything.

25And you husbands must love your wives with the same love Christ showed the church. He gave up his life for her 26to make her holy and clean, washed by baptism and God's word.* 27He did this to present her to himself as a glorious church without a spot or wrinkle or any other blemish. Instead, she will be holy and without fault. 28In the same way, husbands ought to love their wives as they love their own bodies. For a man is actually loving himself when he loves his wife. 29No one hates his own body but lovingly cares for it, just as Christ cares for his body, which is the church. 30And we are his body.

5:26 Greek *having cleansed her by the washing of water with the word.*

5:21-33 When our life is out of control, family tensions and conflict are common. Paul tells us that the home should be a place where love and mutual respect are shown. Husbands and wives should love each other and be sensitive to each other's needs, showing the same love Christ showed the church. The painful consequences of our addiction are felt most deeply by our family. By selfishly seeking to meet our own needs through addictive behavior, we have neglected and hurt the people it was our responsibility to love and support. Rebuilding family relationships is one of the most important tasks we face in recovery. As we admit the nature of our wrongs and seek to make amends to our loved ones, we can begin to reestablish a family atmosphere of love and mutual respect.
6:1-4 Paul directed both parents and children to show love toward one another. Children are to honor their parents. The widespread disrespect shown toward parents today leads to deep emotional scars both in parents and children. Paul also warned parents to treat their children with love and respect. Through ridicule and neglect parents can create resentment that may scar their children for life. Whether we are parents or children who have failed, we need to admit our failures and seek to make amends wherever possible.
6:10-12 While we may be firmly grounded in sound doctrine and accept our responsibility to live a godly life, we must be aware of the fierce, invisible warfare Satan wages against us. Many of our struggles with addiction could be the result of direct attacks by spiritual enemies. Since we continue to struggle with a dependency that once rendered us powerless, we need to admit our inability to manage our life. Then as we turn our life and will over to God, he will stand with us in the battle.
6:13-20 Notice that each piece of spiritual armor (except the sword) is defensive in nature. As recovering addicts, we need to improve our conscious contact with God, to know him better, and to surround ourselves with truth, righteousness, faith, and prayer. These will protect us against the assault of hostile spiritual forces. The forces arrayed against us are powerful, but the weapons God gives us are adequate for our defense. Part of that armor—the shoes—enables us to share the Good News of God's delivering power with others, giving hope to them while strengthening our own recovery.

³¹As the Scriptures say, "A man leaves his father and mother and is joined to his wife, and the two are united into one."* ³²This is a great mystery, but it is an illustration of the way Christ and the church are one. ³³So again I say, each man must love his wife as he loves himself, and the wife must respect her husband.

CHAPTER 6
Children and Parents
Children, obey your parents because you belong to the Lord, for this is the right thing to do. ²"Honor your father and mother." This is the first of the Ten Commandments that ends with a promise. ³And this is the promise: If you honor your father and mother, "you will live a long life, full of blessing."*

⁴And now a word to you fathers. Don't make your children angry by the way you treat them. Rather, bring them up with the discipline and instruction approved by the Lord.

Slaves and Masters
⁵Slaves, obey your earthly masters with deep respect and fear. Serve them sincerely as you would serve Christ. ⁶Work hard, but not just to please your masters when they are watching. As slaves of Christ, do the will of God with all your heart. ⁷Work with enthusiasm, as though you were working for the Lord rather than for people. ⁸Remember that the Lord will reward each one of us for the good we do, whether we are slaves or free.

⁹And in the same way, you masters must treat your slaves right. Don't threaten them; remember, you both have the same Master in heaven, and he has no favorites.

The Whole Armor of God
¹⁰A final word: Be strong with the Lord's mighty power. ¹¹Put on all of God's armor so that you will be able to stand firm against all strategies and tricks of the Devil. ¹²For we are not fighting against people made of flesh and blood, but against the evil rulers and authorities of the unseen world, against those mighty powers of darkness who rule this world, and against wicked spirits in the heavenly realms.

¹³Use every piece of God's armor to resist the enemy in the time of evil, so that after the battle you will still be standing firm. ¹⁴Stand your ground, putting on the sturdy belt of truth and the body armor of God's righteousness. ¹⁵For shoes, put on the peace

5:31 Gen 2:24. **6:2-3** Exod 20:12; Deut 5:16.

STEP

10

Dealing with Anger
BIBLE READING: Ephesians 4:26-27
We continued to take personal inventory and when we were wrong promptly admitted it.
Many of us have a hard time dealing with anger. Some of us have a history of rage, so we try to stifle our feelings. Others of us stuff down the feelings of anger, pretending they don't exist, because we were never allowed to express them in the past. If some of our problems stem from not knowing how to express anger properly, we may try to avoid dealing with it altogether. We may try to "put it off" and hope it goes away. Evaluating how to deal with anger appropriately is an important part of our daily inventory.

The apostle Paul said, "'Don't sin by letting anger gain control over you.' Don't let the sun go down while you are still angry, for anger gives a mighty foothold to the Devil" (Ephesians 4:26-27). One key is to have daily time limits for handling our anger—time to find ways to express the feelings and then let them go.

Dealing with anger promptly is important because when it is left to fester, it becomes bitterness. Bitterness is anger that has been buried and given time to grow. The Bible warns us: "Get rid of all bitterness, rage, anger, harsh words, and slander, as well as all types of malicious behavior. Instead, be kind to each other, tenderhearted, forgiving one another, just as God through Christ has forgiven you" (Ephesians 4:31-32).

Alcoholics Anonymous teaches that we should never allow ourselves to become too hungry, angry, lonely, or tired. We can help accomplish this by promptly dealing with our anger when it occurs. *Turn to page 355, 1 Timothy 4.*

that comes from the Good News, so that you will be fully prepared.* [16]In every battle you will need faith as your shield to stop the fiery arrows aimed at you by Satan.* [17]Put on salvation as your helmet, and take the sword of the Spirit, which is the word of God. [18]Pray at all times and on every occasion in the power of the Holy Spirit. Stay alert and be persistent in your prayers for all Christians everywhere.

[19]And pray for me, too. Ask God to give me the right words as I boldly explain God's secret plan that the Good News is for the Gentiles, too.* [20]I am in chains now for preaching this message as God's ambassador. But pray that I will keep on speaking boldly for him, as I should.

Final Greetings

[21]Tychicus, a much loved brother and faithful helper in the Lord's work, will tell you all about how I am getting along. [22]I am sending him to you for just this purpose. He will let you know how we are, and he will encourage you.

[23]May God give you peace, dear brothers and sisters,* and love with faith, from God the Father and the Lord Jesus Christ. [24]May God's grace be upon all who love our Lord Jesus Christ with an undying love.

6:15 Or *For shoes, put on the readiness to preach the Good News of peace with God.* **6:16** Greek *by the evil one.*
6:19 Greek *explain the mystery of the gospel.* **6:23** Greek *brothers.*

PHILIPPIANS

THE BIG PICTURE

A. JOY IN THE MIDST OF DIFFICULT CIRCUMSTANCES (1:1-30)
B. THE SECRET OF VICTORIOUS LIVING (2:1-30)
C. HAVING A VICTORIOUS FOCUS (3:1-21)
D. FINDING A JOYFUL FELLOWSHIP (4:1-23)

As a missionary and a traveling pastor, Paul sometimes had to depend on others for financial support. The Philippian church, which Paul planted during his second missionary journey, had supported him for ten years. They were compassionate people whose commitment to Christ and support of Christ's work were well known.

Paul wrote this letter to thank the Philippians and to challenge them to remain true to Christ and joyful in their circumstances. Wholeness of life, he reminded them, does not come from material things or pleasant circumstances. Genuine joy, meaning, and satisfaction come as we follow Christ and help others to grow spiritually.

Paul knew what he was talking about. He wrote this encouraging letter while facing a trial in Rome that, for all he knew, might lead to his execution. Paul had been both rich and poor, comfortable and in pain, healthy and sick, popular and the target of mobs. He had learned to be content, even joyful, no matter what his physical circumstances.

The letter to the Philippians has much to say to us. Our life had become unmanageable, and we had hurt people we loved. We had come to the end of our rope. Though the worst is behind us, we still must contend with day-to-day frustration, anger, and conflict. Yet despite our painful circumstances, Christ can be our joy. Recovery will probably never be pleasant, but at the same time we need to remember that we have God helping us. Because of that, we can have joy. The secret of being full of joy can be found by getting to know Christ better and making him the center of our life each day.

THE BOTTOM LINE

PURPOSE: To thank the Philippian believers for their support of Paul's ministry and to encourage them. AUTHOR: The apostle Paul. AUDIENCE: The believers in Philippi, a city in Macedonia. DATE WRITTEN: Around A.D. 61–62. SETTING: Paul, a prisoner in Rome, wrote this warm letter to the believers at Philippi after they sent him a generous gift. KEY VERSE: "Keep putting into practice all you learned from me and heard from me and saw me doing, and the God of peace will be with you" (4:9). KEY PEOPLE AND RELATIONSHIPS: Paul with Timothy, Epaphroditus, and the Philippian believers.

RECOVERY THEMES

The Importance of Humility: When we turn our life over to God, we experience the power of his Holy Spirit at work within us. He changes our life and gives us the control we once lacked. But a long time in successful recovery can make us prone to pride. We may begin to forget the source of our power and start to feel self-sufficient. The letter to the Philippians reminds us to be humble, to adopt the attitude of Christ, who, though he was God, "did not demand and cling to his rights as God" (2:6). Recovery must always involve humility.

Recovery Leads to True Joy: Our life has been unmanageable and out of control. When we admit our powerlessness and turn our life over to God, we not only start the recovery process but also take the first steps toward finding true joy. We can have joy even during the tough times—because real joy does not come from outward circumstances but from inward strength. Joy comes from knowing Christ personally and from depending on his strength and power on a daily basis.

Recovery Requires Sacrifice: A sure sign of progress in recovery is when we begin to care about those around us who are still in bondage to their addiction. As Christ suffered and died so we might have life, we must sacrifice for others as well. It takes maturity to lay aside our own interests and agenda in order to share the message of hope and recovery with others. But such sacrifices are part of recovery. Staying self-absorbed can set us up for pride and relapse; carrying the message of recovery to others will always strengthen us.

Fighting the Real Enemies: As we struggle through the recovery process, it is common to have conflicts with other people. We are sometimes in pain, and it can be very easy to turn against the people who are causing that pain. The believers at Philippi sometimes "picked at each other." But as this letter reminds us, our battles should not be waged against one another. We need to concentrate our energy against much greater enemies—our powerful dependency and destructive pride.

CHAPTER 1
Greetings from Paul

This letter is from Paul and Timothy, slaves of Christ Jesus.

It is written to all of God's people in Philippi, who believe in Christ Jesus, and to the elders* and deacons.

²May God our Father and the Lord Jesus Christ give you grace and peace.

1:1 Greek *overseers.*

Paul's Thanksgiving and Prayer

³Every time I think of you, I give thanks to my God. ⁴I always pray for you, and I make my requests with a heart full of joy ⁵because you have been my partners in spreading the Good News about Christ from the time you first heard it until now. ⁶And I am sure that God, who began the good work within you, will continue his work until it is finally fin-

---

1:3-11 Paul told the Philippians that he had been praying for them, which would have greatly encouraged those early believers. Our spiritual awakening will lead us to feel a growing concern for people in need. As we share the message of hope with others, we should also pray for their progress as part of serving them. Our prayers for other people struggling with addiction will significantly impact their spiritual growth. As we let them know we are behind them, not only will they grow in their faith, but we will be encouraged to persevere in recovery.

1:12-14 In retrospect, Paul could see that God had allowed the events of his life, both good and bad, to help him spread the Good News. If we take an honest look at our life, we may find the same to be true. Through our painful addiction we have gained the perspective needed to share the message of hope with others. Our personal story of deliverance is an essential tool for reaching others in need of recovery. As with Paul, our painful past and God's powerful deliverance open the door to our serving God by helping others.

1:19-24 We cannot lose if we belong to God. Whether we live or die, we know we will win in the end. During times of relapse and failure we may be tempted to give up on life completely. Paul's primary motivation for persevering was his deep concern for others who still needed to hear the Good News of God's loving power. No matter how bad things are, if we trust God, he will come through for us. We will then have one more victory story to share with others. No matter how deeply we have failed or how many times we have fallen, God can still use us to save the lives of others just like us. There is always a reason to live.

ished on that day when Christ Jesus comes back again. ⁷It is right that I should feel as I do about all of you, for you have a very special place in my heart. We have shared together the blessings of God, both when I was in prison and when I was out, defending the truth and telling others the Good News. ⁸God knows how much I love you and long for you with the tender compassion of Christ Jesus. ⁹I pray that your love for each other will overflow more and more, and that you will keep on growing in your knowledge and understanding. ¹⁰For I want you to understand what really matters, so that you may live pure and blameless lives until Christ returns. ¹¹May you always be filled with the fruit of your salvation*—those good things that are produced in your life by Jesus Christ—for this will bring much glory and praise to God.

Paul's Joy That Christ Is Preached

¹²And I want you to know, dear brothers and sisters,* that everything that has happened to me here has helped to spread the Good News. ¹³For everyone here, including all the soldiers in the palace guard, knows that I am in chains because of Christ. ¹⁴And because of my imprisonment, many of the Christians* here have gained confidence and become more bold in telling others about Christ.

¹⁵Some are preaching out of jealousy and rivalry. But others preach about Christ with pure motives. ¹⁶They preach because they love me, for they know the Lord brought me here to defend the Good News. ¹⁷Those others do not have pure motives as they preach about Christ. They preach with selfish ambition, not sincerely, intending to make my chains more painful to me. ¹⁸But whether or not their motives are pure, the fact remains that the message about Christ is being preached, so I rejoice. And I will continue to rejoice. ¹⁹For I know that as you pray for me and as the Spirit of Jesus Christ helps me, this will all turn out for my deliverance.

Paul's Life for Christ

²⁰For I live in eager expectation and hope that I will never do anything that causes me shame, but that I will always be bold for Christ, as I have been in the past, and that my life will always honor Christ, whether I

1:11 Greek *the fruit of righteousness.* **1:12** Greek *brothers.*
1:14 Greek *brothers in the Lord.*

Perseverance

READ PHILIPPIANS 1:2-6

Sometimes we may feel like giving up the struggle. We try to persevere, only to fall once again. We take two steps forward but then stumble backward. We feel condemned, and we fear that even God may give up on us. At times there are so many difficulties, so many issues to work through, so many patterns in our life that have to be changed, that we begin to feel as if we are going crazy.

God acknowledges the difficulties we face, but he also promises us victory in the end. The apostle Paul wrote: "Overwhelming victory is ours through Christ, who loved us. And I am convinced that nothing can ever separate us from his love. Death can't, and life can't. The angels can't, and the demons can't. Our fears for today, our worries about tomorrow, and even the powers of hell can't keep God's love away. . . . Nothing in all creation will ever be able to separate us from the love of God that is revealed in Christ Jesus our Lord" (Romans 8:37-39). Paul also said, "I am sure that God, who began the good work within you, will continue his work until it is finally finished on that day when Christ Jesus comes back again" (Philippians 1:6).

When we feel as if we are going crazy and don't think we can handle life, God is there. He is determined not to give up on us. We can rely on his persistent love. God has promised to keep working on us until we are whole. There will still be tough times, but with his help we can handle them, one day at a time. ***Turn to page 335, Colossians 3.***

live or I die. ²¹For to me, living is for Christ, and dying is even better. ²²Yet if I live, that means fruitful service for Christ. I really don't know which is better. ²³I'm torn between two desires: Sometimes I want to live, and sometimes I long to go and be with Christ. That would be far better for me, ²⁴but it is better for you that I live.

²⁵I am convinced of this, so I will continue with you so that you will grow and experience the joy of your faith. ²⁶Then when I return to you, you will have even more reason to boast about what Christ Jesus has done for me.

Live as Citizens of Heaven

²⁷But whatever happens to me, you must live in a manner worthy of the Good News about Christ, as citizens of heaven. Then, whether I come and see you again or only hear about you, I will know that you are standing side by side, fighting together for the Good News. ²⁸Don't be intimidated by your enemies. This will be a sign to them that they are going to be destroyed, but that you are going to be saved, even by God himself. ²⁹For you have been given not only the privilege of trusting in Christ but also the privilege of suffering for him. ³⁰We are in this fight together. You have seen me suffer for him in the past, and you know that I am still in the midst of this great struggle.

CHAPTER 2
Unity through Humility

Is there any encouragement from belonging to Christ? Any comfort from his love? Any fellowship together in the Spirit? Are your hearts tender and sympathetic? ²Then make me truly happy by agreeing wholeheartedly with each other, loving one another, and working together with one heart and purpose.

³Don't be selfish; don't live to make a good impression on others. Be humble, thinking of others as better than yourself. ⁴Don't think only about your own affairs, but be interested in others, too, and what they are doing.

Christ's Humility and Exaltation

⁵Your attitude should be the same that Christ Jesus had. ⁶Though he was God, he did not demand and cling to his rights as God. ⁷He made himself nothing;* he took the humble position of a slave and appeared in human form.* ⁸And in human form he obediently humbled himself even

2:7a Or *He laid aside his mighty power and glory.* **2:7b** Greek *and was born in the likeness of men and was found in appearance as a man.*

2:1-4 We are never an island unto ourself; we are a part of a whole, a member of Christ's body. If we are part of a loving community, when others hurt, we hurt; when we hurt, others hurt. Early in the recovery process we may need to concentrate on our own welfare. But as we grow, we have to move beyond self-centeredness and become interested in others. Part of making amends to people we have harmed is showing them that we have changed. As we love others, we will find that others will love us. As our relationships grow stronger, our addiction will lose its grip on us.

2:5-11 Jesus Christ is our ideal model for humility in obedience and service. Our thoughts, attitudes, and actions are to be patterned after Christ. His willingness to humbly obey his Father is a great example for us. As we take an honest moral inventory of our life, we must humbly admit our faults so we can begin to change our destructive patterns. If we follow Jesus Christ in humility, learning to admit our failures without hesitation, nothing will be able to stop our recovery.

2:12-18 Obedience to God's program is one of the requirements for spiritual growth. But how can we lead a clean, innocent life like he wants us to? We have already admitted that we are powerless over our addiction. God not only asks us to live a godly life, he also provides us with the power to do it. He works in us, giving us the desire and the ability to obey him. As we get to know God by reading the Bible and spending time with him in prayer, he can transform us from the inside out so we can shine brightly for him.

2:25-28 Believing in Christ is not always easy. As Epaphroditus clearly demonstrated, we need stamina to do the work and a servant's attitude to succeed in our spiritual battles. We must give ourself to the cause of Christ, putting others' needs before our personal comforts. As we carry the message of salvation and recovery to fellow strugglers despite difficulties and ridicule, we realize that when we give up our desires in order to meet the needs of others, we also leave behind the burden of our addiction. As we serve others, we build meaningful relationships and a strong foundation for permanent recovery. By helping others, we help ourselves.

further by dying a criminal's death on a cross. ⁹Because of this, God raised him up to the heights of heaven and gave him a name that is above every other name, ¹⁰so that at the name of Jesus every knee will bow, in heaven and on earth and under the earth, ¹¹and every tongue will confess that Jesus Christ is Lord, to the glory of God the Father.

Shine Brightly for Christ

¹²Dearest friends, you were always so careful to follow my instructions when I was with you. And now that I am away you must be even more careful to put into action God's saving work in your lives, obeying God with deep reverence and fear. ¹³For God is working in you, giving you the desire to obey him and the power to do what pleases him.

¹⁴In everything you do, stay away from complaining and arguing, ¹⁵so that no one can speak a word of blame against you. You are to live clean, innocent lives as children of God in a dark world full of crooked and perverse people. Let your lives shine brightly before them. ¹⁶Hold tightly to the word of life, so that when Christ returns, I will be proud that I did not lose the race and that my work was not useless. ¹⁷But even if my life is to be poured out like a drink offering to complete the sacrifice of your faithful service (that is, if I am to die for you), I will rejoice, and I want to share my joy with all of you. ¹⁸And you should be happy about this and rejoice with me.

Paul Commends Timothy

¹⁹If the Lord Jesus is willing, I hope to send Timothy to you soon. Then when he comes back, he can cheer me up by telling me how you are getting along. ²⁰I have no one else like Timothy, who genuinely cares about your welfare. ²¹All the others care only for themselves and not for what matters to Jesus Christ. ²²But you know how Timothy has proved himself. Like a son with his father, he has helped me in preaching the Good News. ²³I hope to send him to you just as soon as I find out what is going to happen to me here. ²⁴And I have confidence from the Lord that I myself will come to see you soon.

Paul Commends Epaphroditus

²⁵Meanwhile, I thought I should send Epaphroditus back to you. He is a true

STEP 7

Into the Open

BIBLE READING: Philippians 2:5-9
We humbly asked him to remove our shortcomings.
Because of our pride, we may hide behind defenses during the recovery process. We may hide behind our good reputation, our important position, or a delusion of our superiority. We may feel such inner shame that we go overboard to cover up with a self-righteous public identity. Those of us who have tried to protect ourself in these ways will need a dramatic change of attitude.

The apostle Paul wrote: "Your attitude should be the same that Christ Jesus had. Though he was God, he did not demand and cling to his rights as God. He made himself nothing; he took the humble position of a slave and appeared in human form. And in human form he obediently humbled himself even further by dying a criminal's death on a cross. Because of this, God raised him up to the heights of heaven and gave him a name that is above every other name" (Philippians 2:5-9). The author of Hebrews wrote: "We do this by keeping our eyes on Jesus, on whom our faith depends from start to finish. He was willing to die a shameful death on the cross because of the joy he knew would be his afterward. Now he is seated in the place of highest honor beside God's throne in heaven" (Hebrews 12:2).

We can ask God to change our attitudes. When he deals with our pride, we will be able to stop hiding behind our reputation. We can allow ourself to become "anonymous," each of us known as just another person struggling with addiction. When we humbly yield ourself to God in recovery, he promises us future honor and the restoration of our good name. *Turn to page 435, 1 John 5.*

brother, a faithful worker, and a courageous soldier. And he was your messenger to help me in my need. 26Now I am sending him home again, for he has been longing to see you, and he was very distressed that you heard he was ill. 27And he surely was ill; in fact, he almost died. But God had mercy on him—and also on me, so that I would not have such unbearable sorrow.

28So I am all the more anxious to send him back to you, for I know you will be glad to see him, and that will lighten all my cares. 29Welcome him with Christian love* and with great joy, and be sure to honor people like him. 30For he risked his life for the work of Christ, and he was at the point of death while trying to do for me the things you couldn't do because you were far away.

CHAPTER 3
The Priceless Gain of Knowing Christ

Whatever happens, dear brothers and sisters,* may the Lord give you joy. I never get tired of telling you this. I am doing this for your own good.

2Watch out for those dogs, those wicked men and their evil deeds, those mutilators who say you must be circumcised to be saved. 3For we who worship God in the Spirit* are the only ones who are truly circumcised. We put no confidence in human effort. Instead, we boast about what Christ Jesus has done for us.

4Yet I could have confidence in myself if anyone could. If others have reason for confidence in their own efforts, I have even more! 5For I was circumcised when I was eight days old, having been born into a pure-blooded Jewish family that is a branch of the tribe of Benjamin. So I am a real Jew if there ever was one! What's more, I was a member of the Pharisees, who demand the strictest obedience to the Jewish law. 6And zealous? Yes, in fact, I harshly persecuted the church. And I obeyed the Jewish law so carefully that I was never accused of any fault.

7I once thought all these things were so very important, but now I consider them worthless because of what Christ has done. 8Yes, everything else is worthless when compared with the priceless gain of knowing Christ Jesus my Lord. I have discarded everything else, counting it all as garbage, so that I may have Christ 9and become one with him. I no longer count on my own goodness or

2:29 Greek *in the Lord.* **3:1** Greek *brothers;* also in 3:13, 17. **3:3** Or *in spirit;* some manuscripts read *worship by the Spirit of God.*

3:2-3 The world is full of deceivers. We must be especially alert for those who offer recovery plans that exclude God. The false teachers Paul mentioned demanded that Gentile Christians obey the Jewish law of circumcision in order to be saved. The apostle stood against this claim, reminding the Philippians that only God through Jesus Christ could bring them deliverance. This message is for us, too. If people claim we don't need God for a successful recovery, we should walk the other way. Programs that depend on our actions will never succeed for long. Until we admit that we are powerless to help ourself, our recovery won't succeed.

3:4-11 Paul made a detailed inventory of his past behaviors—including his religious activities—and found nothing worth hanging on to. He threw out his past life and replaced it with his new life in Christ. We should engage in an honest inventory of our heritage and accomplishments as Paul did. As we compare the value of our past accomplishments to the power offered by Christ, we will find the new life God offers is the obvious choice. Our personal inventory helps us discover that the things of this world can't satisfy our eternal needs—only God can.

3:17-21 On the human level, we need to pattern our life after those who, despite difficulties, have successfully lived for Christ. Those who fail to examine themselves end up spending all their efforts living only for themselves, enslaved by destructive habits and dependencies. Full recovery, however, can be experienced by trusting Jesus Christ and following in his steps. Some of us may wonder if we will ever get beyond the pain we experience on a daily basis. But even if the pain remains throughout our life, we will be changed completely when Jesus Christ returns.

4:1-3 Since we know with certainty what our ultimate destiny is, we can confidently face the hardships of life. Paul set a good example for how to grow spiritually and encourage others in their growth. To encourage these two Christian women to reestablish a harmonious relationship, he complimented them on their previous service to God. He was assuming that they were humble enough to take criticism and change for the better. When we keep a close watch on our own life, as Paul did his, we will be better able to hold others accountable to their recovery commitment.

my ability to obey God's law, but I trust Christ to save me. For God's way of making us right with himself depends on faith. ¹⁰As a result, I can really know Christ and experience the mighty power that raised him from the dead. I can learn what it means to suffer with him, sharing in his death, ¹¹so that, somehow, I can experience the resurrection from the dead!

Pressing toward the Goal

¹²I don't mean to say that I have already achieved these things or that I have already reached perfection! But I keep working toward that day when I will finally be all that Christ Jesus saved me for and wants me to be. ¹³No, dear brothers and sisters, I am still not all I should be,* but I am focusing all my energies on this one thing: Forgetting the past and looking forward to what lies ahead, ¹⁴I strain to reach the end of the race and receive the prize for which God, through Christ Jesus, is calling us up to heaven.*

¹⁵I hope all of you who are mature Christians will agree on these things. If you disagree on some point, I believe God will make it plain to you. ¹⁶But we must be sure to obey the truth we have learned already.

¹⁷Dear brothers and sisters, pattern your lives after mine, and learn from those who follow our example. ¹⁸For I have told you often before, and I say it again with tears in my eyes, that there are many whose conduct shows they are really enemies of the cross of Christ. ¹⁹Their future is eternal destruction. Their god is their appetite, they brag about shameful things, and all they think about is this life here on earth. ²⁰But we are citizens of heaven, where the Lord Jesus Christ lives. And we are eagerly waiting for him to return as our Savior. ²¹He will take these weak mortal bodies of ours and change them into glorious bodies like his own, using the same mighty power that he will use to conquer everything, everywhere.

CHAPTER 4

Dear brothers and sisters,* I love you and long to see you, for you are my joy and the reward for my work. So please stay true to the Lord, my dear friends.

Paul's Final Thoughts

²And now I want to plead with those two women, Euodia and Syntyche. Please,

3:13 Some manuscripts read *I am not all I should be.*
3:14 Or *from heaven.* 4:1 Greek *brothers;* also in 4:8.

STEP

6

Attitudes and Actions

BIBLE READING: Philippians 3:12-14
We were entirely ready to have God remove all these defects of character. Getting "entirely ready" to have God remove "all" our defects of character sounds impossible. In reality we know that such perfection is out of human reach. This is another way of saying that we are going to do our best to work toward a lifelong goal that no one ever reaches until eternity.

The apostle Paul expressed a similar thought: "I don't mean to say that I have already achieved these things or that I have already reached perfection! But I keep working toward that day when I will finally be all that Christ Jesus saved me for and wants me to be. . . . Forgetting the past and looking forward to what lies ahead, I strain to reach the end of the race and receive the prize for which God, through Christ Jesus, is calling us up to heaven" (Philippians 3:12-14).

This combination of a positive attitude and energetic effort is part of the mystery of our cooperation with God. Paul said: "Be even more careful to put into action God's saving work in your lives, obeying God with deep reverence and fear. For God is working in you, giving you the desire to obey him and the power to do what pleases him" (Philippians 2:12-13).

We will need to practice these steps the rest of our life. We don't have to demand perfection of ourself; it is enough to keep moving ahead as best we can. We can look forward to our rewards with the hope of becoming all that God intends us to be. God will strengthen and encourage us as we do so. *Turn to page 511, Psalm 51.*

because you belong to the Lord, settle your disagreement. ³And I ask you, my true teammate,* to help these women, for they worked hard with me in telling others the Good News. And they worked with Clement and the rest of my co-workers, whose names are written in the Book of Life.

⁴Always be full of joy in the Lord. I say it again—rejoice! ⁵Let everyone see that you are considerate in all you do. Remember, the Lord is coming soon.

⁶Don't worry about anything; instead, pray about everything. Tell God what you need, and thank him for all he has done. ⁷If you do this, you will experience God's peace, which is far more wonderful than the human mind can understand. His peace will guard your hearts and minds as you live in Christ Jesus.

⁸And now, dear brothers and sisters, let me say one more thing as I close this letter. Fix your thoughts on what is true and honorable and right. Think about things that are pure and lovely and admirable. Think about things that are excellent and worthy of praise. ⁹Keep putting into practice all you learned from me and heard from me and saw me doing, and the God of peace will be with you.

Paul's Thanks for Their Gifts

¹⁰How grateful I am, and how I praise the Lord that you are concerned about me again. I know you have always been concerned for me, but for a while you didn't have the chance to help me. ¹¹Not that I was ever in need, for I have learned how to get along happily whether I have much or little. ¹²I know

how to live on almost nothing or with everything. I have learned the secret of living in every situation, whether it is with a full stomach or empty, with plenty or little. ¹³For I can do everything with the help of Christ who gives me the strength I need. ¹⁴But even so, you have done well to share with me in my present difficulty.

¹⁵As you know, you Philippians were the only ones who gave me financial help when I brought you the Good News and then traveled on from Macedonia. No other church did this. ¹⁶Even when I was in Thessalonica you sent help more than once. ¹⁷I don't say this because I want a gift from you. What I want is for you to receive a well-earned reward because of your kindness.

¹⁸At the moment I have all I need—more than I need! I am generously supplied with the gifts you sent me with Epaphroditus. They are a sweet-smelling sacrifice that is acceptable to God and pleases him. ¹⁹And this same God who takes care of me will supply all your needs from his glorious riches, which have been given to us in Christ Jesus. ²⁰Now glory be to God our Father forever and ever. Amen.

Paul's Final Greetings

²¹Give my greetings to all the Christians there. The brothers who are with me here send you their greetings. ²²And all the other Christians send their greetings, too, especially those who work in Caesar's palace.

²³May the grace of the Lord Jesus Christ be with your spirit.

4:3 Greek *true yokefellow*, or *loyal Syzygus.*

4:4-9 True happiness can be found in every situation of life when we recognize that God is at work and always in control. Because Christ is with us and his return is certain, we can act calmly in pain and difficulty. Peace and joy come when we focus on those things that provide lasting value to our life. The more we commit ourself to knowing God's will through prayer and study of his Word, the better prepared we are to help ourself and others in the process of recovery.

4:12-13 Some of us may wonder if we will ever experience peace again. Our battle against addiction seems endless and hard. We continually find ourself in helpless situations. When we get discouraged and recognize that recovery is too hard for us to achieve alone, we can claim these verses for renewed hope. God wants us to make progress in recovery, and he has the power to help us do it. As we entrust our life to God, we can make progress in recovery with the help of Christ, who gives us the strength we need. With God, nothing is impossible!

4:15-20 Paul's relationship with the Philippian believers was characterized by mutual respect and sharing—important qualities in any strong relationship, including our relationships in recovery. Paul was a respected Christian leader in the early church. Many in his position would have had difficulty accepting the Philippians' help and might have refused it. It is sometimes difficult to accept help from others. Perhaps we feel they really don't understand where we are coming from or are just trying to manipulate us, doing things that make them feel good about themselves. If we hope to succeed in recovery, however, we need to follow Paul's example. He joyfully received the help from the Philippian believers and, as a result, he stood firm through tough, lonely times.

READ PHILIPPIANS 4:10-14

GOD grant me the serenity to accept the things I cannot change the courage to change the things I can and the wisdom to know the difference AMEN

Serenity is having an inner calm in the midst of the ups and downs of life. It involves learning to be content with the things in our life that cannot be changed.

Some of us have never accepted the hurtful circumstances of our life. We may be living in denial to avoid the pain. We continue to struggle against the painful realities, to rebel against who we are or what has happened to us. Others of us have accepted the bad, even to the point of feeling that it's normal and comfortable. Therefore, we repeat the destructive cycle of behavior.

The apostle Paul wrote: "I have learned how to get along happily whether I have much or little. I know how to live on almost nothing or with everything. I have learned the secret of living in every situation, whether it is with a full stomach or empty, with plenty or little" (Philippians 4:11-12). When Paul wrote this, he was in a Roman prison waiting to hear if he would be executed. And yet we hear no whining or complaining. Instead, he learned to accept the circumstances he could not change.

The process of recovery is a time of learning to find serenity while also accepting life as it is. Life isn't always fair. It isn't predictable or controllable. It can be wonderfully rich in some ways and terribly difficult in others. When we become willing to face the hurt in our life and consider how we have reacted to it, then our discomfort can lead us to break the destructive cycle. Then we can learn to be content with the things we cannot change. ***Turn to page 333, Colossians 1.***

COLOSSIANS

THE BIG PICTURE
A. THE POWER OF JESUS CHRIST (1:1–2:23)
B. CHRIST'S POWER WITHIN US (3:1–4:18)

Colossians is a letter about the greatness of Christ. Since their conversion, the believers in the city of Colosse had heard many theories about salvation, all of which diminished Christ in some way. Some people had faith in angels, some in rituals, and others in various religious philosophies or practices. Paul wrote to correct them all: Christ is God in the flesh and the only one sufficient to save us from sin and its destructive power.

In this letter Paul included practical advice about how the believers were to live. He called them to adhere to the truth, to live sexually pure lives, to live in peace with their friends and neighbors, and to live in dependence on God. Paul did not expect the Colossians to accomplish these things on their own. He emphasized that when we seek to do God's will, we can depend on God's help. Our actions can be energized by the greatest power in the universe—the power of God in Jesus Christ.

Recovery is easier when we lean on others, but ultimately God is the only one who can rescue us completely. We need God's power to begin the process of healing in recovery. The same power that made salvation possible makes it possible for us to recover. We can trust Christ to save us, and we can trust his power to help us with our struggles as we live each day as it comes.

THE BOTTOM LINE

PURPOSE: To show us that Christ is the only real source of power in our life. AUTHOR: The apostle Paul. AUDIENCE: The believers at Colosse, a city in Asia Minor. DATE WRITTEN: Around A.D. 60, while Paul was in prison in Rome. SETTING: Paul was writing to a church that he had never visited. It had been started by some of his converts, including a man named Epaphras. KEY VERSES: "For in Christ the fullness of God lives in a human body, and you are complete through your union with Christ. He is the Lord over every ruler and authority in the universe" (2:9-10). KEY PEOPLE AND RELATIONSHIPS: Paul with Timothy, Tychicus, Onesimus, John Mark, and Epaphras.

RECOVERY THEMES

Recovery Is a Lifelong Process: We may long for a day when we will be totally free from the bondage of our past—a day when recovery will be complete and we can go on with our life. But recovery is a lifelong process, with daily challenges to maintain contact with our powerful and loving God. From this letter to the Colossian believers, we learn that our life with Christ is not just a onetime rescue operation but a lifelong commitment.

True Recovery Involves Faith in God: One danger we face after a period of successful recovery is the tendency to forget how much we need God. It is easy to start thinking we can go it alone, depending on rules or formulas for success. Paul warned the Colossians about this danger, urging them to live in daily contact and communication with God. It is true that with maturity comes strength of character, but it is not true that we can end our need for faith in God. Self-sufficiency got us into trouble in the first place, and it can lead us to relapse as well. If we are to experience true recovery, we need to acknowledge our ongoing need for faith in God.

Jesus Is Lord of the Universe: The entire universe is being held together by the power of Jesus Christ. He is the supreme ruler and Lord of all creation. He is the reflection of the invisible God. He is eternal, preexistent, omnipotent, and equal with the Father. He is also the Lord of every successful recovery. What a privilege to depend not merely on some anonymous "higher Power," but on the highest Power of all! How incredible that he invites each of us to have a personal relationship with him!

Healthy Relationships: An important part of the recovery process involves making amends to the people we have wronged. This letter to the Colossians gives us practical guidance in this area. Paul calls us to live according to the principles of selfless love and to mutually respect all the people in our life. If we treat others in ways that build them up, our relationships will grow stronger and support us in the recovery process.

CHAPTER 1
Greetings from Paul

This letter is from Paul, chosen by God to be an apostle of Christ Jesus, and from our brother Timothy.

²It is written to God's holy people in the city of Colosse, who are faithful brothers and sisters* in Christ.

May God our Father give you grace and peace.

Paul's Thanksgiving and Prayer

³We always pray for you, and we give thanks to God the Father of our Lord Jesus Christ, ⁴for we have heard that you trust in Christ Jesus and that you love all of God's people. ⁵You do this because you are looking forward to the joys of heaven—as you have been ever since you first heard the truth of the Good News. ⁶This same Good News that came to you is going out all over the world. It is changing lives everywhere, just as it changed yours that very first day you heard and understood the truth about God's great kindness to sinners.

⁷Epaphras, our much loved co-worker, was the one who brought you the Good News. He is Christ's faithful servant, and he is helping us in your place.* ⁸He is the one who told us about the great love for others that the Holy Spirit has given you.

⁹So we have continued praying for you ever since we first heard about you. We ask

1:2 Greek *faithful brothers.* **1:7** Greek *he is ministering on your behalf;* other manuscripts read *he is ministering on our behalf.*

1:11-14 As always, Paul was careful to point out that our strength and power come not from ourself but from God. Only God's "glorious" power at work within us can strengthen us and give us "patience and endurance" for recovery. We have already admitted that we are powerless over our dependency. By recognizing that God has the power to restore us, we can begin to think more positively about recovery.

1:15-17 These verses describe God in Jesus Christ, our higher power. As the Creator of our world, he has the means to rebuild our life, no matter how broken it is. In fact, the entire universe would dissolve if he stopped holding it together. Even people who seem to have things under control could not exist a moment longer if it weren't for the power of God extended on their behalf. We all need God and his power, whether we admit it or not. God is our infinite power source, and he can provide all the power we need to pursue recovery.

1:20-23 When our life is unmanageable and out of control, we are God's enemies, and our thoughts and actions separate us from him. But God through Christ's death on the cross reaches out to make us his friends. When we turn our life and our will over to him, he brings us into the very presence of God and makes us blameless before God!

GOD grant me the serenity to accept the things I cannot change the courage to change the things I can and the wisdom to know the difference AMEN

Many of us in recovery are learning to think and act in new ways. We may find it hard to recognize true wisdom, even when it's staring us in the face.

We may need some guidelines to help us identify wisdom in our thoughts and choices. According to the Bible, there are two aspects of wisdom: the spiritual and the practical. Spiritual wisdom gives insight into the true nature of things. Paul said: "We ask God to give you a complete understanding of what he wants to do in your lives, and we ask him to make you wise with spiritual wisdom. Then . . . you will learn to know God better and better" (Colossians 1:9-10). Special wisdom is also sometimes given "that your hearts will be flooded with light so that you can understand the wonderful future he has promised to those he called" (Ephesians 1:18).

Godly wisdom can be evaluated by its qualities. The Bible tells us that God's wisdom is "first of all pure. It is also peace loving, gentle at all times, and willing to yield to others. It is full of mercy and good deeds. It shows no partiality and is always sincere" (James 3:17).

On the practical level, our wisdom can be judged by whether or not our actions conform to God's instructions. God's instructions were given to us because they naturally lead to healthy living. Following them, we can find the wisdom we need to walk toward wholeness. This can be one of the standards we use in our continuing daily inventory. *Turn to page 365, 2 Timothy 4.*

God to give you a complete understanding of what he wants to do in your lives, and we ask him to make you wise with spiritual wisdom. ¹⁰Then the way you live will always honor and please the Lord, and you will continually do good, kind things for others. All the while, you will learn to know God better and better.

¹¹We also pray that you will be strengthened with his glorious power so that you will have all the patience and endurance you need. May you be filled with joy, ¹²always thanking the Father, who has enabled you to share the inheritance that belongs to God's holy people, who live in the light. ¹³For he has rescued us from the one who rules in the kingdom of darkness, and he has brought us into the Kingdom of his dear Son. ¹⁴God has purchased our freedom with his blood* and has forgiven all our sins.

Christ Is Supreme

¹⁵Christ is the visible image of the invisible God. He existed before God made anything at all and is supreme over all creation.* ¹⁶Christ is the one through whom God created everything in heaven and earth. He made the things we can see and the things we can't see—kings, kingdoms, rulers, and authorities. Everything has been created through him and for him. ¹⁷He existed before everything else began, and he holds all creation together.

¹⁸Christ is the head of the church, which is his body. He is the first of all who will rise from the dead,* so he is first in everything. ¹⁹For God in all his fullness was pleased to live in Christ, ²⁰and by him God reconciled everything to himself. He made peace with everything in heaven and on earth by means of his blood on the cross. ²¹This includes you who were once so far away from God. You

1:14 Some manuscripts do not include *with his blood.* **1:15** Greek *He is the firstborn of all creation.* **1:18** Greek *He is the beginning, the firstborn from the dead.*

were his enemies, separated from him by your evil thoughts and actions, [22]yet now he has brought you back as his friends. He has done this through his death on the cross in his own human body. As a result, he has brought you into the very presence of God, and you are holy and blameless as you stand before him without a single fault. [23]But you must continue to believe this truth and stand in it firmly. Don't drift away from the assurance you received when you heard the Good News. The Good News has been preached all over the world, and I, Paul, have been appointed by God to proclaim it.

Paul's Work for the Church

[24]I am glad when I suffer for you in my body, for I am completing what remains of Christ's sufferings for his body, the church. [25]God has given me the responsibility of serving his church by proclaiming his message in all its fullness to you Gentiles. [26]This message was kept secret for centuries and generations past, but now it has been revealed to his own holy people. [27]For it has pleased God to tell his people that the riches and glory of Christ are for you Gentiles, too. For this is the secret: Christ lives in you, and this is your assurance that you will share in his glory. [28]So everywhere we go, we tell everyone about Christ. We warn them and teach them with all the wisdom God has given us, for we want to present them to God, perfect* in their relationship to Christ. [29]I work very

hard at this, as I depend on Christ's mighty power that works within me.

CHAPTER 2

I want you to know how much I have agonized for you and for the church at Laodicea, and for many other friends who have never known me personally. [2]My goal is that they will be encouraged and knit together by strong ties of love. I want them to have full confidence because they have complete understanding of God's secret plan, which is Christ himself. [3]In him lie hidden all the treasures of wisdom and knowledge.

[4]I am telling you this so that no one will be able to deceive you with persuasive arguments. [5]For though I am far away from you, my heart is with you. And I am very happy because you are living as you should and because of your strong faith in Christ.

Freedom from Rules and New Life in Christ

[6]And now, just as you accepted Christ Jesus as your Lord, you must continue to live in obedience to him. [7]Let your roots grow down into him and draw up nourishment from him, so you will grow in faith, strong and vigorous in the truth you were taught. Let your lives overflow with thanksgiving for all he has done.

[8]Don't let anyone lead you astray with empty philosophy and high-sounding nonsense that come from human thinking and from the evil powers of this world,* and not from Christ. [9]For in Christ the fullness of

1:28 Or *mature.* **2:8** Or *from the basic principles of this world;* also in 2:20.

1:28-29 An essential part of rebuilding our life is to carry the message of our recovery in Jesus Christ to others. We were far away from God, yet he provided not only the solution to our problem but also the power to change. That is news worth sharing! We may be afraid to do this at first, but the power available for our recovery is also available to help us share our story.

2:6-7 The same faith that we exercised when we turned our life over to God must continue daily as we walk with and obey him. Paul urges us to improve our conscious contact with God so that his power will be at work within us, filling us with joy and thanksgiving. Without God's power nourishing us, we are at the mercy of our destructive habits and dependency.

2:9-10 When we tried to change through our own efforts, we realized just how powerless we were. It was then that we realized the truth found in Paul's statement—that everything we need is found not in ourself, or even in other people, but in Jesus Christ. A recovery that is not built on the person and power of Jesus Christ will always be incomplete.

2:11-15 The power of Christ is able to restore us to sanity and help us overcome our destructive patterns from the past. Since he has authority over every other power, including the power of evil in our life, Jesus can set us free. Our freedom is not just from the physical bondage of the past but also from the spiritual bondage of our old sinful nature. In Christ we can experience the life of peace, joy, and victory that God intends for us.

2:20-23 There are many recovery programs with strict rules to follow. Perhaps we have chosen the programs with the most rules to try to break free from our bondage. "We just need to try harder," we tell ourself. But Paul tells us that we won't find success in our own strength or rules, which lead us away from the only adequate power source—God. He is the only one with the power to transform us and help us conquer evil and rebuild our life.

God lives in a human body,* [10]and you are complete through your union with Christ. He is the Lord over every ruler and authority in the universe.

[11]When you came to Christ, you were "circumcised," but not by a physical procedure. It was a spiritual procedure—the cutting away of your sinful nature. [12]For you were buried with Christ when you were baptized. And with him you were raised to a new life because you trusted the mighty power of God, who raised Christ from the dead.

[13]You were dead because of your sins and because your sinful nature was not yet cut away. Then God made you alive with Christ. He forgave all our sins. [14]He canceled the record that contained the charges against us. He took it and destroyed it by nailing it to Christ's cross. [15]In this way, God disarmed the evil rulers and authorities. He shamed them publicly by his victory over them on the cross of Christ.

[16]So don't let anyone condemn you for what you eat or drink, or for not celebrating certain holy days or new-moon ceremonies or Sabbaths. [17]For these rules were only shadows of the real thing, Christ himself. [18]Don't let anyone condemn you by insisting on self-denial. And don't let anyone say you must worship angels, even though they say they have had visions about this. These people claim to be so humble, but their sinful minds have made them proud. [19]But they are not connected to Christ, the head of the body. For we are joined together in his body by his strong sinews, and we grow only as we get our nourishment and strength from God.

[20]You have died with Christ, and he has set you free from the evil powers of this world. So why do you keep on following rules of the world, such as, [21]"Don't handle, don't eat, don't touch." [22]Such rules are mere human teaching about things that are gone as soon as we use them. [23]These rules may seem wise because they require strong devotion, humility, and severe bodily discipline. But they have no effect when it comes to conquering a person's evil thoughts and desires.

CHAPTER 3
Living the New Life

Since you have been raised to new life with Christ, set your sights on the realities of

2:9 Greek *in him dwells all the fullness of the Godhead bodily.*

Self-Protection

READ COLOSSIANS 3:1-4

The world doesn't get any better just because we are in recovery! We still have to pay our bills, deal with people, and face the stressful changes that recovery can bring. There are pressures beyond our control that will tend to make us anxious or wear us down if we aren't careful to protect ourself from the world's onslaught.

The apostle Paul gave us a strategy to help guard against the troubles of daily life. He wrote: "Let heaven fill your thoughts. Do not think only about things down here on earth" (Colossians 3:2). The apostle also wrote: "Don't worry about anything; instead, pray about everything. Tell God what you need, and thank him for all he has done. If you do this, you will experience God's peace, which is far more wonderful than the human mind can understand. His peace will guard your hearts and minds as you live in Christ Jesus" (Philippians 4:6-7).

The idea of God guarding us from the evil we face in life is comforting. God's peace is promised only if we routinely turn every worry and need over to him and develop a grateful attitude. When we turn our worries over to God's care, we will discover his protection and experience the inner peace that passes all understanding. *Turn to page 347, 2 Thessalonians 3.*

heaven, where Christ sits at God's right hand in the place of honor and power. ²Let heaven fill your thoughts. Do not think only about things down here on earth. ³For you died when Christ died, and your real life is hidden with Christ in God. ⁴And when Christ, who is your* real life, is revealed to the whole world, you will share in all his glory.

⁵So put to death the sinful, earthly things lurking within you. Have nothing to do with sexual sin, impurity, lust, and shameful desires. Don't be greedy for the good things of this life, for that is idolatry. ⁶God's terrible anger will come upon those who do such things. ⁷You used to do them when your life was still part of this world. ⁸But now is the time to get rid of anger, rage, malicious behavior, slander, and dirty language. ⁹Don't lie to each other, for you have stripped off your old evil nature and all its wicked deeds. ¹⁰In its place you have clothed yourselves with a brand-new nature that is continually being renewed as you learn more and more about Christ, who created this new nature within you. ¹¹In this new life, it doesn't matter if you are a Jew or a Gentile,* circumcised or uncircumcised, barbaric, uncivilized,* slave, or free. Christ is all that matters, and he lives in all of us.

¹²Since God chose you to be the holy people whom he loves, you must clothe yourselves with tenderhearted mercy, kindness, humility, gentleness, and patience. ¹³You must make allowance for each other's faults and forgive the person who offends you. Remember, the Lord forgave you, so you must forgive others. ¹⁴And the most important piece of clothing you must wear is love. Love is what binds us all together in perfect harmony. ¹⁵And let the peace that comes from Christ rule in your hearts. For as members of one body you are all called to live in peace. And always be thankful.

¹⁶Let the words of Christ, in all their richness, live in your hearts and make you wise. Use his words to teach and counsel each other. Sing psalms and hymns and spiritual songs to God with thankful hearts. ¹⁷And whatever you do or say, let it be as a representative of the Lord Jesus, all the while giving thanks through him to God the Father.

Instructions for Christian Households

¹⁸You wives must submit to your husbands, as is fitting for those who belong to the Lord. ¹⁹And you husbands must love your wives and never treat them harshly.

²⁰You children must always obey your parents, for this is what pleases the Lord. ²¹Fathers, don't aggravate your children. If you do, they will become discouraged and quit trying.

²²You slaves must obey your earthly masters in everything you do. Try to please them all the time, not just when they are watching you. Obey them willingly because of your reverent fear of the Lord. ²³Work hard and cheerfully at whatever you do, as though you were working for the Lord rather than for people. ²⁴Remember that the Lord will give you an inheritance as your reward, and the Master you are serving is Christ. ²⁵But if you do what is wrong, you will be paid back for the wrong you have done. For God has no favorites who can get away with evil.

3:4 Some manuscripts read *our.* **3:11a** Greek *Greek.* **3:11b** Greek *Barbarian, Scythian.*

3:1-3 Paul isn't urging us to deny the harsh realities of life; he is simply reminding us of where our focus should be. When our eyes are on Christ, we see this life from a different perspective. We realize that there is hope, even when everything seems dark and hopeless. As we look with an eternal perspective, the struggles of recovery don't disappear; rather, they are seen in the proper light. They no longer have the terrifying power that they once did. When we keep our eyes on Christ and his promises for recovery, no obstacle is too great for us to overcome.

3:9-11 To make progress in recovery it is essential that we take a personal inventory and then make amends to the people we have hurt. This involves shedding our denial and being honest about our failures. As we recognize our character flaws and seek to change with God's help, we begin to live a new kind of life. This new kind of life with God at the center involves taking an honest personal inventory regularly. Although we will never reach perfection in this life, by noting our progress, we affirm the new life that God is creating within us through Jesus Christ.

3:12-13 Paul urges us to maintain our relationships with other people. Our addiction has probably destroyed or severely strained all our important relationships, and we have a lot of work to do on this front. We need to make amends where necessary, seek forgiveness from those we have hurt, and forgive those who have hurt us. Obviously, there are some situations where we cannot, or should not, directly involve the people we have harmed. In such cases Paul urges caution, telling us to be gentle and not to hold grudges. As we seek to make amends, our actions are to be governed by the principle of selfless love.

CHAPTER 4

You slave owners must be just and fair to your slaves. Remember that you also have a Master—in heaven.

An Encouragement for Prayer

²Devote yourselves to prayer with an alert mind and a thankful heart. ³Don't forget to pray for us, too, that God will give us many opportunities to preach about his secret plan—that Christ is also for you Gentiles. That is why I am here in chains. ⁴Pray that I will proclaim this message as clearly as I should.

⁵Live wisely among those who are not Christians, and make the most of every opportunity. ⁶Let your conversation be gracious and effective so that you will have the right answer for everyone.

Paul's Final Instructions and Greetings

⁷Tychicus, a much loved brother, will tell you how I am getting along. He is a faithful helper who serves the Lord with me. ⁸I have sent him on this special trip to let you know how we are doing and to encourage you. ⁹I am also sending Onesimus, a faithful and much loved brother, one of your own people. He and Tychicus will give you all the latest news.

¹⁰Aristarchus, who is in prison with me, sends you his greetings, and so does Mark, Barnabas's cousin. And as you were instructed before, make Mark welcome if he comes your way. ¹¹Jesus (the one we call Justus) also sends his greetings. These are the only Jewish Christians among my co-workers; they are working with me here for the Kingdom of God. And what a comfort they have been!

¹²Epaphras, from your city, a servant of Christ Jesus, sends you his greetings. He always prays earnestly for you, asking God to make you strong and perfect, fully confident of the whole will of God. ¹³I can assure you that he has agonized for you and also for the Christians in Laodicea and Hierapolis.

¹⁴Dear Doctor Luke sends his greetings, and so does Demas. ¹⁵Please give my greetings to our Christian brothers and sisters* at Laodicea, and to Nympha and those who meet in her house.

¹⁶After you have read this letter, pass it on to the church at Laodicea so they can read it, too. And you should read the letter I wrote to them. ¹⁷And say to Archippus, "Be sure to carry out the work the Lord gave you."

¹⁸Here is my greeting in my own handwriting—PAUL.

Remember my chains.

May the grace of God be with you.

4:15 Greek *brothers.*

4:2-3 Paul encouraged the Colossian believers to devote themselves to prayer. This is good advice for us, too. As we pray, we acknowledge our need for God and are reminded to keep our eyes on him. As we make prayer a daily priority, we are to thank God for his help, and we become increasingly aware of his activity in our life. When we are feeling weak, we can still come to God in prayer, and he will empower us to "keep at it." As we turn to God in prayer, we embrace the power sufficient to meet all our needs in recovery.

FIRST THESSALONIANS

THE BIG PICTURE

Paul and his companions Silas and Timothy first traveled to Thessalonica on their second missionary journey (see Acts 17:1-4). Many people there who had worshiped idols turned their lives over to God, and for this Paul commended them. The believers in Thessalonica had turned from depending on material things and empty rituals to serving the living and true God.

Their new lives of faith were not easy, though. Many of their friends and relatives opposed their faith. Despite the positive changes God had made in them, some people harassed and mocked them. This same persecution forced Paul and his companions to leave Thessalonica. After he left, Paul became concerned about the new believers who had remained there. Were they grounded enough in their new faith in God? Would they relapse into old patterns of belief and practice? Paul sent Timothy to check on them, and, encouraged by Timothy's report, Paul sent them this letter of encouragement.

When we meet with opposition in recovery, we can identify with Paul and the believers at Thessalonica. Friends and family members may not understand our faith; old habits may be a source of pressure, pushing us from within to return to our old ways. But we can be encouraged by the progress we have already made. God's power is at work within us. We don't have to quit just because we face opposition.

THE BOTTOM LINE

PURPOSE: To commend the believers in Thessalonica for their trust in God, to encourage them to continue trusting, and to reassure them that Christ would return. AUTHOR: The apostle Paul. AUDIENCE: The believers in Thessalonica, a city in Macedonia. DATE WRITTEN: About A.D. 50–51, during Paul's second missionary journey. SETTING: The church in Thessalonica was only two or three years old when Paul wrote this letter. The believers there needed to mature spiritually, and they needed help in understanding what to expect at the return of Christ. KEY VERSE: "For you are all children of the light and of the day; we don't belong to darkness and night" (5:5). KEY PEOPLE AND RELATIONSHIPS: Paul with the believers at Thessalonica and with Timothy.

RECOVERY THEMES

God Is Our Source of Hope: If we have placed our trust in Christ to save us from sin, we will live with him forever—we have eternal life. But we can hope in more than just life beyond the grave; we can also hope in what God brings to our life in the present. The power that raised Jesus Christ from the dead is nothing less than the power of God—the God to whom we have entrusted our life. With this kind of power available to us, there is always hope!

Recovery Is a Way of Life: Paul challenged the Thessalonians to live at all times in humble anticipation of Christ's coming—to live each day as if it were important. In a similar way, we need to live one day at a time, realizing that we will never complete the recovery process in this life. We need to live responsibly, working and living in dependence on God at all times. We are always in recovery; when we become complacent and forget that fact, we set ourself up for relapse.

Commitment That Overcomes Obstacles: We are all flawed human beings with numerous limitations and problems. Because of this, we will always face obstacles to our continued recovery. Living in this world means we need to stand firm in our commitment to recovery, knowing that the Holy Spirit empowers us with God's strength. Although God's power is available to all of us, God will not do the work of recovery for us. To make progress, we must ask for his help and commit ourself to the task.

CHAPTER 1
Greetings from Paul

This letter is from Paul, Silas,* and Timothy.

It is written to the church in Thessalonica, you who belong to God the Father and the Lord Jesus Christ.

May his grace and peace be yours.

The Faith of the Thessalonian Believers

²We always thank God for all of you and pray for you constantly. ³As we talk to our God and Father about you, we think of your faithful work, your loving deeds, and your continual anticipation of the return of our Lord Jesus Christ.

⁴We know that God loves you, dear brothers and sisters,* and that he chose you to be his own people. ⁵For when we brought you the Good News, it was not only with words but also with power, for the Holy Spirit gave you full assurance that what we said was true. And you know that the way we lived among you was further proof of the truth of our message. ⁶So you received the message with joy from the Holy Spirit in spite of the severe suffering it brought you. In this way, you imitated both us and the Lord. ⁷As a result, you yourselves became an example to all the Christians in Greece.* ⁸And now the word of the Lord is ringing out from you to people everywhere, even beyond Greece, for wherever we go we find people telling us about your faith in God. We don't need to tell them about it, ⁹for they themselves keep talking about the wonderful welcome you gave us and how you turned away from idols

1:1 Greek *Silvanus.* **1:4** Greek *brothers.* **1:7** Greek *Macedonia and Achaia,* the northern and southern regions of Greece; also in 1:8.

1:2-3 Paul is thankful for the Thessalonian believers and their love for each other, their faithful work, and their hope in Christ's return. The triad of faith, love, and hope summarizes the Christian life (see 1 Corinthians 13:13). *Faith* in an all-powerful God is demonstrated by living one day at a time. *Love* is shown as principles of truth are demonstrated through sacrificial service to others. *Hope* carries us through the hard times as we depend on God.

1:4-6 The Thessalonians had been restored to productive roles in God's Kingdom and had gained freedom from bondage to idols because they believed in Jesus Christ and experienced his transforming power in their lives. This same power—our higher Power—makes all the difference between a doomed do-it-yourself recovery and true, God-centered recovery. When we recognize our powerlessness and entrust our life to God, we allow God's infinite resources to work on our behalf.

1:7-9 The Thessalonian believers had experienced spiritual awakening through belief in Jesus Christ. As they imitated his ways, despite the persecution it brought them, they became examples that led many in the surrounding area to experience the salvation offered by God. An essential part of recovery is sharing the good news of God's powerful deliverance with others—a natural outflow of our salvation experience. As God delivers us from our dependency, we can give hope to others by sharing our story. We will not only inspire hope in others, but we will also be personally encouraged as we recall all that God has done for us.

to serve the true and living God. [10]And they speak of how you are looking forward to the coming of God's Son from heaven—Jesus, whom God raised from the dead. He is the one who has rescued us from the terrors of the coming judgment.

CHAPTER 2
Paul Remembers His Visit

You yourselves know, dear brothers and sisters,* that our visit to you was not a failure. [2]You know how badly we had been treated at Philippi just before we came to you and how much we suffered there. Yet our God gave us the courage to declare his Good News to you boldly, even though we were surrounded by many who opposed us. [3]So you can see that we were not preaching with any deceit or impure purposes or trickery.

[4]For we speak as messengers who have been approved by God to be entrusted with the Good News. Our purpose is to please God, not people. He is the one who examines the motives of our hearts. [5]Never once did we try to win you with flattery, as you very well know. And God is our witness that we were not just pretending to be your friends so you would give us money! [6]As for praise, we have never asked for it from you or anyone else. [7]As apostles of Christ we certainly had a right to make some demands of you, but we were as gentle among you as a mother* feeding and caring for her own children. [8]We loved you so much that we gave you not only God's Good News but our own lives, too.

[9]Don't you remember, dear brothers and sisters, how hard we worked among you? Night and day we toiled to earn a living so that our expenses would not be a burden to anyone there as we preached God's Good News among you. [10]You yourselves are our witnesses—and so is God—that we were pure and honest and faultless toward all of you believers. [11]And you know that we treated each of you as a father treats his own children. [12]We pleaded with you, encouraged you, and urged you to live your lives in a way that God would consider worthy. For he called you into his Kingdom to share his glory.

[13]And we will never stop thanking God that when we preached his message to you, you didn't think of the words we spoke as being just our own. You accepted what we said as the very word of God—which, of course, it was. And this word continues to work in you who believe.

[14]And then, dear brothers and sisters, you suffered persecution from your own countrymen. In this way, you imitated the believers in God's churches in Judea who, because of their belief in Christ Jesus, suffered from their own people, the Jews.

[15]For some of the Jews had killed their own prophets, and some even killed the Lord Jesus. Now they have persecuted us and driven us out. They displease God and oppose everyone [16]by trying to keep us from preaching the Good News to the Gentiles, for fear some might be saved. By doing this, they continue to pile up their sins. But the anger of God has caught up with them at last.

Timothy's Good Report about the Church

[17]Dear brothers and sisters, after we were separated from you for a little while (though our hearts never left you), we tried very hard to come back because of our intense longing to see you again. [18]We wanted very much to come, and I, Paul, tried again and again, but Satan prevented us. [19]After all, what gives us hope and joy, and what is our proud reward and crown? It is you! Yes, you will bring us much joy as we stand together before our Lord Jesus when he comes back again. [20]For you are our pride and joy.

2:1 Greek *brothers;* also in 2:9, 14, 17. **2:7** Some manuscripts read *we were as infants among you; we were as a mother.*

2:3-12 Paul did not minister in Thessalonica for personal gain. Yet to discredit Paul, his enemies charged him with that very thing. The apostle recalled his ministry among them, showing that he had gained nothing from it. Paul's work among the Thessalonians had been motivated by his sincere love and empathy. In recovery we are to carry the message of hope to others. But before getting involved in others' lives, we need to examine our motives. Are we helping other people for personal gain or because we are sincerely concerned about them? We should make this question an integral part of our personal moral inventory.

2:19-20 Paul had discovered the message of hope in the gospel of Jesus Christ. As he grew in faith, he joyfully shared it with others. Paul's ministry helped not only the Thessalonians, but it also helped Paul. As he saw the Thessalonians grow spiritually, he experienced incredible joy in his own life. Just as their sorrow had been his sorrow, their victory became his victory. The Thessalonians became Paul's "reward and crown" and "pride and joy." The common bond that we share with others in Christ can be a source of great joy and encouragement as we continue in recovery.

CHAPTER 3

Finally, when we could stand it no longer, we decided that I should stay alone in Athens, ²and we sent Timothy to visit you. He is our co-worker for God and our brother in proclaiming the Good News of Christ. We sent him to strengthen you, to encourage you in your faith, ³and to keep you from becoming disturbed by the troubles you were going through. But, of course, you know that such troubles are going to happen to us Christians. ⁴Even while we were with you, we warned you that troubles would soon come—and they did, as you well know.

⁵That is why, when I could bear it no longer, I sent Timothy to find out whether your faith was still strong. I was afraid that the Tempter had gotten the best of you and that all our work had been useless. ⁶Now Timothy has just returned, bringing the good news that your faith and love are as strong as ever. He reports that you remember our visit with joy and that you want to see us just as much as we want to see you. ⁷So we have been greatly comforted, dear brothers and sisters,* in all of our own crushing troubles and suffering, because you have remained strong in your faith. ⁸It gives us new life, knowing you remain strong in the Lord.

⁹How we thank God for you! Because of you we have great joy in the presence of God. ¹⁰Night and day we pray earnestly for you, asking God to let us see you again to fill up anything that may still be missing in your faith.

¹¹May God himself, our Father, and our Lord Jesus make it possible for us to come to you very soon. ¹²And may the Lord make your love grow and overflow to each other and to everyone else, just as our love overflows toward you. ¹³As a result, Christ will make your hearts strong, blameless, and holy when you stand before God our Father on that day when our Lord Jesus comes with all those who belong to him.

CHAPTER 4
Live to Please God

Finally, dear brothers and sisters,* we urge you in the name of the Lord Jesus to live in a way that pleases God, as we have taught you. You are doing this already, and we encourage you to do so more and more. ²For you remember what we taught you in the name of the Lord Jesus. ³God wants you to be holy, so you should keep clear of all sexual sin. ⁴Then each of you will control your body* and live in holiness and honor—⁵not in lustful passion as the pagans do, in their ignorance of God and his ways.

⁶Never cheat a Christian brother in this matter by taking his wife, for the Lord

---

3:7 Greek *brothers.* **4:1** Greek *brothers;* also in 4:10, 13. **4:4** Or *will know how to take a wife for himself;* Greek reads *will know how to possess his own vessel.*

3:2-4 Paul made it clear that troubles are to be expected in life, even a life of recovery in Christ. When we trust God, we cannot expect everything to go smoothly. God never promised to miraculously remove our dependency, though he may do so on rare occasions. God stands with us as we face our problems, giving us strength to confront each new challenge. Realizing that we will always have troubles in this life can help us to survive the hard times in the recovery process. As we face the struggles inherent to all humans, we can count on God's presence with us.

3:6-8 Timothy returned with good news from Thessalonica. The spiritual well-being of the Thessalonians was a great encouragement to Paul, and it helped him make it through his own tough times. Our relationships with others in recovery can be an essential source of mutual help. When we are down, the successes of others can lift us up. When we are up, our joy can lift others out of their despair. As we share our life with one another, we will build each other up and provide the needed encouragement for successful recovery.

3:11-13 Paul concluded this portion of his letter with a short prayer for the Thessalonian believers. Paul prayed that these spiritually transformed people would continue to mature in their love for God. He requested that their new love for God would "grow and overflow" to others. Paul's prayer for these believers can be a model for us as we seek to encourage others in recovery. We can continually lift others to God in prayer and then rejoice as we see God transforming their lives.

4:3-8 The Bible paints a clear picture of what God wants us to be like. Here we are given characteristics we will exemplify if we are following God's will. Passages like this can serve as a measuring stick for us as we take our personal inventory. If we don't measure up to God's standards, we must admit our failures to him and allow him to change us. As we entrust our life to him, we will begin to see the positive characteristics growing in our life.

avenges all such sins, as we have solemnly warned you before. ⁷God has called us to be holy, not to live impure lives. ⁸Anyone who refuses to live by these rules is not disobeying human rules but is rejecting God, who gives his Holy Spirit to you.

⁹But I don't need to write to you about the Christian love* that should be shown among God's people. For God himself has taught you to love one another. ¹⁰Indeed, your love is already strong toward all the Christians* in all of Macedonia. Even so, dear brothers and sisters, we beg you to love them more and more. ¹¹This should be your ambition: to live a quiet life, minding your own business and working with your hands, just as we commanded you before. ¹²As a result, people who are not Christians will respect the way you live, and you will not need to depend on others to meet your financial needs.

The Hope of the Resurrection

¹³And now, brothers and sisters, I want you to know what will happen to the Christians who have died so you will not be full of sorrow like people who have no hope. ¹⁴For since we believe that Jesus died and was raised to life again, we also believe that when Jesus comes, God will bring back with Jesus all the Christians who have died.

¹⁵I can tell you this directly from the Lord: We who are still living when the Lord returns will not rise to meet him ahead of those who are in their graves. ¹⁶For the Lord himself will come down from heaven with a commanding shout, with the call of the archangel, and with the trumpet call of God. First, all the Christians who have died will rise from their graves. ¹⁷Then, together with them, we who are still alive and remain on the earth will be caught up in the clouds to meet the Lord in the air and re-

main with him forever. ¹⁸So comfort and encourage each other with these words.

CHAPTER 5

I really don't need to write to you about how and when all this will happen, dear brothers and sisters.* ²For you know quite well that the day of the Lord will come unexpectedly, like a thief in the night. ³When people are saying, "All is well; everything is peaceful and secure," then disaster will fall upon them as suddenly as a woman's birth pains begin when her child is about to be born. And there will be no escape.

⁴But you aren't in the dark about these things, dear brothers and sisters, and you won't be surprised when the day of the Lord comes like a thief. ⁵For you are all children of the light and of the day; we don't belong to darkness and night. ⁶So be on your guard, not asleep like the others. Stay alert and be sober. ⁷Night is the time for sleep and the time when people get drunk. ⁸But let us who live in the light think clearly, protected by the body armor of faith and love, and wearing as our helmet the confidence of our salvation. ⁹For God decided to save us through our Lord Jesus Christ, not to pour out his anger on us. ¹⁰He died for us so that we can live with him forever, whether we are dead or alive at the time of his return. ¹¹So encourage each other and build each other up, just as you are already doing.

Paul's Final Advice

¹²Dear brothers and sisters, honor those who are your leaders in the Lord's work. They work hard among you and warn you against all that is wrong. ¹³Think highly of them and give them your wholehearted love because of their work. And remember to live peaceably with each other.

4:9 Greek *brotherly love.* **4:10** Greek *the brothers.* **5:1** Greek *brothers;* also in 5:4, 12, 14, 25, 26, 27.

4:13-18 Apparently the Thessalonian believers were afraid that believers who died before Jesus returned would lose the opportunity of sharing in Christ's glorious reign. Paul explained that dead Christians would be raised and share in the fellowship and reign of Jesus in God's Kingdom. We all have this hope in our future as well. All believers can be sure that they will have a special part to play when Christ returns. It doesn't matter whether we are dead or alive; God's plan includes us.

5:1-11 Paul warns us that God will hold all people accountable for their attitudes and actions. This day of the Lord will come unexpectedly, so we need to stay alert and ready at all times. This is especially important for those of us who procrastinate, thinking we can start recovery anytime. God wants us to act immediately to receive his forgiveness and power to help us change. Those of us who belong to God will give evidence of our faith by acting in ways that testify to God's work in our life. If we entrust our life to God and seek to follow his will, we have nothing to fear. If we continue to do things our own way, rejecting God's plan of salvation, this day of accountability will be our day of doom.

[14]Brothers and sisters, we urge you to warn those who are lazy. Encourage those who are timid. Take tender care of those who are weak. Be patient with everyone.

[15]See that no one pays back evil for evil, but always try to do good to each other and to everyone else.

[16]Always be joyful. [17]Keep on praying. [18]No matter what happens, always be thankful, for this is God's will for you who belong to Christ Jesus.

[19]Do not stifle the Holy Spirit. [20]Do not scoff at prophecies, [21]but test everything that is said. Hold on to what is good. [22]Keep away from every kind of evil.

5:26 Greek *with a holy kiss.*

Paul's Final Greetings

[23]Now may the God of peace make you holy in every way, and may your whole spirit and soul and body be kept blameless until that day when our Lord Jesus Christ comes again. [24]God, who calls you, is faithful; he will do this.

[25]Dear brothers and sisters, pray for us.

[26]Greet all the brothers and sisters in Christian love.*

[27]I command you in the name of the Lord to read this letter to all the brothers and sisters.

[28]And may the grace of our Lord Jesus Christ be with all of you.

5:14-28 Paul leaves us with his final good advice. If we follow these instructions with God's help, we will be well on our way in the recovery process. We are called to minister to others, a part of recovery that gives hope to others and reinforces our own success. Paul tells us to rebuild our relationships by repaying the wrongs of others with kindness. We are called to live a joyful life, always prayerful, continually seeking God's will. We are reminded of the gift of the Holy Spirit, God's continual helping presence in our life. God gives us what we need to succeed in recovery. Our part is to participate in the good plan he has set out for us.

SECOND THESSALONIANS

THE BIG PICTURE

A. GREETINGS (1:1-2)

B. COMMENDATIONS IN THE MIDST OF PERSECUTION (1:3-12)

C. CORRECTION CONCERNING THE DAY OF THE LORD (2:1-17)

D. ENCOURAGEMENT FOR PRAYER AND A DISCIPLINED LIFE (3:1-15)

E. CONCLUDING REMARKS (3:16-18)

The messages we receive are not always the messages that were sent. Paul's first letter to the Thessalonians had made an impact on its readers, but it wasn't the impact the apostle intended. Paul had affirmed that Jesus would return soon. In response, some of the people assumed that they should stop everything and wait for Christ to return. Some even stopped working, expecting that they would no longer need food and other supplies.

Not every believer in Thessalonica thought that way; many continued to act responsibly even as they anticipated Christ's return. But this only added to the tension among church members. The diligent ones felt pressure to pick up the slack left by the others. The lazy ones claimed they were living a life of true faith. After hearing about this problem, Paul sent the Thessalonians this second letter.

Though Paul wrote to correct his audience's misunderstanding, he commended them for their faithfulness to God. He was confident, because of their commitment to doing God's will, that God would help them resolve this issue. Paul's message was simple. He urged them to be content with their situation and disciplined about fulfilling their responsibilities.

Second Thessalonians is a good reminder for us in recovery. While we have turned our life over to God and look forward to the day when all our problems will be behind us, we have to live here and now. Being in recovery does not mean we can neglect our family, work, or friends. Continuing with the responsibilities God has given us helps us get our life back to normal. Recovery involves taking on our responsibilities, not laying them aside.

THE BOTTOM LINE

PURPOSE: To encourage the Thessalonian believers to fulfill their day-to-day responsibilities while anticipating Christ's return. AUTHOR: The apostle Paul. AUDIENCE: The church at Thessalonica, a city in Macedonia. DATE WRITTEN: About A.D. 51–52, during Paul's second missionary journey; shortly after he had written 1 Thessalonians. SETTING: Some of these young believers had misunderstood Paul's first letter; they thought that Christ was to return at any moment, and they used that assumption as an excuse for being lazy and disruptive while waiting for Christ to return. KEY VERSE: "May the Lord bring you into an ever deeper understanding of the love of God and the endurance that comes from Christ" (3:5). KEY PEOPLE AND RELATIONSHIPS: Paul with Silas, Timothy, and the believers at Thessalonica.

RECOVERY THEMES

God Is the Source of Our Hope: Sometimes we take our eyes off God and focus too much on recovery. We tell ourself that if we only keep up our resolve, all will be well. But when we place our hope in anything other than God, we set ourself up for relapse. Part of the reason we are in recovery is that we recognized that our life had become unmanageable and that we needed God's help. If we depend on resolve alone, we will eventually get so tired of our burdens that we will want to quit. But if we depend on God, he will provide us with the strength and joy we need to persevere.

The Importance of Perseverance: Some of the believers in Thessalonica were sitting back and waiting for the return of Christ. Their lazy, indifferent attitude toward the concerns of everyday life kept them from living responsibly. They soon became a burden to others. Entrusting our life to God does not give us license to just sit around. We must continue to put forth effort, trusting God to sustain us and bring about the desired result of recovery. Our dependence on God is a partnership with him; he doesn't become our slave. Expecting him to do all the work leads to relapse and will alienate the people who have to pick up after us.

God's Reassuring Power and Presence: We live in a time when evil seems to be on the increase, as it was in Thessalonica. From the New Testament we know that until Christ returns, evil will continue to increase. But we don't need to be surprised or afraid; God is sovereign over the earth, no matter how evil our world becomes. As we consciously work on our relationship with God and continue to turn our life and will over to him, he promises to guard us from evil. We can have victory over the evil in our life by remaining faithful to God and obeying him.

CHAPTER 1
Greetings from Paul
This letter is from Paul, Silas,* and Timothy.

It is written to the church in Thessalonica, you who belong to God our Father and the Lord Jesus Christ.

²May God our Father and the Lord Jesus Christ give you grace and peace.

Encouragement during Persecution
³Dear brothers and sisters,* we always thank God for you, as is right, for we are thankful that your faith is flourishing and you are all growing in love for each other. ⁴We proudly tell God's other churches about your endurance and faithfulness in all the persecutions and hardships you are suffering. ⁵But God will use this persecution to show his justice. For he will make you worthy of his Kingdom, for which you are suffering, ⁶and in his justice he will punish those who persecute you. ⁷And God will provide rest for you who are being persecuted and also for us when the Lord Jesus appears from heaven. He will come with his mighty angels, ⁸in flaming fire, bringing judgment on those

1:1 Greek *Silvanus.* **1:3** Greek *Brothers.*

1:3-5 Paul rejoiced that the Thessalonians were maturing in their faith. Their hardships were an important impetus to their spiritual growth. Paul reminds us that hardships are learning opportunities. Most of us would not be in recovery except for the pain caused by our dependency. Just as God used hardships to inspire growth among the Thessalonians, he does the same with us. Painful situations force us to admit that we cannot make it without God. When we realize that we are powerless, we can begin to rebuild our life on the only sure foundation—Jesus Christ.
1:5-8 We often look upon difficulty as something to avoid at all costs. We run from painful situations, however, only to be trapped by other serious problems. Sometimes the desire to escape pain is the foundation for our destructive addiction and compulsion. As we learn to face painful circumstances with God's help, we will be freed from the addictive habit we once used as an escape. Hardships can become an impetus for spiritual growth, not a cause for failure and relapse.
1:9-10 Everlasting destruction refers not to complete annihilation but to eternal separation from God's healing presence and glorious power. The Thessalonians escaped such a terrible fate by committing their lives to God. We have the same opportunity—beginning the process of faith that leads to emotional, physical, and spiritual recovery.
2:3-10 Paul warned the Thessalonians of an evil power at work in the world. These new believers had experienced the work of this oppressor during their years as idol worshipers. We experience that same evil power at work in our addiction, compulsion, or other dysfunctional behavior. We can rejoice that when Jesus Christ returns, he will completely overcome the evil powers in this world. And if we entrust our life to him now, he will begin his delivering work in our life right away.

who don't know God and on those who refuse to obey the Good News of our Lord Jesus. [9]They will be punished with everlasting destruction, forever separated from the Lord and from his glorious power [10]when he comes to receive glory and praise from his holy people. And you will be among those praising him on that day, for you believed what we testified about him.

[11]And so we keep on praying for you, that our God will make you worthy of the life to which he called you. And we pray that God, by his power, will fulfill all your good intentions and faithful deeds. [12]Then everyone will give honor to the name of our Lord Jesus because of you, and you will be honored along with him. This is all made possible because of the undeserved favor of our God and Lord, Jesus Christ.*

CHAPTER 2
Events prior to the Lord's Second Coming

And now, brothers and sisters,* let us tell you about the coming again of our Lord Jesus Christ and how we will be gathered together to meet him. [2]Please don't be so easily shaken and troubled by those who say that the day of the Lord has already begun. Even if they claim to have had a vision, a revelation, or a letter supposedly from us, don't believe them. [3]Don't be fooled by what they say.

For that day will not come until there is a great rebellion against God and the man of lawlessness is revealed—the one who brings destruction.* [4]He will exalt himself and defy every god there is and tear down every object of adoration and worship. He will position himself in the temple of God, claiming that he himself is God. [5]Don't you remember that I told you this when I was with you? [6]And you know what is holding him back, for he can be revealed only when his time comes.

[7]For this lawlessness is already at work secretly, and it will remain secret until the one who is holding it back steps out of the way. [8]Then the man of lawlessness will be revealed, whom the Lord Jesus will consume with the breath of his mouth and destroy by the splendor of his coming. [9]This evil man will come to do the work of Satan with counterfeit power and signs and miracles. [10]He will use every kind of wicked deception to fool those who are on their way to destruction because they refuse to believe the truth

1:12 Or *of our God and the Lord Jesus Christ.* **2:1** Greek *brothers;* also in 2:13, 15. **2:3** Greek *the son of destruction.*

Self-Protection

READ 2 THESSALONIANS 3:1-8

Many of us know what it is like to be a burden to others. It is a common side effect of being controlled by an addiction or compulsive behavior. Sometimes our behavior has made us lose our job. As a result, we have found ourself in financial need. This humiliation can affect our family in many ways. We may have caused our loved ones great stress and shame because we haven't provided for their needs.

The apostle Paul taught us to follow this standard: "For you know that you ought to follow our example. We were never lazy when we were with you. We never accepted food from anyone without paying for it. We worked hard day and night" (2 Thessalonians 3:7-8). "This should be your ambition: to live a quiet life, minding your own business and working with your hands. . . . As a result, people . . . will respect the way you live, and you will not need to depend on others to meet your financial needs" (1 Thessalonians 4:11-12).

It is important for us to think about how our irresponsibility has affected others. Much pain may have been caused by our failure to provide for our family's needs. We need to reflect on how this failure has caused us to lose their respect and trust. The shame of not facing this aspect of our life can be terribly discouraging. Once we face this and become willing to make amends, our sense of self-respect will improve significantly. This step will help us get rid of some of our daily stresses, freeing us to proceed further with recovery. *Turn to page 389, Hebrews 10.*

that would save them. [11]So God will send great deception upon them, and they will believe all these lies. [12]Then they will be condemned for not believing the truth and for enjoying the evil they do.

Believers Should Stand Firm

[13]As for us, we always thank God for you, dear brothers and sisters loved by the Lord. We are thankful that God chose you to be among the first* to experience salvation, a salvation that came through the Spirit who makes you holy and by your belief in the truth. [14]He called you to salvation when we told you the Good News; now you can share in the glory of our Lord Jesus Christ.

[15]With all these things in mind, dear brothers and sisters, stand firm and keep a strong grip on everything we taught you both in person and by letter.

[16]May our Lord Jesus Christ and God our Father, who loved us and in his special favor gave us everlasting comfort and good hope, [17]comfort your hearts and give you strength in every good thing you do and say.

CHAPTER 3
Paul's Request for Prayer

Finally, dear brothers and sisters,* I ask you to pray for us. Pray first that the Lord's message will spread rapidly and be honored wherever it goes, just as when it came to you. [2]Pray, too, that we will be saved from wicked and evil people, for not everyone believes in the Lord. [3]But the Lord is faithful; he will make you strong and guard you from the evil one.* [4]And we are confident in the Lord that you are practicing the things we commanded you, and that you always will. [5]May the Lord bring you into an ever deeper understanding of the love of God and the endurance that comes from Christ.

An Exhortation to Proper Living

[6]And now, dear brothers and sisters, we give you this command with the authority of our Lord Jesus Christ: Stay away from any Christian* who lives in idleness and doesn't follow the tradition of hard work we gave you. [7]For you know that you ought to follow our example. We were never lazy when we were with you. [8]We never accepted food from anyone without paying for it. We worked hard day and night so that we would not be a burden to any of you. [9]It wasn't that we didn't have the right to ask you to feed us, but we wanted to give you an example to follow. [10]Even while we were with you, we gave you this rule: "Whoever does not work should not eat."

2:13 Some manuscripts read *God chose you from the very beginning.* **3:1** Greek *brothers;* also in 3:6, 13. **3:3** Or *from evil.* **3:6** Greek *brother;* also in 3:15.

2:15-16 Paul praised the Thessalonians for their exemplary faith and encouraged them to stand firm and keep a strong grip on the truths they had been taught. We must do the same if we hope to make progress in recovery. If we cannot face the truth about our own life, we cannot even begin the process. We need to recognize that we are powerless and that we need God's help to survive and grow spiritually. Recognizing this truth is a foundational step toward recovery.

3:1-2 Paul drew his readers into his life and ministry by asking them to pray for him. He didn't set himself above them but shared how he needed their prayers, just as he needed God's power for continued safety. Paul shows us how his own survival was tied to the spiritual growth of others. As the Thessalonians prayed for Paul, they shared in his life—his struggles and his victories. As Paul experienced deliverance, they rejoiced and were strengthened by God's clear answers to their prayers. Our relationships in recovery yield mutual encouragement in similar ways.

3:6-10 Apparently many of the Thessalonian believers had stopped working in anticipation of Christ's return. Their false understandings had led them to live irresponsibly. So Paul told these believers to get back to work. If they refused to work, they would have to face the consequence—they shouldn't eat. Since God has promised to help us in recovery, we might be tempted to think we can sit idly by and watch it happen. This is not the case. We need to participate in the plan God has for us. If we don't take the necessary steps of faith, we will have to face the consequence—failed recovery.

3:11-13 Some Thessalonians had begun to meddle in other people's business. This practice is extremely destructive to the process of recovery. Not only does it breed discouragement among the people being bothered, but it also keeps us from examining our own life as we should. Instead of taking inventory of our own life, we focus on the lives of others. Paul exhorted the Thessalonians to set things straight and to live in the power of God. If they didn't, their gossiping lifestyle would cause them to shrink away from their own recovery, while also discouraging others.

[11]Yet we hear that some of you are living idle lives, refusing to work and wasting time meddling in other people's business. [12]In the name of the Lord Jesus Christ, we appeal to such people—no, we command them: Settle down and get to work. Earn your own living. [13]And I say to the rest of you, dear brothers and sisters, never get tired of doing good.

[14]Take note of those who refuse to obey what we say in this letter. Stay away from them so they will be ashamed. [15]Don't think of them as enemies, but speak to them as you would to a Christian who needs to be warned.

Paul's Final Greetings

[16]May the Lord of peace himself always give you his peace no matter what happens. The Lord be with you all.

[17]Now here is my greeting, which I write with my own hand—PAUL. I do this at the end of all my letters to prove that they really are from me.

[18]May the grace of our Lord Jesus Christ be with you all.

FIRST TIMOTHY

THE BIG PICTURE

A. A CALL TO SOUND DOCTRINE (1:1-20)
B. A CALL TO ORDER AMONG THE BELIEVERS (2:1–4:16)
C. A CALL TO PROPER RELATIONSHIPS (5:1–6:2)
D. A CALL TO SPIRITUAL DISCERNMENT (6:3-21)

Paul and Timothy had a special relationship. Timothy came to faith in Christ as a result of Paul's ministry, and he quickly joined the apostle's traveling team. As they traveled and ministered together, the two became as close as father and son. As Timothy matured in his faith, Paul sent him to lead the church in Ephesus. As a young minister, Timothy faced many challenges and problems. Paul wrote this letter to counsel and encourage his young protégé.

Although this letter is personal in nature, Paul included in it a wealth of advice about how to deal with problems in the church. He also painted a clear picture of what the Christian church should be like. Every church, for example, should have sound spiritual teaching, faithful worship, strong leadership, dedication to God's Word, and caring ministries. These characteristics are what make a church community a place of redemption and healing.

Recovery is a long-term process. In the search for wholeness we need a safe, nurturing environment in which we can set things straight and build a new life for ourself. Professional counselors or recovery groups are limited in this respect. We need to find a more permanent context for our long-term care and support.

The ideal context for this kind of help is a healthy church community. Not all churches, however, qualify for this distinction. An ideal church provides loving accountability, like the church described in this letter. A church should be a hospital for the hurting, a place where old wounds can heal and lives can be rebuilt. We all need a healthy church family to help us in the long-term process of recovery.

THE BOTTOM LINE

PURPOSE: To encourage Timothy, a young minister of the gospel, at a time when he was facing difficult circumstances. AUTHOR: The apostle Paul. AUDIENCE: Timothy. DATE WRITTEN: Around A.D. 64, just before Paul was imprisoned in Rome. SETTING: Timothy was one of Paul's closest friends. Paul had sent him to help the church at Ephesus and was now writing to offer him practical advice on issues Timothy was facing. KEY VERSE: "Cling tightly to your faith in Christ, and always keep your conscience clear" (1:19). KEY PEOPLE AND RELATIONSHIPS: Paul with Timothy.

RECOVERY THEMES

The Truth Brings Healing: Paul urged Timothy to preserve the Christian faith and to speak only the truth. Timothy was opposing false teachers who were trying to undermine his work. The only weapons he had were the truth about Christ and a godly lifestyle that backed up everything he taught. Paul knew that only the truth about God in Jesus Christ could bring healing and recovery to broken people, and he wanted Timothy to be convinced of that as well. It is still true: Only Jesus Christ offers us true freedom. Our job is to defend and share the message of God's healing power through belief in Christ. We can do this by speaking the truth about God's power and by backing up our words with our transformed life.

The Importance of Discipline: Paul urged Timothy to discipline himself. Self-discipline does not negate our need for God's power, just as God's gracious help does not negate our need for self-discipline. Both are necessary in a successful recovery program. We need to stay in good spiritual and emotional condition in order to receive the powerful help that God offers us. We must continue to take personal inventory and right the wrongs we uncover. We also must involve ourself in activities that increase our conscious contact with God. These disciplines will encourage our spiritual growth and keep us on track in recovery.

God Works through People: An important part of recovery involves our relationships with other people. Paul gave Timothy specific instructions on how to relate to the people in his church. Paul's advice relates to our relationships as well, especially as we carry the message of hope to others. Caring for each other demonstrates God's power at work within us and also reminds us of how we were cared for when we entered recovery.

Taking Inventory Leads to Wise Conduct: Recovery always takes place in the context of relationships. So taking our personal inventory in the recovery process must lead us to make improvements in how we relate to others. We may not be in a position of leadership, but we are always an example to others. When we are taking inventory on a regular basis, everyone wins: We do because we grow; others do because they are encouraged. A successful recovery will lead to the healing of our broken relationships.

CHAPTER 1
Greetings from Paul

This letter is from Paul, an apostle of Christ Jesus, appointed by the command of God our Savior and by Christ Jesus our hope.

²It is written to Timothy, my true child in the faith.

May God our Father and Christ Jesus our Lord give you grace, mercy, and peace.

Warnings against False Teachings

³When I left for Macedonia, I urged you to stay there in Ephesus and stop those who are teaching wrong doctrine. ⁴Don't let people waste time in endless speculation over myths and spiritual pedigrees.* For these things only cause arguments; they don't help people live a life of faith in God.* ⁵The purpose of my instruction is that all the Christians there would be filled with love that comes from a pure heart, a clear conscience, and sincere faith.

⁶But some teachers have missed this whole point. They have turned away from these things and spend their time arguing and talking foolishness. ⁷They want to be known as teachers of the law of Moses, but they don't know what they are talking about, even though they seem so confident. ⁸We know these laws are good when they are used as God intended. ⁹But they were not made for people who do what is right. They are for people who are disobedient and rebellious, who are ungodly and sinful, who consider nothing sacred and defile what is holy, who murder their father

1:4a Greek *in myths and endless genealogies, which cause speculation.* **1:4b** Greek *a stewardship of God in faith.*

1:3-7 Apparently false teachers in Ephesus were claiming that certain knowledge and activities were necessary for salvation. Their teachings were dividing the believers, and some of them claimed to have special knowledge. This also led the believers away from the essentials of the faith and the only way to salvation—faith in Jesus Christ. Many today claim to have solutions for recovery, and many of their programs assume we can accomplish recovery without God's help. We must heed Paul's exhortation and steer clear of people who teach such things. Only God has the power to deliver us.

TIMOTHY

When we have found a good friend, we have found a treasure. This is especially true as we struggle through the stages of recovery. We need people who are faithful and willing to persevere with us through the hard times. We need the love and acceptance that only true friends can offer. The friendship between young Timothy and the apostle Paul brought significant support and encouragement to both men.

Paul described Timothy as a faithful brother with a solid reputation. Timothy was devoted to Paul and shared many of the triumphant victories in Paul's ministry. But Timothy didn't stay around only when things were going well. He persevered with Paul during the difficult times of imprisonment, torture, and mockery. Their years of shared ministry grew into a lifelong friendship.

Paul referred to Timothy with admiration in many of his letters. He called him "my beloved and trustworthy child in the Lord" (1 Corinthians 4:17) and "my fellow worker" (Romans 16:21). In his letter to the Philippians, Paul referred to Timothy with the highest praise and said that he had been "like a son" to him (Philippians 2:22). In his letters to Timothy, Paul expressed great affection for him. Paul's personal involvement in Timothy's ministry was evident when Paul reminded him "to fan into flames the spiritual gift God gave you when I laid my hands on you" (2 Timothy 1:6).

Timothy was never known as a charismatic or strong leader. He was apparently somewhat timid and afraid to confront his people, especially the older men. But he was faithful and persevered in his ministry despite his fears and trials. Paul supported Timothy in his ministry, realizing that God had called this young man into special service for him. Despite his weaknesses, Timothy was used by God to build the church and to encourage his more charismatic co-worker, Paul.

Recovery requires that we allow people into our life for both support and accountability. We need to ask God for "Timothys"—people who have integrity, who can be trusted, and who will stand by us through anything. When we find our Timothys, we will be better equipped to face the trials of recovery.

STRENGTHS AND ACCOMPLISHMENTS:
- Timothy had an excellent reputation for his faithfulness.
- He was a special friend to the apostle Paul.
- He stood by Paul even in the most difficult circumstances.
- He was a faithful minister of the gospel.

WEAKNESSES AND MISTAKES:
- Timothy struggled with his youth and timidity.
- He had stomach problems, possibly related to anxiety.

LESSONS FROM HIS LIFE:
- Our fears and inadequacies need not stop us from serving God.
- Good friendships are extremely valuable, especially in recovery.

KEY VERSES:
"Finally, when we could stand it no longer, we decided that I should stay alone in Athens, and we sent Timothy to visit you. He is our co-worker for God and our brother in proclaiming the Good News of Christ. We sent him to strengthen you, to encourage you in your faith, and to keep you from becoming disturbed by the troubles you were going through" (1 Thessalonians 3:1-3).

Timothy is first named in Acts 16:1-5 and is mentioned at various other points in the book. He is the recipient of Paul's letters 1 and 2 Timothy. He is also mentioned in Romans 16:21; 1 Corinthians 4:17; 16:10-11; 2 Corinthians 1:1, 19; Philippians 1:1; 2:19-23; Colossians 1:1; 1 Thessalonians 1:1-10; 3:2-6; Philemon 1:1; and Hebrews 13:23.

---

or mother or other people. ¹⁰These laws are for people who are sexually immoral, for homosexuals and slave traders, for liars and oath breakers, and for those who do anything else that contradicts the right teaching ¹¹that comes from the glorious Good News entrusted to me by our blessed God.

Paul's Gratitude for God's Mercy
¹²How thankful I am to Christ Jesus our Lord for considering me trustworthy and appointing me to serve him, ¹³even though I used to scoff at the name of Christ. I hunted down his people, harming them in every way I could. But God had mercy on me because I did it in ignorance and unbelief. ¹⁴Oh, how

kind and gracious the Lord was! He filled me completely with faith and the love of Christ Jesus.

[15]This is a true saying, and everyone should believe it: Christ Jesus came into the world to save sinners—and I was the worst of them all. [16]But that is why God had mercy on me, so that Christ Jesus could use me as a prime example of his great patience with even the worst sinners. Then others will realize that they, too, can believe in him and receive eternal life. [17]Glory and honor to God forever and ever. He is the eternal King, the unseen one who never dies; he alone is God. Amen.

Timothy's Responsibility

[18]Timothy, my son, here are my instructions for you, based on the prophetic words spoken about you earlier. May they give you the confidence to fight well in the Lord's battles. [19]Cling tightly to your faith in Christ, and always keep your conscience clear. For some people have deliberately violated their consciences; as a result, their faith has been shipwrecked. [20]Hymenaeus and Alexander are two examples of this. I turned them over to Satan so they would learn not to blaspheme God.

CHAPTER 2
Instructions about Worship

I urge you, first of all, to pray for all people. As you make your requests, plead for God's mercy upon them, and give thanks. [2]Pray this way for kings and all others who are in authority, so that we can live in peace and quietness, in godliness and dignity. [3]This is good and pleases God our Savior, [4]for he wants everyone to be saved and to understand the truth. [5]For there is only one God and one Mediator who can reconcile God and people. He is the man Christ Jesus. [6]He gave his life to purchase freedom for everyone. This is the message that God gave to the world at the proper time. [7]And I have been chosen—this is the absolute truth—as a preacher and apostle to teach the Gentiles about faith and truth.

[8]So wherever you assemble, I want men to pray with holy hands lifted up to God, free from anger and controversy. [9]And I want women to be modest in their appearance. They should wear decent and appropriate clothing and not draw attention to themselves by the way they fix their hair or by wearing gold or pearls or expensive clothes. [10]For women who claim to be devoted to

---

1:18-20 Paul commanded Timothy to fight God's battles well. In one sense this continued his earlier thoughts about upholding God's truth against false teachers. Yet the real battle was not in the realm of ideas; it involved acting in ways that reflected a close relationship with God. Paul told Timothy to cling to his faith and keep his conscience clear. He was to live in ways that showed God's power. Our beliefs are important, too, but we must go beyond *thinking* the right things to *doing* the right things. That is where God's real battles are won. Our commitment to recovery is evidenced when we take the necessary steps, some of them painful, and live out our relationship with God, showing others the comfort and deliverance that can be found in him.

2:1-2 Here Paul shows why prayer is essential for establishing a peaceful context for spiritual growth. Through prayer, both public and private, order and peace are promoted and strengthened. Prayer involves thanksgiving for God's blessings and intercession for others. It is one of the assets we often overlook as we work our program. We can easily become so focused on our own activities that we forget to turn to God for help. Prayer improves our conscious contact with God. Regular prayer also reminds us that we are helpless without God's continual and powerful help.

2:3-5 That God wants everyone to be saved is encouraging news. No matter how hopeless our life may seem, how bad we have been, or how badly others have treated us, God wants us to come to him. The truth is that all of us are separated from God by sin until we give our life to Christ, the one who bridges the gulf between man and God. God gives us power for recovery when we confess our powerlessness and ask Jesus for forgiveness, salvation, and assistance.

3:1-7 Paul described the prospective leader as someone who has self-control, spiritual maturity, and strong management of his own family. The home is the most reliable proving ground for potential leaders. It is also the place where we can give evidence of our progress in recovery. Since our family members have probably been hurt by our dependency, it is essential that we make amends to them. Sometimes it is hardest to restore our closest relationships. But successful recovery always involves the people in our family and leads to the restoration of broken family relationships.

God should make themselves attractive by the good things they do.

¹¹Women should listen and learn quietly and submissively. ¹²I do not let women teach men or have authority over them. Let them listen quietly. ¹³For God made Adam first, and afterward he made Eve. ¹⁴And it was the woman, not Adam, who was deceived by Satan, and sin was the result. ¹⁵But women will be saved through childbearing* and by continuing to live in faith, love, holiness, and modesty.

CHAPTER 3
Leaders in the Church

It is a true saying that if someone wants to be an elder,* he desires an honorable responsibility. ²For an elder must be a man whose life cannot be spoken against. He must be faithful to his wife.* He must exhibit self-control, live wisely, and have a good reputation. He must enjoy having guests in his home and must be able to teach. ³He must not be a heavy drinker or be violent. He must be gentle, peace loving, and not one who loves money. ⁴He must manage his own family well, with children who respect and obey him. ⁵For if a man cannot manage his own household, how can he take care of God's church?

⁶An elder must not be a new Christian, because he might be proud of being chosen so soon, and the Devil will use that pride to make him fall.* ⁷Also, people outside the church must speak well of him so that he will not fall into the Devil's trap and be disgraced.

⁸In the same way, deacons must be people who are respected and have integrity. They must not be heavy drinkers and must not be greedy for money. ⁹They must be committed to the revealed truths of the Christian faith and must live with a clear conscience. ¹⁰Before they are appointed as deacons, they should be given other responsibilities in the church as a test of their character and ability. If they do well, then they may serve as deacons.

¹¹In the same way, their wives* must be respected and must not speak evil of others. They must exercise self-control and be faithful in everything they do.

¹²A deacon must be faithful to his wife, and he must manage his children and

2:15 Or *will be saved by accepting their role as mothers,* or *will be saved by the birth of the Child.* **3:1** Greek *overseer;* also in 3:2. **3:2** Greek *be the husband of one wife;* also in 3:12. **3:6** Or *he might fall into the same judgment as the Devil.* **3:11** Or *the women deacons.* The Greek word can be translated *women* or *wives.*

STEP

10

Spiritual Exercises

BIBLE READING: 1 Timothy 4:7-8

We continued to take personal inventory and when we were wrong promptly admitted it.

It is amazing what human beings can achieve through consistent disciplined effort. How many times have we watched seasoned gymnasts or other athletes and marveled at the ease with which they performed? We realize that they developed those abilities through rigorous training, which is what sets the true athletes apart from the spectators. Continuing our regular personal inventory requires similar self-discipline.

Paul wrote to Timothy: "Spend your time and energy in training yourself for spiritual fitness. Physical exercise has some value, but spiritual exercise is much more important" (1 Timothy 4:7-8). The word translated "exercise" referred specifically to the disciplined training done by gymnasts in Paul's day.

Spiritual strength and agility come only through practice. We need to develop our spiritual muscles through consistent effort and daily discipline. Continuing to take our personal inventory is one of the disciplines we need to develop. Like the athlete, we can motivate ourself to continue in disciplined routines by looking forward to our reward. This kind of discipline "promises a reward in both this life and the next" (1 Timothy 4:8). Results won't happen overnight. But as we continue practicing these disciplines each day, we will eventually reap the benefits. *Turn to page 363, 2 Timothy 2.*

household well. [13]Those who do well as deacons will be rewarded with respect from others and will have increased confidence in their faith in Christ Jesus.

The Truths of Our Faith

[14]I am writing these things to you now, even though I hope to be with you soon, [15]so that if I can't come for a while, you will know how people must conduct themselves in the household of God. This is the church of the living God, which is the pillar and support of the truth.

[16]Without question, this is the great mystery of our faith:

Christ* appeared in the flesh
and was shown to be righteous by the Spirit.*

He was seen by angels
and was announced to the nations.
He was believed on in the world
and was taken up into heaven.*

CHAPTER 4
Warnings against False Teachers

Now the Holy Spirit tells us clearly that in the last times some will turn away from what we believe; they will follow lying spirits and teachings that come from demons. [2]These teachers are hypocrites and liars. They pretend to be religious, but their consciences are dead.*

[3]They will say it is wrong to be married and wrong to eat certain foods. But God created those foods to be eaten with thanksgiving by people who know and believe the truth. [4]Since everything God created is good, we

3:16a Greek *Who;* some manuscripts read *God.* 3:16b Or *in his spirit.* 3:16c Greek *in glory.* 4:2 Greek *are seared.*

3:16 Paul had been reminding the Thessalonian believers that the way to godly living is never easy. We all know this. We have already recognized that we cannot do it alone. Even with God's powerful help, each step of confession and healing can be painful. Yet Jesus Christ has paid the debt for our sins and failures. He has paved the way for our recovery and will stand beside us each step of the way. As difficult as the recovery process may be, Jesus Christ can give us the power to start over. He already has been resurrected to a new life; he now offers us the same.

4:1-5 One of the errors Paul warned Timothy about was religiously motivated self-denial. What is wrong with this? Isn't it self-indulgence that gets most of us in trouble in the first place? Paul pointed out that the pleasures offered by God should be enjoyed with thanksgiving and not rejected in the name of spirituality. Some recovery leaders have called their followers to give up all forms of pleasure to purge their lives of the tendency toward addiction. If we have tried this, however, we know that deprivation leads to a deeper hunger and an eventual relapse. God has given us many legitimate earthly pleasures. When we learn how to replace our enslaving dependency with wholesome activities, we will be less tempted to escape life through our addiction.

4:7-10 Paul warned Timothy not to argue about insignificant issues and tells him to focus on training himself for spiritual fitness. In recovery it is easy to get sidetracked by new ideas and solutions to our problems or the strengths and weaknesses of certain programs over others. We can keep spiritually fit only by taking regular moral inventory, admitting our failures, and seeking to make amends to those we have wronged. We can make progress in recovery only if we are willing to take the first steps and train hard.

4:11-16 Timothy is admonished to share the Good News of new life in Christ through word and deed. We sometimes forget that the most effective way to share our story of deliverance is to live it. Nothing we say can witness as powerfully to God's power as the changes people can see in us and in our actions. Some people will always question the legitimacy of what we say, but no one can question the evidence of a transformed life. When we entrust our life to God, we can experience the transforming power promised through Jesus Christ. Allowing God to change us is the best way to help others enter the path of recovery.

5:1-2 Paul reminded Timothy to treat all people, young and old, with respect. He reminds us of the importance of healthy relationships in the Christian community. Sound doctrine, proper worship, and godly leadership are all important, but unless we treat people with love and respect, the church will never be a place where people in recovery can grow. The courtesy and affection requested by Paul will make the Christian community a place where healing can take place and lives can be rebuilt.

5:3-10 Paul made it clear that the Christian community was to show special attention to their widows. Paul's directions here reflect God's concern for the helpless and rejected in society. This is encouraging to us because we all know what it feels like to be helpless and rejected. But God wants us to be included among his people; there is a place for everyone in his church. No matter who we are or what we have done, we are accepted on the basis of our faith in Jesus Christ. God reaches out to us, as helpless and rejected as we may be, and calls each one of us to be part of his family.

should not reject any of it. We may receive it gladly, with thankful hearts. ⁵For we know it is made holy by the word of God and prayer.

A Good Servant of Christ Jesus

⁶If you explain this to the brothers and sisters,* you will be doing your duty as a worthy servant of Christ Jesus, one who is fed by the message of faith and the true teaching you have followed. ⁷Do not waste time arguing over godless ideas and old wives' tales. Spend your time and energy in training yourself for spiritual fitness. ⁸Physical exercise has some value, but spiritual exercise is much more important, for it promises a reward in both this life and the next. ⁹This is true, and everyone should accept it. ¹⁰We work hard and suffer much* in order that people will believe the truth, for our hope is in the living God, who is the Savior of all people, and particularly of those who believe.

¹¹Teach these things and insist that everyone learn them. ¹²Don't let anyone think less of you because you are young. Be an example to all believers in what you teach, in the way you live, in your love, your faith, and your purity. ¹³Until I get there, focus on reading the Scriptures to the church, encouraging the believers, and teaching them.

¹⁴Do not neglect the spiritual gift you received through the prophecies spoken to you when the elders of the church laid their hands on you. ¹⁵Give your complete attention to these matters. Throw yourself into your tasks so that everyone will see your progress. ¹⁶Keep a close watch on yourself and on your teaching. Stay true to what is right, and God will save you and those who hear you.

CHAPTER 5

Never speak harshly to an older man,* but appeal to him respectfully as though he were your own father. Talk to the younger men as you would to your own brothers. ²Treat the older women as you would your mother, and treat the younger women with all purity as your own sisters.

Advice about Widows, Elders, and Slaves

³The church should care for any widow who has no one else to care for her. ⁴But if she has children or grandchildren, their first responsibility is to show godliness at home and repay their parents by taking care of them. This is something that pleases God very much.

4:6 Greek *brothers.* **4:10** Some manuscripts read *and strive.* **5:1** Or *an elder.*

STEP 12

Talking the Walk

BIBLE READING: 1 Timothy 4:14-16

Having had a spiritual awakening as the result of these steps, we tried to carry this message to others and to practice these principles in all our affairs.

When we realize everything we have gained by following the Twelve Steps, it will be natural to want to share this life-giving message with others. If we think back to the time before we entered recovery, we will probably recall that we didn't respond very well to "preaching." Yet we also realize that there are people in our life who could be helped by our message. That is why we need to communicate our story, but do it with sensitivity.

The apostle Paul taught Timothy that to get the gospel message across, he was not only to teach others but also be an example by putting his beliefs into practice. Paul said: "Give your complete attention to these matters. Throw yourself into your tasks so that everyone will see your progress. Keep a close watch on yourself and on your teaching. Stay true to what is right, and God will save you and those who hear you" (1 Timothy 4:15-16). When we practice the principles of the Twelve Steps, others will be watching and notice the changes. This will open the doors for us to share our story.

Every addict is a precious lost soul whom God loves and wants to rescue. "If anyone among you wanders away from the truth . . . the one who brings that person back will save that sinner from death and bring about the forgiveness of many sins" (James 5:19-20). *Turn to page 373, Titus 3.*

5But a woman who is a true widow, one who is truly alone in this world, has placed her hope in God. Night and day she asks God for help and spends much time in prayer. 6But the widow who lives only for pleasure is spiritually dead. 7Give these instructions to the church so that the widows you support* will not be criticized.

8But those who won't care for their own relatives, especially those living in the same household, have denied what we believe. Such people are worse than unbelievers.

9A widow who is put on the list for support must be a woman who is at least sixty years old and was faithful to her husband.* 10She must be well respected by everyone because of the good she has done. Has she brought up her children well? Has she been kind to strangers? Has she served other Christians humbly?* Has she helped those who are in trouble? Has she always been ready to do good?

11The younger widows should not be on the list, because their physical desires will overpower their devotion to Christ and they will want to remarry. 12Then they would be guilty of breaking their previous pledge. 13Besides, they are likely to become lazy and spend their time gossiping from house to house, getting into other people's business and saying things they shouldn't. 14So I advise these younger widows to marry again, have children, and take care of their own homes. Then the enemy will not be able to say anything against them. 15For I am afraid that some of them have already gone astray and now follow Satan.

16If a Christian woman has relatives who are widows, she must take care of them and not put the responsibility on the church. Then the church can care for widows who are truly alone.

17Elders who do their work well should be paid well,* especially those who work hard at both preaching and teaching. 18For the Scripture says, "Do not keep an ox from eating as it treads out the grain." And in another place, "Those who work deserve their pay!"*

19Do not listen to complaints against an elder unless there are two or three witnesses to accuse him. 20Anyone who sins should be rebuked in front of the whole church so that others will have a proper fear of God.

21I solemnly command you in the presence of God and Christ Jesus and the holy angels to obey these instructions without taking sides or showing special favor to anyone. 22Never be in a hurry about appointing an elder. Do not participate in the sins of others. Keep yourself pure.

23Don't drink only water. You ought to drink a little wine for the sake of your stomach because you are sick so often.

24Remember that some people lead sinful lives, and everyone knows they will be judged. But there are others whose sin will not be revealed until later. 25In the same way, everyone knows how much good some people do, but there are others whose good deeds won't be known until later.

CHAPTER 6
Christians who are slaves should give their masters full respect so that the name of God and his teaching will not be shamed. 2If your master is a Christian, that is no excuse for being disrespectful. You should work all the harder because you are helping another believer* by your efforts.

False Teaching and True Riches
Teach these truths, Timothy, and encourage everyone to obey them. 3Some false teachers may deny these things, but these are the sound, wholesome teachings of the Lord Jesus Christ, and they are the foundation for a godly life. 4Anyone who teaches any-

---

5:7 Or *so the church;* Greek reads *so they.* **5:9** Greek *was the wife of one man.* **5:10** Greek *Has she washed the feet of saints?* **5:17** Greek *should be worthy of double honor.* **5:18** Deut 25:4; Luke 10:7. **6:2** Greek *a brother.*

5:19-20 Paul called Timothy to confront his fellow church leaders who were living sinful lives. By confronting them about their failures, Timothy would save them from the consequences that continued disobedience would bring them on judgment day. This advice to confront wrongdoers is a call to tough love. Sometimes we must do the same for the people we love. As we notice the growing power of people's addictive behaviors, we can say something before they hit bottom. In so doing, we will give them the opportunity to admit their helplessness and receive God's transforming help.

6:3-5 Paul warned Timothy about those who spread false teachings among the believers. The apostle wanted to protect the message of free salvation offered by Jesus Christ from the distorting lies of money-hungry charlatans. Paul's advice is valuable for us in recovery. Recovery through any

thing different is both conceited and ignorant. Such a person has an unhealthy desire to quibble over the meaning of words. This stirs up arguments ending in jealousy, fighting, slander, and evil suspicions. 5These people always cause trouble. Their minds are corrupt, and they don't tell the truth. To them religion is just a way to get rich.

6Yet true religion with contentment is great wealth. 7After all, we didn't bring anything with us when we came into the world, and we certainly cannot carry anything with us when we die. 8So if we have enough food and clothing, let us be content. 9But people who long to be rich fall into temptation and are trapped by many foolish and harmful desires that plunge them into ruin and destruction. 10For the love of money is at the root of all kinds of evil. And some people, craving money, have wandered from the faith and pierced themselves with many sorrows.

Paul's Final Instructions

11But you, Timothy, belong to God; so run from all these evil things, and follow what is right and good. Pursue a godly life, along with faith, love, perseverance, and gentleness. 12Fight the good fight for what we believe. Hold tightly to the eternal life that God has given you, which you have confessed so well before many witnesses. 13And I command you before God, who gives life to all, and before Christ Jesus, who gave a good testimony before Pontius Pilate, 14that you obey his commands with all purity. Then no one can find fault with you from now until our Lord Jesus Christ returns. 15For at the right time Christ will be revealed from heaven by the blessed and only almighty God, the King of kings and Lord of lords. 16He alone can never die, and he lives in light so brilliant that no human can approach him. No one has ever seen him, nor ever will. To him be honor and power forever. Amen.

17Tell those who are rich in this world not to be proud and not to trust in their money, which will soon be gone. But their trust should be in the living God, who richly gives us all we need for our enjoyment. 18Tell them to use their money to do good. They should be rich in good works and should give generously to those in need, always being ready to share with others whatever God has given them. 19By doing this they will be storing up their treasure as a good foundation for the future so that they may take hold of real life.

20Timothy, guard what God has entrusted to you. Avoid godless, foolish discussions with those who oppose you with their so-called knowledge. 21Some people have wandered from the faith by following such foolishness.

May God's grace be with you all.

---

power other than God's through Jesus Christ is false. Only God can deliver us from our sins and weaknesses. Anyone claiming to have another solution to our problems likely has something to gain from the program being offered. Only God's solution through Jesus Christ can heal our deepest wounds, and the power he offers is free of charge.

6:17-19 Paul warned Timothy about the pitfall of trusting in money. Some of us may have already experienced the emptiness of such misplaced trust. We may have thought that wealth could buy solutions to all our problems. We now know, however, that money cannot deliver us from the power of our dependency. Whether we are rich or poor, the pull of our addiction can be overcome only when we admit our helplessness and turn to God for help. The only way to a successful life in God's eyes is to pursue godliness. By taking steps of faith in God we can experience his help in the recovery process and renewed life.

REFLECTIONS ON

FIRST

TIMOTHY

✲*insights* ABOUT GOD'S LAW

In **1 Timothy 1:8-11** Paul pointed out that God's law is intended to convict us of our sins and lead us to admit our helplessness and receive his forgiveness. It is not primarily a set of rules for us to live by. It is true that recovery involves acknowledging that there are healthy boundaries for our actions. But recovery will never be successful by observing the Old Testament law, which is beyond our ability to keep (see Acts 15:10). Attempting to do so will lead to frustration and guilt, which will stymie rather than encourage us in recovery. We need to use the law as a means for discovering how helpless we are. Then we can entrust our life to God and trust him to help us take each new step in recovery.

✲*insights* ABOUT GOD'S TRANSFORMING POWER

In **1 Timothy 1:12-17** Paul recounted how he had once done everything he could to stop the growth of the early Christian community. But God mercifully intervened in Paul's life, transforming him into one of the most dynamic leaders of the early Christian church. As he shared his story, his previous status as an enemy made his message all the more powerful. The amazing changes in his life testified to God's transforming power. Some of us may feel that we will never be able to impact the lives of others. We may feel that we are so terrible that we are beyond the point of recovery. But God can change us no matter who we are or what we have done. As we share our story of deliverance, others will receive hope as they see what God has done in our life.

SECOND TIMOTHY

THE BIG PICTURE

A. GREETINGS (1:1-2)
B. ENCOURAGEMENT TO PERSEVERE (1:3–2:26)
   1. The Need to Be Faithful (1:3-18)
   2. The Reality of Hardships (2:1-13)
   3. The Need to Behave Responsibly (2:14-26)
C. EXHORTATIONS CONCERNING THE LAST DAYS (3:1–4:8)
D. PAUL SHARES HIS OWN PERSONAL NEEDS (4:9-22)

When a loved one is about to die, we strain to hear any whispered words of blessing or advice, knowing they will be the last. When an important person is at death's door, people crowd around for words of enduring wisdom. In this letter Paul wrote his final words of blessing, advice, and comfort. It is Paul's deathbed communication to Timothy, his son in the faith.

As he wrote this letter, Paul was awaiting his execution in a Roman prison. He expected the end to come soon, so he penned these words of advice and encouragement to his young protégé in Ephesus. He wanted to make sure that Timothy had all the tools he needed to be an effective minister of the gospel.

Paul told Timothy to develop his relationship with God and to serve God faithfully. Paul knew that Timothy would face many problems as a church leader, so he encouraged Timothy to persevere. He challenged the young minister to be faithful to his duties, to use the gifts God had given him, to hold on to the truth of God's Word, to teach others, and to be willing to suffer for the sake of Christ.

Paul had made mistakes in the past, but that didn't disqualify him from helping Timothy. Neither do our mistakes disqualify us from reaching out to others. God gives each of us something to share from our experiences in life. Paul had much to pass on to Timothy. Through our recovery, God has given us important insights from which others can benefit. Sharing those insights with others is an important part of our own journey toward wholeness.

THE BOTTOM LINE

PURPOSE: To encourage a faithful but discouraged Timothy in continuing to do God's work. AUTHOR: The apostle Paul. AUDIENCE: Timothy, a young minister of the gospel. DATE WRITTEN: Sometime between A.D. 66 and 67, shortly before Paul's death during the reign of Emperor Nero. SETTING: When Paul wrote this letter, he was in prison; only his friend Luke was with him. This is a very personal letter, showing Paul's vulnerability and loneliness as he faced death. It also reveals his inner strength as he continued, even in his desperate situation, to encourage young Timothy. KEY VERSE: "Run from anything that stimulates youthful lust. Follow anything that makes you want to do right. Pursue faith and love and peace, and enjoy the companionship of those who call on the Lord with pure hearts" (2:22). KEY PEOPLE AND RELATIONSHIPS: Paul, with Timothy, Luke, and Mark.

RECOVERY THEMES

God's Way Can Be Difficult: We don't like giving up destructive behaviors because it is painful, and the changes required for recovery are often especially painful. Some of us would rather suffer in a known situation than risk moving into the unknown world of recovery. As it was for Timothy, so it is with us: Our growth involves some pain, but we can be confident that the sacrifices we make will be ultimately worthwhile. Knowing that there will be hard times in recovery can help us face them and persevere in the healing process.

The Importance of Faithfulness: We can count on opposition as we pursue recovery, but that is not all bad. Opposition can clue us in to the fact that important changes are taking place in our life. Not everyone likes to see us change, even if those changes are good and healthy. Some people may be afraid that they are losing an old friend. Others may begin to feel guilty about their own dependency and try to stop our progress. We don't have to figure out why people want to stand in our way; our job is to be faithful to our program of recovery and spiritual growth. Paul was faithful to God, and he called Timothy to follow his example. God calls each of us to do the same.

The Power of God's Word: One of the primary sources of strength and guidance for us in recovery is God's Word. Paul challenged Timothy to know what God's Word says and means (2:15). He described how God's Word helps us as it teaches us what is true, makes us realize what is wrong in our life, points us in the right direction, and helps us do what is right (3:16). Our praying and thinking are to focus on God's Word, for it equips us to live as God wants us to live.

CHAPTER 1
Greetings from Paul

This letter is from Paul, an apostle of Christ Jesus by God's will, sent out to tell others about the life he has promised through faith in Christ Jesus.

²It is written to Timothy, my dear son.

May God our Father and Christ Jesus our Lord give you grace, mercy, and peace.

Encouragement to Be Faithful

³Timothy, I thank God for you. He is the God I serve with a clear conscience, just as my ancestors did. Night and day I constantly remember you in my prayers. ⁴I long to see you again, for I remember your tears as we parted. And I will be filled with joy when we are together again.

⁵I know that you sincerely trust the Lord,

1:5 We all learn from our parents and pass on the lessons we learn—good or bad—to our children. We blame our parents for our defects of character and weep because we have passed those same defects on to our children. But we can stop the cycle of passing destructive traits from one generation to the next by turning our life over to God. Timothy's mother and grandmother were models of faith and passed their faith on to Timothy. As we obey God, we will model a transformed life to our children. As they see the power of our vibrant faith in God, they will be likely to follow in our steps. Like Timothy's mother and grandmother, we will be able to rejoice in our godly children.

1:7-14 Timothy did not have all the character traits normally expected of a leader. He may have been fearful and timid at times, but Paul said that God gives "power, love, and self-discipline." Paul told Timothy not to let his weakness stop him from ministering to others. His success was not based on his ability, skill, or courage; it was based on the Holy Spirit's power working in him. In recovery we don't have the inherent strength, courage, and self-discipline needed to overcome our dependency. Through God's power, however, we can succeed in recovery.

1:15-18 Paul was in prison when he wrote this letter; he had been deserted by most of his friends and followers. His friend Onesiphorus, however, stood with Paul even though it was risky. Onesiphorus teaches us how to show loyalty and love to someone in need. Like Paul, we may have been abandoned by our friends as we entered recovery. We may also know how Paul must have felt toward his loyal friend. We may have an Onesiphorus in our life, too. Realizing how essential these people are to our recovery encourages us to take every opportunity to be a loyal friend to others. This is part of sharing the message of hope with others and helping them toward recovery.

2:1-2 Paul didn't tell Timothy just to be strong; he told him to be strong in Christ Jesus. The apostle knew that Timothy could never succeed in his ministry by depending on his own strength. He needed the only power sufficient for godly living—God. The truth that God gives us the power to live a transformed life is good news, and we need to pass it on to others! That is what recovery is all about. As each of us hears about and experiences God's power, we pass the word on to others. In this way others receive God's gracious help, and we discover the joy of helping others and growing in our faith.

for you have the faith of your mother, Eunice, and your grandmother, Lois. ⁶This is why I remind you to fan into flames the spiritual gift God gave you when I laid my hands on you. ⁷For God has not given us a spirit of fear and timidity, but of power, love, and self-discipline. ⁸So you must never be ashamed to tell others about our Lord. And don't be ashamed of me, either, even though I'm in prison for Christ. With the strength God gives you, be ready to suffer with me for the proclamation of the Good News.

⁹It is God who saved us and chose us to live a holy life. He did this not because we deserved it, but because that was his plan long before the world began—to show his love and kindness to us through Christ Jesus. ¹⁰And now he has made all of this plain to us by the coming of Christ Jesus, our Savior, who broke the power of death and showed us the way to everlasting life through the Good News. ¹¹And God chose me to be a preacher, an apostle, and a teacher of this Good News.

¹²And that is why I am suffering here in prison. But I am not ashamed of it, for I know the one in whom I trust, and I am sure that he is able to guard what I have entrusted to him* until the day of his return.

¹³Hold on to the pattern of right teaching you learned from me. And remember to live in the faith and love that you have in Christ Jesus. ¹⁴With the help of the Holy Spirit who lives within us, carefully guard what has been entrusted to you.

¹⁵As you know, all the Christians who came here from the province of Asia have deserted me; even Phygelus and Hermogenes are gone. ¹⁶May the Lord show special kindness to Onesiphorus and all his family because he often visited and encouraged me. He was never ashamed of me because I was in prison. ¹⁷When he came to Rome, he searched everywhere until he found me. ¹⁸May the Lord show him special kindness on the day of Christ's return. And you know how much he helped me at Ephesus.

CHAPTER 2
A Good Soldier of Christ Jesus
Timothy, my dear son, be strong with the special favor God gives you in Christ Jesus. ²You have heard me teach many things that have been confirmed by many reliable witnesses. Teach these great truths to trustworthy people who are able to pass them on to others.

1:12 Or *what has been entrusted to me.*

STEP 10

Perseverance
BIBLE READING: 2 Timothy 2:1-8
We continued to take personal inventory and when we were wrong promptly admitted it.
Recovery is a lifelong process. There will be times when we grow weary and want to throw in the towel. We will experience pain, fear, and a host of other emotions. We will win some battles but lose others in the war to achieve wholeness. We may get discouraged at times when we can't see any progress, even though we have been working hard. But if we persevere through it all, we can maintain the ground we have gained.

The apostle Paul used three illustrations to teach about perseverance. He wrote to Timothy: "Endure suffering along with me, as a good soldier of Christ Jesus. And as Christ's soldier, do not let yourself become tied up in the affairs of this life, for then you cannot satisfy the one who has enlisted you in his army. Follow the Lord's rules for doing his work, just as an athlete either follows the rules or is disqualified and wins no prize. Hardworking farmers are the first to enjoy the fruit of their labor. Think about what I am saying. The Lord will give you understanding in all these things" (2 Timothy 2:3-7).

Like a soldier, we are in a war that we can win only if we fight to the end. Like an athlete, we must train for a new way of life and follow the steps of recovery to the finish line. Like a farmer, we must do our work in every season and then wait patiently until we see growth. If we stop working our program before reaching the goal, we may lose everything we have fought, trained, and worked hard for. *Turn to page 403, James 1.*

[3]Endure suffering along with me, as a good soldier of Christ Jesus. [4]And as Christ's soldier, do not let yourself become tied up in the affairs of this life, for then you cannot satisfy the one who has enlisted you in his army. [5]Follow the Lord's rules for doing his work, just as an athlete either follows the rules or is disqualified and wins no prize. [6]Hardworking farmers are the first to enjoy the fruit of their labor. [7]Think about what I am saying. The Lord will give you understanding in all these things.

[8]Never forget that Jesus Christ was a man born into King David's family and that he was raised from the dead. This is the Good News I preach. [9]And because I preach this Good News, I am suffering and have been chained like a criminal. But the word of God cannot be chained. [10]I am willing to endure anything if it will bring salvation and eternal glory in Christ Jesus to those God has chosen.

[11]This is a true saying:

If we die with him,
  we will also live with him.
[12]If we endure hardship,
  we will reign with him.
If we deny him,
  he will deny us.
[13]If we are unfaithful,
  he remains faithful,
  for he cannot deny himself.

2:19a Num 16:5. **2:19b** See Isa 52:11.

An Approved Worker

[14]Remind everyone of these things, and command them in God's name to stop fighting over words. Such arguments are useless, and they can ruin those who hear them. [15]Work hard so God can approve you. Be a good worker, one who does not need to be ashamed and who correctly explains the word of truth. [16]Avoid godless, foolish discussions that lead to more and more ungodliness. [17]This kind of talk spreads like cancer. Hymenaeus and Philetus are examples of this. [18]They have left the path of truth, preaching the lie that the resurrection of the dead has already occurred; and they have undermined the faith of some.

[19]But God's truth stands firm like a foundation stone with this inscription: "The Lord knows those who are his,"* and "Those who claim they belong to the Lord must turn away from all wickedness."*

[20]In a wealthy home some utensils are made of gold and silver, and some are made of wood and clay. The expensive utensils are used for special occasions, and the cheap ones are for everyday use. [21]If you keep yourself pure, you will be a utensil God can use for his purpose. Your life will be clean, and you will be ready for the Master to use you for every good work.

[22]Run from anything that stimulates youthful lust. Follow anything that makes you want to do right. Pursue faith and love

---

2:3-7 Recovery and spiritual growth are never easy. Progress requires that we follow principles of disciplined faith on a daily basis. Like soldiers we need to put aside the obstacles to our spiritual growth—our dependency, our pursuit of pleasure, our denial. Like athletes we need to follow the rules for healthy living—God's will for our life. Like farmers we need to work hard—persevering through the tough times. If we follow these examples, God will work in our life and help us win life's hard battles. He will reward us with understanding and a rich harvest of blessings.

2:15 Paul told Timothy to work hard to receive God's approval by diligently studying God's Word to discover God's will for him in both attitude and action. We cannot know God's will unless we know what the Bible says. Since recovery is dependent upon our following God's will, we need to study his Word to discover how God wants us to live. This will enable us to follow his instructions for rebuilding our broken life.

2:22 Paul's advice to Timothy is appropriate for us too. We need to run from the places and situations that are likely to tempt us. We should avoid spending time with people who will lead us to relapses. Instead, we should be with people who will encourage us and support our progress in recovery and spiritual growth. If we don't have friends or activities that support our recovery, we need to seek out and get involved in a community of godly and supportive people.

3:1-9 These verses describe people we should not imitate. Sadly, under the influence of our addiction, however, many of us fit this description. We lived selfishly, with little thought for the other people in our life. Many of us may be suffering the consequences for our actions right now, feeling alone, lost, and abandoned. Paul made it clear that these attitudes and actions have severe consequences as most of us have already discovered. By continuing to take inventory of our attitudes and actions, we can uncover our destructive character traits and ask God to transform us. With the help God offers through Jesus Christ, we can become new people.

READ 2 TIMOTHY 4:5-15

GOD grant me the serenity to accept the things I cannot change the courage to change the things I can and the wisdom to know the difference AMEN

In recovery we all struggle to move out of a difficult past and into a healthier future. Our energy can easily be misspent trying to rewrite the past—a hopeless task. In the recovery process we need to honestly evaluate our life, including everything in the past, and then concentrate our energy on rebuilding a new life.

Jesus said, "You will know the truth, and the truth will set you free" (John 8:32). The path to freedom always leads to the truth, even the truth about the past. The apostle Paul once wrote to young Timothy: "Alexander the coppersmith has done me much harm, but the Lord will judge him for what he has done" (2 Timothy 4:14). Paul stated the truth about someone who had hurt him but leaves the matter in God's hands. We, too, need to honestly accept the things that have been done to us and then let them go, leaving them in God's hands.

We cannot change our past, yet it is hard to accept the truth about it. It is hard to face the things that others have done to us and all the mistakes we have made.

Elsewhere Paul examined his past, honestly reviewing his earthly accomplishments, his wrongs, his mistakes, his family, his gains, and his losses. It was from this broad perspective that he could write these words: "I don't mean to say that I have already achieved these things or that I have already reached perfection! But I keep working toward that day when I will finally be all that Christ Jesus saved me for and wants me to be" (Philippians 3:12). When we face the truth about our past, we can finally let it go. Then we can journey into a healthier future. *Turn to page 371, Titus 2.*

and peace, and enjoy the companionship of those who call on the Lord with pure hearts.

23Again I say, don't get involved in foolish, ignorant arguments that only start fights. 24The Lord's servants must not quarrel but must be kind to everyone. They must be able to teach effectively and be patient with difficult people. 25They should gently teach those who oppose the truth. Perhaps God will change those people's hearts, and they will believe the truth. 26Then they will come to their senses and escape from the Devil's trap. For they have been held captive by him to do whatever he wants.

CHAPTER 3
The Dangers of the Last Days

You should also know this, Timothy, that in the last days there will be very difficult times.

2For people will love only themselves and their money. They will be boastful and proud, scoffing at God, disobedient to their parents, and ungrateful. They will consider nothing sacred. 3They will be unloving and unforgiving; they will slander others and have no self-control; they will be cruel and have no interest in what is good. 4They will betray their friends, be reckless, be puffed up with pride, and love pleasure rather than God. 5They will act as if they are religious, but they will reject the power that could make them godly. You must stay away from people like that.

6They are the kind who work their way into people's homes and win the confidence of* vulnerable women who are burdened with the guilt of sin and controlled by many desires. 7Such women are forever following new teachings, but they never understand

3:6 Greek *and take captive.*

the truth. [8]And these teachers fight the truth just as Jannes and Jambres fought against Moses. Their minds are depraved, and their faith is counterfeit. [9]But they won't get away with this for long. Someday everyone will recognize what fools they are, just as happened with Jannes and Jambres.

Paul's Charge to Timothy

[10]But you know what I teach, Timothy, and how I live, and what my purpose in life is. You know my faith and how long I have suffered. You know my love and my patient endurance. [11]You know how much persecution and suffering I have endured. You know all about how I was persecuted in Antioch, Iconium, and Lystra—but the Lord delivered me from all of it. [12]Yes, and everyone who wants to live a godly life in Christ Jesus will suffer persecution. [13]But evil people and impostors will flourish. They will go on deceiving others, and they themselves will be deceived.

[14]But you must remain faithful to the things you have been taught. You know they are true, for you know you can trust those who taught you. [15]You have been taught the holy Scriptures from childhood, and they have given you the wisdom to receive the salvation that comes by trusting in Christ Jesus. [16]All Scripture is inspired by God and is useful to teach us what is true and to make us realize what is wrong in our lives. It straightens us out and teaches us to do what is right. [17]It is God's way of preparing us in every way, fully equipped for every good thing God wants us to do.

CHAPTER 4

And so I solemnly urge you before God and before Christ Jesus—who will someday judge the living and the dead when he appears to set up his Kingdom: [2]Preach the word of God. Be persistent, whether the time is favorable or not. Patiently correct, rebuke, and encourage your people with good teaching.

[3]For a time is coming when people will no longer listen to right teaching. They will follow their own desires and will look for teachers who will tell them whatever they want to hear. [4]They will reject the truth and follow strange myths.

[5]But you should keep a clear mind in every situation. Don't be afraid of suffering for the Lord. Work at bringing others to Christ. Complete the ministry God has given you.

Paul's Final Words

[6]As for me, my life has already been poured out as an offering to God. The time of my death is near. [7]I have fought a good fight, I have finished the race, and I have remained faithful. [8]And now the prize awaits me—the crown of righteousness that the Lord, the righteous Judge, will give me on that great day of his return. And the prize is not just for me but for all who eagerly look forward to his glorious return.

[9]Please come as soon as you can. [10]Demas has deserted me because he loves the things of this life and has gone to Thessalonica. Crescens has gone to Galatia, and Titus has gone to Dalmatia. [11]Only Luke is with me.

3:14-17 Paul reminded Timothy of the wonderful resource that God has left us—the Bible. It is the ultimate guide to help us realize what is wrong in our life. It is the only accurate measuring tool available to help us make an honest moral inventory. It reveals God's program for healthy living and shows us how to relate properly and unselfishly to God and to other people. God's Word offers more than just good advice. It promises God's powerful help to all who turn to him with a humble heart. Our recovery will benefit when we take the time to understand it and apply it to our life.

4:1-5 Paul strongly encouraged Timothy to share the Good News of Jesus Christ with others. This is an integral part of Christian living. The good news of recovery in Christ is also something to be shared. In fact, strong and permanent recovery is impossible unless we make sharing our story an integral part of our life. By sharing what God has done for us we can offer new life to other needy people and be encouraged to persevere in our own recovery. We will build strong relationships with others as we walk through recovery with them. This will lead to the healthy community life necessary to support our recovery on a permanent basis.

4:6-8 Paul left his young protégé with these reflections to encourage him as he struggled to live a godly life. Paul had fought hard to live for God and had suffered greatly for the sake of the gospel. Now he could look forward to the wonderful reward he would receive in God's presence. Giving Timothy an eternal perspective would help him approach the tough times with the hope of future blessings. We are given this same hope. It is not easy to walk the path of recovery and spiritual growth. We will experience painful times as we recognize our desperate need for God. We will experience rejection as we seek to share our hope with others. But God rewards our faithfulness and perseverance with eternal peace and joy.

Bring Mark with you when you come, for he will be helpful to me. [12]I sent Tychicus to Ephesus. [13]When you come, be sure to bring the coat I left with Carpus at Troas. Also bring my books, and especially my papers.*

[14]Alexander the coppersmith has done me much harm, but the Lord will judge him for what he has done. [15]Be careful of him, for he fought against everything we said.

[16]The first time I was brought before the judge, no one was with me. Everyone had abandoned me. I hope it will not be counted against them. [17]But the Lord stood with me and gave me strength, that I might preach the Good News in all its fullness for all the Gentiles to hear. And he saved me from certain death.* [18]Yes, and the Lord will deliver me from every evil attack and will bring me safely to his heavenly Kingdom. To God be the glory forever and ever. Amen.

Paul's Final Greetings

[19]Give my greetings to Priscilla and Aquila and those living at the household of Onesiphorus. [20]Erastus stayed at Corinth, and I left Trophimus sick at Miletus.

[21]Hurry so you can get here before winter. Eubulus sends you greetings, and so do Pudens, Linus, Claudia, and all the brothers and sisters.*

[22]May the Lord be with your spirit. Grace be with you all.

4:13 Greek *especially the parchments.* **4:17** Greek *from the mouth of a lion.* **4:21** Greek *brothers.*

4:11 Mark had forsaken Paul and Barnabas during their first missionary journey (see Acts 13:13), so Paul did not allow his participation in the second journey, resulting in the separation of Paul and Barnabas (Acts 15:36-41). Though Mark had failed miserably earlier, it is clear in this passage that his relationship with Paul had been fully restored. Mark's recovery from a past mistake can encourage all who have failed and wondered whether recovery was even possible. Mark wrote the Gospel of Mark, which has touched the lives of millions over the past twenty centuries. No matter how great our failures in the past, God can use us in amazing ways if we entrust our life—failures and all—to him.

4:16-18 Paul recalled his loneliness during his first Roman imprisonment. He remembered how God had stayed with him even after all his human companions had forsaken him. Only God could strengthen him and bring him deliverance when he was a helpless prisoner. Some of us know what it is like to be forsaken by our friends. Under the influence of our addiction we may have destroyed healthy family relationships. And when we entered recovery, the friends who supported our addiction soon left us. We don't have to face the dark days of recovery alone; God is always with us. As we grow in our faith, God will provide the healthy relationships we need to support our progress.

TITUS

THE BIG PICTURE

A. THREATS TO THE TRUTH ABOUT GOD'S GRACE (1:1-16)
B. SOUND TEACHINGS WITH RESPECT TO GOD'S GRACE (2:1–3:11)
  1. Applying God's Truth to Various Age-Groups (2:1-10)
  2. God's Grace As a Motivation for Godly Living (2:11–3:8)
  3. Applying God's Truth to the Problem of Legalism (3:9-11)
C. FINAL PERSONAL REMARKS (3:12-15)

Paul wrote this letter to Titus, a young pastor on the island of Crete. Titus faced two primary problems in his church. On the one hand, some claimed that immoral living was all right because God's grace was sufficient for forgiveness. On the other hand, there were those who claimed that acceptance by God came through obeying God's laws. Paul encouraged Titus to confront both groups for undermining God's gracious gift of forgiveness in Christ.

Paul solved Titus's dual problem by reminding him of the importance of God's grace. When we discover the amazing grace that God has bestowed on us, we will feel an incredible sense of gratitude. This will motivate us to delight in obeying God's will for our life, not to live immorally because our forgiveness is guaranteed. God is not a harsh taskmaster whose favor depends on our slavish obedience to his rules. He is a gracious Father who offers us a relationship with him, both now and throughout eternity. We can live a godly life out of gratitude to God because he loves and forgives us.

The fact that God is gracious and forgiving is essential to recovery. We already know that we are powerless against sin and our dependency. We have all failed many times over. We don't need to be afraid to admit our sins and failures to our gracious God. He will forgive us and help us start over again. Because God is gracious, we can continue our honest self-examination without fear. God will never write us off for our failures and mistakes. God accepts us just as we are.

THE BOTTOM LINE

PURPOSE: To encourage Titus to be faithful in applying the grace of God to various circumstances. AUTHOR: The apostle Paul. AUDIENCE: Titus, a pastor on the island of Crete. DATE WRITTEN: Between Paul's first and second Roman imprisonments (A.D. 63–66). SETTING: Titus pastored the believers on the island of Crete, a place well known for its immorality. Also, a group of Jewish legalists had made inroads into the church. Titus thus had to deal with both immorality and legalism. KEY VERSES: "For the grace of God has been revealed, bringing salvation to all people. And we are instructed to turn from godless living and sinful pleasures. We should live in this evil world with self-control, right conduct, and devotion to God" (2:11-12). KEY PEOPLE AND RELATIONSHIPS: Paul with Titus.

RECOVERY THEMES

The Blessings of God's Grace: Salvation through Jesus Christ is good news! This is especially true because God offers it to us freely even though we do not deserve it. This Good News goes beyond God's offer to pay for our sins; God also seeks to transform us so that we can live day by day with the reality of his power inside us. We don't need to be afraid as we come before God, regardless of our sinful past or our failures. Our relationship with God is not based on our success at following his laws. It is based on his gracious provision for the forgiveness of our sins—Jesus Christ. As we entrust our life to God, he forgives us and empowers us to live according to his perfect will.

The Importance of Accountability: We can never make much progress in recovery when we are isolated from others. Developing healthy relationships goes right along with turning our life over to God. On our own, we are helpless against the power of our dependency. God often uses other people to give us the help and encouragement we need to persevere. Paul urged Titus to be accountable to others. By depending on others, he was able to stand firm and reflect God's love and power in his life. Relationships that hold us accountable can give us the courage to do as Titus did.

Recovery Requires Sacrifice: When we enter into recovery, we also enter into new relationships. As we see in this letter, there is an order to all our relationships. Everyone's role is important, and if we are going to be faithful to our role, we must make sacrifices for others. Recovery, like salvation, can begin with a selfish motive. We tend to focus on our own problems and needs. But a healthy recovery moves beyond this self-focus to reach out to others. Each of us has something to share. We must make the sacrifices necessary to be helpful to others in need of recovery.

CHAPTER 1
Greetings from Paul

This letter is from Paul, a slave of God and an apostle of Jesus Christ. I have been sent to bring faith to those God has chosen and to teach them to know the truth that shows them how to live godly lives. ²This truth gives them the confidence of eternal life, which God promised them before the world began—and he cannot lie. ³And now at the right time he has revealed this Good News, and we announce it to everyone. It is by the command of God our Savior that I have been trusted to do this work for him.

⁴This letter is written to Titus, my true child in the faith that we share.

May God the Father and Christ Jesus our Savior give you grace and peace.

Titus's Work in Crete

⁵I left you on the island of Crete so you could complete our work there and appoint elders in each town as I instructed you. ⁶An elder must be well thought of for his good life. He must

---

1:4-5 Paul had planted churches on the island of Crete, and Titus was to finish Paul's work. He was to strengthen the believers and appoint leaders. Paul recognized that Titus could not do everything alone. He probably also recognized that having a single leader is never ideal. Organizations that revolve around one person are likely to reflect the flaws of their leader. A leadership group provides balance. If church or recovery leaders try to control everything without sharing the responsibilities and power with others, we should wonder whether they are there to help other people or themselves. We need to steer clear of this kind of situation.

1:6-9 These character traits for church leaders make no mention of social standing, financial resources, or professional accomplishments. Church leaders must be good spouses and parents; they need to have good reputations; they need to be humble, patient, self-controlled, hospitable, sensible, and fair. No one can buy these character traits; no one can demand them. We get them only by entrusting our life to God and seeking his will. God can help these character traits grow in our life, regardless of our circumstances. Whether we are a respected millionaire or a homeless addict, God can transform us into someone worthy of being a church leader.

1:10-14 Paul encouraged Titus to confront both the Cretans, who abused God's grace by living in sin, and the Jewish legalists, who denied God's grace by requiring believers to do good works to earn salvation. Paul's primary concern was with the legalists, since they undermined a life of grace with their rules and traditions (see Mark 7:1-8). Legalism makes obedience to rules and traditions more important than our personal and transforming relationship with God. It falsely assumes that we can be good under our own power. In recovery we recognize our powerlessness. We cannot change without God's power, so we need to trust him to help us. Paul was defending two of the basic tenets of recovery: our powerlessness and God's sufficiency.

READ TITUS 2:11-14

GOD grant me the serenity to accept the things I cannot change the courage to change the things I can and the wisdom to know the difference AMEN

No matter how terrible our past has been, we can make changes for the better in our mind, body, and spirit.

Some of us may have come to the conclusion that we just can't change. But if we are willing to place our life in God's hands, there is always hope for positive change and a bright future. The apostle Paul wrote: "Now may the God of peace make you holy in every way, and may your whole spirit and soul and body be kept blameless until that day when our Lord Jesus Christ comes again. God, who calls you, is faithful; he will do this" (1 Thessalonians 5:23-24).

"For the grace of God has been revealed, bringing salvation to all people. And we are instructed to turn from godless living and sinful pleasures. We should live in this evil world with self-control, right conduct, and devotion to God, while we look forward to that wonderful event when the glory of our great God and Savior, Jesus Christ, will be revealed. He gave his life to free us from every kind of sin, to cleanse us, and to make us his very own people, totally committed to doing what is right" (Titus 2:11-14).

God has promised us a wonderful future! In the present, he can keep us from constantly falling into sin if we call on him. Our willingness to let go of the things we cannot change in our past will free us to make positive changes for a healthy future. ***Turn to page 469, Revelation 21.***

---

be faithful to his wife,* and his children must be believers who are not wild or rebellious. ⁷An elder* must live a blameless life because he is God's minister. He must not be arrogant or quick-tempered; he must not be a heavy drinker, violent, or greedy for money. ⁸He must enjoy having guests in his home and must love all that is good. He must live wisely and be fair. He must live a devout and disciplined life. ⁹He must have a strong and steadfast belief in the trustworthy message he was taught; then he will be able to encourage others with right teaching and show those who oppose it where they are wrong.

¹⁰For there are many who rebel against right teaching; they engage in useless talk and deceive people. This is especially true of those who insist on circumcision for salvation. ¹¹They must be silenced. By their wrong teaching, they have already turned whole families away from the truth. Such teachers

only want your money. ¹²One of their own men, a prophet from Crete, has said about them, "The people of Crete are all liars; they are cruel animals and lazy gluttons." ¹³This is true. So rebuke them as sternly as necessary to make them strong in the faith. ¹⁴They must stop listening to Jewish myths and the commands of people who have turned their backs on the truth.

¹⁵Everything is pure to those whose hearts are pure. But nothing is pure to those who are corrupt and unbelieving, because their minds and consciences are defiled. ¹⁶Such people claim they know God, but they deny him by the way they live. They are despicable and disobedient, worthless for doing anything good.

CHAPTER 2
Promote Right Teaching
But as for you, promote the kind of living that reflects right teaching. ²Teach the older men

1:6 Or *have only one wife,* or *be married only once;* Greek reads *be the husband of one wife.* **1:7** Greek *overseer.*

to exercise self-control, to be worthy of respect, and to live wisely. They must have strong faith and be filled with love and patience.

3Similarly, teach the older women to live in a way that is appropriate for someone serving the Lord. They must not go around speaking evil of others and must not be heavy drinkers. Instead, they should teach others what is good. 4These older women must train the younger women to love their husbands and their children, 5to live wisely and be pure, to take care of their homes, to do good, and to be submissive to their husbands. Then they will not bring shame on the word of God.

6In the same way, encourage the young men to live wisely in all they do. 7And you yourself must be an example to them by doing good deeds of every kind. Let everything you do reflect the integrity and seriousness of your teaching. 8Let your teaching be so correct that it can't be criticized. Then those who want to argue will be ashamed because they won't have anything bad to say about us.

9Slaves must obey their masters and do their best to please them. They must not talk back 10or steal, but they must show themselves to be entirely trustworthy and good. Then they will make the teaching about God our Savior attractive in every way.

11For the grace of God has been revealed, bringing salvation to all people. 12And we are instructed to turn from godless living and sinful pleasures. We should live in this evil world with self-control, right conduct, and devotion to God, 13while we look forward to that wonderful event when the glory of our great God and Savior, Jesus Christ, will be revealed. 14He gave his life to free us from every kind of sin, to cleanse us, and to make us his very own people, totally committed to doing what is right. 15You must teach these things and encourage your people to do them, correcting them when necessary. You have the authority to do this, so don't let anyone ignore you or disregard what you say.

2:1-5 Paul called on older men and women to take a special role in the Christian community— to be role models, teaching others by the way they lived. Many of us have experienced the importance of having a godly mentor to encourage us. The most helpful recovery groups have a healthy mix of people, with sponsors who provide encouragement through their words and their actions. As we grow spiritually and progress in recovery, we can become a healthy role model to others in need of recovery. As they see our transformed life and hear our story of deliverance through Christ, they will be encouraged to take the steps necessary to restore their lives.

2:6 Paul told Titus to encourage the young people in his church to "live wisely." Young people are often blind to the consequences of certain activities. They tend to act first and think later. Many of us were very shortsighted when we became involved in our addiction. We probably started out innocently enough, using alcohol or other addictive substances socially. We didn't think through the possible consequences before we took the first dangerous steps toward addiction. Now we are reaping the painful consequences of our unwise choices. If we think before we act and conform our actions to God's will, we will build a meaningful future.

2:11-15 When we realize how much God loves us and that he provides the power for us to live a godly life, we are motivated to entrust our life to him and seek his will. The proper response to God's grace is right conduct. The Bible never considered guilt and fear appropriate motivations for righteousness. We obey God because he loves us and desires to help us succeed. Seeing God as accepting, gracious, and compassionate instead of harsh, condemning, and punitive is critical for our spiritual growth. We don't need to fear God because of our sins. He still loves us and will help us rebuild our life when we admit our failures to him. This can give us hope as we work through recovery.

3:3 We, too, were "foolish and disobedient" and became a slave to our dependency; we were filled with resentment, envy, and hate. But God delivered us from this through his Son, Jesus Christ. Our broken life is the black backdrop against which the bright jewels of God's mercy and gracious salvation are displayed. None of us deserves God's mercy and grace. He loves us simply because he chooses to, more in spite of us than because we deserve it. This truth makes it easier to admit our powerlessness and commit our life to God. No matter how terrible our past, God is willing to forgive and transform us.

3:4-8 Notice the terms that describe God's grace: "kindness and love" (3:4), "mercy" (3:5), and "great kindness" (3:7). We are justified by God's grace, declared "not guilty" in God's eyes by virtue of belonging to Christ. This takes us off the performance treadmill, relieving us of the need to measure up to God's standards. Some of us have spent our life trying to measure up. We bear the guilt of failing to fulfill the unrealistic ideals of our parents, teachers, or bosses. The resulting anger and pain have helped to drive our addiction. But God accepts us just as we are. He doesn't expect us to be perfect; he knows we cannot do it alone. When he calls us to holy living, he also provides the power and direction we need to build a new life.

CHAPTER 3
Do What Is Good

Remind your people to submit to the government and its officers. They should be obedient, always ready to do what is good. ²They must not speak evil of anyone, and they must avoid quarreling. Instead, they should be gentle and show true humility to everyone.

³Once we, too, were foolish and disobedient. We were misled by others and became slaves to many wicked desires and evil pleasures. Our lives were full of evil and envy. We hated others, and they hated us.

⁴But then God our Savior showed us his kindness and love. ⁵He saved us, not because of the good things we did, but because of his mercy. He washed away our sins and gave us a new life through the Holy Spirit.* ⁶He generously poured out the Spirit upon us because of what Jesus Christ our Savior did. ⁷He declared us not guilty because of his great kindness. And now we know that we will inherit eternal life. ⁸These things I have told you are all true. I want you to insist on them so that everyone who trusts in God will be careful to do good deeds all the time. These things are good and beneficial for everyone.

Paul's Final Remarks and Greetings

⁹Do not get involved in foolish discussions about spiritual pedigrees* or in quarrels and fights about obedience to Jewish laws. These kinds of things are useless and a waste of time. ¹⁰If anyone is causing divisions among you, give a first and second warning. After that, have nothing more to do with that person. ¹¹For people like that have turned away from the truth. They are sinning, and they condemn themselves.

¹²I am planning to send either Artemas or Tychicus to you. As soon as one of them arrives, do your best to meet me at Nicopolis as quickly as you can, for I have decided to stay there for the winter. ¹³Do everything you can to help Zenas the lawyer and Apollos with their trip. See that they are given everything they need. ¹⁴For our people should not have unproductive lives. They must learn to do good by helping others who have urgent needs.

¹⁵Everybody here sends greetings. Please give my greetings to all of the believers who love us.

May God's grace be with you all.

3:5 Greek *He saved us through the washing of regeneration and renewing of the Holy Spirit.* 3:9 Greek *discussions and genealogies.*

STEP 12

Never Forget

BIBLE READING: Titus 3:1-5
Having had a spiritual awakening as the result of these steps, we tried to carry this message to others and to practice these principles in all our affairs.
As we get further along in recovery, the memory of how bad our life really was may begin to fade. Do we vividly remember what we once were? Can we humbly recall the dark emotions that filled our soul? Do we have true compassion and genuine sympathy for those to whom we try to carry the message?

When we take the message of recovery to others, we must never forget where we came from and how we got where we are. Paul told Titus: "Once we, too, were foolish and disobedient. We were misled by others and became slaves to many wicked desires and evil pleasures. . . . But then God our Savior showed us his kindness and love. He saved us, not because of the good things we did, but because of his mercy. He washed away our sins and gave us a new life through the Holy Spirit" (Titus 3:3-5).

As we share our message, let us never forget the following truths: We were once a slave, just as others are today. Our heart was filled with the confusion and painful emotions that others still feel. We were saved because of the love and kindness of God, not because we were good enough. We must also remember that we can stay free because God is with us, upholding us every step of the way. *Turn to page 419, 1 Peter 4.*

PHILEMON

THE BIG PICTURE

A. GREETINGS (1:1-3)
B. PAUL COMMENDS PHILEMON (1:4-7)
C. PAUL REQUESTS CONSIDERATION FOR ONESIMUS (1:8-21)
D. CONCLUDING REMARKS (1:22-25)

There were millions of slaves in the Roman Empire; Onesimus was one of them. He was owned by a kind Christian leader named Philemon. Out of desperation, Onesimus stole from his master and ran away. But as so often happens, his attempt at a solution only added to his problem. According to the law, a runaway slave could be branded on the forehead or even executed.

Onesimus hid in Rome, and while there he met Paul. Through the apostle's influence, Onesimus came to believe in Jesus Christ. Paul, himself a prisoner at the time, wrote to his friend Philemon to tell him of Onesimus's conversion. The apostle begged Philemon to forgive Onesimus and welcome him home as a "beloved brother." We do not know how Philemon responded, but it seems reasonable to assume that he forgave Onesimus.

We all know what it's like to be a slave. We have been enslaved to an addictive substance, to other people, to compulsive behavior, and even to the injuries of our past. Slavery of any kind takes away our dignity and humanity, turning us into a mere tool in the hands of our master. We know the utter powerlessness we felt in that condition.

Paul's letter to Philemon reminds us that God still loves us. God cares for us, just as he cared for Onesimus, no matter what we have done in the past. God can step into the middle of our unmanageable life and bring us real hope for the future. As long as we do our part—facing our powerlessness, turning our life over to God, confessing our sins, and seeking to make amends—we can count on a life of freedom.

THE BOTTOM LINE

PURPOSE: To convince Philemon, a slave owner, to forgive a slave for running away. AUTHOR: The apostle Paul. AUDIENCE: Philemon, a believer in the early church. DATE WRITTEN: About A.D. 60, during Paul's imprisonment in Rome. SETTING: Slavery was common in the Roman Empire, even among the new believers. Paul did not speak directly against slavery, but he did take a radical step by calling the slave Onesimus "a beloved brother" (1:16). KEY VERSE: "Onesimus [whose name means 'useful'] hasn't been of much use to you in the past, but now he is very useful to both of us" (1:11). KEY PEOPLE AND RELATIONSHIPS: Paul with Onesimus and Philemon.

RECOVERY THEMES

God Cares for the Dispossessed: Onesimus was one of the rejects of his society. As a slave, he had no worth apart from what he was able to do for his master. When he intensified his problems by stealing and running away, his value was diminished even further—he was worthless. But to God he was highly valued; no one is ever worthless in the eyes of God. God's values are different from ours: he cares deeply about all people who have been broken and dispossessed. No matter what we have done in the past, he calls us to himself and offers us recovery and hope.

The Necessity of Forgiveness: Anyone in the Roman Empire would have expected Onesimus to be condemned to death for what he had done. But from God's perspective, Onesimus was deemed worthy of forgiveness because of his relationship with Jesus Christ. The foundation of the change in Onesimus's life was the forgiveness he would receive from God. And the foundation of his continued relationship with Philemon was the forgiveness he received from his master. The forgiveness granted by God and by others is what makes recovery possible. We can rejoice that when we entrust our life to God, he forgives us and transforms our life. Then he helps us make amends to the people we have harmed, paving the way for our forgiveness and restoration.

Greetings from Paul

This letter is from Paul, in prison for preaching the Good News about Christ Jesus, and from our brother Timothy.

It is written to Philemon, our much loved co-worker, ²and to our sister Apphia and to Archippus, a fellow soldier of the cross. I am also writing to the church that meets in your house.

³May God our Father and the Lord Jesus Christ give you grace and peace.

Paul's Thanksgiving and Prayer

⁴I always thank God when I pray for you, Philemon, ⁵because I keep hearing of your trust in the Lord Jesus and your love for all of God's people. ⁶You are generous because of your faith. And I am praying that you will really put your generosity to work, for in so doing you will come to an understanding of all the good things we can do for Christ. ⁷I myself have gained much joy and comfort from your love, my brother, because your

1:3-9 Before bringing up the problem of the runaway Onesimus, Paul established his lines of communication with Philemon. The apostle showed an appreciation for Philemon and a real concern for his family. Paul's example can help us in recovery. Sometimes we must confront others about their dependency or deal with another touchy problem. As we face confrontation, we need to make sure we value the people involved and take the time to establish strong lines of communication. If we jump in too soon, they may feel that we are just trying to hurt them. If we prove our love beforehand, however, they will be more receptive to what we say.

1:10-13 Onesimus had been reconciled to God and had experienced God's forgiveness. But the fact that God had forgiven him did not exempt him from the consequences of his earlier actions. He still had to return to Philemon to make amends for his wrongs. Restitution is one of the hardest parts of recovery. Our actions have painful consequences; they hurt other people. Even after we have been reconciled to God, we still need to make amends to the people we have wronged. We can be sure that God will stand with us in the process. Onesimus returned to his master bearing Paul's letter. There is no record of the outcome of Onesimus's return, but it is unlikely that this letter would have survived had Philemon not taken Paul's advice to forgive Onesimus.

1:14-17 Both Onesimus and Philemon had a responsibility. Onesimus had to do what he could to make amends to Philemon; Philemon was responsible to accept the overtures of the repentant Onesimus. Old resentments had to be set aside, and Philemon was called upon to forgive and accept his repentant new brother in Christ. If we have wronged others, we need to take clear steps toward making amends. It is equally important, however, that we forgive someone who humbly seeks to make amends to us. Bearing grudges against others is destructive to the people we turn away; it also fills us with unresolved bitterness, hindering our progress in recovery.

1:18-21 With the phrase "charge me for it," Paul was asking Philemon to charge Onesimus's debt against Paul's account. Philemon was to welcome Onesimus back into his household as if Paul was the one returning. Paul intervened to arrest the progression of resentment and brokenness in this relationship. This is a beautiful illustration of what God does for us through Jesus Christ. God charges all our sins and failures to the account of Jesus Christ, who has paid the price through his death on the cross. Then God joyfully receives us into his family, just as he would welcome his own Son (see 2 Corinthians 5:21).

kindness has so often refreshed the hearts of God's people.

Paul's Appeal for Onesimus

[8]That is why I am boldly asking a favor of you. I could demand it in the name of Christ because it is the right thing for you to do, [9]but because of our love, I prefer just to ask you. So take this as a request from your friend Paul, an old man, now in prison for the sake of Christ Jesus.

[10]My plea is that you show kindness to Onesimus. I think of him as my own son because he became a believer as a result of my ministry here in prison. [11]Onesimus* hasn't been of much use to you in the past, but now he is very useful to both of us. [12]I am sending him back to you, and with him comes my own heart.

[13]I really wanted to keep him here with me while I am in these chains for preaching the Good News, and he would have helped me on your behalf. [14]But I didn't want to do anything without your consent. And I didn't want you to help because you were forced to do it but because you wanted to. [15]Perhaps you could think of it this way: Onesimus ran away for a little while so you could have him back forever. [16]He is no longer just a slave; he is a beloved brother, especially to me. Now he will mean much more to you, both as a slave and as a brother in the Lord.

[17]So if you consider me your partner, give him the same welcome you would give me if I were coming. [18]If he has harmed you in any way or stolen anything from you, charge me for it. [19]I, Paul, write this in my own handwriting: "I will repay it." And I won't mention that you owe me your very soul!

[20]Yes, dear brother, please do me this favor for the Lord's sake. Give me this encouragement in Christ. [21]I am confident as I write this letter that you will do what I ask and even more!

[22]Please keep a guest room ready for me, for I am hoping that God will answer your prayers and let me return to you soon.

Paul's Final Greetings

[23]Epaphras, my fellow prisoner in Christ Jesus, sends you his greetings. [24]So do Mark, Aristarchus, Demas, and Luke, my co-workers.

[25]The grace of the Lord Jesus Christ be with your spirit.

11 *Onesimus* means "useful."

Unfinished Business

BIBLE READING: Philemon 1:13-16

We made direct amends to such people wherever possible, except when to do so would injure them or others.

Sometimes we need to complete unfinished business before we can move forward toward new opportunities in life. Some of us may have left trails of broken laws and relationships—things we need to address before moving on.

Our new life does not excuse us from past obligations. While the apostle Paul was in prison, he led a runaway slave named Onesimus to a new life in Christ. Then Paul sent him back to his master, even though Onesimus faced possible death for his offense. Since his previous master was a friend of Paul's and a Christian brother, they hoped that Onesimus would be forgiven.

Onesimus carried a letter from Paul to his master, which read: "I really wanted to keep [Onesimus] here with me. . . . But I didn't want to do anything without your consent. . . . Onesimus ran away for a little while so you could have him back forever. He is no longer just a slave; he is a beloved brother. . . . If he has harmed you in any way or stolen anything from you, charge me for it" (Philemon 1:13-16, 18).

Before we can move ahead to a new future, we must face the unfinished business of the past. This includes offering to pay back what we owe, coming clean before the law, and going back to the people from whom we ran away. We can't assume forgiveness from people, although we can hope for it. In some cases we may be surprised to find pardon and release from the bondage of our past. *Turn to page 415, 1 Peter 2.*

HEBREWS

THE BIG PICTURE

A. THE SUPERIORITY OF JESUS AS OUR POWER FOR RECOVERY (1:1–10:18)
  1. He Is More Powerful Than the Angels (1:1–2:18)
  2. He Is Greater Than Moses and Joshua (3:1–4:13)
  3. He Surpasses Everything in the Old Covenant Priesthood (4:14–7:28)
  4. His New Covenant Is Superior (8:1–10:18)
B. THE FREEING POWER OF FAITH AND HUMILITY (10:19–13:25)
  1. Faith Needed in Hard Times (10:19-39)
  2. Faith Seen in Old Testament Times (11:1-40)
  3. Faithfulness and the Loving Discipline of God (12:1-29)
  4. Faithfulness and the Trustworthy Foundation of Christ (13:1-25)

All of us have felt the tug of old habits or our former lifestyle. We have known the frustration it creates as we long for the familiar, even if it is destructive. Perhaps at times the challenge of recovery seems too hard for us. Our old life beckons, tempting us with familiar sources of comfort.

Many of the Jewish Christians of the first century thought about returning to the Jewish faith. Some of Jesus' teachings didn't seem to line up with the teachings of the Jewish rabbis. Was Jesus really the Messiah? Did following him mean they had to give up their old, familiar forms of worship? Would it be wrong to go back to their old beliefs and traditions? Did it make sense to follow this "new way" when it led to harsh persecution?

The writer of Hebrews dealt with the doubts of Jewish believers by showing how salvation in Jesus Christ is clearly superior to the way of the Jewish law. The Jewish readers are told to hold on to their new faith, to encourage each other, and to look forward to Jesus the Messiah's return. They are warned of the consequences of rejecting the salvation offered by God through Christ and reminded of the blessings promised to those who trust him.

Entering recovery requires that we entrust our life to God through Jesus Christ and follow his ways. From time to time we will almost certainly feel tempted to return to our former lifestyle. But God is the only one who can empower us in recovery. When we give our life to him, we take the leap of faith necessary to begin the process of recovery.

THE BOTTOM LINE

PURPOSE: To demonstrate the wisdom of following Christ and the foolishness of looking elsewhere for salvation. AUTHOR: The author is unknown; but Paul, Luke, Barnabas, Apollos, Silas, Philip, Priscilla, and others have been suggested as possibilities. AUDIENCE: Jewish believers. DATE WRITTEN: Probably shortly before the destruction of the Jerusalem Temple in A.D. 70. SETTING: Hebrews was written to encourage Jewish believers who were being severely persecuted. They needed to be reassured that Jesus was who he claimed to be—the Son of God and the promised Messiah. KEY VERSE: "The Son reflects God's own glory, and everything about him represents God exactly" (1:3). KEY PEOPLE AND RELATIONSHIPS: Jesus Christ, along with many men and women of faith.

RECOVERY THEMES

The Primacy of Jesus Christ: The book of Hebrews describes Jesus as God. It explains that Jesus is the ultimate power and authority in the universe, superior to any and every other leader in history. He is the full and complete revelation of God to us. And Jesus is the one who can forgive our sins. Christ is the center of our hope and trust, and for that reason he is our only real hope for recovery.

God Delivers the Powerless: Because Jesus was the perfect sacrifice, he fulfilled all that the Old Testament sacrifices represented—he was the means of God's complete forgiveness of our sins. That means every sin can be forgiven completely—past, present, and future. Through Christ, God did for us what we could not do. Jesus removed the barrier of sin between us and God so we could have access to God's very presence. Christ's complete sacrifice removed the guilt that accompanied our sins. Through his sacrificial death and powerful resurrection, he has delivered the powerless!

The Necessity of Faith: Faith is "the confident assurance that what we hope for is going to happen. It is the evidence of things we cannot yet see" (11:1). Recovery is based on faith—our confident trust that God will help us do what we are powerless to do. As we place our trust in God, he will transform us with his power. He has promised this to all who believe.

The Importance of Perseverance: It is one thing to know that recovery is a lifelong process; it is another to persevere when obstacles and problems block our way. The first readers of the book of Hebrews experienced incredible persecution for their faith. But the writer assured them that they would be able to endure it if they did not give up or turn back. We need to pray for the strength to endure, because perseverance is essential to any successful recovery.

CHAPTER 1
Jesus Christ Is God's Son

Long ago God spoke many times and in many ways to our ancestors through the prophets. ²But now in these final days, he has spoken to us through his Son. God promised everything to the Son as an inheritance, and through the Son he made the universe and everything in it. ³The Son reflects God's own glory, and everything about him represents God exactly. He sustains the universe by the mighty power of his command. After he died to cleanse us from the stain of sin, he sat down in the place of honor at the right hand of the majestic God of heaven.

Christ Is Greater Than the Angels

⁴This shows that God's Son is far greater than the angels, just as the name God gave him is far greater than their names. ⁵For God never said to any angel what he said to Jesus:

"You are my Son.
   Today I have become your Father.*"

And again God said,

"I will be his Father,
   and he will be my Son."*

⁶And then, when he presented his honored* Son to the world, God said, "Let all the angels of God worship him."* ⁷God calls his angels

1:5a Or *Today I reveal you as my Son.* Ps 2:7. **1:5b** 2 Sam 7:14. **1:6a** Greek *firstborn.* **1:6b** Deut 32:43.

1:1-2 Jesus Christ, the Son of God, is God's final and most perfect revelation. Yet God the Son shaped the original creation as well. As "the Alpha and the Omega—the beginning and the end" (Revelation 1:8), he is the only Power capable of the re-creation and transformation we seek in recovery. As the heir of all the treasures of heaven and earth, Jesus Christ stands ready and able to help those who come to him with empty hands, acknowledging their needs and problems.

1:3 There is a vast difference between the divine infinite Being (God) and limited human beings. The only way a person can come to understand something of God's glory and power is to get to know Jesus Christ by faith. Christ is simultaneously both an incredibly powerful expression of God's person and the one who lovingly entered sinful human existence to redeem and renew needy souls. When we acknowledge how powerless we are to save ourself, we can then come to the only power who can accomplish what we cannot—God in Jesus Christ.

1:4-6 The Jews greatly esteemed angels as servants of God, largely because of their role in the Old Testament. But as glorious as angels are, there is still no comparison between the angels and Jesus Christ. Christ is clearly superior in his person and in his works; he also has a unique relationship with the heavenly Father as his Son. It is into this wonderful Father-child relationship that he draws us (Hebrews 2:11). Through Jesus we have access to the Father who loves us and cares for our every need tenderly and with infinite wisdom (see Galatians 4:6; Ephesians 2:18). This is good news indeed!

"messengers swift as the wind,
and servants made of flaming fire."*

8But to his Son he says,

"Your throne, O God, endures forever
and ever.
Your royal power is expressed in
righteousness.
9You love what is right and hate what
is wrong.
Therefore God, your God, has anointed
you,
pouring out the oil of joy on you more
than on anyone else."*

10And,

"Lord, in the beginning you laid the
foundation of the earth,
and the heavens are the work of your
hands.
11Even they will perish, but you remain
forever.
They will wear out like old clothing.
12You will roll them up like an old coat.
They will fade away like old clothing.
But you are always the same;
you will never grow old."*

13And God never said to an angel, as he did to
his Son,

"Sit in honor at my right hand
until I humble your enemies,
making them a footstool under your
feet."*

14But angels are only servants. They are spirits sent from God to care for those who will
receive salvation.

CHAPTER 2
A Warning against Drifting Away

So we must listen very carefully to the truth
we have heard, or we may drift away from it.
2The message God delivered through angels
has always proved true, and the people were
punished for every violation of the law and
every act of disobedience. 3What makes us
think that we can escape if we are indifferent
to this great salvation that was announced by
the Lord Jesus himself? It was passed on* to us
by those who heard him speak, 4and God
verified the message by signs and wonders
and various miracles and by giving gifts of the
Holy Spirit whenever he chose to do so.

Jesus, the Man

5And furthermore, the future world we are
talking about will not be controlled by angels. 6For somewhere in the Scriptures it says,

"What is man that you should think of
him,
and the son of man* that you should
care for him?
7For a little while you made him lower
than the angels,
and you crowned him with glory and
honor.*
8You gave him authority over all things."*

Now when it says "all things," it means
nothing is left out. But we have not yet seen
all of this happen. 9What we do see is Jesus,
who "for a little while was made lower than
the angels" and now is "crowned with glory
and honor" because he suffered death for us.
Yes, by God's grace, Jesus tasted death for

1:7 Ps 104:4. 1:8-9 Ps 45:6-7. 1:10-12 Ps 102:25-27. 1:13 Ps 110:1. 2:3 Or *and confirmed.* 2:6 Or *Son of Man.*
2:7 Some manuscripts add *You put him in charge of everything you made.* 2:6-8 Ps 8:4-6.

2:1-3 This is the first of many "warning" passages in Hebrews. By it, the author sought to alert
the Jewish readers to the subtle danger of drifting back into their former lifestyle in Judaism. In
recovery, too, there is always the danger of falling back into old ways. This passage makes clear
the consequences of our decisions: There will be either just punishment for ignoring the opportunity Christ offers for recovery, or wonderful salvation by trusting God and receiving his special
favor and transforming power.
2:5-8 The writer of Hebrews used Psalm 8:4-6 most likely because of its reference to the "Son of
Man." In Psalm 8 itself it is not obvious that these verses are messianic (referring to Christ); they
seem to refer to humanity's status: "lower than the angels," yet having "authority over all things."
The writer of Hebrews adds a new twist by applying these verses to Christ. As the Son of Man,
Christ was lower than the angels for a time, but now is exalted to a position of authority over all
things. He went before us and now gives us hope for our future. No matter how difficult things
are for us now, our eternal destiny is to rule in heaven with Christ if we believe in him.
2:8-14 Believers who are in recovery are on the way to an eternity with God, moving through
difficult territory where Christ has already been. It was God's great love and grace that led Jesus
to his death; by his death salvation was made available to all. It is also God's grace that leads us
through suffering in recovery. Often it is only through the refining fire of suffering that we achieve
balance and true holiness. When we suffer, we can be sure that Jesus is with us, that he went
before us, and that God will use our pain for his purposes.

everyone in all the world. [10]And it was only right that God—who made everything and for whom everything was made—should bring his many children into glory. Through the suffering of Jesus, God made him a perfect leader, one fit to bring them into their salvation.

[11]So now Jesus and the ones he makes holy have the same Father. That is why Jesus is not ashamed to call them his brothers and sisters.* [12]For he said to God,

"I will declare the wonder of your name
    to my brothers and sisters.*
I will praise you among all your people."

[13]He also said, "I will put my trust in him." And in the same context he said, "Here I am—together with the children God has given me."*

[14]Because God's children are human beings—made of flesh and blood—Jesus also became flesh and blood by being born in human form. For only as a human being could he die, and only by dying could he break the power of the Devil, who had the power of death. [15]Only in this way could he deliver those who have lived all their lives as slaves to the fear of dying.

[16]We all know that Jesus came to help the descendants of Abraham, not to help the angels. [17]Therefore, it was necessary for Jesus to be in every respect like us, his brothers and sisters, so that he could be our merciful and faithful High Priest before God. He then could offer a sacrifice that would take away the sins of the people. [18]Since he himself has gone through suffering and temptation, he is able to help us when we are being tempted.

CHAPTER 3
Jesus Is Greater Than Moses

And so, dear brothers and sisters who belong to God* and are bound for heaven, think about this Jesus whom we declare to be God's Messenger and High Priest. [2]For he was faithful to God, who appointed him, just as Moses served faithfully and was entrusted with God's entire house. [3]But Jesus deserves far more glory than Moses, just as a person who builds a fine house deserves more praise than the house itself. [4]For every house has a builder, but God is the one who made everything.

[5]Moses was certainly faithful in God's house, but only as a servant. His work was an illustration of the truths God would reveal later. [6]But Christ, the faithful Son, was in charge of the entire household. And we are God's household, if we keep up our courage and remain confident in our hope in Christ. [7]That is why the Holy Spirit says,

"Today you must listen to his voice.
[8]Don't harden your hearts against him
    as Israel did when they rebelled,
    when they tested God's patience in the
        wilderness.

2:11 Greek *his brothers;* also in 2:17. **2:12** Greek *my brothers.* Ps 22:22. **2:13** Isa 8:17-18. **3:1** Greek *And so, holy brothers.*

2:17-18 When we are depressed or struggling in recovery, we may feel that nobody cares about us or understands what we are going through. No person has ever gone to greater lengths to identify with us than Jesus Christ; though he was limitless God, he subjected himself to all our human limitations. He lived in our world as a human being and suffered as we do—therefore he understands our pain and suffering from personal experience. He has been where we are, and he is both eager and able to help us.

3:1 The writer of Hebrews reminded his readers that they were God's special people, set apart, chosen for heaven. Periodically in our recovery work we need to remember who we are and where we are headed. Before we began recovery, our past controlled our present. Now in recovery, because of the faith we exercise, our future sets the direction and tone of our life. As often as we need to, we can affirm who we are in Christ and the glorious destiny that awaits us.

3:2-6 Christ's superiority to Moses was underlined by comparing the positions held by each. Christ was like a builder of a fine house (as Creator), while Moses was like the house itself or even a servant in that house. God may use many means to help us in recovery: therapists, recovery groups, pastors, sponsors, books, meetings, tapes, journaling, prayer. But God lovingly controls the reconstruction of our life. In that knowledge we can find comfort, confidence, and joy.

3:7–4:13 In this second and more extended "warning" (see note on 2:1-3), readers are cautioned to avoid the mistake made by the Israelites who received the law at Mount Sinai. In spite of all their spiritual privileges and visual awareness of God's awesome power, they still refused to exercise faith and enter the Promised Land that God graciously offered. Many of us have made a similar mistake upon entering recovery. Either we don't persevere, or we don't anchor our recovery in Christ, the only true source of healing. All of Scripture, including the book of Hebrews, is geared toward helping us put our full trust in God as he is revealed in Jesus Christ.

⁹There your ancestors tried my patience,
even though they saw my miracles for
forty years.
¹⁰So I was angry with them, and I said,
'Their hearts always turn away from me.
They refuse to do what I tell them.'
¹¹So in my anger I made a vow:
'They will never enter my place of
rest.'"*

¹²Be careful then, dear brothers and sisters.*
Make sure that your own hearts are not evil
and unbelieving, turning you away from the
living God. ¹³You must warn each other
every day, as long as it is called "today," so
that none of you will be deceived by sin and
hardened against God. ¹⁴For if we are faithful
to the end, trusting God just as firmly as
when we first believed, we will share in all
that belongs to Christ. ¹⁵But never forget the
warning:

"Today you must listen to his voice.
Don't harden your hearts against him
as Israel did when they rebelled."*

¹⁶And who were those people who rebelled against God, even though they heard
his voice? Weren't they the ones Moses led
out of Egypt? ¹⁷And who made God angry
for forty years? Wasn't it the people who
sinned, whose bodies fell in the wilderness?
¹⁸And to whom was God speaking when he
vowed that they would never enter his place
of rest? He was speaking to those who disobeyed him. ¹⁹So we see that they were not
allowed to enter his rest because of their unbelief.

CHAPTER 4
Promised Rest for God's People
God's promise of entering his place of rest
still stands, so we ought to tremble with fear

that some of you might fail to get there. ²For
this Good News—that God has prepared a
place of rest—has been announced to us just
as it was to them. But it did them no good
because they didn't believe what God told
them.* ³For only we who believe can enter
his place of rest. As for those who didn't believe, God said,

"In my anger I made a vow:
'They will never enter my place of
rest,'"*

even though his place of rest has been ready
since he made the world. ⁴We know it is
ready because the Scriptures mention the
seventh day, saying, "On the seventh day
God rested from all his work."* ⁵But in the
other passage God said, "They will never enter my place of rest."* ⁶So God's rest is there
for people to enter. But those who formerly
heard the Good News failed to enter because
they disobeyed God. ⁷So God set another
time for entering his place of rest, and that
time is today. God announced this through
David a long time later in the words already
quoted:

"Today you must listen to his voice.
Don't harden your hearts against
him."*

⁸This new place of rest was not the land of
Canaan, where Joshua led them. If it had
been, God would not have spoken later
about another day of rest. ⁹So there is a special rest* still waiting for the people of God.
¹⁰For all who enter into God's rest will find
rest from their labors, just as God rested
after creating the world. ¹¹Let us do our best
to enter that place of rest. For anyone who
disobeys God, as the people of Israel did, will
fall.

3:7-11 Ps 95:7-11. **3:12** Greek *brothers.* **3:15** Ps 95:7-8. **4:2** Some manuscripts read *they didn't share the faith of those who listened [to God].* **4:3** Ps 95:11. **4:4** Gen 2:2. **4:5** Ps 95:11. **4:7** Ps 95:7-8. **4:9** Or *Sabbath rest.*

4:1-3 God is always ready, willing, and able to fulfill his promises of freedom and rest. Only one
thing stops him—our unbelief or lack of faith. God wants us to receive wonderful blessings and
freedom from our dependency, but these can only be received by faith. Just as the Jews of Moses'
day didn't believe what God told them, sometimes we allow the difficulties of the present to
cause us to doubt God's promises. Recovery is hard, painful work at times. When the going seems
the hardest, we must consciously fix our mind on God's promises. Faith in Christ, not in our own
efforts, is the only way to true recovery.
4:4-11 Though God is by no means presently inactive, he, in a very real sense, entered his "rest"
at the end of the Creation (Genesis 2:1-3). The writer understood David's renewed offer of rest in
Psalm 95 to mean that the special rest was not secured when Joshua and Israel entered
the Promised Land. Therefore, God's offer of rest, which certainly includes the goals of recovery
(peace with God, self, and others; healthy relationships; the ability to cope with life) remains available to those who pursue it with faith and perseverance.

¹²For the word of God is full of living power. It is sharper than the sharpest knife, cutting deep into our innermost thoughts and desires. It exposes us for what we really are. ¹³Nothing in all creation can hide from him. Everything is naked and exposed before his eyes. This is the God to whom we must explain all that we have done.

Christ Is Our High Priest

¹⁴That is why we have a great High Priest who has gone to heaven, Jesus the Son of God. Let us cling to him and never stop trusting him. ¹⁵This High Priest of ours understands our weaknesses, for he faced all of the same temptations we do, yet he did not sin. ¹⁶So let us come boldly to the throne of our gracious God. There we will receive his mercy, and we will find grace to help us when we need it.

CHAPTER 5

Now a high priest is a man chosen to represent other human beings in their dealings with God. He presents their gifts to God and offers their sacrifices for sins. ²And because he is human, he is able to deal gently with the people, though they are ignorant and wayward. For he is subject to the same weaknesses they have. ³That is why he has to offer sacrifices, both for their sins and for his own sins. ⁴And no one can become a high priest simply because he wants such an honor. He has to be called by God for this work, just as Aaron was.

⁵That is why Christ did not exalt himself to become High Priest. No, he was chosen by God, who said to him,

"You are my Son.
Today I have become your Father.*"

⁶And in another passage God said to him,

"You are a priest forever
in the line of Melchizedek."*

⁷While Jesus was here on earth, he offered prayers and pleadings, with a loud cry and tears, to the one who could deliver him out of death. And God heard his prayers because of his reverence for God. ⁸So even though Jesus was God's Son, he learned obedience from the things he suffered. ⁹In this way, God qualified him as a perfect High Priest, and he became the source of eternal salvation for all those who obey him. ¹⁰And God designated him to be a High Priest in the line of Melchizedek.

A Call to Spiritual Growth

¹¹There is so much more we would like to say about this. But you don't seem to listen, so it's hard to make you understand. ¹²You have been Christians a long time now, and you ought to be teaching others. Instead, you need someone to teach you again the basic things a beginner must learn about the Scriptures.* You are like babies who drink only milk and cannot eat solid food. ¹³And a person who is living on milk isn't very far along in the Christian life and doesn't know much about doing what is right. ¹⁴Solid food

5:5 Or *Today I reveal you as my Son.* Ps 2:7. 5:6 Ps 110:4. 5:12 Or *about the oracles of God.*

4:12-13 During hard times our faith tends to dwindle; we may grow angry and harden our heart to the truth about ourself. The antidote to this problem is the living Word of God, which has power to penetrate even the deepest denial. This is good news for those of us struggling to overcome a dysfunctional lifestyle and having a tendency to distort reality. God knows everything about us, even the things we try to hide from ourself. We can count on him, through his Word, to expose the problems and needs we will face in recovery.

5:4-10 Like any high priest, Jesus Christ had to be chosen for his role. But Christ was a different priest from the Jewish priests descended from Aaron. Jesus is the final (and eternal) High Priest in the line of Melchizedek (see 7:1-21; Psalm 110:4). To prepare for that unique calling, Jesus, the perfect High Priest (see Hebrews 13:8), had to go through a painful growing and learning process (see Luke 2:52) that culminated in his death on the cross. His success in that process lends us great hope as we pursue recovery. He is the one who goes before us and has prepared the way, and he is with us in every step we take.

5:11-13 The writer interrupted his discussion of Melchizedek to warn the people about the spiritual dynamics underlying their immaturity in Christ. Having adequate time to grow and change was not the problem. But the people (like many of us today) continued to manifest childlike behavior instead of growing to spiritual adulthood. Sometimes in recovery it takes a long time to see any progress. But this passage suggests that growth is the norm, even though it is often slow. If we don't see any progress in our recovery over time, we should seek to find out why.

is for those who are mature, who have trained themselves to recognize the difference between right and wrong and then do what is right.

CHAPTER 6

So let us stop going over the basics of Christianity* again and again. Let us go on instead and become mature in our understanding. Surely we don't need to start all over again with the importance of turning away from evil deeds and placing our faith in God. ²You don't need further instruction about baptisms, the laying on of hands, the resurrection of the dead, and eternal judgment. ³And so, God willing, we will move forward to further understanding.

⁴For it is impossible to restore to repentance those who were once enlightened—those who have experienced the good things of heaven and shared in the Holy Spirit, ⁵who have tasted the goodness of the word of God and the power of the age to come—⁶and who then turn away from God. It is impossible to bring such people to repentance again because they are nailing the Son of God to the cross again by rejecting him, holding him up to public shame.

⁷When the ground soaks up the rain that falls on it and bears a good crop for the farmer, it has the blessing of God. ⁸But if a field bears thistles and thorns, it is useless. The farmer will condemn that field and burn it.

⁹Dear friends, even though we are talking like this, we really don't believe that it applies to you. We are confident that you are meant for better things, things that come with salvation. ¹⁰For God is not unfair. He will not forget how hard you have worked for him and how you have shown your love to him by caring for other Christians, as you still do. ¹¹Our great desire is that you will keep right on loving others as long as life lasts, in order to make certain that what you hope for will come true. ¹²Then you will not become spiritually dull and indifferent. Instead, you will follow the example of those who are going to inherit God's promises because of their faith and patience.

God's Promises Bring Hope

¹³For example, there was God's promise to Abraham. Since there was no one greater to swear by, God took an oath in his own name, saying:

¹⁴ "I will certainly bless you richly,
    and I will multiply your descendants
        into countless millions."*

¹⁵Then Abraham waited patiently, and he received what God had promised.

¹⁶When people take an oath, they call on someone greater than themselves to hold them to it. And without any question that oath is binding. ¹⁷God also bound himself with an oath, so that those who received the

6:1 Or *the basics about Christ.* 6:14 Gen 22:17.

5:14 Spiritual growth, eventual maturity, and balance can happen only through application—acting on what we know to be true. As we meditate on God's Word, we will do the right things; the more we do what is right, the more it becomes second nature to us. Like an athlete, we need to discipline our body, training it to do what it should through making right choices, which leads to spiritual and emotional maturity.

6:4-8 This section refers either to believers who turned from their salvation or to unbelievers who came close to salvation but then turned away. Either way, the agricultural analogy brings out the truth that if there is real spiritual life, there will be some evidence of it. In recovery, let us look for and cherish any and all signs of growth, even if they are small—green shoots where before there was dry, barren ground. If we are seeking wholeness through faith in Christ, we can be assured that there will, in good time, be fruit.

6:9-12 In confronting his readers regarding their spiritual lethargy (see 5:11-14), the writer's words were strong and direct, though here he still chose to be positive and think the best about them. He knew from the past how hard they had worked. But he also faced the reality of their immaturity and challenged them to persevere in spiritual growth and recovery with patient faith. In our recovery we sometimes need to be corrected and challenged. This passage gives us an example of how to confront when necessary and yet be open to correction from the people who love us.

6:13-20 Abraham, the father of the Jewish nation, exemplified patient faith. After waiting for many years, he finally received his promised son, Isaac, the first of many descendants (Genesis 12:1-3; 22:16-18). Abraham's persevering faith (see 11:8-19) was anchored in God's promises, which were based on God's unchanging nature. Like Abraham, we can trust God's promises and find absolute security in the resurrected Christ, who is our High Priest and who connects us with the living God.

promise could be perfectly sure that he would never change his mind. [18]So God has given us both his promise and his oath. These two things are unchangeable because it is impossible for God to lie. Therefore, we who have fled to him for refuge can take new courage, for we can hold on to his promise with confidence.

[19]This confidence is like a strong and trustworthy anchor for our souls. It leads us through the curtain of heaven into God's inner sanctuary. [20]Jesus has already gone in there for us. He has become our eternal High Priest in the line of Melchizedek.

CHAPTER 7
Melchizedek Is Compared to Abraham
This Melchizedek was king of the city of Salem and also a priest of God Most High. When Abraham was returning home after winning a great battle against many kings, Melchizedek met him and blessed him. [2]Then Abraham took a tenth of all he had won in the battle and gave it to Melchizedek. His name means "king of justice." He is also "king of peace" because *Salem* means "peace." [3]There is no record of his father or mother or any of his ancestors—no beginning or end to his life. He remains a priest forever, resembling the Son of God.

[4]Consider then how great this Melchizedek was. Even Abraham, the great patriarch of Israel, recognized how great Melchizedek was by giving him a tenth of what he had taken in battle. [5]Now the priests, who are descendants of Levi, are commanded in the law of Moses to collect a tithe from all the people, even though they are their own rela-

tives.* [6]But Melchizedek, who was not even related to Levi, collected a tenth from Abraham. And Melchizedek placed a blessing upon Abraham, the one who had already received the promises of God. [7]And without question, the person who has the power to bless is always greater than the person who is blessed.

[8]In the case of Jewish priests, tithes are paid to men who will die. But Melchizedek is greater than they are, because we are told that he lives on. [9]In addition, we might even say that Levi's descendants, the ones who collect the tithe, paid a tithe to Melchizedek through their ancestor Abraham. [10]For although Levi wasn't born yet, the seed from which he came was in Abraham's loins when Melchizedek collected the tithe from him.

[11]And finally, if the priesthood of Levi could have achieved God's purposes—and it was that priesthood on which the law was based—why did God need to send a different priest from the line of Melchizedek, instead of from the line of Levi and Aaron?*

[12]And when the priesthood is changed, the law must also be changed to permit it. [13]For the one we are talking about belongs to a different tribe, whose members do not serve at the altar. [14]What I mean is, our Lord came from the tribe of Judah, and Moses never mentioned Judah in connection with the priesthood.

Christ Is like Melchizedek
[15]The change in God's law is even more evident from the fact that a different priest, who is like Melchizedek, has now come. [16]He became a priest, not by meeting the old re-

7:5 Greek *their brothers, who are descendants of Abraham.* **7:11** Greek *according to the order of Aaron.*

7:1-3 The discussion returned to Melchizedek (see 5:6-10). These ideas may have been too deep for the original readers to fully understand in their state of spiritual infancy, but the writer thought it was crucial that they try to understand. Aspects of Melchizedek's life (Genesis 14:18-20) were amazingly parallel to events in the life of Christ. This was to emphasize that Christ truly did qualify as a priest in the line of Melchizedek (see 6:20) and thus as our perpetual anchor for recovery and reconciliation.
7:4-10 Abraham recognized Melchizedek as greater than himself, and thus he was obviously greater than any of Abraham's descendants, including Levi and the priests who descended from him. The priesthood Christ came from—the priesthood of Melchizedek—is actually older (implying more stability) than that of Aaron. Such stability can be a great comfort to a person in the turmoil of recovery. Our life may seem to fall apart and circumstances may constantly change, but Christ, our perfect High Priest, will never change.
7:11-19 The new priesthood of Christ was desperately needed because the Levitical priesthood and the Mosaic law were incapable of producing true spiritual maturity. A better priesthood, a better law, and a better hope for living in a growing relationship with God were necessary. Christ's qualification as High Priest came not because of tribal descent but because of his resurrection to new life. The Mosaic law could not make people right with God. Only Christ could do that. In our recovery, Jesus will work his lasting changes in our life.

quirement of belonging to the tribe of Levi, but by the power of a life that cannot be destroyed. [17]And the psalmist pointed this out when he said of Christ,

"You are a priest forever
in the line of Melchizedek."*

[18]Yes, the old requirement about the priesthood was set aside because it was weak and useless. [19]For the law made nothing perfect, and now a better hope has taken its place. And that is how we draw near to God.

[20]God took an oath that Christ would always be a priest, but he never did this for any other priest. [21]Only to Jesus did he say,

"The Lord has taken an oath
and will not break his vow:
'You are a priest forever.'"*

[22]Because of God's oath, it is Jesus who guarantees the effectiveness of this better covenant.

[23]Another difference is that there were many priests under the old system. When one priest died, another had to take his place. [24]But Jesus remains a priest forever; his priesthood will never end. [25]Therefore he is able, once and forever, to save* everyone who comes to God through him. He lives forever to plead with God on their behalf.

[26]He is the kind of high priest we need because he is holy and blameless, unstained by sin. He has now been set apart from sinners, and he has been given the highest place of honor in heaven. [27]He does not need to offer sacrifices every day like the other high priests. They did this for their own sins first and then for the sins of the people. But Jesus did this once for all when he sacrificed himself on the cross. [28]Those who were high priests under the law of Moses were limited by human weakness. But after the law was given, God appointed his Son with an oath, and his Son has been made perfect forever.

CHAPTER 8
Christ Is Our High Priest

Here is the main point: Our High Priest sat down in the place of highest honor in heaven, at God's right hand. [2]There he ministers in the sacred tent, the true place of worship that was built by the Lord and not by human hands.

[3]And since every high priest is required to offer gifts and sacrifices, our High Priest must make an offering, too. [4]If he were here on earth, he would not even be a priest, since there already are priests who offer the gifts required by the law of Moses. [5]They serve in a place of worship that is only a copy, a shadow of the real one in heaven. For when Moses was getting ready to build the Tabernacle, God gave him this warning: "Be sure that you make everything according to the design I have shown you here on the mountain."* [6]But our High Priest has been given a ministry that is far superior to the ministry of those who serve under the old laws, for he is the one who guarantees for us a better covenant with God, based on better promises.

[7]If the first covenant had been faultless, there would have been no need for a second covenant to replace it. [8]But God himself found fault with the old one when he said:

"The day will come, says the Lord,
when I will make a new covenant
with the people of Israel and Judah.
[9]This covenant will not be like the one
I made with their ancestors

7:17 Ps 110:4. **7:21** Ps 110:4. **7:25** Or *able to save completely.* **8:5** Exod 25:40; 26:30.

7:20-26 God's unchanging oath regarding Christ's priesthood stated prophetically in Psalm 110:4 meant that Christ's priesthood was forever and was related to a better and final covenant. This permanence means that Christ will see our recovery through to the end, that he is always available to help, and that he is always our perfect model for godly living.

8:1-6 Christ, our High Priest, sits at the highest place of honor in heaven—God's right hand. This is the true place of worship, built by God, not by human hands like the Tabernacle, which was only a copy of the real worship place in heaven. Through Christ's death and resurrection the limited, earthly priesthood gave way to the perfect, heavenly priesthood. This heavenly priesthood is far superior: It is based on better promises and guarantees the needed resources for recovery.

8:7-13 Six centuries before Christ died on the cross to provide a new way for us to relate to God (see Luke 22:20), the prophet Jeremiah predicted that a "new covenant," totally unlike the Old Testament law, was needed to breach the separation between God and humans (Jeremiah 31:31-34). Thus, rather than turning back to the old legalistic ways of Judaism, the readers should have been aware that God's old program had been on its way out for a long time. They were looking for recovery in the wrong place. There is only one way to experience recovery and reconciliation—through faith in Jesus Christ.

when I took them by the hand
    and led them out of the land of Egypt.
They did not remain faithful to my
        covenant,
    so I turned my back on them, says the
        Lord.
¹⁰ But this is the new covenant I will make
    with the people of Israel on that day,
        says the Lord:
I will put my laws in their minds
    so they will understand them,
and I will write them on their hearts
    so they will obey them.
I will be their God,
    and they will be my people.
¹¹ And they will not need to teach their
        neighbors,
    nor will they need to teach their family,
        saying, 'You should know the Lord.'
For everyone, from the least to the greatest,
    will already know me.
¹² And I will forgive their wrongdoings,
    and I will never again remember their
        sins."*

¹³When God speaks of a new covenant, it means he has made the first one obsolete. It is now out of date and ready to be put aside.

CHAPTER 9
Old Rules about Worship

Now in that first covenant between God and Israel, there were regulations for worship and a sacred tent here on earth. ²There were two rooms in this tent. In the first room were a lampstand, a table, and loaves of holy bread on the table. This was called the Holy Place. ³Then there was a curtain, and behind the curtain was the second room called the Most

Holy Place. ⁴In that room were a gold incense altar and a wooden chest called the Ark of the Covenant, which was covered with gold on all sides. Inside the Ark were a gold jar containing some manna, Aaron's staff that sprouted leaves, and the stone tablets of the covenant with the Ten Commandments written on them. ⁵The glorious cherubim were above the Ark. Their wings were stretched out over the Ark's cover, the place of atonement. But we cannot explain all of these things now.

⁶When these things were all in place, the priests went in and out of the first room* regularly as they performed their religious duties. ⁷But only the high priest goes into the Most Holy Place, and only once a year, and always with blood, which he offers to God to cover his own sins and the sins the people have committed in ignorance. ⁸By these regulations the Holy Spirit revealed that the Most Holy Place was not open to the people as long as the first room and the entire system it represents were still in use.

⁹This is an illustration pointing to the present time. For the gifts and sacrifices that the priests offer are not able to cleanse the consciences of the people who bring them. ¹⁰For that old system deals only with food and drink and ritual washing—external regulations that are in effect only until their limitations can be corrected.

Christ Is the Perfect Sacrifice

¹¹So Christ has now become the High Priest over all the good things that have come. He has entered that great, perfect sanctuary in heaven, not made by human hands and not part of this created world. ¹²Once for all time

8:8-12 Jer 31:31-34. 9:6 Greek *first tent*; also in 9:8.

8:10-13 The new covenant established by God through Jesus Christ is exciting. God would write his laws on his people's hearts, giving them a new desire to obey him. They would have a special, close relationship with God and new fellowship with other believers. God would forgive their past sins and character defects. In Christ, we can receive spiritual and emotional healing and have all the help necessary for a successful recovery.
9:1-10 The regulations for worship in the Old Testament were striking and powerfully symbolized the painful consequences of sin. But the old sacrificial system was effective on a short-term basis and was not a permanent solution to the sin problem. It could not produce immediate personal access to God or a clear conscience. These regulations sufficed until God's final and complete revelation arrived in the person of Jesus Christ. Again we see that for those of us in need of recovery and spiritual transformation, Christ is the only viable option. Only through him can God effect permanent changes in our life.
9:11-15 There was absolutely no comparison between the ongoing sacrifices of the earthly Temple in Jerusalem and the sacrifice provided by Christ, our great High Priest and mediator. Christ accomplished what the Old Testament sacrificial system never could—once and for all, he completed redemption. Trusting the work that Christ did is the only way to have complete forgiveness, a clear conscience, and eternal life. Now when we put our faith in Christ, we are free to joyfully know and serve God.

he took blood into that Most Holy Place, but not the blood of goats and calves. He took his own blood, and with it he secured our salvation forever.

¹³Under the old system, the blood of goats and bulls and the ashes of a young cow could cleanse people's bodies from ritual defilement. ¹⁴Just think how much more the blood of Christ will purify our hearts from deeds that lead to death so that we can worship the living God. For by the power of the eternal Spirit, Christ offered himself to God as a perfect sacrifice for our sins. ¹⁵That is why he is the one who mediates the new covenant between God and people, so that all who are invited can receive the eternal inheritance God has promised them. For Christ died to set them free from the penalty of the sins they had committed under that first covenant.

¹⁶Now when someone dies and leaves a will, no one gets anything until it is proved that the person who wrote the will* is dead.* ¹⁷The will goes into effect only after the death of the person who wrote it. While the person is still alive, no one can use the will to get any of the things promised to them.

¹⁸That is why blood was required under the first covenant as a proof of death. ¹⁹For after Moses had given the people all of God's laws, he took the blood of calves and goats, along with water, and sprinkled both the book of God's laws and all the people, using branches of hyssop bushes and scarlet wool. ²⁰Then he said, "This blood confirms the covenant God has made with you."* ²¹And in the same way, he sprinkled blood on the sacred tent and on everything used for worship. ²²In fact, we can say that according to the law of Moses, nearly everything was purified by sprinkling with blood. Without the shedding of blood, there is no forgiveness of sins.

²³That is why the earthly tent and everything in it—which were copies of things in heaven—had to be purified by the blood of animals. But the real things in heaven had to be purified with far better sacrifices than the blood of animals.

²⁴For Christ has entered into heaven itself to appear now before God as our Advocate.* He did not go into the earthly place of worship, for that was merely a copy of the real Temple in heaven. ²⁵Nor did he enter heaven to offer himself again and again, like the earthly high priest who enters the Most Holy Place year after year to offer the blood of an

---

Self-Protection

READ HEBREWS 10:23-34

Recovery is not a battle anyone wins alone. We help each other to think and live in new ways. Alone, we are vulnerable to temptation; together, we form a shield of protection for one another.

The apostle Paul wrote: "In every battle you will need faith as your shield to stop the fiery arrows aimed at you by Satan" (Ephesians 6:16). Faith here refers to trusting in Christ for salvation. In general terms it also means being steadfast in our convictions. This can apply to our convictions about God's wisdom in the Bible or our confidence in the Twelve Steps. The shield of faith was likened to the shields carried by Roman soldiers, which covered the entire body. To advance in battle, a group of soldiers would assemble together, making a wall of shields for protection as they moved forward.

In like manner, we are told to stick together. The writer of Hebrews wrote: "Let us not neglect our meeting together, as some people do, but encourage and warn each other" (Hebrews 10:25). We are to take our place in a fellowship of people that provides us with the mutual protection we need to stand firm in recovery.

We need to assemble with others who share the common beliefs helpful in recovery. Our encouragement of one another, our shared faith in God and his Word, and the principles of the Twelve Steps will be a form of strength and protection as we advance in the recovery process. ***Turn to page 393, Hebrews 12.***

9:16a Or *covenant.* **9:16b** Or *Now when someone makes a covenant, it is necessary to ratify it with the death of a sacrifice.* **9:20** Exod 24:8. **9:24** Greek *on our behalf.*

animal. ²⁶If that had been necessary, he would have had to die again and again, ever since the world began. But no! He came once for all time, at the end of the age, to remove the power of sin forever by his sacrificial death for us.

²⁷And just as it is destined that each person dies only once and after that comes judgment, ²⁸so also Christ died only once as a sacrifice to take away the sins of many people. He will come again but not to deal with our sins again. This time he will bring salvation to all those who are eagerly waiting for him.

CHAPTER 10
Christ's Sacrifice Once for All

The old system in the law of Moses was only a shadow of the things to come, not the reality of the good things Christ has done for us. The sacrifices under the old system were repeated again and again, year after year, but they were never able to provide perfect cleansing for those who came to worship. ²If they could have provided perfect cleansing, the sacrifices would have stopped, for the worshipers would have been purified once for all time, and their feelings of guilt would have disappeared.

³But just the opposite happened. Those yearly sacrifices reminded them of their sins

10:5-7 Ps 40:6-8.

year after year. ⁴For it is not possible for the blood of bulls and goats to take away sins. ⁵That is why Christ, when he came into the world, said,

"You did not want animal sacrifices and
    grain offerings.
But you have given me a body so that
    I may obey you.
⁶No, you were not pleased with animals
    burned on the altar
or with other offerings for sin.
⁷Then I said, 'Look, I have come to do your
    will, O God—
just as it is written about me in the
    Scriptures.'"*

⁸Christ said, "You did not want animal sacrifices or grain offerings or animals burned on the altar or other offerings for sin, nor were you pleased with them" (though they are required by the law of Moses). ⁹Then he added, "Look, I have come to do your will." He cancels the first covenant in order to establish the second. ¹⁰And what God wants is for us to be made holy by the sacrifice of the body of Jesus Christ once for all time.

¹¹Under the old covenant, the priest stands before the altar day after day, offering sacrifices that can never take away sins. ¹²But our High Priest offered himself to God

9:27-28 Hope for the future must be based on our facing the reality of the past and present. Death (and the following judgment) is the ultimate reality of this life; even Jesus Christ, in his humanity, died! But because of his resurrection he is able to offer salvation and spare believers from the fear of judgment. This blend of reality and hope through faith can calm our fearful heart as we struggle with recovery issues. We can face any sin, any character defect, any hurt, knowing that Christ's sacrifice is completely sufficient to offer cleansing and new life.

10:3-10 As this section on the superiority of the new covenant (8:1–10:18) ends, the writer asserts that the ineffective repetition of old covenant sacrifices has now been replaced by Christ's coming and offering himself once and for all in accord with God's will. To not pursue recovery by faith in Christ is to openly reject the superior nature of God's will for history and for individual human lives. If we reject God's offer of salvation and transformation through Jesus Christ, we are rejecting the only means available to sustain us in permanent recovery.

10:19-25 This climactic section of Hebrews (10:19–13:25) begins with a summary of the argument for Christ's superiority, then shifts its emphasis to the transformed attitudes. Since Christ is the final redemptive sacrifice and great High Priest, we can enjoy the full privileges he has secured for us: personal access to God through Christ without an elaborate system, full assurance of our faith and salvation, hope for the future, and encouragement from other people of faith. Through Christ and a community of believers we can receive everything necessary for successful recovery.

10:24-25 Sometimes in recovery we may pull away from healthy relationships or fall into codependent or negative situations that undermine our recovery. These verses remind us that relationships with other believers are crucial to our spiritual growth; godly people can encourage us and hold us accountable. No one can stand alone for long in the recovery process. If we run from healthy relationships, we are running straight toward a painful relapse.

10:26-39 This "warning" summarizes the only way to a wholehearted pursuit of emotional and spiritual healing. First we can find release by repenting of sinful patterns and receiving forgiveness. Then we can take positive steps by strengthening our healthy behavioral patterns and attitudes, particularly our faith in God.

as one sacrifice for sins, good for all time. Then he sat down at the place of highest honor at God's right hand. ¹³There he waits until his enemies are humbled as a footstool under his feet. ¹⁴For by that one offering he perfected forever all those whom he is making holy.

¹⁵And the Holy Spirit also testifies that this is so. First he says,

¹⁶ "This is the new covenant I will make
  with my people on that day, says the
    Lord:
 I will put my laws in their hearts
  so they will understand them,
 and I will write them on their minds
  so they will obey them."

¹⁷Then he adds,

 "I will never again remember
  their sins and lawless deeds."*

¹⁸Now when sins have been forgiven, there is no need to offer any more sacrifices.

A Call to Persevere

¹⁹And so, dear brothers and sisters,* we can boldly enter heaven's Most Holy Place because of the blood of Jesus. ²⁰This is the new, life-giving way that Christ has opened up for us through the sacred curtain, by means of his death for us.*

²¹And since we have a great High Priest who rules over God's people, ²²let us go right into the presence of God, with true hearts fully trusting him. For our evil consciences have been sprinkled with Christ's blood to make us clean, and our bodies have been washed with pure water.

²³Without wavering, let us hold tightly to the hope we say we have, for God can be trusted to keep his promise. ²⁴Think of ways to encourage one another to outbursts of love and good deeds. ²⁵And let us not neglect our meeting together, as some people do, but encourage and warn each other, especially now that the day of his coming back again is drawing near.

²⁶Dear friends, if we deliberately continue sinning after we have received a full knowledge of the truth, there is no other sacrifice that will cover these sins. ²⁷There will be nothing to look forward to but the terrible expectation of God's judgment and the raging fire that will consume his enemies. ²⁸Anyone who refused to obey the law of Moses was put to death without mercy on

10:16-17 Jer 31:33-34. **10:19** Greek *brothers.*
10:20 Greek *his flesh.*

STEP **2**

Hope in Faith

BIBLE READING: Hebrews 11:1-10
We came to believe that a Power greater than ourselves could restore us to sanity.
Step Two is often referred to as "the hope step." In coming to believe that a Power greater than ourself can restore us to sanity, we will remember what it was like to live sanely and have the faith to hope that sanity can return.

"What is faith?" the Bible asks. "It is the confident assurance that what we hope for is going to happen. It is the evidence of things we cannot yet see" (Hebrews 11:1). How can we be confident that something we want is going to happen, especially if all of our hopes have been dashed? How can we risk believing that the life we hope for is waiting for us around the bend?

The Bible tells us that the key is in the nature of the higher Power we look to. We are told that "anyone who wants to come to him must believe that there is a God and that he rewards those who sincerely seek him" (Hebrews 11:6). If we see God as one who is reaching out to help us, we will be more eager to look for him. If our faith has not matured to that point yet, we can ask for help. One man came to Jesus asking him to help his young son who was afflicted by a demon. He said to Jesus, "'Have mercy on us and help us. Do something if you can.' 'What do you mean, "If I can"?' Jesus asked. 'Anything is possible if a person believes.' The father instantly replied, 'I do believe, but help me not to doubt!'" (Mark 9:22-24). We can start by asking God to help us have more faith. Then we can ask him for the courage to hope for a better future. *Turn to Step Three, page 21, Matthew 11.*

the testimony of two or three witnesses. 29Think how much more terrible the punishment will be for those who have trampled on the Son of God and have treated the blood of the covenant as if it were common and unholy. Such people have insulted and enraged the Holy Spirit who brings God's mercy to his people.

30For we know the one who said,

"I will take vengeance.
I will repay those who deserve it."

He also said,

"The Lord will judge his own people."*

31It is a terrible thing to fall into the hands of the living God.

32Don't ever forget those early days when you first learned about Christ. Remember how you remained faithful even though it meant terrible suffering. 33Sometimes you were exposed to public ridicule and were beaten, and sometimes you helped others who were suffering the same things. 34You suffered along with those who were thrown into jail. When all you owned was taken from you, you accepted it with joy. You knew you had better things waiting for you in eternity.

35Do not throw away this confident trust in the Lord, no matter what happens. Remember the great reward it brings you! 36Patient endurance is what you need now, so you will continue to do God's will. Then you will receive all that he has promised.

37 "For in just a little while,
the Coming One will come and not
delay.
38 And a righteous person will live by faith.
But I will have no pleasure in anyone
who turns away."*

39But we are not like those who turn their backs on God and seal their fate. We have faith that assures our salvation.

CHAPTER 11
Great Examples of Faith

What is faith? It is the confident assurance that what we hope for is going to happen. It is the evidence of things we cannot yet see. 2God gave his approval to people in days of old because of their faith.

3By faith we understand that the entire universe was formed at God's command, that what we now see did not come from anything that can be seen.

4It was by faith that Abel brought a more acceptable offering to God than Cain did. God accepted Abel's offering to show that he was a righteous man. And although Abel is long dead, he still speaks to us because of his faith.

5It was by faith that Enoch was taken up to heaven without dying—"suddenly he disappeared because God took him."* But before he was taken up, he was approved as pleasing to God. 6So, you see, it is impossible to please God without faith. Anyone who wants to come to him must believe that there is a God and that he rewards those who sincerely seek him.

7It was by faith that Noah built an ark to save his family from the flood. He obeyed God, who warned him about something that had never happened before. By his faith he condemned the rest of the world and was made right in God's sight.

8It was by faith that Abraham obeyed when God called him to leave home and go to another land that God would give him as his inheritance. He went without knowing where he was going. 9And even when he

10:30 Deut 32:35-36. **10:37-38** Hab 2:3-4. **11:5** Gen 5:24.

11:5-7 Enoch was unique (along with Elijah; 2 Kings 2) in that he did not die (11:5; Genesis 5:21-24). Noah also played a unique role with the ark, the Flood, and earth's new beginning (Genesis 6–9). These two Old Testament characters illustrate the utter necessity of having faith and being right in God's sight. As we trust and depend on God for each aspect of the recovery process, we can be confident that such trust pleases God and will be rewarded with his powerful help.
11:8-19 Abraham fathered the Jewish nation and repeatedly lived by faith as he encountered circumstances that seemed to undermine the fulfillment of God's promises. Sometimes in recovery it seems like forever before we see any changes. At such times we can remind ourself that people of God who are most famous for their faith had to persevere without seeing visible results. We can trust that God will come through for us, even when the struggle seems to go on forever. Abraham had to wait most of his lifetime to see God's promises even partially fulfilled.
11:20-31 The writer demonstrates that many people between the life of Abraham and Israel's entrance into the Promised Land exhibited exemplary faith. God accomplishes his purposes because of the faith of his people. As we trust him with every aspect of our life and recovery, he will accomplish the healing that is surely his will for us. If we trust in God, nothing is impossible!

reached the land God promised him, he lived there by faith—for he was like a foreigner, living in a tent. And so did Isaac and Jacob, to whom God gave the same promise. ¹⁰Abraham did this because he was confidently looking forward to a city with eternal foundations, a city designed and built by God.

¹¹It was by faith that Sarah together with Abraham was able to have a child, even though they were too old and Sarah was barren. Abraham believed that God would keep his promise.* ¹²And so a whole nation came from this one man, Abraham, who was too old to have any children—a nation with so many people that, like the stars of the sky and the sand on the seashore, there is no way to count them.

¹³All these faithful ones died without receiving what God had promised them, but they saw it all from a distance and welcomed the promises of God. They agreed that they were no more than foreigners and nomads here on earth. ¹⁴And obviously people who talk like that are looking forward to a country they can call their own. ¹⁵If they had meant the country they came from, they would have found a way to go back. ¹⁶But they were looking for a better place, a heavenly homeland. That is why God is not ashamed to be called their God, for he has prepared a heavenly city for them.

¹⁷It was by faith that Abraham offered Isaac as a sacrifice when God was testing him. Abraham, who had received God's promises, was ready to sacrifice his only son, Isaac, ¹⁸though God had promised him, "Isaac is the son through whom your descendants will be counted."* ¹⁹Abraham assumed that if Isaac died, God was able to bring him back to life again. And in a sense, Abraham did receive his son back from the dead.

²⁰It was by faith that Isaac blessed his two sons, Jacob and Esau. He had confidence in what God was going to do in the future.

²¹It was by faith that Jacob, when he was old and dying, blessed each of Joseph's sons and bowed in worship as he leaned on his staff.

²²And it was by faith that Joseph, when he was about to die, confidently spoke of God's bringing the people of Israel out of Egypt. He was so sure of it that he commanded them to carry his bones with them when they left!

11:11 Some manuscripts read *It was by faith that Sarah was able to have a child, even though she was too old and barren. Sarah believed that God would keep his promise.* **11:18** Gen 21:12.

Faith

READ HEBREWS 12:1-4

Our addiction interferes with our ability to win in the race of life. Many of us feel like a loser who has just dropped out of the race. Faith in God can give us the motivation to run the race, with a real chance at winning life's rewards.

Hebrews 11 has been called the "Hall of Faith." It mentions a long list of people whose lives were used by God because of their faith. The next chapter begins this way: "Since we are surrounded by such a huge crowd of witnesses to the life of faith, let us strip off every weight that slows us down, especially the sin that so easily hinders our progress. And let us run with endurance the race that God has set before us" (Hebrews 12:1).

This illustration referred to the ancient Olympic games. In Bible times men wore flowing robes. Before an event, the athletes would strip off their robes and lay them aside to run without encumbrance. If someone tried to compete in his robe, he would get tangled up, losing both the race and the prize.

It is God's will for us to win the race of life. The robe of our recurring sins needs to be laid aside. There will be pain from the exertion, but we are told to pace ourself and bear the pain with patience. And remember, others who have run the same race and finished well are cheering us on! *Turn to page 395, Hebrews 12.*

23It was by faith that Moses' parents hid him for three months. They saw that God had given them an unusual child, and they were not afraid of what the king might do.

24It was by faith that Moses, when he grew up, refused to be treated as the son of Pharaoh's daughter. 25He chose to share the oppression of God's people instead of enjoying the fleeting pleasures of sin. 26He thought it was better to suffer for the sake of the Messiah than to own the treasures of Egypt, for he was looking ahead to the great reward that God would give him. 27It was by faith that Moses left the land of Egypt. He was not afraid of the king. Moses kept right on going because he kept his eyes on the one who is invisible. 28It was by faith that Moses commanded the people of Israel to keep the Passover and to sprinkle blood on the doorposts so that the angel of death would not kill their firstborn sons.

29It was by faith that the people of Israel went right through the Red Sea as though they were on dry ground. But when the Egyptians followed, they were all drowned.

30It was by faith that the people of Israel marched around Jericho seven days, and the walls came crashing down.

31It was by faith that Rahab the prostitute did not die with all the others in her city who refused to obey God. For she had given a friendly welcome to the spies.

32Well, how much more do I need to say? It would take too long to recount the stories of the faith of Gideon, Barak, Samson, Jephthah, David, Samuel, and all the prophets. 33By faith these people overthrew kingdoms, ruled with justice, and received what God had promised them. They shut the mouths of lions, 34quenched the flames of fire, and escaped death by the edge of the sword. Their weakness was turned to strength. They became strong in battle and put whole armies to flight. 35Women received their loved ones back again from death.

But others trusted God and were tortured, preferring to die rather than turn from God and be free. They placed their hope in the resurrection to a better life. 36Some were mocked, and their backs were cut open with whips. Others were chained in dungeons. 37Some died by stoning, and some were sawed in half; others were killed with the sword. Some went about in skins of sheep and goats, hungry and oppressed and mistreated. 38They were too good for this world. They wandered over deserts and mountains, hiding in caves and holes in the ground.

39All of these people we have mentioned received God's approval because of their faith, yet none of them received all that God had promised. 40For God had far better things in mind for us that would also benefit them, for they can't receive the prize at the end of the race until we finish the race.*

CHAPTER 12
God's Discipline Proves His Love
Therefore, since we are surrounded by such a huge crowd of witnesses to the life of faith, let us strip off every weight that slows us down, especially the sin that so easily hinders our

11:40 Greek for us, for they apart from us can't finish.

11:32-39 The writer continues the list of Old Testament people who demonstrated powerful faith and received God's approval. Clearly, even in Old Testament times faith was not just a strict obedience to Mosaic law; it was heartfelt trust in a personal God. The readers would know that many before them had faced difficult times and persevered by faith. When we feel our faith faltering, it is good to remember others who have gone before us. We can turn both to the Bible and to other Christians in recovery for real-life testimonies of how God works powerfully through faith.
12:14-29 This is the last of the "warnings" throughout Hebrews (see 2:1-4; 3:7–4:13; 5:11–6:12; 10:26-39). In effect, the writer was confronting his readers about their apparent defection from Christ to Judaism and the Mosaic law. After exhorting the readers not to squander God's grace, the writer considers the serious consequences of rejecting faith in Christ and the recovery he offers. Our choices have eternal consequences! If we reject Christ, we also reject the only means for eternal salvation and recovery from our destructive dependency.
12:15 When we deal with difficult circumstances or face painful recovery issues, we may grow angry or bitter. Sometimes we don't perceive our own bitterness taking root; we need others to point it out to us. The feelings are understandable, especially if we have been victimized; allowing ourself to feel them can be a first step in recovery. But we need to forgive and to release the injustices and hurts to God in order to experience his overwhelming forgiveness (see Matthew 18:21-35). When we hang on to our bitterness, we not only hinder our own healing but also hurt others along the way.

progress. And let us run with endurance the race that God has set before us. ²We do this by keeping our eyes on Jesus, on whom our faith depends from start to finish.* He was willing to die a shameful death on the cross because of the joy he knew would be his afterward. Now he is seated in the place of highest honor beside God's throne in heaven. ³Think about all he endured when sinful people did such terrible things to him, so that you don't become weary and give up. ⁴After all, you have not yet given your lives in your struggle against sin.

⁵And have you entirely forgotten the encouraging words God spoke to you, his children? He said,

"My child, don't ignore it when the Lord
    disciplines you,
    and don't be discouraged when he
    corrects you.
⁶For the Lord disciplines those he loves,
    and he punishes those he accepts as his
    children."*

⁷As you endure this divine discipline, remember that God is treating you as his own children. Whoever heard of a child who was never disciplined? ⁸If God doesn't discipline you as he does all of his children, it means that you are illegitimate and are not really his children after all. ⁹Since we respect our earthly fathers who disciplined us, should we not all the more cheerfully submit to the discipline of our heavenly Father and live forever*?

¹⁰For our earthly fathers disciplined us for a few years, doing the best they knew how. But God's discipline is always right and good for us because it means we will share in his holiness. ¹¹No discipline is enjoyable while it is happening—it is painful! But afterward there will be a quiet harvest of right living for those who are trained in this way.

¹²So take a new grip with your tired hands and stand firm on your shaky legs. ¹³Mark out a straight path for your feet. Then those who follow you, though they are weak and lame, will not stumble and fall but will become strong.

A Call to Listen to God

¹⁴Try to live in peace with everyone, and seek to live a clean and holy life, for those who are not holy will not see the Lord. ¹⁵Look after each other so that none of you will miss out on the special favor of God. Watch out

12:2 Or *Jesus, the Originator and Perfecter of our faith.*
12:5-6 Prov 3:11-12. **12:9** Or *really live.*

Faith

READ HEBREWS 12:5-11
Some phases of our recovery may be very painful. We may feel that we are being punished for our failures. We may assume that bad things are happening to us because we are bad. And we may even begin to believe that God doesn't love us.

It may hurt when God disciplines us, but this in itself displays his love for us. The Bible says: "'My child, don't ignore it when the Lord disciplines you. . . . For the Lord disciplines those he loves, and he punishes those he accepts as his children.' As you endure this divine discipline, remember that God is treating you as his own children. Whoever heard of a child who was never disciplined? . . . God's discipline is always right and good for us because it means we will share in his holiness. No discipline is enjoyable while it is happening—it is painful! But afterward there will be a quiet harvest of right living for those who are trained in this way" (Hebrews 12:5-7, 10-11).

Recovery is a time of correction, a time of facing problems and character flaws and changing incorrect beliefs. There may be seasons when we do have to pay for our past. God will use these times to redirect our life toward something better. His correction isn't arbitrary or abusive, but it is still painful. Knowing that God's discipline demonstrates his love for us can be comforting in the midst of our pain. It helps to remember that his love will allow only that which is for our ultimate good.
Turn to page 407, James 3.

that no bitter root of unbelief rises up among you, for whenever it springs up, many are corrupted by its poison. [16]Make sure that no one is immoral or godless like Esau. He traded his birthright as the oldest son for a single meal. [17]And afterward, when he wanted his father's blessing, he was rejected. It was too late for repentance, even though he wept bitter tears.

[18]You have not come to a physical mountain, to a place of flaming fire, darkness, gloom, and whirlwind, as the Israelites did at Mount Sinai when God gave them his laws. [19]For they heard an awesome trumpet blast and a voice with a message so terrible that they begged God to stop speaking. [20]They staggered back under God's command: "If even an animal touches the mountain, it must be stoned to death."* [21]Moses himself was so frightened at the sight that he said, "I am terrified and trembling."*

[22]No, you have come to Mount Zion, to the city of the living God, the heavenly Jerusalem, and to thousands of angels in joyful assembly. [23]You have come to the assembly of God's firstborn children, whose names are written in heaven. You have come to God himself, who is the judge of all people. And you have come to the spirits of the redeemed in heaven who have now been made perfect. [24]You have come to Jesus, the one who mediates the new covenant between God and people, and to the sprinkled blood, which graciously forgives instead of crying out for vengeance as the blood of Abel did.

[25]See to it that you obey God, the one who is speaking to you. For if the people of Israel did not escape when they refused to listen to Moses, the earthly messenger, how terrible our danger if we reject the One who speaks to us from heaven! [26]When God spoke from Mount Sinai his voice shook the earth, but now he makes another promise: "Once again I will shake not only the earth but the heavens also."* [27]This means that the things on earth will be shaken, so that only eternal things will be left.

[28]Since we are receiving a Kingdom that cannot be destroyed, let us be thankful and please God by worshiping him with holy fear and awe. [29]For our God is a consuming fire.

CHAPTER 13
Concluding Words

Continue to love each other with true Christian love.* [2]Don't forget to show hospitality to strangers, for some who have done this have entertained angels without realizing it! [3]Don't forget about those in prison. Suffer with them as though you were there yourself. Share the sorrow of those being mistreated, as though you feel their pain in your own bodies.

[4]Give honor to marriage, and remain faithful to one another in marriage. God will surely judge people who are immoral and those who commit adultery.

[5]Stay away from the love of money; be satisfied with what you have. For God has said,

"I will never fail you.
    I will never forsake you."*

[6]That is why we can say with confidence,

"The Lord is my helper,
    so I will not be afraid.
What can mere mortals do to me?"*

[7]Remember your leaders who first taught you the word of God. Think of all the good

---

12:20 Exod 19:13.   **12:21** Deut 9:19.   **12:26** Hag 2:6.   **13:1** Greek *with brotherly love.*   **13:5** Deut 31:6, 8.   **13:6** Ps 118:6.

12:22-24 There is a wonderful reward waiting for those who, by faith in Christ, have endured in the recovery process. The references to Mount Zion, Jerusalem, angels, the firstborn, God, mediation, and blood were intended to show that the new covenant and Christ offer the very things that the readers mistakenly sought by returning to Judaism. Again we see that full spiritual recovery is available only through faith in Jesus Christ.

13:1-6 The writer lists practical commands for faithfulness in service to others—to strangers, prisoners, those who are suffering, and to our spouse. We are also warned about the love of money. Perhaps the readers were seriously struggling in these areas, even as many professing believers struggle today. Many of us with a dysfunctional background struggle to determine which behaviors and attitudes are acceptable; God's clear standards can guide us. We can be confident that God's presence and power are available to help us practice right living.

13:7, 17 Many of us in recovery may have difficulty dealing with authority figures. Apparently the readers of Hebrews, in returning to Judaism, were ignoring their spiritual leaders. So the writer admonished his readers to imitate the faith and lifestyle of their leaders and to obey them and not cause them sorrow. In our recovery work, let us remember the importance of leaders in our life, especially those who model godliness and are concerned about our spiritual growth.

that has come from their lives, and trust the Lord as they do.

[8]Jesus Christ is the same yesterday, today, and forever. [9]So do not be attracted by strange, new ideas. Your spiritual strength comes from God's special favor, not from ceremonial rules about food, which don't help those who follow them.

[10]We have an altar from which the priests in the Temple on earth have no right to eat. [11]Under the system of Jewish laws, the high priest brought the blood of animals into the Holy Place as a sacrifice for sin, but the bodies of the animals were burned outside the camp. [12]So also Jesus suffered and died outside the city gates in order to make his people holy by shedding his own blood. [13]So let us go out to him outside the camp and bear the disgrace he bore. [14]For this world is not our home; we are looking forward to our city in heaven, which is yet to come.

[15]With Jesus' help, let us continually offer our sacrifice of praise to God by proclaiming the glory of his name. [16]Don't forget to do good and to share what you have with those in need, for such sacrifices are very pleasing to God.

[17]Obey your spiritual leaders and do what they say. Their work is to watch over your souls, and they know they are accountable to God. Give them reason to do this joyfully and not with sorrow. That would certainly not be for your benefit.

[18]Pray for us, for our conscience is clear and we want to live honorably in everything we do. [19]I especially need your prayers right now so that I can come back to you soon.

[20-21]And now, may the God of peace, who brought again from the dead our Lord Jesus, equip you with all you need for doing his will. May he produce in you, through the power of Jesus Christ, all that is pleasing to him. Jesus is the great Shepherd of the sheep by an everlasting covenant, signed with his blood. To him be glory forever and ever. Amen.

[22]I urge you, dear brothers and sisters,* please listen carefully to what I have said in this brief letter.

[23]I want you to know that our brother Timothy is now out of jail. If he comes here soon, I will bring him with me to see you.

[24]Give my greetings to all your leaders and to the other believers there. The Christians from Italy send you their greetings.

[25]May God's grace be with you all.

13:22 Greek *brothers.*

13:8, 15-16 Even if our human leaders were to fail or be abusive, Jesus Christ is totally consistent and trustworthy. He will always be there for us, no matter what. As that kind of God and friend, Christ deserves to receive the new covenant equivalent of old covenant sacrifices: (1) praise for who he is and what he has done; (2) good works of service; and (3) sharing with others in need (see 13:2-3). These activities all support an essential step in our ongoing recovery—telling others what God has done in our life and reaching out to people in need.

13:20-25 The letter to the Hebrews concludes with a double benediction. The first is a summary prayer, asking for the power of Christ's resurrection to enable the readers to do God's will and please him. Unlike some human fathers, God the Father readily helps his children to succeed by equipping them to do his will. This leads beautifully to the final concept of the letter—grace. God will provide us with what we need to overcome our dependency, according to his grace and mercy.

REFLECTIONS ON

HEBREWS

✳insights ABOUT THE PERSON OF CHRIST

Hebrews 1:7-13 quotes from several messianic psalms, showing that even though angels are powerful spirits, Christ's power and glory are far greater because of: Christ's clear right to rule as messianic King; his power over Creation and the final re-creation when it occurs; and his current status of honor beside the Father. Christ can provide all the resources necessary for our recovery when we entrust our life to his greatness and his loving plan for us.

It would be terrifying to admit our failures to a perfect God if Jesus wasn't our High Priest. But we see in **Hebrews 4:14–5:3** that Jesus became a man and is able to deal gently with our weaknesses because he understands our problems. Unlike the human priests, Jesus Christ, the ultimate High Priest, has already been glorified in heaven. He suffered the same temptations we do, but did not sin; yet he became the sacrifice for the sins of the world. That combination of glory and understanding beckons us to pray confidently and continually for God's grace and mercy. The first steps in recovery involve admitting powerlessness over our problems, acknowledging that only God can restore us, and turning our will and life over to God. Hebrews 4:14-16 gives us the scriptural confidence that as we work those steps, God can and will give us the mercy and grace we need.

✳insights ABOUT ANGELS

Although Jesus is far superior to the angels, in **Hebrews 1:14** we are also told that angels are involved in helping God's people. Angels are God's servants who constantly serve and protect those who have already entered the process of recovery through faith in Christ. We may also interpret this verse to mean that God's "guardian angels" are somehow watching over all those who will yet receive salvation by faith.

✳insights ABOUT GOD'S TRANSFORMING POWER

In **Hebrews 2:4** the power of God to confirm the message of salvation through "signs and wonders" is tremendously impressive. In the apostles' generation (see 2 Corinthians 12:12), which was drawing to a close, miracles were more the rule in the newborn church than the exception. Though miraculous healings and immediate transformations may still happen today, it seems more likely that recovery is often a long process, even for committed believers with great faith. Nevertheless, the signs and wonders God demonstrated in the past remind us that he still works just as powerfully, though perhaps in different ways. The "gifts of the Holy Spirit" God assigns to us may have more to do with perseverance or a new ability to resist temptation, but they are no less miraculous than an immediate healing by God.

✳insights ABOUT ACCOUNTABILITY AND RESPONSIBILITY

Most of **Hebrews 3:7-13** is a paraphrase of Psalm 95:7-11. The writer was reminding his Jewish audience of the mistakes their ancestors had made, recalling how they had been unfaithful to God and had suffered the painful consequences. The writer used past events to show his readers that they would be held accountable to live out their faith in whatever context God placed them. Most recovery programs incorporate this kind of accountability through such things as attending meetings and working with sponsors. These verses underline the importance of such measures, especially obeying the living God, to whom we are most accountable.

In **Hebrews 3:14-19** the writer confirms the need to act immediately as well as the necessity to accept full responsibility for wrong actions. The urgency to act immediately is underlined here by the emphasis on "today" in Psalm 95:7. The importance of taking responsibility becomes clear as we see that the Israelites truly had no one to blame but themselves for their sojourn in the wilderness. Acting immediately and taking responsibility for our life are both crucial aspects of the recovery process.

insights ABOUT TRUE FAITH

In **Hebrews 11:1-3, 39-40** we find that faith blends our trust in the dependability of God working in the unseen spiritual realm and our reliance upon the evidence of God's past actions in the real world. Those who want a vibrant spiritual life must live by such faith (11:2). Amazingly, by trusting and obeying God, we can still make a place for ourself in the "Hall of Faith." The day of induction is still in the future! Seeking approval from other people is a constant battle for some of us in recovery. We need to remember that we cannot please everyone. We will make progress only when we stop trying to please others and put our trust in God, following his will for our life.

    Hebrews 12:1-3 shows us that many "witnesses," including some very unlikely candidates, have already "won" the race of faith along the rocky road of recovery. The author of Hebrews advises us to strip off our weights and sins that hinder us—chemical dependencies, immoral sex, unbalanced work habits, even false religious activities—and focus on Christ every step of the way, knowing that Jesus suffered a shameful death for us and emerged victorious (see 4:14-15). Such perseverance in faith can help us face the reality of delayed gratification and prevent burnout in recovery.

insights ABOUT GOD'S DISCIPLINE

We are reminded in **Hebrews 12:5-10** that true discipline is a form of loving correction, not hateful destruction. Many of us have suffered painful consequences because of our dependency. We may have become angry and wondered why God allowed us to suffer so deeply. Often, painful consequences are used by God for discipline. But God does not allow us to suffer because he wants revenge or he wants to destroy us. He allows us to suffer because he loves us. Sometimes harsh discipline is the only way to break through our denial and get us into recovery. As we look back, we can realize that our most painful days led to our first steps in recovery. Through the pain we realized how powerless we were and turned to God for help. By allowing us to suffer, God was leading us into a vital relationship with himself.

JAMES

THE BIG PICTURE

A. WISDOM: THE FOUNDATION OF RECOVERY (1:1-27)
B. FAITH: THE SUBSTANCE OF RECOVERY (2:1-26)
C. SELF-CONTROL: SETTING BOUNDARIES IN RECOVERY (3:1-18)
D. HUMILITY: THE ATTITUDE OF RECOVERY (4:1-17)
E. GIVING OF OURSELF: THE EVIDENCE OF RECOVERY (5:1-20)

When we think of hypocrisy, we tend to think of those who overtly live inconsistent lives, people who live in constant denial. Yet in one way or another we are all hypocrites at times. This is true in the church community as well as in our recovery group. We have all said that we believe in something, only to prove by our actions that we really don't!

James—the half brother of Jesus and one of the leaders of the Jerusalem church—wrote bluntly against hypocrisy. He recognized that being human means that we tend to hear God's Word without putting it into practice. His goal was simple: to get his audience, and all believers, to face their denial and start acting on what they claim to believe.

James challenged his readers to be full of wisdom, faith, forgiveness, self-control, and generosity to others. He encouraged them to not rely on mind games or tricks but to simply do what God asked them to do. If their progress started anywhere, it started with an admission that they were responsible to obey God. Only then could they conquer denial and forge ahead with the activities and attitudes that reflected God's will.

It is easy to buy into a recovery program in principle but never take the steps necessary for progress. James reminds us that just saying we believe God can help us is not enough. We need to show our faith and commitment by taking actual steps of faith. If we don't take active steps toward recovery, we will never move forward in the process.

THE BOTTOM LINE

PURPOSE: To show God's people how to live. AUTHOR: James, the half brother of Jesus. AUDIENCE: Probably primarily the Jewish believers living in Gentile communities outside of Palestine. DATE WRITTEN: This short letter was probably written between A.D. 44 and A.D. 49, before the Jerusalem Council held in A.D. 50 (Acts 15:1-35). SETTING: James wrote to the persecuted believers who were once part of the church in Jerusalem. He wanted to encourage them to live out their faith in everyday life. KEY VERSE: "Confess your sins to each other and pray for each other so that you may be healed" (5:16). KEY PEOPLE AND RELATIONSHIPS: James with his audience.

RECOVERY THEMES

The Importance of Action: If faith can be alive, it can also be dead. Dead faith is belief that does not prove itself in action. It claims to be something when it is not. Turning our life over to God always involves action. If we simply say that we have entrusted our life to God but do not make amends to others or confess our wrongs, then we are only fooling ourself. Effective recovery involves following through on our profession of faith and good intentions.

Gaining Strength from Hard Trials: Strength of character comes from patiently facing life's problems. Since most of us try to avoid our problems, how can we develop strength of character? We can learn to welcome trials and problems as opportunities to pray for wisdom, to ask God to give us patience, and to learn to depend on him. When we turn to God in times of trial, he can teach us the lessons we need to grow spiritually and make progress in recovery.

True Recovery Leads to Wise Speech: One of the hardest things for us to control is our tongue (1:26). James gives us very practical advice about how to handle our tongue. We are to ask God for wisdom, be slow to speak, and listen more than we talk. Since our speech is a reflection of what is in our heart, we can check our speech for clues to our inner strengths and weaknesses. As we take our personal inventory and confess our sins to God, he will begin to change us inside. Only then will we find our inner change reflected in our words.

CHAPTER 1
Greetings from James
This letter is from James, a slave of God and of the Lord Jesus Christ.

It is written to Jewish Christians scattered among the nations.*

Greetings!

Faith and Endurance
[2]Dear brothers and sisters,* whenever trouble comes your way, let it be an opportunity for joy. [3]For when your faith is tested, your endurance has a chance to grow. [4]So let it grow, for when your endurance is fully developed, you will be strong in character and ready for anything.

[5]If you need wisdom—if you want to know what God wants you to do—ask him, and he will gladly tell you. He will not resent your asking. [6]But when you ask him, be sure that you really expect him to answer, for a doubtful mind is as unsettled as a wave of the sea that is driven and tossed by the wind. [7]People like that should not expect to receive anything from the Lord. [8]They can't make up their minds. They waver back and forth in everything they do.

[9]Christians who are* poor should be glad,

1:1 Greek *To the twelve tribes in the dispersion.* **1:2** Greek *brothers;* also in 1:16, 19. **1:9** Greek *The brother who is.*

1:2-4 Difficulties and temptations are facts of life for everyone, particularly those of us with a background of addiction, abuse, or other dysfunction. We may be tempted to return to our destructive behaviors. As we face difficult times, though, our attitude can make all the difference. James tells us to be happy as we face difficulties and temptations. This is hardly a natural reaction to a painful situation. Seeing our trials as building blocks to God's work in our life, however, may help us change our negative attitude toward tough times. We can have joy during these trials because through them we learn patience, an essential ingredient for successful recovery.

1:5 How many times have we scolded ourself for making unwise decisions? All of us have made wrong choices that have led us into trouble, ultimately affecting our relationship with God and with others. When we ask God for wisdom, he is more than willing to give it. Since God is the source of all wisdom, we can make fewer unwise decisions by turning to him for guidance. In recovery we are told to improve our conscious contact with God so we can better know his will for us. This can be achieved by studying God's Word and praying regularly.

1:19-20 Who or what is in control of our life? Is it God? Is it other people? Is it a controlling dependency or compulsion or an overpowering emotion? The issue of control is vital to our spiritual growth and recovery. For some of us, the emotion of anger is overpowering. James advises us to listen before we speak, to have self-control, and to be patient, not letting anger control our actions in any situation. We may be angry over our past as well as over current events. To control our anger, we need to give our life over to God. Even when we feel out of control, he can help us maintain our composure. He can give us the strength and wisdom to think and listen before we speak or act.

for God has honored them. ¹⁰And those who are rich should be glad, for God has humbled them. They will fade away like a flower in the field. ¹¹The hot sun rises and dries up the grass; the flower withers, and its beauty fades away. So also, wealthy people will fade away with all of their achievements.

¹²God blesses the people who patiently endure testing. Afterward they will receive the crown of life that God has promised to those who love him. ¹³And remember, no one who wants to do wrong should ever say, "God is tempting me." God is never tempted to do wrong, and he never tempts anyone else either. ¹⁴Temptation comes from the lure of our own evil desires. ¹⁵These evil desires lead to evil actions, and evil actions lead to death. ¹⁶So don't be misled, my dear brothers and sisters.

¹⁷Whatever is good and perfect comes to us from God above, who created all heaven's lights.* Unlike them, he never changes or casts shifting shadows. ¹⁸In his goodness he chose to make us his own children by giving us his true word. And we, out of all creation, became his choice possession.

Listening and Doing

¹⁹My dear brothers and sisters, be quick to listen, slow to speak, and slow to get angry. ²⁰Your anger can never make things right in God's sight.

²¹So get rid of all the filth and evil in your lives, and humbly accept the message God has planted in your hearts, for it is strong enough to save your souls.

²²And remember, it is a message to obey, not just to listen to. If you don't obey, you are only fooling yourself. ²³For if you just listen and don't obey, it is like looking at your face in a mirror but doing nothing to improve your appearance. ²⁴You see yourself, walk away, and forget what you look like. ²⁵But if you keep looking steadily into God's perfect law—the law that sets you free—and if you do what it says and don't forget what you heard, then God will bless you for doing it.

²⁶If you claim to be religious but don't control your tongue, you are just fooling yourself, and your religion is worthless. ²⁷Pure and lasting religion in the sight of God our Father means that we must care for orphans and widows in their troubles, and refuse to let the world corrupt us.

1:17 Greek *from above, from the Father of lights.*

STEP

10

Looking in the Mirror

BIBLE READING: James 1:21-25

We continued to take personal inventory and when we were wrong promptly admitted it.

How many times do we look in the mirror each day? Suppose we looked in the mirror and found that we had mustard smeared around our mouth. Wouldn't we immediately wash our face and clean up the problem? In the same way, we need to routinely look at ourself in our "spiritual mirror," the Bible. Then if anything is wrong, we can take the proper steps to fix it.

James uses a similar illustration to show how God's Word should be like a spiritual mirror in our life. He said: "And remember, it is a message to obey, not just to listen to. If you don't obey, you are only fooling yourself. For if you just listen and don't obey, it is like looking at your face in a mirror but doing nothing to improve your appearance. You see yourself, walk away, and forget what you look like. But if you keep looking steadily into God's perfect law—the law that sets you free—and if you do what it says and don't forget what you heard, then God will bless you for doing it" (James 1:22-25).

This illustration supports the sensibleness of making a routine personal inventory. As we examine our life, we need to respond with immediate action if something has changed since we last looked. If we put off taking care of a problem, it may soon slip our mind. Just as we would think it foolish to go all day knowing there is mustard on our face, it is not logical to notice a problem that could lead to a fall and not correct it promptly. *Turn to page 431, 1 John 1.*

CHAPTER 2
A Warning against Prejudice

My dear brothers and sisters,* how can you claim that you have faith in our glorious Lord Jesus Christ if you favor some people more than others?

²For instance, suppose someone comes into your meeting* dressed in fancy clothes and expensive jewelry, and another comes in who is poor and dressed in shabby clothes. ³If you give special attention and a good seat to the rich person, but you say to the poor one, "You can stand over there, or else sit on the floor"— well, ⁴doesn't this discrimination show that you are guided by wrong motives?

⁵Listen to me, dear brothers and sisters. Hasn't God chosen the poor in this world to be rich in faith? Aren't they the ones who will inherit the Kingdom he promised to those who love him? ⁶And yet, you insult the poor man! Isn't it the rich who oppress you and drag you into court? ⁷Aren't they the ones who slander Jesus Christ, whose noble name you bear?

⁸Yes indeed, it is good when you truly obey our Lord's royal command found in the Scriptures: "Love your neighbor as yourself."* ⁹But if you pay special attention to the rich, you are committing a sin, for you are guilty of breaking that law.

¹⁰And the person who keeps all of the laws except one is as guilty as the person who has broken all of God's laws. ¹¹For the same God who said, "Do not commit adultery," also said, "Do not murder."* So if you murder someone, you have broken the entire law, even if you do not commit adultery.

¹²So whenever you speak, or whatever you do, remember that you will be judged by the law of love, the law that set you free. ¹³For there will be no mercy for you if you have not been merciful to others. But if you have been merciful, then God's mercy toward you will win out over his judgment against you.

Faith without Good Deeds Is Dead

¹⁴Dear brothers and sisters, what's the use of saying you have faith if you don't prove it by your actions? That kind of faith can't save anyone. ¹⁵Suppose you see a brother or sister who needs food or clothing, ¹⁶and you say, "Well, good-bye and God bless you; stay warm and eat well"—but then you don't give that person any food or clothing. What good does that do?

¹⁷So you see, it isn't enough just to have faith. Faith that doesn't show itself by good deeds is no faith at all—it is dead and useless.

¹⁸Now someone may argue, "Some people have faith; others have good deeds." I say, "I can't see your faith if you don't have good deeds, but I will show you my faith through my good deeds."

¹⁹Do you still think it's enough just to believe that there is one God? Well, even the demons believe this, and they tremble in terror! ²⁰Fool! When will you ever learn that faith that does not result in good deeds is useless?

²¹Don't you remember that our ancestor Abraham was declared right with God because of what he did when he offered his son Isaac

2:1 Greek *brothers;* also in 2:5, 14. **2:2** Greek *synagogue.* **2:8** Lev 19:18. **2:11** Exod 20:13-14; Deut 5:17-18.

2:1-9 Since participation in recovery may lead to rejection by others, the process can be painful. Old friends may reject us for trying to escape our bondage. Sometimes a Christian community or society at large may reject us, treating us like unworthy outcasts because of their prejudice. We all need acceptance. Jesus intended for the Christian community to graciously accept and love people whether they are wealthy and influential or poor and homeless. We need to welcome outcasts who are honestly struggling with their problems. Jesus calls us to treat others just as we want them to treat us (see Matthew 7:12).

2:14-26 Faith, the cornerstone of recovery, needs to be accompanied by action. Some of us may have found it easy to admit we needed God's help, but when called upon to actively prove our faith, we refused. We all have made commitments that we failed to back up with our actions. James left us this powerful reminder: "Faith that doesn't show itself by good deeds is no faith at all—it is dead and useless" (2:17). If we believe in the principles of recovery but refuse to act upon them, we are not in recovery. If we believe God can help us but refuse to obey his will, we prove that our faith is dead. True faith in God expresses itself in committed actions; our actions need to back up our words if we want to succeed in recovery.

3:1-2 James was deeply aware of the destructive power of words. We all are guilty of offending others by our words or actions. When we offend someone, we need to ask forgiveness and make amends for the wrongs we have committed. This is an essential part of the recovery process. Sometimes a quiet change of behavior can be the most effective way to make amends. By treating others with respect, we can slowly rebuild the trust we have destroyed. As we follow God's program for healthy living, we can learn to encourage, instead of offend, others with our words and deeds.

JAMES & JUDE

It is difficult to live up to the high standards set by older brothers and sisters. It can be equally difficult, and sometimes more painful, to live down the embarrassing reputation of an older sibling. James and Jude had to deal with both challenges. Their older half brother, Jesus, was both perfect and embarrassing.

It is probable that Mary, their mother, had always told James and Jude that Jesus was unique. But it is doubtful that they had any idea just how special Jesus was. One thing is certain: Jesus must have been a hard act to follow. It must have been difficult for James, Jude, and the rest of their siblings to feel close to their wonderful, though different, big half brother. The situation probably became even worse after their father, Joseph, died. As the oldest child, Jesus probably had to take on the role of substitute dad.

After Jesus' public ministry began, James and Jude took a stand-back-and-watch attitude. One day Jesus would do great miracles and be acclaimed as a hero. The next he would present a convicting message and offend the powerful religious and political authorities. He claimed to be not only the promised Messiah, but also God himself! At this point, James and Jude probably thought that their half brother had gone off the deep end. In the end, Jesus was sentenced to death.

James and Jude had lost their father, Joseph, when they were young. Now they had lost their famous, though embarrassing, older sibling. Could the family recover? The resurrection of Jesus brought the resounding answer: *yes!* After Jesus rose from the dead, he overcame the doubts of his younger half brothers who later became leaders in the early church. Their relationships with Jesus had been restored. Both brothers are remembered for the books in the Bible they wrote.

The transforming power of Christ's resurrection is still available to us today. As we read of the painful trial and death of Jesus, we see God's loving sacrifice on our behalf. As we claim his resurrection and experience its power in our life, we discover that the power that transformed James and Jude can transform us, too.

STRENGTHS AND ACCOMPLISHMENTS:
- James and Jude apparently wanted to understand and know Jesus.
- Both grew beyond the relational problems that surely existed in their family.
- Both became effective leaders and writers.

WEAKNESSES AND MISTAKES:
- James and Jude did not really understand Jesus until after his resurrection.
- They became disillusioned with Jesus' claims when he faced opposition.

LESSONS FROM THEIR LIVES:
- Finding our own identity when following gifted siblings can be painful.
- Even the confused and disillusioned can regain trust and hope.
- Recovery offers hope for restoring broken relationships.

KEY VERSE:
[Jesus said,] "Anyone who does the will of my Father in heaven is my brother and sister and mother!" (Matthew 12:50).

James and Jude are named or alluded to in the Gospels and Acts 1:14. James is mentioned in Acts 15; 21; Galatians 2; the book of James; and Jude 1:1. Jude's name is found in Jude 1:1.

---

on the altar? ²²You see, he was trusting God so much that he was willing to do whatever God told him to do. His faith was made complete by what he did—by his actions. ²³And so it happened just as the Scriptures say: "Abraham believed God, so God declared him to be righteous."* He was even called "the friend of God."* ²⁴So you see, we are made right with God by what we do, not by faith alone.

²⁵Rahab the prostitute is another example

of this. She was made right with God by her actions—when she hid those messengers and sent them safely away by a different road. ²⁶Just as the body is dead without a spirit, so also faith is dead without good deeds.

CHAPTER 3
Controlling the Tongue
Dear brothers and sisters,* not many of you should become teachers in the church, for

2:23a Gen 15:6. **2:23b** See Isa 41:8. **3:1** Greek *brothers;* also in 3:10.

we who teach will be judged by God with greater strictness.

²We all make many mistakes, but those who control their tongues can also control themselves in every other way. ³We can make a large horse turn around and go wherever we want by means of a small bit in its mouth. ⁴And a tiny rudder makes a huge ship turn wherever the pilot wants it to go, even though the winds are strong. ⁵So also, the tongue is a small thing, but what enormous damage it can do. A tiny spark can set a great forest on fire. ⁶And the tongue is a flame of fire. It is full of wickedness that can ruin your whole life. It can turn the entire course of your life into a blazing flame of destruction, for it is set on fire by hell itself.

⁷People can tame all kinds of animals and birds and reptiles and fish, ⁸but no one can tame the tongue. It is an uncontrollable evil, full of deadly poison. ⁹Sometimes it praises our Lord and Father, and sometimes it breaks out into curses against those who have been made in the image of God. ¹⁰And so blessing and cursing come pouring out of the same mouth. Surely, my brothers and sisters, this is not right! ¹¹Does a spring of water bubble out with both fresh water and bitter water? ¹²Can you pick olives from a fig tree or figs from a grapevine? No, and you can't draw fresh water from a salty pool.

True Wisdom Comes from God

¹³If you are wise and understand God's ways, live a life of steady goodness so that only good deeds will pour forth. And if you don't brag about the good you do, then you will be truly wise! ¹⁴But if you are bitterly jealous and there is selfish ambition in your hearts, don't brag about being wise. That is the worst kind of lie. ¹⁵For jealousy and selfishness are not God's kind of wisdom. Such things are earthly, unspiritual, and motivated by the Devil. ¹⁶For wherever there is

3:3-12 The tongue is difficult to control, but what it does is extremely important. Like a rudder that steers a ship or a bit that directs a horse, our tongue does much to control and shape our life. Our speech may have destroyed our relationships, which caused us great pain. Our tongue may be out of control, enslaved to our destructive dependency. If this is so, our recovery must include yielding our tongue to God's control. Even when we feel powerless to control our destructive words, God can still tame our tongue. As he transforms our heart, our words will soon begin to reflect this change. God can then use our words to heal our relationships and encourage others in the recovery process.

3:13-18 Wisdom is essential to recovery. It must, however, be godly wisdom, not earthly wisdom. Earthly wisdom leads to selfishness and pride, invariably causing confusion and strife. True wisdom is based on the knowledge of God. It brings peace and leads to selfless living and faith that works; it never distinguishes between groups of people but treats everyone with respect and love. Godly wisdom allows us to admit our failures and rebuild our life from the ashes of defeat. It frees us from our destructive dependency; it helps us live for others and builds relationships that will support our recovery.

4:1-4 A right relationship with God is essential to the recovery process. Most of us would like to receive the freedom God offers, but we generally make mistakes that hold us back: (1) We try to gain our freedom by working hard. We forget to ask God for help and thus never receive the life that God wants to give us; (2) if we do ask God for help, we ask with wrong motives. We ask for his blessings to satisfy our personal pleasure, ignoring the fact that seeking friendship with the world makes us God's enemies. God wants to give us abundant lives so we can tell others about him. We experience the freedom God offers by drawing close to and asking for his guidance and help.

4:6-10 Most of us have a hard time modeling submission and humility—qualities that are essential to the recovery process because they show dependence on God and a willingness to be guided by him. Satan's pride—and our adoption of it—opposes God's program for healthy and godly living. As many of us know from experience, the way of pride and selfishness only leads to confusion and strife. True contentment comes only when we submit our life to God and his program. As we admit our failures and humbly seek to do God's will, we will draw closer to God. As we draw close to God, the grip of our dependency will weaken, and he will lift us up to rebuild our life.

4:11-12 Many Christian communities are rendered ineffective because of self-righteous criticism. People become critical of anyone who doesn't measure up to their ideals of perfection. Some of us may have experienced this kind of destructive criticism as our addiction became public. Perhaps we even left a church community for that very reason. Sadly, some of us are also guilty of criticizing others. We may look down on people who make slower progress than we do in the recovery process. We must maintain healthy humility. No one is perfect except God; only he is in a position to judge others (see Romans 14:10-12). We need to focus on our own faults, including our tendency to criticize others. If we don't, our recovery is at risk.

jealousy and selfish ambition, there you will find disorder and every kind of evil.

¹⁷But the wisdom that comes from heaven is first of all pure. It is also peace loving, gentle at all times, and willing to yield to others. It is full of mercy and good deeds. It shows no partiality and is always sincere. ¹⁸And those who are peacemakers will plant seeds of peace and reap a harvest of goodness.

CHAPTER 4
Drawing Close to God

What is causing the quarrels and fights among you? Isn't it the whole army of evil desires at war within you? ²You want what you don't have, so you scheme and kill to get it. You are jealous for what others have, and you can't possess it, so you fight and quarrel to take it away from them. And yet the reason you don't have what you want is that you don't ask God for it. ³And even when you do ask, you don't get it because your whole motive is wrong—you want only what will give you pleasure.

⁴You adulterers! Don't you realize that friendship with this world makes you an enemy of God? I say it again, that if your aim is to enjoy this world, you can't be a friend of God. ⁵What do you think the Scriptures mean when they say that the Holy Spirit, whom God has placed within us, jealously longs for us to be faithful*? ⁶He gives us more and more strength to stand against such evil desires. As the Scriptures say,

"God sets himself against the proud,
   but he shows favor to the humble."*

⁷So humble yourselves before God. Resist the Devil, and he will flee from you. ⁸Draw close to God, and God will draw close to you. Wash your hands, you sinners; purify your hearts, you hypocrites. ⁹Let there be tears for the wrong things you have done. Let there be sorrow and deep grief. Let there be sadness instead of laughter, and gloom instead of joy. ¹⁰When you bow down before the Lord and admit your dependence on him, he will lift you up and give you honor.

Warning against Judging Others

¹¹Don't speak evil against each other, my dear brothers and sisters.* If you criticize each other and condemn each other, then

4:5 Or *the spirit that God placed within us tends to envy,* or *the Holy Spirit, whom God has placed within us, opposes our envy.* 4:6 Prov 3:34. 4:11 Greek *brothers.*

Wisdom

READ JAMES 3:13-18

When we get caught up in catering to our addiction, it is almost like we are two different people—as if there are two of us tied up together. The Bible recognizes this dual nature in each of us. One part yearns for good, and the other part is drawn toward corrupt desires and animal passions. The Bible describes a kind of "worldly" wisdom that justifies destructive behavior and leads to disorder, instability, and confusion.

We need to beware of this type of wisdom, which is characterized by jealousy and selfishness. James wrote: "For jealousy and selfishness are not God's kind of wisdom. Such things are earthly, unspiritual, and motivated by the Devil. For wherever there is jealousy and selfish ambition, there you will find disorder and every kind of evil" (James 3:15-16).

This kind of thinking causes us to focus on what others are and have. It makes us envy others so much that we are always dissatisfied. It is easy to become so consumed by our own desires that we become inconsiderate of others, often hurting the people we love. This type of wisdom is inspired by the Devil and will lead to our ultimate destruction, since Satan's "purpose is to steal and kill and destroy" (John 10:10).

If our thoughts are still dominated by jealousy and selfishness, we need to ask God to replace our earthly wisdom with his godly wisdom. We can trust him to change our mind and our life. ***Turn to page 413, 1 Peter 1.***

you are criticizing and condemning God's law. But you are not a judge who can decide whether the law is right or wrong. Your job is to obey it. ¹²God alone, who made the law, can rightly judge among us. He alone has the power to save or to destroy. So what right do you have to condemn your neighbor?

Warning about Self-Confidence

¹³Look here, you people who say, "Today or tomorrow we are going to a certain town and will stay there a year. We will do business there and make a profit." ¹⁴How do you know what will happen tomorrow? For your life is like the morning fog—it's here a little while, then it's gone. ¹⁵What you ought to say is, "If the Lord wants us to, we will live and do this or that." ¹⁶Otherwise you will be boasting about your own plans, and all such boasting is evil.

¹⁷Remember, it is sin to know what you ought to do and then not do it.

CHAPTER 5
Warning to the Rich

Look here, you rich people, weep and groan with anguish because of all the terrible troubles ahead of you. ²Your wealth is rotting away, and your fine clothes are moth-eaten rags. ³Your gold and silver have become worthless. The very wealth you were counting on will eat away your flesh in hell.* This treasure you have accumulated will stand as evidence against you on the day of judgment. ⁴For listen! Hear the cries of the field workers whom you have cheated of their pay. The wages you held back cry out against you. The cries of the reapers have reached the ears of the Lord Almighty.

⁵You have spent your years on earth in luxury, satisfying your every whim. Now your hearts are nice and fat, ready for the slaughter. ⁶You have condemned and killed good people who had no power to defend themselves against you.

Patience in Suffering

⁷Dear brothers and sisters,* you must be patient as you wait for the Lord's return. Consider the farmers who eagerly look for the rains in the fall and in the spring. They patiently wait for the precious harvest to ripen. ⁸You, too, must be patient. And take courage, for the coming of the Lord is near.

⁹Don't grumble about each other, my brothers and sisters, or God will judge you. For look! The great Judge is coming. He is standing at the door!

¹⁰For examples of patience in suffering, dear brothers and sisters, look at the prophets who spoke in the name of the Lord. ¹¹We give great honor to those who endure under suffering. Job is an example of a man who endured patiently. From his experience we see how the Lord's plan finally ended in good, for he is full of tenderness and mercy.

¹²But most of all, my brothers and sisters, never take an oath, by heaven or earth or anything else. Just say a simple yes or no, so that you will not sin and be condemned for it.

5:3 Or *will eat your flesh like fire.* **5:7** Greek *brothers;* also in 5:9, 10, 12, 19.

5:1-5 Some of us may wonder why we have to give up our pursuit of pleasure. Often people living for wealth and pleasure seem to be happier than we are. James reminded his audience that a selfish lifestyle inevitably leads to painful consequences. Some of us have already experienced the pain and emptiness brought on by selfish pleasures. A selfish lifestyle never yields lasting joy and peace; it always leads to some kind of bondage. When we make God's will our own and follow his program, we experience freedom and become a blessing to others.

5:7-11 We have all probably asked ourself this question: Why are these terrible things happening to me? This question might become especially urgent after we have entered the recovery process. We may recognize that God used our sufferings to get us started in our program, but why does he allow suffering to continue? Recovery is a painful, lifelong process. Just as our addiction didn't appear overnight, recovery will also take time. We need to learn patience as we take small steps forward, planting the seeds that will yield a harvest of healing and restoration. God will nurture the seeds we have planted, transforming our life from the inside.

5:13-15 Since God has the power to heal us spiritually, emotionally, and physically, prayer is one of the most powerful tools available to us in recovery. When we pray to God, we call upon that power and display our faith that he can help us. Prayer is essential in the process of putting our broken life into God's caring and capable hands. He is more than able to help us and guide us to blessings and peace. When our life seems out of control and we are in despair, we can begin the healing process by bringing our problems to God. He is listening, and he has the power to rebuild even the most shattered life.

The Power of Prayer

¹³Are any among you suffering? They should keep on praying about it. And those who have reason to be thankful should continually sing praises to the Lord.

¹⁴Are any among you sick? They should call for the elders of the church and have them pray over them, anointing them with oil in the name of the Lord. ¹⁵And their prayer offered in faith will heal the sick, and the Lord will make them well. And anyone who has committed sins will be forgiven.

¹⁶Confess your sins to each other and pray for each other so that you may be healed. The earnest prayer of a righteous person has great power and wonderful results. ¹⁷Elijah was as human as we are, and yet when he prayed earnestly that no rain would fall, none fell for the next three and a half years! ¹⁸Then he prayed for rain, and down it poured. The grass turned green, and the crops began to grow again.

Restore Wandering Believers

¹⁹My dear brothers and sisters, if anyone among you wanders away from the truth and is brought back again, ²⁰you can be sure that the one who brings that person back will save that sinner from death and bring about the forgiveness of many sins.

STEP 3

Single-Minded Devotion

BIBLE READING: James 4:7-10
We made a decision to turn our will and our life over to the care of God.
We may have already chosen to follow God, letting him define the overall direction of our life. Even so, many of us still try to keep parts of our heart hidden from God. We have devoted these parts of ourself to gratifying our addiction, to doing things that are contrary to the will of God. This sets us up for living a double life, which can fill us with guilt, shame, and instability.

Even those of us who have given our heart to God face new temptations and decisions every day. James was addressing believers when he wrote: "So humble yourselves before God. Resist the Devil, and he will flee from you. Draw close to God, and God will draw close to you" (James 4:7-8).

If we choose to live a double life, we may begin to doubt whether God hears us at all. As James wrote: "A doubtful mind is as unsettled as a wave of the sea that is driven and tossed by the wind. People like that should not expect to receive anything from the Lord. They can't make up their minds. They waver back and forth in everything they do" (James 1:6-8).

When we resist the Devil at every turn and draw close to God, he will draw close to us. When we open the hidden portions of our heart and begin to make choices in favor of recovery, we will soon grow confident that God desires to help us. *Turn to page 517, Psalm 61.*

REFLECTIONS ON

JAMES

*insights ABOUT TRUE FAITH

We see in **James 1:6-8** that all truly wise decisions are rooted in a vital faith in God. Faith "is the confident assurance that what we hope for is going to happen. It is the evidence of things we cannot yet see" (Hebrews 11:1). God wants us to make progress in recovery. When we ask God to help us make wise decisions, we can do so without any trace of doubt, fully believing that whatever we ask for in faith will be granted. God will supply the wisdom we need to make the right decisions for successful recovery.

*insights ABOUT HONEST CONFESSION

As we try to make an honest personal inventory, some of us may have nothing to measure our attitudes or actions against. We may never have had any good role models to follow. In **James 1:22-25** we are reminded that God's Word functions like a mirror in our life. As we read it, we are given a clear picture of what God wants us to be like. It shows us where we don't measure up to God's standards and provides a measuring stick for our personal inventory. But James also warns us not to stop after that inventory. We should not look into God's Word only to walk away and forget what we saw there. To make real progress in recovery we need to enlist God's help and take concrete steps to live according to God's Word.

Admitting our faults to God and to a trustworthy person is an essential step in the recovery process. When we share our faults with others, we give them the opportunity to uphold us in prayer. James reminds us in **James 5:16-20** that confession is an important part of our personal prayer life. God invites us to confess our sins and failures to him through prayer. When we bring our sins and defects of character before God, he starts the healing process in us. Prayer is never a waste of time; it yields amazing results! God responds powerfully when we display our faith by sharing our problems with him.

FIRST PETER

THE BIG PICTURE

A. SUFFERING IS A VALUABLE PART OF LIFE (1:1-25)
B. LIVING HONESTLY AS WE WORK AT RELATIONSHIPS (2:1-10)
C. HOW TO LIVE WELL IN A DIFFICULT WORLD (2:11–4:6)
D. THE HOPE OF ULTIMATE RESTORATION (4:7–5:14)

Peter's audience was made up of hurting people. They were suffering persecution from unbelievers in the form of rejection and, in many cases, outright physical abuse. The price they paid for their beliefs included everything from broken relationships to physical pain and rejection.

Peter wrote to encourage them. The wonderful part of his message lay in the perspective he offered his audience. In response to their cries of anguish he did not say, "There must be something wrong with you" or "Pray harder and your problems will go away." Neither did he flippantly promise them an easy road ahead. Instead, he gave them this hope: They belonged to God, and he would never fail them. These words offer the same hope to us.

Most of us would agree that suffering is one of the most difficult parts of life to accept, much less understand. Though we wish we were exempt or cushioned from life's harsh blows, pain is a reality. All of us suffer, and suffering is part of recovery. We must accept the fact that we will hurt from time to time.

God equips us to live at peace in the midst of tough times. We obtain God's powerful help when we hold fast to Christ and live according to his will. This does not mean that our troubles will vanish because we believe in God. Rather, it means that God will surround us with his love when problems seem overwhelming. The way out of the storm is to take comfort in God's presence and persevere through it. As we do, God will use the trials to bring about our growth.

THE BOTTOM LINE

PURPOSE: To show us how to live well in a shattered and hopeless world. AUTHOR: The apostle Peter. AUDIENCE: Jewish Christians who were suffering persecution for their faith. DATE WRITTEN: Around A.D. 64, just prior to Nero's persecutions of the early Christians. SETTING: This letter was written when Peter and other Christians were being tortured and martyred for their faith. The believers faced opposition from both Jewish and secular authorities. KEY VERSE: "You are not slaves; you are free. But your freedom is not an excuse to do evil. You are free to live as God's slaves" (2:16). KEY PEOPLE AND RELATIONSHIPS: Peter with Silas and with John Mark.

RECOVERY THEMES

God's Way Can Be Painful: Part of the reason we may be afraid of recovery is that we know the changes God asks us to make will be painful. There was pain in our old way of life, but we usually found ways to escape it. When we enter the recovery process, we also decide to face our pain head-on. Turning our life over to God, taking moral inventory, making amends, and allowing God to remove our defects are all painful steps. But because they are part of God's plan, they will also lead to joy and wholeness.

Nothing Is Hopeless with God: As we struggle in recovery, we may begin to feel helpless. We might be tempted to throw up our hands and say, "What's the use?" But *feeling* helpless is different from *being* helpless. We are never really helpless, for with God, help is close at hand. We are not without hope, for God is the source of all hope. When we struggle with despair, this letter reminds us to turn our life over to God and totally depend on his power. God will never leave us to face our trials alone.

The Importance of Relationships: Accepting Jesus Christ as our Savior makes us part of God's family. We enter into a community that has Jesus Christ as its founder and leader. Everyone in this community is related; no one stands alone. All healing and recovery take place in the context of relationships with others. Peter teaches us how to manage those relationships: with loyalty, care, and humility, praying that we will become what God wants us to be.

CHAPTER 1
Greetings from Peter

This letter is from Peter, an apostle of Jesus Christ.

I am writing to God's chosen people who are living as foreigners in the lands of Pontus, Galatia, Cappadocia, the province of Asia, and Bithynia. ²God the Father chose you long ago, and the Spirit has made you holy. As a result, you have obeyed Jesus Christ and are cleansed by his blood.

May you have more and more of God's special favor and wonderful peace.

The Hope of Eternal Life

³All honor to the God and Father of our Lord Jesus Christ, for it is by his boundless mercy that God has given us the privilege of being born again. Now we live with a wonderful expectation because Jesus Christ rose again from the dead. ⁴For God has reserved a priceless inheritance for his children. It is kept in heaven for you, pure and undefiled, beyond the reach of change and decay. ⁵And God, in his mighty power, will protect you until you receive this salvation, because you are trusting him. It will be revealed on the last day for

---

1:7 The refiner would heat the gold in the fire in order to separate the worthless and impure dross from the precious and beautiful gold. The dross would be skimmed off until the refiner could see his image in the liquid gold. God uses the fiery trials and tribulations in our life to purify and beautify our faith so that one day he will see clearly his image in us. This truth offers great comfort to those of us who struggle to make sense of a past marked by suffering. We can be confident that God will separate something priceless from the dross of our experiences.

1:8-9 Turning our will and our life over to God is a critical step in the recovery process. During our most painful trials, we may fail to see God with us. Yet Peter suggests that, strange as it may seem at the time, surrendering to God in difficult times can be a joyful experience. If we trust that God will use our trials to further the process of healing in our life, even the tough times can become times of celebration.

1:10-13 The good news of God's forgiveness in Christ flows from a plan that took God centuries to complete. Now that it is complete, we can count on God's continuing kindness as we trust in him until Jesus returns. We don't have to wonder if we are being tricked into believing something that isn't true. Centuries of history and numerous promises stand behind the revelation of God through Jesus Christ. As we turn our life and will over to him, we can be sure that his power is sufficient for a successful recovery.

1:17-20 It is impossible for us to earn God's favor and acceptance. Many people misunderstand Peter's counsel to reverently fear God; they think it means that God is looking to catch us in sin to punish us, so we should be afraid of him. Actually, if we perceive God and ourself correctly, we see that God knows we can't measure up on our own. He accepts our limitations, forgives our sins, seeks to help us learn from our mistakes, and helps us progress toward a more godly life.

all to see. 6So be truly glad!* There is wonderful joy ahead, even though it is necessary for you to endure many trials for a while.

7These trials are only to test your faith, to show that it is strong and pure. It is being tested as fire tests and purifies gold—and your faith is far more precious to God than mere gold. So if your faith remains strong after being tried by fiery trials, it will bring you much praise and glory and honor on the day when Jesus Christ is revealed to the whole world.

8You love him even though you have never seen him. Though you do not see him, you trust him; and even now you are happy with a glorious, inexpressible joy. 9Your reward for trusting him will be the salvation of your souls.

10This salvation was something the prophets wanted to know more about. They prophesied about this gracious salvation prepared for you, even though they had many questions as to what it all could mean. 11They wondered what the Spirit of Christ within them was talking about when he told them in advance about Christ's suffering and his great glory afterward. They wondered when and to whom all this would happen.

12They were told that these things would not happen during their lifetime, but many years later, during yours. And now this Good News has been announced by those who preached to you in the power of the Holy Spirit sent from heaven. It is all so wonderful that even the angels are eagerly watching these things happen.

A Call to Holy Living

13So think clearly and exercise self-control. Look forward to the special blessings that will come to you at the return of Jesus Christ. 14Obey God because you are his children. Don't slip back into your old ways of doing evil; you didn't know any better then. 15But now you must be holy in everything you do, just as God—who chose you to be his children—is holy. 16For he himself has said, "You must be holy because I am holy."*

17And remember that the heavenly Father to whom you pray has no favorites when he judges. He will judge or reward you according to what you do. So you must live in reverent fear of him during your time as foreigners here on earth. 18For you know that

Hope

READ 1 PETER 1:3-7

Life is rough. We must constantly struggle against the sin inherent in our mortal body. We live with the realities of pain, sickness, and death. We live in a world that is constantly decaying. Even if we turn our life over to God, what is there to look forward to?

Peter tells us: "Now we live with a wonderful expectation because Jesus Christ rose again from the dead. For God has reserved a priceless inheritance for his children. It is kept in heaven for you. . . . And God, in his mighty power, will protect you until you receive this salvation, because you are trusting him. It will be revealed on the last day for all to see. So be truly glad! There is wonderful joy ahead, even though it is necessary for you to endure many trials for a while" (1 Peter 1:3-6).

Paul offers this encouragement: "Since we are his children, we will share his treasures—for everything God gives to his Son, Christ, is ours, too. But if we are to share his glory, we must also share his suffering. Yet what we suffer now is nothing compared to the glory he will give us later. For all creation is waiting eagerly for that future day when God will reveal who his children really are" (Romans 8:17-19). These promises are for us! *Turn to page 417, 1 Peter 3.*

1:6 Or *So you are truly glad.* **1:16** Lev 11:44-45; 19:2; 20:7.

God paid a ransom to save you from the empty life you inherited from your ancestors. And the ransom he paid was not mere gold or silver. [19]He paid for you with the precious lifeblood of Christ, the sinless, spotless Lamb of God. [20]God chose him for this purpose long before the world began, but now in these final days, he was sent to the earth for all to see. And he did this for you.

[21]Through Christ you have come to trust in God. And because God raised Christ from the dead and gave him great glory, your faith and hope can be placed confidently in God. [22]Now you can have sincere love for each other as brothers and sisters* because you were cleansed from your sins when you accepted the truth of the Good News. So see to it that you really do love each other intensely with all your hearts.*

[23]For you have been born again. Your new life did not come from your earthly parents because the life they gave you will end in death. But this new life will last forever because it comes from the eternal, living word of God. [24]As the prophet says,

"People are like grass that dies away;
    their beauty fades as quickly as the
        beauty of wildflowers.
The grass withers,
    and the flowers fall away.
[25]But the word of the Lord will last
    forever."*

And that word is the Good News that was preached to you.

CHAPTER 2

So get rid of all malicious behavior and deceit. Don't just pretend to be good! Be done with hypocrisy and jealousy and backstabbing. [2]You must crave pure spiritual milk so that you can grow into the fullness of your salvation. Cry out for this nourishment as a baby cries for milk, [3]now that you have had a taste of the Lord's kindness.

Living Stones for God's House

[4]Come to Christ, who is the living cornerstone of God's temple. He was rejected by the people, but he is precious to God who chose him.

[5]And now God is building you, as living stones, into his spiritual temple. What's more, you are God's holy priests, who offer the spiritual sacrifices that please him because of Jesus Christ. [6]As the Scriptures express it,

"I am placing a stone in Jerusalem,*
    a chosen cornerstone,
and anyone who believes in him
    will never be disappointed.*"

[7]Yes, he is very precious to you who believe. But for those who reject him,

"The stone that was rejected by the
        builders
    has now become the cornerstone."*

[8]And the Scriptures also say,

"He is the stone that makes people
        stumble,
    the rock that will make them fall."*

1:22a Greek *can have brotherly love.* **1:22b** Some manuscripts read *with a pure heart.* **1:24-25** Isa 40:6-8. **2:6a** Greek *in Zion.* **2:6b** Or *will never be put to shame.* Isa 28:16. **2:7** Ps 118:22. **2:8** Isa 8:14.

2:2-3 Here Peter pinpointed an insight for helping us resist sin: We can live a godly life because we have tasted of God's kindness. To the extent that we experience God's love (which often comes through our relationships with other people), we won't want to sin because we will see that it isn't good for us, and it grieves God's Spirit. This puts the focus in recovery work not on improving outward behavior (which is more the result) but on seeking to please God and experience more of his kindness. We can come to him with all our needs, and he will fill our heart with the love we crave.
2:9-10 The Christian's true identity is no longer that of a sinner but that of a holy saint. We are no longer a slave, but a chosen priest of the King. We have been called out of the darkness of our dependency to receive God's healing love so we can share it with others who are hurting.
2:11 Sin is alluring because there is pleasure in it. Many of us have struggled with the temptation to escape the painful realities of life by turning to the "pleasures" of alcohol, drugs, food, sex, work, money, or even religious activity. Yet sooner or later we realized that these pleasures, when used wrongly, fought against the well-being of our soul. By seeing ourself as an "alien" on earth with our real home in heaven, we can learn to delay gratification, which leads to wisdom—and recovery.
2:15 The testimony of a changed life is a far better witness of God's grace than a lecture is. When hurting people who haven't yet started in recovery see how God has brought us through our challenges to a place of increased growth and contentment, they may want to know what God can do for them.

They stumble because they do not listen to God's word or obey it, and so they meet the fate that has been planned for them.

⁹But you are not like that, for you are a chosen people. You are a kingdom of priests, God's holy nation, his very own possession. This is so you can show others the goodness of God, for he called you out of the darkness into his wonderful light.

¹⁰ "Once you were not a people;
    now you are the people of God.
Once you received none of God's mercy;
    now you have received his mercy."*

¹¹Dear brothers and sisters, you are foreigners and aliens here. So I warn you to keep away from evil desires because they fight against your very souls. ¹²Be careful how you live among your unbelieving neighbors. Even if they accuse you of doing wrong, they will see your honorable behavior, and they will believe and give honor to God when he comes to judge the world.*

Respecting People in Authority

¹³For the Lord's sake, accept all authority— the king as head of state, ¹⁴and the officials he has appointed. For the king has sent them to punish all who do wrong and to honor those who do right.

¹⁵It is God's will that your good lives should silence those who make foolish accusations against you. ¹⁶You are not slaves; you are free. But your freedom is not an excuse to do evil. You are free to live as God's slaves. ¹⁷Show respect for everyone. Love your Christian brothers and sisters.* Fear God. Show respect for the king.

Slaves

¹⁸You who are slaves must accept the authority of your masters. Do whatever they tell you—not only if they are kind and reasonable, but even if they are harsh. ¹⁹For God is pleased with you when, for the sake of your conscience, you patiently endure unfair treatment. ²⁰Of course, you get no credit for being patient if you are beaten for doing wrong. But if you suffer for doing right and are patient beneath the blows, God is pleased with you. ²¹This suffering is all part of what God has called you to. Christ, who suffered for you, is your example. Follow in his steps. ²²He never sinned, and he never deceived anyone. ²³He did not retaliate when he was insulted. When he suffered, he did not threaten to get

2:10 Hos 1:6, 9; 2:23. **2:12** Or *on the day of visitation.*
2:17 Greek *Love the brotherhood.*

A Servant's Heart

BIBLE READING: 1 Peter 2:18-25
We made direct amends to such people wherever possible, except when to do so would injure them or others.
At this point in recovery, most of us have experienced some major changes in our attitudes. At one time, we were so consumed by our addiction that we thought only of ourself, failing to show any consideration for others. This step focuses on the interests and needs of others.

The apostle Paul taught: "Don't be selfish; don't live to make a good impression on others. Be humble, thinking of others as better than yourself. Don't think only about your own affairs, but be interested in others, too, and what they are doing" (Philippians 2:3-4). Whether we make amends directly to others or choose not to because of the injury it would cause, we should be concerned with protecting others from pain and suffering.

There may be situations in which we will suffer if we go back to make amends. This is part of the work of recovery, and the potential pain should not deter us. The apostle Peter wrote: "If you suffer for doing right and are patient beneath the blows, God is pleased with you. . . . Christ, who suffered for you, is your example. Follow in his steps. He never sinned, and he never deceived anyone. He did not retaliate when he was insulted. When he suffered, he did not threaten to get even. He left his case in the hands of God, who always judges fairly" (1 Peter 2:20-23).

This step can be very difficult as we face the painful consequences of past actions. During this time we need to turn our life over to God, who always judges justly. *Turn to Step Ten, page 243, Romans 5.*

even. He left his case in the hands of God, who always judges fairly. ²⁴He personally carried away our sins in his own body on the cross so we can be dead to sin and live for what is right. You have been healed by his wounds! ²⁵Once you were wandering like lost sheep. But now you have turned to your Shepherd, the Guardian of your souls.

CHAPTER 3
Wives
In the same way, you wives must accept the authority of your husbands, even those who refuse to accept the Good News. Your godly lives will speak to them better than any words. They will be won over ²by watching your pure, godly behavior.

³Don't be concerned about the outward beauty that depends on fancy hairstyles, expensive jewelry, or beautiful clothes. ⁴You should be known for the beauty that comes from within, the unfading beauty of a gentle and quiet spirit, which is so precious to God. ⁵That is the way the holy women of old made themselves beautiful. They trusted God and accepted the authority of their husbands. ⁶For instance, Sarah obeyed her husband, Abraham, when she called him her master. You are her daughters when you do what is right without fear of what your husbands might do.

Husbands
⁷In the same way, you husbands must give honor to your wives. Treat her with under-

standing as you live together. She may be weaker than you are, but she is your equal partner in God's gift of new life. If you don't treat her as you should, your prayers will not be heard.

All Christians
⁸Finally, all of you should be of one mind, full of sympathy toward each other, loving one another with tender hearts and humble minds. ⁹Don't repay evil for evil. Don't retaliate when people say unkind things about you. Instead, pay them back with a blessing. That is what God wants you to do, and he will bless you for it. ¹⁰For the Scriptures say,

"If you want a happy life and good days,
  keep your tongue from speaking evil,
  and keep your lips from telling lies.
¹¹ Turn away from evil and do good.
  Work hard at living in peace with
    others.
¹² The eyes of the Lord watch over those
    who do right,
  and his ears are open to their prayers.
But the Lord turns his face
  against those who do evil."*

Suffering for Doing Good
¹³Now, who will want to harm you if you are eager to do good? ¹⁴But even if you suffer for doing what is right, God will reward you for it. So don't be afraid and don't worry. ¹⁵Instead, you must worship Christ as Lord of

3:10-12 Ps 34:12-16.

2:23-24 Not only does Jesus show us how to deal with suffering, but he also suffered for us. He received the ultimate punishment for our sins so we wouldn't have to. Instead of facing terrible punishment, we can receive his mercy. He desires to set us free from bondage and heal us from the devastating effects of our sins.

3:1-7 God's design for marriage is for the wife to respect her husband and the husband to be sensitive and loving toward his wife. Husband and wife are to receive through each other the blessings of God's loving grace and guiding truth. This sounds wonderful, but, as anyone who is married knows, it can be hard and painful! It requires being vulnerable, resolving conflicts, and being confronted with the truth even when it hurts. Working through such difficulties is part of God's plan for helping us mature.

3:8-11 The Christian community is to be like a healthy, loving family. Some of us who come from a dysfunctional family may not know what this means, but Peter spelled it out: people share their hurts and find sympathy; they humbly express their needs and receive loving care; they forgive one another rather than plot revenge; they pray for each other; they are careful not to say things that will unnecessarily hurt others; they can be honest about who they are; they seek to do good for one another; and they try to live in peace by resolving conflicts with each other. These same qualities are ideal for helping us with the recovery process.

3:13-17 We all know what it feels like to be hurt by someone we are trying to help, or to have someone falsely accuse us of wrongdoing. It is not uncommon in recovery for people to misunderstand us and resist the changes we are trying to make. The challenge in such situations is to be patient and maintain quiet trust in God's promises. If we persevere in doing what is right, God will reward us.

your life. And if you are asked about your Christian hope, always be ready to explain it. ¹⁶But you must do this in a gentle and respectful way. Keep your conscience clear. Then if people speak evil against you, they will be ashamed when they see what a good life you live because you belong to Christ. ¹⁷Remember, it is better to suffer for doing good, if that is what God wants, than to suffer for doing wrong!

¹⁸Christ also suffered when he died for our sins once for all time. He never sinned, but he died for sinners that he might bring us safely home to God. He suffered physical death, but he was raised to life in the Spirit.*

¹⁹So he went and preached to the spirits in prison—²⁰those who disobeyed God long ago when God waited patiently while Noah was building his boat. Only eight people were saved from drowning in that terrible flood.* ²¹And this is a picture of baptism, which now saves you by the power of Jesus Christ's resurrection. Baptism is not a removal of dirt from your body; it is an appeal to God from* a clean conscience.

²²Now Christ has gone to heaven. He is seated in the place of honor next to God, and all the angels and authorities and powers are bowing before him.

CHAPTER 4
Living for God
So then, since Christ suffered physical pain, you must arm yourselves with the same attitude he had, and be ready to suffer, too. For if you are willing to suffer for Christ, you have decided to stop sinning. ²And you won't spend the rest of your life chasing after evil desires, but you will be anxious to do the will of God. ³You have had enough in the past of the evil things that godless people enjoy—their immorality and lust, their feasting and drunkenness and wild parties, and their terrible worship of idols.

⁴Of course, your former friends are very surprised when you no longer join them in the wicked things they do, and they say evil things about you. ⁵But just remember that they will have to face God, who will judge everyone, both the living and the dead. ⁶That is why the Good News was preached even to those who have died—so that although their bodies were punished with death, they could still live in the spirit as God does.

3:18 Or *spirit.* **3:20** Greek *saved through water.*
3:21 Or *for.*

Honesty
READ 1 PETER 3:10-17

Lying can become a way of life. We may even have lied to ourself, pretending we don't have any problems with lying. We may have learned to cover up our problems by becoming excellent liars. But when we choose to face reality, we will see the unhappiness caused by our lies and how they have hurt us and our loved ones. Only when we stop lying can God begin to bring blessing and change into our life.

Think about these verses: "Do any of you want to live a life that is long and good? Then watch your tongue! Keep your lips from telling lies!" (Psalm 34:12-13). "If you want a happy life and good days, keep your tongue from speaking evil, and keep your lips from telling lies" (1 Peter 3:10). "Don't lie to each other, for you have stripped off your old evil nature and all its wicked deeds. In its place you have clothed yourselves with a brand-new nature that is continually being renewed as you learn more and more about Christ, who created this new nature within you" (Colossians 3:9-10).

There are great benefits to honesty. What other virtue is accompanied by such promises? Telling the truth is vital to recovery. Since lying may be second nature to us, it may be difficult to change. Part of any successful recovery involves guarding our lips and our thoughts from lies that will hurt us and others. Since lying may have been a lifelong way of coping, we must accept that learning to tell the truth may involve hard work. *Turn to page 425, 2 Peter 1.*

7The end of the world is coming soon. Therefore, be earnest and disciplined in your prayers. 8Most important of all, continue to show deep love for each other, for love covers a multitude of sins. 9Cheerfully share your home with those who need a meal or a place to stay.

10God has given gifts to each of you from his great variety of spiritual gifts. Manage them well so that God's generosity can flow through you. 11Are you called to be a speaker? Then speak as though God himself were speaking through you. Are you called to help others? Do it with all the strength and energy that God supplies. Then God will be given glory in everything through Jesus Christ. All glory and power belong to him forever and ever. Amen.

Suffering for Being a Christian

12Dear friends, don't be surprised at the fiery trials you are going through, as if something strange were happening to you. 13Instead, be very glad—because these trials will make you partners with Christ in his suffering, and afterward you will have the wonderful joy of sharing his glory when it is displayed to all the world.

14Be happy if you are insulted for being a Christian, for then the glorious Spirit of God will come upon you. 15If you suffer, however, it must not be for murder, stealing, making trouble, or prying into other people's affairs. 16But it is no shame to suffer for being a Christian. Praise God for the privilege of being called by his wonderful name! 17For the time has come for judg-

---

4:8 Real love for others requires that we face our own sinfulness and consider the well-being of those we have wronged in the past. In many cases this means humbly and sincerely asking the people we have offended for forgiveness; sometimes we may need to take the further step of making amends.

4:10-11 Unfortunately, many of us don't realize that God has given each of us special and unique abilities. Discovering these is a part of recovery. It is a process of learning to esteem ourself and receive respect and encouragement from God and from other people. Then we can pass on God's blessings to others, relying on his strength to enable us to use the gifts he has given us.

4:12-13 Peter returned to a central theme of his letter: We should not only expect to experience trials, but we should also rejoice in them. Through our difficult circumstances we receive opportunities to share in Christ's sufferings as well as in his glory. This theme offers great hope for those of us in recovery, because it affirms that our suffering has a purpose. Through it, God will draw us close and transform us into the person he intended us to be.

4:14-16 We need wisdom to know the difference between suffering because of our own sins and suffering for doing what is right. If we ask for wisdom, God will grant it (see James 1:5). When we suffer because of our own sins, we naturally feel ashamed; it is then we need divine courage to change. When we are persecuted for our Christian conduct or godly character, we can rejoice in that suffering; in this case, we need divine serenity to help us accept the things we cannot change.

5:1-4 Several qualities are necessary for a Christian leader: the willingness to care for others, a desire to serve others, and the ability to lead by example rather than force. We may have grown up surrounded by leaders who embodied none of these principles, and now we are in a position of leadership at work, at church, or in our family. How do we avoid following the negative models that have influenced us? Jesus has provided the best example for us to follow. To become the type of person God wants us to be, we must submit to Christ's leadership and allow his grace, peace, and wisdom to flow through us.

5:7 God cares about our troubles. He watches over us and is continually concerned about our welfare! If we truly believed this, we would turn our worries over to him. However, many of us find it hard to trust God so completely. Because of our past, we may have trouble believing that anyone is that concerned about us. We may have found that if we didn't worry about our problems, no one would. One way to increase our level of trust in God is to find a friend further along in recovery and Christian maturity with whom we can learn to trust. As we are able to share our concerns with caring people, we can consciously remind ourself that God's concern is like our friends'— only much wider and deeper.

5:8-9 Satan is ultimately responsible for the evil that happens to us. Whether he tempts us to relapse in recovery or kicks us when we are already down, Satan is lurking and prowling about. We are commanded to be careful and stand firm against Satan. We are not alone; others are suffering like we are and fighting the same battles. Meeting with others in recovery will help us see that victory over addiction is attainable and that we are not alone in the battle.

5:10-11 God's promise to us when we fall down or are suffering is that he will restore us, set us in a good and secure place, and use the difficulties we have been through to make us stronger than ever! It is this hope that gives us the courage to persevere in our journey of recovery.

ment, and it must begin first among God's own children. And if even we Christians must be judged, what terrible fate awaits those who have never believed God's Good News? 18And

> "If the righteous are barely saved,
>   what chance will the godless and
>   sinners have?"*

19So if you are suffering according to God's will, keep on doing what is right, and trust yourself to the God who made you, for he will never fail you.

CHAPTER 5
Advice for Elders and Young Men

And now, a word to you who are elders in the churches. I, too, am an elder and a witness to the sufferings of Christ. And I, too, will share his glory and his honor when he returns. As a fellow elder, this is my appeal to you: 2Care for the flock of God entrusted to you. Watch over it willingly, not grudgingly—not for what you will get out of it, but because you are eager to serve God. 3Don't lord it over the people assigned to your care, but lead them by your good example. 4And when the head Shepherd comes, your reward will be a never-ending share in his glory and honor.

5You younger men, accept the authority of the elders. And all of you, serve each other in humility, for

> "God sets himself against the proud,
>   but he shows favor to the humble."*

6So humble yourselves under the mighty power of God, and in his good time he will honor you. 7Give all your worries and cares to God, for he cares about what happens to you.

8Be careful! Watch out for attacks from the Devil, your great enemy. He prowls around like a roaring lion, looking for some victim to devour. 9Take a firm stand against him, and be strong in your faith. Remember that your Christian brothers and sisters* all over the world are going through the same kind of suffering you are.

10In his kindness God called you to his eternal glory by means of Jesus Christ. After you have suffered a little while, he will restore, support, and strengthen you, and he will place you on a firm foundation. 11All power is his forever and ever. Amen.

4:18 Prov 11:31. **5:5** Prov 3:34. **5:9** Greek *your brothers.*

s T E P
12

The Narrow Road

BIBLE READING: 1 Peter 4:1-4
Having had a spiritual awakening as the result of these steps, we tried to carry this message to others and to practice these principles in all our affairs.
We probably came into recovery because we'd had enough! We'd had enough of the pain, the lies, and the destruction that resulted from our addictive behavior. One day at a time, we learned the principles on the road to recovery. Now we are at a place we weren't sure we could ever reach—Step Twelve. Now we are encouraged to share the message with others—even though not everyone will welcome it.

Peter pointed out: "You have had enough in the past of the evil things that godless people enjoy—their immorality and lust, their feasting and drunkenness and wild parties. . . . Of course, your former friends are very surprised when you no longer join them in the wicked things they do, and they say evil things about you" (1 Peter 4:3-4).

Jesus said: "You can enter God's Kingdom only through the narrow gate. The highway to hell is broad, and its gate is wide for the many who choose the easy way. But the gateway to life is small, and the road is narrow, and only a few ever find it" (Matthew 7:13-14).

Our message won't be accepted by the masses. The people on the "highway to hell" won't eagerly restrict themselves to the clearly defined steps on the road to recovery. But for those who do listen, our story could be the difference between life and death for them. *End of the Twelve Step reading plan.*

Peter's Final Greetings

¹²I have written this short letter to you with the help of Silas,* whom I consider a faithful brother. My purpose in writing is to encourage you and assure you that the grace of God is with you no matter what happens.

¹³Your sister church here in Rome* sends you greetings, and so does my son Mark. ¹⁴Greet each other in Christian love.*

Peace be to all of you who are in Christ.

5:12 Greek *Silvanus*. **5:13** Greek *The elect one in Babylon.* Babylon was probably a code name for Rome. **5:14** Greek *with a kiss of love.*

REFLECTIONS ON

FIRST PETER

✴*insights* ABOUT THE PERSON OF GOD

As the apostle greeted his friends in **1 Peter 1:1-2,** he reminded them of how they were related to the triune God: They were chosen by God the Father, cleansed by the blood of Jesus Christ, and renewed by the Holy Spirit, who was at work in their hearts. On the basis of God's work in our life, we can be confident that he will bless us richly and grant us increasing freedom from anxiety and fear. Becoming free from anxiety is a process that continues as we trust him (1:8).

In **1 Peter 1:3-6** the apostle praised our Father God for the free gift of his loving grace. All who receive God's gift become his children and belong together in his family and have a "priceless inheritance." All who trust in him share the hope of eternal life with God. This hope gives us the strength to persevere in recovery with joy, despite the difficult and painful circumstances we face.

1 Peter 2:4-6 leaves us with two wonderful promises upon which we can build our life and recovery: We are acceptable to God because of Jesus, and God will never disappoint us if we trust in him. With these truths as our foundation, we can live to please God. As we join other believers in Christ's Spirit of love, together we can create a place where others feel safe and included.

✴*insights* ABOUT THE DANGER OF RELAPSE

In **1 Peter 1:14-17** the apostle warned his readers about the temptation to give up on their faith. Peter knew how it felt to slip back into old ways. Once he boldly proclaimed that he was willing to die in Jesus' defense. A few hours later he denied knowing Jesus just to save his reputation (see Matthew 26:31-35, 69-75). The only way to keep from slipping back into sinful and unhealthy patterns is to maintain a conscious and sober awareness of our identity: We are children of a holy God. Like children, we are weak and dependent, but the Father we depend on is strong, loving, just, and perfect.

✴*insights* ABOUT OUR NEW LIFE IN CHRIST

In **1 Peter 1:23-25** the apostle contrasts the new life we have in Christ with the natural life our parents gave us. Even the most positive legacy from our natural parents will fade and decay, for from them we inherited the dysfunctions of a sinful human race. But the life God gives us increases in beauty and lasts forever. God's promises to save us will never fail.

In **1 Peter 2:1** the apostle tells us to avoid five destructive behaviors: hanging on to hatred and malicious behavior; pretending to be good when there is unacknowledged sin in our heart; not being honest about our feelings and behavior; being jealous of others instead of making the best of our own situation; and talking about people behind their backs instead of directly to them. Peter knew that doing these things would hurt us and hinder the growth of loving and intimate relationships. We must examine our heart and continue to work toward the recovery goals of forgiveness, honesty, contentment, and openness.

In **1 Peter 4:1-5** we are called to follow Christ's example, resisting the sinful pleasures that come our way and focusing instead on living according to God's will. The sins Peter listed here can exert incredible power over us when they become the central focus of our life. To break free of an addictive lifestyle, we have to cut ourself off from past practices and sometimes even from past relationships. To "just say no" alone won't set us free. We also need to say yes to God and redirect our energy to our recovery activities and, eventually, to the recovery of others.

✳insights ABOUT PERSEVERING THROUGH TRIALS

In **1 Peter 2:21-23** it is clear that persevering through difficulty and pain is the God-ordained path to maturity. God does not ask us to endure anything that he did not endure himself in Christ. Like us, Jesus was tempted by our enemy and was offered the pleasures of this world. He also suffered deeply at the hands of unjust people. Like Jesus, we can respond to injustice with faith that entrusts matters into God's hands, knowing that ultimately he will bring about justice.

In **1 Peter 4:19** we are encouraged to keep doing what is right, even if we are suffering. We may have been persecuted by old friends who want us to return to our old lifestyle. Perhaps family members are afraid of the changes we are making and are hindering our progress. As we face these trials we can trust that God will be faithful to us and remember that he can use even our painful experiences for our good. God wants us to continue in recovery. So if we are suffering for our work in recovery, we need to keep on doing what we know to be right. No matter what obstacles may be placed in our way, God will never desert us, once we have entrusted our life to him.

SECOND PETER

THE BIG PICTURE

A. A WORD OF BLESSING (1:1-2)
B. GOD HAS EVERYTHING WE NEED (1:3-21)
C. THE PERIL WITHIN: BEWARE! (2:1-22)
D. HOPE FOR TOMORROW; PURPOSE FOR TODAY (3:1-18)

Peter's audience had a problem. False teachers were moving into church fellowships and promoting wrong ideas about God. In many of these early churches a majority of the people were uneducated. They were easily swayed by the eloquence of traveling false teachers who intentionally deceived the people, using lies and half-truths to manipulate the believers for the teachers' own ends.

The apostle Peter sent warnings to his readers: Watch out for false teachers; remember that they will have to give account for their errors; recognize false teachers by their deeds; and remember the price they will pay for misleading people. Peter wanted his readers to experience the life-changing power of God in their lives, and that would mean avoiding man-made substitutes. How could Peter's audience follow Christ if they believed all kinds of false teachings about him?

The challenge Peter left them went beyond a mere warning, however. He included a plan of action: "May God bless you with his special favor and wonderful peace as you come to know Jesus, our God and Lord, better and better. As we know Jesus better, his divine power gives us everything we need for living a godly life" (1:2-3).

Why do the pains, disappointments, and sins of life bring us down? Why do we hurt those we love the most? Perhaps we will never learn the answers to those questions. But 2 Peter does tell us how to change: Get to know God. The God of the universe has made himself available to us on a personal level. As we get to know him, he will help us overcome our shortcomings and replace them with self-control, kindness, love, forgiveness, perseverance, patience, and peace.

THE BOTTOM LINE

PURPOSE: To help his readers keep their focus on God's grace and truth. AUTHOR: The apostle Peter. AUDIENCE: All believers everywhere. DATE WRITTEN: Around A.D. 66–67, a few years after 1 Peter was written. SETTING: Peter was probably writing from Rome, giving encouragement and warning to people he did not expect to see again. He wanted them to watch out for false teachings and to be faithful to God and one another. KEY VERSE: "As we know Jesus better, his divine power gives us everything we need for living a godly life. He has called us to receive his own glory and goodness!" (1:3). KEY PEOPLE AND RELATIONSHIPS: Peter with Paul and with the church at large.

RECOVERY THEMES

True Recovery Involves Surrender to God: In recovery, some people say that we have the power to heal ourself. That false idea is fed by our own wishful thinking. We wish we had the power within ourself to overcome our problems. This idea also assumes that recovery is a simple process. But for recovery to be successful, it must involve our entire self—our heart, our mind, our spirit, and our will—being handed over to God's rule. Recovery is never an easy and painless process. It demands complete commitment and surrender to God. But if we are willing to entrust our life to God, we will discover the joy and peace that God intends for each of us.

God Is Our Help and Hope: Peter wrote to people who were facing severe opposition. The Roman emperor Nero had begun heavy persecution of Christians, and many would soon face death at his hands. At the same time, false ideas about God threatened their new faith. Peter helped them face these assaults on their faith by reminding them to keep their eyes on God, the only reliable source of help and hope. As we focus on God, we will find new hope no matter what circumstances we face. Then, as we persevere through tough times, our behavior will show that God is working powerfully in our life.

The Importance of Perseverance: God does not require that we suddenly become perfect. He knows we will slip and fall at times. But, as Peter warned his audience, we must be careful not to get tangled up in our sins to the point of becoming enslaved again. This only adds to our burden of guilt and makes the recovery process much more difficult. Making progress depends on perseverance. With God's help we can get up and get back on track as soon as possible, no matter what our circumstances. When we confess our sins to God and accept his free gift of forgiveness, we will grow closer to God, who loves us and promises to be with us. God helps us to persevere through the tough times and experience his joy in the process.

CHAPTER 1
Greetings from Peter
This letter is from Simon* Peter, a slave and apostle of Jesus Christ.

I am writing to all of you who share the same precious faith we have, faith given to us by Jesus Christ, our God and Savior, who makes us right with God.

²May God bless you with his special favor and wonderful peace as you come to know Jesus, our God and Lord,* better and better.

Growing in the Knowledge of God
³As we know Jesus better, his divine power gives us everything we need for living a godly life. He has called us to receive his own glory and goodness! ⁴And by that same mighty power, he has given us all of his rich and wonderful promises. He has promised that you will escape the decadence all around you caused by evil desires and that you will share in his divine nature.

⁵So make every effort to apply the benefits of these promises to your life. Then your faith will produce a life of moral excellence. A life of moral excellence leads to knowing God better. ⁶Knowing God leads to self-control. Self-control leads to patient endurance, and patient endurance leads to godliness. ⁷Godliness leads to love for other Christians,* and fi-

1:1 Greek *Simeon*. **1:2** Or *come to know God and Jesus our Lord*. **1:7** Greek *brotherly love*.

1:1-2 Peter greeted his readers by reminding them of the gift of forgiveness and new life they had received through faith in Jesus Christ. It is a gift because no one can claim to be worthy of the salvation God offers through Christ (see Ephesians 2:8-9). Truly God is good! Experiencing God's kindness and peace depends on knowing him. Sometimes we expect peace to come before we make healthy choices, but Peter reminds us that grace and peace come when we concentrate on getting to know God. We can take concrete steps to improve our conscious contact with God through prayer and meditation on his Word.
1:3-4 One of the most comforting by-products of faith is the simple awareness that we possess everything we need to live a full and meaningful life. How do we experience this provision? By participating in God's nature through faith and by growing through practice into all that he has designed us to be. The past is part of who we are, the future is securely in God's hands, and today is filled with opportunities to grow in our understanding of love, forgiveness, truth, and grace! Just as parents provide for their children's needs, so God supplies all that we need, including the ability to rise above our circumstances and temptations.
2:1-12 Here we are reminded of the consequences of rejecting God's program and leading others away from the truth. Perhaps this describes the way we were before entering recovery. Thankfully, God has provided us with the help we need to start again and rebuild our life according to his will. The consequences of the self-centered pursuit of pleasure and power are terrible. It is good to be reminded every so often of what we have been delivered from—"a swift and terrible end."

nally you will grow to have genuine love for everyone. [8]The more you grow like this, the more you will become productive and useful in your knowledge of our Lord Jesus Christ. [9]But those who fail to develop these virtues are blind or, at least, very shortsighted. They have already forgotten that God has cleansed them from their old life of sin.

[10]So, dear brothers and sisters,* work hard to prove that you really are among those God has called and chosen. Doing this, you will never stumble or fall away. [11]And God will open wide the gates of heaven for you to enter into the eternal Kingdom of our Lord and Savior Jesus Christ.

Paying Attention to Scripture

[12]I plan to keep on reminding you of these things—even though you already know them and are standing firm in the truth. [13]Yes, I believe I should keep on reminding you of these things as long as I live. [14]But the Lord Jesus Christ has shown me that my days here on earth are numbered and I am soon to die.* [15]So I will work hard to make these things clear to you. I want you to remember them long after I am gone.

[16]For we were not making up clever stories when we told you about the power of our Lord Jesus Christ and his coming again. We have seen his majestic splendor with our own eyes. [17]And he received honor and glory from God the Father when God's glorious, majestic voice called down from heaven, "This is my beloved Son; I am fully pleased with him." [18]We ourselves heard the voice when we were there with him on the holy mountain.

[19]Because of that, we have even greater confidence in the message proclaimed by the prophets. Pay close attention to what they wrote, for their words are like a light shining in a dark place—until the day Christ appears and his brilliant light shines in your hearts.* [20]Above all, you must understand that no prophecy in Scripture ever came from the prophets themselves* [21]or because they wanted to prophesy. It was the Holy Spirit who moved the prophets to speak from God.

CHAPTER 2
The Danger of False Teachers
But there were also false prophets in Israel, just as there will be false teachers among you. They will cleverly teach their destructive

1:10 Greek *brothers.* **1:14** Greek *I must soon put off this earthly tent.* **1:19** Or *until the day dawns and the morning star rises in your hearts.* **1:20** Or *is a matter of one's own interpretation.*

Self-Control

READ 2 PETER 1:2-9

We would love to have self-control! But trying to find it within ourself can become as much of an obsession as our primary addiction. The more we try to get a hold on it, the more elusive it seems.

According to Peter, self-control is one step in the middle of a larger progression: "May God bless you with his special favor and wonderful peace as you come to know Jesus, our God and Lord, better and better. As we know Jesus better, his divine power gives us everything we need for living a godly life. He has called us to receive his own glory and goodness! And by that same mighty power, he has given us all of his rich and wonderful promises. He has promised that you will escape the decadence all around you caused by evil desires and that you will share in his divine nature. So make every effort to apply the benefits of these promises to your life. Then your faith will produce a life of moral excellence. A life of moral excellence leads to knowing God better. Knowing God leads to self-control. Self-control leads to patient endurance, and patient endurance leads to godliness. Godliness leads to love for other Christians, and finally you will grow to have genuine love for everyone" (2 Peter 1:2-7).

Self-control is something that comes as we grow closer to God. As we take one step at a time, one day at a time, God will give us his own character, including self-control. *Turn to page 433, 1 John 2.*

heresies about God and even turn against their Master who bought them. Theirs will be a swift and terrible end. ²Many will follow their evil teaching and shameful immorality. And because of them, Christ and his true way will be slandered. ³In their greed they will make up clever lies to get hold of your money. But God condemned them long ago, and their destruction is on the way.

⁴For God did not spare even the angels when they sinned; he threw them into hell,* in gloomy caves* and darkness until the judgment day. ⁵And God did not spare the ancient world—except for Noah and his family of seven. Noah warned the world of God's righteous judgment. Then God destroyed the whole world of ungodly people with a vast flood. ⁶Later, he turned the cities of Sodom and Gomorrah into heaps of ashes and swept them off the face of the earth. He made them an example of what will happen to ungodly people. ⁷But at the same time, God rescued Lot out of Sodom because he was a good man who was sick of all the immorality and wickedness around him. ⁸Yes, he was a righteous man who was distressed by the wickedness he saw and heard day after day.

⁹So you see, the Lord knows how to rescue godly people from their trials, even while punishing the wicked right up until the day of judgment. ¹⁰He is especially hard on those who follow their own evil, lustful desires and who despise authority. These people are proud and arrogant, daring even to scoff at the glorious ones* without so much as trembling. ¹¹But the angels, even though they are far greater in power and strength than these false teachers, never speak out disrespectfully against* the glorious ones.

¹²These false teachers are like unthinking animals, creatures of instinct, who are born to be caught and killed. They laugh at the terrifying powers they know so little about, and they will be destroyed along with them. ¹³Their destruction is their reward for the harm they have done. They love to indulge in evil pleasures in broad daylight. They are a disgrace and a stain among you. They revel in deceitfulness while they feast with you. ¹⁴They commit adultery with their eyes, and their lust is never satisfied. They make a game of luring unstable people into sin. They train themselves to be greedy; they are doomed and cursed. ¹⁵They have wandered off the right road and followed the way of Balaam son of Beor,* who loved to earn money by doing wrong. ¹⁶But Balaam was stopped from his mad course when his donkey rebuked him with a human voice.

¹⁷These people are as useless as dried-up springs of water or as clouds blown away by the wind—promising much and delivering nothing. They are doomed to blackest darkness. ¹⁸They brag about themselves with empty, foolish boasting. With lustful desire as their bait, they lure back into sin those who have just escaped from such wicked living. ¹⁹They promise freedom, but they themselves are slaves to sin and corruption. For you are a slave to whatever controls you. ²⁰And when people escape from the wicked ways of the world by learning about our Lord and Savior Jesus Christ and then get tangled up with sin and become its slave again, they are worse off than before. ²¹It would be better if they had never known the right way to live than to know it and then reject the holy commandments that were given to them. ²²They make these proverbs come true: "A dog returns to its vomit,"* and "A washed pig returns to the mud."

CHAPTER 3
The Day of the Lord Is Coming

This is my second letter to you, dear friends, and in both of them I have tried to stimulate your wholesome thinking and refresh your memory. ²I want you to remember and understand what the holy prophets said long ago and what our Lord and Savior commanded through your apostles.

2:4a Greek *Tartaros.* 2:4b Some manuscripts read *chains of gloom.* 2:10 *The glorious ones* are probably evil angels; also in 2:11. 2:11 Greek *never bring blasphemous judgment from the Lord against.* 2:15 Other manuscripts read *Bosor.* 2:22 Prov 26:11.

2:13-22 An important part of recovery is setting appropriate boundaries. People who do not have our best interests at heart abound, even in the Christian community. Peter emphasized the need for discernment. Apparently, the church in Peter's day was plagued by those who once professed faith in Christ but then "added to" the simple truth of the gospel. They advocated "freedom," but that freedom was really only a license to become enslaved to sin once again. Setting healthy boundaries for behavior involves knowing God's truth and allowing neither the false teachings of others nor our own sinful inclinations to lead us astray.

[3]First, I want to remind you that in the last days there will be scoffers who will laugh at the truth and do every evil thing they desire. [4]This will be their argument: "Jesus promised to come back, did he? Then where is he? Why, as far back as anyone can remember, everything has remained exactly the same since the world was first created."

[5]They deliberately forget that God made the heavens by the word of his command, and he brought the earth up from the water and surrounded it with water. [6]Then he used the water to destroy the world with a mighty flood. [7]And God has also commanded that the heavens and the earth will be consumed by fire on the day of judgment, when ungodly people will perish.

[8]But you must not forget, dear friends, that a day is like a thousand years to the Lord, and a thousand years is like a day. [9]The Lord isn't really being slow about his promise to return, as some people think. No, he is being patient for your sake. He does not want anyone to perish, so he is giving more time for everyone to repent. [10]But the day of the Lord will come as unexpectedly as a thief. Then the heavens will pass away with a terrible noise, and everything in them will disappear in fire, and the earth and everything on it will be exposed to judgment.*

[11]Since everything around us is going to melt away, what holy, godly lives you should be living! [12]You should look forward to that day and hurry it along—the day when God will set the heavens on fire and the elements will melt away in the flames. [13]But we are looking forward to the new heavens and new earth he has promised, a world where everyone is right with God.

[14]And so, dear friends, while you are waiting for these things to happen, make every effort to live a pure and blameless life. And be at peace with God.

[15]And remember, the Lord is waiting so that people have time to be saved. This is just as our beloved brother Paul wrote to you with the wisdom God gave him— [16]speaking of these things in all of his letters. Some of his comments are hard to understand, and those who are ignorant and unstable have twisted his letters around to mean something quite different from what he meant, just as they do the other parts of Scripture—and the result is disaster for them.

Peter's Final Words

[17]I am warning you ahead of time, dear friends, so that you can watch out and not be carried away by the errors of these wicked people. I don't want you to lose your own secure footing. [18]But grow in the special favor and knowledge of our Lord and Savior Jesus Christ.

To him be all glory and honor, both now and forevermore. Amen.

3:10 Some manuscripts read *will be burned up.*

3:3-9 It is difficult to wait on God, particularly when he seems so slow in bringing about our healing. Why doesn't God return for us now? Why does he allow further suffering and frustration? The answer is simple yet profoundly full of love: God is patient! He wants all to come to him and discover the only true way of salvation and life. As we wait, we can trust that it is always for a good purpose.

3:10-16 We live in a world that encourages and rewards our active lifestyle. We are doers and fixers, arrangers and controllers. We seek to bolster our sense of self-esteem by the things we do. When Christ returns, however, who we *are* will be far more important than what we *do*. Peter reminds us that as we wait for this day, we are called to be God's people. It is good to take time to ask, Am I enjoying the privilege of being? In all my doing, have I lost sight of what's important—the kind of person I am, and the person I am becoming?

REFLECTIONS ON

SECOND PETER

*insights ABOUT OUR ROLE IN RECOVERY

When we entrust our life to God, we might wonder if there is any part for us to play. In **2 Peter 1:5-11** we are reminded that God expects us to do our part in the recovery process. As we actively seek change in our life, we will share in God's nature and receive the ability to think new thoughts and formulate new behavior patterns. "Work hard to prove that you really are among those God has called and chosen," Peter urges. "Doing this, you will never stumble or fall away. And God will open wide the gates of heaven for you to enter into the eternal Kingdom of our Lord and Savior Jesus Christ."

It is easy to remember the painful moments of life—the disappointments and the people who disappointed us. It is sometimes harder to remember the many blessings we receive in small ways each day. In **2 Peter 1:12-18** the apostle reminded his readers that they could overcome the pain of past trials by focusing on God: his power and his coming again, his splendor and his majesty. Peter wanted to etch the truth of God's amazing love into their minds. We must work through our painful memories (they do not disappear on their own!), but as we do, we can also reflect on God's majesty and amazing love. As we recall the good things God has done, the painful memories will begin to fade.

*insights ABOUT GOD'S TRUTH

God's truth is dependable; our human perspective often is not. In **2 Peter 1:19-21** the apostle made this distinction clear. God's truth is not weak or questionable; it is not a theory waiting to be proven false. God's truth is certain and can be counted on. In recovery a central question is, Are we ready to believe what God says? Or do we prefer the perspective of fallible people, the messages ingrained in our minds from past events, the doubts instilled by friends not yet in recovery? As we take God's Word to heart, we come to understand more and more of the truth—about God, about ourself, and about our future in Christ.

FIRST JOHN

THE BIG PICTURE

A. INTRODUCTION
(1:1–2:2)

B. RECOVERY FROM FALSE
THINKING: OBEDIENCE
(2:3-27)

C. RECOVERY FROM FALSE
THINKING: THE WORK OF
CHRIST (2:28–4:6)

D. RECOVERY FROM FALSE
THINKING: THE GIFTS OF GOD
(4:7–5:5)

E. CONCLUSION: ASSURANCE OF
SPIRITUAL RECOVERY (5:6-21)

False spiritual teachers were a big problem in the early church. Because there was no New Testament that new believers could refer to, many churches fell prey to pretenders who taught their own ideas and advanced themselves as leaders. John wrote this letter to set the record straight on some important issues, particularly concerning the identity of Jesus Christ.

Because John's letter was about the basics of faith in Christ, it helped his readers take inventory of their faith. It helped them answer the question, Are we true believers? John told them that they could tell by looking at their actions: Loving one another was evidence of God's presence in their lives. But if they bickered and fought all the time, or were selfish and did not look out for one another, they were revealing that they, in fact, did not know God.

That did not mean they had to be perfect. John also recognized that believing involved admitting our sins and seeking God's forgiveness. Depending on God for cleansing from sin and freedom from guilt through admitting our wrongs against others and making amends was also important in getting to know God.

God's recovery program requires us to make amends because this is essential to successful recovery. John's letter challenges us to treat others with respect and dignity as we grow spiritually. People transformed by Christ will show it in how they treat others. In a similar way, we will progress in recovery only as far as we right the wrongs we have committed against others. It takes humility and commitment to live at peace with others, but it is a price worth paying as we seek God's blessings.

THE BOTTOM LINE

PURPOSE: To set boundaries on the content of faith and to give believers assurance of their salvation. AUTHOR: The apostle John. AUDIENCE: Circulated through an unnamed group of early churches. DATE WRITTEN: Probably between A.D. 85 and 96. SETTING: John was the only surviving apostle when he wrote this circular letter. He was living in Ephesus, supervising the churches of Asia Minor. KEY VERSE: "I write this to you who believe in the Son of God, so that you may know you have eternal life" (5:13). KEY PEOPLE AND RELATIONSHIPS: John, with the believers to whom he wrote.

RECOVERY THEMES

God Desires Our Recovery: One of the ways God cares for us is by listening to us. When Satan (called the "Accuser" in Revelation 12:10) plants thoughts of hopelessness in our mind and tells us that we have gone too far for God to forgive us, John urges us not to give up hope. Jesus Christ, our advocate, has already paid the penalty for any and every sin we have done or could do. We do not need to shy away from asking Christ to plead our case; he has already won it.

The Invitation to Love: One of the evidences of salvation in a person's life is love for others—shown in action, not just words. An important part of recovery is being willing to extend God's love to others as God has shown his love toward us. He loved us while we were in the middle of insanity—we did not have to clean up our act to get him to love us. Through us he wants to love others in the midst of their insanity, using us to carry the message of God's love and forgiveness to them. God loves us enough to free us from bondage and use us to show his love toward others in need of recovery.

The Importance of Boundaries: The false teachers whom John corrected said that the people could throw off all moral restraints because what they did "in the body" did not matter. Those who listened to that message were becoming indifferent to sin and returning to old, sinful habits. They were relapsing into immorality and thinking it was all right. John pointed out that there are boundaries around what we believe and that Jesus Christ is the focus. Anything that leads us away from Christ is outside the boundaries. Staying focused on Christ is the most essential part of our spiritual growth and the only means for successful recovery.

CHAPTER 1
Introduction
The one who existed from the beginning* is the one we have heard and seen. We saw him with our own eyes and touched him with our own hands. He is Jesus Christ, the Word of life. ²This one who is life from God was shown to us, and we have seen him. And now we testify and announce to you that he is the one who is eternal life. He was with the Father, and then he was shown to us. ³We are telling you about what we ourselves have actually seen and heard, so that you may have fellowship with us. And our fellowship is with the Father and with his Son, Jesus Christ.

⁴We are writing these things so that our* joy will be complete.

Living in the Light
⁵This is the message he has given us to announce to you: God is light and there is no darkness in him at all. ⁶So we are lying if we say we have fellowship with God but go on living in spiritual darkness. We are not living in the truth. ⁷But if we are living in the light of God's presence, just as Christ is, then we have fellowship with each other, and the blood of Jesus, his Son, cleanses us from every sin.

⁸If we say we have no sin, we are only fooling ourselves and refusing to accept the truth.

1:1 Greek *What was from the beginning.* **1:4** Some manuscripts read *your.*

1:1-4 John wrote to assure those who doubted the value of their faith in God. He showed that faith in Christ is intellectually, socially, and emotionally satisfying. Spiritual recovery takes place only where there is a healthy balance among the intellectual, social, and emotional aspects of life, all centered on genuine faith in God. Dealing with our shortcomings and making amends where possible means facing all our shortcomings—in all areas of our life.

1:5-7 There is a strong contrast between the light in the Christian life and the darkness in a life controlled by sin. If we live in sin while claiming to be a Christian, we are lying and will never successfully navigate the recovery process. Honest, accurate self-examination and personal inventory of our spiritual state are crucial. Choosing to live in the light—continually acknowledging our flaws as the light reveals them—results in a cleansed conscience and fulfilling relationships.

2:3-6 How can we be sure that we belong to Christ? Our assurance is validated by our continuing desire to obey God's will for us. Those who claim to be saved but continually disobey God are liars. We cannot make progress in recovery unless we are willing to submit to God's program for godly living. That means continuing our personal inventory, promptly admitting our wrongs to others, and confessing our sins to God. As we learn to love God more and more, our actions will show it.

2:7-11 Another distinctive mark of our faith is loving others. Hatred toward others is a sure sign that recovery has not yet begun. Light and darkness cannot exist in the same heart. The absence of love will keep us in the dark and prove a severe hindrance to progress in recovery. Love is never weak or compromising; it is the evidence of emotional strength. The love God gives us provides the energy to approach those we have harmed and to make amends when possible.

9But if we confess our sins to him, he is faithful and just to forgive us and to cleanse us from every wrong. 10If we claim we have not sinned, we are calling God a liar and showing that his word has no place in our hearts.

CHAPTER 2

My dear children, I am writing this to you so that you will not sin. But if you do sin, there is someone to plead for you before the Father. He is Jesus Christ, the one who pleases God completely.* 2He is the sacrifice for our sins. He takes away not only our sins but the sins of all the world.

3And how can we be sure that we belong to him? By obeying his commandments. 4If someone says, "I belong to God," but doesn't obey God's commandments, that person is a liar and does not live in the truth. 5But those who obey God's word really do love him. That is the way to know whether or not we live in him. 6Those who say they live in God should live their lives as Christ did.

A New Commandment

7Dear friends, I am not writing a new commandment, for it is an old one you have always had, right from the beginning. This commandment—to love one another—is the same message you heard before. 8Yet it is also new. This commandment is true in Christ and is true among you, because the darkness is disappearing and the true light is already shining.

9If anyone says, "I am living in the light," but hates a Christian brother or sister,* that person is still living in darkness. 10Anyone who loves other Christians* is living in the light and does not cause anyone to stumble. 11Anyone who hates a Christian brother or sister is living and walking in darkness. Such a person is lost, having been blinded by the darkness.

12I am writing to you, my dear children, because your sins have been forgiven because of Jesus.

13I am writing to you who are mature because you know Christ, the one who is from the beginning.

I am writing to you who are young because you have won your battle with Satan.

14I have written to you, children, because you have known the Father.

2:1 Greek *Jesus Christ, the righteous.* 2:9 Greek *his brother;* also in 2:11. 2:10 Greek *his brother.*

STEP 10

Recurrent Sins

BIBLE READING: 1 John 1:8-10

We continued to take personal inventory and when we were wrong promptly admitted it.

We may feel awkward about bringing our recurrent sins before God. We may be embarrassed by the number of times we have had to deal with the same issues— issues that stubbornly refuse to be washed away. We may imagine that God is collecting a long list of repeated offenses to be used against us.

The apostle John wrote: "If we say we have no sin, we are only fooling ourselves and refusing to accept the truth. But if we confess our sins to him, he is faithful and just to forgive us and to cleanse us from every wrong. [And it is perfectly proper for God to do this for us because Christ died to wash away our sins.] If we claim we have not sinned, we are calling God a liar and showing that his word has no place in our hearts" (1 John 1:8-10).

To confess means to agree with God that what he declares to be wrong really is wrong. This means we need to recognize our wrongs when they occur. John says that God will forgive us and cleanse us of *every* wrong. Each time we confess a sin it is washed away. Our life is like a slate that has been wiped clean. Our sins are not recorded on some celestial list; they are gone forever! Even when we make the same mistakes over and over again, God keeps forgiving us if we are truly repentant. Some areas of our life need more cleaning than others! God doesn't get angry when we come back to him repeatedly. There is no need to feel awkward. God wants us to come to him every time we sin. *Turn to Step Eleven, page 149, John 3.*

I have written to you who are mature because you know Christ, the one who is from the beginning.

I have written to you who are young because you are strong with God's word living in your hearts, and you have won your battle with Satan.

15Stop loving this evil world and all that it offers you, for when you love the world, you show that you do not have the love of the Father in you. 16For the world offers only the lust for physical pleasure, the lust for everything we see, and pride in our possessions. These are not from the Father. They are from this evil world. 17And this world is fading away, along with everything it craves. But if you do the will of God, you will live forever.

18Dear children, the last hour is here. You have heard that the Antichrist is coming, and already many such antichrists have appeared. From this we know that the end of the world has come. 19These people left our churches because they never really belonged with us; otherwise they would have stayed with us. When they left us, it proved that they do not belong with us. 20But you are not like that, for the Holy Spirit has come upon you,* and all of you know the truth. 21So I am writing to you not because you don't know the truth but because you know the difference between truth and falsehood. 22And who is the great liar? The one who says that Jesus is not the Christ. Such people are antichrists, for they have denied the Father and the Son. 23Anyone who denies the Son doesn't have the Father either. But anyone who confesses the Son has the Father also.

24So you must remain faithful to what you have been taught from the beginning. If you do, you will continue to live in fellowship with the Son and with the Father. 25And in this fellowship we enjoy the eternal life he promised us.

26I have written these things to you because you need to be aware of those who want to lead you astray. 27But you have received the Holy Spirit,* and he lives within you, so you don't need anyone to teach you what is true. For the Spirit teaches you all things, and what he teaches is true—it is not a lie. So continue in what he has taught you, and continue to live in Christ.

28And now, dear children, continue to live in fellowship with Christ so that when he returns, you will be full of courage and not shrink back from him in shame. 29Since we know that God is always right, we also know that all who do what is right are his children.

CHAPTER 3
Living as Children of God
See how very much our heavenly Father loves us, for he allows us to be called his children, and we really are! But the people who belong to this world don't know God, so

2:20 Greek *But you have an anointing from the Holy One.* 2:27 Greek *the anointing.*

2:24-27 Belief in Jesus as the Son of God and reliance upon the Holy Spirit within us will guard us against being deceived by false doctrines. The quest for new, sophisticated solutions to the consequences of sin and despair only leads to new kinds of enslavement to cultic religions, substance abuse, or codependency. Historical Christianity gives us the only perspective of ourself and the world that leads to true freedom from the enslavement of sin because only the Christian faith asserts that Jesus took upon himself the penalty for our sins.
2:28–3:3 Many of us struggle with shame. John tells us that as we live in Christ, trusting him for forgiveness and walking with him consistently, we will have no reason to be ashamed when Christ returns. We can rest assured that we are loved and acceptable because God himself has made us his children. As his children, we long to be with him and to be like him. The ultimate step in recovery is for this longing to be fulfilled. In the meantime, the knowledge that Jesus is coming again provides powerful motivation to live a godly life and to know God better through prayer and meditation on his Word.
3:4-9 As we take moral inventory of our life, let's face the essence of sin honestly: It is breaking God's law, doing things our own way rather than God's way. Once we commit our life to God, he gives us a new nature that is no longer comfortable with sin. We still sin, but we no longer make it a practice. We know that Jesus gave his life on the cross for our sins, so now we desire to please him because we have a new nature. Whereas before—in our sins, codependency, and/or addiction—we continued with little sense of wrongdoing, now we know better. In recovery we constantly affirm that we have God's power to break old patterns.
3:10-20 Using Cain and Abel as examples, John underscored the importance of love. Having true love means being willing to make sacrifices for the ones we love. In recovery the best way to express our love for God is to be willing to make amends for the wrongs we have done to others. Our actions toward others, not just our words, will reveal what's in our heart.

they don't understand that we are his children. ²Yes, dear friends, we are already God's children, and we can't even imagine what we will be like when Christ returns. But we do know that when he comes we will be like him, for we will see him as he really is. ³And all who believe this will keep themselves pure, just as Christ is pure.

⁴Those who sin are opposed to the law of God, for all sin opposes the law of God. ⁵And you know that Jesus came to take away our sins, for there is no sin in him. ⁶So if we continue to live in him, we won't sin either. But those who keep on sinning have never known him or understood who he is.

⁷Dear children, don't let anyone deceive you about this: When people do what is right, it is because they are righteous, even as Christ is righteous. ⁸But when people keep on sinning, it shows they belong to the Devil, who has been sinning since the beginning. But the Son of God came to destroy these works of the Devil. ⁹Those who have been born into God's family do not sin, because God's life is in them. So they can't keep on sinning, because they have been born of God. ¹⁰So now we can tell who are children of God and who are children of the Devil. Anyone who does not obey God's commands and does not love other Christians* does not belong to God.

Love One Another

¹¹This is the message we have heard from the beginning: We should love one another. ¹²We must not be like Cain, who belonged to the evil one and killed his brother. And why did he kill him? Because Cain had been doing what was evil, and his brother had been doing what was right. ¹³So don't be surprised, dear brothers and sisters,* if the world hates you.

¹⁴If we love our Christian brothers and sisters, it proves that we have passed from death to eternal life. But a person who has no love is still dead. ¹⁵Anyone who hates another Christian* is really a murderer at heart. And you know that murderers don't have eternal life within them. ¹⁶We know what real love is because Christ gave up his life for us. And so we also ought to give up our lives for our Christian brothers and sisters. ¹⁷But if anyone has enough money to live well and sees a brother or sister in need and refuses to help—how can God's love be in that person?

3:10 Greek *his brother.* **3:13** Greek *brothers;* also in 3:14, 16. **3:15** Greek *his brother.*

Forgiveness

READ 1 JOHN 2:1-6

At times we may feel as if we are the worst sinner on earth. We just seem to keep doing the same bad things over and over. We feel guilty! Can God just wink at our sins and pretend that everything is all right? How can he repeatedly forgive us for committing the same wrongs?

The apostle John said: "My dear children, I am writing this to you so that you will not sin. But if you do sin, there is someone to plead for you before the Father. He is Jesus Christ, the one who pleases God completely. He is the sacrifice for our sins. He takes away not only our sins but the sins of all the world" (1 John 2:1-2).

God takes sin very seriously. As a righteous judge, he can't just ignore sin and act as if it doesn't matter. But he forgives us completely and repeatedly. The words used here are legal terms. Jesus is our advocate, our defense attorney in a court of law, who intercedes for us, the lawbreakers. But he is not only the defense attorney; he is also "the sacrifice for our sins." This means that Jesus' death has been accepted by the court as admissible payment for all of our sins. We are all guilty. The sentence is death! But our sentence has already been paid by Jesus. When we bring our sins to Jesus, he goes back to the judge, his Father, on our behalf, reminding him that our sentence has already been paid. *Turn to page 447, Jude 1.*

[18]Dear children, let us stop just saying we love each other; let us really show it by our actions. [19]It is by our actions that we know we are living in the truth, so we will be confident when we stand before the Lord, [20]even if our hearts condemn us. For God is greater than our hearts, and he knows everything.

[21]Dear friends, if our conscience is clear, we can come to God with bold confidence. [22]And we will receive whatever we request because we obey him and do the things that please him. [23]And this is his commandment: We must believe in the name of his Son, Jesus Christ, and love one another, just as he commanded us. [24]Those who obey God's commandments live in fellowship with him, and he with them. And we know he lives in us because the Holy Spirit lives in us.

CHAPTER 4
Discerning False Prophets

Dear friends, do not believe everyone who claims to speak by the Spirit. You must test them to see if the spirit they have comes from God. For there are many false prophets in the world. [2]This is the way to find out if they have the Spirit of God: If a prophet acknowledges that Jesus Christ became a human being, that person has the Spirit of God. [3]If a prophet does not acknowledge Jesus, that person is not from God. Such a person has the spirit of the Antichrist. You have heard that he is going to come into the world, and he is already here.

[4]But you belong to God, my dear children. You have already won your fight with these false prophets, because the Spirit who lives in you is greater than the spirit who lives in the world. [5]These people belong to this world, so they speak from the world's viewpoint, and the world listens to them. [6]But we belong to God; that is why those who know God listen to us. If they do not belong to God, they do not listen to us. That is how we know if someone has the Spirit of truth or the spirit of deception.

Loving One Another

[7]Dear friends, let us continue to love one another, for love comes from God. Anyone who loves is born of God and knows God. [8]But anyone who does not love does not know God—for God is love.

[9]God showed how much he loved us by sending his only Son into the world so that we might have eternal life through him. [10]This is real love. It is not that we loved God, but that he loved us and sent his Son as a sacrifice to take away our sins.

[11]Dear friends, since God loved us that much, we surely ought to love each other. [12]No one has ever seen God. But if we love each other, God lives in us, and his love has been brought to full expression through us.

[13]And God has given us his Spirit as proof that we live in him and he in us. [14]Furthermore, we have seen with our own eyes and now testify that the Father sent his Son to be

---

4:1-6 No religious system can be true if it denies that Jesus was God in a human body. A clear view of who Jesus is will help us develop a relationship with God; through prayer and studying his Word we can know what his will is and how to accomplish it in our life. Even if other people don't understand or accept our new way of life, as we walk with God, we can know that he who lives in our heart is stronger than our past and our present struggles with sin.

4:7-12 Recovery depends upon God's gifts, and the most important among them is the provision of a Savior. The Father loves us enough to have sent his Son to save us. As we grow to be more like him, we also grow in our ability to love others with sacrificial love. Many of us feel the recovery process would be greatly expedited if only we could see God. But God is usually seen only through his people when they love one another. That is why it is so important for us to restore relationships with the people we have harmed. That is also why we need the fellowship of believers—because we desperately need the love they offer.

4:16–5:3 John spoke again about the importance of love. True Christianity is characterized by loving relationships in which there is no fear. Experiencing such relationships—first with God, then with other believers—is at the heart of recovery. We can trust God wholly, without fear, because the punishment for our sins has already taken place (through Christ). Where love reigns, we can be open and vulnerable with fellow believers, trusting that our honesty will not be used to hurt us. Mature Christian love delights in helping others. It creates an environment in which we can develop accountability and a new sense of responsibility toward ourself and others.

5:6-13 How can we who are committed to recovery know that we are actually achieving it in a way that pleases God? Scripture tells us that we can look for certain evidence: Belief that Jesus is the Son of God and commitment to obey him are two sources of assurance. Another is the witness of the Holy Spirit, who points to Christ in our life. God gives us a sense of rightness as we maintain contact with him through prayer and study of his Word and as we obey his revealed will.

the Savior of the world. ¹⁵All who proclaim that Jesus is the Son of God have God living in them, and they live in God. ¹⁶We know how much God loves us, and we have put our trust in him.

God is love, and all who live in love live in God, and God lives in them. ¹⁷And as we live in God, our love grows more perfect. So we will not be afraid on the day of judgment, but we can face him with confidence because we are like Christ here in this world.

¹⁸Such love has no fear because perfect love expels all fear. If we are afraid, it is for fear of judgment, and this shows that his love has not been perfected in us. ¹⁹We love each other* as a result of his loving us first.

²⁰If someone says, "I love God," but hates a Christian brother or sister,* that person is a liar; for if we don't love people we can see, how can we love God, whom we have not seen? ²¹And God himself has commanded that we must love not only him but our Christian brothers and sisters, too.

CHAPTER 5
Faith in the Son of God

Everyone who believes that Jesus is the Christ is a child of God. And everyone who loves the Father loves his children, too. ²We know we love God's children if we love God and obey his commandments. ³Loving God means keeping his commandments, and really, that isn't difficult. ⁴For every child of God defeats this evil world by trusting Christ to give the victory. ⁵And the ones who win this battle against the world are the ones who believe that Jesus is the Son of God.

⁶And Jesus Christ was revealed as God's Son by his baptism in water and by shedding his blood on the cross*—not by water only, but by water and blood. And the Spirit also gives us the testimony that this is true. ⁷So we have these three witnesses*—⁸the Spirit, the water, and the blood—and all three agree. ⁹Since we believe human testimony, surely we can believe the testimony that comes from God. And God has testified about his Son. ¹⁰All who believe in the Son of God know that this is true. Those who don't believe this are actually calling God a liar because they don't believe what God has testified about his Son.

¹¹And this is what God has testified: He has

4:19 Or *We love him;* Greek reads *We love.* **4:20** Greek *brother;* also in 4:21. **5:6** Greek *This is he who came by water and blood.* **5:7** Some very late manuscripts add *in heaven—the Father, the Word, and the Holy Spirit, and these three are one. And we have three witnesses on earth.*

Eyes of Love

BIBLE READING: 1 John 5:11-15

We humbly asked him to remove our shortcomings.

Most of us probably aren't used to getting the things we ask for. How can we have confidence that God will hear our prayers? How do we know he will answer when we ask him to remove our shortcomings?

The apostle Paul wrote: "Long ago, even before he made the world, God loved us and chose us in Christ to be holy and without fault in his eyes" (Ephesians 1:4). God's primary goal is to make us holy—that is, to form his character in us. Looking through the eyes of love, he already sees us as we will be when his work is done. Then he works out his goals for us in the arena of everyday life. The Bible tells us: "God's discipline is always right and good for us because it means we will share in his holiness" (Hebrews 12:10). Our holiness—the removal of our shortcomings—is God's will for each of us. The apostle John wrote: "We can be confident that he will listen to us whenever we ask him for anything in line with his will. And if we know he is listening when we make our requests, we can be sure that he will give us what we ask for" (1 John 5:14-15).

It is clearly God's will to have our sinful shortcomings removed. And he has promised to give us anything we ask for in line with his will. Therefore, we can have full confidence that God will remove our shortcomings in his time. *Turn to Step Eight, page 33, Matthew 18.*

given us eternal life, and this life is in his Son. [12]So whoever has God's Son has life; whoever does not have his Son does not have life.

Conclusion

[13]I write this to you who believe in the Son of God, so that you may know you have eternal life. [14]And we can be confident that he will listen to us whenever we ask him for anything in line with his will. [15]And if we know he is listening when we make our requests, we can be sure that he will give us what we ask for.

[16]If you see a Christian brother or sister* sinning in a way that does not lead to death, you should pray, and God will give that person life. But there is a sin that leads to death, and I am not saying you should pray for those who commit it. [17]Every wrong is sin, but not all sin leads to death.

[18]We know that those who have become part of God's family do not make a practice of sinning, for God's Son holds them securely, and the evil one cannot get his hands on them. [19]We know that we are children of God and that the world around us is under the power and control of the evil one. [20]And we know that the Son of God has come, and he has given us understanding so that we can know the true God. And now we are in God because we are in his Son, Jesus Christ. He is the only true God, and he is eternal life.

[21]Dear children, keep away from anything that might take God's place in your hearts.*

5:16 Greek *your brother.* **5:21** Greek *keep yourselves from idols.*

5:16-19 Another evidence of spiritual recovery is godly discernment—the spiritual capacity to know right from wrong. This power of discernment is lost in codependent relationships; regaining it is at the heart of the recovery process. Until we see ourself as God sees us, our moral inventory will be flawed and self-excusing.

5:20-21 John concludes his letter by reminding us who the true God is and warning us not to let anything take God's place in our heart. He cautions against entertaining any false ideas about God. We can know the true God through his Son, Jesus Christ. Recovery involves eliminating all wrong ideas about God, any material substitutes for him, and all controlling sins. Recovery means putting God in his rightful place as the absolute Lord of our life. Someone has said, "Only Jesus Christ is able to control a person's life without destroying it." In a restored relationship with God, the submission of our life and will to his control is the way back to sanity.

REFLECTIONS ON

FIRST JOHN

✳insights ABOUT CONFESSION AND FORGIVENESS

Accurate personal inventory normally leads to an awareness of sin. We are assured in **1 John 1:8-10** that if we confess our sins, we will experience the forgiveness and cleansing God has provided through the blood shed by his Son, Jesus Christ. The lesson is simple: Confession must precede cleansing. Confession should be followed by a willingness to change and make amends where possible.

In most recovery situations, whether the need is for cleansing from sin or for deliverance from the trauma of abuse or codependence, honest self-evaluation will lead to an admission of powerlessness. We see in **1 John 2:1-2** that we can turn to the greatest resource and advocate of all— Jesus Christ. Because he received the full force of God's anger against sin, we in recovery need not live in fear of God's anger for our past transgressions. Trusting that Christ suffered for our sins, we can now come to the Father freely, with complete trust that we will be accepted unconditionally.

✳*insights* ABOUT THE DANGER OF WORLDLY VALUES

In **1 John 2:15-17** we are reminded that the more we are wrapped up in this world and its attractions, the harder it will be to establish spiritual goals for our life. If we feed our desires with what the world offers, we starve ourself spiritually. The best way to avoid entanglement with worldly values is to "feed" our spirits by seeking God through prayer and meditation on his Word. Then we will discover his will and his help in redirecting our life.

✳*insights* ABOUT THE IMPORTANCE OF RIGHT BELIEFS

In **1 John 2:18-23** we learn that an important aspect of recovery is commitment to right beliefs. As we rely on the Holy Spirit to know the truth, we are able to recognize the spirit of antichrist. The critical doctrinal issue for John was that of the deity of Jesus Christ. One cannot genuinely profess belief in God while denying his Son. Full spiritual recovery cannot take place unless we recognize Jesus as the Son of God and the higher power who can restore us to sane living.

We are told in **1 John 5:4-5** that if we believe in Jesus and live by faith, we are equipped to triumph over the negative influences of our hostile world. For those of us who trust Christ with our life, recovery is not only possible but certain. Neither addictive behaviors nor abusive people can dominate where God has promised the power to overcome.

✳*insights* ABOUT ASSURANCE IN SALVATION AND RECOVERY

In **1 John 4:13-15** we are told that assurance of salvation comes from believing that Jesus is the Son of God, because that ability to believe is proof that God himself, through the Holy Spirit, is living in us. Confession of who Christ is is both the evidence and the expression of a genuine faith. It is more than intellectual belief; believing that Christ is the Son of God and Savior of the world leads us to confession of sin and commitment to live for God. We do this as we take responsibility for our life and deal with our past failures and broken relationships.

In **1 John 5:14-15** we see that another encouraging sign of true recovery is answered prayer. It is gratifying to know that when we pray according to the will of God, he has promised to hear and to answer us. Our greatest resources for recovery are the Word of God, by which we learn God's will, and prayer, through which we talk to God and present our needs to him.

SECOND JOHN

THE BIG PICTURE

A. SALUTATION (1:1-3)

B. RECOVERY WITH LOVE AND OBEDIENCE (1:4-6)

C. RECOVERY WITH TRUTH AND VIGILANCE (1:7-11)

D. CONCLUDING REMARKS (1:12-13)

Recovery is a fragile process. Without vigilance and encouragement from others, we live with the prospect of relapse. In the face of this, we need help from others who have courage and sensitivity toward our situation. Harsh "reprogramming" will not help us, but neither will friends who flatter us with falsely positive words. Diligence together with faithful support is what we need.

This letter is a highly personal one that deals with the kinds of issues that are addressed more broadly in 1 John. The tone is warm and pastoral. John wrote this letter with a twofold purpose: to commend and to encourage "the chosen lady," his addressee. She had already demonstrated her faithfulness to God; she did not need to be corrected. But John did not want her to trip over the obstacles ahead that might threaten her continued service to God.

In balancing commendation and encouragement, John proves to be a wise counselor and a splendid example to all of us in recovery. We need to recognize and affirm each other's past successes. At the same time, we must be willing to point out the hazards ahead when we see them, sharing our hard-won wisdom as warnings for the unwary. Pointing out the obstacles ahead and encouraging one another to be careful are the loving things to do. Thus, this letter underscores the critical importance of carrying the message of recovery to others.

THE BOTTOM LINE

PURPOSE: To commend the chosen lady and to encourage her to continue teaching others about Christ.
AUTHOR: The apostle John. AUDIENCE: "The chosen lady" and her children. DATE WRITTEN: Probably written before 1 John, sometime near A.D. 90. SETTING: The woman to whom John wrote was probably involved in one of the churches that John oversaw, although it is uncertain whether the "chosen lady" was an individual; John may have been writing to a local church. KEY VERSE: "If someone comes to your meeting and does not teach the truth about Christ, don't invite him into your house or encourage him in any way" (1:10). KEY PEOPLE AND RELATIONSHIPS: John, with the chosen lady and her children.

RECOVERY THEMES

The Importance of Boundaries: John urged this special lady to be careful about those whom she let into her life. Like David, who in Psalm 101 vowed not to allow deceitful people to stay in his house, she was not to allow false teachers into her home. In fact, she was not to encourage them in any way. Sometimes we think that out of fairness we need to listen to everyone, but there are dangers in this attitude. We must carefully set limits on whom we listen to if we are to protect ourself in recovery and in our spiritual growth.

The Challenge to Love: Loving one another is the most basic act of obedience to God. It is also an important ingredient in recovery. As we recover, we may tend to focus inward or become self-centered. Loving others will not only please God, but it will go a long way toward healing our relationships.

Greetings

This letter is from John the Elder.*

It is written to the chosen lady and to her children,* whom I love in the truth, as does everyone else who knows God's truth—²the truth that lives in us and will be in our hearts forever.

³May grace, mercy, and peace, which come from God our Father and from Jesus Christ his Son, be with us who live in truth and love.

Live in the Truth

⁴How happy I was to meet some of your children and find them living in the truth, just as we have been commanded by the Father.

⁵And now I want to urge you, dear lady, that we should love one another. This is not a new commandment, but one we had from the beginning. ⁶Love means doing what God has commanded us, and he has commanded us to love one another, just as you heard from the beginning.

⁷Many deceivers have gone out into the world. They do not believe that Jesus Christ came to earth in a real body. Such a person is a deceiver and an antichrist. ⁸Watch out, so that you do not lose the prize for which we* have been working so hard. Be diligent so that you will receive your full reward. ⁹For if you wander beyond the teaching of Christ, you will not have fellowship with God. But if you continue in the teaching of Christ, you will have fellowship with both the Father and the Son.

¹⁰If someone comes to your meeting and does not teach the truth about Christ, don't invite him into your house or encourage him in any way. ¹¹Anyone who encourages him becomes a partner in his evil work.

Conclusion

¹²Well, I have much more to say to you, but I don't want to say it in a letter. For I hope to visit you soon and to talk with you face to face. Then our joy will be complete.

¹³Greetings from the children of your sister,* chosen by God.

1a Greek *From the elder.* **1b** Or *the church God has chosen and her members,* or *the chosen Kyria and her children.* **8** Some manuscripts read *you.* **13** Or *from the members of your sister church.*

1:4-6 Note the wise approach John used here: First he commended this woman and her children for their faithfulness; then he exhorted them to act according to Christian love; finally he followed his exhortation with an explanation. There is a sequential pattern for helping others: encouragement, exhortation, and explanation. Even though we are teaching truths established by the authority of God's Word, sharing the Good News must still be done in ways that will communicate to people. An initial commendation will edify and build rapport; exhortation will communicate the truth or confront a problem; and an explanation will establish the truth and build relationships.
1:7-9 Clear boundaries for belief and practice are essential for spiritual growth and effective recovery. Many of us have been deceived and pulled into unhealthy relationships, damaging habits, or false religions. People may even have tried to convince us that such things would lead to recovery. We need to be aware of the subtle lies and distortions of truth some people use to deceive us. The best way to avoid being deceived is to anchor our faith in God's Word and seek his will for us through prayer. Faith in God through Jesus Christ is the only viable means for successful recovery.
1:10-11 With heresy on the rise, John warned believers not to allow those with suspect doctrinal views to infiltrate the Christian community. He did not want new believers who had made a good beginning in the Christian faith to be led astray. We also need godly people in our life—people like John—who can warn us about false teachings and dangerous activities. If we don't have relationships that hold us accountable, we need to develop them. All of us are susceptible to being deceived and led astray. Building healthy relationships with wise and godly people is vital to any successful recovery program.

THIRD JOHN

THE BIG PICTURE

A. SALUTATION (1:1)

B. GAIUS: A CASE FOR COMMENDATION (1:2-8)

C. DIOTREPHES: A CASE FOR CONFRONTATION (1:9-10)

D. DEMETRIUS: A CASE FOR CONGRATULATION (1:11-12)

E. CONCLUDING REMARKS (1:13-15)

We know little about Gaius except that he was generous and hospitable and highly regarded by the apostle John. Apparently, Gaius took it upon himself to provide free room and board for traveling pastors and missionaries. In a day when most preachers had to travel from town to town with no regular means of support, the service Gaius provided was greatly needed. John wrote this letter to commend him and to warn him to watch out for a self-important spiritual teacher named Diotrephes. John challenged Gaius not to be influenced by Diotrephes's bad example and to warn others about him, too.

Aside from his warning about Diotrephes, John was primarily concerned with encouraging his friend Gaius. This reminds us that the simple act of including others in our life and sharing ourself with them is especially pleasing to God. One of the reasons God places people in our life is so we can support and encourage them. As we reach out to help others, we will discover that we, too, are blessed and strengthened in a special way.

Hospitality doesn't have to be complicated. It can mean setting an extra place at the table, offering a ride, giving a hug or a handshake, or speaking a word of greeting. We all need a little support sometimes; it is part of the process of recovery to open up and support one another as we face our struggles. How affirming it is to be shown some hospitality or to be invited into someone else's life. Hospitality can be such a simple act; yet it is a potent way to show love, appreciation, and support, and each of us has some of it to share.

THE BOTTOM LINE

PURPOSE: To commend Gaius for his hospitality and to encourage him in his faithfulness. AUTHOR: The apostle John. AUDIENCE: Gaius, a prominent believer, perhaps from Derbe in Asia Minor. DATE WRITTEN: Around A.D. 90. SETTING: Like 1 and 2 John, 3 John was probably written from Ephesus and circulated among the churches in Asia Minor. KEY VERSE: "Dear friend, don't let this bad example influence you. Follow only what is good. Remember that those who do good prove that they are God's children, and those who do evil prove that they do not know God" (1:11). KEY PEOPLE AND RELATIONSHIPS: John with Gaius, with Diotrephes, and with Demetrius.

RECOVERY THEMES

Pride Leads to Relapse: Diotrephes refused to humble himself before others and decided that he alone would be the boss. His arrogant attitude disqualified him from the leadership role he coveted. One of the vices we face in recovery is pride. As we experience success, it is all too easy to feel as if we have arrived. We begin to think we are self-sufficient and superior to others. A word to the wise: Pride and self-sufficiency often lead to relapse.

The Importance of Helping Others: In contrast to Diotrephes, Gaius and Demetrius were commended for their faithful service to others. They had generously shared with others, both in hospitality and in their teaching of the truth, without complaint. In their own ways they were carrying the message of God's transforming power to people who were still in bondage. John did not take them for granted; he commended them for their service. Today they live on as godly examples for each of us to follow.

Greetings

This letter is from John the Elder.*

It is written to Gaius, my dear friend, whom I love in the truth.

²Dear friend, I am praying that all is well with you and that your body is as healthy as I know your soul is. ³Some of the brothers recently returned and made me very happy by telling me about your faithfulness and that you are living in the truth. ⁴I could have no greater joy than to hear that my children live in the truth.

Caring for the Lord's Workers

⁵Dear friend, you are doing a good work for God when you take care of the traveling teachers* who are passing through, even though they are strangers to you. ⁶They have told the church here of your friendship and your loving deeds. You do well to send them on their way in a manner that pleases God. ⁷For they are traveling for the Lord* and accept nothing from those who are not Christians.* ⁸So we ourselves should support them so that we may become partners with them for the truth.

⁹I sent a brief letter to the church about this, but Diotrephes, who loves to be the leader, does not acknowledge our authority. ¹⁰When I come, I will report some of the things he is doing and the wicked things he is saying about us. He not only

1 Greek *From the elder.* **5** Greek *the brothers;* also in verse 10. **7a** Greek *the Name.* **7b** Greek *from Gentiles.*

1:1-4 Recovery is a process that involves our total being. Spiritual difficulties are often intimately tied to personal problems or physical disorders, and resolving these problems may be key to restoring both spiritual and physical health. Conversely, neglecting our spiritual needs may contribute to our physical and emotional problems. As we make honest and fearless inventory of our life, we need to examine how our unhealthy spiritual condition contributes to our physical problems.

1:5-8 John commended Gaius for his hospitality toward the Christian teachers who periodically passed through town. Hospitality is a special gift and often overlooked. Some of us may feel that we're not good at sharing our faith with others and wonder if there is any way we can encourage others in recovery. Hospitality is one way to show others what God has done for us. By quietly serving others in our home, we show them that we have become new people. They may wonder how it happened, which would open a natural opportunity for us to share our faith in God. Opening our home to others may also give needy people a place to relax and explore the truth about themselves.

1:9-11 Confrontation is a necessary part of the recovery process, but it scares many of us. Here John dealt with an individual who was hurting people in the Christian community. He warned Gaius and his fellow believers about Diotrephes and told them not to let his bad example influence them. We may know people who are trying to stop our recovery. We may need to confront them, which may be difficult and painful. We need to be honest with other people and break free of them if they are trying to make us reject God's will for our life. God wants us to make progress in recovery; he will help us deal wisely with the people who stand in our way.

1:11-12 Having a good role model is an important part of effective recovery. John urged Gaius to follow good examples and to avoid imitating anyone who was doing evil. This means that we should put relationships that lead us back into our dependency on hold for a while and build relationships with people who model a godly lifestyle and will encourage us in recovery. Since God desires our success in recovery, he will help us build healthy relationships in our life.

refuses to welcome the traveling teachers, he also tells others not to help them. And when they do help, he puts them out of the church.

¹¹Dear friend, don't let this bad example influence you. Follow only what is good. Remember that those who do good prove that they are God's children, and those who do evil prove that they do not know God. ¹²But everyone speaks highly of Demetrius, even truth itself. We ourselves can say the same for him, and you know we speak the truth.

Conclusion

¹³I have much to tell you, but I don't want to do it in a letter. ¹⁴For I hope to see you soon, and then we will talk face to face.

¹⁵May God's peace be with you.

Your friends here send you their greetings. Please give my personal greetings to each of our friends there.

JUDE

THE BIG PICTURE

A. A CAUTION TO BELIEVERS (1:1-16)

B. A CHALLENGE TO BELIEVERS (1:17-25)

Jude wrote this letter to young believers who had left their old life behind to follow Christ. They had made spiritual and moral commitments to do what God wanted them to do. But some false teachers claimed that believers could live however they wanted because God had already paid for their sins. Consequently, many new believers were tempted to go back to their old destructive lifestyle.

Jude urged his readers to stand up for the truth and not fall back into their old way of life. He explained that the false teachers were wrong; it did matter how they lived, and their actions did have consequences. They could not go back to their old, sinful ways without paying a terrible price.

Pressures to return to our addiction surround us, but perhaps at no time are they more difficult to resist than when they come from other people. There will always be people who make us feel like giving up on recovery. Some try to get us to give in just a little. "Just take one drink," they say. Others discourage us by their contempt for us or lack of hope that we will ever change.

It pays to recognize and stand up for God's truth. Our addiction is like a hungry lion, devouring whatever it touches. God has gone to great lengths to help us and wants us to succeed even more than we do. When we trust him fully and faithfully obey his will for our life, we will experience the freedom from bondage that he wants for us.

THE BOTTOM LINE

PURPOSE: To warn believers of the dangers of false teachings about God. AUTHOR: Jude, the brother of James and half brother of Jesus. AUDIENCE: All believers everywhere. DATE WRITTEN: Probably around A.D. 65–70. SETTING: From the beginning the church had been threatened by false teachers. Jude wrote this letter to caution all believers not to accept just any teaching about God but to defend the truth they had received from the apostles. KEY VERSES: "But you, dear friends, must continue to build your lives on the foundation of your holy faith. And continue to pray as you are directed by the Holy Spirit. Live in such a way that God's love can bless you as you wait for the eternal life that our Lord Jesus Christ in his mercy is going to give you" (1:20-21). KEY PEOPLE AND RELATIONSHIPS: Jude with his audience.

RECOVERY THEMES

The Importance of Action: This letter is a call to action, a call to "defend the truth" (1:3). Recovery is an active, not a passive, process. Once we are over the crises that led us into recovery, there is always the temptation to sit back and relax. But actively repenting and confessing our sins, taking regular inventory, making amends, and asking God to remove our defects of character are all part of the recovery process. We need to persevere in the process of recovery, always taking action toward wholeness.

Carrying the Message to Others: Because following Jesus is not a solitary activity, Jude urged his audience to intervene in one another's lives. He told them to be merciful and gently confront others, keeping them from falling prey to destructive beliefs and activities. Recovery always involves us with other people. We cannot become stabilized in recovery unless we make carrying the message of hope to others an integral part of our life. We will discover that as we share our story of deliverance, we will gain new strength to persevere in our own struggle.

Greetings from Jude

This letter is from Jude, a slave of Jesus Christ and a brother of James.

I am writing to all who are called to live in the love of God the Father and the care of Jesus Christ.

²May you receive more and more of God's mercy, peace, and love.

The Danger of False Teachers

³Dearly loved friends, I had been eagerly planning to write to you about the salvation we all share. But now I find that I must write about something else, urging you to defend the truth of the Good News.* God gave this unchanging truth once for all time to his holy people. ⁴I say this because some godless people have wormed their way in among you, saying that God's forgiveness allows us to live immoral lives. The fate of such people was determined long ago, for they have turned against our only Master and Lord, Jesus Christ.

⁵I must remind you—and you know it well—that even though the Lord* rescued the whole nation of Israel from Egypt, he later destroyed every one of those who did not remain faithful. ⁶And I remind you of the angels who did not stay within the limits of authority God gave them but left the place where they belonged. God has kept them chained in prisons of darkness, waiting for the day of judgment. ⁷And don't forget the cities of Sodom and Gomorrah and their neighboring towns, which were filled with sexual immorality and every kind of sexual perversion. Those cities were destroyed by fire and are a warning of the eternal fire that will punish all who are evil.

⁸Yet these false teachers, who claim author-

3 Greek *to contend for the faith.* 5 Some manuscripts read *Jesus.*

1:3-7 Problems don't usually attack us head-on; they often come when we least expect them. Sometimes we are completely unaware of the dangers that certain people, ideas, or activities pose to us. Jude warned his readers about people who would try to lead them away from true faith in Jesus Christ by claiming that God's grace set them free to do whatever they wanted. Our society often proclaims a similar message: Boundaries to behavior are limiting and destructive. Most of us have discovered firsthand, however, that this teaching leads to painful bondage. We should take Jude's warning seriously. We should avoid people and activities that could lead us back into slavery. The only road to freedom is God's program for healthy living.

1:14-16 Jude reminded his readers that the false teachers among them would suffer terrible consequences for their selfish and sinful lifestyle. We may be tempted to follow our old friends back into the "pleasures" of our old sinful habits. Jude's warning can help us turn away from any such temptations. If we take part in destructive activities, we will be enslaved and then destroyed. If we plant seeds of righteousness by following God's will, we will receive God's blessings and help. True freedom can be found only through a vibrant relationship with God.

1:17-23 God's Word is reliable and true. It warns us about people who might try to hinder our spiritual growth. When we learn to expect such people, we can prepare to stand firm against the temptations they offer us. By learning to recognize our weaknesses and walk humbly, depending on the Holy Spirit's guidance, we can shun the things that tear us down. When we encourage others in recovery, the story we tell must be clear and consistent with our lifestyle. We can share God's message of hope by showing others the kind of selfless love that God has already shown to us. We cannot live this way under our own power; we can do it only by receiving the power God offers through his Holy Spirit.

ity from their dreams, live immoral lives, defy authority, and scoff at the power of the glorious ones.* ⁹But even Michael, one of the mightiest of the angels, did not dare accuse Satan of blasphemy, but simply said, "The Lord rebuke you." (This took place when Michael was arguing with Satan about Moses' body.) ¹⁰But these people mock and curse the things they do not understand. Like animals, they do whatever their instincts tell them, and they bring about their own destruction. ¹¹How terrible it will be for them! For they follow the evil example of Cain, who killed his brother. Like Balaam, they will do anything for money. And like Korah, they will perish because of their rebellion.

¹²When these people join you in fellowship meals celebrating the love of the Lord, they are like dangerous reefs that can shipwreck you.* They are shameless in the way they care only about themselves. They are like clouds blowing over dry land without giving rain, promising much but producing nothing. They are like trees without fruit at harvesttime. They are not only dead but doubly dead, for they have been pulled out by the roots. ¹³They are like wild waves of the sea, churning up the dirty foam of their shameful deeds. They are wandering stars, heading for everlasting gloom and darkness.

¹⁴Now Enoch, who lived seven generations after Adam, prophesied about these people. He said,

"Look, the Lord is coming
    with thousands of his holy ones.
¹⁵ He will bring the people of the world
    to judgment.
He will convict the ungodly of all the
        evil things
    they have done in rebellion
and of all the insults that godless sinners
    have spoken against him."*

¹⁶These people are grumblers and complainers, doing whatever evil they feel like. They are loudmouthed braggarts, and they flatter others to get favors in return.

A Call to Remain Faithful

¹⁷But you, my dear friends, must remember what the apostles of our Lord Jesus Christ told you, ¹⁸that in the last times there would be scoffers whose purpose in life is to enjoy themselves in every evil way imaginable. ¹⁹Now they are here, and they are the ones

8 *The glorious ones* are probably evil angels. **12** Or *they are contaminants among you,* or *they are stains.* **14-15** The quotation comes from the Apocrypha: Enoch 1:9.

Accountability

READ JUDE 1:20-23

As we grapple with our addiction we are likely to avoid honest communication with others about our problems. It is important, however, that we return to the relationships that will help us face the truth. Paul spoke of the value of honesty: "So put away all falsehood and 'tell your neighbor the truth' because we belong to each other" (Ephesians 4:25). Jude, the half brother of Jesus, reminded his readers that they were to deal honestly and directly with those who were doing wrong: "Show mercy to those whose faith is wavering. . . . There are still others to whom you need to show mercy, but be careful that you aren't contaminated by their sins" (Jude 1:22-23).

Jesus even gave specific instructions for dealing with people who have done wrong but persist in denying it: "If another believer sins against you, go privately and point out the fault. If the other person listens and confesses it, you have won that person back. But if you are unsuccessful, take one or two others with you and go back again, so that everything you say may be confirmed by two or three witnesses. If that person still refuses to listen, take your case to the church. If the church decides you are right, but the other person won't accept it, treat that person as a pagan or a corrupt tax collector" (Matthew 18:15-17).

Accountability and honesty in our relationships are essential to successful recovery. When we make ourself accountable to others, the caring influence of godly friends can help keep us on the right track. They can provide us with an objective perspective, helping us to admit the truth. We often become isolated as a result of our shame or fear that we will be rejected if we ever reveal who we really are. Admitting our wrongs to trustworthy people helps break down the isolation. ***Turn to page 455, Revelation 3.***

who are creating divisions among you. They live by natural instinct because they do not have God's Spirit living in them.

[20]But you, dear friends, must continue to build your lives on the foundation of your holy faith. And continue to pray as you are directed by the Holy Spirit.* [21]Live in such a way that God's love can bless you as you wait for the eternal life that our Lord Jesus Christ in his mercy is going to give you. [22]Show mercy to those whose faith is wavering. [23]Rescue others by snatching them from the flames of judgment. There are still others to whom you need to show mercy, but be careful that you aren't contaminated by their sins.*

A Prayer of Praise

[24]And now, all glory to God, who is able to keep you from stumbling, and who will bring you into his glorious presence innocent of sin and with great joy. [25]All glory to him, who alone is God our Savior, through Jesus Christ our Lord. Yes, glory, majesty, power, and authority belong to him, in the beginning, now, and forevermore. Amen.

20 Greek *Pray in the Holy Spirit.* **23** Greek *mercy, hating even the clothing stained by the flesh.*

REVELATION

THE BIG PICTURE

A. JOHN'S PAIN AND GOD'S GLORY (1:1-20)

B. THE NEED FOR RECOVERY AMONG THE CHURCHES (2:1–3:22)

C. GOD'S GLORIOUS POWER—HOPE FOR RECOVERY (4:1–5:14)

D. GOD'S WRATH TOWARD UNBELIEF AND DENIAL (6:1–16:21)

E. BABYLON'S GRAND APPEARANCE AND FIERCE JUDGMENT (17:1–18:24)

F. CHRIST'S VICTORY, RULE, AND FINAL JUDGMENT (19:1–20:15)

G. THE NEW HEAVENS AND NEW EARTH (21:1–22:21)

From beginning to end, the book of Revelation is about struggle. In its opening chapters are John's seven dictated letters from the resurrected Christ to seven churches. Each church had its own struggles, but some had deeper problems than others. In each letter Jesus urged his people to cling to him and do what they knew to be right. The ones who listened he called overcomers.

The rest of the book contains the story of another dramatic struggle: God's plan to rid the world of sin and its destructive consequences. John describes when Jesus will return in glory to conquer Satan and restore his broken world, vindicating God's people and judging the wicked. All people will get their dues when Christ returns. Believers will receive eternal joy; unbelievers, unending separation from God. In the end, God will rebuild what has been broken by sin. He will introduce a new heaven and a new earth.

The book of Revelation ends with Christ as victor over all. All that he said will come true; all that he taught will be proven right; all who followed him will be vindicated; and all who rejected him will be judged. God will have his way. He wants nothing more than to have us stand beside him as victors! We face struggles in recovery; God knows that. Through this book he urges us to not give up but to believe in him and to overcome. As he renews our broken world, he will make our broken life new and perfect as well.

THE BOTTOM LINE

PURPOSE: To give hope to believers and warn them not to compromise their loyalty to God. AUTHOR: The apostle John. AUDIENCE: Seven churches in Asia Minor. DATE WRITTEN: Probably about A.D. 95, during the Roman emperor Domitian's persecution of Christians. SETTING: John, who was in exile on the island of Patmos, wrote to the seven churches to urge them to devote themselves to Christ. KEY VERSE: "Look! Here I stand at the door and knock. If you hear me calling and open the door, I will come in, and we will share a meal as friends" (3:20). KEY PLACES: Patmos, seven cities in Asia Minor, Babylon, and the New Jerusalem. KEY PEOPLE: John, the risen Christ, and members of the churches of Asia Minor.

RECOVERY THEMES

God Is Over All: God is sovereign. He is greater than any other power in the universe—including our dependency. Nothing can compare to him. When we look at the abuse we may have suffered as children or at the pain we have caused others, we may feel powerless to change things or make amends. But John wrote this book to assure us that though evil may seem to win today's battles, God is all-powerful and will assert his power for his people. Ultimately all things will be made new in Christ. As we submit our life to God, he will begin the process of renewal right away.

God Is the Source of Our Hope: We may feel helpless and about to give up all hope. But the book of Revelation reveals to us the ultimate source of hope—Jesus Christ. He is coming again and will deal with the problems of our sin-tattered world, restoring what is broken and dealing with the injustices around us. Life is never hopeless, regardless of what has happened to us or what we have done. We can focus on God's love, grace, and forgiveness. He has made our restoration possible through Christ, and he will return to complete his task of universal renewal. If we are looking to Christ, we can claim our hope despite the difficult circumstances we may face.

The Pain of Consequences: Something in every one of us cries out for justice. When evil and injustice prosper, we may become angry and think that people ultimately get away with their selfish and wicked deeds. But in reality God will judge all wicked actions. Those who openly defy him will face awful consequences in the end. Those who turn to him for forgiveness need not fear the future day of judgment. Judgment is an awful thing, but the pain of sin's consequences can motivate us to turn our life over to God and obediently follow his plan.

Justice Belongs to God: Being in recovery does not release us from our sense of justice. As we deal with the wrongs we have done, we may feel that others are not dealing with theirs and that we have legitimate grudges to harbor. While these feelings are natural, they are not godly and endanger our recovery. The book of Revelation makes it clear that justice belongs to God; he alone has the right to avenge the wrongs of others. What's more, he alone has the power to change their lives. Anger and bitterness make recovery more difficult than it already is. Part of giving our life and our will over to God is releasing the bitterness we feel toward others.

CHAPTER 1
Prologue

This is a revelation from* Jesus Christ, which God gave him concerning the events that will happen soon. An angel was sent to God's servant John so that John could share the revelation with God's other servants. ²John faithfully reported the word of God and the testimony of Jesus Christ—everything he saw.

³God blesses the one who reads this prophecy to the church, and he blesses all who listen to it and obey what it says. For the time is near when these things will happen.

John's Greeting to the Seven Churches

⁴This letter is from John to the seven churches in the province of Asia. Grace and peace from the one who is, who always was, and who is still to come; from the sevenfold Spirit* before his throne; ⁵and from Jesus Christ, who is the faithful witness to these things, the first to rise from the dead, and the commander of all the rulers of the world.

All praise to him who loves us and has freed us from our sins by shedding his blood for us. ⁶He has made us his Kingdom and his priests who serve before God his Father. Give

1:1 Or *of.* 1:4 Greek *the seven spirits.*

1:1-2 The book of Revelation describes what will happen in the future. It looks forward to the time of Christ's return, when our new life in Christ will be perfected. It also tells about the hard battle God will fight to restore our world from the destructive consequences of sin. Many of this book's symbols are difficult to interpret, but one message comes through clearly: No matter how bad things are right now, God has a solution! Jesus Christ will return to re-create our broken and polluted world. He will give us a new body and a healed heart. God has already started his healing in us through our relationship with Christ; he will complete this task when he returns to rule.
1:4-6 The powerful work of Jesus Christ is the only valid foundation for recovery. Christ shed his redemptive blood on the cross to free us from bondage to sin, past abuse, destructive habits, compulsions, and addictions. God loved us enough to send his Son to die on our behalf. But, praise God, Jesus rose from the dead, conquering death forever! Through him we can rise to new life. No matter who we are or what we have done, God has solutions for our problems. Through Christ, we have been made citizens of his eternal Kingdom (see Philippians 3:20); therefore we can look forward to an eternity of joy and being in God's presence.

to him everlasting glory! He rules forever and ever! Amen!

⁷Look! He comes with the clouds of heaven. And everyone will see him—even those who pierced him. And all the nations of the earth will weep because of him. Yes! Amen!

⁸"I am the Alpha and the Omega—the beginning and the end," says the Lord God. "I am the one who is, who always was, and who is still to come, the Almighty One."

Vision of the Son of Man

⁹I am John, your brother. In Jesus we are partners in suffering and in the Kingdom and in patient endurance. I was exiled to the island of Patmos for preaching the word of God and speaking about Jesus. ¹⁰It was the Lord's Day, and I was worshiping in the Spirit.* Suddenly, I heard a loud voice behind me, a voice that sounded like a trumpet blast. ¹¹It said, "Write down what you see, and send it to the seven churches: Ephesus, Smyrna, Pergamum, Thyatira, Sardis, Philadelphia, and Laodicea."

¹²When I turned to see who was speaking to me, I saw seven gold lampstands. ¹³And standing in the middle of the lampstands was the Son of Man.* He was wearing a long robe with a gold sash across his chest. ¹⁴His head and his hair were white like wool, as white as snow. And his eyes were bright like flames of fire. ¹⁵His feet were as bright as bronze refined in a furnace, and his voice thundered like mighty ocean waves. ¹⁶He held seven stars in his right hand, and a sharp two-edged sword came from his mouth. And his face was as bright as the sun in all its brilliance.

¹⁷When I saw him, I fell at his feet as dead. But he laid his right hand on me and said, "Don't be afraid! I am the First and the Last. ¹⁸I am the living one who died. Look, I am alive forever and ever! And I hold the keys of death and the grave.* ¹⁹Write down what you have seen—both the things that are now happening and the things that will happen later. ²⁰This is the meaning of the seven stars you saw in my right hand and the seven gold lampstands: The seven stars are the angels of* the seven churches, and the seven lampstands are the seven churches.

CHAPTER 2

The Message to the Church in Ephesus

"Write this letter to the angel of* the church in Ephesus. This is the message from the one who holds the seven stars in his right hand, the one who walks among the seven gold lampstands:

²"I know all the things you do. I have seen your hard work and your patient endurance. I know you don't tolerate evil people. You have examined the claims of those who say they are apostles but are not. You have discovered they are liars. ³You have patiently suffered for me without quitting. ⁴But I have this complaint against you. You don't love me or each other as you did at first! ⁵Look how far you have fallen from your first love! Turn back to me again and work as

1:10 Or *in spirit.* 1:13 Or *one who looked like a man;* Greek reads *one like a son of man.* See Dan 7:13. 1:18 Greek *and Hades.* 1:20 Or *the messengers for.* 2:1 Or *the messenger for;* also in 2:8, 12, 18.

1:7-8 The future coming of Jesus Christ will be desperately painful for those who refuse to believe and follow him. The terrifying consequences of their denial will be eternal judgment (see 20:11-15). On the other hand, if we pursue recovery by faith in Christ, we can rejoice in the new life his return will bring. God is "the beginning and the end" of all things. We can have hope because God is in control of our past, present, and future.

1:9-11 John suffered a great deal for Christ and persevered through it all. All the pain and exile had not embittered him toward God; the apostle still worshiped God faithfully. John was worshiping when he received the visions recorded in this book. It is easy to become discouraged as we work our program. Some people may reject us because we are trying to change or because we have problems. We know what it's like to be looked down upon. John's example provides encouragement to persevere despite the difficulties we face. If we give up now, we face sure disaster in the future. If we stick with recovery, God will help us to build a new life.

2:1-7 Christ addressed the church in Ephesus first. It was the largest congregation and probably responsible for planting the other churches (see Acts 19:1, 10). John began on a positive note by commending the Ephesian believers for their perseverance through hardship. Then he confronted the more painful realities and challenged his readers to repent and rekindle their love, which had waned. Confrontations are best made in the context of love. We need to begin our conversations by building others up and showing that we care. After laying the groundwork lovingly, we can better communicate the more painful messages.

you did at first. If you don't, I will come and remove your lampstand from its place among the churches. 6But there is this about you that is good: You hate the deeds of the immoral Nicolaitans, just as I do.

7"Anyone who is willing to hear should listen to the Spirit and understand what the Spirit is saying to the churches. Everyone who is victorious will eat from the tree of life in the paradise of God.

The Message to the Church in Smyrna

8"Write this letter to the angel of the church in Smyrna. This is the message from the one who is the First and the Last, who died and is alive:

9"I know about your suffering and your poverty—but you are rich! I know the slander of those opposing you. They say they are Jews, but they really aren't because theirs is a synagogue of Satan. 10Don't be afraid of what you are about to suffer. The Devil will throw some of you into prison and put you to the test. You will be persecuted for 'ten days.' Remain faithful even when facing death, and I will give you the crown of life.

11"Anyone who is willing to hear should listen to the Spirit and understand what the Spirit is saying to the churches. Whoever is victorious will not be hurt by the second death.

The Message to the Church in Pergamum

12"Write this letter to the angel of the church in Pergamum. This is the message from the one who has a sharp two-edged sword:

13"I know that you live in the city where that great throne of Satan is located, and yet you have remained loyal to me. And you refused to deny me even when Antipas, my faithful witness, was martyred among you by Satan's followers. 14And yet I have a few complaints against you. You tolerate some among you who are like Balaam, who showed Balak how to trip up the people of Israel. He taught them to worship idols by eating food offered to idols and by committing sexual sin. 15In the same way, you have some Nicolaitans among you—people who follow the same teaching and commit the same sins. 16Repent, or I will come to you suddenly and fight against them with the sword of my mouth.

17"Anyone who is willing to hear should listen to the Spirit and understand what the Spirit is saying to the churches. Everyone who is victorious will eat of the manna that has been hidden away in heaven. And I will give to each one a white stone, and on the stone will be engraved a new name that no one knows except the one who receives it.

The Message to the Church in Thyatira

18"Write this letter to the angel of the church in Thyatira. This is the message from the Son of God, whose eyes are bright like flames of fire, whose feet are like polished bronze:

19"I know all the things you do—your love, your faith, your service, and your patient endurance. And I can see your constant improvement in all these

---

2:8-11 The church in Smyrna was the closest of the other six to Ephesus, and it was experiencing similar hardships. This small Christian community was suffering from unrelenting oppression by Satan and his evil spiritual forces. John's vision reminded the believers that their perseverance through dangerous times would be rewarded with the crown of life for their faithfulness. We too are called to persevere through the tough times. As we entrust our life to God and obey him, he will slowly transform us. At Christ's return, we will receive a new body and a cleansed heart—a completely new life!

2:12-17 The church in Pergamum had remained intensely loyal to Jesus Christ through a satanic onslaught. But some in the church had given in to sexual misconduct. Such relational and spiritual dysfunctions threatened to undermine, or at least neutralize, the testimony of this Christian community. Sometimes great victories in recovery can be neutralized by small mistakes. We need to be consistent in our walk with God, making sure that all areas of our life are yielded to his control. Ignoring even the smallest sin or bad habit could lead to our undoing.

2:18-29 The church in Thyatira was commended for its acts of faith, love, and patience, and it was encouraged to persevere in doing them. But a serious spiritual cancer was growing in their midst—a self-styled prophetess named Jezebel was encouraging a profligate lifestyle. God punished this woman harshly to show how much he wanted to protect his people from her evil influence. This gives us some idea of how dangerous it is to have relationships with people who might lead us astray. We need to choose our relationships carefully. Dysfunctional relationships may lead us away from God and quickly destroy our progress in recovery.

things. [20]But I have this complaint against you. You are permitting that woman—that Jezebel who calls herself a prophet—to lead my servants astray. She is encouraging them to worship idols, eat food offered to idols, and commit sexual sin. [21]I gave her time to repent, but she would not turn away from her immorality. [22]Therefore, I will throw her upon a sickbed, and she will suffer greatly with all who commit adultery with her, unless they turn away from all their evil deeds. [23]I will strike her children dead. And all the churches will know that I am the one who searches out the thoughts and intentions of every person. And I will give to each of you whatever you deserve. [24]But I also have a message for the rest of you in Thyatira who have not followed this false teaching ('deeper truths,' as they call them—depths of Satan, really). I will ask nothing more of you [25]except that you hold tightly to what you have until I come.

[26]"To all who are victorious, who obey me to the very end, I will give authority over all the nations. [27]They will rule the nations with an iron rod and smash them like clay pots. [28]They will have the same authority I received from my Father, and I will also give them the morning star! [29]Anyone who is willing to hear should listen to the Spirit and understand what the Spirit is saying to the churches.

CHAPTER 3
The Message to the Church in Sardis

"Write this letter to the angel of* the church in Sardis. This is the message from the one who has the sevenfold Spirit* of God and the seven stars:

"I know all the things you do, and that you have a reputation for being alive—but you are dead. [2]Now wake up! Strengthen what little remains, for even what is left is at the point of death. Your deeds are far from right in the sight of God. [3]Go back to what you heard and believed at first; hold to it firmly and turn to me again. Unless you do, I will come upon you suddenly, as unexpected as a thief.

[4]"Yet even in Sardis there are some who have not soiled their garments with evil deeds. They will walk with me in white, for they are worthy. [5]All who are victorious will be clothed in white. I will never erase their names from the Book of Life, but I will announce before my Father and his angels that they are mine. [6]Anyone who is willing to hear should listen to the Spirit and understand what the Spirit is saying to the churches.

The Message to the Church in Philadelphia

[7]"Write this letter to the angel of the church in Philadelphia. This is the message from the one who is holy and true. He is the one who has the key of David. He opens doors, and no one can shut them; he shuts doors, and no one can open them.

[8]"I know all the things you do, and I have opened a door for you that no one can shut. You have little strength, yet you obeyed my word and did not deny me. [9]Look! I will force those who belong to Satan—those liars who say they are Jews but are not—to come and bow down at your feet. They will acknowledge that you are the ones I love.

[10]"Because you have obeyed my command to persevere, I will protect you from the great time of testing that will come upon the whole world to test those who belong to this world. [11]Look, I am coming quickly. Hold on to what you have, so that no one will take away

3:1a Or *the messenger for;* also in 3:7, 14. 3:1b Greek *the seven spirits.*

3:1-6 The believers in Sardis were, for the most part, just going through the motions of being spiritual. They were warned to make immediate changes or they would suffer painful consequences. Fortunately, some believers in Sardis stood firm in their faith, and they would be rewarded accordingly. With God's help, it is possible to stand firm even when everyone around us is falling away. We don't have to follow the crowd or be a victim of our environment; we can follow God instead. As we do, he will bless us and write our name in the Book of Life.
3:7-13 The church in Philadelphia was not strong, but it had remained obedient to God and stood firm against satanic oppression. So Christ promised this church protection from the greatest time of tribulation that would ever come upon the whole world. He encouraged them to persevere, promising that they would live forever with Christ in his new Jerusalem. This promise has been greatly delayed, but that doesn't make it any less secure (see 21:1–22:21). We have this same hope if we entrust our life to God through faith in Jesus Christ. Though the years of recovery may seem long, our hope in God's eternal deliverance is just as certain.

your crown. [12]All who are victorious will become pillars in the Temple of my God, and they will never have to leave it. And I will write my God's name on them, and they will be citizens in the city of my God—the new Jerusalem that comes down from heaven from my God. And they will have my new name inscribed upon them. [13]Anyone who is willing to hear should listen to the Spirit and understand what the Spirit is saying to the churches.

The Message to the Church in Laodicea

[14]"Write this letter to the angel of the church in Laodicea. This is the message from the one who is the Amen—the faithful and true witness, the ruler* of God's creation:

[15]"I know all the things you do, that you are neither hot nor cold. I wish you were one or the other! [16]But since you are like lukewarm water, I will spit you out of my mouth! [17]You say, 'I am rich. I have everything I want. I don't need a thing!' And you don't realize that you are wretched and miserable and poor and blind and naked. [18]I advise you to buy gold from me—gold that has been purified by fire. Then you will be rich. And also buy white garments so you will not be shamed by your nakedness. And buy ointment for your eyes so you will be able to see. [19]I am the one who corrects and disciplines everyone I love. Be diligent and turn from your indifference.

[20]"Look! Here I stand at the door and knock. If you hear me calling and open the door, I will come in, and we will share a meal as friends. [21]I will invite everyone who is victorious to sit with me on my throne, just as I was victorious and sat with my Father on his throne. [22]Anyone who is willing to hear should listen to the Spirit and understand what the Spirit is saying to the churches."

3:14 Or *the source.*

3:14-21 The believers in Laodicea were engaged in full-blown denial. Though they portrayed themselves as being self-sustaining and having no needs, Christ saw their situation differently. To him they were spiritually blind and destitute. But, worst of all, they were spiritually indifferent—lukewarm. Sometimes after making progress in recovery we grow indifferent to our new lifestyle. We forget how desperate we were before entering recovery and that God is the one who set us free. We begin to long for things that will lead us back into bondage. We can avoid that long slide backward by taking honest moral inventory and getting back on track.

4:1-3 The apostle John saw this spectacular scene in God's heavenly throne room (4:1–5:14) while he was a prisoner on the island of Patmos. We may also be living in bondage, feeling hopelessly entrapped and distant from help or deliverance. But like John, we can draw close to God even when the world around us is dark and foreboding. John's vision of heaven gave him the hope he needed to face the lonely days ahead. And the record the apostle left us can give us hope during hard times, too. Even when we are alone and helpless, God is still with us, and we can draw near to him. God's grace and power are never limited by the circumstances we are in.

4:4-8 Two principles from this passage can encourage us as we work toward recovery: (1) The fact that the twenty-four elders represent the people of God shows that believers are honored significantly by God in heaven; (2) the diverse appearances of the four living beings implies that God wants all of us to be unique, utilizing our special characteristics for his glory. God values us because he created us; each of us has unique gifts to use in his service and for his glory. These truths can encourage us as we deal with the problems and pressures of the recovery process.

4:8-11 God is worthy of our continuous praise. Even the great spiritual beings in heaven fervently praised God. As we make God a daily focus in our life and offer him our gratitude and praise, we will discover new freedom from our problems and dependency. Our painful circumstances will begin to fade away in the light of his glorious love and power. God is greater and more powerful than anything we have to face. We can entrust our life to him, follow his will, and then praise him for the amazing things he will do in our life.

5:1-7 Many of us know the tremendous pain of not being able to live up to our perfectionistic goals. Expecting absolute perfection in this life is unrealistic. In heaven, however, perfection will be the norm. Even there, though, initially there was no one worthy to open the scroll of revelation and judgment. The Lamb—Jesus Christ—is the only one worthy to open the scroll. He is perfect and has conquered sin and death through his death and resurrection. Because of him, we can overcome our sins and dependency. Christ will open the scroll, beginning the process of recovery for our broken and sinful world. If we entrust our life to him, he will begin the same process of restoration in our life. Someday, by God's grace and power, we will be made perfect.

CHAPTER 4
Worship in Heaven

Then as I looked, I saw a door standing open in heaven, and the same voice I had heard before spoke to me with the sound of a mighty trumpet blast. The voice said, "Come up here, and I will show you what must happen after these things." ²And instantly I was in the Spirit,* and I saw a throne in heaven and someone sitting on it! ³The one sitting on the throne was as brilliant as gemstones—jasper and carnelian. And the glow of an emerald circled his throne like a rainbow. ⁴Twenty-four thrones surrounded him, and twenty-four elders sat on them. They were all clothed in white and had gold crowns on their heads. ⁵And from the throne came flashes of lightning and the rumble of thunder. And in front of the throne were seven lampstands with burning flames. They are the seven spirits* of God. ⁶In front of the throne was a shiny sea of glass, sparkling like crystal.

In the center and around the throne were four living beings, each covered with eyes, front and back. ⁷The first of these living beings had the form of a lion; the second looked like an ox; the third had a human face; and the fourth had the form of an eagle with wings spread out as though in flight. ⁸Each of these living beings had six wings, and their wings were covered with eyes, inside and out. Day after day and night after night they keep on saying,

"Holy, holy, holy is the Lord God
    Almighty—
the one who always was, who is, and
    who is still to come."

⁹Whenever the living beings give glory and honor and thanks to the one sitting on the throne, the one who lives forever and ever, ¹⁰the twenty-four elders fall down and worship the one who lives forever and ever. And they lay their crowns before the throne and say,

¹¹ "You are worthy, O Lord our God,
    to receive glory and honor and power.
For you created everything,
    and it is for your pleasure that they
        exist and were created."

CHAPTER 5
The Lamb Opens the Scroll

And I saw a scroll in the right hand of the one who was sitting on the throne. There

4:2 Or *in spirit.* **4:5** See 1:4 and 3:1, where the same expression is translated *the sevenfold Spirit.*

Love

READ REVELATION 3:14-22

We may feel like love just doesn't seem to work for us. We may wonder if we are doing something wrong. Perhaps we have problems loving because we are disconnected from the source of true love.

The apostle John wrote: "Dear friends, let us continue to love one another, for love comes from God. . . . But anyone who does not love does not know God— for God is love" (1 John 4:7-8).

Jesus said: "I am giving you a new commandment: Love each other. Just as I have loved you, you should love each other" (John 13:34). Trying to love without first receiving God's love is like trying to water something with a hose that's disconnected from the faucet. When we receive God's unconditional love, we can begin to love ourself. We are then told to love others as we love ourself and as Jesus has loved us. There is a boundless reservoir of love available to us; but without receiving the love of God in Christ, we will quickly run dry.

Jesus is waiting for us to open our heart and receive his love. He said: "Look! Here I stand at the door and knock. If you hear me calling and open the door, I will come in, and we will share a meal as friends" (Revelation 3:20). Love is waiting. We receive it when we open up to the love God offers us. *Turn to page 471, Revelation 22.*

was writing on the inside and the outside of the scroll, and it was sealed with seven seals. [2]And I saw a strong angel, who shouted with a loud voice: "Who is worthy to break the seals on this scroll and unroll it?" [3]But no one in heaven or on earth or under the earth was able to open the scroll and read it.

[4]Then I wept because no one could be found who was worthy to open the scroll and read it. [5]But one of the twenty-four elders said to me, "Stop weeping! Look, the Lion of the tribe of Judah, the heir to David's throne,* has conquered. He is worthy to open the scroll and break its seven seals."

[6]I looked and I saw a Lamb that had been killed but was now standing between the throne and the four living beings and among the twenty-four elders. He had seven horns and seven eyes, which are the seven spirits* of God that are sent out into every part of the earth. [7]He stepped forward and took the scroll from the right hand of the one sitting on the throne. [8]And as he took the scroll, the four living beings and the twenty-four elders fell down before the Lamb. Each one had a harp, and they held gold bowls filled with incense—the prayers of God's people!

[9]And they sang a new song with these words:

"You are worthy to take the scroll
  and break its seals and open it.
For you were killed, and your blood has
    ransomed people for God
  from every tribe and language and
    people and nation.

[10]And you have caused them to become
  God's Kingdom and his priests.
  And they will reign* on the earth."

[11]Then I looked again, and I heard the singing of thousands and millions of angels around the throne and the living beings and the elders. [12]And they sang in a mighty chorus:

"The Lamb is worthy—the Lamb who
    was killed.
  He is worthy to receive power and
    riches
  and wisdom and strength
  and honor and glory and blessing."

[13]And then I heard every creature in heaven and on earth and under the earth and in the sea. They also sang:

"Blessing and honor and glory and power
  belong to the one sitting on the throne
  and to the Lamb forever and ever."

[14]And the four living beings said, "Amen!" And the twenty-four elders fell down and worshiped God and the Lamb.

CHAPTER 6
The Lamb Breaks the First Six Seals
As I watched, the Lamb broke the first of the seven seals on the scroll. Then one of the four living beings called out with a voice that sounded like thunder, "Come!" [2]I looked up and saw a white horse. Its rider carried a bow, and a crown was placed on his head. He rode out to win many battles and gain the victory.

5:5 Greek *the root of David.* **5:6** See note on 4:5. **5:10** Some manuscripts read *they are reigning.*

5:9-10 By shedding his blood on the cross, Jesus Christ, the Lamb, made salvation possible for all. But God does far more than deliver us from our sins and dependency. He promises to make us part of his team for restoring and maintaining his world. We will be members of God's kingdom of priests. As soon as we entrust our life to God and seek to follow his will, we can begin our priestly duties. This involves sharing our story of deliverance and calling others to faith in Jesus Christ—the only power available for true recovery.

5:11-14 In these final verses of John's description of the heavenly throne room, praise for the divine Lamb spills over from heaven to the rest of the created realm. No matter how much unbelief and sin dominate the earthly scene today, a time will come when all will honor God. Such praise will necessarily include the admission of guilt, responsibility, and unbelieving denial by many (see Philippians 2:9-11). We don't have to wait until Christ returns to acknowledge his lordship in our life. We can do it today and begin to enjoy the immediate benefits of a vital relationship with God through Jesus Christ.

6:1-8 Jesus Christ, the Lamb, begins opening the scroll (see 5:1), setting in motion the events leading to God's victory over sin and death. War, famine, and disease will be rampant during the period of the first four seals. The first steps toward God's cosmic restoration lead through painful times. Millions of people will die as God deals with the sin that dominates our world. God often leads us through periods of pain as we suffer the consequences of our behavior, but he does so for our ultimate good. Even though he allows us to suffer for a time, he plans for our restoration and recovery. Sometimes the trials brought on by our dependency are the only way God can teach us how helpless we are and how much we need him.

[3]When the Lamb broke the second seal, I heard the second living being say, "Come!" [4]And another horse appeared, a red one. Its rider was given a mighty sword and the authority to remove peace from the earth. And there was war and slaughter everywhere.

[5]When the Lamb broke the third seal, I heard the third living being say, "Come!" And I looked up and saw a black horse, and its rider was holding a pair of scales in his hand. [6]And a voice from among the four living beings said, "A loaf of wheat bread or three loaves of barley for a day's pay.* And don't waste* the olive oil and wine."

[7]And when the Lamb broke the fourth seal, I heard the fourth living being say, "Come!" [8]And I looked up and saw a horse whose color was pale green like a corpse. And Death was the name of its rider, who was followed around by the Grave.* They were given authority over one-fourth of the earth, to kill with the sword and famine and disease* and wild animals.

[9]And when the Lamb broke the fifth seal, I saw under the altar the souls of all who had been martyred for the word of God and for being faithful in their witness. [10]They called loudly to the Lord and said, "O Sovereign Lord, holy and true, how long will it be before you judge the people who belong to this world for what they have done to us? When will you avenge our blood against these people?" [11]Then a white robe was given to each of them. And they were told to rest a little longer until the full number of their brothers and sisters*—their fellow servants of Jesus—had been martyred.

[12]I watched as the Lamb broke the sixth seal, and there was a great earthquake. The sun became as dark as black cloth, and the moon became as red as blood. [13]Then the stars of the sky fell to the earth like green figs falling from trees shaken by mighty winds. [14]And the sky was rolled up like a scroll and taken away. And all of the mountains and all of the islands disappeared. [15]Then the kings of the earth, the rulers, the generals, the wealthy people, the people with great power, and every slave and every free person—all hid themselves in the caves and among the rocks of the mountains. [16]And they cried to the mountains and the rocks, "Fall on us and hide us from the face of the one who sits on the throne and from the wrath of the Lamb. [17]For the great day of their wrath has come, and who will be able to survive?"

CHAPTER 7
God's People Will Be Preserved
Then I saw four angels standing at the four corners of the earth, holding back the four winds from blowing upon the earth. Not a leaf rustled in the trees, and the sea became as smooth as glass. [2]And I saw another angel coming from the east, carrying the seal of the living God. And he shouted out to those four angels who had been given power to injure land and sea, [3]"Wait! Don't hurt the land or

---

6:6a Greek *A choinix of wheat for a denarius, and 3 choinix of barley for a denarius.* **6:6b** Or *hurt.* **6:8a** Greek *by Hades.* **6:8b** Greek *death.* **6:11** Greek *their brothers.*

6:9-11 The opening of the fifth seal reveals those who have died in God's service; they are waiting for God to avenge their unjust deaths. God tells them that they will have to wait because still other martyrs will join them. Many of us have suffered abuse in the past. Perhaps the abuse we suffered is at the root of our present problems and dependency. We may desire revenge against people who have wronged us. Maybe we blame others for our addiction. Like the martyrs of Revelation, we must let God avenge the wrongs done to us. When we release our bitterness and forgive our abusers, we will make progress in recovery. Ultimately we are responsible for our addiction, whatever other factors may be involved.

6:12-17 The opening of the sixth seal is followed by a huge earthquake and amazing phenomena in the sky. Those who don't believe in Christ will want to die, mistakenly thinking they can escape God's terrible judgment. Sadly, their hearts are so hard that though they recognize God, they will not repent and turn to him in faith (see 9:20-21) and they will be destroyed. Continuing in denial about our destructive dependency or compulsion will lead to a similar end. If we refuse to recognize God's rule in our life, we will inevitably head toward deeper bondage and ultimate destruction. God wants to give us a meaningful and joyful life, but to receive this gift we need to accept his program for godly living.

7:1-3 As difficult as things will be during the period of the seals, God will protect those who belong to him. They will be "sealed" with God's sign of ownership and protection. Perhaps this seal is similar to the seal of the Holy Spirit now present in the lives of all who believe in Jesus Christ (see Ephesians 1:13-14; 4:30). This seal signifies an eternal relationship with God. We can begin our eternal relationship with God right now if we accept God's loving forgiveness through Jesus Christ and submit our life to his will.

the sea or the trees until we have placed the seal of God on the foreheads of his servants."

⁴And I heard how many were marked with the seal of God. There were 144,000 who were sealed from all the tribes of Israel:

⁵ from Judah	12,000
from Reuben	12,000
from Gad	12,000
⁶ from Asher	12,000
from Naphtali	12,000
from Manasseh	12,000
⁷ from Simeon	12,000
from Levi	12,000
from Issachar	12,000
⁸ from Zebulun	12,000
from Joseph	12,000
from Benjamin	12,000

Praise from the Great Multitude

⁹After this I saw a vast crowd, too great to count, from every nation and tribe and people and language, standing in front of the throne and before the Lamb. They were clothed in white and held palm branches in their hands. ¹⁰And they were shouting with a mighty shout, "Salvation comes from our God on the throne and from the Lamb!"

¹¹And all the angels were standing around the throne and around the elders and the four living beings. And they fell face down before the throne and worshiped God. ¹²They said,

"Amen! Blessing and glory and wisdom
    and thanksgiving and honor and power
    and strength
belong to our God forever and forever.
    Amen!"

¹³Then one of the twenty-four elders asked me, "Who are these who are clothed in white? Where do they come from?"

¹⁴And I said to him, "Sir, you are the one who knows."

Then he said to me, "These are the ones coming out of the great tribulation. They washed their robes in the blood of the Lamb and made them white. ¹⁵That is why they are standing in front of the throne of God, serving him day and night in his Temple. And he who sits on the throne will live among them and shelter them. ¹⁶They will never again be hungry or thirsty, and they will be fully protected from the scorching noontime heat. ¹⁷For the Lamb who stands in front of the throne will be their Shepherd. He will lead them to the springs of life-giving water. And God will wipe away all their tears."

CHAPTER 8
The Lamb Breaks the Seventh Seal

When the Lamb broke the seventh seal, there was silence throughout heaven for about half an hour. ²And I saw the seven angels who stand before God, and they were given seven trumpets.

³Then another angel with a gold incense burner came and stood at the altar. And a great quantity of incense was given to him to mix with the prayers of God's people, to be offered on the gold altar before the throne. ⁴The smoke of the incense, mixed with the prayers of the saints, ascended up to God from the altar where the angel had poured them out. ⁵Then the angel filled the incense burner with fire from the altar and threw it down upon the earth; and thunder crashed, lightning flashed, and there was a terrible earthquake.

7:9-14 This vast multitude from all races and nations is the harvest Christ envisioned from his great commission (see Matthew 28:19). They are truly thankful and worshipful toward God, greatly appreciating the salvation and recovery he has promised. The white garments they wear speak not only of the purity of their lifestyle but also of their redemption through the blood of Christ. By entering recovery, admitting our sins and failures, accepting God's forgiveness through Jesus Christ, and obeying God we can join this joyful throng of people who have been saved by God's wonderful grace.

7:15-17 This majestic passage describes the heavenly relationship between Christ and his people. They will serve him constantly, and he will always protect them. All their other needs will be met by Christ, the Lamb, who is also the Shepherd. In such a close and secure relationship, all the tears of painful oppression, loss, and misunderstanding will be wiped away. What wonderful hope these verses offer! By trusting in Jesus Christ, we can hope for a future filled with joy and peace.

8:1-2 The opening of the seventh seal on the scroll of judgment brings a short period of silence throughout heaven, offering people the chance to prepare for the incredibly difficult time ahead. Sometimes in recovery we get these "silence before the storm" experiences. Things may be good at the moment, but we sense that difficult times lie ahead. We can use these quiet times to get ready for what is to come by continuing with our honest personal inventory and giving our life—problems and all—to God. If God is with us, no future trial or testing will be too great to overcome.

The First Four Trumpets

6Then the seven angels with the seven trumpets prepared to blow their mighty blasts.

7The first angel blew his trumpet, and hail and fire mixed with blood were thrown down upon the earth, and one-third of the earth was set on fire. One-third of the trees were burned, and all the grass was burned.

8Then the second angel blew his trumpet, and a great mountain of fire was thrown into the sea. And one-third of the water in the sea became blood. 9And one-third of all things living in the sea died. And one-third of all the ships on the sea were destroyed.

10Then the third angel blew his trumpet, and a great flaming star fell out of the sky, burning like a torch. It fell upon one-third of the rivers and on the springs of water. 11The name of the star was Bitterness.* It made one-third of the water bitter, and many people died because the water was so bitter.

12Then the fourth angel blew his trumpet, and one-third of the sun was struck, and one-third of the moon, and one-third of the stars, and they became dark. And one-third of the day was dark and one-third of the night also.

13Then I looked up. And I heard a single eagle crying loudly as it flew through the air, "Terror, terror, terror to all who belong to this world because of what will happen when the last three angels blow their trumpets."

CHAPTER 9

The Fifth Trumpet Brings the First Terror

Then the fifth angel blew his trumpet, and I saw a star that had fallen to earth from the sky, and he was given the key to the shaft of the bottomless pit. 2When he opened it, smoke poured out as though from a huge furnace, and the sunlight and air were darkened by the smoke.

3Then locusts came from the smoke and descended on the earth, and they were given power to sting like scorpions. 4They were told not to hurt the grass or plants or trees but to attack all the people who did not have the seal of God on their foreheads. 5They were told not to kill them but to torture them for five months with agony like the pain of scorpion stings. 6In those days people will seek death but will not find it. They will long to die, but death will flee away!

7The locusts looked like horses armed for battle. They had gold crowns on their heads, and they had human faces. 8Their hair was long like the hair of a woman, and their teeth were like the teeth of a lion. 9They wore armor made of iron, and their wings roared like an army of chariots rushing into battle. 10They had tails that stung like scorpions, with power to torture people. This power was given to them for five months. 11Their king is the angel from the bottomless pit; his name in Hebrew is *Abaddon*, and in Greek, *Apollyon*—the Destroyer.

12The first terror is past, but look, two more terrors are coming!

The Sixth Trumpet Brings the Second Terror

13Then the sixth angel blew his trumpet, and I heard a voice speaking from the four horns of the gold altar that stands in the presence of God. 14And the voice spoke to the sixth angel who held the trumpet: "Release the four angels who are bound at the great Euphrates River." 15And the four angels who had been

8:11 Greek *Wormwood.*

8:6-13 At the blowing of the first four trumpets, the people of our dysfunctional and sinful world will suffer the terrible consequences for their sins and the sins of their ancestors. There is a day of reckoning for all who reject God. Many of us have experienced similar days of reckoning in our own life. Our attitudes and actions led to periods of great suffering. When we shed our denial and confess our sins, however, Jesus Christ will deliver us from our powerful dependency and help us escape these terrible judgments.

9:1-4 As the fifth trumpet blows, a locust plague will be unleashed. Unlike regular locusts, however, these creatures will attack people, not plants. God will not allow these creatures to harm everyone—just those not protected by God's seal. As we seek recovery with God's help, we can be secure knowing that God is able and willing to protect us. He may allow hard times into our life to help us grow. If we continue to trust and obey him, he won't allow us to be destroyed by sin and its terrible consequences.

9:13-21 As the sixth trumpet blows, a demonically led army will slaughter one-third of the remaining population of the world (see 6:8). Certainly circumstances would seem completely hopeless to most inhabitants of the earth at this point. They could either humble themselves and begin recovery by faith, or sink into depressed denial. Sadly, only a few will accept God's gracious offer of forgiveness at that late stage. We have a similar choice before us today as we face the destructive, painful consequences of our sins. We can either give up and fall into deeper bondage, or we can recognize how helpless we are and receive God's gift of deliverance and recovery. The choice is ours!

prepared for this hour and day and month and year were turned loose to kill one-third of all the people on earth. [16]They led an army of 200 million mounted troops—I heard an announcement of how many there were.

[17]And in my vision, I saw the horses and the riders sitting on them. The riders wore armor that was fiery red and sky blue and yellow. The horses' heads were like the heads of lions, and fire and smoke and burning sulfur billowed from their mouths. [18]One-third of all the people on earth were killed by these three plagues—by the fire and the smoke and burning sulfur that came from the mouths of the horses. [19]Their power was in their mouths, but also in their tails. For their tails had heads like snakes, with the power to injure people.

[20]But the people who did not die in these plagues still refused to turn from their evil deeds. They continued to worship demons and idols made of gold, silver, bronze, stone, and wood—idols that neither see nor hear nor walk! [21]And they did not repent of their murders or their witchcraft or their immorality or their thefts.

CHAPTER 10
The Angel and the Small Scroll
Then I saw another mighty angel coming down from heaven, surrounded by a cloud, with a rainbow over his head. His face shone like the sun, and his feet were like pillars of fire. [2]And in his hand was a small scroll, which he had unrolled. He stood with his right foot on the sea and his left foot on the land. [3]And he gave a great shout, like the roar of a lion. And when he shouted, the seven thunders answered.

[4]When the seven thunders spoke, I was about to write. But a voice from heaven called to me: "Keep secret what the seven thunders said. Do not write it down."

[5]Then the mighty angel standing on the sea and on the land lifted his right hand to heaven. [6]And he swore an oath in the name of the one who lives forever and ever, who created heaven and everything in it, the earth and everything in it, and the sea and everything in it. He said, "God will wait no longer. [7]But when the seventh angel blows his trumpet, God's mysterious plan will be fulfilled. It will happen just as he announced it to his servants the prophets."

[8]Then the voice from heaven called to me again: "Go and take the unrolled scroll from the angel who is standing on the sea and on the land."

[9]So I approached him and asked him to give me the little scroll. "Yes, take it and eat it," he said. "At first it will taste like honey, but when you swallow it, it will make your stomach sour!" [10]So I took the little scroll from the hands of the angel, and I ate it! It was sweet in my mouth, but it made my stomach sour. [11]Then he said to me, "You must prophesy again about many peoples, nations, languages, and kings."

CHAPTER 11
The Two Witnesses
Then I was given a measuring stick, and I was told, "Go and measure the Temple of God and the altar, and count the number of worshipers. [2]But do not measure the outer courtyard, for it has been turned over to the nations. They will trample the holy city for 42 months.

10:1-4 As the mighty angel from heaven shouts out the contents of the additional scroll, John assumes that he is to record it. But God prevents him from doing so. This episode reminds us that along with honesty, we need God-directed discretion. In recovery we are told to make amends to those we have wronged, except when doing so would injure them or others. Sometimes we need to refrain and be discreet because telling our whole story or seeking restoration might damage someone else. God can help us use discretion, but the guiding principle is love. We need to do what is best for others, not just what is best for ourself.

10:8-10 John was told to eat the scroll, much as the prophet Ezekiel had been instructed to do in the Old Testament (Ezekiel 2:8; 3:1-3). The scroll would be sweet in his mouth but bitter in his stomach. God's Word can sometimes work that way. It contains a sweet message of deliverance for all who repent, but it also calls us to account for our sinful actions. If we abide by the wise boundaries that God has set for us, his Word is filled with promises of joy and peace. If, on the other hand, we choose to reject God's program, his Word will be filled with predictions of eternal judgment.

11:1-13 These two witnesses serve as God's prophets. During their 1,260-day ministry, they will be empowered and protected by God. They will then be killed by the beast from the pit. God's two prophets are treated even more despicably than Christ, who was at least given a decent burial (see Matthew 27:57-61). In three and a half days, however, God will raise them from the dead, showing that even death cannot thwart his plans. No obstacle is so great that God has to abandon his plan for the world and its people. We can be confident that God wants us to experience effective recovery. So if we trust him and follow his plan, no obstacle will be too great for us to overcome.

³And I will give power to my two witnesses, and they will be clothed in sackcloth and will prophesy during those 1,260 days."

⁴These two prophets are the two olive trees and the two lampstands that stand before the Lord of all the earth. ⁵If anyone tries to harm them, fire flashes from the mouths of the prophets and consumes their enemies. This is how anyone who tries to harm them must die. ⁶They have power to shut the skies so that no rain will fall for as long as they prophesy. And they have the power to turn the rivers and oceans into blood, and to send every kind of plague upon the earth as often as they wish.

⁷When they complete their testimony, the beast that comes up out of the bottomless pit will declare war against them. He will conquer them and kill them. ⁸And their bodies will lie in the main street of Jerusalem,* the city which is called "Sodom" and "Egypt," the city where their Lord was crucified. ⁹And for three and a half days, all peoples, tribes, languages, and nations will come to stare at their bodies. No one will be allowed to bury them. ¹⁰All the people who belong to this world will give presents to each other to celebrate the death of the two prophets who had tormented them.

¹¹But after three and a half days, the spirit of life from God entered them, and they stood up! And terror struck all who were staring at them. ¹²Then a loud voice shouted from heaven, "Come up here!" And they rose to heaven in a cloud as their enemies watched.

¹³And in the same hour there was a terrible earthquake that destroyed a tenth of the city. Seven thousand people died in that earthquake. And everyone who did not die was terrified and gave glory to the God of heaven.

¹⁴The second terror is past, but look, now the third terror is coming quickly.

11:8 Greek *the great city.*

The Seventh Trumpet Brings the Third Terror

¹⁵Then the seventh angel blew his trumpet, and there were loud voices shouting in heaven: "The whole world has now become the Kingdom of our Lord and of his Christ, and he will reign forever and ever."

¹⁶And the twenty-four elders sitting on their thrones before God fell on their faces and worshiped him. ¹⁷And they said,

"We give thanks to you, Lord God Almighty,
  the one who is and who always was,
for now you have assumed your great power
  and have begun to reign.
¹⁸ The nations were angry with you,
  but now the time of your wrath has come.
It is time to judge the dead and reward your servants.
You will reward your prophets and your holy people,
  all who fear your name, from the least to the greatest.
And you will destroy all who have caused destruction on the earth."

¹⁹Then, in heaven, the Temple of God was opened and the Ark of his covenant could be seen inside the Temple. Lightning flashed, thunder crashed and roared; there was a great hailstorm, and the world was shaken by a mighty earthquake.

CHAPTER 12
The Woman and the Dragon

Then I witnessed in heaven an event of great significance. I saw a woman clothed with the sun, with the moon beneath her feet, and a crown of twelve stars on her head. ²She was

---

11:15-18 The sounding of the seventh trumpet accompanies a proclamation of God's control over his Kingdom. Many among the nations of the earth have been angry with God without just cause, but now God's righteous anger will be released. Those who have committed themselves to God will be rewarded, while those who have turned their backs on him will be judged. The same principle holds true for us. If we reject God and his plan for us, we will have to face his terrible anger. If we commit our life to God, he will lovingly heal us.

12:1-14 The birth of Christ and Satan's opposition to it are graphically depicted here. Jesus the Messiah was born into this world to implement God's plan for its restoration. Satan had planted sin into God's good creation by tempting Adam and Eve. Since Jesus was born to reverse the effects of that sin, Satan did all he could to destroy the infant Savior. Thankfully, Satan failed and the future ruler of the world completed his earthly mission. As much as Satan tries to thwart God's plan for the world's recovery, he will not be able to. Our personal recovery is an important part of God's plan for cosmic recovery. If we entrust our life to God and obey him, he will certainly complete the task of recovery in our life.

pregnant, and she cried out in the pain of labor as she awaited her delivery.

³Suddenly, I witnessed in heaven another significant event. I saw a large red dragon with seven heads and ten horns, with seven crowns on his heads. ⁴His tail dragged down one-third of the stars, which he threw to the earth. He stood before the woman as she was about to give birth to her child, ready to devour the baby as soon as it was born.

⁵She gave birth to a boy who was to rule all nations with an iron rod. And the child was snatched away from the dragon and was caught up to God and to his throne. ⁶And the woman fled into the wilderness, where God had prepared a place to give her care for 1,260 days.

⁷Then there was war in heaven. Michael and the angels under his command fought the dragon and his angels. ⁸And the dragon lost the battle and was forced out of heaven. ⁹This great dragon—the ancient serpent called the Devil, or Satan, the one deceiving the whole world—was thrown down to the earth with all his angels.

¹⁰Then I heard a loud voice shouting across the heavens,

"It has happened at last—the salvation and power and kingdom of our God, and the authority of his Christ! For the Accuser has been thrown down to earth—the one who accused our brothers and sisters* before our God day and night. ¹¹And they have defeated him because of the blood of the Lamb and because of their testimony. And they were not afraid to die. ¹²Rejoice, O heavens! And you who live in the heavens, rejoice! But terror will come on the earth and the sea. For the Devil has come down to you in great anger, and he knows that he has little time."

¹³And when the dragon realized that he had been thrown down to the earth, he pursued the woman who had given birth to the child. ¹⁴But she was given two wings like those of a great eagle. This allowed her to fly to a place prepared for her in the wilderness, where she would be cared for and protected from the dragon* for a time, times, and half a time.

¹⁵Then the dragon tried to drown the woman with a flood of water that flowed from its mouth. ¹⁶But the earth helped her by opening its mouth and swallowing the river that gushed out from the mouth of the dragon. ¹⁷Then the dragon became angry at the woman, and he declared war against the rest of her children—all who keep God's commandments and confess that they belong to Jesus.

The Beast out of the Sea

¹⁸Then he stood* waiting on the shore of the sea.

CHAPTER 13

And now in my vision I saw a beast rising up out of the sea. It had seven heads and ten horns, with ten crowns on its horns. And written on each head were names that blasphemed God. ²This beast looked like a leopard, but it had bear's feet and a lion's mouth! And the dragon gave him his own power and throne and great authority.

³I saw that one of the heads of the beast seemed wounded beyond recovery—but the fatal wound was healed! All the world marveled at this miracle and followed the beast in awe. ⁴They worshiped the dragon for giving the beast such power, and they worshiped the beast. "Is there anyone as great as the beast?" they exclaimed. "Who is able to fight against him?"

⁵Then the beast was allowed to speak great blasphemies against God. And he was given authority to do what he wanted for forty-two months. ⁶And he spoke terrible words of blasphemy against God, slandering his name and all who live in heaven, who are his temple. ⁷And the beast was allowed to wage war against God's holy people and to overcome them. And he was given authority to rule

12:10 Greek *brothers.* **12:14** Greek *the serpent;* also in 12:15. See 12:9. **12:18** Some manuscripts read *Then I stood,* and some translations put this entire sentence into 13:1.

13:1-10 These are some of Satan's primary representatives. For a time, God will allow them free rein in the world as they battle all who trust Christ. Ever since Jesus Christ walked this earth, Satan has sought to lead people away from the delivering power God offers. These creatures are an intensified form of the spirit of antichrist already active in our world. We will face opposition as we seek recovery from addiction and its power. Satan doesn't want us to succeed at recovery; he only wants to destroy us. Despite the power Satan wields in our world, he cannot remove us from God's loving care. When we trust in God to help us and obey him, our recovery is assured. Satan and his henchmen will be powerless.

over every tribe and people and language and nation. ⁸And all the people who belong to this world worshiped the beast. They are the ones whose names were not written in the Book of Life, which belongs to the Lamb who was killed before the world was made.

⁹Anyone who is willing to hear should listen and understand. ¹⁰The people who are destined for prison will be arrested and taken away. Those who are destined for death will be killed. But do not be dismayed, for here is your opportunity to have endurance and faith.

The Beast out of the Earth

¹¹Then I saw another beast come up out of the earth. He had two horns like those of a lamb, and he spoke with the voice of a dragon. ¹²He exercised all the authority of the first beast. And he required all the earth and those who belong to this world to worship the first beast, whose death-wound had been healed. ¹³He did astounding miracles, such as making fire flash down to earth from heaven while everyone was watching. ¹⁴And with all the miracles he was allowed to perform on behalf of the first beast, he deceived all the people who belong to this world. He ordered the people of the world to make a great statue of the first beast, who was fatally wounded and then came back to life. ¹⁵He was permitted to give life to this statue so that it could speak. Then the statue commanded that anyone refusing to worship it must die.

¹⁶He required everyone—great and small, rich and poor, slave and free—to be given a mark on the right hand or on the forehead. ¹⁷And no one could buy or sell anything without that mark, which was either the name of the beast or the number representing his name. ¹⁸Wisdom is needed to understand this. Let the one who has understanding solve the number of the beast, for it is the number of a man.* His number is 666.*

CHAPTER 14
The Lamb and the 144,000

Then I saw the Lamb standing on Mount Zion, and with him were 144,000 who had his name and his Father's name written on their foreheads. ²And I heard a sound from heaven like the roaring of a great waterfall or the rolling of mighty thunder. It was like the sound of many harpists playing together.

³This great choir sang a wonderful new song in front of the throne of God and before the four living beings and the twenty-four elders. And no one could learn this song except those 144,000 who had been redeemed from the earth. ⁴For they are spiritually undefiled, pure as virgins,* following the Lamb wherever he goes. They have been purchased from among the people on the earth as a special offering* to God and to the Lamb. ⁵No falsehood can be charged against them; they are blameless.

The Three Angels

⁶And I saw another angel flying through the heavens, carrying the everlasting Good News to preach to the people who belong to this world—to every nation, tribe, language, and people. ⁷"Fear God," he shouted. "Give glory to him. For the time has come when he will sit as judge. Worship him who made heaven and earth, the sea, and all the springs of water."

⁸Then another angel followed him through the skies, shouting, "Babylon is fallen—that great city is fallen—because she

---

13:18a Or *of humanity.* **13:18b** Some manuscripts read *616.* **14:4a** Greek *they are virgins who have not defiled themselves with women.* **14:4b** Greek *as firstfruits.*

13:11-18 Another creature representing Satan rises from the earth. It looks like a lamb, Satan's attempt to copy the appearance of Christ, the Lamb (see 5:6). This creature's miracles copy the amazing deeds that were performed by God's two witnesses (see 11:5-6). Satan is trying to deceive people into thinking this lamb represents the true God. He is trying to sell a counterfeit in order to lead people away from the true deliverer—Jesus Christ. Satan uses this same strategy today. Numerous recovery plans claim to offer deliverance, but only God can truly deliver. If we seek help from any other source, Satan has succeeded in leading us away from the only real Power that can save us. We need to be on guard against the counterfeit solutions that Satan puts before us.

14:1-20 In these verses we see some of the blessings enjoyed by those who trust in Christ; then we see the terrible consequences of rejecting him. The deliverance that God offers us through Jesus Christ is good news. We are called to rejoice in God's infinite rule, praising him for his greatness. If we refuse to acknowledge God's rule and do things our own way, we are headed toward complete destruction. But when we persevere in our faith in Jesus Christ, God will reward us with eternal rest.

seduced the nations of the world and made them drink the wine of her passionate immorality."

[9]Then a third angel followed them, shouting, "Anyone who worships the beast and his statue or who accepts his mark on the forehead or the hand [10]must drink the wine of God's wrath. It is poured out undiluted into God's cup of wrath. And they will be tormented with fire and burning sulfur in the presence of the holy angels and the Lamb. [11]The smoke of their torment rises forever and ever, and they will have no relief day or night, for they have worshiped the beast and his statue and have accepted the mark of his name. [12]Let this encourage God's holy people to endure persecution patiently and remain firm to the end, obeying his commands and trusting in Jesus."

[13]And I heard a voice from heaven saying, "Write this down: Blessed are those who die in the Lord from now on. Yes, says the Spirit, they are blessed indeed, for they will rest from all their toils and trials; for their good deeds follow them!"

The Harvest of the Earth

[14]Then I saw the Son of Man* sitting on a white cloud. He had a gold crown on his head and a sharp sickle in his hand.

[15]Then an angel came from the Temple and called out in a loud voice to the one sitting on the cloud, "Use the sickle, for the time has come for you to harvest; the crop is ripe on the earth." [16]So the one sitting on the cloud swung his sickle over the earth, and the whole earth was harvested.

[17]After that, another angel came from the Temple in heaven, and he also had a sharp sickle. [18]Then another angel, who has power to destroy the world with fire, shouted to the angel with the sickle, "Use your sickle now to gather the clusters of grapes from the vines of the earth, for they are fully ripe for judgment." [19]So the angel swung his sickle on the earth and loaded the grapes into the great winepress of God's wrath. [20]And the grapes were trodden in the winepress outside the city, and blood flowed from the winepress in a stream about 180 miles* long and as high as a horse's bridle.

CHAPTER 15
The Song of Moses and of the Lamb

Then I saw in heaven another significant event, and it was great and marvelous. Seven angels were holding the seven last plagues, which would bring God's wrath to completion. [2]I saw before me what seemed to be a crystal sea mixed with fire. And on it stood all the people who had been victorious over the beast and his statue and the number representing his name. They were all holding harps that God had given them. [3]And they were singing the song of Moses, the servant of God, and the song of the Lamb:

"Great and marvelous are your actions,
  Lord God Almighty.
Just and true are your ways,
  O King of the nations.*
[4]Who will not fear, O Lord, and glorify
    your name?
  For you alone are holy.
All nations will come and worship
    before you,
  for your righteous deeds have been
    revealed."

The Seven Bowls of the Seven Plagues

[5]Then I looked and saw that the Temple in heaven, God's Tabernacle, was thrown wide open! [6]The seven angels who were holding the bowls of the seven plagues came from the Temple, clothed in spotless white linen* with gold belts across their chests. [7]And one of the four living beings handed each of the seven angels a gold bowl filled with the terrible wrath of God, who lives forever and forever. [8]The Temple was filled with smoke from God's glory and power. No one could enter the Temple until the seven angels had completed pouring out the seven plagues.

14:14 Or *one who looked like a man;* Greek reads *one like a son of man.* **14:20** Greek *1,600 stadia* [296 kilometers]. **15:3** Some manuscripts read *King of the ages;* other manuscripts read *King of the saints.* **15:6** Some manuscripts read *in bright and sparkling stone.*

15:1–16:21 The seven angels with the bowls of God's judgment are portrayed in these chapters. God's wrath against the unbelieving world will be complete (see 6:17; 11:18) when the angels pour out their bowls of plagues over the earth. The day of reckoning will surely arrive, even though those in denial live as though things will continue forever just as they are. We cannot live forever in bondage to sin or a powerful addiction. There will be a day when we have to face the truth about our life. We have the choice to submit our life to God and his good plan before the bottom drops out from under us.

CHAPTER 16

Then I heard a mighty voice shouting from the Temple to the seven angels, "Now go your ways and empty out the seven bowls of God's wrath on the earth."

²So the first angel left the Temple and poured out his bowl over the earth, and horrible, malignant sores broke out on everyone who had the mark of the beast and who worshiped his statue.

³Then the second angel poured out his bowl on the sea, and it became like the blood of a corpse. And everything in the sea died.

⁴Then the third angel poured out his bowl on the rivers and springs, and they became blood. ⁵And I heard the angel who had authority over all water saying, "You are just in sending this judgment, O Holy One, who is and who always was. ⁶For your holy people and your prophets have been killed, and their blood was poured out on the earth. So you have given their murderers blood to drink. It is their just reward." ⁷And I heard a voice from the altar saying, "Yes, Lord God Almighty, your punishments are true and just."

⁸Then the fourth angel poured out his bowl on the sun, causing it to scorch everyone with its fire. ⁹Everyone was burned by this blast of heat, and they cursed the name of God, who sent all of these plagues. They did not repent and give him glory.

¹⁰Then the fifth angel poured out his bowl on the throne of the beast, and his kingdom was plunged into darkness. And his subjects ground their teeth in anguish, ¹¹and they cursed the God of heaven for their pains and sores. But they refused to repent of all their evil deeds.

¹²Then the sixth angel poured out his bowl on the great Euphrates River, and it dried up so that the kings from the east could march their armies westward without hindrance. ¹³And I saw three evil spirits that looked like frogs leap from the mouth of the dragon, the beast, and the false prophet. ¹⁴These miracle-working demons caused all the rulers of the world to gather for battle against the Lord on that great judgment day of God Almighty.

¹⁵"Take note: I will come as unexpectedly as a thief! Blessed are all who are watching for me, who keep their robes ready so they will not need to walk naked and ashamed."

¹⁶And they gathered all the rulers and their armies to a place called *Armageddon* in Hebrew.

¹⁷Then the seventh angel poured out his bowl into the air. And a mighty shout came from the throne of the Temple in heaven, saying, "It is finished!" ¹⁸Then the thunder crashed and rolled, and lightning flashed. And there was an earthquake greater than ever before in human history. ¹⁹The great city of Babylon split into three pieces, and cities around the world fell into heaps of rubble. And so God remembered all of Babylon's sins, and he made her drink the cup that was filled with the wine of his fierce wrath. ²⁰And every island disappeared, and all the mountains were leveled. ²¹There was a terrible hailstorm, and hailstones weighing seventy-five pounds* fell from the sky onto the people below. They cursed God because of the hailstorm, which was a very terrible plague.

CHAPTER 17

The Great Prostitute

One of the seven angels who had poured out the seven bowls came over and spoke to me. "Come with me," he said, "and I will show you the judgment that is going to come on the great prostitute, who sits on many waters. ²The rulers of the world have had immoral relations with her, and the people who belong to this world have been made drunk by the wine of her immorality."

³So the angel took me in spirit* into the wilderness. There I saw a woman sitting on a scarlet beast that had seven heads and ten horns, written all over with blasphemies against God. ⁴The woman wore purple and scarlet clothing and beautiful jewelry made of gold and precious gems and pearls. She held in her hand a gold goblet full of obscenities and the impurities of her immorality.

16:21 Greek *1 talent* [34 kilograms]. **17:3** Or *in the Spirit.*

17:1–19:5 Just as the previous chapters portray God's judgment of those who refuse to believe in Christ, these chapters foretell God's conquest over Satan's henchmen. Even Satan's power will be overthrown by God when the time is right. The Devil's representatives will be called to account for the suffering they imposed on God's people. God's team will always win out in the end. To be on the winning side, we need to admit our need for God and trust him to deliver us from the power of sin. That way we won't weep when the evil powers in this world are destroyed; we will rejoice.

5A mysterious name was written on her forehead: "Babylon the Great, Mother of All Prostitutes and Obscenities in the World." 6I could see that she was drunk—drunk with the blood of God's holy people who were witnesses for Jesus. I stared at her completely amazed.

7"Why are you so amazed?" the angel asked. "I will tell you the mystery of this woman and of the beast with seven heads and ten horns. 8The beast you saw was alive but isn't now. And yet he will soon come up out of the bottomless pit and go to eternal destruction. And the people who belong to this world, whose names were not written in the Book of Life from before the world began, will be amazed at the reappearance of this beast who had died.

9"And now understand this: The seven heads of the beast represent the seven hills of the city where this woman rules. They also represent seven kings. 10Five kings have already fallen, the sixth now reigns, and the seventh is yet to come, but his reign will be brief. 11The scarlet beast that was alive and then died is the eighth king. He is like the other seven, and he, too, will go to his doom. 12His ten horns are ten kings who have not yet risen to power; they will be appointed to their kingdoms for one brief moment to reign with the beast. 13They will all agree to give their power and authority to him. 14Together they will wage war against the Lamb, but the Lamb will defeat them because he is Lord over all lords and King over all kings, and his people are the called and chosen and faithful ones."

15And the angel said to me, "The waters where the prostitute is sitting represent masses of people of every nation and language. 16The scarlet beast and his ten horns—which represent ten kings who will reign with him—all hate the prostitute. They will strip her naked, eat her flesh, and burn her remains with fire. 17For God has put a plan into their minds, a plan that will carry out his purposes. They will mutually agree to give their authority to the scarlet beast, and so the words of God will be fulfilled. 18And this woman you saw in your vision represents the great city that rules over the kings of the earth."

CHAPTER 18
The Fall of Babylon

After all this I saw another angel come down from heaven with great authority, and the earth grew bright with his splendor. 2He gave a mighty shout, "Babylon is fallen—that great city is fallen! She has become the hideout of demons and evil spirits, a nest for filthy buzzards, and a den for dreadful beasts. 3For all the nations have drunk the wine of her passionate immorality. The rulers of the world have committed adultery with her, and merchants throughout the world have grown rich as a result of her luxurious living."

4Then I heard another voice calling from heaven, "Come away from her, my people. Do not take part in her sins, or you will be punished with her. 5For her sins are piled as high as heaven, and God is ready to judge her for her evil deeds. 6Do to her as she has done to your people. Give her a double penalty for all her evil deeds. She brewed a cup of terror for others, so give her twice as much as she gave out. 7She has lived in luxury and pleasure, so match it now with torments and sorrows. She boasts, 'I am queen on my throne. I am no helpless widow. I will not experience sorrow.' 8Therefore, the sorrows of death and mourning and famine will overtake her in a single day. She will be utterly consumed by fire, for the Lord God who judges her is mighty."

9And the rulers of the world who took part in her immoral acts and enjoyed her great luxury will mourn for her as they see the smoke rising from her charred remains. 10They will stand at a distance, terrified by her great torment. They will cry out, "How terrible, how terrible for Babylon, that great city! In one single moment God's judgment came on her."

11The merchants of the world will weep and mourn for her, for there is no one left to buy their goods. 12She bought great quantities of gold, silver, jewels, pearls, fine linen, purple dye, silk, scarlet cloth, every kind of perfumed wood, ivory goods, objects made of expensive wood, bronze, iron, and marble. 13She also bought cinnamon, spice, incense, myrrh, frankincense, wine, olive oil, fine flour, wheat, cattle, sheep, horses, chariots, and slaves—yes, she even traded in human lives.

14"All the fancy things you loved so much are gone," they cry. "The luxuries and splendor that you prized so much will never be yours again. They are gone forever."

15The merchants who became wealthy by selling her these things will stand at a distance, terrified by her great torment. They will weep and cry. ¹⁶"How terrible, how terrible for that great city! She was so beautiful—like a woman clothed in finest purple and scarlet linens, decked out with gold and precious stones and pearls! ¹⁷And in one single moment all the wealth of the city is gone!"

And all the shipowners and captains of the merchant ships and their crews will stand at a distance. ¹⁸They will weep as they watch the smoke ascend, and they will say, "Where in all the world is there another city like this?" ¹⁹And they will throw dust on their heads to show their great sorrow. And they will say, "How terrible, how terrible for the great city! She made us all rich from her great wealth. And now in a single hour it is all gone."

²⁰But you, O heaven, rejoice over her fate. And you also rejoice, O holy people of God and apostles and prophets! For at last God has judged her on your behalf.

²¹Then a mighty angel picked up a boulder as large as a great millstone. He threw it into the ocean and shouted, "Babylon, the great city, will be thrown down as violently as I have thrown away this stone, and she will disappear forever. ²²Never again will the sound of music be heard there—no more harps, songs, flutes, or trumpets. There will be no industry of any kind, and no more milling of grain. ²³Her nights will be dark, without a single lamp. There will be no happy voices of brides and grooms. This will happen because her merchants, who were the greatest in the world, deceived the nations with her sorceries. ²⁴In her streets the blood of the prophets was spilled. She was the one who slaughtered God's people all over the world."

CHAPTER 19
Songs of Victory in Heaven

After this, I heard the sound of a vast crowd in heaven shouting, "Hallelujah! Salvation is from our God. Glory and power belong to him alone. ²His judgments are just and true. He has punished the great prostitute who corrupted the earth with her immorality, and he has avenged the murder of his servants." ³Again and again their voices rang, "Hallelujah! The smoke from that city ascends forever and forever!"

⁴Then the twenty-four elders and the four living beings fell down and worshiped God, who was sitting on the throne. They cried out, "Amen! Hallelujah!"

ˢᵀᴱᴾ **4**

God's Mercy

BIBLE READING: Revelation 20:11-15
We made a searching and fearless moral inventory of ourselves.

We may wish we could avoid taking moral inventory; it's normal to want to hide from personal examination. But in our heart we probably sense that a day will come when we will have to face the truth about ourself and our life.

The Bible tells us there is a day coming when an inventory will be made of every life. No one will be able to hide. In John's vision he saw "a great white throne, and I saw the one who was sitting on it. The earth and sky fled from his presence, but they found no place to hide. I saw the dead, both great and small, standing before God's throne. And the books were opened, including the Book of Life. And the dead were judged according to the things written in the books, according to what they had done. . . . And anyone whose name was not found recorded in the Book of Life was thrown into the lake of fire" (Revelation 20:11-12, 15).

It is best to do our own earthly moral inventory now so we can be ready for the one to come. Anyone whose name is in the Book of Life will be saved, including all whose sins have been atoned for by the death of Jesus. Those who refuse God's offer of mercy are left to be judged on the basis of their own deeds recorded in "the books." No one will pass that test! Perhaps now is a good time to make sure that our name is in the right book. Knowing that our sins are covered with God's forgiveness can help us examine our life fearlessly and honestly. *Turn to Step Five, page 157, John 8.*

⁵And from the throne came a voice that said, "Praise our God, all his servants, from the least to the greatest, all who fear him."

⁶Then I heard again what sounded like the shout of a huge crowd, or the roar of mighty ocean waves, or the crash of loud thunder: "Hallelujah! For the Lord our God, the Almighty, reigns. ⁷Let us be glad and rejoice and honor him. For the time has come for the wedding feast of the Lamb, and his bride has prepared herself. ⁸She is permitted to wear the finest white linen." (Fine linen represents the good deeds done by the people of God.)

⁹And the angel said, "Write this: Blessed are those who are invited to the wedding feast of the Lamb." And he added, "These are true words that come from God."

¹⁰Then I fell down at his feet to worship him, but he said, "No, don't worship me. For I am a servant of God, just like you and other brothers and sisters* who testify of their faith in Jesus. Worship God. For the essence of prophecy is to give a clear witness for Jesus.*"

The Rider on the White Horse

¹¹Then I saw heaven opened, and a white horse was standing there. And the one sitting on the horse was named Faithful and True. For he judges fairly and then goes to war. ¹²His eyes were bright like flames of fire, and on his head were many crowns. A name was written on him, and only he knew what it meant. ¹³He was clothed with a robe dipped in blood, and his title was the Word of God. ¹⁴The armies of heaven, dressed in pure white linen, followed him on white horses. ¹⁵From his mouth came a sharp sword, and with it he struck down the nations. He ruled them with an iron rod, and he trod the winepress of the fierce wrath of almighty God. ¹⁶On his robe and thigh was written this title: King of kings and Lord of lords.

¹⁷Then I saw an angel standing in the sun, shouting to the vultures flying high in the sky: "Come! Gather together for the great banquet God has prepared. ¹⁸Come and eat the flesh of kings, captains, and strong warriors; of horses and their riders; and of all humanity, both free and slave, small and great."

¹⁹Then I saw the beast gathering the kings of the earth and their armies in order to fight against the one sitting on the horse and his army. ²⁰And the beast was captured, and with him the false prophet who did mighty miracles on behalf of the beast—miracles that deceived all who had accepted the mark of the beast and who worshiped his statue. Both the beast and his false prophet were thrown alive into the lake of fire that burns with sulfur. ²¹Their entire army was killed by the sharp sword that came out of the mouth of the one riding the white horse. And all the vultures of the sky gorged themselves on the dead bodies.

CHAPTER 20
The Thousand Years

Then I saw an angel come down from heaven with the key to the bottomless pit and a heavy chain in his hand. ²He seized the dragon—that old serpent, the Devil, Satan—and bound him in chains for a thousand years. ³The angel threw him into the bottomless pit, which he then shut and locked so Satan could not deceive the nations anymore until the thousand years were finished. Afterward he would be released again for a little while.

⁴Then I saw thrones, and the people sitting on them had been given the authority to judge. And I saw the souls of those who had been beheaded for their testimony about

19:10a Greek *brothers*. **19:10b** Or *is the message confirmed by Jesus.*

19:6–20:10 Here we see a glimpse of Christ, the conquering King. He will return to deliver all those who believe in him. Though great human armies led by Satan and his representatives will gather to resist, there will be no contest. Jesus Christ will ride to an overwhelming victory. As Christ triumphs over Satan and his armies, he will vindicate our individual battles against sin and addiction. What a glorious day that will be! All our efforts to overcome our dependency will be supported by Christ's final conquest over sin and evil. Satan and his helpers will be bound forever!
20:11-15 At the climactic "white throne" judgment, those who reject God will face eternal consequences. Believers in Christ, however, will be shown amazing grace. Most of us expect our judgment to be based upon whether or not we are guilty. At this judgment, though, everyone is guilty. The people who have believed in Christ will be forgiven. Those who have chosen to go their own way are headed to a place of eternal torment. No matter who we are or how terrible our past, we can have our name written in the Book of Life. We cannot earn a place in that book; we can only receive it as a gift. By admitting our failures, entrusting our life to God in Jesus Christ, and building a new life according to God's will, we become a member of God's family.

GOD grant me the serenity
to accept the things I cannot change
the courage to change the things I can
and the wisdom to know the difference
AMEN

As we think about making changes in our life, we may find ourself dwelling on the defects in our character.

Removing our defects may seem to be an overwhelming task, despite the fact that God has promised to do the work. Perhaps if we could just catch a glimpse of life beyond recovery, our hope would be revived. The apostle Paul wrote: "And I am sure that God, who began the good work within you, will continue his work until it is finally finished on that day when Christ Jesus comes back again" (Philippians 1:6).

The apostle John wrote: "I heard a loud shout from the throne, saying, 'Look, the home of God is now among his people! He will live with them, and they will be his people. God himself will be with them. He will remove all of their sorrows, and there will be no more death or sorrow or crying or pain. For the old world and its evils are gone forever.' And the one sitting on the throne said, 'Look, I am making all things new!' And then he said to me, 'Write this down, for what I tell you is trustworthy and true.' And he also said, 'It is finished! I am the Alpha and the Omega—the Beginning and the End. To all who are thirsty I will give the springs of the water of life without charge!'" (Revelation 21:3-6).

There is hope for all of us, no matter how terrible our past or the problems we face today. Someday all our defects will be gone; all things will be made new; the thirst of our soul will be quenched by the Water of Life. *Turn to page 555, Psalm 111.*

Jesus, for proclaiming the word of God. And I saw the souls of those who had not worshiped the beast or his statue, nor accepted his mark on their forehead or their hands. They came to life again, and they reigned with Christ for a thousand years. [5]This is the first resurrection. (The rest of the dead did not come back to life until the thousand years had ended.) [6]Blessed and holy are those who share in the first resurrection. For them the second death holds no power, but they will be priests of God and of Christ and will reign with him a thousand years.

The Defeat of Satan

[7]When the thousand years end, Satan will be let out of his prison. [8]He will go out to deceive the nations from every corner of the earth, which are called Gog and Magog. He will gather them together for battle—a mighty host, as numberless as sand along the shore. [9]And I saw them as they went up on the broad plain of the earth and surrounded God's people and the beloved city. But fire from heaven came down on the attacking armies and consumed them.

[10]Then the Devil, who betrayed them, was thrown into the lake of fire that burns with sulfur, joining the beast and the false prophet. There they will be tormented day and night forever and ever.

The Final Judgment

[11]And I saw a great white throne, and I saw the one who was sitting on it. The earth and sky fled from his presence, but they found no place to hide. [12]I saw the dead, both great and small, standing before God's throne. And the books were opened, including the Book of Life. And the dead were judged

according to the things written in the books, according to what they had done. ¹³The sea gave up the dead in it, and death and the grave* gave up the dead in them. They were all judged according to their deeds. ¹⁴And death and the grave were thrown into the lake of fire. This is the second death—the lake of fire. ¹⁵And anyone whose name was not found recorded in the Book of Life was thrown into the lake of fire.

CHAPTER 21
The New Jerusalem
Then I saw a new heaven and a new earth, for the old heaven and the old earth had disappeared. And the sea was also gone. ²And I saw the holy city, the new Jerusalem, coming down from God out of heaven like a beautiful bride prepared for her husband.

³I heard a loud shout from the throne, saying, "Look, the home of God is now among his people! He will live with them, and they will be his people. God himself will be with them.* ⁴He will remove all of their sorrows, and there will be no more death or sorrow or crying or pain. For the old world and its evils are gone forever."

⁵And the one sitting on the throne said, "Look, I am making all things new!" And then he said to me, "Write this down, for what I tell you is trustworthy and true." ⁶And he also said, "It is finished! I am the Alpha and the Omega—the Beginning and the End. To all who are thirsty I will give the springs of the water of life without charge! ⁷All who are victorious will inherit all these blessings, and I will be their God, and they will be my children. ⁸But cowards who turn away from me, and unbelievers, and the corrupt, and murderers, and the immoral, and those who practice witchcraft, and idol worshipers, and all liars—their doom is in the lake that burns with fire and sulfur. This is the second death."

⁹Then one of the seven angels who held the seven bowls containing the seven last plagues came and said to me, "Come with me! I will show you the bride, the wife of the Lamb."

¹⁰So he took me in spirit* to a great, high mountain, and he showed me the holy city, Jerusalem, descending out of heaven from God. ¹¹It was filled with the glory of God and sparkled like a precious gem, crystal clear like

20:13 Greek *and Hades;* also in 20:14. **21:3** Some manuscripts read *God himself will be with them, their God.* **21:10** Or *in the Spirit.*

21:1-7 What hope this scene gives us! Ever since the first sin in the Garden of Eden, God has been working to restore his earth to its original perfection. He even sent his Son to suffer and die to overcome the power of sin and death and to begin the process of healing in those who love him. It is God's will to make old things new; he will make a new heaven and a new earth for his people! By following his will for our life, we become part of God's plan of restoration. He will free our soul from its bondage to sin. We can receive him into our life today and begin this restoration process without delay.

21:7-8 At the conclusion of these wonderful promises of restoration, we are reminded that some will mourn at Christ's return. Those who have rejected God by their selfish and ungodly living will be thrown into the lake of fire. If we remain enslaved to our dependency, we are headed for that terrible end. Rejecting God's offer of healing will lead to an eternity of suffering—the second death. But we can choose to stop being controlled by ungodly people and destructive substances and put our life into God's hands. Only he has the power to deliver us from the power of sin and addiction. If we rely on him, he can restore our life and make us part of his plan for restoring his created world.

21:10-27 The new Jerusalem is portrayed as the radiant bride of the Lamb (see 21:2). The eternal city has twelve gates, representing the twelve tribes of Israel (see 7:4-8), and twelve foundation stones, representing the twelve apostles of Christ. Thus, the city—the bride—represents the people of God. We as the community of faith are members of the church—the bride of Christ. What a wonderful picture of grace! No matter how many mistakes we have made in the past, God forgives us through Christ, and we are brought into intimate relationship with God. We can begin this healing relationship with God today by giving our life to him.

22:1-5 The book of Revelation climaxes here, portraying the eternal state as a new and better Garden of Eden. God will re-create his broken creation. God's healing power will be easily accessible and intimate, and face-to-face relationships with God will be the norm. God's presence will bring light to everything, making cruelty and deception impossibilities in his new world. What can only be a dream in our present sinful world will then be eternal reality. What a source of hope this picture is for us! No matter how bad our life may be now, there is hope for the future. If we accept the wonderful offer of salvation that God holds out to us through Jesus Christ, we will someday be a part of that blessed world.

jasper. [12]Its walls were broad and high, with twelve gates guarded by twelve angels. And the names of the twelve tribes of Israel were written on the gates. [13]There were three gates on each side—east, north, south, and west. [14]The wall of the city had twelve foundation stones, and on them were written the names of the twelve apostles of the Lamb.

[15]The angel who talked to me held in his hand a gold measuring stick to measure the city, its gates, and its wall. [16]When he measured it, he found it was a square, as wide as it was long. In fact, it was in the form of a cube for its length and width and height were each 1,400 miles.* [17]Then he measured the walls and found them to be 216 feet thick* (the angel used a standard human measure).

[18]The wall was made of jasper, and the city was pure gold, as clear as glass. [19]The wall of the city was built on foundation stones inlaid with twelve gems: the first was jasper, the second sapphire, the third agate, the fourth emerald, [20]the fifth onyx, the sixth carnelian, the seventh chrysolite, the eighth beryl, the ninth topaz, the tenth chrysoprase, the eleventh jacinth, the twelfth amethyst.

[21]The twelve gates were made of pearls— each gate from a single pearl! And the main street was pure gold, as clear as glass.

[22]No temple could be seen in the city, for the Lord God Almighty and the Lamb are its temple. [23]And the city has no need of sun or moon, for the glory of God illuminates the city, and the Lamb is its light. [24]The nations of the earth will walk in its light, and the rulers of the world will come and bring their glory to it. [25]Its gates never close at the end of day because there is no night. [26]And all the nations will bring their glory and honor into the city. [27]Nothing evil will be allowed to enter—no one who practices shameful idolatry and dishonesty—but only those whose names are written in the Lamb's Book of Life.

CHAPTER 22

And the angel showed me a pure river with the water of life, clear as crystal, flowing from the throne of God and of the Lamb, [2]coursing down the center of the main street. On each side of the river grew a tree of life, bearing twelve crops of fruit,* with a fresh crop each month. The leaves were used for medicine to heal the nations.

21:16 Greek *12,000 stadia* [2,220 kilometers].
21:17 Greek *144 cubits* [65 meters]. **22:2** Or *12 kinds of fruit.*

Forgiveness

READ REVELATION 22:1-5

We all suffer from brokenness in our life, in our relationship with God, and in our relationships with others. Brokenness tends to weigh us down and can easily lead us back into our addiction. Recovery isn't complete until all the areas of brokenness are healed.

God's ultimate plan for us and our world involves our complete healing. In Revelation the apostle John saw a vision of a new heaven and new earth where this ultimate healing will take place: "And the angel showed me a pure river with the water of life, clear as crystal, flowing from the throne of God and of the Lamb. . . . On each side of the river grew a tree of life. . . . The leaves were used for medicine to heal the nations" (Revelation 22:1-2).

Although we know that God will heal all things when he returns to rule, we still need to work toward healing the brokenness right now. Jesus taught: "So if you are standing before the altar in the Temple, offering a sacrifice to God, and you suddenly remember that someone has something against you, leave your sacrifice there beside the altar. Go and be reconciled to that person. Then come and offer your sacrifice to God" (Matthew 5:23-24).

Giving and receiving forgiveness is an essential part of our present healing. This requires that we make peace—with God, within ourself, and with others whom we have alienated. Once we go through the process of making amends, we must keep our mind and heart open to anyone we may have overlooked. God will often remind us of relationships that need attention. When these come to mind, we should stop everything and go to those we have offended and seek to repair the damage.
Turn to page 481, Psalm 8.

³No longer will anything be cursed. For the throne of God and of the Lamb will be there, and his servants will worship him. ⁴And they will see his face, and his name will be written on their foreheads. ⁵And there will be no night there—no need for lamps or sun—for the Lord God will shine on them. And they will reign forever and ever.

⁶Then the angel said to me, "These words are trustworthy and true: 'The Lord God, who tells his prophets what the future holds, has sent his angel to tell you what will happen soon.'"

Jesus Is Coming

⁷"Look, I am coming soon! Blessed are those who obey the prophecy written in this scroll."

⁸I, John, am the one who saw and heard all these things. And when I saw and heard these things, I fell down to worship the angel who showed them to me. ⁹But again he said, "No, don't worship me. I am a servant of God, just like you and your brothers the prophets, as well as all who obey what is written in this scroll. Worship God!"

¹⁰Then he instructed me, "Do not seal up the prophetic words you have written, for the time is near. ¹¹Let the one who is doing wrong continue to do wrong; the one who is vile, continue to be vile; the one who is good, continue to do good; and the one who is holy, continue in holiness."

22:16 Greek *I am the root and offspring of David.*

¹²"See, I am coming soon, and my reward is with me, to repay all according to their deeds. ¹³I am the Alpha and the Omega, the First and the Last, the Beginning and the End."

¹⁴Blessed are those who wash their robes so they can enter through the gates of the city and eat the fruit from the tree of life. ¹⁵Outside the city are the dogs—the sorcerers, the sexually immoral, the murderers, the idol worshipers, and all who love to live a lie.

¹⁶"I, Jesus, have sent my angel to give you this message for the churches. I am both the source of David and the heir to his throne.* I am the bright morning star."

¹⁷The Spirit and the bride say, "Come." Let each one who hears them say, "Come." Let the thirsty ones come—anyone who wants to. Let them come and drink the water of life without charge. ¹⁸And I solemnly declare to everyone who hears the prophetic words of this book: If anyone adds anything to what is written here, God will add to that person the plagues described in this book. ¹⁹And if anyone removes any of the words of this prophetic book, God will remove that person's share in the tree of life and in the holy city that are described in this book.

²⁰He who is the faithful witness to all these things says, "Yes, I am coming soon!" Amen! Come, Lord Jesus!

²¹The grace of the Lord Jesus be with you all.

22:20-21 It is unhealthy to harbor unrealistic dreams about a future that will never come about. But it is very healthy for us to anchor our new life and recovery in the certainty of Christ's return. By trusting Christ with our future, we can better deal with our past and live a more productive present. Like the apostle John, we can pray for Christ to return soon, because we know for certain that he will come. This will not only give us hope to persevere during tough times; it will deepen our personal relationship with him. As we trust in him and possess the hope of meeting him face to face, we will grow closer to him. Then Christ's unconditional acceptance and unlimited power will continually undergird us in recovery.

PSALMS

AND

PROVERBS

PSALMS

THE BIG PICTURE

A. PSALMS OF PREPARATION
   AND PROMISE (1–41)
B. PSALMS OF PETITION
   AND PRESERVATION (42–72)
C. PSALMS OF PROBLEMS
   AND POWER (73–89)
D. PSALMS OF PERIL AND
   PROTECTION (90–106)
E. PSALMS OF PERFECTION
   AND PRAISE (107–150)

It is impossible to adequately summarize the richness contained in the book of Psalms. It was Israel's hymnal, containing hymns of praise to God for personal and national salvation, and contains the laments of God's people in difficult situations. It was Israel's prayer book. The psalmists looked to God in moments of private despair and times of national suffering. Amidst their difficulties, they found release by lifting their heartfelt laments and praises to God.

The psalms are for us, too. They are brimming with honest emotion. Through them we can pour out our anguish and adoration, our suffering and confessions, our hopes and fears. Through some we may openly question God's actions or his apparent lack of action. Through others we might express our pain, heartache, and discouragement. Through still others we may praise God as he frees us from oppression and sin. Each psalm is an expression of the heart. None of them is a neat little package of answers tied up with a pretty bow. They are living documents, a collection of spiritual diaries from people who honestly sought God's gracious help.

We will find that the psalms may be read at many different levels, depending on the problems we face. They may function as deterrents to keep us out of trouble, as guides to help us through our problems, as reminders of the one who actually delivers us, or as beacons of hope to encourage us in perplexing or painful situations. Through the psalms we share in the hopes and failures of the entire human race. Yet as we read them, we are also ushered into the very presence of our loving and merciful God.

THE BOTTOM LINE

PURPOSE: To demonstrate that God is holy and loving and intimately involved in every aspect of our human experience. AUTHORS: David wrote seventy-three psalms; Asaph wrote twelve; the sons of Korah wrote nine; Solomon wrote two; Heman (with the sons of Korah), Ethan, and Moses each wrote one; fifty-one psalms are anonymous. AUDIENCE: The people of Israel. DATE WRITTEN: The psalms were written between 1440 and 586 B.C. SETTING: Though the psalms are not generally concerned with recording history, many of them were inspired by historical events. KEY VERSE: "Let everything that lives sing praises to the LORD! Praise the LORD!" (150:6). KEY PLACE: The Temple in Jerusalem. KEY PEOPLE: David, Asaph, Solomon, Heman, the sons of Korah, Ethan, and Moses.

RECOVERY THEMES

Truth Brings Healing: Above everything else, the psalmists were honest about their experiences and feelings. Again and again they testified to God's faithfulness in hearing and responding to their words of honest confession or praise. It is so easy to try and hedge on the truth, even when we pray to God. This, however, is always a dead end. Only the truth can bring us into the kind of relationship with God that will result in true healing. When we face the truth about our sins and failures and recognize that we are powerless over them, God will meet us where we are and guide us in the path of recovery and healing.

Legitimate Doubts and Complaints: Most of us act as if doubt is an unforgivable sin. We do everything we can to hide it from God. But God knows all about our doubts. The psalmists were honest about their doubts and brought them straight to God. They were also honest in their complaints. There is a place for complaining before God—it helps us to bring our raw feelings and doubts out into the open. But just as the psalmists did, we will find that our complaining is followed by an affirmation of faith. If we hide our doubts about God, we will be sure to drift away from him. But if we honestly express them to him, even complaining about his apparent failures in our life, we will discover that our faith is renewed. As happened with the psalmists, our complaints will be followed by words of praise.

God's Power of Deliverance: We can count on the fact that God is all-powerful, and he always chooses to act at the best possible time. God is sovereign over every situation. The psalmists testify repeatedly that God is able to overcome the despair and pain in life and that he is always in control. This kind of faith didn't come easily to them. They struggled with this truth, often questioning God's presence in their lives, just as we do. But in the end, their questions were always replaced by praises that affirmed the fact of God's powerful presence.

The Necessity of Forgiveness: Many of the psalms are intense prayers asking God for forgiveness. What the psalmists discovered was that they could be open and honest before God about their failures, emotions, and weaknesses, because God had promised to forgive them. As we experience God's forgiveness, we move away from our dependencies and feelings of alienation and guilt and into an intimate and loving relationship with God. God's antidote to our past failures—no matter how terrible our sins—is always forgiveness!

BOOK ONE (Psalms 1–41)

PSALM 1

¹Oh, the joys of those
  who do not follow the advice of the
    wicked,
  or stand around with sinners,
  or join in with scoffers.
²But they delight in doing everything the
    LORD wants;
  day and night they think about his
    law.
³They are like trees planted along the
    riverbank,
  bearing fruit each season without fail.
Their leaves never wither,
  and in all they do, they prosper.

⁴But this is not true of the wicked.
  They are like worthless chaff, scattered
    by the wind.
⁵They will be condemned at the time
    of judgment.
  Sinners will have no place among the
    godly.

⁶For the LORD watches over the path of the
    godly,
  but the path of the wicked leads
    to destruction.

PSALM 2

¹Why do the nations rage?
  Why do the people waste their time
    with futile plans?

1:1-6 Turning our will over to God means turning away from the kind of people who draw us into temptation. There is no better source for wisdom and direction than the Word of God. When we fail to study and apply God's Word, we tend to drift through life. We are tossed around by every new fad or philosophy that comes our way. Recognizing our sins and being willing to change our sinful habits is the only way to avoid God's judgment. God wants to help us live a godly life. But if we refuse to work on removing the character defects that slow the recovery process, we will certainly suffer the consequences.

2:1-6 If God is in charge of the world, why do we continually try to do things our own way? Fighting God's program is useless and foolish. Many turn from God because they think it involves becoming his slave. But if we reject God's rule in our life, we will invariably become a slave to someone or something else. The foolish man who rejects God's rule soon falls into a prison of sin and destruction. The only way we can be in tune with God's plan and receive his help is to accept his loving rule in our life.

2 The kings of the earth prepare for battle;
    the rulers plot together
against the Lord
    and against his anointed one.
3 "Let us break their chains," they cry,
    "and free ourselves from this slavery."

4 But the one who rules in heaven laughs.
    The Lord scoffs at them.
5 Then in anger he rebukes them,
    terrifying them with his fierce fury.
6 For the Lord declares, "I have placed
    my chosen king on the throne
in Jerusalem, my holy city.*"

7 The king proclaims the Lord's decree:
"The Lord said to me, 'You are my
    son.*
    Today I have become your Father.*
8 Only ask, and I will give you the nations
    as your inheritance,
    the ends of the earth as your
    possession.
9 You will break them with an iron rod
    and smash them like clay pots.'"

10 Now then, you kings, act wisely!
    Be warned, you rulers of the earth!
11 Serve the Lord with reverent fear,
    and rejoice with trembling.
12 Submit to God's royal son, or he will
    become angry,
    and you will be destroyed in the midst
    of your pursuits—
    for his anger can flare up in an
    instant.

But what joy for all who find protection
    in him!

PSALM 3

*A psalm of David, regarding the time David fled
from his son Absalom.*

1 O Lord, I have so many enemies;
    so many are against me.

2 So many are saying,
    "God will never rescue him!"
                                    *Interlude**

3 But you, O Lord, are a shield around me,
    my glory, and the one who lifts my
    head high.
4 I cried out to the Lord,
    and he answered me from his holy
    mountain.   *Interlude*

5 I lay down and slept.
    I woke up in safety,
    for the Lord was watching over me.
6 I am not afraid of ten thousand enemies
    who surround me on every side.

7 Arise, O Lord!
    Rescue me, my God!
Slap all my enemies in the face!
    Shatter the teeth of the wicked!

8 Victory comes from you, O Lord.
    May your blessings rest on your people.
                                    Interlude

PSALM 4

*For the choir director: A psalm of David, to be
accompanied by stringed instruments.*

1 Answer me when I call,
    O God who declares me innocent.
Take away my distress.
    Have mercy on me and hear my prayer.

2 How long will you people ruin my
    reputation?
    How long will you make these
    groundless accusations?
    How long will you pursue lies?
                                    Interlude

3 You can be sure of this:
    The Lord has set apart the godly for
    himself.
    The Lord will answer when I call to
    him.

2:6 Hebrew *on Zion, my holy mountain.* **2:7a** Or *Son;* also in 2:12. **2:7b** Or *Today I reveal you as my son.* **3:2** Hebrew
Selah. The meaning of this word is uncertain, though it is probably a musical or literary term. It is rendered *Interlude*
throughout the Psalms.

3:1-4 Even David, a righteous man, recognized problems in his life that had become unmanageable. When we fail, even our friends sometimes begin to think we are beyond God's help. David, however, knew otherwise. He looked to God for help and encouragement. Calling out to God to increase our knowledge of him is one of the most important steps in the recovery process.
3:5-8 God comforted David so much that he could sleep in the face of his troubles. What is more, David's worries and anxieties vanished when he focused his thoughts fully on God; he could view life as though all of his problems had been eliminated. By placing his problems in God's hands, David had made the most important step toward solving them. True deliverance and happiness come when we acknowledge God as our helper and the source of our strength.

4 Don't sin by letting anger gain control
over you.
Think about it overnight and remain
silent.   *Interlude*
5 Offer proper sacrifices,
and trust in the LORD.

6 Many people say, "Who will show us
better times?"
Let the smile of your face shine on us,
LORD.
7 You have given me greater joy
than those who have abundant harvests
of grain and wine.

8 I will lie down in peace and sleep,
for you alone, O LORD, will keep me
safe.

PSALM 5

For the choir director: A psalm of David, to be
accompanied by the flute.

1 O LORD, hear me as I pray;
pay attention to my groaning.
2 Listen to my cry for help, my King and
my God,
for I will never pray to anyone but you.
3 Listen to my voice in the morning, LORD.
Each morning I bring my requests to
you and wait expectantly.

4 O God, you take no pleasure in
wickedness;
you cannot tolerate the slightest sin.
5 Therefore, the proud will not be allowed
to stand in your presence,
for you hate all who do evil.

6 You will destroy those who tell lies.
The LORD detests murderers and
deceivers.

7 Because of your unfailing love, I can enter
your house;
with deepest awe I will worship at your
Temple.
8 Lead me in the right path, O LORD,
or my enemies will conquer me.
Tell me clearly what to do,
and show me which way to turn.

9 My enemies cannot speak one truthful
word.
Their deepest desire is to destroy others.
Their talk is foul, like the stench from an
open grave.
Their speech is filled with flattery.
10 O God, declare them guilty.
Let them be caught in their own traps.
Drive them away because of their many
sins,
for they rebel against you.

11 But let all who take refuge in you rejoice;
let them sing joyful praises forever.
Protect them,
so all who love your name may be filled
with joy.
12 For you bless the godly, O LORD,
surrounding them with your shield
of love.

PSALM 6

For the choir director: A psalm of David, to be
accompanied by an eight-stringed instrument.*

6:TITLE Hebrew *with stringed instruments; according to the sheminith.*

4:4-5 Turning our will over to God is not a onetime experience; it is a moment-by-moment decision to keep our mind fixed on doing God's will. Today we don't sacrifice animals on an altar to
please God, but we can offer God our life as a living sacrifice. In order to do this, we must seek
out and then follow God's plan for holy and healthy living.
4:6-8 Many people around us cannot see God at work in our life; they see only our past failures.
But as we seek God and with his help make changes, our success in recovery will allow others to
see God's power. True joy comes from God—a joy that is greater than all the gladness the world
can produce. Nothing will bring us more peaceful nights of sleep than the knowledge that God
is with us and helping us to progress in recovery.
5:1-7 We have probably tried just about everything to escape our slavery to destructive habits.
David understood how foolish it was to look for help from anything or anyone else but God. One
by one, he brought his needs daily to God. David understood that God would not accept the
prayers of one who was trusting in himself and continuing in his sin. When we trust God for help
in our moment-by-moment walk of obedience, his wall of protection surrounds us wherever we
go and whatever we do.
5:8-12 David requested God's guidance because he knew that God's plan for him was the only
way to avoid the destructive traps he faced. Our old friends, like David's enemies, will tell us the
big lie—that one more sin won't hurt us. Their words sound good, but their lives prove that they
are slaves to sin and that they are headed for destruction. In the midst of these snares of the
world, we can always find protection by trusting in God.

¹O LORD, do not rebuke me in your anger
or discipline me in your rage.
²Have compassion on me, LORD, for I am
weak.
Heal me, LORD, for my body is in agony.
³I am sick at heart.
How long, O LORD, until you restore me?

⁴Return, O LORD, and rescue me.
Save me because of your unfailing love.
⁵For in death, who remembers you?
Who can praise you from the grave?

⁶I am worn out from sobbing.
Every night tears drench my bed;
my pillow is wet from weeping.
⁷My vision is blurred by grief;
my eyes are worn out because of all
my enemies.

⁸Go away, all you who do evil,
for the LORD has heard my crying.
⁹The LORD has heard my plea;
the LORD will answer my prayer.
¹⁰May all my enemies be disgraced and
terrified.
May they suddenly turn back in shame.

PSALM 7

*A psalm of David, which he sang to the LORD
concerning Cush of the tribe of Benjamin.*

¹I come to you for protection, O LORD
my God.
Save me from my persecutors—
rescue me!
²If you don't, they will maul me like a lion,
tearing me to pieces with no one to
rescue me.

³O LORD my God, if I have done wrong
or am guilty of injustice,
⁴if I have betrayed a friend
or plundered my enemy without cause,

7:12 Hebrew *he.*

⁵then let my enemies capture me.
Let them trample me into the ground.
Let my honor be left in the dust.

Interlude

⁶Arise, O LORD, in anger!
Stand up against the fury of my enemies!
Wake up, my God, and bring justice!
⁷Gather the nations before you.
Sit on your throne high above them.
⁸The LORD passes judgment on the nations.
Declare me righteous, O LORD,
for I am innocent, O Most High!
⁹End the wickedness of the ungodly,
but help all those who obey you.
For you look deep within the mind and
heart,
O righteous God.

¹⁰God is my shield,
saving those whose hearts are true and
right.
¹¹God is a judge who is perfectly fair.
He is angry with the wicked every day.

¹²If a person does not repent,
God* will sharpen his sword;
he will bend and string his bow.
¹³He will prepare his deadly weapons
and ignite his flaming arrows.

¹⁴The wicked conceive evil;
they are pregnant with trouble
and give birth to lies.
¹⁵They dig a pit to trap others
and then fall into it themselves.
¹⁶They make trouble,
but it backfires on them.
They plan violence for others,
but it falls on their own heads.

¹⁷I will thank the LORD because he is just;
I will sing praise to the name of the
LORD Most High.

6:1-5 Although we might want instant relief from the anguish of temptation, it doesn't usually come immediately. But when we realize that we are powerless over our dependency or compulsion, we have taken the first step toward recovery. Once we have acknowledged that God has the power to help us, we have taken the second step. Knowing about these important steps, however, is never enough to help us avoid destruction. We need to act on them, too.
6:6-10 Even though we may be suffering greatly, we can have confidence that God answers our prayers. God will always hear our petitions and rescue us. We should be as bold as David is here, claiming victory at the end of his prayer. Prayer should not be a last-ditch tactic; it should be the basis for our battles for recovery.
7:11-16 God is patient, but there is a limit to how long he will tolerate those who continue to rebel against him. When we choose to live in ways that run counter to God's program, we will quickly discover that our problems only grow worse. The plans we make to achieve personal success at the expense of others will destroy us in the end. We will only fall prey to our own schemes (see 9:15).

PSALM 8

*For the choir director: A psalm of David, to be
accompanied by a stringed instrument.* *

¹O LORD, our Lord, the majesty of your
name fills the earth!
Your glory is higher than the heavens.

²You have taught children and nursing
infants
to give you praise.*
They silence your enemies
who were seeking revenge.

³When I look at the night sky and see the
work of your fingers—
the moon and the stars you have set
in place—
⁴what are mortals that you should think
of us,
mere humans that you should care for us?*
⁵For you made us only a little lower than
God,*
and you crowned us with glory and
honor.
⁶You put us in charge of everything you
made,
giving us authority over all things—
⁷the sheep and the cattle
and all the wild animals,
⁸the birds in the sky, the fish in the sea,
and everything that swims the ocean
currents.

⁹O LORD, our Lord, the majesty of your
name fills the earth!

PSALM 9

*For the choir director: A psalm of David, to be sung
to the tune "Death of the Son."*

¹I will thank you, LORD, with all my heart;
I will tell of all the marvelous things
you have done.
²I will be filled with joy because of you.
I will sing praises to your name, O Most
High.

³My enemies turn away in retreat;
they are overthrown and destroyed
before you.
⁴For you have judged in my favor;
from your throne, you have judged
with fairness.

⁵You have rebuked the nations and
destroyed the wicked;
you have wiped out their names
forever.
⁶My enemies have met their doom;
their cities are perpetual ruins.
Even the memory of their uprooted
cities is lost.

⁷But the LORD reigns forever,
executing judgment from his throne.
⁸He will judge the world with justice
and rule the nations with fairness.

8:TITLE Hebrew *according to the gittith.* **8:2** As in Greek version; Hebrew reads *to show strength.* **8:4** Hebrew *what is
man that you should think of him, the son of man that you should care for him?* **8:5** Or *a little lower than the angels;*
Hebrew reads *Elohim.*

8:3-9 Many of our problems are rooted in our low self-esteem. Perhaps we were never listened to
as children. Or maybe we were abused by people who had authority over us. Whatever the roots of
our problems, we are now probably overly sensitive to the attacks of others. We see here that God
has made us to be fantastic beings with great honor and authority. We should never sell ourselves
short. Self-esteem should be based on what God thinks of us—not on what others say about us.
9:1-6 As we experience God's help and begin to change our life for the better, we have the
responsibility to carry the message of deliverance to others so their lives can be changed, too.
As we allow God to help us overcome the defects in our character, others will see what God has
done for us and may also receive the gift of hope. Our painful struggles with our addictions and
compulsions and our victories through God's help can be a source of encouragement and guidance to others whose lives are headed toward destruction.
9:15-20 The people who set traps for others will ultimately be trapped themselves. God ensures
that such people do not succeed in the long run. Those who realize they need God's help and
turn to him will receive it; those who try to control their problems alone will ultimately fail. If we
think we are in control of our own destiny or the destinies of others, we have a terrible surprise
in store. One day God will step in and demonstrate who is truly in control. Since God is ultimately
in control, the only wise plan to follow is God's plan.
10:1-11 God sometimes seems far away when temptation is strong. In truth, he is never far
from us. Temptation sometimes becomes strongest when our godless friends seem to be able to
do things without getting trapped the way we do. We tend to follow along and end up in trouble. We need to realize that even though our friends seem to do well and be in control at the
moment, they are headed for serious trouble; they just don't realize it yet. We need to make sure
that the apparent successes of others don't lead us away from God's program for healthy living.

⁹The LORD is a shelter for the oppressed,
a refuge in times of trouble.
¹⁰Those who know your name trust in you,
for you, O LORD, have never abandoned
anyone who searches for you.

¹¹Sing praises to the LORD who reigns in
Jerusalem.*
Tell the world about his unforgettable
deeds.
¹²For he who avenges murder cares for the
helpless.
He does not ignore those who cry to him
for help.

¹³LORD, have mercy on me.
See how I suffer at the hands of those
who hate me.
Snatch me back from the jaws of death.
¹⁴Save me, so I can praise you publicly at
Jerusalem's gates,
so I can rejoice that you have rescued me.

¹⁵The nations have fallen into the pit they
dug for others.
They have been caught in their own trap.
¹⁶The LORD is known for his justice.
The wicked have trapped themselves in
their own snares.

                                    *Quiet Interlude**

¹⁷The wicked will go down to the grave.*
This is the fate of all the nations who
ignore God.
¹⁸For the needy will not be forgotten forever;
the hopes of the poor will not always be
crushed.

¹⁹Arise, O LORD!
Do not let mere mortals defy you!
Let the nations be judged in your
presence!
²⁰Make them tremble in fear, O LORD.
Let them know they are merely human.

                                            Interlude

PSALM 10

¹O LORD, why do you stand so far away?
Why do you hide when I need you the
most?
²Proud and wicked people viciously oppress
the poor.
Let them be caught in the evil they plan
for others.
³For they brag about their evil desires;
they praise the greedy and curse the
LORD.

9:11 Hebrew *Zion;* also in 9:14. 9:16 Hebrew *Higgaion
Selah.* The meaning of this phrase is uncertain.
9:17 Hebrew *to Sheol.*

Self-Perception

READ PSALM 8:1-9

We develop our sense of self-perception
by noticing how the important people in
our life see us. If we grew up in a dysfunctional family, their skewed view of us
probably warped our ability to see ourself
as we truly are in God's eyes. Understanding how God sees us and the value he has
placed on us can help us overcome the
negative self-perception that many of us
have developed.

King David was amazed as he thought
about how much God valued him. He
said, "What are mortals that you should
think of us, mere humans that you should
care for us? For you made us only a little
lower than God, and you crowned us
with glory and honor. You put us in
charge of everything you made, giving us
authority over all things" (Psalm 8:4-6).
"How precious are your thoughts about
me, O God! They are innumerable! I can't
even count them; they outnumber the
grains of sand! And when I wake up in
the morning, you are still with me!"
(Psalm 139:17-18). God demonstrated
how precious we are in his sight by sending Jesus to give his life for us.

God wants us to realize how precious
we are to him and to see ourself in the
light of his love. Consider this: If God
considered us worthy of giving up the
most precious thing he had (his only
Son), what does that say about how
valuable we are to him? ***Turn to page 497,
Psalm 32.***

⁴These wicked people are too proud to
    seek God.
They seem to think that God is
    dead.
⁵Yet they succeed in everything they do.
They do not see your punishment
    awaiting them.
They pour scorn on all their enemies.
⁶They say to themselves, "Nothing bad
    will ever happen to us!
We will be free of trouble forever!"

⁷Their mouths are full of cursing, lies,
    and threats.
Trouble and evil are on the tips
    of their tongues.
⁸They lurk in dark alleys,
    murdering the innocent who
    pass by.

They are always searching
    for some helpless victim.
⁹Like lions they crouch silently,
    waiting to pounce on the helpless.
Like hunters they capture their victims
    and drag them away in nets.
¹⁰The helpless are overwhelmed and
    collapse;
they fall beneath the strength of the
    wicked.
¹¹The wicked say to themselves, "God
    isn't watching!
He will never notice!"

¹²Arise, O LORD!
Punish the wicked, O God!
Do not forget the helpless!
¹³Why do the wicked get away with
    cursing God?
How can they think, "God will never
    call us to account"?

¹⁴But you do see the trouble and grief
    they cause.
You take note of it and punish them.
The helpless put their trust in you.
You are the defender of orphans.

¹⁵Break the arms of these wicked, evil
    people!
Go after them until the last one is
    destroyed!
¹⁶The LORD is king forever and ever!
Let those who worship other gods
    be swept from the land.

¹⁷LORD, you know the hopes of the
    helpless.
Surely you will listen to their cries and
    comfort them.
¹⁸You will bring justice to the orphans and
    the oppressed,
so people can no longer terrify them.

PSALM 11
For the choir director: A psalm of David.

¹I trust in the LORD for protection.
    So why do you say to me,
"Fly to the mountains for safety!
²   The wicked are stringing their bows
    and setting their arrows in the
    bowstrings.
They shoot from the shadows at those
    who do right.
³The foundations of law and order have
    collapsed.
What can the righteous do?"

⁴But the LORD is in his holy Temple;
    the LORD still rules from heaven.
He watches everything closely,
    examining everyone on earth.
⁵The LORD examines both the righteous
    and the wicked.
He hates everyone who loves violence.
⁶He rains down blazing coals on the
    wicked,
punishing them with burning sulfur
    and scorching winds.
⁷For the LORD is righteous, and he loves
    justice.
Those who do what is right will see
    his face.

10:13-18 Even when it appears that God is blind to the evil deeds of others, we can be sure that one day he will respond with judgment. Those who drag others into sin will be judged harshly by God (see Luke 17:1-3). At times God works quietly behind the scenes, helping those who admit their helplessness to overcome the enemies and problems they face. When we humble ourself and put our trust in God, we can have hope that one day God will give us a full recovery.

11:1-3 Security from temptation can only be found in God; running elsewhere for help—to merely human sources and programs—will never do any long-term good. If we turn only to human resources for help, the people and situations that endanger us will cause us to fall when we are most vulnerable. They will destroy us when the human resources we depend on are unavailable. God is always with us. If we put our trust in him, we will never be without the means to overcome temptation.

PSALM 12

For the choir director: A psalm of David, to be accompanied by an eight-stringed instrument. *

[1] Help, O LORD, for the godly are fast disappearing!
The faithful have vanished from the earth!
[2] Neighbors lie to each other,
speaking with flattering lips and insincere hearts.
[3] May the LORD bring their flattery to an end
and silence their proud tongues.
[4] They say, "We will lie to our hearts' content.
Our lips are our own—who can stop us?"

[5] The LORD replies, "I have seen violence done to the helpless,
and I have heard the groans of the poor.
Now I will rise up to rescue them,
as they have longed for me to do."
[6] The LORD's promises are pure,
like silver refined in a furnace,
purified seven times over.

[7] Therefore, LORD, we know you will protect the oppressed,
preserving them forever from this lying generation,
[8] even though the wicked strut about,
and evil is praised throughout the land.

PSALM 13

For the choir director: A psalm of David.

[1] O LORD, how long will you forget me? Forever?
How long will you look the other way?

12:TITLE Hebrew *according to the sheminith.*

[2] How long must I struggle with anguish in my soul,
with sorrow in my heart every day?
How long will my enemy have the upper hand?

[3] Turn and answer me, O LORD my God!
Restore the light to my eyes, or I will die.
[4] Don't let my enemies gloat, saying, "We have defeated him!"
Don't let them rejoice at my downfall.

[5] But I trust in your unfailing love.
I will rejoice because you have rescued me.
[6] I will sing to the LORD
because he has been so good to me.

PSALM 14

For the choir director: A psalm of David.

[1] Only fools say in their hearts,
"There is no God."
They are corrupt, and their actions are evil;
no one does good!

[2] The LORD looks down from heaven
on the entire human race;
he looks to see if there is even one with real understanding,
one who seeks for God.
[3] But no, all have turned away from God;
all have become corrupt.
No one does good,
not even one!

[4] Will those who do evil never learn?
They eat up my people like bread;
they wouldn't think of praying to the LORD.

12:5-8 We need not worry about the harm that liars may bring us. God has promised to protect us from those who try to destroy us. People make a grave mistake if they don't understand that God is not like us—his words are pure. He never deceives, nor does he ever fail to keep his promises. God has offered to protect us from the wicked if we but ask. If we really want to avoid tempting situations, God offers us his protection.

13:1-6 The recovery process is often long, with seemingly interminable stretches of spiritual barrenness. At times we may be convinced that God has forgotten us completely. We may feel overwhelmed by our problems and baffled that God has done nothing to help. David began this psalm with similar feelings. Then he demonstrated a helpful way of dealing with the temptation to give in to discouragement. We can turn our focus away from our problems and on to God. When we turn our thoughts to God, we will see that he is already at work in us to complete the recovery process and to fill us with joy.

14:1-3 Our refusal to believe in God is the first step toward failure in recovery. Unless we can accept that there is a God who is concerned about us, there is no hope for us. The psalmist gave us a good term to describe the people who refuse to believe in God—*fools*. The world is filled with evil-minded fools, but we don't have to be like them. We prove we are not such people by deciding to turn our will over to God.

5 Terror will grip them,
    for God is with those who obey him.
6 The wicked frustrate the plans of the
        oppressed,
    but the LORD will protect his people.

7 Oh, that salvation would come from
        Mount Zion to rescue Israel!
    For when the LORD restores his people,
    Jacob will shout with joy, and Israel
        will rejoice.

PSALM 15
A psalm of David.

1 Who may worship in your sanctuary, LORD?
    Who may enter your presence on your
        holy hill?

2 Those who lead blameless lives
    and do what is right,
    speaking the truth from sincere hearts.
3 Those who refuse to slander others
    or harm their neighbors
    or speak evil of their friends.
4 Those who despise persistent sinners,
    and honor the faithful followers of
        the LORD
    and keep their promises even when it hurts.
5 Those who do not charge interest on the
        money they lend,
    and who refuse to accept bribes to
        testify against the innocent.

Such people will stand firm forever.

PSALM 16
A psalm of David.

1 Keep me safe, O God,
    for I have come to you for refuge.

2 I said to the LORD, "You are my Master!
    All the good things I have are from you."
3 The godly people in the land
    are my true heroes!
    I take pleasure in them!
4 Those who chase after other gods will be
        filled with sorrow.
    I will not take part in their sacrifices
    or even speak the names of their gods.

5 LORD, you alone are my inheritance, my
        cup of blessing.
    You guard all that is mine.
6 The land you have given me is a pleasant
        land.
    What a wonderful inheritance!

7 I will bless the LORD who guides me;
    even at night my heart instructs me.
8 I know the LORD is always with me.
    I will not be shaken, for he is right
        beside me.

9 No wonder my heart is filled with joy,
    and my mouth* shouts his praises!
    My body rests in safety.
10 For you will not leave my soul among
        the dead*
    or allow your godly one* to rot in the
        grave.
11 You will show me the way of life,
    granting me the joy of your presence
    and the pleasures of living with you
        forever.

PSALM 17
A prayer of David.

1 O LORD, hear my plea for justice.
    Listen to my cry for help.

16:9 As in Greek version; Hebrew reads *glory*. **16:10a** Hebrew *in Sheol*. **16:10b** Or *your Holy One*.

15:1-3 If we want to experience recovery, we must be committed to honesty, integrity, and right living. We must quit lying to ourself and to others, and we must stop doing things that hurt other people. These are all essential elements of any effective personal inventory if we hope to bring reconciliation to our relationships.
16:1-6 Strength and security come from God alone; he is the only one who can restore us to right living. We can often draw strength from those who are trying to do God's will. As we recover, we can offer that strength to others. If we look to God as the source of our strength and joy, he will never disappoint us. People and other sources of pleasure will let us down, but God will not.
16:7-11 As we seek through prayer and meditation to improve our relationship with God, we will find in his Word not only peace of mind and heart but also good counsel that will keep us from falling into sin. Knowing that God is with us and that he will never abandon us should be a constant source of joy and peace. An important principle of recovery is realizing that God is with us—here and now—and that he promises to be with us through all eternity.
17:1-5 Taking a careful personal inventory of our life is absolutely necessary for complete recovery. If we refuse to examine our life, we will encounter numerous obstacles that will stand in the way of our recovery program. As we learn to live as we should, we can have confidence that God will respond to our cries for help. We must follow through on our commitment by avoiding involvement with the people who draw us toward the evil things that have overwhelmed us in the past.

Pay attention to my prayer,
    for it comes from an honest heart.
²Declare me innocent,
    for you know those who do right.

³You have tested my thoughts and
        examined my heart in the night.
    You have scrutinized me and found
        nothing amiss,
    for I am determined not to sin in
        what I say.
⁴I have followed your commands,
    which have kept me from going along
        with cruel and evil people.
⁵My steps have stayed on your path;
    I have not wavered from following you.

⁶I am praying to you because I know you
        will answer, O God.
    Bend down and listen as I pray.
⁷Show me your unfailing love in
        wonderful ways.
    You save with your strength
    those who seek refuge from their
        enemies.
⁸Guard me as the apple of your eye.
    Hide me in the shadow of your wings.
⁹Protect me from wicked people who
        attack me,
    from murderous enemies who
        surround me.

¹⁰They are without pity.
    Listen to their boasting.
¹¹They track me down, surround me,
    and throw me to the ground.
¹²They are like hungry lions, eager to tear
        me apart—
    like young lions in hiding, waiting for
        their chance.

¹³Arise, O LORD!
    Stand against them and bring them
        to their knees!
    Rescue me from the wicked with your
        sword!
¹⁴Save me by your mighty hand, O LORD,
    from those whose only concern is
        earthly gain.
    May they have their punishment in full.
    May their children inherit more of the
        same,

and may the judgment continue to
    their children's children.

¹⁵But because I have done what is right,
    I will see you.
    When I awake, I will be fully satisfied,
    for I will see you face to face.

PSALM 18

For the choir director: A psalm of David, the servant
of the LORD. He sang this song to the LORD on the
day the LORD rescued him from all his enemies and
from Saul.

¹I love you, LORD; you are my strength.
²The LORD is my rock, my fortress, and
        my savior;
    my God is my rock, in whom I find
        protection.
    He is my shield, the strength of my
        salvation, and my stronghold.
³I will call on the LORD, who is worthy
        of praise,
    for he saves me from my enemies.

⁴The ropes of death surrounded me;
    the floods of destruction swept over me.
⁵The grave* wrapped its ropes around me;
    death itself stared me in the face.
⁶But in my distress I cried out to the LORD;
    yes, I prayed to my God for help.
    He heard me from his sanctuary;
    my cry reached his ears.

⁷Then the earth quaked and trembled;
    the foundations of the mountains
        shook;
    they quaked because of his anger.
⁸Smoke poured from his nostrils;
    fierce flames leaped from his mouth;
    glowing coals flamed forth from him.
⁹He opened the heavens and came down;
    dark storm clouds were beneath his
        feet.
¹⁰Mounted on a mighty angel,* he flew,
    soaring on the wings of the wind.
¹¹He shrouded himself in darkness,
    veiling his approach with dense rain
        clouds.
¹²The brilliance of his presence broke
        through the clouds,
    raining down hail and burning coals.

18:5 Hebrew *Sheol.* **18:10** Hebrew *a cherub.*

18:6-15 The psalmist used very graphic language here to show how serious God is about helping those who turn to him for help. The psalmist knew that he would be delivered—not because
he was strong or deserving of God's help but because God loved him and was powerful enough
to arouse all the forces of nature to help him. If God is on our side, no enemy is too great. We can
always experience victory by depending on God's delivering hand.

13 The LORD thundered from heaven;
 the Most High gave a mighty shout.*
14 He shot his arrows and scattered his
 enemies;
 his lightning flashed, and they were
 greatly confused.
15 Then at your command, O LORD,
 at the blast of your breath,
 the bottom of the sea could be seen,
 and the foundations of the earth were
 laid bare.

16 He reached down from heaven and
 rescued me;
 he drew me out of deep waters.
17 He delivered me from my powerful
 enemies,
 from those who hated me and were
 too strong for me.
18 They attacked me at a moment when
 I was weakest,
 but the LORD upheld me.
19 He led me to a place of safety;
 he rescued me because he delights
 in me.
20 The LORD rewarded me for doing right;
 he compensated me because of my
 innocence.
21 For I have kept the ways of the LORD;
 I have not turned from my God to
 follow evil.
22 For all his laws are constantly before me;
 I have never abandoned his principles.
23 I am blameless before God;
 I have kept myself from sin.
24 The LORD rewarded me for doing right,
 because of the innocence of my hands
 in his sight.

25 To the faithful you show yourself faithful;
 to those with integrity you show
 integrity.
26 To the pure you show yourself pure,
 but to the wicked you show yourself
 hostile.

27 You rescue those who are humble,
 but you humiliate the proud.
28 LORD, you have brought light to my life;
 my God, you light up my darkness.
29 In your strength I can crush an army;
 with my God I can scale any wall.

30 As for God, his way is perfect.
 All the LORD's promises prove true.
 He is a shield for all who look to him
 for protection.
31 For who is God except the LORD?
 Who but our God is a solid rock?
32 God arms me with strength;
 he has made my way safe.
33 He makes me as surefooted as a deer,
 leading me safely along the mountain
 heights.
34 He prepares me for battle;
 he strengthens me to draw a bow of
 bronze.
35 You have given me the shield of your
 salvation.
 Your right hand supports me;
 your gentleness has made me great.
36 You have made a wide path for my feet
 to keep them from slipping.

37 I chased my enemies and caught them;
 I did not stop until they were
 conquered.
38 I struck them down so they could not
 get up;
 they fell beneath my feet.
39 You have armed me with strength for the
 battle;
 you have subdued my enemies under
 my feet.
40 You made them turn and run;
 I have destroyed all who hated me.
41 They called for help, but no one came
 to rescue them.
 They cried to the LORD, but he refused
 to answer them.

18:13 As in Greek version (see also 2 Sam 22:14); Hebrew adds *raining down hail and burning coals*.

18:16-19 When the psalmist realized his helplessness and turned his life over to God, God came to his aid. Many of us have known this truth as a theological principle, but now we are beginning to experience it in our own life. We also are given a clear warning in these verses. Our enemies or temptations always attack us when we are most vulnerable. A careful moral inventory helps us see what our weaknesses are and when temptation will most likely attack. Then we need to evaluate the situations we encounter and decide which ones should be avoided.

18:37-42 We cannot fight the battles between us and our dependency alone. Although at times we may feel that our efforts are overcoming the things that cripple and destroy us, we soon realize that it is God who gives us the strength to fight these battles. Once we bring God into our battles, we begin to experience victory in the places where we were defeated in the past. God alone can guarantee a permanent victory.

⁴²I ground them as fine as dust carried by
the wind.
I swept them into the gutter like dirt.

⁴³You gave me victory over my accusers.
You appointed me as the ruler over
nations;
people I don't even know now serve me.
⁴⁴As soon as they hear of me, they submit;
foreigners cringe before me.
⁴⁵They all lose their courage
and come trembling from their
strongholds.

⁴⁶The LORD lives! Blessed be my rock!
May the God of my salvation be
exalted!
⁴⁷He is the God who pays back those who
harm me;
he subdues the nations under me
⁴⁸   and rescues me from my enemies.
You hold me safe beyond the reach of
my enemies;
you save me from violent opponents.
⁴⁹For this, O LORD, I will praise you among
the nations;
I will sing joyfully to your name.
⁵⁰You give great victories to your king;
you show unfailing love to your
anointed,
to David and all his descendants
forever.

PSALM 19

For the choir director: A psalm of David.

¹The heavens tell of the glory of God.
The skies display his marvelous
craftsmanship.
²Day after day they continue to speak;
night after night they make him
known.

³They speak without a sound or a word;
their voice is silent in the skies;*
⁴yet their message has gone out to all the
earth,
and their words to all the world.

The sun lives in the heavens
where God placed it.
⁵It bursts forth like a radiant bridegroom
after his wedding.
It rejoices like a great athlete
eager to run the race.
⁶The sun rises at one end of the heavens
and follows its course to the other
end.
Nothing can hide from its heat.

⁷The law of the LORD is perfect,
reviving the soul.
The decrees of the LORD are trustworthy,
making wise the simple.
⁸The commandments of the LORD are
right,
bringing joy to the heart.
The commands of the LORD are clear,
giving insight to life.
⁹Reverence for the LORD is pure,
lasting forever.
The laws of the LORD are true;
each one is fair.
¹⁰They are more desirable than gold,
even the finest gold.
They are sweeter than honey,
even honey dripping from the comb.
¹¹They are a warning to those who hear
them;
there is great reward for those who
obey them.

¹²How can I know all the sins lurking in
my heart?
Cleanse me from these hidden faults.

19:3 Or *There is no speech or language where their voice is not heard.*

18:43-50 The successes that God gives us can be a strong encouragement to others. In recovery we are called upon to share our victories with others. As we do, we will also be carrying the message of his saving power and love to those who are listening. This may be all it takes to give them the courage to go on. They will see God's transforming power in our life and begin to hope that God can do the same for them. Because of who God is and what he does for us, we should constantly give him thanks and praise for the way he helps us.
19:1-6 No one can rightly say that he or she has never heard about God (see Romans 1:20). His power can be seen throughout our physical world. Even the sun, though silent in the skies, declares every day what God has done. All humans benefit from the sun, and, whether they like it or not, they cannot hide from the message it declares to all the world. God is not a figment of our imagination. He is with us right now, and he desires to help us through the recovery process.
19:7-11 Adhering to God's laws will produce wholeness in our life. Applying God's truth revives our inner being and gives insight—even to the least of us—into how we should live. His Word is not a burden that robs us of the good things of life (see Matthew 11:29-30). Instead, it transforms us and replaces our discouragement with joy.

¹³Keep me from deliberate sins!
    Don't let them control me.
    Then I will be free of guilt
        and innocent of great sin.

¹⁴May the words of my mouth and the
        thoughts of my heart
    be pleasing to you,
    O Lord, my rock and my redeemer.

PSALM 20

For the choir director: A psalm of David.

¹In times of trouble, may the Lord respond
        to your cry.
    May the God of Israel* keep you safe
        from all harm.
²May he send you help from his sanctuary
    and strengthen you from Jerusalem.*
³May he remember all your gifts
    and look favorably on your burnt
        offerings.   *Interlude*

⁴May he grant your heart's desire
    and fulfill all your plans.
⁵May we shout for joy when we hear of
        your victory,
    flying banners to honor our God.
    May the Lord answer all your prayers.

⁶Now I know that the Lord saves his
        anointed king.
    He will answer him from his holy
        heaven
    and rescue him by his great power.
⁷Some nations boast of their armies and
        weapons,*
    but we boast in the Lord our God.
⁸Those nations will fall down and collapse,
    but we will rise up and stand firm.

⁹Give victory to our king, O Lord!
    Respond to our cry for help.

PSALM 21

For the choir director: A psalm of David.

¹How the king rejoices in your strength,
        O Lord!
    He shouts with joy because of your
        victory.
²For you have given him his heart's desire;
    you have held back nothing that he
        requested.   *Interlude*

³You welcomed him back with success and
        prosperity.
    You placed a crown of finest gold on
        his head.
⁴He asked you to preserve his life,
    and you have granted his request.
    The days of his life stretch on forever.
⁵Your victory brings him great honor,
    and you have clothed him with
        splendor and majesty.
⁶You have endowed him with eternal
        blessings.
    You have given him the joy of being
        in your presence.
⁷For the king trusts in the Lord.
    The unfailing love of the Most High
        will keep him from stumbling.

⁸You will capture all your enemies.
    Your strong right hand will seize all
        those who hate you.
⁹You will destroy them as in a flaming
        furnace
    when you appear.
    The Lord will consume them in his
        anger;
    fire will devour them.
¹⁰You will wipe their children from the face
        of the earth;
    they will never have descendants.
¹¹Although they plot against you,
    their evil schemes will never succeed.

20:1 Hebrew *of Jacob.* **20:2** Hebrew *Zion.* **20:7** Hebrew *chariots and horses.*

20:1-3 The psalmist counted on God's presence at all times to protect him, especially when his problems were most intense. The Bible is full of stories of people who were helped by God in times of trouble: Abraham, Joseph, Moses, Joshua, David, Peter, Paul. If God helped all these people when they needed him, he can also protect all of us. Knowing we need his help, we must remain steadfast in our decision to turn our will and our life over to his care.
20:4-9 God is more than able to give us our greatest desires—even recovery from the consequences of our past mistakes (see Ephesians 3:20). Unlike those who trust in their own power to overcome their problems, we can place our trust in God. As a result, we have hope in the future because God will help us when we call out to him.
21:1-6 As we thoroughly evaluate our life, we realize that our strength comes from God as we seek him through prayer and meditation. He wants to give each of us a life that has eternal value and meaning. As we experience this, we will begin to understand that true joy is an outgrowth of being in God's presence. This should motivate us to spend time with God through prayer and meditation. We need to draw close to him, not just for what he can do for us but for who he is.

¹²For they will turn and run
    when they see your arrows aimed
      at them.

¹³We praise you, LORD, for all your glorious
    power.
    With music and singing we celebrate
    your mighty acts.

PSALM 22

*For the choir director: A psalm of David, to be sung
to the tune "Doe of the Dawn."*

¹My God, my God! Why have you forsaken
    me?
    Why do you remain so distant?
    Why do you ignore my cries for help?
²Every day I call to you, my God, but you
    do not answer.
    Every night you hear my voice, but
    I find no relief.

³Yet you are holy.
    The praises of Israel surround your
    throne.
⁴Our ancestors trusted in you,
    and you rescued them.
⁵You heard their cries for help and saved
    them.
    They put their trust in you and were
    never disappointed.

⁶But I am a worm and not a man.
    I am scorned and despised by all!
⁷Everyone who sees me mocks me.
    They sneer and shake their heads,
    saying,
⁸"Is this the one who relies on the LORD?
    Then let the LORD save him!
    If the LORD loves him so much,
    let the LORD rescue him!"

22:18 Hebrew *cast lots.*

⁹Yet you brought me safely from my
    mother's womb
    and led me to trust you when I was
    a nursing infant.
¹⁰I was thrust upon you at my birth.
    You have been my God from the
    moment I was born.
¹¹Do not stay so far from me,
    for trouble is near,
    and no one else can help me.
¹²My enemies surround me like a herd
    of bulls;
    fierce bulls of Bashan have hemmed
    me in!
¹³Like roaring lions attacking their prey,
    they come at me with open mouths.
¹⁴My life is poured out like water,
    and all my bones are out of joint.
    My heart is like wax,
    melting within me.
¹⁵My strength has dried up like sunbaked
    clay.
    My tongue sticks to the roof of my
    mouth.
    You have laid me in the dust and left
    me for dead.

¹⁶My enemies surround me like a pack
    of dogs;
    an evil gang closes in on me.
    They have pierced my hands and feet.
¹⁷I can count every bone in my body.
    My enemies stare at me and gloat.
¹⁸They divide my clothes among
    themselves
    and throw dice* for my garments.

¹⁹O LORD, do not stay away!
    You are my strength; come quickly
    to my aid!

22:1-5 We all have experienced feelings of abandonment. The words in the first verse were repeated by Jesus Christ as he hung on the cross, indicating that even he experienced isolation from God the Father (see Matthew 27:46; Mark 15:34). When we feel cut off from God, we may be tempted to question his existence or doubt that he is able to rescue us. At such times, we must rely on facts not feelings. We must remember who God is and what he has done for us in the past.

22:6-11 When things aren't going well, we may experience low self-esteem, feeling like a "worm." But God cares for us and will help us. Others may mock us, doubting that God can really save us. We should ignore these people because we know God is there to rescue us. He has helped before, ever since our birth, and he will surely continue to help us through the low points in our life.

22:12-21 For many of us, these verses describe the results of our addiction. People may torment us, making fun of our problems. The physical pain described here reminds us of the effects of drugs or alcohol, or the symptoms of withdrawal. When we seek recovery, we have the help of a God who understands our pain. Jesus Christ experienced similar conditions during his earthly life; he also had to face death. He was surrounded, crucified, gawked at, and stripped of his dignity. Jesus knows how we feel, and he is with us through each step in the recovery process.

²⁰ Rescue me from a violent death;
  spare my precious life from these dogs.
²¹ Snatch me from the lions' jaws,
  and from the horns of these wild oxen.

²² Then I will declare the wonder of your
    name to my brothers and sisters.
  I will praise you among all your people.
²³ Praise the LORD, all you who fear him!
  Honor him, all you descendants of Jacob!
  Show him reverence, all you
    descendants of Israel!
²⁴ For he has not ignored the suffering
    of the needy.
  He has not turned and walked away.
  He has listened to their cries for help.

²⁵ I will praise you among all the people;
  I will fulfill my vows in the presence
    of those who worship you.
²⁶ The poor will eat and be satisfied.
  All who seek the LORD will praise him.
  Their hearts will rejoice with everlasting
    joy.
²⁷ The whole earth will acknowledge the
    LORD and return to him.
  People from every nation will bow
    down before him.
²⁸ For the LORD is king!
  He rules all the nations.

²⁹ Let the rich of the earth feast and worship.
  Let all mortals—those born to die—
    bow down in his presence.
³⁰ Future generations will also serve him.
  Our children will hear about the
    wonders of the Lord.
³¹ His righteous acts will be told to those
    yet unborn.
  They will hear about everything he
    has done.

PSALM 23
A psalm of David.

¹ The LORD is my shepherd;
  I have everything I need.

²⁴:4 Or *the darkest valley.* **24:6** Hebrew *of Jacob.*

² He lets me rest in green meadows;
  he leads me beside peaceful streams.
³   He renews my strength.
  He guides me along right paths,
    bringing honor to his name.

⁴ Even when I walk
    through the dark valley of death,*
  I will not be afraid,
    for you are close beside me.
  Your rod and your staff
    protect and comfort me.

⁵ You prepare a feast for me
    in the presence of my enemies.
  You welcome me as a guest,
    anointing my head with oil.
  My cup overflows with blessings.
⁶ Surely your goodness and unfailing love
    will pursue me
  all the days of my life,
  and I will live in the house of the LORD
    forever.

PSALM 24
A psalm of David.

¹ The earth is the LORD's, and everything
    in it.
  The world and all its people belong
    to him.
² For he laid the earth's foundation on
    the seas
  and built it on the ocean depths.

³ Who may climb the mountain of the LORD?
  Who may stand in his holy place?
⁴ Only those whose hands and hearts are pure,
  who do not worship idols
  and never tell lies.
⁵ They will receive the LORD's blessing
  and have right standing with God their
    savior.
⁶ They alone may enter God's presence
  and worship the God of Israel.*
                                    Interlude

23:1-6 God is our shepherd, and he knows what we need even better than we do. God wants us to have what is best for us. As long as we make him our shepherd, he will lead us to places of safety. He knows how to direct us away from places where we may be tempted to stumble. Even when we fall, he can deliver us from our failure, pain, and suffering. God will help us avoid the places where we have stumbled in the past and guide as we journey toward recovery.
24:1-2 Some of us may feel that there is no power great enough to deliver us from the terrible circumstances we have fallen into. In these verses, however, we see a God who has enough power to create and control the entire universe. We know from his Word that God desires to support us in the process of recovery from sin and its terrible consequences. God is more than able to help us overcome our dependency and lead us to freedom. We must bring our failures to him and ask him to help us deal with our defects of character.

7 Open up, ancient gates!
  Open up, ancient doors,
  and let the King of glory enter.
8 Who is the King of glory?
  The LORD, strong and mighty,
  the LORD, invincible in battle.
9 Open up, ancient gates!
  Open up, ancient doors,
  and let the King of glory enter.
10 Who is the King of glory?
  The LORD Almighty—
  he is the King of glory.   *Interlude*

PSALM 25

A psalm of David.

1 To you, O LORD, I lift up my soul.
2   I trust in you, my God!
  Do not let me be disgraced,
    or let my enemies rejoice in my defeat.
3 No one who trusts in you will ever be
    disgraced,
  but disgrace comes to those who try
    to deceive others.

4 Show me the path where I should walk,
  O LORD;
  point out the right road for me to follow.
5 Lead me by your truth and teach me,
  for you are the God who saves me.
  All day long I put my hope in you.

6 Remember, O LORD, your unfailing love
    and compassion,
  which you have shown from long ages past.
7 Forgive the rebellious sins of my youth;
  look instead through the eyes of your
    unfailing love,
  for you are merciful, O LORD.

8 The LORD is good and does what is right;
  he shows the proper path to those who
    go astray.
9 He leads the humble in what is right,
  teaching them his way.

10 The LORD leads with unfailing love and
    faithfulness
  all those who keep his covenant and
    obey his decrees.

11 For the honor of your name, O LORD,
  forgive my many, many sins.
12 Who are those who fear the LORD?
  He will show them the path they
    should choose.
13 They will live in prosperity,
  and their children will inherit the
    Promised Land.
14 Friendship with the LORD is reserved for
    those who fear him.
  With them he shares the secrets of his
    covenant.
15 My eyes are always looking to the LORD
    for help,
  for he alone can rescue me from the
    traps of my enemies.

16 Turn to me and have mercy on me,
  for I am alone and in deep distress.
17 My problems go from bad to worse.
  Oh, save me from them all!
18 Feel my pain and see my trouble.
  Forgive all my sins.
19 See how many enemies I have,
  and how viciously they hate me!
20 Protect me! Rescue my life from them!
  Do not let me be disgraced, for I trust
    in you.
21 May integrity and honesty protect me,
  for I put my hope in you.

22 O God, ransom Israel
  from all its troubles.

PSALM 26

A psalm of David.

1 Declare me innocent, O LORD,
  for I have acted with integrity;

25:1-7 When we place our faith in God, we can trust him to care for us and help us overcome the things in our life that would destroy us. We need to ask him to show us how to live according to his truth. Because of his great love and compassion, he will forgive our past sins when we ask him to. And while forgiveness for our sins is important, it is also important for us to forgive others who have harmed us. As we forgive others, we can release our anger and focus on our own recovery.
25:8-10 We need to let God change us, yet we cannot expect him to work his transformation in our life if we are still proud and unwilling to admit that we are helpless apart from him. The first step in recovery is humbly admitting that we are powerless over our dependency. Only after we do this can we experience God's healing work in our life.
26:1-7 Even if we stumble, we must keep trying to live an honest and open life, doing all we can to discover and fulfill God's will for us. We don't have to fear God's judgment, since he loves us— even with all our faults. As we seek God's will for us, we also need to avoid the people who will lead us back into our destructive lifestyle. Nothing good can come from trying to associate with those who formerly dragged us down. We also need to avoid the situations and activities that could tempt us and lead to an eventual fall.

I have trusted in the LORD without
    wavering.
2 Put me on trial, LORD, and cross-
    examine me.
  Test my motives and affections.
3 For I am constantly aware of your
    unfailing love,
  and I have lived according to your
    truth.

4 I do not spend time with liars
  or go along with hypocrites.
5 I hate the gatherings of those who
    do evil,
  and I refuse to join in with the
    wicked.

6 I wash my hands to declare my
    innocence.
  I come to your altar, O LORD,
7 singing a song of thanksgiving
  and telling of all your miracles.
8 I love your sanctuary, LORD,
  the place where your glory shines.

9 Don't let me suffer the fate of sinners.
  Don't condemn me along with
    murderers.
10 Their hands are dirty with wicked
    schemes,
  and they constantly take bribes.

11 But I am not like that; I do what is right.
  So in your mercy, save me.
12 I have taken a stand,
  and I will publicly praise the LORD.

PSALM 27
A psalm of David.

1 The LORD is my light and my salvation—
  so why should I be afraid?
  The LORD protects me from danger—
  so why should I tremble?

2 When evil people come to destroy me,
  when my enemies and foes attack me,
  they will stumble and fall.
3 Though a mighty army surrounds me,
  my heart will know no fear.
  Even if they attack me,
  I remain confident.

4 The one thing I ask of the LORD—
  the thing I seek most—
  is to live in the house of the LORD all the
    days of my life,
  delighting in the LORD's perfections
  and meditating in his Temple.
5 For he will conceal me there when
    troubles come;
  he will hide me in his sanctuary.
  He will place me out of reach on a
    high rock.
6 Then I will hold my head high,
  above my enemies who surround me.
  At his Tabernacle I will offer sacrifices
    with shouts of joy,
  singing and praising the LORD with
    music.

7 Listen to my pleading, O LORD.
  Be merciful and answer me!
8 My heart has heard you say, "Come and
    talk with me."
  And my heart responds, "LORD, I am
    coming."
9 Do not hide yourself from me.
  Do not reject your servant in anger.
  You have always been my helper.
  Don't leave me now; don't abandon me,
  O God of my salvation!
10 Even if my father and mother abandon me,
  the LORD will hold me close.

11 Teach me how to live, O LORD.
  Lead me along the path of honesty,
  for my enemies are waiting for me
    to fall.

27:11-14 Because temptations press in around us, we need to learn how God wants us to act in the midst of such pressures. He wants to become the stabilizing factor in our life. Apart from him we have no power against the things that once put us in bondage. We must determine, one day at a time, to follow God, patiently and confidently waiting for him to protect and lead us.

28:1-5 The decision to turn our life over to God for his care is an important step in recovery. We won't find the answers to life's problems anywhere else. The best way to avoid the judgment that will fall on those who lead others astray is to stay away from them. If we don't avoid the people and situations of our past failures, we will almost always get trapped by the same old mistakes and dependencies.

28:6-9 God expects us to do our part in recovery, but we know that only he can empower us to stand against the pressures that seem to drive us back into our old ways. Knowing that God is our strength and will give us victory over our bad habits should fill our heart with great joy and encouragement. Even when we feel we are powerless and can't go on, God is waiting for us to run into his open and powerful arms.

¹²Do not let me fall into their hands.
  For they accuse me of things I've never
    done
  and breathe out violence against me.
¹³Yet I am confident that I will see the
    LORD's goodness
  while I am here in the land of the
    living.

¹⁴Wait patiently for the LORD.
  Be brave and courageous.
  Yes, wait patiently for the LORD.

PSALM 28
A psalm of David.

¹O LORD, you are my rock of safety.
  Please help me; don't refuse to
    answer me.
  For if you are silent,
  I might as well give up and die.
²Listen to my prayer for mercy
  as I cry out to you for help,
  as I lift my hands toward your holy
    sanctuary.

³Don't drag me away with the wicked—
  with those who do evil—
  those who speak friendly words to their
    neighbors
  while planning evil in their hearts.
⁴Give them the punishment they so richly
    deserve!
  Measure it out in proportion to their
    wickedness.
  Pay them back for all their evil deeds!
  Give them a taste of what they have
    done to others.
⁵They care nothing for what the LORD has
    done
  or for what his hands have made.
  So he will tear them down like old
    buildings,
  and they will never be rebuilt!

⁶Praise the LORD!
  For he has heard my cry for mercy.
⁷The LORD is my strength, my shield from
    every danger.
  I trust in him with all my heart.
  He helps me, and my heart is filled with
    joy.
  I burst out in songs of thanksgiving.

⁸The LORD protects his people
  and gives victory to his anointed king.
⁹Save your people!
  Bless Israel, your special possession!
  Lead them like a shepherd,
  and carry them forever in your arms.

STEP **11**

Thirst for God

BIBLE READING: Psalm 27:1-6
**We sought through prayer and medita-
tion to improve our conscious contact
with God, praying only for knowledge
of his will for us and the power to carry
that out.**
Most of us initially turn to God for the
help he can give us, namely, his power to
free us from the power of our dependency.
We may be surprised to find that, as time
passes, we turn to God out of a desire to
be near him. As we discover how wonderful he is and how much he loves us, we
draw near to him because of the joy we
experience in his presence.

King David gave us a glimpse into his
relationship with God, saying, "The one
thing I ask of the LORD—the thing I seek
most—is to live in the house of the LORD
all the days of my life, delighting in the
LORD's perfections and meditating in his
Temple. For he will conceal me there
when troubles come; he will hide me
in his sanctuary. He will place me out
of reach on a high rock. Then I will hold
my head high, above my enemies who
surround me. At his Tabernacle I will offer
sacrifices with shouts of joy, singing and
praising the LORD with music" (Psalm
27:4-6).

David found great joy by improving
his conscious contact with God. God
is always there, but we are not always
aware of his presence. Our relationship
with God usually begins with his meeting
our desperate needs. But when we begin
to focus on getting to know God as an
end in itself, we will discover that he will
give us what we have always desired—the
joy of being close to our loving Creator.
Then we will see that he can be trusted
with every area of our life. *Turn to page 519,
Psalm 65.*

PSALM 29

A psalm of David.

¹Give honor to the LORD, you angels;
  give honor to the LORD for his glory
    and strength.
²Give honor to the LORD for the glory
    of his name.
  Worship the LORD in the splendor
    of his holiness.

³The voice of the LORD echoes above
    the sea.
  The God of glory thunders.
  The LORD thunders over the mighty sea.
⁴The voice of the LORD is powerful;
  the voice of the LORD is full of majesty.
⁵The voice of the LORD splits the mighty
    cedars;
  the LORD shatters the cedars of Lebanon.
⁶He makes Lebanon's mountains skip
    like a calf
  and Mount Hermon* to leap like a
    young bull.
⁷The voice of the LORD strikes with
    lightning bolts.
⁸The voice of the LORD makes the desert
    quake;
  the LORD shakes the desert of Kadesh.
⁹The voice of the LORD twists mighty oaks*
    and strips the forests bare.
  In his Temple everyone shouts, "Glory!"

¹⁰The LORD rules over the floodwaters.
  The LORD reigns as king forever.
¹¹The LORD gives his people strength.
  The LORD blesses them with peace.

PSALM 30

A psalm of David, sung at the dedication of the Temple.

¹I will praise you, LORD, for you have
    rescued me.
  You refused to let my enemies triumph
    over me.
²O LORD my God, I cried out to you for
    help,
  and you restored my health.
³You brought me up from the grave,
    O LORD.
  You kept me from falling into the pit
    of death.

⁴Sing to the LORD, all you godly ones!
  Praise his holy name.
⁵His anger lasts for a moment,
  but his favor lasts a lifetime!
  Weeping may go on all night,
  but joy comes with the morning.

⁶When I was prosperous I said,
  "Nothing can stop me now!"
⁷Your favor, O LORD, made me as secure
    as a mountain.
  Then you turned away from me, and
    I was shattered.

⁸I cried out to you, O LORD.
  I begged the Lord for mercy, saying,
⁹"What will you gain if I die,
  if I sink down into the grave?
  Can my dust praise you from the grave?
  Can it tell the world of your
    faithfulness?
¹⁰Hear me, LORD, and have mercy on me.
  Help me, O LORD."

¹¹You have turned my mourning into joyful
    dancing.
  You have taken away my clothes of
    mourning and clothed me with joy,
¹²that I might sing praises to you and not
    be silent.
  O LORD my God, I will give you thanks
    forever!

29:6 Hebrew *Sirion,* another name for Mount Hermon. **29:9** Or *causes the deer to writhe in labor.*

29:1-9 In this psalm we are reminded of God's great power over the natural world. Yet even though his majesty is greater than any words can describe, he knows and loves each one of us. Knowing how powerless we are over the problems we face should make us realize that we need to turn our life over to him, the one who is all-powerful. He is the only one able and willing to help us.
30:1-5 What joy and gratitude we feel when God picks us up and does not allow our problems to defeat or destroy us! One of the hard lessons to learn during recovery is how to delay gratification. We may go through some long, dark nights struggling with temptation before we experience the joy of victory. But the Lord will not let our enemy triumph over us. When we do finally overcome, the joy of success will only be that much sweeter.
30:6-9 Sometimes we may be in the most danger when everything in our life is going well. We tend to become overconfident; we think nothing can happen to us. But pride and arrogance usually come before a fall. Sometimes God allows us to go our own way and suffer the consequences so we will learn that we can't make it alone. We will succeed in recovery only when we learn to rely completely on God and follow his recovery program.

PSALM 31

For the choir director: A psalm of David.

¹O LORD, I have come to you for
protection;
don't let me be put to shame.
Rescue me, for you always do what
is right.
²Bend down and listen to me;
rescue me quickly.
Be for me a great rock of safety,
a fortress where my enemies cannot
reach me.

³You are my rock and my fortress.
For the honor of your name, lead me
out of this peril.
⁴Pull me from the trap my enemies set
for me,
for I find protection in you alone.
⁵I entrust my spirit into your hand.
Rescue me, LORD, for you are a faithful
God.

⁶I hate those who worship worthless idols.
I trust in the LORD.
⁷I am overcome with joy because of your
unfailing love,
for you have seen my troubles,
and you care about the anguish of
my soul.
⁸You have not handed me over to my
enemy
but have set me in a safe place.

⁹Have mercy on me, LORD, for I am in
distress.
My sight is blurred because of my tears.
My body and soul are withering away.
¹⁰I am dying from grief;
my years are shortened by sadness.
Misery* has drained my strength;
I am wasting away from within.
¹¹I am scorned by all my enemies
and despised by my neighbors—
even my friends are afraid to come
near me.

When they see me on the street,
they turn the other way.
¹²I have been ignored as if I were dead,
as if I were a broken pot.
¹³I have heard the many rumors about me,
and I am surrounded by terror.
My enemies conspire against me,
plotting to take my life.

¹⁴But I am trusting you, O LORD,
saying, "You are my God!"
¹⁵My future is in your hands.
Rescue me from those who hunt me
down relentlessly.
¹⁶Let your favor shine on your servant.
In your unfailing love, save me.
¹⁷Don't let me be disgraced, O LORD,
for I call out to you for help.
Let the wicked be disgraced;
let them lie silent in the grave.
¹⁸May their lying lips be silenced—
those proud and arrogant lips that
accuse the godly.

¹⁹Your goodness is so great!
You have stored up great blessings
for those who honor you.
You have done so much for those who
come to you for protection,
blessing them before the watching
world.
²⁰You hide them in the shelter of your
presence,
safe from those who conspire against
them.
You shelter them in your presence,
far from accusing tongues.

²¹Praise the LORD,
for he has shown me his unfailing love.
He kept me safe when my city was
under attack.
²²In sudden fear I had cried out,
"I have been cut off from the LORD!"
But you heard my cry for mercy
and answered my call for help.

31:10 Or *Sin.*

31:9-13 These verses reflect the heavy toll that sin takes on our life. When we fall into its bondage, everything begins to fall apart. Friends and neighbors avoid us, afraid to come near us. The psalmist understood how we might feel when caught in the trap of sin and continual failure. But he also knew that God is merciful and ready to help us when we call out to him. God is willing to forgive and empower us if we will only look to him for help.
31:19-22 Old friends can drag us down with their "accusing tongues," sometimes without meaning to do so. God can protect us from harm if we allow him to take control of our life. In our distress we may wrongly assume that we are alone; yet God is always there, answering our cries for help. No situation is too tough for God to handle. If we rely on him, he will guide us away from our old life of sin and toward recovery, hiding us "in the shelter of [his] presence."

²³ Love the LORD, all you faithful ones!
　　For the LORD protects those who are
　　　loyal to him,
　　but he harshly punishes all who are
　　　arrogant.
²⁴ So be strong and take courage,
　　all you who put your hope in the LORD!

PSALM 32
A psalm of David.

¹ Oh, what joy for those
　　whose rebellion is forgiven,
　　whose sin is put out of sight!
² Yes, what joy for those
　　whose record the LORD has cleared of
　　　sin,
　　whose lives are lived in complete
　　　honesty!

³ When I refused to confess my sin,
　　I was weak and miserable,
　　and I groaned all day long.
⁴ Day and night your hand of discipline
　　was heavy on me.
　　My strength evaporated like water in
　　　the summer heat.　　　　*Interlude*

⁵ Finally, I confessed all my sins to you
　　and stopped trying to hide them.
　I said to myself, "I will confess my
　　　rebellion to the LORD."
　　And you forgave me! All my guilt is
　　　gone.　　　　*Interlude*

⁶ Therefore, let all the godly confess their
　　rebellion to you while there is time,
　　that they may not drown in the
　　　floodwaters of judgment.

⁷ For you are my hiding place;
　　you protect me from trouble.
　　You surround me with songs of victory.
　　　　　　　　　　　　Interlude

⁸ The LORD says, "I will guide you along the
　　best pathway for your life.
　　I will advise you and watch over you.
⁹ Do not be like a senseless horse or mule
　　that needs a bit and bridle to keep it
　　　under control."

¹⁰ Many sorrows come to the wicked,
　　but unfailing love surrounds those
　　　who trust the LORD.
¹¹ So rejoice in the LORD and be glad, all
　　you who obey him!
　　Shout for joy, all you whose hearts
　　　are pure!

PSALM 33
¹ Let the godly sing with joy to the LORD,
　　for it is fitting to praise him.
² Praise the LORD with melodies on the
　　　lyre;
　　make music for him on the ten-stringed
　　　harp.
³ Sing new songs of praise to him;
　　play skillfully on the harp and sing
　　　with joy.

⁴ For the word of the LORD holds true,
　　and everything he does is worthy
　　　of our trust.
⁵ He loves whatever is just and good,
　　and his unfailing love fills the earth.

⁶ The LORD merely spoke,
　　and the heavens were created.

32:1-4 When we get serious about our past sins, admitting each of them and seeking to make amends, we will probably find that most people are willing to forgive us. Making amends for our past failures and reconciling our relationships is an important part of the recovery process. We see in this psalm that being reconciled to God begins as we admit our sins to him. He will forgive us; we can count on it! When we try to hide our sins from God, our life becomes dysfunctional and miserable. Our inner beings become tied up in knots, and we once again begin to lose control. Why fight it? Confessing our sins to God is the first step toward having a joyful heart.

32:5-9 Like David, we need to confess our sins before God and admit them to the people we have wronged. By doing so, we set a good example for others who are also having a hard time admitting their sins to God. We also set our heart free of the destructive grip of guilt and can reestablish the healthy relationships we all need for a full recovery. God wants to give us a full and productive life, but we must respond willingly to his commands.

33:1-11 Such a powerful God is worthy of our trust and praise. The God who spoke the universe into existence is able to re-create us, and he is filled with tender love for us. He can heal us of the defects that have brought such destruction to us and the people we love. All he asks is that we turn our life over to him so he can work these changes in us.

34:1-7 When we experience deliverance through God's power, it should be natural for us to praise him and share the good news with others. If we care about other people who suffer as we did, we would be selfish not to tell how God has delivered us. Boasting about our God and the help he has given us is one kind of boasting that is good. This kind of godly boasting will not only encourage others in the recovery process, but it will also strengthen our faith in God.

He breathed the word,
and all the stars were born.
⁷He gave the sea its boundaries
and locked the oceans in vast reservoirs.

⁸Let everyone in the world fear the LORD,
and let everyone stand in awe of him.
⁹For when he spoke, the world began!
It appeared at his command.

¹⁰The LORD shatters the plans of the nations
and thwarts all their schemes.
¹¹But the LORD's plans stand firm forever;
his intentions can never be shaken.

¹²What joy for the nation whose God is the
LORD,
whose people he has chosen for his
own.

¹³The LORD looks down from heaven
and sees the whole human race.
¹⁴From his throne he observes
all who live on the earth.
¹⁵He made their hearts,
so he understands everything they do.
¹⁶The best-equipped army cannot save a
king,
nor is great strength enough to save a
warrior.
¹⁷Don't count on your warhorse to give you
victory—
for all its strength, it cannot save you.

¹⁸But the LORD watches over those who fear
him,
those who rely on his unfailing love.
¹⁹He rescues them from death
and keeps them alive in times of
famine.

²⁰We depend on the LORD alone to save us.
Only he can help us, protecting us like
a shield.
²¹In him our hearts rejoice,
for we are trusting in his holy name.
²²Let your unfailing love surround us,
LORD,
for our hope is in you alone.

PSALM 34

*A psalm of David, regarding the time he pretended
to be insane in front of Abimelech, who sent him
away.*

¹I will praise the LORD at all times.
I will constantly speak his praises.
²I will boast only in the LORD;
let all who are discouraged take heart.
³Come, let us tell of the LORD's greatness;
let us exalt his name together.

Honesty

READ PSALM 32:1-11

Living a lie is miserable. We may know from personal experience the heavy burden of trying to hide a secret life. If we are avoiding God and withdrawing from people because we fear being found out, we are living in needless agony.

Moses understood the price one must pay for trying to live a lie. He prayed, "We wither beneath your anger; we are overwhelmed by your fury. You spread out our sins before you—our secret sins—and you see them all. We live our lives beneath your wrath. We end our lives with a groan" (Psalm 90:7-9). David showed us the other side. "Oh, what joy for those whose rebellion is forgiven, whose sin is put out of sight! Yes, what joy for those whose record the LORD has cleared of sin, whose lives are lived in complete honesty! When I refused to confess my sin, I was weak and miserable, and I groaned all day long. Day and night your hand of discipline was heavy on me. My strength evaporated like water in the summer heat. Finally, I confessed all my sins to you and stopped trying to hide them. I said to myself, 'I will confess my rebellion to the LORD.' And you forgave me! All my guilt is gone. Therefore, let all the godly confess their rebellion to you while there is time, that they may not drown in the floodwaters of judgment" (Psalm 32:1-6).

Why should we live with the weight of dishonesty when relief is available to us? God already knows our secret sins anyway. Why continue to suffer needless agony when we can be set free? ***Turn to page 505, Psalm 42.***

4 I prayed to the LORD, and he answered me,
   freeing me from all my fears.
5 Those who look to him for help will be
   radiant with joy;
   no shadow of shame will darken their
   faces.
6 I cried out to the LORD in my suffering,
   and he heard me.
   He set me free from all my fears.
7 For the angel of the LORD guards all who
   fear him,
   and he rescues them.

8 Taste and see that the LORD is good.
   Oh, the joys of those who trust in him!
9 Let the LORD's people show him reverence,
   for those who honor him will have all
   they need.
10 Even strong young lions sometimes go
   hungry,
   but those who trust in the LORD will
   never lack any good thing.

11 Come, my children, and listen to me,
   and I will teach you to fear the LORD.
12 Do any of you want to live
   a life that is long and good?
13 Then watch your tongue!
   Keep your lips from telling lies!
14 Turn away from evil and do good.
   Work hard at living in peace with
   others.

15 The eyes of the LORD watch over those
   who do right;
   his ears are open to their cries for help.
16 But the LORD turns his face against those
   who do evil;
   he will erase their memory from the
   earth.

17 The LORD hears his people when they call
   to him for help.
   He rescues them from all their troubles.
18 The LORD is close to the brokenhearted;
   he rescues those who are crushed in
   spirit.

19 The righteous face many troubles,
   but the LORD rescues them from each
   and every one.
20 For the LORD protects them from harm—
   not one of their bones* will be broken!

34:20 Hebrew *protects him from harm—not one of his bones.*

21 Calamity will surely overtake the wicked,
   and those who hate the righteous will
   be punished.
22 But the LORD will redeem those who serve
   him.
   Everyone who trusts in him will be
   freely pardoned.

PSALM 35
A psalm of David.

1 O LORD, oppose those who oppose me.
   Declare war on those who are
   attacking me.
2 Put on your armor, and take up your
   shield.
   Prepare for battle, and come to my aid.
3 Lift up your spear and javelin
   and block the way of my enemies.
Let me hear you say,
   "I am your salvation!"

4 Humiliate and disgrace those trying
   to kill me;
   turn them back in confusion.
5 Blow them away like chaff in the wind—
   a wind sent by the angel of the LORD.
6 Make their path dark and slippery,
   with the angel of the LORD pursuing
   them.
7 Although I did them no wrong,
   they laid a trap for me.
Although I did them no wrong,
   they dug a pit for me.
8 So let sudden ruin overtake them!
   Let them be caught in the snare they
   set for me!
   Let them fall to destruction in the pit
   they dug for me.

9 Then I will rejoice in the LORD.
   I will be glad because he rescues me.
10 I will praise him from the bottom of my
   heart:
   "LORD, who can compare with you?
Who else rescues the weak and helpless
   from the strong?
   Who else protects the poor and needy
   from those who want to rob them?"

11 Malicious witnesses testify against me.
   They accuse me of things I don't even
   know about.

34:8-14 If we have gone through life trusting in our own judgment, we may find it hard to commit ourself to God and his plan for us. But when we trust the Lord and honor him, he has promised to supply all our needs. He has the power and the wisdom we need to have victory in our struggles over sin and temptation.

¹²They repay me with evil for the good I do.
   I am sick with despair.
¹³Yet when they were ill,
   I grieved for them.
 I even fasted and prayed for them,
   but my prayers returned unanswered.
¹⁴I was sad, as though they were my friends
      or family,
   as if I were grieving for my own mother.

¹⁵But they are glad now that I am in trouble;
   they gleefully join together against me.
 I am attacked by people I don't even
      know;
   they hurl slander at me continually.
¹⁶They mock me with the worst kind of
      profanity,
   and they snarl at me.

¹⁷How long, O Lord, will you look on and
      do nothing?
   Rescue me from their fierce attacks.
   Protect my life from these lions!
¹⁸Then I will thank you in front of the
      entire congregation.
   I will praise you before all the people.

¹⁹Don't let my treacherous enemies
   rejoice over my defeat.
 Don't let those who hate me without cause
   gloat over my sorrow.
²⁰They don't talk of peace;
   they plot against innocent people
   who are minding their own business.
²¹They shout that they have seen me doing
      wrong.
   "Aha," they say. "Aha!
   With our own eyes we saw him do it!"

²²O LORD, you know all about this.
   Do not stay silent.
   Don't abandon me now, O Lord.
²³Wake up! Rise to my defense!
   Take up my case, my God and my Lord.
²⁴Declare me "not guilty," O LORD my God,
      for you give justice.
   Don't let my enemies laugh about me
      in my troubles.

²⁵Don't let them say, "Look! We have what
      we wanted!
   Now we will eat him alive!"

²⁶May those who rejoice at my troubles
   be humiliated and disgraced.
 May those who triumph over me
   be covered with shame and dishonor.

²⁷But give great joy to those
   who have stood with me in my defense.
 Let them continually say, "Great is the
      LORD,
   who enjoys helping his servant."
²⁸Then I will tell everyone of your justice
      and goodness,
   and I will praise you all day long.

PSALM 36

For the choir director: A psalm of David, the servant of the LORD.

¹Sin whispers to the wicked, deep within
      their hearts.
   They have no fear of God to restrain
      them.
²In their blind conceit,
   they cannot see how wicked they really
      are.
³Everything they say is crooked and
      deceitful.
   They refuse to act wisely or do what
      is good.
⁴They lie awake at night, hatching sinful
      plots.
   Their course of action is never good.
   They make no attempt to turn from
      evil.

⁵Your unfailing love, O LORD, is as vast
      as the heavens;
   your faithfulness reaches beyond the
      clouds.
⁶Your righteousness is like the mighty
      mountains,
   your justice like the ocean depths.
 You care for people and animals alike,
      O LORD.

35:17-28 In this psalm David expressed feelings of desperation; he felt that God had forgotten him. At times we feel the same. But when relief comes, we should, like David, encourage others who are having the same desperate feelings by telling them of God's goodness. The whole world seems to conspire against us when we are fighting to stay free from our dependency and compulsions. We need to keep crying out to God for his wisdom and power to help us continue to do what is right. When those who have stood with us see our progress, they will rejoice with us as we tell them about the goodness of the Lord.

36:1-4 Sins and repeated failures have taken a toll on our life. Sometimes we aren't fully aware of how deceitful we have been or how much damage our sin has done to us and to others. That is why it is important to examine our life carefully as we take moral inventory so that God can begin to help us change the things that need to be changed.

⁷ How precious is your unfailing love,
  O God!
All humanity finds shelter
  in the shadow of your wings.
⁸ You feed them from the abundance
  of your own house,
  letting them drink from your rivers
  of delight.
⁹ For you are the fountain of life,
  the light by which we see.

¹⁰ Pour out your unfailing love on those
  who love you;
  give justice to those with honest hearts.
¹¹ Don't let the proud trample me;
  don't let the wicked push me around.
¹² Look! They have fallen!
  They have been thrown down, never
  to rise again.

PSALM 37
A psalm of David.

¹ Don't worry about the wicked.
  Don't envy those who do wrong.
² For like grass, they soon fade away.
  Like springtime flowers, they soon
  wither.

³ Trust in the LORD and do good.
  Then you will live safely in the land
  and prosper.
⁴ Take delight in the LORD,
  and he will give you your heart's
  desires.

⁵ Commit everything you do to the LORD.
  Trust him, and he will help you.
⁶ He will make your innocence as clear as
  the dawn,
  and the justice of your cause will shine
  like the noonday sun.

⁷ Be still in the presence of the LORD,
  and wait patiently for him to act.
Don't worry about evil people who
  prosper
  or fret about their wicked schemes.

⁸ Stop your anger!
  Turn from your rage!
  Do not envy others—
  it only leads to harm.
⁹ For the wicked will be destroyed,
  but those who trust in the LORD will
  possess the land.

¹⁰ In a little while, the wicked will disappear.
  Though you look for them, they will be
  gone.
¹¹ Those who are gentle and lowly will
  possess the land;
  they will live in prosperous security.

¹² The wicked plot against the godly;
  they snarl at them in defiance.
¹³ But the Lord just laughs,
  for he sees their day of judgment coming.

¹⁴ The wicked draw their swords
  and string their bows
to kill the poor and the oppressed,
  to slaughter those who do right.
¹⁵ But they will be stabbed through the
  heart with their own swords,
  and their bows will be broken.

¹⁶ It is better to be godly and have little
  than to be evil and possess much.
¹⁷ For the strength of the wicked will be
  shattered,
  but the LORD takes care of the godly.

¹⁸ Day by day the LORD takes care of the
  innocent,
  and they will receive a reward that
  lasts forever.
¹⁹ They will survive through hard times;
  even in famine they will have more
  than enough.

²⁰ But the wicked will perish.
  The LORD's enemies are like flowers
  in a field—
  they will disappear like smoke.

²¹ The wicked borrow and never repay,
  but the godly are generous givers.

37:1-7 Do not worry about or envy those who seem to get away with doing wrong things. Their moments of glory will soon be over, and like grass, they will soon "fade away." We need to do things that have lasting value—faithfully serving God and helping the people around us. God's formula for our success is that we develop a relationship with him and determine to serve him in everything we do. Then, in God's perfect timing, we will experience the true joy God promises and freedom from the guilt heaped upon us by others.
37:27-31 God's plan for godly living is the only means to a healthy life. If we really desire to follow God, we must "turn from evil" and saturate our mind with the truth of his Word. God's truth should be the foundation for our life. It helps us to know right from wrong and to make wise decisions. Living according to God's program will lead to healthy relationships and freedom from the dependencies that bind us.

22 Those blessed by the LORD will inherit
the land,
but those cursed by him will die.

23 The steps of the godly are directed by
the LORD.
He delights in every detail of their lives.
24 Though they stumble, they will not fall,
for the LORD holds them by the hand.

25 Once I was young, and now I am old.
Yet I have never seen the godly
forsaken,
nor seen their children begging for
bread.
26 The godly always give generous loans
to others,
and their children are a blessing.

27 Turn from evil and do good,
and you will live in the land forever.
28 For the LORD loves justice,
and he will never abandon the godly.

He will keep them safe forever,
but the children of the wicked will
perish.
29 The godly will inherit the land
and will live there forever.

30 The godly offer good counsel;
they know what is right from wrong.
31 They fill their hearts with God's law,
so they will never slip from his path.

32 Those who are evil spy on the godly,
waiting for an excuse to kill them.
33 But the LORD will not let the wicked
succeed
or let the godly be condemned when
they are brought before the judge.

34 Don't be impatient for the LORD to act!
Travel steadily along his path.
He will honor you, giving you the land.
You will see the wicked destroyed.

35 I myself have seen it happen—
proud and evil people thriving like
mighty trees.

36 But when I looked again, they were gone!
Though I searched for them, I could not
find them!

37 Look at those who are honest and good,
for a wonderful future lies before those
who love peace.
38 But the wicked will be destroyed;
they have no future.

39 The LORD saves the godly;
he is their fortress in times of trouble.
40 The LORD helps them,
rescuing them from the wicked.
He saves them,
and they find shelter in him.

PSALM 38

*A psalm of David, to bring us to the LORD's
remembrance.*

1 O LORD, don't rebuke me in your anger!
Don't discipline me in your rage!
2 Your arrows have struck deep,
and your blows are crushing me.

3 Because of your anger, my whole body
is sick;
my health is broken because of my sins.
4 My guilt overwhelms me—
it is a burden too heavy to bear.
5 My wounds fester and stink
because of my foolish sins.
6 I am bent over and racked with pain.
My days are filled with grief.
7 A raging fever burns within me,
and my health is broken.
8 I am exhausted and completely crushed.
My groans come from an anguished
heart.

9 You know what I long for, Lord;
you hear my every sigh.
10 My heart beats wildly, my strength fails,
and I am going blind.
11 My loved ones and friends stay away,
fearing my disease.
Even my own family stands at a
distance.

38:1-8 God's judgment against our sinful habits may seem very harsh, but even his toughest
discipline is intended for our ultimate good. Sin has consequences; God allows us to experience
the painful results of our sins in order to encourage us to turn to him. Our suffering will only
worsen unless we turn from our sins and commit our life to God. Only he can help us overcome
our sinful habits and reestablish our relationships. We would be wise to learn from our suffering
rather than be destroyed by it.
38:11-22 As we fall deeper into our addictions, our loved ones and friends may turn away
from us, which can make the people who approve of our dependency and problems even more
powerful in our life. We may find that being with these people draws us deeper and deeper into
a destructive trap. If we hope to recover, we need to avoid the people who want us to remain
trapped by our sinful habits. If everyone else has abandoned us, we may find this hard to do.

¹²Meanwhile, my enemies lay traps
for me;
they make plans to ruin me.
They think up treacherous deeds all
day long.
¹³But I am deaf to all their threats.
I am silent before them as one who
cannot speak.
¹⁴I choose to hear nothing,
and I make no reply.

¹⁵For I am waiting for you, O LORD.
You must answer for me, O Lord my
God.
¹⁶I prayed, "Don't let my enemies gloat
over me
or rejoice at my downfall."
¹⁷I am on the verge of collapse,
facing constant pain.
¹⁸But I confess my sins;
I am deeply sorry for what I have done.
¹⁹My enemies are many;
they hate me though I have done
nothing against them.
²⁰They repay me evil for good
and oppose me because I stand for
the right.

²¹Do not abandon me, LORD.
Do not stand at a distance, my God.
²²Come quickly to help me, O Lord my
savior.

PSALM 39
For Jeduthun, the choir director: A psalm of David.

¹I said to myself, "I will watch what I do
and not sin in what I say.
I will curb my tongue
when the ungodly are around me."
²But as I stood there in silence—
not even speaking of good things—
the turmoil within me grew to the
bursting point.

³My thoughts grew hot within me
and began to burn,
igniting a fire of words:
⁴"LORD, remind me how brief my time
on earth will be.
Remind me that my days are numbered,
and that my life is fleeing away.
⁵My life is no longer than the width of
my hand.
An entire lifetime is just a moment
to you;
human existence is but a breath."
Interlude

⁶We are merely moving shadows,
and all our busy rushing ends in
nothing.
We heap up wealth for someone else
to spend.

⁷And so, Lord, where do I put my hope?
My only hope is in you.
⁸Rescue me from my rebellion,
for even fools mock me when I rebel.
⁹I am silent before you; I won't say a word.
For my punishment is from you.
¹⁰Please, don't punish me anymore!
I am exhausted by the blows from your
hand.
¹¹When you discipline people for their
sins,
their lives can be crushed like the life
of a moth.
Human existence is as frail as breath.
Interlude

¹²Hear my prayer, O LORD!
Listen to my cries for help!
Don't ignore my tears.
For I am your guest—
a traveler passing through,
as my ancestors were before me.
¹³Spare me so I can smile again
before I am gone and exist no more.

We should begin by looking to God for help and seek godly companions. Staying close to God demands that we confess our sins and do what is right. This should then lead to healthy relationships in our life.

39:1-7 At times we may become frustrated and explode in anger just as David did in this psalm. We should not be afraid to do this. If we feel afraid, alone, and abandoned, we should voice our feelings of anger and confusion. As we do this, we are admitting our helplessness. This is the first step in turning to God, through whom we can gain a true perspective on life. God is never threatened by our strong emotions. It is our apathy and pride that disturb him the most.

39:8-13 As we suffer God's punishment in our life, there is no point in trying to escape it. The only wise thing to do is beg for mercy. When God reproves us for our sins, we soon learn that everything we hold dear—our family and friends, even our life—is ultimately under his divine control. Rather than trying to rationalize our sins, we need to confess them. God is ready and willing to forgive anyone who comes to him with a humble heart. In confessing our sins and failures to God, we are taking an important step in the process of recovery.

PSALM 40
For the choir director: A psalm of David.

¹I waited patiently for the LORD to
    help me,
  and he turned to me and heard
    my cry.
²He lifted me out of the pit of despair,
    out of the mud and the mire.
He set my feet on solid ground
    and steadied me as I walked along.
³He has given me a new song to sing,
    a hymn of praise to our God.
Many will see what he has done and
    be astounded.
  They will put their trust in the
    LORD.

⁴Oh, the joys of those who trust the
    LORD,
  who have no confidence in the
    proud,
  or in those who worship idols.
⁵O LORD my God, you have done many
    miracles for us.
  Your plans for us are too numerous
    to list.
If I tried to recite all your wonderful
    deeds,
  I would never come to the end of
    them.

⁶You take no delight in sacrifices or
    offerings.
  Now that you have made me listen,
    I finally understand—
  you don't require burnt offerings or
    sin offerings.
⁷Then I said, "Look, I have come.
  And this has been written about me
    in your scroll:
⁸I take joy in doing your will, my God,
  for your law is written on my heart."

⁹I have told all your people about your
    justice.
  I have not been afraid to speak out,
    as you, O LORD, well know.
¹⁰I have not kept this good news hidden
    in my heart;
  I have talked about your faithfulness
    and saving power.
I have told everyone in the great
    assembly
  of your unfailing love and
    faithfulness.

¹¹LORD, don't hold back your tender
    mercies from me.
  My only hope is in your unfailing
    love and faithfulness.
¹²For troubles surround me—
    too many to count!
They pile up so high
    I can't see my way out.
They are more numerous than the
    hairs on my head.
  I have lost all my courage.

¹³Please, LORD, rescue me!
  Come quickly, LORD, and help me.
¹⁴May those who try to destroy me
    be humiliated and put to shame.
May those who take delight in my
    trouble
  be turned back in disgrace.
¹⁵Let them be horrified by their shame,
    for they said, "Aha! We've got him
    now!"

¹⁶But may all who search for you
    be filled with joy and gladness.
May those who love your salvation
    repeatedly shout, "The LORD is
    great!"

¹⁷As for me, I am poor and needy,
    but the Lord is thinking about me
    right now.
You are my helper and my savior.
  Do not delay, O my God.

40:1-5 God's timing is always worth waiting for. If we look to him for help, he will rescue us from destruction and despair and from the things that hold us down. He will also bring stability to our life so we can move forward again with confidence and joy. If we are to experience God's best for our life (which far exceeds anything we can imagine), we need to rely on him alone and avoid any entanglements with those who could lead us away from God and his plan for us.

40:11-17 Recovery is rarely a once-and-for-all thing. The psalmist apparently experienced deliverance from depression (40:1), but then a few verses later he expressed frustration at his numerous troubles (40:12). Every time he felt entrapped, he called out to God for help. This is an important lesson for us to learn as we struggle on the road to full recovery. God will respond as many times as we call out to him. We, however, should never use this as an excuse to return to our sin time and time again. We need to do what we can to avoid the people and situations that we know will lead us into trouble.

PSALM 41

For the choir director: A psalm of David.

¹Oh, the joys of those who are kind to the
poor.
The LORD rescues them in times of
trouble.
²The LORD protects them
and keeps them alive.
He gives them prosperity
and rescues them from their enemies.
³The LORD nurses them when they are sick
and eases their pain and discomfort.

⁴"O LORD," I prayed, "have mercy on me.
Heal me, for I have sinned against you."
⁵But my enemies say nothing but evil
about me.
"How soon will he die and be
forgotten?" they ask.
⁶They visit me as if they are my friends,
but all the while they gather gossip,
and when they leave, they spread it
everywhere.
⁷All who hate me whisper about me,
imagining the worst for me.
⁸"Whatever he has, it is fatal," they say.
"He will never get out of that bed!"
⁹Even my best friend, the one I trusted
completely,
the one who shared my food,
has turned against me.

¹⁰LORD, have mercy on me.
Make me well again, so I can pay them
back!

¹¹I know that you are pleased with me,
for you have not let my enemy triumph
over me.
¹²You have preserved my life because I am
innocent;
you have brought me into your
presence forever.

¹³Bless the LORD, the God of Israel,
who lives forever from eternal ages
past.
Amen and amen!

Book Two (Psalms 42–72)

PSALM 42

*For the choir director: A psalm of the descendants
of Korah.*

¹As the deer pants for streams of water,
so I long for you, O God.
²I thirst for God, the living God.
When can I come and stand before
him?
³Day and night, I have only tears for
food,
while my enemies continually taunt
me, saying,
"Where is this God of yours?"

⁴My heart is breaking
as I remember how it used to be:
I walked among the crowds of worshipers,
leading a great procession to the house
of God,
singing for joy and giving thanks—
it was the sound of a great
celebration!

41:1-3 As we work through the process of recovery, it is easy to become blind to the needs of others as we focus on our own needs and feelings. Recovery demands that we reach out to help others in need. Because of the things we have suffered, we are uniquely gifted to help other people seeking freedom from their dependency. As we reach out to others, we will experience God's help when we are emotionally down or physically sick, or when we face seemingly hopeless situations.

41:4-9 Many people wish us well as we seek to recover. Others, however, seem to hover over us, constantly trying to predict our next failure. We will feel pressure from such people when our relationship with God is weak. At such vulnerable moments, our enemies may seem hard at work trying to ruin our life through deception, lies, and discouraging words. We must keep focused on God; he will never let us down.

42:1-3 We probably developed many destructive appetites during our days of rebellion against God. The solution to this problem is to make God the only object of our desires. The psalmist paints a beautiful picture of the person who longs to be close to God. The language he uses could easily describe the craving we feel for our addiction. We need to realize that only God can satisfy our deepest needs and that our addiction will never bring us real satisfaction. It may temporarily numb the pain, but in the end it will destroy us. If we turn to God, he will help us to change our desires. We can learn to make him the object of our heart's deepest longings.

43:1-5 As we work through the recovery process, those who are ungodly may treat us unfairly. During such times we must look to God, our only dependable source of strength and encouragement. As we turn our life over to him and seek his wisdom and strength, we will find the help we need. We must learn, as the psalmist did, to find strength by reading God's Word and allowing him to restore our joy. As our relationship with God grows stronger, we will discover the means for reconciling our broken relationships.

5 Why am I discouraged?
   Why so sad?
I will put my hope in God!
   I will praise him again—
   my Savior and 6my God!

Now I am deeply discouraged,
   but I will remember your kindness—
from Mount Hermon, the source of the
      Jordan,
   from the land of Mount Mizar.
7 I hear the tumult of the raging seas
   as your waves and surging tides
      sweep over me.

8 Through each day the LORD pours his
      unfailing love upon me,
   and through each night I sing his
      songs,
   praying to God who gives me life.

9 "O God my rock," I cry,
   "Why have you forsaken me?
Why must I wander in darkness,
   oppressed by my enemies?"
10 Their taunts pierce me like a fatal
      wound.
   They scoff, "Where is this God
      of yours?"

11 Why am I discouraged?
   Why so sad?
I will put my hope in God!
   I will praise him again—
   my Savior and my God!

PSALM 43
1 O God, take up my cause!
   Defend me against these ungodly
      people.
   Rescue me from these unjust liars.
2 For you are God, my only safe haven.
   Why have you tossed me aside?
Why must I wander around in darkness,
   oppressed by my enemies?

3 Send out your light and your truth;
   let them guide me.
Let them lead me to your holy mountain,
   to the place where you live.
4 There I will go to the altar of God,
   to God—the source of all my joy.
I will praise you with my harp,
   O God, my God!

5 Why am I discouraged?
   Why so sad?
I will put my hope in God!
   I will praise him again—
   my Savior and my God!

Hope

READ PSALM 42:1-11

During bad times we may get lost in our memories of the "good old days." We may struggle with conflicting emotions, teetering between the extremes of depression and hope.

The psalmist reflected these emotions when he said to himself, "My heart is breaking as I remember how it used to be: I walked among the crowds of worshipers, leading a great procession to the house of God, singing for joy and giving thanks—it was the sound of a great celebration! Why am I discouraged? Why so sad? I will put my hope in God! . . . I will remember your kindness. . . . I hear the tumult of the raging seas as your waves and surging tides sweep over me. Through each day the LORD pours his unfailing love upon me, and through each night I sing his songs, praying to God who gives me life. . . . Why am I discouraged? Why so sad? I will put my hope in God! I will praise him again—my Savior and my God!" (Psalm 42:4-8, 11).

Look how the psalmist improved his conscious contact with God. He talked to himself, commanding his emotions to "hope in God!" He repeated "I will praise him again," even though he didn't feel like it at the time. In the dark times he sang songs, thought about God's steadfast love, and prayed. We can do these things, too. *Turn to page 547, Psalm 103.*

PSALM 44

For the choir director: A psalm of the descendants of Korah.

¹ O God, we have heard it with our own
    ears—
  our ancestors have told us
of all you did in other days,
  in days long ago:
² You drove out the pagan nations
  and gave all the land to our ancestors;
you crushed their enemies,
  setting our ancestors free.
³ They did not conquer the land with their
    swords;
  it was not their own strength that gave
    them victory.
It was by your mighty power that they
    succeeded;
  it was because you favored them and
    smiled on them.

⁴ You are my King and my God.
  You command victories for your
    people.*
⁵ Only by your power can we push back our
    enemies;
  only in your name can we trample our
    foes.
⁶ I do not trust my bow;
  I do not count on my sword to save me.
⁷ It is you who gives us victory over our
    enemies;
  it is you who humbles those who hate
    us.
⁸ O God, we give glory to you all day long
  and constantly praise your name.

Interlude

⁹ But now you have tossed us aside in
    dishonor.
  You no longer lead our armies to battle.
¹⁰ You make us retreat from our enemies
  and allow them to plunder our land.
¹¹ You have treated us like sheep waiting
    to be slaughtered;
  you have scattered us among the
    nations.
¹² You sold us—your precious people—for
    a pittance.
  You valued us at nothing at all.

44:4 Hebrew *for Jacob.*

¹³ You have caused all our neighbors to
    mock us.
  We are an object of scorn and derision
    to the nations around us.
¹⁴ You have made us the butt of their jokes;
  we are scorned by the whole world.
¹⁵ We can't escape the constant humiliation;
  shame is written across our faces.
¹⁶ All we hear are the taunts of our mockers.
  All we see are our vengeful enemies.

¹⁷ All this has happened despite our loyalty
    to you.
  We have not violated your covenant.
¹⁸ Our hearts have not deserted you.
  We have not strayed from your path.
¹⁹ Yet you have crushed us in the desert.
  You have covered us with darkness
    and death.

²⁰ If we had turned away from worshiping
    our God
  or spread our hands in prayer to
    foreign gods,
²¹ God would surely have known it,
  for he knows the secrets of every
    heart.
²² For your sake we are killed every day;
  we are being slaughtered like sheep.

²³ Wake up, O Lord! Why do you sleep?
  Get up! Do not reject us forever.
²⁴ Why do you look the other way?
  Why do you ignore our suffering
    and oppression?
²⁵ We collapse in the dust,
  lying face down in the dirt.
²⁶ Rise up! Come and help us!
  Save us because of your unfailing love.

PSALM 45

For the choir director: A psalm of the descendants of Korah, to be sung to the tune "Lilies." A love song.

¹ My heart overflows with a beautiful
    thought!
  I will recite a lovely poem to the king,
  for my tongue is like the pen of a
    skillful poet.

² You are the most handsome of all.
  Gracious words stream from your lips.
  God himself has blessed you forever.

44:1-7 There are always valuable lessons to be learned from our spiritual predecessors. Those who have progressed farther in the struggle of life and recovery can share how God brought them help and deliverance. The victories God has given others should encourage us, but we must put into practice the principles they share. If we don't act on what we learn, we will never experience the victories they have told us about.

³Put on your sword, O mighty warrior!
    You are so glorious, so majestic!
⁴In your majesty, ride out to victory,
    defending truth, humility, and justice.
    Go forth to perform awe-inspiring
        deeds!
⁵Your arrows are sharp,
    piercing your enemies' hearts.
  The nations fall before you,
    lying down beneath your feet.

⁶Your throne, O God,* endures forever and
        ever.
    Your royal power is expressed in justice.
⁷You love what is right and hate what is
        wrong.
    Therefore God, your God, has anointed
        you,
    pouring out the oil of joy on you more
        than on anyone else.
⁸Your robes are perfumed with myrrh,
        aloes, and cassia.
    In palaces decorated with ivory,
    you are entertained by the music of
        harps.
⁹Kings' daughters are among your
        concubines.
    At your right side stands the queen,
    wearing jewelry of finest gold from
        Ophir!

¹⁰Listen to me, O royal daughter; take to
        heart what I say.
    Forget your people and your homeland
        far away.
¹¹For your royal husband delights in your
        beauty;
    honor him, for he is your lord.
¹²The princes of Tyre* will shower you with
        gifts.
    People of great wealth will entreat your
        favor.

¹³The bride, a princess, waits within her
        chamber,
    dressed in a gown woven with gold.

¹⁴In her beautiful robes, she is led to the
        king,
    accompanied by her bridesmaids.
¹⁵What a joyful, enthusiastic procession
    as they enter the king's palace!

¹⁶Your sons will become kings like their
        father.
    You will make them rulers over many
        lands.

¹⁷I will bring honor to your name in every
        generation.
    Therefore, the nations will praise you
        forever and ever.

PSALM 46

*For the choir director: A psalm of the descendants
of Korah, to be sung by soprano voices.* A song.*

¹God is our refuge and strength,
    always ready to help in times of
        trouble.
²So we will not fear, even if earthquakes
        come
    and the mountains crumble into the
        sea.
³Let the oceans roar and foam.
    Let the mountains tremble as the waters
        surge!   *Interlude*

⁴A river brings joy to the city of our God,
    the sacred home of the Most High.
⁵God himself lives in that city; it cannot
        be destroyed.
    God will protect it at the break of day.
⁶The nations are in an uproar,
    and kingdoms crumble!
  God thunders,
    and the earth melts!

⁷The LORD Almighty is here among us;
    the God of Israel* is our fortress.
                                                    Interlude

⁸Come, see the glorious works of the LORD:
    See how he brings destruction upon the
        world

45:6 Or *Your divine throne.* **45:12** Hebrew *The daughter of Tyre.* **46:TITLE** Hebrew *according to alamoth.* **46:7** Hebrew
of Jacob; also in 46:11.

46:1-6 God is more than able to protect us no matter how strong the pull of temptation might
be. If we try to resist temptation in our own strength, we have good reason to fear. But if God is
with us, we have no reason to be afraid. God's river of mercy and strength flows just for us when
we are weak and thirsty. No power can draw us out of the circle of his protection once we take
refuge in him.
46:7-11 God, the commander of the heavenly armies, is here among us. If we put our life in his
hands, we can rest, confident that he will protect us. He knows our weaknesses and can strengthen
us in the needed areas, helping us to overcome the attacks we face each day. Our enemies may be
strong, but God is far more powerful than anything that might assail us.

9 and causes wars to end throughout the
earth.
He breaks the bow and snaps the spear
in two;
he burns the shields with fire.

10 "Be silent, and know that I am God!
I will be honored by every nation.
I will be honored throughout the
world."

11 The LORD Almighty is here among us;
the God of Israel is our fortress.

Interlude

PSALM 47

*For the choir director: A psalm of the descendants
of Korah.*

1 Come, everyone, and clap your hands
for joy!
Shout to God with joyful praise!
2 For the LORD Most High is awesome.
He is the great King of all the earth.
3 He subdues the nations before us,
putting our enemies beneath our feet.
4 He chose the Promised Land as our
inheritance,
the proud possession of Jacob's
descendants, whom he loves.

Interlude

5 God has ascended with a mighty shout.
The LORD has ascended with trumpets
blaring.
6 Sing praise to God, sing praises;
sing praise to our King, sing praises!

7 For God is the King over all the earth.
Praise him with a psalm!
8 God reigns above the nations,
sitting on his holy throne.
9 The rulers of the world have gathered
together.
They join us in praising the God
of Abraham.
For all the kings of the earth belong
to God.
He is highly honored everywhere.

PSALM 48

A psalm of the descendants of Korah. A song.

1 How great is the LORD,
and how much we should praise him
in the city of our God,
which is on his holy mountain!
2 It is magnificent in elevation—
the whole earth rejoices to see it!
Mount Zion, the holy mountain,*
is the city of the great King!
3 God himself is in Jerusalem's towers.
He reveals himself as her defender.

4 The kings of the earth joined forces
and advanced against the city.
5 But when they saw it, they were stunned;
they were terrified and ran away.
6 They were gripped with terror,
like a woman writhing in the pain
of childbirth
7 or like the mighty ships of Tarshish
being shattered by a powerful east
wind.

8 We had heard of the city's glory,
but now we have seen it ourselves—
the city of the LORD Almighty.
It is the city of our God;
he will make it safe forever.   *Interlude*

9 O God, we meditate on your unfailing
love
as we worship in your Temple.
10 As your name deserves, O God,
you will be praised to the ends of the
earth.
Your strong right hand is filled with
victory.
11 Let the people on Mount Zion rejoice.
Let the towns of Judah be glad,
for your judgments are just.

12 Go, inspect the city of Jerusalem.*
Walk around and count the many
towers.
13 Take note of the fortified walls,
and tour all the citadels,
that you may describe them
to future generations.

48:2 Or *Mount Zion, in the far north;* Hebrew reads *Mount Zion, the heights of Zaphon.* 48:12 Hebrew *Zion.*

47:1-9 Victories, great and small, should be shared with others who are struggling. The psalmist made it a goal to encourage others, reminding them how good and powerful God is and inviting them to join him in praising our awesome God.
48:9-14 We must worship God and meditate on how he has brought us victory over the problems that once held us in bondage and defeat. An important part of the recovery process involves seeking God through prayer and meditation, actions that help us to develop confidence in God. We are told to meditate on God's unfailing love for us. He will be our guide and strength as we face the struggles of recovery.

14 For that is what God is like.
   He is our God forever and ever,
   and he will be our guide until we die.

PSALM 49

For the choir director: A psalm of the descendants of Korah.

1 Listen to this, all you people!
   Pay attention, everyone in the world!
2 High and low,
   rich and poor—listen!
3 For my words are wise,
   and my thoughts are filled with insight.
4 I listen carefully to many proverbs
   and solve riddles with inspiration from
      a harp.

5 There is no need to fear when times
      of trouble come,
   when enemies are surrounding me.
6 They trust in their wealth
   and boast of great riches.
7 Yet they cannot redeem themselves from
      death*
   by paying a ransom to God.
8 Redemption does not come so easily,
   for no one can ever pay enough
9 to live forever
   and never see the grave.

10 Those who are wise must finally die,
   just like the foolish and senseless,
   leaving all their wealth behind.
11 The grave is their eternal home,
   where they will stay forever.
   They may name their estates after
      themselves,
   but they leave their wealth to others.
12 They will not last long despite their
      riches—
   they will die like the animals.
13 This is the fate of fools,
   though they will be remembered
      as being so wise.   *Interlude*

49:7 Or *no one can redeem the life of another.*

14 Like sheep, they are led to the grave,
   where death will be their shepherd.
   In the morning the godly will rule over
      them.
   Their bodies will rot in the grave,
   far from their grand estates.
15 But as for me, God will redeem my life.
   He will snatch me from the power
      of death.   *Interlude*

16 So don't be dismayed when the wicked
      grow rich,
   and their homes become ever more
      splendid.
17 For when they die, they carry nothing
      with them.
   Their wealth will not follow them into
      the grave.
18 In this life they consider themselves
      fortunate,
   and the world loudly applauds their
      success.
19 But they will die like all others before
      them
   and never again see the light of day.
20 People who boast of their wealth don't
      understand
   that they will die like the animals.

PSALM 50

A psalm of Asaph.

1 The mighty God, the LORD, has spoken;
   he has summoned all humanity from
      east to west!
2 From Mount Zion, the perfection of
      beauty,
   God shines in glorious radiance.
3 Our God approaches with the noise
      of thunder.
   Fire devours everything in his way,
   and a great storm rages around
      him.
4 Heaven and earth will be his witnesses
   as he judges his people:

49:5-13 We need to respect our addictions and compulsions, remembering how they once caused us to lose control. But we do not need to fear them, because God won't allow our destruction as long as we trust in him and follow his program for godly living. The only way we can repay God for his deliverance is to show gratitude and share the good news with others. Although some may seem to prosper and escape the consequences of their wrongdoings in this life, they will leave all their wealth behind and face judgment in the next (see 37:12-17). This should be a warning to us not to spend too much time envying others (37:1).
50:1-6 These verses portray God's judgment of the wicked with powerful images of thunder and fire. Judgment is coming to those who refuse to recognize God's authority. God is good, but he must deal with those who have harmed others or he would not be a just God after all. Because he is just, we need to take careful inventory of our life, doing our best to right all the wrongs we have committed.

5 "Bring my faithful people to me—
　　those who made a covenant with me
　　　　by giving sacrifices."
6 Then let the heavens proclaim his
　　justice,
　　for God himself will be the judge.
　　　　　　　　　　　　　　　Interlude

7 "O my people, listen as I speak.
　　Here are my charges against you,
　　　　O Israel:
　　I am God, your God!
8 I have no complaint about your sacrifices
　　or the burnt offerings you constantly
　　　　bring to my altar.
9 But I want no more bulls from your
　　barns;
　　I want no more goats from your pens.
10 For all the animals of the forest are
　　mine,
　　and I own the cattle on a thousand
　　　　hills.
11 Every bird of the mountains
　　and all the animals of the field belong
　　　　to me.
12 If I were hungry, I would not mention
　　it to you,
　　for all the world is mine and everything
　　　　in it.
13 I don't need the bulls you sacrifice;
　　I don't need the blood of goats.
14 What I want instead is your true thanks
　　to God;
　　I want you to fulfill your vows to the
　　　　Most High.
15 Trust me in your times of trouble,
　　and I will rescue you,
　　and you will give me glory."

16 But God says to the wicked:
　　"Recite my laws no longer,
　　and don't pretend that you
　　　　obey me.
17 For you refuse my discipline
　　and treat my laws like trash.
18 When you see a thief, you help him,
　　and you spend your time with
　　　　adulterers.
19 Your mouths are filled with wickedness,
　　and your tongues are full of lies.
20 You sit around and slander a brother—
　　your own mother's son.
21 While you did all this, I remained
　　silent,
　　and you thought I didn't care.
　　But now I will rebuke you,
　　listing all my charges against you.
22 Repent, all of you who ignore me,
　　or I will tear you apart,
　　and no one will help you.
23 But giving thanks is a sacrifice that truly
　　honors me.
　　If you keep to my path,
　　I will reveal to you the salvation
　　　　of God."

PSALM 51

For the choir director: A psalm of David, regarding the time Nathan the prophet came to him after David had committed adultery with Bathsheba.

1 Have mercy on me, O God,
　　because of your unfailing love.
　　Because of your great compassion,
　　blot out the stain of my sins.
2 Wash me clean from my guilt.
　　Purify me from my sin.

50:16-23 People who deceive, slander, lie, and encourage others to follow immoral lifestyles cannot ignore God's Word for long. God sees what goes on, and, just because he is silent does not mean he doesn't care. One day he will present his case against them, and judgment will follow. The way to avoid such an end is to worship God with thanksgiving and follow him in what he says in his Word.

51:5-9 If we fail to admit and confess our sins, they will continue to burden us with destructive guilt and rob us of joy. We need to learn to confess and forsake our sins immediately. Then we need to seek God's wisdom as to how we can make amends for the wrongs we have done to others. We won't be able to progress in the recovery process or reach out to others until we seek forgiveness for our past failures. Some people may not readily forgive us, but we can be sure God will.

51:10-13 David had already seen what happened when God removed his Spirit from King Saul—it was the beginning of his bitter downfall (1 Samuel 15–19). David wrote this psalm of repentance after he committed adultery with Bathsheba and then arranged for her husband's death (2 Samuel 11–12). On the surface, David's sins were far worse than Saul's. Why did God forgive David and offer him restoration? David was humble and broken about his sin. He admitted it and asked for God's help and forgiveness. Saul was never willing to admit his sins; he continued in denial. If we try to hide or deny our sins, we are in grave danger of judgment. But if we are sensitive to our sins and humbly seek God's forgiveness, there is hope for us, no matter how great our past sins. God will remove any taint of guilt and restore our joy.

³For I recognize my shameful deeds—
  they haunt me day and night.
⁴Against you, and you alone, have
    I sinned;
  I have done what is evil in your
    sight.
  You will be proved right in what you say,
    and your judgment against me is just.

⁵For I was born a sinner—
  yes, from the moment my mother
    conceived me.
⁶But you desire honesty from the heart,
  so you can teach me to be wise in my
    inmost being.

⁷Purify me from my sins,* and I will be
    clean;
  wash me, and I will be whiter than
    snow.
⁸Oh, give me back my joy again;
  you have broken me—
    now let me rejoice.
⁹Don't keep looking at my sins.
  Remove the stain of my guilt.
¹⁰Create in me a clean heart, O God.
  Renew a right spirit within me.
¹¹Do not banish me from your presence,
  and don't take your Holy Spirit from
    me.
¹²Restore to me again the joy of your
    salvation,
  and make me willing to obey you.
¹³Then I will teach your ways to sinners,
  and they will return to you.
¹⁴Forgive me for shedding blood, O God
    who saves;
  then I will joyfully sing of your
    forgiveness.
¹⁵Unseal my lips, O Lord,
  that I may praise you.

¹⁶You would not be pleased with sacrifices,
  or I would bring them.
  If I brought you a burnt offering,
    you would not accept it.
¹⁷The sacrifice you want is a broken
    spirit.
  A broken and repentant heart, O God,
    you will not despise.

¹⁸Look with favor on Zion and help her;
  rebuild the walls of Jerusalem.
¹⁹Then you will be pleased with worthy
    sacrifices
  and with our whole burnt offerings;
  and bulls will again be sacrificed on
    your altar.

51:7 Hebrew *Purify me with the hyssop branch.*

S T E P

Healing the Brokenness

BIBLE READING: Psalm 51:16-19
**We were entirely ready to have God
remove all these defects of character.**
If we have sincerely practiced the previous
steps, we have probably found enough
pain inside ourself to break our heart.
Facing the fact that brokenness is part
of the human condition can be crushing.
But if we have arrived at this point, it is
probably a sign that we are ready for God
to change us.

As a young man, King David wasn't
ready for God to change his character
because he didn't recognize that it had
defects. He prayed, "Don't let me suffer
the fate of sinners. . . . I am not like that;
I do what is right. So in your mercy, save
me" (Psalm 26:9-11). He approached
God on the basis of his own merit.

It wasn't until later in his life when he
was confronted with his sins of adultery
and murder that he was able to say, "For I
was born a sinner—yes, from the moment
my mother conceived me" (Psalm 51:5).
He also said, "You would not be pleased
with sacrifices, or I would bring them. . . .
The sacrifice you want is a broken spirit.
A broken and repentant heart, O God,
you will not despise" (Psalm 51:16-17).

Jesus taught that "God blesses those
who mourn, for they will be comforted"
(Matthew 5:4). God isn't looking for
evidence of how good we are or how
hard we try. He only wants us to mourn
over our sins and admit our brokenness.
Then he will not ignore our needs but
will forgive us, comfort us, and cleanse
us. *Turn to Step Seven, page 115, Luke 11.*

PSALM 52

For the choir director: A psalm of David, regarding the time Doeg the Edomite told Saul that Ahimelech had given refuge to David.

¹You call yourself a hero, do you?
     Why boast about this crime of yours,
     you who have disgraced God's people?
²All day long you plot destruction.
     Your tongue cuts like a sharp razor;
     you're an expert at telling lies.
³You love evil more than good
     and lies more than truth.   *Interlude*

⁴You love to say things that harm others,
     you liar!
⁵But God will strike you down once and
     for all.
     He will pull you from your home
     and drag you from the land of the
     living.   *Interlude*

⁶The righteous will see it and be amazed.
     They will laugh and say,
⁷"Look what happens to mighty warriors
     who do not trust in God.
     They trust their wealth instead
     and grow more and more bold in their
     wickedness."

⁸But I am like an olive tree,
     thriving in the house of God.
     I trust in God's unfailing love
     forever and ever.
⁹I will praise you forever, O God,
     for what you have done.
     I will wait for your mercies
     in the presence of your people.

PSALM 53

For the choir director: A meditation of David.

¹Only fools say in their hearts,
     "There is no God."

They are corrupt, and their actions are evil;
     no one does good!

²God looks down from heaven
     on the entire human race;
     he looks to see if there is even one with
     real understanding,
     one who seeks for God.
³But no, all have turned away from God;
     all have become corrupt.
     No one does good,
     not even one!

⁴Will those who do evil never learn?
     They eat up my people like bread;
     they wouldn't think of praying to God.
⁵But then terror will grip them,
     terror like they have never known
     before.
     God will scatter the bones of your enemies.
     You will put them to shame, for God
     has rejected them.

⁶Oh, that salvation would come from
     Mount Zion to rescue Israel!
     For when God restores his people,
     Jacob will shout with joy, and Israel will
     rejoice.

PSALM 54

For the choir director: A meditation of David, regarding the time the Ziphites came and said to Saul, "We know where David is hiding." To be accompanied by stringed instruments.

¹Come with great power, O God, and
     rescue me!
     Defend me with your might.
²O God, listen to my prayer.
     Pay attention to my plea.

³For strangers are attacking me;
     violent men are trying to kill me.
     They care nothing for God.   *Interlude*

52:5-9 In the past we may have valued people for the enjoyment and excitement we experienced while we were with them. We lived for the pleasure and fun of the present moment. With time, however, it became clear that such a lifestyle always led to painful long-term consequences. We see in this psalm that God is able and willing to snatch us out of the dangerous situations we may have gotten ourselves into. A consistent prayer life can help us keep the right perspective about the world and give us patience and hope as we look to the future.

53:1-6 Believing in God is essential in the recovery journey. Ignoring God's plan for healthy living brings only trouble and suffering. We have become prisoners of our own desires, powerless to escape without God's help. Seeing the damage that rebellion has done should cause us to spend time in prayer. Our own powerlessness should serve as a constant reminder of our need for God's powerful presence in our life.

54:1-7 We will almost certainly face opposition from people who don't understand what recovery is all about or who feel threatened by it. The words of this psalm should be our prayer for deliverance at such times. God is our rescuer and helper, who will cause our enemies to fall into their own traps. Our response to God's deliverance from those who are against us should be worship and thanks.

⁴But God is my helper.
  The Lord is the one who keeps me alive!
⁵May my enemies' plans for evil be turned
    against them.
  Do as you promised and put an end
    to them.

⁶I will sacrifice a voluntary offering to you;
  I will praise your name, O Lord,
    for it is good.
⁷For you will rescue me from my troubles
  and help me to triumph over my
    enemies.

PSALM 55

*For the choir director: A psalm of David, to be
accompanied by stringed instruments.*

¹Listen to my prayer, O God.
  Do not ignore my cry for help!
²Please listen and answer me,
  for I am overwhelmed by my troubles.
³My enemies shout at me,
  making loud and wicked threats.
  They bring trouble on me,
    hunting me down in their anger.

⁴My heart is in anguish.
  The terror of death overpowers me.
⁵Fear and trembling overwhelm me.
  I can't stop shaking.
⁶Oh, how I wish I had wings like a dove;
  then I would fly away and rest!
⁷I would fly far away
  to the quiet of the wilderness.
                                    Interlude
⁸How quickly I would escape—
  far away from this wild storm
    of hatred.

⁹Destroy them, Lord, and confuse their
    speech,
  for I see violence and strife in the city.
¹⁰Its walls are patrolled day and night
    against invaders,
  but the real danger is wickedness
    within the city.
¹¹Murder and robbery are everywhere there;

threats and cheating are rampant
    in the streets.

¹²It is not an enemy who taunts me—
  I could bear that.
  It is not my foes who so arrogantly insult
    me—
  I could have hidden from them.
¹³Instead, it is you—my equal,
  my companion and close friend.
¹⁴What good fellowship we enjoyed
  as we walked together to the house
    of God.

¹⁵Let death seize my enemies by surprise;
  let the grave* swallow them alive,
    for evil makes its home within them.

¹⁶But I will call on God,
  and the Lord will rescue me.
¹⁷Morning, noon, and night
  I plead aloud in my distress,
  and the Lord hears my voice.
¹⁸He rescues me and keeps me safe
  from the battle waged against me,
    even though many still oppose me.
¹⁹God, who is king forever,
  will hear me and will humble them.
                                    Interlude
  For my enemies refuse to change their
    ways;
  they do not fear God.

²⁰As for this friend of mine, he betrayed me;
  he broke his promises.
²¹His words are as smooth as cream,
  but in his heart is war.
  His words are as soothing as lotion,
    but underneath are daggers!

²²Give your burdens to the Lord,
  and he will take care of you.
  He will not permit the godly to slip
    and fall.

²³But you, O God, will send the wicked
  down to the pit of destruction.
  Murderers and liars will die young,
    but I am trusting you to save me.

55:15 Hebrew *let Sheol.*

55:16-19 During recovery our relationship with God is extremely important. At times he may
be the only friend we have. David was confident that God would rescue and deliver him from
his problems. He also depended on God to keep him safe from others who opposed him. With
God as our friend and helper, there is hope for recovery no matter what circumstances we have
to face.
55:20-22 David's anguish caused him to think about the pain he had suffered at the betrayal
of an old friend. Old friends may say all the right words, but deep down they probably want us
to continue practicing destructive habits with them. The solution for David, and for us, is to give
our burdens to God. He is able to strengthen us, encourage us, and keep us from falling.

PSALM 56

For the choir director: A psalm of David, regarding the time the Philistines seized him in Gath. To be sung to the tune "Dove on Distant Oaks."

¹O God, have mercy on me.
   The enemy troops press in on me.
   My foes attack me all day long.
²My slanderers hound me constantly,
   and many are boldly attacking me.
³But when I am afraid,
   I put my trust in you.
⁴O God, I praise your word.
   I trust in God, so why should I be
      afraid?
   What can mere mortals do to me?

⁵They are always twisting what I say;
   they spend their days plotting ways
      to harm me.
⁶They come together to spy on me—
   watching my every step, eager to kill
      me.
⁷Don't let them get away with their
      wickedness;
   in your anger, O God, throw them
      to the ground.

⁸You keep track of all my sorrows.
   You have collected all my tears in your
      bottle.
   You have recorded each one in your
      book.

⁹On the very day I call to you for help,
   my enemies will retreat.
   This I know: God is on my side.*
¹⁰O God, I praise your word.
   Yes, LORD, I praise your word.
¹¹I trust in God, so why should I be
      afraid?
   What can mere mortals do to me?

¹²I will fulfill my vows to you, O God,
   and offer a sacrifice of thanks for your
      help.

56:9 Or *By this I will know that God is on my side.*

¹³For you have rescued me from death;
   you have kept my feet from slipping.
So now I can walk in your presence,
      O God,
   in your life-giving light.

PSALM 57

For the choir director: A psalm of David, regarding the time he fled from Saul and went into the cave. To be sung to the tune "Do Not Destroy!"

¹Have mercy on me, O God, have mercy!
   I look to you for protection.
I will hide beneath the shadow of your
      wings
   until this violent storm is past.

²I cry out to God Most High,
   to God who will fulfill his purpose
      for me.
³He will send help from heaven to save me,
   rescuing me from those who are out to
      get me.   *Interlude*
My God will send forth his unfailing love
   and faithfulness.

⁴I am surrounded by fierce lions
   who greedily devour human prey—
whose teeth pierce like spears and arrows,
   and whose tongues cut like swords.

⁵Be exalted, O God, above the highest
      heavens!
   May your glory shine over all the earth.

⁶My enemies have set a trap for me.
   I am weary from distress.
They have dug a deep pit in my path,
   but they themselves have fallen into it.
                              Interlude

⁷My heart is confident in you, O God;
   no wonder I can sing your praises!
⁸Wake up, my soul!
   Wake up, O harp and lyre!
   I will waken the dawn with my song.

56:8-13 As we keep our thoughts focused on God and trust him, we will find, as the psalmist did, that God is on our side. Even when our struggles are most difficult, God knows all our pain, and he will do his part. We, however, must fulfill our responsibilities of being obedient to God's revealed will. His program is always best for us in the long run.

57:1-3 When we understand the mercy and unfailing love of God, we find comfort in turning to him in times of trouble, knowing that he will surround us with his protection until the storm is past. God is faithful and will always be there for us. Understanding and acting upon this truth are essential for progressing in recovery.

57:7-11 Here the psalmist demonstrates an important principle for recovery: After experiencing God's help, we should be thankful and share what God has done for us with others. In fact, this should be the natural response of our grateful hearts. This will not only encourage others in the recovery process but also help in our own journey toward recovery.

⁹I will thank you, Lord, in front of all the
people.
  I will sing your praises among the
  nations.
¹⁰For your unfailing love is as high as the
heavens.
  Your faithfulness reaches to the clouds.

¹¹Be exalted, O God, above the highest
heavens.
  May your glory shine over all the earth.

PSALM 58

*For the choir director: A psalm of David, to be sung
to the tune "Do Not Destroy!"*

¹Justice—do you rulers know the meaning
of the word?
  Do you judge the people fairly?
²No, all your dealings are crooked;
  you hand out violence instead of
  justice.
³These wicked people are born sinners;
  even from birth they have lied and
  gone their own way.
⁴They spit poison like deadly snakes;
  they are like cobras that refuse to listen,
⁵ignoring the tunes of the snake charmers,
  no matter how skillfully they play.

⁶Break off their fangs, O God!
  Smash the jaws of these lions, O LORD!
⁷May they disappear like water into thirsty
ground.
  Make their weapons useless in their
  hands.*
⁸May they be like snails that dissolve into
slime,
  like a stillborn child who will never see
  the sun.
⁹God will sweep them away, both young
and old,
  faster than a pot heats on an open flame.

¹⁰The godly will rejoice when they see
injustice avenged.
  They will wash their feet in the blood
  of the wicked.

¹¹Then at last everyone will say,
  "There truly is a reward for those who
  live for God;
  surely there is a God who judges justly
  here on earth."

PSALM 59

*For the choir director: A psalm of David, regarding
the time Saul sent soldiers to watch David's house
in order to kill him. To be sung to the tune "Do
Not Destroy!"*

¹Rescue me from my enemies, O God.
  Protect me from those who have come
  to destroy me.
²Rescue me from these criminals;
  save me from these murderers.

³They have set an ambush for me.
  Fierce enemies are out there waiting,
  though I have done them no wrong,
  O LORD.
⁴Despite my innocence, they prepare
to kill me.
  Rise up and help me! Look on my
  plight!
⁵O LORD God Almighty, the God of Israel,
  rise up to punish hostile nations.
  Show no mercy to wicked traitors.
                                    Interlude

⁶They come at night,
  snarling like vicious dogs
  as they prowl the streets.
⁷Listen to the filth that comes from their
mouths,
  the piercing swords that fly from their
  lips.
  "Who can hurt us?" they sneer.

⁸But LORD, you laugh at them.
  You scoff at all the hostile nations.
⁹You are my strength; I wait for you to
rescue me,
  for you, O God, are my place of safety.
¹⁰In his unfailing love, my God will come
and help me.
  He will let me look down in triumph
  on all my enemies.

58:7 Or *Let them be trodden down and wither like grass.* The meaning of the Hebrew is uncertain.

58:1-5 The world is unfair and unjust. We shouldn't expect everything to go our way; nor should
we allow our anger at apparent injustices to cause us to compromise. Regardless of how others
act, God still expects us to make amends for the mistakes we have made. He is the only one in the
position to ultimately judge whether things are fair or unfair.
59:1-4 Our enemies may not be people—they may be alcohol or some other addictive substance,
abuse, pornography, or a dysfunctional family. Whatever our enemies are, we should realize that
they are capable of destroying us. The wisest thing we can do is to call out to God for help. He is
the only one really capable of helping and protecting us; he is our "place of safety in the day of
distress" (59:16).

11 Don't kill them, for my people soon
forget such lessons;
stagger them with your power, and
bring them to their knees,
O Lord our shield.
12 Because of the sinful things they say,
because of the evil that is on their lips,
let them be captured by their pride,
their curses, and their lies.
13 Destroy them in your anger!
Wipe them out completely!
Then the whole world will know
that God reigns in Israel.*　　　*Interlude*

14 My enemies come out at night,
snarling like vicious dogs
as they prowl the streets.
15 They scavenge for food
but go to sleep unsatisfied.*

16 But as for me, I will sing about your power.
I will shout with joy each morning
because of your unfailing love.
For you have been my refuge,
a place of safety in the day of distress.

17 O my Strength, to you I sing praises,
for you, O God, are my refuge,
the God who shows me unfailing love.

PSALM 60

*For the choir director: A psalm of David useful for
teaching, regarding the time David fought Aram-
naharaim and Aram-zobah, and Joab returned and
killed twelve thousand Edomites in the Valley of
Salt. To be sung to the tune "Lily of the Testimony."*

1 You have rejected us, O God, and broken
our defenses.
You have been angry with us; now
restore us to your favor.

2 You have shaken our land and split it
open.
Seal the cracks before it completely
collapses.
3 You have been very hard on us,
making us drink wine that sent us
reeling.
4 But you have raised a banner for those
who honor you—
a rallying point in the face of attack.
　　　　　　　　　　　　　　　Interlude

5 Use your strong right arm to save us,
and rescue your beloved people.
6 God has promised this by his holiness*:
"I will divide up Shechem with joy.
I will measure out the valley of
Succoth.
7 Gilead is mine,
and Manasseh is mine.
Ephraim will produce my warriors,
and Judah will produce my kings.
8 Moab will become my lowly servant,
and Edom will be my slave.
I will shout in triumph over the
Philistines."

9 But who will bring me into the fortified
city?
Who will bring me victory over
Edom?
10 Have you rejected us, O God?
Will you no longer march with our
armies?
11 Oh, please help us against our enemies,
for all human help is useless.
12 With God's help we will do mighty
things,
for he will trample down our foes.

59:13 Hebrew *in Jacob.* **59:15** Or *and growl if they don't get enough.* **60:6** Or *in his sanctuary.*

60:1-4 When God shows his anger because of our sins, we feel both rejected and overwhelmed. It is at such times that we need to repent and renew our fellowship with him. The consequences of our sins and mistakes often hurt others as well, and we ought to be sensitive to that fact and do our best to make amends. Discipline is never easy to take, but in the midst of it, God provides us with the direction we need to regain his favor and protection. He has revealed his program for spiritual recovery in his Word.

61:1-8 Wherever we are, whatever circumstances we face, we can turn to God for help. He will hear our prayer and protect us with his divine presence. He is our safety and our refuge. We can confidently ask him for help because he has proven himself to be a deliverer of those who love him who are under enemy attack. He is our loving protector, who blesses us and gives our life meaning as we fulfill our vows to live for him daily.

62:1-8 When we face problems that we cannot overcome alone, the wisest thing to do is wait quietly for God to defend us. We will never totally escape our problems and temptations, but God is with us at all times. He is more than capable of overcoming our most powerful adversaries—all we have to Is ask him. We can rely on him not only for deliverance in times of trouble but also for strength when things are going well and our guard is down. As we realize these truths, we should encourage others to place their confidence in God. As we reach out to help others, we are strengthened by sharing with them the good news of God's salvation.

PSALM 61

For the choir director: A psalm of David, to be accompanied by stringed instruments.

¹O God, listen to my cry!
  Hear my prayer!
²From the ends of the earth,
  I will cry to you for help,
  for my heart is overwhelmed.
 Lead me to the towering rock of safety,
³ for you are my safe refuge,
  a fortress where my enemies cannot
    reach me.
⁴Let me live forever in your sanctuary,
  safe beneath the shelter of your wings!
                                    Interlude

⁵For you have heard my vows, O God.
  You have given me an inheritance
    reserved for those who fear your
    name.

⁶Add many years to the life of the king!
  May his years span the generations!
⁷May he reign under God's protection
    forever.
  Appoint your unfailing love and
    faithfulness to watch over him.

⁸Then I will always sing praises to your
    name
  as I fulfill my vows day after day.

PSALM 62

For Jeduthun, the choir director: A psalm of David.

¹I wait quietly before God,
  for my salvation comes from him.
²He alone is my rock and my salvation,
  my fortress where I will never be
    shaken.

³So many enemies against one man—
  all of them trying to kill me.
 To them I'm just a broken-down wall
  or a tottering fence.
⁴They plan to topple me from my high
    position.
  They delight in telling lies about me.
 They are friendly to my face,
  but they curse me in their hearts.
                                    Interlude

⁵I wait quietly before God,
  for my hope is in him.
⁶He alone is my rock and my salvation,
  my fortress where I will not be shaken.
⁷My salvation and my honor come from
    God alone.
  He is my refuge, a rock where no enemy
    can reach me.

STEP 3

Giving Up Control

BIBLE READING: Psalm 61:1-8

We made a decision to turn our will and our life over to the care of God.

The thought of turning our will and our life over can be attractive. When we give in to our dependencies and compulsions, aren't we giving control over to another power? Aren't we in some way giving up personal responsibility for our life? When we are overwhelmed and want to escape, our addiction can make us feel strong, safe, attractive, powerful, happy. So, in a sense, we are very comfortable with the thought of giving up control of our will and our life.

We can take steps to change our focus and turn our life over to God instead of reverting to the hiding places of the past. The apostle Paul touched on this contrast when he said, "Don't be drunk with wine, because that will ruin your life. Instead, let the Holy Spirit fill and control you" (Ephesians 5:18).

When we are overwhelmed and in need of some kind of escape, we have a new place to turn. King David declared, "The LORD is a shelter for the oppressed, a refuge in times of trouble. Those who know your name trust in you, for you, O LORD, have never abandoned anyone who searches for you" (Psalm 9:9-10).

David also wrote, "From the ends of the earth, I will cry to you for help, for my heart is overwhelmed. Lead me to the towering rock of safety, for you are my safe refuge, a fortress where my enemies cannot reach me" (Psalm 61:2-3). *Turn to Step Four, page 15, Matthew 7.*

8 O my people, trust in him at all times.
  Pour out your heart to him,
  for God is our refuge. *Interlude*

9 From the greatest to the lowliest—
  all are nothing in his sight.
  If you weigh them on the scales,
  they are lighter than a puff of air.
10 Don't try to get rich
  by extortion or robbery.
  And if your wealth increases,
  don't make it the center of your life.

11 God has spoken plainly,
  and I have heard it many times:
  Power, O God, belongs to you;
12   unfailing love, O Lord, is yours.
  Surely you judge all people
  according to what they have done.

PSALM 63

A psalm of David, regarding a time when David was in the wilderness of Judah.

1 O God, you are my God;
  I earnestly search for you.
  My soul thirsts for you;
  my whole body longs for you
  in this parched and weary land
  where there is no water.

2 I have seen you in your sanctuary
  and gazed upon your power and
  glory.
3 Your unfailing love is better to me than
  life itself;
  how I praise you!
4 I will honor you as long as I live,
  lifting up my hands to you in prayer.
5 You satisfy me more than the richest
  of foods.
  I will praise you with songs of joy.

6 I lie awake thinking of you,
  meditating on you through the night.
7 I think how much you have helped me;
  I sing for joy in the shadow of your
  protecting wings.

8 I follow close behind you;
  your strong right hand holds me
  securely.

9 But those plotting to destroy me will
  come to ruin.
  They will go down into the depths
  of the earth.
10 They will die by the sword
  and become the food of jackals.

11 But the king will rejoice in God.
  All who trust in him will praise him,
  while liars will be silenced.

PSALM 64

For the choir director: A psalm of David.

1 O God, listen to my complaint.
  Do not let my enemies' threats
  overwhelm me.
2 Protect me from the plots of the wicked,
  from the scheming of those who
  do evil.
3 Sharp tongues are the swords they
  wield;
  bitter words are the arrows they aim.
4 They shoot from ambush at the innocent,
  attacking suddenly and fearlessly.
5 They encourage each other to do evil
  and plan how to set their traps.
  "Who will ever notice?" they ask.
6 As they plot their crimes, they say,
  "We have devised the perfect plan!"
  Yes, the human heart and mind are
  cunning.

7 But God himself will shoot them down.
  Suddenly, his arrows will pierce them.
8 Their own words will be turned against
  them, destroying them.
  All who see it happening will shake
  their heads in scorn.
9 Then everyone will stand in awe,
  proclaiming the mighty acts of God,
  realizing all the amazing things he
  does.

63:1-5 The more difficult our life is and the more severe the temptations we face, the more important God becomes to us. When we are at our weakest, God's power takes on added significance for us. We begin to discover how precious his compassionate care toward us really is. He is worthy of all our praise, for only he can satisfy our deepest longings.

64:7-10 God knows exactly where our enemies are, and thus he is able to help us thwart their attacks. Our part in the recovery process is to turn our life and will over to God for his care. He can't help us without our cooperation. As we allow God to work on our behalf, others will be amazed at what he has done for us. As we share the good news of God's marvelous deeds, our victories will be cause for the hope and celebration of others, too.

65:5-13 God is more than able to respond to our need for deliverance because he is the one God who made the majestic mountains of this world. If he can take care of the earth and water it, bringing forth bountiful harvests, we can be sure he can take care of us.

¹⁰ The godly will rejoice in the LORD
    and find shelter in him.
And those who do what is right
    will praise him.

PSALM 65

For the choir director: A psalm of David. A song.

¹ What mighty praise, O God,
    belongs to you in Zion.
We will fulfill our vows to you,
²   for you answer our prayers,
    and to you all people will come.
³ Though our hearts are filled with sins,
    you forgive them all.
⁴ What joy for those you choose to bring
    near,
    those who live in your holy courts.
What joys await us
    inside your holy Temple.

⁵ You faithfully answer our prayers with
    awesome deeds,
    O God our savior.
You are the hope of everyone on earth,
    even those who sail on distant seas.
⁶ You formed the mountains by your power
    and armed yourself with mighty
    strength.
⁷ You quieted the raging oceans
    with their pounding waves
    and silenced the shouting of the
    nations.
⁸ Those who live at the ends of the earth
    stand in awe of your wonders.
From where the sun rises to where it sets,
    you inspire shouts of joy.

⁹ You take care of the earth and water it,
    making it rich and fertile.
The rivers of God will not run dry;
    they provide a bountiful harvest
    of grain,
    for you have ordered it so.
¹⁰ You drench the plowed ground with rain,
    melting the clods and leveling the
    ridges.
You soften the earth with showers
    and bless its abundant crops.
¹¹ You crown the year with a bountiful
    harvest;
    even the hard pathways overflow with
    abundance.
¹² The wilderness becomes a lush pasture,
    and the hillsides blossom with joy.
¹³ The meadows are clothed with flocks
    of sheep,
    and the valleys are carpeted with grain.
    They all shout and sing for joy!

STEP 11

Joy in God's Presence

BIBLE READING: Psalm 65:1-4
**We sought through prayer and medita-
tion to improve our conscious contact
with God, praying only for knowledge
of his will for us and the power to carry
that out.**
Most of us need to desire something
before we will wholeheartedly seek after
it. Until we realize how much God loves
us and cares about the details of our life,
we probably won't have the desire to pray
to him. Until we sincerely believe that he
has completely forgiven us, we will be
ashamed to face him. If we hold to our
misconceptions about God, this step will
be a formidable chore rather than a joy.

The life of King David should give us
hope. After he had come face to face with
his own sinfulness, he was able to sing,
"What mighty praise, O God, belongs to
you in Zion. We will fulfill our vows to you,
for you answer our prayers, and to you all
people will come. Though our hearts are
filled with sins, you forgive them all. What
joy for those you choose to bring near,
those who live in your holy courts. What
joys await us inside your holy Temple"
(Psalm 65:1-4). God wants us to be like
those who lived and served in his Temple,
walking freely into his presence. He wants
us to know that we are welcome and
valued before him. (See also Matthew
10:29-31.)

God is always present with us and can
be a source of joy and happiness for us
now. We can look forward to spending
time with him and living in his presence
every day. *Turn to page 549, Psalm 105.*

PSALM 66

For the choir director: A psalm. A song.

¹ Shout joyful praises to God, all the earth!
² Sing about the glory of his name!
Tell the world how glorious he is.
³ Say to God, "How awesome are your deeds!
Your enemies cringe before your mighty power.
⁴ Everything on earth will worship you;
they will sing your praises,
shouting your name in glorious songs."
Interlude

⁵ Come and see what our God has done,
what awesome miracles he does for his people!
⁶ He made a dry path through the Red Sea,*
and his people went across on foot.
Come, let us rejoice in who he is.
⁷ For by his great power he rules forever.
He watches every movement of the nations;
let no rebel rise in defiance. *Interlude*

⁸ Let the whole world bless our God
and sing aloud his praises.
⁹ Our lives are in his hands,
and he keeps our feet from stumbling.
¹⁰ You have tested us, O God;
you have purified us like silver melted in a crucible.
¹¹ You captured us in your net
and laid the burden of slavery on our backs.
¹² You sent troops to ride across our broken bodies.
We went through fire and flood.
But you brought us to a place of great abundance.

¹³ Now I come to your Temple with burnt offerings
to fulfill the vows I made to you—
¹⁴ yes, the sacred vows you heard me make
when I was in deep trouble.

¹⁵ That is why I am sacrificing burnt offerings to you—
the best of my rams as a pleasing aroma.
And I will sacrifice bulls and goats.
Interlude

¹⁶ Come and listen, all you who fear God,
and I will tell you what he did for me.
¹⁷ For I cried out to him for help,
praising him as I spoke.
¹⁸ If I had not confessed the sin in my heart,
my Lord would not have listened.
¹⁹ But God did listen!
He paid attention to my prayer.

²⁰ Praise God, who did not ignore my prayer
and did not withdraw his unfailing love from me.

PSALM 67

For the choir director: A psalm, to be accompanied by stringed instruments. A song.

¹ May God be merciful and bless us.
May his face shine with favor upon us.
Interlude
² May your ways be known throughout the earth,
your saving power among people everywhere.
³ May the nations praise you, O God.
Yes, may all the nations praise you.

⁴ How glad the nations will be, singing for joy,
because you govern them with justice
and direct the actions of the whole world. *Interlude*
⁵ May the nations praise you, O God.
Yes, may all the nations praise you.

⁶ Then the earth will yield its harvests,
and God, our God, will richly bless us.
⁷ Yes, God will bless us,
and people all over the world will fear him.

66:6 Hebrew *the sea.*

66:1-7 When God demonstrates his power and his care for us, we need to share what he has done with others. We are not alone in our troubles. Some of our struggling friends face the same problems we do. Seeing us praise God for his deliverance can become a source of hope and inspiration for them as they seek victory over their dependencies.

67:1-7 We are called to share with others the good news of God's powerful deliverance and his plan of salvation for all. This should not be thought of as a chore to avoid. It should be a natural expression of our joy at being delivered from forces too powerful for us to handle alone. Without God's help, we could never resist the tempting call of our addictions. But with his help we can live with freedom and joy. Let us celebrate and spread the news of God's powerful deliverance!

PSALM 68

For the choir director: A psalm of David. A song.

¹Arise, O God, and scatter your
    enemies.
    Let those who hate God run for
    their lives.
²Drive them off like smoke blown by the
    wind.
    Melt them like wax in fire.
    Let the wicked perish in the presence
    of God.
³But let the godly rejoice.
    Let them be glad in God's presence.
    Let them be filled with joy.

⁴Sing praises to God and to his name!
    Sing loud praises to him who rides
    the clouds.
    His name is the LORD—
    rejoice in his presence!

⁵Father to the fatherless, defender of
    widows—
    this is God, whose dwelling is holy.
⁶God places the lonely in families;
    he sets the prisoners free and gives
    them joy.
    But for rebels, there is only famine
    and distress.

⁷O God, when you led your people from
    Egypt,
    when you marched through the
    wilderness,   *Interlude*
⁸the earth trembled, and the heavens
    poured rain
    before you, the God of Sinai,
    before God, the God of Israel.
⁹You sent abundant rain, O God,
    to refresh the weary Promised
    Land.
¹⁰There your people finally settled,
    and with a bountiful harvest, O God,
    you provided for your needy people.

¹¹The Lord announces victory,
    and throngs of women shout the
    happy news.
¹²Enemy kings and their armies flee,
    while the women of Israel divide the
    plunder.

¹³Though they lived among the sheepfolds,
    now they are covered with silver and
    gold,
    as a dove is covered by its wings.
¹⁴The Almighty scattered the enemy kings
    like a blowing snowstorm on Mount
    Zalmon.

¹⁵The majestic mountains of Bashan
    stretch high into the sky.
¹⁶Why do you look with envy, O rugged
    mountains,
    at Mount Zion, where God has chosen
    to live,
    where the LORD himself will live
    forever?

¹⁷Surrounded by unnumbered thousands
    of chariots,
    the Lord came from Mount Sinai into
    his sanctuary.
¹⁸When you ascended to the heights,
    you led a crowd of captives.
    You received gifts from the people,
    even from those who rebelled against
    you.
    Now the LORD God will live among us
    here.

¹⁹Praise the Lord; praise God our savior!
    For each day he carries us in his arms.
                                  Interlude
²⁰Our God is a God who saves!
    The Sovereign LORD rescues us from
    death.

²¹But God will smash the heads of his
    enemies,
    crushing the skulls of those who love
    their guilty ways.
²²The Lord says, "I will bring my enemies
    down from Bashan;
    I will bring them up from the depths
    of the sea.
²³You, my people, will wash your feet in
    their blood,
    and even your dogs will get their share!"

²⁴Your procession has come into view,
    O God—
    the procession of my God and King
    as he goes into the sanctuary.

68:1-6 There is no security for those who act like rebels in opposition to God. When life has beaten us down, God wants us to know we can find a loving family among his people. He himself is like a father to us, a loving deliverer who sets us free from the traps in which we are caught.
68:24-31 When God helps us gain control over our inner enemies, praise should naturally flow from our lips. The best gifts we can bring to God are our life and our praise. As we thank God for delivering us from our dependencies and problems, others will be encouraged to admit their need for God and call out to him for help.

25 Singers are in front, musicians are behind;
　　with them are young women playing
　　　tambourines.
26 Praise God, all you people of Israel;
　　praise the LORD, the source of Israel's
　　　life.
27 Look, the little tribe of Benjamin leads
　　the way.
　Then comes a great throng of rulers
　　from Judah
　and all the rulers of Zebulun and
　　Naphtali.

28 Summon your might, O God.
　　Display your power, O God, as you
　　　have in the past.
29 The kings of the earth are bringing tribute
　　to your Temple in Jerusalem.
30 Rebuke these enemy nations—
　　these wild animals lurking in the reeds,
　　this herd of bulls among the weaker
　　　calves.
　Humble those who demand tribute from
　　us.*
　Scatter the nations that delight in war.
31 Let Egypt come with gifts of precious
　　metals;
　　let Ethiopia* bow in submission to God.
32 Sing to God, you kingdoms of the earth.
　　Sing praises to the Lord.　　　*Interlude*

33 Sing to the one who rides across the
　　ancient heavens,
　　his mighty voice thundering from the
　　　sky.
34 Tell everyone about God's power.
　　His majesty shines down on Israel;
　　his strength is mighty in the heavens.
35 God is awesome in his sanctuary.
　　The God of Israel gives power and
　　　strength to his people.

　Praise be to God!

PSALM 69

For the choir director: A psalm of David, to be sung to the tune "Lilies."

1 Save me, O God,
　　for the floodwaters are up to my neck.
2 Deeper and deeper I sink into the mire;
　　I can't find a foothold to stand on.
　I am in deep water,
　　and the floods overwhelm me.
3 I am exhausted from crying for help;
　　my throat is parched and dry.
　My eyes are swollen with weeping,
　　waiting for my God to help me.

4 Those who hate me without cause
　　are more numerous than the hairs
　　　on my head.
　These enemies who seek to destroy me
　　are doing so without cause.
　They attack me with lies,
　　demanding that I give back what
　　　I didn't steal.

5 O God, you know how foolish I am;
　　my sins cannot be hidden from you.
6 Don't let those who trust in you stumble
　　because of me,
　　O Sovereign LORD Almighty.
　Don't let me cause them to be humiliated,
　　O God of Israel.
7 For I am mocked and shamed for your
　　sake;
　　humiliation is written all over my
　　　face.
8 Even my own brothers pretend they
　　don't know me;
　　they treat me like a stranger.

9 Passion for your house burns within me,
　　so those who insult you are also
　　　insulting me.
10 When I weep and fast before the LORD,
　　they scoff at me.

68:30 Or *Humble them until they submit, bringing pieces of silver as tribute.* **68:31** Hebrew *Cush.*

69:1-4, 13 As he wrote this psalm, David felt as if his problems were drowning him. It seemed that everyone was attacking him and no one was around to take his side. We often feel the same desperation as we work through the process of recovery. In times like these, we should do what David did—cry out to God for help, submit to his will, and entrust our life to his care.
69:5-8 David knew how important it was to recognize his sins and to admit them to God. This is an essential step toward recovery in our own life. We must accept responsibility for what we have done in the past. Then, like David, we should turn to God for forgiveness and restoration.
69:9-12 David's visible repentance and desire to change his life brought him intense ridicule. He became a laughingstock among those who opposed God. Even the town drunks ridiculed him. As we confess our failures and turn our life over to God, we may experience similar scorn. We may deserve some of the ridicule we receive; it may take people awhile to believe that the changes in our life are real. During such trials we should remember that God is more concerned about rebuilding our character than he is about restoring our reputation.

¹¹ When I dress in sackcloth to show sorrow,
  they make fun of me.
¹² I am the favorite topic of town gossip,
  and all the drunkards sing about me.

¹³ But I keep right on praying to you, LORD,
  hoping this is the time you will show
  me favor.
 In your unfailing love, O God,
  answer my prayer with your sure
  salvation.
¹⁴ Pull me out of the mud;
  don't let me sink any deeper!
 Rescue me from those who hate me,
  and pull me from these deep waters.
¹⁵ Don't let the floods overwhelm me,
  or the deep waters swallow me,
  or the pit of death devour me.

¹⁶ Answer my prayers, O LORD,
  for your unfailing love is wonderful.
 Turn and take care of me,
  for your mercy is so plentiful.
¹⁷ Don't hide from your servant;
  answer me quickly, for I am in deep
  trouble!
¹⁸ Come and rescue me;
  free me from all my enemies.

¹⁹ You know the insults I endure—
  the humiliation and disgrace.
 You have seen all my enemies
  and know what they have said.
²⁰ Their insults have broken my heart,
  and I am in despair.
 If only one person would show some pity;
  if only one would turn and comfort me.
²¹ But instead, they give me poison for food;
  they offer me sour wine to satisfy my
  thirst.

²² Let the bountiful table set before them
  become a snare,
  and let their security become a trap.
²³ Let their eyes go blind so they cannot see,
  and let their bodies grow weaker and
  weaker.
²⁴ Pour out your fury on them;
  consume them with your burning
  anger.
²⁵ May their homes become desolate
  and their tents be deserted.

69:35 Hebrew *Zion.*

²⁶ To those you have punished, they add
  insult to injury;
 they scoff at the pain of those you
  have hurt.
²⁷ Pile their sins up high,
  and don't let them go free.
²⁸ Erase their names from the Book of Life;
  don't let them be counted among the
  righteous.

²⁹ I am suffering and in pain.
 Rescue me, O God, by your saving
  power.
³⁰ Then I will praise God's name with
  singing,
 and I will honor him with
  thanksgiving.
³¹ For this will please the LORD more than
  sacrificing an ox
 or presenting a bull with its horns and
  hooves.
³² The humble will see their God at work
  and be glad.
 Let all who seek God's help live in joy.
³³ For the LORD hears the cries of his needy
  ones;
 he does not despise his people who are
  oppressed.

³⁴ Praise him, O heaven and earth,
  the seas and all that move in them.
³⁵ For God will save Jerusalem*
  and rebuild the towns of Judah.
 His people will live there
  and take possession of the land.
³⁶ The descendants of those who obey him
  will inherit the land,
 and those who love him will live there
  in safety.

PSALM 70
*For the choir director: A psalm of David, to bring us
to the LORD's remembrance.*

¹ Please, God, rescue me!
  Come quickly, LORD, and help me.
² May those who try to destroy me
  be humiliated and put to shame.
 May those who take delight in my
  trouble
  be turned back in disgrace.

70:1-5 This prayer by David is short and to the point. He cried out to God for help in the face
of an emergency. It is possible to pray at any time, and it is especially appropriate when faced
with a sudden temptation or dilemma. For many of us, prayer is the last solution we think of
in times of trouble. We try any number of human solutions before looking to God for help. We
would be wise to always pray about everything (see Philippians 4:6).

³ Let them be horrified by their shame,
  for they said, "Aha! We've got him
    now!"
⁴ But may all who search for you
  be filled with joy and gladness.
May those who love your salvation
  repeatedly shout, "God is great!"
⁵ But I am poor and needy;
  please hurry to my aid, O God.
You are my helper and my savior;
  O LORD, do not delay!

PSALM 71

¹ O LORD, you are my refuge;
  never let me be disgraced.
² Rescue me! Save me from my enemies, for
    you are just.
  Turn your ear to listen and set me free.
³ Be to me a protecting rock of safety,
  where I am always welcome.
Give the order to save me,
  for you are my rock and my fortress.

⁴ My God, rescue me from the power of the
    wicked,
  from the clutches of cruel oppressors.
⁵ O Lord, you alone are my hope.
  I've trusted you, O LORD, from
    childhood.
⁶ Yes, you have been with me from birth;
  from my mother's womb you have
    cared for me.
No wonder I am always praising you!

⁷ My life is an example to many,
  because you have been my strength and
    protection.
⁸ That is why I can never stop praising you;
  I declare your glory all day long.

⁹ And now, in my old age, don't set me
    aside.
  Don't abandon me when my strength is
    failing.
¹⁰ For my enemies are whispering against me.
  They are plotting together to kill me.
¹¹ They say, "God has abandoned him.
  Let's go and get him,
  for there is no one to help him now."

¹² O God, don't stay away.
  My God, please hurry to help me.
¹³ Bring disgrace and destruction on those
    who accuse me.
  May humiliation and shame cover
    those who want to harm me.

¹⁴ But I will keep on hoping for you to help
    me;
  I will praise you more and more.
¹⁵ I will tell everyone about your
    righteousness.
  All day long I will proclaim your saving
    power,
  for I am overwhelmed by how much
    you have done for me.
¹⁶ I will praise your mighty deeds,
  O Sovereign LORD.
  I will tell everyone that you alone are
    just and good.

¹⁷ O God, you have taught me from my
    earliest childhood,
  and I have constantly told others about
    the wonderful things you do.
¹⁸ Now that I am old and gray,
  do not abandon me, O God.
Let me proclaim your power to this new
    generation,
  your mighty miracles to all who come
    after me.

¹⁹ Your righteousness, O God, reaches to the
    highest heavens.
  You have done such wonderful things.
  Who can compare with you, O God?
²⁰ You have allowed me to suffer much
    hardship,
  but you will restore me to life again
  and lift me up from the depths of the
    earth.
²¹ You will restore me to even greater honor
  and comfort me once again.

²² Then I will praise you with music on the
    harp,
  because you are faithful to your
    promises, O God.
  I will sing for you with a lyre,
  O Holy One of Israel.

71:1-8 The psalmist often described God as his refuge or protecting rock—a place of safety in times of difficulty and trial. The psalmist gave heartfelt praise for God's protection from birth. His life was an example to many. One way we can show the reality of God's power to others is to praise and thank him for his deliverance. Let us learn from David's praise and pass the same lesson on to the people around us.

71:9-12 We all face difficult times, especially as we undergo the recovery process. As we struggle with our dependency, our strength often drains to its lowest possible level. When we are powerless, we should seek God's watchful care. He has the power we need to overcome even the most devastating problems.

23 I will shout for joy and sing your praises,
   for you have redeemed me.
24 I will tell about your righteous deeds
      all day long,
   for everyone who tried to hurt me
      has been shamed and humiliated.

PSALM 72
A psalm of Solomon.

1 Give justice to the king, O God,
   and righteousness to the king's son.
2 Help him judge your people in the right
      way;
   let the poor always be treated fairly.
3 May the mountains yield prosperity
      for all,
   and may the hills be fruitful,
   because the king does what is right.
4 Help him to defend the poor,
   to rescue the children of the needy,
   and to crush their oppressors.
5 May he live* as long as the sun shines,
   as long as the moon continues in
      the skies.
   Yes, forever!
6 May his reign be as refreshing as the
      springtime rains—
   like the showers that water the earth.
7 May all the godly flourish during his reign.
   May there be abundant prosperity until
      the end of time.

8 May he reign from sea to sea,
   and from the Euphrates River* to the
      ends of the earth.
9 Desert nomads will bow before him;
   his enemies will fall before him in the
      dust.
10 The western kings of Tarshish and the
      islands
   will bring him tribute.
   The eastern kings of Sheba and Seba
   will bring him gifts.
11 All kings will bow before him,
   and all nations will serve him.

12 He will rescue the poor when they cry
      to him;
   he will help the oppressed, who have
      no one to defend them.

13 He feels pity for the weak and the needy,
   and he will rescue them.
14 He will save them from oppression and
      from violence,
   for their lives are precious to him.

15 Long live the king!
   May the gold of Sheba be given
      to him.
   May the people always pray for him
   and bless him all day long.
16 May there be abundant crops throughout
      the land,
   flourishing even on the mountaintops.
   May the fruit trees flourish as they do
      in Lebanon,
   sprouting up like grass in a field.
17 May the king's name endure forever;
   may it continue as long as the sun
      shines.
   May all nations be blessed through him
   and bring him praise.

18 Bless the LORD God, the God of Israel,
   who alone does such wonderful things.
19 Bless his glorious name forever!
   Let the whole earth be filled with his
      glory.
   Amen and amen!

20 (This ends the prayers of David son
      of Jesse.)

BOOK THREE (Psalms 73–89)
PSALM 73
A psalm of Asaph.

1 Truly God is good to Israel,
   to those whose hearts are pure.

2 But as for me, I came so close to the edge
      of the cliff!
   My feet were slipping, and I was almost
      gone.
3 For I envied the proud
   when I saw them prosper despite their
      wickedness.
4 They seem to live such a painless life;
   their bodies are so healthy and strong.
5 They aren't troubled like other people
   or plagued with problems like everyone
      else.

72:5 As in Greek version; Hebrew reads *May they fear you.*   **72:8** Hebrew *the river.*

72:12-14 God acts on behalf of those who have no power to free themselves from their problems. He helps those who are oppressed and have no one to defend them. He has great love and compassion for those who are weak and needy. As we face our addiction, we know what it means to be powerless. Alone, we are helpless to overcome the temptations of our dependency. But with God's help, there is always hope for us. His power can help us overcome any problems we face, and he wants to see us through the hard times to a new life of freedom and joy.

⁶They wear pride like a jeweled necklace,
  and their clothing is woven of cruelty.
⁷These fat cats have everything
  their hearts could ever wish for!
⁸They scoff and speak only evil;
  in their pride they seek to crush others.
⁹They boast against the very heavens,
  and their words strut throughout the
  earth.
¹⁰And so the people are dismayed and
  confused,
  drinking in all their words.
¹¹"Does God realize what is going on?" they
  ask.
  "Is the Most High even aware of what is
  happening?"
¹²Look at these arrogant people—
  enjoying a life of ease while their riches
  multiply.

¹³Was it for nothing that I kept my heart
  pure
  and kept myself from doing wrong?
¹⁴All I get is trouble all day long;
  every morning brings me pain.

¹⁵If I had really spoken this way,
  I would have been a traitor to your
  people.
¹⁶So I tried to understand why the wicked
  prosper.
  But what a difficult task it is!
¹⁷Then one day I went into your sanctuary,
  O God,
  and I thought about the destiny of the
  wicked.
¹⁸Truly, you put them on a slippery path
  and send them sliding over the cliff to
  destruction.
¹⁹In an instant they are destroyed,
  swept away by terrors.
²⁰Their present life is only a dream
  that is gone when they awake.

74:2 Hebrew *Mount Zion.*

When you arise, O Lord,
  you will make them vanish from this life.

²¹Then I realized how bitter I had become,
  how pained I had been by all I had seen.
²²I was so foolish and ignorant—
  I must have seemed like a senseless
  animal to you.
²³Yet I still belong to you;
  you are holding my right hand.
²⁴You will keep on guiding me with your
  counsel,
  leading me to a glorious destiny.
²⁵Whom have I in heaven but you?
  I desire you more than anything on
  earth.
²⁶My health may fail, and my spirit may
  grow weak,
  but God remains the strength of my
  heart;
  he is mine forever.

²⁷But those who desert him will perish,
  for you destroy those who abandon you.
²⁸But as for me, how good it is to be near
  God!
  I have made the Sovereign LORD my
  shelter,
  and I will tell everyone about the
  wonderful things you do.

PSALM 74
A psalm of Asaph.

¹O God, why have you rejected us forever?
  Why is your anger so intense against
  the sheep of your own pasture?
²Remember that we are the people you
  chose in ancient times,
  the tribe you redeemed as your own
  special possession!
  And remember Jerusalem,* your home
  here on earth.

73:13-20 The psalmist had begun to wonder whether following God's program was worth it.
It seemed to him that evil people were happy and prosperous. It didn't seem to make sense. But
then the psalmist came to his senses as he thought about the destiny of the wicked. God's justice
will ultimately be served. We all know that our addiction seemed to work for a while, but with
time, it became destructive. God's plan is the only recovery program leading to wholeness and
eternal life with him. We would be wise to follow his plan no matter how difficult it may seem to
us at present.
73:21-24 The psalmist had begun to think that God was unjust and had a hard time believing
that God was loving and good. In these verses, however, he realized how foolish he had been.
God was waiting to restore his relationship with the doubting psalmist. We need God's help if
we want to succeed in recovery. But if we cannot believe that God is good, we will hardly be able
to entrust him with our life. Like the psalmist, we need to realize that God does love us and that
his plan for us is for the best. If we trust in God and seek to follow his will for us, he will keep on
guiding us with his good counsel.

³Walk through the awful ruins of the city;
  see how the enemy has destroyed your
    sanctuary.
⁴There your enemies shouted their
    victorious battle cries;
  there they set up their battle standards.
⁵They chopped down the entrance
  like woodcutters in a forest.
⁶With axes and picks,
  they smashed the carved paneling.
⁷They set the sanctuary on fire, burning
    it to the ground.
  They utterly defiled the place that bears
    your holy name.
⁸Then they thought, "Let's destroy
    everything!"
  So they burned down all the places
    where God was worshiped.

⁹We see no miraculous signs
  as evidence that you will save us.
 All the prophets are gone;
  no one can tell us when it will end.
¹⁰How long, O God, will you allow our
    enemies to mock you?
  Will you let them dishonor your name
    forever?
¹¹Why do you hold back your strong right
    hand?
  Unleash your powerful fist and deliver
    a deathblow.

¹²You, O God, are my king from ages past,
  bringing salvation to the earth.
¹³You split the sea by your strength
  and smashed the sea monster's heads.
¹⁴You crushed the heads of Leviathan
  and let the desert animals eat him.
¹⁵You caused the springs and streams to
    gush forth,
  and you dried up rivers that never run dry.
¹⁶Both day and night belong to you;
  you made the starlight* and the sun.
¹⁷You set the boundaries of the earth,
  and you make both summer and winter.

74:16 Or *moon;* Hebrew reads *light.*

¹⁸See how these enemies scoff at you, LORD.
  A foolish nation has dishonored your
    name.
¹⁹Don't let these wild beasts destroy your
    doves.
  Don't forget your afflicted people
    forever.

²⁰Remember your covenant promises,
  for the land is full of darkness and
    violence!
²¹Don't let the downtrodden be constantly
    disgraced!
  Instead, let these poor and needy ones
    give praise to your name.

²²Arise, O God, and defend your cause.
  Remember how these fools insult you
    all day long.
²³Don't overlook these things your enemies
    have said.
  Their uproar of rebellion grows ever
    louder.

PSALM 75

*For the choir director: A psalm of Asaph, to be sung
to the tune "Do Not Destroy!" A song.*

¹We thank you, O God!
  We give thanks because you are near.
  People everywhere tell of your mighty
    miracles.

²God says, "At the time I have planned,
  I will bring justice against the wicked.
³When the earth quakes and its people
    live in turmoil,
  I am the one who keeps its foundations
    firm.   *Interlude*

⁴"I warned the proud, 'Stop your
    boasting!'
  I told the wicked, 'Don't raise your
    fists!
⁵Don't lift your fists in defiance at the
    heavens
  or speak with rebellious arrogance.'"

74:12-23 God has proven himself over and over as a God who is able to deliver us. He has shown his power by his control over our enemies, over ferocious animals, and over nature itself. We therefore can call on him and be confident that he is able to overcome all the problems we face. He will be faithful to his Word, watching over us even as we walk through the darkest valleys in this life.

75:1-5 Once we turn our life and will over to God, we begin to see evidence of his care for us. But pride is a powerful enemy. It keeps us from turning to God or others to get help and perpetuates our tendency for denial. God shows the wrath of his judgment against the proud and boastful, who consider themselves self-sufficient. We were never created to stand alone and make our own way in life. God created us to fit into his plan for the created universe. God's program for righteous and healthy living has been given for our benefit and joy.

⁶For no one on earth—from east or west,
  or even from the wilderness—
  can raise another person up.
⁷It is God alone who judges;
  he decides who will rise and who will
    fall.
⁸For the LORD holds a cup in his hand;
  it is full of foaming wine mixed with
    spices.
 He pours the wine out in judgment,
  and all the wicked must drink it,
    draining it to the dregs.

⁹But as for me, I will always proclaim what
  God has done;
  I will sing praises to the God of Israel.*

¹⁰For God says, "I will cut off the strength
  of the wicked,
  but I will increase the power of the godly."

PSALM 76

*For the choir director: A psalm of Asaph, to be
accompanied by stringed instruments. A song.*

¹God is well known in Judah;
  his name is great in Israel.
²Jerusalem* is where he lives;
  Mount Zion is his home.
³There he breaks the arrows of the enemy,
  the shields and swords and weapons
    of his foes.   *Interlude*

⁴You are glorious and more majestic
  than the everlasting mountains.*
⁵The mightiest of our enemies have been
  plundered.
  They lie before us in the sleep of death.
  No warrior could lift a hand against us.
⁶When you rebuked them, O God of Jacob,
  their horses and chariots stood still.

⁷No wonder you are greatly feared!
  Who can stand before you when
    your anger explodes?
⁸From heaven you sentenced your
    enemies;
  the earth trembled and stood silent
    before you.
⁹You stand up to judge those who do evil,
  O God,
  and to rescue the oppressed of the
    earth.   *Interlude*

¹⁰Human opposition only enhances your
  glory,
  for you use it as a sword of judgment.*

¹¹Make vows to the LORD your God, and
  fulfill them.
  Let everyone bring tribute to the
    Awesome One.
¹²For he breaks the spirit of princes
  and is feared by the kings of the
    earth.

PSALM 77

For Jeduthun, the choir director: A psalm of Asaph.

¹I cry out to God without holding back.
  Oh, that God would listen to me!
²When I was in deep trouble,
  I searched for the Lord.
 All night long I pray, with hands lifted
    toward heaven, pleading.
  There can be no joy for me until he
    acts.
³I think of God, and I moan,
  overwhelmed with longing for his
    help.   *Interlude*

⁴You don't let me sleep.
  I am too distressed even to pray!

75:9 Hebrew *of Jacob.* 76:2 Hebrew *Salem,* another name for Jerusalem. 76:4 As in Greek version; Hebrew reads
than mountains filled with beasts of prey. 76:10 The meaning of the Hebrew is uncertain.

75:6-10 Our desire to be greater than others is another great enemy of our soul. The psalmist understood that it was God who elevates one person and demotes another. We must leave issues of promotion in God's hands. His promise to punish the wicked is given first to cause them to turn away from their evil ways and also to assure those who suffer at the hands of wicked people that God hasn't forgotten them.

76:11-12 As we think about the people we have harmed and make plans for reconciliation, we need to follow through on our plans. We often make promises to act but then fail to do so. If we expect to reconcile our relationships, we need to follow through on our promises. The same principle holds true with God. If we make a promise to him, refusing to follow through will only lead to further pain and separation from him. God expects us to fulfill our vows. All relationships are based on trust. Unless we learn to be trustworthy, our relationships will be shaky, and our efforts in recovery are doomed to failure.

77:1-4 As he wrote these verses, the psalmist became so distressed that he couldn't even pray! The same thing often happens to us. When we are discouraged, we need to be more persistent in our prayers. God is the only one who can really help us. When our life is out of control, God is able to help us slow down and put the pieces back together again.

5 I think of the good old days, long since
    ended,
6   when my nights were filled with joyful
      songs.
    I search my soul and think about the
      difference now.
7 Has the Lord rejected me forever?
    Will he never again show me favor?
8 Is his unfailing love gone forever?
    Have his promises permanently failed?
9 Has God forgotten to be kind?
    Has he slammed the door on his
      compassion?   *Interlude*

10 And I said, "This is my fate,
    that the blessings of the Most High
      have changed to hatred."
11 I recall all you have done, O LORD;
    I remember your wonderful deeds
      of long ago.
12 They are constantly in my thoughts.
    I cannot stop thinking about them.

13 O God, your ways are holy.
    Is there any god as mighty as you?
14 You are the God of miracles and wonders!
    You demonstrate your awesome power
      among the nations.
15 You have redeemed your people by your
      strength,
    the descendants of Jacob and of Joseph
      by your might.   *Interlude*

16 When the Red Sea* saw you, O God,
    its waters looked and trembled!
    The sea quaked to its very depths.
17 The clouds poured down their rain;
    the thunder rolled and crackled in the
      sky.
    Your arrows of lightning flashed.
18 Your thunder roared from the whirlwind;
    the lightning lit up the world!
    The earth trembled and shook.
19 Your road led through the sea,
    your pathway through the mighty
      waters—
    a pathway no one knew was there!
20 You led your people along that road like
      a flock of sheep,
    with Moses and Aaron as their
      shepherds.

77:16 Hebrew *the waters.*

PSALM 78
A psalm of Asaph.

1 O my people, listen to my teaching.
    Open your ears to what I am saying,
2   for I will speak to you in a parable.
    I will teach you hidden lessons from our
      past—
3   stories we have heard and know,
    stories our ancestors handed down to us.
4 We will not hide these truths from our
      children
    but will tell the next generation about
      the glorious deeds of the LORD.
    We will tell of his power and the
      mighty miracles he did.
5 For he issued his decree to Jacob;
    he gave his law to Israel.
  He commanded our ancestors
    to teach them to their children,
6 so the next generation might know
      them—
    even the children not yet born—
    that they in turn might teach their
      children.
7 So each generation can set its hope anew
      on God,
    remembering his glorious miracles
    and obeying his commands.
8 Then they will not be like their
      ancestors—
    stubborn, rebellious, and unfaithful,
    refusing to give their hearts to God.

9 The warriors of Ephraim, though fully
      armed,
    turned their backs and fled when the
      day of battle came.
10 They did not keep God's covenant,
    and they refused to live by his law.
11 They forgot what he had done—
    the wonderful miracles he had shown
      them,
12   the miracles he did for their ancestors
      in Egypt, on the plain of Zoan.
13 For he divided the sea before them and
      led them through!
    The water stood up like walls beside
      them!
14 In the daytime he led them by a cloud,
    and at night by a pillar of fire.

78:9-12 God's people, although well equipped to defeat their enemies in the Promised Land, failed to carry out God's commands. When they should have boldly pressed forward, they ran from the conflict like cowards. This failure was undoubtedly prompted by the fact that they forgot God's past acts of power on behalf of his people. When we fail to believe in God's power, because of either unbelief or pride, we are bound to fail.

15 He split open the rocks in the wilderness
   to give them plenty of water, as from
   a gushing spring.
16 He made streams pour from the rock,
   making the waters flow down like a
   river!

17 Yet they kept on with their sin,
   rebelling against the Most High in the
   desert.
18 They willfully tested God in their hearts,
   demanding the foods they craved.
19 They even spoke against God himself,
   saying,
   "God can't give us food in the desert.
20 Yes, he can strike a rock so water gushes
   out,
   but he can't give his people bread and
   meat."
21 When the LORD heard them, he was
   angry.
   The fire of his wrath burned against
   Jacob.
   Yes, his anger rose against Israel,
22   for they did not believe God
   or trust him to care for them.
23 But he commanded the skies to open—
   he opened the doors of heaven—
24   and rained down manna for them to
   eat.
   He gave them bread from heaven.
25   They ate the food of angels!
   God gave them all they could hold.
26 He released the east wind in the heavens
   and guided the south wind by his
   mighty power.
27 He rained down meat as thick as dust—
   birds as plentiful as the sands along the
   seashore!
28 He caused the birds to fall within their
   camp
   and all around their tents.
29 The people ate their fill.
   He gave them what they wanted.
30 But before they finished eating this food
   they had craved,
   while the meat was yet in their mouths,

31 the anger of God rose against them,
   and he killed their strongest men;
   he struck down the finest of Israel's
   young men.
32 But in spite of this, the people kept on
   sinning.
   They refused to believe in his miracles.
33 So he ended their lives in failure
   and gave them years of terror.

34 When God killed some of them, the rest
   finally sought him.
   They repented and turned to God.
35 Then they remembered that God was
   their rock,
   that their redeemer was the Most High.
36 But they followed him only with their
   words;
   they lied to him with their tongues.
37 Their hearts were not loyal to him.
   They did not keep his covenant.
38 Yet he was merciful and forgave their sins
   and didn't destroy them all.
   Many a time he held back his anger
   and did not unleash his fury!
39 For he remembered that they were merely
   mortal,
   gone in a moment like a breath of
   wind, never to return.

40 Oh, how often they rebelled against him
   in the desert
   and grieved his heart in the wilderness.
41 Again and again they tested God's
   patience
   and frustrated the Holy One of Israel.
42 They forgot about his power
   and how he rescued them from their
   enemies.
43 They forgot his miraculous signs in Egypt,
   his wonders on the plain of Zoan.
44 For he turned their rivers into blood,
   so no one could drink from the streams.
45 He sent vast swarms of flies to consume
   them
   and hordes of frogs to ruin them.
46 He gave their crops to caterpillars;
   their harvest was consumed by locusts.

78:17-33 God's anger against his rebellious people increased because they continually complained and refused to trust him to deliver them from their wilderness experience. We should pray that this won't happen to us. In spite of our unbelief, God is still merciful to us, giving us benefits we don't deserve (Exodus 16:4-5; Numbers 11:31). The people had all they could ever want, but because they still rebelled against him, God sent a plague that terrified them and cut down many of them in the prime of their lives (Numbers 11:32-33). Rebellion will cause our life to end in failure, too.
78:34-39 God knows that we are human, with all the imperfections and frailties of mortal beings. He is compassionate toward us, forgiving our sins and often turning away his judgment as he did to his people in the wilderness. His goodness should encourage us and make us more willing to commit our life to him.

47 He destroyed their grapevines with hail
and shattered their sycamores with
sleet.
48 He abandoned their cattle to the hail,
their livestock to bolts of lightning.
49 He loosed on them his fierce anger—
all his fury, rage, and hostility.
He dispatched against them
a band of destroying angels.
50 He turned his anger against them;
he did not spare the Egyptians' lives
but handed them over to the plague.
51 He killed the oldest son in each Egyptian
family,
the flower of youth throughout the
land of Egypt.*
52 But he led his own people like a flock
of sheep,
guiding them safely through the
wilderness.
53 He kept them safe so they were not afraid;
but the sea closed in upon their
enemies.
54 He brought them to the border of his holy
land,
to this land of hills he had won for them.
55 He drove out the nations before them;
he gave them their inheritance by lot.
He settled the tribes of Israel into their
homes.

56 Yet though he did all this for them,
they continued to test his patience.
They rebelled against the Most High
and refused to follow his decrees.
57 They turned back and were as faithless as
their parents had been.
They were as useless as a crooked bow.
58 They made God angry by building altars
to other gods;
they made him jealous with their idols.
59 When God heard them, he was very
angry,
and he rejected Israel completely.
60 Then he abandoned his dwelling at Shiloh,
the Tabernacle where he had lived
among the people.
61 He allowed the Ark of his might to be
captured;
he surrendered his glory into enemy
hands.

78:51 Hebrew *in the tents of Ham.*

62 He gave his people over to be butchered
by the sword,
because he was so angry with his own
people—his special possession.
63 Their young men were killed by fire;
their young women died before
singing their wedding songs.
64 Their priests were slaughtered,
and their widows could not mourn
their deaths.
65 Then the Lord rose up as though waking
from sleep,
like a mighty man aroused from a
drunken stupor.
66 He routed his enemies
and sent them to eternal shame.*
67 But he rejected Joseph's descendants;
he did not choose the tribe of Ephraim.
68 He chose instead the tribe of Judah,
Mount Zion, which he loved.
69 There he built his towering sanctuary,
as solid and enduring as the earth
itself.
70 He chose his servant David,
calling him from the sheep pens.
71 He took David from tending the ewes
and lambs
and made him the shepherd of Jacob's
descendants—
God's own people, Israel.
72 He cared for them with a true heart
and led them with skillful hands.

PSALM 79
A psalm of Asaph.

1 O God, pagan nations have conquered
your land, your special possession.
They have defiled your holy Temple
and made Jerusalem a heap of ruins.
2 They have left the bodies of your servants
as food for the birds of heaven.
The flesh of your godly ones
has become food for the wild animals.
3 Blood has flowed like water all around
Jerusalem;
no one is left to bury the dead.
4 We are mocked by our neighbors,
an object of scorn and derision to those
around us.

78:59-64 Sin has devastating consequences. God loves us, but our persistent disobedience
sometimes causes him to turn away from us and allow our enemies to defeat us. If we are wise,
we will understand what has happened, admit our sins and failures, and commit our life again
to God's care and control.

⁵O LORD, how long will you be angry with
us? Forever?
How long will your jealousy burn like
fire?
⁶Pour out your wrath on the nations that
refuse to recognize you—
on kingdoms that do not call upon
your name.
⁷For they have devoured your people Israel,*
making the land a desolate wilderness.
⁸Oh, do not hold us guilty for our former
sins!
Let your tenderhearted mercies quickly
meet our needs,
for we are brought low to the dust.
⁹Help us, O God of our salvation!
Help us for the honor of your name.
Oh, save us and forgive our sins
for the sake of your name.
¹⁰Why should pagan nations be allowed
to scoff,
asking, "Where is their God?"
Show us your vengeance against the
nations,
for they have spilled the blood of your
servants.
¹¹Listen to the moaning of the prisoners.
Demonstrate your great power by
saving those condemned to die.

¹²O Lord, take sevenfold vengeance on our
neighbors
for the scorn they have hurled at you.
¹³Then we your people, the sheep of your
pasture,
will thank you forever and ever,
praising your greatness from generation
to generation.

PSALM 80

*For the choir director: A psalm of Asaph, to be sung
to the tune "Lilies of the Covenant."*

¹Please listen, O Shepherd of Israel,
you who lead Israel* like a flock.

O God, enthroned above the cherubim,
display your radiant glory
² to Ephraim, Benjamin, and Manasseh.
Show us your mighty power.
Come to rescue us!

³Turn us again to yourself, O God.
Make your face shine down upon us.
Only then will we be saved.

⁴O LORD God Almighty,
how long will you be angry and reject
our prayers?
⁵You have fed us with sorrow
and made us drink tears by the
bucketful.
⁶You have made us the scorn of
neighboring nations.
Our enemies treat us as a joke.

⁷Turn us again to yourself, O God
Almighty.
Make your face shine down upon us.
Only then will we be saved.
⁸You brought us from Egypt as though
we were a tender vine;
you drove away the pagan nations
and transplanted us into your
land.
⁹You cleared the ground for us,
and we took root and filled the land.
¹⁰The mountains were covered with our
shade;
the mighty cedars were covered with
our branches.
¹¹We spread our branches west to the
Mediterranean Sea,
our limbs east to the Euphrates
River.*
¹²But now, why have you broken down
our walls
so that all who pass may steal our
fruit?
¹³The boar from the forest devours us,
and the wild animals feed on us.

79:7 Hebrew *Jacob.* **80:1** Hebrew *Joseph.* **80:11** Hebrew *west to the sea, . . . east to the river.*

79:5-13 As we face hard times, we need to be open to the possibility that God may be allowing
our difficulties so we will turn from sin. If that is true, we need to plead for God's mercy and
forgiveness so we can be restored to wholeness. God delivers us from the controlling influences of
our life not merely to give us freedom but also to bring him honor and to have others recognize
his greatness. It is our responsibility to spread the good news of God's deliverance.

80:9-13 God does marvelous works for us. He frees us from bondage, removes barriers from our
life, and firmly establishes us, doing all he can to help us grow and prosper spiritually. When we
begin to act as if we don't need God, he may cut us back down to size and allow our
enemies—internal or external—to take advantage of us. Recovery is a lifelong process. Our relationship with God should also last a lifetime. We need to realize that without God's help, we are
in danger of falling, even when we seem to be doing well. Our progress in recovery and our relationship with God need our constant attention.

14 Come back, we beg you, O God Almighty.
　Look down from heaven and see our
　　plight.
Watch over and care for this vine
15 　that you yourself have planted,
　this son you have raised for yourself.
16 For we are chopped up and burned by our
　　enemies.
　May they perish at the sight of your frown.
17 Strengthen the man you love,
　the son of your choice.
18 Then we will never forsake you again.
　Revive us so we can call on your name
　　once more.

19 Turn us again to yourself, O LORD God
　　Almighty.
　Make your face shine down upon us.
　Only then will we be saved.

PSALM 81

*For the choir director: A psalm of Asaph, to be
accompanied by a stringed instrument.*　*

1 Sing praises to God, our strength.
　Sing to the God of Israel.*
2 Sing! Beat the tambourine.
　Play the sweet lyre and the harp.
3 Sound the trumpet for a sacred feast
　when the moon is new,
　when the moon is full.
4 For this is required by the laws of Israel;
　it is a law of the God of Jacob.
5 He made it a decree for Israel*
　when he attacked Egypt to set us free.

I heard an unknown voice that said,
6 "Now I will relieve your shoulder of its
　　burden;
　I will free your hands from their heavy
　　tasks.
7 You cried to me in trouble, and I saved you;
　I answered out of the thundercloud.

I tested your faith at Meribah,
　when you complained that there was
　　no water.　　　　　　　*Interlude*

8 "Listen to me, O my people, while I give
　you stern warnings.
　O Israel, if you would only listen!
9 You must never have a foreign god;
　you must not bow down before a false
　　god.
10 For it was I, the LORD your God,
　who rescued you from the land of
　　Egypt.
　Open your mouth wide, and I will fill
　it with good things.

11 "But no, my people wouldn't listen.
　Israel did not want me around.
12 So I let them follow their blind and
　　stubborn way,
　living according to their own desires.
13 But oh, that my people would listen
　　to me!
　Oh, that Israel would follow me,
　walking in my paths!
14 How quickly I would then subdue their
　　enemies!
　How soon my hands would be upon
　　their foes!
15 Those who hate the LORD would cringe
　　before him;
　their desolation would last forever.
16 But I would feed you with the best
　of foods.
　I would satisfy you with wild honey
　　from the rock."

PSALM 82

A psalm of Asaph.

1 God presides over heaven's court;
　he pronounces judgment on the judges:

81:TITLE Hebrew *according to the gittith.*　**81:1** Hebrew *of Jacob.*　**81:5** Hebrew *for Joseph.*

80:14-19 When we are beaten down, we must plead for God's mercy and his restorative work in our life. Even though we feel overwhelmed by our suffering, we should remember that God can end all that caused us so much pain. As he strengthens and restores us to wholeness, he wants us to share the good news about deliverance with others. As we share the message of God's deliverance, others will begin to hope in God's power, and we will be strengthened as well by the hope we bring to others. **81:6-10** With great power, God takes the burdens away from his people and delivers them when they cry out to him. God warns us over and over not to allow any person or thing to take his place in our life. Trusting any resource or power other than God is foolishness. He is far more powerful than any other possible means of deliverance. Only he can satisfy our deepest needs; all we need to do is look to him for help. **82:1-4** God executes judgment among his people and holds accountable particularly those who deal unfairly with the helpless and the destitute. Many will have to answer for things they have done that caused others to stumble and become addicted to a harmful, controlling influence. If we have led others astray, part of making amends may be to help them face their problems and to share the good news of God's deliverance with them.

2 "How long will you judges hand down
  unjust decisions?
  How long will you shower special favors
  on the wicked?   *Interlude*

3 "Give fair judgment to the poor and the
  orphan;
  uphold the rights of the oppressed and
  the destitute.
4 Rescue the poor and helpless;
  deliver them from the grasp of evil
  people.
5 But these oppressors know nothing;
  they are so ignorant!
And because they are in darkness,
  the whole world is shaken to the core.
6 I say, 'You are gods
  and children of the Most High.
7 But in death you are mere men.
  You will fall as any prince,
  for all must die.'"

8 Rise up, O God, and judge the earth,
  for all the nations belong to you.

PSALM 83

A psalm of Asaph. A song.

1 O God, don't sit idly by,
  silent and inactive!
2 Don't you hear the tumult of your enemies?
  Don't you see what your arrogant
  enemies are doing?
3 They devise crafty schemes against your
  people,
  laying plans against your precious ones.
4 "Come," they say, "let us wipe out Israel
  as a nation.
  We will destroy the very memory of its
  existence."
5   This was their unanimous decision.
  They signed a treaty as allies against you—
6   these Edomites and Ishmaelites,
  Moabites and Hagrites,

7   Gebalites, Ammonites, and Amalekites,
  and people from Philistia and Tyre.
8 Assyria has joined them, too,
  and is allied with the descendants
  of Lot.   *Interlude*

9 Do to them as you did to the Midianites
  or as you did to Sisera and Jabin at the
  Kishon River.
10 They were destroyed at Endor,
  and their decaying corpses fertilized
  the soil.
11 Let their mighty nobles die as Oreb and
  Zeeb did.
  Let all their princes die like Zebah and
  Zalmunna,
12 for they said, "Let us seize for our own use
  these pasturelands of God!"

13 O my God, blow them away like whirling
  dust,
  like chaff before the wind!
14 As a fire roars through a forest
  and as a flame sets mountains ablaze,
15 chase them with your fierce storms;
  terrify them with your tempests.
16 Utterly disgrace them
  until they submit to your name,
  O LORD.
17 Let them be ashamed and terrified forever.
  Make them failures in everything
  they do,
18 until they learn that you alone are called
  the LORD,
  that you alone are the Most High,
  supreme over all the earth.

PSALM 84

*For the choir director: A psalm of the descendants
of Korah, to be accompanied by a stringed
instrument.**

1 How lovely is your dwelling place,
  O LORD Almighty.

84:TITLE Hebrew *according to the gittith.*

83:1-8 Encountering problems in our life should motivate us to call out to God for help. All
the forces of evil seem to conspire against us as we face temptation. God doesn't want us to fail;
he is there to help us. But we need to become aware of the things that weaken and defeat us.
By avoiding them, we will find temptation easier to deal with. God's program for healthy living
is designed for this very thing—to lead us away from temptation.
83:13-18 Nothing can stand against God. He created everything that exists, and he alone is
sovereign over all the world. When we are trying to live for him, our enemies are his enemies,
and we can count on him to deal with them in our behalf.
84:1-4 Beauty is found wherever the all-powerful God resides. Although God rules with great
power, he also cares for the seemingly insignificant things of the world—even sparrows and swallows. True blessing and joy come to us when we choose to live in his presence. As we entrust our
life to God and do our best to follow his will for us, we will discover the blessings of living in the
presence of our righteous and loving God.

²I long, yes, I faint with longing
  to enter the courts of the LORD.
With my whole being, body and soul,
  I will shout joyfully to the living God.
³Even the sparrow finds a home there,
  and the swallow builds her nest
  and raises her young—
  at a place near your altar,
  O LORD Almighty, my King and my God!
⁴How happy are those who can live in your
    house,
  always singing your praises.   *Interlude*

⁵Happy are those who are strong in the
    LORD,
  who set their minds on a pilgrimage
    to Jerusalem.
⁶When they walk through the Valley
    of Weeping,*
  it will become a place of refreshing
    springs,
  where pools of blessing collect after
    the rains!
⁷They will continue to grow stronger,
  and each of them will appear before
    God in Jerusalem.*

⁸O LORD God Almighty, hear my prayer.
  Listen, O God of Israel.*   *Interlude*

⁹O God, look with favor upon the king,
    our protector!
  Have mercy on the one you have
    anointed.

¹⁰A single day in your courts
  is better than a thousand anywhere else!
I would rather be a gatekeeper in the
    house of my God
  than live the good life in the homes
    of the wicked.
¹¹For the LORD God is our light and
    protector.
  He gives us grace and glory.
No good thing will the LORD withhold
  from those who do what is right.
¹²O LORD Almighty,
  happy are those who trust in you.

PSALM 85

For the choir director: A psalm of the descendants of Korah.

¹LORD, you have poured out amazing
    blessings on your land!
  You have restored the fortunes of
    Israel.*
²You have forgiven the guilt of your
    people—
  yes, you have covered all their sins.

                                    Interlude

³You have withdrawn your fury.
  You have ended your blazing anger.
⁴Now turn to us again, O God of our
    salvation.
  Put aside your anger against us.
⁵Will you be angry with us always?
  Will you prolong your wrath to distant
    generations?
⁶Won't you revive us again,
  so your people can rejoice in you?
⁷Show us your unfailing love, O LORD,
  and grant us your salvation.

⁸I listen carefully to what God the LORD
    is saying,
  for he speaks peace to his people, his
    faithful ones.
  But let them not return to their foolish
    ways.
⁹Surely his salvation is near to those who
    honor him;
  our land will be filled with his glory.

¹⁰Unfailing love and truth have met
    together.
  Righteousness and peace have kissed!
¹¹Truth springs up from the earth,
  and righteousness smiles down from
    heaven.
¹²Yes, the LORD pours down his blessings.
  Our land will yield its bountiful
    crops.
¹³Righteousness goes as a herald before
    him,
  preparing the way for his steps.

84:6 Hebrew *valley of Baca.* **84:7** Hebrew *Zion.* **84:8** Hebrew *of Jacob.* **85:1** Hebrew *of Jacob.*

84:8-12 A single day in the presence of God is far better than a thousand lifetimes apart from him. The security, peace, and love that God offers are greater than anything we could receive from people. When we find that the initial pleasures of our addiction have faded and the promises of our dependency haven't come true, we can turn to God, and he will fill our soul with true happiness.
85:1-3 It is hard enough to deal with the sins that have us entrapped; how much worse we make it by having to live with a bad conscience. Great relief comes when God helps us regain control and we realize that he has forgiven our sins. All we need to do is confess our sins to God and accept the forgiveness he offers.

PSALM 86

A prayer of David.

¹Bend down, O LORD, and hear my prayer;
  answer me, for I need your help.
²Protect me, for I am devoted to you.
  Save me, for I serve you and trust you.
  You are my God.
³Be merciful, O Lord,
  for I am calling on you constantly.
⁴Give me happiness, O Lord,
  for my life depends on you.
⁵O Lord, you are so good, so ready to
    forgive,
  so full of unfailing love for all who ask
    your aid.
⁶Listen closely to my prayer, O LORD;
  hear my urgent cry.
⁷I will call to you whenever trouble strikes,
  and you will answer me.

⁸Nowhere among the pagan gods is there
    a god like you, O Lord.
  There are no other miracles like yours.
⁹All the nations—and you made each
    one—
  will come and bow before you, Lord;
  they will praise your great and holy
    name.
¹⁰For you are great and perform great
    miracles.
  You alone are God.

¹¹Teach me your ways, O LORD,
  that I may live according to your truth!
  Grant me purity of heart,
  that I may honor you.
¹²With all my heart I will praise you, O Lord
    my God.
  I will give glory to your name forever,

¹³for your love for me is very great.
  You have rescued me from the depths
    of death*!

¹⁴O God, insolent people rise up against me;
  violent people are trying to kill me.
  And you mean nothing to them.
¹⁵But you, O Lord, are a merciful and
    gracious God,
  slow to get angry,
  full of unfailing love and truth.
¹⁶Look down and have mercy on me.
  Give strength to your servant;
  yes, save me, for I am your servant.
¹⁷Send me a sign of your favor.
  Then those who hate me will be put
    to shame,
  for you, O LORD, help and comfort me.

PSALM 87

A psalm of the descendants of Korah. A song.

¹On the holy mountain stands the city
    founded by the LORD.
² He loves the city of Jerusalem
    more than any other city in Israel.*
³O city of God,
    what glorious things are said of you!
                                    Interlude

⁴I will record Egypt* and Babylon among
    those who know me—
  also Philistia and Tyre, and even distant
    Ethiopia.*
  They have all become citizens of
    Jerusalem!
⁵And it will be said of Jerusalem,*
  "Everyone has become a citizen here."
  And the Most High will personally bless
    this city.

86:13 Hebrew *of Sheol.* **87:2** Hebrew *He loves the gates of Zion more than all the dwellings of Jacob.* **87:4a** Hebrew *Rahab,* the name of a mythical sea monster that represents chaos in ancient literature. The name is used here as a poetic name for Egypt. **87:4b** Hebrew *Cush.* **87:5** Hebrew *Zion.*

86:1-5 Even though we may be trying to serve and trust God, we still may be bound by addictions and problems from which we need deliverance. Sometimes the answers don't come quickly, and though we pray constantly, nothing seems to happen. We may become impatient and begin to wonder if God will ever act. God will ultimately respond with forgiveness and compassion to all who call upon him. Sometimes, though, we may have to wait awhile before we experience changes in our life.
86:11-17 We only know God's will as we seek to know him through prayer and the study of his Word. The more we know about God, the more we know what he expects of us. As we get to know God better, we will discover that he gives us not only direction but also the strength and encouragement we need to walk the pathway he has chosen for us.
87:1-7 Because of God's kindness, we all can be citizens of Jerusalem, the city for which God had special love and concern. In the Old Testament, Jerusalem was known as God's dwelling place on earth and the seat of his rule. Since the coming of Jesus Christ, God comes to dwell in our heart. He loves us and longs to direct our decisions and actions through his Holy Spirit. It is a privilege to be called God's beloved and to be considered citizens of his Kingdom. It means he cares for us and wants us to enjoy living in his presence.

⁶When the LORD registers the nations,
   he will say, "This one has become a
      citizen of Jerusalem."   *Interlude*

⁷At all the festivals, the people will sing,
   "The source of my life is in Jerusalem!"

PSALM 88

*For the choir director: A psalm of the descendants
of Korah, to be sung to the tune "The Suffering of
Affliction." A psalm of Heman the Ezrahite. A song.*

¹O LORD, God of my salvation,
   I have cried out to you day and night.
²Now hear my prayer;
   listen to my cry.
³For my life is full of troubles,
   and death draws near.
⁴I have been dismissed as one who is dead,
   like a strong man with no strength left.
⁵They have abandoned me to death,
   and I am as good as dead.
 I am forgotten,
   cut off from your care.
⁶You have thrust me down to the
      lowest pit,
   into the darkest depths.
⁷Your anger lies heavy on me;
   wave after wave engulfs me.   *Interlude*

⁸You have caused my friends to loathe me;
   you have sent them all away.
 I am in a trap with no way of escape.
⁹   My eyes are blinded by my tears.
 Each day I beg for your help, O LORD;
   I lift my pleading hands to you for
      mercy.
¹⁰Of what use to the dead are your
      miracles?
   Do the dead get up and praise you?
                                 Interlude

¹¹Can those in the grave declare your
      unfailing love?
   In the place of destruction, can they
      proclaim your faithfulness?
¹²Can the darkness speak of your miracles?
   Can anyone in the land of forgetfulness
      talk about your righteousness?

¹³O LORD, I cry out to you.
   I will keep on pleading day by day.
¹⁴O LORD, why do you reject me?
   Why do you turn your face away from me?
¹⁵I have been sickly and close to death since
      my youth.
   I stand helpless and desperate before
      your terrors.
¹⁶Your fierce anger has overwhelmed me.
   Your terrors have cut me off.
¹⁷They swirl around me like floodwaters all
      day long.
   They have encircled me completely.
¹⁸You have taken away my companions and
      loved ones;
   only darkness remains.

PSALM 89

A psalm of Ethan the Ezrahite.

¹I will sing of the tender mercies of the
      LORD forever!
   Young and old will hear of your
      faithfulness.
²Your unfailing love will last forever.
   Your faithfulness is as enduring as the
      heavens.

³The LORD said, "I have made a solemn
      agreement with David, my chosen
      servant.
   I have sworn this oath to him:
⁴'I will establish your descendants as kings
      forever;
   they will sit on your throne from now
      until eternity.'"   *Interlude*

⁵All heaven will praise your miracles, LORD;
   myriads of angels will praise you for
      your faithfulness.
⁶For who in all of heaven can compare
      with the LORD?
   What mightiest angel is anything like
      the LORD?
⁷The highest angelic powers stand in awe
      of God.
   He is far more awesome than those who
      surround his throne.

88:1-5 All of us who have struggled with an addiction know what it means to feel hopeless and overwhelmed by troubles. It is comforting to know that God listens to our cries. We are privileged to have the Bible, which tells us about God and his power to help us when we call out to him. No situation is hopeless for those who call out to God. When we feel helpless and abandoned, we need to look to God and hope in his deliverance.

88:6-12 In these verses, the psalmist felt that God's anger was heavily upon him. It is important to remember that God allows us to stumble and fall, giving us opportunities to learn personally about the consequences of sin. But we should also remember that God does not cause us to fall. Natural consequences should be expected when we sin. If we are suffering because of our sins and failures, we should use the opportunity to learn from the past and turn to God.

8 O LORD God Almighty!
   Where is there anyone as mighty as
      you, LORD?
   Faithfulness is your very character.

9 You are the one who rules the oceans.
   When their waves rise in fearful
      storms, you subdue them.
10 You are the one who crushed the great
      sea monster.*
   You scattered your enemies with your
      mighty arm.
11 The heavens are yours, and the earth is
      yours;
   everything in the world is yours—you
      created it all.
12 You created north and south.
   Mount Tabor and Mount Hermon
      praise your name.
13 Powerful is your arm!
   Strong is your hand!
   Your right hand is lifted high in
      glorious strength.
14 Your throne is founded on two strong
      pillars—righteousness and justice.
   Unfailing love and truth walk before
      you as attendants.
15 Happy are those who hear the joyful call
      to worship,
   for they will walk in the light of your
      presence, LORD.
16 They rejoice all day long in your
      wonderful reputation.
   They exult in your righteousness.
17 You are their glorious strength.
   Our power is based on your favor.
18 Yes, our protection comes from the
      LORD,
   and he, the Holy One of Israel, has
      given us our king.

19 You once spoke in a vision to your
      prophet and said,
   "I have given help to a warrior.
   I have selected him from the common
      people to be king.

20 I have found my servant David.
   I have anointed him with my holy oil.
21 I will steady him,
   and I will make him strong.
22 His enemies will not get the best of him,
   nor will the wicked overpower him.
23 I will beat down his adversaries before him
   and destroy those who hate him.
24 My faithfulness and unfailing love will be
      with him,
   and he will rise to power because of me.
25 I will extend his rule from the
      Mediterranean Sea in the west
   to the Tigris and Euphrates rivers in the
      east.*
26 And he will say to me, 'You are my Father,
   my God, and the Rock of my salvation.'
27 I will make him my firstborn son,
   the mightiest king on earth.
28 I will love him and be kind to him
      forever;
   my covenant with him will never end.
29 I will preserve an heir for him;
   his throne will be as endless as the
      days of heaven.
30 But if his sons forsake my law
   and fail to walk in my ways,
31 if they do not obey my decrees
   and fail to keep my commands,
32 then I will punish their sin with the rod,
   and their disobedience with beating.
33 But I will never stop loving him,
   nor let my promise to him fail.
34 No, I will not break my covenant;
   I will not take back a single word I said.
35 I have sworn an oath to David,
   and in my holiness I cannot lie:
36 His dynasty will go on forever;
   his throne is as secure as the sun,
37   as eternal as the moon,
   my faithful witness in the sky!"
                              Interlude

38 But now you have rejected him.
   Why are you so angry with the one you
      chose as king?

89:10 Hebrew *Rahab*, the name of a mythical sea monster that represents chaos in ancient literature. **89:25** Hebrew
I will set his hand on the sea, his right hand on the rivers.

89:11-18 God created and sustains everything that exists. He is extremely powerful, and he
displays righteousness, truth, justice, and unfailing love. When we are powerless, it only makes
sense to turn to God. He has the power we need to overcome our dependencies. As we remain
close to him and do his will, we will experience deliverance and discover true freedom.

89:38-45 Although God at times may seem to abandon his people and act toward them in anger,
he is just doing what he promised to do. He said he would bless us if we obey and punish us if we
disobey. We sometimes find it hard to understand why God lets some people be seemingly in
perfect control of their life, while we are hopelessly out of control. Deep down, we know the
answer: Unless God is in control of a person's life, nothing of ultimate good will ever come of it.

39 You have renounced your covenant with
 him,
  for you have thrown his crown in the
   dust.
40 You have broken down the walls
   protecting him
  and laid in ruins every fort defending
   him.
41 Everyone who comes along has robbed
   him
  while his neighbors mock.
42 You have strengthened his enemies
   against him
  and made them all rejoice.
43 You have made his sword useless
  and have refused to help him in battle.
44 You have ended his splendor
  and overturned his throne.
45 You have made him old before his time
  and publicly disgraced him.   *Interlude*

46 O LORD, how long will this go on?
  Will you hide yourself forever?
  How long will your anger burn like fire?
47 Remember how short my life is,
  how empty and futile this human
   existence!
48 No one can live forever; all will die.
  No one can escape the power of the
   grave.   *Interlude*

49 Lord, where is your unfailing love?
  You promised it to David with a faithful
   pledge.
50 Consider, Lord, how your servants are
   disgraced!
  I carry in my heart the insults of so
   many people.
51 Your enemies have mocked me, O LORD;
  they mock the one you anointed
   as king.

52 Blessed be the LORD forever!
  Amen and amen!

BOOK FOUR (Psalms 90–106)
PSALM 90
A prayer of Moses, the man of God.

1 Lord, through all the generations
  you have been our home!

2 Before the mountains were created,
  before you made the earth and the
   world,
  you are God, without beginning or end.
3 You turn people back to dust, saying,
  "Return to dust!"
4 For you, a thousand years are as yesterday!
  They are like a few hours!
5 You sweep people away like dreams that
   disappear
  or like grass that springs up in the
   morning.
6 In the morning it blooms and flourishes,
  but by evening it is dry and withered.
7 We wither beneath your anger;
  we are overwhelmed by your fury.
8 You spread out our sins before you—
  our secret sins—and you see them all.
9 We live our lives beneath your wrath.
  We end our lives with a groan.

10 Seventy years are given to us!
  Some may even reach eighty.
  But even the best of these years are filled
   with pain and trouble;
  soon they disappear, and we are gone.
11 Who can comprehend the power of your
   anger?
  Your wrath is as awesome as the fear
   you deserve.
12 Teach us to make the most of our time,
  so that we may grow in wisdom.

13 O LORD, come back to us!
  How long will you delay?
  Take pity on your servants!
14 Satisfy us in the morning with your
   unfailing love,
  so we may sing for joy to the end
   of our lives.
15 Give us gladness in proportion to our
   former misery!
  Replace the evil years with good.
16 Let us see your miracles again;
  let our children see your glory at work.
17 And may the Lord our God show us his
   approval
  and make our efforts successful.
  Yes, make our efforts successful!

90:10-12 Remembering that life is short and often filled with sorrow, we should ask God how
he wants us to spend our days and concentrate on making our life count for something. We have
wasted enough time creating our own problems. We should focus now on growing in wisdom
and making positive changes in our life so we can accomplish things for God.
90:13-17 Our restoration to wholeness and health depends on our cooperation with God. Only
he can give us the power to be what we ought to be. But God won't force changes on us; we
must want to change. We must begin through prayer and Bible study. We can ask God to make
us willing to change and to give us the strength to follow through with action.

PSALM 91

¹Those who live in the shelter of the Most
  High
  will find rest in the shadow of the
  Almighty.
²This I declare of the LORD:
  He alone is my refuge, my place of
  safety;
  he is my God, and I am trusting him.
³For he will rescue you from every trap
  and protect you from the fatal plague.
⁴He will shield you with his wings.
  He will shelter you with his feathers.
  His faithful promises are your armor
  and protection.
⁵Do not be afraid of the terrors of the
  night,
  nor fear the dangers of the day,
⁶nor dread the plague that stalks in
  darkness,
  nor the disaster that strikes at
  midday.
⁷Though a thousand fall at your side,
  though ten thousand are dying
  around you,
  these evils will not touch you.
⁸But you will see it with your eyes;
  you will see how the wicked are
  punished.

⁹If you make the LORD your refuge,
  if you make the Most High your
  shelter,
¹⁰no evil will conquer you;
  no plague will come near your
  dwelling.
¹¹For he orders his angels
  to protect you wherever you go.
¹²They will hold you with their hands
  to keep you from striking your foot
  on a stone.
¹³You will trample down lions and
  poisonous snakes;
  you will crush fierce lions and serpents
  under your feet!

¹⁴The LORD says, "I will rescue those who
  love me.
  I will protect those who trust in my
  name.
¹⁵When they call on me, I will answer;
  I will be with them in trouble.
  I will rescue them and honor them.
¹⁶I will satisfy them with a long life
  and give them my salvation."

PSALM 92

A psalm to be sung on the LORD's Day. A song.

¹It is good to give thanks to the LORD,
  to sing praises to the Most High.
²It is good to proclaim your unfailing
  love in the morning,
  your faithfulness in the evening,
³accompanied by the harp and lute
  and the harmony of the lyre.
⁴You thrill me, LORD, with all you have
  done for me!
  I sing for joy because of what you
  have done.

⁵O LORD, what great miracles you do!
  And how deep are your thoughts.
⁶Only an ignorant person would not
  know this!
  Only a fool would not understand it.
⁷Although the wicked flourish like weeds,
  and evildoers blossom with success,
  there is only eternal destruction ahead
  of them.
⁸But you are exalted in the heavens.
  You, O LORD, continue forever.
⁹Your enemies, LORD, will surely perish;
  all evildoers will be scattered.

¹⁰But you have made me as strong as
  a wild bull.
  How refreshed I am by your power!
¹¹With my own eyes I have seen the
  downfall of my enemies;
  with my own ears I have heard the
  defeat of my wicked opponents.

91:1-4 When we discover that we are powerless to fight our addiction alone, we become weak like little children. We feel helpless to protect ourself, caught in a whirlwind of our own making. We turn to God our rescuer because there is nowhere else to go. How comforting to know that when we cry out, God will rescue us and protect us as a mother bird protects her young. Our powerful defender will never fail us if we turn to him for shelter and safety.
91:10-16 We will escape danger because God protects us as his chosen ones. Sometimes his protection comes through angels, who are given the responsibility of caring for us and keeping us safe. Sometimes God may use other, more natural, means. As we cry out to him for help, he will be with us in our troubles and rescue us. Ultimately, he will bring us into his eternal presence forever.
92:1-4 It is a necessary part of recovery to praise God for all he has done for us, to proclaim his unfailing love and his faithfulness to us. He brings us abiding joy. As we experience his faithfulness in our life, praise and thanks should be our natural responses. Our praise will serve as a declaration to others of God's power to deliver us from the bondage of addiction.

¹²But the godly will flourish like palm
    trees
    and grow strong like the cedars
    of Lebanon.
¹³For they are transplanted into the LORD's
    own house.
    They flourish in the courts of our God.
¹⁴Even in old age they will still produce
    fruit;
    they will remain vital and green.
¹⁵They will declare, "The LORD is just!
    He is my rock!
    There is nothing but goodness
    in him!"

PSALM 93

¹The LORD is king! He is robed in majesty.
    Indeed, the LORD is robed in majesty
    and armed with strength.
    The world is firmly established;
    it cannot be shaken.

²Your throne, O LORD, has been established
    from time immemorial.
    You yourself are from the everlasting
    past.
³The mighty oceans have roared, O LORD.
    The mighty oceans roar like thunder;
    the mighty oceans roar as they pound
    the shore.
⁴But mightier than the violent raging
    of the seas,
    mightier than the breakers on the
    shore—
    the LORD above is mightier than these!
⁵Your royal decrees cannot be changed.
    The nature of your reign, O LORD,
    is holiness forever.

PSALM 94

¹O LORD, the God to whom vengeance
    belongs,
    O God of vengeance, let your glorious
    justice be seen!

94:7 Hebrew *of Jacob.*

²Arise, O judge of the earth.
    Sentence the proud to the penalties
    they deserve.
³How long, O LORD?
    How long will the wicked be allowed
    to gloat?
⁴Hear their arrogance!
    How these evildoers boast!
⁵They oppress your people, LORD,
    hurting those you love.
⁶They kill widows and foreigners
    and murder orphans.
⁷"The LORD isn't looking," they say,
    "and besides, the God of Israel*
    doesn't care."

⁸Think again, you fools!
    When will you finally catch on?
⁹Is the one who made your ears deaf?
    Is the one who formed your eyes
    blind?
¹⁰He punishes the nations—won't he also
    punish you?
    He knows everything—doesn't he
    also know what you are doing?
¹¹The LORD knows people's thoughts,
    that they are worthless!

¹²Happy are those whom you discipline,
    LORD,
    and those whom you teach from
    your law.
¹³You give them relief from troubled times
    until a pit is dug for the wicked.
¹⁴The LORD will not reject his people;
    he will not abandon his own special
    possession.
¹⁵Judgment will come again for the
    righteous,
    and those who are upright will have
    a reward.

¹⁶Who will protect me from the wicked?
    Who will stand up for me against
    evildoers?

93:1-5 The Lord is more powerful than the mighty oceans. Surely such a God is able to help us exercise control over our universe—our life. He always keeps his promises. Since he has said he will help us if we turn to him, we can count on it.
94:8-10 The voice of the tempter says, "No one will know or care if we have just one more moment of pleasure." Here we are reminded that God is neither deaf nor blind. Neither are the people who know us well. "Just one more" always translates into a disastrous downfall. Remembering that God knows what we are doing and that he cares about us should encourage us to stand against the temptations we face.
94:16-23 In the final analysis, we can count on no one but God to stand up for us against our enemies. He is our fortress and mighty rock. When we stumble into temptation, he is there to keep us from falling. Because he is our defender, he does not allow sin to destroy us beyond hope. Knowing that God is so intimately involved in our life should encourage us to live for him.

¹⁷ Unless the LORD had helped me,
  I would soon have died.
¹⁸ I cried out, "I'm slipping!"
  and your unfailing love, O LORD,
    supported me.
¹⁹ When doubts filled my mind,
  your comfort gave me renewed hope
    and cheer.

²⁰ Can unjust leaders claim that God is
    on their side—
  leaders who permit injustice by their
    laws?
²¹ They attack the righteous
  and condemn the innocent to death.
²² But the LORD is my fortress;
  my God is a mighty rock where I can
    hide.
²³ God will make the sins of evil people fall
    back upon them.
  He will destroy them for their sins.
  The LORD our God will destroy them.

PSALM 95
¹ Come, let us sing to the LORD!
  Let us give a joyous shout to the rock
    of our salvation!
² Let us come before him with
    thanksgiving.
  Let us sing him psalms of praise.
³ For the LORD is a great God,
  the great King above all gods.
⁴ He owns the depths of the earth,
  and even the mightiest mountains are
    his.
⁵ The sea belongs to him, for he made it.
  His hands formed the dry land, too.

⁶ Come, let us worship and bow down.
  Let us kneel before the LORD our maker,
⁷   for he is our God.
  We are the people he watches over,
    the sheep under his care.

  Oh, that you would listen to his voice today!
⁸ The LORD says, "Don't harden your hearts
    as Israel did at Meribah,
  as they did at Massah in the wilderness.

⁹ For there your ancestors tried my
    patience;
  they courted my wrath though they
    had seen my many miracles.
¹⁰ For forty years I was angry with them,
    and I said,
  'They are a people whose hearts turn
    away from me.
  They refuse to do what I tell them.'
¹¹ So in my anger I made a vow:
  'They will never enter my place
    of rest.'"

PSALM 96
¹ Sing a new song to the LORD!
  Let the whole earth sing to the LORD!
² Sing to the LORD; bless his name.
  Each day proclaim the good news that
    he saves.
³ Publish his glorious deeds among the
    nations.
  Tell everyone about the amazing things
    he does.
⁴ Great is the LORD! He is most worthy
    of praise!
  He is to be revered above all the gods.
⁵ The gods of other nations are merely
    idols,
  but the LORD made the heavens!
⁶ Honor and majesty surround him;
  strength and beauty are in his
    sanctuary.

⁷ O nations of the world, recognize the
    LORD;
  recognize that the LORD is glorious
    and strong.
⁸ Give to the LORD the glory he deserves!
  Bring your offering and come to
    worship him.
⁹ Worship the LORD in all his holy
    splendor.
  Let all the earth tremble before him.
¹⁰ Tell all the nations that the LORD is king.
  The world is firmly established and
    cannot be shaken.
  He will judge all peoples fairly.

95:1-7 We all know how frightening it is to lose control of our life. For this very reason, we may hesitate to entrust ourself to God. Can he be trusted? God wants us to remember that when we surrender our life to him, he regards us with the same concern that a kind shepherd feels for his sheep. If a watchful shepherd is around, the sheep have little to fear.

96:1-9 The way we live demonstrates what we believe about God. If we stay in our prison of sin, we show that we are either unaware of God's power to save us or indifferent about him and the help he offers. If we seek his help to escape the bondage of sin and share the joyful news of recovery with others, we show our gratitude to God and reveal the beauty of a changed life. The world is filled with "remedies" for our problems. Many of them are helpful, but none can offer us the power we need for real change. Only God is mighty enough to offer that kind of help.

11 Let the heavens be glad, and let the earth
rejoice!
Let the sea and everything in it shout
his praise!
12 Let the fields and their crops burst forth
with joy!
Let the trees of the forest rustle with
praise 13before the LORD!
For the LORD is coming!
He is coming to judge the earth.
He will judge the world with righteousness
and all the nations with his truth.

PSALM 97

1 The LORD is king! Let the earth rejoice!
Let the farthest islands be glad.
2 Clouds and darkness surround him.
Righteousness and justice are the
foundation of his throne.
3 Fire goes forth before him
and burns up all his foes.
4 His lightning flashes out across the world.
The earth sees and trembles.
5 The mountains melt like wax before the
LORD,
before the Lord of all the earth.
6 The heavens declare his righteousness;
every nation sees his glory.
7 Those who worship idols are disgraced—
all who brag about their worthless gods—
for every god must bow to him.
8 Jerusalem* has heard and rejoiced,
and all the cities of Judah are glad
because of your justice, LORD!
9 For you, O LORD, are most high over all
the earth;
you are exalted far above all gods.

10 You who love the LORD, hate evil!
He protects the lives of his godly people
and rescues them from the power of the
wicked.
11 Light shines on the godly,
and joy on those who do right.
12 May all who are godly be happy in the
LORD
and praise his holy name!

97:8 Hebrew *Zion.* 99:2 Hebrew *Zion.*

PSALM 98

A psalm.

1 Sing a new song to the LORD,
for he has done wonderful deeds.
He has won a mighty victory
by his power and holiness.
2 The LORD has announced his victory
and has revealed his righteousness
to every nation!
3 He has remembered his promise to love
and be faithful to Israel.
The whole earth has seen the salvation
of our God.

4 Shout to the LORD, all the earth;
break out in praise and sing for joy!
5 Sing your praise to the LORD with the
harp,
with the harp and melodious song,
6 with trumpets and the sound of the
ram's horn.
Make a joyful symphony before the LORD,
the King!

7 Let the sea and everything in it shout his
praise!
Let the earth and all living things
join in.
8 Let the rivers clap their hands in
glee!
Let the hills sing out their songs of joy
9 before the LORD.
For the LORD is coming to judge the
earth.
He will judge the world with justice,
and the nations with fairness.

PSALM 99

1 The LORD is king!
Let the nations tremble!
He sits on his throne between the cherubim.
Let the whole earth quake!
2 The LORD sits in majesty in Jerusalem,*
supreme above all the nations.
3 Let them praise your great and awesome
name.
Your name is holy!

97:10-12 God desires to help us, and he wants us to hate our sin as he does. He helps those who hate evil and want to please him. God has placed a very close link between happiness and holiness. If we want real joy, we need to commit our life to the Lord and his program for joyful and holy living.
98:1-3 God revealed his power to the whole world by rescuing the people of Israel. Today he shows his power by delivering us from our addiction and hopeless problems. We can win impossible battles, just as the Israelites did, because God is powerful and active in our life. Having found victory, we can share with others our stories of God's deliverance. This will give them the hope and wisdom they need to experience God's help in their own lives.

4 Mighty king, lover of justice,
  you have established fairness.
You have acted with justice
  and righteousness throughout Israel.*
5 Exalt the LORD our God!
  Bow low before his feet, for he is holy!

6 Moses and Aaron were among his priests;
  Samuel also called on his name.
They cried to the LORD for help,
  and he answered them.
7 He spoke to them from the pillar of cloud,
  and they followed the decrees and
    principles he gave them.
8 O LORD our God, you answered them.
  You were a forgiving God,
  but you punished them when they
    went wrong.

9 Exalt the LORD our God
  and worship at his holy mountain
    in Jerusalem,
  for the LORD our God is holy!

PSALM 100
A psalm of thanksgiving.

1 Shout with joy to the LORD, O earth!
2   Worship the LORD with gladness.
  Come before him, singing with joy.
3 Acknowledge that the LORD is God!
  He made us, and we are his.
  We are his people, the sheep of his pasture.

4 Enter his gates with thanksgiving;
  go into his courts with praise.
  Give thanks to him and bless his name.
5 For the LORD is good.
  His unfailing love continues forever,
  and his faithfulness continues to each
    generation.

99:4 Hebrew *Jacob.*

PSALM 101
A psalm of David.

1 I will sing of your love and justice.
  I will praise you, LORD, with songs.
2 I will be careful to live a blameless life—
  when will you come to my aid?
I will lead a life of integrity
  in my own home.
3 I will refuse to look at
  anything vile and vulgar.
I hate all crooked dealings;
  I will have nothing to do with them.
4 I will reject perverse ideas
  and stay away from every evil.
5 I will not tolerate people who slander
    their neighbors.
  I will not endure conceit and pride.

6 I will keep a protective eye on the godly,
  so they may dwell with me in safety.
Only those who are above reproach
  will be allowed to serve me.
7 I will not allow deceivers to serve me,
  and liars will not be allowed to enter
    my presence.
8 My daily task will be to ferret out criminals
  and free the city of the LORD from their
    grip.

PSALM 102
*A prayer of one overwhelmed with trouble, pouring
out problems before the LORD.*

1 LORD, hear my prayer!
  Listen to my plea!
2 Don't turn away from me
  in my time of distress.
Bend down your ear
  and answer me quickly when I call to you,
3   for my days disappear like smoke,
  and my bones burn like red-hot coals.

99:1-9 Even though God is a God of love, he is also holy and righteous. His love causes him to show mercy toward us, but his holiness means that we can't please him if we continue in sin. We must not presume upon God's loving and forgiving nature, for he also loves justice. Continuing in sin will result in terrible consequences. Our experiences of God's delivering power should motivate us to live for him with all our strength.
100:1-5 We always have reasons to rejoice: We live in God's presence, under his continual care, and we experience his love each day. Each time we come into his presence, our heart should be filled with gratitude and praise. God never stops showering us with his love; he always keeps his promise to help us when we call on him.
101:1-5 Staying free from the sin that used to entrap us depends on our staying close to God and staying away from every evil. It is vital that we not waste our time following a recovery program that tries to undermine our faith in God. We must learn to be discerning about the activities we become involved in. Like the psalmist, we must not tolerate anyone in our life who does not value the things of God and who may slander us because of our faith in Christ.
102:1-7 When we are heartsick and beaten down by the events of life, we can run to God with our urgent requests. At times we may lose our appetite and feel pain like red-hot coals in our

⁴My heart is sick, withered like grass,
  and I have lost my appetite.
⁵Because of my groaning,
  I am reduced to skin and bones.
⁶I am like an owl in the desert,
  like a lonely owl in a far-off wilderness.
⁷I lie awake,
  lonely as a solitary bird on the roof.
⁸My enemies taunt me day after day.
  They mock and curse me.
⁹I eat ashes instead of my food.
  My tears run down into my drink
¹⁰because of your anger and wrath.
  For you have picked me up and thrown
  me out.
¹¹My life passes as swiftly as the evening
  shadows.
  I am withering like grass.

¹²But you, O LORD, will rule forever.
  Your fame will endure to every
  generation.
¹³You will arise and have mercy on
  Jerusalem*—
  and now is the time to pity her,
  now is the time you promised to help.
¹⁴For your people love every stone in her
  walls
  and show favor even to the dust in her
  streets.
¹⁵And the nations will tremble before the
  LORD.
  The kings of the earth will tremble
  before his glory.
¹⁶For the LORD will rebuild Jerusalem.
  He will appear in his glory.
¹⁷He will listen to the prayers of the
  destitute.
  He will not reject their pleas.

¹⁸Let this be recorded for future
  generations,
  so that a nation yet to be created will
  praise the LORD.
¹⁹Tell them the LORD looked down
  from his heavenly sanctuary.
  He looked to the earth from heaven

²⁰ to hear the groans of the prisoners,
  to release those condemned to die.
²¹And so the LORD's fame will be celebrated
  in Zion,
  his praises in Jerusalem,
²²when multitudes gather together
  and kingdoms come to worship the
  LORD.

²³He has cut me down in midlife,
  shortening my days.
²⁴But I cried to him, "My God, who lives
  forever,
  don't take my life while I am still
  so young!
²⁵In ages past you laid the foundation
  of the earth,
  and the heavens are the work of your
  hands.
²⁶Even they will perish, but you remain
  forever;
  they will wear out like old clothing.
  You will change them like a garment,
  and they will fade away.
²⁷But you are always the same;
  your years never end.
²⁸The children of your people
  will live in security.
  Their children's children
  will thrive in your presence."

PSALM 103
A psalm of David.

¹Praise the LORD, I tell myself;
  with my whole heart, I will praise
  his holy name.
²Praise the LORD, I tell myself,
  and never forget the good things
  he does for me.
³He forgives all my sins
  and heals all my diseases.
⁴He ransoms me from death
  and surrounds me with love and tender
  mercies.
⁵He fills my life with good things.
  My youth is renewed like the eagle's!

102:13 Hebrew *Zion;* also in 102:16.

---

bones. Our energy—our very life—withers like grass under the scorching sun. When there is no other solution, God is still able to deliver us. We need to admit our powerlessness in the situation and trust God to help us through the pain.
102:17-22 God responds to people who are downtrodden and in distress. Sometimes we may feel that God is too busy or too distant, but he is always intimately concerned about us and will not reject our requests. He wants us to have a joyful and meaningful relationship with him—that's what he created us for! When we admit our helplessness and turn to God, he will come through for us in one way or another. Then our only natural response to him will be one of joyful praise; we should also want to tell others about what God has done for us.

⁶The LORD gives righteousness
and justice to all who are treated
unfairly.
⁷He revealed his character to Moses
and his deeds to the people of Israel.
⁸The LORD is merciful and gracious;
he is slow to get angry and full of
unfailing love.
⁹He will not constantly accuse us,
nor remain angry forever.
¹⁰He has not punished us for all our sins,
nor does he deal with us as we deserve.
¹¹For his unfailing love toward those who
fear him
is as great as the height of the heavens
above the earth.
¹²He has removed our rebellious acts
as far away from us as the east is from
the west.
¹³The LORD is like a father to his children,
tender and compassionate to those
who fear him.
¹⁴For he understands how weak we are;
he knows we are only dust.
¹⁵Our days on earth are like grass;
like wildflowers, we bloom and die.
¹⁶The wind blows, and we are gone—
as though we had never been here.
¹⁷But the love of the LORD remains forever
with those who fear him.
His salvation extends to the children's
children
¹⁸ of those who are faithful to his covenant,
of those who obey his commandments!

¹⁹The LORD has made the heavens his
throne;
from there he rules over everything.
²⁰Praise the LORD, you angels of his,
you mighty creatures who carry out his
plans,
listening for each of his commands.
²¹Yes, praise the LORD, you armies of angels
who serve him and do his will!

²²Praise the LORD, everything he has created,
everywhere in his kingdom.
As for me—I, too, will praise the LORD.

PSALM 104

¹Praise the LORD, I tell myself;
O LORD my God, how great you are!
You are robed with honor and with
majesty;
² you are dressed in a robe of light.
You stretch out the starry curtain of the
heavens;
³ you lay out the rafters of your home
in the rain clouds.
You make the clouds your chariots;
you ride upon the wings of the wind.
⁴The winds are your messengers;
flames of fire are your servants.

⁵You placed the world on its foundation
so it would never be moved.
⁶You clothed the earth with floods of water,
water that covered even the mountains.
⁷At the sound of your rebuke, the water
fled;
at the sound of your thunder, it fled
away.
⁸Mountains rose and valleys sank
to the levels you decreed.
⁹Then you set a firm boundary for the seas,
so they would never again cover the
earth.

¹⁰You make the springs pour water into
ravines,
so streams gush down from the
mountains.
¹¹They provide water for all the animals,
and the wild donkeys quench their
thirst.
¹²The birds nest beside the streams
and sing among the branches of the
trees.

103:13-18 As a loving father cares for his children, God has compassion on all who call on him. He is sensitive to our needs and treats us lovingly because he understands our weaknesses and the transitory nature of our life. God's love never ceases for those who fear him. By obediently serving him now, we can be assured that his love will touch not only our own life but also the lives of our children and grandchildren.

104:1-26 God created us as well as this world and all its creatures. He created the world to function according to his plan. God also created us to function best—to live joyful and healthy lives—when we do things his way. When we follow our own path, we will suffer painful consequences. If we seek to live according to God's program revealed in the Bible, we will discover the way to live in peace and harmony with God, other people, and the world we live in.

104:27-35 God controls the destinies of all beings; every living being depends on him for food and life. We need to realize that if we withdraw ourself from God's presence, from his control and care, we are without hope, just as the natural world would be without hope if God should withdraw himself from it.

¹³ You send rain on the mountains from
    your heavenly home,
and you fill the earth with the fruit
    of your labor.
¹⁴ You cause grass to grow for the cattle.
    You cause plants to grow for people
        to use.
    You allow them to produce food from
        the earth—
¹⁵   wine to make them glad,
    olive oil as lotion for their skin,
    and bread to give them strength.
¹⁶ The trees of the LORD are well cared
    for—
    the cedars of Lebanon that he
        planted.
¹⁷ There the birds make their nests,
    and the storks make their homes
        in the firs.
¹⁸ High in the mountains are pastures
    for the wild goats,
    and the rocks form a refuge for rock
        badgers.*
¹⁹ You made the moon to mark the
    seasons
    and the sun that knows when to set.
²⁰ You send the darkness, and it becomes
    night,
    when all the forest animals prowl about.
²¹ Then the young lions roar for their food,
    but they are dependent on God.
²² At dawn they slink back
    into their dens to rest.
²³ Then people go off to their work;
    they labor until the evening shadows
        fall again.

²⁴ O LORD, what a variety of things you have
    made!
    In wisdom you have made them all.
    The earth is full of your creatures.
²⁵ Here is the ocean, vast and wide,
    teeming with life of every kind,
    both great and small.
²⁶ See the ships sailing along,
    and Leviathan, which you made to play
        in the sea.
²⁷ Every one of these depends on you
    to give them their food as they need it.
²⁸ When you supply it, they gather it.
    You open your hand to feed them,
    and they are satisfied.
²⁹ But if you turn away from them, they
    panic.
    When you take away their breath,
        they die
    and turn again to dust.

104:18 Or *coneys,* or *hyraxes.*

Forgiveness

READ PSALM 103:1-22

We may have a hard time believing in
God's forgiveness. We may think, *After
all I've done, I don't think anyone can
completely forgive me.* Maybe we feel that
we have done such horrible things or hurt
people so badly that there's no way our
sins could ever be blotted out entirely.
Even if we could be forgiven, who could
ever *forget* the things we have done?

When we think of people we know—
the people we have hurt—perhaps these
fears are well founded. But when it comes
to forgiveness from God, we need to
remember that his ways are higher than
our ways. The psalmist wrote, "[God] has
not punished us for all our sins, nor does
he deal with us as we deserve. For his
unfailing love toward those who fear him
is as great as the height of the heavens
above the earth. He has removed our rebellious acts as far away from us as the east is
from the west" (Psalm 103:10-12). God
has said, "Come now, let us argue this
out. . . . No matter how deep the stain of
your sins, I can remove it. I can make you
as clean as freshly fallen snow. Even if you
are stained as red as crimson, I can make
you as white as wool" (Isaiah 1:18).
"I—yes, I alone—am the one who blots
out your sins for my own sake and will
never think of them again" (Isaiah 43:25).

Part of the recovery process is accepting
complete forgiveness from God. When we
come to God through the atoning blood
of Jesus Christ, his forgiveness is complete.
We may keep track of our failures, adding
every one to the long list we have written
out against ourself. But God doesn't keep
lists of our past sins; in his eyes we are
clean. ***Turn to page 595, Proverbs 15.***
Turn to page 595, Proverbs 15.

30 When you send your Spirit, new life is
   born
   to replenish all the living of the earth.

31 May the glory of the LORD last forever!
   The LORD rejoices in all he has made!
32 The earth trembles at his glance;
   the mountains burst into flame at his
   touch.
33 I will sing to the LORD as long as I live.
   I will praise my God to my last
   breath!
34 May he be pleased by all these thoughts
   about him,
   for I rejoice in the LORD.
35 Let all sinners vanish from the face
   of the earth;
   let the wicked disappear forever.
   As for me—I will praise the LORD!

   Praise the LORD!

PSALM 105
1 Give thanks to the LORD and proclaim
   his greatness.
   Let the whole world know what he
   has done.
2 Sing to him; yes, sing his praises.
   Tell everyone about his miracles.
3 Exult in his holy name;
   O worshipers of the LORD, rejoice!
4 Search for the LORD and for his strength,
   and keep on searching.
5 Think of the wonderful works he has done,
   the miracles and the judgments he
   handed down,
6 O children of Abraham, God's servant,
   O descendants of Jacob, God's chosen
   one.
7 He is the LORD our God.
   His rule is seen throughout the land.
8 He always stands by his covenant—
   the commitment he made to a
   thousand generations.

9 This is the covenant he made with
   Abraham
   and the oath he swore to Isaac.
10 He confirmed it to Jacob as a decree,
   to the people of Israel as a never-
   ending treaty:
11 "I will give you the land of Canaan
   as your special possession."

12 He said this when they were few in
   number,
   a tiny group of strangers in Canaan.
13 They wandered back and forth between
   nations,
   from one kingdom to another.
14 Yet he did not let anyone oppress
   them.
   He warned kings on their behalf:
15 "Do not touch these people I have
   chosen,
   and do not hurt my prophets."
16 He called for a famine on the land
   of Canaan,
   cutting off its food supply.
17 Then he sent someone to Egypt ahead
   of them—
   Joseph, who was sold as a slave.
18 There in prison, they bruised his feet
   with fetters
   and placed his neck in an iron collar.
19 Until the time came to fulfill his word,
   the LORD tested Joseph's character.
20 Then Pharaoh sent for him and set him
   free;
   the ruler of the nation opened his
   prison door.
21 Joseph was put in charge of all the king's
   household;
   he became ruler over all the king's
   possessions.
22 He could instruct the king's aides as he
   pleased
   and teach the king's advisers.

105:5-15 God always keeps his word. He fulfills all his promises. God promised Abraham and Jacob that their descendants would inherit the land of Canaan. Generations after Jacob's death, the Israelites entered Canaan. Sometimes God's promises take time to be fulfilled. In recovery we often grow impatient with our slow progress. At times we may think the entire process is hopeless and be tempted to give up. We need to realize that recovery takes time, but this does not mean God is not working on our behalf. We should also remember that the benefits of our efforts in recovery will touch not only our own life but also the lives of our descendants. Let us embrace God's recovery promises for the long haul.

105:39-45 God is able to care for his people. He responds to our prayers—even our complaints—and meets all our needs that no one else could possibly fill. His ultimate purpose is to make us faithful and obedient to his laws. As he helps us be faithful and obedient to his plan, he will fill us with joy. These verses are of special comfort to us in recovery. As we admit our faults to God, we can know that he is listening. As we seek to live according to his will, he will fill us with joy and fulfillment. As we entrust our life to God, we can be sure we are in good hands.

²³ Then Israel arrived in Egypt;
  Jacob lived as a foreigner in the land
    of Ham.
²⁴ And the LORD multiplied the people
    of Israel
  until they became too mighty for their
    enemies.
²⁵ Then he turned the Egyptians against the
    Israelites,
  and they plotted against the LORD's
    servants.

²⁶ But the LORD sent Moses his servant,
  along with Aaron, whom he had
    chosen.
²⁷ They performed miraculous signs among
    the Egyptians,
  and miracles in the land of Ham.
²⁸ The LORD blanketed Egypt in darkness,
  for they had defied his commands
    to let his people go.
²⁹ He turned the nation's water into blood,
  poisoning all the fish.
³⁰ Then frogs overran the land;
  they were found even in the king's
    private rooms.
³¹ When he spoke, flies descended on the
    Egyptians,
  and gnats swarmed across Egypt.
³² Instead of rain, he sent murderous hail,
  and flashes of lightning overwhelmed
    the land.
³³ He ruined their grapevines and fig trees
  and shattered all the trees.
³⁴ He spoke, and hordes of locusts came—
  locusts beyond number.
³⁵ They ate up everything green in the
    land,
  destroying all the crops.
³⁶ Then he killed the oldest child in each
    Egyptian home,
  the pride and joy of each family.

³⁷ But he brought his people safely out
  of Egypt, loaded with silver and
    gold;
  there were no sick or feeble people
    among them.
³⁸ Egypt was glad when they were gone,
  for the dread of them was great.
³⁹ The LORD spread out a cloud above them
    as a covering
  and gave them a great fire to light the
    darkness.
⁴⁰ They asked for meat, and he sent them
    quail;
  he gave them manna—bread from
    heaven.

STEP 11

Finding God

BIBLE READING: Psalm 105:1-9

We sought through prayer and meditation to improve our conscious contact with God, praying only for knowledge of his will for us and the power to carry that out.

As we work through the Twelve Steps, we spend a lot of time looking back. We often think about the wrong things we have done in the past. As we proceed in the recovery process, we will need strength to move along the path God wants us to follow. Part of this strength will come as we visualize God's constant presence with us.

The psalmist wrote, "Give thanks to the LORD and proclaim his greatness. Let the whole world know what he has done. . . . Think of the wonderful works he has done, the miracles and the judgments he handed down. . . . He is the LORD our God. His rule is seen throughout the land. He always stands by his covenant—the commitment he made to a thousand generations" (Psalm 105:1, 5-8).

From now on when we look back, we should concentrate on seeing the "wonderful works he has done" and remember "the miracles and the judgments he handed down." We can look around to find his goodness "throughout the land" and look forward to the fulfillment of his promises. In prayer, we should thank God for what he has done, seek him for the strength we need today, and ask him to fulfill his promises for tomorrow. In meditation, we need to remember our victories, ponder God's presence with us today, and consider his faithfulness and the hope he gives us for tomorrow. *Turn to page 559, Psalm 119.*

⁴¹ He opened up a rock, and water gushed out
  to form a river through the dry and
    barren land.
⁴² For he remembered his sacred promise
  to Abraham his servant.
⁴³ So he brought his people out of Egypt
    with joy,
  his chosen ones with rejoicing.
⁴⁴ He gave his people the lands of pagan
    nations,
  and they harvested crops that others
    had planted.
⁴⁵ All this happened so they would follow
    his principles
  and obey his laws.

Praise the LORD!

PSALM 106
¹ Praise the LORD!

Give thanks to the LORD, for he is good!
  His faithful love endures forever.
² Who can list the glorious miracles of the
    LORD?
  Who can ever praise him half enough?
³ Happy are those who deal justly with
    others
  and always do what is right.

⁴ Remember me, too, LORD, when you show
    favor to your people;
  come to me with your salvation.
⁵ Let me share in the prosperity of your
    chosen ones.
  Let me rejoice in the joy of your people;
  let me praise you with those who are
    your heritage.

⁶ Both we and our ancestors have sinned.
  We have done wrong! We have acted
    wickedly!
⁷ Our ancestors in Egypt
  were not impressed by the LORD's
    miracles.

They soon forgot his many acts of
    kindness to them.
  Instead, they rebelled against him at
    the Red Sea.*
⁸ Even so, he saved them—
  to defend the honor of his name
  and to demonstrate his mighty power.
⁹ He commanded the Red Sea* to divide,
  and a dry path appeared.
  He led Israel across the sea bottom that
    was as dry as a desert.
¹⁰ So he rescued them from their enemies
  and redeemed them from their foes.
¹¹ Then the water returned and covered
    their enemies;
  not one of them survived.
¹² Then at last his people believed his
    promises.
  Then they finally sang his praise.

¹³ Yet how quickly they forgot what he had
    done!
  They wouldn't wait for his counsel!
¹⁴ In the wilderness, their desires ran wild,
    testing God's patience in that dry
    land.
¹⁵ So he gave them what they asked for,
  but he sent a plague along with it.
¹⁶ The people in the camp were jealous
    of Moses
  and envious of Aaron, the LORD's holy
    priest.
¹⁷ Because of this, the earth opened up;
  it swallowed Dathan
  and buried Abiram and the other
    rebels.
¹⁸ Fire fell upon their followers;
  a flame consumed the wicked.

¹⁹ The people made a calf at Mount Sinai*;
  they bowed before an image made
    of gold.
²⁰ They traded their glorious God
  for a statue of a grass-eating ox!

106:7 Hebrew *at the sea, the sea of reeds.* **106:9** Hebrew *sea of reeds;* also in 106:22. **106:19** Hebrew *at Horeb,* another name for Sinai.

106:6-12 The psalmist reflected on the failures of the present generation in Israel and the mistakes of past generations. In recovery we must do the same. Our failures are often closely tied to the mistakes of our parents and grandparents. We need to look back and forgive those who have hurt us. Then we should honestly assess our own mistakes, taking responsibility for them and seeking forgiveness from those we have hurt. Just as God revealed his goodness by rescuing the Israelites from their enemies, he will forgive us and support us in the recovery process.
106:13-15 We all get discouraged when we fail. Like the people of Israel, we sometimes have very short memories. We learn a lesson one day, only to forget it the next. After failing repeatedly, we need to remember that God has pulled us through in the past, and he is able and willing to do it again. God is always willing to help us if we are sincerely sorry and truly desire to change. We must be careful, however, not to test God's patience to the breaking point. If we sin willfully, we will suffer the consequences.

²¹ They forgot God, their savior,
who had done such great things in
Egypt—
²² such wonderful things in that land,
such awesome deeds at the Red Sea.
²³ So he declared he would destroy them.
But Moses, his chosen one, stepped
between the LORD and the people.
He begged him to turn from his anger
and not destroy them.

²⁴ The people refused to enter the pleasant
land,
for they wouldn't believe his promise
to care for them.
²⁵ Instead, they grumbled in their tents
and refused to obey the LORD.
²⁶ Therefore, he swore
that he would kill them in the
wilderness,
²⁷ that he would scatter their descendants
among the nations,
exiling them to distant lands.

²⁸ Then our ancestors joined in the worship
of Baal at Peor;
they even ate sacrifices offered to the
dead!
²⁹ They angered the LORD with all these
things,
so a plague broke out among them.
³⁰ But Phinehas had the courage to step in,
and the plague was stopped.
³¹ So he has been regarded as a righteous
man
ever since that time.

³² At Meribah, too, they angered the LORD,
causing Moses serious trouble.
³³ They made Moses angry,*
and he spoke foolishly.

³⁴ Israel failed to destroy the nations in the
land,
as the LORD had told them to.
³⁵ Instead, they mingled among the pagans
and adopted their evil customs.
³⁶ They worshiped their idols,
and this led to their downfall.
³⁷ They even sacrificed their sons
and their daughters to the demons.
³⁸ They shed innocent blood,
the blood of their sons and daughters.

By sacrificing them to the idols of
Canaan,
they polluted the land with murder.
³⁹ They defiled themselves by their evil
deeds,
and their love of idols was adultery
in the LORD's sight.

⁴⁰ That is why the LORD's anger burned
against his people,
and he abhorred his own special
possession.
⁴¹ He handed them over to pagan nations,
and those who hated them ruled over
them.
⁴² Their enemies crushed them
and brought them under their cruel
power.
⁴³ Again and again he delivered them,
but they continued to rebel against him,
and they were finally destroyed by their
sin.
⁴⁴ Even so, he pitied them in their distress
and listened to their cries.
⁴⁵ He remembered his covenant with them
and relented because of his unfailing
love.
⁴⁶ He even caused their captors
to treat them with kindness.

⁴⁷ O LORD our God, save us!
Gather us back from among the nations,
so we can thank your holy name
and rejoice and praise you.

⁴⁸ Blessed be the LORD, the God of Israel,
from everlasting to everlasting!
Let all the people say, "Amen!"

Praise the LORD!

BOOK FIVE (Psalms 107–150)
PSALM 107
¹ Give thanks to the LORD, for he is good!
His faithful love endures forever.
² Has the LORD redeemed you? Then speak
out!
Tell others he has saved you from your
enemies.
³ For he has gathered the exiles from many
lands,
from east and west, from north and
south.

106:33 Hebrew *They embittered his spirit.*

106:40-46 God hates sin. When we continue in our sinful ways, we shouldn't expect him to be
pleased with us. God's judgment sometimes follows swiftly and may come from unexpected
sources. Our sins will eventually destroy us. Yet God never abandons us forever. His goal is still to
free us from the bondage of our sins.

⁴Some wandered in the desert,
   lost and homeless.
⁵Hungry and thirsty,
   they nearly died.
⁶"LORD, help!" they cried in their trouble,
   and he rescued them from their
   distress.
⁷He led them straight to safety,
   to a city where they could live.
⁸Let them praise the LORD for his great love
   and for all his wonderful deeds to them.
⁹For he satisfies the thirsty
   and fills the hungry with good things.

¹⁰Some sat in darkness and deepest gloom,
   miserable prisoners in chains.
¹¹They rebelled against the words of God,
   scorning the counsel of the Most High.
¹²That is why he broke them with hard
   labor;
   they fell, and no one helped them rise
   again.
¹³"LORD, help!" they cried in their trouble,
   and he saved them from their distress.
¹⁴He led them from the darkness and
   deepest gloom;
   he snapped their chains.
¹⁵Let them praise the LORD for his great
   love
   and for all his wonderful deeds to them.
¹⁶For he broke down their prison gates of
   bronze;
   he cut apart their bars of iron.

¹⁷Some were fools in their rebellion;
   they suffered for their sins.
¹⁸Their appetites were gone,
   and death was near.
¹⁹"LORD, help!" they cried in their trouble,
   and he saved them from their distress.
²⁰He spoke, and they were healed—
   snatched from the door of death.
²¹Let them praise the LORD for his great love
   and for all his wonderful deeds to them.
²²Let them offer sacrifices of thanksgiving
   and sing joyfully about his glorious
   acts.

²³Some went off in ships,
   plying the trade routes of the world.
²⁴They, too, observed the LORD's power
   in action,
   his impressive works on the deepest
   seas.
²⁵He spoke, and the winds rose,
   stirring up the waves.
²⁶Their ships were tossed to the heavens
   and sank again to the depths;
   the sailors cringed in terror.
²⁷They reeled and staggered like drunkards
   and were at their wits' end.
²⁸"LORD, help!" they cried in their trouble,
   and he saved them from their distress.
²⁹He calmed the storm to a whisper
   and stilled the waves.
³⁰What a blessing was that stillness
   as he brought them safely into harbor!
³¹Let them praise the LORD for his great love
   and for all his wonderful deeds to them.
³²Let them exalt him publicly before the
   congregation
   and before the leaders of the nation.

³³He changes rivers into deserts,
   and springs of water into dry land.
³⁴He turns the fruitful land into salty
   wastelands,
   because of the wickedness of those
   who live there.
³⁵But he also turns deserts into pools
   of water,
   the dry land into flowing springs.
³⁶He brings the hungry to settle there
   and build their cities.
³⁷They sow their fields, plant their
   vineyards,
   and harvest their bumper crops.
³⁸How he blesses them!
   They raise large families there,
   and their herds of cattle increase.
³⁹When they decrease in number and
   become impoverished
   through oppression, trouble, and
   sorrow,

107:10-20 When we reject God and his plan, we live in spiritual darkness; we are like prisoners in chains. God punishes evil acts with heavy penalties, including God's divine punishment and the natural consequences of disobedience. The psalmist's announcement of punishment, however, should not leave us in despair; his comments end on a hopeful note. If we come to our senses and ask God for his deliverance, he will help us escape from bondage and heal us.
107:23-32 Sometimes we may feel that we are in a small ship plowing through stormy seas and about to go under. Bad memories and a sense of failure make our world seem dark and hopeless. The longer the storm rages, the more we fear and lose all hope of rescue. But when we cry out to God in our trouble, he will turn our storm-tossed life into a calm and peaceful sea and restore our joy. We must turn to him for help, follow his plan for healthy living, and patiently await his deliverance.

⁴⁰ the LORD pours contempt on their princes,
    causing them to wander in trackless
    wastelands.
⁴¹ But he rescues the poor from their distress
    and increases their families like vast
    flocks of sheep.
⁴² The godly will see these things and be glad,
    while the wicked are stricken silent.
⁴³ Those who are wise will take all this
    to heart;
    they will see in our history the faithful
    love of the LORD.

PSALM 108
A psalm of David. A song.

¹ My heart is confident in you, O God;
    no wonder I can sing your praises!
Wake up, my soul!
²   Wake up, O harp and lyre!
    I will waken the dawn with my song.
³ I will thank you, LORD, in front of all the
    people.
    I will sing your praises among the nations.
⁴ For your unfailing love is higher than the
    heavens.
    Your faithfulness reaches to the clouds.
⁵ Be exalted, O God, above the highest
    heavens.
    May your glory shine over all the earth.

⁶ Use your strong right arm to save me,
    and rescue your beloved people.
⁷ God has promised this by his holiness*:
    "I will divide up Shechem with joy.
    I will measure out the valley of Succoth.
⁸ Gilead is mine,
    and Manasseh is mine.
 Ephraim will produce my warriors,
    and Judah will produce my kings.
⁹ Moab will become my lowly servant,
    and Edom will be my slave.
    I will shout in triumph over the
    Philistines."

108:7 Or *in his sanctuary.*

¹⁰ But who will bring me into the fortified
    city?
    Who will bring me victory over Edom?
¹¹ Have you rejected us, O God?
    Will you no longer march with our
    armies?
¹² Oh, please help us against our enemies,
    for all human help is useless.
¹³ With God's help we will do mighty
    things,
    for he will trample down our foes.

PSALM 109
For the choir director: A psalm of David.

¹ O God, whom I praise,
    don't stand silent and aloof
² while the wicked slander me
    and tell lies about me.
³ They are all around me with their hateful
    words,
    and they fight against me for no reason.
⁴ I love them, but they try to destroy me—
    even as I am praying for them!
⁵ They return evil for good,
    and hatred for my love.

⁶ Arrange for an evil person to turn on him.
    Send an accuser to bring him to trial.
⁷ When his case is called for judgment,
    let him be pronounced guilty.
    Count his prayers as sins.
⁸ Let his years be few;
    let his position be given to someone
    else.
⁹ May his children become fatherless,
    and may his wife become a widow.
¹⁰ May his children wander as beggars;
    may they be evicted from their ruined
    homes.
¹¹ May creditors seize his entire estate,
    and strangers take all he has earned.
¹² Let no one be kind to him;
    let no one pity his fatherless children.

108:1-5 Morning is a wonderful time to praise God. Now that we are in recovery, our nights may seem long, but each addiction-free day should fill our heart with joy. We should let our joy spill out as a message of hope to others in need. Our testimony of God's faithfulness may lead others to the joy we are beginning to experience in the process of recovery.

108:6-13 There is no resource for true recovery other than the strength offered by our gracious God. It is futile to rely on anyone else for our victory, since God alone can give us the power to overcome our dependencies and compulsions. Ultimately he is the one who conquers our enemies and helps us do "mighty things." We must admit our powerlessness and turn our life over to his care and direction.

109:1-5 We all know what it feels like to be condemned by others—sometimes unjustly. Sometimes we are attacked by painful memories of the abuse we may have suffered. It is then we need to turn to God for relief. He will fill our heart with his love and help us to forgive those who speak hateful words against us. We can rest in him and do our best to love those who hurt us.

13 May all his offspring die.
   May his family name be blotted out
      in a single generation.
14 May the LORD never forget the sins of his
      ancestors;
   may his mother's sins never be erased
      from the record.
15 May these sins always remain before the
      LORD,
   but may his name be cut off from
      human memory.
16 For he refused all kindness to others;
   he persecuted the poor and needy,
   and he hounded the brokenhearted
      to death.
17 He loved to curse others;
   now you curse him.
  He never blessed others;
   now don't you bless him.
18 Cursing is as much a part of him as his
      clothing,
   or as the water he drinks,
   or the rich food he eats.
19 Now may his curses return and cling
      to him like clothing;
   may they be tied around him like a
      belt.

20 May those curses become the LORD's
      punishment for my accusers
   who are plotting against my life.
21 But deal well with me, O Sovereign
      LORD,
   for the sake of your own reputation!
  Rescue me because you are so faithful
      and good.
22   For I am poor and needy,
   and my heart is full of pain.
23 I am fading like a shadow at dusk;
   I am falling like a grasshopper that is
      brushed aside.
24 My knees are weak from fasting,
   and I am skin and bones.

110:2 Hebrew *Zion.*

25 I am an object of mockery to people
      everywhere;
   when they see me, they shake their heads.

26 Help me, O LORD my God!
   Save me because of your unfailing love.
27 Let them see that this is your doing,
   that you yourself have done it, LORD.
28 Then let them curse me if they like,
   but you will bless me!
  When they attack me, they will be
      disgraced!
   But I, your servant, will go right on
      rejoicing!
29 Make their humiliation obvious to all;
   clothe my accusers with disgrace.
30 But I will give repeated thanks to the
      LORD,
   praising him to everyone.
31 For he stands beside the needy,
   ready to save them from those who
      condemn them.

PSALM 110
A psalm of David.

1 The LORD said to my Lord,
   "Sit in honor at my right hand
  until I humble your enemies,
   making them a footstool under your
      feet."

2 The LORD will extend your powerful
      dominion from Jerusalem*;
   you will rule over your enemies.
3 In that day of battle,
   your people will serve you willingly.
  Arrayed in holy garments,
   your vigor will be renewed each day
      like the morning dew.
4 The LORD has taken an oath and will not
      break his vow:
   "You are a priest forever in the line
      of Melchizedek."

109:21-31 It takes great humility to entrust our life to God. One of the most difficult parts of recovery, as God's children, is to admit how helpless we are to overcome our powerful dependency alone. We have all discovered what happens when we try to do things our own way: We become enslaved to our own desires and appetites. Dependence on God and his program is the only road to true freedom. We need to remember, however, that although God calls us to be childlike in spirit, he does not want us to be childish in behavior.
111:9-10 God ransomed his people, the Israelites, first by making a covenant with them and then by delivering them time after time from their enemies. God has ransomed us, too, from the penalty of our sins by paying a very dear price—his own Son! God made this ultimate sacrifice so we, unworthy though we are, can be restored to godly and joyful lives. This should encourage us as we seek recovery. God wants it to happen even more than we do! That's why we can safely entrust our life into his hands. God has proven how strongly he desires our recovery by giving his own Son to suffer on our behalf.

READ PSALM 111:1-10

GOD grant me the serenity to accept the things I cannot change the courage to change the things I can and the wisdom to know the difference AMEN

When we lack wisdom, the storms of life can be devastating. When we find our life is in pieces, we may realize that we have acted unwisely and want to change, but where do we start?

"Reverence for the LORD," the psalmist wrote, "is the foundation of true wisdom. The rewards of wisdom come to all who obey him" (Psalm 111:10). God has given us clear instructions for our life in his Word. When we have reverence for God and are willing to accept his instructions as the basis for all of our decisions, we have a good starting point.

Jesus said, "Anyone who listens to my teaching and obeys me is wise, like a person who builds a house on solid rock. Though the rain comes in torrents and the floodwaters rise and the winds beat against that house, it won't collapse, because it is built on rock" (Matthew 7:24-25). Listening to what the Bible says is the next step toward walking in wisdom. Filling our mind with God's instructions will help lead us to follow them. This will also help us turn away from the things forbidden by God. The book of Job tells us, "The fear of the LORD is true wisdom; to forsake evil is real understanding" (Job 28:28).

Turning our life over to God is a wise move! Like most aspects of recovery, walking in wisdom is a process that we grow into. These three elements are the groundwork: reverence for God, listening to his instructions, and following them. ***Turn to page 571, Psalm 139.***

---

⁵The Lord stands at your right hand
   to protect you.
   He will strike down many kings in the
      day of his anger.
⁶He will punish the nations
   and fill them with their dead;
he will shatter heads
   over the whole earth.
⁷But he himself will be refreshed from
      brooks along the way.
   He will be victorious.

PSALM 111
¹Praise the LORD!

I will thank the LORD with all my heart
   as I meet with his godly people.
²How amazing are the deeds of the LORD!
   All who delight in him should ponder
      them.
³Everything he does reveals his glory and
      majesty.
   His righteousness never fails.

⁴Who can forget the wonders he performs?
   How gracious and merciful is our LORD!
⁵He gives food to those who trust him;
   he always remembers his covenant.
⁶He has shown his great power to his
      people
   by giving them the lands of other nations.
⁷All he does is just and good,
   and all his commandments are trust-
      worthy.
⁸They are forever true,
   to be obeyed faithfully and with
      integrity.
⁹He has paid a full ransom for his people.
   He has guaranteed his covenant with
      them forever.
   What a holy, awe-inspiring name he has!
¹⁰Reverence for the LORD is the foundation
      of true wisdom.
   The rewards of wisdom come to all who
      obey him.

   Praise his name forever!

PSALM 112

¹Praise the LORD!

Happy are those who fear the LORD.
　　Yes, happy are those who delight in
　　doing what he commands.
²Their children will be successful everywhere;
　　an entire generation of godly people
　　will be blessed.
³They themselves will be wealthy,
　　and their good deeds will never be
　　forgotten.
⁴When darkness overtakes the godly, light
　　will come bursting in.
　　They are* generous, compassionate,
　　and righteous.
⁵All goes well for those who are generous,
　　who lend freely and conduct their
　　business fairly.
⁶Such people will not be overcome by evil
　　circumstances.
　　Those who are righteous will be long
　　remembered.
⁷They do not fear bad news;
　　they confidently trust the LORD to care
　　for them.
⁸They are confident and fearless
　　and can face their foes triumphantly.
⁹They give generously to those in need.
　　Their good deeds will never be forgotten.
　　They will have influence and honor.
¹⁰The wicked will be infuriated when they
　　see this.
　　They will grind their teeth in anger;
　　they will slink away, their hopes thwarted.

PSALM 113

¹Praise the LORD!

Yes, give praise, O servants of the LORD.
　　Praise the name of the LORD!

²Blessed be the name of the LORD
　　forever and ever.
³Everywhere—from east to west—
　　praise the name of the LORD.
⁴For the LORD is high above the nations;
　　his glory is far greater than the heavens.

⁵Who can be compared with the LORD
　　our God,
　　who is enthroned on high?
⁶Far below him are the heavens and the
　　earth.
　　He stoops to look,
⁷and he lifts the poor from the dirt
　　and the needy from the garbage dump.
⁸He sets them among princes,
　　even the princes of his own people!
⁹He gives the barren woman a home,
　　so that she becomes a happy mother.

Praise the LORD!

PSALM 114

¹When the Israelites escaped from Egypt—
　　when the family of Jacob left that
　　foreign land—
²the land of Judah became God's
　　sanctuary,
　　and Israel became his kingdom.

³The Red Sea* saw them coming and
　　hurried out of their way!
　　The water of the Jordan River turned
　　away.
⁴The mountains skipped like rams,
　　the little hills like lambs!

⁵What's wrong, Red Sea, that made you
　　hurry out of their way?
　　What happened, Jordan River, that you
　　turned away?
⁶Why, mountains, did you skip like rams?
　　Why, little hills, like lambs?

112:4 Greek version reads *The LORD is.*　**114:3** Hebrew *the sea;* also in 114:5.

112:5-10 Our best chance of success in overcoming our habits, our bad thought patterns, and the hurts in our life is to keep our eyes on God. Making good changes in our life won't make everyone happy. Some of our old enemies—and our old friends who used to lead us astray—will wonder why we no longer relate to them as we did. Some of them may even criticize us or think we are snobbish. As a result, we may find the process of recovery lonely at first. In times like these, we must look to God, who is always with us. With his help we will find new relationships that will strengthen us and learn how to reconcile our old relationships so they will support us in the recovery process.
113:5-9 Only God can restore us to sanity and right living, and he alone can lift us up. We may not sit "among princes," but we can return to society with dignity when we allow God to help us regain control of our life.
114:1-6 There is no end to the miracles God can perform on behalf of those who seek refuge in him. To bring courage to his readers, the psalmist listed some of God's amazing acts of deliverance in Israel's history. As we face difficulties, we can recall events of God's deliverance—in biblical history or in our own life. This will give us the hope we need to persevere in recovery; it will help us entrust our life into God's hands without reservation. God is truly awesome, worthy of our respect, obedience, and praise.

[7]Tremble, O earth, at the presence of the
Lord,
at the presence of the God of Israel.*
[8]He turned the rock into pools of water;
yes, springs of water came from solid
rock.

PSALM 115
[1]Not to us, O LORD, but to you goes all the
glory
for your unfailing love and faithfulness.
[2]Why let the nations say,
"Where is their God?"
[3]For our God is in the heavens,
and he does as he wishes.
[4]Their idols are merely things of silver and
gold,
shaped by human hands.
[5]They cannot talk, though they have
mouths,
or see, though they have eyes!
[6]They cannot hear with their ears,
or smell with their noses,
[7] or feel with their hands,
or walk with their feet,
or utter sounds with their throats!
[8]And those who make them are just like
them,
as are all who trust in them.

[9]O Israel, trust the LORD!
He is your helper; he is your shield.
[10]O priests of Aaron, trust the LORD!
He is your helper; he is your shield.
[11]All you who fear the LORD, trust the
LORD!
He is your helper; he is your shield.

[12]The LORD remembers us,
and he will surely bless us.
He will bless the people of Israel
and the family of Aaron, the priests.

114:7 Hebrew *of Jacob.* **116:3** Hebrew *of Sheol.*

[13]He will bless those who fear the LORD,
both great and small.
[14]May the LORD richly bless
both you and your children.
[15]May you be blessed by the LORD,
who made heaven and earth.
[16]The heavens belong to the LORD,
but he has given the earth to all
humanity.
[17]The dead cannot sing praises to the LORD,
for they have gone into the silence of
the grave.
[18]But we can praise the LORD
both now and forever!

Praise the LORD!

PSALM 116
[1]I love the LORD because he hears
and answers my prayers.
[2]Because he bends down and listens,
I will pray as long as I have breath!
[3]Death had its hands around my throat;
the terrors of the grave* overtook me.
I saw only trouble and sorrow.
[4]Then I called on the name of the LORD:
"Please, LORD, save me!"
[5]How kind the LORD is! How good he is!
So merciful, this God of ours!
[6]The LORD protects those of childlike faith;
I was facing death, and then he saved me.
[7]Now I can rest again,
for the LORD has been so good to me.
[8]He has saved me from death,
my eyes from tears,
my feet from stumbling.
[9]And so I walk in the LORD's presence
as I live here on earth!
[10]I believed in you, so I prayed,
"I am deeply troubled, LORD."

115:1-8 God is the only real resource for recovery. We have probably tried a number of recovery plans, but if God is not a central part of our program, we won't experience a lasting recovery. Some of us look for help in every new fad that comes along. If we don't ask God for help, all the recovery resources are useless—they are only man-made plans, as powerless as idols. Recovery is never easy. If we hear of a plan that is easy or quick, someone is probably just after our money. God alone knows what we need and has the power to lift us out of our painful circumstances and give us a life of meaning and joy. His program is our only way to a healthy life.
116:1-9 How wonderful that God hears and answers the prayers of those who turn to him in distress! When we were in the grip of our dependency or addiction, we may have been blind to the fact that we were in danger of losing our reputation, our friends, or even our life. But then we called out to the Lord, and he saved us. The natural response to this realization should be praise to God.
116:10-19 We will never be able to repay God for what he has done for us. But we can at least show our gratitude by fulfilling the promises we made to him when we called out to him for help. God thinks of us as his precious children, so we should thank him by keeping our promises to him. This may include making sure everyone knows it is God who deserves the credit for our deliverance.

¹¹ In my anxiety I cried out to you,
"These people are all liars!"
¹² What can I offer the LORD
for all he has done for me?
¹³ I will lift up a cup symbolizing his
salvation;
I will praise the LORD's name for
saving me.
¹⁴ I will keep my promises to the LORD
in the presence of all his people.

¹⁵ The LORD's loved ones are precious
to him;
it grieves him when they die.
¹⁶ O LORD, I am your servant;
yes, I am your servant, the son of your
handmaid,
and you have freed me from my
bonds!
¹⁷ I will offer you a sacrifice of thanksgiving
and call on the name of the LORD.
¹⁸ I will keep my promises to the LORD
in the presence of all his people,
¹⁹ in the house of the LORD,
in the heart of Jerusalem.

Praise the LORD!

PSALM 117
¹ Praise the LORD, all you nations.
Praise him, all you people of the earth.
² For he loves us with unfailing love;
the faithfulness of the LORD endures
forever.

Praise the LORD!

PSALM 118
¹ Give thanks to the LORD, for he is good!
His faithful love endures forever.

² Let the congregation of Israel repeat:
"His faithful love endures forever."
³ Let Aaron's descendants, the priests,
repeat:
"His faithful love endures forever."
⁴ Let all who fear the LORD repeat:
"His faithful love endures forever."

⁵ In my distress I prayed to the LORD,
and the LORD answered me and
rescued me.
⁶ The LORD is for me, so I will not be
afraid.
What can mere mortals do to me?
⁷ Yes, the LORD is for me; he will help me.
I will look in triumph at those who
hate me.
⁸ It is better to trust the LORD
than to put confidence in people.
⁹ It is better to trust the LORD
than to put confidence in princes.
¹⁰ Though hostile nations surrounded me,
I destroyed them all in the name of the
LORD.
¹¹ Yes, they surrounded and attacked me,
but I destroyed them all in the name
of the LORD.
¹² They swarmed around me like bees;
they blazed against me like a roaring
flame.
But I destroyed them all in the name
of the LORD.
¹³ You did your best to kill me, O my
enemy,
but the LORD helped me.
¹⁴ The LORD is my strength and my song;
he has become my victory.
¹⁵ Songs of joy and victory are sung in the
camp of the godly.
The strong right arm of the LORD has
done glorious things!
¹⁶ The strong right arm of the LORD is raised
in triumph.
The strong right arm of the LORD has
done glorious things!
¹⁷ I will not die, but I will live
to tell what the LORD has done.
¹⁸ The LORD has punished me severely,
but he has not handed me over to
death.

¹⁹ Open for me the gates where the
righteous enter,
and I will go in and thank the LORD.

118:22-25 God's ways are not the same as our ways. What people may cast aside as unfit for use, God uses to do awe-inspiring work. This can be true for us, too. We may feel that our life is beyond repair or that God would never use us for anything significant. God often uses the most unlikely people to work his greatest miracles, proving to the world that he is at work. As willing vessels of God's power, we can be transformed to impact others far beyond our wildest dreams. To do this, we must entrust our life to God.
119:9-16 Obedience to God's Word produces wholeness; it seems only logical that we should do all we can to follow it. This is a significant part of seeking God's will for us. In the Bible, God has left clear guidelines for how he expects us to live. He has also promised that he will help us to carry out his will if we only ask him. Studying and applying God's Word should become a joyful experience that will implant God's truth firmly in our mind and heart.

²⁰ Those gates lead to the presence of the
LORD,
and the godly enter there.
²¹ I thank you for answering my prayer
and saving me!

²² The stone rejected by the builders
has now become the cornerstone.
²³ This is the LORD's doing,
and it is marvelous to see.
²⁴ This is the day the LORD has made.
We will rejoice and be glad in it.
²⁵ Please, LORD, please save us.
Please, LORD, please give us success.
²⁶ Bless the one who comes in the name
of the LORD.
We bless you from the house of the
LORD.
²⁷ The LORD is God, shining upon us.
Bring forward the sacrifice and put
it on the altar.
²⁸ You are my God, and I will praise you!
You are my God, and I will exalt you!

²⁹ Give thanks to the LORD, for he is good!
His faithful love endures forever.

PSALM 119
¹ Happy are people of integrity,
who follow the law of the LORD.
² Happy are those who obey his decrees
and search for him with all their
hearts.
³ They do not compromise with evil,
and they walk only in his paths.
⁴ You have charged us
to keep your commandments carefully.
⁵ Oh, that my actions would consistently
reflect your principles!
⁶ Then I will not be disgraced
when I compare my life with your
commands.
⁷ When I learn your righteous laws,
I will thank you by living as I should!
⁸ I will obey your principles.
Please don't give up on me!

⁹ How can a young person stay pure?
By obeying your word and following
its rules.
¹⁰ I have tried my best to find you—
don't let me wander from your
commands.
¹¹ I have hidden your word in my heart,
that I might not sin against you.

119 This psalm is a Hebrew acrostic poem; there are
22 stanzas, one for each letter of the Hebrew alphabet.
The 8 verses within each stanza begin with the Hebrew
letter of its section.

STEP 11

Powerful Secrets

BIBLE READING: Psalm 119:1-11
**We sought through prayer and medita-
tion to improve our conscious contact
with God, praying only for knowledge
of his will for us and the power to carry
that out.**
The secrets we hide have enormous power
in our life. How many of our addictive/
compulsive behaviors have been hidden
or covered up? When we took the step
and admitted the exact nature of our
addiction to another person, we were
probably amazed at the way the addiction
lost its power as it was exposed. The power
of hidden behaviors and secrets can work
for us as well as against us.

The psalmist wrote this prayer to God:
"I have hidden your word in my heart,
that I might not sin against you" (Psalm
119:11). If we "hide" God's Word in our
heart by memorizing and meditating on it,
we will find new power to keep our mind
and heart clean.

The power of secrets will also work to
our advantage in our prayer life. Jesus
taught us that "when you pray, go away
by yourself, shut the door behind you,
and pray to your Father secretly. Then
your Father, who knows all secrets, will
reward you" (Matthew 6:6). When we
begin to spend time shut away with God
in prayer and meditation, we'll find that
power working for us. *Turn to Step Twelve,
page 85, Mark 16.*

¹²Blessed are you, O LORD;
  teach me your principles.
¹³I have recited aloud
  all the laws you have given us.
¹⁴I have rejoiced in your decrees
  as much as in riches.
¹⁵I will study your commandments
  and reflect on your ways.
¹⁶I will delight in your principles
  and not forget your word.

¹⁷Be good to your servant,
  that I may live and obey your word.
¹⁸Open my eyes to see
  the wonderful truths in your law.
¹⁹I am but a foreigner here on earth;
  I need the guidance of your commands.
  Don't hide them from me!
²⁰I am overwhelmed continually
  with a desire for your laws.
²¹You rebuke those cursed proud ones
  who wander from your commands.
²²Don't let them scorn and insult me,
  for I have obeyed your decrees.
²³Even princes sit and speak against me,
  but I will meditate on your principles.
²⁴Your decrees please me;
  they give me wise advice.

²⁵I lie in the dust, completely discouraged;
  revive me by your word.
²⁶I told you my plans, and you answered.
  Now teach me your principles.
²⁷Help me understand the meaning of your
  commandments,
  and I will meditate on your wonderful
  miracles.
²⁸I weep with grief;
  encourage me by your word.
²⁹Keep me from lying to myself;
  give me the privilege of knowing your
  law.
³⁰I have chosen to be faithful;
  I have determined to live by your
  laws.
³¹I cling to your decrees.
  LORD, don't let me be put to shame!
³²If you will help me,
  I will run to follow your commands.

³³Teach me, O LORD,
  to follow every one of your principles.

³⁴Give me understanding and I will obey
  your law;
  I will put it into practice with all my
  heart.
³⁵Make me walk along the path of your
  commands,
  for that is where my happiness is
  found.
³⁶Give me an eagerness for your decrees;
  do not inflict me with love for money!
³⁷Turn my eyes from worthless things,
  and give me life through your word.*
³⁸Reassure me of your promise,
  which is for those who honor you.
³⁹Help me abandon my shameful ways;
  your laws are all I want in life.
⁴⁰I long to obey your commandments!
  Renew my life with your goodness.

⁴¹LORD, give to me your unfailing love,
  the salvation that you promised me.
⁴²Then I will have an answer for those who
  taunt me,
  for I trust in your word.
⁴³Do not snatch your word of truth from me,
  for my only hope is in your laws.
⁴⁴I will keep on obeying your law
  forever and forever.
⁴⁵I will walk in freedom,
  for I have devoted myself to your
  commandments.
⁴⁶I will speak to kings about your decrees,
  and I will not be ashamed.
⁴⁷How I delight in your commands!
  How I love them!
⁴⁸I honor and love your commands.
  I meditate on your principles.

⁴⁹Remember your promise to me,
  for it is my only hope.
⁵⁰Your promise revives me;
  it comforts me in all my troubles.
⁵¹The proud hold me in utter contempt,
  but I do not turn away from your law.
⁵²I meditate on your age-old laws;
  O LORD, they comfort me.
⁵³I am furious with the wicked,
  those who reject your law.
⁵⁴Your principles have been the music
  of my life
  throughout the years of my pilgrimage.

119:37 Some manuscripts read *in your ways.*

119:17-24 With God's guidance, we can learn truths from his Word that will lead us safely through the uncharted territories of life. Because God rebukes those who do not follow his teaching, we need to seek his forgiveness for those times we have strayed from his commands. We must not let our problems inhibit our study of God's Word. Without God's wisdom and guidance, we lack the insight we need to experience a successful recovery.

⁵⁵ I reflect at night on who you are, O LORD,
and I obey your law because of this.
⁵⁶ This is my happy way of life:
obeying your commandments.

⁵⁷ LORD, you are mine!
I promise to obey your words!
⁵⁸ With all my heart I want your blessings.
Be merciful just as you promised.
⁵⁹ I pondered the direction of my life,
and I turned to follow your statutes.
⁶⁰ I will hurry, without lingering,
to obey your commands.
⁶¹ Evil people try to drag me into sin,
but I am firmly anchored to your law.
⁶² At midnight I rise to thank you
for your just laws.
⁶³ Anyone who fears you is my friend—
anyone who obeys your
commandments.
⁶⁴ O LORD, the earth is full of your unfailing
love;
teach me your principles.

⁶⁵ You have done many good things for me,
LORD,
just as you promised.
⁶⁶ I believe in your commands;
now teach me good judgment and
knowledge.
⁶⁷ I used to wander off until you disciplined
me;
but now I closely follow your word.
⁶⁸ You are good and do only good;
teach me your principles.
⁶⁹ Arrogant people have made up lies about me,
but in truth I obey your
commandments with all my heart.
⁷⁰ Their hearts are dull and stupid,
but I delight in your law.
⁷¹ The suffering you sent was good for me,
for it taught me to pay attention to
your principles.
⁷² Your law is more valuable to me
than millions in gold and silver!

⁷³ You made me; you created me.
Now give me the sense to follow your
commands.
⁷⁴ May all who fear you find in me a cause
for joy,
for I have put my hope in your word.
⁷⁵ I know, O LORD, that your decisions are
fair;
you disciplined me because I needed it.
⁷⁶ Now let your unfailing love comfort me,
just as you promised me, your servant.
⁷⁷ Surround me with your tender mercies
so I may live,
for your law is my delight.
⁷⁸ Bring disgrace upon the arrogant people
who lied about me;
meanwhile, I will concentrate on your
commandments.
⁷⁹ Let me be reconciled
with all who fear you and know your
decrees.
⁸⁰ May I be blameless in keeping your
principles;
then I will never have to be ashamed.

⁸¹ I faint with longing for your salvation;
but I have put my hope in your word.
⁸² My eyes are straining to see your
promises come true.
When will you comfort me?
⁸³ I am shriveled like a wineskin in the
smoke, exhausted with waiting.
But I cling to your principles and
obey them.
⁸⁴ How long must I wait?
When will you punish those who
persecute me?
⁸⁵ These arrogant people who hate your
law
have dug deep pits for me to fall
into.
⁸⁶ All your commands are trustworthy.
Protect me from those who hunt me
down without cause.

119:57-64 In recovery we are called to seek out God's will for our life. The Bible should be the first place we look. Yet we must not merely listen to his Word and study his principles. We also need to take appropriate action once God's will is known (see James 1:22-25). If we learn God's will but fail to act on it, we are no better off than we were before. Recovery demands that we act—now!
119:71-72 We should be thankful when God disciplines us for our sins. Painful as it may be, discipline drives us back to his truth, which is far more valuable than all the riches of this world. God wants only what is best for us. We would be wise to learn from God's discipline rather than fight it. It is given for our betterment, not our destruction.
119:73-77 As we obey God's revealed commands, people will begin to see the changes in our life and praise God. All of God's work—even his discipline—is done because of his goodness and faithfulness. God wants us to live joyfully. We need to seek God's will and do our best, with his help, to follow it. As God transforms us, we will become a living testimony of God's power to transform broken lives.

87 They almost finished me off,
but I refused to abandon your
commandments.
88 In your unfailing love, spare my life;
then I can continue to obey your decrees.

89 Forever, O LORD,
your word stands firm in heaven.
90 Your faithfulness extends to every
generation,
as enduring as the earth you created.
91 Your laws remain true today,
for everything serves your plans.
92 If your law hadn't sustained me with joy,
I would have died in my misery.
93 I will never forget your commandments,
for you have used them to restore my
joy and health.
94 I am yours; save me!
For I have applied myself to obey your
commandments.
95 Though the wicked hide along the way
to kill me,
I will quietly keep my mind on your
decrees.
96 Even perfection has its limits,
but your commands have no limit.

97 Oh, how I love your law!
I think about it all day long.
98 Your commands make me wiser than my
enemies,
for your commands are my constant
guide.
99 Yes, I have more insight than my teachers,
for I am always thinking of your
decrees.
100 I am even wiser than my elders,
for I have kept your commandments.
101 I have refused to walk on any path of evil,
that I may remain obedient to your
word.
102 I haven't turned away from your laws,
for you have taught me well.
103 How sweet are your words to my taste;
they are sweeter than honey.
104 Your commandments give me
understanding;
no wonder I hate every false way of life.

105 Your word is a lamp for my feet
and a light for my path.

106 I've promised it once, and I'll promise
again:
I will obey your wonderful laws.
107 I have suffered much, O LORD;
restore my life again, just as you
promised.
108 LORD, accept my grateful thanks
and teach me your laws.
109 My life constantly hangs in the balance,
but I will not stop obeying your law.
110 The wicked have set their traps for me
along your path,
but I will not turn from your
commandments.
111 Your decrees are my treasure;
they are truly my heart's delight.
112 I am determined to keep your principles,
even forever, to the very end.

113 I hate those who are undecided about you,
but my choice is clear—I love your law.
114 You are my refuge and my shield;
your word is my only source of hope.
115 Get out of my life, you evil-minded
people,
for I intend to obey the commands
of my God.
116 LORD, sustain me as you promised, that
I may live!
Do not let my hope be crushed.
117 Sustain me, and I will be saved;
then I will meditate on your principles
continually.
118 But you have rejected all who stray from
your principles.
They are only fooling themselves.
119 All the wicked of the earth are the scum
you skim off;
no wonder I love to obey your decrees!
120 I tremble in fear of you;
I fear your judgments.

121 Don't leave me to the mercy of my enemies,
for I have done what is just and right.
122 Please guarantee a blessing for me.
Don't let those who are arrogant
oppress me!
123 My eyes strain to see your deliverance,
to see the truth of your promise fulfilled.
124 I am your servant;
deal with me in unfailing love,
and teach me your principles.

119:124-128 Until we turn to God for help, we will never be rescued or have sure guidance for our life. Following God's plan for recovery will not be easy, but we can count on his help. Like the psalmist, we should ask God to teach us his principles. When we are under pressure, we may be tempted to abandon God's principles. Before returning to our old, destructive behaviors, we should turn to God, asking him to help us do what is right. God wants us to recover. He is willing to provide not only the plan but also the encouragement we need to follow it.

125 Give discernment to me, your servant;
  then I will understand your decrees.
126 LORD, it is time for you to act,
  for these evil people have broken your
    law.
127 Truly, I love your commands
  more than gold, even the finest gold.
128 Truly, each of your commandments is
    right.
  That is why I hate every false way.

129 Your decrees are wonderful.
  No wonder I obey them!
130 As your words are taught, they give
    light;
  even the simple can understand them.
131 I open my mouth, panting expectantly,
  longing for your commands.
132 Come and show me your mercy,
  as you do for all who love your name.
133 Guide my steps by your word,
  so I will not be overcome by any evil.
134 Rescue me from the oppression of evil
    people;
  then I can obey your commandments.
135 Look down on me with love;
  teach me all your principles.
136 Rivers of tears gush from my eyes
  because people disobey your law.

137 O LORD, you are righteous,
  and your decisions are fair.
138 Your decrees are perfect;
  they are entirely worthy of our trust.
139 I am overwhelmed with rage,
  for my enemies have disregarded your
    words.
140 Your promises have been thoroughly
    tested;
  that is why I love them so much.
141 I am insignificant and despised,
  but I don't forget your
    commandments.
142 Your justice is eternal,
  and your law is perfectly true.
143 As pressure and stress bear down on me,
  I find joy in your commands.
144 Your decrees are always fair;
  help me to understand them, that
    I may live.
145 I pray with all my heart; answer me,
    LORD!
  I will obey your principles.

146 I cry out to you; save me,
  that I may obey your decrees.
147 I rise early, before the sun is up;
  I cry out for help and put my hope
    in your words.
148 I stay awake through the night,
  thinking about your promise.
149 In your faithful love, O LORD, hear my
    cry;
  in your justice, save my life.
150 Those lawless people are coming near
    to attack me;
  they live far from your law.
151 But you are near, O LORD,
  and all your commands are true.
152 I have known from my earliest days
  that your decrees never change.

153 Look down upon my sorrows and
    rescue me,
  for I have not forgotten your law.
154 Argue my case; take my side!
  Protect my life as you promised.
155 The wicked are far from salvation,
  for they do not bother with your
    principles.
156 LORD, how great is your mercy;
  in your justice, give me back my life.
157 Many persecute and trouble me,
  yet I have not swerved from your
    decrees.
158 I hate these traitors
  because they care nothing for your
    word.
159 See how I love your commandments,
    LORD.
  Give back my life because of your
    unfailing love.
160 All your words are true;
  all your just laws will stand forever.

161 Powerful people harass me without cause,
  but my heart trembles only at your
    word.
162 I rejoice in your word
  like one who finds a great treasure.
163 I hate and abhor all falsehood,
  but I love your law.
164 I will praise you seven times a day
  because all your laws are just.
165 Those who love your law have great
    peace
  and do not stumble.

119:153-160 As we entrust our life to God, he restores us to wholeness. We can be sure that he will stand with us and protect us from those who persecute us. We can count on him to encourage us when the recovery process becomes difficult or painful. As we seek out God's will in his Word, we will discover the joyful truth: He is willing and able to restore us to wholeness!

166 I long for your salvation, LORD,
  so I have obeyed your commands.
167 I have obeyed your decrees,
  and I love them very much.
168 Yes, I obey your commandments and
  decrees,
  because you know everything I do.

169 O LORD, listen to my cry;
  give me the discerning mind you
  promised.
170 Listen to my prayer;
  rescue me as you promised.
171 Let my lips burst forth with praise,
  for you have taught me your
  principles.
172 Let my tongue sing about your word,
  for all your commands are right.
173 Stand ready to help me,
  for I have chosen to follow your
  commandments.
174 O LORD, I have longed for your
  salvation,
  and your law is my delight.
175 Let me live so I can praise you,
  and may your laws sustain me.
176 I have wandered away like a lost sheep;
  come and find me,
  for I have not forgotten your
  commands.

PSALM 120

A song for the ascent to Jerusalem.

1 I took my troubles to the LORD;
  I cried out to him, and he answered
  my prayer.
2 Rescue me, O LORD, from liars
  and from all deceitful people.
3 O deceptive tongue, what will God
  do to you?
  How will he increase your
  punishment?
4 You will be pierced with sharp arrows
  and burned with glowing coals.

5 How I suffer among these scoundrels
  of Meshech!
  It pains me to live with these people
  from Kedar!
6 I am tired of living here
  among people who hate peace.
7 As for me, I am for peace;
  but when I speak, they are for war!

PSALM 121

A song for the ascent to Jerusalem.

1 I look up to the mountains—
  does my help come from there?
2 My help comes from the LORD,
  who made the heavens and the
  earth!

3 He will not let you stumble and fall;
  the one who watches over you will
  not sleep.
4 Indeed, he who watches over Israel
  never tires and never sleeps.

5 The LORD himself watches over you!
  The LORD stands beside you as your
  protective shade.
6 The sun will not hurt you by day,
  nor the moon at night.
7 The LORD keeps you from all evil
  and preserves your life.
8 The LORD keeps watch over you as you
  come and go,
  both now and forever.

PSALM 122

*A song for the ascent to Jerusalem. A psalm
of David.*

1 I was glad when they said to me,
  "Let us go to the house of the
  LORD."
2 And now we are standing here
  inside your gates, O Jerusalem.
3 Jerusalem is a well-built city,
  knit together as a single unit.
4 All the people of Israel—the LORD's
  people—
  make their pilgrimage here.
  They come to give thanks to the name
  of the LORD
  as the law requires.
5 Here stand the thrones where judgment
  is given,
  the thrones of the dynasty of David.

6 Pray for the peace of Jerusalem.
  May all who love this city prosper.
7 O Jerusalem, may there be peace within
  your walls
  and prosperity in your palaces.
8 For the sake of my family and friends,
  I will say,
  "Peace be with you."

121:1-8 God alone is able to give us victory over our dependency. He watches over us day and night, placing us under his umbrella of protection. He guards us against the dangers that threaten to destroy our life and keeps us from evil.

9 For the sake of the house of the LORD
    our God,
  I will seek what is best for you,
    O Jerusalem.

PSALM 123
A song for the ascent to Jerusalem.

1 I lift my eyes to you,
    O God, enthroned in heaven.
2 We look to the LORD our God for his
    mercy,
    just as servants keep their eyes on
      their master,
    as a slave girl watches her mistress
      for the slightest signal.

3 Have mercy on us, LORD, have mercy,
    for we have had our fill of contempt.
4 We have had our fill of the scoffing of
    the proud
    and the contempt of the arrogant.

PSALM 124
A song for the ascent to Jerusalem. A psalm of David.

1 If the LORD had not been on our side—
    let Israel now say—
2 if the LORD had not been on our side
    when people rose up against us,
3 they would have swallowed us alive
    because of their burning anger
      against us.
4 The waters would have engulfed us;
    a torrent would have overwhelmed us.
5 Yes, the raging waters of their fury
    would have overwhelmed our very lives.

6 Blessed be the LORD,
    who did not let their teeth tear us
      apart!
7 We escaped like a bird from a hunter's
    trap.
  The trap is broken, and we are free!
8 Our help is from the LORD,
    who made the heavens and the earth.

126:1 Hebrew *Zion.*

PSALM 125
A song for the ascent to Jerusalem.

1 Those who trust in the LORD are as secure
    as Mount Zion;
    they will not be defeated but will
      endure forever.
2 Just as the mountains surround and
    protect Jerusalem,
    so the LORD surrounds and protects
      his people, both now and forever.
3 The wicked will not rule the godly,
    for then the godly might be forced
      to do wrong.
4 O LORD, do good to those who are good,
    whose hearts are in tune with you.
5 But banish those who turn to crooked
    ways, O LORD.
  Take them away with those who do
    evil.
  And let Israel have quietness and
    peace.

PSALM 126
A song for the ascent to Jerusalem.

1 When the LORD restored his exiles
    to Jerusalem,*
    it was like a dream!
2 We were filled with laughter,
    and we sang for joy.
  And the other nations said,
    "What amazing things the LORD has
      done for them."
3 Yes, the LORD has done amazing things
    for us!
  What joy!

4 Restore our fortunes, LORD,
    as streams renew the desert.
5 Those who plant in tears
    will harvest with shouts of joy.
6 They weep as they go to plant their
    seed,
    but they sing as they return with the
      harvest.

124:1-8 Without God, there is no hope of deliverance and freedom. If he is not helping us fight our battles, we will be overwhelmed by our powerful addiction. We should respond to God's gracious deliverance by praising him for what he has done for us. This is the first step toward sharing the good news of God's love and power with others.
126:1-6 This psalm was written in response to the return of the Jewish exiles from captivity. God enabled his people to recover from their many sins by leading them through a period of painful exile. During this exile, they confessed their sins and returned to God. Then God allowed them to return to their homeland. This can be our story too. As we experience God's restoration, our tears will turn to joy and we can sing our own songs of praise. Change never comes overnight, but God promises to complete the transformation in our life when the time is right.

PSALM 127

A song for the ascent to Jerusalem. A psalm of Solomon.

¹Unless the LORD builds a house,
    the work of the builders is useless.
Unless the LORD protects a city,
    guarding it with sentries will do no
        good.
²It is useless for you to work so hard
    from early morning until late at night,
anxiously working for food to eat;
    for God gives rest to his loved ones.

³Children are a gift from the LORD;
    they are a reward from him.
⁴Children born to a young man
    are like sharp arrows in a warrior's
        hands.
⁵How happy is the man whose quiver is
        full of them!
    He will not be put to shame when he
        confronts his accusers at the city gates.

PSALM 128

A song for the ascent to Jerusalem.

¹How happy are those who fear the LORD—
    all who follow his ways!
²You will enjoy the fruit of your labor.
    How happy you will be! How rich your
        life!
³Your wife will be like a fruitful vine,
    flourishing within your home.
And look at all those children!
    There they sit around your table
    as vigorous and healthy as young olive
        trees.
⁴That is the LORD's reward
    for those who fear him.

⁵May the LORD continually bless you from
        Zion.
    May you see Jerusalem prosper as long
        as you live.
⁶May you live to enjoy your grandchildren.
    And may Israel have quietness and
        peace.

PSALM 129

A song for the ascent to Jerusalem.

¹From my earliest youth my enemies have
        persecuted me—
    let Israel now say—
²from my earliest youth my enemies have
        persecuted me,
    but they have never been able to finish
        me off.
³My back is covered with cuts,
    as if a farmer had plowed long furrows.
⁴But the LORD is good;
    he has cut the cords used by the
        ungodly to bind me.

⁵May all who hate Jerusalem*
    be turned back in shameful defeat.
⁶May they be as useless as grass on a
        rooftop,
    turning yellow when only half grown,
7   ignored by the harvester,
    despised by the binder.
⁸And may those who pass by refuse to give
        them this blessing:
    "The LORD's blessings be upon you;
    we bless you in the LORD's name."

PSALM 130

A song for the ascent to Jerusalem.

¹From the depths of despair, O LORD,
    I call for your help.
²Hear my cry, O Lord.
    Pay attention to my prayer.

³LORD, if you kept a record of our sins,
    who, O Lord, could ever survive?
⁴But you offer forgiveness,
    that we might learn to fear you.

⁵I am counting on the LORD;
    yes, I am counting on him.
    I have put my hope in his word.
⁶I long for the Lord
    more than sentries long for the dawn,
    yes, more than sentries long for the
        dawn.

129:5 Hebrew *Zion.*

127:1 As we seek to rebuild our life, we must make sure God is involved in the building process. Without him, we have no hope for success. The forces that tear at our life are too strong for us to handle alone. Yet God is able to protect us as the rebuilding goes on, and he will direct us each step of the way. Recovery programs that fail to keep God at the center of our life will only lead to disappointment and deeper suffering. Unless God is supporting us in the recovery process, all our efforts are useless.

130:1-8 When we cry out to God, we want quick answers. We should be thankful that God does not respond on the basis of our worthiness. If he did, we would receive nothing but judgment. God forgives us of every kind of sin so we might worship him with a thankful heart. He desires our recovery from the sinful forces that beset us; he will deliver us when we call out to him.

7 O Israel, hope in the LORD;
    for with the LORD there is unfailing
        love
    and an overflowing supply of
        salvation.
8 He himself will free Israel
    from every kind of sin.

PSALM 131

*A song for the ascent to Jerusalem. A psalm
of David.*

1 LORD, my heart is not proud;
    my eyes are not haughty.
I don't concern myself with matters too
        great
    or awesome for me.
2 But I have stilled and quieted myself,
    just as a small child is quiet with its
        mother.
    Yes, like a small child is my soul
        within me.

3 O Israel, put your hope in the LORD—
    now and always.

PSALM 132

A song for the ascent to Jerusalem.

1 LORD, remember David
    and all that he suffered.
2 He took an oath before the LORD.
    He vowed to the Mighty One of
        Israel,*
3 "I will not go home;
    I will not let myself rest.
4 I will not let my eyes sleep
    nor close my eyelids in slumber
5   until I find a place to build a house
        for the LORD,
    a sanctuary for the Mighty One
        of Israel."
6 We heard that the Ark was in
        Ephrathah;
    then we found it in the distant
        countryside of Jaar.
7 Let us go to the dwelling place of the
        LORD;
    let us bow low before him.
8 Arise, O LORD, and enter your sanctuary,
    along with the Ark, the symbol of
        your power.

132:2 Hebrew *of Jacob;* also in 132:5. 132:13 Hebrew *Zion.*

9 Your priests will be agents of salvation;
    may your loyal servants sing for joy.
10 For the sake of your servant David,
    do not reject the king you chose for
        your people.
11 The LORD swore to David
    a promise he will never take back:
"I will place one of your descendants
        on your throne.
12 If your descendants obey the terms
        of my covenant
    and follow the decrees that I teach
        them,
    then your royal line will never end."

13 For the LORD has chosen Jerusalem*;
    he has desired it as his home.
14 "This is my home where I will live
        forever," he said.
    "I will live here, for this is the place
        I desired.
15 I will make this city prosperous
    and satisfy its poor with food.
16 I will make its priests the agents of
        salvation;
    its godly people will sing for joy.
17 Here I will increase the power of David;
    my anointed one will be a light for my
        people.
18 I will clothe his enemies with shame,
    but he will be a glorious king."

PSALM 133

*A song for the ascent to Jerusalem. A psalm
of David.*

1 How wonderful it is, how pleasant,
    when brothers live together in
        harmony!
2 For harmony is as precious as the fragrant
        anointing oil
    that was poured over Aaron's head,
    that ran down his beard
    and onto the border of his robe.
3 Harmony is as refreshing as the dew
        from Mount Hermon
    that falls on the mountains of Zion.
And the LORD has pronounced his
        blessing,
    even life forevermore.

133:1-3 Reconciling our human relationships is an important part of the recovery process. We need the people in our life to give us encouragement to overcome our pain and to stand with us against the temptations we face. There is nothing quite like human fellowship and friendship, and God wants to bless us through other people. The kind of friends most helpful to us in recovery are those who are trying to live godly lives.

PSALM 134

A song for the ascent to Jerusalem.

¹Oh, bless the LORD, all you servants of the LORD,
you who serve as night watchmen in the house of the LORD.
²Lift your hands in holiness,
and bless the LORD.

³May the LORD, who made heaven and earth,
bless you from Jerusalem.*

PSALM 135

¹Praise the LORD!

Praise the name of the LORD!
Praise him, you who serve the LORD,
² you who serve in the house of the LORD,
in the courts of the house of our God.
³Praise the LORD, for the LORD is good;
celebrate his wonderful name with music.
⁴For the LORD has chosen Jacob for himself,
Israel for his own special treasure.

⁵I know the greatness of the LORD—
that our Lord is greater than any other god.
⁶The LORD does whatever pleases him
throughout all heaven and earth,
and on the seas and in their depths.
⁷He causes the clouds to rise over the earth.
He sends the lightning with the rain
and releases the wind from his storehouses.
⁸He destroyed the firstborn in each Egyptian home,
both people and animals.
⁹He performed miraculous signs and wonders in Egypt;
Pharaoh and all his people watched.
¹⁰He struck down great nations
and slaughtered mighty kings—
¹¹ Sihon king of the Amorites,
Og king of Bashan,
and all the kings of Canaan.
¹²He gave their land as an inheritance,
a special possession to his people Israel.

134:3 Hebrew *Zion.*

¹³Your name, O LORD, endures forever;
your fame, O LORD, is known to every generation.
¹⁴For the LORD will vindicate his people
and have compassion on his servants.

¹⁵Their idols are merely things of silver and gold,
shaped by human hands.
¹⁶They cannot talk, though they have mouths,
or see, though they have eyes!
¹⁷They cannot hear with their ears
or smell with their noses.
¹⁸And those who make them are just like them,
as are all who trust in them.

¹⁹O Israel, praise the LORD!
O priests of Aaron, praise the LORD!
²⁰O Levites, praise the LORD!
All you who fear the LORD, praise the LORD!
²¹The LORD be praised from Zion,
for he lives here in Jerusalem.

Praise the LORD!

PSALM 136

¹Give thanks to the LORD, for he is good!
His faithful love endures forever.
²Give thanks to the God of gods.
His faithful love endures forever.
³Give thanks to the Lord of lords.
His faithful love endures forever.

⁴Give thanks to him who alone does mighty miracles.
His faithful love endures forever.
⁵Give thanks to him who made the heavens so skillfully.
His faithful love endures forever.
⁶Give thanks to him who placed the earth on the water.
His faithful love endures forever.
⁷Give thanks to him who made the heavenly lights—
His faithful love endures forever.
⁸ the sun to rule the day,
His faithful love endures forever.
⁹ and the moon and stars to rule the night.
His faithful love endures forever.

135:1-13 Knowing that God has chosen us as his own should give us the confidence to call on him when we are in trouble. All through the Old Testament we see evidence of God working to save his people. Because God is all-powerful and "does whatever pleases him" throughout the earth, he can help us when we call on him. In his greatness, no problem is too great for him to solve.

10 Give thanks to him who killed the
   firstborn of Egypt.
      His faithful love endures forever.
11 He brought Israel out of Egypt.
      His faithful love endures forever.
12 He acted with a strong hand and powerful
   arm.
      His faithful love endures forever.
13 Give thanks to him who parted the
   Red Sea.*
      His faithful love endures forever.
14 He led Israel safely through,
      His faithful love endures forever.
15   but he hurled Pharaoh and his army
   into the sea.
      His faithful love endures forever.
16 Give thanks to him who led his people
   through the wilderness.
      His faithful love endures forever.

17 Give thanks to him who struck down
   mighty kings.
      His faithful love endures forever.
18 He killed powerful kings—
      His faithful love endures forever.
19   Sihon king of the Amorites,
      His faithful love endures forever.
20   and Og king of Bashan.
      His faithful love endures forever.
21 God gave the land of these kings as an
   inheritance—
      His faithful love endures forever.
22   a special possession to his servant Israel.
      His faithful love endures forever.

23 He remembered our utter weakness.
      His faithful love endures forever.
24 He saved us from our enemies.
      His faithful love endures forever.
25 He gives food to every living thing.
      His faithful love endures forever.

26 Give thanks to the God of heaven.
      His faithful love endures forever.

PSALM 137

1 Beside the rivers of Babylon, we sat and wept
   as we thought of Jerusalem.*
2 We put away our lyres,
   hanging them on the branches of the
   willow trees.

3 For there our captors demanded a song
   of us.
   Our tormentors requested a joyful
   hymn:
   "Sing us one of those songs of
   Jerusalem!"
4 But how can we sing the songs of the
   LORD
   while in a foreign land?

5 If I forget you, O Jerusalem,
   let my right hand forget its skill upon
   the harp.
6 May my tongue stick to the roof of my
   mouth
   if I fail to remember you,
   if I don't make Jerusalem my highest
   joy.

7 O LORD, remember what the Edomites did
   on the day the armies of Babylon
   captured Jerusalem.
   "Destroy it!" they yelled.
   "Level it to the ground!"
8 O Babylon, you will be destroyed.
   Happy is the one who pays you back
   for what you have done to us.
9 Happy is the one who takes your babies
   and smashes them against the rocks!

PSALM 138

A psalm of David.

1 I give you thanks, O LORD, with all my
   heart;
   I will sing your praises before the gods.
2 I bow before your holy Temple as I
   worship.
   I will give thanks to your name
   for your unfailing love and faithfulness,
   because your promises are backed
   by all the honor of your name.
3 When I pray, you answer me;
   you encourage me by giving me the
   strength I need.

4 Every king in all the earth will give you
   thanks, O LORD,
   for all of them will hear your words.
5 Yes, they will sing about the LORD's ways,
   for the glory of the LORD is very great.

136:13 Hebrew *sea of reeds;* also in 136:15. **137:1** Hebrew *Zion;* also in 137:3.

136:16-26 Struggling with a powerful addiction might be compared to walking through
a wilderness. But if we entrust our life to him, God is able to lead us to victory, just as he led
the Israelites through the wilderness. God never abandons us when we are humbled by our
enemies—whether internal or external. Instead, he frees us from their clutches because his
faithful love for us "endures forever."

⁶Though the LORD is great, he cares for
the humble,
but he keeps his distance from the
proud.

⁷Though I am surrounded by troubles,
you will preserve me against the anger
of my enemies.
You will clench your fist against my angry
enemies!
Your power will save me.
⁸The LORD will work out his plans for my
life—
for your faithful love, O LORD, endures
forever.
Don't abandon me, for you made me.

PSALM 139

For the choir director: A psalm of David.

¹O LORD, you have examined my heart
and know everything about me.
²You know when I sit down or stand up.
You know my every thought when far
away.
³You chart the path ahead of me
and tell me where to stop and rest.
Every moment you know where I am.
⁴You know what I am going to say
even before I say it, LORD.
⁵You both precede and follow me.
You place your hand of blessing on
my head.
⁶Such knowledge is too wonderful for me,
too great for me to know!

⁷I can never escape from your spirit!
I can never get away from your presence!

⁸If I go up to heaven, you are there;
if I go down to the place of the dead,*
you are there.
⁹If I ride the wings of the morning,
if I dwell by the farthest oceans,
¹⁰even there your hand will guide me,
and your strength will support me.
¹¹I could ask the darkness to hide me
and the light around me to become
night—
¹² but even in darkness I cannot hide
from you.
To you the night shines as bright as day.
Darkness and light are both alike to
you.

¹³You made all the delicate, inner parts
of my body
and knit me together in my mother's
womb.
¹⁴Thank you for making me so wonderfully
complex!
Your workmanship is marvelous—and
how well I know it.
¹⁵You watched me as I was being formed
in utter seclusion,
as I was woven together in the dark
of the womb.
¹⁶You saw me before I was born.
Every day of my life was recorded in
your book.
Every moment was laid out
before a single day had passed.

¹⁷How precious are your thoughts about
me,* O God!
They are innumerable!

139:8 Hebrew *to Sheol.* **139:17** Or *How precious to me are your thoughts.*

138:6-8 God responds favorably to humility, but he keeps his distance from the proud, who think they have no need of him. When we remain humble and seek his face, he will renew our strength and give us power over our enemies. How wonderful to know that the Lord is working out his plans for our life, and he will never fail us.
139:6-12 God is everywhere. We can never escape from his presence. Such knowledge should keep us from falling into sin and encourage us to follow him, knowing he is there to help us. He is not limited by space, nor is he limited by time. He is with us day and night to strengthen and support us.
139:13-18 The power of our dependency is often rooted in low self-esteem. These verses reveal an exciting fact: Each of us is an amazing creature—"wonderfully complex"! More than that, God is constantly thinking about us! We are so precious to him that he has recorded every day of our life in a book. We may have been taught, in one way or another, that we were no good. We began to believe this message, and now we have fallen into various destructive methods to deal with the pain. When we see ourself as God sees us, much of the pain that drives our dependency will fall away.
140:1-5 We need God's protection against those who might cause our destruction. Some people like to stir up trouble and may trap us and entice us to return to the poisonous dependency that led to our downfall in the first place. More than ever, we need God to keep us from being caught in their hidden snares. We are never out of the danger zone and may never totally escape the siren call of our addiction. We must commit ourself to staying close to God, the only one who can keep us safe.

READ PSALM 139:1-16

GOD grant me the serenity to accept the things I cannot change the courage to change the things I can and the wisdom to know the difference AMEN

Many of us have spent our life trying to be someone we are not. Our addictive/compulsive behaviors may be only a desperate attempt to escape from ourself. Maybe we have difficulty accepting our personality, our appearance, our handicap, or even our talents.

Perhaps we spend our energy and time trying to be what other people want us to be because we feel that who we are is not enough. We may do all we can to separate from our inner being because we are so deeply ashamed of who we are. Self-hatred is a defect of character that needs to be removed. It breeds the sin of covetousness—that is, longing to be in someone else's situation or have what they have. The psalmist wrote, "Thank you for making me so wonderfully complex! Your workmanship is marvelous—and how well I know it" (Psalm 139:14). Saying we are God's "workmanship" means that we are unique and beautiful masterpieces—works of divine poetry. Beauty and value are designed into the very fiber of our being by virtue of our Creator.

One important step in the recovery process is to allow God to remove our self-hatred, helping us to value ourself for who we are. We have been miraculously created, and we are treasured by God. This has been true since the time we were in our mother's womb, long before we could *do* anything to earn it! As we begin to see how unique and special we are—embraced and accepted by God himself—our strides toward recovery should grow faster and longer. ***Turn to page 583, Proverbs 2.***

---

¹⁸ I can't even count them;
   they outnumber the grains of sand!
 And when I wake up in the morning,
   you are still with me!

¹⁹ O God, if only you would destroy the
   wicked!
   Get out of my life, you murderers!
²⁰ They blaspheme you;
   your enemies take your name in vain.
²¹ O LORD, shouldn't I hate those who hate
   you?
   Shouldn't I despise those who resist
   you?
²² Yes, I hate them with complete hatred,
   for your enemies are my enemies.

²³ Search me, O God, and know my heart;
   test me and know my thoughts.
²⁴ Point out anything in me that offends
   you,
   and lead me along the path of
   everlasting life.

PSALM 140
For the choir director: A psalm of David.

¹ O LORD, rescue me from evil people.
   Preserve me from those who are
   violent,
² those who plot evil in their hearts
   and stir up trouble all day long.
³ Their tongues sting like a snake;
   the poison of a viper drips from
   their lips.   *Interlude*

⁴ O LORD, keep me out of the hands of the
   wicked.
   Preserve me from those who are
   violent,
   for they are plotting against me.
⁵ The proud have set a trap to catch me;
   they have stretched out a net;
   they have placed traps all along
   the way.   *Interlude*

⁶ I said to the LORD, "You are my God!"
   Listen, O LORD, to my cries for mercy!

7 O Sovereign LORD, my strong savior,
  you protected me on the day of battle.
8 LORD, do not give in to their evil desires.
  Do not let their evil schemes succeed,
    O God.   *Interlude*

9 Let my enemies be destroyed
  by the very evil they have planned for
    me.
10 Let burning coals fall down on their
    heads,
  or throw them into the fire,
  or into deep pits from which they can't
    escape.
11 Don't let liars prosper here in our land.
  Cause disaster to fall with great force
    on the violent.

12 But I know the LORD will surely help those
    they persecute;
  he will maintain the rights of the poor.
13 Surely the godly are praising your name,
  for they will live in your presence.

PSALM 141
A psalm of David.

1 O LORD, I am calling to you. Please hurry!
  Listen when I cry to you for help!
2 Accept my prayer as incense offered to
    you,
  and my upraised hands as an evening
    offering.

3 Take control of what I say, O LORD,
  and keep my lips sealed.
4 Don't let me lust for evil things;
  don't let me participate in acts of
    wickedness.
  Don't let me share in the delicacies
    of those who do evil.

5 Let the godly strike me!
  It will be a kindness!
  If they reprove me, it is soothing medicine.
    Don't let me refuse it.

  But I am in constant prayer
    against the wicked and their deeds.

6 When their leaders are thrown down from
    a cliff,
  they will listen to my words and find
    them pleasing.
7 Even as a farmer breaks up the soil and
    brings up rocks,
  so the bones of the wicked will be
    scattered without a decent burial.

8 I look to you for help, O Sovereign LORD.
  You are my refuge; don't let them
    kill me.
9 Keep me out of the traps they have set
    for me,
  out of the snares of those who do evil.
10 Let the wicked fall into their own snares,
  but let me escape.

PSALM 142
*A psalm of David, regarding his experience in the
cave. A prayer.*

1 I cry out to the LORD;
  I plead for the LORD's mercy.
2 I pour out my complaints before him
  and tell him all my troubles.
3 For I am overwhelmed,
  and you alone know the way I should
    turn.
  Wherever I go,
    my enemies have set traps for me.
4 I look for someone to come and help me,
  but no one gives me a passing
    thought!
  No one will help me;
    no one cares a bit what happens to me.
5 Then I pray to you, O LORD.
  I say, "You are my place of refuge.
  You are all I really want in life.
6 Hear my cry,
    for I am very low.
  Rescue me from my persecutors,
    for they are too strong for me.
7 Bring me out of prison
    so I can thank you.
  The godly will crowd around me,
    for you treat me kindly."

141:1-10 When the flaming desire for our addiction is upon us, we need God's help to put out the fire. God can take away our desire for destructive and evil things. When temptation is so strong that we can't stand up against it, God will help us find a way to escape (see 1 Corinthians 10:13). We should not hesitate to call a Christian friend for prayer and support when we feel weak. During times of stress, we need to allow God to be our defender, to keep us safe from the snares of evil people.

142:1-7 Suffering should drive us to God, not to despair. We should freely express our feelings to God about the trials we experience. Many former friends don't really care what happens to us, but God cares about us. Surrendering our life to him is the thing to do when our dependencies begin to get the better of us. God is our place of refuge. Only he can help us escape from the bondage of our sins and surround us with godly people who can encourage and strengthen us.

PSALM 143

A psalm of David.

¹Hear my prayer, O LORD;
 listen to my plea!
 Answer me because you are faithful
 and righteous.
²Don't bring your servant to trial!
 Compared to you, no one is perfect.
³My enemy has chased me.
 He has knocked me to the ground.
 He forces me to live in darkness like
 those in the grave.
⁴I am losing all hope;
 I am paralyzed with fear.
⁵I remember the days of old.
 I ponder all your great works.
 I think about what you have done.
⁶I reach out for you.
 I thirst for you as parched land thirsts
 for rain.   *Interlude*

⁷Come quickly, LORD, and answer me,
 for my depression deepens.
 Don't turn away from me,
 or I will die.
⁸Let me hear of your unfailing love to me
 in the morning,
 for I am trusting you.
 Show me where to walk,
 for I have come to you in prayer.
⁹Save me from my enemies, LORD;
 I run to you to hide me.
¹⁰Teach me to do your will,
 for you are my God.
 May your gracious Spirit lead me forward
 on a firm footing.
¹¹For the glory of your name, O LORD,
 save me.
 In your righteousness, bring me out
 of this distress.
¹²In your unfailing love, cut off all my
 enemies
 and destroy all my foes,
 for I am your servant.

PSALM 144

A psalm of David.

¹Bless the LORD, who is my rock.
 He gives me strength for war
 and skill for battle.
²He is my loving ally and my fortress,
 my tower of safety, my deliverer.
 He stands before me as a shield, and I take
 refuge in him.
 He subdues the nations* under me.

³O LORD, what are mortals that you should
 notice us,
 mere humans that you should care
 for us?
⁴For we are like a breath of air;
 our days are like a passing shadow.

⁵Bend down the heavens, LORD, and come
 down.
 Touch the mountains so they billow
 smoke.
⁶Release your lightning bolts and scatter
 your enemies!
 Release your arrows and confuse them!
⁷Reach down from heaven and rescue me;
 deliver me from deep waters,
 from the power of my enemies.
⁸Their mouths are full of lies;
 they swear to tell the truth, but they lie.

⁹I will sing a new song to you, O God!
 I will sing your praises with a
 ten-stringed harp.
¹⁰For you grant victory to kings!
 You are the one who rescued your
 servant David.
¹¹Save me from the fatal sword!
 Rescue me from the power of my
 enemies.
 Their mouths are full of lies;
 they swear to tell the truth, but they lie.

¹²May our sons flourish in their youth
 like well-nurtured plants.
 May our daughters be like graceful pillars,
 carved to beautify a palace.

144:2 Some manuscripts read *my people.*

143:5-12 Our addiction often makes it hard to think of anything but the present. We may have lost all hope, and our depression is deepening. It is very important in recovery that we recall times in the past when God helped us overcome our addiction. As we spend time in prayer, his gracious Spirit will lead us forward and show us how to live.
144:3-8 One mystery we will never understand in this life is why God would ever concern himself with us. The greater mystery is how he could ever love us when we are overwhelmed by destructive addictions or compulsions. Why is God so good to us? Why does he continually rescue us? It is God's nature to do this—he is a loving, gracious, and merciful God. He wants the best for his creation. We need to act on God's promises to us and rejoice in his unlimited kindness.

¹³May our farms be filled
with crops of every kind.
May the flocks in our fields multiply
by the thousands,
even tens of thousands,
¹⁴ and may our oxen be loaded down
with produce.
May there be no breached walls, no
forced exile,
no cries of distress in our squares.
¹⁵Yes, happy are those who have it like this!
Happy indeed are those whose God
is the LORD.

PSALM 145
A psalm of praise of David.

¹I will praise you, my God and King,
and bless your name forever and ever.
²I will bless you every day,
and I will praise you forever.
³Great is the LORD! He is most worthy
of praise!
His greatness is beyond discovery!

⁴Let each generation tell its children
of your mighty acts.
⁵I will meditate* on your majestic,
glorious splendor
and your wonderful miracles.
⁶Your awe-inspiring deeds will be on every
tongue;
I will proclaim your greatness.
⁷Everyone will share the story of your
wonderful goodness;
they will sing with joy of your
righteousness.

⁸The LORD is kind and merciful,
slow to get angry, full of unfailing love.
⁹The LORD is good to everyone.
He showers compassion on all his
creation.
¹⁰All of your works will thank you, LORD,
and your faithful followers will bless you.
¹¹They will talk together about the glory
of your kingdom;

they will celebrate examples of your
power.
¹²They will tell about your mighty deeds
and about the majesty and glory
of your reign.
¹³For your kingdom is an everlasting
kingdom.
You rule generation after generation.

The LORD is faithful in all he says;
he is gracious in all he does.*
¹⁴The LORD helps the fallen
and lifts up those bent beneath their
loads.
¹⁵All eyes look to you for help;
you give them their food as they
need it.
¹⁶When you open your hand,
you satisfy the hunger and thirst
of every living thing.

¹⁷The LORD is righteous in everything he
does;
he is filled with kindness.
¹⁸The LORD is close to all who call on him,
yes, to all who call on him sincerely.
¹⁹He fulfills the desires of those who fear
him;
he hears their cries for help and rescues
them.
²⁰The LORD protects all those who love him,
but he destroys the wicked.

²¹I will praise the LORD,
and everyone on earth will bless his
holy name
forever and forever.

PSALM 146
¹Praise the LORD!

Praise the LORD, I tell myself.
²I will praise the LORD as long as I live.
I will sing praises to my God even with
my dying breath.

³Don't put your confidence in powerful
people;
there is no help for you there.

145:5 Some manuscripts read *They will speak.* **145:13** The last two lines of 145:13 are not found in many of the ancient manuscripts.

145:1-7 Praise is an effective weapon against the temptations of our dependency. Keeping our mind focused on God and praising him are helpful weapons against our addiction. Our praise of God's work in our life can bring joy and encouragement to others.
145:8-13 God showers us with his gifts and often withholds the judgment we deserve. Although he hates our sin, he does not react with anger. Instead, he shows us great compassion. Someday all creation will recognize what God has done and will praise him. We are part of the host that will be examples of his great power, especially his work of deliverance in our own life.

4 When their breathing stops, they return
to the earth,
and in a moment all their plans come
to an end.
5 But happy are those who have the God
of Israel* as their helper,
whose hope is in the LORD their God.
6 He is the one who made heaven and
earth,
the sea, and everything in them.
He is the one who keeps every promise
forever,
7   who gives justice to the oppressed
and food to the hungry.
The LORD frees the prisoners.
8   The LORD opens the eyes of the blind.
The LORD lifts the burdens of those bent
beneath their loads.
The LORD loves the righteous.
9 The LORD protects the foreigners
among us.
He cares for the orphans and widows,
but he frustrates the plans of the
wicked.

10 The LORD will reign forever.
O Jerusalem,* your God is King in every
generation!

Praise the LORD!

PSALM 147

1 Praise the LORD!

How good it is to sing praises to our God!
How delightful and how right!
2 The LORD is rebuilding Jerusalem
and bringing the exiles back to Israel.
3 He heals the brokenhearted,
binding up their wounds.
4 He counts the stars
and calls them all by name.
5 How great is our Lord! His power is absolute!
His understanding is beyond
comprehension!

146:5 Hebrew *of Jacob.* **146:10** Hebrew *Zion.*

6 The LORD supports the humble,
but he brings the wicked down into
the dust.

7 Sing out your thanks to the LORD;
sing praises to our God, accompanied
by harps.
8 He covers the heavens with clouds,
provides rain for the earth,
and makes the green grass grow in
mountain pastures.
9 He feeds the wild animals,
and the young ravens cry to him for food.
10 The strength of a horse does not impress
him;
how puny in his sight is the strength
of a man.
11 Rather, the LORD's delight is in those who
honor him,
those who put their hope in his
unfailing love.

12 Praise the LORD, O Jerusalem!
Praise your God, O Zion!
13 For he has fortified the bars of your gates
and blessed your children within you.
14 He sends peace across your nation
and satisfies you with plenty of the
finest wheat.
15 He sends his orders to the world—
how swiftly his word flies!
16 He sends the snow like white wool;
he scatters frost upon the ground like
ashes.
17 He hurls the hail like stones.
Who can stand against his freezing cold?
18 Then, at his command, it all melts.
He sends his winds, and the ice thaws.

19 He has revealed his words to Jacob,
his principles and laws to Israel.
20 He has not done this with any other nation;
they do not know his laws.

Praise the LORD!

146:5-9 God made all things and cares about all his creation, even the most lowly. He gives justice to the oppressed, feeds the hungry, and frees the prisoners. He alone can restore us to sanity when sin has caused us to lose control of our life. We may think no one else cares about us, but we can be assured that God does. He even watches over those who have no one else to care for them.
147:2-11 God can restore us to wholeness again. We need to turn to him instead of withering away in our remorse. There is always hope when we honor God in our life because there is nothing greater than God's power. He is able to heal us and provide for all our needs and is never overwhelmed by the dependency that we call our enemy.
147:12-20 God is our defender and peacemaker, the one who meets all of our needs. Since he is the creator and sustainer of all nature, we should have no doubt about his ability to care for us once we commit our life to him. He is worthy of our trust.

PSALM 148

¹Praise the LORD!

Praise the LORD from the heavens!
   Praise him from the skies!
²Praise him, all his angels!
   Praise him, all the armies of heaven!
³Praise him, sun and moon!
   Praise him, all you twinkling stars!
⁴Praise him, skies above!
   Praise him, vapors high above the clouds!
⁵Let every created thing give praise to the
      LORD,
   for he issued his command, and they
      came into being.
⁶He established them forever and forever.
   His orders will never be revoked.

⁷Praise the LORD from the earth,
   you creatures of the ocean depths,
⁸fire and hail, snow and storm,
   wind and weather that obey him,
⁹mountains and all hills,
   fruit trees and all cedars,
¹⁰wild animals and all livestock,
   reptiles and birds,
¹¹kings of the earth and all people,
   rulers and judges of the earth,
¹²young men and maidens,
   old men and children.
¹³Let them all praise the name of the LORD.
   For his name is very great;
   his glory towers over the earth and
      heaven!
¹⁴He has made his people strong,
   honoring his godly ones—
   the people of Israel who are close to him.

Praise the LORD!

PSALM 149

¹Praise the LORD!

Sing to the LORD a new song.
   Sing his praises in the assembly of the
      faithful.

149:2 Hebrew *Zion.*

²O Israel, rejoice in your Maker.
   O people of Jerusalem,* exult in your
      King.
³Praise his name with dancing,
   accompanied by tambourine and
      harp.
⁴For the LORD delights in his people;
   he crowns the humble with salvation.
⁵Let the faithful rejoice in this honor.
   Let them sing for joy as they lie on
      their beds.
⁶Let the praises of God be in their
      mouths,
   and a sharp sword in their hands—
⁷to execute vengeance on the nations
   and punishment on the peoples,
⁸to bind their kings with shackles
   and their leaders with iron chains,
⁹to execute the judgment written
   against them.
   This is the glory of his faithful
      ones.

Praise the LORD!

PSALM 150

¹Praise the LORD!

Praise God in his heavenly dwelling;
   praise him in his mighty heaven!
²Praise him for his mighty works;
   praise his unequaled greatness!
³Praise him with a blast of the trumpet;
   praise him with the lyre and harp!
⁴Praise him with the tambourine and
      dancing;
   praise him with stringed instruments
      and flutes!
⁵Praise him with a clash of cymbals;
   praise him with loud clanging
      cymbals.
⁶Let everything that lives sing praises
   to the LORD!

Praise the LORD!

148:1-14 God deserves our praise for all the good we receive day by day. Not the least of these benefits is the help he gives us in restoring our life to health and sanity. There was a time when we felt out of control; now God is making us strong. That should give us ample reason to join the rest of the universe in a chorus of ceaseless praise.

149:1-9 It should not be hard to commit our life to God. He is the one who gives us salvation and helps the humble and needy—people just like us. Knowing that he cares for us should cause us to rejoice and sing his praises. God always wants the best for us. All we need to do is turn our life over to him.

150:1-6 One of the best ways to praise God is with our life, including submitting to his will for us and sharing the Good News with others. All of us are recipients of God's loving forgiveness and restoration. Every living creature—each of us—has ample reason to praise our wonderful and gracious God. "Let everything that lives sing praises to the LORD! Praise the LORD!"

REFLECTIONS ON PSALMS

insights INTO GOD'S PROTECTION

In **Psalm 4:1-3** David rejoiced about God's powerful protection. In times of distress our merciful God is the perfect haven of rest. He is listening, and he hears our cries for help. God wants us to put our trust in him. We insult him when we trust in our own resources or anything else to deliver us from our problems. When we turn our will and life over to God, we become his own chosen ones, whom he promises to hear when we call out to him.

In **Psalm 7:3-11** David looked to God to defend him against the slanderous judgments of his enemies. Those who attack us or try to undermine the recovery process through lies are not just our enemies; they are God's enemies, too. We can count on him to deal with our common enemies if we are doing what we can to avoid temptation. We ought to hate the things God hates. We don't need to try to defend our choices when we are choosing the right paths; God has promised to be our defense.

In **Psalm 18:30-36** David praised God for his ability to protect those who looked to him for help. God will protect us if we are willing to admit our weaknesses and depend on him. He will empower us to do what is right in difficult situations and give us the ability to walk without stumbling, even when the path is slippery. God also equips his people for spiritual warfare, enabling us to use the shield of salvation and other powerful weapons. If we will only ask him to help us, God will protect us from temptations that could lead to our defeat.

In **Psalm 27:1-6** David praised God for the protection and hope he provided. We have nothing to fear in this life if we put our complete trust in God as our guide, deliverer, and protector. With God on our side, there is no need for us to be drawn away by the evil people who formerly led us astray. If we maintain our close contact with God, we can be assured that when problems come, he will watch over us, make our way secure, and draw us even closer to himself.

In **Psalm 31:1-5** David's words exhibit his dependence on God in times of danger and stress. God is our strong refuge, our rock of safety—the one we can turn to when we feel overwhelmed by temptations and dangers. Because we know he will always do what is right, we can with confidence turn our will and our life over to his care.

In **Psalm 56:1-7** David trusted God to take care of him during a time of great danger. When we are terrified by tempting or dangerous circumstances, we need to turn our life and our will over to God. We need to trust him and his promises. He is able to strengthen us so we won't fall again. Sometimes the enemy we face is obvious. At other times the attacks are very subtle, so we need to be careful.

insights INTO GOD'S DELIVERANCE

David probably wrote **Psalm 9:7-14** soon after a great victory over the Philistines. David praised God for delivering him from powerful enemies. God is merciful; he is always ready to help those who are oppressed by their enemies. In God's perfect timing, those who are oppressed will find comfort and encouragement if they put their trust in him. Because God never forsakes those who trust him, we should praise him and tell others that he has rescued us. As we remember his faithfulness to us in our times of distress, we will be able to take this message of encouragement to others.

After lamenting the oppressive acts of wicked people, David, in **Psalm 14:4-7,** expressed his confidence that God could deliver him from their clutches. Many of our problems may have been caused by someone else. Someone may have taken advantage of us without considering our feelings. We can find comfort in two facts. First, God will judge the people who have hurt us; we don't have to hold on to our anger and hatred. Second, God is with us; he is there to see us through the recovery process from beginning to end. In his perfect timing God will rescue us.

David wrote **Psalm 18:1-5** soon after God delivered him from his enemies. God is more than able to deliver us from our problems. He is our source of strength, our rock, and the one on whom we must rely as we seek freedom from our bondage. The psalmist learned that his decision to cry out to God for help was a wise choice. We, too, can experience God's deliverance. We should start by admitting our helplessness, the first step in recovery. Then we can look to God to give us the help we need to overcome our dependency.

In **Psalm 31:14-18** the psalmist shared his confidence that God alone could deliver him from his troubles. He also realized that without God's help he would suffer humiliation. God is the only one able to solve our problems. He is willing to help us overcome the people and situations that once dragged us down. We need to make sure he is at the center of our life as we continue in recovery.

In **Psalm 42:4-11** the psalmist honestly shared his feelings of depression. He felt God had forsaken him. Then he declared his faith in God and again put his hope in God. He struggled with his emotions—between despair and faith—and he was always honest about his feelings. In the process of recovery, we may experience times of deep depression. But God wants us to remember that even as floods of trouble pour over us, we should keep trusting him. We should feel free to express our feelings to God. As we spill out our complaints to him, he will pour over us waves of his steadfast love.

In **Psalm 57:4-6** David witnessed God's faithful help and love in times of trouble. Our dependencies and compulsions are never easy to handle. In fact, without God's help, they are impossible to handle. But God is far more powerful than all our internal and external enemies combined. He rules over heaven and earth and is able and willing to thwart the plans of our enemies.

David wrote **Psalm 60:6-12** during a time of war and affirmed that his help came from God alone. We can turn to God for deliverance because he has promised to help us. God reminds us that we still belong to him, no matter how great our failures in the past. He still offers a good life for any who are willing to do their best to follow his divine program. He can still give us victory if we allow him to help us fight our battles against temptation.

In **Psalm 76:1-12** we learn that God is able to overcome even the most powerful opposition we might face. He can use evil deeds to bring about his own plans for good. God's power is far greater than we can imagine. He is able to overcome even our greatest problems. All we need to do is turn our dependency over to him and entrust our life to his care. When he fights for us, none of our enemies—past, present, or future—can stand against us.

In **Psalm 104:19-24** the psalmist praised God for his amazing control over the created world. God uses the sun to regulate the days and nights and the moon to mark the seasons. Such power and control over the physical world should encourage us that when we commit our life to God, we have committed ourself to someone who has the power to help us.

In **Psalm 109:16-20** David spoke to God about the undeserved attacks he was forced to endure. All of us have suffered injustice; we all know the feelings that accompany innocent suffering. When we are hurt without just cause, we may be tempted to lash out in revenge. This will never resolve our pain or hurts. We need to let go of our anger; it will only lead to more suffering. We can trust God to work his justice according to his timetable. God will ultimately return the same kind of evil done to the innocent to those who are guilty. God is the best judge; judgment against the sins of others is best left up to him.

*insights INTO GOD'S FORGIVENESS

In **Psalm 103:8-12** David praised God for his great love and kindness. We should be encouraged by the knowledge that God loves us enough to not only forgive our sins but also put them behind him forever—"as far . . . as the east is from the west." We have all failed; our mistakes have hurt other people and damaged or destroyed our relationships. Sometimes others have a hard time forgiving us, even when we seek to make amends. God, on the other hand, is waiting to forgive us. All we have to do is confess our sins and turn our life over to him. Knowing that God has forgiven us should give us the courage to continue seeking reconciliation with the people we have wronged.

*insights INTO THE VALUE OF CONFESSION

In **Psalm 15:1-5** David reflected on how God's way of doing things leads to stability and peace. If we want to progress in recovery, we must never compromise with sin, whether it's our own or someone else's. No matter how painful it might be, we must confess the sin in our life or, in some cases, confront others with theirs. Many times our sins have caused a great deal of pain and loss to the people close to us. We need to become more sensitive to the wrongs we have committed and be specific in our personal inventory. This will help us escape the cycle of sin we are caught in and protect the people we love from further hurt.

In **Psalm 18:25-29** David recognized God's desire to bestow mercy on those who are merciful toward others and repentant of their sins. When we are ready to admit our wrongs to God and to others and when we show mercy to others, God is merciful toward us. We do great harm to ourselves and to others when we are too proud to admit our failures. But God is always ready to help us when we acknowledge who he is.

In **Psalm 19:12-14** David asked God to reveal any hidden sins in his life—to break through any denial he might have. He was taking a moral inventory and asked God to help him do this with absolute honesty. Because we tend to be blind to our sinful disposition, we need God to clarify our thinking—to reveal any sin that is working its deception within us and to keep us from deliberately doing wrong. When our thought life is right with God, our actions will be right also.

In **Psalm 38:9-16** the psalmist recognized how hideous he had become because of his sins. He turned to the only one who was listening—indeed, the only one who could help—God. The longer we remain in sin, the more disabled we become. Our heart pounds in fear, our energy ebbs away, and our ability to see ourselves as we really are becomes distorted. Even our closest friends and family members steer clear of us for fear we might drag them down. We must recognize how helpless we are in the face of our problems and turn to God for help. He is always ready to give us a helping hand.

David wrote **Psalm 51:16-19** after being convicted of adultery with Bathsheba. He realized that no number of sacrifices would cover his sins if he wasn't sorry for what he had done. He knew that God would grant him forgiveness if he honestly confessed his sins. We don't earn forgiveness from God. He is happy to give it to us if we only admit our failures and seek to make changes in our life. God is concerned more with our heartfelt attitudes than outward acts of repentance that do not reflect our true feelings. God is never fooled by these insincere acts of repentance. He wants us to take responsibility for our sins and seek forgiveness and restoration. There is always hope for us if we are willing to repent, as David did, and seek God's forgiveness. God is looking for people with humble hearts, not perfect records.

insights INTO THE VALUE OF PRAISE

In **Psalm 30:10-12** David concluded his request for deliverance with words of praise to God. Staying close to God through prayer and meditation is an important part of recovery. God wants us to succeed in recovery—he wants it even more than we do. He wants us to have a meaningful life filled with purpose and joy. When God helps us, we should not hesitate to praise him; like David, we should "sing praises to [God] and not be silent." Praising God out loud is an excellent way to tell others about God's work in our life. Sharing our experiences of deliverance will encourage others to persevere in recovery as well as strengthen our own resolves.

After experiencing God's deliverance, David spoke in **Psalm 40:9-10** about how he shared this good news with others. The news about our deliverance needs to be shared with others who are struggling. God is righteous, faithful, and able to deliver others from their bondage, just as he delivered us. As we share our victories with others, we will discover that not only will they be encouraged, but we will be strengthened as well.

Through **Psalm 111:1-8** the psalmist illustrated what it means to fulfill Step Twelve in recovery. God's work in our life has a twofold purpose: to accomplish our deliverance from bondage and to demonstrate God's power to others who need his help. Sharing the good news of God's deliverance will help others and will also strengthen us, giving us the encouragement we need to avoid relapses.

In **Psalm 112:1-4** the psalmist sang out in exuberant praise to God. When we decide to turn our life over to God and commit ourself to do his will, we will experience the joy this passage speaks of. Our children and grandchildren, too, will reap the benefits of a godly heritage. When times get tough and we are unsure of what to do, God will reveal his path to us. For our part, we need to tell others about what God has given us. This will not only bring hope to other hurting people; it will also strengthen our own program for recovery.

PROVERBS

THE BIG PICTURE

A. PROLOGUE: THE PURPOSE AND WAY OF WISDOM (1:1-7)
B. SOLOMON CHALLENGES YOUNG PEOPLE TO WISE BEHAVIOR (1:8–9:18)
C. SOLOMON CHALLENGES ALL PEOPLE TO WISE LIVING (10:1–24:34)
D. WISDOM FOR PEOPLE IN LEADERSHIP (25:1–31:9)
E. EPILOGUE: THE WOMAN OF WISDOM (31:10-31)

Common sense—the idea sounds so folksy and simple. Oddly enough, however, we seem to have less and less of it. Perhaps it's because we are too busy or distant to learn from our parents and grandparents. Just as common sense is rare, godly wisdom is also a quality hard to find. The book of Proverbs can be a helpful resource to fill the void left by the lack of wisdom and common sense in society today. By reading and heeding the wise words of Proverbs, we can avoid many common destructive mistakes that come so naturally from our ignorance, denial, and pride.

Although he made numerous costly mistakes, Solomon was the wisest person who ever lived. Because Solomon valued wisdom so highly, he collected many wise proverbs and compiled them into a guidebook of insight and counsel. Solomon was by no means the only wise man of his day. Agur and Lemuel, also known for their wisdom, are credited with the book's final chapters.

Solomon was particularly aware of the need for young people to develop proper priorities, boundaries, and behavior patterns. But young people were not Solomon's only concern. His collection of wisdom is invaluable to people of all ages and occupations. King Hezekiah later found the collection so important that he assigned his men to edit an installment of Solomon's proverbs (see 25:1), speaking to issues such as honesty, limits, and healthy relationships.

As dysfunctional thinking and relationships become more prevalent in society, the godly wisdom offered by Proverbs is desperately needed. Its precious nuggets of life-changing counsel are there for us to discover and use. All of us, no matter how great our failures or hurts, can proceed far down the path of healing by following the God-given wisdom of Proverbs.

THE BOTTOM LINE

PURPOSE: To offer God-given wisdom for protection against dysfunctional behaviors and ungodly practices. AUTHOR: Solomon collected or wrote most of the book; Agur and Lemuel were responsible for the final chapters. AUDIENCE: The people of Israel. DATE WRITTEN: Much of the book was compiled during Solomon's reign (970–930 B.C.); it probably took its final form during Hezekiah's reign (715–686 B.C.). SETTING: This is a book of wise sayings related to the priorities and problems of everyday life. KEY VERSE: "Fear of the LORD is the beginning of knowledge. Only fools despise wisdom and discipline" (1:7). KEY PEOPLE AND RELATIONSHIPS: Parents and children, husbands and wives, leaders and citizens, people and God, with warnings against unhealthy and sinful relationships.

RECOVERY THEMES

The Importance of Common Sense: Any good recovery program is filled with common sense and wisdom. If our addictive behavior has roots in our early life, we may have missed the opportunity of learning both common sense and wisdom. In recovery we seek to learn what we have missed; the book of Proverbs is a primary source. In contrast to a person with common sense is the fool, who is portrayed as a stubborn, willful person who either hates or ignores God. Our own path of recovery should be paved with the common sense found in Proverbs.

The Power of Priorities: We all have priorities, whether we're aware of them or not. So it's never a question of having priorities but rather of straightening them out. A big part of the recovery process involves sorting out our priorities, turning them over to God, and getting them to line up with his will. As our priorities become reflections of God's will, we will progress in recovery and avoid destructive relapses. The book of Proverbs contains wisdom and practical advice that reflect God's desires for us. If we follow this advice, we will discover a significant part of God's will for our life.

The Role of Boundaries: A big part of setting personal boundaries in our life is knowing how and when to say no. Solomon recorded for us a large number of situations where saying no is the wisest option—family situations, sexual situations, monetary situations, business situations, and social situations. As we take these proverbs and make them a part of us, we will develop clearer boundaries and have a better sense of when we should say no.

Building Healthy Relationships: The recovery process will only be as successful as the health of our relationships. We may have the best of intentions, but if we are surrounded with unhealthy relationships, we are headed nowhere. The book of Proverbs gives us sound advice for building healthy relationships with friends, family, and co-workers. We are called to be consistent and tactful and to use self-discipline. If we hope to build the kind of relationships that will help us love and follow God, high moral standards are essential, for us and for those close to us.

CHAPTER 1
The Purpose of Proverbs

These are the proverbs of Solomon, David's son, king of Israel.

²The purpose of these proverbs is to teach people wisdom and discipline, and to help them understand wise sayings. ³Through these proverbs, people will receive instruction in discipline, good conduct, and doing what is right, just, and fair. ⁴These proverbs will make the simpleminded clever. They will give knowledge and purpose to young people.

⁵Let those who are wise listen to these proverbs and become even wiser. And let those who understand receive guidance ⁶by exploring the depth of meaning in these proverbs, parables, wise sayings, and riddles.

⁷Fear of the LORD is the beginning of knowledge. Only fools despise wisdom and discipline.

A Father's Exhortation: Acquire Wisdom

⁸Listen, my child,* to what your father teaches you. Don't neglect your mother's teaching. ⁹What you learn from them will crown you with grace and clothe you with honor.

¹⁰My child, if sinners entice you, turn your back on them! ¹¹They may say, "Come and join us. Let's hide and kill someone! Let's ambush the innocent! ¹²Let's swallow them alive as the grave swallows its victims. Though they are in the prime of life, they will go down into the pit of death. ¹³And the loot we'll get! We'll fill our houses with all kinds of

1:8 Hebrew *my son;* also in 1:10, 15.

1:2-9 The purpose for writing down these proverbs was to teach people foundational principles in wisdom, discipline, and good conduct and in doing what is right, just, and fair. The first step to attaining this kind of wisdom is the hardest: trusting and showing reverence ("fear") for God. This means admitting that we need help and then allowing God to guide and care for us (see 3:5; 9:10; 14:26-27; 15:16, 33; 19:23).

1:20-23 Wisdom is personified here, calling out to all who would choose to follow her. There is no real secret to obtaining wisdom; all we have to do is ask for it. "If you need wisdom—if you want to know what God wants you to do—ask him, and he will gladly tell you. He will not resent your asking" (James 1:5). Unlike experience, which we never get until *after* we need it, God's wisdom is available to us as soon as we are willing to listen to him and obey his plan for our life.

GOD grant me the serenity to accept the things I cannot change the courage to change the things I can and the wisdom to know the difference AMEN

In recovery we come to realize that we are influenced by the people close to us. We welcome the support of those who are farther along the road to recovery. We may rely heavily on the encouragement of our sponsor or others who are supportive of our new way of life.

We will also come to see the negative influence of associating with people who are still living the kind of life from which we are trying to escape. Part of our self-inventory may include considering those with whom we choose to spend our time and how these decisions contribute to our progress in recovery. In Proverbs we are told that "wisdom will enter your heart, and knowledge will fill you with joy. Wise planning will watch over you. Understanding will keep you safe. Wisdom will save you from evil people, from those whose speech is corrupt. These people turn from right ways to walk down dark and evil paths. They rejoice in doing wrong, and they enjoy evil" (Proverbs 2:10-14). We are encouraged to "follow the steps of good men instead, and stay on the paths of the righteous. For only the upright will live in the land, and those who have integrity will remain in it. But the wicked will be removed from the land, and the treacherous will be destroyed" (Proverbs 2:20-22).

Are we exercising wisdom by following the steps of those who are living the kind of life we truly desire? If we do this, we will find our life filled with joy. We will also be spared the loss and destruction that await those who continue down darkened pathways and do not enter into recovery. *Turn to page 585, Proverbs 3.*

---

things! ¹⁴Come on, throw in your lot with us; we'll split our loot with you."

¹⁵Don't go along with them, my child! Stay far away from their paths. ¹⁶They rush to commit crimes. They hurry to commit murder. ¹⁷When a bird sees a trap being set, it stays away. ¹⁸But not these people! They set an ambush for themselves; they booby-trap their own lives! ¹⁹Such is the fate of all who are greedy for gain. It ends up robbing them of life.

Wisdom Shouts in the Streets

²⁰Wisdom shouts in the streets. She cries out in the public square. ²¹She calls out to the crowds along the main street, and to those in front of city hall. ²²"You simpletons!" she cries. "How long will you go on being simpleminded? How long will you mockers relish your mocking? How long will you fools fight the facts? ²³Come here and listen to me! I'll pour out the spirit of wisdom upon you and make you wise.

²⁴"I called you so often, but you didn't come. I reached out to you, but you paid no attention. ²⁵You ignored my advice and rejected the correction I offered. ²⁶So I will laugh when you are in trouble! I will mock you when disaster overtakes you—²⁷when calamity overcomes you like a storm, when you are engulfed by trouble, and when anguish and distress overwhelm you.

²⁸"I will not answer when they cry for help. Even though they anxiously search for me, they will not find me. ²⁹For they hated knowledge and chose not to fear the LORD. ³⁰They rejected my advice and paid no attention when I corrected them. ³¹That is why they must eat the bitter fruit of living their own way. They must experience the full terror of the path they have chosen. ³²For they are simpletons who turn away from me—to death. They are fools, and their own complacency will destroy them. ³³But all who listen to me will live in peace and safety, unafraid of harm."

CHAPTER 2
The Benefits of Wisdom

My child,* listen to me and treasure my instructions. [2]Tune your ears to wisdom, and concentrate on understanding. [3]Cry out for insight and understanding. [4]Search for them as you would for lost money or hidden treasure. [5]Then you will understand what it means to fear the LORD, and you will gain knowledge of God. [6]For the LORD grants wisdom! From his mouth come knowledge and understanding. [7]He grants a treasure of good sense to the godly. He is their shield, protecting those who walk with integrity. [8]He guards the paths of justice and protects those who are faithful to him.

[9]Then you will understand what is right, just, and fair, and you will know how to find the right course of action every time. [10]For wisdom will enter your heart, and knowledge will fill you with joy. [11]Wise planning will watch over you. Understanding will keep you safe.

[12]Wisdom will save you from evil people, from those whose speech is corrupt. [13]These people turn from right ways to walk down dark and evil paths. [14]They rejoice in doing wrong, and they enjoy evil as it turns things upside down. [15]What they do is crooked, and their ways are wrong.

[16]Wisdom will save you from the immoral woman, from the flattery of the adulterous woman. [17]She has abandoned her husband and ignores the covenant she made before God. [18]Entering her house leads to death; it is the road to hell.* [19]The man who visits her is doomed. He will never reach the paths of life.

[20]Follow the steps of good men instead, and stay on the paths of the righteous. [21]For only the upright will live in the land, and those who have integrity will remain in it. [22]But the wicked will be removed from the land, and the treacherous will be destroyed.

CHAPTER 3
Trusting in the LORD

My child,* never forget the things I have taught you. Store my commands in your heart, [2]for they will give you a long and satisfying life. [3]Never let loyalty and kindness get away from you! Wear them like a necklace; write them deep within your heart. [4]Then you will find favor with both God and people, and you will gain a good reputation.

[5]Trust in the LORD with all your heart; do not depend on your own understanding. [6]Seek his will in all you do, and he will direct your paths.

[7]Don't be impressed with your own wisdom. Instead, fear the LORD and turn your back on evil. [8]Then you will gain renewed health and vitality.

[9]Honor the LORD with your wealth and with the best part of everything your land produces. [10]Then he will fill your barns with grain, and your vats will overflow with the finest wine.

[11]My child, don't ignore it when the LORD disciplines you, and don't be discouraged when he corrects you. [12]For the LORD corrects those he loves, just as a father corrects a child* in whom he delights.

2:1 Hebrew *My son.* **2:18** Hebrew *to the spirits of the dead.* **3:1** Hebrew *My son;* also in 3:11, 21. **3:12** Hebrew *a son.*

2:1-9 Wisdom is like a hidden treasure that is found only by those who search for it. God will grant us wisdom and good sense. He will also protect us and instruct us on how to make good decisions. We may not have made great decisions in the past, and now we may be suffering the consequences of those decisions. But when we put our trust in God, he will guide us in the decisions we should make in order to experience a full recovery.

2:20-22 While we may try to do good, our dependencies are utterly evil. We know what our addictions have cost us: our jobs, friends, families, health, sanity. Now we want to change our life patterns to escape our enslavement. God tells us here that if we get on the right track, we can still enjoy life to the fullest. We may be tempted at times to stray from the path of recovery, but here we are reminded that our addictions will eventually lead to destruction. Recovery is the only real option we have.

3:5-6 What a promise! God will guide us on the right pathway of life if we put our trust in him rather than try to do it on our own. Putting God first means turning our life and will over to him. Surrendering to his leadership is humbling, but it is the only way for us to lead a good life.

3:11-12 When God disciplines us, he is not doing so because he hates us or likes to see us suffer. He is correcting us because he loves us and doesn't want us to go any farther into our sin. Those of us who have had abusive parents may not be able to easily grasp the concept of a loving, nurturing God, because the parental figures we have known were anything but loving. To help us see the true nature of God, we need to look to the Gospels and examine the love Jesus had for others. When we understand that Jesus and God are one and the same, we can more readily understand that God loves us and has our best interests in mind as he disciplines us.

GOD grant me the serenity to accept the things I cannot change the courage to change the things I can and the wisdom to know the difference AMEN

None of us set out to become addicted to something. We were seeking something else—escape from pain, perhaps, or something to make up for our losses and brokenness—or maybe we had a subconscious desire for self-destruction.

Unfortunately, the things we turned to could not satisfy our deepest needs or desires. Our needs are legitimate. What must be changed is the tendency to go the wrong way to try to meet those needs. The Bible says, "My child, don't lose sight of good planning and insight. Hang on to them, for they fill you with life and bring you honor and respect. They keep you safe on your way and keep your feet from stumbling" (Proverbs 3:21-23).

Godly wisdom leads to great benefits in life. As we seek wisdom, we will find the other things we desire. "Happy is the person who finds wisdom and gains understanding. For the profit of wisdom is better than silver, and her wages are better than gold. Wisdom is more precious than rubies; nothing you desire can compare with her. She offers you life in her right hand, and riches and honor in her left. She will guide you down delightful paths; all her ways are satisfying" (Proverbs 3:13-17). As we change our focus and begin to seek after wisdom, we will find our life more fulfilled and secure. Godly wisdom will also help us avoid the destructive paths we have previously taken as we tried to fulfill our unmet needs and desires. ***Turn to page 587, Proverbs 4.***

---

¹³Happy is the person who finds wisdom and gains understanding. ¹⁴For the profit of wisdom is better than silver, and her wages are better than gold. ¹⁵Wisdom is more precious than rubies; nothing you desire can compare with her. ¹⁶She offers you life in her right hand, and riches and honor in her left. ¹⁷She will guide you down delightful paths; all her ways are satisfying. ¹⁸Wisdom is a tree of life to those who embrace her; happy are those who hold her tightly.

¹⁹By wisdom the LORD founded the earth; by understanding he established the heavens. ²⁰By his knowledge the deep fountains of the earth burst forth, and the clouds poured down rain.

²¹My child, don't lose sight of good planning and insight. Hang on to them, ²²for they fill you with life and bring you honor and respect. ²³They keep you safe on your way and keep your feet from stumbling. ²⁴You can lie down without fear and enjoy pleasant dreams. ²⁵You need not be afraid of disaster or the destruction that comes upon the wicked, ²⁶for the LORD is your security. He will keep your foot from being caught in a trap.

²⁷Do not withhold good from those who deserve it when it's in your power to help them. ²⁸If you can help your neighbor now, don't say, "Come back tomorrow, and then I'll help you."

²⁹Do not plot against your neighbors, for they trust you. ³⁰Don't make accusations against someone who hasn't wronged you.

³¹Do not envy violent people; don't copy their ways. ³²Such wicked people are an abomination to the LORD, but he offers his friendship to the godly.

³³The curse of the LORD is on the house of the wicked, but his blessing is on the home of the upright.

³⁴The LORD mocks at mockers, but he shows favor to the humble.

³⁵The wise inherit honor, but fools are put to shame!

CHAPTER 4
A Father's Wise Advice

My children,* listen to me. Listen to your father's instruction. Pay attention and grow wise, ²for I am giving you good guidance. Don't turn away from my teaching. ³For I, too, was once my father's son, tenderly loved by my mother as an only child.

⁴My father told me, "Take my words to heart. Follow my instructions and you will live. ⁵Learn to be wise, and develop good judgment. Don't forget or turn away from my words. ⁶Don't turn your back on wisdom, for she will protect you. Love her, and she will guard you. ⁷Getting wisdom is the most important thing you can do! And whatever else you do, get good judgment. ⁸If you prize wisdom, she will exalt you. Embrace her and she will honor you. ⁹She will place a lovely wreath on your head; she will present you with a beautiful crown."

¹⁰My child,* listen to me and do as I say, and you will have a long, good life. ¹¹I will teach you wisdom's ways and lead you in straight paths. ¹²If you live a life guided by wisdom, you won't limp or stumble as you run. ¹³Carry out my instructions; don't forsake them. Guard them, for they will lead you to a fulfilled life.

¹⁴Do not do as the wicked do or follow the path of evildoers. ¹⁵Avoid their haunts. Turn away and go somewhere else, ¹⁶for evil people cannot sleep until they have done their evil deed for the day. They cannot rest unless they have caused someone to stumble. ¹⁷They eat wickedness and drink violence!

¹⁸The way of the righteous is like the first gleam of dawn, which shines ever brighter until the full light of day. ¹⁹But the way of the wicked is like complete darkness. Those who follow it have no idea what they are stumbling over.

²⁰Pay attention, my child, to what I say. Listen carefully. ²¹Don't lose sight of my words. Let them penetrate deep within your heart, ²²for they bring life and radiant health to anyone who discovers their meaning.

²³Above all else, guard your heart, for it affects everything you do.*

²⁴Avoid all perverse talk; stay far from corrupt speech.

²⁵Look straight ahead, and fix your eyes on what lies before you. ²⁶Mark out a straight path for your feet; then stick to the path and stay safe. ²⁷Don't get sidetracked; keep your feet from following evil.

CHAPTER 5
Avoid Immoral Women

My son, pay attention to my wisdom; listen carefully to my wise counsel. ²Then you will learn to be discreet and will store up knowledge.

³The lips of an immoral woman are as sweet as honey, and her mouth is smoother than oil. ⁴But the result is as bitter as poison, sharp as a double-edged sword. ⁵Her feet go down to death; her steps lead straight to the grave.* ⁶For she does not care about the path to life. She staggers down a crooked trail and doesn't even realize where it leads.

4:1 Hebrew *My sons.* 4:10 Hebrew *My son;* also in 4:20. 4:23 Hebrew *for from it flow the springs of life.* 5:5 Hebrew *to Sheol.*

4:11-19 We are all influenced by our environment. We become like our friends. That is why we are warned here to stay away from those who do evil deeds. It is easy to become desensitized to sin. If we spend too much time with people who have few moral boundaries, we will begin to think and act as they do. Slipping back into our dependency will be a very natural thing. However, by spending time with godly people, we will find the encouragement we need to continue in recovery and enjoy the life God intended for us.

4:23-27 The warning to guard our heart is also a warning to not give in to the temptation of sinful pleasures of any kind. Indulging in sin is pleasurable at first, but in the end its promise is empty and bitter. Sin may satisfy short-term desires, but its consequences are long term. Returning to our addiction may make us feel better for the moment, but it will damage (maybe even undo) our progress in the recovery process.

5:1-23 Sexual temptation is often very hard to resist, even if we are aware of the dangers and consequences of promiscuous sex. Sex outside of marriage is against God's law, whether we are married or not. Throughout the book of Proverbs there are warnings against promiscuity (see 2:16-19; 6:25-35; 7:6-27; 22:14; 23:27-28). Unfaithfulness can destroy family life and physical health, and it may result in pregnancy. If sex is among our addictions, we must *run* from any situations where we might be tempted to sin. We should also seek help from a support group or a counselor.

GOD grant me the serenity to accept the things I cannot change the courage to change the things I can and the wisdom to know the difference AMEN

Some people grew up in a family where they received wise advice and where wisdom was modeled and taught by their parents. But if we haven't, we may feel like the rest of the human race has passed us by. Some of us feel anger, resentment, and shame because we had little guidance and never learned how to make wise choices. We may ask ourselves, Shouldn't someone have shown me the way? Ideally, all of us should have had wise and godly instruction. The book of Proverbs records a father's godly instruction to his son: "For I, too, was once my father's son, tenderly loved by my mother. . . . My father told me, 'Take my words to heart. . . . Learn to be wise, and develop good judgment. Don't forget or turn away from my words. Don't turn your back on wisdom, for she will protect you. Love her, and she will guard you'" (Proverbs 4:3-6).

For those of us who were neglected and given little or no guidance by our parents, it's not too late. We have a Father in heaven who is eager to give us the wisdom we need. James advised: "If you need wisdom—if you want to know what God wants you to do—ask him, and he will gladly tell you" (James 1:5). Our heavenly Father loves us tenderly, as a parent should. He is always there for us, waiting to give us the wisdom we need whenever we ask for it. *End of the Serenity Prayer reading plan.*

Many of us grew up in a dysfunctional family. Our parents scarcely seemed to care about us at all, let alone provide wise guidance for us. This deprivation can leave us wondering how we can fill the void in our life.

---

[7]So now, my sons, listen to me. Never stray from what I am about to say: [8]Run from her! Don't go near the door of her house! [9]If you do, you will lose your honor and hand over to merciless people everything you have achieved in life. [10]Strangers will obtain your wealth, and someone else will enjoy the fruit of your labor. [11]Afterward you will groan in anguish when disease consumes your body, [12]and you will say, "How I hated discipline! If only I had not demanded my own way! [13]Oh, why didn't I listen to my teachers? Why didn't I pay attention to those who gave me instruction? [14]I have come to the brink of utter ruin, and now I must face public disgrace."

[15]Drink water from your own well— share your love only with your wife.* [16]Why spill the water of your springs in public, having sex with just anyone?* [17]You should reserve it for yourselves. Don't share it with strangers.

[18]Let your wife be a fountain of blessing for you. Rejoice in the wife of your youth. [19]She is a loving doe, a graceful deer. Let her breasts satisfy you always. May you always be captivated by her love. [20]Why be captivated, my son, with an immoral woman, or embrace the breasts of an adulterous woman?

[21]For the LORD sees clearly what a man does, examining every path he takes. [22]An evil man is held captive by his own sins; they are ropes that catch and hold him. [23]He will die for lack of self-control; he will be lost because of his incredible folly.

5:15 Hebrew *Drink water from your own cistern, flowing water from your own well.* **5:16** Hebrew *Why spill your springs in public, your streams in the streets?*

CHAPTER 6
Lessons for Daily Life

My child,* if you co-sign a loan for a friend or guarantee the debt of someone you hardly know—²if you have trapped yourself by your agreement and are caught by what you said—³quick, get out of it if you possibly can! You have placed yourself at your friend's mercy. Now swallow your pride; go and beg to have your name erased. ⁴Don't put it off. Do it now! Don't rest until you do. ⁵Save yourself like a deer escaping from a hunter, like a bird fleeing from a net.

⁶Take a lesson from the ants, you lazybones. Learn from their ways and be wise! ⁷Even though they have no prince, governor, or ruler to make them work, ⁸they labor hard all summer, gathering food for the winter. ⁹But you, lazybones, how long will you sleep? When will you wake up? I want you to learn this lesson: ¹⁰A little extra sleep, a little more slumber, a little folding of the hands to rest—¹¹and poverty will pounce on you like a bandit; scarcity will attack you like an armed robber.

¹²Here is a description of worthless and wicked people: They are constant liars, ¹³signaling their true intentions to their friends by making signs with their eyes and feet and fingers. ¹⁴Their perverted hearts plot evil. They stir up trouble constantly. ¹⁵But they will be destroyed suddenly, broken beyond all hope of healing.

¹⁶There are six things the LORD hates—no, seven things he detests:
¹⁷ haughty eyes,
 a lying tongue,
 hands that kill the innocent,
¹⁸ a heart that plots evil,
 feet that race to do wrong,
¹⁹ a false witness who pours out lies,
 a person who sows discord among
  brothers.

²⁰My son, obey your father's commands, and don't neglect your mother's teaching. ²¹Keep their words always in your heart. Tie them around your neck. ²²Wherever you walk, their counsel can lead you. When you sleep, they will protect you. When you wake up in the morning, they will advise you. ²³For these commands and this teaching are a lamp to light the way ahead of you. The correction of discipline is the way to life.

²⁴These commands and this teaching will keep you from the immoral woman, from the smooth tongue of an adulterous woman. ²⁵Don't lust for her beauty. Don't let her coyness seduce you. ²⁶For a prostitute will bring you to poverty, and sleeping with another man's wife may cost you your very life. ²⁷Can a man scoop fire into his lap and not be burned? ²⁸Can he walk on hot coals and not blister his feet? ²⁹So it is with the man who sleeps with another man's wife. He who embraces her will not go unpunished.

³⁰Excuses might be found for a thief who steals because he is starving. ³¹But if he is caught, he will be fined seven times as much as he stole, even if it means selling everything in his house to pay it back.

³²But the man who commits adultery is an utter fool, for he destroys his own soul. ³³Wounds and constant disgrace are his lot. His shame will never be erased. ³⁴For the woman's husband will be furious in his jealousy, and he will have no mercy in his day of vengeance. ³⁵There is no compensation or bribe that will satisfy him.

CHAPTER 7
Another Warning about Immoral Women

Follow my advice, my son; always treasure my commands. ²Obey them and live! Guard my teachings as your most precious possession.* ³Tie them on your fingers as a reminder. Write them deep within your heart.

⁴Love wisdom like a sister; make insight a beloved member of your family. ⁵Let them hold you back from an affair with an immoral woman, from listening to the flattery of an adulterous woman.

6:1 Hebrew *My son.* 7:2 Hebrew *as the apple of your eye.*

6:16-19 The seven things God hates are things that stand against recovery. They violate our well-being. Haughtiness is being too proud to begin recovery by admitting we need God's help (Step One). Lying is failing to take inventory of our life and admit our wrongs (Steps Four and Five). Plotting evil is going in the opposite direction of those who repent of their sins and ask God to cleanse their heart (Steps Six and Seven). Murder is the opposite of asking forgiveness and making amends (Steps Eight and Nine). Racing to do wrong is the opposite of being eager to do right by seeking to know God and do his will (Step Eleven). Bearing false witness and sowing discord among brothers are contrary to carrying the true message of peace to those who are hurting (Step Twelve).

⁶I was looking out the window of my house one day ⁷and saw a simpleminded young man who lacked common sense. ⁸He was crossing the street near the house of an immoral woman. He was strolling down the path by her house ⁹at twilight, as the day was fading, as the dark of night set in. ¹⁰The woman approached him, dressed seductively and sly of heart. ¹¹She was the brash, rebellious type who never stays at home. ¹²She is often seen in the streets and markets, soliciting at every corner.

¹³She threw her arms around him and kissed him, and with a brazen look she said, ¹⁴"I've offered my sacrifices and just finished my vows. ¹⁵It's you I was looking for! I came out to find you, and here you are! ¹⁶My bed is spread with colored sheets of finest linen imported from Egypt. ¹⁷I've perfumed my bed with myrrh, aloes, and cinnamon. ¹⁸Come, let's drink our fill of love until morning. Let's enjoy each other's caresses, ¹⁹for my husband is not home. He's away on a long trip. ²⁰He has taken a wallet full of money with him, and he won't return until later in the month."

²¹So she seduced him with her pretty speech. With her flattery she enticed him. ²²He followed her at once, like an ox going to the slaughter or like a trapped stag, ²³awaiting the arrow that would pierce its heart. He was like a bird flying into a snare, little knowing it would cost him his life.

²⁴Listen to me, my sons, and pay attention to my words. ²⁵Don't let your hearts stray away toward her. Don't wander down her wayward path. ²⁶For she has been the ruin of many; numerous men have been her victims. ²⁷Her house is the road to the grave.* Her bedroom is the den of death.

CHAPTER 8
Wisdom Calls for a Hearing

Listen as wisdom calls out! Hear as understanding raises her voice! ²She stands on the hilltop and at the crossroads. ³At the entrance to the city, at the city gates, she cries aloud, ⁴"I call to you, to all of you! I am raising my voice to all people. ⁵How naive you are! Let me give you common sense. O foolish ones, let me give you understanding. ⁶Listen to me! For I have excellent things to tell you. Everything I say is right, ⁷for I speak the truth and hate every kind of deception. ⁸My advice is wholesome and good. There is nothing crooked or twisted in it. ⁹My words are plain to anyone with understanding, clear to those who want to learn.

¹⁰"Choose my instruction rather than silver, and knowledge over pure gold. ¹¹For wisdom is far more valuable than rubies. Nothing you desire can be compared with it.

¹²"I, Wisdom, live together with good judgment. I know where to discover knowledge and discernment. ¹³All who fear the LORD will hate evil. That is why I hate pride, arrogance, corruption, and perverted speech. ¹⁴Good advice and success belong to me. Insight and strength are mine. ¹⁵Because of me, kings reign, and rulers make just laws. ¹⁶Rulers lead with my help, and nobles make righteous judgments.

¹⁷"I love all who love me. Those who search for me will surely find me. ¹⁸Unending riches, honor, wealth, and justice are mine to distribute. ¹⁹My gifts are better than the purest gold, my wages better than sterling silver! ²⁰I walk in righteousness, in paths of justice. ²¹Those who love me inherit wealth, for I fill their treasuries.

²²"The LORD formed me from the beginning, before he created anything else. ²³I was appointed in ages past, at the very first, before the earth began. ²⁴I was born before the oceans were created, before the springs bubbled forth their waters. ²⁵Before the mountains and the hills were formed, I was born—²⁶before he had made the earth and fields and the first handfuls of soil.

²⁷"I was there when he established the heavens, when he drew the horizon on the oceans. ²⁸I was there when he set the clouds above, when he established the deep fountains of the earth. ²⁹I was there when he set the limits of the seas, so they would not

7:27 Hebrew *to Sheol.*

8:22-36 Solomon portrayed wisdom as a personal being who existed with God before the earth was created and who was the "architect" for Creation. This may be an allusion to Jesus the Messiah, who, according to the book of John, was the Word that not only "already existed . . . in the beginning with God," but "was God," and "created everything there is" (John 1:1-3). Colossians 1:16 says that "Christ is the one through whom God created everything in heaven and earth." Those who in faith listen to Christ and follow his wisdom will find eternal life and favor with God (see John 5:24). Following Christ's instructions for our life is our only means of recovery.

spread beyond their boundaries. And when he marked off the earth's foundations, ³⁰I was the architect at his side. I was his constant delight, rejoicing always in his presence. ³¹And how happy I was with what he created—his wide world and all the human family!

³²"And so, my children,* listen to me, for happy are all who follow my ways. ³³Listen to my counsel and be wise. Don't ignore it.

³⁴"Happy are those who listen to me, watching for me daily at my gates, waiting for me outside my home! ³⁵For whoever finds me finds life and wins approval from the LORD. ³⁶But those who miss me have injured themselves. All who hate me love death."

CHAPTER 9

Wisdom has built her spacious house with seven pillars. ²She has prepared a great banquet, mixed the wines, and set the table. ³She has sent her servants to invite everyone to come. She calls out from the heights overlooking the city. ⁴"Come home with me," she urges the simple. To those without good judgment, she says, ⁵"Come, eat my food, and drink the wine I have mixed. ⁶Leave your foolish ways behind, and begin to live; learn how to be wise."

⁷Anyone who rebukes a mocker will get a smart retort. Anyone who rebukes the wicked will get hurt. ⁸So don't bother rebuking mockers; they will only hate you. But the wise, when rebuked, will love you all the more. ⁹Teach the wise, and they will be wiser. Teach the righteous, and they will learn more.

¹⁰Fear of the LORD is the beginning of wisdom. Knowledge of the Holy One results in understanding.

¹¹Wisdom will multiply your days and add years to your life. ¹²If you become wise, you will be the one to benefit. If you scorn wisdom, you will be the one to suffer.

Folly Calls for a Hearing

¹³The woman named Folly is loud and brash. She is ignorant and doesn't even know it. ¹⁴She sits in her doorway on the heights overlooking the city. ¹⁵She calls out to men going by who are minding their own business. ¹⁶"Come home with me," she urges the simple. To those without good judgment, she says, ¹⁷"Stolen water is refreshing; food eaten in secret tastes the best!" ¹⁸But the men don't realize that her former guests are now in the grave.*

CHAPTER 10
The Proverbs of Solomon

The proverbs of Solomon:

A wise child* brings joy to a father; a foolish child brings grief to a mother.

²Ill-gotten gain has no lasting value, but right living can save your life.

³The LORD will not let the godly starve to death, but he refuses to satisfy the craving of the wicked.

⁴Lazy people are soon poor; hard workers get rich.

⁵A wise youth works hard all summer; a youth who sleeps away the hour of opportunity brings shame.

⁶The godly are showered with blessings; evil people cover up their harmful intentions.

⁷We all have happy memories of the godly, but the name of a wicked person rots away.

⁸The wise are glad to be instructed, but babbling fools fall flat on their faces.

⁹People with integrity have firm footing, but those who follow crooked paths will slip and fall.

¹⁰People who wink at wrong cause trouble, but a bold reproof promotes peace.*

¹¹The words of the godly lead to life; evil people cover up their harmful intentions.

¹²Hatred stirs up quarrels, but love covers all offenses.

¹³Wise words come from the lips of people with understanding, but fools will be punished with a rod.

8:32 Hebrew *my sons.* **9:18** Hebrew *in Sheol.* **10:1** Hebrew *son;* also in 10:1b. **10:10** As in Greek version; Hebrew reads *but babbling fools fall flat on their faces.*

9:7-8 When someone tries to help us and correct us, we have two choices. We can either listen and learn as the wise person does, or we can get angry and rebel as the mocker does. To mock and hate those who are concerned for us is to deny that we have a problem. If we are wise, we will be honest enough to admit that we have a problem and we need help. This attitude enables recovery. Mockers will reject good advice and be overtaken by their sins.
10:6 In this and many of the proverbs Solomon contrasts good and evil people by the way they live and the consequences they suffer. This basic principle is repeated often: Moral living is good for us. One key to doing what is right is having an accurate self-concept. As we begin to see ourself as God sees us, we see that we are loved and valued, and we will want to apply the principles of wisdom to our life.

¹⁴Wise people treasure knowledge, but the babbling of a fool invites trouble.

¹⁵The wealth of the rich is their fortress; the poverty of the poor is their calamity.

¹⁶The earnings of the godly enhance their lives, but evil people squander their money on sin.

¹⁷People who accept correction are on the pathway to life, but those who ignore it will lead others astray.

¹⁸To hide hatred is to be a liar; to slander is to be a fool.

¹⁹Don't talk too much, for it fosters sin. Be sensible and turn off the flow!

²⁰The words of the godly are like sterling silver; the heart of a fool is worthless.

²¹The godly give good advice, but fools are destroyed by their lack of common sense.

²²The blessing of the LORD makes a person rich, and he adds no sorrow with it.

²³Doing wrong is fun for a fool, while wise conduct is a pleasure to the wise.

²⁴The fears of the wicked will all come true; so will the hopes of the godly.

²⁵Disaster strikes like a cyclone, whirling the wicked away, but the godly have a lasting foundation.

²⁶Lazy people are a pain to their employer. They are like smoke in the eyes or vinegar that sets the teeth on edge.

²⁷Fear of the LORD lengthens one's life, but the years of the wicked are cut short.

²⁸The hopes of the godly result in happiness, but the expectations of the wicked are all in vain.

²⁹The LORD protects the upright but destroys the wicked.

³⁰The godly will never be disturbed, but the wicked will be removed from the land.

³¹The godly person gives wise advice, but the tongue that deceives will be cut off.

³²The godly speak words that are helpful, but the wicked speak only what is corrupt.

CHAPTER 11

The LORD hates cheating, but he delights in honesty.

²Pride leads to disgrace, but with humility comes wisdom.

³Good people are guided by their honesty; treacherous people are destroyed by their dishonesty.

⁴Riches won't help on the day of judgment, but right living is a safeguard against death.

⁵The godly are directed by their honesty; the wicked fall beneath their load of sin.

⁶The godliness of good people rescues them; the ambition of treacherous people traps them.

⁷When the wicked die, their hopes all perish, for they rely on their own feeble strength.

⁸God rescues the godly from danger, but he lets the wicked fall into trouble.

⁹Evil words destroy one's friends; wise discernment rescues the godly.

¹⁰The whole city celebrates when the godly succeed; they shout for joy when the godless die.

¹¹Upright citizens bless a city and make it prosper, but the talk of the wicked tears it apart.

¹²It is foolish to belittle a neighbor; a person with good sense remains silent.

¹³A gossip goes around revealing secrets, but those who are trustworthy can keep a confidence.

¹⁴Without wise leadership, a nation falls; with many counselors, there is safety.

¹⁵Guaranteeing a loan for a stranger is dangerous; it is better to refuse than to suffer later.

¹⁶Beautiful women obtain wealth, and violent men get rich.

¹⁷Your own soul is nourished when you are kind, but you destroy yourself when you are cruel.

10:25 A building's foundation keeps it from falling in a storm or strong wind. Without a solid, lasting foundation, tall buildings wouldn't last very long. We encounter all sorts of "storms" along the road to recovery. Whether or not we can stand fast through the many storms we encounter depends on the strength of our "foundation" of faith. Our foundation—that is, our trust in God—will support and steady us so we can get through even the toughest cyclones. When we encounter difficulties, it is a real challenge to weather the storms and learn what God is teaching us through them. For people of faith, such trials are opportunities for personal growth (see James 1:2-4).

11:1-3 These verses underscore the importance of being honest. In recovery, we need to be honest—with ourself and with others. We need to honestly admit that we can't control our addiction (Step One). We need to be honest as we compile our moral inventory (Steps Four and Ten), and we need to honestly admit to God and others exactly what we have done wrong (Step Five).

¹⁸Evil people get rich for the moment, but the reward of the godly will last.

¹⁹Godly people find life; evil people find death.

²⁰The LORD hates people with twisted hearts, but he delights in those who have integrity.

²¹You can be sure that evil people will be punished, but the children of the godly will go free.

²²A woman who is beautiful but lacks discretion is like a gold ring in a pig's snout.

²³The godly can look forward to happiness, while the wicked can expect only wrath.

²⁴It is possible to give freely and become more wealthy, but those who are stingy will lose everything.

²⁵The generous prosper and are satisfied; those who refresh others will themselves be refreshed.

²⁶People curse those who hold their grain for higher prices, but they bless the one who sells to them in their time of need.

²⁷If you search for good, you will find favor; but if you search for evil, it will find you!

²⁸Trust in your money and down you go! But the godly flourish like leaves in spring.

²⁹Those who bring trouble on their families inherit only the wind. The fool will be a servant to the wise.

³⁰The godly are like trees that bear life-giving fruit, and those who save lives are wise.

³¹If the righteous are rewarded here on earth, how much more true that the wicked and the sinner will get what they deserve!

CHAPTER 12

To learn, you must love discipline; it is stupid to hate correction.

²The LORD approves of those who are good, but he condemns those who plan wickedness.

³Wickedness never brings stability; only the godly have deep roots.

⁴A worthy wife is her husband's joy and crown; a shameful wife saps his strength.

⁵The plans of the godly are just; the advice of the wicked is treacherous.

⁶The words of the wicked are like a murderous ambush, but the words of the godly save lives.

⁷The wicked perish and are gone, but the children of the godly stand firm.

⁸Everyone admires a person with good sense, but a warped mind is despised.

⁹It is better to be a nobody with a servant than to be self-important but have no food.

¹⁰The godly are concerned for the welfare of their animals, but even the kindness of the wicked is cruel.

¹¹Hard work means prosperity; only fools idle away their time.

¹²Thieves are jealous of each other's loot, while the godly bear their own fruit.

¹³The wicked are trapped by their own words, but the godly escape such trouble.

¹⁴People can get many good things by the words they say; the work of their hands also gives them many benefits.

¹⁵Fools think they need no advice, but the wise listen to others.

¹⁶A fool is quick-tempered, but a wise person stays calm when insulted.

¹⁷An honest witness tells the truth; a false witness tells lies.

¹⁸Some people make cutting remarks, but the words of the wise bring healing.

¹⁹Truth stands the test of time; lies are soon exposed.

²⁰Deceit fills hearts that are plotting evil; joy fills hearts that are planning peace!

²¹No real harm befalls the godly, but the wicked have their fill of trouble.

11:24-25 Some of us may wonder how we can be expected to give anything away. We may have lost everything, or perhaps we just feel too empty and tired to reach out. It might be refreshing to realize that we have a special gift to give others in recovery—encouragement. When we share our victories, and even our failures, others will be strengthened for their battles ahead. That is what Step Twelve is all about. As we share our message with others who are in recovery, they will gain the insight and encouragement they need for their own success. We, in turn, will be encouraged to stay away from our dependency because of what our recovery has come to mean to others.

12:15 Changing patterns of behavior that led us into bondage or recovering from emotional trauma requires the help of people we trust and respect (see 12:26; 15:22; 19:20). We cannot live successfully alone. Wise people listen to good advice from others; fools do not. Growing toward spiritual and emotional maturity is a process that requires the help of trustworthy people who can guide us with care and hold us accountable as we try to make changes.

12:16 It is foolish to lose our temper when we are insulted. We demonstrate maturity by using self-control and staying calm. By doing so, we can lovingly offer needed correction to the offender, provide a chance to build intimacy in the relationship, and keep our heart free of resentment.

²²The LORD hates those who don't keep their word, but he delights in those who do.

²³Wise people don't make a show of their knowledge, but fools broadcast their folly.

²⁴Work hard and become a leader; be lazy and become a slave.

²⁵Worry weighs a person down; an encouraging word cheers a person up.

²⁶The godly give good advice to their friends;* the wicked lead them astray.

²⁷Lazy people don't even cook the game they catch, but the diligent make use of everything they find.

²⁸The way of the godly leads to life; their path does not lead to death.

CHAPTER 13

A wise child* accepts a parent's discipline; a young mocker refuses to listen.

²Good people enjoy the positive results of their words, but those who are treacherous crave violence.

³Those who control their tongue will have a long life; a quick retort can ruin everything.

⁴Lazy people want much but get little, but those who work hard will prosper and be satisfied.

⁵Those who are godly hate lies; the wicked come to shame and disgrace.

⁶Godliness helps people all through life, while the evil are destroyed by their wickedness.

⁷Some who are poor pretend to be rich; others who are rich pretend to be poor.

⁸The rich can pay a ransom, but the poor won't even get threatened.

⁹The life of the godly is full of light and joy, but the sinner's light is snuffed out.

¹⁰Pride leads to arguments; those who take advice are wise.

¹¹Wealth from get-rich-quick schemes quickly disappears; wealth from hard work grows.

¹²Hope deferred makes the heart sick, but when dreams come true, there is life and joy.

¹³People who despise advice will find themselves in trouble; those who respect it will succeed.

¹⁴The advice of the wise is like a life-giving fountain; those who accept it avoid the snares of death.

¹⁵A person with good sense is respected; a treacherous person walks a rocky road.

¹⁶Wise people think before they act; fools don't and even brag about it!

¹⁷An unreliable messenger stumbles into trouble, but a reliable messenger brings healing.

¹⁸If you ignore criticism, you will end in poverty and disgrace; if you accept criticism, you will be honored.

¹⁹It is pleasant to see dreams come true, but fools will not turn from evil to attain them.

²⁰Whoever walks with the wise will become wise; whoever walks with fools will suffer harm.

²¹Trouble chases sinners, while blessings chase the righteous!

²²Good people leave an inheritance to their grandchildren, but the sinner's wealth passes to the godly.

²³A poor person's farm may produce much food, but injustice sweeps it all away.

²⁴If you refuse to discipline your children, it proves you don't love them; if you love your children, you will be prompt to discipline them.

²⁵The godly eat to their hearts' content, but the belly of the wicked goes hungry.

12:26 Or *The godly are cautious in friendship,* or *the godly are freed from evil.* The meaning of the Hebrew is uncertain.
13:1 Hebrew *son.*

13:6 It should not surprise us that evil deeds destroy people, and sin results in painful consequences. Drug or alcohol abuse will destroy the body; lying will ruin a person's reputation; gambling will put one in the poorhouse. To avoid the inevitable results of sinful behavior, we need to commit our life to the Lord, who is able to give us victory over our addictions and compulsions. Following God's way leads to happiness and gives positive direction to our life.
13:9 Leaving a destructive past to join a recovery program based on God's principles is like walking out of the darkness and into the light. Those who enter the light see their need for help and the reality of a loving God who wants to help them. They can no longer hide their deeds in the darkness of denial and deceit. They must honestly deal with the issues the light has exposed.
13:20 Since we become like the company we keep, it is important to have wise, godly friends we respect. Being involved in a support group is so important to personal growth and recovery. When we are struggling in a certain area, it's helpful to know that we are not alone and that others share our pain. It also helps to see fellow strugglers model the qualities that will help us overcome our obstacles—honesty, perseverance, and accountability.

CHAPTER 14

A wise woman builds her house; a foolish woman tears hers down with her own hands.

²Those who follow the right path fear the LORD; those who take the wrong path despise him.

³The talk of fools is a rod for their backs,* but the words of the wise keep them out of trouble.

⁴An empty stable stays clean, but no income comes from an empty stable.

⁵A truthful witness does not lie; a false witness breathes lies.

⁶A mocker seeks wisdom and never finds it, but knowledge comes easily to those with understanding.

⁷Stay away from fools, for you won't find knowledge there.

⁸The wise look ahead to see what is coming, but fools deceive themselves.

⁹Fools make fun of guilt, but the godly acknowledge it and seek reconciliation.

¹⁰Each heart knows its own bitterness, and no one else can fully share its joy.

¹¹The house of the wicked will perish, but the tent of the godly will flourish.

¹²There is a path before each person that seems right, but it ends in death.

¹³Laughter can conceal a heavy heart; when the laughter ends, the grief remains.

¹⁴Backsliders get what they deserve; good people receive their reward.

¹⁵Only simpletons believe everything they are told! The prudent carefully consider their steps.

¹⁶The wise are cautious* and avoid danger; fools plunge ahead with great confidence.

¹⁷Those who are short-tempered do foolish things, and schemers are hated.

¹⁸The simpleton is clothed with folly, but the wise person is crowned with knowledge.

¹⁹Evil people will bow before good people; the wicked will bow at the gates of the godly.

²⁰The poor are despised even by their neighbors, while the rich have many "friends."

²¹It is sin to despise one's neighbors; blessed are those who help the poor.

²²If you plot evil, you will be lost; but if you plan good, you will be granted unfailing love and faithfulness.

²³Work brings profit, but mere talk leads to poverty!

²⁴Wealth is a crown for the wise; the effort of fools yields only folly.

²⁵A truthful witness saves lives, but a false witness is a traitor.

²⁶Those who fear the LORD are secure; he will be a place of refuge for their children.

²⁷Fear of the LORD is a life-giving fountain; it offers escape from the snares of death.

²⁸A growing population is a king's glory; a dwindling nation is his doom.

²⁹Those who control their anger have great understanding; those with a hasty temper will make mistakes.

³⁰A relaxed attitude lengthens life; jealousy rots it away.

³¹Those who oppress the poor insult their Maker, but those who help the poor honor him.

³²The wicked are crushed by their sins, but the godly have a refuge when they die.

³³Wisdom is enshrined in an understanding heart; wisdom is not* found among fools.

³⁴Godliness exalts a nation, but sin is a disgrace to any people.

³⁵A king rejoices in servants who know what they are doing; he is angry with those who cause trouble.

14:3 Hebrew *a rod of pride.* **14:16** Hebrew *The wise fear.* **14:33** As in Greek version; Hebrew lacks *not.*

14:15 Trusting God to direct us through the advice of others is an important step in recovery. Solomon, however, gave a wise note of caution here: Don't trust others blindly. A healthy trust in others is developed gradually and carefully. This can only happen as we determine when it is safe for us to be vulnerable and if the guidance we are receiving is godly. If any advice is contrary to the truth revealed in the Bible, it should be disregarded, no matter who gave it.

14:26-27 "Fear of the LORD" is integral in any twelve-step program. Steps Two, Three, Six, Seven, and Eleven all have to do directly with trusting God and drawing closer to him. God will give us strength and power that we never could have experienced if we had refused to follow his plan for us. He is our security, our strength, and our source of life. If we haven't given our life to Jesus yet, we must do it now. Any hope of recovery depends on a relationship with him.

15:14 We must be careful what we feed our mind. If we are "hungry for truth," we will not only live according to God's plan, but we will also love and study his Word, which is "more valuable . . . than millions in gold and silver!" (Psalm 119:72). When our thoughts dwell on unhealthy things—things that draw us away from God—we are feeding on "trash." Filling our mind with evil thoughts, words, or images will only hinder us in the recovery process. Instead, we are commanded to "think about things that are pure and lovely and admirable. Think about things that are excellent and worthy of praise" (Philippians 4:8).

CHAPTER 15

A gentle answer turns away wrath, but harsh words stir up anger.

²The wise person makes learning a joy; fools spout only foolishness.

³The LORD is watching everywhere, keeping his eye on both the evil and the good.

⁴Gentle words bring life and health; a deceitful tongue crushes the spirit.

⁵Only a fool despises a parent's discipline; whoever learns from correction is wise.

⁶There is treasure in the house of the godly, but the earnings of the wicked bring trouble.

⁷Only the wise can give good advice; fools cannot do so.

⁸The LORD hates the sacrifice of the wicked, but he delights in the prayers of the upright.

⁹The LORD despises the way of the wicked, but he loves those who pursue godliness.

¹⁰Whoever abandons the right path will be severely punished; whoever hates correction will die.

¹¹Even the depths of Death and Destruction* are known by the LORD. How much more does he know the human heart!

¹²Mockers don't love those who rebuke them, so they stay away from the wise.

¹³A glad heart makes a happy face; a broken heart crushes the spirit.

¹⁴A wise person is hungry for truth, while the fool feeds on trash.

¹⁵For the poor, every day brings trouble; for the happy heart, life is a continual feast.

¹⁶It is better to have little with fear for the LORD than to have great treasure with turmoil.

¹⁷A bowl of soup with someone you love is better than steak with someone you hate.

¹⁸A hothead starts fights; a cool-tempered person tries to stop them.

¹⁹A lazy person has trouble all through life; the path of the upright is easy!

²⁰Sensible children bring joy to their father; foolish children despise their mother.

²¹Foolishness brings joy to those who have no sense; a sensible person stays on the right path.

²²Plans go wrong for lack of advice; many counselors bring success.

²³Everyone enjoys a fitting reply; it is wonderful to say the right thing at the right time!

²⁴The path of the wise leads to life above; they leave the grave* behind.

²⁵The LORD destroys the house of the proud, but he protects the property of widows.

Self-Protection

READ PROVERBS 15:16-33

In recovery we learn new ways of seeing things, new ways of responding, and new guidelines for making decisions. Our old patterns of thinking and living didn't work very well. Now that we are establishing new patterns, we will need wise counselors. They will listen as we share our struggles with them, and they will supply the support and wisdom we need.

King Solomon gave this advice: "Plans go wrong for lack of advice; many counselors bring success" (Proverbs 15:22). "With many counselors, there is safety" (Proverbs 11:14). King David looked to God's Word for counsel saying, "Your decrees please me; they give me wise advice" (Psalm 119:24). Isaiah prophesied about Jesus the Messiah, saying, "For a child is born to us, a son is given to us. And the government will rest on his shoulders. These will be his royal titles: Wonderful Counselor, Mighty God, Everlasting Father, Prince of Peace" (Isaiah 9:6). God is our ultimate source of wise counsel.

When we surround ourself with dependable and wise counselors, we are developing a safety net. Good counsel can come from the Bible and from godly people. When we admit our wrongs to other people, they can become a source of counsel for us. They may be professionals who understand addiction and recovery. They may be people who know us and measure their advice by godly principles. Or perhaps they are people who have experienced what we are now going through. Find someone! But above all, trust in God as your ultimate source of wise counsel. *End of the Recovery Principal reading plan.*

15:11 Hebrew *Sheol and Abaddon.* **15:24** Hebrew *Sheol.*

²⁶The LORD despises the thoughts of the wicked, but he delights in pure words.

²⁷Dishonest money brings grief to the whole family, but those who hate bribes will live.

²⁸The godly think before speaking; the wicked spout evil words.

²⁹The LORD is far from the wicked, but he hears the prayers of the righteous.

³⁰A cheerful look brings joy to the heart; good news makes for good health.

³¹If you listen to constructive criticism, you will be at home among the wise.

³²If you reject criticism, you only harm yourself; but if you listen to correction, you grow in understanding.

³³Fear of the LORD teaches a person to be wise; humility precedes honor.

CHAPTER 16

We can gather our thoughts, but the LORD gives the right answer.

²People may be pure in their own eyes, but the LORD examines their motives.

³Commit your work to the LORD, and then your plans will succeed.

⁴The LORD has made everything for his own purposes, even the wicked for punishment.

⁵The LORD despises pride; be assured that the proud will be punished.

⁶Unfailing love and faithfulness cover sin; evil is avoided by fear of the LORD.

⁷When the ways of people please the LORD, he makes even their enemies live at peace with them.

⁸It is better to be poor and godly than rich and dishonest.

⁹We can make our plans, but the LORD determines our steps.

¹⁰The king speaks with divine wisdom; he must never judge unfairly.

¹¹The LORD demands fairness in every business deal; he sets the standard.

¹²A king despises wrongdoing, for his rule depends on his justice.

¹³The king is pleased with righteous lips; he loves those who speak honestly.

¹⁴The anger of the king is a deadly threat; the wise do what they can to appease it.

¹⁵When the king smiles, there is life; his favor refreshes like a gentle rain.

¹⁶How much better to get wisdom than gold, and understanding than silver!

¹⁷The path of the upright leads away from evil; whoever follows that path is safe.

¹⁸Pride goes before destruction, and haughtiness before a fall.

¹⁹It is better to live humbly with the poor than to share plunder with the proud.

²⁰Those who listen to instruction will prosper; those who trust the LORD will be happy.

²¹The wise are known for their understanding, and instruction is appreciated if it's well presented.

²²Discretion is a life-giving fountain to those who possess it, but discipline is wasted on fools.

²³From a wise mind comes wise speech; the words of the wise are persuasive.

²⁴Kind words are like honey—sweet to the soul and healthy for the body.

²⁵There is a path before each person that seems right, but it ends in death.

²⁶It is good for workers to have an appetite; an empty stomach drives them on.

²⁷Scoundrels hunt for scandal; their words are a destructive blaze.

²⁸A troublemaker plants seeds of strife; gossip separates the best of friends.

15:31-32 If we really want to learn and grow, we must be willing to be held accountable by receiving constructive criticism from others (see 13:18; 15:5; 25:12). For many of us it is hard to receive reproof because even when it is shared in love, it hurts. Our tendency may be to ignore correction to avoid the hurt or to collapse emotionally because we are devastated by a word of constructive criticism. We would be wise to ask for feedback from people we respect so we can learn from our mistakes and grow in understanding and maturity.

16:2 We are incredibly good at rationalizing our actions and motives so that others don't know why we are doing things. This is dangerous because soon we may begin to believe what we are telling others. For those of us who have a drinking problem, for instance, it is easy to deny it. We claim that we really don't need to drink or that we only drink to be social. We may even have "proved" to everyone that we don't have a problem—everyone, that is, except God. He knows all our actions, our motives, and our excuses. He is the only one who can make full recovery possible.

16:9 It is important that we entrust the future to God, but we also need to make plans—for our steps in recovery, for our retirement savings, for our life. Responsible trust in God means taking action to secure what we need in life, while letting God's Word and his Spirit guide us in our preparations. Saying "God will provide" and then sitting passively, waiting for God to take care of us, is often an excuse for laziness. We need to get moving and let God direct our steps in the process.

²⁹Violent people deceive their companions, leading them down a harmful path.

³⁰With narrowed eyes, they plot evil; without a word, they plan their mischief.

³¹Gray hair is a crown of glory; it is gained by living a godly life.

³²It is better to be patient than powerful; it is better to have self-control than to conquer a city.

³³We may throw the dice, but the LORD determines how they fall.

CHAPTER 17

A dry crust eaten in peace is better than a great feast with strife.

²A wise slave will rule over the master's shameful sons and will share their inheritance.

³Fire tests the purity of silver and gold, but the LORD tests the heart.

⁴Wrongdoers listen to wicked talk; liars pay attention to destructive words.

⁵Those who mock the poor insult their Maker; those who rejoice at the misfortune of others will be punished.

⁶Grandchildren are the crowning glory of the aged; parents are the pride of their children.

⁷Eloquent speech is not fitting for a fool; even less are lies fitting for a ruler.

⁸A bribe seems to work like magic for those who give it; they succeed in all they do.

⁹Disregarding another person's faults preserves love; telling about them separates close friends.

¹⁰A single rebuke does more for a person of understanding than a hundred lashes on the back of a fool.

¹¹Evil people seek rebellion, but they will be severely punished.

¹²It is safer to meet a bear robbed of her cubs than to confront a fool caught in folly.

¹³If you repay evil for good, evil will never leave your house.

¹⁴Beginning a quarrel is like opening a floodgate, so drop the matter before a dispute breaks out.

¹⁵The LORD despises those who acquit the guilty and condemn the innocent.

¹⁶It is senseless to pay tuition to educate a fool who has no heart for wisdom.

¹⁷A friend is always loyal, and a brother is born to help in time of need.

¹⁸It is poor judgment to co-sign a friend's note, to become responsible for a neighbor's debts.

¹⁹Anyone who loves to quarrel loves sin; anyone who speaks boastfully* invites disaster.

²⁰The crooked heart will not prosper; the twisted tongue tumbles into trouble.

²¹It is painful to be the parent of a fool; there is no joy for the father of a rebel.

²²A cheerful heart is good medicine, but a broken spirit saps a person's strength.

²³The wicked accept secret bribes to pervert justice.

²⁴Sensible people keep their eyes glued on wisdom, but a fool's eyes wander to the ends of the earth.

²⁵A foolish child* brings grief to a father and bitterness to a mother.

²⁶It is wrong to fine the godly for being good or to punish nobles for being honest!

²⁷A truly wise person uses few words; a person with understanding is even-tempered.

²⁸Even fools are thought to be wise when they keep silent; when they keep their mouths shut, they seem intelligent.

17:19 Or *who builds up defenses;* Hebrew reads *who makes a high gate.* **17:25** Hebrew *son.*

16:33 There is no such thing as luck. Everything that happens to us, even the seemingly random roll of the dice, is under the watchful eye and guiding hand of our sovereign God. It is a challenge to our faith to trust that God is truly in control and that he cares about all the details of our life. But it is encouraging to remember that "God causes everything to work together for the good of those who love God and are called according to his purpose for them" (Romans 8:28).

17:9 The last thing we need to hear in recovery is how badly we have messed up our life. We are well aware of our mistakes and are ashamed of things we have done. But by confessing our sins and repenting, we receive God's forgiveness and cleansing. He has forgotten our sins and has removed them "as far away from us as the east is from the west" (Psalm 103:12). If God has forgiven and forgotten our past mistakes, we have no need to be reminded of them. If friends bring up the past, we need to ignore them and not feel guilty for what we have done. The guilt we feel may drag us back into our old lifestyle.

17:17 A true friend will stick beside us during the hard times. Without a relationship with that kind of friend, recovery and growth can't take place. We all need to be able to express our needs and concerns to someone who will care, pray, and encourage us in our efforts to change.

CHAPTER 18

A recluse is self-indulgent, snarling at every sound principle of conduct.

²Fools have no interest in understanding; they only want to air their own opinions.

³When the wicked arrive, contempt, shame, and disgrace are sure to follow.

⁴A person's words can be life-giving water; words of true wisdom are as refreshing as a bubbling brook.

⁵It is wrong for a judge to favor the guilty or condemn the innocent.

⁶Fools get into constant quarrels; they are asking for a beating.

⁷The mouths of fools are their ruin; their lips get them into trouble.

⁸What dainty morsels rumors are—but they sink deep into one's heart.

⁹A lazy person is as bad as someone who destroys things.

¹⁰The name of the LORD is a strong fortress; the godly run to him and are safe.

¹¹The rich think of their wealth as an impregnable defense; they imagine it is a high wall of safety.

¹²Haughtiness goes before destruction; humility precedes honor.

¹³What a shame, what folly, to give advice before listening to the facts!

¹⁴The human spirit can endure a sick body, but who can bear it if the spirit is crushed?

¹⁵Intelligent people are always open to new ideas. In fact, they look for them.

¹⁶Giving a gift works wonders; it may bring you before important people!

¹⁷Any story sounds true until someone sets the record straight.

¹⁸Casting lots can end arguments and settle disputes between powerful opponents.

¹⁹It's harder to make amends with an offended friend than to capture a fortified city. Arguments separate friends like a gate locked with iron bars.

²⁰Words satisfy the soul as food satisfies the stomach; the right words on a person's lips bring satisfaction.

²¹Those who love to talk will experience the consequences, for the tongue can kill or nourish life.

²²The man who finds a wife finds a treasure and receives favor from the LORD.

²³The poor plead for mercy; the rich answer with insults.

²⁴There are "friends" who destroy each other, but a real friend sticks closer than a brother.

CHAPTER 19

It is better to be poor and honest than to be a fool and dishonest.

²Zeal without knowledge is not good; a person who moves too quickly may go the wrong way.

³People ruin their lives by their own foolishness and then are angry at the LORD.

⁴Wealth makes many "friends"; poverty drives them away.

⁵A false witness will not go unpunished, nor will a liar escape.

⁶Many beg favors from a prince; everyone is the friend of a person who gives gifts!

⁷If the relatives of the poor despise them, how much more will their friends avoid them. The poor call after them, but they are gone.

⁸To acquire wisdom is to love oneself; people who cherish understanding will prosper.

⁹A false witness will not go unpunished, and a liar will be destroyed.

¹⁰It isn't right for a fool to live in luxury or for a slave to rule over princes!

¹¹People with good sense restrain their anger; they earn esteem by overlooking wrongs.

¹²The king's anger is like a lion's roar, but his favor is like dew on the grass.

¹³A foolish child* is a calamity to a father; a nagging wife annoys like a constant dripping.

19:13 Hebrew *son;* also in 19:27.

18:1 The self-indulgent person lacks the ability to delay gratification. If we are self-indulgent, we end up satisfying our whims but never meeting our real needs. Rather than demanding our own way, it is healthier to take the time to reflect on what is truly important to us and to appropriately seek to have those needs met.

18:12 When we are filled with pride, we cannot see our weaknesses. We build walls of denial that are almost impregnable. If we cannot admit our faults, they will never be corrected, and we will suffer the consequences. On the other hand, humility opens the door for correction. When we honestly evaluate our life, we can see our weaknesses and take steps to improve and correct them. This may be painful now, but it will be much more bearable than the pain of a life destroyed by a dependency and a compulsion.

¹⁴Parents can provide their sons with an inheritance of houses and wealth, but only the LORD can give an understanding wife.

¹⁵A lazy person sleeps soundly—and goes hungry.

¹⁶Keep the commandments and keep your life; despising them leads to death.

¹⁷If you help the poor, you are lending to the LORD—and he will repay you!

¹⁸Discipline your children while there is hope. If you don't, you will ruin their lives.

¹⁹Short-tempered people must pay their own penalty. If you rescue them once, you will have to do it again.

²⁰Get all the advice and instruction you can, and be wise the rest of your life.

²¹You can make many plans, but the LORD's purpose will prevail.

²²Loyalty makes a person attractive. And it is better to be poor than dishonest.

²³Fear of the LORD gives life, security, and protection from harm.

²⁴Some people are so lazy that they won't even lift a finger to feed themselves.

²⁵If you punish a mocker, the simple-minded will learn a lesson; if you reprove the wise, they will be all the wiser.

²⁶Children who mistreat their father or chase away their mother are a public disgrace and an embarrassment.

²⁷If you stop listening to instruction, my child, you have turned your back on knowledge.

²⁸A corrupt witness makes a mockery of justice; the mouth of the wicked gulps down evil.

²⁹Mockers will be punished, and the backs of fools will be beaten.

CHAPTER 20
Wine produces mockers; liquor leads to brawls. Whoever is led astray by drink cannot be wise.

²The king's fury is like a lion's roar; to rouse his anger is to risk your life.

³Avoiding a fight is a mark of honor; only fools insist on quarreling.

⁴If you are too lazy to plow in the right season, you will have no food at the harvest.

⁵Though good advice lies deep within a person's heart, the wise will draw it out.

⁶Many will say they are loyal friends, but who can find one who is really faithful?

⁷The godly walk with integrity; blessed are their children after them.

⁸When a king judges, he carefully weighs all the evidence, distinguishing the bad from the good.

⁹Who can say, "I have cleansed my heart; I am pure and free from sin"?

¹⁰The LORD despises double standards of every kind.

¹¹Even children are known by the way they act, whether their conduct is pure and right.

¹²Ears to hear and eyes to see—both are gifts from the LORD.

¹³If you love sleep, you will end in poverty. Keep your eyes open, and there will be plenty to eat!

¹⁴The buyer haggles over the price, saying, "It's worthless," then brags about getting a bargain!

¹⁵Wise speech is rarer and more valuable than gold and rubies.

¹⁶Be sure to get collateral from anyone who guarantees the debt of a stranger. Get a deposit if someone guarantees the debt of a foreigner.*

¹⁷Stolen bread tastes sweet, but it turns to gravel in the mouth.

¹⁸Plans succeed through good counsel; don't go to war without the advice of others.

¹⁹A gossip tells secrets, so don't hang around with someone who talks too much.

²⁰If you curse your father or mother, the lamp of your life will be snuffed out.

20:16 An alternate reading in the Hebrew text is *the debt of an adulterous woman;* compare 27:13.

19:19 If we rescue impatient friends from their problems once, we will probably rescue them again and again. They will become used to being rescued and will live irresponsibly without suffering the consequences of their behavior. We may even become codependent, addicted to the pattern of avoiding our own needs and gaining a sense of importance by helping others in their need. This harms us and the people who need our help. Though it is painful to do, we must let others feel the effects of their addiction. The pain of those experiences may bring them to admit their problems and seek recovery.

20:9 None of us is without sin, but we can receive God's forgiveness through confession and repentance. An important step in recovery involves taking a moral inventory of our life, which is a big job! Many of our sins were committed unconsciously and will require real soul-searching to uncover. Since we have such a strong tendency to sin, we will need to take several inventories. We can be sure, however, that each time we confess our sins to God, he will be faithful in forgiving us.

²¹An inheritance obtained early in life is not a blessing in the end.

²²Don't say, "I will get even for this wrong." Wait for the LORD to handle the matter.

²³The LORD despises double standards; he is not pleased by dishonest scales.

²⁴How can we understand the road we travel? It is the LORD who directs our steps.

²⁵It is dangerous to make a rash promise to God before counting the cost.

²⁶A wise king finds the wicked, lays them out like wheat, then runs the crushing wheel over them.

²⁷The LORD's searchlight penetrates the human spirit,* exposing every hidden motive.

²⁸Unfailing love and faithfulness protect the king; his throne is made secure through love.

²⁹The glory of the young is their strength; the gray hair of experience is the splendor of the old.

³⁰Physical punishment cleanses away evil;* such discipline purifies the heart.

CHAPTER 21

The king's heart is like a stream of water directed by the LORD; he turns it wherever he pleases.

²People may think they are doing what is right, but the LORD examines the heart.

³The LORD is more pleased when we do what is just and right than when we give him sacrifices.

⁴Haughty eyes, a proud heart, and evil actions are all sin.

⁵Good planning and hard work lead to prosperity, but hasty shortcuts lead to poverty.

⁶Wealth created by lying is a vanishing mist and a deadly trap.*

⁷Because the wicked refuse to do what is just, their violence boomerangs and destroys them.

⁸The guilty walk a crooked path; the innocent travel a straight road.

⁹It is better to live alone in the corner of an attic than with a contentious wife in a lovely home.

¹⁰Evil people love to harm others; their neighbors get no mercy from them.

¹¹A simpleton can learn only by seeing mockers punished; a wise person learns from instruction.

¹²The Righteous One* knows what is going on in the homes of the wicked; he will bring the wicked to disaster.

¹³Those who shut their ears to the cries of the poor will be ignored in their own time of need.

¹⁴A secret gift calms anger; a secret bribe pacifies fury.

¹⁵Justice is a joy to the godly, but it causes dismay among evildoers.

¹⁶The person who strays from common sense will end up in the company of the dead.

¹⁷Those who love pleasure become poor; wine and luxury are not the way to riches.

¹⁸Sometimes the wicked are punished to save the godly, and the treacherous for the upright.

¹⁹It is better to live alone in the desert than with a crabby, complaining wife.

²⁰The wise have wealth and luxury, but fools spend whatever they get.

20:27 Or *The human spirit is the LORD's searchlight.* **20:30** The meaning of the Hebrew is uncertain. **21:6** As in Greek version; Hebrew reads *mist for those who seek death.* **21:12** Or *The righteous man.*

20:22 Seeking revenge against people who have hurt us will never satisfy our anger; it will only add fuel to the fire. The cycle of retribution often lasts a long time, sometimes for years after both parties have forgotten the origin of the conflict. To overcome our anger, we need to start the process of forgiveness right away. We may need to confront our offender in love and seek to resolve the conflict through mutual understanding. If reconciliation is not possible, it is best to give the matter to God and his ultimate justice. Either way, we need to put the sin behind us and move on with our life.

20:27 God intends for our conscience to be like a searchlight that illuminates our life, helping us take our moral inventory. When exposing sin, the godly conscience doesn't condemn and blame, but it doesn't overlook sin either. Instead it realizes that sin is not good for us and it causes pain to others. When we feel that something is not right about our actions, our conscience is probably speaking to us, shining its light on our sins. Once we know that sins are there, we can confess them, repent, and be forgiven.

21:5 Recovery is spelled P-A-T-I-E-N-C-E! We often feel as if we are plodding along, just one short step at a time. Sometimes we even have to repeat steps we have already completed. To experience real change in our life will almost always be a slow process. It takes time to put the principles of recovery into practice. A "quick fix" recovery program will not have lasting results because it will never give us the time we need to make the steps an integral part of our life.

²¹Whoever pursues godliness and unfailing love will find life, godliness, and honor.

²²The wise conquer the city of the strong and level the fortress in which they trust.

²³If you keep your mouth shut, you will stay out of trouble.

²⁴Mockers are proud and haughty; they act with boundless arrogance.

²⁵The desires of lazy people will be their ruin, for their hands refuse to work. ²⁶They are always greedy for more, while the godly love to give!

²⁷God loathes the sacrifice of an evil person, especially when it is brought with ulterior motives.

²⁸A false witness will be cut off, but an attentive witness will be allowed to speak.

²⁹The wicked put up a bold front, but the upright proceed with care.

³⁰Human plans, no matter how wise or well advised, cannot stand against the LORD.

³¹The horses are prepared for battle, but the victory belongs to the LORD.

CHAPTER 22

Choose a good reputation over great riches, for being held in high esteem is better than having silver or gold.

²The rich and the poor have this in common: The LORD made them both.

³A prudent person foresees the danger ahead and takes precautions; the simpleton goes blindly on and suffers the consequences.

⁴True humility and fear of the LORD lead to riches, honor, and long life.

⁵The deceitful walk a thorny, treacherous road; whoever values life will stay away.

⁶Teach your children to choose the right path, and when they are older, they will remain upon it.

⁷Just as the rich rule the poor, so the borrower is servant to the lender.

⁸Those who plant seeds of injustice will harvest disaster, and their reign of terror will end.

⁹Blessed are those who are generous, because they feed the poor.

¹⁰Throw out the mocker, and fighting, quarrels, and insults will disappear.

¹¹Anyone who loves a pure heart and gracious speech is the king's friend.

¹²The LORD preserves knowledge, but he ruins the plans of the deceitful.

¹³The lazy person is full of excuses, saying, "If I go outside, I might meet a lion in the street and be killed!"

¹⁴The mouth of an immoral woman is a deep pit; those living under the LORD's displeasure will fall into it.

¹⁵A youngster's heart is filled with foolishness, but discipline will drive it away.

¹⁶A person who gets ahead by oppressing the poor or by showering gifts on the rich will end in poverty.

Thirty Sayings of the Wise

¹⁷Listen to the words of the wise; apply your heart to my instruction. ¹⁸For it is good to keep these sayings deep within yourself, always ready on your lips. ¹⁹I am teaching you today—yes, you—so you will trust in the LORD. ²⁰I have written thirty sayings for you, filled with advice and knowledge. ²¹In this way, you may know the truth and bring an accurate report to those who sent you.

²²Do not rob the poor because they are poor or exploit the needy in court. ²³For the LORD is their defender. He will injure anyone who injures them.

²⁴Keep away from angry, short-tempered people, ²⁵or you will learn to be like them and endanger your soul.

²⁶Do not co-sign another person's note or put up a guarantee for someone else's loan. ²⁷If you can't pay it, even your bed will be snatched from under you.

²⁸Do not steal your neighbor's property by moving the ancient boundary markers set up by your ancestors.

²⁹Do you see any truly competent workers? They will serve kings rather than ordinary people.

22:6 The most important part of being parents is teaching our children to follow a godly lifestyle. If children learn to respect authority and obey God while they are young, they will stay on that path when they are older. We may have grown up in a dysfunctional family where godly values were shunned or laughed at, and now we can see how that led to our codependent lifestyle. But our children deserve better; they need all the advantages of a moral and loving family environment.

22:17-19 Here Solomon repeated one of his favorite themes in Proverbs: Trust in the Lord. He alone is the source of perfect love and truth. It is only by surrendering to him that we can experience true love and discover how our life should be lived.

CHAPTER 23

When dining with a ruler, pay attention to what is put before you. ²If you are a big eater, put a knife to your throat, ³and don't desire all the delicacies—deception may be involved.

⁴Don't weary yourself trying to get rich. Why waste your time? ⁵For riches can disappear as though they had the wings of a bird!

⁶Don't eat with people who are stingy; don't desire their delicacies. ⁷"Eat and drink," they say, but they don't mean it. They are always thinking about how much it costs. ⁸You will vomit up the delicious food they serve, and you will have to take back your words of appreciation for their "kindness."

⁹Don't waste your breath on fools, for they will despise the wisest advice.

¹⁰Don't steal the land of defenseless orphans by moving the ancient boundary markers, ¹¹for their Redeemer is strong. He himself will bring their charges against you.

¹²Commit yourself to instruction; attune your ears to hear words of knowledge.

¹³Don't fail to correct your children. They won't die if you spank them. ¹⁴Physical discipline may well save them from death.*

¹⁵My child,* how I will rejoice if you become wise. ¹⁶Yes, my heart will thrill when you speak what is right and just.

¹⁷Don't envy sinners, but always continue to fear the LORD. ¹⁸For surely you have a future ahead of you; your hope will not be disappointed.

¹⁹My child, listen and be wise. Keep your heart on the right course. ²⁰Do not carouse with drunkards and gluttons, ²¹for they are on their way to poverty. Too much sleep clothes a person with rags.

²²Listen to your father, who gave you life, and don't despise your mother's experience when she is old. ²³Get the truth and don't ever sell it; also get wisdom, discipline, and discernment. ²⁴The father of godly children has cause for joy. What a pleasure it is to have wise children.* ²⁵So give your parents joy! May she who gave you birth be happy.

²⁶O my son, give me your heart. May your eyes delight in my ways of wisdom. ²⁷A prostitute is a deep pit; an adulterous woman is treacherous.* ²⁸She hides and waits like a robber, looking for another victim who will be unfaithful to his wife.

²⁹Who has anguish? Who has sorrow? Who is always fighting? Who is always complaining? Who has unnecessary bruises? Who has bloodshot eyes? ³⁰It is the one who spends long hours in the taverns, trying out new drinks. ³¹Don't let the sparkle and smooth taste of wine deceive you. ³²For in the end it bites like a poisonous serpent; it stings like a viper. ³³You will see hallucinations, and you will say crazy things. ³⁴You will stagger like a sailor tossed at sea, clinging to a swaying mast. ³⁵And you will say, "They hit me, but I didn't feel it. I didn't even know it when they beat me up. When will I wake up so I can have another drink?"

CHAPTER 24

Don't envy evil people; don't desire their company. ²For they spend their days plotting violence, and their words are always stirring up trouble.

23:14 Hebrew *from Sheol.* **23:15** Hebrew *My son;* also in 23:19. **23:24** Hebrew *a wise son.* **23:27** Hebrew *is a narrow well.*

23:4-5 Perhaps the most common and unrecognized addiction in our culture today is greed or materialism. Many people weary themselves trying to get more and more money so they can buy more goods and do more things. The pleasure that money buys is only temporary; it doesn't satisfy the longings of our heart. The wise learn the secret of delayed gratification and resist the greedy impulses that bring quick and fleeting pleasure. Instead they seek to have their needs met through a healthy relationship with God and with others.

23:10-11 Unfortunately, those of us who were not adequately cared for as children often get taken advantage of as adults. Because we have been abandoned, neglected, or violated by people who were supposed to love and care for us, we have trouble discerning when it's safe to trust others. We often allow others to abuse our rights so we will be liked. We need help learning to set boundaries to protect us from people who might take advantage of our vulnerability. We need to look for godly people who will help us draw healthy boundaries in our life.

23:26-35 Three thousand years haven't changed the fact that alcohol and sex are still two of the most alluring and destructive addictions. They promise pleasure and escape from our troubles, but in the end they result in shame and embarrassment. The only real escape from our troubles, including alcohol abuse and sexual sin, is Jesus Christ. When we turn our life over to him and turn from our sins, addictions, and dependencies, we are freed to pursue a godly lifestyle. The temptations will still be there, but now we have God working with us to help us resist them. He will help us persevere in our recovery program.

³A house is built by wisdom and becomes strong through good sense. ⁴Through knowledge its rooms are filled with all sorts of precious riches and valuables.

⁵A wise man is mightier than a strong man,* and a man of knowledge is more powerful than a strong man. ⁶So don't go to war without wise guidance; victory depends on having many counselors.

⁷Wisdom is too much for a fool. When the leaders gather, the fool has nothing to say.

⁸A person who plans evil will get a reputation as a troublemaker. ⁹The schemes of a fool are sinful; everyone despises a mocker.

¹⁰If you fail under pressure, your strength is not very great.

¹¹Rescue those who are unjustly sentenced to death; don't stand back and let them die. ¹²Don't try to avoid responsibility by saying you didn't know about it. For God knows all hearts, and he sees you. He keeps watch over your soul, and he knows you knew! And he will judge all people according to what they have done.

¹³My child,* eat honey, for it is good, and the honeycomb is sweet to the taste. ¹⁴In the same way, wisdom is sweet to your soul. If you find it, you will have a bright future, and your hopes will not be cut short.

¹⁵Do not lie in wait like an outlaw at the home of the godly. And don't raid the house where the godly live. ¹⁶They may trip seven times, but each time they will rise again. But one calamity is enough to lay the wicked low.

¹⁷Do not rejoice when your enemies fall into trouble. Don't be happy when they stumble. ¹⁸For the LORD will be displeased with you and will turn his anger away from them.

¹⁹Do not fret because of evildoers; don't envy the wicked. ²⁰For the evil have no future; their light will be snuffed out.

²¹My child, fear the LORD and the king, and don't associate with rebels. ²²For you will go down with them to sudden disaster. Who knows where the punishment from the LORD and the king will end?

More Sayings of the Wise
²³Here are some further sayings of the wise:

It is wrong to show favoritism when passing judgment. ²⁴A judge who says to the wicked, "You are innocent," will be cursed by many people and denounced by the nations. ²⁵But blessings are showered on those who convict the guilty.

²⁶It is an honor to receive an honest reply.

²⁷Develop your business first before building your house.

²⁸Do not testify spitefully against innocent neighbors; don't lie about them. ²⁹And don't say, "Now I can pay them back for all their meanness to me! I'll get even!"

³⁰I walked by the field of a lazy person, the vineyard of one lacking sense. ³¹I saw that it was overgrown with thorns. It was covered with weeds, and its walls were broken down. ³²Then, as I looked and thought about it, I learned this lesson: ³³A little extra sleep, a little more slumber, a little folding of the hands to rest—³⁴and poverty will pounce on you like a bandit; scarcity will attack you like an armed robber.

CHAPTER 25
More Proverbs of Solomon
These are more proverbs of Solomon, collected by the advisers of King Hezekiah of Judah.

²It is God's privilege to conceal things and the king's privilege to discover them.

³No one can discover the height of heaven, the depth of the earth, or all that goes on in the king's mind!

⁴Remove the dross from silver, and the

24:5 As in Greek version; Hebrew reads *A wise man is strength.* **24:13** Hebrew *My son;* also in 24:21.

24:8 This verse is not saying that planning and doing evil are the same thing. But evil actions are born of wrong motives. It is wise to take a moral inventory, not just of our actions but also of our motives. Confessing a sinful *action* is like pulling a weed but leaving the roots; it will reappear in time. Confessing a sinful *motive* is like pulling a weed out by its roots; the source of the trouble is gone.

24:15-16 Recovery is a process of being restored again and again. Though we may be tripped up by sin or fall down many times, those who belong to God will have the strength and help to get up again and move forward. God is forgiving and patient with us in our failings, and he is quick to help us back on our feet.

24:30-34 Just as financial poverty comes to those who are lazy, emotional impoverishment comes to those who neglect to work on themselves. As we work on our life, weeding out destructive patterns and sowing the principles of recovery, we will reap a harvest of growth and recovery. Those of us who are lazy, however, will find our soul overgrown with weeds.

sterling will be ready for the silversmith. [5]Remove the wicked from the king's court, and his reign will be made secure by justice.

[6]Don't demand an audience with the king or push for a place among the great. [7]It is better to wait for an invitation than to be sent to the end of the line, publicly disgraced!

Just because you see something, [8]don't be in a hurry to go to court. You might go down before your neighbors in shameful defeat. [9]So discuss the matter with them privately. Don't tell anyone else, [10]or others may accuse you of gossip. Then you will never regain your good reputation.

[11]Timely advice is as lovely as golden apples in a silver basket.

[12]Valid criticism is as treasured by the one who heeds it as jewelry made from finest gold.

[13]Faithful messengers are as refreshing as snow in the heat of summer. They revive the spirit of their employer.

[14]A person who doesn't give a promised gift is like clouds and wind that don't bring rain.

[15]Patience can persuade a prince, and soft speech can crush strong opposition.

[16]Do you like honey? Don't eat too much of it, or it will make you sick!

[17]Don't visit your neighbors too often, or you will wear out your welcome.

[18]Telling lies about others is as harmful as hitting them with an ax, wounding them with a sword, or shooting them with a sharp arrow.

[19]Putting confidence in an unreliable person is like chewing with a toothache or walking on a broken foot.

[20]Singing cheerful songs to a person whose heart is heavy is as bad as stealing someone's jacket in cold weather or rubbing salt in a wound.

[21]If your enemies are hungry, give them food to eat. If they are thirsty, give them water to drink. [22]You will heap burning coals on their heads, and the LORD will reward you.

[23]As surely as a wind from the north brings rain, so a gossiping tongue causes anger!

[24]It is better to live alone in the corner of an attic than with a contentious wife in a lovely home.

[25]Good news from far away is like cold water to the thirsty.

[26]If the godly compromise with the wicked, it is like polluting a fountain or muddying a spring.

[27]Just as it is not good to eat too much honey, it is not good for people to think about all the honors they deserve.

[28]A person without self-control is as defenseless as a city with broken-down walls.

CHAPTER 26

Honor doesn't go with fools any more than snow with summer or rain with harvest.

[2]Like a fluttering sparrow or a darting swallow, an unfair curse will not land on its intended victim.

[3]Guide a horse with a whip, a donkey with a bridle, and a fool with a rod to his back!

[4]When arguing with fools, don't answer their foolish arguments, or you will become as foolish as they are.

[5]When arguing with fools, be sure to answer their foolish arguments, or they will become wise in their own estimation.

[6]Trusting a fool to convey a message is as foolish as cutting off one's feet or drinking poison!

[7]In the mouth of a fool, a proverb becomes as limp as a paralyzed leg.

[8]Honoring a fool is as foolish as tying a stone to a slingshot.

[9]A proverb in a fool's mouth is as dangerous as a thornbush brandished by a drunkard.

[10]An employer who hires a fool or a bystander is like an archer who shoots recklessly.

25:17 We have all known "cling-ons," people who cling to anyone who seems to care for them. Generally, they have been deprived of understanding, love, and respect. The "clingee" ends up feeling suffocated and pulls away, which confirms the cling-on's original insecurity. New and loving relationships in themselves don't make up for our past negative relationships. Recovery from childhood deprivations is a process that must also include working through past issues. Otherwise, our new relationships will follow the same destructive patterns as those in the past.

25:20 People who are troubled need empathy, not just halfhearted attempts to cheer them up. By showing that we understand and sincerely care about their feelings, we comfort them and give them the strength to make needed changes in their life.

¹¹As a dog returns to its vomit, so a fool repeats his folly.

¹²There is more hope for fools than for people who think they are wise.

¹³The lazy person is full of excuses, saying, "I can't go outside because there might be a lion on the road! Yes, I'm sure there's a lion out there!"

¹⁴As a door turns back and forth on its hinges, so the lazy person turns over in bed.

¹⁵Some people are so lazy that they won't lift a finger to feed themselves.

¹⁶Lazy people consider themselves smarter than seven wise counselors.

¹⁷Yanking a dog's ears is as foolish as interfering in someone else's argument.

¹⁸Just as damaging as a mad man shooting a lethal weapon ¹⁹is someone who lies to a friend and then says, "I was only joking."

²⁰Fire goes out for lack of fuel, and quarrels disappear when gossip stops.

²¹A quarrelsome person starts fights as easily as hot embers light charcoal or fire lights wood.

²²What dainty morsels rumors are—but they sink deep into one's heart.

²³Smooth* words may hide a wicked heart, just as a pretty glaze covers a common clay pot.

²⁴People with hate in their hearts may sound pleasant enough, but don't believe them. ²⁵Though they pretend to be kind, their hearts are full of all kinds of evil. ²⁶While their hatred may be concealed by trickery, it will finally come to light for all to see.

²⁷If you set a trap for others, you will get caught in it yourself. If you roll a boulder down on others, it will roll back and crush you.

²⁸A lying tongue hates its victims, and flattery causes ruin.

CHAPTER 27
Don't brag about tomorrow, since you don't know what the day will bring.

²Don't praise yourself; let others do it!

³A stone is heavy and sand is weighty, but the resentment caused by a fool is heavier than both.

⁴Anger is cruel, and wrath is like a flood, but who can survive the destructiveness of jealousy?

⁵An open rebuke is better than hidden love!

⁶Wounds from a friend are better than many kisses from an enemy.

⁷Honey seems tasteless to a person who is full, but even bitter food tastes sweet to the hungry.

⁸A person who strays from home is like a bird that strays from its nest.

⁹The heartfelt counsel of a friend is as sweet as perfume and incense.

¹⁰Never abandon a friend—either yours or your father's. Then in your time of need, you won't have to ask your relatives for assistance. It is better to go to a neighbor than to a relative who lives far away.

¹¹My child,* how happy I will be if you turn out to be wise! Then I will be able to answer my critics.

¹²A prudent person foresees the danger ahead and takes precautions. The simpleton goes blindly on and suffers the consequences.

¹³Be sure to get collateral from anyone who guarantees the debt of a stranger. Get a deposit if someone guarantees the debt of an adulterous woman.

¹⁴If you shout a pleasant greeting to your neighbor too early in the morning, it will be counted as a curse!

¹⁵A nagging wife is as annoying as the constant dripping on a rainy day. ¹⁶Trying to stop her complaints is like trying to stop the wind or hold something with greased hands.

¹⁷As iron sharpens iron, a friend sharpens a friend.

¹⁸Workers who tend a fig tree are allowed to eat its fruit. In the same way, workers who protect their employer's interests will be rewarded.

26:23 As in Greek version; Hebrew reads *Burning.* 27:11 Hebrew *My son.*

26:11 We almost invariably repeat the patterns of the past; our old problems revisit us again and again. It is easy to slip back into our addiction; that is why we need to be diligent in the recovery process. When we relax in our recovery program, we are setting ourself up for a relapse into our old lifestyle. Only through perseverance will we be able to overcome our dependency.

27:10 Friends are an important resource in recovery. We need people to whom we can be accountable and to whom we can turn in times of need—friends who are honest with us and have our best interests at heart. Just as we want our friends to stick by us in times of crisis, we should also support them when they need help. If we are there for others, we will have our own support network in place whenever we need help.

¹⁹As a face is reflected in water, so the heart reflects the person.

²⁰Just as Death and Destruction* are never satisfied, so human desire is never satisfied.

²¹Fire tests the purity of silver and gold, but a person is tested by being praised.

²²You cannot separate fools from their foolishness, even though you grind them like grain with mortar and pestle.

²³Know the state of your flocks, and put your heart into caring for your herds, ²⁴for riches don't last forever, and the crown might not be secure for the next generation. ²⁵After the hay is harvested, the new crop appears, and the mountain grasses are gathered in, ²⁶your sheep will provide wool for clothing, and your goats will be sold for the price of a field. ²⁷And you will have enough goats' milk for you, your family, and your servants.

CHAPTER 28

The wicked run away when no one is chasing them, but the godly are as bold as lions.

²When there is moral rot within a nation, its government topples easily. But with wise and knowledgeable leaders, there is stability.

³A poor person who oppresses the poor is like a pounding rain that destroys the crops.

⁴To reject the law is to praise the wicked; to obey the law is to fight them.

⁵Evil people don't understand justice, but those who follow the LORD understand completely.

⁶It is better to be poor and honest than rich and crooked.

⁷Young people who obey the law are wise; those who seek out worthless companions bring shame to their parents.

⁸A person who makes money by charging interest will lose it. It will end up in the hands of someone who is kind to the poor.

⁹The prayers of a person who ignores the law are despised.

¹⁰Those who lead the upright into sin will fall into their own trap, but the honest will inherit good things.

¹¹Rich people picture themselves as wise, but their real poverty is evident to the poor.

¹²When the godly succeed, everyone is glad. When the wicked take charge, people go into hiding.

¹³People who cover over their sins will not prosper. But if they confess and forsake them, they will receive mercy.

¹⁴Blessed are those who have a tender conscience,* but the stubborn are headed for serious trouble.

¹⁵A wicked ruler is as dangerous to the poor as a lion or bear attacking them.

¹⁶Only a stupid prince will oppress his people, but a king will have a long reign if he hates dishonesty and bribes.

¹⁷A murderer's tormented conscience will drive him into the grave. Don't protect him!

¹⁸The honest will be rescued from harm, but those who are crooked will be destroyed.

¹⁹Hard workers have plenty of food; playing around brings poverty.

²⁰The trustworthy will get a rich reward. But the person who wants to get rich quick will only get into trouble.

²¹Showing partiality is never good, yet some will do wrong for something as small as a piece of bread.

²²A greedy person tries to get rich quick, but it only leads to poverty.

²³In the end, people appreciate frankness more than flattery.

²⁴Robbing your parents and then saying, "What's wrong with that?" is as serious as committing murder.

²⁵Greed causes fighting; trusting the LORD leads to prosperity.

27:20 Hebrew *Sheol and Abaddon.* **28:14** Hebrew *those who fear.*

27:20 The desire referred to here is lust or greed—for things like sexual gratification, materialism, power, or prestige. Although satisfying these desires can be pleasurable, it is not fulfilling in the long run because these are false substitutes for deeper needs such as love, intimacy, and security. As time passes we will need more and more of our "drugs" of choice to make us feel good, and we will gradually become enslaved to our impulses.
27:21 One way to evaluate our self-perception is to note our responses when others praise us. If we discount compliments, this probably means that we suffer from a poor self-image. If we gloat in the praise we receive, we probably have an inflated self-image. The healthy response to praise is to receive it graciously and balance it with a humble awareness of our weaknesses.
28:13 This verse contains wisdom essential to recovery and change. We must proceed with recovery by honestly assessing our mistakes, confessing our wrongs to God and to one another, resolving to avoid such mistakes in the future, and asking God to change our heart. It is humbling to admit and confess our sins, and it is alarming to commit to change; but that's the only way we can recover from our dependency and get another chance at life.

²⁶Trusting oneself is foolish, but those who walk in wisdom are safe.

²⁷Whoever gives to the poor will lack nothing. But a curse will come upon those who close their eyes to poverty.

²⁸When the wicked take charge, people hide. When the wicked meet disaster, the godly multiply.

CHAPTER 29

Whoever stubbornly refuses to accept criticism will suddenly be broken beyond repair.

²When the godly are in authority, the people rejoice. But when the wicked are in power, they groan.

³The man who loves wisdom brings joy to his father, but if he hangs around with prostitutes, his wealth is wasted.

⁴A just king gives stability to his nation, but one who demands bribes destroys it.

⁵To flatter people is to lay a trap for their feet.

⁶Evil people are trapped by sin, but the righteous escape, shouting for joy.

⁷The godly know the rights of the poor; the wicked don't care to know.

⁸Mockers can get a whole town agitated, but those who are wise will calm anger.

⁹If a wise person takes a fool to court, there will be ranting and ridicule but no satisfaction.

¹⁰The bloodthirsty hate the honest, but the upright seek out the honest.

¹¹A fool gives full vent to anger, but a wise person quietly holds it back.

¹²If a ruler honors liars, all his advisers will be wicked.

¹³The poor and the oppressor have this in common—the LORD gives light to the eyes of both.

¹⁴A king who is fair to the poor will have a long reign.

¹⁵To discipline and reprimand a child produces wisdom, but a mother is disgraced by an undisciplined child.

¹⁶When the wicked are in authority, sin increases. But the godly will live to see the tyrant's downfall.

¹⁷Discipline your children, and they will give you happiness and peace of mind.

¹⁸When people do not accept divine guidance, they run wild. But whoever obeys the law is happy.

¹⁹For a servant, mere words are not enough—discipline is needed. For the words may be understood, but they are not heeded.

²⁰There is more hope for a fool than for someone who speaks without thinking.

²¹A servant who is pampered from childhood will later become a rebel.

²²A hot-tempered person starts fights and gets into all kinds of sin.

²³Pride ends in humiliation, while humility brings honor.

²⁴If you assist a thief, you are only hurting yourself. You will be punished if you report the crime, but you will be cursed if you don't.

²⁵Fearing people is a dangerous trap, but to trust the LORD means safety.

²⁶Many seek the ruler's favor, but justice comes from the LORD.

²⁷The godly despise the wicked; the wicked despise the godly.

CHAPTER 30
The Sayings of Agur

The message of Agur son of Jakeh. An oracle.*

I am weary, O God; I am weary and worn out, O God.* ²I am too ignorant to be human, and I lack common sense. ³I have not mastered human wisdom, nor do I know the Holy One.

30:1a Or *son of Jakeh from Massa.* **30:1b** The Hebrew can also be translated *The man declares this to Ithiel, to Ithiel and to Ucal.*

29:15, 17 Children cannot grow up to be responsible adults if they are never disciplined, corrected, and held accountable for their actions. Children who are not held accountable fail to learn how to protect themselves from the negative influences of sin. Children who are punished inconsistently, in anger, or in the absence of a loving relationship will become rebellious toward authority and will resist accountability (see 22:15; 23:13-14). We must be consistent and fair in disciplining our children if they are to reap the benefits.
29:23 Pride always sets us up for humiliation. Pride tells us, "I'm strong; I don't need anyone's help." It blinds us to our weaknesses and prevents us from seeking the people and the help we need. Humility says, "I need improvement; could you help me?" Those of us who maintain a humble perspective, realizing that we are weak and vulnerable, will look for the help and support we need for a successful recovery. Humility will protect us from the devastation of a relapse.

⁴Who but God goes up to heaven and comes back down? Who holds the wind in his fists? Who wraps up the oceans in his cloak? Who has created the whole wide world? What is his name—and his son's name? Tell me if you know!

⁵Every word of God proves true. He defends all who come to him for protection. ⁶Do not add to his words, or he may rebuke you, and you will be found a liar. ⁷O God, I beg two favors from you before I die. ⁸First, help me never to tell a lie. Second, give me neither poverty nor riches! Give me just enough to satisfy my needs. ⁹For if I grow rich, I may deny you and say, "Who is the LORD?" And if I am too poor, I may steal and thus insult God's holy name.

¹⁰Never slander a person to his employer. If you do, the person will curse you, and you will pay for it.

¹¹Some people curse their father and do not thank their mother. ¹²They feel pure, but they are filthy and unwashed. ¹³They are proud beyond description and disdainful. ¹⁴They devour the poor with teeth as sharp as swords or knives. They destroy the needy from the face of the earth.

¹⁵The leech has two suckers that cry out, "More, more!"* There are three other things—no, four!—that are never satisfied:
¹⁶ the grave,
  the barren womb,
  the thirsty desert,
  the blazing fire.

¹⁷The eye that mocks a father and despises a mother will be plucked out by ravens of the valley and eaten by vultures.

¹⁸There are three things that amaze me—no, four things I do not understand:
¹⁹ how an eagle glides through the sky,
  how a snake slithers on a rock,
  how a ship navigates the ocean,
  how a man loves a woman.
²⁰Equally amazing is how an adulterous woman can satisfy her sexual appetite, shrug her shoulders, and then say, "What's wrong with that?"

²¹There are three things that make the earth tremble—no, four it cannot endure:
²² a slave who becomes a king,
  an overbearing fool who prospers,
²³ a bitter woman who finally gets a
    husband,
  a servant girl who supplants her mistress.

²⁴There are four things on earth that are small but unusually wise:
²⁵ Ants—they aren't strong,
  but they store up food for the winter.
²⁶ Rock badgers*—they aren't powerful,
  but they make their homes among the
    rocky cliffs.
²⁷ Locusts—they have no king,
  but they march like an army in ranks.
²⁸ Lizards—they are easy to catch,
  but they are found even in kings'
    palaces.

²⁹There are three stately monarchs on the earth—no, four:
³⁰ the lion, king of animals, who won't turn
    aside for anything,
³¹ the strutting rooster,
  the male goat,
  a king as he leads his army.

³²If you have been a fool by being proud or plotting evil, don't brag about it—cover your mouth with your hand in shame.

³³As the beating of cream yields butter, and a blow to the nose causes bleeding, so anger causes quarrels.

30:15 Hebrew *two daughters who cry out, "Give, give!"* **30:26** Or *coneys,* or *hyraxes.*

30:5 The words of God, including these principles in Proverbs, are true and offer protection to those who live by them. Living by God's truth demands that we honestly admit our need for God's wisdom and that we seek to live by it. This will not be easy, and it may not be popular. But walking in God's light will place us under God's protection and care, a necessity for any successful recovery.

30:11-12 It is easier to blame others for our problems than it is to admit them. Many of our problems do have roots in the failures of others. Our parents may have failed to love and discipline us as they should have. But these problems have been compounded by bad decisions that we have made. Our sufferings are usually caused by a combination of factors, including the sins of others and our own sins. We cannot change the failures of others. We cannot blame our mother or father for our wrong choices. Blame does nothing to speed up our recovery process. We can, however, change our own attitudes and actions that have perpetuated the suffering. Maturity comes as we take responsibility for our problems by forgiving those who have wronged us and by seeking forgiveness for our own sins.

CHAPTER 31
The Sayings of King Lemuel

These are the sayings of King Lemuel, an oracle* that his mother taught him.

²O my son, O son of my womb, O son of my promises, ³do not spend your strength on women, on those who ruin kings.

⁴And it is not for kings, O Lemuel, to guzzle wine. Rulers should not crave liquor. ⁵For if they drink, they may forget their duties and be unable to give justice to those who are oppressed. ⁶Liquor is for the dying, and wine for those in deep depression. ⁷Let them drink to forget their poverty and remember their troubles no more.

⁸Speak up for those who cannot speak for themselves; ensure justice for those who are perishing. ⁹Yes, speak up for the poor and helpless, and see that they get justice.

A Wife of Noble Character

¹⁰Who can find a virtuous and capable wife? She is worth more than precious rubies. ¹¹Her husband can trust her, and she will greatly enrich his life. ¹²She will not hinder him but help him all her life.

¹³She finds wool and flax and busily spins it. ¹⁴She is like a merchant's ship; she brings her food from afar. ¹⁵She gets up before dawn to prepare breakfast for her household and plan the day's work for her servant girls. ¹⁶She goes out to inspect a field and buys it; with her earnings she plants a vineyard.

¹⁷She is energetic and strong, a hard worker. ¹⁸She watches for bargains; her lights burn late into the night. ¹⁹Her hands are busy spinning thread, her fingers twisting fiber.

²⁰She extends a helping hand to the poor and opens her arms to the needy.

²¹She has no fear of winter for her household because all of them have warm* clothes. ²²She quilts her own bedspreads. She dresses like royalty in gowns of finest cloth.

²³Her husband is well known, for he sits in the council meeting with the other civic leaders.

²⁴She makes belted linen garments and sashes to sell to the merchants.

²⁵She is clothed with strength and dignity, and she laughs with no fear of the future. ²⁶When she speaks, her words are wise, and kindness is the rule when she gives instructions. ²⁷She carefully watches all that goes on in her household and does not have to bear the consequences of laziness.

²⁸Her children stand and bless her. Her husband praises her: ²⁹"There are many virtuous and capable women in the world, but you surpass them all!"

³⁰Charm is deceptive, and beauty does not last; but a woman who fears the Lord will be greatly praised. ³¹Reward her for all she has done. Let her deeds publicly declare her praise.

31:1 Or *of Lemuel, king of Massa.* **31:21** As in Greek version; Hebrew *scarlet.*

31:10-31 Some women compare themselves to the wife described in this chapter and feel inadequate. Actually, the woman of Proverbs 31 is a description of the *ideal* wife. No wife has ever or will ever completely measure up to all these standards. A wife should not fall into the perfectionist's trap of striving to measure up to these ideal standards. This will inevitably lead to frustration and despair. Instead, a woman should accept herself for who she is and commit to allowing God to transform her more and more into his likeness. As she grows to be more like him, she will naturally exhibit many of the characteristics of this ideal wife.

REFLECTIONS ON

PROVERBS

✳*insights* INTO OUR RELATIONSHIPS WITH GOD AND OTHERS

As we see in **Proverbs 1:29-33,** many people choose to live as they please. They give in to their sinful impulses without thinking about God's will for them. It is foolish to fall to temptations just to feel good momentarily or escape emotional pain for a while. That path will only lead to addiction and fear. It will also lead us away from God, the only one who can really satisfy our deepest needs. The path to secure freedom and peace is narrow and requires listening to God's wisdom and exercising self-control. Recovery is a process, not a "quick fix."

According to **Proverbs 10:4-5,** there is little hope for people who are not willing to work hard. Recovery from damaged emotions or addictive patterns is hard work. It requires persevering through each step in the process. But in recovery we will discover that effort alone is not sufficient. We need the faith to reach out and seize the opportunities that God brings our way. God shows his grace and goodness to us by providing chances for us to exercise our faith. He will also provide us with his spiritual support, wisdom, and encouragement as we seek to obey his will for our life.

Proverbs 12:25 reminds us of the value of encouragement. When people feel troubled or burdened, few things can help them more than a few words of encouragement. We don't necessarily need to give them a pep talk or an it's-gonna-be-all-right speech. Just letting them know that we are there for them and that we love them and are praying for them may be all they need. Real comfort comes from feeling understood, not from hollow words and cliches.

In **Proverbs 13:17** we are reminded of the importance of reliable communication. It is an essential ingredient in any successful recovery program. We need to be honest with ourself, God, and those who are helping us. If we hold anything back, others will not be able to help us completely. If we keep any areas of our addiction hidden, it will ruin the progress we have already made. Just as a war can't be won with inaccurate intelligence reports, giving inaccurate information in recovery will keep us from conquering our dependency.

We see in **Proverbs 14:2** that sin brings dishonor to God. This is one of the most important motivations we have for seeking recovery from our dependency. If we are truly seeking after God, we will want to obey and honor him. Like children who want to please their parents, we should want to recover so we can please God, our heavenly Father.

✳*insights* FOR EVERYDAY LIFE AND RECOVERY

The words in **Proverbs 10:24** speak of a self-fulfilling prophecy: What we expect to happen will happen. How we look at life often affects what actually happens in our life. If we assume that our chances for recovery are hopeless, we have already doomed our recovery program to failure. But if we approach recovery with a positive outlook, trusting in God to see us through, we will progress in the recovery process.

Proverbs 13:11 emphasizes the importance of hard work. Just as hard work can produce material riches, it can also produce spiritual riches. Yet few are willing to persevere through pain and difficulty until the job is done. It is easier to roll the dice and go for the "quick fix." There are no shortcuts to recovery or maturity. The roads to these goals are long, with many small steps that need to be taken over and over again.

As we see in **Proverbs 13:16,** it is wise to process our thoughts and feelings before we act (see also 14:8). Acting on impulses can get us into trouble. Those struggling with addictions to things like drugs, food, sex, work, gambling, or shopping know this well. These kinds of addictions start when we give in to impulses that make us feel good for the moment. The only problem is that the moment doesn't last because the impulsive behaviors don't meet our real needs. It is important to evaluate our real needs and find constructive ways to meet those needs so we can get past our addictive behaviors and find peace.

One thing in life is sure: We will face constant change. As we live in our changing world, it is important that we learn to accept the things that we cannot change. **Proverbs 14:30** reminds us of how important it is for us to find emotional serenity in this life. This is impossible if we fail to accept the things that we cannot change or control. We cannot change the past, but we must make peace with it by seeking to be forgiven and then to forgive others. True, it is easier to remain a victim of the past and seethe with jealousy or bitterness over those who were given advantages that we weren't given. Yet as we are freed from our past, we can put more energy into making positive changes for the future.

The eyes and ears that Solomon was talking about in **Proverbs 20:12** are called perception and understanding. Accurately sensing what is going on within us and around us is the beginning of recovery from an addictive or unhealthy lifestyle in which pain and feelings were avoided or repressed. Only by allowing the painful realities of our life to touch us will we be able to admit we need help and begin the healing process of recovery.

We would be wise to listen to the warning in **Proverbs 20:25.** Impulsive promises to change don't work because they are not made wholeheartedly. They come from people who know what they should do but don't really want to change. Counting the cost involves seriously examining what the promise requires of us and then being willing to fulfill the promise. If we don't want to change but realize that we probably need to, it is helpful to ask God to make us willing to change. It is only when we totally want to follow through with our promises that we will be able to.

We often look with envy at people who indulge in sinful pleasures. **Proverbs 23:17-18** warns us to avoid the temptation to do this. Such people do whatever they choose without regard for how their actions affect others (see 24:1, 19-20). They seem to have easy and pleasurable lives. Those who live righteously, however, seem to have it harder—at least initially. But as they move along the pathway to godly living, they have more fulfilling and meaningful lives. There is also an eternal perspective to be considered: Those who follow God will receive blessings in heaven, but those who live for themselves will face eternal separation from God.

TOPICAL INDEX

This index locates the notes, profiles, devotionals, and recovery themes related to key issues in recovery. Page numbers are provided to make it easy to find all the features listed. Related issues are named in parentheses to make an expanded study on any topic a simple task. For additional information, see the other specialized indexes that follow this topical index: Index to Recovery Profiles, Index to Twelve Step Devotionals, Index to Recovery Principle Devotionals, Index to Serenity Prayer Devotionals, Index to Recovery Reflections.

CODEPENDENCY

COMFORT *(see also* Holy Spirit, Peace)

COMMITMENTS *(see also* Promises, Relationships)

COMMUNICATION *(see also* Criticism, Gossip, Witnessing)

COMMUNITY *(see* Fellowship)

COMPASSION *(see* Love, Service)

COMPLACENCY *(see* Procrastination)

COMPLAINING *(see* Contentment)

COMPROMISE *(see also* Peer Pressure)

CONFESSION *(see* Forgiveness, Repentance)

CONFORMITY *(see* Peer Pressure)

CONFRONTATION

CONSCIENCE (*see also* Guilt)

CONSEQUENCES (*see also* Judgment)

CONTENTMENT (*see also* Peace)

CONTROL (*see* Self-Control)

COUNSELORS (*see* Mentors)

COURAGE (*see also* Fear)

CRITICISM (*see also* Blame, Communication)

DECEPTION

FAITHFULNESS (see also Commitments, Marriage)

FALL (see Relapse, Sin)

FALSE GODS (see Idolatry)

FALSE TEACHINGS (see Deception)

FAMILY (see also Inheritance, Marriage, Parenting)

FAVORITISM (see Partiality)

FEAR (see also Worry)

FELLOWSHIP (*see also* Accountability, Mentors)

FORGIVENESS (*see also* Repentance, Restoration)

FREEDOM (*see also* Choices, Bondage)

PROFILES

TWELVE STEP DEVOTIONALS

RECOVERY PRINCIPLE DEVOTIONALS

SERENITY PRAYER DEVOTIONAL

RECOVERY THEMES IN . . .

FRIENDSHIP (see also Mentors, Peer Pressure)

NOTES

PROFILES

TWELVE STEP DEVOTIONALS

RECOVERY PRINCIPLE DEVOTIONALS

SERENITY PRAYER DEVOTIONAL

RECOVERY THEMES IN . . .

FUN (*see* Enjoyment)

GIVING (*see* Service)

GOD'S POWER

GOD'S SUFFICIENCY (*see* God's Power)

GOD'S WILL (*see also* Guidance)

GOD'S WORD (*see also* Guidance, Wisdom)

GOSSIP (*see also* Communication, Lying)

GRACE (*see also* Legalism)

GRATITUDE (*see also* Praise)

GREED (*see also* Materialism)

HOMOSEXUALITY (*see* Sexuality)

HONESTY (*see also* Lying, Truth)

HOPE

HOPELESSNESS

HOSPITALITY (*see also* Service)

HUMILITY (*see also* Pride)

LOYALTY (see Faithfulness, Friendship)

LUST

LYING (see also Denial, Honesty, Truth)

MARRIAGE (see also Friendship, Relationships)

MATERIALISM (see also Greed)

MEDITATION (see also Prayer)

MENTORS (see also Accountability, Friendship)

PERSISTENCE (*see* Perseverance)

POWERLESSNESS (*see also* Hopelessness)
NOTES

PRAISE (*see also* Celebration, Gratitude, Worship)
NOTES

RECONCILIATION (*see also* Relationships, Restoration)

REDEMPTION (*see also* Salvation)

REJECTION (*see also* Discouragement)

RELAPSE

RELATIONSHIPS (*see also* Marriage)

SCRIPTURE (see God's Word)

SELF-CENTEREDNESS (see Selfishness)

SELF-CONFIDENCE (see Self-Esteem)

SELF-CONTROL (see also Delayed Gratification, Patience)

SELF-DECEPTION (see Denial)

SELF-DEFENSE (see Self-Protection)

SELF-DESTRUCTION (see Self-Hatred)

SELF-DISCIPLINE (see also Perseverance, Self-Control)

SELF-ESTEEM (see also Self-Hatred)

SELF-EXAMINATION (see Inventory)

SELF-HATRED (see also Self-Esteem)

SELF-IMAGE (see Self-Esteem)

SELFISHNESS (see also Greed, Materialism)

SHAME

SHARING (see Witnessing)

SIN (see also Character Defects)

SLAVERY (see Bondage)

SORROW (see Sadness)

SPONSORS (see Mentors)

SUBMISSION (see also Obedience)

SUFFERING (see also Discouragement, Sadness)

TWELVE STEP DEVOTIONALS

RECOVERY THEMES IN . . .

WORRY (*see also* Fear)

NOTES

RECOVERY PRINCIPLE DEVOTIONAL

SERENITY PRAYER DEVOTIONAL

WORSHIP (*see also* Celebration, Praise, Prayer)

NOTES

INDEX TO
RECOVERY PROFILES

INDEX TO
TWELVE STEP DEVOTIONALS

INDEX TO
RECOVERY PRINCIPLE DEVOTIONALS

INDEX TO
SERENITY PRAYER DEVOTIONALS

INDEX TO
RECOVERY REFLECTIONS

LEADING YOU TO THE SOURCE OF T̲R̲U̲E̲ RECOVERY— GOD HIMSELF

If you enjoy the New Testament, check out the full Bible! You'll discover fascinating 12-step notes on almost every page. Explore recovery themes at the beginning of each book. And enjoy 12-step devotions, serenity prayer devotions, and much more in *The Life Recovery Bible* – the complete recovery manual.

Dr. David Stoop and Stephen Arterburn, two nationally respected authorities in Christian recovery, have edited this life-changing Bible.

Get your copy of *The Life Recovery Bible* today wherever Bibles are sold.

TYNDALE

www.newlivingtranslation.com